TEXAS

COMPLETELY REVISED 4TH EDITION

the TexasMonthly®
guidebooks

TEXAS

COMPLETELY REVISED 4TH EDITION

Contributors

Marjie Mugno Acheson   Frances Lowe
Janet Boyanton   Johnnye Montgomery
Nancy Cornell   Eric O'Keefe
Nancy Haston Foster   Robert Rafferty
Joanne Harrison   Richard Zelade
Candace Leslie

Gulf Publishing Company
Houston, Texas

Gulf Publishing Company
Book Division
P.O. Box 2608 ☐ Houston, Texas 77252-2608

10 9 8 7 6 5 4 3 2 1

Library of Congress Cataloging-in-Publication Data

The Texas monthly guidebooks / in collaboration with Marjie Mugno
   Acheson . . . [et al.]. — Completely rev. 4th ed.
      p.   cm. — (The Texas monthly guidebooks)
   Includes bibliographical references and index.
   ISBN 0-87719-317-7 (acid-free paper)
      1. Texas—Guidebooks.   I. Mugno, Marjie.   II. Series.
F384.3.T435   1998
917.6404'63—dc21   97-38567
                                                                         CIP

Printed on Acid-Free Paper (∞)

Printed in the United States of America.

Texas Monthly is a registered trademark of Mediatex Communications Corp.

To Ann Ruff,
a travel writer who explored the nooks and crannies of Texas
and lovingly shared the joys of her travels with her readers.

Contents

Contributing Writers, viii

Acknowledgments, ix

Please Read This First! xi

EAST TEXAS **1**

Big Thicket National Preserve, 1; Brenham, 1; Bryan/College Station, 4; Carthage, 8; Center, 10; Chappell Hill, 12; Conroe, 14; Crockett, 17; Henderson, 19; Houston, 21; Huntsville, 61; Independence, 64; Jasper, 65; Jefferson, 66; Kilgore, 70; Livingston, 72; Longview, 73; Lufkin, 75; Marshall, 78; Mexia, 83; Mount Pleasant, 84; Mount Vernon, 86; Nacogdoches, 87; Navasota, 92; Orange, 94; Palestine, 98; Paris, 102; Pittsburg, 106; Quitman, 109; Rosenberg-Richmond, 110; Rusk, 113; San Augustine, 116; Sulphur Springs, 117; Texarkana, 120; Tyler, 125; Washington, 131; Woodville, 132

CENTRAL TEXAS **135**

Austin, 135; Bandera, 169; Bastrop, 171; Belton, 173; Boerne, 175; Brady, 178; Brownwood, 180; Buchanan Dam, 182; Burnet, 184; Castroville, 186; Columbus, 188; Comfort, 191; Fredericksburg, 193; Georgetown, 199; Gonzales, 201; Hico, 204; Highland Lakes, 206; Johnson City, 207; Kerrville, 208; Killeen, 212; La Grange, 215; Lampasas, 218; Llano, 220; Lockhart, 222; Marble Falls, 224; Mason, 226; New Braunfels, 229; Round Rock, 238; Round Top, 239; Salado, 242; San Antonio, 245; San Marcos, 281; Seguin, 285; Stephenville, 289; Taylor, 291; Temple, 292; Uvalde, 296; Waco, 299; Wimberley, 307

METROPLEX/NORTH CENTRAL TEXAS 310

Addison, 310; Arlington, 314; Bonham, 322; Clifton, 326;
Corsicana, 327; Dallas, 330; Denison, 377; Denton, 381;
Farmers Branch, 385; Fort Worth, 387; Gainesville, 418;
Garland, 421; Glen Rose, 423; Granbury, 426; Grand
Prairie, 429; Grapevine, 434; Greenville, 439; Hillsboro, 442;
Irving, 445; McKinney, 452; Mesquite, 454; Plano, 457;
Richardson, 462; Sherman, 466; Terrell, 470;
Weatherford, 472

SOUTH TEXAS 475

Beaumont, 475; Brazosport, 481; Brownsville, 486; Clear Lake
Area, 497; Corpus Christi, 500; Del Rio, 515; Galveston, 521;
Goliad, 539; Harlingen, 543; Kingsville, 548; Laredo, 552;
McAllen, 561; Port Aransas, 571; Port Arthur, 578; Port
Lavaca, 584; Rockport and Fulton, 588; South Padre Island
and Port Isabel, 594; Victoria, 603; Weslaco, 608; West
Columbia, 610

PANHANDLE 613

Abilene, 613; Albany, 622; Amarillo, 623; Breckenridge, 639;
Canyon, 641; Dalhart, 644; Eastland, 646; Fritch, 647;
Graham, 649; Jacksboro, 650; Lubbock, 652; Mineral
Wells, 669; Quanan, 671; Snyder, 673; Sweetwater, 675;
Wichita Falls, 678

WEST TEXAS 686

Alpine, 686; Big Bend National Park, 690; Big Bend Ranch
State Park, 698; Big Spring, 699; Colorado City, 703;
El Paso, 705; Fort Davis, 729; Fort Stockton, 734; Guadalupe
Mountains National Park, 736; Lajitas and Terlingua, 738;
Langtry, 741; Midland, 742; Monahans, 750; Odessa, 752;
Ozona, 758; Pecos, 759; San Angelo, 760; Sonora, 769

Index 772

CONTRIBUTING WRITERS

Marjie Mugno Acheson
Central Texas

Janet Boyanton
Northeast Texas

Nancy Cornell
Fort Worth and Surrounding Area

Nancy Haston Foster
San Antonio and Surrounding Area

Joanne Harrison
Houston and Surrounding Area

Candace Leslie
Bryan/College Station and Beaumont Areas

Frances Lowe
Panhandle

Johnnye Montgomery
West Central Texas

Eric O'Keefe
West Texas and Crockett County

Robert Rafferty
Metroplex and Texas Coast

Richard Zelade
Austin and Surrounding Area

ACKNOWLEDGMENTS

This book was a team effort: It was researched and written by eleven contributors from across the state. These contributing writers would like to thank the hundreds of people who helped them gather their information, especially the congenial contacts in the various chambers of commerce and convention and visitors bureaus. Without their assistance this book could not live up to its reputation as the biggest, most complete, and most accurate guide to Texas.

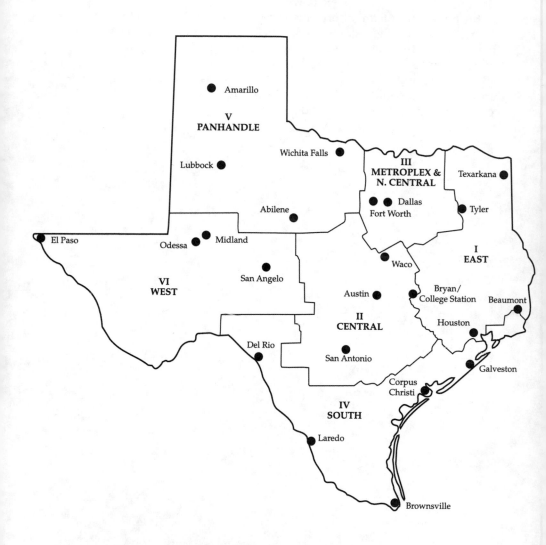

Amarillo

V
PANHANDLE

Wichita Falls

III
METROPLEX &
N. CENTRAL

Texarkana

Lubbock

Dallas
Fort Worth

Tyler

Abilene

El Paso

Odessa Midland

I
EAST

Waco

San Angelo

Bryan/
College Station

Beaumont

VI
WEST

Austin

Houston

II
CENTRAL

Del Rio

Galveston

San Antonio

Corpus
Christi

IV
SOUTH

Laredo

Brownsville

PLEASE READ THIS FIRST!

ORGANIZATION OF THIS GUIDE

This book is divided into six regions: East Texas, Central Texas, Metroplex/ North Texas, South Texas, the Panhandle, and West Texas. Wherever possible, we used geographical and topographical features that are usually thought of as boundaries, such as the pine forests of East Texas, the desert and mountains of West Texas, the semitropics of the south, and the plains of the Panhandle in the north (see map p. x). Aside from these, it is almost impossible to set exact limits to adjoining regions that take into account the overlaps of history, traditions, cultures, and lifestyles. The index at the back of the book will be your best bet in locating a particular city.

THINGS CHANGE

The information in this book is as current as we could make it at the time the book went to press. However, it took a long time to research, write, edit, print, and distribute this book. In the meantime, things have been changing.

To help you avoid any inconvenience caused by changes, we've included telephone numbers in the listings whenever possible. A call before you go might save you a little irritation, especially if you have to travel any distance. Remember, however, phone numbers change, too. If you have trouble reaching a listing, check the phone book or call Information.

HOW TO READ THE LISTINGS

Each city's listing begins with the name of the county in which it is located, the 1990 census figure or the best estimate of the city's current population, and (in parenthesis) the telephone area code.

For most short distances, mileages given were actually checked. Where this was not possible, mileages given were generally provided by knowledgeable local sources or taken from the Texas Department of Transportation's official highway map. These may differ slightly from your actual driving mileage.

SYMBOLS USED IN THIS BOOK

Restaurant Guide

The following symbols indicate the cost of a typical meal for one person, exclusive of drinks, tax, and tip:

$:	under $7
$$:	$8 to $17
$$$:	$18 to $25
$$$$:	over $25

The word **"bar"** at the end of a restaurant listing indicates that the establishment serves liquor and mixed drinks.

Accommodation Guide

Unless otherwise specified, the rate symbols used are for a double room (two people in a room without regard to the bed arrangement). In places with seasonal rates, such as in the resort areas along the coast, the rate symbol is for a double in high season. Off-season rates are usually lower. Always ask about discount rates.

$:	under $45
$$:	$46–$60
$$$:	$61– $80
$$$$:	$81–$100
$$$$$:	over $100

Wheelchair Accessibility Symbols

W: This place is accessible to persons in wheelchairs; the entrance is at least 32 inches wide and there are no more than two steps at the entrance. Not all facilities (restrooms, elevators, etc.) are accessible, however.
W variable: This place is only partially accessible.
W+: This place and all its major facilities are accessible.
No symbol: This place is accessible only with great difficulty or not at all.

Credit Cards

AE	American Express
DIS	Discover
MC	MasterCard
V	Visa
Cr	All major credit cards
No Cr	No credit cards

East Texas

BIG THICKET NATIONAL PRESERVE

At one time the Big Thicket was just that—millions of acres of dense woodlands, streams, marshes, and thick undergrowth that stood like an impenetrable jungle barrier across East Texas. When civilization arrived with its roads and towns and the lumber and oil industries, every year the Thicket shrunk. In order to save a small part of what was left, the Big Thicket National Preserve was established by an act of Congress in 1974.

Today the Thicket consists of eight separate woodlands units with 84,000 acres and more to be added with four water corridors. It offers opportunities for nature study, hiking, boating, canoeing, and fishing. One way to enjoy the Thicket the easy way is to take Timber Ridge Tours, P.O. Box 115, Kountze 77625, 409-246-3107 and cruise the Neches River. A fee is charged. Also, visit the Big Thicket Visitor Information Station on TX 420, 2.9 miles off US 69/287, seven miles north of Kountze. Open Wednesday 10:30–5:00, Thursday–Tuesday 9–5. Visitor Station and two trails W.

The Thicket has been called "the biological crossroads of North America" and has its own unique collection of flora and fauna, including rare plants. For information: Superintendent, The Big Thicket National Preserve, 3785 Milam, Beaumont 77701 409-246-2337.

BRENHAM

Washington County Seat • 13,000 • (409)
Established in 1844, Brenham is the heart and soul of the county where the Texas Declaration of Independence was signed. History buffs will not want to miss a chance to explore this area. Nature lovers will find many exciting attractions in this agriculture-based community. Wildflowers, especially the state's official bluebonnets, are abundant in the spring.

TOURIST SERVICES

WASHINGTON COUNTY CHAMBER OF COMMERCE
314 S. Austin (77833) • 836-3695, 1-888-BRENHAM, fax 836-2540, web site: www.brenhamtx.org • Monday–Friday 8:30–5, Saturday 10–3, Sunday 12–3 • W
This is an official Texas Visitor Information Center so you can pick up free visitor guides, city and county maps, and brochures from around the state. To

1

enhance your visit to Brenham and Washington County there are souvenir postcards, bluebonnet seeds, videos, driving tour tapes, maps, and more.

HISTORIC PLACES

Among the numerous antebellum and Victorian homes and buildings in Washington County is the **Giddings-Wilkin House (1843)** at 805 Crockett, the oldest home in Brenham. It is open by appointment for group tours only through the Heritage Society of Washington County (836-1690) which has its offices in the house. Also open by appointment through the Heritage Society is the **Giddings-Stone Mansion (1869)** at 204 E. Stone St., listed on the National Register of Historic Places. Many other homes are open for group tours by appointment. **The Citadel,** located on US 290 just west of Loop 577, was the former Brenham Country Club. Built in 1923, it is said to be architect Alfred Finn's crowning achievement after the San Jacinto Monument, and the only art deco country club in Texas. For tours, parties, and seminars, call 800-636-9463.

OTHER POINTS OF INTEREST

BLUE BELL CREAMERIES

S. Horton St. (Loop FM 577 East) • 836-7977 or 800-327-8135 • Tours on weekdays only, call for hours • $2, seniors $1.50 • W variable
They've been making ice cream here since 1911, and they must be doing it right because it's now one of the most popular brands in Texas. Tours of about 45 minutes are offered year-round on weekdays and include two short films and a view of the ice-cream-making process followed by a dip of your favorite flavor. On Saturdays, you can visit the Country Store gift shop and ice cream parlor and browse among a great selection of upscale country merchandise.

BRENHAM HERITAGE MUSEUM

105 S. Market Historic Downtown• 830-8445 • Wednesday 1–4, Thursday–Saturday 10–4• $1 donation • W variable
Permanent exhibits illustrate the diverse history of the community with special rare exhibits throughout the year. See the 1879 Silsby Steam Fire Engine housed in an interactive exterior display building.

MONASTERY MINIATURE HORSES

Monastery of St. Clare • *Take TX 105 nine miles east to just past intersection with FM 2193* **• 836-9652 • Daily 2–4 or by appointment • Donation: adults $3, children $1 • W variable**
The contemplative nuns of St. Clare help sustain their monastery by raising, showing, and selling miniature horses. There are usually about 60 of these tiny horses on display, and yes, you may pet them. Also a ceramics studio and gift shop. Special events in May and September.

ELLISON'S GREENHOUSES

107 E. Stone • 836-6011 • Friday and Saturday 9:30–2:30; weekday group tours by appointment • Adults $2, children 50¢ • W
Just imagine miles and miles of mums, aisle after aisle of azaleas, rows and rows of begonias, and during November—poinsettias! poinsettias! poinsettias! Here is Mother Nature in bloom year round, and the weekend before Thanksgiving is the fabulous Poinsettia Festival.

UNITY THEATRE
On the Courthouse Square between Main and Alamo (Historic Downtown)
830-8358 • $10 reserved seating, call for brochure and schedule • W
Using both professional and amateur talent, Unity Theatre produces a variety of plays and musicals in February, April, July, October, and December.

COLLEGES AND UNIVERSITIES
BLINN COLLEGE
902 College Street, between Jackson and Blinn Blvd. • 830-4000 • Campus walking tours by appointment (830-4152), closed on college holidays
W variable
Founded in 1883, Blinn became the first county-owned public junior college in Texas in 1927. Today it has three campuses (including one in Bryan/College Station) and an enrollment of 7,000.

SHOPPING
ANTIQUES, GIFTS, AND APPAREL
The Washington County Chamber of Commerce provides a brochure and map listing many delightful shops and antique stores.

SIDE TRIPS
LAKE SOMERVILLE
Take TX 36 northwest about 14 miles • 535-7763 or 596-1122 • Open at all times • Fees in some areas
This 11,460-acre lake has seven parks: four operated by the U.S. Army Corps of Engineers, one by the city of Somerville, and two by the Texas Parks and Wildlife Dept. About 500 acres of shoreline are developed for picnicking, camping, swimming, fishing, and all water sports.
See also, Chappell Hill, Independence, Washington.

ANNUAL EVENTS
May
MAIFEST
Fireman's Park, N. Park St. (TX 36N) • Three days prior to Mother's Day Admission • W
For more than 100 years this German folk festival has been held in Brenham. Festivities include two parades, two coronations, and the wonderful Antique Carousel is open. Count on plenty of food and entertainment.

September
WASHINGTON COUNTY FAIR
Washington County Fairgrounds, Horton St. E. (FM 577) and Independence 836-4112 • Usually in mid-September • Admission • W variable
Held since 1869, this is the oldest county fair in the state. All the fair ingredients are here: the grand champion livestock, cooking and other contests, quarter horse show, carnival, star entertainment, and three nights of rodeo.

RESTAURANTS

($ = under $7, $$ = $8–$17, $$$ = $18–$25, $$$$ = over $25 for one person excluding drinks, tax, and tip.)

K&G STEAKHOUSE

2209 S. Market near Becker Dr. • 836-7950 • Breakfast, lunch, and dinner Tuesday–Sunday, dinner only Monday • $–$$ • AE, MC, V • W

They've been serving up steaks here since 1966, and now some seafood, chicken, and quail. Lunch buffet. Children's plate. No-smoking area. Bar.

TEJAS CAFE & BAR

2104 S. Market near Becker Dr. • 836-9554 • Sunday–Thursday 11–10:30, Friday and Saturday 11 A.M.–11:30 P.M. • $–$$ • AE, MC, V • W

For a true taste of Texas try the chicken-fried steak, or sample the fajitas, burgers, ribs, grilled shrimp, or chicken platter, or fresh salad. No-smoking area. Bar.

MUST BE HEAVEN

107 W. Alamo St. • 830-8536 • Monday–Saturday 8–5 • AE, MC, V, DIS • W

Ice cream, soups, sandwiches on fresh baked bread, homemade pies. After eating here, you'll surely know that Brenham "must be heaven!"

ACCOMMODATIONS

($ = under $45, $$ = $46–$60, $$$ = $61–$80, $$$$= $81–$100, $$$$$ = over $100) Room tax 11%

HOTELS/MOTELS

There are eight convenient and economical choices in Brenham, including a Holiday Inn Express, Best Western, and Ramada Limited. For a complete list and phone numbers, call the Washington County Chamber of Commerce (836-3695 or 1-888-BRENHAM). Pets OK at some. Several have pools. Rates range from $ to $$$$$.

BED AND BREAKFASTS

More than 30 bed and breakfast inns are found in and around Brenham. Call the Washington County Chamber of Commerce (836-3695 or 1-888-BRENHAM) for a complete list. Pets OK at several. Fishing and boating at some. Many offer fine views of countryside, lakes, miniature horses, and other livestock. Rates are $$–$$$$$.

BRYAN/COLLEGE STATION

Bryan: Brazos County Seat • 58,000 • (409)
College Station: Brazos County • 60,221 (409)

These two cities have grown together, so the only things separating them now are the city limits. Bryan, on the north, has the county courthouse and diversified industry. College Station is the home of Texas A&M University. Both cities benefit from the university.

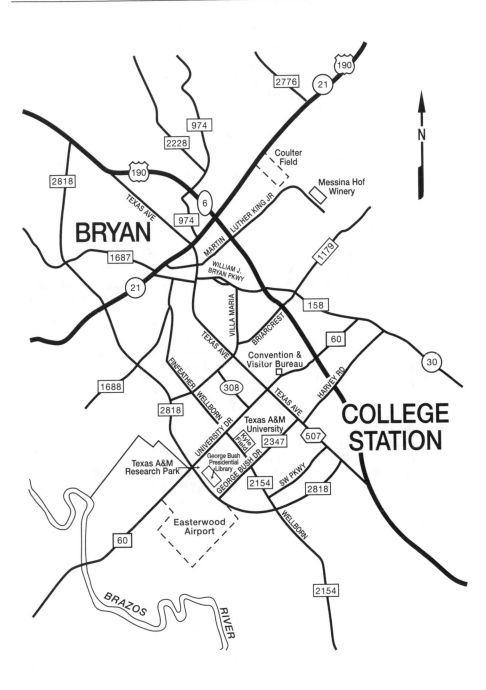

TOURIST SERVICES

BRYAN/COLLEGE STATION CONVENTION AND VISITORS BUREAU

College Station • 715 University Dr. E. (77840) • 260-9898 or 800-777-8292 • W+
A free historic guide to the area is available with highlights of historic buildings in the commercial and residential sections of Bryan, the older buildings on
the campus of Texas A&M, and other historic places in Brazos County.

MUSEUMS

BRAZOS MUSEUM OF NATURAL SCIENCES AND HISTORY

Bryan • Brazos Center, 3232 Briarcrest Dr. • 776-2195 • Monday–Friday 8–5;
Saturday 10–5 • Adults $3, senior citizens and students $2.50, museum
members $2, children 10 and under free • W
Exhibits explore the sciences and present the history of the Brazos Valley.
Small nature trail on grounds.

GEORGE BUSH PRESIDENTIAL LIBRARY AND MUSEUM

College Station • 1000 George Bush Drive (P.O. Box 10410, 77842) • 260-9552
Monday–Saturday 9:30–5; Sunday 12–5. Closed Thanksgiving, Christmas,
New Year's • Adults $3, senior citizens and students $2.50, children 16 and
under free • W
Newly opened in November 1997, this is the tenth presidential library administered by the National Archives. It holds 36,000,000 pages of official and personal papers, more than 1,000,000 audiovisual records, and 40,000 artifacts that doc-
ument President Bush's long public career. Visitors can experience the unique
influences and challenges that formed George Bush's life and presidency.

OTHER POINTS OF INTEREST

MESSINA HOF WINE CELLARS

Bryan • *Take TX 21 east 2 miles past TX 6 to Wallis Rd., then turn south on
Wallis Rd. and follow signs to winery* • 778-9463 • $3
The name is derived from the combination of the owners' winemaking heritage from Messina, Italy, and Hof, Germany. Retail sales and tasting room in
the elegant visitor's center are open Monday through Friday 8:30–5:30, and
weekday tours are at 1 P.M. Saturday tours are 10–5 and Sunday 12–4. Many
special events are held during the year including a grape stomp in mid-April.

SPORTS AND ACTIVITIES

Golf

BRYAN GOLF COURSE

206 W. Villa Maria Rd. • 823-0126 • 18-hole course. Greens fee: weekdays
$11, weekends $13

COLLEGES AND UNIVERSITIES

TEXAS A&M UNIVERSITY

College Station • Main entrance off Texas Ave. (Bus. TX 6) south of
University Dr. (FM 60) • Information Center in lobby of Rudder Tower on

Joe Routt Blvd. • 845-5851 • W variable • Visitor parking across street from Rudder Tower

When it came to picking a location for the state's first public institution of higher learning back in the 1870s, the state commissioners chose a site on the open prairie five miles south of Bryan. They did this to keep the students away from the immoral influence of Bryan's saloons and gambling halls. Originally an all-male military college, today women make up more than 40% of the student body, and enrollment in the Corps of Cadets is optional. Enrollment in the ten academic colleges making up the university has surpassed the 40,000 mark, making this one of the ten largest universities in the nation. Visitors will find a multimedia presentation on the university and its academic programs at the Information Center. A map and a visitor's guide are also available here. In addition to going to an A&M football game—if you can get a ticket—and watching other intercollegiate sports, visitors are also welcome at the concerts, plays by the Theatre Arts Department's Aggie Players and traveling theater groups, movies, and other performances held on campus. You can find out what's going on and buy tickets in the Tower lobby.

PERFORMING ARTS

STAGECENTER
Bryan • 701 N. Main (P.O. Box 6166, 77805) • 823-4297

A community theater group that puts on about five or six plays a year ranging from Shakespeare to Neil Simon. Tickets for adults are about $8.

ARTS COUNCIL OF THE BRAZOS VALLEY
College Station • 111 University Drive E, Suite 217 • 268-2787

A broad assortment of community groups offers a wealth of arts, entertainment, exhibitions and other cultural activities. Many, such as the Brazos Valley Symphony Orchestra, Stage Center and the Brazos Valley Chorale, function under the umbrella of the arts council which will provide information and calendars of upcoming events.

RESTAURANTS

($ = under $7, $$ = $8–$17, $$$ = $18–$25, $$$$ = over $25 for one person excluding drinks, tax, and tip.)

CAFE ECCELL
College Station • 101 Church • 846-7908 • Monday–Thursday 11–10, Friday–Saturday 11–11, Sunday 8 A.M.–10 P.M. • $–$$ • Cr • W

This casual spot has long been popular with both college and community patrons. All menu items are freshly made, from the wood-fired pizza, seafood entrees, and vegetarian dishes to the home baked breads and desserts.

THE KAFFEE KLATSCH
Bryan • 106 North Ave. • 846-4360 • Lunch only Monday–Saturday. Closed Sunday • $ • MC, V • W

This small restaurant is located in the Garden District, an old building renovated to house several fine shops in a garden atmosphere. The blackboard selections change daily and may include Texas *crepes,* homemade chicken salad, *quiche,* or a gumbo. They also serve desserts and coffee during the afternoon. Tea time 3–5.

THE TEXAN

Bryan • 3204 S. College • 822-3588 • Dinner Wednesday–Saturday. Closed Sunday • Reservations suggested • $$–$$$$ • Cr • W

The appearance is deceptively modest for a restaurant that offers *escargot, tempura* shrimp, Alaskan king crab, and lobster among its long list of entrées. The chef-owner's gourmet cooking has made this a place for fine dining for more than 20 years. Bar.

ACCOMMODATIONS

($ = under $45, $$ = $46–$60, $$$ = $61–$80, $$$$ = $81–$100, $$$$$ = over $100) Room tax 13%

COLLEGE STATION HILTON AND CONFERENCE CENTER

801 University Dr. E. • 693-7500 or 800-HILTONS (800-445-8667) • $$$–$$$$$ W+ 16 rooms • No-smoking rooms

This 11-story hotel and conference center offers 303 units that include 3 suites ($$$$$) and 26 no-smoking rooms. Cable TV. Room phones (charge for local calls). Fire sprinklers in rooms. Pets OK. Free airport transportation. Café and seafood restaurant. Lobby bar and lounge. Outdoor pool, exercise room. Guest memberships in local health club. Gift shop.

HAMPTON INN

College Station • 320 S. Texas Ave. (Bus TX 6) • 846-0184 or 800-HAMPTON (800-426-7866) • $ • W+ 7 rooms • No-smoking rooms

The four-story Hampton has 135 rooms including 37 no-smoking. Fire sprinklers in rooms. Cable TV with HBO, The Movie Channel, and pay channel. Room phones (no charge for local calls). Pets OK. Free transportation to airport and University. Outdoor heated pool. Guest memberships available in local health club. Free light breakfast and coffee. Free newspaper.

BED AND BREAKFASTS

The number of bed and breakfast accommodations is growing. Contact the Convention and Visitors Bureau for a current listing. 260-9898 or 800-777-8292.

CARTHAGE

Panola County Seat • 6,496 • (903)

Founded in 1848 as a log cabin village, it underwent slow growth until the gas fields were developed after World War II. Today it is a center for gas and oil processing, petrochemicals, lumber mills, meat packing and chicken processing, and lignite mining.

TOURIST SERVICES

PANOLA COUNTY CHAMBER OF COMMERCE

300 W. Panola, 75633 • 693-6634 • W

MUSEUMS

HERITAGE HALL MUSEUM
St. Mary and W. Sabine, on the square • 693-8689 • Call for hours
Admission • W first floor only
   This museum, in the upstairs of the old First National Bank Building, traces the history of the county and includes memorabilia of three of Panola County's most famous sons: singers Jim Reeves and Tex Ritter, and historian Walter Prescott Webb. Downstairs is the Texas Tea Room, where light lunches are served Monday through Friday by volunteers from the county Heritage Society.

TEX RITTER MUSEUM
300 W. Panola • 693-6634 (Chamber of Commerce) • Call for hours
   Memorabilia of the Country and Western Hall of Fame honoree and cowboy star Tex Ritter fill this small museum located in a traditional southern plantation home.

HISTORIC PLACES

OLD PANOLA COUNTY JAIL MUSEUM
110 N. Shelby
   This was the county jail from 1891 until the new jail was built in 1953. Restored to its original condition, it currently houses a genealogical library and a display of war memorabilia.

OTHER POINTS OF INTEREST

JIM REEVES MEMORIAL
US 79 about 3 miles east of town • W
   A life-sized statue of Country and Western singer Jim Reeves marks his grave in this two-acre memorial park. Reeves was at the top of the C&W charts when he was killed in an airplane crash near Nashville, Tennessee, on July 31, 1964.

COLLEGES AND UNIVERSITIES

PANOLA COLLEGE
1109 W. Panola • 693-2000 • W
   Approximately 1,300 students are enrolled in academic and occupational programs. Visitors are welcome at sports events, the several drama department productions each year, and musical concerts and recitals.

SIDE TRIPS

MARTIN CREEK LAKE STATE PARK
Take TX 149 to Beckville, then County Rd. 256 to lake **• 836-4336 • Open at all times • $3 per vehicle**
   A 5,020-acre lake built by Texas Utilities for generator cooling, but also open for fishing and boating. Picnic areas and a boat ramp are available.

LAKE MURVAUL

Take TX 315 southwest to Clayton then south (left) on FM 1970 to entrance to lake • 693-9301 (Marina) • Open at all times • Free

A 3,820-acre lake with facilities for boating, fishing, waterskiing, and swimming. Also RV and tent campsites and lakeside cottages for rent.

ANNUAL EVENTS

December

CHRISTMAS PARADE AND FESTIVAL OF LIGHTS

First Monday night in December • 693-6634

Over 100 entries are featured in this annual Christmas parade.

CENTER

Shelby County Seat • 5,900 • (409)

It became the county seat in 1866 when a new law required that the county seat be centrally located in the county. And, that's also how Center got its name. Center is also in the heart of the infamous "Neutral Ground." After the Louisiana Purchase, the United States and Spain were unable to agree on the boundary between Louisiana and Texas, and in 1806 this territory was declared "neutral," which really meant all outlaws could roam at will. It was 1821 before it became part of the United States and law and order returned.

TOURIST SERVICES

SHELBY COUNTY CHAMBER OF COMMERCE

321 Shelbyville St. (75935) • 598-3682 • W

Walking tour of historic places brochure available.

MUSEUMS

SHELBY COUNTY MUSEUM

230 Pecan, just off the square • 598-3613 • Tuesday–Saturday 2–5 • Free • W

Exhibits tell the history of the county and East Texas. Among the items on display are antique farm and ranch equipment and furnishing from an old-time doctor's office.

HISTORIC PLACES

SHELBY COUNTY COURTHOUSE

Town Square • 598-3682 • Free

Built in 1885, it was designed by an Irish architect, John J. E. Gibson, who made it with turrets and towers to resemble a Norman castle in his native Ireland. The only one of its kind, it is complete with hidden staircase behind the judge's bench. It's listed in the National Register of Historic Places.

SIDE TRIPS

NATIONAL HALL OF FAME CEMETERY OF FOXHOUNDS

Take TX 87 south to Shelbyville, then FM 417 to FM 2694 to Boles Field
Open at all times • Free
Texans still follow the foxhound's song and talk lovingly of a good hound dog's voice. The all-time great dogs are buried in Boles Field with a ceremony that includes good hunting stories about these beloved hounds.

SABINE NATIONAL FOREST

With 160,609 acres, this national forest has seven U.S. Forest Service recreation areas, the closest entrance is 11 miles southeast on TX 87. For information write: USDA Forest Service, P.O. Box 227, Hemphill 75948, or call 409-787-3870.

TOLEDO BEND RESERVOIR

This huge impoundment of the Sabine River forms part of the border between Texas and Louisiana. A joint project of both states, it is 65 miles long, covers 185,000 acres, and has 1,200 miles of shoreline, making it the largest lake in Texas. In addition to the Sabine River Authority parks are commercial camps, resorts, and marinas. Write the Sabine River Authority, Route 1, Box 270, Burkeville 75932, or call 565-2273.

ANNUAL EVENTS

October

EAST TEXAS POULTRY FESTIVAL

Downtown • 598-3682 (Chamber of Commerce) • First weekend in October • $2 entry button good for 3 days. Five years and under free
Once a year everything goes "fowl" in Center as the county honors its largest industry—poultry. In addition to a fun run, a carnival, concerts, arts and crafts and plenty of fried chicken, a highlight is the broiler show and auction raising money for area youth programs.

ACCOMMODATIONS

($ = under $45, $$ = $46–$60, $$$ = $61–$80, $$$$ = $81–$100, $$$$$ = over $100)
Room tax 11%

LAKE COUNTRY INN

701 San Augustine St. at junction of TX 7 and 96 • 598-2431 • $ • No-smoking rooms • W 1 room
Built on one level, it offers 40 rooms including 10 no-smoking. Senior discounts. Cable TV with 4 movie channels. Room phones (no charge for local calls). Pets OK. Restaurant and private club. 24-hour tanning salon.

BEST WESTERN CENTER INN

1005 Hurst St. at US 87N and 96N • 598-3384 • $–$$ • No-smoking rooms W 1 room
This Best Western has 72 suites and rooms, some with refrigerators and microwaves, and some no-smoking. Cable TV with HBO. Room phones (local calls free). 24-hour restaurant. Free coffee. Outdoor pool.

Bed and Breakfast

PINE COLONY INN

500 Shelbyville St. • 598-7700 • $–$$$ • No-smoking rooms
This two-story historic hotel offers 12 no-smoking rooms including two kitchenette suites, two suites and four singles. All have private baths. All furnished in antiques. Cable TV and phones (local calls free) in each room. No pets. Full country breakfast included.

CHAPPELL HILL

Washington County • 310 • (409)
Most of Main Street in this village has been designated a National Historic District. Chappell Hill was founded in 1847 by Mary Haller, who sold off 100 acres she owned as town lots. She then appointed her husband, Jacob, as the postmaster, and she named the town after her grandfather, Robert Wooding Chappell. Settlers from prominent families of the Old South built plantations in the area. It soon became an educational center with two colleges, but the Civil War and yellow fever decimated the population. More than 25 buildings and homes bear historical markers.

TOURIST SERVICES

CHAPPELL HILL HISTORICAL SOCIETY

P.O. Box 211 (77426) • 836-6033 (leave a message)
The society coordinates tours of the Chappell Hill Historical Museum, Rock Store, library, and church. $3. Tour includes a short video on the history of the folk-art wall hangings at the Rock Store.

WASHINGTON COUNTY CHAMBER OF COMMERCE

314 S. Austin Street (Brenham 77833) • 836-3695 or 800-225-3695, fax 836-2540
The chamber coordinates group tours of the historic homes and properties and offers a brochure and map of the area and complete information about events in Chappell Hill.

MUSEUMS

CHAPPELL HILL HISTORICAL SOCIETY MUSEUM

Church and Poplar • 836-6033 • Wednesday–Saturday 10–4, Sunday 1–4 and by appointment • $1 donation • W
Housed in an old school building, the museum has six rooms of exhibits that bring to life the plantation economy, the Civil War period, and other fascinating topics.

THE ROCK STORE MUSEUM

Main and Cedar • 836-6033 • Open by chance or appointment • W
Folk-art wall hangings depict early Chappell Hill in stitchery in this old store built in 1869. A short video is shown during the tour.

HISTORIC PLACES

THE BROWNING PLANTATION

Rt. 1, Box 339, 77426 • 836-6144 or 713-626-9592 (Houston)

This two-story home, a fine example of Greek Revival architecture, was built in 1857. At one time almost a total wreck, this home, now stands as one of the finest restorations in Texas. You won't believe the "before" photographs. It is also a bed and breakfast with four rooms, two with private baths, no smoking, no pets, no children under 12 ($$$$).

THE STAGECOACH INN

Main and Chestnut • 836-9515 • Tours by appointment • $5

The inn was built in 1850 by Jacob and Mary Chappell Haller, the founders of Chappell Hill. Many noted Texans stopped here when traveling from Houston to Austin or to Waco. The home is filled with museum-quality antiques and many whimsical touches. It is also a bed and breakfast with six rooms ($$$$).

MULBERRY HOUSE

Cedar Street, east of FM 1155 • 830-1311

Restored Queen Anne-style home listed on the National Register of Historic Places. Beautiful landscaped grounds. Group tours with refreshments by appointment. Also a bed and breakfast with five rooms ($$$$).

ANNUAL EVENTS

April

BLUEBONNET FESTIVAL

Main St. • 836-3695 or 800-225-3695 (Washington County Chamber of Commerce) • First or second weekend in April • Free • W variable

Features more than 125 arts and crafts exhibits, antique-collectibles vendors, entertainment, delicious food, hay ride tours (fee), and a children's activity corner.

October

SCARECROW FESTIVAL

Main St. • 836-3695 or 800-225-3695 (Washington County Chamber of Commerce) • Weekends in mid-October • Free • W variable

Everybody pitches in and the whole town is festooned with scarecrows for the entire month of October. More than 125 arts and crafts booths, vintage collectibles, barbecue and county-style food, pumpkin decorating contest for kids, hay ride tours (fee), and a children's activity corner add to fall festivities.

ACCOMMODATIONS

($ = under $45, $$ = $46–$60, $$$ = $61–$80, $$$$ = $81–$100, $$$$$ over $100)

Bed and Breakfasts

In addition to the Browning Plantation, Stagecoach Inn, and Mulberry House (*see* Historic Places), there are several other bed and breakfast accommodations in the area. Call the Washington County Chamber of Commerce for a complete list and map.

CONROE

Montgomery County Seat • 32,290 • (409)

Conroe was born in 1881 when lumberman, Issac Conroe, a former Union Army captain, constructed a short wooden tram to link his sawmill with the International and Great Northern Railroad. This junction became "Conroe's Switch." Shortly, the Gulf, Colorado, and Santa Fe Railroad was built to intersect with Conroe's Switch, and the town became a major shipping point. By 1889 Conroe was the county seat and Issac Conroe its first postmaster.

During the early 1900s Conroe was hard hit in the lumber and farming business, but salvation arrived on June 4, 1932, when George W. Strake hit oil and started the Conroe Field. The Conroe Field is still producing, and even though the boom days are long gone, the town is still growing.

Just east of Conroe on TX 105 is the community of **Cut 'n Shoot.** The name is derived from the quote "cut around the corner and shoot through the bushes." Cut 'n Shoot made the big time in 1983 as the home of Debra Sue Maffett, Miss America that year.

TOURIST SERVICES

GREATER CONROE CHAMBER OF COMMERCE

101 W. Phillips at Pacific (P.O. Box 2347, 77305) • 800-283-6645 • 746-6644 • W

The Chamber's Visitor and Convention Bureau also operates an Information Depot (539-2502) on the I-45 access road north of TX 105. If going north on I-45, take the TX 105 exit. If southbound, exit at TX 105 and make a u-turn to the northbound access road.

POINTS OF INTEREST

LAKE CONROE

Take TX 105 west 7 miles • 588-1111 (San Jacinto River Authority) • Open at all times • Free • W variable

This 20,985-acre lake was originally viewed as a reserve water supply for Houston when the dam was completed in 1973, but since then it has become a prime recreation area offering excellent facilities for fishing, sailing, water skiing, and other water sports. The lake has 150 miles of shoreline, the northern 50 being in the Sam Houston National Forest. The other 100 miles are fringed with marinas, campgrounds, public boat ramps, boat rentals, homes, and resort centers. Dinner, brunch, cocktail and sightseeing cruises are available Thursday through Sunday on the *Southern Empress* paddlewheeler located at TX 105 and Beachwalk Blvd. (800-324-2229).

W. GOODRICH JONES STATE FOREST

Take I-45 south to FM 1488, then west about 2.5 miles • 273-2261 • Open at all times • Free • W variable

Named for the founder of the Texas Forestry Association, this 1,725-acre forest provides facilities for hiking, swimming, picnicking, and fishing. It also includes a marked self-guided nature trail. The **Sweetleaf Nature Trail** is open Monday through Friday 8–5, and free guidebooks to the trail are available at the entrance. If the gate is locked or there are no guidebooks, try the office on the north side of FM 1488.

J-MAR FARMS

Exit 91 off I-45 • 856-8595 or 800-636-8595 • Daily, spring and summer 9–6, fall and winter 9–5 • Adults $6, children 2–12 $5.50, under 2 free • W variable
Petting farm and playground featuring more than 200 animals, along with pony rides, fishing, hay rides, paddle boats and lots of family fun. Admission fee is all inclusive.

PERFORMING ARTS

CRIGHTON THEATRE

234 N. Main • 756-1226 • Admission depends on event • W
Built in 1935, this restored theater is now the center for the Crighton Community Players that stage eight productions a year. Also, it is the stage for music and dance productions.

SIDE TRIPS

MONTGOMERY

Take TX 105 west approximately 17 miles
Founded in 1837, Montgomery boomed before the Civil War and was the county seat. Now just a quaint hamlet, Montgomery offers a step back into the past with its restored homes and buildings and antique shops. Tours are held in April and December. Contact the Montgomery Historical Society, P.O. Box 513, Montgomery 77356.

SAM HOUSTON NATIONAL FOREST

Take I-45 north to FM 1375, then west to entrance to Kaygal Recreation Area
344-6205 • Open at all times • Free • W variable
There are several recreation areas in this 160,443-acre national forest that spreads across parts of Montgomery, San Jacinto, and Walker counties. The Kaygal area on Lake Conroe is closest to Conroe. Facilities are available here for hiking, biking, camping (fee), horseback riding, fishing, boating, and other water sports. For information write: Raven District Office, Sam Houston National Forest, P.O. Box 393, New Waverly 77358.

ANNUAL EVENTS

October/November

TEXAS RENAISSANCE FESTIVAL

Plantersville. *Take TX 105 west past Montgomery to Plantersville, then south (left) on FM 1774 for about 6 miles (see **Navasota**)*

October

CAJUN CATFISH FESTIVAL

Downtown on the square • 539-6009 • Mid-October • Admission • W

This three-day festival is a Cajun blast of music, food, dancing, and games. A 5-K fun run, bingo, kids' games, arts and crafts, and a lot of community spirit make this festival a terrific event.

ACCOMMODATIONS

($ = under $45, $$ = $46–$60, $$$ = $61–$80, $$$$ = $81–$100, $$$$$ over $100)
Room tax 10.25%

APRIL SOUND COUNTRY CLUB AND RESORT

TX 105 about 9 miles west (P.O. Box 253, 77305) • 800-41ROOMS (417-6667), 588-1101 • $$–$$$$$ • W+ 1 room in Villa

The resort, with one- and two-story facilities, offers 9 hotel-type rooms in the Villa ($$–$$$) and 64 one- to three-bedroom condos in the rental pool ($$$–$$$$$). Cable TV. Room phones (no charge for local calls). Pets limited (check in advance). Eighteen-hole and 9-hole golf courses, 17-court tennis center (4 covered courts, 9 outdoor lighted courts), 2 adult outdoor pools, family outdoor pool, children's outdoor wading pool, Jacuzzi, sauna. Temporary memberships available at racquetball/health club in Conroe. Restaurant and lounge. Marina with boat rentals. Boat slips are available on first come, first served basis.

DEL LAGO RESORT AND CONFERENCE CENTER

Take TX 105 about 12 miles west to Walden Rd., then right to resort **(600 Del Lago Blvd., Montgomery 77356) • 582-6100 or in Texas 800-833-3078, outside Texas 800-558-1317 • $$$–$$$$$ • W variable • No-smoking rooms**

The 21-story Del Lago Resort has 310 units that are all suites and include 16 no-smoking units. Two-bedroom golf course cottages, villas with private boat slips. Cable TV. Room phones (charge for local calls). No pets. Restaurant and lounge. Eighteen-hole championship golf course, 11 lighted tennis courts, health spa, heated outdoor pool, saunas, steambath, Jacuzzi. Marina with boat rentals. Children's recreation program. All facilities are open to nonmembers on a fee basis.

HOLIDAY INN—RAMADA LTD.

1601 I-45S at TX 75 (Frazier St. exit) • 756-8941 or 800-HOLIDAY (800-465-4329) • $–$$ • W+ 2 rooms • No-smoking rooms

This two-story Holiday Inn has completely refurbished the main section with the older section becoming a Ramada Ltd. with less frills and lower rates. The Holiday Inn has cable TV with HBO and pay channel. Room phones (charge for local calls). Pets OK. Restaurant. Club (guests automatically members). Outdoor pool.

Other Accommodations

For a complete listing of accommodations including bed and breakfasts and lakeside condo rentals as well as motels, contact the Chamber of Commerce at 746-6644.

CROCKETT

Houston County Seat • 7,550 • (409)
Crockett was incorporated as the third county seat in Texas on December 29, 1837, just six months after Texas became a Republic. The townsite was a gift from A. E. Gossett and his father Elijah, both veterans of the Battle of San Jacinto. The Gossetts named the new county for Sam Houston and the town for David Crockett, the Tennessee scout who was a neighbor of Elijah's in Tennessee. Tradition says Crockett camped here in 1836 on his way to the Alamo and was recognized by Elijah.

TOURIST SERVICES

HOUSTON COUNTY CHAMBER OF COMMERCE
1100 Edminston Drive (P.O. Box 307, 75835) • 1-888-269-2359
www.crockett.org • 544-2359 • W

HISTORIC PLACES

DOWNS-ALDRICH HOUSE

206 N. 7th • 544-4804 • Wednesday, Saturday, and Sunday 2–4 or by appointment through Chamber of Commerce • Adults $2, students $1, children 50¢
Built in the 1890s by J. E. Downes, this imposing two-and-a-half-story frame house is a combination of Queen Anne and Eastlake styles. It is listed in the National Register of Historic Places.

MONROE-CROOK HOUSE

709 E. Houston • 544-2359 • Wednesday 9:30–11:30, Saturday and Sunday 2–4 Adults $2, students $1, children 50¢
This elegant Greek Revival house was built in 1854 by a grand nephew of President James Monroe. It is also listed in the National Register of Historic Places.

SIDE TRIPS

CADDOAN MOUNDS STATE HISTORICAL PARK

Take TX 21 north about 28 miles **• 1-409-858-3218 • Open Friday–Monday 10–6 • Admission • W variable**
Here is an informative and thought-provoking look at the most sophisticated prehistoric Indian culture in Texas with interpretive exhibits, audio-visual program, and one-mile self-guided tour around the reconstructed dwelling, mounds, and village area. Excavations reveal occupations of the site since 6,000 B.C.

DAVY CROCKETT NATIONAL FOREST

Take TX 7 east about 20 miles to Ratcliff Recreation Area **• 544-2046 • Open at all times • Free • W variable**
This forest spreads over more than 161,000 acres in Houston and Trinity counties. The 45-acre Ratcliff Lake has facilities for tent camping, picnic area, swimming beach, bathhouse, amphitheater, interpretive forest walk, and a hiking trail. There is a fee for campers and swimmers. **The Four C National Recreation Trail** begins its 20-mile marked hike at the Ratcliff Recreation Area and ends at the Neches Bluff Observation Site. A canoe trail is also available at the

Big Slough Wilderness Area six miles north of Ratcliff off Forest Service Road 517. For information write: District Ranger, U.S. Forest Service, 1240 E. Loop 304, Crockett 75835.

HOUSTON COUNTY LAKE
Take FM 229 west about 7 miles and follow signs • **544-8466 (Crockett Family Resort)** • **Free** • **W variable**
This small 1,282-acre lake is proud of its "Big Bass" records. The Crockett Family Resort offers camping, clubhouse, cabins, swimming, restaurant, and marina ($).

MISSION TEJAS STATE HISTORICAL PARK
Take TX 21 northeast about 21 miles to Park Rd. 44 • **1-409-687-2394, Web site: http://www.tpwd.state.tx.us** • **Open seven days 8–5 for day use** • **Admission W variable**
This 118-acre park contains a log replica of the first Spanish mission building in East Texas. Spanish Franciscan priests founded Mission *San Francisco de los Tejas* in 1690 to protect Texas from French encroachment. Plagued with troubles, the mission moved several times and finally gave up and moved to San Antonio in 1731 after Spain withdrew its military support. Also in the park is the restored **Rice Family Log Cabin,** a dogtrot home built in 1828. Tent and trailer camping available (fee), nature trail, hiking, playground, and picnic areas.

ANNUAL EVENTS
February

LOVEFEST
Take TX 19 about 14 miles south to Lovelady • **544-1359 (Chamber of Commerce)** • **Second Saturday of February**
The place to be on Saint Valentine's Day is Lovelady with its chili cookoff, big arts and crafts show, and a great hometown parade.

September
WORLD'S CHAMPION FIDDLER'S FESTIVAL
Ponth Ag-Arena and Crockett Civic Center off Loop 304E • **544-2359 (Chamber of Commerce)** • **Second weekend in June**
This contest has been going on for more than 50 years. The fiddling goes on at the Ponth Ag-Arena, and the arts and crafts and food booths are in the Crockett Civic Center. A fun-run and additional entertainment are part of the weekend.

October
GRAPELAND PEANUT FESTIVAL
Second weekend in October
Arts and crafts, food, Peanut Queen Contest, and peanuts.

RESTAURANTS
($ = under $7, $$ = $8–$17, $$$ = $18–$25, $$$$ = over $25 for one person excluding drinks, tax, and tip.)

WOODEN NICKEL

Loop 304E just north of TX 21 • 544-8011 • Lunch and dinner
Tuesday–Saturday, Sunday lunch only. Closed Monday • $–$$ • AE, MC, V
W • Children's menu

This rustic building was originally an art gallery and some of the original works still decorate the walls. The menu includes barbecue, steaks, burgers, and a Mexican food buffet.

ACCOMMODATIONS

($ = under $45, $$ = $46–$60, $$$ = $61–$80, $$$$ = $81–$100, $$$$$ = over $100)
Room tax 13%

CROCKETT INN

1600 Loop 304SE, between TX 19 and US 287 • 1-800-633-9518 or 544-5611
$ • No-smoking rooms

This two-story motel has 86 units including 4 suites and 12 no-smoking rooms. Cable TV. Small pets OK. Restaurant. Private club (guests automatically members, temporary membership available for non-guests). Outdoor pool, Jacuzzi.

Bed and Breakfasts

COUNTRY BLESSINGS

Rt. 3, Box 80-H • 544-7329 • $$$ • MC, V • W variable

This handsome country home rests on 42 acres north of Crockett (ask for directions) and offers three rooms with baths as well as pastures and a creek for roaming. Breakfast specialties include egg and sausage casserole and home-made cinnamon rolls. Turned-down bed service and bedside evening refreshments offer a touch of elegance. No smoking and no pets or children under 12 are allowed.

WARFIELD HOUSE

712 East Houston Avenue • 544-4037 or 888-988-8800 • $$$–$$$$

This elegant Prairie-style house offers 4 guest rooms, each with private bath. All are beautifully furnished in fine antiques. No children under 12 are allowed, no pets, and no smoking inside the house. Breakfast is served in the formal dining room. Swimming pool and spa are available to guests.

HENDERSON

Rusk County Seat • 11,139 • (903)

Founded in 1843, the town was named for J. Pickney Henderson, who went on to become the first governor of Texas. Forestry and agriculture were the major props of the economy in the early years until wildcatter C. M. "Dad" Joiner brought in the "Daisy Bradford Number 3" about six miles west of town in 1930, opening up the great East Texas Oil Field. The Joe Roughneck Monument in Pioneer Park was erected by Lone Star Steel in 1956 as a tribute to the working men in the oil fields, known in their trade as "rough-necks." The park is equipped with derrick-covered picnic tables. Now the county's diversified income is based on oil and gas, lignite coal mining, agriculture, forestry, and light industry.

TOURIST SERVICES

TOURIST DEVELOPMENT DEPT., RUSK COUNTY CHAMBER OF COMMERCE
201 N. Main (75652) • 657-5528 • W

MUSEUMS

DEPOT MUSEUM AND CHILDREN'S DISCOVERY CENTER
514 N. High, behind the library • 657-4303 • Monday–Friday 9–12, 1–5. Saturday 9–1. Closed Sunday • Adults $2, children $1 • W+

One of the prize exhibits on the museum's grounds is the "Arnold Outhouse." This ornate, Victorian-style three-holer, built in 1908, has been awarded the historical landmark designation by the Texas Historical Commission, the first outhouse to be so recognized in Texas. Also outside on the grounds is the Walling Log Cabin, built in 1841 and furnished with antiques from that time. The museum, housed in a restored 1901 Missouri-Pacific Depot, is divided into two parts: a history museum, which traces the county's development, and a children's learning center. Children must be accompanied by an adult.

HISTORIC PLACES

HOWARD-DICKENSON HOUSE
501 S. Main • 657-6925 or 657-5528 (Chamber of Commerce)
Monday–Friday 1–5 or by appointment • Admission $1

Built in 1855 by James and David Howard, this house was the first brick home in the county. Sam Houston, first president of the Republic and a cousin of the wife of David Howard, was a frequent visitor to the house in its early years. Houston's campaign trunk is displayed in the house. Furnishings are from the 1860 to 1900 period.

SPORTS AND ACTIVITIES

OAK HILL RACEWAY
Take TX 43 northeast to FM 1716, then north (left) to track, approximately 10 miles from town • 643-2850 • Admission depends on event • W variable

Both motorcycle races and high-speed go-cart races are held here during the March-through-November season.

SHOPPING

B&E LINEN MANUFACTURING OUTLET STORE
700 W. Main • 657-2210

All the linens manufactured by this company are for the kitchen and dining room. Bargain hunters will find tables heaped with a selection of linen placemats, napkins, tablecloths, aprons, pot holders, and coasters.

FAULKNER'S ANTIQUES
108 TX 64 • 657-3481

The Faulkners are direct importers, making several trips to England each year to buy antiques for their shop.

SIDE TRIPS

MARTIN CREEK STATE PARK

Take TX 43 northeast approximately 19 miles to FM 1716, turn right and follow signs to lake • **836-4336** • **Open at all times** • **$3 per vehicle per day**
  (*see* Carthage)

LAKE STRIKER

Take US 79 southwest about 18 miles to lake signs, then south (left) to lake **854-2404 (Marina)** • **Open at all times** • **Free**
  A 2,400-acre power plant lake open for recreational use. Facilities for fishing, boating, waterskiing, picnicking, and camping. Fee.

ANNUAL EVENTS

April

DEPOT MUSEUM QUILT SHOW

514 N. High • **657-4303** • **Usually second weekend in April** • **Free** • **W+**
  This has been called the "best quilt show between Dallas and Houston." Between 150 and 200 quilts are on display, and expert quilters are on hand to demonstrate their craft and answer questions.

HOUSTON

Harris County Seat • **1,697,759** • **(713) and (281) All numbers (713) unless otherwise noted.**
  The name of this, Texas' largest city, was the first word spoken from the surface of the moon in 1969. Houstonians would say that's only fitting. The can-do city's climb to planetary prominence began, improbably enough, with a newspaper ad. In 1836, two flamboyant entrepreneurs, John and Augustus Allen, purchased land along Buffalo Bayou. They shrewdly christened it Houston for the hero of San Jacinto, the decisive battle in Texas's fight for independence from Mexico. They drew up a fancy map, and the legislature voted the town capital of the new Republic. Overnight Houston became the most important town in Texas, yet it was virtually uninhabited.
  Claims that the town had direct access to the Gulf of Mexico were much exaggerated. When the steamship, the *Laura M,* poked its way laboriously through the muck of Buffalo Bayou in 1838 to prove the stream navigable, it missed the "city" entirely. In 1839 Houston's unceasing mud and yellow fever epidemics sent the government to Austin. Survival looked gloomy indeed. But eventually, because the city's bayou was the only east-west waterway in the area, the Allen's sales pitch that Houston would become "the great interior commercial emporium of Texas" proved true.
  By 1840 Houston was shipping mules, cotton, cattle, and sugar cane from the Brazos Valley to Galveston. Twenty years later, the city's economy was based on "white gold," and Houston became a major competitor in the world market for cotton.

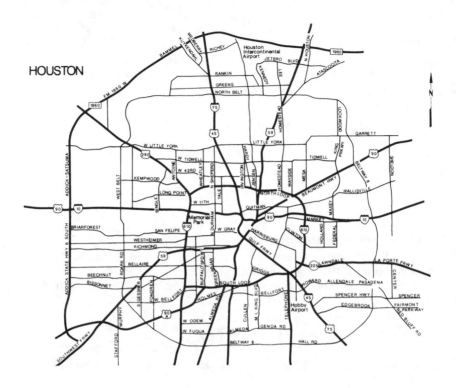

The next great hurdle was to establish a railroad center, and Houston was soon the city where "eleven railroads meet the sea." Even the Civil War did not halt Houston's growth.

Houston's rival for the largest city in Texas was Galveston, The Queen City of the Gulf. But, one dreadful day in September 1900, The Great Storm practically wiped Galveston from the face of the earth. It never recovered, and Houston was the star in Texas' crown.

Black Gold! The next year sealed Houston's destiny to become one of America's great cities. The world's second gusher broke through the Beaumont salt dome and Spindletop changed Houston, Texas, the nation, and the world. Oil! Black gold! By 1906, Houston boasted 30 oil companies, 7 banks, and 25 newspapers.

Even as the cotton market collapsed in 1914, a 100-year dream came true. Officially opened, the Ship Channel snaked its way 51 miles to the Gulf. Heavy industry and hustlers of all sorts soon arrived. In the years just after World War I, Houston shipped more than 194,000 barrels of oil a day, plus tons of agricultural goods. Even in the Great Depression, not one Houston bank failed, and a federal grant to deepen the Ship Channel added to the economy. By 1936, the city's centennial, its grain elevators were full and the prices of oil and cotton were on the rise. The post-World War II era brought more boom days, and by 1948 Houston's port was second only to New York. Petrochemical plants, steel mills, shipyards, and natural gas lines cranked up Houston's economy, and its list of millionaires grew apace.

The '60s saw the Texas Medical Center becoming a leader in cancer treatment and heart surgery, and Houston became the home of the Space Program. Houstonians put astronauts on the moon and dollars in the city's pockets. Space was, and is, good business for the area. By the end of the '60s, Houston's mud and mosquitoes had become 450 square miles of concrete. Stubbornly rejecting any zoning ordinances, city officials semi-mendaciously pointed out that traffic flow was as efficient as cities with zoning. Developers built with little restraint, and Houstonians called no zoning freedom.

In the mid-'80s the price of oil plummeted, and the oil-based economy was shattered. Business had been so good for so long, a major economic crisis was unbelievable. Even though the entire state was affected, Houston was in shock. After several years of doom and gloom, during which the faint-hearted fled, Houston's natural optimism and can-do attitude came bubbling back. The now more-diverse economy is solid and on the rise. A downtown renaissance is underway, and the city has even applied to host the Olympics. Author James Street once described Houston as, "An air-conditioned tower of Babel, anchored on gold, gall and guts." He had that right—just ask any Houstonian.

TOURIST SERVICES

Tour information for specific points of interest (e.g., the Astrodome, the Port of Houston) is listed with the entries for those sights.

GRAY LINE TOURS

602 Sampson • 223-8800 Monday–Friday 8 to 5

Besides general tours of the city, Gray Line offers special packages that focus on the Johnson Space Center and Galveston.

GREATER HOUSTON CONVENTION AND VISITORS BUREAU

801 Congress • 227-4422 • Web site: http://www.houston.com/

Whether you're on your own or with a group of hundreds, this office has all sorts of printed material and brochures on local sights, along with personalized service to help plan your outings.

WALKING TOUR

622-2081 • Third Sunday of each month at 2 P.M. • Admission

Offered by the Houston chapter of the American Institute of Architects, it begins from the lobby of the Hyatt Regency Hotel at 1200 Louisiana and takes about three hours and covers more than 50 buildings and public spaces in the downtown area. Reservations are suggested.

BIRD'S-EYE VIEW

SAN JACINTO MONUMENT

See Other Points of Interest.

RENAISSANCE HOUSTON HOTEL
Greenway Plaza (Southwest Freeway at Edloe) • 629-1200

The City Lights lounge on the Stouffer's 20th floor (*see* Accommodations) provides one of the more centrally located views of Houston. To the east is downtown; to the west the Galleria and the "mini-downtown" along Post Oak Blvd.; and to the south is the Astrodome.

TEXAS COMMERCE TOWER

600 Travis • 223-0441 • Closed weekends

From the moment you step off the elevators on the 60th floor of Texas Commerce Tower—at 75 stories, the tallest building in the city—the panorama begins. Being able to look down on most of the other downtown buildings might inspire a feeling of power, but the view goes even farther, providing a sweeping vista from the south to the west.

TRANSCO TOWER

2800 Post Oak Blvd. • 850-8841 • Closed weekends

The 60th floor of the 64-story Transco Tower—the tallest building in the country located outside a downtown area—has been the site of various parties and performances, thus offering a vast horizon as part of the entertainment.

MUSEUMS AND ART GALLERIES

Commercial art galleries are listed under Shopping.

BAYOU BEND

1 Westcott St. • 529-8773 • Admission

The Museum of Fine Arts is proprietor of Bayou Bend that began in 1928 as the residence of the late Ima Hogg and her two brothers. Miss Ima, as she was affectionately known, filled her home with priceless antiques, with many pieces given to the museum. Ownership of the 28-room mansion, its furnishings, and the 14-acre grounds was gradually transferred to the museum by Miss Ima, who died in 1975. Open to the public since 1966, the mansion houses an extensive collection of American decorative arts covering the seventeenth to nineteenth centuries. Tours are conducted in groups of four, and no one under 14 permitted. Children are welcome to tour the grounds and first floor on the second Sunday of every month except March and April.

BLAFFER GALLERY

University of Houston, central campus, Fine Arts Building (Entrance 16 off Cullen Blvd.) • 743-9530 • Open Tuesday–Friday 10–5, Saturday–Sunday 1–5. Closed Monday • Free • W first floor only

The Blaffer Gallery sponsors a continually changing series of exhibitions, ranging from contemporary paintings, sculpture, and photography to old masters. Maps are available that point out the various outdoor sculptures and paintings that enhance the UH campus.

CONTEMPORARY ARTS MUSEUM

5216 Montrose • 526-3129 • Open Tuesday–Thursday 10–9, Friday–Saturday 10–5 and Sunday noon–5. Closed Monday • Free • W

This museum does not have a permanent collection, all the better to represent the diverse nature of contemporary art. Housed in one of the most distinctive buildings in Houston (the exterior is stainless steel), the museum has introduced the city to both new and established artists in a variety of media. The larger exhibitions are staged in the Upper Gallery. The smaller Perspectives Gallery downstairs introduces new artists to the local community. Guided tours of the museum are held on Sunday afternoons at 3. Groups can reserve tours anytime.

FIRE MUSEUM

2403 Milam • 524-2526 • Open Tuesday–Saturday 10–4. Closed Sunday and Monday • Adults $2, children (3–17) $1, seniors $1, students with ID $1 • W

As you might guess, the predominant color in Houston's Fire Museum is red—four-alarm red. Probably the brightest red is on a 1951 coffee wagon that the Fire Department's Ladies Auxiliary operated to bring coffee and doughnuts to fire fighters at multiple-alarm blazes. The building is a former fire station, built in 1898. But some of the equipment contained within predates even the premises. A "water tower" truck, now valued at more than half a million dollars, dates from 1893 (a motor was added to the truck during the 1920s). The Fire Museum is intended to preserve the history of the Houston Fire Department, but contributions of memorabilia have included items from all over the country. Souvenirs are available.

HOUSTON CENTER FOR PHOTOGRAPHY

1441 W. Alabama • 529-4755 • Open Wednesday–Friday 11–5, Saturday and Sunday, noon–5. Closed Monday and Tuesday • Free • W

The nonprofit HCP is a prime showcase for contemporary photography by local, national, and international photographers. Besides a regular series of exhibitions, HCP also sponsors lectures and workshops by a variety of photographic authorities.

HOUSTON POLICE ACADEMY MUSEUM

17000 Aldine-Westfield Rd. • 230-2300 • Open Monday–Friday 8–4. Closed Saturday and Sunday • Free • W

While tracing the development of the city's police department, beginning with the days when Houston was still a frontier town, the Police Academy Museum also breaks down the barriers between police and public by giving a realistic portrayal of police life. The museum, located at the police academy, has amassed a collection of more than 5,000 items. This includes uniforms, weapons, and vehicles. A portion of the academy is part of the guided museum tours.

MENIL COLLECTION

1515 Sul Ross • 525-9400 • Open Wednesday–Sunday 11–7. Closed Monday and Tuesday • Free • W

The fact that it needs its own building to be displayed properly should give some idea of the scope of the collection amassed by the late Dominique de Menil and her late husband, John. Family holdings include more than 10,000 items assembled over 30 years. Works range from rare Paleolithic objects to contemporary works with particular attention to surrealist paintings and sculptures. The collection also has antiquities from the Mediterranean and Asia Minor, objects from Byzantine civilization, and tribal art from Africa and North America.

MUSEUM OF FINE ARTS

1001 Bissonnet • 639-7300 • Open Tuesday–Saturday 10–5, Thursdays 10–9, Sunday 12:15–6 • Adults $3, 18 and under $1.50 (General museum free on Thursdays) • W

If you approach the Museum of Fine Arts from the north, and then from the south, you might think you're heading toward two different buildings. The tall stone columns on the south side, which face Mecom Fountain and the Warwick Hotel, are part of the original structure erected in 1924. But the north entrance, which faces Bissonnet, is a different style of architecture, reflecting the more modern works displayed on that side of the building. Since its opening, the MFA has been the city's primary repository for artworks ranging from antiquity to the modern era. Included in the museum's permanent collection are paintings by Western artist Frederic Remington, early European masters, ancient and medieval art, nineteenth- and twentieth-century decorative arts, oriental art, and pre-Columbian and tribal arts. The museum annually sponsors as many as 20 exhibitions from other museums and major collections from around the world. Lectures, film series, and the Hirsch Library for Art History are also available to the public. Across Bissonnet, at 5101 Montrose, is the **MFA Alfred C. Glassell, Jr., School of Art,** which offers classes in all manner of the visual arts and art history for adults and children, plus an exhibit area for contemporary art. Between the museum and the school is the **Lillie and Hugh Roy Cullen Sculpture Garden.** MFA tours are given at noon Tuesday through Saturday and Sunday at 1:30 pm. For visitors who come to the museum expressly for the tour, there is no charge for admission.

MUSEUM OF NATURAL SCIENCE

1 Hermann Circle Dr. • 639-4629 • Open Monday–Saturday 9–6, Sunday noon–6 • General museum admission: adults $3, children (3–11) $2, seniors $2 (Free Thursday 2–6) • W

Depending on which way you look in the Museum of Natural Science, you're liable to see everything from towering dinosaur skeletons to heavenly bodies. While the museum gives a broad perspective of its subject matter, it also contains extra-admission attractions such as the **Burke Baker Planetarium,** the splendid **Cockrell Butterfly Center;** the **Museum of Medical Science,** which combines with the museum to depict the world inside, around, and above us. The museum maintains extensive exhibits on areas that have played major roles in Houston's development including the **Rice Energy Hall** and the **Isaac Arnold Hall of Space Science.** The models and displays of the **Harry C. Weiss Hall of Petroleum Science and Technology** demonstrate the development of oil from its formation in the earth to its use in modern products. **The Isaac Arnold Hall of Space Science** contains artifacts from the Mercury, Gemini, and Apollo space programs. Just strolling around the museum, you can't miss the 70-foot *Diplodocus* dinosaur skeleton that dominates the main hall. The planetarium offers a series of special presentations recreating the heavens on its domed ceiling and analyzing the different aspects of the universe, from planets to stars to comets. **The Museum of Medical Science** is on the second floor with its popular transparent anatomical mannequin. **The Wortham Imax Theatre,** with its six-story movie screen, is awe-inspiring with its magnificent productions. You can dance in outer space, jump into a volcano, and get drenched in a rain forest. Shows are on the hour from 11–8 on Sunday, 10–8 Monday through Thursday, 10–9 Friday, and 10–10 Saturday. Reservations are recommended. Admission charged.

MUSEUM OF PRINTING HISTORY

324 W. Clay • 522-4652 • Open Tuesday–Sunday 9–5. Closed Monday Free • W

Located in the Graphic Arts Conference Center, the Museum of Printing History is a rare item—just like many of its holdings. Described as the only printing history museum of its kind, the museum lists among its greatest treasures one of nine remaining originals of the *Hykamanto Dharani Scroll* that was printed in Japan more than 1,200 years ago. Other items from the museum's collection (which includes presses and published materials) are of more recent vintage, such as historic newspaper headlines. They tell of such events as the Battle of Waterloo and Abraham Lincoln's assassination. Group tours are available.

RICE MEDIA CENTER

Rice University, entrance 8 off University Blvd. • 527-4894 (527-4853 or 527-4882 for film series information) • Exhibit space closed Saturday and Sunday • $5 film charge • W

The Rice Media Center is best known for the series of classic and contemporary films it screens throughout the year. The center also contains an exhibit space for photography by local, national, and international photographers.

ROTHKO CHAPEL

3000 Yupon • 524-9839 • Open daily 10–6 • Free • W

This octagonal brick structure, located next to the campus of the University of St. Thomas, houses 14 works by the late abstract expressionist painter Mark Rothko. It is considered a multi-denominational place of worship, and many visitors meditate in the chapel's solitude.

OTHER POINTS OF INTEREST

ALLEN'S LANDING

Main at Commerce on Buffalo Bayou

The modest little park at Allen's Landing on the north side of downtown may not look like much, but this site played a significant role in the birth of Houston. It was here that the Allen brothers, John and Augustus, first set foot, in 1836, on the land they would help develop into a thriving city. Allen's Landing is often overlooked among Houston's attractions, but its designation as a park in the mid-1960s helped preserve its place in history.

ANHEUSER-BUSCH BREWERY

775 Gellhorn • 670-1696 (tour office) • 45-minute guided tours offered 9–4 Monday–Saturday. Self-guided tours offered continuously 9–4 Monday–Saturday • Free

It seems like every time someone takes a brewery tour, the first thing they talk about is getting a free beer at the end. Guests of drinking age (21 in Texas) do receive two samples from among the nine different brands produced at the brewery. But there is more to this walk-through than just a couple of drinks. It includes a review of the brewing process from grains to finished product. Information is also provided on the history of Anheuser-Busch, going back to 1861 in St. Louis when Adolphus Busch married Lilly Anheuser and turned her father's struggling brewery into an industry giant.

ARMAND BAYOU NATURE CENTER

8600 Bay Area Blvd. • 474-2551 • Wednesday–Saturday 9–5, Sunday 12–sundown. Closed Monday and Tuesday • Admission • W variable

The largest of the area's nature parks (2,000 acres), Armand Bayou represents a diverse mix of terrains—forest, prairie, and marsh. Besides the trail system, boating on the bayou is also a popular diversion. Visitors can either bring their own boats or take advantage of a free group ride.

ASTRODOME

8400 Kirby Dr. at South Loop 610 • For tours, enter from west gate on Kirby 799-9500 • Tours daily at 11 A.M., 1 and 3 P.M.; no tours on days when events scheduled • Adults $4, children 4–11 $3, under 4 free • W variable

It's now the world's oldest and smallest domed stadium, but the Astrodome, formally the Harris County Domed Stadium, is still one of the most widely known attractions of the city. For now it's home for the Houston Astros (baseball) and events as diverse as bullfights, lacrosse matches, motorcycle races, and rodeos. Opened in 1965, this is the brainchild of the late Roy Hofheinz. Featured on the tours are the press area, the skyboxes, and a slide presentation of the history of the stadium.

CHRIST CHURCH CATHEDRAL

1117 Texas • 222-2593 • W

The Episcopal Christ Church Cathedral, built in 1893, is the city's oldest church still standing on its original site. Noted for its Gothic Revival architecture, the cathedral does not schedule tours. Besides attending regular services, another way to see it is at lunchtime, when **The Cloisters Restaurant** (*see* Restaurants) serves lunch in the church's cloisters section.

DOWNTOWN TUNNEL SYSTEM

There's something growing underneath downtown Houston, and it shows no signs of stopping. But people who work downtown don't seem to mind at all. The tunnel system allows for easier passage between buildings without having to brave the elements or traffic. The system runs under most of the major buildings downtown. With its various branches, it is approximately five miles long, and the city has plans to add more tunnel routes. Access to the tunnels is possible from the lobbies of several major buildings. These tunnels aren't just dark holes under the ground. All sorts of restaurants and shops abound underground and do a heavy business.

EDITH L. MOORE NATURE SANCTUARY

440 Wilchester • 932-1392 • Open daily from sunrise to sunset • Free • W

The Houston Audubon Society presides over this 18-acre plot off Memorial Dr. The animal life is abundant, both on land and in the water. The aquatic life can be observed from a deck at the sanctuary's pond and in Rummel Creek, which runs through the property. The log cabin (complete with screened-in porch) of the late Edith L. Moore now serves as the visitors center and bookstore (932-1408).

HARRIS COUNTY HERITAGE SOCIETY

Sam Houston Park • 1100 Bagby • 655-1912 • Open Monday–Saturday 10–4; Sunday 1–5 • Tours every hour • Admission

The Society maintains a collection of early Texas homes and buildings from the mid-1800s, complete with antique park benches. **The Museum of Texas History,** tracing 150 years of Lone Star life, is also at the site. The Yesteryear Shop sells Texas books and collectibles.

HERMANN PARK

6001 Fannin at Hermann Dr. • 845-1034 • Free • W

Though adjacent to the Texas Medical Center and Rice University, Hermann Park has plenty of attractions to avoid being overshadowed by its highfalutin neighbors. Included in the park's 388 acres are the **Houston Zoo** (see below), the **Museum of Natural Science,** with its **Cockrell Butterfly Center, Burke Baker Planetarium** (*see* Museums and Art Galleries), **Miller Theater** (*see* Performing Arts), a golf course (*see* Sports and Activities), and the **Houston Garden Center.** And if the kids aren't sufficiently astounded by all of that, a miniature train takes passengers on a leisurely circuit of the park.

HOUSTON ARBORETUM AND NATURE CENTER

4501 Woodway • 681-8433 • Open daily 8:30–6 • Free • W

Drivers speeding along the West Loop may not pay much notice to the trees on the east side of the freeway near the Woodway/Memorial exit, but the heavily wooded area is 154 acres devoted to nature in a neighborhood where concrete and steel get most of the attention. Visitors can stroll through the arboretum's five miles of trails. For those needing direction, guided tours are available. The arboretum includes the **Aline McAshan Botanical Hall** with a gift shop and Discovery Room of animals and plant life for kids to examine.

HOUSTON ZOOLOGICAL GARDENS

1513 N. MacGregor in Hermann Park • 523-5888 • Open daily 10–6
Adults $2.50, seniors $2, children 50¢ (free on city holidays) • W

The Houston Zoological Gardens, known more simply as the Houston Zoo, have undergone several changes and expansion in recent years to provide special areas for the various forms of animal and aquatic life and to allow for closer observation by visitors. Highlights include a 41-exhibit aquarium and a large cat facility. The **George R. Brown Education Center** features educational exhibits and auditorium programs. There is a children's zoo as well. A new primate house is underway, plus an extensive modernization program.

JESSE H. JONES PARK

20634 Kenswick. *Take FM 1960 Exit off I-45 to Kenswick* **• 446-8588**
Open daily 8–7, Nature Center 8–5 • Free • W

Jones Park gives a sampling of the swamps that were once prevalent along the Gulf Coast. Four cypress swamps can be viewed from the boardwalk and overlook deck. A fern trail on the park's 154 acres leads to a white, sandy beach on Spring Creek. Guided tours can be reserved in advance, or visitors can use one of the self-guided trails.

MERCER ARBORETUM AND BOTANIC GARDENS

Humble. 22506 Aldine-Westfield Rd. • 443-0176 • Open Monday–Saturday 8–7; Sunday 10–7 • Free • W

Nature has received more help from man here than in most other arboretums, but the effect of the trees and shrubs that have been planted is reminiscent of the densely wooded Big Thicket in East Texas. In addition to trails and a greenhouse, the Arboretum has a meeting room and resource library for public use.

ORANGE SHOW

2401 Munger • 926-6368 • Open Saturday and Sunday noon–5. Summers also: Wednesday–Friday 9–1 (closed December–March) • Adults $1, children under 12 free

Jeff McKissack was obsessed with the orange. He created a maze, museum, steam engine, and narrative exhibits to extol the virtues of what he calls this perfect food. Here is an incredible collection of junk assembled into what is now enchanting folk art.

PORT OF HOUSTON

Board tour boat *Sam Houston* at 7300 Clinton Dr., Gate No. 8 (Clinton exit off East Loop) • Tours Tuesday, Wednesday, Friday, and Saturday at 10 and 2:30; Thursday and Sunday 2:30 only. Advance reservations required. Closed in July • Free

The Port of Houston is one of the primary reasons for Houston's success as a center of commerce. The port, the culmination of the 50-mile Ship Channel from the Gulf of Mexico, is first in the United States in foreign trade and the third largest U.S. seaport in total tonnage. More than 4,000 ships per year call at the port. The 90-minute tours aboard the inspection boat *Sam Houston* give visitors a close-up look at the port's facilities, including the Turning Basin and more than 40 wharves. There is always a lengthy waiting list for the tours, so reservations should be made at least a month in advance. But if you don't want to wait that long, a drive across the East Loop bridge over the Ship Channel gives a good view of the port.

SAM HOUSTON RACE PARK

7575 N. Sam Houston Parkway (Beltway 8) at US 290 • 281-807-7223 Open Tuesday–Friday nights; Saturday and Sunday afternoon during season Admission: adults $3, children under 12 free, seniors $1

After the racing season, the track is open for simulcasts of races from around the world. Betting is permitted. With 250 betting windows, 400 monitors, state-of-the-art sports bars, dining in the club, and stands that hold 25,000 race fans, the Park is worth a visit even if you don't wager.

TEXAS MEDICAL CENTER

Visitor Information Center, 1155 Holcombe • 790-1136 • Tours 10 A.M. Monday–Thursday, 9:30 A.M. and 1 P.M. Friday • Reservations suggested Free • W

One of the most renowned medical complexes in the world, the Medical Center covers approximately 500 acres and includes more than 15 hospitals and medical and nursing schools. It is located south of downtown and is bounded by Holcombe, Fannin, MacGregor, and Outer Belt Dr. The Medical Center attracts patients from around the world who come seeking the services of a medical community that includes heart surgeons Dr. Michael E. DeBakey and Dr. Denton Cooley. Tours include a 35-minute van ride through the complex and a video presentation explaining the Medical Center. Special tours are available for students and large groups.

TRANQUILITY PARK

Downtown in the block bounded by Smith, Walker, Rusk, and Bagby • W

The grassy embankments and gently sloping paved walkways of this park across from City Hall lure many downtown workers to have their lunch outside or simply sit in the sun while the rest of Houston buzzes on by. The park is built around the pools and metallic columns of the **Wortham Fountain.** Named for the Sea of Tranquility base of the first moon landing in 1969, the park is one of the main areas of activity during the Houston Festival in March (*see* Annual Events).

WATER WALL

2800 Post Oak Blvd. at Hidalgo, next to Transco Tower

The Water Wall is a semicircular, 64-foot-high structure that mesmerizes romantic couples and small children. Thousands of gallons of water a minute cascade down both sides of the wall, though the inside of the curved waterfall, fronted by three brick archways, is flowing more often than the outside, which faces the street. The Water Wall and the grassy expanse between it and the Transco Tower are a popular gathering place at night, when the lights on the fountain create a particularly striking effect.

SPORTS AND ACTIVITIES

College Sports

HOUSTON BAPTIST UNIVERSITY (HUSKIES)

Home events for all sports (no football or baseball) are played on campus, 7502 Fondren. Ticket information 774-7661, ext. 341.

RICE UNIVERSITY (OWLS)

Home events for all sports played on campus, 6100 Main. Tickets 527-4068.

TEXAS SOUTHERN UNIVERSITY (TIGERS)

Home sports events played on campus, 3100 Cleburne, except football, played at Robertson Stadium on nearby central campus of University of Houston. Tickets 313-7011.

UNIVERSITY OF HOUSTON (COUGARS)

Home sports events played on campus, 4800 Calhoun, except football played at the Astrodome, Kirby Dr. at South Loop. Tickets 743-9444.

Cycling

ALKEK VELODROME

19008 Samus Rd. (I-10 at Barker-Cypress in Cullen Park) • 578-0858

If city streets or the hike-and-bike trails don't fulfill your cycling needs, try the Alkek Velodrome. The cycling arena meets Olympic specifications—it was built for the 1986 U.S. Olympic Festival and hosted the 1988 U.S. Olympic Trials. The oval outdoor track is 333-⅓ meters long with 33-degree embankments. The velodrome offers open riding 5–9 Mondays and 2–6 Saturdays and Sundays. Track bikes only 5–9 Wednesdays and Fridays. Fees are charged per session, and bikes are available for rent.

Equestrian Sports

WESTHEIMER STABLES

12608 W. Bellfort • 281-495-2293 • Open daily 9–6, weather permitting
This "range" for riders occupies 80 acres of land in west Houston. Charge is $20 per hour for horses and $10 per hour ($6 per half hour) for children's ponies.

Golf

Fees at the city's municipal golf courses are $12 per person on weekdays and $15 per person on weekends. Golf cart rental $18. Fees at private courses that are open to the public (listed below) are higher and vary depending on the course.

Municipal Courses:
Brock Golf Course, 8201 John Ralston Rd., 458-1350
Glenbrook Golf Course, 8101 Bayou Dr., 649-8089
Hermann Park, 6201 Golf Course Dr., 526-0077
Melrose Golf Course, 401 E. Canino Rd., 847-0875
Memorial Golf Course, 6001 Memorial Loop Dr., 862-4033
Sharpstown Golf Course, 6600 Harbor Town, 988-2099
Wortham Golf Course, 7000 Capitol Ave., 921-3227
Private courses open to public:
Bear Creek Golf World, 16001 Clay Rd., 281-859-8188
Treeline Golf Club, 17505 N. Eldridge Parkway, 281-376-1542
Tournament Players Course, 1730 S. Millbend, 281-367-7285
World Houston Golf Course, 4000 Greens Rd., 281-449-8384

Jogging

The Parks and Recreation Department has a system of hike-and-bike trails that covers more than 30 miles through the city. The sections of the system that get the most use are in **Memorial Park,** along Buffalo Bayou leading into downtown, and along **Brays Bayou** in the Southwest. The YMCA and YWCA also offer facilities for joggers: YMCA, 659-5566; YWCA, 868-9922.

Polo

HOUSTON POLO CLUB

8552 Memorial Dr. • 681-8571 for box seat information
Polo can be an expensive sport, but the club's practice matches on Wednesday and Friday afternoons are free and open to the public. Box seats at the regular Sunday matches cost $15, and season tickets are available. The summer season goes from April to July, and the fall season from September to November.

Professional Sports

BASEBALL: HOUSTON ASTROS

Play 81 home games from early April through early October at the Astrodome, Kirby Dr. at South Loop 610. Tickets 799-9555.

BASKETBALL: HOUSTON ROCKETS

Play 41 home games from late October through mid-April at the Summit, Southwest Freeway at Edloe in Greenway Plaza. Tickets 627-2115.

Swimming and Gymnastics

The city's Parks and Recreation Department operates dozens of gymnasiums and swimming pools throughout the city. For information and locations call 845-1000.

Tennis

Besides the public parks' courts, the city has three major tennis centers. The **Homer L. Ford Center,** 5225 Calhoun (747-5466) has 16 lighted courts with availability on a first-come, first-served basis. Fees are $3.50 for a half hour before 5:30 P.M. and $5.50 for one and a half hours after 5:30 and $6 on weekends. **Memorial Park** has 18 lighted courts (861-3765) and **Southwest Tennis Center,** 9506 S. Gessner, has 26 lighted courts (772-0296). Fees are the same, except only $5.50 on weekends.

COLLEGES AND UNIVERSITIES

HOUSTON BAPTIST UNIVERSITY

7502 Fondren • 774-7661

This four-year liberal arts college is run by the Southern Baptist Convention. HBU's strongest areas of study are premed, nursing, and business. Seminars and special classes in management, business, and computers are available to the public through the school's Professional Development Program (995-3222). The collection of antique dolls in the **Museum of American Architecture and Decorative Arts** (774-7661, ext. 2311), located on the second floor of HBU's main building, might be of interest to visitors. Public parking is available inside the main entrance on Fondren. (*See* Sports and Activities—College Sports.)

HOUSTON COMMUNITY COLLEGE SYSTEM

Central campus, 1300 Holman, 713-718-2000 or 281-265-5343 (information)

HCC offers two-year programs covering a variety of fields of study. Most classes are held at night on the campuses of high schools in independent school districts. The system also has half a dozen campuses that feature both day and night classes. HCC's fine arts department stages plays, concerts, and other events in the Heinen Theater, 3517 Austin.

RICE UNIVERSITY

6100 Main • 527-8101

Considered by some the "Harvard of the South," Rice is a privately funded four-year liberal arts college. Though the campus includes the 70,000-seat **Rice Stadium,** academics get the most emphasis, particularly in science and engineering. Cultural offerings on campus that are available to the public are held in the **Rice Media Center and Farish Gallery** (*see* Museums and Art Galleries) and **Hamman Hall** (521-7529). Public parking is available at various lots around campus, though on class days when spaces are at a premium, visitors may have to park near Rice Stadium. (*See also* Sports and Activities—College Sports; Performing Arts.)

TEXAS SOUTHERN UNIVERSITY

3100 Cleburne • 313-7011

TSU is a four-year, state-supported college with predominantly black enrollment. It includes the Thurgood Marshall School of Law. Dramatic works are presented in the **Hannah Hall** auditorium. Credit and non-credit courses are offered in clerical skills and computers by the school's Center for Lifelong Learning (527-7224). To park on campus, visitors must obtain a permit from the security office at the corner of Blodgett and Tierwester. Public parking is in Lot C off Blodgett. (*See also* Sports and Activities—College Sports; Performing Arts—Theater.)

UNIVERSITY OF HOUSTON
4800 Calhoun (University Park campus) • 743-1000

The central campus of the University of Houston is one of the three largest schools in Texas. It is a four-year, state-supported university with graduate schools in engineering, optometry, and pharmacy as well as the Hilton School of Hotel and Restaurant Management (there is a Hilton hotel on campus) and the Bates College of Law. There are also branch campuses at Clear Lake City (2700 Bay Area Blvd. 281-283-7600) and downtown (One Main St., 221-8000). The Fine Arts building, which houses **Dudley Recital Hall** (743-3009) and the **Blaffer Gallery** (*see* Museums and Art Galleries), and the Humanities building, which includes the **Wortham Theater** (*see* Performing Arts), are the sites of most arts events on campus. Both can be reached by taking Entrance 16 to the campus off Cullen Blvd. Metered public parking is available at this entrance and at the main entrance on Calhoun. The Continuing Education Center (743-1060), near the main entrance, offers non-credit courses on many subjects. (*See also* Sports and Activities—College Sports; Performing Arts.)

UNIVERSITY OF ST. THOMAS
3812 Montrose Blvd. • 522-7911

St. Thomas is a private, four-year liberal arts college affiliated with the Catholic Church. The school's drama department stages productions in **Jones Theater** on campus (*see* Performing Arts—Theater). On-street parking is available on the small campus, which covers only a few square blocks.

PERFORMING ARTS

SOCIETY FOR THE PERFORMING ARTS
Offices: 615 Louisiana (Jones Hall for the Performing Arts) • 227-5134

The nonprofit SPA sponsors artists and productions from all areas of the performing arts. Past events have featured touring orchestras, dance companies, operas, and world-renowned guest artists.

Theaters and Performance Halls

JONES HALL FOR THE PERFORMING ARTS
615 Louisiana • 227-3974 • W

Despite losing two of its principal tenants, Houston Ballet and Houston Grand Opera, to the Wortham Theater Center (see below), Jones Hall is still one of the city's most elegant concert halls. Open since 1966, it is the home of the Houston Symphony Orchestra, but this 3,000-seat facility has also hosted such diverse acts as comedians and jazz bands.

MILLER THEATER
Hermann Park • 520-3290 • Always free • W

One of the favorite pastimes of Houstonians in the spring and summer is taking in one of the plays or concerts at the open-air Miller Theater. The covered seating area has a capacity of nearly 1,600 and is free on a first come-first serve basis, but most patrons like to spread out a blanket on the hill behind the covered seats and enjoy the show.

CYNTHIA WOODS MITCHELL PAVILION

2005 Lake Robbins Dr., The Woodlands • 281-364-3010, 281-363-3024 (tickets)

One of the best outdoor venues anywhere, the location hosts well-known performers in all genres. It is also the summer home of the Houston Symphony. The covered seating area holds 3,000 with seated space for another 1,900 outside the canopy and lots of sit-on-the-grass lawn space.

MUSIC HALL

810 Bagby • 247-1000 (City of Houston) or 853-8000 • W

Despite its age, this municipal facility's acoustics have held up well. Concerts, civic functions, and touring theater productions use the 3,000-seat Music Hall.

SOUTHERN STAR AMPHITHEATER

At Six-Flags Astroworld (Kirby at Loop 610) • 799-1466 • W

Part of the Astroworld complex, Southern Star is the site of various pop and rock music concerts. There are 3,000 reserved seats, plus room to spread out a blanket on the grassy area behind the seats. A ticket to an event at Southern Star allows the bearer use of the attractions at Astroworld.

SUMMIT

Southwest Freeway (US 59) at Edloe • 961-9003 • W

The Summit, which is part of the Greenway Plaza business complex, is the home of the Houston Rockets professional basketball team and also hosts such events as major rock concerts and the circus. It can hold as many as 17,500.

WORTHAM THEATER CENTER

510 Preston Blvd. • 237-1439 • W

The Wortham Theater Center is the showpiece of Houston's performance halls. Home to the Houston Grand Opera and Houston Ballet, it includes two theaters, one seating 2,300 and the other 1,100.

Meeting and Convention Facilities

GEORGE R. BROWN CONVENTION CENTER

1001 Convention Center Blvd. (Downtown in area bounded by Dallas, Walker, Jackson/Chenevert Streets and US 59) • 833-8000 • W

The George R. Brown Convention Center, opened in 1987, is the bait with which Houston lures national conventions and other large-scale meetings to the city. The facility has nearly half a million square feet of exhibit space, with three major halls downstairs and one upstairs. The center has a total of 43 meeting rooms and a 31,500-square-foot ballroom.

Dance

HOUSTON BALLET

Most performances in Wortham Theater Center • 523-6300 (administration) 227-2787 (Houston Ticket Center) • Admission • W

The Houston Ballet is in a position of prominence in the world of classical dance. The ballet regularly tours the United States and the world, earning plaudits from England to China. The ballet is based on the tradition of the classics but also tries to maintain a contemporary direction. Among its five productions each year is a performance during the summer at Miller Theater in Hermann Park and a production of *The Nutcracker* at Christmas. The ballet also operates the Houston Ballet Academy, which channels dancers into the ballet's 40-member company.

Music

COLLEGES

Musical programs are frequently presented at **Dudley Recital Hall** (743-3009) on the University of Houston campus and at **Duncan Recital Hall, Shepherd School of Music** (527-4933) at Rice University.

HOUSTON SYMPHONY

Most performances in Jones Hall for the Performing Arts • 224-4240 (marketing), 227-2787 (Houston Ticket Center) • Admission • W

Since its inception in 1913, the Houston Symphony has grown to a 90-plus-member orchestra that goes on U.S. tours every year. But first priority goes to the 18 "concert weekends" given from September through May. Add to that seven pops concerts during the year. In July, the symphony conducts a Summer Festival dedicated to the work of one or more classical composers. Many of the orchestra programs during the subscription season feature guest artists.

Opera

HOUSTON GRAND OPERA

Most performances in the Wortham Theater Center • 237-1439 (administration), 227-2787 (Houston Ticket Center) • Admission • W

HGO productions have spread the company's fame to Broadway—with *Showboat* in 1983, HGO became the first opera company to stage a production on Broadway—but the organization is better known in its hometown. HGO puts on six productions from September through June as well as three performances in the Great Artists Series, in which leading operatic performers give concerts. The Spring Opera Festival in Hermann Park's Miller Theater hosts an opera that's geared toward entertaining the whole family.

Theater

ALLEY THEATER

615 Texas Ave. • 228-9341 (administration), 228-8421 (tickets) • Admission Performances Tuesday–Sunday • W

The city's only resident professional theater (and one of the few in the country) produces 12 plays on its two stages—seven on the Large Stage, which includes seating for about 800, and five on the Arena Stage, which accommodates about 300. Alley productions have attracted acting, writing, and directing talent from all over the world, establishing it as one of the country's top regional theaters.

COUNTRY PLAYHOUSE

12802 Queensbury in Town & Country Center, IH-10 at West Belt • 467-4497 Admission • Performances Friday–Sunday • W

Six productions, with emphasis on comedies and musicals, are staged each year in the Country Playhouse's 234-seat theater.

THE ENSEMBLE
3535 Main • 520-0055 • Performances Thursday–Sunday • Admission • W

While six plays are produced each year on the Ensemble's Large Stage (with seating for about 180), five plays are produced on the Arena Stage (capacity of about 80) in the troupe's *Potpourri* series. The latter group of plays is usually based around a central theme. These works are a mixture of comedies and drama and are mostly by African-American playwrights and are performed by African-American casts.

MAIN STREET THEATER
2540 Times Blvd., 4617 Montrose Blvd.• Box office 524-6706 • Performances Thursday–Sunday • Admission • W

It's not on Main St. anymore (having moved from there in 1982), but it's definitely a theater, staging plays both in the Village and at Chelsea Market in Montrose. The fare is a combination of classics and world-premiere plays (Main Street claims to mount more first-run plays than anyone else in Houston). Six children's plays, scheduled on weekends throughout the year.

RADIO MUSIC THEATER
2623 Colquit • 522-7722 • Performances Thursday–Saturday • Admission • W

The comedy skits of Radio Music Theater are different from those of other performing groups. They are done in the style of radio shows, complete with sound effects and other elements from the medium's "golden age." It's a unique and hilarious variation on the comedy repertory scheme.

RICE PLAYERS
Rice University. Hamman Hall on campus • 527-4040 • Admission • W

Since Rice has no drama department, members of the Rice Players are recruited from the school's students, faculty, and staff. The group stages four productions during the academic year (September–May), two per semester with performances Monday through Saturday. The plays range from the classics to recent off-Broadway hits.

STAGES REPERTORY THEATER
3201 Allen Parkway • 527-8243 • Performances Wednesday–Sunday Admission • W

The plural of the name is accurate, since Stages has two theaters—one seating 140 and the other seating 240. Musicals and other large-scale productions are reserved for the bigger stage, while a combination of classical and modern plays holds forth on the smaller repertory stage. Four to five children's plays each year are part of the *Early Stages* series.

TEXAS SOUTHERN UNIVERSITY
Hannah Hall auditorium on campus • 313-7011 • Performances Thursday–Sunday during academic year • Admission • W

Among the four productions staged each academic year at TSU, a predominantly African-American school, is a drama focusing on African-American life or issues. A mixture of classics and contemporary works makes up the balance of the schedule. Performances Thursday through Sunday.

THEATER SOUTHWEST

3750 S. Gessner • 661-9505 (tickets) • Performances Friday and Saturday, Sunday matinee • Admission
One of the seven plays produced each year at the 90-seat Theater Southwest is the winner of a playwriting contest the theater sponsors for Texas writers. Another locally written work is also usually included in the schedule of comedies and mysteries.

THEATER SUBURBIA

1410 W. 43rd • 682-3525 • Performances Friday and Saturday •Admission • W
Theater Suburbia specializes in Houston premieres of an assortment of mysteries, comedies, and dramas in its 100-seat facility. Some original works are included in the seven productions staged each year. A melodrama is usually presented during the summer.

THEATER UNDER THE STARS

4235 San Felipe (general offices) • 622-8887 • Admission • Most productions staged at Miller Theater in Hermann Park and the Music Hall downtown
The nonprofit TUTS describes itself as the city's "professional civic light opera" company. During their winter season from November through May, TUTS stages four operettas and musicals. One or two shows, also musicals, are put on in Miller Theater in the summer.

UNIVERSITY OF HOUSTON

Wortham Theater on campus • 749-3450 • Admission • W
Included in the five productions staged in UH's Wortham Theater (not to be confused with the Wortham Theater Center downtown) during the academic year are a musical and a mixture of classical and contemporary plays. Performances Friday through Sunday. Besides the 566-seat Wortham, UH also has the Lab Theater, a convertible space that seats up to 170. During the summer, the UH drama department holds a Children's Theater Festival on campus and the Shakespeare Festival in Hermann Park's Miller Theater.

UNIVERSITY OF ST. THOMAS

Jones Theater on campus • 3910 Yoakum • 522-7911 • Admission • W
Though only four plays are produced each academic year at UST, these can range from a Shakespearean drama to a musical comedy. Performances are Wednesday through Saturday. During the summer, the drama department sponsors workshops in acting and playwriting that are open to the public.

Comedy Clubs

COMEDY SHOWCASE

12547 Gulf Freeway (I-45) • 481-1188 • Closed Monday and Tuesday Reservations necessary • Cover • MC, V • W
Most of the performers are locals at this Gulf Freeway club, but some out-of-town comics are also imported to entertain the customers, who normally pack the place on weekends.

LAFFSTOP

1952-A W. Gray • 524-2333 • Reservations necessary • Cover • AE, MC, V • W

The triple bill of comedians at the Laffstop changes each week because many of the performers are touring the national circuit of comedy clubs. The occasional "name" comic comes in, but most of these joke-tellers have achieved no greater heights than a shot on the *Tonight* show.

SHOPPING

Department Stores

When new to a city, a shopper very likely will go to the department stores with the familiar names. Sears, Montgomery Ward, and J. C. Penney are all fixtures in Houston, and the city's growth has attracted such retailers as Macy's, Dillard's, Lord & Taylor, and Saks Fifth Avenue from other parts of the country. The stores listed below established themselves first in Houston or elsewhere in Texas and are mentioned here to acquaint newcomers with them.

FOLEY'S

Various locations • W

Foley's is the big gun among Houston department stores, firmly entrenched as the largest in the state. The stores have retained the name Foley's even though the founders, brothers Pat and James Foley, were bought out in 1917. Besides being a full-line store with everything from clothing to major appliances, Foley's also makes its mark on the community with public seminars on health, cooking, finances, and other subjects.

NEIMAN-MARCUS

2600 Post Oak Blvd. • 621-7100 • 10615 Town & Country Way (Town & Country Village, I-10 at West Belt) • 984-2100 • W

Neiman-Marcus is more commonly associated with Dallas, the city of its birth, but the store has been in Houston since 1955 and moved to the Galleria when the shopping complex opened in 1970. Considered a fashion specialty store that's known for its furs and jewelry, Neiman-Marcus also carries top-of-the-line merchandise in housewares and other, less fashion-oriented departments.

Shopping Centers

THE GALLERIA

5075 Westheimer • 621-1907 • W

While there are many other shopping centers in Houston, this is the *ne plus ultra* with an ice-skating rink and lots of activities beneath a high, arched glass ceiling. The sprawling complex includes major department stores: Macy's, Lord & Taylor, Neiman-Marcus; two hotels; numerous restaurants; and clothing, jewelry, and specialty stores of all descriptions. Opened in 1970 (the Galleria II was added in '78 and Galleria III in '86), the Galleria is fashioned after a shopping plaza in Milan, Italy.

Antiques

HART GALLERIES

2301 S. Voss Rd. • 266-3500 • W

Hart Galleries, begun in 1938 by the late Samuel Hart, is one of the high rollers in the Houston antiques business, handling some of the major estate sales in the city. Jerry Hart and his wife, Wynonne, are now in charge of one of the city's largest showrooms for antiques. Most of the furnishings and accessories are English and continental. Auctions are held monthly.

HEIGHTS STATION ANTIQUES

121 Heights Blvd. • 868-3175

Every nook and cranny of this barnlike structure contains what the proprietors call "country collectibles"—kitchen utensils from the late nineteenth to early twentieth century and cabinets, cupboards, and other furniture that seem to have come directly from a turn-of-the-century farm or ranch home. Many of the furniture pieces are "primitives," made from unfinished wood and used more for their functional value than their appearance. Several dealers exhibit their wares in the building (built in 1915), making Heights Station the kind of place in which an antiques buff can easily spend a few hours.

Art Galleries

HOOKS-EPSTEIN GALLERY

3210 Eastside • 522-9116 • Closed Sunday • W

The gallery describes the art it deals in as "late nineteenth-century and twentieth-century representational American, European, and Latin paintings, sculpture, and works on paper."

MEREDITH LONG GALLERIES

2323 San Felipe • 523-6671 • Closed Sunday and Monday • W

One of the oldest established galleries in the Southwest, Meredith Long focuses on American art of the nineteenth and twentieth centuries (paintings, drawings, and watercolors), with several contemporary works included in the collection.

TEXAS GALLERY

2012 Peden • 524-1593 • Closed Sunday and Monday • W

The name says Texas, but American artists from as far afield as New York and California are also represented here. Eight exhibitions each year include paintings, sculpture, and photography in a variety of styles.

Miscellaneous

BRITISH MARKET

366 Rice Blvd. • 529-9889 • W

Ardent Anglophiles could spend hours meandering through the British Market, which is like a mini-department store of goods from the British Isles. Food, china, cosmetics, books, and recordings are among the wealth of imports. There is also an impressive collection of children's books and toys.

DON'S RECORD SHOP

4900 Bissonnet • 667-9196 • W

Don's has the local record market cornered when it comes to oldies-but-goodies. If a given recording is anywhere in existence and can be special-ordered, Don Janicek's staff can probably lay their hands on it. The inventory includes the latest releases by country and rock bands, but many customers discover that the more obscure titles—whether they be 45s or albums of show tunes, old standards, or whatever—aren't so hard to find at Don's.

DRAMATIKA

3804 S. Shepherd • 528-5457 • W

Dramatika is an outlet for those who thirst for the theater. The shop deals in posters from past and present Broadway and Off-Broadway productions by the hundreds and can handle framing as well.

HOUSTON SPORTS EXCHANGE

5015 Westheimer (Galleria) • 552-1882 • W

Houston Sports Exchange allows you to do more than just root for your favorite team. Wear the colors of just about any pro or college sports team by choosing from the T-shirts, jerseys, jackets, caps, and other paraphernalia in stock. There is also a Ticketmaster outlet in each store.

ICONOGRAPHY

2552 University Blvd. • 529-2630 • W

The cards and stationery at Iconography are certainly unique, daring to go where Hallmark fears to tread. But what makes this place stand out is the assortment of rubber stamps. No mere "Paid" or "Remittance due" stamps here. There are pictures, slogans, pithy quotations, and other designs for jazzing up a letterhead.

JAMES AVERY, CRAFTSMAN, INC.

Various locations • W

The name sounds somewhat pretentious, but it is accurate. The delicately crafted gold and silver jewelry produced in Avery's headquarters in the Central Texas Hill Country has given a Texas twist to the concept of "designer" goods. Rings, bracelets, earrings, belt buckles, and necklaces are included in the collection. Designs range from religious symbols to the overtly Texan—armadillos, oil wells, etc.

SOUTHERN IMPORTERS

4825 San Jacinto • 524-8236

At any given time, Southern Importers could also be known as Holiday Headquarters. With goods that run the gamut from display and floral supplies to costumes and party and seasonal decorations, there is truly something for everyone here.

TEAS NURSERY

4400 Bellaire Blvd. • 664-4400

This family operation is among the oldest businesses in Houston. Some of the work of its founder, Edward Teas, who started the nursery in 1906, is still in evidence. He planted many of the trees at the Rice University campus.

TOOTSIES
4045 Westheimer • 629-9990 • W

When you're talking high fashion in Houston, you're talking Tootsies. The store specializes in women's clothing, accessories, and jewelry by top designers.

THE TOY MAKER
12850 Memorial Dr. • 461-7830 • 2368 Rice Blvd. • 521-2251 • W

With many toy stores becoming a wasteland of "action figures" whose primary purpose is to do battle, it's nice to find a place that specializes in the basics. The Toy Maker shops have a vast selection of dolls and stuffed animals, from the large and cuddly to the small and dainty. Batman and his ilk can be found here, but when there are enough teddy bears and such to cover an entire wall of the store, it's obvious that all the "action" these toys need is a big hug.

WHOLE EARTH PROVISION CO.
2934 S. Shepherd • 526-3883 • Woodway • 467-0234 • W

Whole Earth has developed into an eclectic store. Equipment for the outdoors is only the beginning of the inventory. Children's books and luggage are some of the items geared toward a more upwardly mobile clientele, but much of the merchandise is still slanted toward varying degrees of "roughing it." Flashlights, kayaks, ropes, backpacks—anything and everything for the plucky camper.

WILLIAMS-SONOMA
4076 Westheimer • 622-4161 • 30 Town & Country Village • 465-4775 • W

You've read the catalog, now see the stores. Visiting Williams-Sonoma is like walking through a well-stocked gourmet kitchen. Fine glassware and cookery, pots and serving dishes as long on function as on form, cookbooks, and everyday household items round out the selections along with a fully equipped kitchen for cooking demonstrations.

KIDS' STUFF

CHILDREN'S MUSEUM
1500 Binz • 522-1138 • Open Tuesday–Thursday and Saturday 9–5, Friday and Sunday 1–5 • Admission • W

This is one museum where you won't hear or see the words "do not touch." The Children's Museum thrives on the involvement and active participation of the people it was designed for—namely, kids. As with other museums, there are changing exhibitions. In the past, these have included hands-on demonstrations of the difficulties encountered by the physically disabled. Permanent exhibits help teach children about computers and aspects of life in the everyday world. Memberships to the museum are available.

DISCOVERY ZOO
Houston Zoological Gardens in Hermann Park • 525-3364 • Open daily 10–5:45 • Admission • W

Formerly known as the Children's Zoo, this is still one of the most popular features of the Houston Zoological Gardens (*see* Other Points of Interest). Kids get a chance to pet some of the Discovery Zoo's residents such as the pygmy goats, llamas, and assorted cattle. Visitors also are intrigued by the two large Galapagos tortoises, which have been at the zoo since the late 1920s. The Texas Wildlife Building offers a close-up look at some native nocturnal animals.

FUN PLEX

13700 Beechnut • 530-7777 • Open Monday–Wednesday 8–10, Friday 5–12, Saturday 10–midnight, Sunday noon–10 • Free admission, prices vary for attractions • W

This indoor entertainment complex has a 40-lane bowling center, two 18-hole miniature golf courses, three movie theaters, roller skating rink, video arcades, restaurants, and a play center for children.

SIX-FLAGS ASTROWORLD

9001 Kirby (at South Loop) • 799-1234 • Open daily June–Labor Day, weekends only March, April, and May and September–November. Closed December–March • Adult pass $30.95 plus tax, children 3 and up $15.95 plus tax • W variable

Just across the freeway from the Astrodome, the 75-acre park is part of the sprawling Astrodomain complex. Thrill-seekers who keep up with the latest in amusement park rides have a lot to choose from at Astroworld. The **Texas Cyclone** is rated as one of the best roller coasters in the country. **Thunder River** sends a raftload of people careening through simulated river rapids. An extravagant live stage show is presented for people who like their seats to stay in one place. The **Enchanted Kingdom** area is for younger children, with lots of hands-on activities. Staff members at the guest relations office will accompany handicapped visitors through the park. Adjacent to Astroworld are **Southern Star Amphitheater** (*see* Performing Arts) and **Waterworld** (see below).

WATERWORKS

13700 Beechnut (adjacent to Fun Plex) • 530-3263 • Hours vary depending on season • Admission, season passes available

For smaller children, Waterworks has a kiddie car wash, rain tree, and watermaze. For the bigger kids there are speed slides, innertube slides, and a wavepool, along with sunbathing and shade areas.

WATERWORLD

9001 Kirby (Kirby Dr. at South Loop, adjacent to Astroworld) • 799-1234 June–Labor Day, opens daily at 10 A.M.; March–May and September open weekends only at 10 A.M. • Adults $15.95 plus tax, children 3 and up $12.95 plus tax

Some may feel that Waterworld is tampering with nature by having its own wave machines and water slides. But a beach doesn't have anything to compete with the excitement of racing down a water chute at 40 mph toward "splashdown." **Runaway River** has a series of increasingly precipitous drops into the water. Innertubes are provided at the individual rides or can be rented for the day. More tranquil pools are on hand at Waterworld for those who just want to float in the sun.

SIDE TRIPS

BATTLESHIP TEXAS

San Jacinto Battlegrounds • *From southeast corner of Loop 610, take TX 225 east approximately 15 miles to TX 134, then north (left) and follow signs*

479-2411 • Open daily 10–5 • Adults $5, seniors 65 and up $3, children 6–11 $2.50, under 6 free • W main deck only

Most Texans know the battleship *Texas* as the ship permanently moored on the Ship Channel near the San Jacinto Battlegrounds and San Jacinto Monument. But the former fighting ship has a long and storied past. First commissioned in 1914, the ship is a veteran of two world wars. Today, the *Texas* serves as a museum and memorial to those who served in the military. Wartime artifacts are on display, along with informational material on the ship and its involvement in the defense of the United States. After it was decommissioned in 1948, the ship was presented to the state. The *Texas* underwent a one-year, $6.9 million restoration at a Galveston shipyard and was reopened to the public in 1989.

BRAZOS BEND STATE PARK

Take US 59 south out of Houston, exit Crabb River Rd., follow signs 18 miles to park • 409-553-3243 or 800-792-1112, Web site: http://www.tpwd.state.tx.us/park/parks/htm • Fee per vehicle • W

When the state of Texas bought what once was the Hale Ranch, 4,897 acres of land became available to the public for camping, fishing, and other outdoor recreation. The park has six lakes available for fishing, two with lighted piers. Besides picnic grounds scattered through the park, there are also two permanent picnic pavilions and a dining hall. Reservations are suggested for use of the campgrounds, which have utility hookups. The park also has 15 miles of hike-and-bike trails and an interpretive center to provide visitors with more information. The **George Observatory** is open 3–10 Saturdays. From 3 to 5 P.M. observe the sun using solar telescopes and visit the observatory's exhibit areas. At 5, free passes are given to the floor of the main dome, which houses a 36-inch telescope. Call 639-4634 for astronomical information.

CHAIN-O-LAKES RESORT, CAMPGROUND, AND CONFERENCE CENTER

From US 59 north of Houston, take Washington St. exit into Cleveland. Take FM 787 east approximately 18 miles from Cleveland. Turn right on Daniel Ranch Road • P.O. Box 218, Romayor 77368 • (713) 592-2150 • Open daily 8–5 Admission • W variable

This is a family resort built around a number of small lakes. Some of the activities available are swimming, fishing, volleyball, paddleboat rentals, horseback riding, pony rides for kids, hiking and nature walks, horse-drawn carriage rides, and hayrides on weekends. Accommodations include wilderness camping, RV sites, rustic cabins, and deluxe log cabins with fireplaces. On weekends a bed and breakfast arrangement is available with the log cabins that includes a horse-drawn carriage ride to the nearby **Hilltop Herb Farm Restaurant** for breakfast. This restaurant is open for a Saturday night traditional dinner, Sunday buffet luncheon, and weekend morning breakfasts. All meals are by reservation only. This is a rebirth of the restaurant, greenhouses, formal gardens, and gift shop at the famed Hilltop Herb Farm destroyed by a tornado in 1983. Featured are gourmet dishes prepared with homegrown seasonings and herbs.

LILES SAFARI RANCH

231 McClellan Road • Kingwood 77339. *Take US 59 north from Houston about 20 miles to Kingwood Drive. Turn left and continue to North Harris County College, turn left at McClellan-Sorters Road and look for ranch entrance* • (713) 359-1946 • Open daily 10–5 • Admission

Located on 120 wooded acres, Liles Safari Ranch is home to hundreds of exotic animals, Texas wildlife, and birds. Professional guides tell you all about the animals while you ride in custom-built trams. Meet a buffalo named Bill (what else?), a llama named Tony (what else?), Siberian elk, Himalayan tahr, Russian tur, and many more. Part of the ranch is a wildlife museum, petting zoo, and picnic area.

LYNDON B. JOHNSON SPACE CENTER AND SPACE CENTER HOUSTON

Clear Lake. *Take I-45 about 25 miles southeast of downtown to NASA Road 1 exit, then about 3 miles east*
See Clear Lake: Space Center Houston

SAN JACINTO MONUMENT

3800 Park Rd. (La Porte, in San Jacinto Battleground State Historic Park) *From southeast corner of Loop 610, take TX 225 east approximately 15 miles to TX 134, follow signs* • 479-2431 • Open daily 9–6 • Museum is free; admission to tower elevator: Adults $1.50, children under 12 50¢ • W

The San Jacinto Monument stands on the site of the San Jacinto Battle-grounds, where in 1836 the forces of General Sam Houston defeated the Mexican Army that only a month before had captured the Alamo. In the lobby of the monument is the **San Jacinto Museum of History,** a collection of artifacts from Texas' past. From the top of the 570-foot monument (*see* Bird's-Eye View), the largest masonry structure in the world, a wide area of the Gulf Coast can be viewed, as well as the Houston skyline to the west. In the **Jesse H. Jones Theatre for Texas Studies,** you can see a memorable slide presentation called *Texas Forever! The Battle of San Jacinto* that documents the Texas battle in 1836. Shown hourly from 10 A.M. to 5 P.M. (Admission).

TEXAS LIMITED

567 TC Jester Blvd. (off I-10 in Heights) • For tickets call 522-0574 or Ticketmaster 629-3700, outside Houston 800-578-9991 • Tours Friday–Saturday depart Houston 9:30 A.M., return Houston 5:15 P.M. Third Saturday departs Houston 4 P.M., arrives Houston midnight. Sundays departs Houston 11 A.M., returns Houston 7:30 P.M.

Take a round-trip ride from Houston to Galveston in one of seven refurbished train cars. Spend the extra bucks for a seat in the *Silver Knight* car. It's first class with first class service. Breakfast is served with sweet rolls, coffee, and juice at very reasonable prices, and a full bar is also aboard. It is not a bullet train, but about two hours of easy riding and great relaxation. A nighttime run is offered the third Saturday of the month, and special parties and murder mysteries are held throughout the year.

ANNUAL EVENTS

February

HOUSTON LIVESTOCK SHOW AND RODEO

Astrodome (Kirby at South Loop) • 791-9000 • Mid-February–early March Admission • W variable

The words "Go Texan" take on special significance during the month as would-be cowboys dress in Western garb to help celebrate the largest stock show and second-largest rodeo in the nation. The festivities begin in mid-February with a downtown parade. The main rodeo events are held in the Astrodome, with stock judging in the adjacent Astrohall and Astroarena. The public can also tour the latter two facilities, where the livestock are penned. Celebrity entertainers are booked for the rodeo, with performances daily.

March

AZALEA TRAIL

River Oaks Garden Club • 523-2483 • Dates vary • Admission
Many of the homes and gardens on the annual Azalea Trail are widely separated, so the best means to admire the early spring foliage is by car. The specified homes on the tour are only part of the floral splendor created by the azaleas (as well as other flowers) all over the city.

April

BAYOU CITY ART FESTIVAL

521-0133 • Dates vary • Free
This is Houston at its most eclectic. For one weekend in Spring (usually late April) and again in Fall (usually October), the public can browse through a variety of booths featuring crafts of jewelry, metals, fibers, and graphics. But the unscheduled entertainment can be just as interesting as the wares on display. Once the Westheimer Colony Festivals in Montrose, the Bayou Festivals' locations move between the Memorial Park area and downtown. Call for information.

HOUSTON INTERNATIONAL FESTIVAL

Various locations • 772-4692 or 654-8808 • Last two weekends in April
Admission to some events • W variable
This civic festival spotlights the city's literary, visual, and performing arts. It encompasses several blocks of downtown, with most outdoor activities held in and around City Hall, Sam Houston Park, Tranquility Park, Jones Hall, and other landmarks. Several outdoor stages feature performances of music, dancing, and drama, with an arts and crafts fair added for good measure. During the week prior to these events, such organizations as the Museum of Fine Arts, Alley Theater, and Houston Symphony conduct exhibitions and performances to coincide with the festival.

WORLDFEST/HOUSTON INTERNATIONAL FILM FESTIVAL

Greenway III Theater (Greenway Plaza) • 626-0402 or 629-5129 • Dates vary
Admission • W
Filmmakers from across the United States and several foreign countries enter their works, ranging from short documentaries to full-length features, for this five-day competition. Tickets are available for individual showings or for the duration of the festival.

May

HEIGHTS HOME TOUR

Heights Blvd. • 868-0102 • Mother's Day weekend • Admission

Six to ten homes in the Heights are opened to give visitors some historical perspective on one of the city's oldest neighborhoods. Many of the homes—different houses are featured every year—are of the Victorian period.

PIN OAK CHARITY HORSE SHOW
Great Southwest Equestrian Center, 2501 S. Mason Rd., Katy 77450 281-578-7009 • Admission • W variable
For more than 50 years this has been the annual highlight for the equestrian set. Entries from all over the United States and a few foreign countries compete in events for saddle-bred, hunter-jumper, walking, and other types of horses. More than $200,000 in cash and awards are given. Proceeds benefit Texas Children's Hospital.

June

JUNETEENTH BLUES FESTIVAL
Various locations • 528-6740 • Free
Blues artists from the legendary to the up-and-coming gather to commemorate June 19, 1865, when word of the Emancipation Proclamation reached Texas. Houston performance sites include Miller Theater and Sam Houston Park (near City Hall).

August

HOUSTON JAZZ FESTIVAL
Various locations • 528-6746 • Admission to some events
Houston's jazz culture has its day—or month, rather—in a series of performances and seminars. To keep up with what's going on, check with the Convention & Visitors Bureau, 620-6634.

September

FIESTAS PATRIAS
Various locations • 926-2636 • Admission to some events
A parade, formal ball, and the presentation of a distinguished Mexican-American citizen award are some of the events to celebrate Hispanic heritage and to educate the public both within and outside the city's Hispanic community.

October

GREEK FESTIVAL
Greek Orthodox Cathedral, 3511 Yoakum • 526-5377 • Usually weekend starting with first Friday of October • Free
A festive atmosphere takes over the church grounds, adjacent to the University of St. Thomas campus, for this three-day celebration of Greek traditions. Approximately 30,000 people come each year to enjoy the Greek dances and foods.

TEXAS RENAISSANCE FESTIVAL
45 miles northwest of Houston on FM 1774 between communities of Magnolia and Plantersville • **356-2178 • Runs seven consecutive weekends beginning with first weekend in October • Admission • W variable**
All sorts of foods, entertainment, and crafts await those who make the winding drive into the countryside for this tribute to the Middle Ages. Lords and ladies in

full Renaissance regalia—including King Henry VIII and his court—stroll around the expansive grounds while jugglers, minstrels, and acrobats thread their way through the crowd. Stages are set up for musical and theatrical performances, but unusual impromptu acts attract their own gatherings of onlookers.

BAYOU CITY ART FESTIVAL
See April.

November

THANKSGIVING DAY PARADE
Downtown • Free
If the televised variety just doesn't cut it, head downtown for Houston's version. A procession of floats, marching bands, and visiting dignitaries such as Santa Claus create a holiday atmosphere—Bayou City style.

December

CHRISTMAS CELEBRATIONS
Various locations • 620-6634 (Convention & Visitors Bureau)
Admission to some events
Christmas festivities in Houston take various forms, such as free candlelight tours of the restored nineteenth-century buildings in Sam Houston Park, performances of *The Nutcracker* by the Houston Ballet in Jones Hall, and concerts by the Second Baptist Church's "Singing Christmas Tree"—a choir performing on a massive, tree-shaped steel frame.

RESTAURANTS

($ = under $7, $$ = $8–$17, $$$ = $18–$25, $$$$ = over $25 for one person excluding drinks, tax, and tip.)

American

BRENNAN'S
3300 Smith • 522-9711 • Lunch and dinner daily, Saturday and Sunday brunch 10:30–2 • Cr • $$$–$$$$ • W
Brennan's recreates the romantic feel of the French Quarter with its sunny brick courtyard, elegant dining room, and most of all, some choice creole creations. The seafood gumbo could go head-to-head with those of the best New Orleans kitchens, while the grilled redfish and veal dishes are among the best of several excellent entrées. A signature dish, the Bananas Foster dessert, is simply to die for.

THE CLOISTER
1117 Texas Ave. (at Christ Church Cathedral) • 229-8248 • Lunch only 11–1:30 Monday–Friday • AE • $ • W
As an enticement to get the downtown crowd to use the church facilities, Christ Church Cathedral opens its cloister to the public for some excellent Cajun lunches served up by the owners of Treebeard's. It's a packed house every noon, and on the second and fourth Wednesday, a live jazz ensemble adds to your dining pleasure.

HARD ROCK CAFE

2801 Kirby • 520-1134 • Lunch and dinner daily • $$ • AE, MC, V • W

Rock 'n' roll meets burgers and ribs. The trendy restaurant chain that became known for the celebrities it attracts in London, New York, and Los Angeles has included Houston in its ever-widening circle. The basic American fare on the menu, along with a few good desserts, is serviceable, but the real attraction here is the interior. The Hard Rock Cafe is a storehouse of rock 'n' roll memorabilia—guitars (one of Stevie Ray Vaughn's), articles of clothing, posters, documents, and other museum pieces from the rock era, past and present.

THE HOFBRAU

1803 Shepherd • 869-7074 • Lunch and dinner Monday–Friday, dinner only Saturday and Sunday • $$–$$$ • AE, MC, V • W

It's subject to debate whether the Hofbrau's clientele comes for the good steaks or because they need a fix of Austin-style atmosphere. The steaks range in size from 10 to 24 ounces, and the fries and salad that accompany each selection are generous as well. It's not a big place—but it's a convivial setting for cutting into a hefty T-bone or porterhouse. And if someone strikes up "The Eyes of Texas," more than a few voices will probably join in.

HOUSTON'S

Various locations • 975-1947 • Lunch and dinner daily • $$ • Cr • W

Once seated at Houston's, particularly during peak periods, you are to be congratulated. First, you found a parking space, and second, you didn't mind waiting for a table. This place is popular, and with good reason. It succeeds in both quantity and quality, with excellent prime rib, oversized hamburgers, generous salads, and a variety of soups. Little touches, like chocolate shakes that most soda fountains couldn't match, provide evidence that Houston's pays attention to details.

OLD SAN FRANCISCO STEAK HOUSE

8611 Westheimer • 783-5990 • Open daily for dinner • $$$ • Cr • W

Old San Francisco is set in the atmosphere of an ornate turn-of-the century saloon, reminiscent of California's famed Barbary Coast. The famous "Girl on the Red Velvet Swing" adds a real flavor of the Old West as she entertains the guests with her acrobatics. And for more real flavor, try the steaks and prime rib. But, you can also enjoy your seafood favorites with fresh fish purchased daily. Just don't eat too much of that block of aged Swiss cheese and sourdough breads placed on the table when you are first seated.

TREEBEARD'S

315 Travis • 225-2160 • Lunch only Monday–Friday. Closed Saturday and Sunday • $ • AE

Few places downtown are better for a deliciously filling lunch than Treebeard's. Steaming bowls of shrimp *etouffee*, sausage and shrimp *jambalaya, chili,* and chicken *gumbo* are spicy, but not so much as to kill the taste of the vegetables in these everything-but-the-kitchen-sink concoctions. Treebeard's also serves lunch at The Cloister in Christ Church Cathedral, 1117 Travis, downtown.

Asian

DONG TING

611 Stuart • 527-0005 • Lunch and dinner Monday–Friday, dinner only Saturday. Closed Sunday • $$–$$$ • Cr • W

Though the menu is somewhat smaller than its principal competitors, Dong Ting is easily among the top Chinese restaurants in Houston. The understatedly opulent surroundings are among many attractions of eating here. The attractive decor and the well-chosen Hunan-accented menu make dining here a treat. *Lah yah* (duck) headlines the smoked dishes, the specialty of the house, which also include chicken and pork variations.

GOLDEN ROOM

1209 Montrose • 524-9614 • Lunch and dinner Monday–Friday; Saturday dinner only; closed Sunday • $$ • Cr

The appetizers such as Thai toast (triangles of bread with a topping of ground pork, shrimp, onion, and garlic and a peanut-oil dressing for dipping) and *sate* (skewered strips of beef or pork) are fine, and the traditional *Phat Thai* is, too. But the standouts are the curries, which are simultaneously cool, smooth, spicy, and flavorful.

NIPPON

4464 Montrose • 523-3939 • Lunch and dinner daily • $$ • Cr • W variable

This Japanese restaurant has something of the air of a country inn about it. There is a small dining room, as well as a sushi bar. Tranquility and neighborhood friendliness are the watchwords here.

Barbecue

GOODE CO. BARBECUE

5109 Kirby, 522-2530 and 8911 Katy Freeway • 464-1901 • Open daily, lunch and dinner • AE, DC, MC, V • W

Down-home Texas teams up in fine style here with what is arguably the best barbecue in Houston. Mesquite-smoked ribs and brisket are served up with a tangy sauce. You probably have the spices Jim Goode rubs into the chicken in your own kitchen, but just try to duplicate it. Links are also first rate, so a combination plate is definitely in order.

LUTHER'S

Various locations • Open daily for lunch and dinner • $–$$ • Cr • W

We would think that the odds are not in Luther's favor. With so many locations, the product is bound to suffer. And when the product is barbecue, which Texans hold dear to their hearts, there would seem to be precious little margin for error. But Luther's beef, chicken, ribs, and links all have a nice flavor and the hamburgers are better than average.

OTTO'S

5502 Memorial Dr. • 864-8526 • Closed Sunday • $ • No Cr • W

Houston's barbecue *cognoscenti* know about Otto's. It may have been overshadowed by larger, better-advertised operations, but this modest restaurant on Memorial Dr. (if you don't look, you'll miss it) still has some of the tenderest, best-flavored beef and ribs around. There are also hamburgers to be had, all presented in a simple, cafeteria-style arrangement. If you want other endorsements for Otto's, you need look no further than the autographed photos on its walls from local and national celebrities who can be counted among Otto's patrons.

Continental

CAFE ANNIE

1728 Post Oak Blvd. • 840-1111 • Lunch and dinner Monday–Saturday. Closed Sunday • $$$$ • Cr • W

Cafe Annie is elegant in the best sense of the word. Small without being cramped, formal but still comfortable. It is an ideal environment for enjoying such dishes as roast duckling, redfish, or sauteed lamb. All in all, the atmosphere is so romantic that one almost expects Fred Astaire and Ginger Rogers to come dancing through during dessert.

LA TOUR D'ARGENT

2011 Ella Blvd. • 864-9864 • Lunch and dinner Monday–Friday, dinner only Saturday. Closed Sunday • $$$$ • Cr • W

Even on the busiest nights at La Tour d'Argent, it's still a toss-up which is in greater number—customers or the animal heads and skins mounted on the walls. This is the city's oldest log cabin, yet with the hunting motif, patrons still consider La Tour d'Argent a good place for a romantic dinner. The restaurant's French cuisine and the rustic setting are an interesting and successful mix.

LA MORA

912 Lovett Blvd. • 522-7412 • Lunch Monday–Friday, dinner Tuesday–Saturday. Closed Sunday and Monday • $$$ • AE, MC, V • W

This Italian menu has a pure Tuscan accent: hearty grilled meats and bean dishes get as much emphasis as pasta does. A selection of splendid *antipasti* needs only a basket of bread and a glass of red wine to make a delicious meal.

MAXIM'S

3735 Richmond • 877-8899 • Lunch and dinner Monday–Friday, dinner only Saturday. Closed Sunday • $$$–$$$$ • Cr • W

Restaurant hounds may not be dropping Maxim's name as often as they do Tony's, but a visit to the ornate structure in Greenway Plaza could hardly be considered slumming. Matronly waitresses add a homey touch to these opulent surroundings, serving top-drawer meals of chicken, veal, and other dishes. There is also a choice of main-course salads, so you can eat light while trying to figure out which power broker is at the next table.

ROTISSERIE FOR BEEF AND BIRD

2200 Wilcrest • 977-9524 • Lunch Monday–Friday, dinner Monday–Saturday. Closed Sunday • $$$–$$$$ • AE, MC, V • W

From appetizer to dessert, the Rotisserie for Beef and Bird excels at serving a unique meal with style and finesse. Beef and fowl receive equal billing and equal attention in the kitchen, which for every sirloin, ribeye, and T-bone produces a just-as-savory goose, pheasant, or quail. Prime rib is also a staple of the menu, as are assorted seafood dishes.

TONY'S

1801 Post Oak Blvd. • 622-6778 • Monday–Saturday, dinner only. Closed Sunday • $$$$ • Cr • W

This is Tony with both a capital T and a small t. Tony's is tony because it is the place to see and be seen in Houston. The lords and ladies of local society make frequent visits, and their presence is duly noted in the gossip columns. The Tony of the name, meanwhile, is owner Tony Vallone, who backs up his restaurant's high-profile reputation with some excellent continental dishes. Swordfish, snapper, veal, and Grand Marnier soufflé are just a few examples of the cuisine that has many other Houston restaurants envious.

VARGO'S

2401 Fondren • 782-3888 • Monday–Saturday, dinner only. Closed Sunday $$$–$$$$ • Cr • W

Vargo's has the most pastoral setting of any Houston restaurant. The dining room, with floor-to-ceiling windows on three sides, overlooks a small lake surrounded by dense gardens. After watching some of the graceful swans that populate the lake, it may be unsettling to order roast duckling, but prime rib, snapper *amandine,* or *filet mignon* are equally flavorful alternatives. As you're driving in, keep a lookout for the peacocks that roam the grounds.

Delis and Sandwiches

ANTONE'S

Various locations • Closed Sunday • $ • No Cr • W

It's surprising that a large percentage, if not most, of Antone's customers come in simply for the poorboy sandwiches, since foodstuffs are imported from all over the world. The poorboys are pretty basic, but Antone's sells hundreds in a day. As long as you're there, take a look around at the wines, cheeses, and other international goods.

BUTERA'S

4621 Montrose • 520-8426 • Open daily • $–$$ • Cr • W

Butera's combines the churn-'em-out technique of a fast-food restaurant with the dizzying variety of a quality deli, and it is under the latter category that it qualifies. Be prepared to wait in line, but you'll need that time to decide what to order from the large chalkboard that lists soups, salads, quiches, and sandwiches. There is a sea of imported beers and wines, plus such tempting morsels as cookies and cheesecake for dessert.

JAMES CONEY ISLAND

Various locations • Open daily • $ • No Cr • W

The hot dogs served with mustard, *chili,* cheese, and onions have been an institution in Houston since 1923, and the combination has never changed, nor has the *chili.* As John Wayne said, "This is damn good chili." As the city has grown, so has James Coney Island, with restaurants all over town. The menu now includes *chili* pie, hamburgers, and kosher sandwiches, but the dogs will always be the mainstay, as will those large wooden chairs that resemble school desks.

Hamburgers

GOODE CO. HAMBURGERS & TAQUERIA

4902 Kirby • 520-9153 • Open daily • $ • AE, DC, MC, V • W

After making it big in barbecue and before diving into seafood, Jim Goode decided to do a number on a traditional favorite (hamburgers) and a Juanny-come-lately (*fajitas*). The results are outstanding. The one-third-pound and half-pound burgers and the flavorful *fajitas* are served cafeteria-style, with fixings on a do-it-yourself basis. At lunchtime, the indoor dining room quickly overflows into the outdoor patio.

Italian

DAMIAN'S CUCINA ITALIANA

3011 Smith • 522-0439 • Lunch and dinner Monday–Friday. Saturday dinner only. Closed Sunday • $$–$$$ • Cr • W

Restaurants run in the Mandola family. After helping create D'Amico *Ristorante Italiano* (see below), Damian opened his own place in early 1984. Brother Tony has two oyster bars and was in on the formative years of the Ninfa's Mexican restaurant chain, while brother Vincent runs Nino's (see below; named for their father). Damian does the tradition proud with chicken, veal, seafood, and pasta dishes that attract some appreciative diners from nearby downtown.

D'AMICO RISTORANTE ITALIANO

2407 Westheimer • 524-5551 • Lunch and dinner Monday–Saturday. Closed Sunday • $$$ • Cr • W

Within a few years of its opening, in late 1977, D'Amico had become a top-flight Italian restaurant and is still willing to take on all comers in its position as one of the city's most popular spots for dining out. The appetizer called "straw and hay"—green and white pasta with mushrooms and ham in a cream sauce—is an excellent lead-in to one of the chicken, veal, or seafood dishes. For dessert, try the *cassata*. Now that's Italian!

THE GREAT CARUSO

10001 Westheimer • 780-4900 • Dinner only Tuesday–Sunday. Closed Mondays • $$$ • Cr. • W

Dinner at the Great Caruso is an event. The restaurant's name only gives a hint of the operatic theme. It is decorated in the style of a turn-of-the-century opera house and is filled with all types of operatic memorabilia. A stage for live entertainment is supplemented by a cadre of singing waiters. The seafood selection includes such exotic fare as squid, swordfish, and octopus, while steak, veal, and prime rib are prepared in a manner befitting a fine restaurant.

NINO'S

2817 S. Dallas • 522-5120 • Monday–Friday, dinner only. Lunch and dinner Saturday. Closed Sunday • $$–$$$ • Cr • W

Nino's calls itself "down home Italian," and that's certainly truth in advertising. A product of one of the city's most industrious restaurant families (*see* Damian's), Nino's puts the Italian touch to ribeye, shrimp, trout, and other dishes. Specialties include *ravioli* and *lasagna*. And don't feel you're lacking imagination by ordering pizza. You may never go back to the franchise variety.

PIZZERIA UNO

7531 Westheimer • 780-8866 • Open daily • $–$$ • AE, MC, V • W
   Houston had seen deep-dish pizza before this, but not like the genuine article found here. The delicious crust deserves endless praise, and gets it from Frank Sinatra, Henry Mancini, and Sonny Bono. An assortment of fresh ingredients is piled on, with cheese complimenting rather than dominating the mix.

Mexican

CADILLAC BAR

1802 Shepherd • 862-2020 • Lunch and dinner daily • $$ • Cr • W
   The Cadillac Bar has that "lived-in" look. Guests are free to write on the walls while straw mannequins hanging in the windows watch over them. Notice that the menu has a few out-of-the-ordinary items, such as roast or fried quail and *cabrito* (the latter when available). The *tacos al carbon,* Cadillac omelette, or snapper Veracruz are more mainstream but still worthy of note. The menu prices are listed in both dollars and pesos, even though the Cadillac Bar doesn't take pesos. If you care to comment, leave a note on the wall.

NINFA'S

Various locations • Lunch and dinner daily • $$ • Cr • W
   In 1973, Ninfa Laurenzo, a widowed mother of five, opened a small Mexican restaurant on Houston's east side to support her family. Within the next decade she had not only expanded her operation to all parts of the city but also had revolutionized Mexican food as Houstonians knew it. Combining a flair for getting her name before the public (note the *Ninfaritas* and *tacos a la Ninfa* on the menu) with some delicious recipes, she took Mexican food into the big time. Some old patrons prefer the original location, at 2704 Navigation, for its ambiance.

PAPPASITO'S

Various locations • Lunch and dinner daily • $$ • AE, MC, V • W
   The Pappas family, owners of Pappas Seafood House and other restaurants, makes a bold foray into Mexican food and comes out a winner. The *fajitas al carbon* provide a pound of flavorful skirt steak and flour *tortillas,* allowing the customers to roll their own. Pappasito's also features charbroiled swordfish, baked red snapper, and broiled shrimp with onions and spices. These places are known almost as much for the long wait for a table (up to two hours) as they are for the food.

Other Ethnic

AMÉRICAS

1800 Post Oak Blvd • 961-1492 • Monday–Friday lunch and dinner; Saturday dinner only; closed Sunday • $$$ • Cr • W
   Notice the last four digits of the phone number. These people think of everything. The literally fantastic decor probably would qualify as an installation at the Contemporary Arts Museum. The food is a fascinating melange of dishes from all over the Western Hemisphere—some bizarre, some surprising, just about all wonderful. The charcoal-grilled vegetables are a special treat. When they recommend reservations, believe them.

SAMMY'S

5825 Richmond • 780-0065 • Lunch and dinner daily • $$ • Cr • W

Lebanese food is the province of Sammy's, and customers needn't explore the menu very far to hit upon some great food. The best choices among the appetizers are *mezza* (a collection of Lebanese hors d'oeuvres) and *homos bi tahini* (a Mideastern dip). Each of these would be enough for a meal for two people but, if you want to venture further, try the *shish tawook* (broiled boneless chicken) or *falafel* plate (no briefer way to describe them can be found than "vegetable burgers").

Seafood

CAPTAIN BENNY'S HALFSHELL

Various locations • Lunch and dinner Monday–Saturday. Closed Sunday $–$$ • No Cr • W

Captain Benny's attracts attention by its appearance. Each restaurant is shaped like a boat, appearing to have run aground along the city's major thoroughfares. The quarters can get somewhat cramped, especially during lunch, but that's because the crab, oysters, gumbo, and shrimp can't be beat for being quick and good.

GOODE CO. TEXAS SEAFOOD

2621 Westpark • 523-7154 • Lunch and dinner daily • $$ • AE, C, V • W

Jim Goode doesn't have to go far to survey his restaurant empire. After successes with barbecue and hamburger places on Kirby Dr., Goode Co. Texas Seafood is another winner. The mesquite-grilled dinners—rainbow trout, swordfish, shrimp, and other selections—are the most succulent, savory items on the menu. The fried fare, which includes oysters, catfish, shrimp, and frog legs, is also praiseworthy, making good on his attempt to emulate the 1950s-era seafood joints that populated the Gulf Coast.

LANDRY'S ON WESTHEIMER

8816 Westheimer • 975-7873 • Lunch and dinner daily • $$ • Cr • W

The intent here is to capture the spirit of New Orleans, or at least the noise. Consider it done. The place is loud, but in a boisterous, fun-loving way. Gumbo, blackened redfish, and shrimp all have sufficient kick to them, and the fried fish and beans and rice are recommended for those looking for something delicious but a bit more bland.

PAPPAS SEAFOOD HOUSE

Various locations • Lunch and dinner daily • $$ • AE, MC, V • W

Fresh fish by the boatload is what each Pappas Seafood House specializes in. If the shrimp doesn't get you, the redfish will. Or maybe the trout or the oysters. Any or all of the above have helped make Pappas one of the most popular seafood restaurants in the city. And don't miss the key lime pie for dessert.

SHANGHAI RED'S

8501 Cypress • 926-6666 • Lunch and dinner daily • $$$ • Cr • W variable

The Turning Basin from Shanghai Red's put the maritime center in an attractive romantic light. But, take a good look at Shanghai Red's itself—a large, ramshackle building that resembles an abandoned mill. There's more charm. Seafood is done best with swordfish, blackened redfish, and Cajun popcorn shrimp.

ACCOMMODATIONS

($ = under $45, $$ = $46–$60, $$$ = $61–$80, $$$$ = $81–$100, $$$$$ = over $100)
Room tax 15%

ADAM'S MARK

**2900 Briarpark Dr. at Westheimer in the southwest • 978-7400 or
800-444-ADAM (800-444-2326), e-mail: cro.adamsmark@ internetmci.com
$$$$–$$$$$ • W+ 4 rooms • No-smoking rooms**
The ten-story Adam's Mark offers 604 units including 49 suites ($$$$$), and
two floors of no-smoking rooms. Children 18 and under free in room with par-
ents. AARP senior discount and package plans available. Fire sprinklers in
rooms. Cable TV with HBO. Room phones (charge for local calls). No pets. Two
restaurants with room service. Three lounges, one with entertainment. Indoor-
outdoor pool with exercise room and indoor whirlpool. Free transportation to
the Galleria. One-day dry cleaning. Free self-parking.

HOLIDAY INN CROWNE PLAZA

**2222 West Loop 610 South near the Galleria • 961-7272 or 800-327-6213, Web
site http://www.holiday-inn.com/ • $$$$–$$$$$ • W+ 20 rooms • No-smoking
rooms**
The 23-story Crowne Plaza offers 477 units including six suites ($$$$$) and 80
no-smoking rooms. Children 19 and under free in room with parents. AARP
senior discount and package plans available. Fire sprinklers in rooms and room
fire intercom system. Cable TV with Showtime. Room phones (charge for local
calls). No pets allowed. Two restaurants, room service. Bar. Indoor pool with
whirlpool and exercise room. Public golf course nearby (Memorial Park). One-
day dry cleaning. Free newspaper. Free transportation within a three-mile
radius. Garage parking with fee.

DOUBLETREE HOTEL

**15747 John F. Kennedy Blvd. near Intercontinental Airport • 442-8000 or 800-
528-0444, Web site http://www.doubletreehotels.com/DoubleT/Reserv.htm
$$$$–$$$$$ • W+ 8 rooms • No-smoking rooms**
The seven-story Doubletree is built around a lush courtyard with 315 units,
including 12 suites ($$$$$) and 90 no-smoking rooms. Children 17 and under
free in room with parents. AARP senior discount and package plans available.
Cable TV with pay movie channel. Room phones (charge for local calls).
Restaurant, two lounges. Outdoor pool and whirlpool, exercise room. Guest
membership at World Houston Golf Course. One-day dry cleaning. Free news-
paper. Free airport transportation. Free self-parking.

EMBASSY SUITES HOTEL

**9090 Southwest Freeway on the southwest side of the Galleria • 995-0123 or
800-553-3417, Web site http://www.embassy-suites.com/embassydocs/
about.html • $$$$ • W+ 4 rooms • No-smoking rooms**
The Embassy Suites offer 243 units of two-room suites with 112 no-smoking
suites. Children 12 and under free in room with parents. AARP senior discount.
Room fire sprinklers and room fire intercom system. No pets. Cable TV with
HBO. Room phones (charge for local calls). Kitchens equipped with coffeemak-
ers, microwave ovens, refrigerators. Free cocktail reception each weekday with

hors d'oeurves and continental breakfast every morning. An indoor pool, sauna, and steam room. One-day dry cleaning. Free newspaper. Free van service to Sharpstown Mall and the Galleria. Free self-parking.

FOUR SEASONS

1300 Lamar in downtown • 650-1300 or 800-332-3442 • $$$$$ • W+ 4 rooms No-smoking rooms

The 30-story Four Seasons offers 399 units including 12 suites ($$$$$) and 13 floors of non-smoking rooms. The top ten floors of the Four Seasons are apartments. Children 18 and under free in room with parents. Package plans. Fire sprinklers in rooms and room fire intercom system. Cable TV with HBO. Room phones (charge for local calls). Pets OK (deposit required). Three restaurants with room service. Two clubs. Outdoor heated pool, indoor whirlpool, exercise room. Free downtown transportation. Valet parking with a $11 daily charge. One-day dry cleaning. The Park Shopping Mall is across the street. The Four Seasons is considered one of the most posh hotels in Houston.

HOBBY AIRPORT HILTON

8181 Airport Blvd. in southeast • 645-3000 or 800-695-2740 nationwide, Web site http://www.hilton.com/reservations/index.html • $$$–$$$$$ • W+ 4 rooms • No-smoking rooms

The Hilton has nine stories plus three stories of cabana units, making a total of 310 units including 32 suites ($$$$$) and five floors of no-smoking rooms. Children any age free in room with parents. AARP senior discount and package plans available. Fire sprinklers in rooms with room fire intercom system. No pets. Cable TV with Spectradyne. Room phones (charge for local calls). Two restaurants with room service. Two lounges. Outdoor pool, exercise room. One-day dry cleaning. Free newspaper. Free Hobby Airport transportation. Free self-parking.

J. W. MARRIOTT

5150 Westheimer across from the Galleria • 961-1500 or in Texas 800-392-5477, outside Texas 800-228-9290, Web site http://www.hyatt.com./TravelWeb/mc/common/marriott.html • $$$$$ • W+ 4 rooms • No-smoking rooms

This 23-story J. W. Marriott offers 494 units including four suites ($$$$$) and 148 no-smoking rooms. Children 12 and under free in room with parents. AARP senior discount and package plans available. Fire sprinklers in rooms. Pets OK (deposit required). Cable TV with HBO and Spectradyne. Room phones (charge for local calls). Restaurant with room service. Lobby bar with entertainment. Health club with an indoor-outdoor pool, exercise room, sauna, racquetball courts, steam room, outdoor tennis courts. Concierge floor. One-day dry cleaning. Free newspaper. Free self-parking underground.

HOTEL SOFITEL

18700 Kennedy Blvd. close to Intercontinental Airport • 445-9000 or in Texas 800-231-4612, worldwide 800-221-4542 • $$$$$ • W+ 4 rooms • No-smoking rooms

This eight-story French-style hotel offers 337 rooms including ten suites ($$$$$) and four floors of no-smoking rooms. Children 14 and under free in room with parents. AARP senior discount and package plans available. Fire sprinklers in rooms. No pets. Cable TV with HBO and Spectradyne. Room phones (charge for local calls). Two restaurants with room service. Lounge. Outdoor pool with two whirlpools, exercise room. Free newspaper with room service. One-day dry cleaning. Free airport transportation. Free self-parking.

HYATT REGENCY

1200 Louisiana in downtown • 654-1234 or 800-233-1234, Web site http://www.hyatt.com/ • $$$$$ • W+ 10 rooms • No-smoking rooms

The 30-story Hyatt Regency offers 958 units which include 52 suites ($$$$$) and 550 no-smoking rooms. Children 18 and under stay free in room with parents. AARP senior discount and package plans available. Pets OK. Cable TV with HBO, Showtime and The Movie Channel. Room phones (charge for local calls). Four restaurants including the revolving Spindletop Restaurant. Room service. Two bars with entertainment. Outdoor heated pool, exercise room. Free membership in the YMCA just down the street. Some rooms with coffeemakers. Airport terminal in the hotel. Free newspaper. One-day dry cleaning. Valet parking with fee.

LA COLOMBE D'OR

3410 Montrose Blvd. in the Museum District • 524-7999 • $$$$$

This six-room European-style chalet is in one of the city's grand old historic mansions. One child allowed free in room with parents. AARP senior discount. Bridal packages available. Pets OK. Room phones (charge for local calls). Cable TV with HBO. Restaurant. One-day dry cleaning. Free continental breakfast with newspaper served in the room. Free parking. The restaurant cuisine is French inspired, splendid, and expensive.

LANCASTER HOTEL

701 Texas Ave. in the downtown theater district • 228-9500 or 800-231-0336 $$$$$ • W+ 6 rooms • No-smoking rooms

This 12-story historic hotel has 93 units including two floors of no-smoking rooms. Children 16 and under free in room with parents. Package plans. Fire sprinklers in rooms. Pets OK. Cable TV. Room phones (charge for local calls). Restaurant with room service. Bar. Guest membership in the Texas Club (a fitness club) two blocks away. One-day dry cleaning. Valet parking ($5). Reminiscent of a small elegant European hotel. Restaurant/bar popular with the theater crowd.

THE RED LION

2525 West Loop 610 South at Westheimer in the Galleria Area • 961-3000 or 800-AT TEXAS (800-288-3927), Web site: http://www.hyatt.com/TravelWeb/ rl/common/redlion.html • $$$$ • W+ 4 rooms • No-smoking rooms

The 15-story Red Lion (once the Sheraton Grand) offers 319 rooms with 25 suites ($$$$$) and 75 no-smoking rooms. Children 18 and under free in room with parents. AARP senior discount and package plans available. Fire sprinklers and room fire intercom system. No pets. Cable TV with pay channels. Room phones (charge for local calls). Restaurant with room service. Sports bar. Outdoor pool and whirlpool with exercise room and sauna. One-day dry cleaning. Free newspaper. Free self-parking.

RITZ-CARLTON

919 Briar Oaks Lane near the Galleria • 840-7600 or 800-241-3333, Web site http://www.hyatt.com./TravelWeb/rz/common/ritz.html• $$$$$
W+ 2 rooms • No-smoking rooms

The 11-story Ritz-Carlton offers 232 rooms including 25 suites, some with a jacuzzi ($$$$$+) and eight floors of no-smoking rooms. Children 18 and under free in room with parents. Package plans. Cable TV with HBO. Room phones (charge for local calls). Two restaurants plus a lounge with piano bar and dancing. Outdoor heated pool and exercise room. Guest memberships available for golf and health club. Concierge floor. One-day dry cleaning. Free newspaper. Valet parking. Very elegant hotel famed for afternoon High Tea. Here is really "putting on the ritz."

RENAISSANCE GREENWAY PLAZA

6 Greenway Plaza East off Southwest Freeway at Edloe next to the Summit and Greenway Plaza • 629-1200 or 800-HOTELS-1 (800-468-3571) • $$$$$
W+ 8 rooms • No-smoking rooms

The 20-story Stouffers offers 389 units including nine suites ($$$$$) and 110 no-smoking rooms. Children 18 and under free in room with parents. AARP senior discount and package plans available. Fire sprinklers and room fire intercom system. Pets under 20 pounds OK. Cable TV with HBO. Room phones (charge for local calls). Restaurant with room service. Lounge with entertainment. City Lights Club on the roof with great view. Outdoor pool and whirlpool, exercise room, and sauna. Guest membership in the Houston City Club with health facilities. Free self-parking or valet (fee) parking. One-day dry cleaning. Free transportation within a five-mile radius. Free newspaper. Coffeemakers in rooms.

WESTIN OAKS

5011 Westheimer • *See* Westin Galleria

WESTIN GALLERIA

5060 W. Alabama in the Galleria • 960-8100 or 800-228-3000, Web site http://www.westin.com/listings/index.html • $$$$$ • W+ 10 rooms
No-smoking rooms

The 24-story Westin Galleria and 21-story Westin Oaks offer 900 units including 52 suites ($$$$$+) and two floors of non-smoking rooms. Children 18 and under free in room with parents. AARP senior discount. Pets OK. Cable TV with pay channels. Room phones (charge for local calls). Seven restaurants. Three clubs. Two outdoor pools, jogging track, tennis, miniature golf, and access (for a fee) to the University Club in the Galleria, which includes squash and racquetball courts and other exercise facilities. Concierge service. One-day dry cleaning. Free self-parking underground or pay valet parking. The hotels are connected to the fabulous Galleria business and shopping complex that offers more than 250 stores, movie theaters, restaurants, art galleries, and an indoor ice-skating rink.

WOODLANDS INN AND COUNTRY CLUB

2301 N. Millbend Dr. *27 miles north of Houston on I-45 at Woodlands Parkway exit* • **Write P.O. Box 4000, The Woodlands, Texas, 77387 281-367-1100 or in Texas 800-533-3052, outside Texas 800-433-2624 • $$$$ W+ 8 rooms • No-smoking rooms**

The two-story Woodlands offers 268 units situated on several sprawling, heavily wooded acres with 40 no-smoking rooms. Children 12 and under stay free in room with parents. AARP senior discount and package plans available. Pets OK with a charge. Cable TV with Showtime. Room phones (charge for local calls). Three restaurants. Lounge. Three golf courses, 24 lighted tennis courts, two full health spas, two swimming pools. Shopping center. One-day dry cleaning. Parking is free, but there is a $20 charge for transportation to the airport. The Cynthia Miller Pavilion, with its many outstanding concerts, is a nearby attraction.

WYNDHAM WARWICK

5701 S. Main • 526-1991 or 800-822-4200 • $$$$ • W+ 10 rooms No-smoking rooms

The 12-story historic Wyndham Warwick offers 310 rooms that include 48 suites ($$$$$). Children 17 and under free in room with parents. AARP senior discount and package plans available. Fire sprinklers in rooms. No pets. Cable TV with HBO. Room phones (charge for local calls). Two restaurants with room service. Lobby lounge. Outdoor pool, exercise room, and sauna. Free transportation to the Texas Medical Center and downtown. One-day dry cleaning. Self-parking or valet parking. Located between downtown and the Medical Center, the Warwick is within walking distance of the Museum of Fine Arts, the Contemporary Arts Museum, and Rice University.

Bed and Breakfast

ANGEL ARBOR BED & BREAKFAST

848 Heights Blvd. • 868-4654 • $$–$$$ • No-smoking in house

Angel Arbor has four bedrooms, four baths and a honeymoon cottage. Antique furnishings are throughout the house, and a full breakfast is served. This unique bed and breakfast is housed in a Victorian mansion on the National Register of Historic Places and hosts Murder Mystery Dinner Parties. Infants and children over 12 welcome.

THE LOVETT INN

501 Lovett Blvd. • 522-5224 • $$–$$$ • No-smoking in house

The Lovett Inn has six bedrooms, each with private bath and queen-size beds. Built in 1924, this grand home is furnished with antiques, but there are phones and TV sets in each room. All rooms overlook the pool, spa, and lovely garden. A buffet continental breakfast is served.

HUNTSVILLE

Walker County Seat • 34,592 • (409)

The city was founded as an Indian trading post in the mid-1830s by a frontiersman named Pleasant Gray, who named it after his former home of Huntsville, Alabama. When the county was created in 1846, it was named for U.S. Senator Robert J. Walker of Mississippi, who was in favor of Texas annexation. But Robert J. Walker was sympathetic to the Union in the Civil War, so in 1863 the county was renamed after another Walker, Captain Samuel H., who was a noted Texas Ranger killed during the Mexican War. Sam Houston called Huntsville his home and is buried here.

TOURIST SERVICES

HUNTSVILLE-WALKER COUNTY CHAMBER OF COMMERCE

1327 11th St. (P.O. Box 538, 77342) • 295-8113 • W

SAM HOUSTON STATUE AND HUNTSVILLE VISITORS CENTER

34000 TX 75 (P.O. Box 1230, 77342) • 291-9726 • Monday–Saturday 10–6, Sunday 12–6 • Free • W

MUSEUMS

SAM HOUSTON MEMORIAL MUSEUM COMPLEX

1836 Sam Houston Ave. • 294-1832 • Open Tuesday–Sunday 9–5. Closed Monday • Free • W variable

A beautifully landscaped 15-acre park full of history and Sam Houston memorabilia contains seven intriguing buildings including the main museum, Sam Houston's law office, a pioneer kitchen, a blacksmith shop, the War and Peace House, Sam Houston's home "Woodland," and the Steamboat House where Houston died in 1863. Check at the museum for tour times. Gift shop.

TEXAS PRISON MUSEUM

1113 12th Street • 295-2155 • Open Tuesday–Friday noon–5, Saturday 9–5, Sunday 2–5 • Adults $2, children $1.50 • W+

Huntsville is the site of the oldest prison in Texas, "The Walls," and its list of inmates reads like a Who's Who in crime. This museum is the only one of its kind in Texas, and you can see "Old Sparky," the Texas electric chair used to electrocute 361 inmates from 1924 to 1964, plus many unique items.

HISTORIC PLACES

Historic buildings include: the **Collard Log House** (1834) on 19th St. across from Sam Houston Park, the **Rogers-Baird House** (1845) at 1418 University, the **Austin College Building** (1852) on the campus of Sam Houston State University, and the **Ward Home** (1870) now the Junction Restaurant at 2641 11th. The **Gibbs-Powell Home** at 1228 11th is the only one open for tours Saturday 10–4.

SAM HOUSTON'S GRAVE AND MONUMENT

Oakwood Cemetery • Ave. I and 9th
   The monument bears Andrew Jackson's tribute, "The world will take care of Houston's fame." The two-block-long street to the cemetery, Spur 94, is the shortest Texas highway in the state.

OTHER POINTS OF INTEREST

HUNTSVILLE STATE PARK

Take I-45 south approximately 8 miles to Park Rd. 40 **• 295-5644 • Open 8–5 for day use, at all times for camping • Fee per vehicle • W variable**
   This 2,083-acre park lies in the piney woods of the Sam Houston National Forest and includes **Lake Raven.** Facilities include boat launching ramps, lighted fishing piers, 11 miles of hiking and nature trails, picnic area, camping (fee), and canoe and pedal boat rentals. Water skiing prohibited.

SPORTS AND ACTIVITIES

Golf

COUNTRY CAMPUS

TX 19 northeast of town • 291-0008 • 9-hole course. Greens fee: weekdays $9, weekends and holidays $10.50, senior citizens weekdays $5.80, weekends and holidays $7.40.

Scuba Diving

BLUE LAGOON

Take I-45 north 6 miles and take Exit 123 east 4 miles **• 291-6111 or Houston 281-376-3157 • Admission**
   Called "The Texas Cozumel," Blue Lagoon is a scuba diver's paradise. This lagoon is a place run by divers for divers. It has rest rooms, concessions, camping, air-fill station, picnic tables, and first-aid station (including oxygen). To make sure this is strictly for divers, no swimming is allowed, no pets, no small children, and cliff-jumping will result in expulsion. Weekends 8–dark, weekdays May–October, 10–6.

COLLEGES AND UNIVERSITIES

SAM HOUSTON STATE UNIVERSITY (SHSU)

Sam Houston and Bowers • 294-1111 • W+ but not all areas
Visitor parking marked
   Founded in 1879, SHSU was the first state-supported teacher-training institute west of the Mississippi. The university now has more than 12,000 students. Visitors are welcome to intercollegiate athletic events, plays, and concerts. Check the planetarium for its monthly shows.

SIDE TRIPS

LAKE LIVINGSTON

Take US 190 east about 24 miles **• 365-2292 (Trinity River Authority) Open at all times • Free • W variable (***See* **Livingston)**

SAM HOUSTON NATIONAL FOREST

344-6205 • Open at all times • Free • W variable

Huntsville sits just northwest of this vast 160,443-acre forest. The nearest recreation area to Huntsville is the **Stubblefield Lake Recreation Area.** Also in the forest is the 27-mile **Lone Star Hiking Trail.** For information write: District Ranger, Sam Houston National Forest, P.O. Box 393, New Waverly 77358.

ANNUAL EVENTS

April

GENERAL SAM HOUSTON FOLK FESTIVAL

Sam Houston Memorial Complex and the Sam Houston State University Campus • 800-289-0389 • Third weekend in April • $5 • W

The colorful contrasts of Texas are reflected within the various cultural groups who gather to show, tell, and entertain through foods, crafts, music, dance, and costumed characters telling stories of their role in Texas history.

RESTAURANTS

($ = under $7, $$ = $8–$17, $$$ = $18–$25, $$$$ = over $25 for one person excluding drinks, tax, and tip.)

JUNCTION RESTAURANT

2641 11th • 291-2183 • Lunch and dinner daily • $–$ • Cr • W call ahead Children's plates

This charming restaurant in a historic landmark offers prime rib, steaks, chicken, and seafood, plus a wide selection of light meals. Bar.

NEW ZION MISSIONARY BAPTIST CHURCH

Exit 114 off I-45 east on FM 1374 one mile. **Restaurant next to church 295-7394 • Tuesday, Wednesday, and Thursday 8–7, Friday and Saturday 8–8. Closed Sunday and Monday • $ • W+**

Some of the finest in East Texas barbecue has to be here in this modest dining room. Don't miss the all-you-can-eat family-style meals.

ACCOMMODATIONS

($ = under $45, $$ = $46–$60, $$$ = $61–$80, $$$$ = $81–$100, $$$$$ = over $100)
Room tax 10%

LA QUINTA

1407 I-45, just north of TX 30 • 295-6454 • $$–$$$ • W+ 1 room No-smoking rooms

This two-story motel has 120 rooms. Cable TV with HBO, pay channel, and Nintendo in rooms. Room phones. Restaurant and lounge. Outdoor pool, picnic area. All rooms have coffeemakers. Free "First Light" continental breakfast.

Bed and Breakfast

THE WHISTLER

906 Avenue M • 295-2834 or (713) 524-0011 • $$$$ • No-smoking

Just two blocks from the center of Huntsville is a secluded Greek Revival mansion (circa 1859) that is the epitome of the Old South. It offers six rooms, each with private bath, and all furnished in beautiful antiques. Breakfast is usually served in the elegant dining room on the family china and crystal. No children. No pets.

INDEPENDENCE

Washington County • 140 • (409)

Founded in 1824 by John P. Coles, a member of one of Stephen F. Austin's original 300 families, the site was originally Coles Settlement. (Coles' log cabin is now restored at the entrance of Old Baylor Park.) The name was changed to honor the signing of the Texas Declaration of Independence at nearby Washington-on-the-Brazos. It became an educational center, and the ruins of Baylor Female College and Baylor University are located in Old Baylor Park. But, Independence lost the election for county seat to Brenham by three votes, the railroad bypassed it, and the colleges moved. Now it is a crossroads community with several interesting sights.

MUSEUMS

TEXAS BAPTIST HISTORICAL CENTER MUSEUM

Intersection of FM 50 and FM 390 • 836-5117 • Wednesday–Saturday 10–4. Sunday 1–5 by reservation only • Free (donations) • W

The original adobe church was destroyed by fire and the present church built in 1872. The museum contains a collection of records of the church and town, as well as the history of Baptists in Texas.

POINTS OF INTEREST

THE ANTIQUE ROSE EMPORIUM

9300 Lueckmeyer Rd., Brenham 77833, FM 50 approximately .4 miles south of FM 390 • 836-5548 • Monday–Saturday 9–6, Sunday 11–5:30. Closed on major holidays • Free • W

More than 200 varieties of old garden roses are grown here with some documented to have been grown during the Republic of Texas. The gardens of annuals, perennials, and roses are at their peak from mid-March through mid-May. Fall Festival of Roses in November. Newsletter and catalog available.

EARLY HOMES OF INDEPENDENCE

FM 390/FM 50 area • 836-0548 • Saturday and Sunday during March and April, 1:30–4:30. Other dates by appointment • W variable

Step back in time and experience several rare Texas Colonial buildings. Tours are offered of two of the earliest homes of Washington County and a rural one-room schoolhouse.

JASPER

Jasper County Seat • 8,500 • (409)
With woods covering almost 90% of the county, it is no surprise that Jasper is called "The Jewel of the Forest." The city began as Bevil's settlement in 1824. In 1835 the name was changed to Jasper in honor of Sergeant William Jasper, a hero of the American Revolution and member of Francis Marion's famed regiment. The county was one of the original 23 counties created in 1836 by the Republic of Texas and was named after the city. The weekly newspaper, the *Jasper News Boy,* one of the oldest in Texas, has been published continuously since 1865.

TOURIST SERVICES

JASPER CHAMBER OF COMMERCE
246 E. Milam (75951) • 384-2762, Web site: www.inu.net/Jasper

HISTORIC PLACES

The 1890 **Beaty-Orton House,** 200 S. Main St., is a restored Victorian home on the National Register of Historic Places. For tours, call 383-6138.

The **Jasper County Courthouse,** on the square in downtown Jasper, was built in 1889 and restored in 1993. It is the only courthouse in the state to replace its clock tower after an absence of 36 years. Guided tours given by the Jasper Historical Commision, Monday–Friday. Free. Call 384-6441.

SHOPPING

ANTIQUES & ARTS SHOWCASE
121 W. Houston • 384-6961
Handmade crafts, kitchen collectibles, glassware, quilts, baskets, large selection pottery, various colors granite ware, American oak furniture, yankee candles and gift items, homemade jams and jellies.

SIDE TRIPS

ANGELINA NATIONAL FOREST
Nearest entrance about 13 miles northwest on TX 63 • 634-7709
Open at all times • Free • W variable
Its 154,916 acres make it the smallest of the national forests in Texas, but it is still big enough to spread across four counties. Adjacent to Lake Sam Rayburn, the forest offers facilities for fishing, boating, water sports, picnicking, and camping (fee), plus a five-and-a-half-mile *Sawmill Hiking Trail.* For information write: Forest Supervisor, Angelina National Forest, P.O. Box 756, Lufkin 75901.

LAKE B. A. STEINHAGEN
Take US 190 west about 12 miles • 384-5231 • Open at all times • Free
W variable
The 705 acres in the **Martin Dies, Jr. State Park,** on the eastern shore of the lake provide facilities for fishing, boating, water sports, and camping (fee). For information write: Martin Dies, Jr. State Park, Route 4, Box 274, Jasper 75951.

LAKE SAM RAYBURN

Take US 96 about 11 miles north to FM 255, then about 8 miles west (left) to dam area • **384-5716 (Army Corps of Engineers)** • **Open at all times** • **Free W variable**

"Mr. Sam's Lake" covers 114,500 acres at normal capacity, making it the largest manmade lake wholly within Texas. It offers 560 miles of shoreline with facilities for boating, fishing, picnicking, and camping (fee), plus many commercial marinas and motels. Rayburn Country Resort and Country Club is the most posh with golf and clubhouse. Call (800-882-1442). For lake information write: U.S. Army Corps of Engineers, Route 3, Box 320, Jasper 75951.

SABINE NATIONAL FOREST

North and east via US 96 • **1-275-2632** • **Open at all times** • **Free** • **W variable** (*See* **Center**)

RESTAURANTS

($ = under $7, $$ = $8–$17, $$$ = $18–$25, $$$$ = over $25 for one person excluding drinks, tax, and tip.)

TEXAS CHARLIE'S FAMILY RESTAURANT

399 S. Wheeler (US 96 in the Greentree Plaza Shopping Center) • **384-4451 Monday–Thursday 11–9, Friday 11–10, Saturday 5:30–10, Sunday buffet 11–2. Saturday 5:30–6. Closed Sunday** • **$–$$** • **Cr** • **W**

You'll find a varied menu with emphasis on barbecue cooked over hickory wood.

ACCOMMODATIONS

($ = under $45, $$ = $46–$60, $$$ = $61–$80, $$$$ = $81–$100, $$$$$ = over $100) Room tax 13%

RAMADA INN

249 E. Gibson (US 190 just west of US 96) • **384-9021 or 800-228-2828** • **$$ W+ 2 rooms** • **No-smoking rooms**

The two-story Ramada offers 100 rooms including a number of no-smoking. Cable TV with HBO. Room phones (charge for local call). Pets OK. Restaurant. Private club (guests automatically members). Outdoor pool. Memberships for guests available in local health club. Free coffee in lobby.

JEFFERSON

Marion County • **2,199** • **(903)**

Founded with the Republic in 1836, the fortunes of Jefferson literally rose and fell with the water in the Big Cypress Bayou. It became an important inland port because of a fluke of nature called the great Red River Raft. This was a monstrous 75-mile jam of debris, downed trees, and silt that over many years had built up so thick it blocked the river above Shreveport. The result was rechanneling of water that made a navigable route from Jefferson's Big Cypress Bayou through Caddo Lake and the Red River to the Mississippi. The town boomed as steamboats from New Orleans brought settlers westward and carried back the products of northeast Texas. Records show that 226 steamboats landed at this port in 1872, when it was at its height. It was just two years later that the Army engineers, using dynamite (that Nobel had invented a few years earlier), cleared the Red River Raft, and the waters returned to their normal channel, making the route to Jefferson impassable for the steamboats. Within a few years, the population of the town fell from about 10,000 to 2,000.

There is another story that goes along with this history that is interesting to tell, even though some historians say it is more myth than fact. Supposedly, Jay Gould wanted the town fathers to give him money and land along the right-of-way as an inducement to bring his railroad to their town. But, content with their prosperous life as an inland port, they refused. Gould then predicted that this decision would mean the end of Jefferson. And it wasn't long after his prediction that the bustling inland port was left high and dry.

Fortunately, many of the old homes that graced the city in its glory days have been restored. Among those responsible for this preservation and restoration are the far-sighted members of the Jesse Allen Wise Garden Club, who started the historic homes tours and purchased and restored the Excelsior Hotel, Jay Gould's private railroad car, and other historic properties. Their efforts have paid off. Exploring the town now is like experiencing a living page of Texas history.

TOURIST SERVICES

MARION COUNTY CHAMBER OF COMMERCE
116 W. Austin (75657) • 665-2672 • Monday–Saturday 9–6 • W+

CYPRESS BAYOU RIVERBOAT RIDES
Hwy. 59 and Cypress River Bridge • 665-2222 • Adults $5.50, children $3.50

One-hour boat tour of Big Cypress Bayou. Usually runs every two hours, starting at 10 A.M., every day in summer and, as weather permits, in winter.

HISTORICAL HOMES TOURS
Chamber of Commerce, 116 W. Austin • 665-2672

There are seven historic homes that are open for tours at some time almost every day (see Historic Places, following). The Chamber of Commerce helps set up your visit to each house.

MULLINS NARRATED TOURS
Austin and Market, across from Jefferson Museum • 665-2857

This is a 40-minute tour of the historic district in a surrey drawn by two horses. By appointment.

MUSEUMS

JEFFERSON HISTORICAL MUSEUM
223 W. Austin at Market • 665-2775 • Daily 9–5, except closed December 24 and 25 • Adults $2, children under 12 $1

The museum, housed in the Old Post Office and Courts Building, was built in 1890 and is listed in the National Register of Historic Places. The basement and three floors are jammed with items relating to the history of the area. Among the more than 3,000 items on display are a 200-year-old loom that still works, a gun collection (approximately displayed in the old marshal's office), and Annie Oakley's boot last. The second-floor courtroom has been turned into an art gallery displaying a number of 16th- to 19th-century paintings. Gift shop.

HISTORIC PLACES

Jefferson is filled with buildings wearing the Texas State Historical Medallion. Following is a list of those normally open for tours.

EXCELSIOR HOTEL

211 W. Austin • 665-2513 • Tours daily 1:00 and 2:00 P.M.
Adults $2, children $1
This is the second oldest hotel in Texas, having been in continuous operation since it was built in 1858. Among its guests were Ulysses S. Grant, Rutherford B. Hayes, and Oscar Wilde. (*See* Accommodations.)

FREEMAN PLANTATION HOUSE

Take TX 49 west approximately 1 mile **• 665-2320 • Tours daily, times vary**
Adults $4, children $1
This is an example of the Greek Revival-style architecture favored by the planters of the area during the antebellum period. Built by slave labor in 1850, it was the center of a 1,000-acre plantation of cotton and sugar cane. It has been painstakingly restored and furnished with authentic furniture of its era.

HOUSE OF THE SEASONS

409 S. Allen • 665-1218 • Tours 10:30 and 1:30 • Adults $5.00
Built in 1872 during the heyday of Jefferson, the house is a fine example of the transition period between Greek Revival and Victorian styles of architecture. A unique feature is the cupola, from which the house gets its name. Each wall contains a different color of stained glass that, when looked through, creates the illusion of a different season.

OTHER POINTS OF INTEREST

CARNEGIE LIBRARY DOLL COLLECTION

301 Lafayette at Market • 665-8911 • Friday 12–5, Saturday 9–5, Sunday 1–5
50¢ admission to doll collection
An extensive collection that traces the history of dolls from primitive to modern times. Built in 1907, the library itself is one of only four libraries in Texas built with funds from the Andrew Carnegie Foundation that is still functioning as a library.

JAY GOULD'S PRIVATE RAILROAD CAR *ATALANTA*

210 W. Austin, across from Excelsior Hotel • 665-2513 • Daily 10–3
Adults $1, children under 12 50¢
It's ironic that financier Jay Gould's private rail car should wind up on display here after his dire prediction that Jefferson would fold up without his railroad. This palace on wheels is grounded now, but its interior is still luxurious. It contains four staterooms, a dining room, and a bathroom with a sterling silver washbasin.

SIDE TRIPS

CADDO LAKE STATE PARK
Take FM 2198 east approximately 12 miles • **679-3351** • **Open daily 8–10 for day use, at all times for camping** • **$2 per vehicle per day** • **W+ but not all areas**
See Marshall.

LAKE O' THE PINES
Take TX 49 northwest to FM 729, then west (left) to lake • **665-2336 (Army Corps of Engineers)** • **Open daily dawn to 10 for day use, at all times for camping** • **Free** • **W variable**
This 18,000-acre lake is excellent for fishing, swimming, boating, and other water sports. In addition to several Army Corps of Engineers parks with campsites (fee) on the lake shore, there are several commercial marinas. For information write: Reservoir Manager, Lake O' The Pines, P.O. Drawer W, Jefferson 75657-0660.

ANNUAL EVENTS

May

JEFFERSON PILGRIMAGE
665-2672 (Chamber of Commerce) • **First weekend in May**
Admission to Homes Tour and some events
The pilgrimage that visitors make is to a number of the stately old homes that each year are opened to the public. Each evening at 8 and Sunday at 3, a play called *The Diamond Bessie Murder Trial*, which has been put on by local citizens annually since 1955, is performed. It is the melodramatic reenactment of the 1877 trial of Abe Rothchild, son of a wealthy diamond merchant, who was accused of murdering his wife, an ex-prostitute. Her real name was Annie Stone, but she was called "Diamond Bessie" because of the many diamonds she wore. (He was finally acquitted.) It is performed at the Jefferson Playhouse at Delta and Henderson streets. The Junior Historians also put on a cabaret-type show several times each day in the Old McGarity Saloon, which they restored, at 61 Dallas St. Other activities include a fun run and a parade.

ACCOMMODATIONS

($ = under $45, $$ = $46–$60, $$$ = $61–$80, $$$$ = $81–$100, $$$$$ = over $100)
Room tax 13%

THE EXCELSIOR HOTEL
211 W. Austin • **665-2513** • **$$–$$$$**
The two-story Excelsior offers 14 rooms that include one suite ($$). Cable TV. No pets. Restaurant serves breakfast only by reservation. This is the second oldest hotel in Texas. It has been restored and furnished with antiques by the Jesse Allen Wise Garden Club. (*See* Historic Places above.)

HOTEL JEFFERSON HISTORIC INN
124 W. Austin • 665-2592 • $$–$$$$
This two-story inn has 23 rooms. TV. No pets. Restaurant open for breakfast only, with free breakfast for guests. Courtesy car to and from nearby airports and train and bus stations. Built in 1861 as a cotton warehouse, the building was later used as livery stable, saloon, skating rink, and hotel. Rooms furnished with antiques.

Bed and Breakfast

More than 50 houses in Jefferson, including some historic homes, offer bed-and-breakfast accommodations. Prices run from $65 to $185 a night, and the breakfasts range from continental to a full "plantation-style" meal. For an up-to-date list, contact the Marion County Chamber of Commerce (see above).

KILGORE

Gregg and Rusk Counties • 11,339 • (903)
From its founding in 1872 until 1930, the economy of this small town was based on cotton and timber. Then in 1930 the huge East Texas Oil Field was discovered, and Kilgore found itself a boom town right in the middle of the oil field. Today oil is still king, but the city's name has also been spread around the world as the home of pianist Van Cliburn and of the Kilgore College Rangerettes, the precision drill and dance team from Kilgore College.

TOURIST SERVICES

KILGORE CHAMBER OF COMMERCE
1100 Stone Rd. (P.O. Box 1582, 75663) • 984-5022 • W

MUSEUMS

EAST TEXAS OIL MUSEUM
Henderson Blvd. (US 259) at Ross on Kilgore College campus • 983-8295
Tuesday–Saturday 9–4 (9–5 June–August), Sunday 2–5. Closed Monday
Adults $4.00, children 3 to 11 $2.50 • W+ but not all areas • Parking lot in rear
Return with us now to those thrilling days of yesteryear when it was discovered that East Texas was sitting on a sea of oil. This museum gives you a chance to step back in time to the oil days. At the heart of the museum is a full-scale boomtown street scene that you walk into and become a part of. At the Boomtown Cinema, the feature is historical footage of the boom period, showing how the wildcatters fought the mud, weather, and frustration to bring in the wells. And as the movie ends you may think a well is coming in right under you, as the floor shakes and the earth rumbles. On the other side of the "street" at the Gladewater Museum, you can join a puppet guide and take a simulated elevator ride 3,800 feet below the surface of the earth directly to the oil deposits,

occasionally stopping en route so your guide can explain the geology of the layers of earth you pass through.

OTHER POINTS OF INTEREST

RANGERETTE SHOWCASE

Broadway at Ross on Kilgore College campus • 983-8273 • Monday–Friday 9–12, 1–5; Saturday 10–12, 1–4 • Free • Parking behind East Texas Oil Museum, 1 block east

The Kilgore College Rangerettes were the originals who brought show business to the gridiron with half-time shows of precision high kicks and dances. The museum displays their props and costumes and thousands of photographs. There is also a 10-minute film of performances of the Rangerettes and the Ranger Band that accompanies them.

WORLD'S RICHEST ACRE

Main and Commerce • Open at all times • Free • W

On this small street corner plot stands one original oil derricks and 12 restored derricks, a restored pumpjack, and a granite monument to the pioneer oil families of Kilgore. At one time there were more than 1,000 wells in downtown Kilgore; and 24 wells, owned by six different operators, were crammed onto just a little over an acre tract at this site. This acre produced over two and a half million barrels of crude oil.

COLLEGES AND UNIVERSITIES

KILGORE COLLEGE

Henderson Blvd. (US 259) between Houston and Laird • 984-8531 • W

There are about 4,500 full-time students enrolled at this junior college. The campus is the site of the Shakespeare Garden, which is a horticultural display of plants mentioned in Shakespeare's plays.

ACCOMMODATIONS

($ = under $45, $$ = $46–$60, $$$ = $61–$80, $$$$ = $81–$100, $$$$$ = over $100)
Room tax 13%

KILGORE COMMUNITY INN

801 US 259, about 4 miles south of I-20 • 984-5501 • $–$$ • No-smoking rooms

The two-story Kilgore Inn has 100 rooms. Cable TV. Room phones. Small pets OK. Restaurant. Private club. Outdoor pool.

BEST WESTERN

1409 US 259, about 3.5 miles south of I-20 • 986-1195 • $–$$ • No-smoking rooms

The two-story Best Western has 40 rooms. Cable TV. Room phones. Outdoor pool.

LIVINGSTON

Polk County Seat • 5,500 • (409)

The town dates from 1846 when Moses L. Choate donated 100 acres for the site and named it for his former home in Alabama. Unfortunately, much of the town's history was lost in a fire that destroyed the downtown area in 1902.

TOURIST SERVICES

POLK COUNTY CHAMBER OF COMMERCE

505 N. Drew (77351) • 327-4929, e-mail: chamber@livingston.net, homepage: www.livingston.net/chamber/ • W

MUSEUMS

POLK COUNTY MEMORIAL MUSEUM

514 W. Mill • 327-8192 • Monday–Friday 12:30–5 • Free (donations) • W

The displays relate local history with the emphasis on the lumber industry. On the same block is the Jonas Davis Cabin and an old steam locomotive.

SIDE TRIPS

ALABAMA-COUSHATTA INDIAN RESERVATION

Take US 190 east about 16 miles (Rt. 3, Box 640, Livingston 77351) • 563-4391 or 800-444-3507 • Tourist facilities and attractions open seven days June–August, reduced schedule March–May and September–November. Call for schedule. Closed December–February • Camping area open at all times Adults $12, children 12 and under $10 • W variable

The people of these two tribes have lived in the Big Thicket area for more than 150 years. Some aided Sam Houston in the Texas War for Independence, and others served in the Confederate Army in the Civil War. Houston was influential in getting them a reservation in the 1850s. In the 1960s the tribal council decided to open the reservation for tourists. With about 500 members of the united tribes living and working here, on the grounds are a museum, an Indian village, a craft and gift shop, and a restaurant. Tribal dances are performed daily during the summer and on weekends in the spring and fall. Camping spaces (fee), from primitive to RV, are set on the reservation's 26-acre Lake Tombigbee.

LAKE LIVINGSTON STATE PARK

Take US 59 south to FM 1988, then west (right) to FM 3126 to the park. Approximately 7 miles from the city • 365-2201 • Open daily for day use, at all times for camping • Fee • W variable

Located on the eastern shore of Lake Livingston, this park offers facilities for boating, fishing, picnicking, swimming, water skiing, hiking, and tent and RV camping (fee). The lake is 52 miles long and has 452 miles of timbered shoreline devoted to recreation. On the western shore is **Wolf Creek Park,** which offers facilities for all outdoor recreation. For information on the state park, write: Route 9, Box 1300, Livingston 77351. For Wolf Creek Park write: P.O. Box 309, Coldspring 77331, 409-653- 4312.

LONGVIEW

Gregg County Seat • 70,311 • (903)

Surveyors laying out the townsite in the early 1870s noted the "long view" from nearby Rock Hill, and that became the town's name. It was a railroad, agriculture, and lumber center until the 1930s, when the huge East Texas Oil Field was discovered and the boom hit. Gregg County has produced more than two-and-a-half billion barrels of oil since then. Following World War II, there was an intensive campaign to attract industry. The result is that Longview is not only an oil and gas center but is also highly industrialized. Which is why it bills itself as "The Action Capital of East Texas."

TOURIST SERVICES

LONGVIEW CONVENTION AND VISITORS BUREAU

401 N. Center St. (75601) • 753-3281 • W

MUSEUMS

GREGG COUNTY HISTORICAL MUSEUM

214 N. Fredonia at Bank • 753-5840 • Tuesday–Saturday 10–4. Closed Sunday, Monday, and major holidays • Adults $2, children $1

This small but well-thought-out museum tells the story of the development of the county from the late 1800s through World War II. Housed in a bank built in 1910, the exhibits include the bank president's office, a teller's cage, and the original bank vault. Other exhibits include the interior of a log cabin, a dentist's office, a schoolroom, and memorabilia of the robbery of a local bank by the Dalton Gang in 1894. There is also a hands-on area for children. Gift shop.

LONGVIEW ART MUSEUM

102 W. College • 753-8103 • Tuesday–Saturday 10–4. Closed Sunday and Monday • Free • W

The emphasis here is on regional and Texas art in all media. The permanent collection represents a major sampling of innovations and styles of traditional American art. Exhibits change approximately every six weeks. The hands-on "Discovery Gallery" is designed to teach both children and adults how to view and evaluate art.

OTHER POINTS OF INTEREST

CARGILL-LONG PARK NATIONAL RECREATION TRAIL

Open at all times • Free • W+

This is a three-and-a-half-mile paved trail through a residential area along an old railroad bed. It's available for walking, jogging, or bicycling. It starts at Hollybrook, about half a block west of Eastman, and ends at US 80. Along the trail are benches, a small playground, and restrooms.

ROTARY PARK FOR SPECIAL POPULATION

East end of Baylor Dr. off McCann • Open daily • Free • W+

Everything here is designed for the handicapped: play structures, fountains, pavilion, and restrooms. For example, there is a ground-level merry-go-round set up so wheelchairs can be rolled on and strapped into place.

COLLEGES AND UNIVERSITIES

LETOURNEAU UNIVERSITY
2100 S. Mobberly • 753-0231 • W

This private Christian university offers degrees in arts and sciences and engineering to about 900 students. The college was founded by R. G. LeTourneau, who invented a number of different types of earth-moving equipment. Models of this equipment and other exhibits relating to the inventor and the school are in the college museum on the third floor of the Student Center. The museum is open Monday through Friday 8–5.

ANNUAL EVENTS

June

ALLEY FEST
Downtown • 237-4040 • Free

This three-day arts and crafts festival features only original arts and crafts. The festival is in its 13th year.

July

GREAT TEXAS BALLOON RACE
Gregg County Airport • 753-3281 (Convention and Visitors Bureau)
Usually early in July • Admission • W

Hot air balloons in a rainbow of colors dot the skies over Longview for this three-day event, as balloonists from all over the country compete for the title of Texas Champion. The term "balloon race" is a misnomer. The events are actually a test of the pilot's skill in maneuvering a hot air balloon from one point to another, which depends entirely on the wind, and dropping a marker on a prescribed target. Scores are measured from the center of the target and speed is not a consideration in scoring. There are usually about a half dozen of these flying-skill tests during the three days, most held in early morning or evening, when the winds are best for flying. Between flights there are a number of on-the-ground events including arts and crafts, airplane exhibits, and evening concerts.

RESTAURANTS

($ = under $7, $$ = $8–$17, $$$ = $18–$25, $$$$ = over $25 for one person excluding drinks, tax, and tip.)

BODACIOUS BARBECUE
227 S. Mobberly • Lunch and dinner Monday–Saturday. Closed Sunday
$ • No Cr

Well-known for its East Texas-style chopped beef. Also sliced beef, ribs and links, sandwiches, plates, or by the pound. Cafeteria style.

ACCOMMODATIONS

($ = under $45, $$ = $46–$60, $$$ = $61–$80, $$$$ = $81–$100, $$$$$ = over $100)
Room tax 13%

LA QUINTA MOTOR INN

502 S. Access Rd. off I-20, exit at Estes Parkway • 757-3663 or 800-531-5900
$$–$$$ • W+ 4 rooms • No-smoking rooms
    This La Quinta has 106 rooms including 53 no-smoking. Satellite TV with Showtime. Room phones (no charge for local calls). Small pets OK. Restaurant adjacent. Outdoor pool. Free coffee in lobby. Free news magazine.

DAYS INN—ALL SUITES

3101 Estes Parkway • 758-1113 or 800-329-7466 • $-$$ • No-smoking rooms
    This Days Inn has 36 suites and 4 rooms. Cable with HBO. Room phones. OK. Restaurant on premises. Complimentary McDonald's breakfast. Outdoor pool.

LUFKIN

Angelina County Seat • 35,000 • (409)
    As the story goes, when the railroad arrived in the early 1880s it was heading through Homer, then the county seat. But some of the railroaders got drunk in Homer and were arrested. Their boss thought this so inhospitable of Homer he bypassed the town and went through Denman Springs instead. Denman Springs immediately decided to rename their town after the railroad boss, E. P. Lufkin. About ten years later the county seat followed the railroad to Lufkin. Lufkin is now the heart of the Texas timber industry.

TOURIST SERVICES

LUFKIN CONVENTION AND VISITORS BUREAU

1615 Chestnut (P.O. Box 1606, 75901) • 634-6644

MUSEUMS

MUSEUM OF EAST TEXAS

503 N. Second at Paul • 639-4434 • Tuesday–Friday 10–5, Saturday and Sunday 1–5. Closed Monday • Free • W
    Housed in a 1905 vintage church, the museum offers a permanent collection of art representing the character, history, and heritage of this part of East Texas; as well as art, science, and history exhibits on loan from many major museums.

TEXAS FORESTRY MUSEUM

1905 Atkinson Dr. (TX 103E) • 632-9535 • Monday–Saturday 10–5, Sunday 1–5 or group tours by appointment • W
    Operated by the Texas Forestry Association, this is the only forestry museum in Texas and one of the largest in the United States. Here is a colorful and historic look at one of Texas' oldest industries—the wood products industry. Exhibits include tools, machinery, a fire lookout tower, ox-drawn logging cart, blacksmith shop, and a complete logging train.

OTHER POINTS OF INTEREST

ELLEN TROUT PARK & ZOO

Loop 287N at Martin Luther King, Jr. Dr. • 633-0399 • Open daily 9–5 in winter, 9–6 in summer • Admission $2, children 12 and under $1, children 3 and under free • W variable

In 1965 some friends sent Lufkin industrialist Walter Trout a gag gift—a hippopotamus. The zoo, now among the finest small-city zoos in the nation, was born. It is set in a park with a 60-acre lake, nature trail, playgrounds, and picnic areas. Ride the Z&OO Railroad with miniature cars pulled by a replica of an 1863 locomotive for a one-mile trip.

MEDFORD COLLECTION OF WESTERN ART

Lufkin City Hall, 300 E. Shepherd • Monday–Friday 8–5 • Free • W

More than 50 paintings by contemporary Western artists, from the collection of Dr. Gail Medford, are on display in the foyer of City Hall.

COLLEGES AND UNIVERSITIES

ANGELINA COLLEGE

US 59S, about 1.5 miles south of Loop 287 • 639-1301 • W+ but not all areas

This two-year community college offers both academic and technical/vocational programs for about 3,000 students. Visitors are welcome to athletic events, concerts, and plays put on at the college by the Angelina Playhouse, a combined college and community theater group.

PERFORMING ARTS

ANGELINA COUNTY EXPOSITION CENTER

Loop 287N and Lake St. • 634-6644 or 637-EXPO (637-3976) • Admission depends on event • W

This clear-span-covered arena is used for rodeos, concerts, horse shows, and other major crowd events.

SIDE TRIPS

ANGELINA NATIONAL FOREST

Nearest entrance about 14 miles southeast via US 69 • 634-7709 • Open at all times • Free • W variable (*See* Jasper)

DAVY CROCKETT NATIONAL FOREST

Take TX 103 west to TX 7 then to Ratcliff Recreation Area • 544-2046 Open at all times • Free • W variable (*See* Crockett)

LAKE SAM RAYBURN

Take TX 103 east to the lake • 384-5716 (Army Corps of Engineers) • Open at all times • Free • W variable (*See* Jasper)

ANNUAL EVENTS

September

TEXAS FOREST FESTIVAL AND SOUTHERN HUSHPUPPY OLYMPICS

Angelina County Exposition Center, Loop 287N and Lake St. • 634-6644
Fourth weekend in September • Admission • W variable

Among the highlights of this festival are the Lumberjack Show, BBQ Cookoff, and carnival. And, contestants come from all parts of the country to try their secret recipes at frying up the tastiest hushpuppies to win $1,000.

RESTAURANTS

($ = under $7, $$ = $8–$17, $$$ = $18–$25, $$$$ = over $25 for one person excluding drinks, tax, and tip.)

ROMA'S ITALIAN RESTAURANT

112 S. First • 637-7227 • Lunch and dinner Monday–Friday, dinner only
Saturday, closed Sunday • $$ • AE, DC, DIS, MC, V • W variable

Located in what was one of Lufkin's earliest clothing stores, this downtown restaurant features a variety of fish, veal, chicken, beef, seafood, and, of course, pasta dishes prepared northern Italian-style. There is a cappuccino bar and a rooftop gathering place for partaking of appetizers, finger foods, and occasional live music.

ACCOMMODATIONS

($ = under $45, $$ = $46–$60, $$$ = $61–$80, $$$$ = $81–$100, $$$$$ = over $100)
Room tax 13%

DAYS INN

2130 S. First • 639-3301 • $$ • W+ 5 rooms • No-smoking rooms

Because of its restaurant, lounge, conference and meeting rooms, this two-story Days Inn is especially popular with wedding and family reunion groups. Half of the 124 rooms are no-smoking. Free television includes regular cable plus HBO and ESPN. Outdoor swimming pool with kiddie pool, same-day dry cleaning service, "Texas-size"continental breakfast. Senior and other discounts. Children 17 and under stay free with parents.

LA QUINTA INN

2119 S. First • 634-3351 or 800-531-5900, fax 634-9475 • $$$ • W+ 2 rooms
No-smoking rooms

This two-story La Quinta has 106 rooms, 74 of which are no-smoking. Select from spacious "Gold Medal" rooms with large decks and expanded bathrooms or the more traditional "King Plus"rooms. Free TV with for-pay first-run movies, free local calls, outdoor pool, and a generous complimentary breakfast. Pets 25 pounds and under OK. Children under 18 stay free in parent's room. Senior discount available.

MARSHALL

Harrison County Seat • 23,682 • (903)

First settled in 1839, this city was named for John Marshall, Chief Justice of the U.S. Supreme Court. In the early 1840s, the commissioners decided that the location of the original county seat was unsanitary, and so they went looking for a new county seat. One of the commissioners, Peter Whetstone, offered some of his own land, but the other commissioners said the site was too dry. In answer, Whetstone first showed them a spring on the land, and then reached into a hollow tree near the spring and brought out a jug of whiskey. After several passes of this "liquid refreshment," the commissioners agreed that Whetstone's land was an ideal location. Whetstone was later shot down in the streets of Marshall during the war between the Regulators and the Moderators, two vigilante groups that were organized to clean up the county and wound up cleaning up each other.

During the Civil War, Marshall played a major role as a center of activity for the Confederacy west of the Mississippi. It was also the home of Lucy Holcomb Pickens, the "Sweetheart of the Confederacy," who was the only woman whose portrait graced Confederate currency. During that war, Marshall was the Confederate capital-in-exile of the state of Missouri, which gave rise to the city's claim that, while most of Texas had only six flags flying over it, Marshall is the "City of Seven Flags."

TOURIST SERVICES

GREATER MARSHALL CHAMBER OF COMMERCE

213 W. Austin at Franklin (P.O. Box 520, 75670) • 935-7868

A Texas Tourist Information Center, open every day, is located near Waskom on I-20 at the Louisiana border about 20 miles east of Marshall.

MUSEUMS

MICHELSON ART MUSEUM

216 N. Bolivar • 935-9480 • Tuesday–Friday 12–4, Saturday and Sunday 1–5. Closed Monday and major holidays • Free • W

Impressionist artist Leo Michelson (1887–1978) spent most of his life in Paris and was awarded the Legion of Honor by the French government in 1937 in recognition of his artistic ability. His works are displayed in museums in Baltimore, Jerusalem, Paris, Riga, San Diego, Tel Aviv, Toulouse, and here in Marshall. This collection was donated to Marshall by Michelson's widow. This small museum displays both Michelson's work and traveling exhibits.

OLD COURTHOUSE MUSEUM

On the Square • 938-2680 • Tuesday–Saturday 9–5, Sunday 1:30–5. Closed Monday • Adults $2, students $1

The displays in each of the 22 rooms in this old county courthouse are built around a theme. Themes range from the Caddo Indian Artifacts Room, where there is an 18,000-year-old Clovis point arrowhead, to the Transportation Collection, which goes from spurs to the space age. There are also tributes to some celebrities from Marshall and Harrison County, including Lady Bird Johnson, football player Y. A. Tittle, journalist Bill Moyers, and boxer George Foreman.

MARSHALL

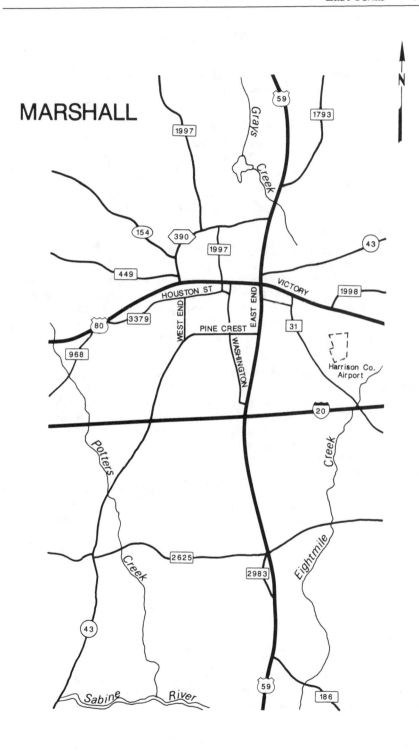

HISTORIC PLACES

ALLEN HOUSE

610 N. Washington • 938-4578 or 938-4198 • Tours by appointment only • $1
Now the home of the Harrison County Conservation Society, this two-story frame house was built in the late 1870s. It is furnished with period furniture.

MAPLECROFT STATE HISTORIC SITE

Travis and Grove • Tours Saturday–Sunday • Adults $2, children $1
Built in the early 1870s, the house was named for the maples planted around it, many of which are still standing. The four-bedroom house is furnished with Persian carpets and Victorian furniture.

OTHER POINTS OF INTEREST

FRANKS DOLL MUSEUM

211 W. Grand (US 80W) near Franklin • 935-3065 • Open by appointment Adults $2.50, children $1.50
The doll museum is housed in a separate building behind the historic Hochwald House, which was built in 1895. Mrs. Clara Franks began her collection a number of years ago with French and German bisque dolls. Today she has more than 1,600 dolls from all over the world, and many related items such as doll furniture, buggies, toys, doll houses, dishes, and trucks.

JOSEY'S RANCH

Take TX 43 north about 5 miles **• 935-5358 • Free • Tours by appointment W variable**
This ranch is the home of the Josey Championship School of Calf Roping and Barrel Racing. Students come here from every state and some foreign countries to learn these rodeo skills. R. E. and Martha Josey have been turning out champions since they first opened the school in 1967. Visitors are welcome, but tours are available only if they aren't too busy with the students.

COLLEGES AND UNIVERSITIES

EAST TEXAS BAPTIST UNIVERSITY

1209 N. Grove • 935-7963 • W variable
Courses of study at this four-year liberal arts school include teacher education and preparation for church ministry. Enrollment averages about 1,400. Visitors are welcome to sports events, dramatic and musical theater productions, and concerts. The library has a rare collection of wood mosaic portraits of 35 presidents of the United States by artist James A. Mason. This collection was donated by Cecil Keyes and is open to the public.

WILEY COLLEGE

Wiley and University • 938-8341 • W variable
The oldest traditionally black institution of higher learning west of the Mississippi, Wiley was founded by the Methodist Church in 1873. The four-year liberal arts college enrolls about 500 students. Visitors are welcome at sports, dramatic, and musical events.

SHOPPING

MARSHALL POTTERY

FM 31 about 4 miles east of downtown • 938-9201 • W

Established in 1896, this is Texas' oldest potter and America's largest manufacturer of red clay pots. In the rear of the store, master potters demonstrate the techniques of pottery making. All the handmade pottery produced by the company is made at this site while the mass production items, like the flower pots, are made at another plant. But everything they make is for sale here, including lower-priced "seconds." And if you want something to use with the pottery, you can probably get it here, too. Under the same roof, almost 20 shops sell everything from real plants and silk flowers to Texas souvenirs and limited-edition prints. The Hungry Potter Restaurant, in the pottery yard, is open for lunch. There is also an RV park.

POTTER'S VILLAGE

Hwy. 59 and Houston St. • 935-4320

A craft and antique mall with everything from gifts and silk flowers to handmade lace. Despite the name there are no active potters here.

SIDE TRIPS

CADDO LAKE STATE PARK

Take TX 43 northeast approximately 14 miles to FM 2198, then east 1 mile to park **• 679-3351 • Open daily 8–10 for day use, at all times for camping weekdays: $3 per vehicle per day, weekends: $4 per vehicle per day • W+ but not all area**

The 32,500-acre lake is a maze of channels and bayous with thousands of acres of cypress groves. The state has marked about 40 miles of "boat roads" in the lake that provide access to fishing spots and other points of interest. The state park is located on the upper end of the lake. Facilities include an interpretive center, picnic areas, playground, fishing pier, recreation hall, campsites for tent and RV camping (fee), cabins (fee), and hiking trail.

T.C. LINDSEY & CO. GENERAL STORE

Take US 80E to FM 1998, turn left and continue east on FM 1998 to FM 134, then right (south) about 2 miles to store at Jonesville **• 687-3382 Monday–Saturday 8–5 • Free**

Still operating, this authentic old-family-owned country store dates from 1847. It is chock-full of dry goods, groceries, feed, antiques, and collectibles. The store has been used as a setting in two Disney movies.

ANNUAL EVENTS

May

STAGECOACH DAYS

On the Square • 935-7868 (Chamber of Commerce) • Third weekend in May Free (admission to some events) • W variable

On Saturday the theme for the festivities comes into play with a parade celebrating the different modes of transportation from the stagecoach to the modern car, and then again with stagecoach rides on the Square. Other activities include a BBQ cookoff, arts and crafts and food fair, rodeo, historic homes tour, free entertainment, and a street dance.

September

CENTRAL EAST TEXAS FAIR

Fairgrounds on W. Houston St. • 935-7868 (Chamber of Commerce)
Monday–Saturday in mid-September • Adults $1, children 50¢ • W variable
All the typical county fair ingredients are here: livestock show, exhibits of arts and crafts, food booths, a carnival, and entertainment.

October

EAST TEXAS FIREANT FESTIVAL

On the Square, at the Civic Center, and around town • 935-7868 (Chamber of Commerce) • Second weekend in October • Free • W variable
When you want to do a parody of the traditional festival, a good way to do it is to dedicate it to the most irritating pest you can find. In this case, it's the fire ant. The result is a fun festival with crazy contests and absurd costumes, including those worn by the festival's mascots, Freddie and Elvira FireAnt. Activities include a FireAnt Calling Contest and a FireAnt Roundup, a chili cookoff in which contestants must swear there is a fire ant somewhere in the pot, a wacky parade, rubber chicken chunking, as well as the more traditional food booths, entertainment, and a street dance.

November/December

WONDERLAND OF LIGHTS

On the Square • 935-7868 (Chamber of Commerce) • Thanksgiving through New Year's
The historic city is lit with 7 million lights for this festival. The six-week festival features a living Christmas tree of area choirs, nightly tours, and a Christmas parade held the first Saturday in December.

ACCOMMODATIONS

($ = under $45, $$ = $46–$60, $$$ = $61–$80, $$$$ = $81–$100, $$$$$ = over $100)
Room tax 13%

BEST WESTERN OF MARSHALL

555 East End Blvd. S. (US 59 exit off I-20) • 935-1941 or 800-528-1234 • $–$$
W+ one room • No-smoking rooms
The two-story Best Western has 100 rooms including one suite ($$$) and 25 no-smoking rooms. Cable TV. Room phones (charge for local calls). Pets OK. Restaurant adjacent. Outdoor pool.

MEXIA

Limestone County • 6,994 • (254)

Founded as a railroad town in 1871, it was named for Mexican General Jose Antonio Mejia, whose son later changed the spelling of the name. Once a follower of Santa Anna, Mejia later took part in an unsuccessful uprising against him and wound up in front of a firing squad. Mejia's family donated the land for the town.

An early distinguished resident was Joseph W. Stubenrauch, a horticulturist and educator who came here in 1876. He developed some 100 new varieties of peaches to make Limestone County one of the largest peach-producing counties in Texas.

The oil boom hit in 1920 and population zoomed from 4,000 to 50,000, many of whom were undesirables. The Texas Rangers were sent in, the boom fizzled, and now peaches are Mexia's claim to fame.

The Chamber of Commerce slogan for Mexia is "A great place however you pronounce it." And they pronounce it Meh-HAY-ah.

TOURIST SERVICES

MEXIA AREA CHAMBER OF COMMERCE

315 N. Sherman (P.O. Box 352, 76667) • 562-5569 • W

GIBBS MEMORIAL LIBRARY

305 E. Rusk (76667) • 562-3231 • www.mexia.com/-gibbs/library.html
gibbs.library@mexia.com • Open Monday–Friday 10–6, Saturday 10–4

Check Web site for tourist information on landmarks like the Old West Museum and Saloon and history of Mexia, which is 40 miles east of Waco.

HISTORIC PLACES

Built in 1898, the **First Presbyterian Church,** N. McKinney and E. Carthage, is the oldest church in town. Not open to the public is the **Blake-Berry-Kidd Home,** 701 N. Red River, that hosted William Jennings Bryan.

OTHER POINTS OF INTEREST

FORT PARKER STATE PARK

Take TX 14 south approximately 7 miles • 562-5751 • **Open daylight hours for day use, overnight for camping • Admission • W variable**

The 1,485-acre park includes 750-acre Lake Fort Parker. Facilities are available for fishing, swimming, boating, hiking, and camping (fee). There is a separate group camp with four dormitories, a recreation hall, staff building, and kitchen that can accommodate up to 96 persons.

LAKE MEXIA

Take US 84 west about 7 miles to FM 2681, then south to park • **Open at all times • W variable**

Most of the shoreline along this 1,200-acre lake is residential. However, there are public facilities for boating, fishing, swimming, and camping (fee). On the west shore is the 30-acre **Booker T. Washington Park** that was set aside in 1898 as a permanent site for celebrating June 19th (Juneteenth), the anniversary of the 1865 Emancipation of Slaves in Texas. The oldest annual Juneteenth celebration in the state is still held here.

RESTAURANT

DRILLIN' RIG

312 N Hwy 14 (at US 84) • 562-6323 • Breakfast (from 5:30 A.M.), lunch, and dinner 364 days a year • Bar • $–$$ • Cr • W variable

Next to a 60-foot replica of a drilling rig, about three blocks west of town, is a one-story, rustic, no-frills restaurant with a diverse menu that includes seafood and steaks. About 100 can be served in the main dining room, and as many in the Black Gold Bar. Country bands sometimes play. The rig, of course, is a salute to Mexia's oil boom days.

MOUNT PLEASANT

Titus County Seat • 12,291 • (903)

There are two stories about how this city was named. The first is a simple explanation that it was named for its pleasant location on beautifully wooded hills. The second is more romantic. It states that before the settlers arrived, the Caddo Indians used to come here for the mineral springs that flowed waters of red, white, and blue. There were mounds in the area constructed by a prehistoric race, so according to the legend the Indians began to call it "Pleasant Mound." This name was translated by the early settlers and eventually became Mount Pleasant.

For more than a decade after the turn of the century, the mineral waters made this a popular health spa centered on the Dellwood Resort Hotel in what is now Dellwood Park.

Today the city's economy is diversified, with farming, ranching, industry, and wholesale and retail trade each contributing to it. A big draw for tourists is the excellent fishing in nearby lakes.

TOURIST SERVICES

MT. PLEASANT—TITUS COUNTY CHAMBER OF COMMERCE

1604 N. Jefferson, P.O. Box 1237 (75455) • 572-8567 • W

POINTS OF INTEREST

LAKE MONTICELLO

Take FM 127 southwest approximately 9 miles **• 572-2398 • Titus County Park Admission $2 • W variable**

This 2,000-acre lake is a power plant cooling lake, so it is virtually a warm-water reservoir, which contributes to its reputation for excellent bass fishing. Titus County Park on the lake has boat ramps, campsites (fee), and picnic areas.

LAKE BOB SANDLIN

Take FM 127 southwest to FM 21, then south to dam **• 572-5531 • Open at all times • $3 per vehicle per day • W variable**

At 9,460 acres, this is the largest lake in the area, and it offers facilities for fishing and most water sports. There are a number of commercial marinas, boat ramps, rental cabins, camping areas, and restaurants around the lake.

LAKE WELSH

Take TX 49 east to FM 1735, then south about 4 miles to lake • 572-6935 (Grocery at campgrounds) • Open at all times • Free • W variable

This is another power company cooling lake. It is an all-year lake, but like Lake Monticello, this 1,500-acre lake's warm water makes it a good choice for fishing in cold months. There are some commercial campgrounds and rental cabins near the lake.

BLUEBIRD TRAILS OF TEXAS

572-7529 • Guided tour $35 per group • Self guided free

This tour takes you on part of a 150-mile trail of bluebird nest boxes that stretch from Texarkana to Huntsville. Baby birds can be seen from mid-April to July.

ANNUAL EVENTS

June

INTERNATIONAL RODEO ASSOCIATION CHAMPIONSHIP RODEO

Rodeo Arena, Greenhill Rd. (FM 2152) about 2½ miles north of I-30
572-1170 • Usually Thursday–Saturday of second week of June
Admission • W

Contestants in this rodeo include some of the top money-winning cowboys of the International Rodeo Association. There is a parade downtown and other entertainment during the rodeo.

September

TITUS COUNTY FAIR

Civic Center grounds, 1800 N. Jefferson (Bus US 271) • 572-8678
Wednesday–Saturday of last week of September • Free • W+
(Civic Center) • Charge for parking

They call it "The Biggest Little Fair in Texas." In addition to the exhibits, carnival, arts and crafts show and contests, livestock show, and entertainment, there is an Ice Cream "Freeze-off" and a Chicken Stew Cookoff.

ACCOMMODATIONS

($ = under $45, $$ = $46–$60, $$$ = $61–$80, $$$$ = $81–$100, $$$$$ over $100)
Room tax 11%

DAYS INN

2501 N. Ferguson, I-30 and US 271 bypass • 577-0152 or 800-325-2525 • $–$$
W+ 2 rooms • No-smoking rooms

This three-story Days Inn has 70 rooms, 35 no-smoking. Satellite TV with HBO. Room phones (no charge for local calls). Restaurant. Outdoor pool.

MOUNT VERNON

Franklin County Seat • 2,219 • (903)

The town of Lone Star was started on this site in 1849. When Franklin County was carved out of Red River County, the town's name was changed to Mount Vernon in honor of George Washington's Virginia home. The county is named after Benjamin Franklin. Not Washington's friend, the famous Ben from Philadelphia, but Benjamin C. Franklin of Texas, who was a hero at the Battle of San Jacinto.

TOURIST SERVICES

FRANKLIN COUNTY CHAMBER OF COMMERCE

109 S. Kaufman (P.O. Box 554, 75457) • 537-4365

HISTORIC PLACES

Mount Vernon has an ongoing program to designate all the historic buildings in the town, and about 40 have been marked with signs on lawns or buildings. Many of these are on Main St. and on Spur 423, which connects Main St. with I-30. The Chamber of Commerce offers a historical homes map.

OTHER POINTS OF INTEREST

LAKE CYPRESS SPRINGS

Take TX 37 south about 6 miles to FM 900, then east (left) about 3 miles to FM 115, then south (right) about 2 miles to lake **• 537-4536 (Franklin County Water District) • Open at all times • Free • W variable**

This 3,400-acre lake has five public parks that offer facilities for swimming, fishing, boating, other water sports, and camping (fee). The shoreline is also well-developed commercially with marinas, restaurants, and rental cabins and houses.

SIDE TRIPS

LAKE BOB SANDLIN

Take TX 37 south to FM 21, then southeast (left) staying on FM 21 to dam **856-7121 (Marina) • Open at all times • Free • W variable**

See Mount Pleasant.

ANNUAL EVENTS

July

FUN FESTIVAL

Lake Cypress Springs Marina and Resort • 537-4365 (Chamber of Commerce) Dates vary • Admission • W variable

This festival starts with a parade downtown on Friday afternoon and a street dance that evening. Events on Saturday include arts and crafts booths, a water-ski show, children's contests, and entertainment.

October

COUNTRY FEST

Town Square • 537-4365 (Chamber of Commerce) • Dates vary • Free
Events include a stew cookoff, arts and crafts booths, a fun run, wing-ding contest, and a recipe contest.

NACOGDOCHES

Nacogdoches County Seat • 32,725 • (409)
It calls itself "the oldest town in Texas." Whether it is *the* oldest is contested, but it is definitely one of the oldest and its history one of the most colorful.

In the early 1700s the Spanish established a series of six missions and two presidios in East Texas. One of these was *Nuestra Señora de Guadalupe de Nacogdoches*. Destined for failure, the missions were abandoned in 1773 and the settlers ordered to move to San Antonio. But, many were unhappy and followed Antonio Gil Y'Barbo back to the Nacogdoches area. In 1779 Y'Barbo built a stone house, now known as the Old Stone Fort, and established a permanent settlement.

Long before the Texas Revolution *empresarios* dreamed of a Texas empire. In 1812 the Magee-Gutierrez revolt was put down by Mexican troops. It was during that revolution the first newspaper was published in Texas in Nacogdoches. In 1819 Dr. James Long led an unsuccessful expedition, and in 1826, Haden Edwards set up the independent state of Fredonia. It lasted only as long as it took Edwards and his followers to scatter when the Mexican troops arrived.

In 1832 the Mexican commander of the area ordered the East Texans to surrender all firearms. They reacted by banding together as a militia and defeating the Mexican garrison at the Battle of Nacogdoches. The land remained part of Mexico, but Mexican troops were never again stationed in East Texas.

One thing common to all of these incidents was that one side or the other was headquartered in the Old Stone Fort.

Four signers of the Texas Declaration of Independence, Haden Edwards, and Frost Thorn, Texas' first millionaire, are buried in the historic Oak Grove cemetery.

Another first for Nacogdoches was Texas' first oil well. Just after the Civil War, Tol Barret hit oil at a depth of 106 feet. But it only produced ten barrels a day and financing was unavailable, so Barret abandoned it.

TOURIST SERVICES

NACOGDOCHES CONVENTION AND VISITORS BUREAU
513 North St. (P.O. Drawer 631918, 75961) • 1-888-564-7351
Cassette tape recorder, tape, and map are available for audio driving tour. These are provided free with a refundable $5 deposit. A walking tour brochure is also free. A "Ghosts of Nacogdoches Trail" guide is available for a small fee.

MUSEUMS

OLD NACOGDOCHES UNIVERSITY

Mound St., on campus of Thomas J. Rusk Middle School • 564-7292
Tuesday–Sunday 1–4, Saturday, 10–4

Built in 1858, this is the only remaining structure of a university that was chartered in 1845 and lasted until 1895. The displays tell the history of the area and include letters from the Marx Brothers, who performed in Nacogdoches early in their career. The building is on the National Register of Historic Places.

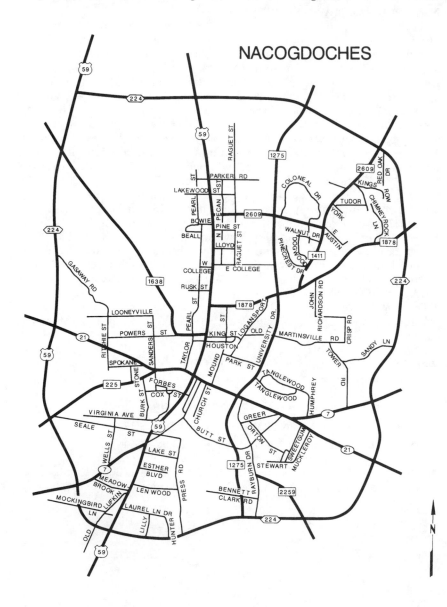

NACOGDOCHES

OLD STONE FORT MUSEUM

**On Stephen F. Austin State University campus, Griffith and Clark • 568-2408
Tuesday–Saturday 9–5, Sunday 1–5. Closed Monday • Free (donations) • W
First floor**

This is a replica of the original Old Stone Fort that stood where Main and Fredonia Streets are now. Built in 1779 by Antonio Gil Y'Barbo, it began as a trading post, but also served as a seat of government, a prison, a newspaper office, and a fort. Nine different flags have flown over this building including those from the three aborted revolutions: the Magee-Gutierrez Expedition of 1812, Dr. Long's Republic in 1819, and the Fredonia Republic. The oath of allegiance to Mexico was administered here to James Bowie, Thomas Rusk, Sam Houston, and David Crockett.

STERNE-HOYA HOME

211 S. Lanana • 560-5426 • Monday–Saturday 9–12, 2–5. Closed Sunday • Free

Adolphus Sterne built this home for his bride in 1828. Sam Houston was baptized a Roman Catholic here in 1833 to comply with Mexican law. Sterne played an important role in the Texas Revolution, and many famous Texans visited this house.

HISTORIC PLACES

INDIAN MOUND

500 Block of Mound St.

This is the last remaining burial mound of several left in this area by the Caddo Indians. Many of the items recovered are on display at the Old Stone Fort.

MILLARD'S CROSSING

**6020 North St. (US 59N) • 564-6631 • Tours Monday–Saturday 9–4,
Sunday 1–4• $3**

This collection of restored nineteenth-century homes and other buildings resembles a small village. The buildings were gathered here under the direction of Lera Thomas, a former member of the U.S. Congress and widow of Congressman Albert Thomas, who served as Representative from Harris County for 29 years.

OLD NORTH CHURCH

US 59N, about 4 miles north of downtown

One of the oldest Protestant churches in Texas still in use, this church was built in 1852 to replace the original built in 1838.

SPORTS AND ACTIVITIES

Golf

WOODLAND HILLS GOLF COURSE

**Bus US 59S, approximately 4 miles south of Loop 224 • 564-2762 • 18-hole
course. Greens fee: weekdays $12.50, weekends and holidays $17.50. Twilight
starts at 2 p.m.• $10**

COLLEGES AND UNIVERSITIES

STEPHEN F. AUSTIN STATE UNIVERSITY

Main entrance: North (Bus US 59) at Vista Dr. • 468-2011 • W variable
Visitor parking on campus with pass from gate guard

This former teacher-training college now offers undergraduate and graduate programs ranging from agribusiness to visual/performing arts to more than 13,000 students. Visitors are welcome at most campus events that are held in Turner Auditorium.

PERFORMING ARTS

LAMPLITE THEATRE

Loop 224 and Old Tyler Rd. • 564-8300 • Admission • W

This community theater presents performances throughout the year.

NACOGDOCHES COUNTY EXPOSITION CENTER

3805 NW Stallings Dr. (Loop 224/US 59) • 564-0849 • Admission • W variable

With a covered arena seating 4,300 and 400 horse stalls, this center is host year-round to rodeos, concerts, horse shows, and special events.

SHOPPING

ANTIQUE AND GIFT SHOPS

The Convention and Visitors Bureau has a free brochure, *Antique Shopping Guide*, listing a dozen or more antique shops throughout the city.

HOOPER-BARR ART STUDIO AND GALLERY

327 E. Main • 560-0050 • Tuesday–Friday 1–6 or by appointment

Mary Hooper, a well-known watercolor artist, and her associate artist, Wanda Barr, have their studio in what was once the Nacogdoches Opera House, where the Marx Brothers performed.

SIDE TRIPS

LAKE NACOGDOCHES

Take FM 225 west about 12 miles • 564-4693 (City Recreation Dept.)
Open at all times • Free • W variable

Two city parks on this 2,210-acre lake offer facilities for boating, fishing, picnicking, swimming, and waterskiing. There is also a nature trail.

ANNUAL EVENTS

June

TEXAS BLUEBERRY FESTIVAL

Various locations in city • (Chamber of Commerce)
Second weekend in June • W variable

This official festival of the Texas Blueberry Growers Association features arts and crafts booths, doll parade, petting zoo, street entertainment, concert in the park, pet parade, art show, and fresh blueberry sales.

October

PINEY WOODS FAIR

**Nacogdoches County Exposition Center, 3805 NW Stallings Dr.
(Loop 224/US 59)• 560-5533 (Chamber of Commerce) • Wednesday–Sunday
in second week of October • Admission • W variable**

Contestants come from surrounding counties for prizes in agricultural, home, and art categories. Exhibits, entertainment, food, and a carnival add to the fun.

RESTAURANTS

($ = under $7, $$ = $8–$17, $$$ = $18–$25, $$$$ = over $25 for one person excluding drinks, tax, and tip.)

THE CALIFORNIAN RESTAURANT AND OYSTER BAR

**342 N. University Dr. • 560-1985 • Lunch and dinner daily • $–$$ • AE,
MC, V • Children's plates**

The emphasis here is on seafood, but the menu also includes roast beef, chicken, hamburgers, soups, and sandwiches. Daily specials and the catch of the day are posted. Private club bar.

LA HACIENDA

**1411 North • 564-6450 • Lunch and dinner daily • $–$$ • Cr
Children's plates**

Located in a comfortable old home built in 1913, this restaurant is unusual in that it separates its Mexican entrées on the menu from the Tex-Mex items. Other entrées include steaks, seafood, and chicken. Private club bar.

ACCOMMODATIONS

*($ = under $45, $$ = $46–$60, $$$ = $61–$80, $$$$ = $81–$100, $$$$$ = over $100)
Room tax 14%*

FREDONIA HOTEL AND CONVENTION CENTER

**200 N. Fredonia • 564-1234 or 800-594-5323 • $$–$$$ • W+ 2 rooms
No-smoking rooms**

Built by citizens of Nacogdoches, the old Fredonia has been beautifully refurbished into a modern hotel with the lobby as the city's living room. Its Cafe Fredonia has a lovely panoramic view in a French atmosphere, and the Nine Flags Bar serves drinks and High Teas. Accommodations are varied from a top level Executive Floor to tropical cabana rooms with poolside ambiance.

HOLIDAY INN

**3400 South Street • 569-8100 or 800-HOLIDAY • $$–$$$ • W+ 2 rooms
No-smoking rooms**

This fine addition to the Nacogdoches motel scene is just minutes from the hub of town. It offers 126 rooms, restaurant, bar with nightly dancing, indoor/outdoor pool and Jacuzzi, and a fully equipped exercise room.

Bed and Breakfast

The Convention and Visitors Bureau (564-7351) will provide you with a list of a variety of bed and breakfasts throughout the city.

HARDEMAN GUEST HOUSE

316 N Church Street • 569-1947 • $$$ • Special weekday and long-term rates available

Built in 1892 on the original Old Washington Square, this National Register home is within walking distance of a number of historic sites. Antiques, paintings, and craft items displayed in the house are available for purchase. Four rooms with private baths are decorated in varying styles. Sumptuous breakfast served following early morning coffee and tea. Smoking limited to porch and yard. Children welcome.

TOL BARRET HOUSE

Rt. 4, Box 9400 (Call for directions) • 569-1249 • $$$

Tol Barret drilled the first oil well in Texas, and his 1848 house is listed in the National Register of Historic Places. One room is available behind the house, two in the nearby Sparks House, and two in the Gate House. All are charmingly furnished and secluded among a tree farm. No pets, no small children.

NAVASOTA

Grimes County • 8,820 • (409)

Settlers from Louisiana, responding to Stephen F. Austin's advertisement for colonists, founded the town in the early 1820s. The railroad bypassed the county seat, Anderson, so Navasota became the center for surrounding plantations. After the Civil War the town was burned by a mob of unpaid Confederate soldiers, and in 1867 a yellow fever epidemic drove half the population away. To prevent another disastrous fire, construction with any material that was not fireproof was banned. The result is that the downtown area survived and is now listed on the National Register of Historic Places.

Downtown on E. Washington Ave. (TX 90) is a statue honoring the French explorer Rene Robert Cavelier, Sieur de La Salle. In March 1687, while searching for the Mississippi River he had discovered on a previous voyage, La Salle was murdered by one of his men.

TOURIST SERVICES

GRIMES COUNTY CHAMBER OF COMMERCE

117 S. La Salle (P.O. Box 530, 77868) • 825-6600 or (800) 252-6642 • W

Pick up a Visitors Packet listing its historic buildings and numerous antique shops, accommodations, restaurants, and attractions.

MUSEUMS

HORLOCK HISTORY CENTER

1215 E. Washington • 825-7615 • Friday, Saturday, Sunday 9–4 • Free

Robert A. Horlock, a prominent businessman, built this Victorian house in the early 1880s. The house is furnished with antiques and artifacts from the area. Rotating museum exhibits.

HISTORIC PLACES

A few of the outstanding historic buildings are **The Bank of Navasota** (1890) at 109 W. Washington, **First Presbyterian Church** (1894) at 302 Nolan, **The Castle Inn** (1893) at 1403 E. Washington, the Greek Revival **Emory Terrell Home** (1904) at 415 E. Johnson, and the **Stewart Davis Home** (1904) at 902 E. Washington featuring cypress columns and a different type of wood in each room.

SPORTS AND ACTIVITIES

Golf

NAVASOTA GOLF COURSE

TX 105 approximately 1 mile west of downtown • 825-7284 • 9-hole course. Greens fee: weekdays $5.50, weekends and holidays $7

SIDE TRIPS

ANDERSON HISTORIC DISTRICT

Take TX 90 north 10 miles
The town dates back to 1834, but as the story goes, the railroad bypassed Anderson—so businesses went to Navasota. The tiny town, which is the Grimes County seat, has been declared a National Historic District. Stop at the **Fanthrop Inn** at Main St. south of Johnson (873-2633, Wednesday–Sunday 9–4, adults $3, children and students $1.50, W variable). You will walk in the footsteps of Zachary Taylor, Robert F. Lee, and Ulysses S. Grant. **The Grimes County Courthouse** sits on the highest of Anderson's seven hills, and its unique double staircase catches your attention. Both the inn and the courthouse are on the National Register of Historic Places.

ANNUAL EVENTS

February

GO TEXAN WEEKEND

Grimes County Fairgrounds • 800-252-6642 • First weekend • Admission (dances only) • W variable
Chili cookoff, dance, exhibits, horseshoes.

May

BLUES FESTIVAL

**800-252-6642 for location and times • Third weekend • Admission
W variable**
Local and regional performers. Street dance, solo and acoustic sessions, workshops, arm wrestling contest.

September

TEXIAN DAYS

**Anderson. Take SH 90 east for 10 miles from Navasota • 800-252-6642
Fourth weekend • Free • W variable**
Historic home tour, Texas Army Encampment, live entertainment, arts and crafts.

October/November

TEXAS RENAISSANCE FESTIVAL

Plantersville. *Take TX 105 east to Plantersville, then south (right) on FM 1774 for six miles* • **356-2178 or 800-458-3435** • **Seven weekends from October through mid-November** • **Admission** • **W variable**

Take a trip back in time with the likes of Robin Hood and his Merrie Men, Henry VIII and his six wives, poets, gypsies, knights in shining armor, and other real and mythical characters in this medieval village. Entertainment surrounds you on six stages and wanders around the grounds. The variety of food is just as interesting as are the guilds (shops).

ACCOMMODATIONS

($ = under $45, $$ = $46–$60, $$$ = $61–$80, $$$$ = $81–$100, $$$$$ = over $100) Room tax 11%

SUPER 8 NAVASOTA INN

818 Loop 6 South • **825-7775 or 800-528-1234** • **$–$$** • **No-smoking rooms**

This two-story motel has 60 rooms including ten no-smoking. Cable TV with the Movie Channel. Room phones (no charge for local calls). Restaurant next door. Lounge. Outdoor pool.

CEDAR CREEK INN

1000 Loop 6 South • **825-8000** • **$** • **W+ 1 room** • **No-smoking rooms**

The two-story Inn has 64 rooms that include ten no-smoking. Cable TV with free in-room movies. Room phones (no charge for local calls). Restaurant and lounge.

Bed and Breakfast

THE CASTLE INN

1403 E. Washington • **825-8051** • **$$–$$$**

This beautiful mansion offers four upstairs rooms, each with private bath. No children under 13. No pets. Downhome Texas breakfast with European flair. Mystery dinners and gourmet dinners by reservation. The Castle was built in 1893 and is furnished with lovely antiques from 1850 to 1870.

ORANGE

Orange County Seat • **19,381** • **(409)**

Texas' easternmost city sits on the border of Louisiana. Established in 1836, it had a variety of names before finally being named Orange for the wild orange groves on the banks of the Sabine River.

Legend has it that the pirate Jean Lafitte used this area as a repair station for his ships in the early 1800s. If so, he was the forerunner of the shipyards that boomed here in World War I and II. This inland port 42 miles up the Sabine River is not as bustling as in those years, but Orange is still a shipping center.

Orange was fortunate to have two great benefactors, Lutcher Stark and Edgar Brown. The philanthropy of these men and their families gave the city some of its cultural centers and what are now historic buildings.

Orange, Beaumont, and Port Arthur are known as The Golden Triangle.

TOURIST SERVICES

GREATER ORANGE CONVENTION AND VISITORS BUREAU

1012 Green Ave. at 10th (77630) • 883-3536 or (800) 528-4906, Web site: www.org-tx.com/chamber, e-mail: orgcvb@exp.net, fax: 886-3247 • W

TEXAS TRAVEL INFORMATION CENTER

I-10 at Louisiana state line • 883-9416 • Open daily 8–5 • W

Trained travel counselors can provide a wealth of free information, official highway maps, and tons of other travel literature on Orange and all of Texas.

MUSEUMS

HERITAGE HOUSE MUSEUM AND HERITAGE HISTORY MUSEUM OF ORANGE COUNTY

905 Division St. just west of Civic Plaza • 886-5385 • Tuesday–Friday 10–4, weekends by appointment • $1 at each museum

Part of this turn-of-the-century home is furnished to reflect the lifestyle of an upper-middle-class family in the early 1900s. The rest is a historical museum relating the history of Orange County. The house is on the National Register of Historic Places.

STARK MUSEUM OF ART

712 Green St. at 7th, Civic Plaza • 883-6661 • Wednesday–Saturday 10–5, Sunday 1–5. Closed Monday, Tuesday, and major holidays • Free • W
Children under 12 must be accompanied by an adult

This award-winning building offers exhibits reflecting the Stark family's interest in land, wildlife, and the American West. Audubon prints, bronze sculptures by Remington and Russell, a collection of Doughty's porcelain birds, and a series of Steuben glass bowls representing each of the fifty states are just a few of the exhibits.

HISTORIC PLACES

LUTCHER MEMORIAL CHURCH BUILDING

(First Presbyterian Church) • 902 W. Green Ave. at 8th, Civic Plaza • 883-2097
Individuals welcome when church is open, tours by appointment only • W

The stained glass windows were made by hand techniques no longer commercially available, much of the marble was imported from Italy, the pews and woodwork are mahogany, and many decorations are overlaid in gold leaf. It took four years (1908–1912) to build this memorial to the H. J. Lutcher family. It was the first public building in the world to be air conditioned.

W. H. STARK HOUSE

Green at 6th, Civic Plaza • Entrance through Carriage House at 610 W. Main
883-0871 • Tuesday–Saturday (10–3). Closed Sunday and Monday
Reservations requested • Children must be 14 and older and accompanied by an adult • $2

This magnificent mansion tells what it was like to be one of the richest families in Texas. The restored 1894 Queen Anne home is the only surviving structure of many fine houses that lined the streets of the neighborhood. The 15-room, three-story home with its many gables, galleries, and distinctive windowed turret reflects the influence of several architectural styles. The house is much as it was when the H. J. Lutcher and H. J. Lutcher Stark families lived here, with all its original furnishings. It is listed in the National Register of Historic Places.

OTHER POINTS OF INTEREST

FARMER'S MERCANTILE

702 W. Division • 883-2941 • Monday–Friday 8–5, Saturday 8–5:30 • Free • W
This old-fashioned general store opened in 1928 and still maintains its early-century atmosphere. You are welcome to just come, browse, and enjoy a bit of nostalgia, or you may shop for kerosene lamps, sausage stuffers, horse collars, hand churns, or any of the hundreds of other farm and ranch items that you won't find at your local discount store.

PINEY WOODS COUNTRY WINES

3400 Willow • *Take exit 875 off I-10 traveling west, take exit 876 traveling east and turn back west at the bayou* • 883-5408 • Monday–Saturday 9–5:30, Sunday 12–5:30 • Winery and vineyard tours by appointment for groups of four or more • $2 • W
This little winery in the woods sells and bottles wines made from local fruits and muscadine grapes. Owner-winemaker Alfred J. Flies offers samples and conversation.

PETROCHEMICAL ROW

FM 1006 south of town
This miles-long complex of plants produces a variety of products derived from petroleum. You are looking at an investment of more than $3 billion.

PERFORMING ARTS

LUTCHER THEATER FOR THE PERFORMING ARTS

707 W. Main, Civic Plaza (P.O. Box 2310, 77630) • 886-5535 or (800) 828-5535 Admission varies with show • W
A modern 1,500-seat theater with productions ranging from touring Broadway shows to celebrity concerts to opera.

SHOPPING

THE HORSEMANS STORE

519 I-10 Freeway, exit 878 • 883-5712 • Monday–Saturday 9–6, Sunday 12–5 • W
For boots and jeans and classy western wear, The Horsemans Store has been outfitting cowboys and cowgirls since 1969.

THE OLD WOOD SHOP

1201 Front St. at 11th by the railroad tracks • 883-4641 • Monday–Friday 9–4, Saturday 9–12 • W
It began operation before Orange had electricity, so old steam-powered woodworking machinery is still here. It is now a crafts shop.

SIDE TRIPS

CLAIBORNE WEST PARK

I-10W between Orange and Vidor • *Traveling west take exit 869; traveling east take exit 864 and cross over at FM 1442* **• 745-2255 • Open at all times Free • W variable**

A 454-acre park that is designed for both recreational use and as a wildlife preserve. There are playgrounds, picnic area, nature and exercise trails, rental canoes, and an outdoor amphitheater.

SUPER GATOR TOURS AIRBOAT RIDES

108 E. Lutcher Dr. I-10 exit 878 • 883-7725 • Open 9–6 daily • Adults $21.95, children $10

Fly like the wind on Stan Floyd's 300 hp, air-cooled engine airboat on the marshes of the Sabine River for an up-close look at nature through areas inaccessible any other way. Each tour lasts a minimum of an hour. Bring your picnic.

ANNUAL EVENTS

May

INTERNATIONAL GUMBO COOKOFF

Downtown Orange by Lamar University and Orange Public Library 883-3536 (Chamber of Commerce) • First weekend in May • Admission W • Pay parking

Cajun cooking has slipped across the border from Louisiana with gumbos made from just about any critter that flies, runs, or swims. Catfish races, drafts show, entertainment, a carnival, plus more add to the fun. Free shuttle buses from Civic Plaza.

RESTAURANTS

($ = under $7, $$ = $8–$17, $$$ = $18–$25, $$$$ = over $25 for one person excluding drinks, tax, and tip.)

SOMEPLACE SPECIAL

Bates Plaza, 6521 IH-10 • 883-8605 • Lunch daily 11–2 • $ • W

Classic cuisine in an elegant atmosphere. Lunch serves up what many claim are the best soups, salads, and sandwiches in the Golden Triangle. Ask about the Sandwich of the Day.

CAJUN COOKERY

2505 I-10, exit 877 • 886-0990 • Sunday–Thursday 11–9, Friday and Saturday 11–10 • $–$$, discounts for 60 and older • W

This is the place for great Cajun-style cuisine without having to go to Louisiana. Salad bar and seafood buffet guarantee that no one will leave hungry.

ACCOMMODATIONS

($ = under $45, $$ = $46–$60, $$$ = $61–$80, $$$$ = $81–$100, $$$$$ = over $100) Room tax 13%

RAMADA INN

**2610 I-10W • 883-0231 or 800-635-5312 • $$ • W+ 2 rooms
No-smoking rooms**
This two-story Ramada has 125 units that include two suites ($$$) and 20 no-smoking rooms. Cable TV. Room phones (no charge for local calls). Pets OK. Restaurant and "most popular" bar in Orange. Outdoor pool. Free newspaper.

PALESTINE

Anderson County Seat • 18,042 • (903)
The town was created in 1846 to comply with the Texas Legislature's law that the county seat should be located within three miles of the center of the county. Palestine (pronounced Palace-steen) was named by a relative of Cynthia Ann Parker, mother of the Comanche Chief Quanah Parker, after the Parker family's original hometown of Palestine, Illinois.
Agriculture, oil, and gas are the mainstays of the local economy.

TOURIST SERVICES

PALESTINE CONVENTION AND VISITORS BUREAU

**US 287/Loop 256 N. (P.O. Box 1177, 75802) • 729-6066 • 723-3014
(800) 659-3484**
Maps and brochures on Palestine and East Texas are available at the Civic Center. Their hours are 8:00 A.M.–5:00 P.M. Monday–Friday.

MUSEUMS

HOWARD HOUSE MUSEUM

1011 N. Perry • 729-2511 or 729-4784 • By appointment only, except usually open during Dogwood Trails (see below) • Free
Located in one of the oldest houses in the city, built in 1851, this museum features a doll collection, a collection of photos of early settlers and events, period furniture, and other items related to the history of the area. The anchor on display is from the *Ruthven,* the last steamer to use the docks at nearby Magnolia when it was a port on the Trinity River.

MUSEUM FOR EAST TEXAS CULTURE

**Crockett and Park in Reagan Park • 723-1914 • Tuesday–Friday 10–4,
Saturday and Sunday 1–4. Closed Monday • Adults $1, children 50¢**
Among the exhibits in this old high school building converted to a museum is, appropriately, a replica of a country classroom with authentic furnishings. There are also exhibits commemorating the major role the railroad played in the growth of the city, and an art center. The museum is set in a 22-acre park.

HISTORIC PLACES

VICTORIAN HOMES

There are several homes in the city that were built in the mid- and late-1800s. These are all private residences, not open to the public. Some of the better examples of Victorian architecture listed by street are: 921 N. Perry (1849); 503 E. Hodges (1896), 517 E. Hodges (1895); the Dr. Edwin Link House (listed in the

National Register of Historic Places) at 925 N. Link (1896), 1003 N. Link (1851); 407 E. Kolstad (1848); 1006 N. Mallard (1895); 215 S. Sycamore (1877), 318 S. Sycamore (1882), 619 S. Sycamore (1886), 715 S. Sycamore (1889), 805 S. Sycamore (1880), 814 S. Sycamore (1891), 1011 S. Sycamore (1892), 1305 S. Sycamore (1894); 220 Reagan (1889); 301 S. Magnolia (1879); 404 S. Royall (1894), 511 S. Royall (1884), and 519 S. Royall (1881).

CHURCHES

Sacred Heart Catholic Church, 503 N. Queen St. and Oak, was built in the 1890s. This High-Victorian Gothic structure is listed in the National Register of Historic Places. The First Presbyterian Church, 410 Ave. A, was built in 1888 of handmade bricks.

OTHER POINTS OF INTEREST

DAVEY DOGWOOD PARK

N. Link St. off US 155 • Open year-round for day use • Free • W variable
Five-and-a-half miles of paved road wind through the natural beauty of rolling hills, clear flowing streams, and an abundance of native dogwood trees in this 400-acre park. Picnic areas. The park is a featured area during the Texas Dogwood Trails each Spring.

NATIONAL SCIENTIFIC BALLOON FACILITY

Take US 287 approximately 5 miles west, next to airport **• 729-0271**
Tours by appointment • Free
Operated by NASA, this facility provides complete balloon operations and engineering support to the U.S. and foreign scientific communities. It has launched scientific balloons for more than 35 universities, 23 other research groups, and 33 foreign groups. Visitors are welcome during launchings, but call in advance or contact the receptionist at the administration building.

PALESTINE COMMUNITY FOREST

Entrance on Armory Rd. off US 287, approximately 2 miles northwest of downtown • 729-2181 (City Parks and Recreation) • Open at all times Free • W variable
A 700-acre forest containing several small lakes offering facilities for boating, fishing, and swimming plus picnic areas, nature trails, exercise course, and athletic fields.

TEXAS STATE RAILROAD STATE HISTORICAL PARK

Palestine depot off US 84 approximately 4 miles east • 683-2561 (in Rusk) or 800-442-8951 (Texas only) • Round trip: adults $15, children 3 to 12 $9
You might say this is a rolling state historical park. At its heart are turn-of-the-century steam locomotives that pull passenger coaches restored to the grandeur characteristic of the time when the railroads were the kings of the nation's transportation system. The 25.5-mile route between Palestine and Rusk is in the state's longest and narrowest park, and it includes some 30 bridges, pine and hardwood forests, and pastureland. It is operated by the Texas Parks and Wildlife Department and dedicated to the preservation of steam locomotives and railroading's golden age. The depots at each end of the line are set in small parks. The Palestine park has picnic tables, a playground, and grills. The

park at Rusk offers campsites with partial and full hook-ups, pavilions for group events, and a small theater in the depot where the railroad's history and other film presentations are offered. The railroad usually runs Saturdays and Sundays only from mid-March through late May, then Thursday through Monday (closed Tuesday and Wednesday) from late May until mid-August, and again on Saturdays and Sundays from mid-August through early November.

The normal schedule calls for a train from Palestine and one from Rusk to depart for the other station at 11 a.m. They meet and pass near the midway point at Menshaw siding, and then arrive at the other depot at 12:30. There's an hour layover for lunch—short-order foods are available at both depots—then both trains start the return trip at 1:30, arriving at their starting depot at 3:00 p.m. Seats are usually sold out well in advance, so reservations are strongly recommended. For current schedules and fares or more information call the numbers listed above or write: Park Superintendent, Texas State Railroad State Historical Park, P.O. Box 39, Rusk TX 75785.

SPORTS AND ACTIVITIES

Golf

MEADOWBROOK COUNTRY CLUB

Country Club Rd. • 723-7530 • 9-hole course. Greens fee for visitors: weekdays $16.25, weekends $21.65

PERFORMING ARTS

PALESTINE COMMUNITY THEATRE

Texas Theater, 217 W. Crawford • 549-2321 • Admission $6 • W

This local theater group puts on about six productions a year including one during the annual Texas Dogwood Trails.

SHOPPING

EILENBERGER'S BUTTER NUT BAKING COMPANY

512 N. John • 729-0881 • W

In business since 1898 and at its current location since 1918, this bakery is famous for its apricot, pecan, and fruit cakes, which are sold worldwide by mail. All baking is done the old-fashioned way with cakes mixed, decorated, and put in and taken out of the oven by hand. While looking over the selection you can have a cup of coffee, a sandwich, or a pastry in the small bake shop restaurant.

SIDE TRIPS

GUS ENGELING WILDLIFE MANAGEMENT AREA

Take US 287 northwest approximately 20 miles **• 928-2251 • Open for day use except during hunts • Contact office for pass**

The more than 10,000 acres in this wildlife habitat offer opportunities for bird watching, hunting, and fishing. Fishing on the more than eight miles of Catfish Creek is free. Fee permits for supervised public hunts for deer and feral hogs are by a lottery conducted by the Texas Parks and Wildlife Department. Permits are available for squirrel and duck hunting at the Area check station on the day of the scheduled hunt. Contact the Area biologist for hunt dates.

LAKE PALESTINE

Take TX 155 northeast approximately 20 miles • **Open at all times**
This 22,500-acre lake is some 18 miles long and has a shoreline of 135 miles. It is popular for boating, fishing, and other water sports. Commercial facilities around the lake include motels, bait and tackle shops, boat ramps, and camping areas. The "Dogwood Classic" professional boat races are held here in May.

ANNUAL EVENTS

March/April

TEXAS DOGWOOD TRAILS

Headquarters in Redlands Bldg., 400 N. Queen • 729-7275
Usually last two weekends in March and first weekend in April
Free (admission to some events) • W variable
Visitors will find marked driving and hiking trails among the dogwoods in Davey Dogwood Park, and an abundance of blooms along the many rural roads that wind through the rolling hills of wooded Anderson County. A number of other activities are tied in with the spring flowering season. These include a downtown parade, an arts and crafts festival at the Civic Center (fee), and a tour of historic homes (fee). Other attractions include a fishing tournament, a chili cookoff, guided tours of the old bakery, a play by the Palestine Community Theater, helicopter, trolley, and miniature train rides, a car show and a BBQ cookoff. Contact the headquarters for a schedule of events.

October

HOT PEPPER FESTIVAL

Various locations downtown • 729-6066 (Chamber of Commerce)
Last Saturday in October • Free • W variable
Events change from year to year, but in the past they have included a bicycle race, live entertainment, a street dance, a car show, chili cookoff, and arts and crafts displays.

December

CHRISTMAS PILGRIMAGE

Various locations • 729-6066 • First weekend in December • Admission
A tour of historic homes.

ACCOMMODATIONS

($ = under $45, $$ = $46–$60, $$$ = $61–$80, $$$$ = $81–$100, $$$$$ = over $100)
Room tax 13%

BEST WESTERN PALESTINE INN

1601 W. Palestine Ave. (US 79) • 723-4655 or 800-528-1234 • $ • W+ 2 rooms
No-smoking rooms
The two-story Best Western has 66 rooms including 15 no-smoking. Cable TV with HBO. Room phones (no charge for local calls). Small pets OK. Restaurant. Outdoor pool.

PARIS

Lamar County Seat • 25,699 • (903)

This is reportedly the second largest city named Paris in the world, immediately behind Paris, France, which it was named after. Founded in 1839, it became the county seat of Lamar County in 1844. Lamar was one of the few Texas counties backing Sam Houston against seceding from the Union. However, once Texas went with the Confederacy, the people supported that cause.

A number of real and semi-mythical figures of the Old West have connections with the city. On his way to the Alamo, Davy Crockett allegedly slept under a tree in the city. The woman outlaw Belle Starr was once a resident in the local jail. Frank James clerked in a local dry goods store for a brief time after his brother Jesse was killed. And John Chisum, one of the great cattle barons of the 1800s, who was portrayed by John Wayne in the movie *Chisum*, lived here for a number of years and is buried here.

The Woman's Christian Temperance Union in Texas was organized here in 1882.

Two disastrous fires, one in 1877 and the other in 1916, wiped out much of the city. As a result, the architecture of downtown Paris today is like that of a 1920s city. It also has a unique downtown plaza with a centerpiece fountain of Italian marble.

TOURIST SERVICES

PARIS CHAMBER OF COMMERCE AND VISITORS CENTER

1651 Clarksville (Bus US 271) at 16th St. SE • 784-2501 • W+

Free *Historical Tour Guide* and a *Visitors Guide* are available.

INDUSTRIAL TOURS

KIMBERLY CLARK

Loop 286 SW and FM 137 (P.O. Box 9000) • 785-7501, ext. 208 • Group tours only, reservations required

This is the Southwestern distribution center for Kimberly Clark and also a plant for the production of Huggies diapers. The one-and-a-half-hour tour includes viewing an introductory film, a visit to the company's collection of Southwestern art, and a tour of the fully automated warehouse that features robot cars and a nine-story retrieval crane. Group tours require at least two-weeks advance notice; no one under 12 and no cameras are permitted.

MUSEUMS

SAMUEL BELL MAXEY HOUSE

812 S. Church at Washington • 785-5716 • Friday 1–5; Saturday 10–5; Sunday 1–5 • Adults $2, children 6 to 12 $1

This house was built in 1866 by Samuel Bell Maxey, an 1846 West Point graduate and lawyer who served as a major general in the Confederate Army and later as a U.S. senator (1875–87). The two-story house is an excellent example of the Greek Revival and Italianate influence. Tours are held every hour on the hour, and visitors can see the original family furniture, memorabilia, clothing, and family heirlooms dating back to 1795. The house is in the National Register of Historic Places.

HISTORIC PLACES

A map of historic buildings is available from the Chamber of Commerce. Most of the buildings in the city date from after the 1916 fire. In fact, Paris boasts the largest concentration of 1916–1917 architecture in the country. However, the following are some of the historic buildings that did survive that fire (most are private residences and not open to the public):

Atkinson-Morris House, 802 Fitzhugh near Tudor, built in 1891; **Daniel Home,** W. Kaufman and 4th St. SW, built in 1876; **First Presbyterian Church,** 410 W. Kaufman near 4th St. SW, built in 1892; **Lightfoot House,** Washington at Church, built in 1876; **Scott-Roden Mansion,** 425 Church St. at Woodlawn, built in 1908; **Wise-Fielding Home,** 418 W. Washington, built in 1889; and **Sante Fe—Frisco Railroad Depot,** 1100 Bonham St., Built in 1911.

OTHER POINTS OF INTEREST

A.M. AND WEMA AIKEN REGIONAL ARCHIVES

Paris Junior College in Rheudasil Learning Center • 784-9164
Monday–Friday 8–5 • Free • W

In addition to the historical archives for Lamar, Red River, Delta, and Fannin counties, there is also a replica of the office of State Senator Aiken as it appeared in the state capitol in Austin, where he served in the legislature for 46 years.

CULBERTSON FOUNTAIN

On the Plaza • Free • W

A gift to the city from J. J. Culbertson to honor the rebuilding of Paris after the 1916 fire, it was completed in 1927. Its triton and basins are of Italian marble embellished with stone carvings. The base and pillars are of Bedford stone and the steps are of Carthage stone. It is the focal point of the plaza, which *Texas Monthly* magazine has called "the prettiest plaza in the state of Texas."

LAKE CROOK

Take US 271 north approximately 3 miles **• Open at all times • Free**
W variable

This 1,226-acre lake has become the local fishing hole since it was overshadowed by the opening of Lake Pat Mayse. Facilities for fishing.

CELEBRATE AMERICA EXCURSION TRAIN

1651 Clarksville Street • 784-2501 • Dates vary • Adults $22.50; children 12 and under $15.00

Journey across the Red River for a two-hour visit in Hugo, Oklahoma.

SPORTS AND ACTIVITIES

Drag Racing

PARIS DRAG STRIP

Take US 82 east approximately 6 miles **• 785-0430 • Admission**

NHRA-sanctioned races are held here on Sunday afternoons from March through May and on Friday evenings June through August.

GOLF

ELK HOLLOW GOLF CLUB

220 Elk Hollow Dr. at 36th St. NE • 785-6585 • 9-hole course. Greens fee: $5 for 18 holes.

COLLEGES AND UNIVERSITIES

PARIS JUNIOR COLLEGE

2400 Clarksville (Bus US 271) at 24th St. SE • 784-9247 (Public Relations) W+ but not all areas • Designated visitor parking

Founded in 1924, the college now has about 2,200 students enrolled in its academic and technical/vocational programs. The Division of Jewelry Technology, Horology, and Gemology is one of only three in the United States. Its professional gemology program is the only scientifically oriented gemology program at a public teaching institution in the country. Most of the activities to which visitors are welcome center around the Fine Arts Department. These include plays, art exhibits, music concerts, and recitals.

PERFORMING ARTS

PARIS MUNICIPAL BAND

784-2501 (Chamber of Commerce)

Formed in 1923, this mixed professional/amateur group claims it is the oldest continuously organized municipal band in the United States. Its big event is the annual free summer concert series that is given every Friday night from the middle of June through the middle of July. The band plays in the formal Peristyle in Bywaters Park, on S. Main about two blocks south of the Plaza, while the concert goers sit on blankets and lawn chairs on the grass.

PARIS COMMUNITY THEATER

Plaza Theater, on the Plaza • 784-0259 • Admission • W

Four or five productions are put on each year by this theater group.

SHOPPING

JUDYE SAFFLE GALLERY CENTER

135 Lamar at 1st St. NE • 785-8446

The gallery features the works of local artists including those of Judye Saffle, who is nationally known for her paintings of wildlife and florals.

PARIS ANTIQUE MALL

Hwy. 24 • 785-0872

Over 50 dealers offer their antiques for sale at this popular antique mall.

REFLECTIONS GLASS AND GIFTS

1445 Clarksville in Williamsburg Shopping Center • 784-8229 • W

This is a studio and gallery for stained and leaded glass, handblown glass, painted glass, and hand-painted decorative items.

SWAIM'S HARDWARE

240 1st St. SW at Austin • 784-3321

An old-fashioned hardware store where the floor is wood, the stock runs from horse riggings to cookware, and the motto is "If we don't have it, it's not made." Outside, on the Austin St. side of the building, is a three-panel mural depicting the history of Paris during the cotton era.

THRASHER'S ART STUDIO

US 271N, 1.9 miles from intersection with Loop 286N • 785-1579 • W

The artist here has a national reputation for Western art including paintings of Texas bluebonnets and wildlife. Originals and limited editions are available.

SIDE TRIPS

BACK SIDE OF NOWHERE

Call for directions • 784-2079 • Tuesday–Saturday tours at 10 and 1–4 on the hour, Sunday 2–4. Closed Monday • Admission

This eclectic farm includes a caboose, a collection of outhouses, a terrapin village and blackberry picking.

GAMBILL GOOSE REFUGE

From northwest Loop 286, take FM 79 for 3.2 miles to FM 2820, then west 2 miles **• 785-7511 (City Parks Dept.) • Open at all times • Free • W variable**

As the story goes, back in the early 1920s a local farmer, John Gambill, nursed an injured wild goose back to health. The following year the tagged goose returned bringing a dozen other geese with it. This inspired Gambill to set up a wild goose sanctuary. Now, thousands of Canadian, snow, and other geese and many varieties of ducks stop over here during the migration season from October to April. The best time to view the birds is while they feed at 7:15 a.m. and 4:45 p.m. The 600-acre refuge adjacent to Lake Gibbons also has facilities for picnicking and fishing.

LAKE PAT MAYSE

Take US 271 north approximately 13 miles, then west on FM 906 for 2 miles **732-3020 • Open at all times • Free • W variable**

Five developed parks dot the 67-mile shoreline of the 5,993-acre Army Corps of Engineers lake. Facilities are available for fishing, swimming, boating, picnicking, and camping (fee). Public hunting is also permitted in the wildlife management area around the lake in season for deer, squirrels, rabbits, quail, ducks, and geese.

TRIDEN'S PRAIRIE

Southwest corner of intersection of US 82 and FM 38 approximately 8 miles west

There's not much to see here except open prairie, but it's worthy of note because this 97-acre slice of land is an undisturbed remnant of the natural grassland that once extended from Texas north to southern Canada. Native grasses and wildflowers have been harvested here, but the land has never been cultivated. Its name is derived from the native, perennial bunchgrass known as long-spiked tridens. This important part of Texas' natural history is being preserved by Texas Garden Clubs, Inc., and the Texas Nature Conservancy.

ANNUAL EVENTS

PARIS BY NIGHT ROAD RALLY

Staging area approximately 3 miles north on US 271 at Lake Crook picnic area • 784-2501 (Chamber of Commerce) • Date varies, usually held every 18 months in fall or spring • Free • W

Members bring their cars here from all over the country to participate in this Sports Car Club of America sanctioned event. On Saturday a display of the cars and an exhibition shows spectators what to look for in the rally. Various stages of the rally are held over the three days.

July

TOUR DE PARIS BICYCLE RALLY

Paris Junior College • 784-2501 (Chamber of Commerce) • Saturday closest to July 14 • Free (entrance fee for race) • W variable

This race draws over 1,500 cyclists from four states.

September

RED RIVER VALLEY FAIR AND EXPOSITION

Paris Fairgrounds, Clement Rd. (between Bus US 271 and Loop 286) 784-2501 (Chamber of Commerce) • 6 days starting Labor Day Admission to some events • Pay parking

A typical county fair with livestock competitions, carnival, chili cookoff, old-time fiddlers contest, entertainment, a fun run, and other sports competitions.

ACCOMMODATIONS

($ = under $45, $$ = $46–$60, $$$ = $61–$80, $$$$ = $81–$100, $$$$$ = over $100) Room tax 13%

BEST WESTERN INN

3755 NE Loop 286 at US 82E • 785-5566 or 800-528-1234 • $ • No-smoking rooms

The two-story Best Western has 80 units including one suite ($$) and 15 no-smoking rooms. Cable TV with HBO. Room phones (charge for local calls). Pets OK. Restaurant. Outdoor pool. Free coffee in lobby. Free newspaper.

PITTSBURG

Camp County Seat • 4,007 • (903)

In 1855 W. H. Pitts settled a tract of land that is now within the corporate limits of the town that was later named after him. Poultry is the biggest industry in the county, and Pittsburg is the world headquarters for Pilgrims Pride Industries, a firm that produces more than 600 million pounds of chicken a year from its plants scattered throughout Texas and nearby states. Livestock, peaches, vegetables, and light industry also contribute significantly to the local economy. The town's claims to fame include being the home of the Ezekiel Airship, which is said to have flown a year before the Wright brothers, and of the regionally popular Pittsburg hot links (a mildly spiced beef and pork sausage). The area is locally called "Great Lakes Country" because there are four lakes surrounding it, each just a short drive away.

TOURIST SERVICES

CAMP COUNTY CHAMBER OF COMMERCE
202 Jefferson • 856-3442 • W

SIDE TRIPS

LAKE BOB SANDLIN
Take TX 11 west to FM 21, then north to dam • 572-5531 • **Open at all times**
$3 per vehicle per day • **W variable**
See Mount Pleasant.

ANNUAL EVENTS

July

PEACH BERRY FESTIVAL
Downtown • 856-3442 • On or around the 4th of July
This festival recognizes local peach and berry growers. Food, fireworks, and fun.

September

CHICKFEST
Downtown • 856-3442 (Chamber of Commerce) • Third weekend in September • Free (Admission to some events) • W variable
Festivities include arts and crafts exhibits, trades day, tennis tournament, tour of homes (fee), pinto bean cooking contest, parade, variety of sports tournaments, entertainment, antique car show, wagon rides, a historical play, street dance, and hot-links eating contest.

OFFBEAT

EZEKIEL AIRSHIP
142 Marshall, Warrick's Restaurant • 856-7881 • Free • W
Around the turn of the century, the Rev. Burrell Cannon was a part-time Baptist preacher, part-time sawmill operator, and part-time inventor. He got his idea for an airship from the description by the Prophet Ezekiel in the Bible of a vehicle that was a sort of "wheel within a wheel" that flew through the air. Cannon set up a stock company and raised $20,000 to build the airship. The ship had large, fabric-covered wings powered by an engine that turned four sets of paddles. Although there are several conflicting stories, reportedly the ship was briefly airborne in an undocumented "test" flight in 1902, a year before the Wright brothers' first flight. That airship was destroyed by a storm while being shipped to the St. Louis World's Trade Fair in 1904. In 1913 a second model crashed, and the Rev. Cannon gave up the project. The 26-by-23 foot

replica on exhibit here was constructed by the Optimist Club based on historical records and an aged photo of the airship.

RESTAURANTS

FRANKLIN'S FOOD STORE RESTAURANT

**115 Jefferson • 856-3681 • Monday–Saturday 11–4. Closed Sunday • $
No Cr • W**

Walk through the grocery store to the unpretentious restaurant in the back,
where they still serve hot links on paper as they have since the 1930s, and you
share tables communal style. They also offer barbecue, chicken, beef stew, and
hamburgers.

PITTSBURG HOT LINKS RESTAURANT

**136 Marshall at Rusk • 856-5765 • Monday–Saturday 9–6. Closed Sunday
$ • No Cr • W**

As the name says, hot links are the specialty here. They are called "hot"
because they are served hot, not because of the spices that are actually mild by
Texas tastes. Place your order at the counter in the rear and buy by the link,
with a minimum of four. Also available are beef stew, chili, chicken-fried steak,
and hamburgers.

WARRICK'S RESTAURANT

**142 Marshall • 856-7881 • Dinner only 7 days • $–$$$ • AE, MC, V • W
Children's plates**

The owners of Pittsburg Hot Links have branched out and opened this din-
ner-only restaurant that offers catfish, seafood, and steaks. The replica of the
Ezekiel Airship is here (see above).

TAYLORS

8–5 six days • 856-0443

Specialty coffees, soda fountain, sandwiches, and ice cream.

CARSON HOUSE INN & GRILL

**302 Mt. Pleasant St. • 856-2468 • Lunch and dinner 6 days • $–$$$
Brunch Sunday**

Chicken-fried steak to grilled salmon, salad bar.

PAPA NACHOS

308 S. Greer Blvd. • 856-7679 • $–$$

Lunch and dinner six days. Good Mexican food at reasonable prices.

POP'S CHICKEN & BURGERS

119 N. Greer Blvd. • 856-2928 • $–$$

Lunch and dinner seven days. Buffet-style home cooking.

QUITMAN

Wood County Seat • 1,684 • (903)

Settled in the 1840s, the town is named in honor of John Anthony Quitman, a lawyer and later a major general in the United States Army, governor of Mississippi, and governor of Mexico for a time after the Mexican War (he was the only American to rule in Montezuma's Palace). Quitman never really lived in Texas, but he brought in a company of volunteers in 1836 to fight in the Texas Revolution and later championed the cause for the annexation of Texas into the Union. For a time it was also the home of James Stephen Hogg, the first native Texan to be elected governor. Also from Wood County was Texas Ranger Captain Bill McDonald, who became famous for his comment, "One riot, one Texas Ranger."

TOURIST SERVICES

QUITMAN CHAMBER OF COMMERCE

101 N. Main, across from courthouse • 763-4411

MUSEUMS

GOVERNOR HOGG SHRINE STATE HISTORICAL PARK

**518 S. Main (TX 37) • 763-2701 • Weekends only, call for hours • Tour $2
W variable**

James Stephen Hogg, born in Rusk in 1851, worked as a farmhand, clerk, printer's devil, typesetter, and country editor. He published the *Quitman Daily News* in the early 1870s. His political career started when he was elected justice of the peace at age 22, then went on to be county attorney and state attorney general. In 1891 he became the first native Texan to be elected governor. Located in this 26-acre park are the Stinson Home, in which James Hogg was married to Sallie Stinson in 1874; the Honeymoon Cottage, and the Miss Ima Hogg Museum, named after their only daughter.

LAKES

Lake Fork Reservoir, on TX 154, has a 27,000-acre lake offering facilities for fishing, boating, swimming, and camping. There are commercial marinas, campgrounds, and motels along its 300 miles of shoreline. For information, call 878-2262.

Lake Quitman, on FM 2966, is an 814-acre county lake offering facilities for fishing, swimming and other water sports, picnicking, and camping. Commercial facilities include marinas, boat rentals, and campsites. For information, call 878-2234.

ANNUAL EVENTS

March or April

DOGWOOD FIESTA

**Various locations • 763-4411 (Chamber of Commerce) • Date varies
Most activities free • W variable**

The dates vary depending on the prediction of when the dogwoods will bloom each year. Activities include an arts and crafts market, a fishing tournament, early Texas homes tour, fun run, coronation of the queen, and a trail ride around nearby Lake Lydia.

August

OLD SETTLERS' REUNION

Governor Hogg Shrine State Historical Park, 518 S. Main (TX 37) • 763-4411 (Chamber of Commerce) • First Wednesday–Saturday in August • Free W variable

Started in 1898, this is believed to be the oldest reunion of its type in the state. The celebration includes gospel singing, old-time country and bluegrass music, an old-time fiddlin' contest, games, and a small carnival.

ROSENBERG-RICHMOND

Fort Bend County • Richmond is County Seat • 27,692 • (281)

Each of these adjoining cities has its own municipal government, but share a joint Chamber of Commerce. Richmond is smaller but older, dating back to 1822 and Stephen F. Austin's Old Three Hundred colony. Their log blockhouse on the bend of the Brazos River looked like a fort, so it became Fort Bend. Settlers from Virginia changed the name to Richmond, but the county is still Fort Bend.

In the late 1880s, Richmond became the site of the "Jaybird-Woodpecker War." The Jaybirds were wealthy white settlers and ex-Confederates, and the Woodpeckers were reconstructionists who controlled local politics with the Black vote. Both sides had been sniping at each other for several years and there had been some killings. The showdown came in a shootout around the courthouse square on August 16, 1889, and several men died. Eventually the governor—backed by the Texas Rangers and State Militia—intervened and ruled in favor of the Jaybirds. The Jaybird Monument at Morton and 4th commemorates the lives lost in the battle.

The Nation Hotel was owned by Carry Nation and her husband. After the battle, the Nations moved to Kansas, where Carry started wielding her hatchet and chopping up saloons.

Rosenberg, settled in the early 1880s, was named after the president of the Gulf, Colorado, and Santa Fe Railroad.

Buried in the Morton Cemetery in Richmond are Mirabeau B. Lamar, the second president of the Republic, and Jane Long, called the "Mother of Texas." Erastus "Deaf" Smith, the famous scout of the Texas War for Independence, is buried somewhere near (local historians say "under") the intersection of Houston and 6th.

TOURIST SERVICES

ROSENBERG-RICHMOND CHAMBER OF COMMERCE

4120 Ave. H (77471) • 342-5464 • W

MUSEUMS

CONFEDERATE MUSEUM

Richmond, 603 Calhoun, 2740 FM 359, north of US 90A • 342-8787
Tuesday and Thursday 10–3, Saturday and Sunday 1–4
Located on the Old South Plantation owned by the descendants of Jane Long, the "Mother of Texas," the museum features more than a thousand Confederate artifacts from the Civil War. An ongoing project is to bring the flavor of Richmond, Virginia, to its Texas namesake. Gift shop.

FORT BEND COUNTY MUSEUM COMPLEX

Richmond, 500 Houston St. between 5th and 6th from Houston to Preston
342-6478 • Tuesday–Friday 10–4, Saturday and Sunday 1–5 • Free
The complex consists of the Fort Bend County Museum, the John H. Moore Home, the Long-Smith Cabin and Decker Park.

FORT BEND COUNTY MUSEUM

500 Houston • Free • W
Featured here are interpretive exhibits covering the county's history from 1822 to 1922. Included is the founding of Fort Bend; the life of Jane Long, who ran a boarding house in town and a plantation outside it; and the life of Mirabeau B. Lamar, the second president of the Republic.

THE JOHN M. MOORE HOME

406 S. 5th • Saturday and Sunday 1–5 • Admission • W
This home was built in 1883 by Congressman Moore for his bride. A "Candlelight Tour" is held here during the Christmas season.

THE LONG-SMITH CABIN

500 Houston • Saturday and Sunday 1–5 • Free • W
This was the home of Thomas Jefferson Smith, a survivor of the Goliad Massacre. Some of the furniture belonged to Jane Long.
In **Decker Park** are several pioneer buildings and the 1896 County Jail. Some are open by appointment through the museum.

HISTORIC PLACES

A historical tour map of Richmond is available from the Chamber of Commerce.

SIDE TRIPS

BRAZOS BEND STATE PARK

From US 59E take FM 762 approximately 20 miles southeast • **(409) 553-3243**
Open daylight hours seven days for day use, at all times for camping • Fee
per vehicle • W
One of the greatest attractions is the George Observatory. The 36-inch telescope is one of the most powerful available to the public in the United States. It is open to visitors Saturday 3–10. Free admission. Fishing, picnicking, hiking, tent and RV camping (fee), and wildlife observation are offered. For information on park facilities write: Park Superintendent, 21901 FM 762, Needville 77461.

GEORGE RANCH HEADQUARTERS

From US 59E take FM 762 approximately 6 miles south (follow signs to Brazos Bend State Park) • 545-9212 • **Call for Seasonal Schedules, tour information, and special event information • Admission • W variable**

This is a 470-acre park in the midst of a 23,000-acre family ranch that was started in 1824. Four generations of the family lived here, and a number of historic buildings have been moved here and restored. There is also a herd of 50 longhorns. Many events are held here all year. Write P.O. Box 1007, Richmond 77469.

ANNUAL EVENTS

May

FORT BEND CZECHFEST

Fort Bend County Fairgrounds, TX 36 about 1 mile south of US 59 • 342-6171 **Friday–Sunday of first full weekend in May • Admission • W variable**

Many of the first Czech settlers originally came here to work on railroads, and they wound up becoming farmers. This festival is held by their descendants. You can eat Czech dishes, watch Czech dances, see an arts and crafts show, plus continuous entertainment and many more events. As they say, "Czech it out!"

October

TEXIAN MARKET DAYS

George Ranch Headquarters • *From US 59E take FM 762 approximately 6 miles south* • 545-9212 • **Fourth weekend in October • Admission • W**

This living history festival revolves around the development of the area from 1824 to the present. It includes tours of the historic buildings, ranching and historical crafts demonstrations, music, and entertainment.

RESTAURANTS

($ = under $7, $$ = $8–$17, $$$ = $18–$25, $$$$ = over $25 for one person excluding drinks, tax, and tip.)

LARRY'S ORIGINAL MEXICAN RESTAURANT

116 US 90A, just east of the bridge • 342-2881 • **Breakfast, lunch, and dinner seven days • $-$$ • AE, MC, V • W • Children's plates**

When the State Department wanted Chinese Premier Chou En Lai to taste Tex-Mex food on his first visit to the States, they brought him here. That was years ago, but Larry's has been pulling in customers with Tex-Mex specialties since 1960. Some steaks and burgers are on the menu. Beer.

QUAIL HOLLOW INN

214 Morton at 3rd • 341-6733 • **Lunch and dinner Tuesday–Saturday, brunch only on Sunday. Closed Monday • Reservations suggested • $$ • AE, MC, V W • Children's plates**

Quail dishes are among the continental cuisine specialties of the Swiss chef/owner. Or, you can also choose from entrees such as fillet of beef Wellington, milk-fed veal, or Karl's Mixed Grill. Bar.

THE SWINGING DOOR

Take FM 359 south about 5 miles • 342-4758 • **Lunch and dinner**
Wednesday–Sunday • **$–$$** • **No Cr** • **W**
  Barbecue is the order of the day-and night-in this rustic restaurant set by a
duck pond. Try the fresh cobblers for the dessert. C&W dances are held on weekends. Bar.

ACCOMMODATIONS

($ under $45, $$ = $46–$60, $$$ = $61–$80, $$$$ = $81–$100, $$$$$ = over $100)
Room tax 13%

BEST WESTERN SUNDOWNER MOTOR INN

28382 SW. Freeway (US 59) at TX 36 • **342-6000 or 800-528-1234** • **$–$$** • **W+ 1**
room • **No-smoking rooms**
  This two-story Best Western has 104 rooms including 15 no-smoking. TV
with free in-room movies. Room phones (no charge for local calls). Pets OK.
Restaurant. Outdoor pool and spa.

EXPRESS INN

26010 SW Freeway (US 59) at FM 2218 • **342-6671** • **$** • **W+ 1 room**
No-smoking rooms
  The two-story Inn has 140 rooms including 10 no-smoking. TV with free in-
room movies. Room phones (no charge for local calls). Pets OK. Restaurant
serves breakfast only. Outdoor pool. Free newspaper.

RUSK

Cherokee County Seat • **4,366** • **(903)**
  Immigration started here after the Cherokee Indians were driven out of the
area in 1838. The city is named for Thomas Jefferson Rusk, who was a signer of
the Texas Declaration of Independence, president of the convention that framed
the first state constitution, and later a United States senator. During the Civil
War a Confederate gun factory and a prisoner of war camp were located here.
This is also the birthplace of the first two native-born governors of Texas, James
Stephen Hogg and Thomas Mitchell Campbell.

TOURIST SERVICES

RUSK CHAMBER OF COMMERCE
415 S. Main (P.O. Box 67, 75785) • **683-4242** • **W**

HISTORIC PLACES

BONNER BANK BUILDING
US 69S at Euclid
  The small building was built in 1865 and was used as the first bank in the
county by F. W. Bonner from 1884 until the financial world collapsed in the
panic of 1893. At various times after that it was used as a cigar factory, school,
shoe shop, mechanic's shop, and an express office.

HISTORIC HOMES

The three best-preserved historic homes in Rusk are all on E. 5th St. All are private residences, not open to the public. **James Perkins Home,** 302 E. 5th; the one-story part of the home was built in 1851, and the two-story wing and Victorian detailing were added in 1883. **Dr. I. K. Frazer Home,** 704 E. 5th; a typical Texas home of the 1850s. Dr. Frazer was the leading physician of Rusk from the 1870s until his death in 1908. **Gregg Family Home,** 808 E. 5th; built in 1847; this dogtrot-style home is one of the oldest in Rusk. It was remodeled in 1919 and 1935.

OLD RUSK PENITENTIARY BUILDING

Ave. A and US 69, Rusk State Hospital

Built in 1878 with sandstone walls two-and-a-half feet thick, this was the main building of the former state prison. The prisoners built the "Old Alcalde" iron ore smelting furnace, which produced iron products used in construction throughout the United States. They also built what is now the Texas State Railroad from Rusk to Palestine. In 1917 the prison was converted to a state hospital for the mentally ill, and the building is now the administrative center for the Rusk State Hospital.

OTHER POINTS OF INTEREST

FAIRCHILD STATE FOREST

Take US 84 west approximately 13 miles to main tract

Originally owned by the state prison system, there are 2,896 acres in six tracts. Small day-use area for fishing and picnicking in main tract.

FOOTBRIDGE GARDEN PARK

E. 5th, 1 block east of town square • Open at all times • Free

Crossing a tree-shaded creek, this footbridge, 4 feet wide and 546 feet long, is believed to be the longest wooden trestle-type bridge in the United States. Originally built in 1861, it was used by the people on the east side of town to get across the boggy valley to downtown in rainy weather. It was replaced by another footbridge in 1889. That one lasted into the 1950s, but then fell into disrepair until it was restored in 1969 using the 1889 planks.

JIM HOGG STATE HISTORIC PARK

US 84 about 2 miles east • 683-4850 • Weekends only, call for hours
$2 per person • W variable

James Stephen Hogg was the first native Texan elected governor. Attractions in the 175-acre park include a museum featuring memorabilia of the Hogg family, a replica of his birthplace, the family cemetery, a playground, picnic areas, and hiking and nature study trails.

RUSK STATE PARK

Take US 84 west approximately 2 miles • 683-5126 • Open at all times • $2 per person • W variable

Comprising 100 acres of mixed pine and hardwood forest around the Rusk depot of the Texas State Railroad (see below), this park offers facilities for overnight camping (fee); fishing in a 15-acre lake stocked with bass, catfish, and perch; and hiking and picnicking. Also here are a playground, paddleboat and rowboat rentals, and two tennis courts.

TEXAS STATE RAILROAD STATE HISTORICAL PARK

Take US 84 west approximately 3.5 miles • 683-2561 or 800-442-8951 (Texas only) • **Round trip: adults $15, children 3–12 $9**

The depots at each end of the line are set in parks. The park at Rusk offers campsites with partial and full hook-ups, pavilions for group events, and a small theater in the depot where the railroad's history and other film presentations are offered.

See Palestine.

PERFORMING ARTS

CHEROKEE CIVIC THEATRE

Cherokee Theater, 116 W. 5th between Main and Sycamore • 683-2131 **Admission • W**

The Cherokee Civic Theater Group usually puts on four productions a year— one in the fall in conjunction with the Indian Summer Festival.

SIDE TRIPS

CADDOAN MOUNDS STATE HISTORIC SITE

Alto. *Take US 69 south approximately 12 miles to Alto, then TX 21 southwest about 6 miles* • 409-858-3218 • **Friday–Monday, call for hours** • **Adults $2, children 6 to 12 $1** • **W variable**

Three Caddo Indian Mounds—two temple mounds and a burial mound dating from about 780 to 1200—were discovered here. There is also a reconstructed Caddo house and a museum that offers a 10-minute slide presentation on the mounds and the artifacts recovered from them. An interpretive trail has exhibits along the way explaining Caddo life, the most sophisticated prehistoric Indian culture in Texas.

ANNUAL EVENTS

October

INDIAN SUMMER FESTIVAL

Downtown Rusk • 683-4242 (Chamber of Commerce) • **Dates vary** • **Adults $2, children 6 to 12 $1** • **W variable**

The atmosphere is old-time county fair with exhibits of woodcrafts, leatherwork, jewelry, pottery, paintings, and other arts and crafts. Plus booths offering traditional Texas food favorites. The Civic Theatre puts on a Broadway musical.

SAN AUGUSTINE

San Augustine County Seat • 2,930 • (409)
Established in 1832, it was the first town after crossing the Sabine River on the Old San Antonio Road (*El Camino Real*) and thus became an eastern gateway to Texas and the Southwest. San Augustine was built on the site of a Spanish mission started in 1716 and abandoned in 1773. Sam Houston was a certified resident while seeking office during the days of the Republic and also as a United States senator. J. Pinckney Henderson, the first governor of Texas, came from here, as did O. M. Roberts, who served as governor from 1879 to 1883. Because of these men and other figures important in the early years, the town is known as "The Cradle of Texas," and it also claims to be the oldest town in Texas. At one time it was also an education center with three universities. Several Protestant church congregations here also lay claim as Texas' oldest. Although a fire destroyed much of the town in 1890, a number of historic homes survived.

TOURIST SERVICES

SAN AUGUSTINE COUNTY CHAMBER OF COMMERCE
611 W. Columbia, 75972 • 275-3610 • W

HISTORIC PLACES

EZEKIEL CULLEN HOUSE
207 Congress • Thursday–Sunday 1–4, or by appointment • 275-3610 (Chamber of Commerce) • Adults $3
Ezekiel Cullen was a judge and a member of the Texas House of Representatives. While in the Texas House, he was mainly responsible for the laws funding public schools with public lands. The Greek Revival-style house, built in 1839, was donated to the Daughters of the Republic of Texas in 1953 by well-known oil man Hugh Roy Cullen, a grandson of Ezekiel. Of special interest are the large double-fan windows at each end of the garret. This garret extends the entire length of the house and is furnished as a ballroom. The house is listed in the National Register of Historic Places and is headquarters for the city's annual Candlelite Tour the second weekend in December.

OTHER HISTORIC PLACES

The **Christ Episcopal Church,** 201 S. Ayish, was organized in 1848 and the present building was erected in 1870 with the original handmade pews still in use. The **Memorial Presbyterian Church,** 205 E. Livingston, was organized in 1838 and the church erected in 1887. Note the handmade pulpit and two handmade pews in the room to the right of the sanctuary. The **Colonel Phillip A. Sublett House** (Sam Houston's law partner) is four miles east on TX 21 and built in 1874. Listed in the National Register of Historic Places are the **Colonel Stephen William Blount House** (1839) at 502 E. Columbia (Colonel Blount was a signer of the Texas Declaration of Independence), the **Matthew Cartwright House** (1839) at 912 Main Street, and the **William Garrett Plantation Home** (during Civil War), one mile west on TX 21.

SIDE TRIPS

ANGELINA NATIONAL FOREST
Take TX 147 south. (*See* **Jasper.**)

LAKE SAM RAYBURN
Take TX 147 south. (*See* **Jasper.**)

MILTON GARRETT HOUSE
11 miles west on TX 21 • (Not open to public)
   Built in 1826, this is the oldest house in San Augustine County and one of the few all-log houses left in East Texas.

SABINE NATIONAL FOREST
Take TX 21 east. (*See* **Center.**)

TOLEDO BEND RESERVOIR
Take TX 21 east. (*See* **Center.**)

ACCOMMODATIONS

($ = under $45, $$ = $46–$60, $$$ = $61–$80, $$$$ = $81–$100, $$$$$ over $100)
Room tax 13%

Bed and Breakfast

MAIN STREET BED & BREAKFAST
409 E. Main • 275-5013 • $$–$$$
   Accommodations include one room with private bath and two with shared bath. Sam Houston is said to have used the property's old well that is still in operation. Generous full country breakfast; snack and beverages always available. No indoor smoking. Children welcome.

THE WADE HOUSE
128 E. Columbia • 275-5489 or 275-2553 • $$–$$$ • V, MC • No-smoking in house
   This bed and breakfast offers five guest rooms, two share a bath. This is not an historic home, but built in the 1940s. Called "The House of Hats" because hats worn by Mrs. Atheniar Wade from the 1930s to the 1970s are displayed. Only children over 12. No pets. Continental breakfast.

SULPHUR SPRINGS

Hopkins County Seat • 14,062 • (903)
   It was originally called Bright Star, and in 1870 the Atkins House on Atkins St. was built in the shape of a five-pointed star as a tribute to the town name. Shortly after, however, the name was changed to Sulphur Springs in an effort to promote the town as a mineral springs health resort. That worked for a while, but soon agriculture took over as the foremost business in the county. Today Hopkins County, with some 350 dairy operations, is the second largest milk-producing county in Texas and the second largest beef-producing county in the state.

TOURIST SERVICES

HOPKINS COUNTY CHAMBER OF COMMERCE
1200 Houston, Civic Center Complex (P.O. Box 347, 75483) • 885-6515 • W

MUSEUMS

HOPKINS COUNTY MUSEUM AND HERITAGE PARK
416 N. Jackson at E. Houston • 885-2387 • Saturday 10–4, Sunday 1–4
Free (donations) • W outside only
The museum, in the 1910 house fronting the park, has displays of regional artifacts. Buildings include a gristmill, old print shop, blacksmith shop, syrup mill, log cabin, and brick plant.

SOUTHWEST DAIRY CENTER
1210 Houston St. • 439-MILK • Monday–Saturday 9–4, Sunday 1–5
Free (donations) • W
This museum has exhibits demonstrating life on an early day dairy farm. In addition, there is a 12-minute video giving an overview of the dairy industry and a bike-riding skeleton that talks about calcium. Guided tours are available.

HISTORIC PLACES

HOPKINS COUNTY COURTHOUSE
Northeast corner of the Square at Jefferson and Church
Open business hours Monday–Friday • Free
Designed by J. Reily Gordon, who also did the imposing courthouses in Waxahachie and Decatur, this three-story granite and sandstone building was erected in 1894. The site of this Romanesque-style building is unusual because it is located in the corner of the Square, rather than in the center of it as are most Texas county courthouses. The rehabilitation of the Square itself is an ongoing city project designed to give it a more park-like atmosphere and to highlight the courthouse.

OTHER POINTS OF INTEREST

MUSIC BOX GALLERY
Public Library, 201 N. Davis at Connelly • 885-4926 • Monday–Friday 9–6,
Saturday 9–12 (ask for admission at library desk)
The collection was started in 1919 when the Belgian royal family gave Leo St. Clair a music box. Now St. Clair's collection of 175 animated and tinkling music boxes, in all shapes and sizes, is owned by the Hopkins County Historical Society and displayed in an upstairs room of the library.

COOPER LAKE STATE PARK
North of Sulphur Springs on FM 3505 • Route 3, Box 741 • 945-5256
Reservations 1-512-389-8900 • Admission
Boating, swimming, hiking, camping and other outdoor activities are available in this state park. The park also has a designated equestrian camping area.

SHOPPING

FACTORY STORES OF AMERICA
614 Radio Rd. at Industrial Dr. • 885-0015
This outlet center has 22 stores carrying many well-known brands.

ANNUAL EVENTS

May

ANNUAL FOLK FESTIVAL
Heritage Park • Dates vary • Admission
This two-day event celebrates the traditional folk ways of East Texas.

June

DAIRY FESTIVAL
Location and dates vary. Milking contests and homemade ice cream contest are among the events held during this two-day celebration.

September

HOPKINS COUNTY FALL FESTIVAL
Civic Center Complex, 1200 Houston • 885-8071 • 8 days starting second Saturday in September • Admission • W+ but not all areas
One of the highlights of this festival is the World Championship Hopkins County Stew Contest held on the final Saturday. Other festival events include an arts and crafts fair, a parade, an antiques auction, livestock show, homemakers' competitions, a fiddlin' contest, a carnival, and a variety of entertainment.

October/November

CENTRAL RODEO ASSOCIATION (CRA) FINALS
Civic Center Complex, 1200 Houston • 885-6515 (Chamber of Commerce)
Dates depend on length of CRA circuit • Admission • W+ but not all areas
The CRA's circuit through the central region starts in Sulphur Springs in the spring, and the top 15 finalists wind up back here in the late fall for these finals.

ACCOMMODATIONS

($ = under $45, $$ = $46–$60, $$$ = $61–$80, $$$$ = $81–$100, $$$$$ = over $100)
Room tax 12%

HOLIDAY INN

1495 E. Industrial • 885-0562 or 800-238-8000 • $$–$$$ • W+ 2 rooms
No-smoking rooms
The two-story Holiday Inn offers 98 rooms, including 40 no-smoking. Cable TV with HBO. Room phones (no charge for local calls). Pets allowed only in smoking rooms. Private club (guests automatically members). Restaurant. Free coffee in lobby. Coffeemakers in some rooms. Outdoor pool.

BEST WESTERN TRAIL DUST INN

1521 Shannon Rd. • 885-7515 • $–$$$$ • W+ 1 room • No-smoking rooms

The Best Western offers 103 rooms, including 30 no-smoking. Cable TV with HBO. Room phones (no charge for local calls). Pets limited. Private club (guests automatically members.) Electronic locks, outdoor pool, and complimentary newspapers in the lobby with a 24-hour restaurant adjacent to the motel. Close to Lake Fork and Cooper Lake. Also, two-room suites available. Movie rental on-site.

TEXARKANA

Texarkana, Texas: Bowie County • 31,656 • (903) • Texarkana, Arkansas: Miller County • 88,476 • (501)

There are a number of stories about how this two-state city got its name. One of the more popular legends credits it to a railroad surveyor who picked the site where two railroads building toward each other from Texas and Arkansas were to meet in 1873. As the story goes, he took a pine board, nailed it up on a tree at the connection point, and wrote on it three letters for Texas, three letters for Arkansas, and three letters for Louisiana (which was just 30 miles south). He ignored Oklahoma, which is about as close in the northwest direction. The result was TEX-ARK-ANA, and he is reported to have said, "This is the name of the town that is to be built here."

Actually what grew here were two cities—one in each state—each with its own city government, but in almost every other way linked together like Siamese twins. An example is the Bi-State Justice Center, which straddles the borderline on State Line Ave. and houses courts and jails for two cities. And

the federal government shows its impartiality with the world's only post office and federal building that has the state line running down the middle of it. Fittingly, the building itself was constructed of Texas pink granite and Arkansas limestone.

One way the cities do differ is in regard to liquor—the Texas side is dry, while just across the line in Arkansas it's partially wet, which adds meaning to the local Chamber of Commerce slogan that says Texarkana is "Twice as Nice."

TOURIST SERVICES

TEXARKANA VISITORS AND CONVENTION BUREAU

819 State Line Dr. (P.O. Box 1468, Texarkana, Tex/Ark 75504) • 792-7191 • W

TEXAS TOURIST INFORMATION CENTER

I-30 west of US 59 • 794-2114 • Open daily 8–5 • W+

This is one of 12 roadside visitor centers operated by the Texas Department of Transportation on key highways entering the state. Trained travel counselors can provide a wealth of free information on Texarkana and the rest of Texas. There is also a steel sculpture of a stylized highway of the future. Further east on I-30, across the state line, is the Arkansas Tourist Bureau (501-772-4301), which is also open seven days a week.

MUSEUMS

REGIONAL ARTS CENTER

**321 W. 4th and Texas • 792-8681 • Tuesday–Friday 10–4, Saturday 12–4
Free • W+**

The center is housed in a three-story building built in 1903 with marble floors and stairs and an open-cage elevator. There is no permanent collection as yet, but in addition to rotating exhibits, there are also regional juried art shows. The facility also includes the studios of artists-in-residence and a small theater for regional and experimental theater productions and workshops.

TEXARKANA HISTORICAL MUSEUM

**219 State Line Ave. at 3rd St. • 793-4831 • Tuesday–Saturday 10–4
Adults $2, senior citizens $1.50, students $1 • W**

Appropriately, the museum is housed in one of the oldest brick buildings in town, the Offenhauser Insurance Company building, erected in 1879 and now listed in the National Register of Historic Places. Permanent exhibits depict the culture of the Caddo Indians, the founding of Texarkana, and its subsequent development through the railroad, timber, and agricultural industries. Upstairs are period rooms of the late 1800s and early 1900s. Special temporary exhibits are arranged about twice a year.

HISTORIC PLACES

DRAUGHN-MOORE HOUSE

**420 Pine St. at 5th • 793-4831 • Tuesday–Saturday 10–4, • Adults $5, senior
citizens $4.50, students $3.50 • W**

This Italianate Victorian house was built in 1884. Called the "Ace of Clubs" house because of its shape, with the interior floor plan consisting of a 40-foot, two-story octagonal rotunda surrounded on three sides by octagonal rooms and on the fourth side by a rectangular wing. Gift shop. It is listed in the National Register of Historic Places.

OTHER HISTORIC HOMES

(The first two listings are private residences, not open to the public). **Brantley-Barkley Home,** 3306 Rice, built in 1880. **Wadley-Monroe House,** 618 Pecan, built in 1895. **Benjamin F. Whitaker House,** 517 Whitaker St., built in 1885. This house is noted for its fine carved woodwork in the entryway, walnut staircases, and heart pine floors. It is listed in the National Register of Historic Places and now houses an antique shop.

OTHER POINTS OF INTEREST

BI-STATE JUSTICE CENTER
State Line and Broad • 798-3000
Resting on the border line between Texas and Arkansas, this building is unique because it is the only Justice Center in two states. It took special legislation in both states to set it up so the location would not become a legal technicality in a trial. As a result, it makes no legal difference if an Arkansas judge hears a case in a court physically located in Texas, or vice versa. And the Texarkana, Arkansas, city police are actually located in Texas. Tours may be arranged.

FIRST UNITED METHODIST CHURCH
400 E. Sixth and Laurel • 501-772-6931
The most impressive part of this church is the stained-glass sanctuary windows, which reflect the history of Methodism. Ask permission at the church office to view the windows from the inside. The church, built in 1904, is listed in the National Register of Historic Places.

PHOTOGRAPHER'S ISLAND
State Line and 5th in front of Post Office
A unique photo setting where you can take pictures of people with one foot in each state.

SCOTT JOPLIN MURAL
3rd and Main on south wall of Ragland's Office Equipment Building
Scott Joplin, the great ragtime composer, was just five years old when Texarkana was established. He grew up here and now is perhaps the city's most famous native son. Although he died in 1916, he was posthumously awarded a special Pulitzer Prize in 1976 for his contributions to American music. The mural depicts both his life and accomplishments.

SPORTS AND ACTIVITIES

Golf

SOUTH HAVEN GOLF COURSE
Line Ferry Rd. (Arkansas) • 501-774-5771 • Eighteen-hole course. Greens fee: weekdays $10, weekends and holidays $12

COLLEGES AND UNIVERSITIES

TEXARKANA COLLEGE

2500 N. Robison Rd. and Tucker • 838-4541 • W+ but not all areas

This two-year junior college offers its 4,000 students both academic and vocational/technical programs. A branch of Texas A&M University shares the campus (2600 N. Robison Rd., 838-6514) offering a limited selection of upper level and graduate courses leading to bachelor's and master's degrees. Visitors are welcome to a variety of performing arts events on the college campus.

PERFORMING ARTS

PEROT THEATRE

219 Main at 3rd • 792-4992 • Admission depends on show • W+

This was the most opulent of the several theaters in Texarkana in the 1920s and 1930s, and the premier showplace of the four-state area. When the competition from television forced it to close in 1977, it was purchased by the city, and after a $2 million restoration project accomplished with donations and grants, it was restored to its former grandeur and reopened as a center for performing arts. The annual Perot Theatre Series runs from September through May and features national and international performing artists. The diverse series ranges from symphony orchestras to the superstars of pop and country music with Broadway shows and ballet in between. The theater's Overnight Package Program offers out-of-towners an orchestra seat, overnight accommodations, and a breakfast for one price. It is booked through participating motels in town. Other events in the theater include Children's Theatre productions and summer productions by the Texarkana Regional Theatre. Tours are available by appointment.

KIDS' STUFF

GOLF & KART WORLD AND BATTING CENTER

State Line Ave., 3 miles north of I-30; Open daily

SIDE TRIPS

CRYSTAL SPRINGS BEACH

Take US 67 west about 2 miles past Maud, approximately 18 miles west of Texarkana **• 585-5246 • Open some weekends in May and daily from Memorial Day to Labor Day • Admission**

This 12-acre spring-fed lake surrounded by sandy beaches offers facilities for swimming, picnicking, and camping. Attractions include a 400-foot waterslide, paddleboats, a cable swing, and the Cannonball Ride.

LAKE WRIGHT PATMAN

Take US 59 southwest approximately 12 miles **• 838-8781**
Open at all times • Free • W variable

The Army Corps of Engineers impounded the Sulphur River to form this 20,300-acre lake. There are a number of commercial facilities and parks along the 165 miles of shoreline. These offer recreational facilities for swimming, fishing, boating, picnicking, and camping (some free, some fee). For information write: Park Manager, P.O. Box 1817, Texarkana 75504.

ANNUAL EVENTS

STRANGE FAMILY BLUEGRASS FESTIVAL

From I-30 or Hwy 59 South, take FM 989 South to FM 2516, turn right to George Thomas Road and follow signs to the Strange Family Park • 792-2481, 838-0361, or 791-0342 • **Wednesday–Sunday of Memorial Day and Labor Day weekends** • **Admission varies by day from $3 to $7; 5-day pass $20** • **W**

Bring your lawn chair and sit under a shade tree and listen to bluegrass bands and artists from all over playing in a natural amphitheater. The festival starts on Wednesday evening, then runs from early afternoon until midnight on Thursday and Friday, and from morning to midnight on Saturday and Sunday. Spaces for RV and tent campers usually open up the week before. No alcoholic beverages permitted in the park.

September/October

FOUR STATES FAIR AND RODEO

Four States Fairgrounds (Arkansas). *Take Loop 245E to Arkansas Blvd. and follow signs to Fairgrounds* • **501-773-2941** • **Mid-September** • **Admission W** • **Usually charge for parking**

The four states are Arkansas, Louisiana, Oklahoma, and Texas, and people come from all of them to take part in the fair and rodeo. In addition to the county fair livestock show, exhibits, and agricultural and home arts contests, there's a parade, the rodeo, a carnival, and performances by nationally known entertainers.

RESTAURANTS

($ = under $7, $$ = $8–$17, $$$ = $18–$25, $$$$ = over $25 for one person excluding drinks, tax, and tip.)

CATTLEMAN'S STEAK HOUSE

4018 State Line • **(501) 774-4481** • **Dinner only Monday–Saturday. Closed Sunday** • **$$** • **Cr** • **W** • **Children's plate**

Steaks, chicken, seafood, and barbecue including barbecued lamb. Beer. Private club for mixed drinks.

ACCOMMODATIONS

($ = under $45, $$ = $46–$60, $$$ = $61–$80, $$$$ = $81–$100, $$$$$ = over $100)
Room tax (Texas) 10%, (Arkansas) 10.5%

LA QUINTA

5201 State Line at Elizabeth • **794-1900 or 800-531-5900** • **$$–$$$$** • **W+ 2 rooms** • **No-smoking**

The two-story La Quinta has 130 rooms, including 91 no-smoking. Cable TV with Showtime. Room phones (no charge for local calls). Small pets OK. Free airport transportation. Outdoor pool. Free coffee in lobby. Coffeemakers in rooms.

TYLER

Smith County Seat • 75,450 • (903)

Incorporated in 1846, the city was named for the tenth president of the United States, John Tyler, who had signed the point resolution under which Texas was admitted to the Union. Although it has a diversified economy based on oil, manufacturing, and agriculture, the city is best known by the name it calls itself: "The Rose Capital of America."

Following the Civil War, a number of nurserymen moved into the area. They found the combination of sandy soil, the annual rainfall that was spread throughout the year, and a long growing season made excellent conditions for growing fruits, especially peaches. They also found it close to ideal for growing

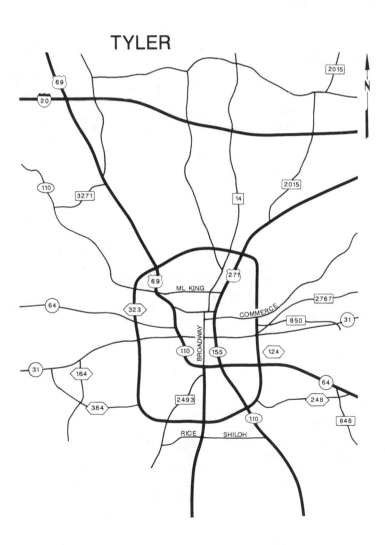

roses and ornamental shrubs, and made this a sideline to their fruit business. It was this diversification that saved them when diseases struck the fruit trees. As the fruit trees died, the growers increased production of rosebushes. By the early 1900s, commercial production of roses was a major industry in Smith County.

For a while, with the discovery of the Great East Texas Oil Field in 1930, roses took a back seat to oil as Tyler became the headquarters for several major oil companies and quickly grew to be the largest urban center in the area, with the population doubling in five years. But the importance of the commercial production of roses was once again acknowledged with the founding of the Texas Rose Foundation in 1945.

Today more than one-third of the commercial, field-grown rosebushes sold in the United States are produced within a 50-mile radius of Tyler. For the up-to-date location of the rose farms contact the Tyler Area Chamber of Commerce (*see* Tourist Services, below).

And as if millions of roses were not enough to beautify the area, Tyler's home gardens are well known for azaleas. Each of these flowers has its own festival with the Azalea and Spring Flower Trail in the spring and the Texas Rose Festival in the Fall (*see* Annual Events, below).

TOURIST SERVICES

TYLER AREA CHAMBER OF COMMERCE
407 N. Broadway at Line (P.O. Box 390, 75710) • 592-1661 • W

MUSEUMS

SMITH COUNTY HISTORICAL MUSEUM
125 S. College St. at Elm • 592-5993 • Call for open times • Free • W

Housed on the first floor of the building that served the city as the Carnegie Public Library from 1904 until 1979, this museum displays artifacts that reflect the history of Tyler and Smith County. These include the interior of a typical log cabin from the time of the Republic of Texas, Civil War items unearthed at the nearby Camp Ford Prison (the largest prisoner of war compound for Union prisoners west of the Mississippi), and Indian artifacts.

GOODMAN-LEGRANDE MUSEUM
624 N. Broadway at Goodman • 531-1286 • Call for open times • Free (donations) • Parking entrance on Bois d'Arc

It was originally called "Bonnie Castle" when it was built as a one-story home in 1859. The second story was added in 1880, and the house was remodeled to its present appearance in 1924. The museum houses Empire-period furnishings, antique medical tools, documents, and early photographs of Tyler and Smith County.

TYLER MUSEUM OF ART
1300 S. Mahon, off Fifth St., adjacent to campus of Tyler Junior College
595-1001 • Call for open times • Free • W

The emphasis here is on changing exhibits of contemporary art by national, international, and regional artists. Other programs at the museum include films, musical and theatrical performances, lectures, and seminars.

HISTORIC PLACES

HISTORIC HOMES

A Tyler Heritage Tour Map of historic buildings is available at the Chamber of Commerce. The following are some of the older homes noted on that tour. All are private residences not open to the public. **Chilton House,** 727 S. Chilton, built in 1888 by Horace Chilton, the first native Texan to serve in the U.S. Senate. **Whiteman House,** 815 S. Broadway, a Victorian-style house built around 1895. **Washington G. Cain House,** 306 S. Fannin, a Victorian cottage built in the 1890s. **Douglas-Holland-Pollard House,** 318 S. Fannin, built around 1872 with additional rooms added around the turn of the century. **Butler House,** 630 S. Fannin, a Queen Anne-style home built in 1898. **Patterson House,** 1311 W. Oakwood, built in 1854, this house was enlarged several times during the years and given its Victorian detailing in 1882. **Ransour House,** 504 E. Charnwood, built around 1865, is one of the oldest remaining structures in Tyler. **Hunt-Miller-Walker House,** 223 E. Charnwood, built about 1861 as a frame house, it was extensively remodeled to its present appearance in 1899.

WHITAKER-MCCLENDON HOUSE

806 W. Houston St. • 592-3533 • Call for reservations • Admission • Open weekends during Azalea and Spring Flower Trail and the Texas Rose Festival

Built in 1880s, this is the birthplace of the White House news correspondent Sara McClendon.

OTHER POINTS OF INTEREST

CALDWELL ZOO

2203 Martin Luther King Blvd., off Gentry Parkway (Bus US 69) • 593-0121 With exception of a few major holidays, it's open daily, April 1–September 30 9:30–6; October 1–March 31 9:30–4:30 • Free • W+

What started as a backyard menagerie at the Caldwell Playschool in 1937 is now one of the better small zoos in Texas. There are more than 800 animals from Texas, Africa, and South America living on the 35 acres, many in miniature recreations of their natural environment. It includes an aquarium, herpetarium (reptiles and amphibians), a petting farm, and a nature trail with six sensory activity stations. All the exhibits are well-marked, in many cases with photos to help visitors spot the species they are reading about among the many species living together in the enclosures. A multimedia slide show about the zoo is shown on weekends. Snack bar and picnic area.

HUDNALL PLANETARIUM

Tyler Junior College campus at east end of E. Lake St. • 510-2249 • Call for schedule and reservations • Admission • W (call ahead)

There are different one-hour shows presented on selected days. Although this is the only large planetarium in East Texas, it only seats about 110, so reservations are advised.

MUNICIPAL ROSE GARDEN

1900 W. Front (TX 31) at Rose Park Dr., on east side of East Texas Fairgrounds
531-1370 • Garden Center Bldg. open daily 8–5, garden open at all times
Free • W

More than 30,000 rosebushes in 500 varieties are displayed in this 14-acre park that is the nation's largest municipal rose garden. A small camellia garden adds additional beauty, and there is also a large greenhouse filled with rare and spectacular tropical plants. Rose bloom season peaks in mid-May each year and continues through the end of October. During the annual Texas Rose Festival, held in October, the Garden Center houses about 120,000 roses featured in the four-day Festival Rose Show.

ROSE MUSEUM

1900 W. Front (TX 31) next to Rose Garden Bldg. • 597-3130 • $3.50 per person

Displays of gowns, photos, and memorabilia of past Texas Rose Festivals, as well as historical value of the rose industry.

TYLER STATE PARK

From Loop 323N, take FM 14 north approximately 8 miles to Park Rd. 16
597-5338 • Open daily 8–10 for day use, at all times for camping
$2 per adult • W+ but not all areas

Situated in the piney woods, this 994-acre park includes a 64-acre spring-fed lake that each year is stocked with trout, making for excellent fall and winter fishing. There is a bathhouse, and swimming is permitted on an unsupervised 400-foot beach. Other facilities include hiking and nature trails, mini-bike trail, picnic areas, boat rentals during the summer season, and both tent and RV campsites (fee). For information and campsite reservations contact: Park Superintendent, Tyler State Park, Route 29, Box 29030, Tyler 75706.

COLLEGES AND UNIVERSITIES

TEXAS COLLEGE

2404 N. Grand Ave., north of Martin Luther King • 593-8311
W, but not all areas

The oldest college in the area, it was established in 1894 by the Colored Methodist Episcopal Church. The school is still church-related and the student body of approximately 600 is still predominantly Black. A four-year liberal arts college, it offers a variety of degree programs with the emphasis on business and social sciences.

TYLER JUNIOR COLLEGE

1400 E. 5th (TX 64E) near Mahon • 510-2200 • W+ but not all areas
Marked visitor parking

Established in 1946, the school now has about 16,000 full- and part-time students enrolled in courses in more than 82 fields ranging from agricultural science to teacher education. The Apache Belles, the school's precision all-women drill team, perform at major sporting events both at the college and all over the country. Hudnall Planetarium is on the campus.

UNIVERSITY OF TEXAS AT TYLER

3900 University Blvd. (Spur 248) at Old Omen Rd. • 566-7000
W+ but not all areas • Marked visitor parking

Opened in 1972 as Tyler State College, it was known under a variety of names until it became part of the University of Texas system in 1979. A two-year upper level and graduate school, it has an enrollment of about 3,600.

PERFORMING ARTS

EAST TEXAS SYMPHONY

Office 911 S. Broadway • 592-1427
This combined professional/amateur orchestra has a season that runs from September through May. Most concerts are performed at Caldwell Auditorium, 120 S. College, and ticket prices range from about $9 to about $20.

TYLER CIVIC THEATRE

400 Rose Park Dr. • 592-0561 • W+ • Admission
Parking at nearby Harvey Convention Center
This community theater group, with a professional director, usually puts on about four productions in a theater-in-the-round during its September-to-June season.

SHOPPING

ANTIQUE SHOPS

There are several antique shops clustered along Vine and on S. Broadway and some of the streets crossing it. A brochure is available at the Chamber of Commerce.

SIDE TRIPS

LAKE PALESTINE

From Loop 323 SW take TX 155 south approximately 15 miles
Open at all times • W variable
A 25,500-acre lake with mostly commercial facilities for boating, fishing, and other water sports. Around the lake are marinas, motels, trailer parks, camping areas, and boat ramps.

LAKE TYLER AND LAKE TYLER EAST

From Loop 323 SE., take TX 110 to Whitehouse, then east on FM 346 to lakes
Open at all times • Free • W variable
These twin municipal lakes cover about 4,800 acres and offer facilities for boating, fishing, swimming, and camping. (Charge for camping)

ANNUAL EVENTS

March/April

AZALEA AND SPRING FLOWER TRAIL

Trail maps available at Chamber of Commerce • 592-1661 (Chamber of Commerce) • Last week of March and first week of April • Trail free (Admission to Home Tour) • W variable
The seven-mile driving trail winds through residential districts where most of the flowers are on display in home gardens. The Tyler Heritage Homes Tour is held during one weekend of the Trail. Usually six private homes of historic significance are open to the public. You drive yourself from home to home and

are given a guided tour of each home. Home Tour tickets run about $7. Other activities normally held during this period include a quilt show, arts and crafts fair, a 10-K and Fun Run, and a Symphony Concert in the park.

September

EAST TEXAS STATE FAIR

East Texas Fairgrounds, 2114 W. Front (TX 31) • 597-2501 • Usually held last full week in September • Admission • W variable

All the ingredients of a county fair are here: livestock shows, arts and crafts exhibits, industrial and agricultural exhibits, entertainment, a carnival midway, and food booths.

October

TEXAS ROSE FESTIVAL

Municipal Rose Garden Center Bldg., 1900 W. Front (TX 31) • 592-1661 (Chamber of Commerce) • Usually third weekend of October • Admission to most events • Parking at nearby Harvey Convention Center • W variable

In keeping with Tyler's title of "The Rose Capital of America," everything comes up roses at this festival. There are rose-adorned floats at the Rose Parade, a Rose Queen coronation, a Rose Show featuring 120,000 roses against a setting of mirrors, walkways, and fountains, The Palette of Roses Art Show, The Queen's Tea in the Rose Garden, and The Rambling Rose Grand March and Dance. An arts and crafts fair is held during this period.

RESTAURANTS

($ = under $7, $$ = $8–$17, $$$ = $18–$25, $$$$ = over $25 for one person excluding drinks, tax, and tip.)

CACE'S SEAFOOD

7011 S. Broadway approximately 2 miles south of Loop 323 • 581-0744 Lunch and dinner seven days • $$–$$$ • Cr • W+ • Children's plates

Seafood in the New Orleans tradition, with entrées in both Cajun and creole cuisine. Seafood has been a Cace family business tradition since Grandpa Cace was an oyster fisherman in New Orleans. Now three members of the family have seafood restaurants in Tyler, Longview, and San Antonio. One way to get a good sample of some of the best on the menu here is to order the Taste of New Orleans combination, which includes oysters Rockefeller, broiled scallops, shrimp Barataria (broiled with artichoke hearts and mushrooms in sherry, butter, and herbs), and redfish amandine. Steaks and chicken also available. No-smoking section. Private club (temporary memberships available).

POTPOURRI HOUSE

2301 S. Broadway in Off Broadway Shopping Center • 592-4171 Lunch only. Closed Sunday • $$ • AE, MC, V • W+

Although it's indoors, the setting is that of a garden courtyard, an atmosphere heightened by stained-glass windows that came from an old church. Dinner entrées include steaks and prime rib, a variety of seafood such as broiled red snapper and beer-batter shrimp, chicken, and several Italian dishes. Live music Friday and Saturday. Entrance area is set up as a gift and antique shop.

ACCOMMODATIONS

($ = under $45, $$ = $46–$60, $$$ = $61–$80, $$$$ = $81–$100, $$$$$ = over $100)
Room tax 13%

LA QUINTA MOTOR INN

1601 Loop 323 W SW. near Professional Dr. • 561-2223 or 800-531-5900
$$–$$$$ • W+ 6 rooms • No-smoking rooms
   This La Quinta has 130 rooms, including 91 no-smoking, in four two-story
buildings. Cable TV with HBO. Room phones (no charge for local calls). Pets
OK. Restaurant adjacent. Outdoor pool. Free coffee in lobby. Coffeemakers in
rooms. Complimentary continental breakfast.

WASHINGTON

Washington County • 265 • (77880) • (409)
   In the early 1820s, Andrew Robinson, Sr., first settler of Stephen F. Austin's
"Old 300," opened a ferry on the Brazos River at the crossing of the La Bahia
Road. This old Spanish road between Goliad and East Texas had been used
since the seventeenth century. In 1834 he laid out the town on his property,
then known as Washington-on-the-Brazos. Here the Texas Declaration of Independence was signed in 1836 in an unfinished building, and the town became
the first capital of the Republic. It became a prime target for Santa Anna, and as
the Mexicans approached, both the new Republic and the townspeople fled. In
1842, the government returned and remained there until 1845. For a time the
town flourished, but the railroad bypassed it, and it was only a memory in 1901
when the Independence Monument was dedicated there.

TOURIST SERVICES

WASHINGTON COUNTY CHAMBER OF COMMERCE

314 S. Austin, Brenham (77833) • 836-3695 or (800) 225-3695, fax 836-2540
   The Chamber offers complete information about historic sites and events and
provides a free brochure with map of the area.

POINTS OF INTEREST

WASHINGTON-ON-THE-BRAZOS STATE HISTORICAL PARK

From TX 105 take FM 1155 1 mile to park • **878-2214 • Open daily 8 until
sundown. • Free • W+ but not all areas**
   This 154-acre park contains much of the historic townsite, a replica of Independence Hall, the Star of the Republic Museum, and Barrington, the restored
home of Anson Jones, the last president of the Republic. Also on the grounds are
an interpretive center, amphitheater, auditorium, picnic area, and nature trail. A
special program is held to celebrate Texas Independence Day, the Sunday closest
to March 2.
   Independence Hall Replica, Star of the Republic Museum (878–2461), and
Barrington (878-2214) are open seven days March–August 10–5;
September–February, Wednesday–Sunday 10–5. Closed Thanksgiving and
Christmas through New Year's Day • Free • W+

Independence Hall is a replica, but archeologists have determined its precise location is on this spot. **Star of the Republic Museum** is a Texas star-shaped museum depicting the colorful history of the Texas Republic. **Barrington** was the residence of Anson Jones, fourth and last president of the Republic, and originally four miles from the park. Despondent over his failure to be elected to the United States Senate, Jones committed suicide in 1858.

WOODVILLE

Tyler County Seat • 2,821 • (409)

Settlers began arriving here in the mid-1830s. In 1846 the county was created and named after President John Tyler, who helped in the annexation of Texas. The town was named for Texas Senator George T. Wood, who later became the second governor of the state. Woodville is the northern gateway to the Big Thicket.

TOURIST SERVICES

TYLER COUNTY CHAMBER OF COMMERCE

201 N. Magnolia (75979) • 283-2632 • Monday–Friday 9–5 • W located in lobby of Woodville Inn

MUSEUMS

ALLAN SHIVERS LIBRARY AND MUSEUM

302 N. Charlton, 2 blocks north of the courthouse • 283-3709 • Monday–Friday 9–5, Saturday 10–2 • Admission $1, students free • W variable

Memorabilia of the former governor's life are exhibited in an 1881 Victorian home that Governor and Mrs. Shivers saved from the wrecking ball, restored, and gave to his hometown. Included are elegant gowns worn by Mrs. Shivers during the period of his governorship (1949–1957), a Freedom Shrine, and Shivers' personal collection of Texana and rare books. The house is furnished with period pieces from the Victorian era.

HERITAGE VILLAGE MUSEUM

Approximately 2 miles west on US 190 (P.O. Box 888, 75979) • 283-2272 or (800) 323-0389 • Open daily 9–5, closed major holidays • Adults $4, children 6–12 $2, seniors $3 • W

The village contains an entire town of restored and reconstructed early Texas buildings, including a log cabin built in 1866, an 1850s general store, blacksmith shop, barbershop, and an 1888 newspaper plant. The 1906 school is now The Pickett House Restaurant (see below). Gift shop features crafts by people from Tyler County. At Christmas, there is a pioneer version of festivities, food, and fun.

SIDE TRIPS

ALABAMA-COUSHATTA INDIAN RESERVATION
Take US 190 west about 16 miles (see **Livingston)**

BIG THICKET NATIONAL PRESERVE
District Office: 507 N. Pine • 283-5824
   Information is available at the District Office and the Chamber of Commerce.
(*See* Big Thicket National Preserve.)

LAKE B. A. STEINHAGEN
Take US 190 east about 15 miles (See **Jasper)**

LAKE TEJAS
*Take US 69 north to Colmesneil, then east (right) on FM 256E approximately
1 mile* **• 837-5757 • Open daily Memorial Day–Labor Day. Swimming: Adults
$2 weekdays, $2.50 weekends; children $1 weekdays, $1.50 weekends. Closed
rest of year • W**
   The two-acre, roped-off swimming area is the main attraction at this 10-acre
lake shaped like Texas. Picnic area, shelters, and camping (fee), pedal boats,
and fishing.

ANNUAL EVENTS

TYLER COUNTY DOGWOOD FESTIVAL
**Various locations • 283-2632 (Chamber of Commerce) • Last two weekends
in March and first weekend in April • Admission to some events
W variable**
   This three-weekend event begins with a Spring Roundup at Heritage Village
featuring games, crafts, and outdoor activities.
   Hundreds of trailriders converge from all direction on Woodville for the
Western Weekend part of this festival. Friday is a trailrider dance, Saturday a
parade, rodeo, and dance. The Dogwood Queen's weekend is the first weekend
in April with a parade, arts and crafts fair, the Queen's Coronation, a historical
pageant, fireworks display, and a dance.

RESTAURANTS

*($ = under $7, $$ = $8–$17, $$$ = $18–$25, $$$$ = over $25 for one person excluding
drinks, tax, and tip.)*

THE HOMESTEAD
Take US 69 south about 8 miles to Hillister and follow signs **• 283-7324 or
283-7244 • Friday and Saturday 5–10, Sunday 11–3, available
Monday–Thursday for special occasions and private parties
Reservations suggested • $–$$ • No Cr • W**
   A restored 1912 home inside a white picket fence with seafood, steaks, and
chicken plus some intriguing desserts. Also antiques and collectibles for sale.

PICKETT HOUSE

Approximately 2 miles west on US 190 in Heritage Village • 283-3371
Monday–Thursday 11–2, Friday and Saturday 11–8, Sunday 11–6 • $–$$ • V,
MC, AE, DIS • W

It's all you can eat boardinghouse-style in this 1907 schoolhouse decorated with a collection of early circus posters. The menu is fried chicken, dumplings, fresh vegetables, stone-ground cornbread, watermelon rind preserves, sassafras tea, and more.

ACCOMMODATIONS

($ = under $45, $$ = $46–$60, $$$ = $61–$80, $$$$ = $81–$100, $$$$$ = over $100)
Room tax 13%

WOODVILLE INN

201 N. Magnolia • 283-3741 • $ • W+ 2 rooms

The two-story motel has 72 rooms. Cable TV. Room phones (no charge for local calls). Restaurant. Private club with automatic memberships for guests. Outdoor pool. No-smoking wing.

Bed and Breakfast

THE GETAWAY

Highway 69 at Hillister • 283-7244 • $$

This two-bedroom cottage is an adjunct to The Homestead Restaurant. Woodburning fireplace.

THE ANTIQUE ROSE

612 Nellius Street • 283-8926 or (800) 386-8926 • $$$ • Reservations by phone only, 2 weeks in advance

This 1862 Southern Plantation Federal-style house in the heart of town offers three rooms with private "water closets" and old-fashioned cast-iron bathtubs. Furnished in turn-of-the-century style, there are also modern amenities such as coffeemakers and ceiling fans. A full breakfast is served in the dining room or sun porch. Airport transportation available.

Central Texas

AUSTIN

Travis County Seat, Capital of Texas • 548,000 • (512)

Austin wasn't founded by Stephen F., although he did endow the city with its most enduring moniker. We can only speculate what its original settlers called the place fifteen or sixteen thousand years ago, but the locals who met Spanish explorers near present-day St. Edward's University in 1709 called themselves *Tickanwatic*, "those most like humans." The Spanish built a mission at Barton Springs in 1730, but retreated back to San Antonio that same year. The Tickanwatics had the place most like Austin to themselves for another century, until the enterprising Jake Harrell set up his tent at the future corner of 1st and Congress in 1838. He built a log stockade very soon thereafter and named the stand "Waterloo."

That fall, vice-president of the Republic of Texas Mirabeau Bonaparte Lamar visited Harrell, because he heard that the buffalo were running on Congress. After shooting his fill, Lamar was impressed and moved to grandiloquence. "This should be the seat of future empire," he pronounced. Shortly after this visit, Lamar succeeded Sam Houston as president of Texas. A government commission was evaluating candidates for the permanent capital of the Republic, and Lamar recommended that the commissioners visit Waterloo. They did, and chose the site accordingly, although the deadly yellow fever epidemic just then abating in Houston might have had something to do with their decision not to go with Sam Houston's choice of Houston.

Once named the Republic's capital, Waterloo became Austin. Work on the new capital began in May 1839. Lamar was eager to get settled in his new seat of empire, so he, his cabinet, and 50 wagonloads of paperwork arrived in October. They were greeted by one log hotel and enough log cabins to house the major branches of government. The president's house and the Capitol had been whitewashed for the occasion.

The Tickanwatics weren't impressed, and most congressmen were afraid to leave their boardinghouse citadels after nightfall. Austin was surrounded by a stockade until 1845. By 1840, Austin had 856 citizens and two newspapers. In 1842, one of Santa Anna's divisions took spring vacation in San Antonio and looked poised to move onto Barton Springs for the summer. That was excuse enough for Sam Houston, who was again president, and he ordered the men of government to congregate in the Bayou City.

Recognizing that paperwork is truly the heart of government, Austin vigilantes placed the state archives under armed guard so that they too would not

135

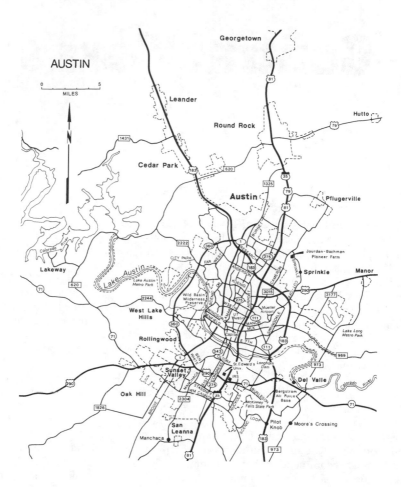

flee to Houston. Houston sent a company of Rangers to retrieve the papers, but stressed that no blood must be shed. The Rangers slid into town on New Year's Eve 1842, impressed the papers, and stole away. The next day, Austin vigilantes trailed the scions of Sam to their campground near Round Rock and rescued the scrolls of democracy. The men of government finally rejoined them here in 1844.

Austin stepped into the modern, reach-out-and-touch-someone age when the first telegraph line began tapping out condolences and compliments in October 1865. The first train came in 1871, on Christmas Day. One can only put off mention of the University of Texas for so long. In 1839, the Congress of the Republic ordered a site set aside for the establishment of a "university of the first class," and then granted their child a 115,000-acre dowry out in West Texas. Congress decided that popular vote should decide the site. The election was finally set for September 6, 1881. Building commenced in Austin in the fall of 1882.

Graduated UT students (we'll leave the burgeoning state government out of this for now) who couldn't bear to leave the city of Barton Springs and Scholz

Garden contributed as much as any other collective body to Austin's steady growth over the years.

Then in 1967, Tracor established an electronics outpost out here in the high-tech wilderness. IBM, Texas Instruments, Motorola, Advanced Micro Devices, Apple, MCC, Sematech, Dell, Samsung, and most of the rest of the siliconized world have followed, and it has been that way ever since.

TOURIST SERVICES

ARMADILLO EXPRESS

Capital Metropolitan Transit Authority • 474-1200 (route and schedule information) • Free

The distinctive, green, trolley-like "Dillos" are a good way to get around downtown and avoid the downtown parking hassle.

AROUND AUSTIN

4831 Spicewood Springs Rd. • 345-6552 • Call for schedule • W

Personalized service to both small groups and convention masses. Take the standard tour of the city, or make up your own (call ahead to make special arrangements). Weekend hill country tours.

AUSTIN CONVENTION AND VISITOR'S BUREAU

201 E. 2nd, near the Convention Center • 478-0098 or 800-888-8287 Open daily • W

Dozens of area pamphlets, brochures, and maps. Travel counseling and other services for large groups. Also kiosk at Robert Mueller Airport. Free guided downtown walking tours.

THE OLD BAKERY EMPORIUM AND HOSPITALITY DESK

1006 Congress • 477-5961 • Monday–Friday 9–4 • W

Provides information, brochures, and advice on Austin-area attractions, as well as information on senior citizens' activities and services. Open Saturdays 10–3 during June, July, August, and December.

WALKING TOURS

CONGRESS AVENUE

"The Avenue," as Congress Avenue is often called, is listed in the National Register of Historic Places. The riotously detailed facades of many of the Avenue's nineteenth- and early twentieth-century buildings have been restored. There are tree-shaded benches to sit on and places to linger, making downtown seem less businesslike. There's much to see and traffic is heavy, so it's best to explore Congress Avenue by foot.

James H. Robertson Building • 416 • (1893)

The Robertson Building is the most richly textured building on Congress Avenue and one of its most exuberant.

Scarbrough Building • 512 at 6th • (1909)

At eight stories, Austin's first skyscraper. The stylish black Art Deco facade was added later. When built, this building had all the latest amenities, including a vacuum-cleaning plant with connections on each floor and a cooling system that circulated air cooled by passage over refrigerated pipes.

Sampson-Hendricks Building • 620-22 at 7th • (1859)

The Avenue's oldest remaining building, built by Abner Cook. Its Italianate design broke new ground in Greek Revival Austin. Excellent craftsmanship.

Walter Tips Building • 712 • (1876)

This Venetian Gothic palace of hardware was the most ambitious building of its type and era in Austin. Jasper Preston, who later designed the Driskill Hotel and supervised construction of the present Capitol, had free rein in designing this $30,000 building. The first three stories are carved limestone, even the Corinthian column capitals.

Paramount Theatre • 713 • (1915)

Sarah Bernhardt played this Renaissance Revival theatre on her swan-song tour. The interior has been expertly restored. Formerly a moving-picture palace, it's now a performing arts theatre.

Millet Opera House • 110 E. 9th • (1878)

Austin's first proper Opera House was first built by C.F. Millet as a hardware warehouse. It was enlarged and remodeled to become an opera house in 1878. The state legislature met here after the "colonial" capitol burned in 1881. The Classic Revival double galleries were added in 1911.

Jacob Larmour Block • 906–922 • (ca. 1876)

Jacob Larmour built nine Greek Revival-style buildings in a row here. Although each had its own distinct detailing, they were all of the same basic design. Six of them still stand, in various stages of restoration. Larmour was said to have a virtual monopoly on the design of most local and state buildings constructed in the 1800s.

The Old Bakery • 1006 • (1876)

Originally built for Charles Lundberg, a Swedish immigrant baker who later organized the Austin National Bank.

OLD PECAN STREET

(E. 6th between Congress and IH-35)

One hundred years ago, nearly every important business in Austin had an office on this stretch of the main artery leading east to Houston. Only after the completion of the present Capitol in 1888 did Congress Avenue displace Pecan Street as Austin's premier business thoroughfare. Thus began a downward slide in fortune. By April 27, 1895, William Sidney Porter observed "East Pecan and the vicinity, once the center of business, where the mild-eyed granger traded eggs and butter for delusive red calico, and drank his cold lemonade in peace, has now risen up and declared itself bold, bad, and hard to curry. Loafing, gambling, fighting, and drinking has invaded this Arcadian spot."

By 1970, Pecan Street had withered away to a string of mostly shabby joints, pawnshops, and shine parlors. The tide began to turn in 1968, when a local architect turned an aging (1881) ex-saloon and bawdy house into an honest townhouse. The Old Pecan Street Café followed in 1972, then all the rest. Most of the old buildings were restored during the 1980s boom.

Old Pecan Street is a Registered Historic District, and new buildings have had to conform in style with the originals. Overly enthusiastic travel writers have called Pecan Street "Austin's Bourbon Street" or "Austin's French Quarter," which it isn't, in age, charm or debauchery. Nonetheless, there's still a lot to see and sample, so park somewhere and hoof it.

Driskill Hotel • 122 at Brazos • (1886)

Jesse Driskill spent $400,000 building his hotel, and the Driskill is as close to majestic as you'll find in Austin. The busts pulling sentinel duty up top are of Jesse and sons A.W. and J.W. Threatened with destruction in the 1960s, the Driskill was saved by the people of Austin. (*See* Accommodations.)

Grove Drug • 209 • (1874)

Originally two-story, the third story and cast-metal Queen Anne bayfront were added around 1898. Passersby today generally overlook the rows of electric light bulbs that run up and down the bayfront. In 1906, their lavish display of electric power drew admirers from all over.

Thaison Building • 410 • (1881)

This plain little brick building first housed William Thaison's Saloon and Billiard Parlor. Its restoration in 1968 commenced the Pecan Street Renaissance.

Paggi's Carriage Shop • 421 • (ca. 1875)

Michael Paggi sold and repaired wagons and carriages here. Because the back side of the building faced on to the Austin City Market, it sports an elegant rear entrance, as do other buildings on the block.

E.H. Carrington Store • 522 • (1870)

An ex-slave, Carrington became a prosperous grocer and leader in the black community. He operated his store here from 1873 until 1907. The second story served as hall for black social affairs.

Old Depot Hotel • 504 E. 5th • (1872)

With the railroad's arrival, depot hotels immediately sprang up. Adjacent to Market Square and a block from the depot, this little limestone complex first operated as the Railroad House.

BIRD'S-EYE VIEW

MT. BONNELL

Crest of Mt. Bonnell Rd.; *turn right on Mt. Bonnell Rd., just before W. 35th dead-ends* **• Open daily • Curfew 10 P.M.**

Mt. Bonnell is one of Austin's oldest tourist attractions. At 785 feet, it's one of the highest points within the Austin city limits.

OASIS CANTINA DEL LAGO

6550 Comanche Trail, off RM 620 • 266-2441 • Open daily • AE, DIS, MC, V W but not all areas

Situated high as it is over the sparkling blue waters of Lake Travis, the Oasis is the perfect place to enjoy the broad western sunset over the lake.

MUSEUMS AND ART GALLERIES

ARCHER M. HUNTINGTON ART GALLERY

Art Building, University of Texas (E. 23rd and San Jacinto) and Harry Ransom Center (W. 21st and Guadalupe) • 471-7324 • Monday–Saturday 9–5, Sunday 1–5 • Free • W call ahead

Generally, several exhibits are on view in each hall. The Huntington Gallery's permanent collection is housed in the Ransom Center. It is composed of Greek and Roman art, nineteenth- and twentieth-century American art (including the

James Michener and C.R. Smith Collections) and contemporary Latin American art, plus 4,000 more paintings and drawings from all periods.

Displays from the permanent collection are supplemented by an assortment of temporary loan exhibits from art centers all over the world. Annual student-faculty exhibit at the Art Building gallery each spring. Guided tours available by appointment.

ATRIUM GALLERY

Moody Hall, St. Edward's University, 3100 S. Congress • 448-8404 Open daily • Free • W
Exhibits change on a regular basis.

AUSTIN MUSEUM OF ART—DOWNTOWN

823 Congress • 495-9224 • Open Tuesday–Sunday • Adults about $3, students about $2, under 12 free • W+
Changing exhibitions of 20th-century art by local, regional, and nationally prominent artists and photographers. Special events, a gift shop, and art school complement the gallery. Also worth visiting is the AMA's Laguna Gloria site (3809 W. 35th, 458-8191, Tuesday–Sunday). Clara Driscoll Sevier, the "Savior of the Alamo," built this Mediterranean-style villa in 1915 on the banks of Lake Austin. Changing exhibitions; allow time for a stroll through the naturally landscaped grounds.

ELISABET NEY MUSEUM

304 E. 44th at Ave. H • 458-2255 • Wednesday–Saturday, 10–5, Sunday 12–5 Free • W but not all areas
Built by Ney in 1892 and one of only four intact nineteenth-century sculptor's studios in the United States. A National Historic Site, it houses the collection of Ney, who lived in Texas from 1873 to 1907. Following her death here, friends and admirers acquired the studio and founded the museum. Ney named her studio *Formosa,* meaning "beautiful," after her old studio in Europe. Dozens of plaster models, marble busts, and bronze statues of European dignitaries and famous Texans make up the collection on display. The grounds are a pleasant escape from bustling downtown Austin. The museum offers classes in sculpture and life drawing, and audiovisual presentations on Ney and her work.

FRENCH LEGATION

802 San Marcos at E. 7th • 472-8180 • Tuesday–Sunday 1–5 • Adults about $3, students $1
Comte Alphonse Dubois de Saligny, His Majesty's *charge d'affaires* to the Republic of Texas from France, had this charming French provincial cottage built in 1841. It was the young capital's most pretentious building. Now a museum operated by the Daughters of the Republic of Texas, it is furnished with nineteenth-century antiques and some of the Count's original effects. The kitchen, with its inventory of pewter utensils and copper pots, is said to be the country's only authentic French creole kitchen.

HARRY RANSOM HUMANITIES RESEARCH CENTER

University of Texas, W. 21st and Guadalupe • 471-8944 • Monday–Friday 9–5 • Free • W

Exhibits from the Ransom Center's vast collections fill both the Ransom Center building and the nearby Academic Center (on the West Mall, W. 23rd and Guadalupe, west of the Tower). Besides showing off the Center's Gutenberg Bible and Huntington Gallery art, the Ransom Center maintains several public exhibition rooms. The **Photography Collection** contains the world's first photograph (taken by Joseph Niepce in 1826), 3,000 pieces of antique camera equipment and more than 5 million prints and negatives. The **Hoblitzelle Theatre Arts Collection** has such diverse items as Harry Houdini posters and correspondence, the Burl Ives collection of folk-music records and the Stanley Marcus collection of Sicilian marionettes.

The **Academic Center's** fourth floor contains several exhibits, the most interesting of which is the **Erle Stanley Gardner Study,** a faithful reconstruction of the author's study in his California ranch home. The creator of Perry Mason donated his professional effects to the University of Texas. The **Chinese Garden and Walkway,** an outdoor porch, contains eighteenth-century Chinese artifacts. The view of the western hills and campus buildings is especially nice up here.

LYNDON B. JOHNSON LIBRARY

University of Texas, 2313 Red River near E. 23rd • Parking on Red River between Manor and E. 26th • 916-5137 • Open daily 9–5 • Tours for groups of 12 or more by appointment • Free • W

The LBJ Library's commanding location atop this high knoll overlooking the UT campus, on equal footing with the Capitol, isn't happenstance. The spirit of the library and museum is best summed up by a 1971 cartoon on display here: Lyndon is portrayed as a larger-than-life wheeler-dealer Texan, hunkered down on a stool-sized version of the museum, asking "D'yuh all mind if I rest on muh laurels?" The exquisite array of ceremonial gifts given Johnson during his sovereignty makes for great window shopping. The historical displays tracing his career make for interesting reading, and political campaign paraphernalia fans will enjoy these displays. A replica of the Oval Office is upstairs. Four stories' worth of the presidential papers are at the core of the temple. Traveling exhibitions, films, concerts, and lectures.

NEILL-COCHRAN HOUSE

2310 San Gabriel at W. 23rd • Parking in rear, off W. 23rd • 478-2335 Wednesday–Sunday 2–5 • Hour-long guided tours, call for hours • Admission

Abner Cook built this graceful Greek Revival manse for George Washington Hill in 1853. In 1856, it became the state Blind Institute. In 1865, it served as a hospital for Yankee prisoners. The house is said to be haunted by patients who died and were buried on the grounds. During the 1880s it became a social center for the state and community elite under the successive ownerships of Andrew Neill and Judge T.B. Cochran. The Colonial Dames of America restored it with a variety of seventeenth- to nineteenth-century antiques. Almost all the doors, doorknobs, windows, shutters, and hinges are original.

O. HENRY MUSEUM

409 E. 5th at Neches • 472-1903 • Wednesday–Sunday 12–5 • Donation

William Sidney "O. Henry" Porter is world-famous for his short stories. What is not generally known is that he was also the editor of the short-lived, humorous Austin weekly, the *Rolling Stone*. He lived in this cottage during that time, and some of his printing equipment stood on the back porch. Some of the furnishings belonged to Porter and his family. Also on display are momentos from his life.

REPUBLIC OF TEXAS MUSEUM

510 E. Anderson • 339-1997 • Open Monday–Friday 10–4, most Saturdays Adults about $2, students 50¢ • W+

Permanent exhibits center on the Republic of Texas period, but rotating exhibits range from then to the present.

TEXAS MEMORIAL MUSEUM

2400 Trinity, on the University of Texas campus • 471-1605 • Monday–Friday 9–5, Saturday 10–5, and Sunday 1–5 • Free • W call ahead

A 30-foot-long fossil mosasaur, gleaming minerals from the Barron Collection, and hand weaponry that spans four centuries are just a few of the permanent exhibitions to be seen. In addition to the many other permanent exhibitions in geology and paleontology, natural history, and anthropology, there are special temporary exhibits. Natural history exhibits concentrate on the flora and fauna of Texas. The museum gift shop sells high-quality imports, museum replicas, books, art objects, and cards.

TEXAS MILITARY FORCES MUSEUM

Camp Mabry, 3500 W. 35th • 406-6967 • Open Wednesday–Sunday Donations • W+

Texas' war heroes and military glory are memorialized here. Jet planes, helicopters, tanks, and artillery are outside. Inside are trucks, jeeps, more artillery and machine guns from various sides and wars, as well as a display of Texans who won the Medal of Honor, dioramas of famous battles, uniforms, rifles and small arms, and other trappings of war and the armed forces.

UMLAUF SCULPTURE GARDEN AND MUSEUM

605 Robert E. Lee Rd., near Zilker Park • 445-5582, Wednesday–Sunday Adults about $3, students about $2

The works of Austin sculptor Charles Umlauf are displayed throughout the garden and the interior of the Umlauf Sculpture Garden and Museum.

HISTORIC PLACES

GOVERNOR'S MANSION

1010 Colorado and W. 11th • 463-5516 • Guided tours Monday–Friday mornings, subject to governor's schedule • Reservations required for groups of 10 or more • Free • W rear entrance

Abner Cook built this stately Greek Revival residence using locally made bricks and Bastrop pine. He had $17,000 with which to work. There was no money left over for furnishings. The first inhabitants, Governor Elisha Pease and family, brought their own when they moved in during the summer of 1856. It is the first and only Governor's mansion the state has ever had, and it is nearer its original condition than any of the three older houses in the U.S. still in use as governors' residences. Museum-quality nineteenth century American and Texas furnishings and works of art furnish the mansion, including the writing desk of Stephen F. Austin. Tours include the six public rooms of the first floor and the grounds.

ST. DAVID'S EPISCOPAL CHURCH

304 E. 7th and San Jacinto • 472-1196

Built in 1854, the current Gothic castle facade dates to 1870. The congregation wanted to build a new sanctuary; failing to collect enough money, they remodelled what they had. Some of the stained-glass windows are genuine Tiffany. The interior is spacious and Victorian. The second-oldest protestant church in Texas and the oldest Episcopal church west of the Mississippi, it has also been called the "Gamblers' Church"; legend has it that some of the money to build the original church came from gamblers.

ST. MARY'S CATHEDRAL

204 E. 10th • 476-6182

It's easy to miss this graceful Gothic church, overshadowed and surrounded by newer, secular structures. Designed by noted architect Nicholas Clayton, St. Mary's was built in 1874. The beautiful stained glass windows from France and Germany were added in the 1890s.

SANTA RITA NO. 1

Trinity and Martin Luther King Jr. • Open 24 hours • Free • W

When it was established in 1883, the University of Texas had an endowment of two million acres of rangeland out on the edge of the Great American Desert with which to support itself. West Texas ranchers paid the University about 5¢ an acre for grazing rights.

Then in 1916, after poking around "out there," UT professor John A. Udden got the harebrained idea that oil just might be lurking somewhere beneath the University's share of the desert floor. Work on an oil derrick finally commenced in 1921, and it was christened Santa Rita, after a priest admonished the well's investors to invoke the name of Santa Rita, the saint of the impossible. The well finally blew in, in 1923, and oil royalties from the dozens of wells that followed have flowed into the Permanent University Fund ever since, totalling several billion dollars. The Santa Rita well was dismantled and shipped to Austin in 1949, and dedicated on Thanksgiving Day 1958, during the annual Longhorn-Aggie clash. It is set in motion for occasional state occasions, and its tape-recorded story plays on and on for the occasional visitor.

STATE CAPITOL COMPLEX

11th and Congress • 463-0063 • Open daily • Free • Parking at intersection's southwest corner • W

The Texas Capitol is one of the nation's largest, a grand Renaissance Revival palace that almost always outshines the mortals who legislate within. Grand as it appears today, the Capitol as originally planned would have been much grander, with four wings instead of two and statues lining the roofline. Those plans called for the use of limestone quarried by state prisoners at Convict Hill in Oak Hill. After the basement and foundation were built, the limestone was deemed unfit for exterior use, and designers made do with the more durable, beautiful, harder-to-cut, and expensive pink granite from Granite Mountain in Marble Falls. The plans were simplified accordingly, and here we have it.

The place is really big; its exquisite wainscoating—oak, pine, cherry, cedar, walnut, ash, mahogany—goes on for seven miles. It used up 15,000 railroad cars of granite. The cornerstone alone roughed out at eight tons. Covering three acres of ground with 8.5 acres of floor space, the Texas Capitol was said to be the world's seventh-largest building at the time of its birth. Paintings and statues of governors and other prominent Texans line the rotunda and halls.

In 1990, work commenced on a massive Capitol-complex restoration project. As state offices proliferated over the years, so had offices in the Capitol building. Big rooms were subdivided, ceilings lowered, etc. It was haphazardly done and sometimes the results were shoddy. The Capitol fire of 1983 and the capitol's centennial called attention to its neglect. In order to create more parking and office space, a huge pit was dug out just north of the Capitol for a 4-story-deep parking garage and office complex called the Capitol Extension. With offices underground, the Capitol could then be restored to its original palatial look and dimensions. The Capitol Extension opened in 1993. It is connected to the 1888 Capitol and other state buildings by tunnels. About two-thirds of the legislature has offices in the Extension. The Extension's design incorporates similar building materials, symbols, and designs from the Capitol building. In 1995, renovations to the 1888 Capitol were completed. The whole Capitol complex project cost $187 million, but was hailed as a work without parallel. Just what a Texan would expect to hear. Most people consider it money well spent, once they have seen it.

Hundreds of pieces of original furnishings and art were restored. Exact replicas of original furniture were created to replace pieces that had been lost. Carpeting, flooring, draperies, and lighting were carefully reproduced. The original Governor's Office on the first floor has been restored to its ca. 1910 appearance, as well as the House and Senate chambers. The Treasurer's Business Office on the first floor, south foyer, once served as the state's bank. Vaults in the north of the room housed the state's money, securities, and other legal tender.

Daily Capitol tours start from the Treasurer's Business Office. These free guided tours take about 45 minutes and run from 8:30 to 4:30 weekdays and 9:30 to 4:30 weekends.

On the southeast corner of the grounds is the restored, German castle-like Old Land Office (1857), now the Capitol Complex Visitors Center (305-8400, open Tuesday through Saturday, free). Employees at the information desk orient visitors to the Capitol complex. Self-guided and scheduled guided tours are available. A 20-minute video presentation about the fascinating history of the Capitol complex is narrated by Texan Walter Cronkite. The Capitol Gift Shop offers a wealth of Capitol and state of Texas memorabilia. The Center also houses several other permanent and rotating exhibits.

STATE CEMETERY

E. 7th and Comal • 463-6023 • Visitors Center open Monday–Saturday 8–5, grounds open daily • Free • W

Stephen F. Austin (the Father of Texas), several governors, and hundreds of Confederate veterans are buried here on two lovely wooded hills. Recently restored.

SYMPHONY SQUARE

Red River and 11th • 476-6090

Three of the four limestone buildings that constitute Symphony Square were moved stone by stone from nearby locations. The **Jeremiah Hamilton Home** is the sole original edifice. Hamilton was the former slave of Reconstruction governor A.J. Hamilton. A carpenter, he was a representative in the 1870 House and a delegate to the 1873 state Republican convention. In 1873, he built this distinctive limestone two-story triangular house, wedged into a triangular plot formed by Waller Creek, 11th and Red River streets. The three buildings moved here are the old **Wilson Mercantile-New Orleans Club** (ca. 1870), the **Hardemann House** (1887), and **Doyle House** (1880). These three buildings frame the creekside amphitheater.

OTHER POINTS OF INTEREST

BARSANA DHAM

RM 1826, about 18 mi. southwest of Austin • Open daily • Free • W+
The Southwest's largest Hindu temple, Barsana Dham is dedicated to Radha Rani, the female form of God. The $2.5 million temple was built along Bear Creek on land that once belonged to Texas' most prominent historian, Walter Prescott Webb. Barsana Dham is the headquarters of the International Society of Divine Love, founded in India in 1975. This site was chosen for its resemblance to holy sites in Barsana, India.

CELIS BREWERY

2431 Forbes Dr. • 835-0884 • Tours Tuesday–Saturday afternoons • Free • W
Belgian brewer Pierre Celis established this American outpost in 1992 and has been winning converts to his authentic Belgian-style beers ever since. Tour the brewery and then sample its wares in the hospitality room.

CONGRESS AVENUE BRIDGE BAT COLONY

Congress Avenue Bridge over Town Lake • Nightly, April–October
Free • W
Congress Avenue Bridge is summer home to North America's largest urban bat colony. About 750,000 of them leave their home under the bridge at dusk nightly to feed on insects. The exodus lasts about 15 minutes as they stream like a river down the Colorado. July and August are the best viewing months. Favored free viewing spots are from atop the Congress Avenue Bridge, the hike-and-bike trail, and the *Austin American-Statesman's* parking lot (305 S. Congress). The Mexican free-tails desert Austin for Mexico with the first cool fronts of autumn.

HILL COUNTRY FLYER

Runs from Cedar Park to Burnet, every Saturday and Sunday,
March–December • 477-8468 • Adults about $25 and up, children about $13
and up, senior citizen discount • Reservations recommended • W with
assistance
This entertaining train runs from Cedar Park through Liberty Hill and Bertram to Burnet. Number 786, a restored Southern Pacific steam locomotive built in 1916, pulls an assortment of cars from the 1920s to the 1950s. Number 786 once hauled freight between Houston and Austin before being retired in 1956. Restored, it re-entered service in 1992.

MCKINNEY FALLS STATE PARK

5808 McKinney Falls Parkway • 243-1643 • Open daily
Admission about $2 • W variable
This stretch of Onion Creek on the southeast edge of Austin has two sets of scenic falls. The creek, with its tall cypress and cedar sentinels, makes for a

scenic stroll, and the remains of the old Thomas McKinney house still stand, near the confluence of Williamson and Onion creeks. Another trail takes you through an ancient Indian campground, one of the oldest yet discovered in Central Texas. Fishing, restrooms, picnic sites, trails, group shelters, primitive and trailer camping sites with hookups (fee), swimming.

NATIONAL WILDFLOWER RESEARCH CENTER

4801 La Crosse Ave. • 292-4200 • Open Tuesday–Sunday • Adults about $4, children and senior citizens about $2 • W

The National Wildflower Research Center shows the ecological and aesthetic importance of native wildflowers and other native plants, trees, and shrubs. Wildflower meadow and restored native prairie, nature trail, and visitors gallery with exhibits that describe North American prairie, desert, and forest ecosystems show medicinal, ceremonial, and agricultural uses of native plants, and tell how to be better stewards of the Earth. Buildings reflect the region's diverse architectural heritage: from Spanish missions to sturdy, boxy German farmhouses to western ranch houses. The stone observation tower offers great Hill Country views.

LAKE AUSTIN

Redbud Trail at Lake Austin Blvd.

A dam was first built here in 1893; its failure in 1900 was the darkest moment in Austin history. It was rebuilt in 1940. Lake Austin, 1,830 acres, provides Austin's drinking water. Boating and swimming are popular pasttimes. **Lake Austin Metropolitan Park** (City Park Rd., off FM 2222 • Open daily • Admission) is a popular access point.

LAKE TRAVIS

Lake Travis, 18,930 acres, has the largest capacity of the seven Highland Lakes. Fishing, boating, scuba-diving, and sailing are popular. Numerous private campgrounds, resorts, and boat launches. Public parks (Admission) include Arkansas Point, Windy Point, Cypress Creek, "Hippie Hollow," Mansfield Dam, Pace Bend, Sandy Creek. Formed by Mansfield Dam, which FM 620 crosses.

TOWN LAKE PARK

Colorado River, from dam to dam • Open daily • W but not all areas

Town Lake Park and Zilker Park are the twin jewels of the Austin Park system. Thousands of Austinites use the 10 mile Walk and Bikeway daily. Hundreds of others fish from favorite spots on the banks. Picnics, concerts, and Fourth of July fireworks go off here. Motorboats not permitted. No swimming; the undercurrents are too dangerous. More than 3,000 trees and shrubs have been planted along the length of the park, many of them endangered Texas species. Come spring, many of them are in radiant bloom: redbuds, peaches, cherries, plums, and so on. You can thank Lady Bird Johnson and the National Recreation Trails System for it all. Ball fields and playgrounds. Public boat launches.

ZILKER PARK

2100 Barton Springs Rd., between Robert E. Lee and Loop 1 (MoPac) 472-4914 • Open daily • Free (parking free on weekends) • W

Four-hundred-acre Zilker Park is best known as the home of **Barton Springs,** Texas' most venerated swimming hole. Picnic tables, playgrounds, ball fields, and group shelters are scattered throughout the park. A miniature train runs through, and you can rent canoes. You can also fish, hike, bike, and run. The **Hillside Theatre** is host to musical and theatrical productions.

Barton Springs is the fourth-largest natural spring in Texas. The spring's non-chlorinated, limestone-filtered water stays at a near-constant 69 degrees. Always a popular Austin swimming hole, the spring at one time also powered sawmills and flour mills.

SPORTS AND ACTIVITIES

Baseball

UNIVERSITY OF TEXAS LONGHORNS

Disch-Falk Field, E. MLK Jr. at Comal, just east of IH-35 • 471-4602
Admission • February–May • W partial

In the old Southwest Conference, the Longhorn baseball team perennially made the post-season playoffs and won the conference championship dozens of times. In 1998, Austin was the largest city in the country without a professional baseball team, but with the Longhorns, no one much cared.

Basketball

UNIVERSITY OF TEXAS LONGHORNS (MEN AND WOMEN)

Erwin Center, 1701 Red River near IH-35 • 471-4602 • Admission
November–March • W+ but not all areas

The Longhorns (male) have their ups and downs from season to season. On the other hand, the Lady Longhorns are always among the best teams in the country.

Fishing

Many local Izaak Waltons fish Town Lake. (But don't eat the fish!) Those smitten with wanderlust may choose between Lake Austin, Lake Long, McKinney Falls State Park, Lake Travis, the Pedernales River, and the rest of the Highland Lakes. You need a Texas fishing license, available at most sporting goods stores.

Football

UNIVERSITY OF TEXAS LONGHORNS

Memorial Stadium, University of Texas, 23rd and San Jacinto • 471-4602
Admission • Late summer, fall • W partial

Collegiate football is a big industry in Austin, just in terms of the numbers of postgame margaritas and enchiladas consumed. What makes the fans' provender more palatable is the fact that it usually follows on the heels of an orange-and-white success down in the pits d'combat.

Golf

The City of Austin operates five golf courses. Each offers a full range of professional services. Fees start at about $12. Each course closes one Monday per month; call ahead to confirm.

Hancock Golf Course • 811 E. 41st • 453-0276
Jimmy Clay and Roy Kizer Golf Courses • 5400 Jimmy Clay Dr. • 444-0999

Lions Municipal Golf Course • 2910 Enfield near Exposition • 477-6963
Morris Williams Golf Course • 4300 Manor, across from airport • 926-1298

Hockey

AUSTIN ICE BATS

Travis County Exposition Center, 7311 Decker Ln. • **927-7825** • **October through mid-spring** • **W partial**

Pro ice hockey came to Austin in 1996 and was an immediate hit. The Ice Bats play in the Western Professional League.

Horse Racing

MANOR DOWNS

Take US 290 east to Manor, follow signs • **272-4042** • **Admission about $2** • **W**

This grade 2 track's quarterhorse season runs from March through early June.

Running

Austin was one of the first cities in Texas to embrace the sport on a commoner's level. There are plenty of 5K-and-up races year-round. The biggie is the *Austin American-Statesman's* Capitol 10,000, held in March or April.

Sailing and Boating

Skiing and pleasure boating are good on all of the Highland Lakes, except Town Lake, where motorboats are prohibited. Lake Travis is excellent for sailing. Boat ramps are found in most public parks, marinas, and campgrounds.

Tennis

The City of Austin has more than 100 courts at more than 25 locations; most are free courts in neighborhood parks. Five tennis centers require reservations and a fee. Lessons are available for groups and individuals of all ages and abilities.

VELOWAY

La Crosse Ave., across from the National Wildflower Research Center, 4801 La Crosse • **Open daily dawn to dusk** • **Free** • **W**

Recreational cyclists and inline skaters use this 5 km paved asphalt loop; runners and walkers cannot. Spring flowers are gorgeous; ride or skate and enjoy them without having to worry about cars.

COLLEGES AND UNIVERSITIES

Although other Texas cities offer a few educational opportunities not found in Austin, on the whole Austin is the greenest of intellectual and educational oases in Texas and the South. The primary watering hole is of course the **University of Texas at Austin,** chief of the University of Texas System's campuses and medical centers. But the University of Texas isn't the only game in town. **Austin Community College,** with over 25,000 students, is bigger than most colleges and universities. **Huston-Tillotson College, St. Edward's University,** and **Concordia University** offer a more personal brand of higher education.

ST. EDWARD'S UNIVERSITY

3001 S. Congress at St. Edward's Dr. • **448-8400** • **W variable**

St. Edward's **Old Main Building** is south Austin's most prominent landmark. It overlooks the city from the crest of a hill three miles south of downtown and is easily visible from there. Nicholas J. Clayton designed the massive
Gothic Revival building, which was built in 1887. It was rebuilt after a fire
destroyed it in 1903.

St. Edwards began in the 1870s as a school for boys. It achieved university
status in 1885. Now a four-year, coed university offering 50 major fields of
study, St. Edwards is still operated by the Catholic Church, but its 3,200 students represent all creeds and ethnic backgrounds.

THE UNIVERSITY OF TEXAS AT AUSTIN

**Main campus boundaries: Guadalupe and Red River, Martin Luther King Jr.
and 26th. Campus closed to public driving and parking on weekdays during
class terms; open weekends and holidays. Free parking and information at
visitors center, Sid Richardson Hall Unit 1, next to the LBJ Library, 2313 Red
River. Center open Monday–Friday 8–5 • 471-1420 • W variable**

It's impossible to speak of Austin without bringing up the University of
Texas. UT-Austin isn't just the 357-acre Main Campus, the 445-acre Brackenridge Tract, the 33-acre Bee Caves Research Center, and the 476-acre J.J. Pickle
Research Campus. And it's more than the 5,000-odd professors and teaching
assistants, 14,000 assorted other staff and 50,000 students. A recent study indi-
cated that UT-Austin, directly or indirectly, generates over $3 billion per year in
the local economy.

Several schools and degree programs rank in or near the top ten nationally.
The combined libraries add up to the sixth largest academic library in the United States.

A guide to UT-Austin could run as many pages as a guide to the city. But the
university hasn't come up with anything like that yet. It has published a number of free maps, brochures, guides, and tours of the university complex which
are of interest to the visitor.

It was 1930 before the university really began to step outside its original 40-
acre square. None of the original buildings still stand. The gothic towers and
ivy-covered brick walls of Old Main gave way to the present Tower in the
1930s. In 1910, Cass Gilbert began to draw up the first comprehensive architectural plan for the university campus, setting the theme for the next half-centu-
ry of UT construction, that of a modified Spanish Renaissance. Many regard
Battle Hall (1911) as the prettiest building on campus. Gilbert followed it with
nearby **Sutton Hall** in 1914. And that's as far as his ambitious plan got. Farmer
Jim Ferguson was governor of Texas by then, and he begrudged the university
every penny it got. When UT's 1930s building boom began, architect Paul Cret
was at the helm. Although his grandiose centerpiece **Tower** drew hisses and
catcalls from many quarters, the rest of Cret's campus masterplan was also
modified Spanish Renaissance. Many of Cret's buildings eventually got built,
although grandeur was often sacrificed to economy. Still, we have the **Home
Economics Building,** with its wrought ironwork and Spanish courtyard; **Garrison Hall,** with its Texas cattle brands and roster of Texas heroes; **Waggener
Hall,** with its decorative cornice and frieze; and the Tex-Deco **Hogg Auditorium.** Only with the construction of the **Academic Center** (now Peter T. Flawn
Academic Center) and the **Business-Economics Building** in the 1960s did the

university begin to break away from the distinctive, graceful, unified look that had been 50 years in the making.

In addition to intercollegiate sports (*see* Sports and Activities), visitors are welcome at music, dance, and dramatic presentations (*see* Performing Arts), and the museums on campus (*see* Museums and Art Galleries). Astronomical observations through a nine-inch telescope are also open to visitors, usually every Saturday night. The telescope is located on the top floor of Painter Hall (24th between Whitis and Speedway; 471-1307 or 471-5007). You can also eat at the Texas Union.

PERFORMING ARTS

PERFORMING ARTS CENTER

University of Texas, E. 23rd at E. Campus Dr. • 471-1444 • W+ but not all areas

The Performing Arts Center is actually a complex consisting of five contiguous buildings built to the tune of $41 million. This includes the 3000-seat **Bass Concert Hall,** the 700-seat **Bates Recital Hall** and the smaller **McCullough Theatre.** Classrooms and offices take up the rest of the space. In the true spirit of the University and the rest of Texas, the Bass Concert Hall is too big for anything but touring Broadway shows, opera, and symphony orchestras. The lighting is computer-controlled and the orchestra pit can be raised and lowered. Bates Recital Hall contains one of the nation's largest tracker organs and is designed for smaller ensembles and soloists. The McCullough Theatre is used for chamber operas, dance programs, and some drama department productions.

AUSTIN LYRIC OPERA

1111 W. 6th • 472-5927

Well-organized and funded, ALO presents international artists and rising young American talent in quality productions meant to "reflect the unique flavor and innovation which is Austin." Several full operas are presented each year in the Bass Concert Hall, in addition to other special events.

AUSTIN SYMPHONY

1101 Red River (Symphony Square) • 476-6064 or 476-4626 (Box office) Admission

The symphony performs in the Bass Concert Hall monthly October through May. During June, July, and August the symphony sponsors a weekend evening concert series featuring local jazz, folk, and rock acts in the Symphony Square outdoor amphitheater.

BALLET AUSTIN

3002 Guadalupe • 476-9051 • Admission

Ballet Austin presents both classical and contemporary works during its fall-to-spring season. *The Nutcracker Suite* is presented each December. Ballet Austin performs at the UT Performing Arts Center.

ESTHER'S FOLLIES
525 E. 6th • 320-0553 • Admission • W
Austin's favorite comedy and irreverence troupe, Esther's Follies has been performing for 20-odd years. Shows change monthly.

HYDE PARK THEATRE
511 W. 43rd • 452-6688 • Admission • W
This cozy arena hosts plays, musical acts, and other live entertainment.

LIVE OAK THEATRE AT THE STATE
719 Congress • 472-5143 • W
This emerging resident professional theatre presents musicals, dramas, comedies, classics, and new works on a seasonal basis. Each December, Live Oak presents its own version of "A Christmas Carol" with original score.

MARY MOODY NORTHEN THEATRE
St. Edward's University, 3001 S. Congress • 448-8484 • Admission • W
St. Edward's productions regularly feature well-known directors and guest stars. Productions have run the gamut from Neil Simon's *The Good Doctor* through Arthur Miller's *The Crucible* to Moliere's *Tartuffe*.

PARAMOUNT THEATRE FOR THE PERFORMING ARTS
713 Congress • 472-5411 • W+
Performances by local and national touring artists: plays, operas, dance, concerts, and standup comedians.

ZACHARY SCOTT THEATRE CENTER
1510 Toomey, off South Lamar • 476-0541 • W
Zachary Scott was the most famous movie star ever to come out of Austin. He died in 1965 and is buried in Austin. The professional resident theater group presents a full, 12-month season. Other non-equity productions are also presented. There are two stages, a 130-seat arena and a 200-seat thrust stage.

SHOPPING

THE ARBORETUM
10000 Research • W
Village-style shopping center adjacent to the Renaissance Hotel. Tenants include Koslow's Furriers, the Sharper Image, Banana Republic, and Higginbottom's.

AUSTIN ANTIQUE MALL
8822 McCann, off Research Blvd. • 459-5900
North Austin's largest concentration of antiques and collectibles dealers. Jewelry, glass, and toys are among the offerings, as well as furniture and *junque*.

AUSTIN COUNTRY FLEA MARKET
9500 US 290E, 5 miles east of IH-35 • 928-2795 • Admission • W
The largest fleamarket in Central Texas, spanning 130 acres with hundreds of covered booths, an open show stage and display and entertainment areas. You can buy fresh produce and pets. Good place to look for Mexican food, herbs, spices, and other ingredients.

BARTON CREEK SQUARE MALL

2901 Capital of Texas Hwy (Loop 360) at Loop 1 (Mo-Pac Expressway)
327-7040 • W+

Dillard's, Foley's, J. C. Penney, Montgomery Ward, and a food court convenient to southwest Austin. Good view of downtown skyline from parking lot.

CENTRAL PARK

4001 N. Lamar • W+

Central Market, Bookstop, the Cadeau, Scarbrough's, Clarksville Pottery, and Dr. Chocolate are among the tenants at this popular new central Austin shopping center.

HIGHLAND MALL

6001 Airport • 454-9656 • W+

This midtown mall has about 120 shops and stores, including Dillard's, Foley's, J. C. Penney, and a food court.

NORTHCROSS MALL

2525 W. Anderson • 451-7466 • W

An ice rink and in-house movie theatre are popular attractions. Oshman's and Beall's are major tenants. Food court. Close to other popular shopping centers.

CENTRAL MARKET

4001 N. Lamar, in the Central Market Center • 206-1000 • W+

You need a map for your first visit, which the store thoughtfully provides. Choose from over 100 varieties of olive oil, 150 varieties of pasta sauces and pestos, 24 kinds of couscous and tabouli, lots of local organic produce and cut flowers. Candies and chocolate from around the world. Central Market Cafe serves hip, healthy food, as well as live music most evenings. Cooking classes and healthy recipes from around the world are offered.

PEOPLE'S RENAISSANCE MARKET

W. 23rd and Guadalupe • W sometimes congested

This block-long stretch of W. 23rd is open year-round to local artists and artisans who make and sell their own wares. On UT football Saturdays and during the Christmas season, the place sucks in an endless stream of buyers and sellers. Jugglers and magicians entertain. Jewelry, paintings, toys, prisms, sculpture, hand-screened T-shirts and the like, all handmade. Painter Walter S. Falk III has sold over 30,000 watercolors here during the last 20 years. Take time to admire the "Austintatious" mural.

Antiques

ATTAL'S SOUTHWEST GALLERY

3310 Red River • 476-3634

Like going through grandmother's attic. You never know what you're going to find: furniture, books, prints, postcards, medicine bottles, Texana, road maps. Furniture leans toward American primitive, rather than fancy European. Attal knows what he's selling; he is one of the area's most-in-demand appraisers. This is not exactly a bargain-hunter's paradise.

WHIT HANKS ANTIQUES

1009 W. 6th • 478-2101 • W+

Over 70 dealers offer American, French, and English furniture, furnishings, and accessories, from Texas primitives to formal French.

Distinctive Shopping Sites

THE CADEAU

2316 Guadalupe, across from UT • 477-7276 • W

Longtime UT area gift shop, with fine china, gourmet kitchenware, linens, fashion accessories, and glassware.

CALLAHAN'S GENERAL STORE

501 Bastrop Hwy. (US 183S) • 385-3452 • W

Originally a feed and seed store, now with hardware and a nursery, kitchen goods, Western wear, boots, and more.

CAPITOL SADDLERY

1614 Lavaca • 478-9309

Made famous by Jerry Jeff Walker's song about bootmaker Charlie Dunn, Capitol Saddlery is an Austin institution. If it's leather and has anything to do with boots or horses, it's crammed in here somewhere. Custom-made boots start at about $600.

CLARKSVILLE POTTERY

4001 N. Lamar, Ste. 200; 9722 Great Hills Trail, Ste. 380 • 454-9079; 794-8580 • W

Austin's most comprehensive pottery shops, with clocks, wind chimes, jewelry, egg separators, match holders, hummingbird feeders, and more. Tortilla warmers and chip-and-dip bowls are popular. Inventory is a good mix of national and local potters.

COWGIRLS AND FLOWERS

508 Walsh • 478-4626

The hippest florists in town, favored for their eclectic and innovative arrangements. Exotic flowers, jewelry, crafts, and arty accent furniture.

DELL FACTORY OUTLET

8801 Research • 728-5656 • Monday–Saturday • W+

Dell personal computers are famous for quality and technical support; this is the cheapest way to get one. Demos, excess, discontinued, and reconditioned desktop systems and notebooks, peripherals, accessories, and software, at varying discounts. Supplies are limited and inventory changes daily.

ECLECTIC ETHNOGRAPHIC GALLERY

916 W. 12th and Lamar • 477-1816

Vintage and contemporary folk arts and craft. Pre-Columbian pottery and shards, African masks, battered Mexican *retablos,* rugs, jewelry, clothing, and toys from places like Africa, India, New Guinea, Peru, Bolivia, and Mexico.

EL INTERIOR

1009 West Lynn • 474-8680

Mexican and Guatemalan folk art, including *santos,* toys and games, furniture, jewelry, clothing, weavings, and pottery. The owner personally buys everything, generally directly from the artisans.

FIRE ISLAND HOT GLASS STUDIO

3104 E. 4th • 389-1100 • W

Visitors are welcome by appointment; you can stand around and watch how your purchases are made. Goblets and perfume bottles are popular. They even make their own glass, using locally produced lime and other locally purchased ingredients.

HILL COUNTRY CELLARS

1700 N. Bell Blvd. in Cedar Park (US 183, just north of RM 1431)
259-2000 • Open daily • W

A tasting room and gift shop are situated on a 5-acre vineyard and winery. A variety of wines and sparkling wines are produced.

NEIMAN MARCUS LAST CALL

Brodie Oaks Shopping Center, S. Lamar at Ben White • 447-0701 • W

The arrival of this "last chance" Neiman's outlet with its radically discounted prices sets many a shopper's heart aflutter; it was one of the most anticipated openings in modern Austin shopping history.

SLAUGHTER-LEFTWICH WINERY

4209 Eck Ln. at Hudson Bend Rd., 1 mile south of Mansfield Dam off
RR 620 • 266-3332

Tasting and sales daily; tours Friday through Sunday. Overlooks Lake Travis. Grapes grown near Lubbock. Chardonnay, Cabernet Sauvignon, Ruby Cabernet, Chenin Blanc.

WHOLE EARTH PROVISION COMPANY

2410 San Antonio; 4006 S. Lamar • 478-1577 • 444-9974

Originally inspired by the hippie-era Whole Earth Catalog, the store has grown with the times and has toys, clothing, shoes, camping, and hiking equipment, maps, books, canoes, and kayaks.

Art Galleries

COUNTRY STORE ART GALLERY

1304 Lavaca • 474-6222 • W

All the cliches in western art will be found here: longhorn statuettes and paintings, cowboys and Indians in various media, bluebonnets, and wildlife scenes. Yet among all the country store clutter, you'll find original works by

Charles Russell, Frederic Remington, and Porfirio Salinas. They hide the Rembrandts and Picassos in the walk-in vault.

RUTH BORINSTEIN GALLERY

3300 Bee Caves Rd. • 306-8848
This art-as-investment gallery has assembled exhibits of works by Miro, Chagall, Dali, Rembrandt, Goya, Lautrec, and Renoir. Within this gallery is **Appaloosa Gallery,** which features southwestern art by artists like R.C. Gorman.

KIDS' STUFF

AUSTIN CHILDREN'S MUSEUM

110 W. 2nd • 472-2494 • Tuesday–Saturday 10–5, Sunday 12–5
Admission about $3 • W
The Children's Museum offers a variety of educational and fun activities for children, for instance, "How and Why" and hands-on "Make and Take" workshops for children and families. Many exhibits are interactive.

AUSTIN NATURE CENTER

301 Nature Center Dr. at Stratford • 327-8181 • Open daily
Donations • W partial
Four Austin habitats are represented: ponds, grasslands, woodlands, and a Hill Country cave. Live wildlife exhibits contain more than 50 native Texas mammals, birds, and reptiles that cannot be returned to the wild because of injury or human upbringing. The Discovery Lab allows hands-on experiences through mini-science labs. The Nature Center is surrounded by an 80-acre Nature Preserve with two miles of trails that cross the Balcones Escarpment.

AUSTIN ZOO

10807 Rawhide Trail, off US 290 • 288-1490 • Open daily, weather permitting
Admission about $4 • W
The Austin Zoo shelters more than 60 exotic and domestic species of mammals, reptiles, and birds. It's kids-oriented, offering hands-on encounters with a variety of animals. Petting corral, dairy barn, pony barn, zoo kitchen and nursery, gift shop, discovery center, aviary, small animal barn, and primate center. Pony and hay rides cost extra.

JOURDAN-BACHMAN PIONEER FARM

11418 Sprinkle Cut-Off Rd. • 837-1215 • Call for hours • Admission
W but not all areas
The Pioneer Farm portrays farm life in Central Texas as it was a century ago. Over 15 reconstructed farm buildings, crop fields, pasture land, and an Indian midden are contained within this 70-acre tract on Walnut Creek in far northeast Austin. Programs and classes such as beekeeping and masonry impart a taste of pioneer life. Originally part of a 2,000-acre cotton plantation established in 1852.

ZILKER ZEPHYR

Zilker Park, 2100 Barton Springs Rd. • Open daily • Admission about $2
Currently Austin's only light-rail system and its most popular form of mass transportation. This miniature train usually runs fuller than any city bus and is a lot more fun. Tour of Zilker Park lasts about 30 minutes.

ANNUAL EVENTS

March

AUSTIN-TRAVIS COUNTY LIVESTOCK SHOW AND RODEO

Texas Exposition and Heritage Center, 7311 Decker Ln. • 928-3710
Usually third week in March, depending on date of Easter, ten days
Admission to some events • W

Livestock and agricultural exhibits, auction, carnival, top country-and-western singers and groups every night, barbecue cookoff, children's barn, and a rodeo.

SOUTH BY SOUTHWEST MUSIC AND MEDIA CONFERENCE

Various locations, mostly downtown • 467-7979 • Usually mid-month
Admission • W

Musicians and music-industry types from all over the world flock to Austin for one of the country's most important music-industry conferences. Around 500 rock, folk, blues, jazz, and pop acts perform during four nights of Music Fest Showcases in leading live-music venues. A trade show, panel discussions, and intensive sessions fill up the daylight hours. A film festival/conference and multimedia conference also take place.

April

TEXAS RELAYS

University of Texas Campus • 471-4602 • Usually first weekend in April,
Friday–Sunday • Admission • W variable

One of the oldest and best track meets around, featuring some of the best high school and college track and field athletes in the world.

October

TEXAS WILDLIFE EXPO

Texas Parks and Wildlife Department headquarters, 4200 Smith School Rd.
389-4472 • Usually first weekend • Free • W

TPWD's annual tribute to hunting, fishing, and the great outdoors in Texas, features events and exhibits for everyone from tree huggers to bow-hunters. Hands-on, how-to outdoors activities, equipment, and products for kids and adults. Climb a wall, catch a fish, shoot clay targets, compete in a biathlon, watch live history reenactments and field dog trials. You can even play game warden and solve a game-law violation.

Late October/Early November

HALLOWEEN/DIA DE LOS MUERTOS

Various locations downtown • October 31–November 1–2 • Some events free

Halloween is Old Pecan Street's biggest night, as the entertainment district is flooded by an ocean of costumes and clubbers. Mexico's Day of the Dead takes on an Austin twist. Related activities include an exhibit of altars, both traditional and *nuevo wavo.* The exhibit is at 419 Congress, home of Mexic-Arte (480-9373).

RESTAURANTS

($ = under $7, $$ = $8–$17, $$$ = $18–$25, $$$$ = over $25 for one person excluding drinks, tax, and tip.)

American

BARBARA ELLEN'S

13129 Hwy 71W at RR 620, in Bee Caves • 263-2385 • Open daily, lunch and dinner • $–$$ • AE, MC, V • W+

Solid American food, southern style, with healthy portions of vegetables and sinful desserts. Don't miss the bathrooms. Convenient to Lake Travis. Bar.

GREEN PASTURES

811 W. Live Oak • 444-4747 • Open daily, lunch and dinner; brunch on Sunday • $–$$$$ • Cr • W

Peacocks strut about the manicured grounds of the large, white Victorian home. The trend continues inside with surroundings and service: vintage southern gentility as found nowhere else in Austin. The classic continental menu has evolved into tastefully executed American gourmet food. The Sunday brunch is still a Texas classic. Bar.

HUT'S HAMBURGERS

807 W 6th • 472-0693 • Open daily, lunch and dinner • $ • AE, MC, V • W+

Hut's hamburgers, chicken-fried steak, and onion rings are among the very best in town.

THE LODGE AT LAKEVIEW

3825-B Lake Austin Blvd. at Enfield Rd. • 476-2473
Open daily, lunch and dinner • $–$$ • Cr • W

Beautiful view of Lake Austin, the Hill Country, and the setting sun. Lakeside decks seat over 400; the dining room is mountain-lodge nostalgic. Mesquite-grilled steaks, gulf seafood, wild game, sandwiches, daily specials. Sunday brunch.

MARTIN'S KUMBAK/DIRTY'S

2808 Guadalupe • 478-0413 • Open daily, lunch and dinner • $ • W

More has been said in print about Dirty's than about any other hamburger joint in Austin. For the full Dirty's experience, go for the O. T. Special, onion rings and/or fries, and a chocolate shake or a cold Shiner beer, then you'll see why the sign outside says "Since 1926." Beer.

TEXAS CHILI PARLOR

1409 Lavaca • 472-2828 • Open daily, lunch and dinner • $
DIS, MC, V • W+

The best place in town to sample the national dish of Texas: straight, in chili pie, smothered over hot dogs and enchiladas, folded into flour tortillas, drizzled over salad greens. Newcomers will enjoy all the beer signs and sundry other *junque* covering the walls and ceiling. Bar.

THREADGILL'S

**6416 N. Lamar • 451-5440 • Open daily, lunch and dinner • $
MC, V • W+**

This gas-station-turned-restaurant's vintage beer sign and clock collection is one of the best in the world. Probably the most neon between Times Square and Las Vegas. The food is Southern, down-home: chicken-fried steak, pork roast, fried chicken, mashed potatoes, black-eyed peas, and lots of other vegetables, plus Louisiana specialties. Bar.

ZOOT

**509 Hearn, 3 blocks west of Mopac • 477-6535 • Open daily for dinner,
Sunday brunch • $$ • Cr • W**

American bistro and wine bar serves over 40 wines by the glass, appetizers, and main courses. Eclectic international menu changes daily; offerings have included bouillabaisse, grilled peppered shrimp with grapefruit and arugula, and beef tenderloin with wild mushroom custard. Local organic produce is extensively used. Many vegetarian offerings. Beer and wine.

Barbecue

IRON WORKS BARBECUE

**100 Red River and E. 1st • 478-4855 • Open Monday–Saturday, lunch and
dinner • $–$$ • AE, MC, V • W+**

Formerly the Weigl Ironworks, barbecue is now the hot item: brisket, sausage, chicken, and meaty beef ribs. Good salad and condiments bar. Rustic interior. Very popular with downtown diners and conveniently next door to the Convention Center.

POK-E-JO'S SMOKEHOUSE

**9828 Great Hills Tr. • 388-1990 • Open daily, lunch and dinner • $
Cr • W+**

Mesquite-smoked beef brisket and ribs, pork loin and ribs, mild and hot sausage, ham, chicken, and turkey. Side dishes are made in house. Good cobbler and banana pudding, if you have any room left. Beer.

SALT LICK

**FM 1826, about 20 mi. west of Austin, across from Camp Ben McCulloch
858-4959 • Open Tuesday–Sunday, lunch and dinner • $–$$ • No Cr • W+**

Pecan-smoked brisket, pork ribs, and sausage, served in a rustic dining hall. Sides of slaw, potato salad, and beans are worthy accompaniments. You can order plates, but groups usually choose to dine family-style. Dry locality; BYOB. The drive from Austin is scenic.

Delicatessen

KATZ'S

**618 W. 6th and Rio Grande • 472-2037 • Open 24 hours, daily • $–$$
Cr • W+**

Katz's is to Austin what the Lone Star Cafe was to New York City. You'll wonder why a corned beef sandwich can cost so much, but once it's in front of you, you'll understand. Katz's comes into its own in those wee, post-clubbing hours, when only a blintz will keep the edge on your finely tuned evening. Bar.

Eclectic, Including Vegetarian

BABY LOUIE'S

1 Jefferson Square, Jefferson and W. 38th • 458-2148 • Open daily for lunch and dinner, weekend brunch • $$ • AE, MC, V • W+

Dishes from around the world include Crab Quesadillas, Steak au Poivre, Goat-Cheese-Stuffed Gulf Shrimp in Red Chile Ancho Sauce, Jamaican-Jerk Chicken. Fresh Fish and Pastas with a variety of sauces and toppings. Desserts such as Flourless Chocolate Cake and Key Lime Pie. Over 30 wines are served by the glass or bottle.

THE BITTER END

311 Colorado • 478-2337 • Open daily for dinner, Monday–Friday for lunch $-$$ • Cr • W

Brewpubs are a recent phenomenon, thanks to the Texas Legislature. The Bitter End's food, much of it cooked in a wood-fired brick oven, is no mere pub grub: robust grilled and roasted meats, pizzas, pastas, plus salads, sandwiches, and appetizers that go well with the beers brewed on-premises.

CAFE AT THE FOUR SEASONS

98 San Jacinto at E. Cesar Chavez • 478-4500 • Open daily $$-$$$ • Cr • W+

Elegant lakeside setting; outdoor patio makes a magnificent Sunday brunch setting. Fish and seafood are prominently featured, along with a smattering of everything else. Alternative cusine menu offers innovative, flavorful dishes low in calories, cholesterol, and fat. Bar.

CASTLE HILL CAFE

1101 W. 5th • 476-0728 • Open Monday–Saturday dinner; Monday–Friday, lunch • $-$$ • AE, MC, V • W+

Menu changes every two weeks to accommodate cusines from around the world, but it has been mostly New Southwestern, Mediterranean, and Asian, meaning appetizers like Lamb Empanadas and Cheese Tortas with Sundried Tomatoes, and entrées like Grilled Pork Tenderloin in a mole-like sauce. Choose between rich or healthy desserts. Beer and wine; good wine selection.

HUDSON'S ON THE BEND

3509 RR 620, 1.5 mi. southwest of Mansfield Dam • 266-1369 • Open daily, dinner only, reservations recommended • $$$ • AE, DC, MC, V • W

Hudson's has brought rabbit, axis deer, javelina, boar, Spanish chorizo, and other exotic ingredients into its eclectic menu. Some dishes are smoked over apple or peach wood fires. All are served in a casually sophisticated, lakeside cottage setting. The drive out is nice, if you come just before sunset. Bar.

JEFFREY'S

1204 W. Lynn • 477-5584 • Open Monday–Saturday, dinner only $$-$$$ • Cr • W+

Jeffrey's is a longtime favorite of many Austin foodies. The menu is an eclectic, innovative mix of continental with American, Southwest, and Asian cuisines. Works by leading Austin artists are featured on the dining room walls.

KERBEY LANE CAFE

3704 Kerbey; 2700 S. Lamar; 12602 Research • 451-1436; 445-4451; 258-7757
Open daily, breakfast, lunch, and dinner • $ • Cr • W+

Healthful food—not health food—is served for vegetarians and carnivores. Local artwork graces the walls. Tex-New Mex dishes are popular items; good burgers, omelettes and breakfasts, and desserts. Late night hours. Bar.

WEST LYNN CAFE

1110 West Lynn • 482-0950 • Open daily, lunch and dinner • $–$$
Cr • W

International vegetarian menu, which includes stir-fry, pasta, Mexican, and curry dishes. Sunday brunch. Good wine list. Lots of plants and original art that changes regularly. Beer and wine.

SHORELINE GRILL

98 San Jacinto, in San Jacinto Center, San Jacinto at E. Cesar Chavez
477-3300 • Open daily for dinner, Monday–Friday for lunch
$$–$$$ • Cr • W+

Casually elegant dining room and patio area offer a beautiful view of Town Lake. Seafood is prominently featured, along with other trend-of-the-moment, internationally inspired appetizers and entrées. During bat season (spring through mid-fall), this is one of the most enjoyable places to watch the Congress Avenue Bridge bats fly out for the evening feed.

Z TEJAS GRILL

1110 W. 6th, 9400 Arboretum • 478-5355, 346-3506 • Open daily, breakfast, lunch, and dinner
$–$$ • Cr • W+

Nouvelle Southwestern cuisine (Navajo Tacos, Grilled Chicken Cotija Pasta) that blends Texas, New Mexico, and Mexico. Bar.

French/Continental

AMANDINE FINE EUROPEAN DESSERTS

917 W. 12th • 476-1976 • Open Monday–Saturday, breakfast and lunch
$ • W+

French bakery that also serves pizzas, soups, continental-style sandwiches, and other light lunch fare, coffee, and cappuccino. Croissants, French pastries, cakes and home-made sorbets. Wedding cakes are a specialty.

THE BELGIAN RESTAURANT

3520 Bee Caves Rd. • 328-0580 • Open daily for dinner;
lunch Monday–Friday • $–$$$ • Cr • W+

Excellent country French cuisine in a romantic atmosphere. A harpist or classical guitarist plays during dinner. Reservations recommended.

CHEZ NOUS

510 Neches • 473-2413 • Open Tuesday–Sunday for dinner; call for lunch hours • $$–$$$ • AE, DC, MC, V • W+

Homey, French food in a bistro-like setting. Most of the menu changes daily, depending on what looks best at the market. Thoughtfully selected wine list; house wines are reasonably priced and available by the glass. Beer also. Free valet parking.

JEAN-PIERRE'S UPSTAIRS

3500 Jefferson at 35th • 454-4811 • Open Monday–Saturday dinner, Monday–Friday lunch • $$–$$$ • Cr • W+
Continental cuisine with a Southwestern accent. Seafood predominates among entrées, but beef, pork, lamb, veal, duck, chicken, quail, and pastas are also presented in a variety of guises.

THE OLD PECAN STREET CAFE

310 E. 6th • Downtown • 478-2491 • Open daily, lunch and dinner $–$$ • Cr • W+
Steaks, seafood, chicken, and pasta, served in one of 6th Street's oldest buildings. Large and luscious array of desserts. Many patrons come for dessert alone. Extensive wine list. Bar. Convenient to the Convention Center.

Italian

BRICK OVEN RESTAURANT

1209 Red River; 10700 Anderson Mill Rd. • 477-7006; 335-1646 • Open Monday–Saturday, lunch and dinner; Sunday, dinner only • $ • Cr • W+
Pizza, lasagna, stromboli, chicken, and other Italian dishes are cooked in a giant wood-fired brick oven in the middle of the main dining room. Bar.

CARMELO'S

504 E. 5th • 477-7497 • Open daily, lunch and dinner • $$–$$$ • Cr • W
Dependable Italian food, convenient to the Convention Center. The rustic old limestone building was originally the Railroad House Hotel. Carmelo's makes its own pastas, and serves veal, poultry, seafood, and beef dishes. Romantic atmosphere. Large dessert selection. Bar.

MEZZALUNA

310 Colorado • 472-6770 • Open daily for dinner, • Monday–Friday for lunch $$ • Cr • W+
Northern Italian-derived food; casual, lively atmosphere. Open kitchen with pizza oven at center stage. Delicious and varied appetizers, plus fish, chicken, beef, pork, and pasta entrées. Tomato sauce isn't ubiquitous. Bar.

TRATTORIA GRANDE

Renaissance Austin Hotel, 9721 Arboretum Blvd. near Research • 343-2626 Open daily, lunch and dinner, weekend brunch • $$–$$$ • Cr • W+
Northern Italian menu, with entrées like baked chicken breast stuffed with spinach and ricotta cheese, topped with tomato cream sauce, or grilled filet of beef with artichokes and capers. Dessert selections are presented on a sterling silver tray. Bar.

Mexican

CAFE SERRANOS

1111 Red River, 3010 W. Anderson Ln. at Shoal Creek; 12636 Research
322-9080, 454-7333; 250-9555 • Open daily, lunch and dinner • $–$$
MC, V • W+

Mesquite-grilled beef and chicken fajitas, fish, shrimp, pork chops, plus Tex-Mex standards served in a setting reminiscent of a Mexican hacienda. Top Shelf Margarita is one of the best in town. Bar.

CHUY'S FINE FOOD

1728 Barton Springs Rd.; 10520 N. Lamar • 474-4452; 836-3218
Open daily, lunch and dinner • $–$$ • Cr • W+

Chuy's pulls out every cliche in the Tex-Mex school of decor: pink and green walls, piñatas, black velvet Elvises, lowriders flying through the sky, hundreds of hubcaps. Customer favorites include taco salad, chiles rellenos, blue corn tortilla enchiladas. Annual green chile festival in the fall. Bar.

EL AZTECA

2600 E. 7th • 477-4701 • Open Monday–Saturday, lunch and dinner
$–$$ • AE, MC, V • W

Eastside eatery reliable for classic Tex-Mex food, with vegetarian entrées as well as chiles rellenos, fajitas, and other standards. Lots of black-velvet paintings and Aztec heroes and heroines. Bar.

FONDA SAN MIGUEL

2330 W. North Loop • 459-4121 • Open daily for dinner, Sunday brunch
$$ • Cr • W+

San Miguel duplicates the pleasures of dining in one of Mexico's great native cuisine restaurants, down to the pleasant patio and dining rooms. La cocina Mexicana is blessed with many foreign influences—French, Italian, Chinese, and German among them—and San Miguel executes it well. Bar.

GUERO'S

1412 S. Congress • 447-7688 • Open daily, breakfast, lunch, and dinner
$ • No Cr • W+

"Guero" is Spanish for light-skinned, which the American owner of this Mexico City-styled taco bar is. The food is authentic Mexican for the most part. Tamales are made here. Full menu as well. Large international beer selection.

LAS MANITAS AVENUE CAFE

211 Congress • 472-9357 • Open daily, breakfast and lunch • $ • MC, V • W+

Interesting clientele. Huevos Motuleños are a refreshing alternative to migas. Daily lunch specials. Most selections from the limited menu will be less greasy than at other places, even the menudo.

MANUEL'S

310 Congress • 472-7555 • Open daily, lunch and dinner • $–$$ • Cr • W+

In addition to Tex-Mex, Manuel's serves interior Mexico-inspired dishes such as Snapper Veracruzano, ceviche y mas. Live music at weekend brunch. Manuel's margaritas get high marks. Bar.

MATT'S EL RANCHO

2613 S. Lamar • 462-9333 • Open Wednesday–Monday, lunch and dinner
$–$$ • Cr • W+
King of Mexican food? Matt's loyal constituency has made Matt Martinez and family millionaires several times over. The food may be more exciting at other restaurants, and the margaritas more potent, but El Rancho's faithful count on a good meal, especially with one of the specialties such as chile relleno, shrimp or fish a la Mexicana. Bar.

MR. NATURAL

1901-B E. Cesar Chavez • 477-5228 • Open Monday–Saturday, breakfast,
lunch, and early dinner • $ • MC, V • W+
Vegetarian Mexican food, juice bar, and whole-wheat bakery. Great licuados. Even strict vegans will be satisfied here.

EL RINCONCITO

1014-E N. Lamar • 476-5277 • Open daily, lunch and dinner • $–$$ • Cr • W+
Interior Mexican food, plus Tex-Mex and Peruvian dishes. Use of black beans, goat cheese, fresh poblano peppers, chipotle peppers, whole-wheat tortillas, jicama, and tomatillos sets this place apart from Austin's hundred-odd Tex-Mex beaneries. Weekend brunch.

TRUDY'S TEXAS STAR

409 W. 30th • 477-0646 • Open daily, breakfast, lunch, and dinner
$ • MC, V • W
Convenient to the UT campus, Trudy's offers a competent array of Tex-Mex and Southern food, efficient service, and late weekend hours. Bar.

Oriental and Indian

CHINA PALACE

6605 Airport • 451-7104 • Open daily, lunch and dinner • $$ • MC, V • W+
The Cantonese/Hunan/Szechuan menu is one of the longest in town, with separate sections dedicated to squid, cuttlefish, and sea cucumber. Hot pots and dim sum. Bar.

KIM PHUNG

7601 N. Lamar • 451-2464 • Open daily, lunch and dinner • $ • V, MC, DIS • W
Chinese dishes are served, but you come for the Vietnamese, especially Pho and Bun. Pho is noodle soup with beef, poultry, or seafood. Bun is noodles served with minced vegetables, and meat or tofu. There are several dozen variations to choose from.

KOREA HOUSE

2700 W. Anderson Ln. • Northwest • 458-2477 • Open daily, lunch and
dinner • $ • Cr • W+
Buried in the back of the Village Shopping Center, Korea House serves typical dishes like bulgokki, doegee kalbi, and kim chee, as well as sushi. Sushi bar.

KYOTO

315 Congress, upstairs • Downtown • 482-9010 • Open Tuesday–Friday for lunch, Monday–Saturday for dinner • $$–$$$ • MC, V
Sushi and other Japanese specialties like sukiyaki, tempura, and teriyaki in this sparsely appointed historic building. Sit at the sushi bar and watch the chefs and your fellow barfish. Bar.

TAJ PALACE

6700 Middle Fiskville Rd., behind Highland Mall • 452-9959
Open daily, lunch and dinner • $–$$ • AE, DC, DIS, MC, V • W+
The Palace's tandoori specialties, which include chicken, lamb, and seafood, are a tasty alternative barbecue fix. There are also the usual curries, fresh-baked breads, and desserts. Extensive vegetarian menu. Great lunchtime buffet. Bar.

TIEN HONG

8301 Burnet • 458-2263 • Open daily, lunch and dinner • $–$$ • Cr • W+
What really sets Tien Hong off from its hundreds of local competitors is the weekend dim sum brunch. Trolley carts are laden with steamed, boiled, and fried savory dumplings, sticky buns, stuffed shrimp, stuffed tofu cubes, and lots more. Bar.

Steaks

DAN MCKLUSKY'S

301 E. 6th; 10000 Research, at the Arboretum • 473-8924; 346-0780
Open daily for dinner, Monday–Friday for lunch on 6th St.; lunch and dinner daily at the Arboretum • $–$$ • Cr • W+
The waiter brings out the raw beef for your inspection before grilling. Side dishes and appetizers don't detract from the experience. The menu also has chicken, lamb chops, fresh fish, and other seafood entrées. Bar.

THE HOFFBRAU

613 W. 6th • 472-0822 • Open Monday–Friday, lunch and dinner • $ • W
Austin's Hoffbrau isn't a beer garden; it's a restaurant serving up grilled steaks (and chicken breasts) and a few simple side dishes in an unpretentious atmosphere. This is the original Hoffbrau, copied by others in Houston and Dallas. Beer.

ACCOMMODATIONS

($ = under $45, $$ = $46–$60, $$$ = $61–$80, $$$$ = $81–$100, $$$$$ = over $100)
Room tax 13%

Downtown

DOUBLETREE GUEST SUITES

303 W. 15th and Lavaca (78701) • 478-7000 or 800-222-TREE • $$$$$
W+ 2 rooms • No-smoking rooms
The 15-story, 189-unit Guest Quarters has one- and two-bedroom suites and four penthouses (all with complete kitchen facilities). It is convenient to both UT and the Capitol. Most rooms are no-smoking. Children under 18 stay free in room with parents. AARP senior discount and package plans available. Fire

sprinklers in rooms and room fire intercom system. Cable TV with HBO and pay channel. Room phones (charge for local calls). Pets OK (deposit). Bar. Restaurant with room service. Outdoor heated pool, exercise room, outdoor whirlpool, sauna. Free newspaper weekdays. Self-service laundry. One-day dry cleaning. Valet inside parking (charge).

DRISKILL HOTEL
604 Brazos at 6th (78701) • 474-5911, in Texas 800-252-9367 • $$$$$
W+ 3 rooms • No-smoking rooms
 LBJ kept a suite here. The grand lobby was once the biggest in Texas, and is still one of the nicest. Ditto the bar, dining room, and the ballrooms. The 12-story hotel has 177 rooms and nine suites ($$$$$+). Two no-smoking floors. Senior discount and package plans available. Fire sprinklers in rooms and room fire intercom system. Cable TV with movies. Room phones (charge for local calls). No pets. Restaurant with room service. Lobby bar and piano bar. Airport transportation (charge). Free coffee in lobby. Free newspaper. One-day dry cleaning. Valet inside parking (charge). Rooms with eastern exposure offer view of Old Pecan Street.

FOUR SEASONS
98 San Jacinto and E. Cesar Chavez (78701) • 478-4500 or 800-332-3442
$$$$$ • W+ 4 rooms • No-smoking rooms
 The 292-room Four Seasons is yards away from the Convention Center. Most rooms are no-smoking with one smoking floor. Family plan available. Children under 18 stay free in room with parents. Fire sprinklers in rooms and room fire intercom system. Cable TV with HBO and movies. Room phones (charge for local calls). Small pets OK. Restaurant with 24-hour room service. Lobby lounge. Outdoor heated pool, indoor whirlpool, saunas, exercise room. Memberships available for guests in health club. Free newspaper with breakfast. One-day dry cleaning. A southwestern theme predominates inside, belying the formal service. Request a lake view. The local rowing clubs are headquartered below and the Hike and Bike Trail runs by.

HOLIDAY INN—TOWN LAKE
20 N. IH-35, southbound feeder road, north bank of Town Lake • 472-8211 or 800-HOLIDAY (800-465-4329) • $$$–$$$$$ • W+ 10 rooms • No-smoking rooms
 Two towers convenient to IH-35, Town Lake, and the Convention Center, with 321 rooms (about 200 no-smoking) and an executive level atop each tower. Children under 18 stay free with parents. AARP discount, package plans. Room fire sprinklers and fire intercom system. Cable TV with HBO and movies. Two phones per room with data ports. Rooms have coffeemaker, iron/ironing board, and hair dryer. Restaurant, room service. Bar. Outdoor heated pool, exercise room, indoor whirlpool, sauna. Free inside parking and airport transportation. One-day dry cleaning.

MARRIOT AT THE CAPITOL
701 E. 11th and IH-35 • 404-6933, 800-228-9290 • $$$$–$$$$$ • W+ 4 rooms
No-smoking rooms
 The 16-story, 365-room Marriot is convenient to the University of Texas, State Capitol, Austin Convention Center, and 6th Street. Amenities include indoor/outdoor heated pool, saunas, whirlpool, exercise room, concierge floor,

restaurant, bar, and gift shop. All rooms have phones with data ports, cable TV with movies, hair dryer, iron/ironingboard, free newspaper. Fire sprinklers in rooms and room fire intercom system. There are 90 rooms designed especially for business travelers. No-smoking rooms. No pets. Negotiable rates.

OMNI HOTEL

700 San Jacinto (78701) • 476-3700 or 800-843-6664 • $$$$$ • W 4 rooms No-smoking rooms

The 14-story, 315-unit Omni includes 24 suites ($$$$$) and five no-smoking floors. Fire sprinklers in rooms and room fire intercom system. Cable TV with pay channels. Room phones (charge for local calls). Restaurant with room service. Lobby bar. Outdoor rooftop pool, exercise room, outdoor heated whirlpool, sauna. Inside parking. Airport transportation. One-day dry cleaning. Unabashedly modern, with lots of glass and chrome and polished red granite, arranged around a 200-foot-tall atrium.

RADISSON HOTEL—TOWN LAKE

111 E. Cesar Chavez and Congress, on Town Lake (78701) • 478-9611 or 800-333-3333 • $$$$ • W+ 1 room • No-smoking rooms

The 12-story Radisson Hotel has 280 rooms including 20 suites ($$$$$) and two no-smoking floors. Children under 12 stay free in room with parents. Senior discount and package plans available. Fire sprinklers in rooms and room fire intercom system. Cable TV with pay channel. Room phones (charge for local calls). Iron/ironing board in rooms. No pets. Restaurant with room service. Bar. Outdoor lakeside pool, exercise room. Airport transportation. Free morning coffee, coffeemakers in rooms. Free newspaper. One-day dry cleaning. Free inside parking. Convenient to the Convention Center. For a good view of Town Lake, ask for a southern exposure. The Town Lake Hike and Bike Trail is seconds away. Great place to watch the Congress Avenue bridge bats.

SHERATON

500 N. IH-35 and 5th (78701) • 480-8181 or 800-325-3535 • $$$$$ • W 3 rooms No-smoking rooms

The 18-story Sheraton is one of Austin's premier hotels, with imported marble, brass, and original art. The 254 units include seven suites ($$$$$) and four no-smoking floors. Children 12 and under stay free with parents. AARP discounts and package plans. Fire sprinklers in rooms and room fire intercom system. Cable TV with HBO and movies. Other amenities include irons/ironing boards, makeup mirrors, in-room coffee service, voice mail, and concierge floor. Room phones (charge for local calls). Bar. Restaurant with room service. Outdoor pool, exercise room, large whirlpool. Covered parking. Convenient to downtown and Convention Center.

North

RED LION HOTEL

6121 N. IH-35 and US 290, 3 miles north of Capitol (78751) • 323-5466 or 800-547-8010 • $$$$$ • W+ 2 rooms • No-smoking rooms

The Red Lion is convenient to Highland Mall, I-35, and the airport. The two wings (seven-story, five-story) contain 300 units, including four suites ($$$$$)

and two no-smoking floors. Children under 18 stay free with parents. Senior discount and package plans. Cable TV with movies. Room phones (charge for local calls). Pets OK. Restaurant with room service. Lounge. Outdoor heated pool, outdoor whirlpool, exercise room. Free coffee in lobby. Free airport shuttle. One-day dry cleaning. Free outdoor parking.

DOUBLETREE HOTEL

6505 N. IH-35, near Highland Mall • 454-3737, 800-222-8733 • $$$–$$$$$
W+ 4 rooms • No-smoking rooms
The six-story, 350-room Doubletree has two no-smoking floors. Children under 18 stay free with parents. Senior discount, package plans. Cable TV and on-command video. Room phones (charge for local calls), data ports. Restaurant, room service. Lounge. Outdoor pool and whirlpool, fitness center, outdoor volleyball court. Free airport transportation. One-day dry cleaning. Self, valet parking. Spanish colonial/Mediterranean ambience.

EMBASSY SUITES

North: 5901 N. IH-35, near Highland Mall (78723); Town Lake: 300 S. Congress, near Town Lake (78704) • 454-8004; 469-9000 or 800-362-2779 $$$$$ • W+ 10 rooms, 8 rooms downtown • No-smoking rooms
Ten stories, approximately 260 suites each location, including four no-smoking floors. Except for the view from your bedroom window, you get the same deal at either location. Children under 12 stay free with parents. Senior discount and package plans. Cable TV with HBO and movies. Room phones (charge for local calls). No pets. Restaurant. Bar. Indoor pool, indoor whirlpool, sauna. Free airport transportation. Coffeemakers, refrigerators, and microwaves in rooms. Free breakfast. Free newspaper. Free cocktails. Self-service laundry and one-day dry cleaning. Free parking.

NORTH HILTON AND TOWERS

6000 Middle Fiskville Rd., between IH-35 and Highland Mall (78752)
451-5757 or 800-445-8667 • $$$–$$$$$ • W+ 5 rooms • No-smoking rooms
Highland Mall is an easy three-minute walk from this 237-unit hotel (nine-story tower and motel-type rooms) with three suites ($$$$$) and about half the rooms no-smoking. Senior discount and family plan. Children under 18 stay free in room. Fire sprinklers in rooms and room fire intercom system. Cable TV with HBO and movies. Room phones (charge for local calls). Pets OK (deposit). Restaurant. Bar. Outdoor heated pool, exercise room. Free airport transportation. One-day dry cleaning. Ask for a room facing west.

RENAISSANCE AUSTIN HOTEL

9721 Arboretum Blvd., near the intersection of Loop 360 and Research (78759)
343-2626 or 800-468-3571 • $$$$$ • W+ 16 rooms • No-smoking rooms
The ten-story, 478-unit Renaissance echoes the spirit of the grand hotels of yesteryear, with lots of marble and granite, a soaring atrium, rare art, attentive service, and fine food. Seven no-smoking floors, 47 suites ($$$$$), and concierge floor. Children under 18 stay free in room with parents. Senior discount. Cable TV with HBO. Room phones (charge for local calls). Fire sprinklers in rooms and room fire intercom system. Restaurants (*see* Restaurants, Trattoria Grande), 24-hour room service. Bar and club. Indoor and outdoor heated pools, indoor

whirlpool, sauna, health club, one-acre lake. Airport transportation (charge). Free wakeup call, coffee, and newspaper. One-day dry cleaning. Gift shop. Some rooms have nice views of the northwest hills. Austin's toniest shopping center, the Arboretum, is next door.

South

HYATT REGENCY HOTEL

208 Barton Springs and Riverside, near S. Congress and south of Town Lake (78704) • 477-1234 or 800-233-1234 • $$$$$ • W+ 4 rooms • No-smoking rooms
At the 17-story 446-unit Hyatt Regency all rooms open onto the atrium lobby. Four no-smoking floors, 17 suites ($$$$$). Senior discount, family plan and package plans available. Children under 18 stay free with parents. Fire sprinklers in rooms and room fire intercom system. Cable TV with HBO and movies. Room phones (charge for local calls) and voice mail. Two restaurants and two lounges. Outdoor pool, outdoor whirlpool. Free airport transportation. Free newspaper weekdays. Self-service laundry and one-day dry cleaning. Free parking. The creek flowing through the Branchwater Lounge downstairs flows into Town Lake. Ask for a lake view. Convenient to Town Lake Hike and Bike Trail and downtown.

OMNI SOUTHPARK

4140 Governor's Row at IH-35 • 488-2222 or 800-433-2241 • $$$$ • W+ 3 rooms No-smoking rooms
Convenient to the new airport, the 313-room Omni is executed in lots of heavy wood, imported marble, leaded and beveled glass, brass, and plants. Cable TV with movies. Restaurant, bar, indoor-outdoor swimming pool, sauna, whirlpool, exercise room, free parking.

Bed and Breakfast Inns

CARRINGTON'S BLUFF

1900 David, off W. MLK Jr. • 479-0638 • $$$–$$$$ • W partial No-smoking rooms
1877 Greek Revival house, eight rooms, near UT. Rooms are furnished with antiques. Lovely gardens. Breakfast served on fine English china. Children over five free in parents' room. Weekly and long-term rates available. Cable TV with premium channels. Room phones, no charge for local calls. Pets OK, with deposit. Free coffee, free newspaper, free breakfast, one-day dry cleaning. Hair dryers and robes in rooms. Afternoon tea.

FAIRVIEW

1304 Newning • 444-4746, 800-310-4746 • $$$$–$$$$$ • No-smoking rooms
Colonial Revival house, six rooms, surrounded by landscaped lawn and gardens, including a rose garden and ancient live oaks. Full breakfast; light afternoon refreshments. Well-behaved children OK. Free cable television and telephone in room. No pets. Free coffee and breakfast.

GOVERNORS' INN

611 W. 22nd • 479-0638 • $$$–$$$$ • W partial • No-smoking rooms

Neo-Classical house close to UT, ten rooms, furnished with antiques. Breakfast and tea served on fine English china. Children over five free in parents' room. Weekly and long-term rates available. Cable TV with premium channels. Room phones, no charge for local calls. No pets. Free coffee, free newspaper, free breakfast, one-day dry cleaning. Hair dryers and robes in rooms. Afternoon tea.

BANDERA

Bandera County Seat • 877 • (830)

There are several stories about how Bandera got its name. According to one, the Treaty of 1732 set a dividing line between Spanish territory and Apache lands at a nearby pass. A banner was placed at the highest point in the pass to remind both sides of the boundary. Since "bandera" means flag or banner in Spanish, the pass became known as Bandera Pass. The other closely related story is that the Spanish general who drove off the Apaches (temporarily) in the 1730s was named Bandera and that the mountains in the area were named in his honor.

About 1852, the first settlers moved in. They made their living cutting the cypress trees along the Medina River and making shingles.

A few miles away is Camp Verde, where the then-secretary of war Jefferson Davis set up the U.S. Army's camel corps in 1856. He imported camels and handlers to test his theory that they would be a dependable means of transportation in the semiarid plains. The experiment had limited success.

Indian troubles continued, so the Texas Rangers set up a patrol route that stretched about 100 miles from San Antonio to Kerrville. Since Bandera was close to the midway point, the town became a focal point for Ranger activities along the road.

Today this tiny Hill Country town still retains its frontier appearance and heritage, billing itself as the "Cowboy Capital of the World." If that isn't a hefty enough title, it has also been designated the "Dude Ranch Capital of the World." In keeping with that, one of the main businesses in Bandera is dude ranching—where tourists can experience first hand a tame version of cowboy and ranch life (*see* Accommodations).

TOURIST SERVICES

BANDERA COUNTY CHAMBER OF COMMERCE

1808 Hwy 16 South (P.O. Box 171, 78003) • 796-3045 or 800-364-3833 • W

MUSEUMS

FRONTIER TIMES MUSEUM

506 13th St • 796-3864 • Monday–Saturday 10–4:30; Sunday 1–4:30
Adults $2, children 6 to 18 25¢ • W

More than 40,000 items in this eclectic, homey museum dedicated to preserving relics of frontier days and a bit more. Artifacts range from old firearms and buggy whips to spearheads and saddles. Great bargain entertainment for kids.

HISTORIC PLACES

More than 30 historic places are listed in a brochure given out by the Chamber of Commerce. Among them the **Bandera County Courthouse** (1890), and an older courthouse (1869) at 12th and Maple, and the **St. Stanislaus Catholic Church** (1876).

SPORTS AND ACTIVITIES

RODEOS

Several area locations • Call 796-3045 (Chamber of Commerce) for details
Held twice weekly from Memorial Day to Labor Day
What would a Cowboy Capital be without rodeos? Call to see where and when. Big one on Memorial Day weekend.

HORSEBACK RIDING

Call 796-3045 (Chamber of Commerce) to see where you can hitch a ride on a mild broncho. Several dude ranches offer day rides.

SIDE TRIPS

HILL COUNTRY STATE NATURAL AREA

Take TX Hwy 173 south to FM 1077 (Dixie Dude Rd.). Approximately 10 miles from town • **796-4413** • **Hours and days vary. Call ahead.**
A 4,753-acre primitive park for hikers and horseback riders.

LOST MAPLES STATE NATURAL AREA

Take TX Hwy 16 west to Medina, then FM 337 to Vanderpool, then north on RR 187 about 4 miles to park • **966-3413** • **Open daily 8–10 for day use; at all times for camping** • **$4 per person ($5 October–November)** • **W variable**
Depending on weather conditions, bigtooth maples usually peak in early November. Park facilities include picnic areas, primitive campsites, RV camping sites, and hiking trails. For information write: Park Superintendent, HC 01, Box 156, Vanderpool 78885.

MEDINA LAKE

Take TX Hwy 16 east to Pipe Creek, then south on FM 1283 to Park Rd. 37. Approximately 22 miles • **(See Castroville)**

ANNUAL EVENTS

MEMORIAL DAY WEEKEND

Various locations • 796-3045 (Chamber of Commerce) • Free • W variable
Activities include a parade, arts and crafts fair, and rodeo.

RESTAURANTS

($ = under $7, $$ = $8–$17, $$$ = $18–$25, $$$$ = over $25 for one person excluding drinks, tax, and tip.)

O.S.T. RESTAURANT

Main and Cypress • 796-3836 • Breakfast, lunch, and dinner daily • $
No Cr • W

This down-home cafe serves Tex-Mex staples, as well as chicken-fried and other steaks.

ACCOMMODATIONS

($ = under $45, $$ = $46–$60, $$$ = $61–$80, $$$$ = $81–$100, $$$$$ = over $100.)
Room tax 12%

BANDERA LODGE
1900 TX Hwy 16S • 796-3093 • $$
Forty-four rooms, cable TV with HBO, room phones (free local calls), pets OK, lounge, restaurant, outdoor pool.

LOST VALLEY RESORT RANCH
On Hwy 16, 2 miles east • 460-8008 • $$–$$$
Forty-eight rooms, some kitchenettes, phones. Eighteen-hole golf course, pool. Golf package.

RIVER OAK INN
1105 Main • 796-7751 • $–$$
Twenty-eight rooms, restaurant.

Dude Ranches and Others

Besides the traditional dude ranches Bandera is known for, you'll also find condos, cabins, RV parks, and bed and breakfasts. Ask Chamber of Commerce for list. Dude ranches typically offer rooms or cottages with meals and activities. Rates run around $$–$$$ per day, but most offer weekly and weekend rates. Among the ranches are **Mayan Ranch** (796-3312), on the Medina River with 67 rooms; **Flying L Guest Ranch** (800-292-5134), with 41 suites and golf course; **Dixie Dude Ranch** (800-375-9255), a working ranch; and **Twin Elm Ranch** (796-3628), on the Medina River. Most all offer horseback riding, hayrides, pool.

BASTROP

Bastrop County Seat • 4,389 • 512
Bastrop is named for Stephen F. Austin's friend, Philip Hendrick Nering Bogel, the self-proclaimed "Baron de Bastrop." The town was established in 1829 on the site of a old Spanish fort, where *El Camino Real* crossed the Colorado River. Three Bastrop men signed the Texas Declaration of Independence, 11 died at the Alamo, and around 60 fought at San Jacinto. Bastrop is part of the "Lost Pines of Texas," an isolated, 70-square-mile forest of Southern pines stranded 80 miles west of the eastern edge of the great pine belt.

The Bastrop Advertiser, published since 1853, is the oldest continuously published weekly in Texas. Lock's Drug Store on Main Street has a turn-of-the-century interior and soda fountain. In 1979, 131 Bastrop buildings and sites were admitted to the National Register of Historic Places. Bastrop has dozens of restored nineteenth- and early twentieth-century commercial buildings and homes to see.

TOURIST SERVICES

BASTROP CHAMBER OF COMMERCE
1009 Main • 321-3419 • Monday–Friday 8–5 • W

MUSEUMS

BASTROP HISTORICAL MUSEUM
702 Main • 321-6177 • Open daily, afternoons only
Adults about $2, children under 12 50¢ • W

The original little red house was built in the 1850s, the brick wings were added in the 1970s to provide exhibit space. Some of the furniture, clothing, dolls, books, and documents on display date back to the Texas Revolution.

BASTROP COUNTY COURTHOUSE AND OLD JAIL
Pine and Water • W

The three-story courthouse, built in 1884, is still in use. The old jail next door, built in 1892, had jailer's quarters on the first floor, cells on the upper floors, and a gallows in the middle. It was used as a jail until 1974.

OTHER POINTS OF INTEREST

BASTROP OPERA HOUSE
709 Spring • 321-6283 • Admission to shows

Built in 1889, the Opera House hosted concerts, touring shows, pageants, graduations, vaudeville, and movies for nearly 90 years. When threatened with demolition, local citizens saved and restored it. Plays and shows are presented on a regular basis, mostly on weekends.

BASTROP STATE PARK
TX 21, about 1 mile east • 321-2101 • Open daily • Admission about $3 per person • W variable (some W+ facilities)

Located in the Lost Pines, this 3,500-acre park has a swimming pool (summer only), golf course, 10-acre lake, hiking trails, picnic tables, tent and RV campsites, and 13 cabins, which may be booked 90 days in advance. Greens fee for the 18-hole golf course is about $10. Call 321-2327. Park Rd. 1 connects with Buescher State Park to the east. Write: Park Superintendent, P.O. Box 518, Bastrop 78602.

LAKE BASTROP
Take TX 95 north about 3 miles to FM 1441, then east to North Shore Recreation Area • 321-3307 • Open daily (South Shore Park usually closed Labor Day through April) • Admission • W variable

This 906-acre lake offers recreational facilities for boating, fishing, swimming, waterskiing, picnicking, and camping.

ACCOMMODATIONS

($ = under $45, $$ = $46–60, $$$ = $61–80, $$$$ = $81–$100, $$$$$-over $100)
Room tax 13%

TAHITIAN VILLAGE INN

In Tahitian Village (a residential development), about 2.5 miles east at East Loop 150 • 321-1135 • $$–$$$ • AE, DIS, MC, V • W+ 1 room

Twenty spacious habitations with microwave, coffeemaker, and refrigerator in several small buildings. Cable TV. Room phones. No pets. Restaurant. Club. Outdoor pool, tennis courts. Write P.O. Box 636, 78602. Pine Forest Golf Course is close by. The course is eighteen holes; greens fee starts at about $20. Call 321-1181.

PFEIFFER HOUSE

1802 Main and Elm • 321-2100 • $$ • No Cr

Restored 1901 Victorian home; three bedrooms with one shared bath. No children. No pets. Wake-up coffee and full breakfast.

BELTON

Bell County Seat • 14,500 • (254)

Belton began as a small fort established by the Texas Rangers in 1836, but it was later abandoned. The city and county were established in 1850 and both named after Peter Hansborough Bell, who was governor then. Belton owed much of its early growth to its location on the Chisholm Trail cattle drives as well as for its stagecoach stop between Dallas and Austin.

TOURIST SERVICES

BELTON AREA CHAMBER OF COMMERCE

412 E. Central (P.O. Box 659, 76513) • 939-3551, Fax 939-1061 • W

MUSEUMS

BELL COUNTY MUSEUM

201 N. Main at 1st Ave. • 933-5243 • Tuesday–Saturday 1–5 Free (donation) • W

Located in the restored 1904 Carnegie Library building, rotating exhibits and other displays depict the history of the county and Central Texas region. A large portion is memorabilia of Miriam A. "Ma" Ferguson, the first woman governor of Texas and a Bell County native.

HISTORIC PLACES

The **Bell County Courthouse,** Main and Central, was designed by J. N. Preston and Sons, the same architects who did Austin's Driskill Hotel, and completed in 1883. It was in the **McWhirter-Kimball House,** 400 N. Pearl, that Martha McWhirter founded her Sanctificationist religion. Some of Belton's wealthiest and best-educated women left their husbands to live here in a form of commune. The movement lasted from 1870 to 1910, and the members retired rich. On the night of May 25, 1874, a mob stormed the **Old Stone Jail,** 210 N.

Pearl, and shot nine horse thieves held in an iron cage. The jail later became a hotel owned by the Sanctificationists.

OTHER POINTS OF INTEREST

BELTON LAKE

Take TX 317 (Main St.) north to FM 439 then west to the lake • 939-2461 (Army Corps of Engineers) • Open at all times • Free • W variable

There are 13 parks along the shoreline of this 12,300-acre lake. Facilities are provided for swimming, boating (including rental), fishing, water skiing, picnicking, and camping (fee). An unusual sight at the lake is an 800-foot mural depicting the history of Texas painted on the dam's emergency spillway executed by the art department of Mary Hardin-Baylor. For information write: Lake Manager, P.O. Box 209, Belton 76513.

STILLHOUSE HOLLOW LAKE

Take US 190 west to Simmonds Rd., then south to lake • 939-2461 (Army Corps of Engineers) • Open at all times • Free • W variable

A 6,430-acre lake with six parks on the shoreline. Facilities are provided for swimming, boating (including rental), fishing, picnicking, and tent camping (fee). The headquarters is on FM 1670 just north of the dam. There is a fishing marina at Stillhouse Park near the dam. For information write: Reservoir Manager, Route 3, Box 3407, Belton 76513.

SPORTS AND ACTIVITIES

LEON VALLEY GOLF COURSE

709 E. 24th • 939-5271 • 18-hole course. Greens fee: weekdays $10.85, weekends $13

COLLEGES AND UNIVERSITIES

UNIVERSITY OF MARY HARDIN-BAYLOR

College and 10th • 939-8642 • W variable

Founded in 1845 by Texas Baptists, it was located at Independence and moved to Belton in 1886. Originally called the Female Department of Baylor University, its name was changed several times, then assumed its present name in 1934. Visitors are welcome at sports events, music department recitals, concerts, theater productions, the annual Easter Pageant, and the **Sid Richardson Museum** in the Mabee Student Center that displays items relating to the university's history.

ANNUAL EVENTS

July

PRCA RODEO AND JULY 4TH CELEBRATION

Bell County Expo Center, South Loop 121, west of IH-35; and Nolan Creek at Confederate Park (off IH-35, Central Ave. exit) • 939-3551 (Chamber of Commerce) • 4 days including July 4 • Rodeo admission about $7.50 W variable

According to local historians, the Fourth of July celebration started in the early 1850s. The rodeo joined the festivities in 1924. The major events take place on July 4 and include a parade, bluegrass music festival, arts and crafts show, carnival, and the rodeo.

RESTAURANTS

($ = under $7, $$ = $8–$17, $$$ = $18–$25, $$$$ = over $25 for one person excluding drinks, tax, and tip.)

FRANK'S LAKEVIEW & ANCHOR CLUB
2207 Lake Rd. • 939-5771 • Open 365 days a year for breakfast, lunch, and dinner • $–$$$ • Cr • W • Children's plates

This family-owned-and-operated landmark began in 1953 when Frank sold soda pop and snow cones to workers building the Belton Dam. (It's only five minutes from town, but call for directions.) Casually elegant with great ambience, it has a 50-foot glassed wall and a sun deck, where you can snack and enjoy the view of the dam, spillway, and Leon River. The extensive menu includes Alaskan King crab legs, lobster, seafood platters, steaks, sandwiches, burgers—and a nice wine list. Diners receive guest cards to the Anchor Club, which has dances on Friday and Saturday.

ACCOMMODATIONS

($ = under $45, $$ = $46–$60, $$$ = $61–$80, $$$$ = $81–$100, $$$$$ = over $100) Room tax 11%

BEST WESTERN RIVER FOREST MOTEL
I-35 (exit 294 B) and 6th Ave. • 939-5711 or 800-528-1234 • $–$$ No-smoking rooms

The one- and two-story motel has 48 units, including one suite and 25 no-smoking rooms. Cable TV. Room phones (free local calls). Pets limited. Outdoor pool, playground. Free continental breakfast in lobby. Hair dryers in all rooms.

Bed and Breakfast

BELLE OF BELTON
1019 N. Main • 939-6478 • $$–$$$

This historic 1893 mansion offers four rooms and two baths all delightfully furnished in antiques. A full breakfast is served in the dining room. No children under 12, no pets, and no smoking in the house.

BOERNE

Kendall County Seat • 5,200 • (830)

Boerne (pronounced "Burney") was named after a German journalist. The first real settlers were a group of German intellectuals who came about 1849 and set up a farm commune. Named after Ludwig Börne, a refugee German political journalist and satirist, the town was settled in 1851.

The county was named after Boerne resident George W. Kendall, who, in 1837, was one of the founders of the *New Orleans Picayune*. Later he became one of the Southwest's biggest sheep raisers on his ranch that encompassed much of the present-day Kendall County.

When the railroad came to town in 1887, it helped turn Boerne into a tourist center for people from San Antonio, some 30 miles away. Today the town has attracted a number of artists, and still attracts tourists who come to enjoy a day in the peaceful old town or to see the nearby caves.

TOURIST SERVICES

GREATER BOERNE AREA CHAMBER OF COMMERCE
One Main Plaza, 78006 • 249-8000

MUSEUMS

KUHLMANN-KING HISTORICAL HOUSE MUSEUM
402 E. Blanco, behind City Hall • 249-2030 • Sunday 1–4 or by appointment
Free (donations accepted) • W

Built between 1885 and 1890, the house contains some period furnishings. Behind the museum is the Archives Building, built around 1900, which contains historical documents on the Boerne area and is usually open Thursdays 9 to 4.

HISTORIC PLACES

There are several historic buildings about town, besides the very obvious one, **Ye Kendall Inn** (*See* Accommodations). Among them are the **Kendall County Courthouse** (at Main and E. San Antonio), and next door an old jail built in 1887, also the **Robert E. Lee House** (S. Main and Evergreen), and **Theis House** (100 block of Newton), which dates back to around 1858.

OTHER POINTS OF INTEREST

CIBOLO WILDERNESS TRAIL & AGRICULTURAL HERITAGE CENTER
City Park at Hwy. 46 • Open daily

Nature trail for hiking. Call 249-2814 for Ag Center days and hours open. Has working blacksmith shop and antique farm equipment. Also Nature Center.

CASCADE CAVERNS
Take I-10 about 3 miles south, then take exit 543 to Cascade Caverns Rd., then follow signs about 3 miles to caverns (226 Cascade Caverns Rd.) • 755-8080
Daily 9–6 (to 5 in winter) • Adults $7.45, children $5.25

These caverns take their name from a waterfall that plunges about 90 feet from a shallow cave containing an underground stream into the main cave. Guided tours take about 45 minutes to an hour to complete. The caverns are about one-third-mile long and the walk is relatively easy. On ground level there's a 105-acre park.

SIDE TRIPS

CAVE WITHOUT A NAME
Take FM 474 east about 6 miles to Kreutzberg Rd., then follow signs about 5 miles to cave (325 Kreutzberg Rd.) • 537-4212 • Wednesday–Monday 9–6, closed Tuesday • Admission

This cave is off the beaten tourist track and a little hard to find. You might want to call first, since this is a big cave but a small operation.

GUADALUPE RIVER STATE PARK

Take TX 46 east about 13 miles to Park Rd. 31, then north about 3 miles to park
438-2656 • **Open daylight hours for day use, at all times for camping**
$4 per person • W variable
The 1,900 acres are cut in two by the Guadalupe River, and its rapids. Facilities available for canoeing, fishing, swimming, hiking, picnicking, and camping (fee). For information write: Park Superintendent, HC 54, Box 2087, Bulverde 78163.

ANNUAL EVENTS

BERGES FEST

Main Plaza • 249-8000 (Chamber of Commerce) • Thursday–Sunday of
Father's Day weekend in June • Admission • W variable
The area's German heritage is emphasized by oompah music and street dances, plus a parade, an arts and crafts fair, entertainment, contests, and children's activities.

RESTAURANTS

($ = under $8, $$ = $8–$18, $$$ = $18–$25, $$$$ = over $25 for one person excluding drinks, tax, and tip.)

COUNTRY SPIRIT

707 S. Main • 249-3607 • Lunch and dinner Wednesday–Monday, closed
Tuesday • $$ • Cr • W
Set in a restored 1870s home, this restaurant offers a variety of entrees from charbroiled shrimp to chicken-fried steak. Bar.

PEACH TREE KOUNTRY KITCHEN

448 S. Main • 249-8583 • Tuesday–Saturday, lunch only • Cr
Victorian tearoom with home cooked meals and linen tablecloths. Walnut chicken breast, *quiche,* cheese rolls, scratch desserts.

PO PO FAMILY RESTAURANT

Take I-10W 7 miles to Welfare exit (exit 533), then west about ½ mile • **537-4194**
Lunch and dinner Tuesday–Sunday • $–$$ • AE, MC, V • W
This old stone house restaurant offers a variety of steaks, chicken, seafood, and all-you-can-eat down-home dinner specials. Outdoor dining available. Bar.

SCUZZI RISTORANTE ITALIANO

128 W. Blanco at Ye Kendall Inn • 249-8886
Lunch and dinner Tuesday–Sunday • $–$$ • Cr
Italian entrées, plus burgers and sandwiches. Located in historic Ye Kendall Inn.

ACCOMMODATIONS

($ = under $45, $$ = $46–$60, $$$ = $61–$80, $$$$ = $81–$100, $$$$$ = over $100)
Room tax 13%

GUADALUPE RIVER RANCH

Take Blanco Rd. (Hwy. 474) northeast 8 miles • **537-4837 or 800-460-2005**
$$–$$$$$ (includes 3 meals)
On 360 acres, 34 rooms, pool, sauna, tennis court, gourmet food.

TAPATIO RESORT AND COUNTRY CLUB

Take Johns Rd. off Main and go about 4.5 miles west following signs. **Box 550, 78006** • **537-4611 or 800-999-3299** • **$$$–$$$$**
The 2-story resort offers 89 rooms, TV, room phones (free local calls), no pets, lounge, restaurant, pool, outdoor spa, sauna, exercise room, 18-hole golf courses, four tennis courts. Most rooms are large with wet bar and patio.

Bed and Breakfast

BORGMAN'S SUNDAY HOUSE BED & BREAKFAST

911 S. Main • **249-9563** • **$$**
The one-story Sunday House Inn has 12 rooms, cable TV, no pets.

YE KENDALL INN

128 W. Blanco on Town Square • **249-2138** • **$$$**
This two-story inn has 13 units including 4 suites all with private baths. Restaurant downstairs (*see* Restaurants), continental breakfast in rooms. Restored hotel built in 1859 and listed in the National Register of Historic Places.

BRADY

McCulloch County Seat • **6,773** • **(915)**
A monument on the courthouse lawn shows a map of Texas with a heart in the middle and the words: Heart of Texas—Brady. Brady is the closest city to the geographic center of Texas. The actual geographic center—"an imaginary point whose coordinates divide the state into four equal areas"—is on a ranch about 20 miles northeast, but that's close enough for Brady.

TOURIST SERVICES

BRADY CHAMBER OF COMMERCE

101 E. 1st St. at Bridge, 76825, one block south of the courthouse • **597-3491, Fax 597-2420, e-mail coc@centex.net**

MUSEUMS

HEART OF TEXAS HISTORICAL MUSEUM

High and Main • **597-3491 (Chamber of Commerce)** • **Saturday–Monday 1–5, or by appointment for large groups** • **Free (donation)** • **W downstairs only (slide show of rest of museum available)**
The museum is housed in the old jail, a three-story castle-like building that served the county from 1910 to 1974, and was restored even to the tint of the paint. Emphasis is on county history and the restored jail cells and gallows.

OTHER POINTS OF INTEREST

BRADY LAKE

Take FM 2028 (17th St.) west about 5 miles, then north (left) on Lake Rd. to park • **597-1823 (Brady Lake Store)** • **Open at all times** • **Free** • **W variable**

This 2,200-acre municipal lake offers facilities for boating, fishing (fishing barge), swimming, waterskiing, picnicking, and camping (fee). There are 20 cabanas for rent. (Reservations: Brady Lake Store.)

SPORTS AND ACTIVITIES

Golf

MUNICIPAL GOLF COURSE

US 87 about 1.5 miles northwest of Town Square • **597-6010** • **9-hole course. Greens fee for 18 or more holes: weekdays $9.74, weekends and holidays $12.99. Municipal swimming pool at same location.**

ANNUAL EVENTS

June

TEXAS STATE MUZZLE LOADING CHAMPIONSHIP

Kenneth Medlock Range, Brady Lake. *Take FM 2028 (17th St.) west about 5 miles, then north (left) on Lake Rd. to range* • **597-3491 (Chamber of Commerce)** • **Usually Wednesday–Sunday early in June** • **Free** • **W**

Although some wear buckskin, fur hats, and other nineteenth-century clothing, most dress casually while competing in the Texas State Muzzle loading Championship. Held at Brady Lake for six days, ending the second full weekend in June, it includes competition in flintlock and percussion rifles and pistols, muskets, and muzzle loading shotguns. (Children compete with their peers.) Also fun to watch: the Frost on the Cactus Shoot (a three-day event ending the second full weekend in March) and the Fall Shoot (a four-day meet ending the first full weekend in October). Interested? Contact Patsy Lohn, TMLRA secretary, at 597-2947.

September

WORLD CHAMPIONSHIP BARBECUE GOAT COOK-OFF

Richards Park, US 87 (Commerce St.) just west of downtown • **597- 3491 (Chamber of Commerce)** • **Friday and Saturday of Labor Day weekend Free** • **W**

More than 100 cooking teams from all over the U.S. and some foreign countries compete here. Continuous entertainment and various contests including the Goat Pill Flip-Off (similar to cow chip throwing) and an Arts and Craft Fair.

RESTAURANTS

($ = under $7, $$ = $8–$17, $$$ = $18–$25, $$$$ = over $25 for one person excluding drinks, tax, and tip.)

LUIGI'S

1104 S. Bridge (Hwy 87) 8 blocks south of the square • 597-2372
Lunch and dinner every day but Tuesday when closed. • Smoking and
no-smoking sections • $–$$ • Cr

Named for its owner, Luigi's features chicken, fish, steaks, and venison as well as Italian dishes and homemade pastries in a one-story, turn-of-the-century cottage, with table linens, candlelight, and a fireplace. Lights twinkle in trees for outside dining, too. Hunters, who flock to the area, bring their quail, dove, wild turkey, and venison for Luigi to cook.

ACCOMMODATIONS

($ = under $45, $$ = $46–$60, $$$ = $61–$80, $$$$ = $81–$100, $$$$$ = over $100)
Room tax 10%

SUNSET INN

US 87S at US 190S • 597-0789 • $–$$ • W+ 1 room • No-smoking rooms

One of the 44 rooms in the one-story inn has a king-sized bed and Jacuzzi; 24 are no-smoking. Cable TV. Room phones (free local calls). Pets OK. Free continental breakfast and coffee in lobby.

Bed and Breakfast

BRADY HOUSE

704 S. Bridge • 597-5265 • $$$ • V, MC, DIS • Children with prior approval
No pets or smoking in house

This antique-filled Craftsman-style home has one suite and two guest rooms with private baths on the second floor. A full breakfast is served family-style. On almost an acre, it's six blocks from downtown, where you'll find the McCulloch County Courthouse, Cafe on the Square, and antique shops.

BROWNWOOD

Brown County Seat • 19,000 • (915)

In 1828, Captain Henry Stephenson Brown led a group of men to this area on a successful raid against the Indians to recover about 500 horses and mules stolen from his ranch near Gonzales. In 1856 the legislature created Brown County to help restrain the Indians by providing the frontier with local government. This was more a gesture than a reality since only two families lived in Brown County at the time.

The county settled down by the time the Santa Fe Railroad arrived in 1885, and by 1920 Brownwood was the largest cotton-buying center west of Fort Worth. Oil was discovered, and a boom was on.

The boom is gone, but Brownwood remains an agriculture center.

TOURIST SERVICES

BROWNWOOD CHAMBER OF COMMERCE

521 E. Baker (P.O. Box 880, 76804) • 646-9535, Fax 643-6686

MUSEUMS

BROWN COUNTY HISTORICAL MUSEUM

500 N. Center, one block northwest of courthouse • 649-8700
Saturday 9–3 or by appointment • Free (donations) • W entrance in rear
   The most interesting point about this museum is the building itself, which is
the fortress-like old county jail built in 1902, making it the oldest public building in the county. Displays depicting the life and history of the county are on
the first floor.

COLLEGES AND UNIVERSITIES

HOWARD PAYNE UNIVERSITY

Austin Ave. (FM 2524) at Coggin • 649-8709 • W variable • Designated
visitor parking
   Founded in 1889, this liberal arts university, owned by the Baptist General
Convention of Texas, reportedly produces more Baptist pastors than any other
university in the state. A major tourist attraction on the campus is **The Douglas
MacArthur Academy of Freedom.** It contains five great halls and two exhibit
rooms depicting man's quest for freedom through western civilization. The
three-story Hall of Christian Civilization contains one of the largest murals in
Texas, a representation of man's relationship to God. The Mediterranean Hall
contains facsimiles of Egyptian statuary and the Rosetta stone. Magna Charta
Hall is a medieval European castle dominated by a mural of the signing of the
Magna Charta. Independence Hall is a faithful copy of the original in Philadelphia. The MacArthur Gallery includes original memorabilia and his famed
corncob pipe. Admission is free and one-hour guided tours are conducted
when the university is in session. Call for times. For groups of 20 or more, call
849-8700 48 hours in advance.

PERFORMING ARTS

BROWNWOOD COLISEUM

500 E. Baker at Carnegie • 646-3586 • Admission • W+
   The circular auditorium is used for everything from symphony concerts to
rodeos, including the Lone Star Fair & Expo/Rattle Snake Show, third weekend
in March; and Baker Street Jazz Festival, first Saturday in October. Nominal
admission for both.

SIDE TRIPS

LAKE BROWNWOOD STATE RECREATION AREA

Take TX 279 northwest about 16 miles to Park Rd. 15, then east about 6 miles
784-5223 • Open daily 8–10 for day use, at all times for camping • Fee
W+ but not all areas
   This 538-acre park, on the shores of the 7,380-acre lake, has facilities for fishing (lighted pier), boating, swimming, waterskiing, picnicking, hiking and
nature study, and camping (fee). Also, cabins, lodges, and a group camp with a
dining hall. For information: Park Superintendent, Route 5, Box 160, 76801.
Contact the Brownwood Chamber of Commerce (646-9535) about commercial
facilities.

ANNUAL EVENTS

September

PECAN VALLEY ART FESTIVAL

Festival Park, Milam Dr. *Take US 377 south to Morris Rd., then east (left) to Burnett, then south (right) to Milam* • **646-9535 (Chamber of Commerce) Third weekend in September • Admission • W variable**

Artists and craftsmen sell all types of artwork. Silent auction Saturday night in Brownwood Coliseum. Bands and entertainment all weekend.

RESTAURANTS

($ = under $7, $$ = $8–$17, $$$ = $18–$25, $$$$ = over $25 for one person excluding drinks, tax, and tip.)

UNDERWOOD'S CAFETERIA

402 W. Commerce (US 67 and 84) • **646-6110** • **Lunch and dinner Thursday–Tuesday. Closed Wednesday** • **$–$$** • **No Cr** • **W** • **Children's plates**

Though still famous for barbecue, Underwood's now has an extensive menu that includes seafood, fried chicken, and weekly specials. It's been in business since 1946.

SECTION HAND STEAKHOUSE

Brady Highway 377 S. • **643-1581** • **Lunch and dinner daily** • **$–$$ Cr • W**

This family restaurant cooks steaks just the way you like them with lots of extras and giant salad bar.

ACCOMMODATIONS

($ = under $45, $$ = $46–$60, $$$ = $61–$80, $$$$ = $81–$100, $$$$$ = over $100) Room tax 13%

GOLD KEY INN

515 E. Commerce • **646-2551** • **$–$$** • **W+ 1 room** • **No-smoking rooms**

This two-story motel has 140 deluxe rooms (85 are no-smoking) with coffeemakers, cable TV, free HBO, and phones (free local calls). Amenities: a hot breakfast buffet in lobby, heated outdoor pool, sauna, hot tub, exercise room, meeting rooms, banquet hall. Fax and copy service available.

BUCHANAN DAM

Llano County • 1,099 • 512

Pronounced BUCK-anan, the town grew with the construction of the dam in the 1930s. The two-mile-long dam consists of a series of arches and is considered the largest multiarch dam in the country. It backs up the Colorado River to form the highest and largest of the Highland Lakes, a 150-mile staircase of seven lakes that ends in Austin with Town Lake. The town is the center for the recreational and residential areas around lakes Ink and Buchanan. (*See* Highland Lakes.)

BUCHANAN DAM MUSEUM

Inside LCRA (Lower Colorado River Authority) building at dam headquarters, TX 29 • Open daily • W

Besides the nice view of Lake Buchanan, the museum has displays on the dam's construction and local history. Visitors can walk along the top of the dam; it is 2 miles long. Tours of the dam are given on weekends during the summer. Call the Lake Buchanan-Inks Lake Chamber of Commerce for latest schedule (512-793-2803). It is located at the same site and is open daily.

POINTS OF INTEREST

INKS LAKE STATE PARK

From Buchanan Dam, take TX 29 east about 2.5 miles to Park Rd. 4, then south (right) to park entrance • **793-2223** • **Admission about $3 per person W variable**

The 1,200-acre park has facilities for boating, fishing, swimming, picnicking, hiking, nature study, and camping in the largest camping area on the Highland Lakes. It is located on Inks Lake, a constant-level lake about four miles long and the second of the Highland Lakes. Write RR2, Box 31, Burnet 78611. The adjacent **Highland Lakes Golf Course** (793-2859) is nine holes, bordering scenic Inks Lake. Greens fee: about $10. Adjoining the park is the **Inks Lake National Fish Hatchery,** where the U.S. Fish and Wildlife Service annually produces over one million channel catfish, largemouth bass, stripers, and paddlefish. The fish are used to stock lakes across Texas and the southwest. Small information center and free brochure outlining a self-guided tour. Picnic area.

LAKE BUCHANAN

The first and highest of the Highland Lakes, Buchanan also has the largest surface area, with 23,060 acres. It is 8 miles across at its widest point and has 192 miles of shoreline. Much of the shoreline is privately owned, but several commercial and public places offer access for fishing, boating, swimming, and other water sports, plus picnicking and camping. The LCRA, Llano County, and Burnet County operate several parks on Lake Buchanan. Many lodges along the lake offer accommodations.

SIDE TRIPS

FALL CREEK VINEYARDS

From Buchanan Dam, proceed west on TX 29, then right onto TX 261, then to FM 2241. At Bluffton, turn north (right) onto FM 2241, to Tow. Vineyard is 2.2 miles beyond Tow Post Office (follow signs) • **915-379-5361 or 476-4477 (Austin office)** • **Open daily** • **Free** • **W variable**

The winery is housed in European-style buildings on the shore of Lake Buchanan. Wines produced include Chardonnay, Sauvignon Blanc, Chenin Blanc, Emerald Riesling, and Zinfandel. Tours, tasting, and sales.

RESTAURANTS

($ = under $7, $$ = $8–$17, $$$ = $18–$25, $$$$ = over $25 for one person excluding drinks, tax, and tip.)

CLUB POCAHONTAS

TX 29 just east of RR 1431 • 793-6128 • Dinner only Wednesday–Sunday. Closed Monday and Tuesday • $$ • MC, V • Children's plates

Specialty is charbroiled steaks, with chicken and fish entrées rounding out the menu. Live music and dancing most nights. Lounge.

ACCOMMODATIONS

There are several lodges, camps, and resorts around the lake offering a variety of accommodations. For a list, contact the Chamber of Commerce.

BURNET

Burnet County Seat • 3,569 • 512

Texas Rangers set up a small outpost nearby in 1848. In 1849, the U.S. Army established Fort Croghan, around which the village of Hamilton Creek grew. Hamilton Creek changed its name in 1852 when it became the seat of newly formed Burnet County, named after David G. Burnet, a provisional president of the Republic of Texas. Burnet became an area trading center after the railroad arrived in 1882, and soon after, a block of marble from a nearby quarry was shipped to Washington, where it was used to represent Texas in the Washington Monument. Burnet (pronounced BURN-it) has been officially designated by the Texas Legislature as the Bluebonnet Capital of Texas, a role it ably plays out each spring in the local Bluebonnet Festival and Highland Lakes Bluebonnet Trail.

TOURIST SERVICES

BURNET CHAMBER OF COMMERCE

705 Buchanan, TX 29 about 1 mile west of US 281 (P.O. Drawer M, 78611) 756-4297

VANISHING TEXAS RIVER CRUISE

From Burnet, take TX 29 west about 3 miles to FM 2341, then north (right) 13.5 miles to dock **(P.O. Box 901, Burnet 78611) • 756-6986 • Closed Tuesdays Reservations required • Adults about $15, children 6–12 about $10 W call ahead**

Enclosed tour boats run scenic, leisurely two-and-a-half-hour cruises year-round on Lake Buchanan and the upper Colorado River. Winter-time cruises offer the sight of American bald eagles that roost along the shoreline. Dinner and sunset cruises run on summer weekends.

MUSEUMS

FORT CROGHAN MUSEUM

703 Buchanan, TX 29, about 1 mile west of US 281 (next to Chamber of Commerce) • 756-8281 • April–October: Thursday–Saturday 10–5, Sunday 1–5 • Admission • W

Fort Croghan was the third of four forts established by the Army in early 1849 to protect frontier settlements from the Indians. The line of forts stretched from Fort Worth to Uvalde. The frontier quickly moved west and the forts went with them; Croghan was abandoned in 1855. None of the original buildings remain; the oldest here is the "Old Powder House," dating from the Civil War, and several other old stone and log buildings moved to the site. The small museum contains local and county history items.

OTHER HISTORIC PLACES

Several of the buildings on the courthouse square are 100 years old, or close to it. The **Badger Building** (1883), Jackson and Pierce, is representative of the type of commercial buildings on the square in the 1880s. It is now a community center and museum. The **Old Burnet County Jail** (1884), Washington and S. Pierce, designed by famed architect F.E. Ruffini, was used as a jail until 1981. Just off the square is the **Old Masonic Lodge Building** (1854), 309 S. Main, built by Logan Vandeveer, a hero at San Jacinto, who had a store downstairs. The Masonic Lodge occupied the upstairs from 1855 to 1969.

OTHER POINTS OF INTEREST

LONGHORN CAVERNS STATE PARK

Take US 281 south about 5 miles to Park Rd. 4, then right (west) about 6 miles to park **(Rt. 2, Box 23, Burnet 78611) • 756-6976 (tour info) or 756-4680**
Open daily year-round except closed December 24 and 25
Adults about $7, children $4
It took at least a million years for water to carve out this cave. Indians and outlaws both used it as a hideout. Confederate gunpowder was manufactured here. In the non-air conditioned 1920s, the Council Room was used as a night-club, when the cavern's constant 64 degree temperature was a lure to customers. The cavern is about 11 miles long, but only a little over a mile is covered in the tour, which lasts about 90 minutes. The walk isn't difficult, but rubber-soled shoes are recommended. The 637-acre park includes a restaurant, gift shop, museum, nature trails, picnic areas, and an observation tower.

ANNUAL EVENTS

April

BLUEBONNET FESTIVAL

Town Square • 756-4297 • Usually second weekend in April • Free
W variable
Held in conjunction with the Highland Lakes Bluebonnet Trail, which guides visitors through the bluebonnets and wildflowers of the Highland Lakes area. Activities include a parade, arts and crafts fair, athletic events, and street dances.

CASTROVILLE

Medina County • 2,159 • (830)

Henri Castro, a Frenchman of Portuguese descent, first came to Texas in 1842. Discovering that the new Republic offered large land grants to anyone who could bring in settlers, he secured a colonization contract which gave him 1.25 million acres. Castroville was his first settlement, established in 1844, mainly by people from the French region of Alsace.

For a time Castroville was the county seat. But, in the 1880s, when local residents refused to pay the price for the railroad to come to town, the railroad bypassed them and developed the town of Hondo. By 1892 Hondo had grown big enough to win the county seat in an election. Castroville settled back into being a small bypassed town, preserving much of its Alsatian heritage, including the unwritten Alsatian dialect (more German than French) that was passed down from generation to generation. And it stayed that way until well after World War II, when visitors started to recognize that this quaint village was the only Alsatian community in the United States. Truly "The Little Alsace of Texas."

The Alsatians built their homes after the pattern of the homes they had left in Europe. Today, more than 90 of these homes still stand, looking as if they would fit in as well on the Rhine River as they do on the Medina. Much of the town is listed as a National Historic District in the National Register of Historic Places.

Each year the people celebrate their heritage with St. Louis Day—named after the king of France who was their patron saint—held the Sunday closest to August 25th, and highlighted by a barbecue and Alsatian sausage feast and entertainment that attracts thousands of visitors.

TOURIST SERVICES

CASTROVILLE CHAMBER OF COMMERCE

802 London at Naples in Public Library (P.O. Box 572, 78009) • 538-3142 or 800-778-6775

"Visitor Guide to Castroville" is available free.

HISTORIC PLACES

LANDMARK INN STATE HISTORIC SITE

402 Florence, off US 90 • 931-2133 • Days and hours vary. Call ahead Admission 50¢ • W

Begun as a one-story combination store and residence in the late 1840s, it became a hotel on the San Antonio-El Paso road in 1863. For years it was a stagecoach stop, and according to tradition, Robert E. Lee and Texas Ranger "Bigfoot" Wallace were among the guests. Today, this is the only historic inn run by the state. There is an interpretive center and an old gristmill on the property, and the inn rooms have been restored to the 1940s era and are available for rent. (*See* Accommodations.)

MOYE CENTER

US 90W • 931-2233 • Free • W

The large, three-story building was built around 1873 as a convent for the Sisters of Divine Providence and as a school. The tiny original St. Louis Catholic Church, built in 1846, is on the grounds.

OLD COUNTY COURTHOUSE
Fiorella St. • Open business hours • Free • W
Built in 1879, it lost its primary function when the county seat went to Hondo in 1892. Now it houses the City Hall.

ST. LOUIS CATHOLIC CHURCH
Houston Square. Angelo St. between Paris and Madrid • 538-2267
Open for services • W
Gothic-style church built in 1868 of native limestone. You can push a button near the entrance to hear a recorded account of the history of the church.

HISTORIC HOMES
There are a number of historic homes in the town that are private residences not open to the public. Among some of the oldest are: the **Seal House** (1844) on Isabella, **Pingenot House** (1845) on Petersburg, **Huth House** (1848) on Florence, **Merian House** (1851) on Angelo, and **Tardé Hotel** (1852) on Fiorella.

OTHER POINTS OF INTEREST

CASTROVILLE REGIONAL PARK
Take Athens south off US 90W to Lisbon, then west (right) to park. **(Box 479, 78009) • 538-2224 • Open at all times • Admission • W variable**
Located on the Medina River, this 126-acre park offers picnic tables, tennis and volleyball courts, Olympic-sized pool, fishing in the river, and camping area (fee).

SIDE TRIPS

MEDINA LAKE
Take FM 471 north about 17 miles to FM 1283, then west (left) to Park Rd. 37, then southwest (left) to lake **• Open at all times • Admission to some areas**
W variable
This 5,575-acre lake once was a state park, but no more. Now commercial facilities include campgrounds, marinas, and cottages for rent.

RESTAURANTS
($ = under $7, $$ = $8–$17, $$$ = $18–$25, $$$$ = over $25 for one person excluding drinks, tax, and tip.)

SAMMY'S RESTAURANT
202 US 90E • 538-2204 • Breakfast, lunch, and dinner daily • $–$$
Cr • W
Probably best known for its chicken-fried steaks, Mexican food, and generous portions.

Other Restaurants

In various historic buildings about town

You can dine in an historic setting in several spots. **The Chantilly** at 309 La Fayette (538-9531), the **Alsatian** at 403 Angelo (931-3260), and **La Normandie** at 1302 Fiorella are currently open, but restaurants come and go, so check ahead.

ACCOMMODATIONS

($ = under $45, $$ = $46–$60, $$$ = $61–$80, $$$$ = $81–$100, $$$$$ = over $100)
Room tax 10%

BEST WESTERN ALSATIAN INN

1650 US 90W • 538-2262 or 800-446-8528 • $$

The two-story Best Western has 40 rooms. Local calls free, small pets OK. Lounge, pool. On hill overlooking town, with nice restaurant view.

LANDMARK INN STATE HISTORIC SITE

402 Florence, off US 90 • 931-2133 • $$ • W+ 1 room

The two-story historic inn has eight rooms, some with private bath. No pets. Restaurants nearby. Built in the mid-1800s, restored to 1940s era.

COLUMBUS

Colorado County Seat • 3,605 • 409

Stephen F. Austin once planned to locate his colony's capital here, but changed his mind in favor of San Felipe on the Brazos. Some colonists settled the site anyway, founding one of the oldest continually occupied Anglo-American settlements in Texas. After the fall of the Alamo in 1836, General Sam Houston's retreating army burned Columbus, leaving Santa Anna scorched earth.

The first district court was held under a spreading live oak tree and was presided over by Judge R.M. Williamson, known as "Three Legged Willie" because he had a withered leg to which he attached a wooden peg leg at the knee. Today Columbus calls itself the "City of Live Oaks," and live oaks grow even in the middle of some streets.

The Magnolia Homes Tour organization has been credited with saving Columbus from the fate of other small Texas towns that let their historic buildings decline and drag the town down with them. In 1961, ten citizens opened four historic homes to the public during the Live Oak Art Club's annual spring art show. It was an immediate success. The Magnolia Homes Tour, now renamed the "Springtime Festival," draws thousands of visitors every May. Their efforts led to a general restoration of the town, making it a treasure trove of historic buildings.

TOURIST SERVICES

COLUMBUS CONVENTION AND VISITORS BUREAU

425 Spring at Milam, on the square in Stafford Opera House • 732-5135 • W

HISTORICAL WALKING TOUR

Downtown historic district • Free • W variable
Self-guided tour starting at the Stafford Opera House, where you can pick up a tour guide from the Visitors Bureau office, Monday–Friday 9–5. The tour may be taken any day, and some museums and historic homes are open on a regular basis.

HISTORIC PLACES

COLORADO COUNTY COURTHOUSE

Walnut (US 90) and Milam • Open Monday–Friday • W
Built in 1890, this brick courthouse had a steeple on top of the clock tower instead of the present copper dome. A storm in 1909 blew the steeple away. The district courtroom has a beautiful stained-glass dome that attracts admirers from across the country. Located on the courthouse grounds is the **Confederate Memorial Museum,** which was originally built as a watertower in 1883 of 400,000 handmade bricks. When the city couldn't destroy it with dynamite, it was turned into a museum by the United Daughters of the Confederacy. Confederate items and local historical memorabilia are displayed. (Open by appointment • Admission • W downstairs only.) The Courthouse District, a 12-block commercial/residential area of downtown, is listed in the National Register of Historic Places.

STAFFORD OPERA HOUSE

425 Spring and Milam, on the square • 732-5135 • Open Monday–Friday Admission • W
In 1886, millionaire cattleman R.E. Stafford hired famed architect Nicholas Clayton to design a building to house his bank on the first floor and a thousand-seat theater on the second. Stafford didn't enjoy his opera house for long; he and brother John were gunned down as the result of a feud on July 7, 1890, the day they laid the cornerstone for the present courthouse. Everything from Shakespeare to magicians played here until the curtain went down in 1916; it next served as a Ford Agency and roller skating rink until the Magnolia Homes Tour bought it in 1972 and began restoration.

MUSEUMS AND HISTORIC HOMES

Columbus has many fine old restored homes, some of which are open to the public on a regular or occasional basis. The **Mary Elizabeth Hopkins Santa Claus Museum** (604 Washington, Thursday through Saturday, admission) is the only known Santa Claus museum in the world, with over 2,000 Santas collected by one person. The **Alley Log Cabin Museum** (1224 Bowie, Thursday through Saturday, free) is an 1836 oak log cabin built by some of Austin's original settlers. It was moved here from its original site on the Colorado River in 1976. The 1860s **Tate-Senftenberg-Brandon House** (616 Walnut), the 1858 **Dilue Rose Harris House** (602 Washington), and the 1872 **Keith-Traylor House** (806 Live Oak) are open by prior arrangement for tour groups. Call the Visitors Bureau (732-5135) for tours and prices.

SPORTS AND ACTIVITIES

Golf

COLUMBUS MUNICIPAL GOLF COURSE

**1617 Walnut (US 90), about .5 mile west of TX 71 • 732-5575 • 9-hole course.
Greens fee about $10.**

SIDE TRIPS

ATTWATER PRAIRIE CHICKEN NATIONAL WILDLIFE REFUGE

*Take TX 71 south to US 90A, then east to FM 3013 at Eagle Lake, then east
(left) about 7 miles to refuge* • 234-3021 • **Open daily dawn to dusk** • **Free
W variable**

During mating season, male prairie chickens make a mating call that sounds
like someone blowing across the mouth of a bottle. You can watch this endangered species' mating dance, and hear the male's "booming" mating call from
late February to early May in this 8,000-acre U.S. Fish and Wildlife Service
refuge. Write P.O. Box 518, Eagle Lake 77434.

ANNUAL EVENTS

May

SPRINGTIME FESTIVAL

**Headquarters in Stafford Opera House, 425 Spring and Milam • 732-5135
Third full weekend in May • Admission • W variable**

Several historic homes are open for the tour, plus the Opera House and museums. Also an arts and crafts show, antiques show and sale, sidewalk café and
biergarten, bike ride, surrey rides, live entertainment, exhibits, and a production at
the Opera House.

RESTAURANTS

*($ = under $7, $$ = $8–$17, $$$ = $18–$25, $$$$ = over $25 for one person excluding
drinks, tax, and tip.)*

HACKEMACK'S HOFBRAUHAS

Take TX 71 north to FM 109, then north (right) about 10 miles to restaurant
**732-6321 • Dinner Thursday–Saturday; open Sundays during the summer
$–$$ • MC, V • W • Children's plates**

If you like wurst, try the *Neu Ulm Bauernschmaus*, with *knackwurst, bratwurst*,
Texas *wurst*, and pork cutlet, plus the trimmings. Other German dishes, plus
charbroiled steaks, chicken, and seafood. Music on Friday and Saturday nights.
Beer and wine.

SCHOEBEL'S RESTAURANT

**2020 Milam at TX 71, just north of I-10 • 732-3485 • Breakfast, lunch, and
dinner daily • DC, MC, V • W • Children's plates**

Texas-style food on a large scale. Charbroiled steaks, seafood, chicken,
some Tex-Mex dishes and a reasonably priced daily buffet. Homemade bread
and pie. No-smoking area. Bar.

ACCOMMODATIONS

($ = under $45, $$ = $46–$60, $$$ = $61–$80, $$$$ = $81–$100, $$$$$ = over $100)
Room tax 8.25%

Bed and Breakfast

GANT GUEST HOUSE
926 Bowie, P.O. Box 112, 78934 • 732-2190 • $$$–$$$$$
   Two bedrooms with shared bath. No children under 12. No pets. No smoking. No credit cards. Cable TV. Continental breakfast. Kitchen privileges. Furnished with antiques. One bedroom was copied for the Texas Room in the DAR Museum in Washington, D.C.

RAUMONDA
1100 Bowie, P.O. Box 112, 78934 • 732-2190 • $$$$
   Three bedrooms, one with private bath, others with bath available. No children under 12. No pets. No smoking. No credit cards. Cable TV. Continental breakfast. Outdoor pool. A two-story Victorian house with three guest rooms, private baths. Two nights minimum on holidays.

COMFORT

Kendall County • 1,593 • 830
   The German immigrants who settled Comfort in 1854 were mostly intellectuals who fled the political persecution and religious beliefs forced upon them in the old country. As a result, the character of this town was different from that of other German settlements in Texas. Whereas founding a church was among the first priorities in other settlements, Comfort's founders had such a disregard for organized religion that 40 years passed before the first church was established. Today, many descendants of the original settlers still live here, and the old spirit of "the less government the better" and "we take care of our own" continues to hold true, to the extent that the town remains unincorporated. The people of Comfort have preserved not only a way of life, but the old town itself. About ten blocks of the original town, including dozens of nineteenth-century buildings, are listed in the National Register of Historic Places as the Comfort Historic District.
   Agriculture and tourism feed the local economy. Several camps line the nearby Guadalupe River, and the town is home to a number of artists and craftspeople.

TOURIST SERVICES

COMFORT CHAMBER OF COMMERCE
7th and High • 995-3131 • Open Friday and Saturday • W

HISTORIC PLACES

   The south side of the 800 block of High St. is one of the most complete nineteenth-century business districts still standing in Texas. The *Guide to Historic Comfort* is useful for exploring downtown and the rest of historic Comfort; it's free and available at the Chamber of Commerce, located in the **Old Comfort**

State Bank, and other local businesses. Other notable buildings on High St. include the **Otto Brinkmann House** (1860), 701 High; the **Ingenhuett/Faust Hotel** (1880), 818 High; **Ingenhuett Store** complex (1880–1900), 828–834 High; and the **Comfort Historical Museum** (1891), 838 High. Originally a blacksmith shop, the museum is open the second Sunday of the month, on special occasions, and by appointment. (Donation.)

On Main St., the **Faltin General Store** (1879, 1907), Main and 7th; **Brinkmann and Sons Store** (1883–1911), 408 7th at Main; and the **Faltin Homestead** (1854), 400 block 7th, between High and Main, are notable.

TREUE DER UNION MONUMENT
High, between 3rd and 4th

The Germans of Comfort opposed slavery and secession. When the Civil War started, some refused to sign the "oath of allegiance" to the Confederacy and openly supported the Union. This led to pillaging and burning of their farms by Confederate supporters. In August 1862, about 65 of these beleaguered Unionists rode south towards Mexico, on the first leg of an escape to join Union forces. They didn't realize that they were being followed by Confederate cavalry, which ambushed them while they were camped on the Nueces River. Nineteen were killed; another 15 were captured and executed. The rest escaped, either to Mexico or back to Comfort. The bodies were left unburied. The bones were gathered up after the war and buried in a common grave here. In 1866, the town erected this monument in tribute to the men who were loyal to the Union. It is believed to be the only monument to the Union in a former Confederate state, outside of national cemeteries.

SHOPPING

COMFORT ART GALLERY
606 High • 995-3633 • W

A co-op gallery exhibiting and selling arts and crafts by local and regional artists.

COMFORT COMMON
818 High • 995-3030

More than a dozen antique and gift shops, located in the old Ingenhuett-Faust Hotel (1880).

INGENHUETT STORE
830 High • 995-2149

An old-fashioned general store selling everything from groceries to farm equipment. One of the oldest commercial businesses in the Hill Country, having been in the same family since 1868.

RESTAURANTS

($ = under $7, $$ = $8–$17, $$$ = $18–$25, $$$$ = over $25 for one person excluding drinks, tax, and tip.)

CYPRESS CREEK INN
TX 27 • 995-3977 • Lunch and dinner Tuesday–Saturday, lunch only Sunday $ • No Cr • W • Children's plates

Homestyle cooking—nothing fancy. Daily specials range from baked pork chops to sausage. Chicken-fried steak, liver and onions, and such on a daily basis. Since 1952. Beer.

ACCOMMODATIONS

($ = under $45, $$ = $46–$60, $$$ = $61–$80, $$$$ = $81–$100, $$$$$ = over $100)

COMFORT COMMON

818 High in Comfort Common • 995-3030 • $$–$$$

B&B with suites and rooms in the hotel and in cottage out back; six lodgings total. No children under 12 on weekends. Call about pets. TV. Restaurant next door provides full breakfast.

THE MEYER BED AND BREAKFAST

845 High • 995-2304 • $$

Nine units (two with kitchenettes). Swimming pool. Fishing in Cypress Creek. Located in what was the Meyers Hotel complex, which began as a stage stop shortly after Comfort was founded.

FREDERICKSBURG

Gillespie County Seat • 7,745 • 830

Many of the German immigrants who settled Texas came under the auspices of the Society for the Protection of German Immigrants in Texas. The society founded New Braunfels in 1845. A year later, Baron Ottfried Hans von Meusebach and 120 colonists moved into Comanche territory to settle near the Pedernales River and founded Fredericksburg, named after Prince Frederick of Prussia. In an incredible feat of diplomacy, Meusebach negotiated a peace treaty with the Comanches, eliminating one of the biggest threats to the fledgling colony. The treaty was generally respected by both sides.

Many descendants of the original settlers still live in the area, and the Germanic heritage is still strong. Many of the shops and restaurants have German names. One church still holds a German-language worship service, and two choirs sing German songs. If you attend the local *Schuetzenfests* (shooting fests) or the *Saengerfests* (singing festivals) you will probably hear as much German spoken as English.

The downtown historic district is listed in the National Register of Historic Places, with over 100 registered buildings and homes. Fredericksburg appreciates its visitors: starting on Main in front of the Vereins Kirche and going east, the first letters of the streets spell out ALL WELCOME (if you use the first two letters of Mesquite). Going west from the same spot, they spell out COME BACK.

Agriculture and tourism feed the local economy, with peaches being one of the main crops. In a good year, about one-fourth of the peaches consumed in Texas are grown here. The various varieties ripen from May through July, and roadside stands selling "just picked" fruit are open all along the main roads during harvest season. Some orchards even let you pick your own.

TOURIST SERVICES

FREDERICKSBURG CHAMBER OF COMMERCE

106 N. Adams (78624) • 997-6523 • Monday–Friday 8–5, Saturday 9–12,
1–5; Sunday 1–5 • W

MUSEUMS

ADMIRAL NIMITZ STATE HISTORICAL PARK

340 E. Main (P.O. Box 777, 78624) • 997-4379 • Daily 8–5
Admission about $3 adults, $2 children • W+

Chester Nimitz, Commander-in-Chief in the Pacific during World War II,
grew up in Fredericksburg and this museum is located in the old "Steamboat
Hotel" once owned by his grandfather. Starting with exhibits about life in old
Fredericksburg, the museum covers Nimitz' life through the war in the Pacific
to his death in 1966. "Hands-on" displays and audiovisual exhibits include a
sound and light presentation of a Pacific theater destroyer battle. In back is the
Japanese Garden of Peace, given by the people of Japan; it includes a replica of
Admiral Togo's study and teahouse. The Pacific History Walk features a collec-
tion of World War II military planes, tanks, and other weapons. Gift shop.

PIONEER MUSEUM COMPLEX

309 W. Main • 997-2835 • Open daily • Adults about $3, children about $1
W but not all areas

The Kammlah house and store, built of stone starting in 1849, anchors the
complex. Its eight rooms are full of period antiques and exhibits about early life
in Gillespie County. Other buildings include the Fassel House (1870s), barn and
smokehouse, a pioneer log cabin, the Weber Sunday House, the old First
Methodist Church (1855), and a firefighting museum, which displays antique
fire-fighting equipment.

VEREINS KIRCHE MUSEUM

Market Square, off 100 block of W. Main, across from Gillespie County
Courthouse • 997-7832, or 997-2835 • Open daily • Adults about $2, students
about $1 • W with assistance

Fredericksburg's best known building, this is a replica of the original *Vereins
Kirche* (People's Church) built by the pioneer settlers in 1847. Its octagonal
shape and conical roof has led it to be called *Die Kaffee-Muehle,* The Coffee Mill.
It holds pioneer artifacts and local historical photos and documents.

HISTORIC PLACES

A self-guided historic tours pamphlet with information on many buildings in
the Historic District is available free from the Fredericksburg Chamber of Commerce. Another valuable source is the Visitors Guide published by the *Fredericksburg Standard-Radio Post.* It's available free at the Chamber of Commerce and
many local businesses.

ST. BARNABAS EPISCOPAL MISSION

605 W. Creek • 997-5762 • Call for appointment • W

Originally built as a house in 1847, it later became an Episcopal Church. The
new church, nearby, was often attended by President Lyndon Johnson.

SCHANDUA HOUSE

111 E. Austin • 997-2835 (Historical Society) • Open by appointment

This little stone house is the only totally authentic restoration in town, down to the lack of electricity and indoor plumbing.

SUNDAY HOUSES

404, 408, 410 W. San Antonio • Not open to the public

Farmers and ranchers built one-room "Sunday" houses so that they would have a place to stay when they came into Fredericksburg on weekends for shopping, social activities and church. The only Sunday House open to visitors is the Weber Sunday House at the Pioneer Museum.

OTHER HISTORIC PLACES

The Historic District is filled with over 100 buildings dating to the town's founding. Some of the more notable examples include: **John Joseph Klingelhoefer House** (1847), S. Acorn and W. Main; **John Peter Tatsch House** (1856), N. Bowie and W. Schubert; **Adam Krieger House** (1848), 512 W. Creek; **Kiehne House** (1850), 407 E. Main; **Schmidt Hotel** (1857), 218 W. Main; **Old St. Mary's Church** (1860s), 300 block W. San Antonio; **Pioneer Library/Old Gillespie County Courthouse** (1882), 115 W. Main; the **Old Jail** (1885), 117 W. San Antonio; **Admiral Nimitz birthplace** (1866), 247 E. Main; and the **Old Fredericksburg Bank** (1889), 120 E. Main.

Two Pilgrimage Walks (accredited by the American *Volkssport* Association) are laid out in the area. A 13-kilometer trek explores the downtown Historic District; the other is a 10-K walk along the scenic, historic southwestern edge of town. Route maps are available at the Chamber of Commerce.

CROSS MOUNTAIN

Two miles north on FM 965

Early settlers found remnants of a wooden cross (probably erected by Spanish missionaries) on this limestone knob. They put up a new cross and named the hill **Kreuzberg** (Cross Mountain). The present illuminated concrete cross is the fourth replacement. A nature trail leads to the summit, which offers a panoramic view of the area.

FORT MARTIN SCOTT

1606 E. Main (US 290) • 997-9895 • Wednesday–Saturday, March–Labor Day; Friday–Sunday rest of year • Admission • W variable

Established by the U.S. Army in 1848 as one of a string of forts along the Texas frontier to protect settlers and travelers. Closed in 1853, it was reopened by the Confederates during the Civil War, then closed for good by the U.S. Cavalry in 1866. The site next became a beer garden, where the first Gillespie County Fair was held, in 1881. It was closed to the public until 1989. The only original building standing is the guardhouse/stockade. Historical reenactments occur monthly. Ongoing archaeological digs and replicas of other fort buildings are being constructed.

SHOPPING

CHARLES BECKENDORF'S GALLERY

519 E. Main • 997-5955 or in Texas 800-369-9004 • W

Said to be the largest one-artist gallery in the country. Beckendorf interprets Texas scenery and wildlife in various media. Originals run from about $300 for a pencil drawing to about $5,000 for a painting. Prints run from $10 to about $600.

HAAS CUSTOM HANDWEAVING

242 E. Main • 997-3175 • W

In the old White Elephant Saloon, Ingrid Haas weaves 100 percent sheep's wool rugs, saddleblankets, and wallhangings on a large handloom. She also stocks specialty items such as Austrian table linens and German lace curtains.

OPA'S SMOKED MEATS

410 S. Washington, about 3 blocks south of Main • 997-3358 • W

A third generation of sausage-makers turns out hickory-smoked meats here; they offer smoked sausage, ham, turkey, bacon and Canadian bacon, beef, and pork. For mail order catalog write P.O. Box 487, 78624.

SCHWETTMANN'S EMPORIUM

305 W. Main • 997-4448

A stuffed zoo, with everything from ostriches to trophy jackalopes. Zebra skins, buffalo rugs, deerskin shoes, and more.

OTHER POINTS OF INTEREST

LADY BIRD JOHNSON MUNICIPAL PARK

About 3 miles southwest on SH 16 (P.O. Box 113, 78624) • 997-4202
Open daily • Free • W variable

This 340-acre park has a swimming pool, volleyball courts and tennis courts, golf course (18-hole, open daily, about $11 and up, call 997-4010), 20-acre lake for boating and fishing, picnic areas, RV and camp sites (fee).

SIDE TRIPS

ENCHANTED ROCK STATE NATURAL AREA

Take FM 965 north about 18 miles • **247-3903** • **Open daily**
Admission about $3 per person• W variable

Enchanted Rock is the best known feature of the Llano Uplift of the Central Mineral Region, a massive dome of Precambrian pink granite covering about 640 acres and rising 425 feet above the bed of Sandy Creek, which flows past the mountain. At more than one billion years, Enchanted Rock is some of the oldest exposed rock in North America. Indians both worshipped and feared the rock, as a holy spot where evil spirits also lived. A hiking trail of moderate difficulty leads to the crest of Enchanted Rock, which offers a spectacular view of the surrounding countryside. Other rock formations in the park are popular with rock climbers. There are other hiking trails, picnic areas, and camp sites. Write Park Superintendent, Rt. 4, Box 170, Fredericksburg 78624.

LUCKENBACH

Take US 290 east about 6 miles to FM 1376, then south (right) to Luckenbach.
About 13 miles from Fredericksburg • **997-3224** • **W variable**

In the 1970s, this tiny hamlet was bought by Hill Country humorist Hondo Crouch, who promoted his town with imaginative events that brought in thousands of visitors. But what made Luckenbach world famous was the song "Luckenbach, Texas," recorded by Texans Waylon Jennings and Willie Nelson. There are usually things going on here (like dances or the annual ladies-only chili cookoff) most weekends from spring to fall, but it might be a good idea to call first.

OBERHELLMANN VINEYARDS

Take TX 16 north about 14 miles • **685-3297** • **Open Saturday** • **Free** • **W**

This winery on the slopes of Bell Mountain produces a variety of wines, including Chardonnays, Rieslings, and Pinot Noir. Complimentary tours and tastings are held every Saturday from Easter to Christmas.

ANNUAL EVENTS
April

EASTER FIRE PAGEANT

Gillespie County Fairgrounds, 3 miles south on TX 16 • **997-6523 (Chamber of Commerce)** • **Saturday night before Easter** • **Admission** • **W**

With a cast of 600, the pageant tells the story of the founding of Fredericksburg and John Meusebach's meeting with the Comanches in 1847 to forge a peace treaty. This leads into a legend associated with the event: some of the children in Fredericksburg were frightened by signal fires set by Indians in the surrounding hills. Adapting an old German story to the New World, their mother told them that the fires were set by the Easter bunny, who was boiling eggs in large kettles over the fires, and that if they went to sleep, they'd find the colored eggs in the morning. So Easter bunnies abound in the pageant. General admission and reserved-seat tickets can be ordered through the Chamber of Commerce.

June

STONEWALL PEACH JAMBOREE

Take US 290 east about 16 miles to Stonewall Rodeo Arena • **997-6523 (Fredericksburg Chamber of Commerce) or 644-9247 (Stonewall Chamber of Commerce)** • **Friday and Saturday of third weekend in June** • **Admission W variable**

This salute naturally includes a peach show and auction, plus a peach pie and cobbler baking contest. Rodeo and dance both nights (admission), parade, fiddler's contest, carnival, and wacky events.

August

GILLESPIE COUNTY FAIR

Gillespie County Fairgrounds, 3 miles on TX 16 • 997-2359 • Fourth weekend in August • Admission about $5 and up • W variable
More than 100 years old, the fair starts with a downtown parade Friday morning. All the usual fair events: livestock show and agricultural exhibits, arts and crafts show, carnival, horse races, contests, and entertainment, including dances.

October

OKTOBERFEST

Market Square • 997-4810 • First weekend in October • Admission to some events • W variable
A bit of Bavaria comes to Texas. Friday night there's the traditional *bierhalle* with music, singing, and dancing. Saturday and Sunday are filled with entertainment, arts and crafts show, children's activities and carnival, and a Saturday night dance featuring a waltz contest.

RESTAURANTS

($ = under $7, $$ = $8–$17, $$$ = $18–$25, $$$$ = over $25 for one person excluding drinks, tax, and tip.)

ALTDORF RESTAURANT

301 W. Main • 997-7774 • Lunch and dinner Wednesday–Monday. Closed Tuesday and the month of January • $–$$ • D, MC, V • W
Located in an 1860 limestone house, Altdorf's dining room is pleasant enough, but in nice weather, choose the outdoor *biergarten*. American-Tex-Mex-German menu, with lots of sandwiches and fingerfoods. Beer and wine.

GEORGE'S OLD GERMAN BAKERY AND RESTAURANT

225 W. Main • 997-9084 • Open Thursday–Monday, breakfast, lunch, and dinner. Closed Tuesday–Wednesday • $–$$ • No Cr • W
Hearty *Deutsche*-Tex breakfasts, sandwiches, and salads, plus a variety of German dishes. Breads and pastries baked on premises.

ACCOMMODATIONS

($ = under $45, $$ = $46–$60, $$$ = $61–$80, $$$$ = $81–$100, $$$$$ = over $100)
Room tax 13%

BARON'S CREEK INN

110 E. Creek • 997-9398, 800-800-4082 • $$$$
B&B in a restored 1911 home in the historic district. Four suites in big house, one Sunday-House-styled guest house.

BE MY GUEST LODGING SERVICE

997-7227
A variety of accommodations in town and out in the country (including ranches), by the day, week, or month.

BED AND BREAKFAST OF FREDERICKSBURG
240 W. Main • 997-4712
Overnight lodging and a full breakfast in old and new local homes.

COUNTRY COTTAGE INN
405 E. Main • 997-8549
Two suites and two single rooms, all with private baths. Full breakfast. Rooms have cable TV, phone, microwave, refrigerator, coffee maker. Inside the historic Kiehne Home.

GASTEHAUST SCHMIDT
231 W. Main • 997-5612, fax 997-8282
Lodging in a wide variety of historic and modern homes and buildings in and around Fredericksburg.

GEORGETOWN

Williamson County Seat • 16,752 • 512
Georgetown was named for George Washington Glasscock, who donated the land for the original townsite in 1848. After the Civil War, the town was a staging area for huge cattle drives north. Georgetown's golden era began in the 1880s, after civic fathers built a spur line from Georgetown to connect with the main line at Round Rock. A building boom ensued, and what remains is now in the National Register of Historic Places. The County Courthouse Square is an excellent example of a Victorian era business district.

TOURIST SERVICES
GEORGETOWN HISTORY AND INFORMATION CENTER
101 W. 7th at Main • 863-5598 • Open daily • W
A brochure, "A Walking Tour of Historic Downtown Georgetown," is available, plus other books and pamphlets.

HISTORIC PLACES
WILLIAMSON COUNTY COURTHOUSE HISTORIC DISTRICT
Almost all the buildings surrounding the courthouse were built during Georgetown's golden era. Oldest building on the square is the small, limestone rubble **Shaffer Saddlery Building** at 711 Main, built in 1870. Other buildings of note are the **M.B. Lockett Building** (1896), 119 W. 7th and Austin; **Lessne-Stone Building** (1884), 102 W. 8th and Main; the **David Love Building** (1883), 706 Austin; and the **Fire Station** (1893), Main and 9th, which has a restored old-time pumper truck. North of the square, at 312 Main, is the **Williamson County Jail,** built in 1888 and still serving its original purpose.

OTHER POINTS OF INTEREST

INNER SPACE CAVERNS

4200 S. IH-35, about 1 mile south of the city at exit 259 • 863-5545 • Memorial Day–Labor Day daily 9–6; rest of year Wednesday–Sunday 10–5 • Closed two weeks before Christmas through Christmas Day • Admission • W

Texas Highway Department drillers taking core samples for a proposed overpass discovered these caverns. Waters of the Edwards Aquifer carved them out over a 100-million-year period. Tours last about an hour and leave every half-hour. An inclined railway car takes you down into the caverns and from there the trip covers less than a mile of relatively easy walking. Be prepared for brief periods of absolute darkness during the sound and light show. Gift shop.

LAKE GEORGETOWN

Take FM 2338 west about 4 miles to entrance road • 863-3016
Open daily • Free entrance • W variable

A 1,310-acre Army Corps of Engineers lake on the North Fork of the San Gabriel River. Visitors Overlook is at the dam on the eastern end, off FM 2338. Three parks provide facilities for boating, fishing, swimming, hiking and primitive camping, picnicking, and RV and tent camping (fee). Write Project Office, Rt. 5, Box 500, Georgetown 78628.

COLLEGES AND UNIVERSITIES

SOUTHWESTERN UNIVERSITY

E. University Ave. and Maple • 863-6511 • W variable

This Methodist-affiliated small university traces its roots back to Rutersville College, chartered by the Republic of Texas in 1840, giving Southwestern claim to being the oldest college in the state. A number of buildings and activities are open to visitors. The **Mood Heritage Museum** in Mood-Bridwell Hall has exhibits on the natural history of the area, plus university history. **Old Main** (1898), now called the Cullen Building, is in the National Register of Historic Places. Visitors are welcome at school athletic events, cultural productions at the **Alma Thomas Fine Arts Center** (863-1378), and the **Kurth-Landrum Golf Course,** a nine-hole course (greens fee about $10, 863-1333).

SHOPPING

MAR-JON CANDLE FACTORY

4411 S. IH-35, about 1 mile south of city at exit 259 • 863-6025
Open daily except holidays • Free • W

More than 300 types of candles in 20 colors and fragrances, and a wide selection of candle holders. The candle wax formulas, colors, and fragrances were developed by Dr. Sherman Lesesne, a chemistry professor at Southwestern University. You can watch the candles being made.

GONZALES

Gonzales County Seat • 6,527 • (830)

Founded in 1825, it earned its major place in history as the town where they fired the first shot of the Texas Revolution.

Named after Don Rafael Gonzales, the governor of the Mexican province of Coahuila and Texas, the 1825 settlement had Indian troubles and to help scare them off, the Mexican government loaned the settlers a small brass cannon. When the Mexicans felt the first stirrings of the Texan revolt in 1835, they tried to get the cannon back. Texan volunteers attacked them on October 2, 1835, under a flag saying "Come and Take It."

The Texas Revolution had begun, and Gonzales had earned its title as the "Lexington of Texas." The following February when Colonel Travis appealed for help, 32 men from Gonzales were the only ones to answer his call, breaking through the Mexican lines to enter the Alamo. General Sam Houston arrived in Gonzales on March 11, 1836, and it was here that he heard the news of the fall of the Alamo. Threatened by Santa Anna's superior force, Houston ordered a scorched-earth retreat, burning Gonzales. This was the beginning of the Runaway Scrape, which ended a month later when the Texans turned on the pursuing Santa Anna and defeated him at the Battle of San Jacinto.

This has always been cattle country. The first brand was recorded here in 1829 and Thornton Chisholm blazed the first Chisholm Trail from Cuero through here to Missouri in 1866.

Cattle is still of major importance to the local economy, but now it has been joined by the production of eggs, broilers, and turkeys, usually ranking number one or two in the state.

TOURIST SERVICES

GONZALES CHAMBER OF COMMERCE AND AGRICULTURE

414 St. Lawrence at St. Joseph (P.O. Box 134, 78629-0134) • 672-6532

Located in the Old County Jail (*see* Museums). A written self-driving tour of historical points of interest is available free. They can also arrange tours.

MUSEUMS

GONZALES MEMORIAL MUSEUM

414 Smith between St. Lawrence and St. Louis • 672-6350 • Tuesday–Saturday 10–12, 1–5; Sunday 1–5. Closed Monday • Free • W

The museum is housed in a classic building of Texas shell-stone and Cordova cream limestone. It was built by the state in 1935 as a memorial to the men who fought in the first battle of the Texas Revolution, as well as the 32 men from Gonzales who answered Travis' call for help and willingly marched off to doom at the Alamo. Featured in the history collection is the 21½-inch, 69-pound, "Come and Take It" cannon.

OLD COUNTY JAIL MUSEUM

414 St. Lawrence • 672-6532 (Chamber of Commerce) • Monday–Friday 8–5, Saturday 8:30–4, Sunday 1–4 • Free

Built in 1887, this three-story brick building was used as the county jail until 1975. Minimally restored, its small cells, walls scarred with initials and dates, and second-floor gallows still give evidence of the horrors of imprisonment. A scattering of artifacts in glass cases on the first floor tell the story of the jail, law enforcement officers from the area, and some local history, including John Wesley Hardin's time in the town. The gallows, which dominates the upstairs, is a reproduction. The building is listed in the National Register of Historic Places. The Chamber of Commerce office is just inside the entrance.

GONZALES PIONEER VILLAGE LIVING HISTORY CENTER

US 183 just north of US 90A • 672-2157 • Friday–Saturday 10–5, Sunday 1–5 in summer; Saturday 10–5, Sunday 1–5 in winter • Tours and demonstrations available for $3–$3.50

Collection of restored structures, including 1870 church, 1860 blacksmith shop, working broom factory, and log cabins that bring history to life. Special programs throughout the year. Just south is Fort Waul, the only earthen enbankment type built by the Confederacy west of the Mississippi.

HISTORIC PLACES

EGGLESTON HOUSE

1300 St. Louis, behind the Memorial Museum • 672-6532 (Chamber of Commerce) • Tuesday–Saturday 10–12, 1–5, Sunday 1–5. Closed Monday Free • W

This log home was built in 1840 by Horace Eggleston.

GONZALES COUNTY COURTHOUSE

St. Louis and St. Joseph (US 183) • 672-2801 (County Clerk) Monday–Friday 8–5 • Free • W

Built in 1895, the three-story red brick building is in the shape of a cross with entrances at the four corners. It is listed in the National Register of Historic Places.

J.B. WELLS HOUSE

829 Mitchell • Group tours available

Built in 1885 of lumber brought by oxcart from Indianola.

SITE OF THE BATTLE OF GONZALES

Take US 183 south to TX 97, then west (right) about 6 miles to monument, then north (right) on paved road around monument to actual battlesite monument on river **• Open at all times • Free • W**

It was here on October 2, 1835, that the Texans fired the first shot of the Texas Revolution, driving off a Mexican cavalry force of about 150 men who had come to take back the Gonzales cannon.

OTHER HISTORIC BUILDINGS

Some of the more interesting buildings are the old **Gonzales College** (1851) at 820 St. Louis, **John Curtis Jones House** (1872) at 108 Hamilton, **Episcopal Church** (1880) at 721 St. Louis, **T.H. Spooner House** (1874) at 207 St. Francis, **Charles T. Rather House** (1892) at 828 St. Louis, **Randle-Rather Building** (1897) at 429 St. George, and the **Lewis-Houston House** (1899) at 619 St. Lawrence. Some of these are private homes and not open to the public except through special tour arrangements.

SIDE TRIPS

BRACHES HOUSE AND SAM HOUSTON OAK

Take US 90A southeast about 10 miles to Peach Creek Bridge, then first road on left past bridge • **Private property not open to the public**

Once a stagecoach station, this plantation house was where Sam Houston rested after burning the town and starting the "Runaway Scrape" ahead of Mexican troops. Santa Anna also stopped over here in his pursuit of the Texans. The house, which can be seen from the road, is listed in the National Register of Historic Places, and the property is one of the settings from the historical novel *True Women* about the region.

NOAH'S LAND WILDLIFE PARK

Take Hwy 304 north about 17 miles • **540-4664** • **Open daily 8:30–5 Adults $6.50, children $4**

Some 400 acres of natural habitat, with over 500 animals, from rhinos to buffalo. Drive-through type where you can feed the animals from the car. Petting zoo, snack bar.

PALMETTO STATE PARK

Take US 183 north about 12 miles, then west (left) on Park Rd. 11 about 2 miles **672-3266** • **Open daily 8–10 for day use, at all times for camping** • **$2 per person** • **W variable**

Located in an area once known as the Ottine Swamp, this 263-acre park resembles a tropical botanical garden. At one time the San Antonio and Aransas Pass Railroad had weekend excursion trips to the Palmetto area for the warm sulphur springs, now vanished. The unusual vegetation here draws naturalists from throughout the state. Recreational facilities include a picnic area, playground, nature trails, fishing, swimming, and campsites (fee). For information write: Park Superintendent, Route 5, Box 201, Gonzales 78629.

OTHER RECREATIONAL AREAS

Lake Wood Recreation Area is off US 90A west fives miles from Gonzales (672-2779). On the Guadalupe River, it has camping, RV, fishing, and water sports. **Independence Park** is on US 183 south of the town, also on the Guadalupe River. Camping, RV, golf.

ANNUAL EVENTS

October

GONZALES "COME AND TAKE IT" DAYS CELEBRATION

Downtown Squares • **672-6532 (Chamber of Commerce)**
First weekend in October • **Free (admission to some events)** • **W**

They commemorate the first shot of the Texas Revolution (October 2, 1835) with this bang-up festival that includes street dances, parade, sports contests, food booths, a reenactment of the "Come and Take It" battle performed at Fort Waul near Pioneer Village, entertainment, and carnival. The museums and some historical buildings are usually open.

November–December

WINTERFEST

Confederate Square, 400 block of St George • 672-6532 (Chamber of Commerce) • Thanksgiving weekend and next weekend • Free • W

The Thanksgiving weekend includes Christmas in Cradle of Texas Independence, Yule Trail, Festival of Lights, historic homes tours, arts and crafts, food, music. Even a Texan Santa arrives via chuck wagon. The next weekend features the candlelight tour of historic homes.

ACCOMMODATIONS

($ = under $45, $$ = $46–$60, $$$ = $61–$80, $$$$ = $81–$100, $$$$$ = over $100) Room tax 11%

COLONIAL INN MOTEL

1721 Sarah DeWitt Dr. (US 90A), about .7 mile east of US 183 • 672-9611 $ • No-smoking rooms

This 2-story inn has 60 units, no-smoking rooms, cable TV, room phones (local calls free), pets OK, free coffee in lobby.

Bed and Breakfast

Several B&B's in area. Call 672-6532 (Chamber of Commerce) for listings.

HICO

Hamilton County • 1,345 • (254)

It rhymes with "eye"—H-eye-co. Settled in 1856 on Honey Creek, Hico was named by an early settler, J.R. Alford, for his hometown in Kentucky. When the Texas Central Railroad was built through the county in 1880, the town moved "to the railroad," relocating three miles away on the north bank of the Bosque River. Incorporated in 1883, and prospering, primarily because of rich farming area, its population soared in 1908 to about 4,000. Though surviving two fires and a flood through the years, the town's future seemed bleak when the railroad left. Downtown was deserted for years.

But thanks to tourism—and some spirited townspeople and merchants—a rejuvenated Hico is prospering once again. See for yourself!

TOURIST SERVICES

THE HICO CHAMBER OF COMMERCE

Call 800-361-HICO. The hotline is answered 10–5 weekdays, 10–9 Saturday, and 1–3 Sunday. When open, information is also available at the Log Cabin Visitor's Center (intersection of US 281 and TX 6).

MUSEUMS

BILLY THE KID MUSEUM

103 Pecan Street • 796-4325 • Weekdays 9–5 and later on Friday and Saturday, or by appointment • Admission: Adults $2, children over 6 $1.

The town has created additional excitement by capitalizing on the lure of Billy the Kid, and you can learn the "true story"—Hico's version of it anyway—at this museum. Locals insist that the infamous outlaw really wasn't killed in New Mexico by Pat Garrett, but he actually lived among them for decades as Brushy Bill Roberts, and died in 1950, at the age of 92, of a heart attack on a downtown street here. Owner Bob Hefner's three books on Billy the Kid are for sale in the museum, along with souvenirs.

(A Billy the Kid Auto Swap Meet at City Park in August and a Billy the Kid Day the first Saturday in April, which even includes a goat-milking contest, keep the mystique alive.)

SHOPPING

Long-deserted limestone buildings Downtown (Pecan Street), as well as an increasing number nearby on TX 6 and US 281, are filled with stores that sell antiques, collectibles, crafts, Western apparel, gourmet coffee, cheeses, and local resident Bobby Kerr's Cowboy art and Western furniture. There are also several tea rooms. Most shops stay open until 9 on Saturday night. (*See* Special Event.) Note the historic mural by artist Style Reed on the First National Bank Building.

SPECIAL EVENT

The main street (Pecan) comes alive with the sound of music each Saturday night, as local musicians congregate to play everything from C&W to bluegrass, to jazz, and rock and roll—and they're great! Held outdoors in the gazebo during warmer months, weather permitting, the free concerts usually begin around 6:30 in the winter and 7 in summer and end before 10. Arrive early for a good seat; this draws a crowd! Horse-drawn carriage rides (free) add to the evening's fun. Hop aboard at Lilly's.

RESTAURANTS

LILLY'S
128 Pecan St. • 796-0999 • Tuesday–Thursday 11–9; Friday and Saturday (kitchen stays open to 9 and all-you-can-eat buffet till 10); Sunday brunch 11–7 (can start ordering from menu at noon) • $–$$ • Cr • W+ • No-smoking room • Children's menu
Noted for Mexican food, but menu is diverse. A fountain and greenery divides two rooms. Providing a nice place for visitors and locals alike to eat helped boost town's appeal during the early days of its resurgence.

ACCOMMODATIONS

INDIAN MOUNTAIN RANCH BED & BREAKFAST
Rt. 1, Box 162-A, Hico 76457 (call for directions) • 796-4060 Fax 796-4090 • $$$$ • W variable • No smoking
This unusual two-story lodge, on top of what formerly was a sacred ritual ground for Native American tribes, has 62 windows, covered porches and balconies, and a Southwestern decor. Three guest rooms plus mezzanine "bunkhouse" sleeps up to 30. Two of the first-floor rooms plus living area are

accessible to handicapped. Rates less ($$$) in off-season. Rooms have phones (no charge for local calls) and fire alarms. Full breakfast for B&B guests; group meals at extra cost. A stone swimming pool, picnic tables, and old-fashioned swings add to the relaxed ambience. Located about five miles from Hico, and around 20 miles from Glen Rose.

HIGHLAND LAKES

The Highland Lakes are a staircase of seven man-made lakes on the Colorado River stretching 150 miles through the Hill Country northwest of Austin down to the Capital City. The lakes are Buchanan, Inks, Lyndon B. Johnson (LBJ), Marble Falls, Travis, Austin, and Town Lake. All but Town Lake are administered by the Lower Colorado River Authority (LCRA), a state agency.

HIGHLAND LAKES BLUEBONNET TRAIL

Austin, Marble Falls, Burnet, Llano, Kingsland • Usually first 2 weekends in April • Free • W variable

The trail winds its way up the Highland Lakes chain, past fields of bluebonnets, historic and scenic sites, and through communities where there are often local festivals and art exhibits.

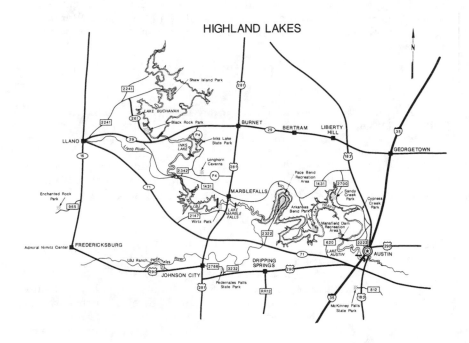

HIGHLAND LAKES

JOHNSON CITY

Blanco County Seat • 1,032 • 830
   Johnson City is named for LBJ's pioneer forebears who settled the area in the mid-1800s. LBJ's grandfather Sam Ealy Johnson, Sr., and great-uncle Tom Johnson made a quick fortune driving Texas beef north after the Civil War. Sam bought land in the Pedernales and Blanco River valleys and set up his ranch headquarters, corrals, and pens where Johnson City now stands. Local ranchers brought their longhorns to the Johnsons' compound, where they assembled the great herds that trudged north up the Chisholm Trail. They were the biggest trail-driving outfit in six counties, driving north several herds of up to 3,000 head each season. In the beginning, a steer that cost $6 to $10 in Texas fetched $30 or $40 at the Kansas railheads. But cattle quickly flooded the market, driving prices down, and the Johnson brothers went bust in 1871. Tom moved on, but Sam stayed and in 1908, his grandson Lyndon was born in nearby Stonewall.

TOURIST SERVICES

JOHNSON CITY CHAMBER OF COMMERCE
404 Main (US 290) • 868-7684 • Monday–Friday 9–5 • W

POINTS OF INTEREST

LYNDON B. JOHNSON NATIONAL HISTORIC PARK
Johnson City Visitors Center, 10th and G, 2 blocks south of US 290 • 868-7128
Open daily 9–5; extended hours in summer. Closed Christmas and New Year's Day • Free • W
   The Johnson City half of this two-part park has President Johnson's boyhood home and the Johnson Settlement, which was part of his grandfather's ranch. A multi-media program on LBJ and Johnson City is presented at the Visitors Center, which also has a gift shop. In 1914, Lyndon's parents moved the family into the modest 1886 frame house, which has been restored and refurnished to its condition as a lived-in home in the 1920s, with toys scattered on the floor of the boys' bedroom. The guided tour takes 20 minutes and leaves every half-hour.
   There's a short walk west to the Johnson Settlement's entrance. A self-guided tour beginning at the Exhibit Center features photographs and audiovisuals to introduce visitors to the history of the settlement and area. The settlement includes the log home of Sam Ealy Johnson, Sr., and his wife Eliza.
   The other half of the park is the LBJ Ranch Unit, which is closed to visitor traffic. Visitor access is limited to National Park Service Tour buses only. Ninety-minute bus tours run from 10 to 4 daily, starting at the LBJ State Historical Park Visitors Center (Take US 290 west 14 miles to Visitors Center in Lyndon B. Johnson State Historical Park • 868-7128, 644-2241 (LBJ Ranch Unit Bus Operations) • W variable). It normally includes the **Junction School,** where Lyndon started attending at age 4, a reconstruction of his birthplace, the Johnson family cemetery where he is buried, the exterior of his Texas White House, and the ranch itself. Because Mrs. Johnson still lives here, and because it's still a working ranch, the tour route varies occasionally. Write Superintendent, P.O. Box 329, 78636.

LYNDON B. JOHNSON STATE HISTORICAL PARK

Take US 290 west 14 miles to main entrance • 644-2252 • Visitors Center open daily 8–5. Closed Christmas • Free • W+ but not all areas

Friends of then-President Johnson purchased this property directly across the Pedernales River from the president's LBJ Ranch and donated it to the Texas Parks and Wildlife Commission, which created the park in recognition of Johnson as a "national and world leader." The Visitors Center of the 700-acre park contains both LBJ and Hill Country memorabilia. A short film about the area is shown approximately 20 minutes before each National Park Service tour bus departs the center for the LBJ Ranch. Also at the center is the Behrens Cabin, a two-room dogtrot cabin built in the 1870s. The Sauer-Beckmann Farmstead is the only living-history farm in a Texas state park. It's open from 8 to 4:30 daily. Park staff in period clothing do farm and household chores as they were done during the period 1915 through 1918. The park also has nature trails, picnic areas, swimming pool, and lighted tennis courts. Write Superintendent, Box 238, Stonewall 78671.

PEDERNALES FALLS STATE PARK

Take FM 2766 east about 10 miles • 868-7304 • Open daily • Admission about $4 per person • W variable

This 4,860-acre park is located on one of the most scenic stretches of the Pedernales River, with more than six miles of river frontage. The Pedernales Falls can be viewed from a scenic overlook at the north end of the park. Swimming, tubing, fishing, picnicking, hiking, biking, primitive camping, and improved campsites, some with hook-ups. Write Park Superintendent, Rt. 1, Box 31A, Johnson City 78636.

KERRVILLE

KERR COUNTY SEAT • 19,134 • 830

With designs on the plentiful cypress trees along the Guadalupe River, Joshua Brown led some shinglemakers here in the early 1840s. The Indians drove them off, but Brown returned in 1848 to establish Brownsborough. When Kerr County was formed in 1856, it was named county seat and renamed Kerrsville; the *s* was soon dropped. The man most prominent in Kerrville's development was Charles A. Schreiner. Born in the Alsace-Lorraine region of France, Schreiner came to San Antonio as a child with his parents. He was a Texas Ranger and a Confederate soldier before opening a country store in Kerrville after the Civil War. By 1900 the Charles Schreiner Company owned more than 600,000 acres of land and had ranching, banking, retail, and wool/mohair marketing interests. Schreiner gambled that angora goats would prosper in the area, and they did, to the extent that Kerrville became the mohair center of the world. A noted philanthropist, his most prominent legacy is Schreiner College. Farming and ranching are still important, but tourism is the area's primary industry today. Many people retire here. Many summer camps for children and adults line the Guadalupe River in the Kerrville/Ingram/Hunt area. About 10,000 children fill the youth camps each summer, so make reservations early for lodging in Kerrville on summer weekends, when parents flock here to visit their kids at camp.

The area has also become a mecca for artists and *aficionados* of the visual arts. There are several art galleries.

TOURIST SERVICES

KERRVILLE AREA CHAMBER OF COMMERCE
1700 Sidney Baker (TX 16), Suite 200 • 792-3535, 800-221-7958
Open Monday–Friday; open Saturdays March–October • W ramp in rear

MUSEUMS

COWBOY ARTISTS OF AMERICA MUSEUM
1550 Bandera Highway. *Take Sidney Baker St. (TX 16) south to Bandera Highway (TX 173), then southeast (left)* • 896-2553 • Open daily
Admission: adults $3, students $1 • W
  Rotating exhibits featuring the paintings and sculpture of the Cowboy Artists of America, which include many of America's leading Western American Realists. The exterior of the 15,000-square-foot building resembles that of a *hacienda*. A noted feature of the interior construction is the 18 boveda brick domes in the main entrance's ceiling. The construction of boveda domes, in which light Mexican brick is positioned without supporting forms or wires, is an art known to only a few Mexican artisans. Gift shop.

HILL COUNTRY MUSEUM
226 Earl Garrett St., next to post office • 896-8633 • Monday–Saturday 10–12, 1–4:30 • Admission about $3 adults, $1.50 students, children under 6 free
  The business Charles Schreiner started in 1869 was a success. In 1879 he decided to build a house worthy of his stature in the community; this turreted mansion was the result. It has been restored to its 1890s appearance and contains furnishings and displays related to the Schreiner family and area history. Listed in the National Register of Historic Places.

HISTORIC PLACES

OLD INGRAM LOOP
Take TX 27 to Ingram, then TX 39. Ingram Loop is south (left) off Highway 39 near the First Presbyterian Church • W variable
  The commercial buildings in old downtown Ingram date to the turn of the century and house a variety of arts, crafts, and antique shops. Across TX 39 from the Ingram Loop is a multipanel mural (on the walls of the Moore Lumberyard) depicting events and eras in Kerr County history. Each of the 15 panels has written commentary.

OTHER POINTS OF INTEREST

HILL COUNTRY ARTS FOUNDATION/POINT THEATRE
Take TX 27 west to TX 39 in Ingram, then west on TX 39 to Hill Country Arts Foundation • 367-5121 • Admission to events • W top level only
  Plays and musicals are presented during the summer in the 700-seat outdoor theater. Productions are held indoors the rest of the year. Art studios are located inside the Arts Foundation Building; art classes are conducted by well-known artists. The gallery features Hill Country artists and is usually open Tuesday–Saturday.

KERRVILLE SCHREINER STATE PARK

2385 Bandera Highway. *Take Sidney Baker St. (TX 16) south to Bandera Highway (TX 173), then southeast (left) about 2.5 miles* • **257-5392**
Open daily • Admission $3 per person • W variable

This 517-acre park on the Guadalupe River has boating, fishing, hiking, picnicking and camping. Swimming in the river is permitted, but no specific or supervised areas are provided.

SPORTS AND ACTIVITIES

Golf

SCOTT SCHREINER MUNICIPAL GOLF COURSE

Country Club Dr. off TX 16, across from football stadium • 257-4982
18-hole course. Greens fee about $10. No reservations.

SHOPPING

JAMES AVERY CRAFTSMAN

FM 783 (Harper Rd.) about 1 mile north of IH-10 exit 505 • 895-1122 • W

The business James Avery started here, in his garage, now has stores all over the southwest and sells nationally by mail. There is a small factory and retail store here. You can see a short video and watch jewelry being made. Write P.O. Box 1367, 78029.

SIDE TRIPS

OLD CAMP VERDE GENERAL STORE

Take TX 16 to TX 173, then southeast (left) about 11 miles • **634-7722**

In 1856, Secretary of War Jefferson Davis set up Camp Verde as home base for the U.S. Army's new camel corps. He imported camels and handlers to test his theory that camels would be a dependable means of transportation over the vast semiarid plains. The experiment met with limited success, but was interrupted by the Civil War. During the war, the camels were neglected and many of them died or wandered off. There's little left of the camp now, but the store, which opened in 1857, has been in operation ever since. A flood swept the original store away around the turn of the century and this one was built. Inside are a hand-carved wooden Indian, plus a selection of Hill Country arts and crafts.

Y.O. RANCH

Take IH-10 west to TX 41 (exit 490) at Mountain Home, then 18 miles south (left) to ranch entrance sign • **800-YO RANCH • Daily tours • Admission • W variable**

A working ranch with cattle, sheep, and goats, plus the cowboys who do all the herding, roping, and all the other daily ranch chores. Founded by Charles Schreiner in 1880, it is home to over 1,000 longhorns, champion quarterhorses, and free-ranging native wildlife, plus exotic animals such as axis deer, American elk, antelope, zebras, giraffes, and ostriches. Several historic buildings have been moved to the ranch and restored, including an 1850s stagecoach stop, Wells Fargo office, and pioneer schoolhouse. In addition to the tours (which include a ranch lunch), you can arrange photo safaris and year-round hunting.

Tours can be customized. There is a summer camp for boys and girls ages 9 to 15. Lodging is available in the lodge or in century-old cabins (11 units). Also a general store, swimming pool, and restaurant. Entrance is by reservation only.

ANNUAL EVENTS
May/June

KERRVILLE FOLK FESTIVAL

Quiet Valley Ranch • *Take TX 16 (Sidney Baker St.) south 9 miles* • 257-3600
About 3 weeks the end of May, beginning of June • Admission • W variable
More than 100 musicians and groups playing folk, blues, soul, and a smattering of other styles make this outdoor festival something to listen to. Many performers are Texas songwriters singing their own songs. Folk Mass on Sundays. Bring lawn chairs to sit on. Single-day and multi-day tickets are available. Many festival-goers camp out.

TEXAS STATE ARTS AND CRAFTS FAIR

Schreiner College, TX 27E • 896-5711 • Memorial Day weekend and following weekend • W variable
Not your ordinary arts and crafts fair. The artists and craftsmen are carefully selected for their work, and the number of exhibitors is limited to 200. Demonstrations and free crafts instruction. Also music, entertainment, and children's area. Pay parking, but free shuttle buses run from the Chamber of Commerce office and major motels and hotels.

October

KERRVILLE FLY-IN

Municipal Airport, TX 27E • 792-3535 • Third weekend in October Admission • W variable
As many as 1,500 planes, including many antique, homebuilt, and experimental, fly in. It's really a convention for members of the Experimental Aircraft Association, but they hold an air show on Saturday that the public can attend.

RESTAURANTS

($ = under $7, $$ = $8–$17, $$$ = $18–$25, $$$$ = over $25 for one person excluding drinks, tax, and tip.)

BILL'S BARBEQUE

1909 Junction Hwy. (TX 27) • 895-5733 • Lunch only Tuesday–Saturday $ • No Cr • W
Brisket, pork ribs and loin, sausage, and chicken. Popular with locals, so get here early.

JOE'S JEFFERSON STREET CAFE

1001 E. Jefferson • 257-2929 • Open for lunch and dinner Monday–Friday, dinner only on Saturday • $–$$ • MC, V, personal checks • W partial
Kinky Friedman is a fan of Joe's, which is locally famous for Southern-style cooking, including chicken-fried steak, fresh vegetables, Cajun dishes, and desserts like peach cobbler. Located in a lovely, restored Victorian-era house.

ACCOMMODATIONS

($ = under $45, $$ = $46–$60, $$$ = $61–$80, $$$$ = $81–$100, $$$$$ = over $100)
Room tax 12%

INN OF THE HILLS RIVER RESORT

1001 Junction Hwy. (TX 27W) at Harper Rd. (FM 783) • 895-5000 or in Texas 800-292-5690 • $$–$$$$ • W+ 1 room • No-smoking rooms

This inn has 200 units including suites and condominium apartments, and 20 no-smoking rooms. Cable TV. Room phones. Small pets OK. Pay transportation to San Antonio airport. Two restaurants. Club with live entertainment nightly. Five pools, lighted tennis and racquetball courts, sauna, whirlpool, exercise room, bowling lanes, putting green, bike and boat rentals. Fishing in stocked lake. Some covered parking. Gift shop.

HOLIDAY INN Y.O. RANCH HOTEL

2033 Sidney Baker (TX 16) about 2 blocks south of IH-10 • 257-4440, in Texas 800-531-2800 • $$$–$$$$$ • W+ 10 rooms • No-smoking rooms

Casually elegant western decor; 200 rooms and suites (150 no-smoking). Children under 18 stay free with parents; special rooms for families with small children. Package plans. Cable TV with movies. Room phones, charge for local calls. Restaurant, room service. Bar. Coffee maker in room. Free newspaper. Pets OK. Indoor pool, outdoor whirlpool. Tennis court. One-day dry cleaning. Adjoins public golf course. Pay transportation to San Antonio airport.

LAZY HILLS GUEST RANCH

Take TX 27 west to entrance, about 2 miles past Ingram, turn right on Henderson Rd. **• 367-5600 or 800-880-0632 • $$$$$ with meals plus 15% service charge • Minimum stay 3 days in summer and over holidays**

There are 25 units in this guest ranch. TV in lobby. No pets. Family-style meals. Outdoor pool, hot tub, tennis courts, sports courts, game room, fishing pond, playground, and horseback riding. Special arrangements for B&B accommodations in fall, winter, and spring.

KILLEEN

Bell County • 70,000 • (254)

When the tracks of the Gulf, Colorado, and Santa Fe Railroad were extended from Temple to Lampasas in the early 1880s, a switching station was set up near the midway point. A settlement grew up and was named for Frank P. Killeen, a senior official of the railroad. Killeen was never far from the legends of the Old West with gunfights in the streets as late as 1910.

In 1941 with World War II, the U.S. Army opened Camp Hood on the city's western rim, which became Fort Hood, a designation the Army gives to bases with a sense of permanence. Killeen became a typical military town with honky tonks, pawn shops, used-car lots, and small businesses that catered to the military.

But times have changed. Killeen is still a military town—a designation it welcomes because it has a strong relationship with what is the largest armor center in the world. But it has grown up and become a bustling city in its own right with a population that makes it the largest city in Bell County.

TOURIST SERVICES

KILLEEN CONVENTION AND VISITORS BUREAU

One Santa Fe Plaza at Gray in old Depot (P.O. Box 548, 76540) • 526-9551
Fax 526-6090 • email - www.gkcc.com • W +

MUSEUMS

FIRST CAVALRY DIVISION MUSEUM

Fort Hood, Bldg. 2218, Battalion Ave. at 56th • Monday–Friday 9–4,
weekends and holidays 12–4. Closed major holidays • Free • W

Organized in Fort Bliss, Texas, in 1921, the First Cavalry Division started out patrolling the Mexican border on horseback. In World War II it fought as infantry, earning the nickname "The First Team" from General Douglas MacArthur. First Cav fought again in Korea, but was converted to Air Cavalry in Vietnam. The Division served as a heavy armored unit during Operations Desert Shield and Desert Storm. The museum tells the history of the unit and traces its cavalry heritage to the Old West. Also of interest is the four-acre vehicle park that includes tanks, equipment, and weapons used by the First Cavalry, including an M1 Abrams tank, one of three displayed in the U.S.

FOURTH INFANTRY DIVISION MUSEUM

Fort Hood, Bldg. 418, Battalion Ave. at 27th • 287-8811 • Monday–Friday 9–4,
Saturday 10–4, Sunday 12–4. Closed major holidays • Free • W

Activated in response to the United States' Declaration of War against Germany in 1917, the 4th Infantry Division participated in four major campaigns of World War I. Again called to serve in World War II, the Division was the first to land at Utah Beach on June 6, 1944, liberated Paris, fought in the Hurtgen Forest, and held the Southern flank when the Germans launched the Battle of the Bulge. Following a Cold War Mission during the 1950s, the 4th deployed to Vietnam in 1966 and fought in the Central Highlands until December 1970. After serving 25 years at Fort Carson, CO, the Division moved to Fort Hood in 1995. Exhibits include audio-visual programs that depict Division history from 1917 to present and an outside display of tanks and weaponry.

OTHER POINTS OF INTEREST

FORT HOOD

Take US 190 west to main gate • 287-1110 • Open at all times • W variable

Named for Confederate General John Bell Hood, commander of Hood's Texas Brigade, the 339-square-mile post has a military population of about 42,000. A good way to visualize the number of vehicles here is to drive Motor Pool Rd. (take Destroyer Blvd. west off Hood Rd. to motor pool area). Besides the two museums, sports facilities and leisure learning classes are open to the public. Also, Fort Hood hosts a spectacular Fourth of July Celebration, with helicopter rapelling, sky diving, exhibitions, entertainment, food, and tank rides, plus an evening fireworks display. Free admission.

There is a map and visitor's center at the main gate of Fort Hood, the only post in the U.S. capable of supporting two full armored divisions. Tourist information can also be obtained from the III Corps Public Affairs Office (287-3703) or via its Web site: www.hood-pao.army.mil.

SPORTS AND ACTIVITIES

Golf

KILLEEN MUNICIPAL GOLF COURSE

Roy Reynolds Dr. south of US 190 Bus and east of the airport • 699-6034
18-hole course. Greens fee: weekdays $8.50, weekends $11.

Tennis

Courts are located at **Longbranch Park,** Rancier (FM 439) at Branch, and
Conder Park, Bus US 190 and Condor. For information call Parks and Recreation at 526-0559.

PERFORMING ARTS

VIVE LES ARTS COMMUNITY THEATRE

Vive Les Arts **Center for the Arts, 3401 S. W.S. Young Dr. • 526-9090**
Admission • W+

This volunteer group with a professional director stages six productions a
season and hosts touring shows and gallery exhibits.

SIDE TRIPS

BELTON LAKE

Take FM 349 to the lake. (*See* **Belton.**)

STILLHOUSE HOLLOW LAKE

Take US 190 east to Simmonds Rd., then south to lake. (*See* **Belton.**)

TOPSEY EXOTIC RANCH AND DRIVE THROUGH PARK

Take US 190 west to FM 1113 and turn north (right), turn west (left) on FM 580
Rt. l, Box 175, Copperas Cove 76522 • 547-3700 • Open daily 9–sundown
Admission • W variable

More than 50 species of wildlife live on the ranch. Most are so gentle they
may be hand-fed with approved feed from the safety of the car.

ANNUAL EVENTS

May

FESTIVAL OF FLAGS

Community Center Grounds and Special Events Center • 286-4626 (Killeen
FOF, Inc.) • Memorial Day weekend • Rodeo admission • W variable

Experience the flavor of Killeen peppered by the many nationalities and cultural heritages represented by Killeen and Fort Hood with food, arts and crafts,
cookoffs, entertainment, art show, military displays, and nightly concerts.

RESTAURANTS

($ = under $7, $$ = $8–$17, $$$ = $18–$25, $$$$ = over $25 for one person excluding
drinks, tax, and tip.)

MUNCHER KIND'L GERMAN RESTAURANT AND CLUB

1519 Florence Rd. in Skyline Plaza • 634-1818 • Dinner only
Monday–Saturday; closed Sunday • Cr • $–$$ • W variable
   Killeen boasts one of the best German restaurants in the area. Don't pass up their specialties, like veal shank and *wiener schnitzel.*

ACCOMMODATIONS

($ = under $45, $$ = $46–$60, $$$ = $61–$80, $$$$ = $81–$100, $$$$$ = over $100)
Room tax 13%

THE PLAZA HOTEL & CONFERENCE CENTER

1721 Central Texas Expressway (at W.S. Youngs) • 634-1555 or 800-633-8756
Fax 519-2945 • $$$ • W + 3 rooms • No-smoking rooms • Cr
   The six-story hotel has 148 rooms, including 12 suites ($$$$$), two presidential suites ($$$$$), and 50 no-smoking rooms. Cable TV, room phones (charge for local calls). Complimentary coffee in lobby. Restaurant open for breakfast, lunch, and dinner weekdays; breakfast and dinner on Saturday, and breakfast and lunch on Sunday. Lounge (DJ Friday and Saturday), outdoor pool, exercize room, meeting facilities. Fax and copier service available. No pets. Free transportation to Killeen Airport.

LA GRANGE

Fayette County Seat • 4,091 • 409
   La Grange's colorful early history includes the legend of "Strap" Buckner. A bear of a man, Buckner settled in the area before the Mexican government granted permission to the Austins to establish an Anglo colony in Texas. "Strap," who could fell a wild bull with one blow, laid down a challenge to fight anyone. The Devil accepted. Their fight lasted three days and knocked down so many trees, that the land was now clear for settling. They battled to a draw, and the angry Devil marked "Strap" for death. Legend or no, Aylkett "Strap" Buckner was killed at the Battle of Velasco in 1832.
   Colonel John H. Moore is credited with actually founding the town. An acclaimed Indian fighter from Tennessee, Moore later became a hero in the Texas Revolution. La Grange became the county seat when Fayette County was formed in 1837. La Grange means "the Meadow." Some say the county was named for the French Marquis de Lafayette and the town named for his country estate. Others say settlers from Tennessee named them after places in their home state. Fighting men like Buckner and Moore were not unusual in this area. The old live oak on the north side of the courthouse square is called the "Muster Oak"; here fighting men gathered to go off to battle in six conflicts, starting with the battle to repel the Mexican invasion of 1842.
   The La Grange area claims a number of firsts in Texas history. Rutersville College, the first Protestant college in the Republic, was built about five miles northeast in 1840. The first rural free delivery (RFD) system in Texas was set up here in 1889. The state's first roadside park was built about 12 miles west in 1933. In more recent times, the city gained unwanted notoriety as the home of the famous, or infamous "Chicken Ranch," the subject of *The Best Little Whorehouse in Texas.*

TOURIST SERVICES

OLD COUNTY JAIL/TOURIST INFORMATION AND CULTURE CENTER

171 S. Main, 1 block south of the courthouse square • 800-524-7264
Open daily • Free • W partial

This vestpocket stone castle was built in 1883 to serve as county jail. It now houses the Chamber of Commerce and the Tourist Information and Culture Center, which features information about Fayette County communities and Fayette County Sheriff history, including Sheriff Jim Flourney, made famous by Marvin Zindler and *The Best Little Whorehouse in Texas*. You can take a tour of the cell block and look through the guards' peepholes. No gallows, but the official La Grange hanging rope is on display.

MUSEUMS

FAISON HOUSE MUSEUM

822 S. Jefferson • 968-5756 • Open by appointment • Admission

The original part of the house was built in 1841. The three front rooms were added in 1855. N.W. Faison was a member of the ill-fated Dawson Company (*see* Monument Hill State Historic Site, below). After spending two years in a Mexican prison, Faison was pardoned by Santa Anna. Faison bought the house in 1866. His family lived here until 1961, and some of the original furniture, paintings, and memorabilia remain.

FAYETTE HERITAGE MUSEUM AND ARCHIVES

855 S. Jefferson, in Public Library • 968-6418 • Open Tuesday 10–6:30, Wednesday–Friday 10–5, Saturday 10–1, Sunday 1–5 • Donations • W downstairs only

Exhibits on county history change two or three times a year. Main displays are upstairs. Large genealogical collection with emphasis on Fayette County.

HISTORIC PLACES

MONUMENT HILL STATE HISTORIC SITE AND KREISCHE HOUSE AND BREWERY STATE HISTORIC SITE

Take US 77 south up bluff to Spur 92, then west (right) to headquarters
968-5658 • Open daily 8–5 • Admission • W+ but not all areas

These two distinct historic sites on 40 acres are administered as one unit. Located on a bluff overlooking the Colorado River, the park offers an excellent bird's-eye view of La Grange. There is a large picnic area.

Monument Hill is marked by a 48-foot-tall stone and bronze monument marking the common grave containing the remains of the men killed in the massacre of Dawson's Company in 1842, and those of the Mier Expedition executed in 1843 in the Black Bean episode. In September 1842, Nicholas Mosby Dawson led a group of 53 men going to join the Texans gathering to fight the Mexican force of General Adrian Woll, who had occupied San Antonio. Dawson's unit was surrounded by about 400 Mexican troops with cannon near San Antonio. Between cannon fire and a cavalry charge, 36 Texans were killed, 15 were captured, and three escaped. The dead were buried in a common grave on the field of battle. A force of 700 Texans sent to repel the Mexican invaders reached the Rio Grande in December. At that point, the force's commander and many of the men followed orders to return to San Antonio. About 300 Texans refused to obey the order to withdraw and attacked the Mexican town of Mier instead. With victory in their grasp, they fell for a ruse by the Mexican commander, who convinced them that they were outnumbered. The Texans surrendered. While being marched as prisoners to Mexico City, 188 Texans escaped, but only five reached Texas. Seven died in the mountains and 176 were recaptured. Santa Anna decreed that one in ten was to be executed. To carry out the order, 159 white beans and 17 black beans were placed in a pot. Those who drew out black beans were shot. In 1847, during the Mexican War, Captain John E. Dusenbery, one of the Mier expedition men who had drawn a white bean, reclaimed the remains of the 17. Shortly after, the remains of Dawson and his men were also retrieved. They were all buried here with military honors on September 18, 1848.

The Kreische House and Brewery have a less morbid history. The brewery was one of the first commercial breweries in Texas when it opened in the 1850s. It operated until the 1880s, and is listed in the National Register of Historic Places. Guided tours of the brewery ruins and the restored house are given each Saturday and Sunday at 2 and 3.

OTHER HISTORIC BUILDINGS

Among the many nineteenth-century buildings are the **Old Library** (1852) at 159 Fannin, **Fire Station** (1881) at N. Franklin and E. Lafayette, **Fayette County Courthouse** (1881) and **St. James Episcopal Church** (1885) at 156 N. Monroe and Colorado. Several nineteenth-century and turn-of-the-century homes are scattered throughout the city.

SIDE TRIPS

FAYETTE LAKE

Take TX 159 toward Fayetteville, about 10 miles from town • **249-3504 (Oak Thicket), 249-3344 (Park Prairie)** • **Admission** • **W variable**

This 2,400-acre lake is a cooling pond for a power-generating plant that also offers boating, fishing, and skiing. The bass fishing is especially good. Oak Thicket and Park Prairie Parks offer camping, nature trails, boat docks, and fishing pier.

ANNUAL EVENTS

FAYETTE COUNTY COUNTRY FAIR

County Fairgrounds, US 77N • **968-5756 (Chamber of Commerce)**
Thursday–Sunday of Labor Day weekend in September • **Admission**
W variable

All the usual country fair events: agricultural and homemaking competitions, carnival, entertainment and dances every night, exhibits, sports tournaments, tractor pull, talent show, barbecue cookoff, and men's cooking contest. Free bus rides are available from downtown.

RESTAURANTS

($ = under $7, $$ = $8–$17, $$$ = $18–$25, $$$$ = over $25 for one person excluding drinks, tax, and tip.)

PRAUSE'S MEAT MARKET AND BBQ
253 W. Travis, on the square • 968-3259 • Monday–Friday 7–5:30, Saturday 5:30–1 • $ • No Cr • W
Go around the meat display cases in the front of the store, place your order, then sit down and enjoy your barbecue at tables in the rear, as folks have been doing around here since 1952.

LAMPASAS

Lampasas County Seat • 7,000 • 512
The Indians used the sulphur springs here for medicinal purposes long before the settlers arrived in the early 1850s. Farmers founded the Farmers' Alliance near here in 1877 to battle ruinous economic conditions. It grew to more than 3,000 chapters, which in 1887 merged with the Farmers' Union. The first state bankers' association formed in the United States was organized here in 1885 and called the Texas State Bankers' Association. In 1882 the Gulf, Colorado and Santa Fe Railroad extended its terminus to Lampasas, and the town became a resort for the medicinal springs. But the boom faded when the railroad moved on west. (Several of the major springs are still flowing in Lampasas.) Now, ranching and manufacturing are major economic factors in this picturesque town, which is enhanced by a creek with shade trees, benches, bridges, 30-foot-high fountains, a gazebo, and ducks.

TOURIST SERVICES

LAMPASAS COUNTY CHAMBER OF COMMERCE
501 E. 2nd (P.O. Box 627, 76550) • 556-5172, Fax 556-2195
Located in the old Santa Fe depot built in 1901.

MUSEUMS

KEYSTONE SQUARE MUSEUM
303 S. Western between E. 2nd and E. 3rd • 556-2224 • Saturday 1–4 (Extended hours during special exhibits) • Free (donations) • W
You can still see the gun loopholes in this 1870s building that houses the memorabilia of local and area history. An annual Quilt Show is held the second weekend in August.

HISTORIC PLACES

A brochure, "Scenic and Historical Driving Tour," is available free from the Chamber of Commerce and at several local businesses.

The **Keystone Hotel** at 404 E. 2nd was originally named the Star Hotel and completed in 1870. Other historic buildings are the **Lampasas County Courthouse** at 4th St. between Oak and Pecan built in 1882, **St. Mary's Episcopal Church** at 4th and Chestnut was built in 1884 and has been in continuous use, and **Silk Stocking Row** on W. 3rd St. Several of these fine residences were built at the turn of the century.

SPORTS AND ACTIVITIES

HANCOCK PARK GOLF COURSE

Hancock Park off US 281 on south side of town • 556-3202 • 18-hole course. Greens fee: weekdays $12.50, weekends and holidays $17.50

SHOPPING

Around the courtyard square, you'll find antiques and crafts in many of the restored buildings that were built in the 1800s. Free concerts (big band to blues) are held every Friday in June; other entertainment year-round.

SIDE TRIPS

TOPSY EXOTIC RANCH AND DRIVE THROUGH PARK

Take US 183 north to FM 580. Turn east (right) to ranch. (*See* **Killeen**.)

ANNUAL EVENTS

SPRING-HO FESTIVAL

Various locations • 556-5172 (Chamber of Commerce) • Second weekend in July, Thursday–Sunday • Free (admission to some events) • W variable

The festival celebrates the importance of the city's underground springs that made it a health resort in the 1880s. Activities are held downtown and at Hancock Park and include every festival event for family fun.

RESTAURANTS

($ = under $7, $$ = $8–$17, $$$ = $18–$25, $$$$ = over $25 for one person excluding drinks, tax, and tip.)

COURTYARD CAFE

402 S. Live Oak • 556-6611 • Open 11 a.m.–2 p.m. Tuesdays and Sunday, 5:30–9 p.m. Wednesday–Thursday, 5:30–10 p.m. Friday and Saturday • $–$$$ MC, V, DIS • W + (elevator)

On the first floor of this restored two-story building that was built in the late 1800s, the cafe has hardwood floors, wood tables, Texas-style lanterns, a Western decor. The menu includes seafood and steaks. Upstairs is a private club with a view of the square. (Nominal fee for guest membership.)

LISA'S SCHNITZEL HOUSE

311 E. 3rd • 556-2660 • Dinner only Tuesday–Saturday. Closed Sunday and Monday • $–$$ • MC, V • Children's plate

Authentic German dishes are the mainstay of the menu including a variety of pork *schnitzels, rouladen* (cabbage rolls), and goulash. Private club with memberships available.

ACCOMMODATIONS

($ = under $45, $$ = $46–$60, $$$ = $61–$80, $$$$ = $81–$100, $$$$$ = over $100) Room tax 7%

Bed and Breakfast

HISTORIC MOSES HUGHES RANCH

Rt. 2, Box 31 (76550). *Take FM 580 seven miles west* **• 556-5923 • $$–$$$ • No Cr**

Deep tranquility and natural beauty surround the two-story, native stone 1856 ranch house on a Hill Country creek. Two bedrooms and one bath are furnished in antiques. Breakfast is included, and all meals can be arranged on request. Your host is a martial arts expert and will give you lessons, or you can just relax in a tube in the creek. No pets, children, or smoking.

LLANO

Llano County Seat • 3,012 • 915

Llano means "plain" in Spanish, and since this is the Hill Country, the name doesn't seem to fit. Some say that Llano is a corruption of the French name given to the Lipan Indians. Spanish explorers named the river "Rio de los Chanas" after the Chanas band of the Tonkawa Indians. Over time, that name may have been corrupted until Chanas evolved into Llano, say others. Neither sounds really convincing, but no one has come up with anything better.

Llano was founded in 1855 and became the county seat a year later. Starting as a farm and ranching community, it suddenly became a boom town in the 1880s because of iron ore deposits discovered in the area. The county is part of the 1.5 billion-acre Llano Uplift, a geological phenomenon packed with a variety of mineral deposits that took more than a billion years to form. In 1886, the Wakefield Iron and Coal Company of Minnesota started mining the iron ore; speculators followed and soon the population swelled to 10,000 in this, the "Pittsburgh of the West." The boom went bust when no nearby source of the coal necessary to make steel was found; shipping coal in or iron ore out was too expensive. Reminders of those days include street names like Bessemer and Pittsburgh, and a number of large homes and business buildings. The granite industry founded here at about the same time prospered, although it has since declined. By 1935, ten quarries and five finishing plants were operating.

The Llano Uplift is a rock hound's wonderland, with amethyst, azurite, dolomite, galena, garnet, quartz, serpentine, traces of gold, and Llanite, a type of brown granite with skyblue crystals and rusty pink feldspar found nowhere else in the world but Llano County. It is farm and ranch country, and Llano attracts hunters, billing itself as the "Deer Capital of Texas." The town is also a contender for the title of Hill Country Barbecue Capital, with several good places to chow down.

TOURIST SERVICES

LLANO COUNTY CHAMBER OF COMMERCE

700 Bessemer (TX 16) (78643), north of the Llano River bridge • 247-5354
Monday–Friday, also Saturdays during deer season • W

Information available on rock hunting and deer hunting leases.

MUSEUMS

LLANO COUNTY HISTORICAL MUSEUM

304 Bessemer (TX 16), at the north end of the Llano River Bridge • 247-3026
June–August: Tuesday–Saturday 10–12, 1:30–5:30, Sunday afternoon; September–May: Wednesday–Saturday 10–12, 1:30–5:30 • Donations • W+

Formerly Bruhl's Drugstore; the marble soda fountain from the 1920s is still here. Many area minerals are on display, photos from Llano's boomtown years, and details on famous residents such as sculptor Frank Teich. Three other local sons are the center of an exhibit devoted to polo.

HISTORIC PLACES

The Llano County Courthouse, Main and Ford, south of the Llano River Bridge, is the centerpiece of Llano's historic district. Built in 1892, it has had no additions over the years. The stock at **Acme Dry Goods** on the courthouse square (109 W. Main) is modern, but the building dates to the 1890s and the store fixtures to the turn of the century. The **Southern Hotel,** 201 W. Main and Berry, was built in 1881 as a stagecoach stop between Mason and Burnet. It now houses the offices of Buttery Hardware, in business here over 100 years. The **Old Llano County Jail,** Oatman St. one block northeast of courthouse, was built in 1895 of local granite. It originally had a red roof, causing its prisoners to refer to it as the "Red Top." It is now a museum, open by appointment; call Chamber of Commerce. Original gallows still in place upstairs.

SPORTS AND ACTIVITIES

Golf

LLANO GOLF COURSE

Llano City Park, FM 152 about 1.5 miles west of courthouse • 247-5100
18-hole course by the Llano River. Greens fee $10 and up. Park also offers swimming pool, playground, picnic area, fishing, campgrounds (fee), and rodeo arena.

ANNUAL EVENTS

June

LLANO COUNTY RODEO

City Park Arena, FM 152 about 1.5 miles west of courthouse • 247-5354
Friday and Saturday of first weekend in June • Admission • W

Professional Rodeo Cowboys' Association (PRCA) rodeo, starts with downtown parade and Friday night dance. Also BBQ cookoff.

RESTAURANTS

($ = under $7, $$ = $8–$17, $$$ = $18–$25, $$$$ = over $25 for one person excluding drinks, tax, and tip.)

COOPER'S OLD TIME PIT BARBECUE

705 W. Young (TX 29W) • 247-3003 • Open daily • $ • No Cr • W
Brisket and other cuts of beef, sausage, pork chops, ribs, and *cabrito* (sometimes) are served. Beans, potato salad, and the trimmings. Beer.

INMAN'S KITCHEN

809 W. Young (TX 29W) • 247-5257 • Tuesday–Saturday, breakfast, lunch, and dinner • $ • MC, V • W
Inman's strongest suit is its turkey sausage, smoked turkey, ham, chicken, and jalapeño sausage. The barbecue is OK, but nothing special. Trimmings, plus breads and pies are made on premises. Very popular during hunting season.

ACCOMMODATIONS

($ = under $45, $$ = $46–$60, $$$ = $61–$80, $$$$ = $81–$100, $$$$$ = over $100)
Room tax 14%

BADU HOUSE

601 Bessemer (TX 16) one block north of the Llano River Bridge • 247-4304 $$$–$$$$$ • AE, MC, V • W partial
This two-story B&B has five rooms with private bath, one suite, all upstairs. Children, pets OK. Continental breakfast. Restaurant open for lunch Tuesday–Saturday, dinner Monday–Saturday. Private club (guests automatically members, temporary memberships for non-guests available). Antiques throughout. Originally a bank when built in 1891 during the iron boom, then converted to a home by N.J. Badu, who discovered Llanite. Largest piece of polished Llanite in the world tops bar. Listed in National Register of Historic Places.

DABBS HOTEL

112 E. Burnet, just off Bessemer on the north bank of the Llano • 247-7905
The last standing railroad hotel in Llano, the Dabbs Hotel opened in 1907 for railroad crewmen who stayed overnight and returned to Austin the next day. Loose, congenial atmosphere. Swimming, fishing, gardens. Huge Southern-style breakfast.

LOCKHART

Caldwell County Seat • 9,415 • 512
In March 1840, a peace meeting in San Antonio between a dozen Comanche chiefs and Republic of Texas peace commissioners turned violent. The Comanches were supposed to turn over about 200 white prisoners at the meeting, but only brought two. The commissioners had brought in the army with a plan to hold the chiefs as hostages for the release of the white captives. When

told they were prisoners, the chiefs fought. All 12 died. Angry Comanches retaliated with a reign of terror that reached its peak in August 1840, when a band of about 600 raided Victoria and the town of Linnville on Lavaca Bay. Loaded with loot and a herd of several thousand stolen horses, they headed north, for home. They were met at Plum Creek, just east of Lockhart today, by about 200 soldiers and militia. The Texans attacked the Indians and won; the Comanches lost over 80 men, the Texans lost one. Never again did the Comanches attack a coastal town or ranch.

When a new county formed in 1848, it was named for one of the Texans at the Battle of Plum Creek, Mathew "Old Paint" Caldwell. The settlement of Plum Creek was named county seat and renamed Lockhart after the man who donated the land for the town.

TOURIST SERVICES

LOCKHART CHAMBER OF COMMERCE

208 E. San Antonio, on the square (P.O. Box 840, 78644) • 398-2818

MUSEUMS

CALDWELL COUNTY MUSEUM

315 E. Market at S. Brazos • 398-2818 (Chamber of Commerce) • Hours vary
Donation
The 1910 county jail is now a museum filled with pioneer furnishings, farm equipment, and other artifacts pertaining to county history. Call the Chamber of Commerce for information.

HISTORIC PLACES

Built in 1893, the three-story limestone Second Empire styled courthouse is the center of the **Caldwell County Courthouse Historic District,** which contains more than six blocks of mostly commercial brick buildings from the turn of the century, when Lockhart grew wealthy off the cotton trade. **Emmanuel Episcopal Church,** 117 N. Church, one block west of the square, (398-3342) was built in 1856. It lays claim to being the oldest continuously used Protestant church building in Texas. The **Dr. Eugene Clark Library,** 217 S. Main (398-3223, open Monday through Saturday), was built in 1900 and is modelled on the Villa Rotunda in Vicenza, Italy. Reportedly the oldest city library in the state. Beautiful stained glass windows. **Brock Log Cabin,** US 183 near Live Oak in city park, is a log cabin built in 1850.

OTHER POINTS OF INTEREST

LOCKHART STATE PARK

Take FM 20 west about 3 miles • 398-3479 • **Open daily 8–10 for day use, at all times for camping • Admission about $2 per person • W variable**
This 257-acre park has a swimming pool, playground, hiking trail, picnic areas, camping, and nine-hole golf course (greens fee). Plum Creek wanders through the park, and there is a rodeo arena. Write Rt. 3, Box 69, Lockhart 78644.

ANNUAL EVENTS

June

CHISHOLM TRAIL ROUNDUP

In City Park, US 183 north of the square • 398-2818 (Chamber of Commerce)
One weekend in middle of June • Admission • W variable

Lockhart was a principal convergence point for herds heading up the old Chisholm Trail, and the first herd up that trail to Kansas was owned by a Lockhart man. There's a carnival, dance every night, parades, sports competitions, chili and barbecue cookoffs, arts and crafts show, Kiwanis Rodeo, and the reenactment of the Battle of Plum Creek. There's no parking at the Park. Shuttle buses run from the courthouse square (fee).

RESTAURANTS

($ = under $7, $$ = $8–$17, $$$ = $18–$25, $$$$ = over $25 for one person excluding drinks, tax, and tip.)

KREUZ MARKET

208 S. Commerce • 398-2361 • Monday–Saturday 7:30–6 • $ • No Cr • W

If you're a barbecue purist who thinks the meat is all-important and eschews the frills, Kreuz is your dream come true. No sauce, beans, potato salad, slaw. Just beef and pork on butcher paper with onions, pickles, and bread or crackers. In addition to the omnipresent brisket, they smoke beef shoulder "clods," prime rib, and whole, bone-in pork loin, which is sliced to order. They make their own sausage. In business since the turn of the century and frequently cited as having the best barbecue in the state. Beer.

MARBLE FALLS

Burnet County • 4,266 • 830

In the 1850s, young Adam R. Johnson came to a place on the Colorado River where it fell about 20 feet over marble ledges. He saw the falls' industrial power potential and started to buy up property and make plans to build an industrial town on the site. But the Civil War interrupted. Johnson became a Confederate General, but was blinded in a battle in Kentucky. His blindness didn't stop him from laying out the town of Marble Falls from memory, aided by his son. When the owners of nearby Granite Mountain donated the granite for the Texas State Capitol Building in Austin, Johnson donated the right-of-way for the railroad to haul the granite. With the railroad in hand, Johnson founded the city of Marble Falls in 1887. The falls have been covered over by Lake Marble Falls, but the Granite Mountain quarry still produces granite for construction projects all over the United States.

TOURIST SERVICES

MARBLE FALLS/LAKE LBJ CHAMBER OF COMMERCE

801 US 281 (78654) • 693-4449 or 800-759-8178 • Open Monday–Friday • W

Located in railroad depot built in 1893.

HISTORIC PLACES

The **Brandt Badger House,** S. 5th and Ave. N, was built in 1888 of granite rubble left over from the Capitol's construction. Upon retirement, former governor of Texas Oran M. Roberts moved into what is now called the **Governor Roberts Cottage** at 819 7th and Main, in 1893. The Roper Hotel, 707 3rd St. and US 281, began life in 1888 as a hotel and remained one until after World War II.

OTHER POINTS OF INTEREST

GRANITE MOUNTAIN

RR 1431 just west of city
It's 866 feet to the summit of this dome of sunset red granite covering 186 acres. Quarrying began here in the 1880s, for construction of the state Capitol. Quarrying continues, and more recently, the stone was used in the Sears Tower in Chicago. Not open to the public.

LAKE LYNDON B. JOHNSON (LBJ)

Take FM 1431 west to Wirtz Dam access road, then south to dam
This 6,300-acre lake is the third of the stair-step Highland Lakes. Both public and commercial facilities around the lake offer the opportunity for boating, fishing, swimming, waterskiing, sailing, picnicking, and camping. The lake is especially popular because the surrounding tree-covered hills and granite cliffs shield it from high winds.

LAKE MARBLE FALLS

Lakeside city park at south end of Ave. H just south of S. 1st St.
Open daily • Free • W variable
A 5.75-mile-long impoundment of the Colorado River, this 780-acre lake is the fourth in the Highland Lakes chain. Facilities are available for boating, fishing, waterskiing, and swimming. There are also commercial campsites.

SCENIC OVERLOOK

Roadside park, US 281 just south of the Colorado River
This park offers a panoramic view of the city and lake. A marker here commemorates Oscar Fox, whose song "The Hills of Home" was inspired by the area.

SPORTS AND ACTIVITIES

Golf

MEADOWLAKES GOLF AND COUNTRY CLUB

Meadowlakes Dr. (continuation of S. Ave. N) • 693-3300
18-hole course. Greens fees over $20. Six tennis courts (fee)

RESTAURANTS

($ = under $7, $$ = $8–$17, $$$ = $18–$25, $$$$ = over $25 for one person excluding drinks, tax, and tip.)

BLUEBONNET CAFE

211 US 281, just north of the bridge • 693-2344 • Breakfast, lunch, and dinner daily • $–$$ • No Cr
The Bluebonnet first opened on Main St. in 1931 and moved out to the highway in 1946, serving up chicken and dumplings as one of the Tuesday lunch

specials ever since. Steaks, liver and onions, Mexican dishes, chicken, catfish, chicken-fried steaks. Breakfast all day. BYOB.

ACCOMMODATIONS

($ = under $45, $$ = $46–$60, $$$ = $61–$80, $$$$ = $81–$100, $$$$$ = over $100)
Room tax 6%

HORSESHOE BAY COUNTRY CLUB RESORT

Take US 281 south just over bridge to FM 2147, then west (right) about 5 miles
598-2511 or in Texas 800-252-9363, outside Texas 800-531-5105 • $$$$$
This resort offers about 200 hotel-style accommodations. Condos and town-houses are also for rent. Cable TV. Room phones. No pets. Restaurant and club. Outdoor pool, beach, marina, three 18-hole golf courses, 18-hole putting course, outdoor lighted and indoor tennis courts, stables.

MASON

Mason County Seat • 2,041 • 915
In the early 1850s the Army built a chain of posts, a day's horseback ride apart, from the Red River to the Rio Grande to protect the frontier from Indian attacks. One of these was Fort Mason. The namesake of the fort is not clear from military records, but it was named for either Lieutenant George T. Mason, killed in the Mexican War, or Brigadier General Richard B. Mason who supervised the construction of the chain of forts. A town grew up around the fort and took its name. The majority of the early settlers came from the German communities around Fredericksburg, Irish immigrants, and from the American Midwest. When the county was formed in 1858, it was also named after the fort, and the town was soon named county seat. After the Civil War the frontier pushed westward and Fort Mason was abandoned (see Museums), but the town lived on.

An internal war hit this area in the mid-1870s. Called the Mason County or Hoo Doo War, it started over cattle rustling and developed into a violent feud between the German and Anglo settlers. About a dozen men were killed in ambushes and mob lynchings before the Texas Rangers moved in and restored order.

Among the many things that set this town apart is its claim to have had the first woman bank president in the state. It is also the hometown of the late Fred Gipson, author of the book "Old Yeller," which Walt Disney made into a movie. Gipson is among the county natives showcased in a room in the library at Post Hill and Schmidt. Mason County is especially well-known among rock hunters as the center of an area loaded with topaz, the Texas gemstone (*see* Sports and Activities). The county is also popular for deer and wild turkey hunting.

TOURIST SERVICES

MASON COUNTY CHAMBER OF COMMERCE

108 Ft. McKavitt, on the square (P.O. Box 156, 76856) • 347-5758 • W

MUSEUMS

FORT MASON OFFICERS QUARTERS

Rainey and Post Hill, about 5 blocks south of the courthouse • 347-5758 (Chamber of Commerce) • Open daily • Free • W

Several men who went down in history as great military leaders in the Civil War were stationed at this fort during its short career (1851–1870). These included George Armstrong Custer, Albert Sidney Johnston, and Robert E. Lee. Colonel Lee was commander here in 1861 when Lincoln called him back to Washington to offer him command of the Union Army being prepared for the upcoming war. After the post was abandoned, the townspeople reused materials from the 23 buildings to construct new buildings in town. This building is a reconstruction of the officers quarters built as a Bicentennial project in 1976 on the original foundation. Exhibits include a miniature of the fort and historical memorabilia.

MASON COUNTY MUSEUM

300 Moody at Bryan • 347-5758 • Free (donations) • W+

The building, constructed in 1887 with stone from Fort Mason buildings, was once a public school. Now it houses both the museum and the senior citizens center. The museum is on the second floor with exhibits that give an overview of the area geology, geography, history, and art. There is a little country schoolhouse behind the main building.

HISTORIC PLACES

MASON HISTORIC DISTRICT

All of the downtown area around the square, Fort Mason, and a large residential neighborhood constitute an historic district listed in the National Register of Historic Places. Many of the buildings on the square have been restored and exemplify a western small town right out of the 1880s. Among the many nineteenth-century buildings in town are the **John Gamel House** (1869) at 104 San Antonio, the **County Jail** (1894) just south of the courthouse, and the **White-Grant House** (1870s) and **Moran House** (1876), both on TX 29 several blocks east of the courthouse. The stores on the square are historical. Hofmann Dry Goods and Grosse Lumber Store have historical markers. They have been in the same family for over 100 years.

SEAQUIST HOME

400 Broad • 347-5413 • By appointment only • $5 person, minimum tour $20

This three-story home is an outstanding example of a Queen Anne Victorian mansion. It has 22 rooms, 15 fireplaces, stained-glass windows, a black walnut staircase made without nails, two-story wraparound galleries, and a third floor ballroom with a balcony for musicians. Made of hand-carved stone and wood, the home was begun in 1891 and renovated to its current form in 1919 by Oscar Seaquist, a Swedish immigrant who had made his fortune as a boot maker. This private home, still in the Seaquist family, is listed in the National Register of Historic Places.

OTHER POINTS OF INTEREST

GENE ZESCH'S CARVINGS

Commercial Bank, 100 Moody, on the square • 347-6324
Open bank hours • Free • W

Zesch does four- to six-inch caricatures in wood and bronze. His subjects are humorous views of today's cowboys and other Western folk as they contend with the joys and calamities of daily life. A large private collection of his work is on display in the Directors' Room at the bank. True to the tradition of Western hospitality, visitors are invited to have a cup of coffee while they view the carvings.

SPORTS AND ACTIVITIES

Bat Watching

ECKERT JAMES RIVER BAT CAVE

FM 1723 to FM 2389 past the Llano River • 347-5758 (Chamber of Commerce)
May–October Thursday–Sunday nights from 6 to 9 • Free

Central Texas is blessed with more than its share of bats, and Mason ranks right up there with the likes of Austin in this regard. An enormous colony of Mexican freetail bats summers near Mason from May to October, and the Nature Conservancy funds a steward's position to assist visitors and care for the site. Budget a casual 30-minute drive to and from town to the cave, and plan to spend at last 90 minutes waiting for the bats to emerge. The bats emerge anywhere from dusk to twilight.

Topaz Hunting

Mason County is one of the few places in the country where topaz can be found. One Mason gem, reportedly the largest gem-quality topaz crystal found in North America, weighs in at 1,296 grams (just under three pounds) and is in the Smithsonian Institution in Washington, D.C.

Two ranches northwest of town regularly permit rockhounds to hunt topaz on their property: the **Seaquist Ranch** (P.O. Box 35, 76856, 347-5413. Pay fees and pick up keys at the Nu-Way Grocery, 347-5713, on the northwest corner of the square in Mason) and the **Hofmann Ranch** (c/o Loeffler, Menard Rt., 76856, 347-6415). Permits cost $10 per day. Improved camp sites are available at the Seaquist Ranch and primitive camping at the Hofmann Ranch (fee). Both ranches are closed to rockhunters during deer hunting season, November to January.

ANNUAL EVENTS

July

MASON COUNTY ROUNDUP

Downtown and Fort Mason Park (south on US 87) • 347-5758 (Chamber of Commerce) • Usually Friday–Saturday of third weekend in July • Free (admission to Rodeo)

Roundup starts with a downtown parade Friday morning. Then follows entertainment and an arts and crafts show on the courthouse lawn, with the rodeo at the park at night followed by a dance.

RESTAURANTS

($ = under $7, $$ = $8–$17, $$$ = $18–$25, $$$$ = over $25 for one person excluding drinks, tax, and tip.)

COOPERS PIT BBQ

Hwy 87 • 347-6897 • 10:30 A.M.–6:30 P.M. • $–$$
    The menu offers open pit barbecue cooked on mesquite wood.

ZAVALA'S CAFE

Hwy 87 North • 347-5365 • Breakfast, lunch, and dinner daily.
Closed Christmas • $ • No Cr • W • Children's plates
    Zavala's has a varied menu including Tex-Mex dishes, hamburgers, and steaks. The *cinco-cinco nachos* are a big local favorite as is the fried catfish on Friday's. The flour tortillas and soups are homemade.

ACCOMMODATIONS

($ = Under $45, $$ = $46–$60, $$$ = $61–$80, $$$$ = $81–$100, $$$$$ = Over $100) Room tax 10%

HASSE HOUSE AND RANCH

Seven miles east of square on TX 29 • 347-6463 or 888-414-2773 • $$$
    Listed in the National Register of Historic Places, the Hasse House is located on a 320-acre working ranch in Art, Texas. House can sleep as many as eight ($$$$$). Kitchen and laundry. Period furniture and woodburning stove. Continental breakfast. Closed during hunting season.

MASON SQUARE BED AND BREAKFAST

Town Square • 347-6398 or 800-369-0405 • $$
    On the north side of courthouse square, smack dab in the middle of Mason, this second-floor bed and breakfast is as convenient as it is comfortable. This section of Mason dates from the late 19th century, and numerous elements from that era are present at the property including the original pressed tin ceiling, Victorian woodwork, oak floors, and stained-glass transoms. Each of the three guest rooms has a private shower and bath. As an added convenience, a common area is also available to guests, complete with refrigerator, dishwasher, microwave, dishes, and utensils. Continental breakfast.

NEW BRAUNFELS

Comal County Seat • 30,700 • 830
    After Texas had gained its independence from Mexico, the new Republic was pictured as a utopia in popular literature in Germany. The appeal of this new country was even greater because in the early 1840s times were hard in Germany. The worn-out soil could not produce enough food for the rapidly growing population and there was a lingering depression. To counter this, several princes and other nobles formed a *Mainzer Adelsverein*, or League of Nobles, to sponsor Germans who wanted to emigrate to Texas. The nobles weren't just being good to their people in this venture. They had been given generous

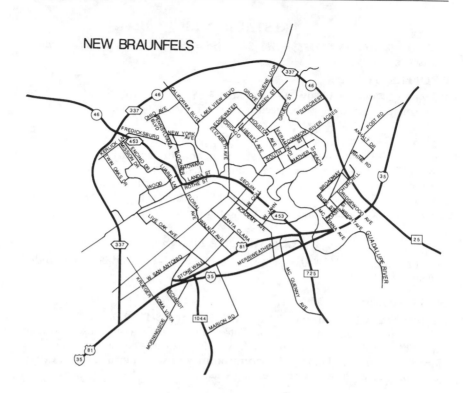

NEW BRAUNFELS

grants of land and other concessions by the Republic of Texas, and had bought
other land which they expected would bring them a profit once the colonies
were established and land values went up. To carry out their plans the nobles
organized the Society for the Protection of German Immigrants in Texas, with
Prince Carl von Solms-Braunfels as its commissioner-general.

Prince Carl arrived in Galveston in July 1844 and soon found the land the
Adelsverein had purchased was too far for his initial colony. So he purchased
1,265 acres (for $1,111) on the Guadalupe River between San Antonio and
Austin near Comal Springs, then called Comal Fountains, in March 1845. Comal
was the name given by the Spanish missionaries because of the pancake-shaped
islands in the river that flowed from the springs. On Good Friday, 1845, Prince
Carl and about 200 of his immigrants founded the town, which they named
after the town in Germany where the prince had his castle.

But if times were bad in Germany, initially they were worse for the new Texans. Within a few months, thousands of them had landed at the port of Indianola, then called Carlsshafen, only to find there was no transport to move
them to New Braunfels. At Indianola, the Germans suffered an epidemic. Many
died and hundreds of others tried to escape by walking to New Braunfels.
Weak and short of supplies, they left a trail of graves. And those who made it to
the colony brought the epidemic with them. Reports on the total number of
deaths vary widely, ranging from 1,000 to 3,000.

Meanwhile, Prince Carl's fiancée, Sophia, Princess of Salm-Salm, refused to
join him in the new land so he went home to marry her and stayed there.

Despite its rought start, and as testimony to the hardiness and persistence of German colonists, by 1850 New Braunfels was the fourth largest city in Texas, exceeded only by Galveston, Houston, and San Antonio. But it never did make money for the *Adelsverein*, which went bankrupt.

German traditions and cultures are still strong in this city, which today sums up its attitude with the slogan "In New Braunfels Ist Das Leben Schon"—which loosely translated means "life is beautiful here."

TOURIST SERVICES

GREATER NEW BRAUNFELS CHAMBER OF COMMERCE

390 S. Seguin at Garden, in the Civic Center complex (P.O. Box 311417, 78131-1417) • 625-2385 or 800-572-2626 • W

In addition to city maps and brochures, they offer a "Visitors Bonus Booklet" containing discount coupons for motels, restaurants, and tourist attractions.

MUSEUMS

HUMMEL MUSEUM

199 Main Plaza • 625-5636 or 800-456-4866 • Monday–Saturday 10–5, Sunday 12–5 • Admission • W+

More than 350 drawings and paintings, the most extensive collection of the works by Sister Maria Innocentia Hummel open to the public anywhere in the world, are on display here. The $8 million collection is on a 12-year lease, by the nonprofit group that runs the museum, from the Nauer family of Switzerland. In addition to the works of art, there are other displays that tell the story of Sister Hummel's life, and a section explaining how the Hummel figurines (based on her work) are made.

MUSEUM OF TEXAS HANDMADE FURNITURE

1370 Church Hill Dr., east off Loop 337W • 629-6504 • Days and hours vary with season. Call ahead • Tour groups by appointment • Adults $3, children 6–12 $1 • W

The central focus of this unique museum is more than 75 of the solid, beautifully crafted furniture items handmade by German cabinet makers in Texas during the mid-nineteenth century. Scores of rare home accessories, such as early English ironstone are also on display. The museum is managed by the local Heritage Society and located in the **Breustedt Haus,** which was built in 1858 and is listed in the National Register of Historic Places.

SOPHIENBURG MUSEUM & ARCHIVES

401 W. Coll at Academy • 629-1572 • Monday–Saturday 10–5, Sunday 1–5. Closed major holidays • Adults $2.50 • W

Prince Carl Von Solms-Braunfels, the founder of New Braunfels, built his administration building on this hilltop site. He planned to build his castle in the New World on this spot, and name it "Sophia's Castle" after his fiancée, Princess Sophia. But Sophia wouldn't come to the wilderness, so he returned to Germany and the castle was never built. The well-designed exhibits tell the story of the German immigrants and their influence on the growth of the state. Archives include photos, maps, records, etc.

HISTORIC PLACES

The Chamber of Commerce offers a free walking-tour map of more than 30 historic buildings dating from 1846 through the early 1900s that are located in the downtown area.

CONSERVATION PLAZA

1300 Church Hill Dr., east off Loop 337W (Conservation Society, P.O. Box 933, 78130) • 629-2943 • W variable

The New Braunfels Conservation Society has brought a number of early buildings to this site. Included are the Baetge House, Forke Store, Welsch Barn, Star Exchange, Jahn House, Haelbig Music Studio, and the one-room Church Hill School built in 1870. These are all in various stages of restoration and are open at irregular times. The Baetge House, built in 1852, is open on a regular basis every Saturday and Sunday 2 to 5 and daily 10 to 5 during Wurstfest. Conservation Society holds a Folklife Festival here the first weekend in May.

GRUENE HISTORIC DISTRICT

Take I-35 north to FM 306 (Canyon Lake exit), then northwest (left) about 1.5 miles to Hunter Rd., then west (left) to Gruene

First of all, it is pronounced Green. Ernest Gruene, one of the original settlers in New Braunfels, moved his family here in 1872. One of his sons, Henry D., became so influential in the small community that eventually the village was renamed after him. Henry's death in 1920, coupled with the coming of the boll weevil and the Depression, turned Gruene into a ghost town. But the ghost came to life again in the mid-1970s when a number of businessmen moved in and restored many of the historic buildings, including **Gruene Hall,** the oldest dance hall in Texas (call 606-1281, it's still a great place to country-western dance). Now part of the city of New Braunfels, the old village has been designated an historic district in the National Register of Historic Places for retaining its ambience as a late nineteenth-century cotton community.

LINDHEIMER HOUSE

491 Comal, on the river • 629-2943 (Conservation Society) • Days and hours vary with season. Call ahead • Admission

Ferdinand Lindheimer, a botanist, served as a guide for the German settlers and was paid in land on the Comal River, where he built this house in 1852. Lindheimer was the first to classify much of the native Texas flora—more than 30 varieties of plants incorporate his name in their botanical titles—and is now known as the father of Texas botany. But after he settled here he spent the next 20 years as editor of the *New-Braunfelser Zeitung*. House is typical Fachwerk construction.

OTHER POINTS OF INTEREST

COMAL RIVER

Public access at Landa Park, Prince Solms Park, Garden St., and Union Ave.

Measuring 3.25 miles from its start at Comal Springs to where it ends by flowing into the Guadalupe River, this river lays claim to being the shortest in Texas. This is a fun river, with tubing a favorite recreation. Landa Park is on the river. Just below it, at Prince Solms Park, is a concrete water slide on the river known as "The Chute" (admission).

LANDA PARK

Landa St. • 608-2160 • Free • W variable

Located on the Comal River, this 196-acre park offers glass-bottom boat rides, boat rentals, swimming in an Olympic-sized pool or a natural spring-fed pool, miniature golf and a regular golf course (*see* Sports and Activities), tubing on the Comal, picnicking, and a playground. You need reservations for picnic tables on weekends from Easter through October. Also on weekends from Easter to Labor Day the park roads are closed, so it becomes a walkers' park. A miniature train ride ($1.50) runs for about a mile through the park. The Wurstfest area (*see* Annual Events) and the Circle Arts Theatre (*see* Performing Arts) are also in the park.

SPORTS AND ACTIVITIES

Golf

NEW BRAUNFELS MUNICIPAL GOLF COURSE

Landa Park, Landa St. • 608-2174 • 18-hole course • Greens fees

SUNDANCE GOLF COURSE

2294 Common at FM 306 • 629-3817 • 18-hole course • Greens fees

Canoeing and Rafting

The stretch of the Guadalupe River between Canyon Lake and New Braunfels is a popular place for canoeing, rafting, and tubing. There are a number of companies along the river that offer everything from guided raft trips to canoe and raft rental, from shuttle service to operating camping cabins and campgrounds for stop-overs on the river. Raft rentals depend on the raft size, the number of people, and whether it's a weekday or weekend, and run from about $12 to $30 per person. Canoes rent for about $30. Deposits are required and shuttle service is extra. Guided raft trips, which last about three hours, cost about $15 for adults and $10 for children 12 and under. Tubes rent for $3 to $5 with a deposit required. Brochures on rental companies and guides at New Braunfels and Canyon Lake are available from the Chamber of Commerce.

Tubing

PRINCE SOLMS PARK

Liberty St. • 608-2165 • Easter–September

This small park, to the east of Landa Park, is one of the places you can enter the Comal River for tubing. To ride your tube through the Tube Chute costs $3.25. Inner tube rentals. (*See* also Other Points of Interest, Comal River, Landa Park; and Sports and Activities, Canoeing and Rafting.)

Tennis

JOHN NEWCOMBE TENNIS RANCH

Take TX 46 west about 3 miles (P.O. Box 310469, 78131) • 625-9105 or in Texas 800-444-6204

This resembles an upscale Hill Country dude ranch, with tennis courts instead of horses. There are 28 courts here. The majority of the instructors are Australian, like owner Newcombe (three-time Wimbledon singles champ), or international professionals. Accommodations range from dorms to motel rooms to family cottages and 2-bedroom condominiums. A variety of package plans available. Also conference center.

T BAR M CONFERENCE CENTER AND TENNIS RANCH

Take TX 46 about 4 miles west of town (P.O. Box 310714, 78131) • 625-7738 or in Texas 800-292-5469

Tennis is not all there is at this 250-acre resort. Facilities include 12 outdoor tennis courts, and indoor and outdoor pools, gymnasium, and jogging trails. Accommodations include rooms and condominiums.

PERFORMING ARTS

CIRCLE ARTS THEATRE

Landa Park, 322 Oakcrest Dr. • 629-6635 • Admission • W

This regional theater puts on about six productions during the year, including a musical in the summer and a melodrama during the Wurstfest.

SHOPPING

BUCK POTTERY

Gruene, in the barn behind the Mercantile Building. *From IH-35 take Canyon Lake exit 306, then left on Hunter Rd., which dead-ends at Gruene Hall.* Mercantile is nearby • 629-7975 • W

Dee Buck produces functional, hand-thrown pottery that he fires in a wood-burning kiln.

GRUENE ANTIQUE COMPANY

Gruene, 1607 Hunter. *Take IH-35 to Canyon Road exit (exit 306), then left on Hunter Rd.* • 629-7781 • W

Southwestern primitives, country antiques, and collectibles are available in what was once Henry Gruene's Mercantile Building and Bank. The old bank vault is still there.

GARDEN RIDGE

17975 I-35. *Take IH-35 south about 9 miles* • 599-5700 • W

Several large buildings on several acres house tons of everything from pottery to furniture to toys. Endless imports require endless walking.

NAEGELIN'S BAKERY

129 S. Seguin • 625-5722 • W

Crave some old-fashioned bakery goodies not cranked out at the supermarket? One of the oldest bakeries in the state, since 1868, Naegelin's is still alive and well in this storefront. Cookies, streudel, coffee cake, bread, they've got it.

NEW BRAUNFELS FACTORY STORES

IH-35 at exit 188 • 620-6806 or 888-SHOP-333 • W+ but not all areas

Bargain hunters set their sights on this factory outlet mall, with about 50 stores selling everything from clothing and shoes to housewares. Westpoint Pepperell Bed, Bath, and Linens Factory Outlet is the large anchor store.

OPA'S HAUS

1600 River Rd., .5 mile north of Loop 337 • 629-1191 • W

Much of the merchandise is imported from Germany, Austria, and Switzerland. This includes from 300 to 500 different authentic German beer steins, more than 100 different German clocks from cuckoo to grandfather, Hummels, lederhosen and dirndls, music boxes, and woodcarvings.

KIDS' STUFF

THE SCHLITTERBAHN

305 W. Austin • 625-2351 • Open daily 10-8 from Memorial Day through Labor Day. Call about other months in season • Adults $21.95, children $17.95 (mid-day tickets less)

Splash away in what lays claim to being Texas' largest waterpark. With 65 acres of water slides, tube chutes, wave pool, surfing wave, kiddie playgrounds, picnic tables, restaurants, and even trees, we won't argue. If you get waterlogged, you can stay overnight at their motel or cottages.

SIDE TRIPS

CANYON LAKE

Take FM 306 north off IH-35 or the River Road north off Loop 337/TX Hwy 46. About 16 miles **• 964-3341 • Open at all times • Free • W variable**

Seven Army Corps of Engineers' parks are on this 8,240-acre lake on the Guadalupe River. Facilities are available for boating, fishing, swimming, waterskiing, scuba diving, picnicking, and camping (fee). Commercial facilities around the lake include motels, restaurants, and marinas. For information write: Canyon Lake Chamber of Commerce, P.O. Box 1435, Canyon Lake 78130 or call 800-528-2104. The River Road route to the lake is the more scenic. It rambles along following the twists and turns of the Guadalupe River, crossing that river in four places. On this route are canoe/raft/tube rentals and campsites.

NATURAL BRIDGE CAVERNS

Take IH-35 south to FM 3009, then west (right) and follow signs to caverns **651-6101 • Open daily 9–4, till 6 in summer • Adults $7, children $5**

Named for the 60-foot natural limestone bridge that spans its entrance, this cavern was discovered in 1960. This U.S. Natural Landmark includes the 50-foot-tall Watchtower, and the hanging Chandelier. Formed over a period of 140 million years, this is still a living cave with many formations growing about a cubic inch every 100 years. Tours leave every 30 minutes and take about one and a fourth hours on a slow and relatively easy walk to show off the half mile of cavern open to the public. Picnic area near the headquarters building.

NATURAL BRIDGE WILDLIFE RANCH

Take IH-35 south to FM 3009, then west (right) and follow signs to Wildlife Ranch **• 438-7400 • Open daily 9–5, till 6:30 in the summer • Adults $6.55, children $4.20**

There are about 600 exotic and native animals in this 200-acre preserve, including Cape buffalo, llamas, ostriches, giraffes, and Texas longhorns. A caged area near the entrance holds primates, bobcats, and exotic birds. There are also petting zoos. Many of the animals come up to the cars to be fed—the ostriches frequently stick their heads in open windows looking for food.

ANNUAL EVENTS

September

COMAL COUNTY FAIR

Comal County Fairgrounds, Common St. • 625-1505 • Wednesday–Sunday late in September • Admission • W variable • Fee for parking

Its billing as the "Largest County Fair in Central Texas" may cause an argument with other county fair holders, but no one can argue about it being one of the oldest. The fair normally opens Wednesday night with a "Night in Old New Braunfels." Then there's a parade, carnival, livestock and homemaker judging, contests, entertainment, a rodeo, a couple of dances, and horse races.

November

WURSTFEST

Wurstfest Grounds at entrance to Land Park, off Landa St. • 625-9167 (Wurstfest Association) • Starts Friday before first Monday in November and runs 10 days through second Sunday • Adults and children over 12 $6, entrance to Wursthalle $3 • W variable • Fee for parking

What started out in 1961 as a one-day "sausage" festival now runs 10 days, draws well over 100,000 visitors from all over the U.S. and many foreign countries, and is probably the best-known Texas version of Munich's famed *Oktoberfest*. It's a salute to the area's German heritage and New Braunfel's most famous product—sausage. Most of the activities revolve around eating and drinking beer, dancing, German-style entertainment or joining sing-alongs and drinking beer. The extra charge to get into Wurstfest Halle is for the special entertainment and dancing to the oompah bands. Other activities include an arts and crafts show, a melodrama and sports tournaments. If you're staying at a local hotel/motel, check on the shuttle bus service (fee).

RESTAURANTS

($ = under $7, $$ = $8–$17, $$$ = $18–$25, $$$$ = over $25 for one person excluding drinks, tax, and tip.)

BAVARIAN VILLAGE

212 W. Austin • 625-0815 • Open year round. Days and hours vary with season. Call ahead • $–$$ • AE, MC, V

Polka on down to the Bavarian Village where collegiates and locals alike enjoy the live polka, brass music, particularly in the summer on the patio. German food and sandwiches.

NEW BRAUNFELS SMOKEHOUSE

TX 81 at TX 46 (P.O. Box 1159, 78131) • 625-2416 • Breakfast, lunch, and dinner daily. • $–$$ • AE, MC, V • W+ • Children's plates

Back in the late 1940s, this was a smokehouse where the farmers and ranchers brought their own meat for smoking. Now it is a restaurant specializing in its own smoked meats. The menu offers choices like sausages (*kolbassa* or *bratwurst*), barbecued beef brisket, barbecued pork ribs, or smoked ham, chicken, or turkey. Also sandwiches and homemade desserts. Gift store and mail order. Wine and beer.

GRISTMILL RESTAURANT

Gruene, 1287 Gruene Rd. *From IH-35 take Canyon Lake exit, then left on Hunter Rd. Located behind Gruene Hall* **• 625-0684 • Lunch and dinner daily $–$$ • AE, MC, V • W+ • Children's plates**

In spite of its name, the building is really a 100-year-old cotton gin, not a grist mill. The ruins are only partially restored, so much of the dining is virtually open-air. The small menu offers smoked sausage, chicken-fried steak, grilled chicken, and a variety of steaks. Also burgers.

KRAUSE'S CAFE

148 S. Castell • 625-7581 • Breakfast, lunch and dinner Monday–Saturday. Closed Sunday, major holidays • $ • DIS, MC, V • W

It started in 1938 and has a basic menu of chili, hamburgers, German dishes, barbecue plates, fried chicken, and steaks. Large selection of pies. Delicatessen. Beer and wine.

PINTO RANCH GRILL

190 S. Seguin • 625-7669 • Open daily lunch and dinner • $–$$ AE, DC, MC, V

Mesquite-grilled entrées in an 1854 old home. Bar.

TREETOPS

444 E. San Antonio • 606-8677 • Lunch and dinner Tuesday–Sunday, closed Monday • $$ • Cr

Casual dining out overlooking the river during warmer months. From burgers to German food and steaks.

ACCOMMODATIONS

($ = under $45, $$ = $46–$60, $$$ = $61–$80, $$$$ = $81–$100, $$$$$ = over $100) Room tax 13%

FAUST HOTEL

240 S. Seguin, south of the Plaza • 625-7791 • $–$$

The four-story hotel has 62 rooms and one suite ($$$$$), cable TV, room phones (local calls free), no pets, lounge. An historic hotel built in 1928 and completely restored to its original elegance. Guest rooms decorated with antiques and no two rooms are alike.

HOLIDAY INN

1051 IH-35E at TX 46 exit • 625-8017 or 800-HOLIDAY (800-465-4329) • $$$ W+ 7 rooms • No-smoking rooms

This two-story Holiday Inn offers 140 units, including two suites ($$$$) and 41 no-smoking rooms. Cable TV with pay channel, room phones (local calls free). Pets OK. Restaurant, pool, playground.

RODEWAY INN

1209 IH-35E at exit 189 (Seguin/Boerne) • 629-6991 or 800-967-1168 • $–$$$
No-smoking rooms
The two-story Rodeway Inn has 130 rooms, including 13 no-smoking. Cable TV. Pets OK. Pool, whirlpool.

Condominiums/Resorts

SCHLITTERBAHN RESORT

305 W. Austin near Liberty, adjacent to Schlitterbahn • 625-2351 • $$–$$$$$
The resort has over 200 units, including motel rooms, cottages, apartments and suites. Restaurant, outdoor pools, hot tubs, playground, water slides, inner tube chute, paddleboats, game room. Discount on Schlitterbahn tickets for guests. Minimum stays on major holiday and busy weekends.

Bed and Breakfast

GRUENE MANSION INN

Gruene, 1275 Gruene Rd. *Take Canyon Rd. exit from IH-35, left on Hunter Rd. then left at Gruene Hall* **• 629-2641 • $$–$$$$$**
Complex includes the Mansion and a number of outbuildings—such as the carriage house, river barn, and corn crib—converted into small apartments. The Victorian mansion on the bluff overlooking Guadalupe River was built in the 1870s and listed in the National Register of Historic Places.

PRINCE SOLMS INN

295 E. San Antonio • 625-9169 or 800-625-9169 • $$$–$$$$$
The two-story B&B inn has eight rooms and two suites. No pets, adults only. Built in 1898, rooms furnished with antiques.

ROUND ROCK

Williamson County • 36,924 • 512
When postal authorities would not accept the name Brushy Creek for the village that grew up here in the late 1840s, the residents decided to name it after a large round rock that served as a landmark for travellers seeking the low-water crossing of Brushy Creek on the Chisholm Trail.

When the International and Great Northern Railroad set its line down slightly east of Round Rock in 1876, much of the town moved to the railroad, leaving a section known as Old Town that now contains many of Round Rock's historic buildings. In 1878, Round Rock gained fame with the shootout that fatally wounded the outlaw Sam Bass. Bass is buried in the old cemetery and the gunfight leading to his death is reenacted each year during Frontier Days, a local annual event held each July.

ROUND ROCK CHAMBER OF COMMERCE

212 E. Main (78664) • 255-5805
Located in the **Palm House Museum**. The Palm House was built in nearby Palm Valley during the 1860s by members of the Palm family. The kitchen and living room have been restored and furnished to look like a typical Swedish settlers' farmhouse of the period.

HISTORIC PLACES

GRAVE OF SAM BASS

Old Round Rock Cemetery, Sam Bass Rd., west of IH-35

Except for one train robbery in which his gang stole $60,000, split six ways, Sam Bass didn't have much success in his short career as a stage and train robber. He held up a number, but generally the pickings were slim, which led him to consider robbing a bank in Round Rock. The robbery never came off, because he was betrayed by one of his gang, who had a deal with the Texas Rangers. In a shootout downtown, Bass was mortally wounded and captured. He died a couple of days later, on his 27th birthday. His exploits and death were written up in dime novels, which made him into a folk hero, a friendly, modern Robin Hood generous with his loot, who never killed a man. Bass and Seaburn Barnes, another gang member killed in the shootout, are buried near the Slave Section.

OTHER HISTORIC PLACES

Several homes and commercial buildings date to the mid-to late-1800s. Two that are listed in the National Register of Historic Places are the **Inn at Brushy Creek** (Cole House, ca. 1860), west of IH-35 at Taylor exit, and the **Captain Nelson Merrill House** (1870), 1300 block of Palm Valley Blvd./TX 79. Other historic buildings include the **Stage Coach Inn** (1853), 900 block of Round Rock Ave.; **4 Chisholm Trail** (1860), **Morrow Building** (1876), N. Mays and E. Main; and the **Reinke Building** (1879), 102 E. Main.

RESTAURANTS

($ = under $7, $$ = $8–$17, $$$ = $18–$25, $$$$ = over $25 for one person excluding drinks, tax, and tip.)

INN AT BRUSHY CREEK

1000 N. IH-35, west of IH-35 at Taylor exit • 255-2555 • Dinner only Thursday–Saturday • Reservations required • $$–$$$ • AE, MC, V W call ahead

Located in 1850s house furnished with antiques. Continental-American menu. Entrées come with Portuguese soup, a hearty tomato-based soup with sausage, cabbage, chunks of potato, and kidney beans. BYOB.

ROUND TOP

Fayette County • 87 • 409

Originally called Townsend because five families by that name settled in the area before the Texas Revolution. In the San Jacinto campaign, the Townsends had four family members in Sam Houston's army, more than any other family in Texas. A Round Top man, Joel Robison, captured Santa Anna. In return for a ride, Santa Anna gave Robison a gold-trimmed vest. It became a Round Top tradition for each local man to wear this elaborate vest at his wedding. The area started to be called Round Top after a distinctive white house with an octagon top, built by a German immigrant in 1847. By the end of the Civil War, the town was almost exclusively German. They built their houses well. Several buildings they put up in the 1850s and 1860s are still in use.

Round Top was just a little backroads town until the 1960s, when it was discovered by several wealthy Texans who bought up and restored many of the old buildings. Through their influence and financial backing, Round Top retained all its old charm, while becoming an oasis of culture centered on the Festival Institute, Henkel Square, and the nearby Winedale Historical Center. Round Top's Fourth of July celebration is one of the oldest—if not the oldest—west of the Mississippi, dating to 1828.

POINTS OF INTEREST

BETHLEHEM LUTHERAN CHURCH

Off TX 237 about 2 blocks south and 1 block west of the courthouse (follow signs) • Free • W

Local cedar and sandstone were used to build this German-style church in 1866. Cedar was also handshaped to make the pipe organ in 1867. Services still held each Sunday.

HENKEL SQUARE

FM 1457, facing the courthouse square • 249-3308 • Open daily 12–5. Closed major holidays • Admission • W variable

The Apothecary Shop of Edward Henkel, who laid out Round Top and was its first mayor, now serves as entrance to a collection of carefully restored buildings dating from the 1820s to the 1870s moved here by the Texas Pioneer Arts Foundation. Included are houses with a superb collection of mostly German-American furnishings, log cabins, and the Haw Creek schoolhouse and church. Docents are available to give details. Several of the foundation's cottages in town have been turned into bed and breakfasts (*See* Accommodations).

FESTIVAL INSTITUTE

Festival Hill, TX 237 approximately .8 mile north of the courthouse square 249-3129 • Grounds open, fee for tour • W variable

In 1971, concert pianist James Dick decided to start a festival institute along the lines of the Berkshire Festival in Massachusetts, where classical musical students could study with masters and put on concerts. The principal buildings are the **Festival Concert Hall,** which seats 1,200, and two Victorian buildings moved to the campus and meticulously restored: the 1885 **Clayton House** and the 1902 **Menke House.** Professional and student concerts are held here all year long. Major concerts occur in May and during the summer festival, which runs every weekend from mid-June through mid-July. An August-to-April season features a concert on one Saturday afternoon per month. The **Menke House** serves as a bed and breakfast for concertgoers and is used for reservations-only gourmet dinners on Saturday evenings; it's best to make reservations for these several months in advance. Tours available by appointment. Write P.O. Drawer 89, 78954 or visit Web site at www.fais.net/~festinst.

WINEDALE INN COMPLEX

Take FM 1457 east off TX 237 to FM 2714, then northeast (left) about one mile **278-3530 • Tours Saturday 9–5, Sunday 12–5, and prior to scheduled events. Monday–Friday by appointment • Adults about $3, students $1 • W grounds only; most buildings require assistance**

This has been a center for the study of ethnic cultures of Central Texas since the grounds and several buildings were donated to the University of Texas by

Miss Ima Hogg in 1967. The 190-acre farmstead dates to 1831, when the Mexican government granted the land to William S. Townsend. Focal point is the **Samuel K. Lewis House,** which Townsend began building in the 1830s; Sam Lewis completed it in the late 1840s. The **McGregor House** was built in 1859; **Hazel's Lone Oak Cottage** was built in 1854. An 1894 barn has been turned into an auditorium. Other farm outbuildings complete the tableau, along with a visitor center, nature trail, and picnic area. The Center is known for annual events such as summer Shakespeare at Winedale, the Winedale Spring Festival, and the Oktoberfest. Write Box 11, Round Top 78954.

ANNUAL EVENTS

April

WINEDALE SPRING FESTIVAL AND TEXAS CRAFTS EXHIBITION

Winedale Historical Center • 278-3530 • Usually first weekend in April
Admission • W variable

Demonstrations of more than a dozen pioneer activities, such as fireplace cooking, goose plucking, and woodcarving. About 40 artists working in various media participate in the Crafts Exhibition. Continuous musical entertainment. Saturday night sees a barbecue chicken dinner (fee) and barn dance. Generally lots of bluebonnets and wildflowers to see as well.

October

WINEDALE OKTOBERFEST

Winedale Historical Center • 278-3530 • Usually first weekend in October
Admission • W variable

Much like Spring Festival. Entertainment emphasizes German music and folk dancers. Antiques fair and local arts and crafts fair held in Round Top at same time.

RESTAURANTS

($ = under $7, $$ = $8–$17, $$$ = $18–$25, $$$$ = over $25 for one person excluding drinks, tax, and tip.)

ROYERS ROUND TOP CAFE

Town Square • 249-3611 • Wednesday–Sunday lunch, dinner • $–$$
No Cr • W

The Houston Chronicle named it best country café in Texas in 1988. Local ingredients are used whenever possible, and they make their own breads, rolls, pies, and such. Country standards like chicken-fried steak and grilled pork chops, plus city favorites like fresh grilled tuna steak and fresh *fettucine.* Various sandwiches, including hamburgers, salads, and soups round out the menu. Beer and wine.

ACCOMMODATIONS

($ = under $45, $$ = $46–$60, $$$ = $61–$80, $$$$ = $81–$100, $$$$$ = over $100)

GASTE HAUS ROUND TOP

P.O. Box 82, 78954 • 249-3308 • $$–$$$

Accommodations in restored nineteenth-century cottages furnished with early Texas antiques. No children under 5. No pets. No smoking in houses.

SALADO

Bell County • Approx. 3,000 • 254

This was the headquarters for Sterling C. Robertson's colony in the early 1830s. Robertson was of Scottish descent and a number of Scots settled this area. It was a small settlement until the impresario's son, Colonel E. Sterling Robertson, moved here from Austin in the 1850s and built a large mansion. Salado College was established in 1860. For a time, Salado was considered as a site for both the state capital and the University of Texas. When the railroad bypassed Salado, the college closed and the population dwindled. In 1950 there were about 200 residents.

A rebirth started in the 1960s and 1970s partly because a number of artists and craftsmen moved here, attracting art galleries and antique shops. Salado is the birthplace of Liz Carpenter, the first newswoman to be staff director and press secretary to a First Lady, Mrs. Lyndon B. Johnson.

TOURIST SERVICES

SALADO CHAMBER OF COMMERCE

Civic Center, Main St. (P.O. Box 81, 76571) • 947-5040, Fax: 947-3126
Monday–Friday 9–5 • W

The Chamber now offices in the Old Red School House. Built in 1923, it has been beautifully restored, thanks to contributions from those fortunate enough to live in this peaceful little hamlet.

DRIVING TOUR TAPES

Rent a drive-yourself tour tape of historical points of interest in either the lobby of the Stagecoach Inn Motel or the Salado Gallery, or write: Bell County Historical Commission, Bell County Courthouse, Belton 76513.

MUSEUMS

CENTRAL TEXAS AREA MUSEUM

Main St. across from Stagecoach Inn (76571) • 947-5232 or 947-9281
(Chamber of Commerce) • Open for special events and by appointment
Free (donations) • W

Housed in a building that's more than 100 years old, the museum traces the history of Central Texas. It also sponsors the Gathering of the Scottish Clans (*See* Annual Events).

HISTORIC PLACES

A large number of the earliest homes are still standing but not open to the public. **Robertson's Home and Plantation** west of town on IH-35S access road. This 22-room house, often called "Sterling's Castle," was built in the mid-1850s and is a rare example of an antebellum plantation complex with house, slave quarters, stables, and family cemetery. Liz Carpenter, whose mother was a Robertson, was born here. **Twelve Oaks** on Center Circle was built in 1867 and boasts 15 rooms and walls 22 inches thick. It's now on the National Register of Historic Places as is the **Levi Tenney House** on Pace Park Dr. east of Main. Built in 1859 for the first president of Salado College, the gun ports in the walls at cellar level are still visible.

SHOPPING

Besides oodles of antique shops and art galleries, Salado's offbeat temptations include Sir Wigglesworth, Bundle of Joy, and the Christmas Shop. Fletcher's Books & Antiques is renowned.

GRACE JONES SHOP
Royal at Main • 947-5555 • W
Grace's selection of ladies high-fashion clothes draws customers from all over the country to her shop in a building that was once the Salado Bank.

SIDE TRIPS

STILLHOUSE HOLLOW LAKE
From IH-35N take FM 1670 northwest to lake (See **Belton**)

ANNUAL EVENTS

November

SCOTTISH FESTIVAL: THE GATHERING OF THE CLANS
Village Green by Stagecoach Inn • 947-5232 (Central Texas Area Museum) or 947-5040 (Chamber of Commerce) • First Saturday and Sunday in November • Admission • W variable
The wee village of Salado becomes a wee part of Scotland on this weekend, as representatives of about 200 clans come from all over the United States. The town is awash with tartans, and the sound of bagpipes is heard everywhere.

December

CHRISTMAS STROLL AND HOMES TOUR
Various locations • Chamber of Commerce • First Saturday and Sunday in December • Admission for home tour only
Usually five historic homes are decorated and open for the tour.

RESTAURANTS

($ = under $7, $$ = $8–$17, $$$ = $18–$25, $$$$ = over $25 for one person excluding drinks, tax, and tip.)

STAGECOACH INN
1 Main • 949-9400 • Lunch 11–4 and dinner 5–9 daily • $$–$$$ Cr • W • Children's plates
Established in the 1850s, it was called the Shady Villa Hotel when Sam Houston slept here and made an anti-secession speech from the balcony. General George Custer and cattlemen Charles Goodnight and Shanghai Pierce were among the many other famous people who reportedly stayed here. About 1944,

it was converted to a restaurant. The menu for the day is still recited by wait-staff, a nice tradition. Can order a one-price meal that includes entrée, salad or appetizer, and dessert. Prime rib, hush puppies, and magnificent strawberry kiss dessert—fantastic!

SALADO MANSION

West side of Main just north of Salado Creek • 947-5157 • Lunch and dinner Tuesday–Thursday, Sunday 11–9; Friday and Saturday 11–10. Closed Monday Reservations requested for 7 or more • $–$$ • AE, MC, V, DIS Bar and lounge

Tex-Mex and Southwestern specialties in 1857 mansion that is listed in the National Register of Historic Places. Casual elegance. Wooden chairs have Texas Star on back. Periodic entertainment on patio (smoking room). Your white carriage awaits in front most nights, weather permitting, or call Good Time Carriage Rides (771-2839).

ACCOMMODATIONS

($ = under $45, $$ = $46–$60, $$$ = $61–$80, $$$$ = $81–$100, $$$$$ = over $100) Room tax 6%

STAGECOACH INN

IH-35N at Salado exit (P.O. Box 97, 76571) • 947-5111 • $$$ No-smoking rooms

In four two-story buildings are 82 units, including two suites ($$$) and 38 no-smoking rooms. Room phones (local calls free). No pets. Coffee shop, private club, whirlpool, two lighted tennis courts, playground. Guest membership available for golf. Adjoins Stagecoach Inn Restaurant (see Restaurants).

Bed and Breakfast

HALLEY HOUSE

N. Main (P.O. Box 125, 76571) • 947-1000 • Fax 947-5508 • $$–$$$$ No smoking in houses

Located next to the Old Red School House, this 1860 Greek Revival home has seven rooms with fine antiques and private baths available, plus three more rooms and baths in Carriage House, and two sleeper sofas (children welcome here) in the Gathering Room. Gourmet buffet served in formal dining room. The Gathering also can easily accommodate meetings for up to 100, and has a kitchenette. (Chamber lists other great B&Bs.)

INN ON THE CREEK

Center Circle off Royal (P.O. Box 858, 76571) • 947-5554 • Fax 947-9198 $–$$$$ • No smoking in inn

Now hosts have 20 guest rooms, 20 baths in six houses around town available for B&B. Great breakfast! Children OK in two cottages; no pets. Original three-story, 1892 B&B has seven rooms, cable TV, and porch overlooking Salado Creek, with walkway to its restaurant in another Victorian house. (It's also open to the public on weekends for dinner with a fixed menu and by reservation.)

SAN ANTONIO

Bexar County Seat • 1,092,300 • (210)

Somehow it seems fitting that old "Bet a Million" Gates demonstrated a new fangled barbed wire invention in San Antonio by penning up some recalcitrant cattle in its downtown streets.

That was way back in the 1870s. But the city is still full of independent critters. What some critics decry as blustery political antics, others find refreshing and even a little healthy. An irrepressible, outspoken diversity that somehow coexists with an undercurrent of urbane tolerance.

Maybe the newspaper headlines and the city council get a little vocal at times, but, hey, that's just San Antonio, say the natives. You might as well sit back and enjoy the show. It's seldom boring and often entertaining. Besides, the city works and some interesting things happen. San Antonio was probably the first major U.S. city to elect a woman mayor, and one of the first to elect a Mexican-American mayor.

This multifaceted individuality, relaxed Mexican lifestyle, and of course that Texan icon, the Alamo, are what fuel the city and one of its biggest industries—tourism. People, including other Texans fleeing plate glass and concrete canyons, gravitate to San Antonio for fiestas, *charreadas,* and a bit of the jalapeño pepper. They enjoy meandering about a downtown that has a sensual,

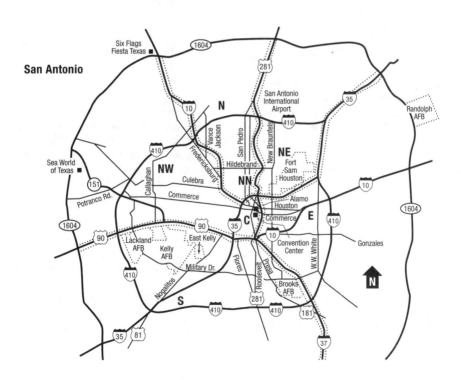

lived-in character, warts and all, and dawdling among those historic old buildings that Big D and H sneered at and insisted San Antonio should have torn down long ago in the name of "progress."

Well, who's laughing now? Because those "backward" San Antonians refused to rush into bulldozing all their older buildings to make merchant bucks, today San Antonio has a viable downtown that other folks pay to come see. The local Conservation Society is one of the most feisty and powerful groups in the country, and has brought the city kudos for its restored River Walk and historic sites.

Geographically, the nation's ninth largest city (population around 1,100,000) looks like your standard overcrowded metropolis with two ringed loops and freeway spokes. But compared to most urban centers, it's relatively easy to get from one side to the other. And the airport is located only about 20 minutes from downtown.

Downtown itself is quite walkable. Practically all the sights are within a mile radius of the hotels. Or hop on the cheap motorized VIA streetcars that make the rounds of tourist spots downtown. Because they've heard so much about it, most people make a beeline for the Alamo first, which is right smack in the middle of town on Alamo Plaza. But that doesn't take more than an hour or so, even if you tarry awhile in the museum and well-landscaped grounds. Actually the heart of San Antonio is the River Walk, a landscaped park area on the San Antonio River just a couple of blocks from the Alamo. The River Walk is lined with sidewalk cafes, shops, hotels, and nightspots, and is a good base of operations to keep going back to, whether for lunch at a cafe table or for Irish ditties and *mariachi* music at nighttime.

Here you'll rub elbows with not only glad-handing conventioneers but also a cross-section of San Antonio—bird colonels, three-piece suit bankers, blue-collar workers, rednecks, politicos, ranchers, artists, and winos. They're all apt to drop by for lunch or spirits.

History . . . Alamo and Missions

The narrow San Antonio River that you can toss a *fajita* across is the very reason for the city's founding. It used to be much wider, and early Spanish settlers coming up from Mexico built their Catholic missions alongside the river in the early 1700s. They built five of them. The first one was the Alamo, which was established as a mission in 1718 (later it became a makeshift fort during the Texas Revolution). SA is the only city in the U.S. to have five old Spanish missions within its confines. (These missions make a pleasant afternoon tour. *See* Historic Places.)

Besides this Spanish heritage, Mexican descendants now actually constitute a slight majority over the Anglo population. So it's a misnomer to speak of them as a minority. Other ethnic influences can be seen in the German breweries, the Victorian King William residential neighborhood, and the quaint French Catholic school architecture. San Antonio is about as old as New Orleans and has much the same ethnic polyglot flavor.

But San Antonio isn't river-oriented like New Orleans. It couldn't be, the river is too scrawny! Historically, it's more tied to the land, being concerned with tending cattle and defending the territory. The Spaniards brought cattle with them, and ranches sprang up all around. SA became a way station for cattle drives and a saloon haven for the roisterous cowboys. As for defense, in the beginning the Spanish built a fort here, and ever since San Antonio has been an inbred military town. Today, there are five military bases (though one is due to be phased out and closed), plus assorted military retirees. Practically every military star from Robert E. Lee to Pershing and Eisenhower spent some time here. Even Teddy Roosevelt trained his Rough Riders in San Antonio.

Then, of course, that ill-fated battle took place at the Alamo in 1836, when a small ragtag band of men (including Davy Crockett and Jim Bowie) fought to their deaths against several thousand Mexican soldiers during Texas' fight for independence. The rough-hewn limestone Alamo is the stuff that legends are made of, and one of the biggest tourist meccas in the nation. It was this disastrous battle at the Alamo that led to the later battle cry of "Remember the Alamo," when Texans finally overpowered the Mexicans at San Jacinto.

Aside from the military, tourism, and agribusiness, Bexar County's other large industry is medicine, with the South Texas Medical Center and University of Texas Health Science Center at San Antonio located in the northwest sector. There is also the growing biotech Texas Research Park. Throw in a little insurance, oil and gas, and computer firms, and you've got the economic base . . . strongly dependent on the feds and governmental defense funding, but less susceptible to the downturns of the oil business.

Add a pinch of creative personae (artists, musicians, and writers find the quality of life simpatico) and educators. SA has the regional University of Texas at San Antonio, the aforementioned UT Health Science Center with its medical schools, Alamo Community College system, and five private colleges.

Terrain and Climate

But what about some practical facts? What's the climate like, and how easy is it to get around? Terrain-wise, the Alamo City is generally flat, with low-slung hills amidst trees. To the south of town lies brush country and to the northwest the Hill Country, a scenic rural area where San Antonians flee for recreation. SA's climate is mild enough to visit year-round, and hot enough in the summer (85–100 degrees) to match the chili. Dress accordingly, casual and informal. If you don't already own them, buy some boots and jeans or Mexican dresses and men's guayabera shirts while visiting. Western stores and Mexican tourist shops abound.

Getting around in San Antonio is comparatively easy. If you're staying in a hotel downtown, you can practically do without a car. Many sites and restaurants are within walking distance. Or ride the special motorized VIA streetcars that periodically stop at tourist sites. For exploring the city's outer limits, the freeway system is good and less the roller derby than Houston's. Get a map however, as some of the older streets wander aimlessly and abruptly change names for no rhyme or reason. In general, the northern part of town is newer, with more affluent suburbs and developments. To the south it is older and less affluent, with more working-class areas and the military bases.

Walking Tour Downtown

Like to walk? We suggest starting at the obvious, the Alamo, at Alamo and Houston streets. From there, go south on Alamo St. several blocks to see the Tower of the Americas (*see* Bird's-Eye View) and HemisFair Park (the Institute of Texan Cultures museum there is excellent). Then cross Alamo St. to the west to the quaint La Villita before ambling down to the River Walk that fronts it. From the River Walk, go up the stairs at Commerce St. and walk westward, taking in Main Plaza, San Fernando Cathedral, and the Spanish Governors' Palace. From there, still heading west, a few blocks farther is Market Square, a huge block encompassing the Mexican market, shops, and Mexican restaurants. While all these sites can be seen briefly in a day's brisk walk, there's so much to see and experience along the way that it's better to break it up into different jaunts.

After all, San Antonio is a place to be savored, and not hurried. Despite its clean city awards and urban developer veneer, it still has pockets where taco frying and boot leather smells waft from mom and pop shops. And streets and plazas that still have a comfortable lived-in feeling, with a bit of respectable dirt. Maybe urbanized San Antonio no longer takes the proverbial siesta, but at least it still takes time out for a catnap or to loll in the healing South Texas sun.

TOURIST SERVICES

Information Centers

SAN ANTONIO CHAMBER OF COMMERCE

602 W. Commerce at Alamo • 229-2100 • Monday–Friday 8:30–5 W side entrance

Don't go here for regular tourist info, go to the Visitor Information Center listed below. But the Chamber has a lot of data and brochures on San Antonio, particularly on business, office buildings, etc. Also has a newcomers' guide for sale.

SAN ANTONIO CONVENTION & VISITORS BUREAU

203 S. St. Mary's at Market • 270-8700 or 800-447-3372 • Monday–Friday 8:30–5 • W

Planning on visiting San Antonio or throwing a convention? Write the bureau at P.O. Box 2277, 78298 for printed brochures. But when you get to the city, go to their Visitor Information Center, listed below, for tourist information.

SAN ANTONIO RIVER ASSOCIATION (PASEO DEL RIO ASSOCIATION)

213 Broadway • 227-4262

Contact them for River Walk facts. They also publish a useful monthly magazine (*Rio*) about happenings on the River Walk. Distributed at hotels and shops along the River Walk.

VISITOR INFORMATION CENTER

317 Alamo Plaza • 270-8748 • Open daily 8:30–6, but subject to change • W

Pop into the center, just across from the Alamo, for all sorts of brochures and help on finding your way about SA. Will tell you about various public tours.

Tours

HORSE 'N CARRIAGE RIDES

Leaves from Alamo Plaza • Daily, roughly 10–6 in the winter, longer hours in the summer

You'll find several horse 'n carriages around Alamo Plaza, chomping at the bit to take you on a whirl. Most charge around $10 per person for a half hour, so it's not cheap. Hours usually depend upon weather and daylight.

YANAGUANA RIVER CRUISES

Leaves from near Market St. Bridge across from Hilton Palacio del Rio Hotel or Rivercenter Mall on the River Walk • 244-5700 • Open daily 9–10, but may vary in winter • Adults $4, children $1

A fun way to see the River Walk—while floating on a barge through the landscaped parkland and shops. Wave to your heart's content at the rest of the tourists. Rain or bad weather may close down this big port on the equally big San Antonio River.

VAN & BUS TOURS

Leaves from Alamo Plaza • Runs daily • Fees vary

Besides the Gray Line Bus Tours below, assorted van and minibus tours also leave from near the Alamo. Ask the Visitor Information Center about the current ones doing business. Fees usually approximate the Gray Line fees for different tours of the city.

GRAY LINE BUS TOURS

Leaves from Alamo Plaza • 226-1706 • Runs daily

Gray Line offers several different tours in their large, air-conditioned buses. Usually leaves morning and afternoon, and lasts about 3½ hours, except for the combination tours. Pick and choose to see the missions, Brackenridge Park, the military bases, or whatever. Buy tickets as they depart from the Alamo.

BIRD'S-EYE VIEW

BRACKENRIDGE SKYRIDE

3883 N. St. Mary's in Brackenridge Park • 736-9534 • Usually open daily 10–5, depending on weather • Adults $2.25, children $1.75

Hang in there on the skyride at Brackenridge Park and you'll see plenty of the downtown skyline and the park itself. Cable cars depart near the zoo entrance. Not for the faint-hearted.

TOWER OF THE AMERICAS

HemisFair Park near E. Market and Bowie • 207-8615 • Sunday–Thursday 9–10, Friday–Saturday 9–11 • Adults $3, children $1 • W

Best panoramic view in San Antonio. Many cities have observation towers, but it is rare to find one that rises so convincingly above all the surrounding buildings. On a clear day the rolling Hill Country stretches away to the north, while San Antonio sprawls out in every direction, and you can see it all from the observation deck. Also a revolving restaurant in the 750-foot tower that offers a spectacular view while dining.

MUSEUMS

HERTZBERG CIRCUS MUSEUM

210 W. Market at S. Presa • 207-7810 • Monday–Saturday 10–5; also Sunday 1–5 during the summer • Adults $2.50, children $1

Circus buffs will find this collection fascinating, but it is not quite as intriguing as the title makes it sound. Posters, photographs, and costumes make up much of the collection, but two favorite exhibits are Tom Thumb's carriage and the detailed model of a circus in the days of the big top.

INSTITUTE OF TEXAN CULTURES

HemisFair Park, Durango at Bowie • 458-2300 • Tuesday–Sunday 9–5 Adults $4, children $2 • W+

Almost every nation and ethnic group that have contributed to Texan myth, lore, history, culture, or progress are represented here in this colorful museum. Standard exhibits include ones on the Spanish, Native Americans, Germans, Tejanos, and African Americans. The exhibits show tools, diaries, lifestyles, farming methods, trades, commerce, and costumes of Texan settlers. There are also frequent slide and film shows and a Texas-oriented gift shop. (*See also* Annual Events—August: Texas Folklife Festival.)

McNAY ART MUSEUM

6000 N. New Braunfels at Austin Hwy. • 824-5368 • Tuesday–Saturday 10–5, Sunday 12–5 • Free • W

The small but remarkable art collection here has been selected with taste and a discerning eye. The treasures run from a brooding head of Christ by El Greco to an exuberant Dufy seascape. Good collection of Post-impressionists, including Gauguin, Cézanne, Picasso, and Van Gogh. Beautiful Spanish-style building and grounds, including an exquisite courtyard, all of which were a bequest of Mrs. Marion Koogler McNay. All in all, one of the top attractions in San Antonio, with both American artists and a top theater arts collection.

MILITARY BASE MUSEUMS

Several of the military bases have military museums open free to the public. Call the bases for directions and hours open, which vary considerably.

Hangar Nine • Brooks Air Force Base • 536-2203 (This base due to close after 2000)

This old hangar houses a flight medicine museum, but does have an actual antique Jenny aircraft like the one Charles Lindbergh flew in his barnstorming days.

Fort Sam Houston • 221-1211

Two museums on the post (*see* Historic Places). One an army military museum with uniforms, swords, guns. The other a medical one, with instruments, uniforms, etc.

Lackland Air Force Base • 671-3055 (museum)

The History and Traditions Museum for recruits and the public. Scale models, engines, and old instrument panels. Some real planes are parked nearby for viewing.

SAN ANTONIO CHILDREN'S MUSEUM

305 E. Houston • 212-4453 • Tuesday–Saturday 9–6; Sunday 12–5 Adults and children $3 • W

Kids Are Us. Interactive exhibits all over. Sit in a real plane cockpit, ring up a cash register sale, or conduct scientific experiments in the city's newest museum for small fries.

SAN ANTONIO MUSEUM OF ART

200 W. Jones between Broadway and St. Mary's • 829-7262
Monday–Saturday 10–5; Sunday noon–5 • Adults $4, children $1.75 • W+

San Antonians like to say they brewed up art in this their flagship museum . . . a stunning, restored, turn-of-the-century brewery building. With room for large traveling exhibits, the permanent collection includes outstanding Mexican folk art (from the Rockefeller and Winn collections), eighteenth- and nineteenth-century American painters, pre-Columbian art, Spanish colonial art, and early Texas furniture.

WITTE MUSEUM

3801 Broadway at Pershing • 357-1900 • Monday–Saturday 10–5 (till 6 in summer), Sunday noon–5 • Adults $4, children $ 1.75 • W

The Witte is an older, comfortable museum that is particularly fun for the kiddies. It's heavy on natural science, history, and anthropology. With sensory, feedback exhibits that let visitors participate, including exhibits on animal senses, dinosaurs, and Texas wildlife. Also has a log cabin and a large exhibit on ancient Texans, the prehistoric Indians of the lower Pecos, and a science treehouse.

TEXAS PIONEERS, TRAIL DRIVERS & RANGERS MUSEUM

3805 Broadway at Tuleta • 822-9011 • Open daily, summer 10–5; winter 11-4 Adults $2, children 50¢

Items from the pioneer and trail-driving days in the cattle industry and from the famed Texas Rangers.

HISTORIC PLACES

ALAMO

On Alamo Plaza, at Alamo and Houston streets • 225-1391
Monday–Saturday 9–5:30, Sunday 10–5:30 (till 6:30 in summer) • Free • W

This popular tourist mecca is located right smack downtown, so you can't miss its familiar postcard facade on Alamo Plaza. It's within easy walking distance from many hotels. The old stone mission-turned-fort and its walled-in compound are kept meticulously by the Daughters of the Republic of Texas. And the landscaped grounds with colorful blooming plants are worth a pleasant stroll just by themselves. But the Alamo chapel and the Long Barrack Museum really don't take that long to see, maybe an hour. The DRT offers short guided tours throughout the day, so just inquire at the desk. First founded in 1718 as a Spanish Catholic mission (called Mission San Antonio de Valero), it became renowned later as a fort during the Texas Revolution. In 1836, a tiny group of men (an estimated 189) died fighting off several thousand Mexican troops in a 13-day siege. They sent out for help, but it never came. The battle itself lasted only a few hours. But at least their defeat bought time for General Sam Houston, who later defeated the Mexicans at San Jacinto to win Texas' independence from Mexico. That's where Texans first hollered, "Remember the Alamo!" (With Hollywood and TV later embellishing the legendary battle with sagas about the likes of Davy Crockett and Jim Bowie, who fought here.)

Also a gift shop with every conceivable Alamo tourist trinket. No food allowed, but there are plenty of eateries across the street on Alamo Plaza. No free public parking, but parking meters and lots are within a block.

FORT SAM HOUSTON

N. New Braunfels Ave. at Grayson (main gate) • 221-1211 • W variable

Still a working army base, Fort Sam is the oldest and most endearing of the local military bases. Dating back to 1876, the base has tree-lined boulevards and old Victorian officers quarters. This is an open post and worth a drive around and a stop at the Quadrangle, the headquarters near the main gate. The limestone Quad is a National Historic Landmark and has a courtyard in the middle where you can brown bag it for lunch amidst wandering deer and tame ducks. Or try the two museums (military and medical) on base (*see* Museums).

KING WILLIAM HISTORIC DISTRICT

Along and around King William • W variable

A walk down King William St., shaded by a canopy of trees, is a trip through Texas' best time tunnel. Many of the old Victorian houses are still used as homes, others are being restored. Since the 1870s, when prosperous San Antonians of German descent (plus a few others) first began to build King William St., it has been one of the city's most fashionable addresses. It is named, incidentally, for King Wilhelm I of Prussia. It would be a pity to drive through this area when you can see so much more on foot. Stop in at 107 King William, headquarters of the San Antonio Conservation Society, to pick up a brief guide to a walking tour of the area. The Steves Homestead at 509 King William is open to visitors (see below).

LA VILLITA

Bounded by S. Alamo, Nueva, S. Presa, and, roughly, the river • 207-8610 Open daily • W variable

Early in this century the area that is now La Villita (the little town) was a crumbling slum. Instead of being allowed to decay, however, the area was rescued in a farsighted effort to preserve a bit of San Antonio's past. Part commercial endeavor and part historical preservation, La Villita is a pleasant strolling area for visitors. If you go, pick up a copy of the walking-tour map distributed by the visitors center (*see* Tourist Services). During Fiesta week (*see* Annual Events: April) La Villita surges with people at A Night in Old San Antonio. Galleries, shops, cafes, and historic sites make La Villita good for relaxed ambling.

Missions

SAN ANTONIO MISSIONS NATIONAL HISTORICAL PARK

South, see individual mission addresses and phones • Open daily 9–5 • Free

San Antonio is rare in that it has five eighteenth-century Spanish missions still standing or restored. Four of them make up the national park and are located in different spots on the San Antonio River south of downtown. (The fifth, but actually the first one built, in 1718, is the Alamo. But it's not in the park and therefore is listed separately.) Many guided tours of the missions leave from near the Alamo (*see* Tourist Services), but if you go by car, just follow the Mission Trail signs beginning downtown by going south on S. Alamo St. (at Market St.).

Take a picnic lunch and make a day of it, or zip through them in an afternoon. If you have less time, at least see Mission San Jose, the largest and the flagship Texas mission. The whole large, walled-in compound is restored and gives you a feel for mission life in the 1700s. With hostile Indians, these missions were far more than Catholic churches, they served as fortlike protection for the village of people within.

Mission Concepción • 807 Mission Rd. at Felisa • 534-1540 • W assistance needed in places

First on the Mission Trail. Collectors of Texan superlatives will be glad to hear that this is one of the oldest unrestored stone churches still in use in the country. Concepción is attractively proportioned, and some of the original frescoes still remain. Mission Concepción was founded in East Texas, but was moved in 1731 to San Antonio.

Mission San Francisco de la Espada • 10040 Espada • 627-2021

Last on the Mission Trail, in a rural setting. The interior of the church, decorated simply so that the carvings of the saints at the front stand out, resembles that of many small southwestern churches. Because Espada is the most distant and smallest of the missions, it retains the air of an isolated agrarian outpost and so is perhaps the most authentic of all.

Mission San Jose • 3200 block of Roosevelt at Napier • 932-1001 W assistance needed in places

Of the four missions, this is the richest in interesting attractions as well as the most extensive. The chapel itself is reconstructed, as is much of the mission, but the ornate carving on the outside of the chapel is largely original. Allow time to wander around the grounds of the mission, established in 1720, to see the Rose Window, the arches of the former convent, the large granary with its squat flying buttresses, and the living quarters. Large Visitors Center.

Mission San Juan Capistrano • 9101 Graf at Ashley • 534-0749

Moved to San Antonio at the same time as Concepción and Espada in 1731. Third on the Mission Trail. San Juan, though in the city, is quite pastoral and charming in its simplicity. Outside of the church is plain except for the silhouette bell tower that is a photo favorite. Fine small museum in the convent on mission life and the Indians. After visiting San Juan, you might want to stop at **Espada Aqueduct** on the way to Mission Espada. The aqueduct was part of the original irrigation system built in the 1730s for the missions, and is supposed to be the only Spanish one left standing.

NAVARRO HISTORICAL SITE

228 S. Laredo at Nueva • 226-4801 • Wednesday–Sunday 10–4 • Adults $2, children $1 • W

José Antonio Navarro, a signer of the 1836 Texas Declaration of Independence, was prominent as a statesman and rancher. His mid-1800s office, residence, and kitchen buildings have been restored for tourists. The buildings, mostly of limestone and adobe, are sparsely furnished. Occasional demonstrations of adobe making.

SOUTHWEST CRAFT CENTER (OLD URSULINE ACADEMY)

300 Augusta at Navarro • 224-1848 • Monday–Saturday 10–5 • Free
W with assistance

This restored Ursuline Academy is now a center for creative artisans and art classes. Perfect place for a stroll about the quaint French architecture buildings (circa 1850–1860s). This was San Antonio's first girls' school, and is located on the banks of the San Antonio River. Art gallery and pleasant serve-yourself lunchroom in an historic setting (Copper Kitchen, Monday through Friday).

SPANISH GOVERNORS' PALACE

105 Military Plaza • 224-0601 • Monday–Saturday 9–5, Sunday 10–5
Adults $1, children 50¢ • W with assistance

The Spanish influence undiluted by layers of Anglo influence is hard to find. The Governors' Palace, built in 1749 and originally the residence of the captain of the presidio, is one place where that influence can be seen clearly. It re-creates a mood typical of southern Spain, with the tranquil courtyard.

STEVES HOMESTEAD

509 King William • 225-5924 • Open daily 10–4:15 • Adults $2, children free

The 1876 Steves Homestead provides a glimpse of the elegance of the King William district. Chatty guides provide a commentary, while the high-ceilinged mansion itself suggests the style of life of the old German section—Sauerkraut Bend.

OTHER POINTS OF INTEREST

ALAMODOME

Located near IH 37 & Market, downtown • 207-3663 • W+

No self-respecting city should be without a dome, so San Antonio went out and built itself one for sports events and conventions. Seats 65,000 ogling souls. You can't miss it. Just look for something that looks like an armadillo lying on its back with its legs sticking up. Call about public tour times.

BRACKENRIDGE PARK

3800 Broadway • See individual site phones (Administrative 207-3000)
Open daily • Free • W variable

Brackenridge Park, the city's largest, fills up regularly on weekends throughout the year. The greenery and plantings account for some of the attraction, but the variety of activities accounts for even more. The Japanese Tea Gardens and the San Antonio Zoo (*see* below) are both in the park, as are a playground, a golf course, and riding stables (*see* Sports and Activities, Riding). Get oriented by taking a skyride which starts near the zoo entrance. Also near the zoo is the depot for the Brackenridge miniature train. The train puffs and chugs through the woods and field, stops at half a dozen of the park's attractions, and ends up where it started following a 20-minute jaunt. Witte Museum is also located in the park at the main entrance.

BUCKHORN HALL OF HORNS

600 Lone Star Blvd. at Mission Rd. • 270-9400 • (due to move in 1998)
Museum open daily 9:30–5 • Adults $5, children $1.75 • W with assistance

This decidedly odd attraction is one of the city's busiest tourist stops. The original Buckhorn was a tavern decorated with horns, including a gigantic chandelier of interlocking antlers. All of these went to the old Lone Star brewery in 1956. They are now on display there together with innumerable mounted animals, including a record longhorn steer. A Hall of Fins is full of fish. Elsewhere on the grounds is the O. Henry house, a stop for those not stimulated by acres of trophy heads. The Buckhorn Hall of Horns is directly on the way back to downtown from the missions and provides a good change of pace from sightseeing, especially for fidgety children. Their parents may be ready for a visit to the Buckhorn bar itself.

FRIEDRICH WILDERNESS PARK

21480 Milsa Rd. at I-10, about 12 miles from Loop 410 • 698-1057
Wednesday–Sunday 8–5 in winter, 8–8 in summer • Free • W
This is really getting out in the great outdoors. It's an unspoiled wilderness park on about 280 acres of Hill Country to the northwest of town. Seven nature trails wind through the park, which is part of the city park system. The Forest Range Trail takes about 30 minutes of easy strolling. The Main Loop Trail is more rugged, while the Water Trail along a creek is tamer. Some wheelchair accessible trails.

HEMISFAIR PARK

Bounded by Alamo St., I-37, Durango, and Market St. • 207-8522 • W
HemisFair Park is a leftover from the 1968 World's Fair in San Antonio. The buildings in it—the Tower of the Americas (*see* Bird's-Eye View), the Institute of Texan Cultures (*see* Museums), the Instituto Cultural Mexicana, the Convention Center, and the Theater for the Performing Arts—draw numerous visitors and conventioneers. The park is a mixture of city and federal buildings, museums, and restaurants, with some parklike areas for walking and a nifty natural wood children's playground.

JAPANESE TEA GARDENS

Brackenridge Park • Entrances at Broadway and Tuleta south of Hildebrand,
and at N. St. Mary's and Mulberry • 207-3000 • Open daily dawn to dusk
Free • W hilly terrain, assistance needed
What's in a name? First this was the Japanese Sunken Garden, then in 1942 it became the Chinese Sunken Garden. Then the Sunken Garden. Now it's the Japanese Tea Gardens. No matter, this carefully tended and well-designed garden does in fact capture some of the precision and tranquility of the Orient. Lotus ponds and, in season, extensive flower displays make it a popular part of Brackenridge Park.

MARKET SQUARE

Bounded by IH-35, Santa Rosa, W. Commerce, and Dolorosa • 207-8600
Area open at all times • W
Market Square covers more than a score of attractions. Restaurants and Mexican shops line the sides of the walkway, off to one side is El Mercado, while at the west end is the Farmers Market. San Antonians can usually find something to celebrate, and when they do the festivities are often here. On most weekends, the central walkway fills up with vendors' booths.

El Mercado • Market Square • W

Here the Mexican tradition of small, individual market stalls, jammed in side by side, thrives. Well, they may not be as tightly packed as in Mexico, but still, there are about 30 shops in the building. Food, gifts, and imports all may be found, with Mexican goods predominating. This is a great place to look for Mexican folk art or cooking utensils such as a tortilla press or a chocolate beater. Usually at good prices too, though compare at various shops.

McALLISTER PARK

Jones-Maltsberger and Buckhorn • 207-3000 • Open daily • Free W variable

Over a square mile of parkland for cycling, jogging, and even soccer playing makes up this large northside park. Once called the Northeast Preserve, McAllister includes barbecue and picnic pavilions where, most weekend afternoons, groups vigorously pummel volleyballs or swat softballs. Reservations for the pavilions can be made with the Parks and Recreation Department. Those who go to a park to avoid anything with wheels, antennae, plastic parts, or digital circuits would do well to come here. Overnight tent camping.

MILITARY BASES

San Antonio is really a military city, what with five military bases located in or just outside the town. Most of them, except Kelly AFB, are open daily to visitors; but check with the security guards before entering the bases.

Ft. Sam Houston (see Historic Places)
Brooks Air Force Base • SE Military Dr. just off I-37 • 536-1110
Kelly Air Force Base • General Hudnell off US 90 • 925-1110 (Due to close 2000)
Lackland Air Force Base • Military Dr. West at US 90 • 671-1110
Randolph Air Force Base • Pat Booker Rd., off IH-35 • 652-1110

PLAZA THEATER OF WAX/RIPLEY'S BELIEVE IT OR NOT

301 Alamo Plaza • 224-9299 • Open daily, 9–10 during summer, fewer hours in winter • Combo ticket, adults $11.95, children $7.95; less for one exhibit

You can catch John Wayne and Elizabeth Taylor here, all waxed up, of course. Ripley's is at same location.

RIVER WALK (PASEO DEL RIO)

Accessible via numerous bridges and entry points; Commerce and Losoya is a major one • 227-4262 • W

Romance, culture, food, and an endless supply of hotels, shops, cafés, and margaritas all exist along the River Walk, the most picturesque part of San Antonio. This landscaped sidewalk along the river is set below street level, and you can either stroll or stop to eat tacos at a sidewalk café. People usually use the River Walk as a base to go back to again and again, whether for respite or nightspot entertainment.

Once there was even a movement to cover over the San Antonio River, use it for waste disposal, and build a highway on the covered top. Fortunately, more visionary spirits prevailed, and today the waterway is as much a hallmark of San Antonio as is the Alamo. The sluggish stream that now makes up the river hardly suggests the flow that was abundant enough to be the main reason for and the main fact of early life in San Antonio. Now it goes virtually unnoticed except along the River Walk. To really see the color of the river, take a barge ride. (See Tours.)

SAN ANTONIO BOTANICAL GARDENS

555 Funston at New Braunfels • 821-5115 • Monday–Sunday 9–6 • Adults $3, children $1 • W

The center has brought together a little plant life from all parts of Texas. There are formal, herb, native Texas, and children's gardens, and even a garden for the blind, all covering about 30 acres with many walkways. Spring of course is prime time, but the center stays open year round. One attraction of this center is that much of it is cultivated in a natural state to look like rural trails. Also has award-winning conservatory and a restaurant in a restored carriage house.

SAN ANTONIO ZOO

Brackenridge Park at 3903 N. St. Mary's St. • 734-7183 • Open daily 9–5, till 6:30 in summer • Adults $6, children $4 • W

The San Antonio Zoo is much more than a children's attraction. Many recognize it as one of the finest zoos in the country because of its natural settings; spectacular bird collection (one of the largest anywhere); unusual animals, including rare antelopes; and imaginative exhibits.

SEA WORLD OF TEXAS

10500 Sea World Dr. (78251). Located 16 miles northwest of downtown San Antonio between Loop 410W and Loop 1604, off TX Hwy. 151 at the intersection of Ellison Dr. and Westover Hills Blvd. • 523-3611 • Open daily during summer, weekends during spring and fall, hours vary • Adults $26.95 plus tax, children 3 to 11 $18.95 plus tax • W+ but not all areas

By now probably everyone has heard of Sea World's star, Shamu, and the companion killer whales who display their acrobatic abilities in shows at the 4,500-seat Shamu Stadium. But Sea World of Texas, the world's largest marine life showplace, is not a one-star attraction. The 250-acre park is filled with shows and exhibits and attractions, so many that they recommend you allow at least eight hours to see everything. One features sea lions, walruses, and otters working together; another, trick water skiers on a 12-acre lake. Exhibits include a marine mammal pool where guests may feed and touch playful dolphins, a shark exhibit, and an exhibit in which penguins live in a recreated Antarctic environment where it snows daily. And this is just part of what there is to see and do. Other attractions are a water park, including a ride that drops five stories, and big name concerts of performers like George Strait and Barbara Mandrell. There are assorted restaurants and shops, a playground for youngsters, and an in-park tram. Admission fee includes all shows. If you plan to go often, a season pass would be in order. Stroller and wheelchair rentals.

SIX FLAGS FIESTA TEXAS

15 miles northwest of downtown at intersection of I-10W and Loop 1604 697-5050 • Open daily during summer, weekends in spring and fall, hours vary • Adults $31, children $21 • W+ but not all areas

San Antonio is turning into theme park mecca, what with both Sea World and Fiesta Texas. This family musical/entertainment park is now run by corporate giant Time Warner's Six Flags, who has brought along its Looney Tunes pal Bugs Bunny. Built on 200 acres of an old rock quarry, with its 100-foot cliffs as a backdrop, the park features Hispanic, German, western, and rock 'n roll areas, with each having separate stages for live music. Plus restaurants to go along with them such as a cantina or barbecue spot. Musical entertainment plays all day long and a big water park area is complete with rides. And speaking of rides, there's the scary kind of really big roller coaster ones. Inquire about season passes.

SOUTH TEXAS MEDICAL CENTER
Covers a large area near the intersection of Wurzbach and Babcock
614-3724 • W variable
Hospitals, innumerable doctors' offices, clinics, and no end of related facilities (including the University of Texas Health Science Center; see Colleges and Universities) make this by far the most complete medical complex in South Texas. The units are mostly independent; no single organization directs the whole complex.

SPORTS AND ACTIVITIES
Baseball
SAN ANTONIO MISSIONS
675-7275 • April–August • Admission
The Missions play in the professional Texas League. They're part of the Los Angeles Dodgers' system.

Basketball
SAN ANTONIO SPURS
Alamodome • 554-7787 • October–April • Admission
Spur mania takes over as San Antonians love their Spurs, *when* they're winning naturally. Since the Alamodome is downtown, parking can be a problem and will cost you. Spurs play in the National Basketball Association.

Golf
All four of the following municipal courses are 18 holes.

BRACKENRIDGE GOLF COURSE • 2315 Avenue B at Mill Race • 226-5612

OLMOS BASIN GOLF COURSE • 7022 N. McCullough at Basin • 826-4041

RIVERSIDE GOLF COURSE • 203 McDonald at Roosevelt • 533-8371

WILLOW SPRINGS GOLF COURSE • E. Houston at Coliseum Rd. • 226-6721

Horse Racing
RETAMA PARK
IH-35, a few miles northeast in Selma • 651-7000 • Admission
Bet on the nags—thoroughbreds and quarterhorses. You'll find a handsome grandstand and facilities, but call ahead for schedule since this, like some other racing parks, has had some financial problems.

Ice Hockey
Several San Antonio teams have played in professional leagues. Check newspaper sports pages.

Horseback Riding

BRACKENRIDGE PARK STABLES • 840 E. Mulberry • 732-8881

Horses may be rented by the hour for rides through the extensive trails of the park.

Jogging

The San Antonio Marathon is run in November; shorter races, most in the 10-kilometer range, are held throughout the year. Jogging trails can be found at these parks.

BRACKENRIDE PARK • See Other Points of Interest.

McCALLISTER PARK • See Other Points of Interest.

MISSION PARK • Joggers can follow a course along the San Antonio River, from mission to mission, through San Antonio history. (See also Historic Places, Missions.)

Swimming

Around 20 municipal pools about the city are open to the public for a small fee. Call 207-3000 for location and info, or check blue telephone pages.

Tennis

Besides numerous free courts at various city parks, there are two good city tennis centers with lighted courts and pro shops. Small hourly fee.

FAIRCHILD TENNIS CENTER • 1214 E. Crockett at Pine • 226-6912

McFARLIN TENNIS CENTER • 1503 San Pedro at Ashby • 732-1223

COLLEGES AND UNIVERSITIES

ALAMO COMMUNITY COLLEGE DISTRICT

Consists of several separate colleges located in various parts of the city, all at the junior college level. These well-populated campuses have all sorts of free lectures and arts performances open to the public. Largest is San Antonio College (see below). St. Philip's is on the east side, and Palo Alto on the south.

SAN ANTONIO COLLEGE

1300 San Pedro at Dewey • 733-2000 • W variable

Being public supported and attended by many working part-time students, this is the largest college in town by enrollment. Centrally located just north of downtown, the campus is the average commuter type, with no dorms, but modern classroom buildings. Started in 1925, SAC, as it is called, is the largest junior college (single campus) in the state. Good library and speakers series. The kids will be fascinated with their planetarium. Parking can be a problem.

INCARNATE WORD UNIVERSITY

4301 Broadway at Hildebrand • 829-6000 • W

One of the older Catholic colleges in town. Very picturesque with its tree-lined acreage and older buildings. Fit for a stroll. Though it's a liberal arts college, it's heavy on health programs, with a strong nursing school. Not surprising, since the same Sisters of Charity who started it in 1881 also founded Santa Rosa Hospital. A highly respected drama department and theater complex. Check out year-round performances.

OUR LADY OF THE LAKE UNIVERSITY

411 SW. 24th St. at Commerce • 434-6711 • W variable

As the name says, OLL is located near a small scenic lake, and some of its comfortable old buildings date back to 1896. One of them, the Sacred Heart Chapel, is an outstanding European style, ornate with marble, gold leaf, and carved wood. Unfortunately, it's not often open to the public. OLL, always alert to community needs, offers a Weekend College and numerous continuing education courses, plus a school of social work.

ST. MARY'S UNIVERSITY

1 Camino Santa Maria near Cincinnati • 436-3011 • W

St. Mary's University enjoys a good reputation for its law and business schools. Although the handsome main building is impressively old, the rest of the campus is more modern. This Catholic university is the oldest college in town, dating from the 1850s when it was opened downtown on the San Antonio River by the Brothers of the Society of Mary. St. Mary's usually fields a watchable basketball team, and its annual outdoor Oyster Bake during Fiesta is popular.

TRINITY UNIVERSITY

715 Stadium Dr., near Hildebrand • 736-7011 • W variable

Probably the most visitable of the city's campuses. From high on its bluffs, it's an ideal spot for viewing the downtown skyline. Brown bag it or eat in the student union. Founded by Presbyterians, Trinity attracts a large number of National Merit Scholars for its relatively small size. Grounds are meticulously landscaped and fit for a long walk or jog. Modernistic buildings, and a fairly affluent student body. Laurie Auditorium is the site of an excellent Distinguished Lecture Series. The series brings in big-name politicians and literary types and is free. But go early to get seats.

UNIVERSITY OF MEXICO AT SAN ANTONIO

HemisFair Park • 222-8626 • W

The University of Mexico maintains this branch as a symbol of the strong cultural ties between San Antonio and Mexico. Courses include Spanish language; Mexican art, culture, and history; and special classes such as business Spanish.

UNIVERSITY OF TEXAS AT SAN ANTONIO

Loop 1604 west of I-10 • 458-4011 • W

UTSA only opened its doors on its campus in the 1970s, but it already has a large enrollment. Its modernistic buildings spring up among the low-slung hill and rock country at the northwest edge of town. Has engineering, science, and business plus the usual liberal arts, and boasts an active Center for Archaeological Research.

UNIVERSITY OF TEXAS HEALTH SCIENCE CENTER AT SAN ANTONIO

7703 Floyd Curl at Medical • 567-7000 • W+

The health science center includes five separate schools: dentistry, biomedical sciences, medicine, allied health sciences, and nursing. The center forms part of the South Texas Medical Center (*see* Other Points of Interest) and is a much used resource for all of South Texas. Visiting displays, such as photography and art. Tours available.

PERFORMING ARTS

ARTS & CULTURAL AFFAIRS HOTLINE

Call city's hotline at 207-2166 for info on current music, theater, literary, dance, museum, and visual arts events.

Theaters and Cultural Centers

ARNESON RIVER THEATRE

On River Walk near Presa, in La Villita • 207-8610

Many events are held in this outdoor theater on the River Walk, particularly in the summer when there's some Mexican entertainment almost every night. Most have admission, but some are free. Outdoor backdrop is pleasant and colorful. No free parking, but parking lots nearby.

CARVER COMMUNITY CULTURAL CENTER

226 N. Hackberry • 207-7211 • Admission to some events • W+

Serves not only as an African-American community center, but also brings outstanding cultural events and artists in for performances and workshops. Look for jazz festivals, gospel singers, art exhibits, dance, etc.

COCKRELL THEATRE FOR THE PERFORMING ARTS

At Convention Center on Market near Bowie • 207-8500 or TicketMaster Admission • W+

This large modernistic auditorium is the site of many big time celebrity performances. Also hosts convention events. Pay parking garage nearby.

GUADALUPE CULTURAL ARTS CENTER

1300 Guadalupe at Brazos • 271-3151 • W theater

Lots of things going on at this Hispanic arts center from art exhibits to films and concerts. Many free, some admission. Sponsors a Latino film festival.

INSTITUTO CULTURAL MEXICANO

600 HemisFair Park • 227-0123 • Free • W

Funded by the Mexican government, the institute brings in Mexican art, films, and musicians. Frequently highlights one specific aspect of Mexico, such as a time period, state, or artist.

MAJESTIC THEATRE

226 E. Houston • 226-3333 • Admission

This elaborate old movie theater has been restored to its heyday, and now hosts the San Antonio Symphony and many touring roadshows and events downtown.

Various Performing Arts

JOSEPHINE THEATRE

339 W. Josephine • 734-4646 • Admission
Local community actors do productions of musicals and comedies.

THE LANDING

Hyatt Regency Hotel, 123 Losoya on River Walk • 223-7266
Open daily • Cover • Cr • W
Live from the River Walk! It's the Jim Cullum Jazz Band with its nationally acclaimed National Public Radio program. You can catch them performing here almost every evening. Small club (in the Hyatt).

SAN ANTONIO OPERA COMPANY

Various locations • 524-9665 • Admission
This local company gives opera samplers at various locations and has helped sponsor small operas and a national touring company production.

SAN ANTONIO PLAYHOUSE

San Pedro Playhouse, 800 W. Ashby at San Pedro • 733-7258
Admission • W
SA Little Theatre, called SALT, does productions with local actors ranging from drama to comedy. Year-round performances at San Pedro Playhouse, an older medium-sized theater with every seat good for viewing. Free parking.

SAN ANTONIO SYMPHONY

222 E. Houston, 78205 • 554-1010 • Admission
Has both classical and pop series to choose from in a season running from fall to spring. The SA Symphony does a professional job in the beautifully restored Majestic Theatre downtown.

TEXAS BACH CHOIR

Various locations • Admission
Local choir gives polished renditions of sacred choral music, such as Bach and other masters. Several concerts each season at different sites.

SHOPPING

Suburban malls abound. Space limits us to the unusual one downtown.

RIVERCENTER MALL

849 E. Commerce, between Bowie and Alamo Plaza • 225-0000 • W+ but not all areas
Dillard's and Foley's are the anchors for about 120 specialty stores and restaurants in this bright, three-level shopping mall on the River Walk extension just a block from the Alamo. Also in the mall is the IMAX Theater with a 6-story screen that shows the 45-minute film *Alamo: The Price of Freedom.* (For schedule and ticket prices call 225-4629.) Two hours free parking is available at the Rivercenter garages on Crockett and Commerce Street. Parking tickets may be validated at any store, with no purchase necessary.

Art Galleries

BLUE STAR ART COMPLEX

Blue Star at S. Alamo

An energetic art district has emerged on the fringe of downtown in an old warehouse district that has been rejuvenated. Called the Blue Star complex, several contemporary art galleries have sprung up in the rough, unfinished warehouse buildings. Blue Star Art Space (227-6960) is one of them.

GALERIA ORTIZ

102 Concho at Market Square • 225-0731 • W

An upscale gallery in the colorful Market Square, DagenBela hones in on Southwestern art, particularly artists such as Gorman and Amado Peña. SA artists are also shown. Also pottery, jewelry, seriagraphs, etchings, and posters. Wide range of prices.

INTERNATIONAL AIRPORT

Airport Blvd. just north of Loop 410 • 824-2424

Art in the airport? Yes, indeed. A large variety of local art is displayed on concourse walls and in a gallery. Particularly regional scenes for tourists.

NANETTE RICHARDSON FINE ART

426 E. Commerce • 224-1550

On street level at the River Walk, this pleasing gallery has traditional art, with a bit of western, plus sculpture and pottery.

RIVER ART GROUP GALLERY

510 Villita at La Villita • 226-8752

An easy place to pop into while touring historic La Villita downtown. This small gallery shows the art of local artists, and ranges from inexpensive to moderate. Oils, watercolors, and pencil drawings. In a restored old home, the shop is a likely place to pick up regional scenes and landscapes.

SOL DEL RIO

1020 Townsend at Ogden • 828-5555

This gallery, which caters to the Alamo Heights crowd, displays a lot of local and regional artists in its nook and cranny rooms. A good bit of it is on the contemporary side, be it ceramics, jewelry, sculpture, paper art, or watercolors.

SOUTHWEST CRAFT CENTER GALLERY

300 Augusta at St. Mary's • 224-1848 • W

Actually there are several gallery rooms here at the restored historic Old Ursuline Academy, now called the Southwest Craft Center. Varied media, such as photography, ceramics, pottery, jewelry, weavings, calligraphy, and sculpture are displayed. Most of it has a contemporary flavor and is work of the center's faculty and students.

TEXAS TRAILS GALLERY

245 Losoya at Commerce • 224-7865

OK pardner, this is where to find some Western art and sculpture, and it's downtown just over the River Walk. Texas scenes, wildlife, landscapes, American Indian and bronzes.

Assorted Stores

Space naturally limits our scope on individual shops. We're only able to mention a representative few to indicate some unusual, regional, offbeat, or craftsman-type places.

ARTISANS' ALLEY

555 Bitters between West and Blanco • 494-3226

A group of galleries, shops, boutiques, and a tearoom, Artisans' Alley brings together varied arts, antiques, collectibles, handmade crafts, plants, macramé, and home accessories.

BOOKSMITHS OF SAN ANTONIO

209 Alamo Plaza • 271-9177

Read all about the fiesty Alamo band and any other Texana your heart desires at this local bookstore where they know their regional lit.

FERGUSON'S MAP

610 W. Sunset • 829-7629

The huge stock of maps is well organized and attractively displayed. Whatever you may need, from topographic maps of the local area to maps for river running or petroleum exploration, Ferguson's either carries or can get it.

LITTLE BOOTS

110 Division • 923-2221

This family of bootmakers does it the old-fashioned way, handcrafting custom-made boots for boot lovers.

KALLISON'S WESTERN WEAR

123 S. Flores • 222-1364

Longtime family store, which used to have a farm and ranch supply, still sells western wear downtown for both working cowboys and cowgirls, not the pseudo variety.

LA VILLITA

Fine artisan's and artist's wares. *See* **Historic Places.**

LEBMAN'S WESTERN WEAR

8701 Perrin-Beitel at Loop 410 • 655-7553

More western wear for both men and women.

LOS PATIOS

2015 NE. Loop 410 at Starcrest • 655-6171 (main office) • W assistance required here and there

Instead of subdividing this gorgeous old estate on the banks of Salado Creek, the owners turned it into a commercial area for shopping and dining in a rural, woodsy setting, and San Antonio is richer for their having done so. The Gazebo restaurant offers informally chic lunch.

LOS PUEBLITOS

202 Produce Row in Market Square • 212-4898

Stylish two-story store in Market Square, with colorful Mexican clothing and other imports for women.

MARKET SQUARE

Great Mexican import selections and bargains at Mexican Market downtown. *See* **Other Points of Interest.**

PARIS HATTERS

119 Broadway • 223-3453

Don't let this old storefront fool you; they know their hats and Stetsons and will custom hang the right hat on your noggin.

SCRIVENER'S

8502 Broadway at Loop 410 • 824-2353 • W

At locally owned Scrivener's you'll find excellent gifts and even a lumber and hardware department and a lunch room, popular with noontime shoppers.

SHEPLERS

6201 NW. Loop 410 at Ingram • 681-8230 • W

Sheplers of Wichita, Kansas, calls itself the world's largest Western store, and with more floor space than many Texas ranchers have grazing land, who's to doubt it? They sell not just clothes but also everything else Western, stopping just short of livestock. How about a rattler's head or hot pink cowgirl boots?

SPURS SOUVENIR SHOP

600 E. Market • 704-6798

It's a given you can't slam dunk like big Dave (the San Antonio Spurs' basketball team's center, David Robinson), but you can buy his jersey and other Spur memorabilia here. Other top NBA players' stuff too.

KIDS' STUFF

See other sections for children's attractions not listed below. Look for Brackenridge Park (*see* Other Points of Interest) and its riding stables (*see* Sports and Activities), skyride (*see* Bird's-Eye View), and zoo (*see* Other Points of Interest). Also the Buckhorn Hall of Horns, Six Flags Fiesta Texas, and Sea World (*see* Other Points of Interest) and the Institute of Texan Cultures and San Antonio Children's Museum (*see* Museums).

BRACKENRIDGE MINIATURE TRAIN

3910 N. St. Mary's at Brackenridge Park • 734-5401 • Open daily. Call about hours, roughly 10–5 in winter, till 9 in summer • Adults $2.25, children $1.75

All aboard! This miniature railroad huffs and puffs through the park woods for three-and-a-half miles. Takes about 20 minutes.

MALIBU CASTLE

3330 Cherry Ridge • 341-6664 • Open daily, hours vary • Different fees for various activities

Two miniature golf courses, plus bumper boats and batting cages.

MALIBU GRAND PRIX

7702 Briaridge • 341-2500 • Open daily, hours vary • Approximately $2.75 per lap plus license fees

Two types of cars (Virage and Mini-Virage) for adults and kids race on the same track.

SPLASHTOWN

3600 IH-35 at Coliseum Rd. • 227-1100 • Open May–September, hours and days vary • Adults $16, children $11 • W

Family water park with water slides, lazy tubing, and big wave.

SIDE TRIPS

NATURAL BRIDGE CAVERNS

Take IH-35 north, then west on FM 3009 **• Approximately 20 miles northeast of San Antonio • 651-6101 • Open daily 9–4, till 6 in the summer • Adults $7, children $5**

Just follow the Natural Bridge Caverns signs. FM 3009 is also called Natural Bridge Caverns Road. Claims to be the largest caverns in Texas. Well suited for family outings.

NATURAL BRIDGE WILDLIFE RANCH

Take IH-35 north, then west on FM 3009; about 20 miles northeast of San Antonio **• 210-438-7400 • Open daily 9–5, till 6:30 in the summer Adults, $6.55, children $4.20**

This is a drive-through zoo on a three-and-a-half-mile road through rugged hill country. The likes of ostriches and buffalo wander around and often come up to the car to be fed. Petting zoo and picnic area. Next to Natural Bridge Caverns, so follow their signs.

LEON SPRINGS

Take I-10 approximately 10 miles northwest of Loop 410 • **W variable**

Leon Springs first appeared in the 1840s as a stage station. In the restored area that was once the heart of Leon Springs, a number of old stone buildings have been developed into a colony of shops, restaurants, and businesses.

ANNUAL EVENTS

January

GREAT COUNTRY RIVER FESTIVAL

Arneson River Theater and River Walk • **Weekend in January, but sometimes held in September** • **227-4262** • **Free** • **W**

Put on your cowboy hat and faded blue jeans, and mosey over to the River Walk for this weekend country and western music festival. Different bands play from barges, stages, and practically hanging from the trees.

February

SAN ANTONIO STOCK SHOW & RODEO

Most events at Joe Freeman Coliseum, Houston and Coliseum St. • **225-5851 Early-February** • **Admission** • **W**

For two weeks, San Antonio goes rodeo-mad. Cowboy hats, always in evidence, multiply noticeably. Stories about prize chickens and steers fill the papers all week. For many, the rodeo is more than entertainment, it is the rancher's equivalent of the doctor's trip to the AMA convention. Many trail rides take place from surrounding points to San Antonio during the week before the rodeo.

March

ST. PATRICK'S DAY FESTIVITIES

River Walk • **227-4262** • **Around March 17** • **Free** • **W**

Well now, if you believe in wearin' the green, then you'll love seeing the San Antonio River dyed green and joining in the bedevilment and good cheer on the River Walk. A parade and green beer.

April

FIESTA

All over the city • **10 days in April** • **Many events free** • **227-5191** • **W variable**

Some compare Fiesta week in San Antonio to Mardi Gras in New Orleans. Parades, fancy dress ball, parties of every description, and a few dozen other events fill the schedule. San Antonians celebrate a fiesta at any excuse, but this one is the granddaddy of them all. One focal event is A Night in Old San Antonio, sponsored by the Conservation Society, where a hundred or so booths at La Villita (S. Presa and Villita streets) offer many kinds of ethnic food. Everybody gets in on the action: military bases have special events, art shows take place, and, as one of the main events, a parade with floats that really float—down the San Antonio River. Fiesta always takes place around April 21.

May

CINCO DE MAYO

Market Square, 514 W. Commerce and downtown • 207-8600 • Free • W

One of the more celebrated Mexican holidays in the city. All sorts of events over the weekend around May 5 (Cinco de Mayo). But look at Market Square for entertainment and food booths.

TEJANO CONJUNTO FESTIVAL

Various parks • 271-3151 • One week in May • Admission for some events

That lively blend of Mexican and German music so special to South Texas, conjunto, blares forth for several days.

June through August

ARNESON RIVER THEATER ENTERTAINMENT

On the River Walk • 207-8610 • Admission

Sit out under the stars on the River Walk. Every night during the summer some Mexican/Spanish musical entertainment is going on at the outdoor Arneson River Theater, beginning at 8:30 P.M.

August

TEXAS FOLKLIFE FESTIVAL

Institute of Texan Cultures, HemisFair Park • 458-2300 • Admission • W with difficulty; many events outdoors

The Texas Folklife Festival, held annually on the ground of the Institute of Texan Cultures (*see* Museums), gives every ethnic group in Texas a chance to show whatever it is proudest of. Music, dancing, and unusual foods just begin the list. Crafts and demonstrations take up lots of space, as do some more or less commercial exhibits of handmade goods. The festival has all the air of a country fair but none of the midway claptrap. Where else can you hear a band of bagpipers and drummers, dressed in kilts, playing "The Eyes of Texas Are Upon Ye"?

September

DIEZ Y SEIS DE SEPTIEMBRE

Various locations • On and around September 16 • Free • W variable

As *norteamericanos* celebrate the Fourth of July, so *mexicanos* celebrate the Sixteenth of September, or Diez y Seis, the anniversary of the call for independence in 1810, which sparked Mexico's struggle for nationhood. Most of the action is at La Villita, Market Square, or along the river.

October

GREEK FUNSTIVAL

St. Sophia Greek Orthodox Church, 2504 N. St. Mary's • 735-5051 Admission • W

The annual Greek Funstival gathers most of the area's Greeks and would-be Greeks for a weekend of dancing, eating, and *retsina* drinking.

OKTOBERFEST
Beethoven Home, 422 Pereida near S. Alamo • 222-1521 • Admission
W but not all areas

In October, just when it is most comfortable to sit out in the evening, the Beethoven *Männerchor* and *Damenchor* sponsor an Oktoberfest. Hundreds of first- and second-generation Germans and friends gather to hear traditional oompah band music and wash down plates of kraut and sausage with foaming mugs of beer.

November

HOLIDAY RIVER PARADE
River Walk • Friday night after Thanksgiving • 227-4262 • Free • W

Get the holiday spirit early. River Walk's gay Christmas lighting is turned on, along with river parade of boats filled with live music.

December

CHRISTMAS FESTIVITIES
River Walk, Market Square and other locations
Weekends in December • Free

Not to miss is the beautifully lit up River Walk with *luminarias* (candles in paper bags) for Fiesta de las Luminarias (227-4262) and choirs. Also check out festivities at Market Square and other locations.

OFFBEAT

BOOTS SCULPTURE
At North Star Mall, Loop 410 at San Pedro

This is the only thing that keeps North Star Mall really bonafide Texan. This giant pair of brown and white boots loom next to the Saks Fifth Avenue store. Thank goodness they didn't tear down our boot sculpture to make way for the New York import, that would have been really gauche. Called *Justin Boots*, the sculpture is by Robert Wade.

TNK ORIENTAL GROCERY, GIFTS
1901 N. New Braunfels • 226-1739

The TNK is worth a morning's entertainment at least, and you can carry home vittles for dinner. This Oriental version of a run-down general store is located near Ft. Sam Houston's main gate, and sports thousands of items in the isles and hanging from the rafters. How about myriad noodles, china, Japanese porcelain cats, or smoked eel? They're all here, plus much, much more.

RESTAURANTS

($ = under $7, $$ = $8–$17, $$$ = $18–$25, $$$$ = over $25 for one person exluding drinks, tax, and tip.)

Restaurants in San Antonio run the usual spectrum of ethnic food, from French and Asian to all-American fare. But naturally there's a predominance of Mexican and Southwestern cuisine, with some of the best being in mom and pop cafés where mama is rolling the tortillas out in the back. One of the bonuses of San Antonio restaurant fare is that much of it is quite moderately priced.

Putting on the Ritz

CHEZ ARDID

1919 San Pedro at Woodlawn • 732-3203 • Dinner Monday–Saturday, closed Sunday • Reservations recommended • $$$$ • AE, MC, V • W

Rarely are service, cuisine, and atmosphere so well matched. The cuisine is French—not that undefined catch-all "continental" but real French. Salmon and rack of lamb are exquisitely cooked, as are fish, beef, and poultry, but Chez Ardid's real strength lies in the union of sauce and food; these are marriages made in heaven. Service is practiced, skilled, and therefore usually unnoticed. Family-run, with a personal interest in every aspect of the operation. Coat and tie suggested. Bar. Elegant setting in a restored urban mansion just north of downtown.

Country Inn

GREY MOSS INN

19010 Scenic Loop Rd. in Grey Forest. *Take TX 16 to Scenic Loop Rd. turn right and go 3 miles.* **Approximately 12 miles northwest of Loop 410 695-8301 • Dinner only daily • Reservations recommended Friday and Saturday • $$$ • AE, MC, V • W with assistance**

What makes a restaurant romantic? How about a history of engagements being proposed (and accepted) there? Not enough? OK, what about a wedding in the grove of trees in front? The inn's rock building, nestled in the woods northwest of San Antonio, has welcomed travelers for almost half a century. The setting is rustic and warm, with semiclassical music filling the air and kerosene lamps on the tables. Steak is the menu's strong point, so there is little reason to order anything else. Pepper steak is especially good. Outdoor patio is pleasant on warm days. Dress isn't formal, but the service is. Bar.

Late Night

EARL ABEL'S

See **American.**

MI TIERRA CAFE AND BAKERY

Market Square, 218 Produce Row near corner of Dolorosa and San Saba 225-1262 • Open daily 24 hours • $–$$ • Cr • W

Hectic, definitely unfancy Mi Tierra never sleeps, with its busy Market Square location. Mexican food at any time of the day or night should be enough to ask for, but a bonus at Mi Tierra is its Mexican bakery, full of *pan dulce* (sweet bread), to eat there or take home. In spite of the endless numbers of tourists, Mi Tierra also brings in native San Antonians who prefer its bustle and ebullience to quieter establishments. Food average. Breakfast shows the kitchen at its best. *Mariachis.* Bar.

American

ANAQUA GRILL

Plaza San Antonio Hotel, 555 S. Alamo at Arceniega • 229-1000 • Breakfast, lunch, and dinner daily. Sunday brunch buffet • Reservations recommended $$$ • Cr • W

Some hotel restaurants are merely mandatory courtesies serving perfunctory food to hungry guests. Not so the distinguished Anaqua Grill. The dining room overlooks the lush fountains and grounds, and the casual elegance combines with the Southwestern cuisine.

BIGA

206 E. Locust at McCullough • 225-0722 • Dinner Monday–Saturday, closed Sunday • $$$–$$$$ • Cr
This old mansion has elegant cuisine in a more casual atmosphere. Eclectic menu blending in southwestern, classic, and Oriental by a trend-setting regional chef.

BOUDRO'S

421 E. Commerce at Presa • 224-8484 • Lunch and dinner daily • $$–$$$ Cr • W
It may sound Cajun and does still have a few Cajun standby's, but now this intimate eatery on the River Walk is more on the Southwestern side. Steaks, seafood, including coconut-battered shrimp and blackened prime rib.

CALICO CAT TEAROOM

418 Villita St. in La Villita • 299-4698 • Lunch Monday–Saturday • $
Cozy up in this restored home in historic La Villita where locals like to chat over lunch. Soups, sandwiches, quiche, and in-house desserts.

CAPPY'S

5011 Broadway at Mary D • 828-9669 • Lunch and dinner daily • $$ • Cr
A favorite of Alamo Heights yuppies and matrons alike, this renovated old lumberyard is casually classic, with plants, wood, and brick. Pecan-crusted catfish and beer-battered shrimp are quite good, as well as the burgers. Bar.

CARRIAGE HOUSE KITCHEN

555 Funston at Botanical Center • 821-6447 • Lunch Tuesday–Sunday $–$$ • No Cr
Going back to the horse 'n carriage days isn't so bad when you can eat lunch in this restored 1896 carriage house with all its polished wood setting. Soups, salads, sandwiches, and some entrées, plus dishy desserts. Part of the San Antonio Botanical Center.

EARL ABEL'S

4210 Broadway at Hildebrand • 822-3358 • Open daily 6:30 A.M.–1 A.M. • $$ Cr • W
Every city has a restaurant that for decades has served prodigious quantities of solidly American food. In San Antonio, it's Earl Abel's. Don't go expecting the latest in *cuisine minceur*, or any kind of "cuisine" for that matter. But when the fried-chicken bug bites you, or when you need a good old American-style steak with French fries and it's not meal time, this is the place.

GUENTHER HOUSE RESTAURANT

129 East Guenther • 227-1061 • Breakfast and lunch daily • $–$$
For a light lunch in an historic setting, try this restored 1860 home in the King William District. Small restaurant is in the basement. Casual, but classy, and

specials, soups, and sandwiches are inexpensive. Run by nearby Pioneer Flour Mills, so you'll find their mixes being used, particularly at breakfast.

JIM'S

Many locations about town • 826-7001 • Breakfast, lunch, and dinner daily $–$$ • Cr • W
No matter where you get lost in town, a Jim's is nearby to rescue you. Despite quantity, these coffee shops manage to serve up good standard meals even into the late hours. Sandwiches, burgers, steaks.

JW STEAKHOUSE

101 Bowie in Marriott Rivercenter Hotel • 223-1000 • Dinner Tuesday–Saturday • $$$–$$$$ • Cr • W+ limited
Befitting the state of the state and cattle country, JW's specializes in steaks in this large highrise corporate hotel. Overlooks river. Casual.

LAS CANARIAS

La Mansion del Rio Hotel, 112 College at St. Mary's • 225-2581 • Lunch Monday–Saturday, dinner daily, Sunday brunch • $$$ • Cr • W
Like most hotels, they may change their menu periodically, but the setting and service in this Spanish-style hotel are always pleasant. Flamenco guitar music many evenings.

LIBERTY BAR

328 E. Josephine near Broadway • 227-1187 • Lunch and dinner daily, Sunday brunch • $$ • AE, MC, V
Maybe it looks like this old wooden building is leaning so much it might fall over any minute. But it hasn't fallen after all these years, and inside is a popular restaurant/bar. Junior leaguers and businessmen alike munch on the sandwiches and politically correct entrées.

LOS PATIOS

2015 NE. Loop 410 at Starcrest • 655-6190 • (The Gazebo) Lunch only daily $$ • Cr
Los Patios is a combination shopping and eating complex on rustic acreage in the northeast part of town. Gazebo has tea room fare. The setting is the thing here. Many tours make a stop here.

POLO'S

401 S. Alamo, Fairmount Hotel • 224-8800 • Breakfast daily, lunch Monday–Friday, dinner Monday–Saturday • $$$–$$$$ • Cr • W
Upscale restaurant in the comfortable elegance of the restored inn-like Fairmount Hotel. Food with a Southwestern flair. Free valet parking.

ZUNI GRILL

511 River Walk • 227-0864 • Breakfast, lunch, and dinner daily • $–$$$ • Cr W (on street level)
Eat indoors or outdoors at this convivial River Walk eatery. Variety of food from sandwiches to Southwestern and Mexican.

Barbecue

COUNTY LINE

111 W. Crockett on River Walk • 229-1941 • Lunch and dinner daily • $$ • Cr
Chomp on huge platters of barbecue and enjoy the outdoors on the River Walk. Another more rustic location on northside.

HICKORY HUT BAR-B-Q

3731 Colony Dr. at I-10 • 696-9134 • Lunch and dinner Monday–Saturday, closed Sunday • $ • Cr
Tender barbecue in this small self-service place on the fringe of Colonies North shopping center. Eat at picnic tables.

Chinese

HSIU YU

8338 Broadway • 828-2273 • Lunch every day except Saturday, dinner daily $$ • Cr
Kung pao chicken and spicy shredded chicken are good in this small restaurant. Crowded at lunch for reasonably priced specials.

TAIPEI

2211 N.W. Military Hwy. • 366-3012 • Lunch and dinner daily • $-$$ • Cr • W+
Dine on Hunan-style menu in classy setting.

Delicatessen

SCHILO'S

424 E. Commerce at Losoya • 223-6692 • Breakfast, lunch and dinner Monday–Saturday, closed Sunday • $-$$ • No Cr
A storefront deli atmosphere prevails here, where generations of San Antonians have come for German-style delicatessen lunches. Sausage, cold-cut sandwiches, Reubens, hot plates, special root beer and non-root beer, and sauerkraut make this a hot spot for lunch. The decor is urban homey. Schilo's is a thoroughly San Antonian tradition, with its noisy and convivial high-ceilinged room. Bar.

French-Continental

CRUMPETS

3920 Harry Wurzbach • 821-5454 • Lunch and dinner daily • $$-$$$ Cr • W
Kind of a tea room with a European flavor. Popular with suburban matrons and the Alamo Heights set who like to meet for lunch. Daily lunch specials in this bustling, informal, yet classy restaurant. Bakery with a line of pastries. Live classical music on certain days. Bar.

THE FIG TREE

515 Paseo de Villita on the River Walk • 224-1976 • Dinner only daily Reservations required • $$$$ • Cr
Everything from the wallpaper to the china, from the pictures to the crystal, goes together to make a warmly elegant ambience. But the food doesn't always

reach the heights that the menu, surroundings, and price lead one to expect. The Fig Tree is definitely for those who do not mind (or whose companies do not mind) parting with over a hundred dollars for dinner for two. Bar.

L'ETOILE

6106 Broadway at Albany • 826-4551 • Lunch and dinner Monday–Saturday, Sunday dinner only • $$–$$$$ • Cr • W with assistance

What? A French restaurant that is not ostentatious? Yes, the clientele may be tony, but the atmosphere here is informal. And surprisingly, the traditional French food can be reasonably priced, with early bird specials. Fresh fish is a specialty, as are the desserts such as chocolate terrine. The black-tie waiters are attentive, but unobtrusively so. Bar.

Greek

DEMO'S

7115 Blanco at Loop 410 • 342-2772 • Lunch and dinner daily • $ • Cr • W

Strictly casual and over-the-counter service in this strip shopping center eatery. But the dishes are authentic and fresh, whether they be *spanokopita*, *baklava*, or *gyros*. Beer and wine.

Italian

ALDO'S RISTORANTE ITALIANO

8539 Fredericksburg Rd. at Wurzbach • 696-2536 • Lunch and dinner Monday–Friday, dinner only Saturday and Sunday • $$$ • Cr • W

Can an Iranian be happy selling northern Italian cuisine to Americans? Of course, if it's Aldo. Aldo's is ensconced in a redecorated older house near the Medical Center. The atmosphere is classy and the service formal, but informal wear will do. Try a candlelit table on the west side for a sunset view. The crab pasta salad is good, as well as the scampi, veal, and snapper.

PAESANO'S

555 E. Basse • 828-9541 • Lunch and dinner daily • $$–$$$ • Cr • W

More sophisticated surroundings in this newer location in an upscale retail center. But same old local movers and shakers go there to banter with owner Joe Cosniac and scarf down some of the same old favorites, such as Shrimp Paesano. Fresh specialty breads. Beer and wine. Also River Walk location.

RUFFINO'S

9802 Colonnade at I-10 • 641-6100 • Dinner daily • $$$ • Cr • W+

Italian and continental food in this restaurant in a modern northwest shopping center.

Japanese

NIKI'S TOKYO INN

819 W. Hildebrand 1 block east of Blanco • 736-5471 • Dinner only Tuesday–Sunday • $$ • AE, MC, V • W

Long time Japanese restaurant in an old house on busy Hildebrand. Both traditional Japanese seating and regular for those with creaky backs. Tasty tempura. Sushi bar.

Mexican

CASA RIO

430 E. Commerce on the River Walk • 225-6718 • Lunch and dinner daily
$–$$ • Cr • W ramp from parking lot; call ahead
Gastronomic merit is not measured by the quantity of food served per day. If it were, Casa Río would rank at the top of the local Mexican restaurant scale. The restaurant's prime River Walk location, not its highly average food, accounts for the influx of tourists. In short, try Casa Río for a Number Two Dinner when you want to sit at the water's edge and don't mind the crowds.

EL MIRADOR

722 S. St. Mary's at Madison • 225-9444 • Breakfast and lunch daily, dinner
Wednesday–Saturday • $–$$ • MC, V
For a no-nonsense, no-frills Mexican lunch near downtown, folksy El Mirador is a good bet. Every day lawyers, businessmen, and ladies in tennis shoes from the nearby King William Historic District fill the tables for El Mirador's hearty lunches. The specialties are the renowned *xochitl* and *azteca* soups, rich Mexican broth-stews of stock, herbs, vegetables, and chicken.

LA FOGATA

2427 Vance Jackson at Addax • 340-1384 • Lunch and dinner daily, breakfast
Saturday–Sunday • $$ • Cr
Mexican food, not Tex-Mex, holds sway here. The menu reads like one at any of thousands of good restaurants in the interior of Mexico. Soft tacos with guacamole, melted cheese in tortillas (*quesadillas*), grilled green onions, and beans (*charro* beans, in a broth with flavors of onion and cilantro) all convince you that this is a close approach to true Mexican dining in San Antonio. The restaurant is simple, good, and popular.

LA FONDA

2415 N. Main at Woodlawn • 733-0621 • Lunch and dinner
Monday–Saturday, closed Sunday • $$ • Cr
Longtime Mexican restaurant. The mild menu is more suited to the white-gloves-at-lunch set and regulars who prefer less spicy Mexican food. Bar.

LA MARGARITA

120 Produce Row at Market Square • 227-7140 • Lunch and dinner daily
$–$$ • Cr • W with assistance
On a visit to busy Market Square and the Mexican Market (El Mercado), you might want to sip a *cerveza* at one of their sidewalk tables and load up on tacos. During peak summer season, the tourists are usually swarming around and the place is crowded and boisterous. Located in an old-fashioned, green and red New Orleans-style building. Bar.

Seafood

KANGAROO COURT

512 River Walk near Commerce • 224-6821 • Breakfast, lunch, and dinner
daily • $–$$ • Cr • W
Old standby River Walk sidewalk café with prime people-watching real estate. The nice thing about Kangaroo Court is that they tolerate your lingering

awhile over suds or a meal to watch the people parade. Sandwiches and seafood. Fried oysters are commendable and the cheesecake is a favorite at this English-style pub. Bar.

SEA ISLAND SHRIMP HOUSE

322 W. Rector at Ahern • 342-7771 • Lunch and dinner Monday–Saturday. Closed Sunday • $$ • Cr • W

A salad and half a dozen oysters make a nice change at lunch for northside diners, and that combination is only one of many. Gumbo, fried fish, and a salad bar are a few of the others. The service, semicafeteria-style, is fast, and the food is far better than most fast-food chains that plague the area. Expect a line at peak lunch time. Beer and wine.

WATER STREET OYSTER BAR

7500 Broadway at Nacogdoches • 829-4853 • Lunch and dinner daily $$–$$$ • Cr

Fine fresh fish menu in casual, yuppie kind of place.

Steaks

BARN DOOR

8400 N. New Braunfels • 824-0116 • Lunch and dinner Monday–Friday and Sunday, Saturday dinner only • $$$–$$$$$ • Cr • W+

Yep, this really is a barn, with hams hanging down from the rafters. Comfortable and busy.

LITTLE RHEIN

231 S. Alamo at Market • 225-2111 • Dinner only daily • $$–$$$ • Cr

With its historic setting, this is one of the better steak restaurants in San Antonio. Let your budget fly out the window and go for some of the juiciest prime beef. The builing is a handsome 1847 rock house. Bar.

SAN FRANCISCO STEAK HOUSE

10223 Sahara at San Pedro • 342-2321 • Dinner only daily • Reservations recommended • $$–$$$ • Cr • W

Growing a little tired of the same old steak and salad bar? Just journey back to the gaudy San Francisco era. Here, in the main dining room, a golden girl climbs aboard a red velvet swing. Oh yes, the food. Meals are preceded by a chance to dig at a huge cheese, and the beef is prime steakhouse. Fancy desserts. Valet parking.

Vietnamese

VIET NAM

3244 Broadway at Natalen • 822-7461 • Lunch and dinner daily • $–$$ AE, MC, V • W

The Vietnamese dishes are uniformly mild and flavorful. Try the crab supreme, a light and inspired noodles mixture which shows the French influence in Indochinese cuisine. More mundane dishes, such as beef and chicken, contain the delicate flavors characteristic of the Far East. The spring rolls are excellent. Everything at this modest restaurant is relaxed and informal. Beer and wine.

ACCOMMODATIONS

Since San Antonio is a big tourist and convention town, downtown is full of quality hotels, most within walking distance of the tourist sites and the River Walk. And innumerable national motel chains are scattered about the city. Both hotels and motels are also concentrated in the north on Loop 410 near the airport, which is only about 20 minutes from downtown. There's a limousine service to downtown hotels from the airport, and some motels have courtesy vans.

Please note that there are many more good city hotels/motels than space allows. We are limited to listing some of the larger major hotels, both downtown and in different geographical areas, along with a few more modest motels, to give a range.

($ = under $45, $$ = $46–$60, $$$ = $61–$80, $$$$ = $81–$100, $$$$$ = over $100)
Room tax 15%

Central

CAMBERLEY SHERATON GUNTER HOTEL

205 E. Houston at St. Mary's • 227-3241 or 800-555-8000 • $$$$$ • W+ some rooms

A lot of business deals went down in this 1909-era 12-story hotel (322 rooms) in the center of downtown on Houston St. It's been renovated and looks quite spiffy and warmly inviting, with its turn-of-the-century warm woods and quality trim in the lobby. Both the bar and restaurants keep this same feeling with wood, brass, and plants. They've also opened the hotel a bit with glassed-in terraces added to the sides. European-style bakery/café. Pool, exercise room. Pay parking.

COURTYARD BY MARRIOTT

600 S. Santa Rosa • 229-9449 or 800-321-2211 • $$$–$$$$ • W+

This chain, a three-story with 149 rooms, is only several blocks from Market Square. Restaurant, pool.

CROWNE PLAZA–ST. ANTHONY

300 E. Travis at Navarro • 227-4392 or 800-227-6963 • $$$$$

People who would not think of staying with the upstarts in the hotel business, such as the Hiltons and Marriotts, have been sojourning at the old-line 10-story St. Anthony (350 rooms) for years. Some of its furniture and elegance are still here, despite several renovations since its beginning in 1909. The classic lobby with columns, ornate ceilings, and antiques is a mainstay, and it's still got a flair few other local hotels have: historic quality that is more gracious. The huge lobby and glassed-in side overlook the landscaped Travis Park, ideal for a stroll and lunch concerts during the summer months. Pool. Pay parking. Senior discount.

FAIRMOUNT HOTEL

401 S. Alamo at Nueva • 224-8800 or 800-642-3363 • $$$$$

This smaller three-story luxury hotel (37 rooms) joined the inn ranks in San Antonio with a lot of fanfare and media attention. The owners moved a 1906 building to this site, where they restored and added onto it. Next to La Villita, a very historical setting. Lots of personal service. Tasteful restaurant and lounge. Valet parking. Senior discount.

HILTON PALACIO DEL RIO HOTEL

200 S. Alamo at Market • 222-1400 or 800-HILTONS (800-445-8667) • $$$$$ W+ some rooms

Among the other San Antonio hotels, the tall 22-story Hilton Palacio del Rio is the oldest one most strongly associated with the River Walk. A restaurant, assorted bars, from sedate to lively, such as Durty Nelly's Pub downstairs, provide plenty of entertainment options. Convention groups are particularly fond of the Hilton, and vice versa. The convention center is right across Alamo St. Small pets are allowed. The Hilton may be a convention hotel, but its latest renovation is quite classy. Pool. Pay parking. Some room discounts.

HOLIDAY INN–CROCKETT HOTEL

320 Bonham at Crockett • 225-6500 or 800-292-1050 • $$$$–$$$$$

It's hard to get much closer to the Alamo than this. This older, seven-story (1909) hotel (206 rooms), restored and spiffed up with an airy skylight literally overlooks the Alamo compound across the street. Somehow the Crockett is friendlier and cozier than some of the bigger hotels. Be forewarned, some rooms are in a motel-like addition next door where the pool is located. Senior discount. Bar and formal dining room. Pay parking. Main hotel and rooms are tastefully furnished.

HOLIDAY INN RIVER WALK

217 N. St. Mary's at College • 224-2500 or 800-HOLIDAY • $$$$$ • W+

This 23-story Holiday (313 rooms) fronts the river, but not the most festive stretch of the River Walk. Bar, restaurant with outside seating. Pay parking. Senior discount.

HYATT REGENCY HOTEL

123 Losoya at Crockett • 222-1234 or 800-233-1234 • $$$$$ • W+ some rooms

One of the city's slickest hotels, the 16-story Hyatt (631 rooms) takes advantage of its River Walk location to the extent of having a little tongue of the river flowing through the lower lobby. Soaring atrium, coffee shop, and pool. Small pets are accepted. Variety of bars, including the popular Landing. Shopping area at River Walk level. Pay parking. Senior discount.

LA MANSION DEL RIO HOTEL

112 College at Presa • 225-2581 or 800-531-7208 • $$$$$ • W+ some rooms

Of all the hotels on the River Walk, the six-story La Mansion (337 rooms) fits in the most naturally. The hotel's Hispanic theme is a quiet celebration of San Antonio's past, especially its founding by the settlers from the Canary Islands. (The main restaurant is Las Canarias.) Some of the spacious rooms have excellent river views. But be wary of rooms near parking garage because of noise. Although not a particularly old hotel, the upscale La Mansion captures the cultural and historical flavor of San Antonio quite effectively. Pets allowed. Pool in pleasant, convivial courtyard. Pay parking. Senior discount.

MARRIOTT RIVER WALK

711 E. River Walk • Enter from Market between S. Alamo and Bowie
224-4555 or 800-648-4462 • $$$$$ • W+ some rooms

The Marriott is a modern, 30-story hotel (500 rooms) conveniently situated across the street from the convention center. It offers a full spectrum of services, from sauna to pool to shops, and is popular for meetings and small- to medium-sized conventions. It has assorted restaurants and bars. Senior discount. Pets accepted. Pay parking, and quick check-out.

MARRIOTT RIVERCENTER

101 Bowie at Commerce • 223-1000 or 800-648-4462 • $$$$$ • W+ some rooms
No-smoking rooms

At 1,000 rooms this 38-story Marriott wins hands down as the big daddy of San Antonio hotels. It's sleek and in the heart of downtown, with 82 suites. Pets are accepted. Indoor parking is either drive yourself or valet. Atrium lounge and restaurants. Heated indoor-outdoor pool, saunas, indoor whirlpool, exercise room. Adjoins Rivercenter Mall with its bustling restaurants and shops.

MENGER HOTEL

204 Alamo Plaza at Crockett • 223-4361 or 800-345-9285 • $$$$–$$$$$
W+ some rooms

The five-story Menger's history stretches back to the 1850s, with colorful guests of cattle barons and U.S. presidents. The splendid front dominates Alamo Plaza. Inside, the new lobby (there is also an old one) is a relaxing place to sit and gaze into the hotel's tropical garden. Next to the new lobby is the historic old lobby, or rotunda, a formal columned room which stretches up three stories. It is easy to see why the Menger was once considered one of the most luxurious hotels in the Southwest. Some of the rooms are new, while others are nostalgic and more reasonably priced. The Menger bar is almost as famous as the rest of the hotel. The hotel has 320 rooms. Pool on patio. Pay parking. Senior discount.

PLAZA SAN ANTONIO BY MARRIOTT

555 S. Alamo at Arceniega • 229-1000 • $$$$$ • W+ some rooms

The Plaza reminds you of the days when a hotel earned a reputation through comfort and service, not advertising. The modern seven-story Plaza (252 rooms) projects the Old World conviction that a guest has a right to be looked after. With its patio, pool, and tennis courts, the attractive Plaza has more facilities than other downtown hotels, and its gardens and grounds make it seem more isolated. The Anaqua Grill serves inventive cuisine in a casually formal setting overlooking the landscaped patio. Senior discount. Pay parking.

RAMADA EMILY MORGAN HOTEL

705 E. Houston • 225-8486 or 800-824-6674 • $$$$

Another hotel (177 rooms) that faces right onto the Alamo complex. In fact, you can sit in your room Jacuzzi and gaze out on the cradle of Texas history. This fine old rococo 12-story building was renovated to house the Emily Morgan, which has a clean, modernistic look of brass inside. Saunas and exercise room. Bar and restaurant. Pay parking. Senior discount.

Northwest and North Central

BEST WESTERN OAK HILLS

7401 Wurzbach at Babcock • 614-9900 • $$ • W+ some rooms

The Oak Hills (223 rooms) sits right in the South Texas Medical Center and so attracts many outpatients and visitors. It also is a popular place for health-related meetings and presentations. A convenient location is the motel's strongest asset. Pets accepted. Pool, restaurant, bar. Free parking. Senior discount.

DOUBLETREE HOTEL

37 N.E. Loop 410 at McCullough • 366-2424 or 800-535-1980 • $$$$$ • W+ some rooms

The five-story Doubletree is a blend of Mexican and Spanish accents. A lofty courtyard is the hotel's centerpiece; less obvious but equally welcome are the solid comfort and generous dimensions of the 290 rooms. Fairly near the airport. Pool, restaurant, bar. Free parking. Senior discount.

EMBASSY SUITES-NORTHWEST

7750 Briaridge near Callaghan and I-10 • 340-5421 or 800-EMBASSY (800-362-2779) • $$$$$

217 rooms, actually suites, in this eight-story hotel, all open onto the huge central atrium, filled with plants and glowing lamps. A breakfast is included in the room rate, as are drinks at the bar in the evening. Most suites come with kitchenettes and bars, as well as more conventional amenities such as TV and use of the pool. The Spanish atmosphere seems natural. Popular bar. Restaurant. Free parking. Senior discount.

HYATT REGENCY HILL COUNTRY RESORT

9800 Hyatt Resort Dr. • 647-1234 or 800-233-1234 • $$$$$ • W+

Two hundred Texas Hill Country acres provide the scenic backdrop setting for this destination resort. And believe it or not, this prime getaway vacation site is on the fringe of the city. The four-story limestone buildings (500 rooms with many suites) look out on greenery, streams, and oak trees. Float down the river in the four-acre water park or opt for tennis or golf. Daily programs for the kids. Health club, jogging paths, restaurants, bars. Sea World is nearby. This is worth a gander, even if you don't stay overnight.

MOTEL 6

9400 Wurzbach • 593-0013 • $

A cut above most Motel 6s, and still the same bargain price. Pool and good location near I-10. Two-story with 117 rooms.

OMNI

9821 Colonnade at I-10 • 691-8888 or 800-843-6664 • $$$$$ • W+

Well-heeled businessmen take their corporate credit cards to the slick 20-story Omni (326 rooms) when they have business on the north side. A popular convention and meeting site. Workout club, restaurants, and pool. Senior discount. Free parking.

SAN ANTONIO AIRPORT HILTON
611 N.W. Loop 410 at San Pedro • 340-6060 or 800-333-3333 • $$$$$ • W+ some rooms
Here, close to north side businesses and to the airport, is a middle-size, solidly comfortable, modern 14-story hotel (387 rooms) with amenities but without frills. An indoor-outdoor swimming pool is a plus. Bar and restaurant. Free parking.

Northeast

COMFORT INN AIRPORT
2635 N.E. Loop 410 at Perrin-Beitel • 653-9110 or 800-221-2222 • $$
Six-story with 203 rooms, cable TV, restaurant, pool. No pets.

COURTYARD BY MARRIOTT/AIRPORT
8615 Broadway • 828-7200 or 800-321-2211 • $$$$ • W+ some rooms
Near airport on east side, this Marriott has 146 rooms. Pool and restaurant.

LA QUINTA WINDSOR PARK
333 NE. Loop 410 at Airport Blvd. • 653-6619 or 800-531-5900 • $$$ • W
Just one of the many La Quintas (198 rooms) sprinkled about town *everywhere*, because San Antonio is corporate headquarters for this businessman-oriented motel chain. Pool. Free parking. Senior discount.

Bed and Breakfast

BED & BREAKFAST HOSTS OF SAN ANTONIO
824-8036 • $–$$$$
Call for info on B&B listings. Breakfast, snacks, and neighborly conversation included in the price.

SAN MARCOS

Hays County Seat • 31,048 • 512
Indians lived near the headwaters of the San Marcos River at least 12,000 years ago. This is one of the oldest continuously inhabited sites in North America. The pure water of the Edwards Underground Reservoir erupts to the surface here through cracks in the limestone associated with the Balcones Fault, producing springs that form the river. The springs' flow have lessened during drought years, but have never failed to produce millions of gallons of water each day. The San Marcos River rises within the San Marcos city limits and merges with the Guadalupe River about 38 miles downstream, near Gonzales. About three miles below its origin, the San Marcos is joined and diluted by the Blanco River. The upper three miles are essentially a large spring running with crystal clear water that maintains a constant year-round temperature of about 71 degrees.

The river was named by Spanish explorers who discovered it on St. Mark's Day. Spanish attempts to establish missions here in the 1700s failed. A colony established in 1807 was abandoned in 1812 because of floods and Indian raids. Anglo settlers who came here in the 1840s had better luck. Among them was General Edward Burleson, a former vice-president of the Republic, who helped set up the town. In 1848, Hays County was formed, named for John Coffee "Jack" Hays, famed captain of the Texas Rangers and nephew of President Andrew Jackson. President Lyndon Johnson earned his college degree here at what is now Southwest Texas State University (SWT). The university, tourism, and light manufacturing drive the local economy.

TOURIST SERVICES

SAN MARCOS CHAMBER OF COMMERCE
202 C.M. Allen Parkway near Hopkins • 396-2495 • W

HISTORIC PLACES

BELVIN STREET HISTORIC DISTRICT
One of San Marcos's earliest residential streets, with a concentration of houses built in the 1880s and 1890s. Listed in the National Register of Historic Places. Of significant architectural interest are the houses at 727, 730, 830, 833, 903, and 1030. These are all private homes, not open to the public.

OTHER POINTS OF INTEREST

AQUARENA CENTER
Aquarena Springs Dr., about .3 mile west of IH-35 exit 206 • 245-7575
Open daily, except Christmas Day • Adults $4, children $3 • W variable
The prolific headsprings of the San Marcos River are the focal point of Aquarena Center, formerly Aquarena Springs. Chief attraction is the glassbottom boat tour (fee) of Spring Lake, formed by hundreds of springs located on the Balcones Fault. Run by Southwest Texas State University as an environmental interpretive center dedicated to preserving the springs and their inhabitants, and explaining their long history, the complex includes an aquarium with native fish, amphibians, plants, and local endangered species like the Texas blind salamander, fountain darter, and San Marcos dwarf salamander. There are also hands-on displays for kids, computer kiosks, and a display of how the Edwards Aquifer works. A short boatride takes you to the other side of the lake, which includes a reproduction of a Kiowa Indian village. Texana Village includes several local historic buildings.

SAN MARCOS RIVER WALKWAY
This path along the river unites three city parks. There are several entrances to the walkway along C.M. Allen Parkway, including one behind the Chamber of Commerce.

WONDER WORLD
Bishop and Prospect on the west side of town. *Take Wonder Dr. exit off IH-35 and follow signs* **• 392-3760 • Open March 1–October 31 • Admission • W**
The cave on which this park is centered was formed by an earthquake in the Balcones Fault, so while it's not as colorful as most of the state's water-formed

caves, it is an interesting sample of the forces of nature at work. Tours leave about every 15 minutes. The 146-foot Texas Observation Tower allows a good view of how the Balcones Fault line looks on the outside, where the Hill Country begins. There is a small wildlife park and petting zoo with Texas and exotic animals. Also miniature train ride and Anti-Gravity House. Picnic areas.

SAN MARCOS FACTORY SHOPS

3939 S. IH-35 • 800-628-9465 • W

Over 100 factory outlet stores, plus a food court, miniature golf course, and children's play area.

COLLEGES AND UNIVERSITIES

SOUTHWEST TEXAS STATE UNIVERSITY (SWT)

LBJ Dr. and University • 245-2111 • W+ but not all areas

Founded in 1903 as a state normal school, SWT is now a full-fledged university; the campus covers 361 acres on a hillside overlooking San Marcos and counts about 20,000 students. President Lyndon B. Johnson received his bachelor's degree and permanent teaching certificate here in 1930. Visitors must obtain a pass at the gate during school hours. Guided campus walking tours are available at the Admissions and Visitors Center, located at the intersection of Guadalupe and Concho streets. LBJ memorabilia is displayed at the Alumni House at LBJ and University drives. In addition to intercollegiate sports, there are theater productions (245-2141), concerts, musical recitals, and dance events, plus occasional art exhibits (245-2611).

SPORTS AND ACTIVITIES

Canoeing and Tubing

T.G. Canoes, about 2 miles out TX 80, 353-3946. Canoe and kayak rentals. **Lions Club Tube Rental,** City Park, Aquarena Springs Dr. and Bugg Ln., 392-8255. May–September, Sunday–Friday 12–7, Saturday 10–7. More than 1,000 inner tubes in a variety of sizes. Shuttle service back from Rio Vista Park, which is about a 90-minute float. Profits go to Lions charities.

Golf

AQUARENA SPRINGS GOLF COURSE

601 University Dr. • 245-7593 • 9-hole course. Greens fee; about $10.

ANNUAL EVENTS

June

TEXAS WATER SAFARI

Aquarena Center, Aquarena Springs Dr., about .3 mile west off IH-35, exit 206 • 396-2495 (Chamber of Commerce) or 357-6113 (Goynes Canoe)
First Saturday in June • Free for spectators • W variable

The "World's Toughest Boat Race," a non-stop 260-mile race down the San Marcos and Guadalupe rivers to Seadrift on the Gulf, begins at Spring Lake.

The boats used are mostly canoes; all are limited to muscle-power propulsion and entrants must carry all supplies with them. Teams have come from as far away as Alaska and England to compete. It usually takes the winners about 36 hours to make it to the coast. The start is interesting, but to see some powerful paddling, find a vantage point farther down the San Marcos.

September

REPUBLIC OF TEXAS CHILYMPIAD

Hays County Civic Center, exit 201 off IH-35 • 396-5400 • Friday–Sunday of third weekend in September • Admission • W variable

The World Championship at Terlingua outranks this state championship, but the Chilympiad is much bigger in size. Hundreds of men's teams gather each year to concoct chili, employing secret recipes and ingredients ranging from armadillo to rattlesnake. Sampling by spectators is encouraged. There's also entertainment, an arts and crafts fair, and a dance every night.

RESTAURANTS

($ = under $7, $$ = $8–$17, $$$ = $18–$25, $$$$ = over $25 for one person exluding drinks, tax, and tip.)

CAFE ON THE SQUARE & BREW PUB

126 N. LBJ • 353-9289 • Open daily, breakfast, lunch, and dinner $–$$ • Cr • W

This cafe and brew pub also has a good collection of vintage Texas beer signs and paraphernalia. American and Tex/Mex breakfasts; lunch and dinner are burgers, sandwiches, steaks, fajitas, wild game, and more exotic fare. Try any of the house brews, or choose from a fairly extensive selection of domestics and imports. Live music.

FUSCHAK'S PIT BAR-B-Q

920 TX 80, east of IH-35 • 353-2712 • Open daily, lunch and dinner • $ • W

Look past the fake log cabin decor and concentrate on the brisket, chicken, and fajita meat. The banana pudding will make puddin' heads happy.

PEPPER'S AT THE FALLS

100 Sessoms Dr. at the dam below Spring Lake • 396-5255 Open daily, lunch and dinner • $–$$ • Cr • W

You come for the view of the San Marcos River, but the food is okay too. Eclectic menu has appetizers, salads, burgers, sandwiches, Tex/Mex, steaks, chicken-fried steak, fried and grilled chicken, catfish, and the other usual suspects.

ACCOMMODATIONS

($ = under $45, $$ = $46–$60, $$$ = $61–$80, $$$$ = $81–$100, $$$$$ = over $100)
Room tax 13%

AQUARENA SPRINGS INN

Aquarena Springs, 601 University Dr. 78666 • 800-893-9466 • June–August $$$–$$$$, lower rest of year

The two-story inn on the grounds of Aquarena Springs has 25 rooms, including one suite ($$$–$$$$). Cable TV. Room phones. No pets. Continental breakfast. Large outdoor pool and wading pool. Coffeemakers in some rooms. Also refurbished 1928 resort with 19 rooms overlooking Spring Lake.

CRYSTAL RIVER INN

326 W. Hopkins near Moore (78666) • 396-3739 • $$$–$$$$$ • Cr
B&B with 11 accommodations in restored 1883 home and two other buildings, 11 have private bath, most have TV and room phones. Children OK by prior arrangement. No pets. Full breakfast. Fountain courtyard. Rose Garden. Close to the courthouse and Belvin Street Historic District.

SEGUIN

Guadalupe County Seat • 18,853 • (830)
A number of cities and towns in Texas are named after heroes of the Texas Revolution, but this is the only one named after a hero who later fought on the other side. Juan Seguin, a Mexican who sided with the Texans, was one of the unsuccessful messengers Colonel Travis sent out through the Mexican lines at the Alamo to request help. Later, Seguin fought against Santa Anna at San Jacinto. Put in charge of the military government of San Antonio, it became his responsibility to arrange for the burial of the ashes of his former comrades at the Alamo.

But as U.S. annexation and a probable war with Mexico grew nearer, rumors spread that Seguin was really a Mexican sympathizer. The rumors and ill-feeling toward him intensified. Finally, when the Mexican Army invaded in 1842, Seguin decided to take his chances with Santa Anna, his old enemy, and fled south of the Rio Grande. Given the choice of joining the Mexican Army or going to prison, he joined the army.

The city of Seguin got its start in 1838 when some members of Matthew "Old Paint" Caldwell's Gonzales Rangers settled here. They called the settlement Walnut Springs, but in 1839, when told there was another Texas town by that name, they changed it to Seguin to honor Juan's role in the Revolution.

Today the city is known for its many pecan and oak trees. The pecans are a major cash crop in the area, while many of the oaks have been around so long— it's estimated some may be 1,000 years old—that they have historical names. These ancient trees fit in well with the downtown historic district that is listed in the National Register of Historic Places.

TOURIST SERVICES

SEGUIN/GUADALUPE COUNTY CHAMBER OF COMMERCE

427 N. Austin (TX Bus. 123) at E. Ireland (P.O. Box 710, 78156)
379-6382 or 800-580-7322 • W
Self-guided walking and driving tour booklet available as well as information about tours conducted by the Seguin Conservation Society.

MUSEUMS AND ART GALLERIES

LOS NOGALES MUSEUM

415 S. River at Live Oak • 379-6382 (Chamber of Commerce)
Open Sundays May–October • Free (donations appreciated)
Built in the 1800s, this adobe pioneer home was restored and operated by the Seguin Conservation Society. Displays artifacts.

HISTORIC PLACES

Besides their regular tour booklet, ask the Chamber of Commerce about their *True Women Tour* brochure/map detailing all of the Seguin places mentioned in the historic novel *True Women* chronicling a Seguin family history and also featured in a TV mini-series.

CAMPBELL LOG CABIN & FIRST CHURCH

211 E. Live Oak • 379-6382 (Chamber of Commerce) • May–October, Sundays 2–5 • Free (donations appreciated)

By 1850, John Campbell had built the first room of this cabin about eight miles southwest of present-day Seguin. It was moved to this site by the Seguin Conservation Society. In the back of the cabin is the First Methodist Church, Seguin's first church.

CONCRETE BUILDINGS

There were more than 100 concrete buildings of various sizes and purposes in Seguin in the late 1800s. They were so numerous the town was sometimes known as "Cement City." The reason behind this was a new formula for concrete developed in the late 1840s by Seguin resident Dr. John E. Park. A few remain, such as the *Sebastopol* (see below), the *Johnson-Smith Home* (1854) at 761 Johnson, and the *St. James Catholic School* (1850) at Camp near Convent.

SEBASTOPOL HOUSE STATE HISTORICAL PARK

704 Zorn at Erkel just off US 90A • 379-4833 • Friday–Sunday 9–4 Adults $2, children $1

Built in the mid-1850s by Colonel Joshua Young, this is one of the best surviving examples of early concrete building in the Southwest. Exhibits explain the construction process. Tours offered.

OTHER HISTORIC BUILDINGS

Hardscrabble, at 513 E. Nolte started out as a dogtrot log cabin around 1838. The **Erskine-Hollaman (Humphreys) House** (1853) at 902 N. Austin was actually built 30 miles away and moved here by oxcart in three pieces in 1867. It is listed in the National Register of Historic Places. **Elm Grove** (1854) at 906 W. Court was built of ship's ballast stones left at Indianola by a French ship and hauled in by oxcart. These are all private residences not open to the public. The apartment house at 203 S. Crockett was originally the **Magnolia Hotel** built in 1842.

OTHER POINTS OF INTEREST

WORLD'S LARGEST PECAN

North side of courthouse, Court and Austin

Measuring five feet by two-and-a-half feet and weighing in at about half a ton, this monster metal-and-cement pecan calls attention to the fact that Guadalupe County produces more than three million pounds of pecans each year.

SPORTS AND ACTIVITIES

MAX STARCKE PARK

TX Bus. 123 at the Guadalupe River • 379-4853
Picnic among towering trees along the river. 18-hole course.

SEGUIN WAVE POOL

Starcke Park East • 401-2480 • Summer season
Ride the waves or play in splash pool. Picnic tables.

COLLEGES AND UNIVERSITIES

TEXAS LUTHERAN UNIVERSITY

1000 W. Court (US 90A) • 379-4161 • W+ but not all areas
Visitor parking areas marked
Founded in Brenham in 1891, the college moved to Seguin in 1912. On the 130-acre campus is the **Fiedler Memorial Museum,** in Langner Hall on Prexy Dr., which emphasizes the geology of the area with exhibits of rocks, minerals, fossils, and archaeology.

PERFORMING ARTS

MID-TEXAS SYMPHONY & ARTS & ENTERTAINMENT SERIES

Jackson Auditorium at Texas Lutheran University • 372-8180 • Admission • W
The Symphony plays six concerts yearly in September–May season. A&E Series of Texas Lutheran brings in national/international shows.

SHOPPING

D&D FARM & RANCH

516 I-10 East near Hwy. 123 • 379-7340 or 800-292-5232
Hey, this is the real thing, probably the biggest store of its kind in the Southwest. Shop for western wear, saddlery, etc.

SIDE TRIPS

LAKE McQUEENEY

Take FM 78 west to FM 725, then north (right) to lake. Approximately 4 miles from town • **557-9900 (Marina) • Open at all times • Free • W variable**
This 396-acre lake is well-known as a haven for water-skiers. Commercial facilities available for boating, fishing, and swimming.

ANNUAL EVENTS

April

TEXAS LADIES STATE CHAMPIONSHIP CHILI COOK-OFF

Starcke Park East • 379-6382 (Chamber of Commerce) • Day in mid-April
Day-long event where the women and their chili are all five-alarm.

July

FREEDOM FIESTA

Max Starcke Park • 379-6382 (Chamber of Commerce) • Thursday–Saturday around July 4 • Free • W variable

Activities include food booths, dances, arts and crafts fair, carnival, and fireworks.

October

GUADALUPE COUNTY FAIR

County Fairgrounds, S. Guadalupe (TX Bus. 123) • 379-6382 (Chamber of Commerce) • Thursday–Sunday of second week in October • Admission. Additional admission to some events • W variable

This typical old-time county fair is more than 100 years old. Parade, livestock judging, dances, and rodeo.

December

A TASTE OF CHRISTMAS PAST

**Sebastopol State Historical Park, at 704 Zorn • 379-4833
First Saturday in December • Free**

Get the Christmas spirit with concerts, choirs, and open house at this historic house all decorated up Victorian style.

RESTAURANTS

DRAGON PLACE

1003 N.W. Hwy. 123 Bypass • 372-2910 • Lunch and dinner daily • $–$$ • Cr
Good Chinese at reasonable prices. Lunchtime crowds.

K & G STEAKHOUSE

3003 N. Hwy. 123 Bypass • 372-3260 • Breakfast, lunch, and dinner daily $–$$ • Cr
Serves up everything from sandwiches to steaks.

ACCOMMODATIONS

*($ = under $45, $$ = $46–$60, $$$ = $61–$80, $$$$ = $81–$100, $$$$$ = over $100)
Room tax 13%*

BEST WESTERN OF SEGUIN

1603 I-10 at Hwy. 46 • 379-9631 or 800-528-1234 • $$
Two-story with 83 rooms, pool, restaurant adjacent. Small pets OK.

HOLIDAY INN

2950 N. TX. 123 Bypass at I-10 • 372-0860 or 800-HOLIDAY (800-465-4329) $$–$$$ • W+ 1 room • No-smoking rooms
This hospitable two-story Holiday Inn has 139 rooms, including satellite TV, lounge, restaurant, pool, exercise room.

STEPHENVILLE

Erath County Seat • 16,100 • (254)

John M. Stephen and about 30 other pioneers settled here in 1855. In 1856 Erath County was created and Stephenville made the county seat. When many of the men went off to the Civil War, the Indian raids increased and didn't stop until early 1870s.

Agriculture is important, but dairy farming accounts for more than half the agricultural income. On the square is the famous cow statue, Moo-La, a life-size model of a Holstein that pays tribute to the dairy industry. Listed as one of the Best 100 Small Towns in America.

TOURIST SERVICES

STEPHENVILLE CHAMBER OF COMMERCE

187 W. Washington (P.O. Box 306, 76401) • 965-5313 or 800-658-6490, Fax 965-3814, e-mail chamber@our-town.com, URL: http://www.our-town.com/local/chofcom/htm • W

MUSEUMS

HISTORICAL HOUSE MUSEUM COMPLEX

525 E. Washington, 4 blocks east of the square • 965-5880 • Friday–Sunday 2–5 • Free (donations) • W variable

Ten restored nineteenth-century structures, complete with period furnishings and tools, make up this complex. The focal point is the **Colonel John D. Berry Cottage,** a two-story English-style cottage built in 1869 of native limestone with a Pennsylvania hex sign design.

SPORTS AND ACTIVITIES

Golf

LEGENDS COUNTRY CLUB

Lingleville Hwy. (TX 8) • 968-2200, Fax 965-4701 • Nonmembers are welcome at this 18-hole course. Greens fee: weekdays $12, weekends and holidays $18.

COLLEGES AND UNIVERSITIES

TARLETON STATE UNIVERSITY

W. Washington (Bus US 377) at Lillian • 968-9000 • W variable Visitor parking areas marked

This university has been part of the Texas A&M University System since 1917. Founded in 1899 by John Tarleton, it is one of the oldest institutions of higher education in Texas. Visitors are welcome at sports events, and also the **Clyde H. Wells Fine Arts Center** located at Lillian and Vanderbilt (968-9131). It offers exhibits, plays, concerts, entertainers, and a film series.

PERFORMING ARTS

CROSS TIMBERS COUNTRY OPRY

SE Loop (US 377E Bypass) about 1 mile east of US 281
965-4575 • Admission • W

They put on family entertainment here every Saturday night starting at 7:30. The variety shows are patterned after the Grand Ol' Opry, with country pickin' and singin' by both local amateur performers and regional professionals. Food, snacks, and soft drinks available from Chuck Wagon.

SIDE TRIPS

HOKA HEY FINE ARTS GALLERY AND FOUNDRY

US 377 southwest near Dublin • 445-2017 • W variable

The nine-foot bronze statue of John Wayne at the International Airport in Los Angeles is an example of the type of work cast at the foundry. Gallery is open daily except holidays, and sculptures by various artists are for sale. Call for tour of foundry. Take time for a Dr Pepper at the Old Doc Soda Shop in the Dr Pepper Bottling Company, 221 S. Patrick St. (445-3466) in Dublin two miles away from Hoka Hey (and 10 miles from Stephenville). This is the only plant that still bottles and sells Dr Pepper with its original formula with pure cane sugar instead of corn syrup!

ANNUAL EVENTS

April

TEXAS GOSPEL SINGING CONVENTION

Stephenville High School Auditorium, 2650 W. Overhill at N. Dale
965-5313 (Chamber of Commerce) • Third Saturday and Sunday in April
Free • W

This annual get-together of gospel singers from Texas and surrounding states has been going on since 1929. Singers include individuals, quartets, choirs, and audience sing-alongs.

ACCOMMODATIONS

($ = under $45, $$ = $46–$60, $$$ = $61–$80, $$$$ = $81–$100, $$$$$ = over $100)
Room tax 13%

HOLIDAY INN

2865 W. Washington (US 377/67W) • 968-5256 or 800-HOLIDAY (800-465-4329)
$$$ • W+ 1 room • No-smoking rooms

The two-story Holiday Inn has 100 units, including two suites ($$$$) and 65 no-smoking rooms. Cable TV. Room phones (local calls free). Pets OK. Restaurant closed after 2 p.m. on Sunday • Free continental breakfast in lobby. Kids under 12 eat free. Night security guard.

Bed and Breakfast

OXFORD HOUSE

563 N. Graham • 965-6885, Fax 965-6885 • No smoking in the house

This grand 1898 house was built by Judge W. J. Oxford, Sr. and it is still in the Oxford family. Oxford House offers four bedrooms, each with private bath and all furnished in family heirlooms. A full breakfast is served. No pets, and children must be supervised.

TAYLOR

Williamson County • 11,971 • 512

Taylor was founded in 1876 with the coming of the International and Great Northern Railway, and was named after Edward Moses Taylor, a railroad official. The railroad brought in settlers—including many Czech and German immigrants—and took out cattle and cotton. The economy really boomed when the Missouri-Kansas-Texas Railroad came through in 1882. By 1900, Taylor was one of the largest inland cotton markets in the world. Cotton is still a major crop for area farmers, with small manufacturing plants taking up the slack.

Bill Pickett is one of Taylor's most interesting celebrities, born on an area ranch in 1870. Pickett, a black cowboy often called "the Dusky Demon," is credited with inventing the rodeo event of "bulldogging," or steer wrestling. He had his own unique style, controlling the steer by sinking his teeth into the animal's upper lip and hanging on like a bulldog as he twisted the neck and brought the steer down. He became a folk hero and travelled the world performing this unusual stunt. In 1971 Pickett was posthumously inducted into the Cowboy Hall of Fame.

Taylor also claims to be "Barbecue Capital of the World," boasting of some of the state's best barbecue joints, places like Louie Mueller's, Rudy Mikeska's (one of the famed barbecuing Mikeska brothers), and local secret places like the Taylor Cafe.

TOURIST SERVICES

TAYLOR CHAMBER OF COMMERCE

1519 N. Main (TX 95), just south of Lake Dr. (P.O. Box 231, 76574) • 352-6364 • W

MUSEUMS

MOODY MUSEUM

114 W. 9th and Talbot • 352-6364 (Chamber of Commerce) • Open special occasions and by appointment • Donation • W downstairs only

Dan Moody, son of Taylor's first mayor, was Texas' youngest attorney general and in 1927, at age 33, he became the youngest governor of Texas. He was born in 1893 in this house, which contains family memorabilia and furnishings.

OTHER HISTORIC PLACES

Taylor had a fire in 1879 that destroyed much of downtown. One of the few frame buildings to survive is the old **Kamp Hotel** (1877) at 101 N. Main, believed to be Taylor's oldest existing structure. Taylor was rebuilt in stone and brick; many downtown buildings date from the 1880s to the early 1900s. Most impressive is the **Taylor National Bank** (1894) 200 N. Main at 2nd, a three-story brick and sandstone construction with some stained glass windows, listed in the National Register of Historic Places. Others include the **First National Bank** (1883) 117 N. Main, **Petersen Hardware Block** (1893) 113–119 W. 2nd, **Eikel-Prewitt Building** (1893) 316 N. Main, and the **Treadgill Building** (1893) 401 N. Main.

ANNUAL EVENTS

August

TAYLOR INTERNATIONAL BARBECUE COOKOFF

Murphy Park • 352-6364 • Third weekend in August • Admission W variable

It's appropriate for the "Barbecue Capital of the World" to hold an international cookoff, even if most of the competitors are from Texas. Free samples of barbecued beef, poultry, pork, lamb, goat, wild game, and what-have-you right off the grills. There's also entertainment, games, and contests.

RESTAURANTS

LOUIE MUELLER'S BARBECUE

206 W. 2nd, just west of Main (TX 95) • 352-6206 • Monday–Saturday 7 to 5:30 or 6:30 • $ • No Cr • W

The green plaster walls and tin ceilings are darkened from years of pit smoke, but don't let that appearance turn you off. There are no frills in this 1905, ex-gymnasium, but from that pit come briskets and sausage that have earned high praise from *Texas Monthly* and *The New York Times*. The meat is served on butcher paper with bread. The extras, like cole slaw, cost extra. Beer.

OLD COUPLAND INN AND DANCE HALL

Take TX 95 approximately 8 miles south to Coupland, then east into town **856-2226 • Thursday–Saturday dinner only • Reservations recommended $–$$ • AE, MC, V • Children's plates**

All-you-can-eat meals make this heaven on earth for some barbecue lovers. You are served family-style with platters of ribs, brisket, chicken and sausage that keep coming as long as you keep eating. They come with potato salad, cole slaw, beans, etc. They also serve all-you-can-eat mesquite-grilled sirloin steak. Beer, wine, BYOB. Next door is an old MKT railroad depot that is now a museum exhibiting Coupland memorabilia.

TEMPLE

Bell County • 53,733 • (254)

When the Gulf, Colorado, and Santa Fe Railroad came to Bell County in 1881, the city of Belton paid a big bonus for the tracks and thought it would be the railroad headquarters. Instead, the railroad moved about eight miles north and set up Temple as its division point.

Temple started out as a rough town with more saloons and brothels than anything else, but the railroad made it a model city. In 1891, a hospital was established to take care of Santa Fe employees. Dr. A. C. Scott, Sr. was appointed chief surgeon in 1892 and held that position until his death in 1940. Dr. Scott and his partner Dr. R. R. White Jr. helped establish King's Daughters Hospital and founded Scott and White Hospital, one of the largest group practice clinics in the United States. Temple now has one of the largest concentrations of medical care in the Southwest.

Two other famous Temple residents were James E. ("Pa") and Miriam A. ("Ma") Ferguson. Both were elected governor. When James was impeached, "Ma" became the first woman governor of Texas (*See* Historic Places).

TOURIST SERVICES

CONVENTION AND VISITORS BUREAU

2 N. Main 76501 • 298-5720, Fax 298-5383

MUSEUMS

CZECH HERITAGE MUSEUM

**Downstairs in SPJST Insurance Co. Building, 520 N. Main at E. French
773-1575 • Open Monday–Friday 8–12, 1–5 • Free**

In 1897 Czechoslovakian immigrants founded the *Slovanska Podporujici Jednota Statu Texas,* the Slavonic Benevolent Order of the State of Texas, a fraternal society providing insurance and social programs. This museum traces the heritage of the Czechs and their contributions to Texas and the United States. The Koliha Collection consists of about 80,000 advertising pens and pencils.

RAILROAD AND PIONEER MUSEUM

**710 Jack Baskin St (corner of Ave. H. and S. 31st) • 298-5172, Fax 298-5171,
e-mail: irving@ci.temple.tx.us • Tuesday–Friday 1–4, Saturday 10–4
Admission $2 adults, $1 seniors, $1 children 5–12, children under 5 free • W**

This restored turn-of-the-century depot was moved here from Moody, Texas. Exhibits trace pioneer life and the significant role of the railroads. It is also a research facility that does educational outreach to schools on pioneer history and railroads. Outside is an old Santa Fe locomotive. Climb aboard and ring the bell!

Both the Moody Santa Fe Depot and Temple Katy Depot (now on East Central) will move to the 8.76-acre downtown depot complex near the much larger Santa Fe Depot when the latter's restoration is completed, hopefully by 1999.

THE SCOTT & WHITE LOG CABIN MEDICAL MUSEUM

**2401 S. 31st (on the south front lawn next to the Special Treatment Center)
771-8205 or 724-3047 • Monday and Wednesday 1–5, except holidays
Free • W+**

Photographs and artifacts depict the history of Scott & White Memorial Hospital and Clinic. Scott & White evolved from a partnership established in 1897 by Dr. A. C. Scott, Sr. and Dr. R. R. White, Jr. Built in 1858, the log cabin was Dr. Scott's study. Evolution of medical treatments the past 100 years is also of interest.

HISTORIC PLACES

FERGUSON HOUSE

518 N. 7th at W. French • Not open to the public

James E. and Miriam A. ("Ma") Ferguson, both of whom served as governor of Texas, built this house in 1907 and lived here until they moved permanently to Austin in 1932. A populist who supported small and tenant farmers and opposed prohibition, James, called "Farmer Jim," was elected governor in 1914 and again in 1916. But strong opposition, fired by his feud with the Board of Regents of the University of Texas who saw him vetoing all appropriations for UT, led to his impeachment and removal from office in 1917. Legally barred from holding office, he ran "Ma" in his place. In 1924 she became the first woman governor in Texas, and she appointed the first woman secretary of state. She was called "Ma" from the initials of her first and middle names. In her reelection bid, "Ma" was defeated by Daniel Moody, the 33-year old attorney general who became the youngest governor of the state. But she ran again in 1932 and won. With a campaign slogan "Two governors for the price of one," it was no secret that James was more governor than "Ma" during her two terms.

NORTH TEMPLE HISTORICAL DISTRICT

The area between 3rd and 13th streets bounded by Nugent on the north and French on the south contains several fine historic homes.

SPORTS AND ACTIVITIES

Golf

SAMMONS GOLF COURSE

2220 W. Ave. D • 778-8282

Located only .25 miles from IH-35 off 49th Street, this course is open from sunup to sundown. Greens fee are $11 weekdays, $14.50 weekends. Tennis courts, fishing, and full-service grilles are also available.

Tennis

PARKS AND RECREATION DEPT.

298-5690 • 21 public courts, 3 soccer, and 7 softball complexes

PERFORMING ARTS

CULTURAL ACTIVITIES CENTER

3011 N. 3rd near Civic Center • 773-9926 • Admission • W+

The 500-seat auditorium and the galleries host concerts, dance, and other performing arts throughout the year. (No charge to view rotating art exhibits.)

TEMPLE CIVIC THEATRE

2413 S. 13th off Loop 363 • 778-4751 • Admission • W

A professional director and technical director and a cast and crew of volunteers put on about 10 productions a year.

SHOPPING

THE ROSEBUD

2010 SW HK Dodgen Loop 363 in Exchange Plaza • 774-1978 • W

This popular ladies shop is famous for its unique styles and personalized service.

SIDE TRIPS

BELTON LAKE

Take FM 2305 (Lake Dr.) northwest to lake (See Belton).

WILDFLOWER TRAILS

In 1989 the state legislature designated Temple as the Wildflower Capital of Texas.

ANNUAL EVENTS

September

TEXAS TRAIN FESTIVAL

Various locations • 298-5172 (Railroad Museum) • Third weekend in September • Admission varies with event • W variable

Temple honors its railroad heritage with activities ranging from a huge model train show and swap meet at the Civic Center to the reenactment of a Civil War battle. See special exhibits and old-time craft demonstrations at the Railroad and Pioneer Museum.

RESTAURANTS

($ = under $7, $$ = $8–$17, $$$ = $18–$25, $$$$ = over $25 for one person excluding drinks, tax, and tip.)

BLUEBONNET CAFE

705 S. 25th, north of Ave. H • 773-6654 • Breakfast, lunch, and dinner Friday–Wednesday. Closed Monday • $ • No Cr • W • Children's plates

This cafe has been serving up southern-style food since 1948. Temple residents boast they cook the best chicken-fried steak in Texas. The menu also offers other steaks, chicken, Mexican dishes, calf's liver, and daily specials.

ACCOMMODATIONS

($ = under $45, $$ = $46–$60, $$$ = $61–$80, $$$$ = $81–$100, $$$$$ = over $100) Room tax 13%

LA QUINTA INN

1604 W. Barton Ave., take exit 301 off IH-35 • 771-2980 or 800-531-5900, Fax 778-7565 • $$–$$$ • W+ 6 rooms • No-smoking rooms

Remodeled in 1997, this three-story motel has 106 units, including two suites ($$$$) and 70 no-smoking rooms. Cable TV with HBO. Phones in room (local calls free). No charge for children under 18 who stay in parent's room. Senior discounts. Pets 25 pounds and below OK. Outdoor pool. Free airport shuttle. Complimentary continental-plus breakfast in lobby. Guests get 10 percent off meals at Shoney's and Grandy's next door. What made staying here unique was the night manager's making sure that a business woman in town alone had returned safely from a late dinner!

UVALDE

Uvalde County Seat • 15,000 • (830)

Two of the more colorful lawmen of the Old West lived here in the 1880s. One was J.K. "King" Fisher, who started out an outlaw and later became a deputy sheriff—although some accounts say he was still a part-time outlaw while a lawman. Often arrested, but never convicted, he dressed flamboyantly and wore two silver-plated revolvers. Bat Masterson called him the best man with a gun in the West. In his outlaw days, he is reported to have posted a popular trail with the sign "This is King Fisher's Road. Take the other!" King, and another notorious Texan, Ben Thompson, were killed in a gunfight in a San Antonio dancehall in 1884. Fisher, who is said to have killed eleven men, is buried in Pioneer Cemetery, N. Park and W. Leona. The other famous lawman was Pat Garrett who lived in Uvalde for a time after he had killed Billy the Kid in New Mexico in 1881.

In more recent times, Uvalde's most famous son was John Nance Garner who was vice president of the United States from 1933 to 1941 (*See* Museums).

Uvalde sits at the crossroads of two highways that span the entire United States: US 90, which runs from Florida to California, and US 83, which goes from Canada to Mexico. Where these highways cross are four squares, one at each corner of this intersection.

The city is sometimes called Tree City USA because of an ordinance protecting oaks that grow in the middle of some streets. It is also famous for its honey and pecans.

TOURIST SERVICES

UVALDE CHAMBER OF COMMERCE/CONVENTION & VISITORS BUREAU
300 E. Main (P.O. Box 706, 78802-0706) • 278-3361 or 800-588-2533

MUSEUMS

GARNER MUSEUM
333 N. Park off US 90W • 278-5018 • Monday–Saturday 9–12, 1–5. Closed Thanksgiving, Christmas • Adults $1, children 50¢ • W

John Nance Garner went to Congress in 1903 when Theodore Roosevelt was president, and he remained a congressman, including serving as Speaker of the House, until 1933 when he started his two terms as vice president (1933–1941) under another Roosevelt—FDR. Garner is often quoted as saying the office of vice president "isn't worth a bucket of warm spit." This is just one of many examples of his Texas forthrightness that fit his nickname "Cactus Jack." This museum is housed in his former home that he gave to the city as a memorial to his wife after her death in 1948. He then moved to the small cottage behind the house, receiving friends from around the world, until he died in 1967, just a few weeks before his 99th birthday. Exhibits of Garner memorabilia include a showcase of 100 gavels sent to him by friends when he broke his gavel during his first day as the new Speaker of the House. Garner is buried in the west end of the City Cemetery, US 90W.

HISTORIC PLACES

UVALDE GRAND OPERA HOUSE
104 W. North St. at N. Getty (US 83) • 278-4184 • Monday–Friday 9–4 Free (Donations) • W+
The two-story brick building was constructed in 1891 at a time when most of the downtown buildings were one-story and wooden. Like most small town opera houses, this one occupied the second floor, upstairs over a store. In 1916 the building was sold to John Nance Garner who used the upstairs bay-windowed room as his office while the theater continued in operation. But it wasn't long after that the whole building was turned into offices. The restored 370-seat Opera House, listed in the National Register of Historic Places, is used for a variety of events throughout the year. Part of it has been set up as a local history museum. Free tours lasting 15–20 minutes are available.

OTHER POINTS OF INTEREST

FIRST STATE BANK OF UVALDE ART COLLECTION
Nopal and Oak • 278-6231 • Monday–Friday 9–3 or by appointment • Free • W
Former Governor Dolph Briscoe is Chairman of the Board of this bank that doubles as an art museum. The collection of art and antiques includes two original Rembrandt etchings, a Gainsborough, and works of most major American Western artists. The antiques include a 1730s mirror owned by Britain's fourth Earl of Sandwich. Guided tours for pre-arranged groups last about 30 minutes.

SIDE TRIPS

GARNER STATE PARK
Take US 83 north 31 miles, turn right on FM 1050 **• 232-6132 • Open daily 8–10 for day use, at all times for camping • $5 per person • W+ but not all areas**
Named for Uvalde's John Nance Garner, vice president under Franklin D. Roosevelt, the 1,420-acre park is along the Frio River, which offers good fishing and swimming. Other recreational facilities include paddleboats for rent, an 18-hole miniature golf course, hike and bike trail, picnic areas, cabins, and campsites (fee). For information write: Park Superintendent, Garner State Park, Rt. 70 Box 599, Concan 78838.

PARK CHALK BLUFF
Take US 83 north about 2 miles to TX 55, then west (left) about 15 miles **278-5515 • Call about hours • Admission • W variable**
About a mile west of here, on May 29, 1861, two of southwest Texas' best known Indian fighters were ambushed and killed by a band of about 20 Indians. Red-bearded Henry Robinson was so well known to the Indians that they had painted his picture on a rock near the Llano River. They scalped both Robinson and his companion, Henry Adams, and also cut off Robinson's red beard. Today there is a campground (fee) in front of the 400-foot high limestone bluff. For information write: Park Chalk Bluff, HCR 33 Box 566, Uvalde 78801.

ANNUAL EVENTS

August

REGIONAL/NATIONAL SAILPLANE COMPETITION

Uvalde Flight Center, Municipal Airport, Garner Field Rd. (FM 1023)
278-3361 (Chamber of Commerce) or 278-4481 • About 10 days early in
August • Free • W variable
Uvalde's excellent soaring weather is one reason that sailplane pilots from across the U.S. and abroad come here for these competitions. Different years will feature different classes of sailplanes taking to the skies. The sailplanes fly hundreds of miles, but you can watch the takeoffs, landings, and some of the patterns they fly over the area.

October

TEXAS BADLAND DAYS FESTIVAL

Uvalde Fairgrounds, US 90 • 278-3361 (Chamber of Commerce)
Third weekend in October • Gate admission includes all events
So you wanna be BAAAD? This festival takes its name from the Southwest Texas Badland area, which includes Uvalde, Del Rio, Eagle Pass, and Bracketville, once roamed and settled by such bad guys and lawmen as Pat Garrett, King Fisher, Billy the Kid, and Judge Roy Bean. Parade, bull riding, food, entertainment.

RESTAURANTS

TOWN HOUSE RESTAURANT

2105 E. Main • 278-2428 • Breakfast, lunch, and dinner daily • $–$$ • Cr
Staple cafe food, with lunch buffet. Anything from chicken-fried and meatloaf to Mexican food and shrimp.

ACCOMMODATIONS

($ = under $45, $$ = $46–$60, $$$ = $61–$80, $$$$ = $81–$100, $$$$$ = over $100)
Room tax 12%

BEST WESTERN CONTINENTAL INN

701 E. Main (US 90) • 278-5671 or 800-528-1234 • $ • W+ 3 rooms
No-smoking rooms
The one- and two-story Best Western's 87 rooms include 28 no-smoking. Cable TV with Showtime. Room phones (local calls free). Pets OK. Restaurant next door. Outdoor pool and playground. Free coffee in lobby.

HOLIDAY INN

920 E. Main (US 90) • 278-4511 or 800-HOLIDAY (800-465-4329) • $$
W+ 1 room • No-smoking rooms
This two-story Holiday Inn has 151 units including four suites ($$$$–$$$$$) and 102 no-smoking rooms. Cable TV. Room phones (charge for local calls). Pets OK. Restaurant, lounge with occasional live entertainment. Outdoor pool. Fax, computer hookups.

WACO

McLennan County Seat • 105,000 • (254)

In 1837 the Texas Rangers established an outpost close to the Brazos River where Indians, including the Waco tribe, had camped for centuries. Called Fort Fisher after the Texas Secretary of War, it was soon abandoned. Neill McLennan established the first permanent settlement in 1849 and named the town for the Waco Indians. Captain Shapley P. Ross of the Texas Rangers bought a riverside tract and opened a ferry and the first hotel. In 1850, McLennan County was created with Waco as the county seat.

Cotton was king in the Brazos River bottomland, so during the Civil War almost every man in the county volunteered for the Confederate Army. Six became generals, and "Sul" Ross, son of Shapley, became one of the South's youngest generals and went on to become governor of Texas from 1887 to 1891. Two other governors from Waco were Richard Coke (1874–1876) and Pat Neff (1912–1925).

During the cattle drives to the north, Waco became a cowboy stop-over with the nickname "Six Shooter Junction." Settlers began moving West, and the ferry did a booming business. A toll bridge opened in 1870, and at the time was the longest suspension bridge in America (*see* Other Points of Interest). The bridge made the city a hub of commerce for years, and this status was reinforced when Waco became a railroad center in 1872.

Baylor University moved here in 1845, and today the town boasts nearly 200 manufacturing plants.

TOURIST SERVICES

WACO TOURIST INFORMATION CENTER

P.O. Box 2570, 76702 • Texas Ranger Hall of Fame Complex, exit 335B off IH-35 750-8696 or 800-922-6386 • Monday–Saturday 8–5, Sunday 9–5 • Free • W+

For 24-hour information on activities and events, dial 752-WACO (752-9226).

BIRD'S-EYE VIEW

LOVERS LEAP

North End of Cameron Park. *Take N. 19th to Parklake Dr., then east to Lovers Leap Rd. to overlook.* **Open at all times • Free • W variable**

Legend is that two Indian lovers, caught in a Romeo and Juliet situation with warring families, leaped to their deaths here. View includes the confluence of the Bosque and Brazos rivers.

MUSEUMS

ART CENTER

1300 College, adjacent to McLennan Community College • 752-4371, Fax 752-3506 • Tuesday–Saturday 10–5, Sunday 1–5. Closed Monday and all major holidays • Free • W+

Located in a Mediterranean-style home overlooking the Brazos and Bosque Rivers, the Art Center has rotating exhibits and frequently hosts traveling exhibits. Gift shop.

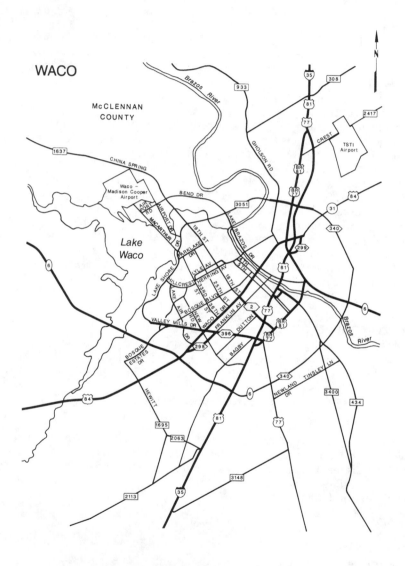

WACO

McCLENNAN
COUNTY

DR PEPPER MUSEUM

300 S. 5th • 757-1024 • Monday–Saturday 10–4, Sunday 12–4
Adults $4, students $2, seniors $3.50 • W+

Remember the slogan "Drink a Bite to Eat at 10-2-4"? The oldest major soft drink in America, Dr Pepper, coined the phrase and sold millions of the fruity drink. It was concocted in 1885 (a year before Coca-Cola) at Morrison's Corner Drug Store in Waco by Dr. Charles C. Alderton who moved his operation to this building in 1906. For years, people said, "Shoot me a Waco" when ordering a Dr Pepper. You can do it again in this charming museum's fountain or order a Dr Pepper float with Blue Bell ice cream.

TEXAS RANGER HALL OF FAME AND MUSEUM

IH-35 exit 335B (P.O. Box 2570, 76702-2570) • 750-8631 or Fax: 750-8629
Daily 9–5. Closed Thanksgiving, Christmas, New Year's Day
Adults $3.75, children 6–12 $1.75, under 6 free • W+

The Texas Ranger Hall of Fame and Museum is the official Texas state hall of fame for the legendary Rangers. They celebrated their 175th anniversary in 1998. The museum features displays drawn from the extensive collections of firearms, badges and Ranger equipment and a multimedia show on the history of the Rangers. The facility has a museum store, adjacent campgrounds, and picnic areas.

HISTORIC PLACES

Historic Waco Foundation offers tours of the following four historic house museums. All feature period furniture, china, and decorative art from the late 1800s. Nominal admission. Hours vary, so call ahead. Closed December, Thanksgiving, and Easter. Group tours by appointment. Contact the Foundation at 753-5166 or write 810 S. 4th.

Earle-Napier-Kinnard House, completed in 1869, is a fine example of Greek Revival architecture, while **East Terrace** (circa 1872) is a classic example of Italianate Villa architecture. Another Greek Revival home is **Fort House** (circa 1868) with an Empire rosewood sleigh bed similar to the one in the White House and believed to have been made by the same cabinet maker. **McCulloch House** was completed in 1872. Of special interest is the Dresden collection of Hallie Neff Wilcox, daughter of former Texas Governor Pat Neff.

OAKWOOD CEMETERY

2124 S. 5th • 754-1631

The final resting place of three Texas governors, two Confederate Army generals, numerous pioneers, and founders of Waco. Note the many angels on the tombstones and red helmet of the Volunteer Firemen Monument.

OTHER POINTS OF INTEREST

CAMERON PARK ZOO

1704 N. 4th • 750-8400 • Monday–Saturday 9–5, Sunday 11–5 (hours vary in winter and bad weather) • Adults $4, seniors $3.50, children (4–12) $2 W variable

The state-of-the-art $10 million natural habitat zoo is in Cameron Park, and includes a cascading waterfall, Tree Top Village, and Sumatran tigers. Cameron Park is one of Texas' largest municipal parks and a wildlife sanctuary.

LAKE BRAZOS

Through the city • 750-5980 • Open at all times • Free • W variable

The lake is actually the stabilized course of the Bosque and Brazos rivers as they go through town, adding up to about 640 surface acres. Much of the shoreline is private property, but there are marinas, restaurants, and other commercial facilities.

WACO LAKE

Northwest edge of city. *Drive west on TX 6/340, US 84, or Lake Brazos Dr. to airport* **• 756-5359 • Open at all times • Free • W variable**

Its 7,260 acres make this the largest lake within city limits in Texas. The Army Corps of Engineers operates six parks with facilities for boating, fishing, swimming, water skiing, picnicking, and camping (fee). Write: Lake Office, Route 10, Box 173G, 76708.

SUSPENSION BRIDGE

University Park Dr. across from Convention Center Complex Open at all times • Free • W

After the Civil War, a group of Waco businessmen got together and built a suspension bridge. With the consultation of John A. Robeling & Sons of Brooklyn Bridge fame, design engineer Thomas M. Griffith, built a 475-foot toll bridge. Opening on January 6, 1870, it was the first bridge across the Brazos River and cost $135,000. It used 2,700,000 Waco bricks and—at the time—was the longest single-span suspension bridge in the United States and the second longest in the world. Because of public protests over the toll, it was sold to the county for $75,000 and then to the city for $1, which quickly made it a free bridge. Now on the National Register of Historic Places, it is open to pedestrians only.

TEXAS SPORTS HALL OF FAME

1108 S. University Parks Dr. (exit 335B off IH-35) • 756-1633 • 10-5 daily Adults $4, seniors and students $3.50, children $2 (under 5 free) • W

Interactive exhibits and displays salute more than 300 legendary Texas sports figures and great moments from their careers. Memorabilia includes Earl Campbell's letter jacket and Martina Navritalova's Wimbledon racket.

SPORTS AND ACTIVITIES

Golf

COTTONWOOD CREEK GOLF COURSE

5200 Bagby • 752-2474 • 18-hole public course. Greens fee: weekdays $10.50, weekends $14.06, twilight (4 P.M.) $8.65

JAMES CONNALLY GOLF COURSE
Aviation Parkway off US 84, northeast of city near TSTC campus • 799-6561
18-hole public course. Greens fee: weekdays $8.75, weekends $12.

Little League Baseball

TEXAS STATE LITTLE LEAGUE BASEBALL CENTER
1612 S. University Parks Dr. • 756-1816 • Free • W variable
    The five-diamond complex is a year-round training center for leaders and youth involved in Texas' Little League Programs. One of the largest Little League tournaments in the nation is held here each August.

Tennis

CHARLIE McCLEARY
1301 Barnard • 750-8662 • 16 lighted courts. $3 per person

Trap and Skeet

WACO SKEET & TRAP
Airport Rd. near Madison Cooper Airport • 753- 2651 • Wednesday–Sunday 1:30 P.M.–dark • Admission plus ammo
    This is one of the largest trap and skeet facilities in Texas. A skeet shoot championship is held the last weekend in May, and another in August.

COLLEGES AND UNIVERSITIES

BAYLOR UNIVERSITY
Take exit 335B off I-35. Wiethorn Visitors Center near main entrance on University Parks Dr. **• 755-1921 • Open Monday–Friday 8–5, Saturday 10–4, Sunday 1–4 • W • Visitor parking**
    Chartered by the Republic of Texas in 1845, Baylor claims to be the state's oldest university, and also the world's largest Baptist university with approximately 12,000 students. Of interest to visitors is **The Armstrong Browning Library,** Speight Ave.between S. 7th and S. 8th (755-3566) with the world's largest collection of materials related to the lives and works of Robert and Elizabeth Barrett Browning. The stained glass windows illustrating their works are spectacular. Open Monday–Friday 9–12 and 2–4, Saturday 9–12. Closed university holidays. **The Strecker Museum of Natural History** (755-1110) is in the Sid Richardson Science Building, but a new **Strecker Museum Complex,** when opened, will have galleries, gift shop, snack bar, and it will trace the story of Central Texas from prehistoric times to the present. Part of the Complex is **Governor Bill and Vara Daniel's Historic Village** (755-1160), open daily. **The Texas Collection,** in the Carroll Library, Speight and S. 5th, is one of the largest collections of Texana in the world. **The Hooper-Schaefer Fine Arts Center,** near the main entrance contains an art gallery/museum and hosts plays, recitals, and concerts. The Baylor bear mascots are at **The Hudson Memorial Bear Plaza,** and visitors are welcome at all Southwest Conference sports events (Tickets: 756-5487).

McLENNAN COMMUNITY COLLEGE

1400 College Dr. • 299-8000 • W+ but not all areas
Designated visitor parking
Visitors are welcome at the college's art gallery, concerts, and plays at the performing arts center, plus sports events.

TEXAS STATE TECHNICAL COLLEGE

Air Base Rd., take Northcrest exit off I-35N and follow signs • 799-3611, ext. 2001 or 800-792-8784 (Campus Information) • W+ but not all areas
It is located on a 2,100-acre former Air Force Base. Visitors might be interested in seeing the old base airfield, the second largest in Texas.

PERFORMING ARTS

HEART O'TEXAS COLISEUM AND FAIRGROUNDS

4601 Bosque Blvd. • 776-1660 • Admission • W+ but not all areas
A multipurpose facility used for major events. It is also the home court for Waco's Wizards, the ice hockey team.

HIPPODROME THEATER (WACO THEATER)

724 Austin • 752-9797 • Admission • W+
Built in 1914, this theater has been restored to its original grandeur when John Wayne, Elvis Presley, and Ann-Margaret performed on its stage. Listed in the National Register of Historic Places. Reopened in 1988 as the home of Waco's performing arts.

WACO CIVIC THEATRE

1517 Lake Air Dr. • 776-1591 • Admission • W
Productions are staged during the fall through spring season.

WACO CONVENTION CENTER

100 Washington at University Parks Dr. • 750-5810 • Admission • W+
This facility hosts everything from conventions to rock concerts and wrestling.

SHOPPING

SIRONIA

1509 Austin Ave. • 754-8009 • Closed Sundays • W variable
This charming shopping mall is filled with small specialty shops offering unique items in food, fashions, jewelry, antiques, gifts, collectibles, art, gardening, and a superb tea room.

KIDS' STUFF

LIONS PARK KIDDIELAND

1716 N. 42nd • 772-4340 • Spring and summer opened daily, but check on hours; closed November–February; rest of year: Saturday 10–10, Sunday 1–10 W variable
This small amusement park includes a train ride around the park, miniature golf, a playground, ten tennis courts, and a public swimming pool.

ANNUAL EVENTS

April

BRAZOS RIVER FESTIVAL
Various locations throughout the city • 753-5166 • Weekend late in April
Admission to some events • W variable
Included among the many activities during the festival are a reenactment of a Civil War battle at Cameron Park, an art show, the Cotton Pageant, and a reenactment of Waco's history.

October

HEART OF TEXAS FAIR & RODEO
The nine-day fair begins the first Friday in October. Information: 776-1660.

December

CHRISTMAS ON THE BRAZOS
Waco Convention Center, 100 Washington at University Parks Dr. • 753-5166
First Saturday and Sunday in month • Admission • W variable
Festivities start with a Christmas Tree lighting in Indian Springs Park Friday night and a parade Saturday morning. A Christmas Bazaar is held at the Convention Center, and an historic homes tour is conducted.

RESTAURANTS

($ = under $7, $$ = $8–$17, $$$ = $18–$25, $$$$ = over $25 for one person excluding drinks, tax, and tip.)

BURGERS & BLUES
215 Mary St. • 752-5837 • Lunch and dinner daily, except Sunday • Bar hours:
7 P.M.–2 A.M. Wednesday–Saturday • $–$$ • Cr • W • Smoking sections
This jumping eatery prides itself on "cool food and hot sax." Catch the live jazz concerts in the bar Wednesday–Saturday from 7 to 2. It's one of the restaurants in a 10,000-square-foot brick one- and two-story warehouse that was built in the 1900s, damaged by a tornado in the 50s, and vacant until restored and recycled in 1995 as an entertainment complex. Find it just off I-35 (at University) near the Hilton.

DIAMOND BACK'S
217 Mary St. • 757-2871, fax 754-2294 • Dinner only 4–10
Monday–Wednesday and 'till 11 Thursday–Saturday • Closed Sunday
$$–$$$ • Cr • W + • Children's menu • Smoking section
Also in the entertainment complex in the warehouse is this upscale restaurant, which is named after the diamondback rattlesnake. (Snake cake is a crab meat and rattlesnake appetizer created by the chef!) New Texas cuisine is featured here. Candlelight dining, linens. Live jazz from 6–8 on Wednesday and Friday.

NINFA'S

**220 S. 3rd. • 757-2050 • Lunch and dinner daily • $–$$$$
Cr • Smoking in bar only • W+ • Children's menu**

Here you'll find strictly Mexican fare, such as *chiles rellenos, tacos al carbon,* and *fajitas.* (No American entrees available.) Lunch specials. If you wish, eat in the bar, which is enhanced by a waterfall. Ninfa's is also in the warehouse.

HEITMILLER STEAKHOUSE

203 Connally Dr. (Exit 343 off I-35) • 829-2651 • Lunch and dinner six days a week (closed Sunday) • $–$$ • Cr • W+ • Children's plates

Family operated and owned, with seating for 300. Steak is a specialty, as you'd expect, but the menu is diverse. Dress casually—and bring the kids!

ELITE CAFE

2132 S. Valley Mills at IH-35, on the Circle • 754-4941 • Lunch and dinner daily • $–$$$ • Cr • W+ • Children's plates

Opened in 1941, this was the first suburban restaurant in town. Filled with '50s memorabilia, the landmark capitalizes on its location at the infamous Circle, selling "I Survived the Circle" T-shirts—along with chicken-fried steak, seafood, and more.

ACCOMMODATIONS

COURTYARD AT MARRIOTT

**101 Washington Ave. • 752-8686 or 800-321-2211, fax: 752-1011
$$$–$$$$ • Cr • W+ 6 rooms**

Take 335 B exit off IH-35 (University Parks Dr.) to this three-story hotel, which opened in 1997. Across from the Waco Convention Center, it has 153 units, including six suites, six handicapped accessible rooms, and 126 no-smoking rooms, all with Cable TV and HBO, coffee makers, irons and ironing boards, hookups for computers; fax service available. Complimentary coffee in lobby and fruit at front desk. Breakfast buffet ($), lounge area. Heated outdoor pool in middle of courtyard, whirlpool, exercise room. No pets. Free airport transportation. Some rooms have river views.

HILTON HOTEL

**113 S. University Parks Dr. • 754-8484 or 800-234-5244, fax: 752-2214
$$$–$$$$ • W+ • No smoking rooms**

The eleven-story Hilton has 199 units including nine for the handicapped, 110 no-smoking rooms, and four suites ($$$$$). All have coffee makers, Cable TV with HBO, room phones (charge for local calls). Dataport phones for computer hookup and fax service upon request. Small (no barking, no biting, housebroken) pets OK with approval. Free airport transportation. A full-service restaurant (brunch on Sunday) and bar. Outdoor pool, whirlpool, tennis court—and fine view of the Brazos River and suspension bridge across the street. Just west of IH-35, it has a walkway connecting it to the Waco Convention Center. No charge for children of any age if occupying same room as parents.

Bed and Breakfast

THE CEDARS

933 Rubydell Lane • Reservations through Be My Guest Bed & Breakfast Service • 776-6708, fax: 776-0934 • $$–$$$ • MC, V • W • Smoking outside only

A country home with a side porch, it has three rooms with private baths available for B&B guests (children included). Members of the same family also offer overnight lodging to guests in three other homes on the 15-acre estate: House by the Creek (two guest rooms with a shared bath), White Stone Cottage (two rooms, private baths), and Shady Hide-a-Way (three rooms, private baths). A full complimentary breakfast. Other B&Bs abound.

WIMBERLEY

Hays County • 2,403 • 512

Founded about 1848, Wimberley has had several names: first Glendale, then Winter's Mill, Cude's Mills, and finally Wimberley Mills after Pleasant Wimberley, who bought the mill complex in 1874. When the post office opened in 1880, the name was shortened to just Wimberley.

The picturesque village is now the center of a resort and retirement area. Wimberley is an unincorporated area, meaning there is no city government. Everything is done by volunteers, with the Chamber of Commerce as the center and guiding light for most activities.

TOURIST SERVICES

WIMBERLEY CHAMBER OF COMMERCE

RR 12 at River Rd. (Box 123, 78676) • 847-2201 • Open daily • W

PLACES OF INTEREST

PIONEER TOWN

7A Ranch Resort. *From RR 12 take River Rd. west 1 mile* **• 847-2517 Memorial Day–Labor Day: open Thursday–Monday; Labor Day–Thanksgiving and March–Memorial Day: Saturday afternoons. Closed December through February • Admission about $2 per car • W variable**

Attractions at this 1880s Western-style town include a scenic ride on a half-size model of an 1873 steam engine (fee). Shops sell folk art, souvenirs, and such. Also ice cream parlor, arcade, opera house, and house made of soda water bottles. The Pioneer Remington Bronze Museum is open by appointment only, but make the appointment, because it has a complete collection of Frederic Remington's bronzes. Write 333 Wayside Dr., 78676.

BLUE HOLE RECREATION CLUB

On Cypress Creek just east of Wimberley School off Old Kyle Rd. • 847-9127 Admission • W variable

Blue Hole has been rated one of the top ten swimming holes in Texas. It is part of a private, family-oriented club in which memberships are required in addition to a daily entrance fee. Reasonably priced weekly and monthly memberships are available. Camping, RV park (fee). Write P.O. Box 331, 78676.

SHOPPING

Several art and antique shops are clustered around the square and spread along RR 12. The Chamber of Commerce offers a free guide map to these.

ANNUAL EVENTS

April–December

FIRST SATURDAY MARKET DAY

Lions Field, RR 2325 just northwest of junction with RR 12 • 847-2201 (Chamber of Commerce) • First Saturday of each month April–December Free; parking fee • W variable

More than 200 vendors offer everything from arts and crafts to antiques to typical flea market items. Lions Club offers barbecue lunch.

October

GOSPEL MUSIC FESTIVAL

Blue Hole Recreation Club, off Old Kyle Rd. • 847-2201 (Chamber of Commerce) or 847-9127 (Blue Hole) • One weekend in early October Donation • W variable

Groups from all over the state gather to make gospel music, from traditional four-part harmony to contemporary played on a synthesizer. It's outdoors, under the cypress trees, so bring blankets or lawnchairs.

RESTAURANTS

JOHN HENRY'S

On the square • 847-5467 • Open daily, lunch and dinner • $$ • AE, DIS, MC, V • W call ahead

Enjoy mesquite-grilled steaks, *fajitas,* seafood, and chicken on the deck overlooking Cypress Creek. Also soups, salads, sandwiches, and burgers. Private club; temporary memberships available.

ACCOMMODATIONS

($ = under $45, $$ = $46–$60, $$$ = $61–$80, $$$$ = $81–$100, $$$$$ = over $100) Room tax 6%

7A RANCH RESORT

From RR 12 take River Rd. west 1 mile **• 847-2517 • $$–$$$$ • AE, DIS, MC, V**

Twenty-six rustic cottages, two 4-room and three 10-room lodges. Some units have cable TV. No room phones. Pets OK in cottages only. Half-mile river frontage for swimming and fishing, outdoor pool, tennis courts. Most cottages have kitchenettes. Weekly rates available. Write 333 Wayside Dr., 78676.

SINGING CYPRESS GARDENS

Mill Race Ln. (P.O. Box 824, 78676) • 847-9344 • $$$–$$$$$ • MC, V, DIS
W+ 1 unit • Mostly no-smoking

B&B with five units of varying size, all with private bath, TV. Some with kitchenettes, jacuzzi. Children allowed in some units. Pets allowed; deposit. Continental breakfast. Complimentary wine. Frontage on Cypress Creek for swimming. Extensive gardens. Walk to town square.

SOUTHWIND BED AND BREAKFAST/CABINS

Three miles from town on FM 3237 (Rt. 2, Box 15, 78676) • 847-5277
$$$–$$$$ • AE, DIS, MC, V

Three rooms with private bath. Outdoor hot tub. Children over 12 welcome. Pets by special arrangement. Full breakfast. Rooms furnished with antiques and reproductions. On wooded hilltop. Also, two secluded cabins with fireplace, whirlpool tub, full kitchen. All rooms no-smoking.

Metroplex/North Central Texas

ADDISON

Dallas County • 10,900 • (972)
Although first settled in 1846, it wasn't until the St. Louis Southwestern Railroad arrived in the early 1880s that it grew into a village. Then it was another 20 years before the town became known as Addison, named after Addison Robertson, who later became the community's postmaster.

The 4.5-square-mile town has only about 10,000 residents, but, on workdays, its daytime business population jumps to around 75,000. That small residential population is a major reason the town can boast that it has more restaurants (well over 100) per capita than any city west of the Mississippi. Its "restaurant row," originally developed to service the daily workday influx, has become a large draw for after-work and weekend diners from Dallas with the Dallas North Tollway, which bisects the town, providing a brief 15-minute trip to and from downtown Dallas.

TOURIST SERVICES

ADDISON TOWN HALL

5300 Belt Line Road (P.O. Box 144, 75001-0144), just east of Montfort Drive
450-7000 • Monday–Friday 8–5 • W
Free brochures, maps, and theatre schedules are among the items available here. The Town Hall is located in the antebellum style home at the rear of the small Prestonwood Place Shopping Center on the south side of Belt Line Road, across from the larger Prestonwood mall.

COMMERCIAL TOURS

CENTER LINE AVIATION TOURS

4545 Eddie Rickenbacker (P.O. Box 667, 75001), at Addison Airport
490-7676 or 490-7045 • Daily 9–6
Flying tours that cover the major sights of Dallas and some of the mid-cities. Thirty-minute tour for $89 a person, 60 minutes $129, 90 minutes $199.

MUSEUMS

CAVANAUGH FLIGHT MUSEUM

4572 Claire Chennault (75228), on east side of Addison Airport (follow signs off Addison Road) • 380-8800 • Monday–Saturday 9–5, Sunday 11–5. Closed Thanksgiving, Christmas, New Year's Day • Adults $5.50, children 6–12 $2.75, 5 and under free • W+

Four hangars hold this growing collection of fully restored military aircraft flown in wars from World War I to Vietnam. Nearly all the warbirds on display are air worthy and are flown on a regular basis. A 30-minute flight in one of the two open-cockpit primary flight trainers costs $110 to $125. Flying in the AT-6 Texas, a closed cockpit advanced flight trainer, costs $200. Warbird passengers must be at least 18 years old and flights must be booked at least 48 hours in advance.

OTHER POINTS OF INTEREST

MARY KAY WORLD HEADQUARTERS AND MUSEUM

16251 Dallas Parkway (75241), on Dallas North Tollway at Westgrove exit 214-687-5889 • Free • W+

The Mary Kay Museum, which relates the Horatio Alger-type history of Mary Kay and her worldwide cosmetics firm, is open for a self-directed tour Monday–Friday 9–5. Conducted tours, available Tuesday–Friday at 9 and 4:30, are by appointment only made at least 48 hours in advance by calling 972-687-5720.

SPORTS AND ACTIVITIES

Ice Skating

ICE CHALET

Prestonwood, 5301 Belt Line (75240), at Tollway • Metro 980-8575 Monday–Saturday 10–9, Sunday noon–6

General skating activities including lessons, hockey, and broomball. Public skating times and fees vary.

ICEOPLEX

15100 Midway Road (75244) • 991-7539 • Public hours vary Adult skating $5.50, children 12 and under $4.50

Two ice rinks open for public skating sessions. Call for schedule.

PERFORMING ARTS

WATERTOWER THEATRE

15650 Addison Road (75248), 3½ blocks north of Belt Line, under the Addison Water Tower • 450-6232 or 800-ADDISON (233-4766) • Tickets about $18 for most productions • W+

This award-winning state-of-the-art theater is designed so both the seating and performance area can be transformed for an elaborate stage presentation or a more intimate theater-in-the-round. The October-to-June season normally features five productions running the gamut from comedies and musicals to new plays and the classics.

SHOPPING

KITTRELL-RIFFKIND ART GLASS

5100 Belt Line Road #820 (75240) • 239-7957 • W
The only all-glass gallery in North Texas, it displays the works of more than 200 artists.

PRESTONWOOD

5301 Belt Line Road (75240), at Dallas North Tollway • Metro 980-4275 • W+
Neiman Marcus, Dillard's, Penney's, Lord and Taylor, and Mervyn's anchor about 130 specialty stores and restaurants in this mall.

ANNUAL EVENTS

September

ADDISON'S OKTOBERFEST

Third weekend (Thursday–Sunday) • Streetside at the Addison Conference and Theatre Center, 15650 Addison Road • 450-7000 or 800-ADDISON (233-4766) • Admission $1, children 3 and under free • W
Considered an authentic re-creation of the celebration in Munich, Germany, this four-day festival features German food, drink, and entertainment, an arts and crafts show, carnival, sing-alongs, a petting zoo, and other children's entertainment.

RESTAURANTS

($ = under $12, $$ = $12–$30, $$$ = over $30 for one person excluding drinks, tax, and tip.)

BLUE MESA GRILL

5100 Belt Line (75240), at Tollway in Village in the Parkway Shopping Center 934-0165 • Lunch and dinner daily • $–$$ • Cr • W+
The innovative Santa Fe cuisine includes the regular mixed grill of beef tenderloin stuffed with Mexican cheeses, blue crab and shrimp cake, and potato chile tart. The seafood mixed grill has chile-basted shrimp, blue crab enchilada Veracruzano, and grilled fish of the day. Vegetarian entrées available. Children's menu. Bar.

CHAMBERLAIN'S STEAK & CHOP HOUSE

5330 Belt Line (75240), east of Tollway between Montfort and Prestonwood 934-2467 • Dinner Monday–Saturday, daily in December only • $$–$$$ Cr • W+
Classic steak and chop house ambiance with a list of entrées heavy on steaks, ranging from a petite filet mignon to a 24-oz. porterhouse. They also serve pork, lamb and veal chops, chicken, and seafood, with occasional wild game specials. Bar.

MAY DRAGON

4848 Belt Line (75244), west of Tollway at Inwood • 392-9998 Lunch and dinner daily • $$ • Cr • W

An upscale Chinese restaurant with the reputation for being one of the best in the Metroplex. The extensive menu offers entrées in a variety of cuisines from Cantonese to Szechuan, all presented in a tradition of fine dining. Bar.

ACCOMMODATIONS

($ = under $80, $$ = $80–$120, $$$ = $121–$180, $$$$ = $181–$250, $$$$$ = over $250)

Room tax 13%

DALLAS MARRIOTT QUORUM

14901 Dallas Parkway (75240), Dallas North Tollway at Belt Line exit, on Tollway west access road south of Belt Line • 661-2800 or 800-228-9290 $$ • W+ 11 rooms • No-smoking rooms

This 12-story Marriott has 548 units including 15 suites ($$$$$) and 425 no-smoking rooms. Senior, weekend, and other discounts and package plans available. Children free in room with parents. Concierge floor. Check in 3 P.M. Check out 1 P.M. Inside access to rooms. Charge for local calls. Cable TV with free HBO and pay channels. Captioned TV, visual alarms, and special phones for the hearing impaired. In-room honor bar. Modem link in rooms. Fire intercom system. Bell service. Room service. Heated indoor/outdoor pool, sauna, exercise room, two lighted tennis and two basketball courts. Free use of fitness center one block away. Business services available weekdays. Gift shop. Self-service laundry. One-day dry cleaning. Free newspaper. Free coffee in lobby mornings. Babysitting available. Restaurants serving all meals (dinner under $12 to $30). Bar. Free parking in garage and outdoor. Valet parking available ($5–$9).

THE GRAND KEMPINSKI DALLAS

15201 Dallas Parkway (75248), Dallas North Tollway at Belt Line exit, on Tollway west access road north of Belt Line • 386-6000 or 800-426-3135 $$$$ • W+ 10 rooms • No-smoking rooms

The 14-story Grand Kempinski has 528 units including 32 suites ($$$$$) and 370 no-smoking rooms. Senior and weekend discounts available. Children up to 17 stay free in room with parents. Concierge floor. Check in 3 P.M. Check out noon. Inside access to rooms. Charge for local calls. Cable TV with pay channels. Visual alarms and special phones for the hearing impaired. Modem link in rooms. Fire intercom system. Bell service. Room service. Indoor and outdoor pools, sauna, lighted tennis courts, indoor racquetball courts, health club. Business services available. Barber, beauty, gift shop and retail stores. Next-day dry cleaning. Free coffee in lobby. Babysitting available. Restaurants serving all meals (dinner $12–$30). Lounge/piano bar and nightclub with dancing. Free outside parking. Self-parking in garage ($1). Valet parking ($9).

LA QUINTA INN AND SUITES DALLAS

14925 Landmark Blvd. (75240), west of Tollway and south of Belt Line 404-0004 or 800-531-5900 • $$ • W+ 5 rooms • No-smoking rooms

This four-story La Quinta has 152 units including 8 suites and 49 no-smoking rooms. Senior, weekend, and other discounts available. Children under 18 stay free in room with parents. Check in 1 P.M. Check out noon. Inside access to rooms. Local phone calls free. Cable TV with Showtime and pay channels. Captioned TV, visual alarms and special phones for the hearing impaired. Modem link in rooms. Coffeemakers in rooms, free coffee in lobby. Outdoor heated pool, exercise room. Self-service laundry. One-day dry cleaning. Free continental breakfast. Restaurants nearby. Outside parking.

ARLINGTON

Tarrant County • 284,000 • (817)

By 1876 Dallas and Fort Worth were well-enough established that the Texas and Pacific Railway decided to build a line connecting them. A mid-route depot site was selected on the prairie and soon residents of the small settlements in the area moved to the new railroad and that depot grew into the frontier town of Arlington, reportedly named after Robert E. Lee's home town in Virginia.

Agriculture was the main industry until the early 1950s when GM opened an auto assembly plant that brought in other industry.

Then, in 1961, Six Flags Over Texas opened as the largest amusement park in the state. Arlington's reputation as an entertainment center was reinforced when the city became home of a major league baseball team in 1971, further enhanced by the 1983 opening of Wet'N Wild, the largest water park in the U.S. (now called Six Flags Hurricane Harbor), and most recently solidified by the opening of The Ballpark in Arlington, the new home of the Texas Rangers and an entertainment complex in itself.

Almost all the hotels offer a free pass to use **The Trolley–Arlington's Entertainment Connection.** This is a fleet of trolley-buses that runs between the hotels and the major attractions in the entertainment district so you don't have to drive (or pay parking fees).

TOURIST SERVICES

ARLINGTON VISITOR INFORMATION CENTER

1905 E. Randol Mill Road (76011) • 461-3888 or 800-342-4305 • W+

Free brochures, maps, and information can be obtained here in person or by a mail or phone request. Travel counselors available daily from 9–5.

COMMERCIAL TOURS

THE BALLPARK IN ARLINGTON TOUR

1000 Ballpark Way (southwest of Six Flags Over Texas) • 273-5098
Adults $5, seniors $4, children 13 and under $3 • Tour ticket booth on
south side of The Ballpark on Randol Mill Road • W variable

Seating 49,292 for a ball game, this ballpark is the home of the Texas Rangers and is an attraction of itself. Depending on game operations, the 50-minute tours may include a visit to the clubhouse, the press box, owner's suite, the dugout and batting cages. On days when the Rangers are at home, tours are run on the hour from 9 to noon, Monday–Friday and 10 to noon on Saturday. No tours on home game Sundays. When the team is away, tours are on the hour, 9–4 Monday–Friday, 10–4 Saturday, and noon to 4 Sundays. A combination ticket for the tour and a visit to the Legends of the Game Baseball Museum costs $10 for adults, $8 for seniors, and $6 for children 6–13. Also in the building are the Children's Learning Center and Sports Legacy–The Gallery of Sports Art (*see* Museums, below).

MUSEUMS

ANTIQUE SEWING MACHINE MUSEUM

804 West Abram • 275-0971 • Monday–Saturday 9:30–5 • Adults $3, seniors $2.50, children $2 (5 and under free)

America's first sewing machine museum features more than 150 vintage machines dating back as far as 1853 and memorabilia depicting the history and development of this important invention. Among the collection are several models by Elias Howe, who patented the first practical sewing machine.

ARLINGTON MUSEUM OF ART

201 West Main at Pecan (76010) • 275-4600 • Wednesday–Saturday 10–5 Free • W

This is an old department store converted to one large main gallery and a smaller gallery on the mezzanine. It emphasizes the works of Texas artists as well as regional, national, and international contemporary art in ten changing exhibits yearly. Gift shop.

FIELDER HOUSE MUSEUM

1616 West Abram St. at Fielder Rd. • 460-4001 • Wednesday–Friday 10–2, Sunday 1:30–4:30, or by appointment • Non-resident adults $5 ($1 discount with receipt from an Arlington business), students and children 6 and over $2, families $10 maximum • W ground floor only, ramp at side

When constructed in 1914, it was one of the first brick homes in the area and the first with indoor plumbing. Exhibits highlight area history and include a replica of a general store, an early 1900s barbershop, a period bedroom, and a basement with an old home laundry and a scale model of a locomotive that once ran between Dallas and Fort Worth. Parking in rear. Picnic tables.

JOHNSON PLANTATION CEMETERY AND LOG CABINS

512 West Arkansas Lane • 460-4001 • Open by appointment • Adults $3, children $2 • W

Several log structures from pioneer communities that predate Arlington have been moved to this site, including two log cabins dating from 1854 and 1858, a one-room school house and a barn. Colonel Middleton Tate Johnson, the Father of Tarrant County, is buried in the small cemetery.

LEGENDS OF THE GAME BASEBALL MUSEUM AND CHILDREN'S LEARNING CENTER

The Ballpark in Arlington, 1000 Ballpark Way • 273-5600 • March–October: Monday–Saturday 9–7, Sunday noon–5; November–February: Tuesday–Saturday 9–5, Sunday noon–5. Closed Monday • Adults $6, seniors $5, children 6–13 $4 • W variable

This museum's exhibits cover the history of baseball from an early eighteenth-century version of the game to the present including items from the Texas League, the Negro Leagues, and the history of the Texas Rangers. Artifacts on loan from the National Baseball Hall of Fame and Museum in Cooperstown, New York, include jerseys worn by Ty Cobb and Babe Ruth, bats used by Lou Gehrig and Ted Williams, and Joe DiMaggio's glove. Fans can sit in a video booth and create a video of themselves doing a play-by-play for a Rangers game. Upstairs, the Children's Learning Center offers kids the opportunity to learn about science and history through interactive activities related to the principles of baseball. Combination ticket covers the museum and the ballpark tour (*see* COMMERCIAL TOURS, above).

RIVER LEGACY LIVING SCIENCE CENTER

701 Northwest Green Oaks Blvd. (76006), at Cooper Street in River Legacy Parks • 860-6752 • Tuesday–Wednesday, Friday–Saturday 9–5, Thursday 9–8. Closed Sunday–Monday • Adults $3, children 2–18 $2, under 2 free • W+

The center features ways for visitors to interact with living exhibits of insects, fish, amphibians, reptiles, and other native wildlife. A ten-minute (TV) "ride" on a river raft takes visitors through the four seasons and covers the history of the Trinity River. Gift shop.

SPORTS LEGACY–THE GALLERY OF SPORTS ART

The Ballpark in Arlington, 1000 Ballpark Way, Suite 122 • 461-1994 Open daily 10–6 and for one hour after Ranger games • Free • W+

Reputed to be the nations' largest art gallery devoted to sports, it features original art, limited edition lithographs, statues, and autograph memorabilia of all sports.

OTHER POINTS OF INTEREST

LAKE ARLINGTON

6300 West Arkansas Lane • 451-6860 • W variable

This 2,250-acre city lake in the southwest corner of the city is popular for boating, sailing, water skiing, and fishing. On its shoreline are two parks and the Lake Arlington Golf Course.

SPORTS AND ACTIVITIES

Baseball

THE TEXAS RANGERS BASEBALL CLUB

The Ballpark in Arlington • 1000 Ballpark Way (southwest of Six Flags Over Texas) • P.O. Box 90111 (76004-3111) • 273-5100 • Tickets $4–$24 Game parking $5 • W+ but not all areas

The Texas Rangers are now a potent force in the American League and contenders against the Dallas Cowboys for the heart of the local sports fans. They play about 80 home games in the season from April until October.

Golf

CHESTER W. DITTO GOLF COURSE

801 Brown Blvd. (76011) • Metro 817-275-5941

Eighteen holes. Green fees: weekdays $10, weekends and holidays $12. Juniors and seniors $6. Open to walk-ins.

LAKE ARLINGTON GOLF COURSE

1516 Green Oaks (76013) • 451-6101

Eighteen holes. Green fees: weekdays $10, weekends and holidays $12. On north end of the lake.

MEADOWBROOK GOLF COURSE
1300 East Dugan (76010) • Metro 817-275-0221
Nine holes. Green fees: weekdays $7, weekends and holidays $8.75. Open to walk-ins.

Tennis

ARLINGTON TENNIS CENTER
500 West Mayfield Road, *from I-20, take Matlock exit then north to Mayfield*
557-5683
Twelve lighted courts. Fee $2.50 per person for 1½ hours.

COLLEGES AND UNIVERSITIES

UNIVERSITY OF TEXAS AT ARLINGTON (UTA)
703 West Nedderman Drive (76019) • 272-2222 • W+ but not all areas
With an enrollment of more than 26,000 students from 80 nations studying in nine academic units, UTA is the second-largest component in the mammoth University of Texas system. The more than 80-building campus traces its history to the one wood-frame building of Arlington College, which was founded in 1895. Visitors are welcome at intercollegiate sports events at **Maverick Stadium** and other athletic facilities. In the Fine Arts complex at Cooper and 2nd are the **Irons Recital Hall, Mainstage Theatre, Studio Theatre,** and the university's two art galleries. The Irons Recital Hall is the setting for concerts nearly every night during the fall and spring semesters (272-3471). Student and other theater groups put on a number of productions in the Mainstage and Studio theaters (272-2650). Call for concert and show schedules. **The Center for Research and Contemporary Art** features national artists in all media, while **Gallery 171** is a student-run gallery. **The Planetarium** (272-2467) offers a show every first Friday of the month (Adults $2, seniors and children $1). There is limited visitor parking near most buildings. Pick up a visitor's pass at the UTA Police Department at 2nd and Davis.

PERFORMING ARTS

ARLINGTON PHILHARMONIC
P.O. Box 201229, 76006 • 275-8965 or Arlington Visitor Information Center 461-3888
This orchestra puts on about four classical and three pops concerts a year at a variety of locations.

JOHNNIE HIGH'S COUNTRY MUSIC REVUE
Arlington Music Hall, 224 North Center Street at Division (P.O. Box 820007, Fort Worth 76182) • Metro 817-226-4400 or 800-540-5127 • Adults: $9 and $10, children under 12 $5 • W variable
Johnnie High, who has been putting on this musical revue in various cities in North Texas for more than 20 years, has made Arlington the permanent home for his troupe. Country music shows Saturdays at 7:30 P.M. and a gospel show every first and third Friday at 7:30.

THEATRE ARLINGTON

305 West Main • 275-7661 • Admission • W side door

This community theater with a professional director usually presents about six productions a year in the intimate 200 seat theater. Productions range from award-winning plays to musicals.

SHOPPING

ANTIQUE SAMPLER MALL

1715 East Lamar • 861-4747 • W

More than 150 dealers display antiques ranging from crystal, jewelry, and quilts to European and American furniture. The tearoom is a popular lunch spot (under $10) and serves afternoon tea by reservation.

ASIAN DISTRICT SHOPS

Strip malls along Pioneer (Spur 303) and Arkansas west of Hwy. 360 W variable

For a cultural adventure as well as a culinary treat, try shopping the Asian shops and bakeries in this area that cater to the more than 10,000 residents of Asian descent, mostly Chinese and Vietnamese, who live in the city. Among the more interesting shops is the **Hong Kong Market** at Pioneer and New York. There are several restaurants in this market center including Arc-en-Ciel (*see* Restaurants, below). Another Asian shop worth a visit is **Pho '95** at 2525 Arkansas Lane.

SIX FLAGS MALL

2911 East Division at Hwy. 360 • 640-1641 • W

Dillards, Foley's, Penney's, and Sears anchor about 115 shops and restaurants and a movie theater. Strollers for rent at Customer Service.

KID'S STUFF

CREATIVE ARTS THEATRE AND SCHOOL (CATS)

1100 West Randol Mill Road • 265-8512 • Adults $7, children $6 • W+

This after-school performing arts school for children and youth (and adults, too) uses student casts for its six productions during the school year and three more in its summer series.

SIX FLAGS HURRICANE HARBOR

1800 East Lamar Blvd. (76006), directly across I-30 from Six Flags Over Texas 265-3356 • Open daily mid-May to mid-August, weekends only early-May to mid-September • Adults $22.96, children 3–9 $18.32, seniors (60+) $13.68, all plus tax. Under 2 free • Parking $5 • Major credit cards accepted

Billed as "America's largest water park," now part of the Six Flags family of parks, this water park offers a wide variety of water activities for both the thrill-seeker and those who just want to float the day away. Among the slides for the daredevils is The Black Hole that zips down through 500 feet of wet black tubes. The Wave Pool offers ocean-sized waves to body-surf, or for something gentler you can tube the quarter-mile Lazy River at 2 mph. Kids' park. Live music shows and music videos, locker rooms, playground, gift shop, tube and raft rentals.

SIX FLAGS OVER TEXAS

I-30 at Hwy. 360 (P.O. Box 90191, 76010) • Metro 817-640-8900 • Open daily mid-May to late August, weekends March–early May and September–October, several weeks in October for Halloween Fright Fest and late November– December for Holiday in the Park (call for schedule) Adults: $31.97, children under 48" tall and seniors (55 and over) $25.99, all plus tax. Under 2 free. Discounted two-consecutive-days tickets available. Varying admissions Halloween and Holiday in the Park • Parking $6 Major credit cards accepted • W variable

This 205-acre theme park attracts more than 3 million visitors a year to its more than 100 rides and shows making it the most popular tourist attraction in the state. Everything is included in the admission except food, souvenirs, video and concession games, and the concerts in the Music Mill. The park is divided into theme sections depicting Texas under the flags of Spain, France, Mexico, the Republic of Texas, the Confederate States of America, and the United States. Thrill rides include The Texas Giant, the world's tallest wooden roller coaster that three times has been voted the top roller coaster in the world; a 17-story parachute drop, and the Log Flume ride that is guaranteed to cool you off on a hot day. An old-style narrow-gauge train circles the park. Looney Tunes Land has a number of rides suited to thrill the littler ones. Many free shows, ranging from stunts to music and animal acts. Concerts by well-known entertainers on selected nights in the 10,000-seat Music Mill Amphitheater. Admission $5–$10.

SIDE TRIPS

KOW BELL INDOOR RODEO

Mansfield. TX Hwy 157 and Mansfield Hwy., about 11 miles south of Arlington (P.O. Box 292, Mansfield 76063) • Metro 817-477-3092 • Saturday– Sunday at 8 P.M. • Adults $4–$6, children under 12 $2–$3 • W variable

The cowboys compete in all the usual rodeo events at this rodeo every weekend year-round. Plus on Monday and Friday nights they have bull riding competitions.

ANNUAL EVENTS

June

TEXAS SCOTTISH FESTIVAL AND HIGHLAND GAMES

Friday–Sunday early in month • Maverick Stadium, University of Texas at Arlington • 654-2293 • Adults $9, children $3.50 • W variable

Lots of kilts and bagpipes provide the authentic Scottish atmosphere for a non-stop flow of events and contests that includes Highland bagpipe and drumming competitions, dance contests, a parade, and USA vs. Canada athletic matches. Scottish food and drink.

RIVERFEST

Friday–Sunday mid-month • River Legacy Park, 703 Northwest Green Oaks 277-9481 • Admission $4 • W variable

This festival offers artisan booths, a children's area, sports area, and continuous entertainment on three stages.

RESTAURANTS

($ = under $12, $$ = $12–$30, $$$ = over $30 for one person excluding drinks, tax, and tip.)

ARC-EN-CIEL

2208 New York Avenue at Pioneer • Metro 817-469-9999 • Lunch and dinner daily • $ • Cr • W

Of the 225 entrées on the menu, about half are Americanized versions of classic dishes from Szechuan and Hunan cuisine, but the rest are authentic Chinese dishes. Order off the menu or sit at your table and select from the large variety of appetizers, entrées, and desserts on the many carts the waitresses wheel around the room. Children's menu. Another location in Garland.

CACHAREL

**2221 East Lamar, northwest of intersection of I-30 and Hwy. 360
Metro 817-640-9981 • Lunch Monday–Friday, dinner Monday–Saturday.
Closed Sunday and major holidays • $$$ • Cr • W+**

Located in the penthouse of the nine-story Brookhollow Two, this entertainment district restaurant offers elegant dining on Country French-American cuisine. The menu changes daily, offering six or seven different appetizers, entrées, and desserts to choose from. For dinner, you may select *à la carte* or have a fixed price three-course dinner for $32.50. Children's menu. Bar. Rated one of the best restaurants in the Metroplex by readers of *Conde Nast Traveler's Magazine*.

FRIDAY'S FRONT ROW SPORTS GRILL

**1000 Ballpark Way, in The Ballpark in Arlington • Metro 265-5192
Lunch and dinner daily • $–$$ • Cr • W+**

An in-the-ballpark restaurant that's definitely above the usual ballpark concession. Not just hamburgers, hot dogs, and sandwiches (in half dozen varieties) but also stone hearth baked pizza and *calzones* and dinner entrées that range from grilled salmon to Kansas City strip steaks. Children's menu. Beer. Located on the "Home Run Porch" in right field.

ACCOMMODATIONS

($ = under $80, $$ = $80–$120, $$$ = $121–$180, $$$$ = $181–$250, $$$$$ = over $250)

Room tax 13%

ARLINGTON COURTYARD BY MARRIOTT

**1500 Nolan Ryan Expressway (76011), south of I-30 • 277-2774 or 800-321-2211
$$ • W+ 8 rooms • No-smoking rooms**

This three-story Courtyard's 147 units include 14 suites ($$–$$$) and 120 no-smoking rooms. Senior, weekend, and other discounts and package plans available. Children 12 and under stay free in room with parents. Check in 4 P.M. Check out noon. Inside access to rooms. Charge for local calls. Cable TV with HBO and pay channels. Visual alarms and special phones for the hearing impaired. Indoor/outdoor pool and exercise room. Fax and copying service. Self-service laundry. One-day dry cleaning. Special hot water dispenser for coffee in room. Free newspaper. Restaurant for breakfast only (under $10). Bar (weekday evenings). Free outside parking.

ARLINGTON HILTON

2401 East Lamar Blvd. (76006), north of I-30 • 640-3322 or 800-527-9332
$$–$$$ • W+ 3 rooms • No-smoking rooms
Among the 310 units in this 16-story Hilton are 26 suites ($$$–$$$$) and 260 no-smoking rooms. Senior and other discounts available. Children under 17 stay free in room with parents. Concierge floor. Check in 3 P.M. Check out noon. Inside access to rooms. Charge for local calls. Cable TV with HBO and pay channels. VCR available. Captioned TV and visual alarms for the hearing impaired. Free coffee in lobby in morning. Modem link in rooms. Bell service. Room service. Indoor/outdoor heated pool, sauna, and exercise room. Fax and copy services available. Gift shop. Self-service laundry. One-day dry cleaning. Free newspaper. Restaurant serving all meals (dinner $12–$30). Lounge with DJ for dancing. Free outside parking.

ARLINGTON HOLIDAY INN

1507 North Watson Road (76006), *take Hwy. 360 north to Avenue K/Brown Blvd., then west* **• $–$$ • W+ 2 rooms • No-smoking rooms**
This five-story inn has 237 rooms of which 100 are no-smoking. Senior discount available. Children under 18 stay free in room with parents. Check in 3 P.M. Check out noon. Inside and some outside access to rooms. Charge for local calls. Cable TV with free premium and pay channels. VCR available. Captioned TV, visual alarms, and special phones for the hearing impaired. Coffeemakers in rooms. Modem link in rooms. Bell service. Room service. Indoor/outdoor heated pool, sauna, exercise room. Fax and copy service. Self-service laundry. One-day dry cleaning. Restaurant serving all meals (dinner $12–$30). Lounge with entertainment and dancing Thursday–Saturday. Free outside parking.

ARLINGTON MARRIOTT

1500 Convention Center Drive (76011), south of I-30 • 261-8200 or 800-442-7275 • $$–$$$ • W+ 20 rooms • No-smoking rooms
The 18-story Marriott has 310 units, including some suites and 150 no-smoking rooms. Weekend discounts and package plans available. Children under 12 stay free in room with parents. Concierge floor. Check in 3 P.M. Check out noon. Inside access to rooms. Charge for local calls. Cable TV with free premium channel and pay channels. Captioned TV, visual alarms, and special phones for the hearing impaired. Wet bars in some rooms. Free coffee available. Modem link in rooms. Fire intercom system. Bell service. Room service. Outdoor pool, exercise room. Guest memberships available for golf and fitness center. Business services available. Gift shop. Self-service laundry. One-day dry cleaning. Free newspaper. Restaurant serving all meals (dinner $12–$30). Bar. Free outside parking or valet parking ($5).

FAIRFIELD INN BY MARRIOTT (ARLINGTON)

2500 East Lamar Blvd. (76006), north of I-30 • 649-5800 or 800-228-2800
$ • W+ 5 rooms • No-smoking rooms
The 109 rooms in this three-story inn include 80 no-smoking rooms. Senior discount available. Children stay free in room with parents. Inside access to rooms. Local phone calls free. Cable TV with HBO. Special phones for the hear-

ing impaired. Coffee in lobby 24 hours. Modem link in rooms. Fire intercom system. Outdoor pool. Fax service available. One-day dry cleaning. Free continental breakfast. Free outside parking.

RADISSON SUITE HOTEL

700 Avenue H East (76011), northeast of intersection of I-30 and Hwy. 360
640-0440 or 800-333-3333 • $$–$$$ • W+ 5 rooms • No-smoking rooms
This seven-story all-suite hotel has 203 suites of which 150 are no-smoking. Senior discount and package plans available. Children under 18 stay free in room with parents. Check in 3 P.M. Check out noon. Inside access to rooms. Charge for local calls. Cable TV with free premium and pay channels. Captioned TV, visual alarms, and special phones for the hearing impaired. Wet bars. Bell service. Room service. Indoor pool and sauna. Guest memberships in health club available. Business services available. Gift shop, beauty and barber shops. One-day dry cleaning. Free breakfast. Free cocktails. Free newspaper. Children's programs. Restaurant serving all meals (dinner $12–$30). Lounge with dancing. Free outside parking. Free transportation within a five-mile radius.

BONHAM

Fannin County Seat • 9,700 • (903)
In 1837, Bailey Inglish, a former sheriff in Arkansas, led a party of settlers to the 1,250-acre land grant he had received from the Republic of Texas. Here they built a log fort for community defense and the settlement grew up around it. At first the town was named Bois d'Arc for the creek that flowed nearby, but after the county seat was moved here in 1843, the name was changed to honor James Butler Bonham, the heroic messenger of the Alamo. A statue of Bonham stands on the courthouse lawn.

Bonham is more famous as the hometown of a more recent Texas notable, Sam Rayburn. Mr. Sam, as he was affectionately known, served 25 consecutive terms in the U.S. House of Representatives and still holds the record for being Speaker of the House longer than any other man.

TOURIST SERVICES

BONHAM CHAMBER OF COMMERCE
110 E. First (75418) • 583-4811

MUSEUMS

FANNIN COUNTY MUSEUM OF HISTORY
One Main St. • 583-8042 • Tuesday and Saturday 10–4 • Free • W some areas
Located in the old Texas and Pacific Railroad depot, this museum displays furniture, clothing, photographs, tools, and other artifacts related to the history of Bonham and of Fannin County. Among the items on exhibit are a rosewood square grand piano shipped from France in the 1880s and a 1916 LaFrance fire truck. The building is on the National Register of Historic Places and has been declared a Texas Historical Landmark.

FORT INGLISH MUSEUM AND PARK

**US 82W (W. Sam Rayburn Dr.) at Chinner St., next to Sam Rayburn Library
583-3441 • April 1–September 1: Tuesday–Saturday 10–4, Sunday 1–4, groups
by appointment. Closed Monday • Free (donations) • W ground floor only**

This is a replica of the first fort built by Bonham pioneer and founder Bailey
Inglish. The original Fort Inglish was one of four frontier forts erected in Fannin
County during the nine years the original county stretched 365 miles from its
present eastern boundary and included all or parts of 26 present-day counties.
The replica is about half the size of the original and contains a small museum
with exhibits of nineteenth-century artifacts. Four restored log cabins from the
1840s are set up as a residence, a blacksmith shop, a general store, and a combination schoolhouse and church. There are also frequent living history demonstrations of pioneer skills.

SAM RAYBURN HOUSE MUSEUM

**US 82W, about 1.5 miles west of Rayburn Libraries • 583-5558
Tuesday–Friday 10–5, Saturday 1–5, Sunday 2–5, holidays 2–5. Closed
Monday, Thanksgiving, Christmas, and New Year's Day • Free (donations)**

Born in Tennessee in 1882, Samuel Taliaferro Rayburn came to Texas with his
parents five years later. His political career began in 1906 with his election to
the Texas House of Representatives. He was elected speaker of the Texas House
in 1911, the youngest man to hold that position. Then he was elected to the U.S.
House in 1912, the first of 25 consecutive terms. In 1940 he was elected speaker
of the House, a position he held almost continuously until his death in 1961.
Notables who attended his funeral included President Kennedy, then Vice President Johnson, and former Presidents Truman and Eisenhower. He is buried in
Willow Wild Cemetery.

Sam Rayburn built this house for his parents in 1916. After their deaths, Sam
and his sister Lucinda lived in the house. The 14-room house has been restored
to the way it was at the time of Sam's death—with the original family furnishing and clothes. Tours include a slide show on "Mr. Sam." Gift shop.

HISTORIC PLACES

The **Scarborough House** at 219 W. Sam Rayburn Dr., a turreted Victorian
mansion built in 1897, is now the Wise Funeral Home, and visitors are welcome
to tour the interior. The oldest house in Bonham is the **Baird House,** 905 N.
Main, which was built in 1857 by slave labor. The **Brownlee House,** 220 W. 6th,
is noted for its Victorian gingerbread. It was built in 1871. The **McClellan-Cun-
ningham House,** 304 W. 7th, is noted for the sunburst design on the gables, a
motif repeated throughout the house. These are private residences, not open to
the public.

OTHER POINTS OF INTEREST

BONHAM HISTORICAL TRAIL

583-8042 (Fannin County Museum)

A driving, hiking, or biking historical trail runs from the original site of Fort
Inglish to the Sam Rayburn House Museum, passing more than 35 historic sites.

A map of the trail can be obtained from the Chamber of Commerce or the Historical Museum.

BONHAM STATE RECREATION AREA

Take SH 78 south about a mile to FM 271, then east about two miles
583-5022 • Open daily 8–10 for day use, all times for camping • $2 per adult, children under 12 free • W+ some areas

This 261-acre park includes a 65-acre lake surrounded by red cedars and hardwoods. Facilities include picnic sites, campsites (fee), group accommodations for rent, playgrounds, unsupervised swimming beach, boat ramp, dock, lighted fishing pier, and a 10-mile mountain bike trail. For information write: Park Superintendent, Route 1, Box 337, Bonham 75418.

LAKE BONHAM RECREATION AREA

Take TX 78 north about 3 miles to FM 898, then northeast to Park Rd. 3, then east to recreation area • 583-8001 (Concessionaire. Closed in winter)
Open daily • Free • W variable

This 1,200-acre lake and recreation area has facilities for boating, fishing, swimming, waterskiing, picnicking, and camping ($8.50 with hookup, $5.50 without, no reservations). There is also a nine-hole golf course and a miniature golf course.

SAM RAYBURN LIBRARY

US 82W (W. Sam Rayburn) at Elphis • Monday–Friday 10–5, Saturday 1–5, Sunday 2–5. Closed Thanksgiving and Christmas • Free • W

In the foyer of this stately structure is the white marble rostrum used by the speaker of the U.S. House of Representatives from 1857 until it was replaced in 1950. Off the lobby is a replica of the speaker's office in Washington, an exact duplicate of the original. Other items of interest on display include a collection of gavels, a 2,500-year-old Grecian urn given Rayburn by the Athens Palace Guard, and a display of political cartoons. In addition to Rayburn's extensive collection of books and records, the library also has the only complete collection of The Congressional Record outside the Library of Congress, covering the First Congress in 1774 to the present.

WILLOW WILD CEMETERY

W. 7th at TX 121 • Open at all times

Sam Rayburn and his family are buried here. His grave, right next to the main entrance road, is marked by a large monument with a gavel and the simple words "Mr. Sam, 1882–1961." Also buried here is Harry Peyton Steger, an editor at Doubleday, who many credit with discovering O. Henry.

SIDE TRIPS

CADDO-LBJ NATIONAL GRASSLANDS AND WILDLIFE MANAGEMENT AREA

Take US 82 east about 16 miles to Honey Grove, then north on FM 100 about 10 miles to the Bois d'Arc Springs Rd. entrance • (817) 627-5475
Free • W variable

This unit of the Caddo-LBJ National Grasslands contains about 13,360 acres and two recreational lakes. Facilities include picnicking, camping (fee), boating, fishing, and a boat ramp. For information write: U.S. Forest Service, Caddo-LBJ National Grasslands, P.O. Box 507, Decatur 76234.

ANNUAL EVENTS

May

BOOTS, BUSTLES AND BUCKBOARDS FESTIVAL

Fort Inglish Park, US 82W • 583-4811 (Chamber of Commerce) • Dates vary. Call for exact dates • Admission • W variable

Activities at this festival include celebrating Victorian and Western history, children's games and contests, a country music review, demonstrations of pioneer skills, tours of historical homes and sites, cowboy poetry reading and wagon rides.

July

KUECKLEHAN RODEO

Kuecklehan Rodeo Arena about 8 miles north on SH 78 • 583-5337 Wednesday–Saturday of last week in July • Admission • W

According to local historians, this is the oldest family-operated rodeo in the state. The Kuecklehan family runs this CRA-sanctioned rodeo every year on their ranch, and cowboys come from all over the Southwest to compete. Entertainment nightly.

October

FANNIN COUNTY FAIR

Fort Inglish Park, US 82W • 583-7453 • Usually Thursday–Saturday of third week in October • Admission • W variable

A typical county fair dating back more than 100 years, with livestock expositions and contests, contests for homemakers, a carnival, and entertainment.

ACCOMMODATIONS

($ = under $45, $$ = $46–$60, $$$ = $61–$80, $$$$ = $81–$100, $$$$$ over $100)

THE CARLETON HOUSE BED & BREAKFAST

803 N. Main • 583-2779 • $$$–$$$$

This two-story bed and breakfast has three guest rooms each with private bath. No room phones. No pets. No elevator.

GRANNY LOU'S BED & BREAKFAST

317 W. Sam Rayburn Dr. • 583-7912 • $$$–$$$$

This three-story has four guest rooms each with private bath. Full breakfast buffet. No room phones. No pets. No elevator.

CLIFTON

Bosque County • 3,500 • (254)

Norwegian immigrants were encouraged to settle in this area in the 1850s by Cleng Peerson, who is called the "Father of Norwegian Immigration in America." Today the area is often called the "Norwegian Capital of Texas." Peerson is buried in the church cemetery at Norse, about 11 miles west.

TOURIST SERVICES

CLIFTON CHAMBER OF COMMERCE

115 N. Ave. D, Suite 100 (76634) • 675-3720, Fax 675-4630, e-mail: clifton. chamber@htcomp.net • web: www.htcomp.net/clifton-chamber

MUSEUMS

BOSQUE MEMORIAL MUSEUM

301 S. Ave. Q at W. 9th • 675-3845 • Open Friday and Saturday 10–5 and Sunday 2–5 • Admission • W ramp at side

Now the largest collection of Norwegian artifacts in the South and Southwest, the museum even includes a log cabin, once the home of Joseph Olson, whose extensive collection was its first contribution. Displays change periodically. See Cleng Peerson's handmade chair, vintage clothing, a weaving loom, handcrafted furniture, a massive stamp collection, and more.

ART GALLERIES/PERFORMING ARTS

THE BOSQUE COUNTY CONSERVATORY OF FINE ARTS

Ave. Q and 9th St. • 675-3724 • Admission to some events

Located in the 1923 three-story, red brick Lutheran College Building, the BCCFA hosts annual art shows, theatrical productions, and cultural events. Nationally recognized area artists such as the late Jim Boren and Melvin Warren, plus Western artist Martin Grelle, sculptor-painter Bruce Greene, and Texana artist George Boutwell are among those showcased.

George Boutwell's **Highview Ranch Gallery** is on SH 6 about four miles south of Clifton. Turn west on the first driveway south of two historical markers. A Memorial Day open house (1 to 6) is a tradition. Call 800-243-4316.

SIDE TRIPS

LAKE WHITNEY AND LAKE WHITNEY STATE PARK

Take FM 219 east about 9 miles to FM 22, then southeast (right) to south end of lake • 694-3189 (Army Corps of Engineers Project Office) **Open Monday–Friday 8–4:30 • Free • W variable**

There are 14 federal parks and Lake Whitney State Park surrounding this 23,560-acre Army Corps of Engineers impoundment. (*At intersection of FM 219 and TX 22, go east (right) 14 miles, then left on FM 433 at stoplight. Go three-fourths of a mile to FM 1244, turn left, and follow road to park gate, 694-3792.*) More than four million visitors come here annually, making it one of the most popular water recreation areas in the nation. Tours of the dam are usually conducted weekdays, but a 24-hour-advance reservation is necessary. Call 694-3191. For information write: Project Engineer, Whitney Project Office, P.O. Box 5038, Laguna Park Station, Clifton 76634-5038. For the park write: P.O. Box 1175, Whitney 76642.

NORSE COUNTRY
West of Clifton, generally along FM 219 and the intersecting FM 182.

Velkommen to Norse Country, which you can explore along **FM 219**–the Cleng Peerson Memorial Highway. In celebration of its heritage, a Norse smorgasbord is usually held on the second Wednesday and Thursday of November at Our Savior's Lutheran Church (675-3962) on FM 182 about three miles north of FM 219. Request an information sheet on how to purchase tickets from the church or Chamber. Reservations are essential, and only ticket orders postmarked during the third week of October will be eligible for a drawing determining who gets a ticket (around $11, adults or children).

The Norwegian Country Christmas, usually on the first Saturday in December, is special, too, and includes a tour of Norwegian homes and historical sites, dancing, folk tales, and story telling. (Confirm all dates with Chamber before traveling.)

Another annual feast that pays homage to the area's heritage is the Lutefisk Dinner, held the first Saturday in December at the local high school approximately 20 miles away in Cranfills Gap. Adults $11, children $6 (Clifton Chamber of Commerce: 675-3720). Order tickets no later than October 1, or you might miss out. St. Olaf Lutheran Church, the old Rock Church, is of special interest here.

ACCOMMODATIONS

($ = under $45, $$ = $46–$60, $$$ = $61–$80, $$$$ = $81–$100, $$$$$ = over $100)

Bed and Breakfast

HEART COTTAGE
Vivian Ender, Rt. 1, Box 217 (Call for directions) • 675-3189 • $$–$$$

This Victorian inspired cottage is perfect for two or four persons. Fully equipped kitchen, TV, country breakfast. Sits on prairie and farmland. The Chamber has information on other B&Bs, including Joann's **Courtney House** in town, **The River's Bend,** a country home on 240 acres overlooking the Bosque River, and Goodnight Station, a hilltop farmhouse.

CORSICANA

Navarro County Seat • 23,000 • (903)

When the county was organized in 1846, it was named for Jose Antonio Navarro, one of the two native Texans who signed the Texas Declaration of Independence. When he was asked to name the town that would be the county seat, Navarro called it Corsicana after his father's birthplace on the island of Corsica.

The oil industry in Texas accidentally got its start in Corsicana in 1894 when the city was drilling for water and struck oil instead. In those pre-automobile days there was limited commercial use for oil, and many considered it more of a nuisance than an asset. But some enterprising businessmen saw the potential and drilled an oil well about 200 feet away from the original discovery well. In 1897, Joseph S. Cullinan, who worked for Standard Oil of Pennsylvania, stopped in Corsicana to see what was going on. By that time, the city had about 1,000 producing wells. Cullinan liked what he saw, arranged financing in the East, and built the first oil refinery west of the Mississippi. It went into operation in December 1898—several months before Spindletop blew its top in 1901. The company Cullinan founded eventually became Mobil Oil. The discovery oil well is located in Petroleum Industrial Park.

Today, in addition to the oil industry, Corsicana is a trading center for a large agricultural area.

TOURIST SERVICES

CORSICANA CHAMBER OF COMMERCE

120 N. 12th near Collin (75110) • 874-4731, Web site www.corsicana.org
e-mail: corsicana.tx.chamber@airmail.net • W

MUSEUMS

PIONEER VILLAGE

912 W. Park at N. 19th (Jester Park) • 654-4846 • Monday–Saturday 9–5,
Sunday 1–5 • Adults 50¢, children 25¢ • W

This village was conceived in order to concentrate and reconstruct the county's surviving historic structures in one location as a display of the area's colorful past. Various heirlooms, antique furnishings, artifacts, and historic collections are housed in the buildings. The oldest building is an 1838 Indian trading post that was originally built near present-day Indian Springs by George Washington Hill, an Indian agent sent to the area by Sam Houston. Also included are blacksmith shops from 1836 and 1890, frontier homes from 1842, 1851, and 1854, a general store from 1851, slave quarters from 1860, and a barn from 1865.

HISTORIC PLACES

HISTORIC HOMES

The Chamber of Commerce has a free map-brochure for a drive-by historical homes tour. All the homes are private and not open to the public. The oldest house in the area, dating from 1847, is now part of the **Roger Q. Mills Home** at 1200 W. 2nd. This home had numerous additions and now contains 15 rooms and eight fireplaces. Also on W. 2nd is the **Judge Simpkins Home** at 514, which was built in 1873 and completely restored, and the impressive **Senator James H. Woods Home** at 504. Built in 1900, the Woods Home is considered a fine example of basic Victorian design. There are several other fine old homes along W. 3rd. These include the **Lemon-Edens Home** (1897) at 745, the **Pace Home** (1894) at 753, the **S. A. Pace Home** (1880) at 1003, and the **Halbert House** (1892) at 1250.

SPORTS AND ACTIVITIES

THE OAKS GOLF COURSE

North of town on US 75 • 872-7252 • 9-hole course. Green fees: weekdays
$8.50, weekends $10

COLLEGES AND UNIVERSITIES

NAVARRO COLLEGE

3200 W. 7th (SH 31W) • 874-6502 • W variable • Marked visitor parking

About 2,100 students are enrolled in the academic and technical/vocational programs at this two-year college. The Arrowhead Room, in the library behind the Administration Building, has a collection of 44,000 Indian arrowheads and art craft pieces. The display is open to the public Monday through Friday 8–5. The Cook Center houses the largest planetarium in Texas, an observatory, and a museum. Star, laser, and other shows are presented. Also scheduled to open in 1997 is the Pearce Civil War Documents collection which includes letters, signatures, photographs, and papers.

PERFORMING ARTS

WAREHOUSE LIVING ARTS CENTER

210 E. Collin near Main • 872-5421 • W

This multipurpose arts facility is the home of the Corsicana Community Playhouse. The nonprofessional theater group puts on about a half-dozen productions a year (admission), ranging from drama to musicals and a melodrama during the annual Derrick Days. The Corsicana Children's Company, a training ground for youngsters interested in dramatics, usually puts on two plays a year. The art gallery in this center hosts dozens of art exhibits and crafts displays throughout the year.

SHOPPING

COLLIN STREET BAKERY

401 W. 7th • 872-8111 • W

A baker named Gus Weidmann from Wiesbaden, Germany, arrived in Corsicana in 1896. He purchased an iron oven on Collin Street, and began baking a fruitcake containing fresh native pecans (27% of the cake) and fancy glacé fruits. Weidmann teamed up with promotion-minded Tom McElwee, built an elite hotel over the bakery, and catered to traveling celebrities. Today, almost a hundred years later, Collin Street Bakery's Deluxe Fruit Cakes are shipped by mail order to customers in every state in the union and to 194 foreign countries—and they still make them from the same recipe Weidmann used when he baked the first one in 1896. Tours are available by appointment.

SIDE TRIPS

AREA LAKES

Lake Navarro Mills, on FM 667, has four Army Corps of Engineers parks on the east end of this 5,070-acre lake. Facilities are available for boating, fishing, swimming, waterskiing, picnicking, and camping (some free, some fee). For information: 578-3211. **Lake Richland-Chambers,** on US 187 southeast, covers 44,752 acres and has facilities for fishing and most water sports. For information: 874-4731. **Lake Halbert Park** at 1600 Lake Halbert is a 145-acre park. Facilities are available for boating, fishing, and flying radio controlled aircraft.

RESTAURANTS

($ = under $7, $$ = $8–$17, $$$ = $18–$25, $$$$ = over $25 for one person excluding drinks, tax, and tip.)

ROY'S CAFE

306 N. Beaton • 874-6791 • Breakfast and lunch Monday–Saturday. Closed Sunday • $ • No Cr • W • Children's plates

The local favorite seems to be the daily lunch specials, which usually give you a choice of several meats, salad, vegetables, a dessert, and beverage for under $5.

ACCOMMODATIONS

($ = under $45, $$ = $46–$60, $$$ = $61–$80, $$$$ = $81–$100, $$$$$ = over $100) Room tax 13%

HOLIDAY INN

2000 S. US 287 • 874-7413 or 800-465-4329 • $$ • W+ 2 rooms No-smoking rooms

This two-story Holiday Inn offers 246 rooms including 45 no-smoking. Cable TV with Showtime. Room phones (no charge for local calls). Restaurant. Private Club open six nights (Guests automatically member, temporary membership for non-guests $4). Outdoor pool. Free newspaper. Self-service laundry.

DALLAS

Dallas County Seat • 1,024,000 • Most area codes 214 (some 972, these exceptions noted in listings)

The question the history of Dallas poses is not how it grew to be the seventh largest city in the United States, but why. How did what is now the nation's largest inland city overcome its lack of the traditional foundations for the growth of a great city, such as a wealth of natural resources or a port or a navigable natural waterway? Dallasites explain the city's growth as the inevitable result of the community's unrelenting can-do attitude, business sense, and an aggressive entrepreneurial spirit which overcame, and continues to overcome, all obstacles. And history seems to bear them out. The citizens have truly learned the fine art of creating advantages where none existed before. Less imaginative interpreters explain it by the crossing of a north-south railroad and an east-west intercontinental railroad in 1873, which tied the city to the extensive rail networks of the Midwest and Northeast. This crucial crossing made Dallas a distribution crossroads that offered cheap rail transport. But no matter which explanation you favor, Dallas has grown dynamically, and "dynamic" is the word for Dallas.

Bryan's Trading Post

The city had its beginning in the early 1840s when John Neely Bryan set up a trading post near the three forks of the Trinity River to sell goods to the Indians. When the Texans forced the Indians to move west, Bryan laid claim to 640 acres and sketched out a town. His dream was to use the Trinity River to make

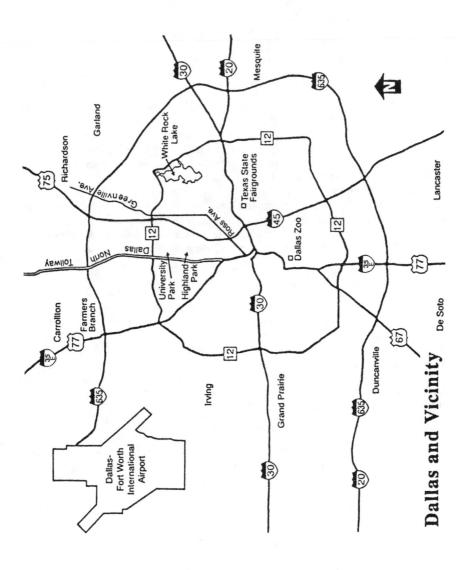

Dallas and Vicinity

his town an inland port with steamboats connecting it to the Gulf of Mexico, 400 miles away. But the river didn't cooperate. It remained contrarily unnavigable. He named his new town after "my friend Dallas." To this day, no one is sure who that friend was. Some believe it was the Vice President of the United States, George Mifflin Dallas, who was for the annexation of Texas. As it turned out, in 1846, after the annexation, the Texas Legislature did name the newly established county in honor of the vice president. But there's no proof that was who Bryan meant when he named the city.

The Crossing of the Railroads

In 1872, when the population was about 1,200, the city fathers lured the Houston and Texas Central Railroad to divert from its planned route and go through Dallas. A year later, the Texas and Pacific line arrived. Dallas suddenly became a major trade center as merchants from Chicago and St. Louis rushed to set up warehouses at this crossing. The population zoomed to around 7,000.

The railroads spurred the first boom and soon that was linked with the agricultural boom, which centered on cotton. Later booms included the oil business. The wells were not even near the city, but the financial and technical support was in Dallas, and the city became the region's business center for the drilling industry with more than 450 oil companies establishing headquarters there at one point. Dallas also became the home base for many insurance companies, banks, and high tech industries.

Dallas Becomes a Fashion Center

In 1907, perhaps drawn by the cosmopolitan ambiance of the city, Neiman Marcus opened an "exclusive woman's ready-to-wear store" in downtown. This store put Dallas on the national fashion map and ultimately on the international fashion map. Building on that tradition, in 1957, two young developers, Trammell Crow and John Stemmons, opened a Home Furnishing Mart, inviting manufacturers and wholesalers to display their products. Over the years this has grown into what is now the Dallas Market Center, the largest wholesale trade complex in the world.

Dallas Becomes Bryan's Dream

In 1965, Dallas and Fort Worth officials agreed to build an airport between the two cities that would serve the entire region. This proved to be the link that would pull together all the disparate cities in the area and consolidate it into one gigantic Metroplex. And with the opening of the giant Dallas/Fort Worth International Airport in 1973, John Neely Bryan's dream of Dallas becoming a major inland port was truly realized.

Driving in Dallas

Aside from morning and evening rush hours during the business week, there's probably less traffic congestion in Dallas than in any city of comparable size. However, parking is a problem, especially downtown. There are plenty of commercial garages and parking lots, but they can be expensive.

DART Buses

If you're staying downtown, you can eliminate the hassles of driving and the expense of parking in the downtown area on weekdays by using the Dallas Area Rapid Transit (DART) shuttle bus system known as the "Rail Runner." This system offers two inexpensive downtown routes which operate Monday–Friday 6 A.M. to 7:30 P.M.

DART Light Rail

Another alternative to driving is the DART Light Rail system, which runs air-conditioned, electric trains that can whisk you in minutes from one place to another along a line that runs roughly north-south through the center of the city. Trains run daily from early morning to late at night, and fares are $1 each way—50 cents each way if both stations are downtown—and day tickets are available for $3. The Light Rail is a boon to visitors who learn the easy steps to use it. To help you take advantage of this transportation, if there is a Light Rail station within easy walking distance it's noted in the listing. Route maps and ticketing instructions are posted at all stations. For more information on both bus and train routes and schedules, call 979-1111.

TOURIST SERVICES

DALLAS CONVENTION & VISITORS BUREAU

1201 Elm Street, Suite 2000 (75270) (DART Light Rail AKARD Station)
746-2677 or 800-C-DALLAS (800-232-5527) for information packet • W+
This bureau serves all the information needs of visitors. Call or write for an information packet. When in Dallas you can pick up information at one of the following **Visitor Information Centers.**

WEST END MARKETPLACE

603 Munger (DART Light Rail WEST END Station) • W
Open Monday–Friday 11–8, Saturday 12–8, Sunday 12–6

DOWNTOWN CENTER

1303 Commerce (DART Light Rail AKARD Station) • W
Open Monday–Friday 8–5, Saturday 9–5, Sunday 11–5

NORTHPARK CENTER

8950 North Central Expressway (DART Light Rail PARK LANE Station)
W+ • Open Monday–Saturday 10–6, Sunday 12–6

THE DALLAS AMBASSADORS

The City of Dallas sponsors The Dallas Ambassadors, young men and women who stroll the downtown streets weekdays from 11:30 A.M. to 6 P.M. to provide assistance to visitors. The Ambassadors carry maps and radios and are easily recognized by their red and blue uniforms.

DALLAS EVENTS HOTLINES

Convention & Visitors Bureau Dallas Events Hotline 746-6679
***Dallas Morning News* Arts and Entertainment Hotline 522-2659**
Department of Parks and Recreation Hotline 670-7070

COMMERCIAL TOUR SERVICES

DALLAS SURREY SERVICES

211 East Colorado (75203) (DART Light Rail WEST END Station) • 946-9911

Horse-drawn surreys operate nightly on Market Street in the West End beginning at about 6:30 P.M., weather permitting. Tours are available to several areas.

GRAY LINE TOURS

5125 Cash Lane (75247) • 630-1000

Gray Line offers several daily scheduled sight-seeing tours with pick-ups at the major hotels. Reservations required.

TOURS DALLAS

P.O. Box 227093 (75222-7093) • 948-8687 • Adults $20, children 6–12 $10

This tour line offers several scenic and historic two-hour mini-van tours. All tours originate at Dealey Plaza in the 400 block of Elm.

WALKIN' AND TALKIN'

528-3453 • Adults $7.50, seniors and students $6.50

Reservations are required for this two-hour walking tour of the downtown business and arts district that highlights art, architecture, and historical information. All tours leave from the West Lobby of El Centro College at Market and Main streets.

INDUSTRY TOURS

MARY KAY COSMETICS MANUFACTURING FACILITY

1339 Regal Row (mailing address: Mary Kay World Headquarters, 16251 Dallas Parkway, 75248) • 972-687-5720 • Free • W

Tours of this facility where a variety of Mary Kay products are prepared are conducted Tuesday–Friday at 10:30 A.M. and 2 P.M. by appointment only. The Mary Kay Museum in the The Mary Kay World Headquarters is also open for tours. (*See* Addison—Other Points of Interest.)

MRS BAIRD'S BAKERY TOUR

5230 Mockingbird (75205), at Central Expressway • 526-7201 • Monday, Wednesday–Thursday 10–4, Friday 10–6 • Call for reservations • Free • W

See how bread and donuts are made while learning the history of this popular Texas bakery on a 45-minute tour. Parking and tour entrance at side facing Central Expressway. Children must be at least six years old.

SELF-GUIDED TOURS

McKINNEY AVENUE TROLLEY

855-0006

With four restored street cars that date back to as early as 1906 (two of which originally serviced passengers in Portugal and Australia), this is more a historic and fun ride than a tour. However, it can get you from the downtown Arts District, near the Dallas Museum of Art, to the restaurants, shops, and nightlife along the McKinney Avenue strip without a car.

SELF-GUIDED WALKING TOURS

The Convention & Visitors Bureau offers a free Downtown Walking Tours map/brochure. The designated tours include a central tour which takes about an hour, and four branch tours: Civic (30 minutes), Farmers Market (30 minutes), Arts District (45 minutes), and West End (30 minutes).

BIRD'S-EYE VIEW

The three places open to the public offering the best panoramic view of the city are the three levels in the 50-story **Reunion Tower** at the **Hyatt Regency Dallas Hotel** (300 Reunion Blvd.). The tower's geodesic dome has been a landmark in the Dallas skyline since it opened in 1978. The lowest level is an observation floor that offers a view for many miles in every direction from both indoor and outdoor viewing areas. On the next level is the hotel's Antares Restaurant with a view that changes as the restaurant rotates at the rate of one revolution every 55 minutes. (*See* Restaurants, below.) At the highest level is the Hyatt's revolving cocktail lounge. You can also get a bird's-eye view of downtown from the Nana Grill on the 27th floor of the **Wyndham Anatole Hotel** (2201 Stemmons Frwy. I-35E) and from Laurel's restaurant on the 20th floor of the **Sheraton Park Central Hotel** (12720 Merit Drive).

FAIR PARK

East of downtown, bounded by Parry Avenue, Cullum Blvd., Fitzhugh Avenue, and Washington Avenue (P.O. Box 159090, 75315) • 670-8400 or 890-2911 (English and Spanish Information Line) • W variable

World Fair buildings are usually constructed based on a short life, ending when the fair closes. Not so with the building put up for the Texas Centennial Exposition of 1936, a world's fair in which Texas celebrated its 100th anniversary of independence from Mexico. For that event, Fair Park was built on the site used for Texas' state fairs since 1886. It was built solidly to remain after the centennial as the heart of state fairs for many years. Now, more than 60 years old, Fair Park has been designated a National Historic Landmark—the largest historical landmark in the state—in recognition of its significant collection of art deco buildings from the 1930s.

Fair Park still lives up to that primary mission, hosting the annual State Fair of Texas every fall (*See* Annual Events, below). But the rest of the year, this 277-acre city park is an attraction itself as a site rich in museums, historic places, and entertainment and sports venues. Admission is free to the grounds, which are open daily except for the week before the state fair and during the fair itself. However, individual admissions are charged to most of the major attractions in the park. Parking is free except during the state fair and some special events. More than six million people visit Fair Park annually.

HALL OF STATE

**3939 Grand Avenue (Dallas Historical Society, P.O. Box 26038, 75226)
421-4500 • Tuesday–Saturday 9–5, Sunday 1–5. Closed Monday
Free, except for special exhibits • W variable**

Built as a centerpiece of the 1936 Texas Centennial, this elegant building is an outstanding example of art deco architecture. Among its features is The Great Hall highlighted by an immense gold seal with symbols representing the six nations of which Texas was a part, and two huge murals depicting major events in the history of the state. The Dallas Historical Society, which is the operator and caretaker of the building, sponsors frequent changing exhibits.

The Museums of Fair Park

AFRICAN-AMERICAN MUSEUM

3536 Grand Avenue (P.O. Box 150153, 75315) • 565-9026 • Tuesday–Thursday 12–5, Friday 12–9, Saturday 10–5, Sunday 1–5. Closed Monday • Free except for occasional special events • W

This is the only museum in the Southwest devoted to the preservation and display of African-American artistic, cultural, and historical materials. It offers a treasury of art and culture that recognizes the vital presence of Black culture in the Metroplex and in the world. A popular monthly event here is "Jazz Under the Dome" every third Friday night (admission). It also sponsors an annual jazz festival in September and the annual Texas Black Invitational Rodeo at Fair Park Coliseum in May.

AGE OF STEAM RAILROAD MUSEUM

1105 Washington Street (P.O. Box 153259, 75315), in northwest corner behind the Centennial Building • 428-0101 • Thursday–Friday 10–3, Saturday–Sunday 11–5. Closed Monday–Wednesday • Adults $3, children 12 and under $1.50

This outdoor collection consists of more than 28 historic pieces of railroad equipment on display, including Dallas' oldest surviving depot, Pullman sleeping cars, lounge cars, and several of the largest and most powerful locomotives in the world.

THE DALLAS AQUARIUM

First Street and Martin Luther King Blvd. (P.O. Box 150113, 75315) • 670-8443 Open daily 9–4:30. Closed Thanksgiving and Christmas • Adults $2, children 3–11 $1, under 3 free • W+

The Aquarium is home to a varied collection of nearly 4,000 freshwater and saltwater species from around the world. Special attractions include shark and piranha feeding on alternate afternoons every day but Monday; an Amazon Flooded Forest Exhibit, which showcases approximately 20 species of fish found in the Amazon River of South America; and The World of Aquatic Diversity Exhibit featuring 25 displays highlighting the bizarre adaptations of a variety of marine and freshwater species.

DALLAS MUSEUM OF NATURAL HISTORY

3535 Grand Avenue (P.O. Box 150349, 75315), just inside the Grand Avenue entrance off Cullum Blvd. • 421-DINO (421-3466) • Open daily 10–5. Closed Thanksgiving and Christmas • Adults $4, children 3 and older $2.50, under 3 free. Free admission Monday 10–1 • W+ but not all areas

"Natural History" in its title means this museum documents the diversity of past and present environments and the changing face of Texas over millions of years. To do this it offers extensive displays and dioramas of Texas wildlife, plants, and minerals. Among its features are The Hall of Prehistoric Texas, which includes a reconstructed dinosaur and the nation's largest prehistoric sea turtle; a working paleontology lab; a City Safari; and a hands-on science discovery center for children.

THE SCIENCE PLACE AND TI FOUNDERS IMAX® THEATER

1318 Second Avenue between Grand and Martin Luther King (P.O. Box 151469, 75315) • 428-5555 • Open daily 9:30–5:30. Closed Christmas • Adults $6, seniors and children 3–12 $3, under 3 free. Extra admission to IMAX Theater and Planetarium • W+ but not all areas

Learn the shocking truth about electricity in the Electric Theater, step inside the body shop to see a real beating heart, or come face-to-face with a (robotic) dinosaur that growls. You can do all this in the hundreds of hands-on exhibits that go to the limit and let you touch and turn and press buttons, making science interactive and fun. And for a real moving movie experience, take in the show at the IMAX Theater, in which an optimum view of the 79-foot dome screen allows the viewers to feel like they're in the film. In a separate building, on First Avenue, about a block away, is **The Science Place Planetarium** which features sky shows Monday–Saturday.

Fair Park Performance and Sports Venues

For schedules and ticket information, call 670-8400 or 890-2911 (English and Spanish Information Line)

Band Shell. Musical concerts and plays are performed in this 4,500-seat amphitheater.

Coca Cola Starplex Amphitheater, 1818 First Avenue, 428-8365. This 20,000-seat amphitheater is the site for about 40 live concerts each year featuring big name entertainers.

Cotton Bowl Stadium, 939-2222. The 72,000-seat stadium is the site of a number of sports events including the Cotton Bowl Football Classic on New Year's Day, the annual football games pitting rivals Grambling and Prairie View A&M and the University of Texas and University of Oklahoma during the State Fair, SMU and other college football games, and the home soccer matches of the Dallas Burn. It also hosts a variety of concerts.

Coliseum, 939-2222. With 7,116 seats, the Coliseum hosts rodeos, horse shows, and other sporting events, including the indoor polo matches of the Dallas Dragoons.

Creative Arts Theatre. This art deco building contains two performance stages, exhibition sites, and a music arena.

Music Hall, 909 First Avenue, 565-2226. The 3,420-seat hall is home for the Dallas Summer Musicals, the opera, ballet, and a variety of concerts. Restaurant.

Other Points of Interest in Fair Park

DALLAS HORTICULTURAL CENTER

3601 Martin Luther King Blvd. (P.O. Box 152537, 75315) • 428-7476 Tuesday–Saturday 10–5, Sunday 1–5. Closed Monday. (Grounds open at all times, access through rear gate.) • Free • W

Among the features on the 7.5 acres of this center are a conservatory, an antique rose garden, a garden featuring plants used for medicinal and culinary purposes, a garden with over 300 varieties of iris, and a Xeriscape garden of native and adapted plants that require minimal supplemental water and maintenance.

TEXAS STAR FERRIS WHEEL

At a little over 212 feet (about 20 stories high), this is the tallest Ferris wheel in North America. Operates only during the State Fair and selected special events.

OTHER MAJOR BUILDINGS IN FAIR PARK

The **Automotive Building, Grand Place, Centennial Hall** and other major buildings in the park not only have important roles as exhibit areas during the State Fair, but are also used during the rest of the year for a variety of exhibits and events, including antique and craft shows and flea markets.

MUSEUMS

AFRICAN-AMERICAN MUSEUM

(*See* Fair Park, above)

AGE OF STEAM RAILROAD MUSEUM

(*See* Fair Park, above)

BIBLICAL ARTS CENTER

**7500 Park Lane at Boedeker (P.O. Box 12727, 75225) • 691-4661
Monday–Saturday 10–5 (Thursday 10–9), Sunday 1–5. Closed Thanksgiving,
Christmas Eve and Day, and New Year's Day • Galleries free. Miracle of
Pentecost Presentation: Adults $3.75, children 6–12 $2, under 6 free • W+**

Nondenominational art that illustrates the Bible is the theme here. Permanent exhibits include a life-sized replica of the Garden Tomb of Christ. The major attraction is the Miracle of Pentecost Presentation, a 30-minute light and sound show highlighting the 124-feet-wide by 20-feet-high oil painting depicting the reception of the Holy Spirit by the Apostles.

THE CONSPIRACY MUSEUM

(See OFFBEAT, below)

DALLAS FIREFIGHTERS MUSEUM

**3801 Parry (75226) at Commerce, across from Fair Park • 821-1500
Monday–Friday 10–4 • Free. Donations accepted • W downstairs only**

The building was a working firehouse from 1907 until 1975. Inside, the museum is packed tight with fire trucks, fire-fighting equipment, photographs, and other memorabilia illustrating the history of the Dallas Fire Department. Displays include the 1936 Texas Centennial Exposition Hook and Ladder Truck and the 1884 Ahrens horse-drawn steam pumper called "Old Tige," after the nickname of W. L. Cabell, mayor of Dallas at the time.

DALLAS MEMORIAL CENTER FOR HOLOCAUST STUDIES

**7900 Northaven Road (75230) in the Jewish Community Center (downstairs)
750-4654 • Monday–Friday 9:30–4:30, Thursday until 9, Sunday 12–4. Closed
Jewish and most national holidays • Recommended donation: Adults $2,
children $1 • W elevator**

Visitors enter this small museum and research library through a boxcar once used to transport people to the concentration camps. Audio tapes are provided for a free self-guided tour that lasts about 45 minutes as it traces in photos and other artifacts that show the horrors of the Holocaust from the first days of the Nazi regime in 1933 through the liberation of the death camps. Films are shown on request.

DALLAS MUSEUM OF ART

1717 North Harwood (75201), between Harwood and St. Paul in the Arts District (DART Light Rail ST. PAUL Station) • 922-1200 • Tuesday–Wednesday, Friday 11–4, Thursday 11–9, Saturday–Sunday 11–5. Closed Monday, Thanksgiving, Christmas, and New Year's Day • No general admission charge for special exhibitions • W+

In 1984, The Arts District was born when this elegant museum opened. In its Art of the Americas collection, there are extensive examples from the lost civilizations of Aztec, Maya, Nasca, and Anasazi, as well as twentieth-century artists such as Church, Sargent, Happer, Benton, O'Keeffe, and Wyeth. Art of Europe includes works by Monet, van Gogh, Gauguin, Degas, Cézanne, and Vuillard. The extensive Arts of Africa collection includes Egyptian, Nubian, and sub-Saharan sculpture. Arts of Asia and the Pacific features beautiful examples of decorative arts from the Japanese Meiji and Edo periods. The pieces in the Contemporary Art collection trace the development from abstract expressionism through pop art to the present. The museum features one of the largest collections of post-1945 art in the Southwest, including masterpieces by Pollock, Johns, Rothko, Stella, and Warhol. The Reves collection, which is a unique showcase for important works by Renoir, Toulouse-Lutrec, Redon, and others, is in a setting patterned after the French Riviera villa of the Reves, who donated the collection. Free tours Tuesday–Friday at 1 P.M. and Saturday–Sunday at 2 P.M. Thursday evenings there is live music, art talks, and even the special exhibitions are free after 5 P.M. Free art activities for children on Saturdays. There are two restaurants in the DMA. Seventeen-Seventeen is an upstairs and upscale dining room open for lunch Tuesday–Sunday and occasionally for dinner (922-1260). The more casual Atrium Café is open for lunch every day the DMA is open and dinner on Thursday evening. Parking in the underground garage is $2.

DALLAS MUSEUM OF NATURAL HISTORY

(*See* Fair Park, above)

DOLLHOUSE MUSEUM OF THE SOUTHWEST

2208 Routh Street (75201), three blocks east of McKinney • 969-5502 Tuesday–Saturday 10–4:30, Sunday 1–4. Closed Monday and major holidays Adults $4, seniors and children under 12 $2

On display are more than a dozen historically accurate miniature houses including a 1900s New York townhouse, a Texas farm, an English bakery, and a sixteenth century French Armorer's shop. Miniature furnishings created by regional professional designers include clocks that can be wound and musical instruments that can be played.

FRONTIERS OF FLIGHT MUSEUM

Love Field at Terminal LB-18 (75235), Cedar Springs at Mockingbird Lane 350-1651 • Monday–Saturday 10–5, Sunday 1–5 • Tours: Adults $2, children under 12 $1

The exhibits here take the visitor through the history of flight from Greek mythology through man's first balloon flights to the space shuttle. The collection includes photographs, models, uniforms, and vintage airplane parts.

INTERNATIONAL MUSEUM OF CULTURES

7500 West Camp Wisdom Road (75236), west of Clark Road, on campus of the International Linguistics Center • 972-709-2406 • Tuesday–Friday 10–5, Saturday–Sunday 1:30–5. Closed Monday • Tour: Adults $2, children $1 • W access on south side

The goal of this museum is to increase understanding of cultural diversity. It does it through exhibits depicting the lives of culturally diverse people living today all around the world. The museum is affiliated with the **International Linguistics Center,** which is next door.

McKINNEY AVENUE CONTEMPORARY

3120 McKinney Avenue (75204) • 953-1212 • W+

This gallery provides exhibition space as part of its interdisciplinary program of art exhibitions, theater performances (in The MAC), concerts, and lectures to showcase the latest developments in all media.

OLD CITY PARK HISTORIC VILLAGE

1717 Gano Street (75215), between Harwood and Ervay streets, just south of I-30 • 421-5141 • Tuesday–Saturday 10–4, Sunday 12–4. Buildings closed Monday, but grounds open • Adults $5, seniors $4, children 3–12 $2. Family maximum $12 • W variable

Step into the past as you stroll the red brick streets and visit more than 35 historic structures that illustrate how people lived in North Texas between 1840 and 1910. In addition to visiting places like a general store, bank, log cabin, Southern colonial mansion, and the Victorian parlors of the George House and Hotel, you can watch the blacksmith, printer, and potter recreate their wares. The park is operated by the Dallas County Heritage Society, which sponsors a number of special events during the year, including Candlelight at Old City Park on several weekends during the Christmas season. Brent Place, a restaurant in an 1876 farmhouse, offers lunch daily (reservations 421-3057).

MEADOWS MUSEUM OF ART

Owens Fine Arts Center, SMU Campus, Bishop Blvd. and Binkley Ave. (75275) • 768-2516 • Monday–Tuesday, Friday–Saturday 10–5, Thursday 10–8, Sunday 1–5. Closed Wednesday and most holidays • Free ($3 donation suggested) • W+

One of the finest and most comprehensive collections of Spanish art outside of Spain and the premier collection of Spanish art in the United States is in this museum. The permanent collection includes major works by some of Europe's greatest painters: Velázquez, Rivera, Zurbarán, Murillo, Goya, Miró, and Picasso. Highlights of the collection include Renaissance altarpieces, monumental Baroque canvases, exquisite rococo oil sketches, polychrome wood sculptures, Impressionist landscapes, Modernist abstractions, and a comprehensive collection of the graphic works of Goya. Free public tours from September–May on Sundays at 2 P.M. and selected Sundays during the summer. **The Elizabeth Meadows Sculpture Garden** (6100 Bishop) displays a collection of major works by such modern masters as Auguste Rodin, Aristide Maillol, Jacques Lipchitz, Henry Moore, David Smith, Claes Oldenburg, and Isamu Noguchi. Open daily 8:30–5. Closed campus holidays.

THE SCIENCE PLACE AND TI FOUNDERS IMAX® THEATER

(*See* Fair Park, above)

THE SIXTH FLOOR MUSEUM

411 Elm Street (75202), at Houston in the West End District (DART Light Rail WEST END Station) • 653-6666 or 653-6659 • Open daily 9–6. Closed Christmas Day • Adults $5, seniors $4, students 12–18 $3, children 6–11 $2, under 6 free • W+ access on north side of building

The original corner window from which Oswald allegedly fired the shots that killed President John F. Kennedy is now encased in glass as one of the many exhibits in this museum which examines JFK's life, times, death, and legacy. The museum is located on the sixth floor of the Dallas County Administration Building (formerly the Texas School Book Depository), the location of the so-called "sniper's perch." JFK's life and death are illustrated through the use of nearly 400 photographs, 45 minutes of documentary film, and other interpretive artifacts and materials. Among the exhibits are a large scale model of Dealey Plaza prepared by the FBI for the Warren Commission in 1964.

(Note: for a differing view of the JFK assassination, *see* The Conspiracy Museum, in OFFBEAT, below.)

TELEPHONE PIONEER MUSEUM OF TEXAS

One Bell Plaza, 208 South Akard Street (75202), at Commerce • 464-4359 Free • W elevator

Here you'll find the story of the past, present, and future of telephone technology told in a number of interactive audiovisual displays. A map brochure available at the entrance leads you through a self-paced tour. Exhibits include life-sized dioramas of the people behind the scenes who make your telephone work today. A theater presentation sums it all up. Kids will enjoy the talking bear and the huge talking telephone. Usually open Tuesday–Friday during business hours, but it is best to call for precise times.

TRAMMELL CROW CENTER

2001 Ross (75201), at Harwood in the Arts District (DART Light Rail PEARL Station) • 979-6348 • W+ but not all areas

The gardens surrounding this 50-story office building feature more than 20 pieces of nineteenth- and twentieth-century bronze sculptures by such artists as Rodin and Maillol. In addition, more than 10,000 square feet of space inside the building is used for art exhibitions.

HISTORIC PLACES

THE BELO MANSION

2101 Ross Avenue (75201), in the Arts District (DART Light Rail PEARL Station) • 969-7066 (Dallas Bar Association) for tours • Free

In the late 1890s, this Neoclassical mansion was constructed for Colonel Alfred H. Belo, founder of the *The Dallas Morning News*, on Ross Avenue, which was then a fashionable street lined with grand homes. By 1926, Ross Avenue was no longer a fashionable address, and the building became a funeral home. The Dallas Bar Foundation bought and meticulously restored the mansion in 1977. Today, it is the lone survivor of those early stately homes and is listed in the National Register of Historic Places. Now known as the Dallas Legal Education Center, the mansion houses the offices of the Dallas Bar Association.

DEALEY PLAZA NATIONAL HISTORIC LANDMARK DISTRICT/KENNEDY ASSASSINATION SITE

Downtown in the West End area around the triple underpass of Elm, Commerce, and Houston streets (DART Light Rail WEST END Station)

Built over the original townsite, the plaza's art deco garden structures were completed in 1940 and named after George Bannerman Dealey, the publisher of *The Dallas Morning News*. In November 1963, President John F. Kennedy was assassinated while passing through the plaza in a motorcade. In 1993, the plaza and the surrounding area were declared a National Historic Landmark District. (*See* The Sixth Floor Museum, above.)

FREEDMAN'S CEMETERY

North of downtown, between Hall, McKinney, and North Central Expressway

The first burials here were slaves prior to the Civil War. When it closed in 1927 there were approximately 18,000 graves in the four-acre plot. In 1989, after several intrusions had already been made by roadways and other private developments, Black Dallas Remembered, Inc. fought city plans to widen a major freeway that would desecrate a large portion of the cemetery. After negotiations, the remains of 1,500 of Dallas' earliest citizens, freed slaves who founded Freedman's Town after the Civil War, were reentered into the property adjacent to the original site. Plans are in progress to build a Freedman's Memorial here.

SWISS AVENUE HISTORIC DISTRICT

Northeast of downtown, Swiss Avenue between La Vista Drive and Fitzhugh Avenue

This neighborhood was among the most prestigious in Dallas in the early 1900s. About a mile of the avenue is listed in the National Register of Historic Places because of the restored grand homes. Of particular note are the 2800 and 2900 blocks, which are called **The Wilson Blocks,** after Frederick P. Wilson who built some of the homes in the late 1890s. For information about tours, call the Historic Preservation League, 821–3290.

THE WEST END HISTORIC DISTRICT

West end of downtown, centered on west end of Market Street from Commerce to Woodall Rodgers Freeway (DART Light Rail WEST END Station)

Part of the original city set up by John Neely Bryan. As the downtown moved further east, this became known as the West End and developed into a factory and warehouse district. Now it is a 20-block historic district that has been transformed into a bustling neighborhood of restaurants, clubs, and shops set in and among the restored buildings. Historic attractions in this district include **"Old Red,"** the 1892 red sandstone courthouse, **Bryan Cabin, Kennedy Memorial, The Sixth Floor Museum,** and its counterpoint, **The Conspiracy Museum.**

OTHER POINTS OF INTEREST

BACHMAN LAKE PARK

3500 Northwest Hwy. (75220). *Take Northwest Hwy. (Loop 12) exit off IH-35E (Stemmons Frwy.) and go east* • **670-4100 (Parks and Recreation Department)**

Fishing is permitted in 205-acre Bachman Lake, which is ringed by a roller skating and jogging track. Other facilities include picnic tables with grills, multipurpose fields, a soccer field, and playground. A concession rents paddle boats. Also the location of the **Bachman Recreation Center** (2750 Bachman Dr. 75220, 670–6266), which offers facilities and programs designed to meet the needs and interests of persons with disabilities aged 6 and up.

BRYAN CABIN

Dallas County Historical Plaza, Elm and Market streets, West End Historic District (DART Light Rail WEST END Station) • W

The tiny log cabin in this large plaza is a reconstruction of a cabin typical of the 1840s when John Neely Bryan settled here. Also on the square is a large tile map of early Dallas County.

DALLAS ARBORETUM AND BOTANICAL GARDENS

8525 Garland Road (75218), on eastern shore of White Rock Lake 327-8263 • Open daily March–October 10–6, November–February 10–5. Closed Thanksgiving, Christmas, and New Year's Day • Adults $6, seniors $5, children 6–12 $3, five and under free. Parking $2 • W variable (Transportation for the mobility impaired and wheelchairs available for loan, free)

Sixty-six acres on the eastern shore of White Rock Lake are devoted to ornamental gardens and the natural woodlands of this oasis in the heart of one of Dallas' oldest neighborhoods. There are a number of special gardens including **The Jonsson Color Garden,** which offers an almost six-acre display of over 15,000 chrysanthemums each fall and one of the nation's largest azalea collections, with more than 2,500 varieties in bloom each spring. A major attraction is **The Degolyer House,** which is listed on the National Register of Historic Places. Completed in 1940, the one-story house encompasses 13 rooms and seven baths in 21,000 square feet. The 4.5 acres of gardens surrounding the house boast a magnolia allée, a rose garden, fountains, and hundreds of annuals. Special events are held every season with the major one being Dallas Blooms, held for about a month in the spring when more than 200,000 flowering bulbs color the gardens.

DALLAS CITY HALL

1500 Marilla (75201), at Ervay (DART Light Rail CONVENTION CENTER Station) • 670-3011 • W+

Famed Architect I. M. Pei designed this building with an inverted front that slopes at a 34-degree angle, which makes its ten levels seem to lean over the street. Sculpture by Henry Moore and a reflecting pool adorn the ceremonial plaza in front which is often used for public events and festivals.

DALLAS MARKET CENTER COMPLEX
2100 Stemmons Frwy., (IH-35E), just north of downtown • 655-6100
W+ but not all areas
This is the world's largest wholesale trade complex with more than a million wholesale buyers attending markets here each year. The center includes eight separate marketing facilities: The World Trade Center, Apparel Mart, Menswear Mart, Trade Mart, Decorative Center, Home Furnishing Mart, Market Hall, and the InfoMart. Only the Market Hall and Infomart are open to the public on a limited basis. **Market Hall,** the largest privately owned exhibition hall in the U.S., is the scene of boat shows, car shows, crafts shows, and numerous other public events. **InfoMart (1950 Stemmons Frwy. • 746-3500 • W+)** is the world's largest high-tech information center, housing offices and showrooms of more than 115 information technology companies. Most of the offices are only open to people in the business; however, the building itself and some of its facilities are open to the public. (Call 746-5678 or 800-232-1022 for schedule of exhibits and events.) The Infomart is housed in a unique building whose glass and lacework arch architecture is designed to resemble London's Crystal Palace, which was built in 1851 for the first World's Fair. Free guided tours Monday–Friday at 11 A.M.

DALLAS NATURE CENTER
7171 Mountain Creek Parkway (75249), southwest near Joe Pool Lake. *Take Mountain Creek exit off IH-20 then south* **• 972-296-1955 • Open daily 7 A.M. to sunset • Free • W visitor center**
Part of this 360-acre wilderness preserve sits on the highest point in Dallas County. It is the habitat for a variety of native wildlife and wildflowers and other plants. Facilities include a Butterfly Garden, seven miles of hiking trails, picnic areas, and a visitor center. The center is also a bird-of-prey rescue facility.

DALLAS PUBLIC LIBRARY
Central Library, 1515 Young Street (75201), downtown (DART Light Rail CONVENTION CENTER Station) • 670-1400 • W+ but not all areas
A vast lending library is just one of the highlights of this central library. It has an outstanding genealogy collection and the largest children's center in the country. It also offers performance space for dance, theater, music, children's shows, films, and lectures; has permanent exhibits of rare books and manuscripts, including a copy of the Declaration of Independence printed by Benjamin Franklin; and features the largest display of Navajo blankets in the country.

DALLAS WORLD AQUARIUM
1801 North Griffin (75202), in the West End District • 720-2224 • Open daily 10–5. Closed Thanksgiving and Christmas • Adults $5, seniors and children 3–12 $3 • W+
Each tank in this privately owned aquarium represents a different dive destination, ranging from British Columbia to Fiji, and each teems with marine life indigenous to that part of the world. Exhibits include bonnet head sharks, stingrays, cuttlefish, seadragons, jellyfish, giant groupers, and a vast assortment of colorful smaller fish that live in the reefs. There is a feeding at one of the exhibits every half-hour from 11 to 4:30. Audio tape tours $2. Restaurant open for lunch.

DALLAS ZOO

650 South R.L. Thornton Frwy (I-35E) (75203), about 3 miles south of downtown. *From I-35E take Marsalis exit and follow zoo signs.* **(DART Light Rail ZOO Station) • 670-8626 (office), 670-5656 (recording) • Open daily 9–5 (can stay until 6) • Adults $5, seniors $4, children 3–11 $2.50, under 3 free Parking $3 • W+ but not all areas**

More than 2,000 mammals, reptiles, amphibians, and birds representing 377 species live in this 100-acre park with many roaming freely in areas designed to be as close to their natural habitat as possible. The zoo is divided into two major areas: Zoo North and the Wilds of Africa. Follow the walkways of **Zoo North** to get a close-up view of rhinos, giraffes, lions, tigers, ocelots, cheetahs, elephants, chimpanzees, red pandas, camels, llamas, wallabies, kangaroos, and many of the more than 700 birds in the zoo's collection. This area also features the Bird and Reptile Building and the Rainforest Aviary, where you can watch brightly colored exotic birds fly all around you. Also here is the Children's Zoo where children can touch and pet a number of smaller wild and domestic animals. The 25-acre **Wilds of Africa** features the six major habitats of Africa. Some of the animals here are mandrill baboons, bongos, zebras, the rare okapi, storks, and lowland gorillas. Part of the exhibit can be seen from the walking trail, but to see it all take the Monorail Safari ($1.50 for ages 3 and up). Live narration is given during the 20-minute ride, and the monorail cars are open on the side facing the exhibit so all have a good view.

JOHN F. KENNEDY MEMORIAL

Memorial Plaza, Main and Market streets, West End Historic District (DART Light Rail WEST END Station) • W

This memorial to our thirty-fifth president was designed by architect Phillip Johnson as a place for meditation. Stark and simple, it consists of four walls, about 30-feet high, open to the sky, creating the effect of an open tomb enclosing a memorial plaque.

NEIMAN MARCUS' ORIGINAL DALLAS STORE

1618 Main (75201), at Ervay Street (DART Light Rail ST. PAUL Station) 573-5800 • Monday–Saturday 10–5:30. Closed Sunday and major holidays • W

In Texas, and just about everywhere else in the world, the name Neiman Marcus stands for a long tradition of sophisticated service and good taste. "The Store" helped put Dallas on the national and international fashion map. This original store is now the flagship of a chain. Among Neiman Marcus' many claims to fame is its annual Christmas catalog, which always includes His and Her gifts that gently spoof its rich customers. A permanent exhibit on the 5th floor tells the history of "The Store." On the 6th floor is the original legendary Zodiac room where Dallas socialites have been lunching for decades.

PIONEER PLAZA CATTLE DRIVE MONUMENT

Young and Griffin streets, between Dallas Convention Center and City Hall (DART Light Rail CONVENTION CENTER Station) • Free • W

Forty-seven larger-than-life-sized bronze longhorn steers move down a rocky bluff through a flowing stream in this plaza park, driven by three cowboys on horseback. Sculpted by Robert Summers of Glen Rose, it's the world's largest bronze monument. The plaza is wide open, so you can walk through it to get a feeling of the immense power of the longhorns that the riders had to control on those legendary cattle drives when the herds numbered in the thousands.

THANKS-GIVING SQUARE

Surrounded by Akard, Ervay, Bryan, and Pacific streets, downtown (DART Light Rail AKARD Station) • Thanks-Giving Square Foundation, P.O. Box 1777, 75221 • 969-1977 • Free • W variable

Architect Phillip Johnson, who designed the John F. Kennedy Memorial (*see* above), designed this tiny triangular park in praise of the universal spirit of the Thanksgiving tradition found in all the world's religions. An island of serenity amidst the bustle of downtown, Thanks-Giving Square includes a 50-foot bell tower with three large bronze bells, a water wall, a reflecting pool, and the spiraling white marble interfaith Chapel of Thanksgiving. There is an entrance to the park from the underground Pedestrianway (*see* OFFBEAT, below).

WHITE ROCK LAKE PARK

8300 Garland Road (75218) • 670-4100 (Parks and Recreation Department)

Facilities in the park's 1,873 acres surrounding the lake include an 11-mile-hike-and-bike trail that follows the water's edge most of the way, play areas, a variety of sports fields, and picnic areas. The **Bath House Cultural Center,** a meeting, exhibition, and performance space, is located in the park on the east side. The Dallas Arboretum and Botanical Gardens adjoins the park on the east. Paddleboats can be rented on the west side of the lake. Canoes and sailboats are permitted on the lake.

SPORTS AND ACTIVITIES

Basketball

DALLAS MAVERICKS

Reunion Arena, 777 Sports Street (75207) (DART Light Rail UNION Station) 939-2800 or 988-9365

An NBA franchise since 1980, the Mavericks play in Reunion Arena from November through April. Tickets $9–$27.

Bicycling

The City of Dallas maintains more than 500 miles of bike trails in the city. Bike Trail Maps are for sale at City Hall for about $2 or by mail for $3.25 (City of Dallas, Department of Transportation, Room 5C-S, 1500 Marilla, 75201). Most bike shops also sell the maps.

College Sports

(See COLLEGES AND UNIVERSITIES/SMU, below.)

Golf

CEDAR CREST PARK GOLF COURSE

1800 Southerland (75203) • 670-7615 • 18 holes. Green fees: weekdays $11, weekends/holidays $14.

L.B. HOUSTON MUNICIPAL GOLF COURSE

11223 Luna Road (75229) • 972-670-6322 • 18 holes.
Green fees: weekdays $13, weekends/holidays $16

GROVER KEETON PARK GOLF COURSE

2323 Jim Miller Road (P.O. Box 17458, 75217) • 670-8784
18 holes. Green fees: weekdays $11, weekends/holidays $14

LONE STAR GOLF CENTER

2101 Walnut Hill (75229) • 972-247-4653 • 9 hole par 3 course. Call for fees

STEVENS PARK GOLF COURSE

1005 North Montclair (75208) • 670-7506 • 18 holes.
Green fees: weekdays $13, weekends $16

TENISON PARK GOLF COURSE

3501 Samuell Blvd. (75223) • 670-1402 • 36 holes.
Green fees: weekdays $13, weekends/holidays $16.

Hockey

DALLAS STARS

Reunion Arena, 777 Sports Street (75207) (DART Light Rail UNION Station)
467-8277
 The Stars play NHL Hockey at the Reunion Arena from September through
April. Tickets $14–$57.50.

Ice Skating

AMERICA'S ICE GARDEN

Plaza of the Americas, 600 North Pearl (75201) (DART Light Rail PEARL
Station) • 922-9800 • Open daily
 This rink is located in the atrium of the Plaza of the Americas office tower
and hotel complex. The $7 admission includes skate rental.

DALLAS ON ICE

700 Munger Avenue (75202), between Market and Record (DART Light Rail
WEST END Station) • 969-RINK (969-7465) • Open daily from Friday after
Thanksgiving to end of February
 Dallas' first outdoor ice rink offers public skating, live ice shows, and is used
as a practice rink for the Dallas Stars. Admission $6. Skate rental $3.

GALLERIA ICE SKATING CENTER

Galleria, 13350 Dallas North Tollway (75240), at LBJ Frwy. (I-635)
972-392-3363 • Open daily
 The rink is located on the lower level of Galleria Mall. Admission $5. Skate
rental $2.50.

ICE CAPADES CHALET

Prestonwood Town Center, 5301 Beltline Road (75240), at Dallas North
Tollway • 972-980-8988 • Open daily
 Admission to this mall rink is $5. Skate rental $2.

Indoor Polo

DALLAS DRAGOONS

Fair Park Coliseum • 520-7656 • Admission
This professional arena polo team usually plays its National Polo League matches on Saturdays year round. Tickets $15.

Soccer

DALLAS BURN

Cotton Bowl, Fair Park • 373-8000 • Admission
The Cotton Bowl is home field for Dallas' newest professional (outdoor) soccer team that competes in the Western Conference. Season is from April–September.

DALLAS SIDEKICKS

Reunion Arena, 777 Sports Street (75207) (DART Light Rail UNION Station) 653-0200
This is Dallas' professional indoor soccer team. Season is from June–September with most games scheduled on weekends. Tickets $7–$22.

Tennis

DALLAS PARKS TENNIS CENTERS

Parks and Recreation Department, City Hall, 1500 Marilla (75201) • 670-4100
The following parks each have a Tennis Center that is city-owned but privately managed. Depending on the park, prime time fees are either $5 or $6 for 1½ hours court time; non-prime fees are $2–$4. There's a $1 reservation fee. The Tennis Centers also offer lessons, ball-machine rentals, and each has a tennis pro shop.

Fair Oaks • 7501 Merriman Pkwy. • 670-1495 • 16 lighted courts
Fretz • 14700 Hillcrest • 972-670-6622 • 15 lighted courts
Kiest • 2324 West Kiest Blvd. • 670-7618 • 16 lighted courts
Samuell-Grand • 6200 East Grand Avenue • 670-1374 • 20 lighted courts
L. B. Houston • 11225 Luna Road • 670-6367 • 16 lighted courts

COLLEGES AND UNIVERSITIES

DALLAS COUNTY COMMUNITY COLLEGE DISTRICT

Headquarters 701 Elm Street (75202) • 860-2135 • W
This district offers a comprehensive two-year program at seven campuses throughout the county enrolling nearly 50,000 students in credit courses leading to associate degrees and a similar number of non-credit students each semester, making it the largest undergraduate institution in Texas and placing it among the six largest community college systems in the nation. Most of the campuses offer visitors student theater, dance, art, and photographic exhibitions. Two of the campuses of this county community college district are in the city of Dallas. At **El Centro College** (Main and Lamar, DART Light Rail WEST END Station, 860-2037) visitors are welcome at the Food and Hospitality Service Department's lunch on Wednesday and dinner on Thursday. The five-course meals are prepared by students in the nationally acclaimed culinary arts program. The cost is $6 per person. Performances at the theater include children's theater productions (978-0110). **Mountain View College** (4849 West Illi-

nois Avenue, 860-8680) is located on 200 acres in the southwestern section of the city. Among the college's programs is the two-year course at the Performing Arts Musical Theatre Conservatory. Students put on live theater performances throughout the year.

SOUTHERN METHODIST UNIVERSITY (SMU)

Hillcrest Avenue, between Mockingbird Lane and Daniel Avenue (75275) 768-2000 • W variable

Dallas' oldest and most prestigious university, SMU was founded in 1911. When the university opened it consisted of two buildings, a 35-member faculty, and 706 students. Today it's a 163-acre campus of red brick buildings with a full-time faculty of close to 500, and about 9,500 students with 68 undergraduate degree programs, 42 master's programs, 18 doctoral programs, and 18 professional degrees. The university is owned by the South Central Jurisdiction of the United Methodist Church; however, from its founding, SMU has been nonsectarian in its teaching.

The premier cultural center on campus is the **Meadows School of Arts/Owens Fine Art Center Complex** at Bishop Blvd. and Binkley Avenue on the west side of the campus (768-3510). The major attraction here is the **Meadows Museum of Art** (*see* Museums, above). In addition, approximately 400 public arts events are held in the school and fine arts complex each year including eight major theater productions, two dance productions, six to eight special exhibitions; and opera, symphony, choral, wind ensemble and organ concerts. Performance facilities include the **Bob Hope Theatre, Greer Garson Theatre, Margo Jones Theatre, Caruth Auditorium, Charles S. Sharp Performing Arts Studio,** and **O'Donnell Lecture/Recital Hall.**

The SMU Mustang football team is part of the 16-member Western Athletic Conference. Home games are held at the **Cotton Bowl Stadium** in Fair Park. With the exception of football and golf, most of the other intercollegiate sports events are held on campus. Men's and women's basketball and women's volleyball are held at **Moody Coliseum,** 6024 Airline Road at Binkley Avenue; tennis in the **Haggar Tennis Stadium,** 3005 Binkley Avenue at Dublin Street; swimming and diving in the **Joe Perkins Natatorium,** 6024 Bishop Blvd. at Binkley Avenue; track and field meets in the **Morrison-Bell Track,** 6001 Airline Road between Mockingbird Lane and Binkley Avenue; and soccer matches at **Westcott Field,** 6001 Airline Road between Mockingbird Lane and Binkley Avenue. For information on all intercollegiate sports, call the Sports and Information Office, 768-2883. For tickets call 768-GAME (768-4263).

PERFORMING ARTS

The Dallas Morning News Arts and Entertainment Hotline 522-2659. Dallas Convention & Visitors Bureau Events Hotline 746-6679.

Theaters and Other Performance Spaces

BOOKER T. WASHINGTON HIGH SCHOOL FOR THE PERFORMING AND VISUAL ARTS

2501 Flora Avenue (75201) (DART Light Rail PEARL Station) • 720-7300 • W

The two performance theaters in this school are used for plays and concerts by the talented students who had to pass a screening to be selected for enrollment.

BRONCO BOWL

2600 Fort Worth Avenue (75211) • 943-1777 • W+ but not all areas

The 3,000-seat arena with a state-of-the-art sound and lighting system hosts concerts by top entertainers and Broadway-style shows. (This eclectic entertainment complex also offers a nightclub with dancing, bowling, billiards, and a games arcade.)

COTTON BOWL STADIUM

(See FAIR PARK, above)

DALLAS CONVENTION CENTER

650 South Griffin (75202) (DART Light Rail CONVENTION CENTER Station) • 658-7000 • W+ but not all areas

When it isn't being used for conventions—and Dallas ranks near the top of the convention cities in the nation—this center's arena and theater are used for live theater and concerts by visiting artists. This is also the home of the **Junior Black Academy** (658-7144), which uses the center theaters for its theatrical and dance productions and the other facilities for its art exhibits.

DALLAS THEATER CENTER/ARTS DISTRICT THEATER

2401 Flora (75201) (DART Light Rail PEARL Station) • 522-8499 W call ahead

This theater is designed to meet the needs of each production in relation to the interaction between the actors and the audience with one of the most flexible arrangements for seating and staging in the nation.

DALLAS THEATER CENTER/KALITA HUMPHREYS THEATER

3626 Turtle Creek Blvd. (75219) • 526-8210 • W call ahead

This theater building was the only theater and one of the last buildings designed by Frank Lloyd Wright. Its square boxes and circular core are reminiscent of Wright's design of the Guggenheim Museum in New York City, which he designed about the same time. The theater hosts a full season of professional theater productions ranging from the classics to musical comedies.

FAIR PARK MUSIC HALL

(See FAIR PARK, above)

MAJESTIC THEATRE

1925 Elm (75201) (DART Light Rail PEARL Station) • 880-0137 • W+

This 1,648-seat theater frequently hosts touring concerts and a Broadway show series as well as dance productions by local groups.

McFARLIN MEMORIAL AUDITORIUM

SMU campus, McFarlin Blvd. and Hillcrest Ave. (75275) • 768-3129 • W+

SMU's largest performance facility hosts year-round activities including classical music concerts, the Willis M. Tate Distinguished Lecture Series, dance performances, screenings, and plays. Concerts and dance performances by internationally acclaimed artists and groups are also held here under the sponsorship of **The International Theatrical Arts Society (TITAS).** For information on TITAS performances call 528-5566.

MORTON H. MEYERSON SYMPHONY CENTER

2301 Flora Street (75201), at Pearl (DART Light Rail PEARL Station)
629-0203 • W+

The musical centerpiece of the Dallas Arts District is home of the Dallas Symphony Orchestra, the Dallas Wind Symphony, and the Turtle Creek Chorale. The 2,062-seat center was named by its principal donor, H. Ross Perot, after one of his top assistants. This is the only symphony center designed by the internationally known architect I. M. Pei. It has won acclaim for both its architectural significance and its acoustics. One of the features of the center is the hand-built $2 million, 4,535-pipe Fisk organ, one of the largest mechanical-action organs ever built for a concert hall.

PEGASUS THEATER

3916 Main Street (75226) • 821-6005 • W+

This small professional theater specializes in original and offbeat comedies with productions year round. Tickets about $12–$15.

POCKET SANDWICH THEATER

5400 East Mockingbird (75206) • 821-1860

A neighborhood theater known for professional-quality productions of all types of plays, but with a leaning toward comedies and melodramas. The sandwich in the name may have come from the sandwiches (and beer, wine, etc.) for sale during the performances.

REUNION ARENA

777 Sport Street (75207) (DART Light Rail UNION Station) • 939-2770 • W+

When it's not being used by the Dallas Mavericks, the Dallas Burn, or Dallas Stars, or for other sports events, this 15,520-seat arena is the frequent site of major pop and country concerts, theatrical events, and even the circus. And there isn't a bad seat in the house. Events line 670-1395.

SAMMONS CENTER FOR THE ARTS

3630 Harry Hines (75219) • 520-7788 • W

The performance spaces here include a hall with performance seating for up to 260 and recital halls. One popular series given here is Sammons Jazz featuring local jazz artists in a relaxed setting for nominal prices. This multi-use facility is also known as a nonprofit arts incubator providing an office home for more than a dozen emerging and midsized nonprofit arts organizations. The building is the converted Turtle Creek Pump Station, which is the oldest public building in Dallas, completed in 1909 and the sole source of water for the city of Dallas until 1930.

SMU THEATERS AND PERFORMANCE SPACES

(See COLLEGES AND UNIVERSITIES/Southern Methodist University, above)

STARPLEX AMPHITHEATER

(See FAIR PARK, above)

TEATRO DALLAS

2204 Commerce (75201) • 741-1135 • W

The works presented here reflect Dallas' rich Hispanic heritage with plays by classical and contemporary Latin American and Hispanic American playwrights. Also dance performances.

THEATRE THREE

2800 Routh Street (75201), in the Quadrangle • 871-3300 • W+

This theater-in-the-round presents year-round productions of a wide variety of plays, musical revues, and occasional children's theater.

Dance

ANITA N. MARTINEZ BALLET FOLKLORICO

4422 Live Oak (75204) • 828-0181

A professional Hispanic dance company that puts on a number of performances each year. Call for schedule.

DALLAS BLACK DANCE THEATRE

2627 Flora Street (75221) • 871-2376

The 12 members of the city's oldest continuously operating dance company perform modern dance by well-known choreographers. Performances are given at the Meyerson Center, the Majestic Theatre, and at other performance spaces in the city.

FORT WORTH DALLAS BALLET

696-3932

This is not a merger of the Fort Worth and Dallas ballet companies, as the name may imply, but rather an expansion of the performances of the professional Fort Worth Ballet to Dallas to fill in the void left when the Dallas Ballet was dissolved in 1988. Dallas performances are usually held at the Music Hall in Fair Park.

Music

DALLAS BACH SOCIETY

P.O. Box 140201, 75214-0201

Not just Bach, but the full range of Baroque and Classical period music is performed under the auspices of this society. Its season runs from September–April with at least one performance each month. Most performances are given in the Morton H. Meyerson Symphony Center.

DALLAS CHAMBER ORCHESTRA

(Office) Sammons Center for the Arts, 3630 Harry Hines Blvd. (75219) 520-3121

This group performs classic works from the seventeenth and eighteenth centuries. Concerts are European style—without a conductor. The orchestra usually performs eight concerts in its September–May season at various locations around the city. Individual tickets: Adults $17, seniors $12, students $10.

DALLAS CLASSIC GUITAR SOCIETY

P.O. Box 190823 (75219) • 528-3733

The greatest classical guitarists in the world have appeared in concert with the society, including: Andres Segovia, John Williams, Julian Bream, and Christopher Parkening. The Society's season runs from September through April with at least one concert each month in two series. The International Series, featuring the best in the world, is held at the Morton H. Meyerson Symphony Center; and the Master Series, which showcases outstanding but lesser known international guitarists, is held at SMU's Caruth Auditorium.

DALLAS JAZZ ORCHESTRA

P.O. Box 743875 (75374) • 644-8833
A 20-piece big band that plays original and traditional big band jazz. It gives a spring and fall concert at the Meyerson Symphony Center and other performances around the city, including free summer concerts on Sunday afternoons in various city parks.

DALLAS OPERA

(Office) The Centrum, 3102 Oak Lawn, Suite 450 (75219)
443-1043 (tickets 443-1000)
Nationally known, the Dallas Opera Company has been staging the classics for more than 40 years. Its November–February season usually features five operas performed at Fair Park Music Hall. Single tickets range from $25 to $104.

DALLAS SYMPHONY ORCHESTRA

Morton H. Meyerson Symphony Center, 2301 Flora Street (75201),
at Pearl (DART Light Rail PEARL Station) • 871-4000 (box office 692-0203)
When the calendar turns over to the year 2000, the Dallas Symphony will celebrate its hundredth anniversary. The Symphony presents a full schedule of programs from late August through May in its Classical and SuperPops Series featuring a variety of guest artists and conductors. It also performs during the summer in the parks and at various events, including the International Summer Music Festival.

DALLAS WIND SYMPHONY

528-5576
The 45-piece orchestra is known as "America's Premier Windband" since it is the only professional civilian wind band active in the nation. Local concerts are at The Meyerson.

DALLAS PUBLIC LIBRARY AFTERNOON CONCERTS

1515 Young Street (75201) • 670-1700 • W+
Outstanding local musicians and singers perform in these free concerts put on in the main library auditorium or in the outside plaza on most Sundays at 3 P.M. every month except November–January.

GREATER DALLAS YOUTH ORCHESTRA

(Office) Sammons Center for the Arts, 3630 Harry Hines Blvd. (75219)
528-7747
The Greater Dallas Youth Orchestra (GDYO) offers a continuum of musical education for young musicians (ages five through high school) who have been selected by competitive auditions. The GDYO puts on four concerts a year in The Meyerson Symphony Center, including the annual "Side-by-Side" concert

with the Dallas Symphony. In addition, depending on age and training, the students may participate in one or more of another half dozen or so concerts as members of the Young Performers Orchestra, the Philharmonic Orchestra, or the Dallas String Ensemble, all of which give concerts in various citywide locations.

SAMMONS JAZZ

(Office) Sammons Center for the Arts, 3630 Harry Hines Blvd. (75219) 520-7788

This is the only ongoing jazz performance series in the Metroplex featuring local jazz artists who play all forms—from swing and bebop to Dixieland and fusion. The sessions are held in Meadows Hall at the Sammons Center the first Wednesday of each month 7 P.M. to 10 P.M. February–December. Tickets $12–$16.

TURTLE CREEK CHORALE

Morton H. Meyerson Symphony Center, 2301 Flora Street (75201), at Pearl (DART Light Rail PEARL Station) • 526-3214

This 200-member male chorus performs concerts ranging from Bach to Broadway. Most performances are in The Meyerson.

Theater

DALLAS SUMMER MUSICALS

(Office) 6013 Berkshire Lane (75225) • 691-7200 (tickets 373-8000)

Every June–August since 1941, this nonprofit organization has brought national touring companies of Broadway shows to the Fair Park Music Hall. Ignoring the seasonal limits of its name, the organization also presents the State Fair Musical and other shows, ranging from Las Vegas-style revues to drama, in the fall and winter.

DEEP ELLUM OPERA COMPANY

501 Second Avenue (75226), at Hickory • 823-2907

This company offers alternative theater. Its August–May season usually includes about seven shows running weekends. The company is located and performs at the Hickory Street Annex Theater.

THE GRYPHON PLAYERS

526-1158

Classical works from Euripides to Shaw and the absurdist theater of Beckett and Ionesco and others are the forte of this company, which uses a variety of performance spaces.

KITCHEN DOG THEATRE

McKinney Avenue Contemporary (The MAC), 312 McKinney Avenue (75204) • 953-1055

Originally formed by students in SMU's Graduate Actor Training Program, this small company has evolved to be the resident company at The MAC. The ensemble is committed to producing works that challenge our moral and social consciences, both classic and original works. They drew their name from Samuel Beckett's *Waiting for Godot*. Tickets $8–$12.

SHAKESPEARE FESTIVAL OF DALLAS

(Office) Sammons Center for the Arts, 3630 Harry Hines Blvd. (75219) 559-2778

With more than a quarter of a century of productions behind it, this is the oldest free Shakespeare festival in the Southwest and the second oldest in the nation, giving up the oldest title only to New York City's festival. Each summer it presents two of the Bard's plays outdoors in Samuell-Grand Park Amphitheater, 6200 East Grand. Performances are Tuesday–Sunday evenings at 8:15 (gates open at 7:30), with the two plays rotating and each play performed three days each week for six weeks. More than 60,000 attend each season. Bring a blanket or lawn chair and insect repellent. During the rest of the year the sponsoring organization offers its Spotlight Series, which features highly acclaimed actors performing unique interpretations of Shakespeare's greatest works, usually in the Majestic Theatre.

SHOPPING

DALLAS FARMERS MARKET

1010 South Pearl (75201) • 939-2808 • Open daily dawn to dusk • W

One of the few remaining farmers markets in the country, it is also one of the largest, consisting of open sheds spread over four city-owned blocks. In the spring and fall the Dallas Chapter of the American Institute of Wine and Food sponsors cooking classes taught by some of Dallas' finest chefs. Classes are held in the Market Resource Kitchen.

GALLERIA

LBJ Frwy. (I-635), at Dallas Parkway North (75240) • 972-702-7100 W+ but not all areas

There are more than 200 stores in this four-level mall including Macy's, Marshall Field's Nordstrom, Saks Fifth Avenue, and Tiffany & Co. Patterned after the barrel-vaulted glass atrium style of the nineteenth-century Galleria Vittorio Emanuele in Milan, Italy, this bright mall also features an indoor ice rink and the attached Westin Hotel.

HIGHLAND PARK VILLAGE

Preston Road at Mockingbird Lane (75205) • 559-2740 • W

One of the first shopping centers in the country when it was built in 1931, the Village has been continuously updated and is now the home of an eclectic collection of shops and restaurants that includes both the ordinary and some prestigious international shops and boutiques that could be equally at home on Los Angeles' Rodéo Drive.

INWOOD TRADE CENTER

Inwood Road (75247), two blocks west of IH-35E • 689-4222 • W variable

This is an example of the many outlet centers in Dallas. Smart shoppers may find some excellent quality products in the stores here at outlet prices. Among the stores are AtCost Warehouse, Accessory Mart, Bottoms Up, Clothes Out Closet, Crate & Barrel Outlet, Design Lighting and Accessories, Designers Group, Far East Menswear, The Real Outlet, Second Base, Shoe Fair, and The Sofa Source.

LOVE FIELD ANTIQUE MALL

6500 Cedar Springs (75235), at Mockingbird, across from the entrance to Love Field • W

The ads for this mall describe it as the largest antique and classic car mall in the United States. There are approximately 250 antique and collectibles dealer booths and a section of classic cars, all under one roof in this air-conditioned 70,000-square-foot building. Whether you're a classic car buff or not, the collection here is worth a visit. Restaurant.

NORTHPARK CENTER

Northwest Hwy. (Loop 12), at North Central Expressway (US 75) (75231) (DART Light Rail PARK LANE Station. Shuttle bus to mall) • 363-7441 • W+ but not all areas

The most popular (and profitable) Neiman Marcus in the chain is located in this mall, along with Abercrombie & Fitch, Lord & Taylor, Barneys New York, Foley's, Dillard's, JC Penney, and more than 150 other specialty stores and restaurants. Northpark Center opened in 1965 and was considered the most elegant mall in Dallas. It has continued to maintain its upscale ambiance for shoppers while, at the same time, attracting non-shoppers to its frequent art displays, activities, and festivities. A Dallas Convention and Visitors Bureau booth is here.

RED BIRD MALL

3662 West Camp Wisdom Road (75237), at US 67 • 296-1491 • W+

While most of the other major malls are in central or north Dallas, this one serves south Dallas and the southern suburbs. Dillard's, Foley's, JC Penney, and Sears anchor over 140 specialty stores.

THE SHOPS AND GALLERIES OF THE CRESCENT

200 Cedar Springs (75201), at Maple • 871-8500 • W

The Crescent, named for its fanlike shape, is a complex of a hotel, an office center, and a small outdoor shopping village that offers a truly distinctive collection of specialty and antique shops, art galleries, and restaurants. Closed Sunday.

WEST END MARKETPLACE

603 Munger Avenue (75202), at Market Street (DART Light Rail WEST END Station) • 748-4801 • W (Elevator entrance on Munger near Planet Hollywood entrance)

Located in the heart of the West End Historic District, this combination shopping and entertainment center includes four floors in three adjoining buildings and houses unique shops, fast food eateries, restaurants, and a multi-nightclub complex. You can buy everything from T-shirts and souvenirs to fine Texas wines and art in various media created by local artists and artisans.

KIDS' STUFF

DALLAS AQUARIUM

(See FAIR PARK, above)

DALLAS CHILDREN'S THEATER
Crescent Theater, 2215 Cedar Springs (75201), at Maple • 978-0110 • W
Most of the dozen productions put on by this professional company each year are family oriented, rather than strictly for children, and they often deal with serious subjects. Performances are also given at El Centro College Theater at Main and Market, downtown.

DALLAS THEATER CENTER TEEN/CHILDREN'S THEATER
Kalita Humphreys Theater, 3636 Turtle Creek (75219) • 526-8210
W call ahead
Children's classics are the favorites among the several productions this company puts on each year. The teens and children in the productions are from the Dallas Theater Center's own theater school.

DALLAS PUPPET THEATRE
2266 Valley View Center (75240) • 972-716-0230 • W
This company of puppeteers puts on about a half-dozen shows a year, mostly lighthearted adaptations of classic children's stories. Shows are aimed at the youngsters, so they are put on weekend afternoons and rarely last more than an hour.

MALIBU FUN CENTER & MALIBU GRAND PRIX
11130 and 11150 Malibu Drive (75229), *take Walnut Hill Ln. exit off Stemmons Frwy. (IH-35E) and go west to Malibu Dr.* • 620-7576 (Fun Center), 247-5318 (Grand Prix) • Open daily, call for hours • Admission free, pay by the game
This side-by-side entertainment complex includes four miniature golf courses, batting cages, video games, bumper boats, and scaled-down racing cars sized for both adults and children 8 and up.

MODEL TRAIN EXHIBIT
Dallas Children's Medical Center, 1935 Motor St. (75235), between Stemmons Frwy. (IH-35E) and Harry Hines Blvd. • 640-2000 • Open daily 5:30 A.M.–10 P.M. Free • W+
The largest permanent model train exhibit in the U.S. is in the lobby of this children's medical center. The $400,000 train exhibit has eight trains running simultaneously over more than 1,000 feet of track, which winds around models of some of America's most famous landmarks, including Mount Rushmore, the Grand Canyon, and even the Dallas skyline. Hospital parking costs $1.50 for the first hour.

VIRTUAL WORLD
9330 North Central Expressway (75231), at Park Ln. in UA Theater Plaza 265-9664
In this digital playworld you can be the pilot, controlling a 30-foot-tall walking tank or flying a souped-up hovercraft in a space race. Prices for the right to be a virtual warrior go from $7–$9. This gives you about 20 minutes of game time, which includes a mission briefing, about 10 minutes of cockpit time, and a mission review. Call for reservations.

OFFBEAT

THE CONSPIRACY MUSEUM

110 South Market (75202), between Main and Commerce, downtown (DART Light Rail WEST END Station) • 741-3040 • Monday–Friday 10–6, Saturday–Sunday 10–7 • Monday–Friday $5 person. Weekends: adults $7, seniors $6, children $3 • W variable

This small, privately funded museum came into existence because so many people rejected the Warren Commission Report that Oswald assassinated President Kennedy. The exhibits present a case for the theory that someone other than Oswald did it. The displays also offer theories on the assassinations and cover-ups of Presidents Lincoln, Garfield, and McKinley, as well as of Bobby Kennedy and Martin Luther King. The museum staff conducts complimentary 30–45 minute walking tours of the JFK assassination area most weekends at 11, 1, and 3.

DALLAS UNDERGROUND PEDESTRIANWAYS AND SKYBRIDGES

Downtown • (Nearest entrance from DART Light Rail AKARD Station) Open normal business hours weekdays • Free • W variable (Elevators at some entrances)

Forget the downtown traffic. On weekdays you can get around much of downtown without crossing a street by using the more than two miles of underground pedestrianway tunnels (and elevated skybridges) that are lined with shops and restaurants. A few exit on the street, but most exit to the lobbies of major office buildings and hotels. One even gets you right into the heart of Thanks-Giving Square.

MEDIEVAL TIMES DINNER AND TOURNAMENT

2021 North Stemmons Frwy. (IH-35E) (75207), at Market Center Blvd. 761-1800 or 800-229-9900 • Tuesday–Saturday evenings, Sunday afternoon. Closed Monday • Adults about $36, seniors about $32, children under 12 about $22 • Reservations recommended • W variable

The year is 1093 and you are the dinner guests in the (air-conditioned) castle of the royal family. As you dine in authentic Middle Ages style, without utensils, you'll witness medieval pageantry, horsemanship, swordplay, falconry, sorcery, and a jousting tournament.

ANNUAL EVENTS

January

SOUTHWESTERN BELL COTTON BOWL CLASSIC

New Year's Day • Cotton Bowl Stadium, Fair Park (Cotton Bowl Classic Association Office, 1300 West Mockingbird Lane, 75356) • 634-7525 Game tickets $40–$50 • Parking $8 • W+ but not all areas (access at Stadium Sections 4–7)

After Dallas entrepreneur J. Curtis Sanford watched SMU battle Stanford in the 1936 Rose Bowl, he decided that Dallas should have a bowl game of its own. The result was this football classic which was started in 1937 and has been played in the same stadium and on the same field for more than 60 years. The two football teams that tangle in the present Classic are selected from the 38 universities that make up the Western Athletic, The PAC 10, and the Big 12—conferences that are spread over 20 states stretching from the Mississippi River to Hawaii.

USA FILM FESTIVAL/KIDFILM FESTIVAL

Saturday and Sunday in mid-month • AMC Glen Lake Theater, 9450 North Central Expressway, at Walnut Hill Ln. (office 2917 Swiss Ave. 75204) 972-395-9034 • Tickets $3 • W

This is the oldest and largest children's film festival in the nation, featuring a diverse line-up of film and videos. Events include appearances by acclaimed TV and film makers.

January–February

DALLAS WINTER BOAT SHOW

Late January–early February • Dallas Market Hall, 2200 Stemmons Frwy. (IH-35E), *take Market Center exit off IH-35E,* **(office P.F. Smith Enterprises, 6220 North Belt Line Rd., Suite 208, Irving 75063) • 972-550-1052 • Adults $6, children under 12 $3, under 3 free • W+**

This show displays hundreds of boats and accessories and always features new models of all types of boats, from 40-foot cruisers to personal watercraft. Most are available at special boat show prices.

February

TRI DELTA CHARITY ANTIQUES SHOW

Thursday–Sunday late in month • Dallas Convention Center, 650 South Griffin, at Young (DART Light Rail CONVENTION CENTER Station) (office P.O. Box 8070, 75205) • 691-9306 • Tickets $8 • W+

Dealers from U.S. and abroad sell fine antiques and art at this popular charity event, which has been presented every February or early March for more than 20 years.

March

DALLAS BLOOMS

All month • Dallas Arboretum and Botanical Gardens, 8525 Garland Road (75218) • 327-8263 • Adults $6, seniors $5, children 6–12 $3, under 5 free. Parking $2 • W variable

When spring comes to Dallas, Dallas Blooms at the arboretum has a spectacular display of more than 200,000 flowering bulbs that color the gardens.

DALLAS NEW CAR AUTO SHOW

Five days in mid-month • Dallas Convention Center, 650 South Griffin, at Young (DART Light Rail CONVENTION CENTER Station) • 939-2700 • W+

This is one of the largest new car shows in the country. Almost all the new models, both domestic and foreign, are on display.

April

USA FILM FESTIVAL

Eight days in mid-month • AMC Glen Lake Theater, 9450 North Central Expressway, at Walnut Hill Ln. (office 2917 Swiss Ave., 75204) • 821-6300 • W

In addition to showings of the best new American and foreign films, this eight-day event includes retrospectives of an outstanding director and actor, and opening and closing night premiers of new works by attending artists. Started in 1971, it is now one of the oldest film festivals in the U.S.

May

ARTFEST

Friday–Sunday of Memorial Day weekend • Fair Park (Artfest c/o The 500, Inc. 11300 North Central Expressway, Suite 415, 75243) • 361-2011 Admission $5 (children under 4 free) • W+

Typically over 800 artists from across the U.S. apply to participate in this three-day event, which draws about 80,000 patrons and is the largest art show and outdoor festival of its kind in the Southwest. Applicants submit works to a jury, which selects about 300 pieces representing all mediums. Activities include live and silent art auctions, continuous musical entertainment, and 5K and 10K runs for adults as well as the kiddie kilometer race for kids. Kids also get to see and participate in free arts and crafts activities and special entertainment.

June

HOOP-IT-UP BONANZA

Saturday and Sunday in mid-month • Record at Ross in the Historic West End District (DART Light Rail WEST END Station) (office 4006 Belt Line Road, Suite 230, 75244) • 972-991-1110 • Free for spectators • W

What started as a popular street basketball tournament in Dallas in 1986 is now a huge charity event running from March through November. More than 50,000 three-man teams enter competitions on a 55-city tour in the U.S. and tours in Europe, Canada, and Mexico. Basketball players of all ages can participate in the amateur three-on-three games with players matched by age, skill, and height. Wheelchair teams are included. The winners advance to regional action then can go on to the World Finals, where the top team meets a team of NBA legends. In Dallas, 300,000 spectators come to see the games. Music and entertainment.

August–September

DALLAS MORNING NEWS DANCE FESTIVAL

Labor Day weekend • Artist Square/Arts District (DART Light Rail ST. PAUL Station) • 953-1977 • Free • W

This weekend extravaganza showcases the dance talent in the Metroplex. It usually includes performances by a number of dance troupes, including the Fort Worth Dallas Ballet, The Anita N. Martinez Ballet Folklorico, The Dallas Black Dance Theater, and the dance students at Booker T. Washington High School.

GRAND PRIX OF DALLAS

Friday–Sunday Labor Day weekend • Downtown around the Reunion Arena (office 3611 Fairmont Street, 75219. 522-5544) • Tickets: 620-PRIX (620-7749) Admission • W

Approximately 100,000 spectators attend this three-day charity event that features a variety of sports-car races over a 1.5 mile, 9 turn temporary street circuit. Races include the Exxon World Sports Car Championship, with cars capable of 200 mph on straightaways.

September

MONTAGE

Saturday–Sunday in mid-month • Arts District (DART Light Rail ST. PAUL Station) • 361-2011 • W

The streets of the Arts District are turned into a showcase for a variety of art forms including theater, music, dance, painting, sculpture, and photography for this outdoor family festival.

September–October

STATE FAIR OF TEXAS

Twenty-four days in late September and early October • Fair Park, east of downtown, bounded by Parry Ave., Cullum Blvd., Fitzhugh Ave., and Washington Ave. (office P.O. Box 150009, 75315) • 565-9931 • Adults $9, seniors and kids under 48-inches tall $5, under 3 free • W variable

With annual attendance figures well over three million, this is the largest state fair in the U.S. It may also have the largest greeter of any state fair. Big Tex, a 52-foot giant cowboy wearing seven-foot-seven-inch-high boots and a five-foot high, 75-gallon cowboy hat, greets all his visitors with a booming "Howdy folks!" The first State Fair was held at this location in 1886. That Fair opened with a downtown parade, and each year that tradition is continued with an opening day parade along Main Street. As with all state fairs, the livestock competitions (with an average of 10,000 entries), agricultural exhibits, cooking contests, and the arts play a continuing role. But there's more, much, much more. In fact, each year they seem to cram in more exhibits, more musical entertainment, more shows, and more demonstrations. Events of each Fair are built around a theme, but almost always feature animal acts, circus acts, puppet shows, U.S. Marine Corps Drum and Bugle Corps and silent Drill Team performances, and free concerts by a variety of well-known entertainers on the Main-Stage. There's also always a major auto show in the Automobile Building, and all the Fair Park museums (*see* Fair Park, above) have extended hours and special exhibits. Plus there's a special musical in the Music Hall, major college football games in the Cotton Bowl, loads of events and activities for kids, and a carnival midway with the tallest Ferris wheel in North America, an 80-year-old carousel, and about 60 other rides.

November–December

CHRISTMAS AT THE ARBORETUM

Late November to after Christmas • Dallas Arboretum and Botanical Gardens, 8525 Garland Road (75218) • 327-8263 • Adults $6, seniors $5, children 6–12 $3, under 5 free. Parking $2 • W variable

The highlight of this month-long event is the tour of the historic 21,000-square-foot DeGolyer House, which is decorated from floor to ceiling with displays of thousands of twinkling lights, trees, and ornaments. The 66 acres of gardens display holiday-colored pansies, hollies, and evergreens.

RESTAURANTS

($ = under $12, $$ = $12–$30, $$$ = over $30 for one person excluding drinks, tax, and tip.)

ADELMO'S RISTORANTE

4537 Cole Avenue (75205), at Knox • 559-0325 • Lunch and dinner Monday–Friday, dinner only Saturday. Closed Sunday and major holidays $$ • Cr • W

A quick scan of the dinner menu will show that this warm little bistro is not your everyday Italian restaurant. Adelmo's creative cuisine is inspired by the eastern Mediterranean region, from France to the Middle East. The most popular specialties of the house include a 20-oz. veal chop and grilled rack of lamb. The owner-operated restaurant is in a charming two-story house with close but cozy seating. Bar.

ALESSIO'S

4117 Lomo Alto (75219), just north of Lemmon Avenue • 521-3585 Lunch Monday–Friday, dinner daily • $$–$$$ • Cr • W

The Northern Italian specialties here include grilled double veal chops steeped in five herbs, *fettucine Genovese,* and *gnocchi* made with Gorgonzola. The decor includes original paintings. Pianist and vocalist on Friday–Saturday. Semi-formal dress requested. Bar.

ANTARES

300 Reunion Blvd. (75207), in Reunion Tower (DART Light Rail UNION Station) • 712-7145 • Lunch Monday–Saturday, brunch Sunday, dinner daily $$ • Cr • W

At 50-stories about the street, the menu runs second to the view, but a close second. The restaurant gently revolves and gives you an enchanting 360-degree panorama of the city in a little less than an hour. The menu, which features New American cuisine, is weighted toward seafood specialties. Bar. Semi-formal in evening.

ANZU

4620 McKinney Avenue, (75205) (DART Light Rail ST. PAUL Station to connect with McKinney Avenue Trolley) • 526-7398 • Lunch Monday–Friday, dinner Monday–Saturday. Closed Sunday, Thanksgiving, Christmas, New Year's Day • $$–$$$ • Cr • W+

Pacific Rim and nouvelle Japanese fare are dominant on the menu with Japanese-influenced staples like *udon* noodles, sushi, sake, and a variety of stir-fry, tempura, and teriyaki dishes. However, in a melding of East meets West, the menu also includes more eclectic choices that loosely fall under the heading of New American cuisine. Intimate booths with a flight of bright-colored origami birds fluttering across the ceiling. Bar.

ARTHUR'S

8350 North Central Expressway (US 75) (75206), at 1000 Campbell Center, *take Caruth-Haven Exit #13* • 361-8833 • Lunch Monday–Friday, dinner Monday–Saturday. Closed Sunday and major holidays • $$ • Cr • W

As it approaches its fiftieth anniversary, Arthur's retains its sedate and classy old-styled dining room with crystal chandeliers, white linens, and candlelight.

And the menu remains much the same as it has been to attract Dallasites for close to half a century with offerings of steaks, seafood, lamb, veal, fowl, and pasta entrées. Live music and dancing nightly in the lounge.

BEAU NASH

2215 Cedar Springs (75201), at McKinney, in Hotel Crescent Court (DART Light Rail ST. PAUL Station to connect with McKinney Avenue Trolley) 871-3240 • Breakfast, lunch, and dinner daily. Closed major holidays $$–$$$ • Cr • W+

This hotel dining room offers casual dining in an elegant setting. The chefs working in the open kitchen prepare dishes that creatively fuse New American cuisine with a touch of northern Italian, such as steak pizza, lobster sandwiches, and angel hair pasta with lump crabmeat. Music Thursday–Saturday evenings. Lounge.

CAFÉ ATHENEE

5365 Spring Valley (75240), at Monfort • 239-8060 • Lunch and dinner Monday–Saturday. Closed Sunday, Thanksgiving, Christmas • $$ • Cr • W+

Romanian (Transylvanian), Greek, and European cuisine in a cozy English library setting may seem incongruous, but this popular restaurant carries it off. Entrées include beef, veal, chicken, pork, seafood, duck, and quail. They make their own breads, pasta, desserts, and Romanian sausage.

CAFÉ PACIFIC

24 Highland Park Village (75205), Mockingbird Lane at Preston Road 526-1170 • Lunch and dinner Monday–Saturday. Closed Sunday, Thanksgiving, Christmas, New Year's Day • $$–$$$ • Cr • W+

To get you off to a pleasant start, there's a complimentary dish of crisp sweet-potato fries. Although there are meat items on the menu, the house is most famous for its seafood specialties. These include shrimp, crab cakes, and the catch-of-the-day special, which may be a culinary delight such as Chilean sea bass or Gulf red snapper. All served in an intimate, sophisticated club-like glass and brass setting. Bar.

CELEBRATION

4503 West Lovers Lane (75209), between Inwood and Lemmon • 351-5681 Lunch and dinner daily. Closed Thanksgiving, Christmas Eve, and Christmas $ • Cr • W+

From the outside it looks like home (a rustic house), and inside, it's as close as you'll get to down-home cooking in a restaurant. Meat loaf, pot roast, southern fried or baked chicken, and other homey mainstays are all on the menu. The unpretentious, hearty meals are served family style, with serve-yourself bowls of salads and loads of southern-style vegetables. And just like at home, most meals even include seconds. Bar.

CHEZ GERARD

4444 McKinney (75205), at Armstrong (DART Light Rail ST. PAUL Station to connect with McKinney Avenue Trolley) • 522-6865 • Lunch Monday–Friday, dinner Monday–Saturday. Closed Sunday and major holidays • $$–$$$ • Cr • W+

This is the type of small, cozy restaurant you'd expect to find in the French countryside, right down to the flowery print wall covering and lace curtains.

And the menu promotes the same feeling of authenticity with substantial, time-honored Gallic recipes interpreted with a respect for tradition combined with a spark of creativity. All elegantly presented and pleasing to the palate. Outdoor dining area. Bar.

CITY CAFÉ

5757 West Lovers Lane (75209), just west of North Dallas Tollway • 351-2233
Lunch and dinner daily. Closed major holidays • $$–$$$ • Cr • W+
It started out as a casual neighborhood restaurant that offered variety to its local customers by changing the menu every two weeks. Except for a few customer favorites, like the famed fresh tomato soup, the City Café still changes the hand-painted menu every two weeks, rotating dishes of seafood, veal, game, beef, pasta, fowl, pork, and lamb. But the biggest change is that the little bistro's reputation for culinary creativity has broadened its following way out of the local area. Bar.

DAKOTA'S

600 North Akard Street (75201), at San Jacinto (DART Light Rail AKARD Station) • 740-4001 • Lunch Monday–Friday, dinner daily • $$–$$$ • Cr W+ elevator
This elegant downtown and downstairs restaurant offers courtyard dining by a cascading waterfall or inside dining in a grill room setting of rich wood paneling and marble. Entrées grilled over native Texas woods highlight the menu of classic American cuisine with a touch of southwest influence. A bargain is the three-course, *prix fixe* twilight menu offered until 6 P.M. for about $16. Bar. Pianist Friday–Saturday evenings.

DEL FRISCO'S DOUBLE EAGLE STEAKHOUSE

5251 Spring Valley Road (75240) • 972-490-9000 • Dinner Monday–Saturday. Closed Sunday, Thanksgiving, Christmas Day • $$–$$$ • Cr • W+
It's not often you'll hear "oohs" and "ahhs" from jaded expense account diners, but those sounds almost become a chorus here as the meat-eaters dig into the thick prime, aged beef that is the hallmark of this chain. The menu reflects the restaurant name with the major items—all steak, steak, steak. They also have a few other items on the menu, including lobster, but they seem almost an afterthought. Warm, classy Texas saloon atmosphere. Bar.

8.0 RESTAURANT AND BAR

2800 Routh Street (75201), in The Quadrangle between McKinney and Laclede • 969-9321 • Lunch and dinner daily. Closed Thanksgiving and Christmas Day • $ • Cr • W
The eclectic menu plays both sides of the cholesterol street with a variety of burgers served with fries on one side and on the other imaginative vegetarian dishes, such as grilled portobello mushrooms with brown rice and a fresh vegetable. Daily blue- and green-plate specials often sell out early. A number of local artists contributed to the funky wall murals. Patio. Bar. Trendy entertainment Thursday–Saturday nights bring in wall-to-wall people.

THE FRENCH ROOM

1321 Commerce Street (75202), at Akard Street in The Adolphus Hotel (DART Light Rail AKARD Station) • 742-8200 or 800-221-9083 (reservations required)

Dinner Monday–Saturday. Closed Sunday and major holidays • $$$ • Cr
W+ special elevator

Opulent. Posh. Sumptuous. Plush. Beautiful. Those are just a few of the
words used to describe The French Room's setting. With its baroque-painted
ceiling, layered tablecloths, drapes, and hand-blown crystal chandeliers of sev-
enteenth century design, the room evokes the sensation of entering a realm in
which King Louis XV would feel at home. The cuisine is neoclassic, that is, clas-
sic French cooking creatively adapted to contemporary American taste. A *prix
fixe* chef's menu with several choices for each course is available for $56 ($82.50
with wine). Semi-formal dress. Bar. Music Friday–Saturday.

INDIA PALACE

12817 Preston Road (75230), *take Preston Road exit 21 off IH-35E*
972-392-0190 • Lunch and dinner daily • $$ • Cr • W

The extensive menu of Northern Indian dishes here gives you a wide choice
of exotic tastes to try. The intense dry heat of the traditional tandoor ovens generates the flavor while retaining the moistness of many of the dishes, such as
the low-fat tandoori chicken. India Palace offers many grilled items using beef,
chicken, and lamb, and numerous vegetarian dishes all imbued with delicate
spices as well as curries and curried dishes. You can call the shots on how spicy
hot you want your food. Bar.

JAVIER'S

**4912 Cole Avenue (75205), between Monticello and Harvard • 521-4211
Dinner daily • $$ • Cr • W**

They've been serving authentic Mexican food here for around 20 years. The
decor is cozy old colonial Mexico, but the cuisine leans more towards modern,
sophisticated Mexico City-style. No Tex-Mex here. Instead there are dishes like
steak prepared with mushrooms and brandy. A little hard to find. Call for
directions. Bar.

JENNIVINE

**3605 McKinney Avenue (75204), between Blackburn Street and Lemmon
Avenue (DART Light Rail ST. PAUL Station to connect with McKinney
Avenue Trolley) • 528-6010 • Lunch and dinner Monday–Saturday. Closed
Sunday and Christmas Day • $$ • Cr • W**

The menu at this charming European-style bistro delightfully wanders
through British, French, Asian, and Southwestern U.S. dishes, often ingeniously
combined. Perhaps to give each of these culinary influences a fair chance, the
menu changes daily. Outdoor dining available. Bar.

LANDMARK CAFE

**3015 Oak Lawn Avenue (75219), at Cedar Springs Road in Melrose Hotel
521-5151 • Breakfast daily, lunch Monday–Friday and Sunday brunch, dinner
Monday–Saturday. Closed Saturday lunch, Sunday dinner. • $$$ • Cr • W+**

The bright and airy dining room, done in mirrors and marble, is the setting
for an eclectic menu featuring what the chef calls New World cuisine—an inno-
vative and creative blending of influences from Mexican, Italian, Cajun, Asian,
and Southwestern cuisines. Specialties include pasta-crusted salmon, beef ten-
derloin, grilled veal medallions, and sizzling shrimp. Especially popular for
business breakfasts and Sunday brunch. Semi-formal dress at dinner. Bar.

LA TRATTORIA LOMBARDI

2916 North Hall Street (75204), near McKinney Avenue • 954-0803 • Lunch Monday–Friday, dinner daily. Closed major holidays • $$–$$$ • Cr • W

For about two decades, old style Italian offerings have been the heart of the menu at this comfortable neighborhood trattoria-style restaurant. Pasta dishes include *Fettucine del Pescatore* (fettucine pasta served with shrimp, scallops, green lip mussels in garlic olive oil and herb sauce) and *Cannelloni Verdi Tricolore* (green cannelloni stuffed with meat and spinach and served with a red and white sauce). Outdoor dining available. Bar.

LAUREL'S

12720 Merit Drive (75251), in Sheraton Park Central Hotel • 851-2021 Dinner Monday–Saturday. Closed Sunday • $$$ • Cr • W+

The view of downtown though the floor-to-ceiling windows of this twentieth-floor North Dallas hotel is just the icing on the cake of the quiet and elegant setting that enhances the menu, featuring a cuisine that melds North and South American recipes. Entrées include steaks, rack of lamb, seafood, veal, and a mixed grill with antelope, lamb, and quail. *Prix fixe* menu, including wine, for about $50. Bar. Pianist or harpist nightly.

THE MANSION ON TURTLE CREEK

2821 Turtle Creek Blvd. (75219), at Gillespie St. in The Mansion on Turtle Creek hotel • 559-2100 or 800-527-5432 • Lunch and dinner daily $$$ • Cr • W

This is the only restaurant in Texas—not just the Metroplex, but all of Texas—to consistently earn a rating of five diamonds from AAA and five stars from Mobil. The restaurant is in a wing of a 1920s-era cattle baron's Italian Renaissance-style mansion converted to this award-winning hotel (*see* Accommodations, below). While opulent, the restaurant's rooms easily create a warm, residential ambiance, since they occupy what was originally the living room, the library, and the glass-walled veranda with a view of the landscaped courtyard. The cuisine is basically Southwestern with a Texas flair and is created by the long-time award-winning Executive Chef Dean Fearing. The menu is also delightfully varied and creative, making superlative use of seasonal, regional ingredients, including Hill Country game, to present offerings going from what are now classic Mansion starters, like tortilla soup and warm lobster taco, to sugarcane-glazed salmon and pan-seared ostrich filet. *Prixe fixe* dinner about $80. Bar. Music nightly. Semi-formal dress for dinner and Sunday brunch.

MEDITERRANEO

18111 Preston Rd. (75252), at Frankford Rd., *take Preston Rd. exit 21 off LBJ Frwy. (IH-635)* **• 972-447-0066 • Lunch Monday–Friday, dinner Monday–Saturday. Closed Sunday and major holidays • $$–$$$ • Cr • W+**

In keeping with its name, the menu features innovative cuisine based on that of Northern Italy and Southern France. The culinary creativity here can be seen in pasta dishes like linguini with smoked scallops, summer vegetables, mushrooms, extra virgin olive oil, and tomato-basil broth; or grilled double cut lamb chops with tomato glaze, herb goat cheese, and whipped potatoes. Bar. Classical guitarist Monday–Thursday dinner.

MIA'S

4322 Lemmon Avenue (75219) • 526-1020 • Lunch and dinner Monday–Saturday. Closed Sunday, Christmas, and New Year's Day • $$ MC, V • W+

This small, family-owned no-frills neighborhood restaurant takes Tex-Mex to new heights. All the classics are here: chimichangas, chiles rellenos, fajitas, flautas, enchiladas, chalupas; it's just that the dishes are all of the same high quality that Mama would serve to her own family. Beer and wine only. Family friendly service and large portions—some of the appetizers could make a meal.

MORTON'S OF CHICAGO

501 Elm Street (75202), in West End Historic District (DART Light Rail WEST END station) • 741-2277 • Dinner only daily. Closed major holidays • $$$ Cr • W call ahead

The dark woods and etched glass decor of this basement restaurant resemble that of a posh Edwardian men's club. No written menu. You order after your server has—usually flawlessly and sometimes passionately— proclaimed the whole list, complete with samples of the offerings of various types and sizes of prime steaks, some lamb, chicken, lobster (the most popular order after steaks), and other choices. Rounding off a meal with a cigar and brandy seems almost *de rigueur* here. Semi-formal dress. Bar. Another location at 14831 Midway in Addison (972-233-5858).

NATURA CAFÉ

2909 McKinney Avenue (75204) (DART Light Rail ST. PAUL Station to connect with McKinney Avenue Trolley) • 855-5483 • Lunch and dinner daily with late breakfast/brunch Saturday–Sunday • $–$$ • AE, MC, V • W

Totally organic, good-for-you food that also pleases the tastebuds is the order of the day here. Lots of imaginative vegetarian dishes, but also nutritionally OK versions of pizza, pasta, pork loin, venison, and other items that may be a healthful no-no elsewhere. Comfortably casual, artsy setting. Bar.

THE OLD WARSAW

2610 Maple Avenue (75201) • 528-0032 • Dinner only daily • $$$ • Cr • W

The "old" in the name has a double meaning since this is one of the oldest Continental restaurants in Dallas. Sticking to the tried-and-true, The Old Warsaw serves traditional French and other European fare like lobster crepes, steak *au poivre, chateaubriand,* braised pheasant, duckling, and rack of lamb. The darkly rich atmosphere of the mirrored room serves as a romantic background for strolling violinists who serenade you while you dine. Semi-formal dress. Bar.

THE PALM

701 Ross Avenue (75202), at Market in the West End Historic District (DART Light Rail WEST END Station) • 698-0474 • Lunch and dinner Monday–Friday, dinner only Saturday–Sunday. Closed Thanksgiving and Christmas Day • $$$ • Cr • W+

It's best known for its huge steaks, but if you want a BIG lobster they can satisfy that hunger, too. They claim that some of the ones they jet in from Maine are big enough to pilot the plane. The decor at this bustling chain steakhouse is simple with sawdust on the floor and colorful cartoon caricatures of local and other celebs on the wall. Besides beef and lobster, the menu also offers veal, seafood, and poultry as well as bountiful pasta dishes. Semi-formal dress. Bar.

PATRIZIO

25 Highland Park Village (75205), at Mockingbird Lane and Preston Road 522-7878 • Lunch and dinner daily. Closed Thanksgiving, Christmas, and New Year's Day • $$ • Cr • W

Oil paintings and oriental rugs set the mood in this Italian *trattoria* which serves traditional pizza and pasta of all kinds that are a cut above most of its competitors. Outdoor dining available. Bar. Another location (Patrizio North) at 1900 Preston Park Blvd. in Plano (972-964-2200).

PEGGY SUE BBQ

6600 Snider Plaza (75205), at Hillcrest and Daniels across from SMU 987-9188 • Lunch and dinner daily. Closed major holidays • $ • MC, V • W

As with any famed barbecue place, the oak-smoked meat is the reason customers come to Peggy Sue's. What's a little unusual here is that you get an extra reward in that the steamed vegetable sides are just as tasty and almost as famous. Beer and wine only. In business for 45 years and the decor pleasantly harks back to its start in the 1950s.

THE PYRAMID ROOM

1717 North Akard (75201), in Fairmont Hotel (DART Light Rail AKARD Station) • 720-2020 • Lunch Monday–Friday, dinner Monday–Saturday, Sunday brunch • $$$ • W+

If one item could sum up and embody the refined cosmopolitan ambiance of this restaurant, it would be the between-course champagne sorbet served in lighted, ice-sculpted cygnets. From the comfortable armchairs set at tables covered with brilliant linens to the glistening silver, the whole setting speaks of opulence and elegance. Continental menu. *Prix fixe* dinner about $36 ($58 with wine) is an excellent value. Music nightly. Semi-formal dress. Bar.

THE RIVIERA

7709 Inwood Road (75209), just south of Lovers Lane • 351-0094 Dinner daily. Closed major holidays • $$$ • Cr • W

Both Southern France and Northern Italy share the real Riviera on the Mediterranean, and the innovative cuisine at this petite restaurant is inspired by the classic dishes of both those sunny regions and the bounty of the sea. While some of the offerings are pure French or pure Italian in origin, most are a joyful blending of the two; like lobster with herbed potato *gnocchi*, marinated tomatoes, grilled red onions, and Dijon sauce. Semi-formal dress. Bar.

RUTH'S CHRIS STEAK HOUSE

5922 Cedar Springs Road (75235), between Inwood Road and Mockingbird Lane, two blocks south of the entrance to Love Field • 902-8080 or 800-544-0808, Ext. 07 • Dinner daily (lunch available two weeks prior to Christmas). Closed Thanksgiving and Christmas Day • $$$ • Cr • W+

The steaks are all aged, never-frozen, corn-fed prime beef. Except for the petite filet, portions are large. All are cooked in specially built broilers at 1700–1800 degrees, to lock in the juices, and served sizzling in melted butter. In addition to beef, the menu offers seafood, including lobster and King crab, lamb and veal chops, and chicken. Cigar-friendly bar. Second location at 17840 North Dallas Parkway, between Trinity Mills and Frankford (972-250-2244 or 800-544-0808 ext. 50).

S & D OYSTER COMPANY

2701 McKinney Avenue (75204), at Boll (DART Light Rail ST. PAUL Station to connect to McKinney Avenue Trolley) • 880-0111 • Lunch and dinner Monday–Saturday. Closed Sunday and major holidays • $$ • MC, V • W

S&D has been serving New Orleans-style seafood in this neighborhood-store setting for more than 20 years. Gumbo, raw oysters on the half shell, oyster loaf, shrimp, and a variety of other fresh Gulf seafood dishes are on the menu. All are simply prepared and you can have most of them broiled, boiled, or fried to your liking. Beer and wine only.

SONNY BRYAN'S SMOKEHOUSE

2202 Inwood Rd. (75235), near Harry Hines Blvd. • 357-7120 • Lunch only daily. Closed major holidays • $ • No Cr • W

With walls tinted by years of pit smoke and an all-pervading aroma of meat and spicy barbecue sauce, this shack is considered by many as a piece of Dallas history. First opened in 1958, it still offers seating in one-armed school desks or outside on picnic tables. More important, it still serves up tender brisket, ribs, and sausage that have pleased customers all these years. Beer only. Other locations at: 302 North Market, in the West End Historic District (744-1610); 325 North St. Paul, in the underground pedestrian tunnel, (979-0103); Macy's third level in Galleria (851-5131); 4701 Frankford at North Dallas Pkwy. (972-447-0102), and in Las Colinas at 4030 North MacArthur Blvd. (972-650-9564).

STAR CANYON

3102 Oak Lawn (75219), in The Centrum at Cedar Springs • 520-STAR (520-7827) • Lunch Monday–Friday, dinner daily. Closed major holidays $$$ • Cr • W+

Its Lone Star setting and Lone Star cuisine are so popular reservations are hard to come by. (If you're from out-of-town, try six weeks in advance.) Among the signature dishes is bone-in cowboy ribeye with red chile onion rings. Other New Texan dishes include roasted chicken with garlic whipped potatoes, grilled quail, grilled coriander-cured venison, and shark steak. All include a palate-pleasing twist, like the black-bean roast banana mash side, which accompanies the pan-seared salmon, and grits laced with bits of littleneck clams, which are served with the pork chops. Bar.

CLUBS AND BARS

Clubs and bars change almost as often as the phases of the moon. For current information about Dallas nightlife see the **Arts and Entertainment Guide** in the Friday edition of *The Dallas Morning News;* and the weekly *Dallas Observer* and *The Met,* which are available free at restaurants, clubs, and tourist attractions throughout the Dallas area. Following is a sampling of the clubs and bars in the city that were up-and-running and popular at the time this book was published. They are broken down by the music type.

Blues

Blue Cat Blues • 2617 Commerce Street in Deep Ellum • 744-CATS (744-2287)
The Bone • 2724 Elm Street in Deep Ellum • 744-BONE (744-2663)
Muddy Waters • 1518 Greenville Avenue • 823-1518

Caribbean

Dread-n-Irie • 2807 Commerce in Deep Ellum • 742-IRIE (742-4743)
Royal Rack Reggae Club • 1906 Greenville Avenue • 824-9733
Tropical Cove • 1820 West Mockingbird Lane • 630-5822

Country

Country 2000 • 10580 Stemmons Frwy. • 654-9595
Red River • 10310 Technology West • 972-263-0404
Sons of Herman Hall • 3414 Elm Street at Exposition • 747-4422
Stampede • 5818 LBJ Frwy. at Preston • 972-701-8081

Dance

Blind Lemon • 2805 Main Street in Deep Ellum • 939-0202
Club Blue Planet • 8796 North Central Expressway at Park Lane • 369-7009
Eden 2000 • 5500 Greenville Avenue • 361-9517
Lakeside • 3100 West Northwest Hwy. • 904-1770
Red Jacket • 3606 Greenville Avenue • 823-8333

Eclectic

Blue Mule • 1701 North Market #105 in West End • 761-0101
Club Clearview • 2806 Elm Street in Deep Ellum • 283-5358
Club Dada • 2720 Elm Street in Deep Ellum • 744-DADA (744-3232)
Dallas Alley • Market at Munger in West End Marketplace
972-988-WEST (972/988-9378)
Lizard Lounge • 2424 Swiss Avenue • 826-4768
Poor Richard's Pub • 1924 Greenville Avenue • 821-9891
Trees • 2709 Elm Street in Deep Ellum • 748-5009
Velvet E • 1906 McKinney at St. Paul • 969-5568

Latino, Tejano

Chances • 9840 North Central Expressway at Walnut Hill • 691-0300
Club Babalu • 2912 McKinney Avenue • 953-0300
Tejano Rodeo • 7331 Gaston Avenue • 321-5540

Jazz

Dreams Club • 7035 Greenville Avenue • 368-4981
Strictly Tabu • 4111 Lomo Alto • 528-5200
Sambucca • 2618 Elm Street • 744-0820
Terilli's • 2815 Greenville Avenue • 827-3993

ACCOMMODATIONS

($ = under $80, $$ = $80–$120, $$$ = $121–$180, $$$$ = $181–$250, $$$$$ = over $250)

Room tax 13%

THE ADOLPHUS

1321 Commerce Street (75202), downtown between Field and Akard (DART Light Rail AKARD Station) • 742-8200 or 800-221-9083 • $$$$–$$$$$ • W + 6 rooms • No-smoking rooms

The 22 floors in this hotel have 431 units including 20 suites ($$$$$) and 210 no-smoking rooms. Weekend discounts available. Children 11 and under stay free in room with parents. Check in 3 P.M. Check out 1 P.M. Inside access to rooms. Charge for local calls. Cable TV with free premium channel and pay TV. VCR available. Captioned TV, visual alarms, and special phones for the hearing impaired. In-room honor bar. Wet bar in suites. Free coffee available. Modem link in rooms. Fire intercom system. Bell service. Room service. Exercise room. Guest memberships available for nearby health club and for tennis and golf. Business services available. Gift shop, beauty shop, barber shop. Free newspaper and magazines. Restaurants serving all meals (*see* Restaurants–The French Room, above). Lounge with entertainment and dancing. Garage valet parking $10. Free downtown transportation available. Afternoon tea in Grand Lobby Monday–Friday 3–5 (reservations suggested). Built in 1912 by beer baron Adolphus Busch, The Adolphus still retains Old World opulence. Rated one of best hotels in the United States in *Conde Nast Traveler's* magazine Readers Choice Awards.

BEST WESTERN MARKET CENTER

2023 Market Center Blvd. (75207), at IH-35E (Stemmons Frwy.) 741-9000 or 800-275-7419 • $–$$$ • W+ 2 rooms • No-smoking rooms

The 98 rooms in this three-story Best Western include 47 no-smoking. Senior and weekend discounts available. Children 16 and under stay free in room with parents. Check in noon. Check out noon. Inside and outside access to rooms. Charge for local calls. Cable TV with HBO. Captioned TV, visual alarms, and special phones for the hearing impaired. Coffeemakers in rooms. Free coffee available in lobby 6:30–9 A.M. Modem link in rooms. Fire intercom system. Bell service. Room service. Outdoor pool. Guest memberships available for health club. Business services available. Self service laundry. One-day dry cleaning. Free continental breakfast. Restaurant serving all meals (dinner under $10). Bar. Free outside parking.

COMFORT INN

8901 R.L. Thornton Freeway (75228), *take Exit 52B from IH-30 East* **• 324-4475 $$$ • W+ 2 rooms • No-smoking rooms**

This two-story inn has 42 units including 4 suites and 20 no-smoking rooms. Senior, weekend, and other discounts available. Children 18 and under stay free in room with parents. Check in 1 P.M. Check out noon. Outside access to rooms. Free local phone calls. Cable TV. Free coffee available. Pool, sauna, exercise room. Self-service laundry. One-day dry cleaning. Free continental breakfast. Free newspaper. Free outside parking.

DALLAS NORTHPARK COURTYARD

10325 North Central Expressway (US 75) (75231), at Meadow Rd. • 739-2500 or 800-321-2211 • $$ • No-smoking rooms

The 160 units in this six-story Courtyard include 24 suites and 13 no-smoking rooms. Children stay free in room with parents. Check in 3 P.M. Check out

1 P.M. Inside access to rooms. Cable TV. Free coffee available. Fire intercom system. Outdoor heated pool, exercise room. Self-service laundry. One-day dry cleaning. Free newspaper. Restaurant serving breakfast only (under $10). Bar Monday–Thursday. Free outside parking.

DALLAS NORTHPARK RESIDENCE INN

10333 North Central Expressway (US 75) (75231), at Meadow Rd. • 450-8220 or 800-331-3131 • $$

There are 103 suites with kitchens in the three floors of this all-suites inn. Children stay free in room with parents. Pets OK ($50 deposit). Check in 3 P.M. Check out noon. Coffeemakers in rooms. Free coffee available. Cable TV. Outdoor heated pool. Sauna. Self-service laundry. One-day dry cleaning. Free continental buffet breakfast. Free transportation for shopping. Free outside parking.

DOUBLETREE HOTEL AT CAMPBELL CENTER

8250 North Central Expressway (US 75) (75206), at Northwest Highway 691-8700 or 800-222-TREE (800-222-8733) • $$ • W+ 8 rooms No-smoking rooms

The 302 units in this 21-story hotel include 19 suites ($$$) and 176 no-smoking rooms. Senior, weekend, and other discounts and package plans available. Children 18 and under stay free in room with parents. Check in 3 P.M. Check out noon. Inside access to rooms. Local phone calls free. Cable TV with pay channels. Visual alarms and special phones for the hearing impaired. Coffeemakers in rooms. Free coffee available. Modem link in rooms. Bell service. Spas, exercise room, tennis court, putting green. Guest memberships available for nearby health clubs. Wine reception Monday–Thursday evenings. Free newspaper. Restaurant serving all meals (dinner $12–$30). Bar. Free outside and garage parking. Diagonally across from Northpark Center Mall with free transportation to the mall. Rooms on upper floors offer view of North Dallas skyline.

DOUBLETREE HOTEL AT LINCOLN CENTRE

5410 LBJ Freeway (IH-635) (75075), at North Dallas Tollway • 972-934-8400 $$$ • W+ 5 rooms • No-smoking rooms

This 20-story hotel has 502 units that include 18 suites ($$$$–$$$$$) and 280 no-smoking rooms. Senior and weekend discounts available. Children stay free in room with parents. Concierge floor. Check in 3 P.M. Check out noon. Inside access to rooms. Charge for local calls. Cable TV with HBO and pay channels. Captioned TV, visual alarms, and special phones for the hearing impaired. Modem link in rooms. Fire intercom system. Bell service. Room service. Outdoor pool, sauna, exercise room. Children's pool. Guest memberships available for health club. Business services available. Gift shop. Retail stores. Self-service laundry. One-day dry cleaning. Free newspaper. Restaurants serving all meals (dinner $12–$30). Bar. Outside parking free, garage self-parking $3, valet parking $5. Free transportation to nearby Galleria Mall.

EMBASSY SUITES HOTEL-DALLAS MARKET CENTER

2727 Stemmons Freeway (IH-35E) (75207), *take Inwood Road exit then West side access road* **• 630-5332 or 800-EMBASSY (800-362-2779) • $$$ • W+ 4 rooms No-smoking rooms**

The 240 suites in this nine-story all-suites hotel include 214 that are no-smoking. Senior and other discounts available. Children under 12 stay free in room with parents. Check in 3 P.M. Check out noon. Inside access to rooms. Charge for local calls. Cable TV with HBO and pay channels. Captioned TV, visual alarms, and special phones for the hearing impaired. Wet bars. Coffeemakers in rooms. Modem link in rooms. Bell service. Room service. Indoor heated pool, sauna, exercise room. Fax and copy services available. Gift shop. Self-service laundry. One-day dry cleaning. Free full breakfast. Free evening cocktails. Free newspaper. Restaurant serving lunch and dinner (dinner under $14). Bar. Free outside parking. Free airport transportation to Love Field and within five-mile radius.

THE FAIRMONT HOTEL

1717 North Akard Street (75201), at Ross in the Arts District (DART Light Rail AKARD Station) • 720-2020 or 800-527-4727 • $$$$ • W+ 8 rooms No-smoking rooms

There are 550 units in this 24-story hotel including 51 suites ($$$$$) and 400 no-smoking rooms. Senior and weekend discounts available. Children 16 and under stay free in room with parents. Check in 3 P.M. Check out 1 P.M. Inside access to rooms. Charge for local calls. Cable TV with pay channels. VCR available. Captioned TV, visual alarms, and special phones for the hearing impaired. Modem link in rooms. Fire intercom system. Bell service. Room service. Outdoor heated Olympic-sized pool. Guest memberships available for health club. Business services available. Barber, beauty, and retail shops. Free newspaper. Restaurants serving all meals (dinner $12 to over $30) (*see* Restaurants-The Pyramid, above). Lounge with entertainment and dancing. Garage valet parking $12. Connected to underground pedestrian walkways that go under much of downtown (*see* Offbeat, above).

HOLIDAY INN SELECT-MOCKINGBIRD LANE

1241 West Mockingbird Lane (75247), at IH-35E • 630-7000 or 800-442-7547 $$–$$$ • W+ 2 rooms • No-smoking rooms

This 13-story inn has 339 units including seven suites ($$$–$$$$$) and 211 no-smoking rooms. Senior, weekend, and other discounts and package plans available. Children 18 and under stay free in room with parents. Concierge floor. Check in 3 P.M. Check out noon. Inside access to rooms. Local phone calls free. Cable TV with HBO and pay channels. Visual alarms and special phones for the hearing impaired. Wet bar. Coffeemakers in rooms. Modem link in rooms. Fire intercom system. Bell service. Room service. Outdoor pool, exercise room. Business services available. Gift shop. Self-service laundry. One-day dry cleaning. Free newspaper. Restaurant serving all meals (dinner $12–$30). Bar. Free outside and garage parking. Free airport transportation to Love Field.

HOTEL ST. GERMAIN

2516 Maple Street (75201), near Cedar Springs Road • 871-2516 • $$$$$

There are only seven suites on the three floors of this European-style luxury hotel. Check in 4 P.M. Check out noon. Inside access to rooms. Charge for local calls. Cable TV with HBO and VCR. Modem link in rooms. Bell service. Room service. Guest memberships available for health club. Business services available. One-day dry cleaning. Free continental breakfast. Free cocktails. Free newspaper. The reservations-only gourmet restaurant serves French/New Orleans cuisine dinner Thursday–Saturday (a la carte over $30, *prix fixe* dinner $65). Free valet parking. Elegant Victorian home built in 1906. Each suite decorated in antiques reminiscent of a French chateaux.

HYATT REGENCY DALLAS

300 Reunion Blvd. (75207), downtown (DART Light Rail UNION Station)
651-1234 or 800-233-1234 • $$–$$$$ • W+ 27 rooms • No-smoking rooms

This downtown 28-story landmark hotel has 939 units that include 25 suites ($$$$$) and 585 no-smoking rooms. Senior, weekend, and other discounts and package plans available. Children 12 and under stay free in room with parents. Concierge floor. Check in 3 P.M. Check out noon. Inside access to rooms. Charge for local calls. Cable TV with HBO and pay channels. Captioned TV, visual alarms, special phones for the hearing impaired. In-room honor bar. Coffeemakers in most rooms. Modem link in rooms. Bell service. Room service. Outdoor heated pool, sauna, exercise room, tennis. Guest memberships available for health club and for golf. Business services available. Gift shop. One-day dry cleaning. Restaurants serving all meals (dinner $12–$30) (*see* Restaurant–Antares, above). Lounge with dancing. Garage valet parking $8. Excellent view of city from upper floor rooms. Includes 50-story Reunion Tower (*see also* Bird's-eye view, above).

MANSION ON TURTLE CREEK

2821 Turtle Creek Blvd. (75219) • 559-2100 or 800-527-5432 • $$$$$ (+13%)
W+ one room • No-smoking rooms

Once the hilltop mansion of a cattle baron, it is the only hotel in Texas to earn the highest five-diamond rating by AAA and five-star rating by Mobil. It is also cited as one of best hotels in the United States in *Conde Nast Traveler's* magazine Readers Choice Awards. The nine-story hotel has 141 units, which include 15 suites and 64 no-smoking rooms. Weekend discounts and package plans are available. Children 14 and under stay free in room with parents. Small pets OK ($50 fee). Check in 3 P.M., Check out noon. Inside access to rooms. Charge for local calls. Cable TV with premium channel and pay channels. VCR available. Captioned TV, visual alarms, and special phones for the hearing impaired. Modem link in rooms. Fire intercom system. Bell service. Room service. Outdoor heated pool, sauna, health club. Guest memberships for tennis and golf available. Business services available. Gift shop. One-day dry cleaning. Babysitting available. Restaurants serving all meals (dinner $30–$50) (*see* Restaurants–Mansion on Turtle Creek, above). Lounge with entertainment and dancing. Valet parking ($12 day). Epitome of luxury and service with spacious, comfortable rooms that have French doors, deep carpets, and furnishing that make you feel as if you're in your own living room.

MELROSE HOTEL

3015 Oak Lawn Avenue (75219), at Cedar Springs Road • 521-5151 or
800-635-7673 (reservations) • $$$–$$$$ • W+ 6 rooms • No-smoking rooms

There are 21 suites ($$$$–$$$$$) and 108 no-smoking rooms among the 184 units in this eight-story hotel. Weekend discounts and package plans available. Children 17 and under stay free in room with parents. Concierge floor. Check in 3 P.M. Check out noon. Inside access to rooms. Charge for local calls. Cable TV with free premium channel and pay channels. VCR available. Visual alarms for the hearing impaired. Wet bars in suites. Coffeemakers for rooms available. Free coffee in lobby weekday mornings. Modem link in rooms. Bell service. Room service. Guest memberships available for nearby health club. Gift shop.

One-day dry cleaning. Free newspaper. Restaurant serving all meals (dinner $12–$30) (*see* Restaurants—The Landmark, above). Bar. Free outdoor parking. Free transportation within three-mile radius.

RADISSON HOTEL AND SUITES

2330 West Northwest Highway (75220), at IH-35E • 351-4477 or 800-254-8744 $$–$$$ • W+ 2 rooms • No-smoking rooms
This eight-story hotel has 198 units including 31 suites ($$$) and 95 no-smoking rooms. Senior, weekend, and other discounts and package plans available. Children 12 and under stay free in room with parents. Small pets OK ($50 deposit). Check in 3 P.M. Check out noon. Inside access to rooms, outside access to suites. Cable TV with free premium channel and pay channels. Captioned TV and visual alarms for the hearing impaired. Free coffee in lobby. Modem link in rooms. Fire intercom system. Bell service. Room service. Outdoor pool, exercise room. Guest memberships available for health club. Self-service laundry. One-day dry cleaning. Free newspaper. Restaurant serving all meals (dinner $9–$19). Lounge. Outside parking. Free airport transportation.

RESIDENCE INN-NORTH CENTRAL

13636 Goldmark Drive (75240), US 75 at Midpark Road • 669-0478 or 800-331-3131 • $$–$$$ • No-smoking suites
This two-story all-suites inn has 70 suites with kitchens of which 45 are no-smoking suites. Senior, weekend, and other discounts available. Children stay free in room with parents. Pets OK ($100 deposit). Check in 3 P.M. Check out noon. Inside access to rooms. Charge for local calls. Cable TV with free premium channel. VCR available. Coffeemakers in rooms. Modem link in rooms. Outdoor heated pool. Business services available. Self-service laundry. One-day dry cleaning. Free continental breakfast. Free newspaper. Restaurant serving dinner. Free outside parking.

RENAISSANCE DALLAS HOTEL

2222 Stemmons Freeway (I-35E) (75207), near Market Center • 631-2222 or 800-892-2233 (in Texas), 800-468-3571 (outside Texas) • $$$–$$$$ • W+ 6 rooms No-smoking rooms
This 30-story hotel has 540 units including 30 suites ($$$$) and 350 no-smoking rooms. Senior discount available. Children 18 and under stay free in room with parents. Concierge floor. Small pets OK. Check in 3 P.M. Check out noon. Inside access to rooms. Charge for local calls. Cable TV with HBO, Disney and pay channels. VCR available. Captioned TV, visual alarms, and special phones for the hearing impaired. In-room honor bar. Coffeemakers in rooms. Fire intercom system. Bell service. Room service. Outdoor heated pool, sauna, exercise room. Guest memberships available for nearby health club. Business services available. Gift shop. One-day dry cleaning. Free newspaper. Babysitting services available. Restaurant serving all meals (dinner $12–$30). Bar. Free outside parking. The pink granite, elliptically shaped hotel is home of what is reportedly the world's longest chandelier, with 7,500 Italian crystals following the winding marble-and-brass staircase up four floors. Excellent view from upper floor rooms.

STONELEIGH HOTEL

2927 Maple Avenue (75201), *take Oaklawn exit off IH-35 to Maple, then right about a mile* **• 871-7111 • $$$–$$$$$ • W+ 3 rooms • No-smoking rooms**

The 11-story Stoneleigh has 153 units of which 18 are suites ($$$$–$$$$$) and 18 are no-smoking. Package plans available. Children stay free in room with parents. Concierge floor. Pets OK. Check in 3 P.M. Check out noon. Inside access to rooms. Charge for local calls. Cable TV with pay channels. VCR available. Captioned TV for the hearing impaired. Free coffee in lobby. Modem link in rooms. Bell service. Room service. Outdoor pool. Guest memberships available for health club. One-day dry cleaning. Babysitting available. Restaurant serving all meals (dinner $25–$30). Bar. Free outdoor and garage parking. Free valet parking available. Free airport transportation.

WESTIN HOTEL

13340 Dallas Parkway (75240), just north of IH-635 in the Galleria Mall 934-9494 or 800-228-3000 • $$$$ • W+ 8 rooms • No-smoking rooms

This 20-story hotel has 431 units which include 13 suites ($$$$$) and some no-smoking rooms. Weekend discounts available. Children 18 and under stay free in room with parents. Concierge floor. Pets OK. Check in 3 P.M. Check out 1 P.M. Inside access to rooms. Cable TV with HBO and pay channels. VCR available. Captioned TV, visual alarms, and special phones for the hearing impaired. In-room honor bar. Coffeemakers in rooms. Modem link in rooms. Fire intercom system. Bell service. Room service. Guest memberships available for health club. Business services available. One-day dry cleaning. Free newspaper. Restaurants serving all meals (dinner $12–$30). Bar. Free outside and covered mall parking, valet parking $12. Built into the west side of the Galleria Mall, which has more than 200 shops, restaurants, a movie theater, and an ice skating rink.

WYNDHAM ANATOLE HOTEL

2201 Stemmons Freeway (IH-35E) (75207), across IH-35E from Dallas Market Center • 748-1200 or 800-WYNDHAM (800-996-3426) • $$$–$$$$ • W+ 5% of rooms • No-smoking rooms

The complex of wings and towers that range from 10 to 27 floors of this hotel includes 1,620 units of which 129 are suites ($$$$$) and 40% are no-smoking rooms. Senior, weekend, and other discounts and package plans available. Concierge floor. Check in 4 P.M. Check out noon. Inside access to rooms. Charge for local calls. Cable TV with free premium channel and pay channels. Captioned TV, visual alarms, and special phones for the hearing impaired. In-room honor bar. Coffeemakers in rooms. Modem link in rooms. Fire intercom system. Bell service. Room service. Two indoor, one outdoor pools; sauna, exercise room, tennis, health club. Business services available. Beauty, barber, and retail shops. One-day dry cleaning. Free newspaper. Playground. Babysitting available. Restaurants serving all meals (dinner $12–$30). Bars/lounge with entertainment and dancing. Free outdoor parking, valet parking $7. Spread over 45 acres, the hotel calls itself a village within the city. Excellent view from upper floors (*see* Bird's Eye View—Nana Grill, above). Self-guided tour brochure for museum-quality art collection scattered throughout hotel that includes the world's largest piece of Wedgwood china and one of the largest private jade collections in the country.

DENISON

Grayson County • 21,505 • (903)

Transportation is important in Denison's history. In the 1850s, Denison was a stop on the route of the Butterfield Stage Line that ran from St. Louis to San Francisco. The stage entered Texas on a ferry raft poled across the Red River by slaves.

In the early 1870s, the town fathers of Sherman, the only town of consequence in Grayson County, paid the Houston and Texas Central to come to their town from the south. But they refused to pay a subsidy to the Missouri, Kansas & Texas Railroad (the "Katy") coming from the north, because they felt that company would have no choice but to make Sherman the destination of its tracks. As often happened when a town refused to pay, in 1872 the Katy crossed the Red River and stopped just north of Sherman to set up its own town, which was named Denison after a railroad vice president.

The railroads created Denison and have played a major role in the city's growth. Dwight David Eisenhower was born in Denison on October 14, 1890, where his family lived briefly while his father worked at the Katy Railroad shops.

Diversification is the key to the city's present success. The broad economic base includes manufacturing and service industries, the medical industry, tourism, agribusiness, and retail trade.

TOURIST SERVICES

DENISON AREA CHAMBER OF COMMERCE

313 W. Woodard near Rusk (P.O. Box 325, 75020-0021) • 465-1551 • W

TEXAS TRAVEL INFORMATION CENTER

US 75N, just south of the Red River Bridge • 465-5577 • Open daily 8–5 • W+

One of 12 roadside visitor centers operated by the Texas Department of Transportation on key highways entering the state. Trained travel counselors can provide a wealth of free information, official highway maps, and tons of other travel literature on Texas.

MUSEUMS

GRAYSON COUNTY FRONTIER VILLAGE

Loy Lake Park. *From US 75 south of town take Loy Lake Rd. exit #67*
463-2487 • May–October: Wednesday– Saturday 10–5, Sunday 2–5. Closed Monday and Tuesday and November through April • Free • W variable

This collection includes frontier homes and structures from the middle of the 1800s containing period furnishings and artifacts. One of the nine structures in the village is the **Davis-Ansley House,** dating from about 1839. Bullet holes in the outer walls are evidence of Indian raids. Among the others are the Greek Revival-style **Bullock-Bass House,** built in the 1850s, which was the first house in the county with glass in its windows; and the **Holder Cabin,** built in 1855, believed to be the area's first schoolhouse. A craft and gift shop is on the premises, and the village is set in a park with a lake, a fishing pier, and a picnic area.

HISTORIC PLACES

Downtown Denison, where brick streets are still prevalent, boasts an 18-block historic district listed in the National Register of Historic Places. A map-brochure outlining a driving tour of historical buildings is available free from the Chamber of Commerce. The following are some of the more interesting historic homes. Most of these are private homes not open to the public.

George Braun House, 421 N. Austin Ave., built in 1882, has a flat roof, projecting tower, and bracketed eaves that are marks of the Italian-villa style. It is listed in the National Register of Historic Places. **Mathis-Knaur House,** 1004 W. Bond, built in 1898, is a fine example of a Queen Anne-style Victorian home. The original part of the **J. K. Miller House,** 1401 W. Walker, was built in 1866. The Butterfield Stagecoach stopped here. **T. V. Munson Home,** 530 W. Hanna at Mirick, built in 1877, was the home of a world-famous grape culturist. Munson is credited with saving much of the French wine industry from ruin. When the French vines were dying, hybrid root stocks developed by Munson were grafted onto them and the French vines survived. The French government awarded him the Legion of Honor. **Hotel Traveler's Home,** 300 E. Main, was built as a store in 1893 by E. M. Kohl. He added the upper story in 1909. Later it was used as a hotel for railroad workers and passengers. It is listed in the National Register of Historic Places.

OTHER POINTS OF INTEREST

EISENHOWER STATE RECREATION AREA

Take US 91 to FM 1310 just south of the Red River, then west (left) 1.8 miles to Park Rd. 20 • 465-1956 • **Open at all times** • **$3 per vehicle per day** **W variable**

This 457-acre park on Lake Texoma offers facilities for fishing from boat and piers, swimming, boating, sailing, and other water sports, plus picnicking, hiking, and camping (fee).

HAGERMAN NATIONAL WILDLIFE REFUGE

Lake Texoma. Refuge headquarters on Refuge Rd. *Turn right off FM 1417 west of Denison* • 786-2826 • **Open at all times** • **Free** • **W variable**

The 11,319 acres of the refuge lie on the Big Mineral arm of Lake Texoma. In addition to being the winter home of several thousand ducks and geese, the refuge also protects many birds and mammals native to north-central Texas and provides food and rest for thousands of migratory waterfowl that travel the Central Flyway between Canada and Mexico each spring and fall. Recreational uses include birdwatching, nature study and photography, picnicking, and fishing and hunting in season. For information write: Refuge Manager, Route 3, Box 123, Sherman 75090.

LAKE TEXOMA AND DENISON DAM

Take US 91 north about 4 miles to the dam • 465-4990 **(Army Corps of Engineers)** • **Open at all times** • **Free** • **W variable**

When completed in 1944, Denison Dam was the largest rolled earthfill dam in the United States. The two-state reservoir covers 89,000 acres in Texas and Oklahoma. Fifty parks, more than 100 picnic areas, and numerous commercial facilities along the lake's 580 miles of shoreline serve more than 12 million visitors annually. Accommodations range from fishing camps to luxury resort hotels. The **Cross Timbers Hiking Trail** winds 14 miles along the shoreline, with both developed and wilderness campsites available. An exhibit at the dam powerhouse recounts the construction of the dam and includes a display of artifacts found when workers dug out the lake. Free tours are conducted weekdays at 1 P.M. For information write: Project Manager, Denison Dam, Rt. 4, Box 493, Denison 75020.

SPORTS AND ACTIVITIES

Golf

GRAYSON COUNTY COLLEGE GOLF COURSE

West Campus, northwest of intersection of FM 691 and FM 1417 • 786-9719
The only golf course in Grayson County open to the public. 18 holes.
Green fees: weekdays $7, weekends $10.

COLLEGES AND UNIVERSITIES

GRAYSON COUNTY COLLEGE

6101 Grayson Dr. *From US 75 south of town take FM 691 west to college*
465-6030 • W variable

This is a two-year college offering both academic and technical/vocational programs. Visitors are welcome at theater productions (which range from children's musicals to dinner theater) and concerts. You can also visit the vineyard located on the West Campus. This vineyard is a memorial to T. V. Munson who developed hundreds of varieties of grapes and has been credited with saving the French wine industry (*see* Historic Places–T. V. Munson Home). It boasts the world's largest collection of hybrid grapes as well as a Viticulture and Enology Center. The school offers continuing education seminars and workshops in grape growing and vineyard management, and a degree program in this field is being developed.

SHOPPING

KATY PLAZA

101 E. Main, at the railroad tracks • 463-7729 • W+

The old Missouri, Kansas & Texas (Katy) Railroad depot has been restored and turned into a small, downtown shopping mall with retail shops, including an art gallery and restaurants.

ANNUAL EVENTS

July

TEXOMA QUARTER HORSE ASSOCIATION RODEO

TQHA Arena, south on Texoma Park Way, between Denison and Sherman
465-1551 (Chamber of Commerce) • Usually third full week in July • Adults
$5, children $3 • W

This rodeo runs Wednesday through Saturday nights.

September–October

U.S. NATIONAL AEROBATIC CHAMPIONSHIPS

Grayson County Airport. *From US 75 south of town take FM 691 west to airport* • **465-1551 (Chamber of Commerce)** • **Last week in September** **Free during week** • **W variable**

Generally about 100 of the top aerobatic fliers from Alaska to Florida fill the sky with heart-stopping maneuvers during this week of competition that marks the culmination of a season of more than 35 regional competitions across the country. They challenge gravity as they do both compulsory and freestyle maneuvers that include nosedives, loops, and tailslides (a tail-first vertical drop). Everything is in view of the spectators, because the sequences are flown in an aerobatic zone over the airport commonly called the "box," an area 3,300 feet long by 3,300 feet wide with a ceiling of 3,500 feet and a bottom varying from 300 feet to 1,500 feet, depending on the pilot's skill category. The winners go on to represent the U.S. in the World Championship competition overseas.

RESTAURANTS

($ = under $7, $$ = $8–$17, $$$ = $18–$25, $$$$ = over $25 for one person excluding drinks, tax, and tip.)

THE POINT RESTAURANT AND CLUB

On Lake Texoma. *Take US 75 north to FM 84, then west about 10 miles and follow signs* • **465-6376** • **Lunch and dinner daily, breakfast Saturday and Sunday** • **$$** • **AE, MC, V** • **W+** • **Children's menu**

Entrées range from catfish fillets and grilled salmon to a New York strip. As part of the entrée accompaniments, you can choose peel-and-eat shrimp in place of a tossed salad. Temporary membership in the private club costs $3 for three days. Good view of the lake from almost every table.

ACCOMMODATIONS

($ = under $45, $$ = $46–$60, $$$ = $61–$80, $$$$ = $81–$100, $$$$$ = over $100) *Room tax 13%*

RAMADA INN

1600 S. Austin, junction of US 75 and 69, just south of downtown • **465-6800 or 800-465-4329** • **$$–$$$** • **W+ 1 room** • **No-smoking rooms**

The two-story Ramada Inn has 100 rooms including 25 no-smoking. Fire sprinklers in rooms. Cable TV with Showtime. Room phones (charge for local calls). Pets OK. Restaurant. Private club open six nights (Guests automatically members, temporary membership for non-guest $3). Outdoor pool. Coffeemaker in room.

DENTON

Denton County Seat • 71,702 • (940)
Both county and city are named for John B. Denton, a frontier preacher, lawyer, and captain in the Texas Rangers in the late 1830s. Killed in an 1841 Indian fight, Denton is buried in the present courthouse lawn.

Denton, established in 1857, is best known as an education center with two major universities: **Texas Woman's University** and the **University of North Texas,** which includes the nation's second-largest school of music. Two Miss Americas, actress Joan Blondell, journalists Jim Lehrer and Bill Moyers, singer Roy Orbison, and sweepstakes winner of $10 million, Bob Castleberry, who went on to serve as mayor, are among the famous people who have lived in Denton.

TOURIST SERVICES

DENTON CONVENTION AND VISITOR BUREAU

414 Parkway at S. Carroll (P.O. Drawer P, 76202) • 382-7895 or 888-381-1818

FEMA (FEDERAL EMERGENCY MANAGEMENT AGENCY) TOUR

800 North Loop 288 • 898-5297 • Monday–Friday 8–4 by reservation Allow 1–2 hours for tour • Free • W
FEMA, used in cases of natural catastrophes such as hurricanes, tornadoes, floods or nuclear warfare, is housed four stories underground.

MUSEUMS

DENTON COUNTY HISTORICAL MUSEUM

Courthouse on the Square, 110 West Hickory • 565-8697 • Tuesday–Saturday 10:30–4:30. Closed Sunday and Monday • Free • W
The building, constructed in 1895–1896, is listed in the National Register of Historic Places. The museum features exhibits depicting city and county history. Gift shop.

HANGAR 10 ANTIQUE AIRPLANE MUSEUM

5088 Sabre Lane, Denton Municipal Airport. *From IH-35, take West Oak exit then right at Airport Rd. (FM 1515)* **• 382-0666 • Monday–Saturday 8–4 • Free**
Named after the location of the first airplane museum in Texas (San Antonio's Brooke Air Force Base), the museum boasts four planes.

HISTORIC PLACES

OAK-HICKORY HISTORIC DISTRICT

W. Oak between Carroll and Normal
Homes on W. Oak are fine examples of Victorian cottages with generous porches, jigsaw work, and tall windows. Among the houses of note are the **May-Wilkirson Home,** built in 1885; the Victorian-style **Lomax Home,** built in 1898; and the **Blewett-Fearce Home,** built in 1900. Private homes, they are not open to the public.

SPORTS AND ACTIVITIES
Golf

Both Texas Woman's University Golf Course and the Radisson Hotel Denton Eagle Point Golf Course are 18-hole courses and open to the public. Call the university or the hotel (see below) for information and green fees.

Tennis
GOLDFIELD TENNIS CENTER
2005 W. Windsor (in North Lakes Park) • 566-8525
Eight lighted courts. Reservations accepted, but Parks and Recreation tennis programs have priority. Fee: $1.75 per person for 1½ hours.

Car Races
NASCAR RACING

Texas Motor Speedway (northwest of intersection of IH-35E and IH-35W, approximately 14 miles south of Denton) • 817-215-8500 • W
There are 60,000 spaces for cars including 600 HC and 7,000 for RVs. Admission fees range from $55–$155.

COLLEGES AND UNIVERSITIES
TEXAS WOMAN'S UNIVERSITY (TWU)
Bell and University • 898-2000 • W+ but not all areas
Visitor parking areas are marked
TWU is a comprehensive public university, primarily for women, established by the Texas Legislature in 1901 as The Girls' Industrial College. Some 9,800 students are enrolled at the main campus here and at the university's health science centers in Dallas and Houston. Through its schools and colleges, the university offers programs leading to bachelor's, master's, and doctoral degrees.

Campus visitors enjoy the **Daughters of the American Revolution Museum** (Human Development Building, 1117 Bell, 898-3201, Monday–Friday, 8–4:30, by appointment. Closed school holidays. Free. W) Displayed are the actual garments or faithful copies of the gowns worn by the wives of the presidents of the Republic of Texas and the governors of Texas. Also, **Texas Woman's University Art Galleries** (Fine Arts Building, 1012 Oakland, 898-2530, Monday–Friday, 9–4. Closed Saturday, Sunday, and school holidays. Free. W), where the East and West Galleries exhibit the works of international, national, and regional artists as well as those of students and faculty. Visitors are also welcome at intercollegiate athletic events, concerts and productions by the Department of Performing Arts, and to the permanent "Texas Women: A Celebration of History" exhibit at the **Blagg-Huey Library**. Another campus attraction is the **Little Chapel-in-the-Woods,** west of Guinn Hall. Dedicated by Eleanor Roosevelt in 1939, all of the artwork was designed by the students. Nearby are the University Gardens.

UNIVERSITY OF NORTH TEXAS (UNT)
Ave. C and Chestnut, *take Ave. D exit from IH-35E* • 565-2000 • W+ but not all areas • Visitor parking areas are marked

Approximately 25,000 students attend classes on UNT's 456-acre campus located at the intersection of IH-35E and IH-35W. It was founded in 1890 in a downtown store and now has nine colleges and schools. The College of Music, home of the famed One O'Clock Jazz Band, is known for its symphony orchestra, a cappella choir, opera theater, and jazz program, which started in 1947 and is the largest university jazz program in the nation. Visitors are welcome at concerts and performances by these groups plus the performing arts productions and intercollegiate sports events.

You may visit the **University of North Texas Art Gallery** (Art Building, one block west of Welch and Mulberry), 565-4005, Monday–Tuesday, 11–8, and Wednesday–Saturday, 11–4. Usually closed Sunday and school holidays. Free.

PERFORMING ARTS

DENTON COMMUNITY THEATER

Campus Theatre, 214 W. Hickory off the downtown square • 382-7014 Admission • W variable

This nonprofessional theater group with a professional directing manager usually puts on about five productions during the fall-and-spring season and a summer musical.

OFFBEAT

FANTASY SUITES

Located in the Ramada Inn (*see* Accommodations), these fantasy suites offer escape to romantic dreams. Each of the luxury suites has a different theme decor such as Geisha Garden and Arabian Nights. Caesar's Court sports marble arches and columns with a draped four-poster bed. A bed replaces car seats in the Pink Cadillac suite featuring a vintage convertible.

SIDE TRIPS

LAKE LEWISVILLE

Take IH-35E south about 8 miles to FM 4071 Justin exit, then east to N. Mill St. **(972) 434-1666 • Open at all times • Free • W variable**

This 23,000-acre Army Corps of Engineers lake draws more than six million visitors a year. Seventeen developed parks surround Lake Lewisville State Park (292-1441), with facilities for boating, fishing, swimming, and other water sports, picnicking, and camping (some free, some fee). For information write: Lake Manager, 1801 N. Mill St., Lewisville 75057, or Lewisville Chamber of Commerce, P.O. Box 416, 75067.

LAKE RAY ROBERTS STATE PARK

Take IH-35E north about 2 miles to FM 455 at Sanger. **The park unit is 10 miles east of IH-35 • 686-2148 • Open at all times • Adults $2, under 12 free W variable**

This 1,397-acre scenic playground is on the south side of Lake Ray Roberts. Camping, boating, swimming, and fishing are available. There is an overnight group pavilion and day-use picnic area as well as a trail for hiking, bicycling, and equestrian use.

ANNUAL EVENTS

April

DENTON ARTS & JAZZ FESTIVAL

**Civic Center Park at Bell and McKinney • 565-0931
(Denton Festival Foundation) • Free • W variable**

Denton, a music town, puts on continuous musical entertainment on four stages during this two-day festival showcasing jazz, pop, rhythm and blues, dance, choral, storytelling, and theater performances. There is a juried arts and crafts show. Proceeds benefit the arts.

September

COUNTY SEAT SATURDAY

Downtown Square • 349-8529 • Free

Awarded 1990's Best Promotional Event in Texas by the Texas Downtwon Association. This one-day event features a pancake breakfast, 5K run, historic exhibits, arts, crafts, music, game and food booths, classic car show, petting zoo, carriage and hay rides.

RESTAURANTS

($ = under $7, $$ = $8–$17, $$$ = $18–$25, $$$$ = over $25 for one person excluding drinks, tax, and tip.)

THE HOMESTEAD

401 S. Locust • 566-3240 • Breakfast and lunch Monday–Saturday 7–2:30, Sunday 9–2:30 • $ • AE, MC, V • W+

Housed in the end building of a Victorian-style shopping center, this restaurant is a popular lunch spot. Daily specials feature traditional homestyle dishes for about $5. No-smoking area.

TEXAS PICKUP

**2101 W. Prairie at Ave. E, across from University of North Texas • 382-1221
Lunch and dinner daily • AE, MC, V • $ • W • Children's menu**

The decor is college casual with old license plates and gas station signs. The menu features large servings of burgers, chili, salads, and more. Beer and wine coolers.

ACCOMMODATIONS

*($ = under $45, $$ = $46–$60, $$$ = $61–$80, $$$$ = $81–$100, $$$$$ = over $100)
Room tax 13%*

HOLIDAY INN

**1500 Dallas Dr. at IH-35E • 387-3511 or 800-465-4329 • $$–$$$ • W+
No-smoking rooms**

This two-story Holiday Inn offers 144 units including four suites ($$$$–$$$$$) and 15 no-smoking rooms. Satellite TV with Showtime and pay channel. No charge for local calls. Restaurant. Outdoor pool.

RADISSON HOTEL DENTON AND EAGLE POINT GOLF COURSE

2211 IH-35E, exit Ave. D • 565-8499 or 800-333-3333 • $$$$–$$$$$ • W+ rooms available • No-smoking rooms

This hotel offers 150 units including six suites ($$$$$), 85 no-smoking rooms, and two fully accessible HC rooms. Cable TV with HBO. Room phones (50¢ for local calls). Coffeemakers in room. Restaurant. Outdoor pool and exercise room.

SUPER 8 MOTEL

620 S. IH-35E, exit 465 • 380-8888 or 800-800-8000 • $$–$$$ • W+ • No-smoking

There are 80 units including 48 no-smoking and four fully accessible HC rooms. Children 12 and under stay free with parents. Cable TV with HBO. Free breakfast. Room phones (no charge for local calls).

FARMERS BRANCH

Dallas County • 25,000 • (972)

This city traces its origin to 1841 when it was part of Peters Colony, a large land grant awarded by the Republic of Texas to the Texas Land and Emigration Company in exchange for bringing in settlers to this vast unoccupied territory. There's not much farming done here anymore since the city is home to more than 3,000 businesses including at least 60 Fortune 500 companies.

TOURIST SERVICES

CITY OF FARMERS BRANCH TOURISM OFFICE

13000 William Dodson Parkway, in City Hall (P.O. Box 819010, 75381-9010) 247-3131 or 800-BRANCH-9 (800-272-6249) • W

This is an administrative office, not a visitor information center. You can pick up brochures and such here during business hours Monday–Friday, but it's best if you write or call in advance and let them send you the information you want.

POINTS OF INTEREST

FARMERS BRANCH HISTORICAL PARK

2540 Farmers Branch Lane at Ford Road (75234-6214), *from IH-635 exit either Denton Drive or Josey Lane and go north to Farmers Branch Lane* **• 406-0183 or 406-0184 • Summer: Monday–Thursday 9:30–8, Saturday–Sunday noon–8. Closed Friday and major holidays. Closes at 6 in winter • Free • W variable**

In this 22-acre tree-shaded park on Farmers Branch Creek are a number of historic buildings that have been restored including **The Gilbert House,** the oldest rock structure in Northeast Texas. Completed in 1857, it has two-foot-thick limestone walls and chestnut plank floors.

KIDS' STUFF

SANDY LAKE AMUSEMENT PARK

1800 Sandy Lake Road at IH-35E (P.O. Box 810536, Dallas 75381) • 242-7449 June–August daily 10–6, April–May and September Wednesday–Sunday 10–6 Admission $2, all amusements extra • W

This 60-acre park offers amusement rides, miniature golf, paddle boats, an arcade, pony rides, and picnic grounds with shade trees and a lake.

ACCOMMODATIONS

(For a double room: $ = under $80, $$ = $81–$120, $$$ = $121–$180, $$$$ =
$181–$250, $$$$$ = over $250)

Room tax 12%

DALLAS MEDALLION

4099 Valley View Lane (Dallas 75244) • 385-9000 or 800-808-1011
(Reservations) • $$$–$$$$ • W+ 7 rooms • No-smoking rooms

This 10-story hotel has 289 units that include seven suites ($$$$) and some
no-smoking rooms. Weekend discount available. Children under 12 stay free in
room with parents. Concierge floor. Pets under 15 pounds OK (large deposit).
Check in 3 P.M. Check out noon. Inside access to rooms. Charge for local calls.
Cable TV with HBO and pay channels. Visual alarms for the hearing impaired.
Modem link in rooms. Fire intercom system. Bell service. Room service. Out-
door pool, exercise room. Two-mile jogging track next door. Business services
available. One-day dry cleaning. Restaurant serving all meals (dinner under
$12). Bar. Free outside parking.

DALLAS PARKWAY HILTON

4801 LBJ Freeway (Dallas 75244-6002) • 661-3600 • $$–$$$ • W+ 5 rooms
No-smoking rooms

The 310 units in this 15-story hotel include 14 suites ($$$) and 217 no-smok-
ing rooms. Senior, weekend, and other discounts and package plans available.
Children 17 and under stay free in room with parents. Check in 3 P.M. Check
out 1 P.M. Inside access to rooms. Charge for local calls. Cable TV with free premium channel. VCR available with advance notice. Captioned TV, visual
alarms, and special phones for the hearing impaired. Free coffee in lobby in
morning. Coffeemakers in suites. Modem link in rooms. Bell service. Room service. Indoor/outdoor heated pool, sauna, exercise room. Guest memberships
available in nearby health club. Business services available weekdays. Gift
shop. One-day dry cleaning. Free newspaper. Restaurant serving all meals (dinner $12–$30). Bar. Free outside parking. Free transportation within five miles.
Located across from the Galleria Mall.

OMNI DALLAS AT PARK WEST

1590 LBJ Freeway (Dallas 75234) • 869-4300 or 800-460-8732 • $–$$$ • W+ 4
rooms • No-smoking rooms

This 12-story Omni has 338 units that include 18 suites ($$–$$$) and 70 no-
smoking rooms. Senior, weekend, and other discounts and package plans avail-
able. Concierge floor. Check in 3 P.M. Check out noon. Inside access to rooms.
Charge for local calls. Cable TV with pay channels. VCR available. Captioned
TV, visual alarms, and special phones for the hearing impaired. Coffeemakers
in rooms. Modem link in rooms. Fire intercom system. Bell service. Room ser-
vice. Outdoor heated pool, sauna, exercise room, jogging track. Membership
available in hotel health club. Business services available. Gift shop. One-day
dry cleaning. Free newspaper. Restaurant serving all meals (dinner $12–$30).
Bar. Free D/FW airport transportation. Valet garage parking ($3). Located on
shore of 125-acre lake.

FORT WORTH

Tarrant County Seat • 475,000 • (817)

The Mexican War was not long over when, in June 1849, Company F, 2nd Dragoons established a frontier outpost on the bluffs overlooking the Trinity River to protect the settlements like Lonesome Dove and Dallas from Indian raids. The post was named in honor of Major General William Jenkins Worth, a hero in the conquest of Mexico City and now head of the U.S. Army in Texas and New Mexico. Worth never got to see the post named after him, dying of cholera in San Antonio about the time the post was being set up. (Worth's heroism was recognized in his home of New York City, too, with a 50-foot tall monument at Broadway and Fifth.) But, by 1853 the frontier had moved further

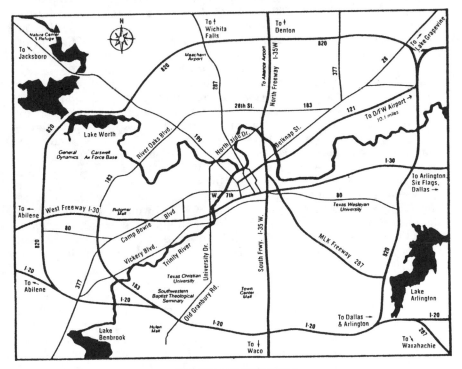

FORT WORTH

west and the soldiers went with it. The settlers moved into the post buildings, which were better than the ramshackle cabins they were living in.

Fort Worth "Steals" the County Seat

The population had reached about 100 by 1856. Among its citizens were a number of town boosters who were dissatisfied that the town of Birdville was the county seat, so they promoted an election to move it to Fort Worth. They won, but the people of Birdville cried "foul" saying Fort Worth had stolen the election by bringing in voters from outside the county. True or not, another election was ordered, but by the time it could be scheduled, it was 1860 and the county government was well entrenched in Fort Worth and nobody wanted to move it again.

Chisholm Trail Makes It a Boom Town

Soon after the Civil War, Texas cattlemen found out that longhorns selling for $5 a head in Texas would fetch $30 or more in northern markets. Thus started the long drives that saw some 10 million head of Texas cattle driven north between 1866 and the mid-1880s. Among the many trails used for the drives was one set up by Jesse Chisholm to the railhead at Abilene, Kansas. The Chisholm Trail ran right through Fort Worth, often right down the main street, causing the town to boom. This was the last stop before crossing into the Oklahoma Indian Territory, so the cowboys stocked up on supplies here and whooped it up a bit before setting out to push the huge herds through the last 300 miles of dust and mud. On the return trip, with the herd sold and their pay burning in their pockets, this was the first Texas town they hit. They usually hit it hard. The favorite place to let off steam was known as Hell's Half Acre—located where the modern Fort Worth/Tarrant County Convention Center now stands. This wide open section of town, made up almost entirely of saloons, gambling houses, and bordellos, was filled with lowlifes who did everything they could to separate the cowboys from their hard-earned dollars.

The townspeople saw solid prosperity just over the horizon when the Texas and Pacific Railroad headed their way in 1873. This would make Fort Worth the railhead instead of Abilene. The population quickly doubled from about 2,000 to 4,000. But then the Panic of 1873 struck, the railroad went bankrupt, and construction stopped 26 miles short. Overnight the population dropped to about 1,000.

It was during this time that a Dallas newspaper, feeding the feud that was growing between the two towns, reported that Fort Worth was so dead a panther had been seen sleeping unmolested in the streets. This insult goaded the people of Fort Worth to action. At first it was a simple thumbing of the nose at Dallas: the fire department adopted a panther for a mascot and many clubs in town added Panther to their names. Then they turned serious. They needed a railroad to survive and if the railroad wouldn't come to them, they'd go out and drag it in.

Dragging In the Railroad

They formed a construction company, reached an agreement with the railroad, and started to lay track. Every business operated with a minimum of help and sent its employees out to work on the right-of-way. The women worked in shifts to feed the men and take care of the mules. They worked under the threat that if the railroad didn't reach Fort Worth before the Texas Legislature adjourned, they would lose the land grant the state would pay the railroad. It's said that when it got down to the last days, the crews just threw down track on ungraded ground, weighing them down with stones. In the meantime, the city council moved the city limits out to meet the tracks, and the ailing representative from Fort Worth had himself carried into the Legislature each day to cast a vote against adjournment.

Their tenacity and spirit paid off. On July 19, 1876, the railroad reached Fort Worth and the city became the end of the trail drives instead of the start. The ranchers soon made it their main shipping point and the city soon became known as "Cowtown." In time, a number of railroads had terminals here, stockyards were built, and in 1902, the big Chicago meat packers, Swift and Armour, built plants here.

Hell's Half Acre

With the cowboys still driving herds to town, Hell's Half Acre continued to be a magnet for them. It was also a hangout for famous outlaws like Butch Cassidy and the Sundance Kid. It was here that Sundance met Etta Place, who later went with them on their ill-fated journey to South America. Hell's Half Acre was pretty well demolished around the time of World War I. It was also around this time that oil was discovered in nearby counties. Hundreds of oil companies set up in the city, and it soon became an oil center. During and after World War II, the defense industry came to town to stay and a number of major corporations followed.

Culture Comes to Cowtown

Culture came to Cowtown starting in the 1930s with a big push from city boosters like millionaires Amon Carter, founder of *The Fort Worth Star-Telegram*, and industrialist Kay Kimbell. Today, in addition to "Cowtown," Fort Worth calls itself "The Museum Capital of the Southwest." Among its numerous museums giving support to that title are such gems as the Amon Carter Museum and the Kimbell Art Museum. The arts also abound with theaters, a symphony, opera, and a botanical garden, and it is the home of the Van Cliburn International Piano Competition, one of the most prestigious musical competitions in the world. Not exactly art, but fun, it is also the home of a zoo, which has been acclaimed as one of America's "Top Five."

As a result, although the city still calls itself Cowtown and the town "Where the West Begins," and continually projects that image to pay tribute to its Old West heritage (businessmen in suits wearing 10-gallon hats and cowboy boots are a common sight), it now might more appropriately be thought of as the home of the sophisticated cowboy.

TOURIST SERVICES

FORT WORTH CONVENTION AND VISITORS BUREAU

415 Throckmorton (76102) at 4th • 336-8791 or 800-433-5747 • Monday–Friday 8:30–5, Saturday 10–4 • W

Everything you want to know about Fort Worth you can find out from the counselors here.

STOCKYARDS VISITOR CENTER

130 East Exchange Avenue, near the Stockyards Station • 624-4741
Monday–Friday 10–6, Saturday 10–7, Sunday noon–6 • W+
Information isn't restricted to the Stockyards. You can find out about attractions, lodging, and dining throughout the city.

COMMERCIAL TOURS

CLASSIC CARRIAGES

336-0400 (Recorded message) • Wednesday–Saturday after 7:30 p.m.
(weather permitting)
Horse-drawn carriage rides through Sundance Square and the downtown area begin at The Worthington Hotel, 200 Main. Up to four people can ride for $20, each additional $5. Pick-ups at other hotels can be arranged.

HELL'S HALF ACRE AND SUNDANCE SQUARE WALKING TOUR

327-1178 • Friday–Saturday mornings at 9:30
A 2½-hour guided walking tour of historic downtown starting at the Radisson Plaza Hotel lobby (100 East 8th Street at Main). $10 per person.

STOCKYARDS TRAILS WALKING TOUR

130 East Exchange Avenue • 625-9715 or Metro 817-988-6877
Monday–Saturday 10–4, Sunday noon–4
An hour guided walk through the Stockyards Historic District leaves from the Stockyards Visitor Center. Adults $7.

INDUSTRY TOURS

MRS. BAIRD'S BAKERY TOUR

7301 South Freeway (76134) at IH-35W South Freeway and Sycamore School Rd.
615-3050 • Monday and Wednesday 10–4, Friday 10–4 • Call for reservations
three weeks in advance • Free • W
See how bread is made while learning the history of this popular Texas bakery. Tour lasts about an hour. Parking is at the front of the plant and the tour starts from the front door. Children must be at least six years old.

SELF-GUIDED WALKING TOURS

The Convention and Visitors Bureau offers a free downtown walking tour map that includes 59 sites. If you follow it all, it covers about three miles and takes about three hours to complete; however, it has sub-tours for art, architecture, and historic sites that cover one to two miles and take one to two hours to complete.

BIRD'S-EYE VIEW

The only panoramic view downtown open to the public is from the **Reata Restaurant** on the 35th floor of the Bank One Building diagonally across from the Convention and Visitors Bureau on Throckmorton between 4th and 5th streets. **Heritage Park,** next to the Tarrant County Courthouse, offers a view of the Trinity Valley and the Stockyards area north of downtown. Not exactly bird's eye, but a good low-level view of downtown can be seen from the grounds of the **Amon Carter Museum.**

MUSEUMS AND ART GALLERIES

AMERICAN AIRLINES C.R. SMITH MUSEUM

4601 Hwy. 360 (76155) at FAA Road, south of Hwy. 183. Southwest of D/FW Airport • 967-1560 • Tuesday 10–7, Wednesday–Saturday 10–6, Sunday 12–5. Closed Monday and major holidays • Free • W+

Through large-screen films viewed from first class airliner seats, interactive displays, hands-on exhibits, and videos, visitors can follow the history and worldwide operations of American Airlines from the 1930s to the present. Included is a close-up look at how an airliner is flown and maintained. Gift shop.

AMON CARTER MUSEUM

3501 Camp Bowie Blvd. (P.O. Box 2365, 76113) at Montgomery and West Lancaster, in the Cultural District • 738-1933 • Tuesday–Saturday 10–5, Sunday 12–5. Closed Monday and major holidays • Free • W+ use side entrance on Camp Bowie Blvd.

The story of Amon G. Carter is one of rags to riches. He came from an impoverished family to become a millionaire and the founder of *The Fort Worth Star-Telegram*. Carter definitely was not into the arts—in an interview he said that in all his life he had only read about a dozen books. But he knew that a great city needed art, and he wanted Fort Worth to be a great city. He started his art collection with the paintings and sculptures of Frederic Remington and Charles M. Russell and other artists of the American West. When he died he left his collection and a foundation to establish this museum. His early collection has been expanded to include all American art and, appropriately, the building that houses it was designed to resemble an American Indian lodge. Among the artists represented are Winslow Homer, William Michael Harnett, Grant Wood, Martin Johnson Heade, and Georgia O'Keefe. The museum also has a photography collection of more than 250,000 prints. Videos on the collections are available for viewing in the museum theater. Free public tours are offered daily at 2 P.M. Museum store.

THE CATTLEMAN'S MUSEUM

1301 West 7th Street (76102) • 332-7064 • Monday–Friday 8:30–4:30. Closed weekends and major holidays • Free • W use rear parking lot entrance

The fascinating story of the development of Texas ranching and the cattle industry is told here on a self-guided tour through multimedia visuals and life-sized dioramas with talking mannequins, including a "Talking Longhorn." Since this museum is in the headquarters of the Texas and Southwestern Cattle Raisers Foundation, it's appropriate that some of the exhibits cover the brand inspectors, the lawmen charged with tracking down cattle thieves.

FIRE STATION NO. 1— 150 YEARS OF FORT WORTH

203 Commerce (76102) at 2nd Street, downtown • 732-1631 (History Department, Fort Worth Museum of Science and History) Daily 9–7 • Free • W

The building that displays the history of Fort Worth itself played a part in that history. On this site, the city's first fire station was built in 1876. Local legend has it that the firemen kept two panthers as mascots to tweak the nose of Dallas for saying Fort Worth was so quiet a panther could sleep downtown without being disturbed. The present structure, which replaced the original building in 1907, is filled with graphics, photographs, documents, and other historical artifacts from the city's history.

FORT WORTH MUSEUM OF SCIENCE AND HISTORY

1501 Montgomery Street (76107) at Crestline, in the Cultural District 732-1631 or Metro 817-654-1356 • Monday 9–5, Tuesday–Thursday 9–8, Friday–Saturday 9–9, Sunday 12–8. Closed Thanksgiving and December 24–25 • General admission: adults $5, seniors $4, children (3–12) $3, under 3 free • W+

The largest museum of its type in the Southwest, it attracts more than a million visitors a year. Nine permanent galleries have exhibitions ranging from dinosaurs to computers, Texas history to the history of medicine. Interactive exhibits for all ages, but special hands-on areas for kids include Kidspace® and the DinoDig® where they dig for dinosaur bones in an outdoor area. Separate admission also charged to the two major permanent attractions: The Noble Planetarium ($3) and the Omni Theater (adults $6, seniors and children 12 and under, $4). The Planetarium shows range from explorations of the heavens and beyond to Laser Magic. The Omni is an IMAX® theater in which the film almost envelops the audience in sight and sound.

KIMBELL ART MUSEUM

3333 Camp Bowie Blvd. (76107) at Arch Adams, in the Cultural District 332-8451 or Metro 817-654-1034 • Tuesday–Thursday and Saturday 10–5, Friday 12–8, Sunday 12–5. Closed Mondays, Thanksgiving, Christmas, New Year's Day • Free except for special exhibits • W+

Kay Kimbell, industrialist and entrepreneur, and his wife, Velma, started collecting art in the 1930s. At Mr. Kimbell's death in 1964, he bequeathed this art collection and his entire personal fortune to establish and maintain a public art museum of the first rank in Fort Worth. His wishes have been well carried out by the foundation that today owns and operates this museum, which has been called "America's Best Small Museum." The permanent collection includes representative paintings by artists such as Gainsborough, Holbein, El Greco, Velázquez, Rembrandt, Cézanne, Picasso, Rubens, Van Dyck, and Monet. Its strongest area of holdings is in European paintings and sculpture from the Renaissance to the mid-20th century, but it also has a substantial collection of Asian arts, Meso-American and African pieces, and Mediterranean antiquities. Even the building housing this museum is widely regarded as one of the most outstanding public art-gallery facilities in the world, especially acclaimed for its use of natural light. A tour featuring highlights of the permanent collection is offered Sundays at 3 P.M. A tour for children aged 5 to 9 years is offered at the same time. Public programs include lectures, classic films, theater, and music presentations. (*See also* Restaurants/The Buffet at the Kimbell, below.) Bookstore.

LOG CABIN VILLAGE

2100 Log Cabin Village Lane (76109) *Take Colonial Parkway off South University Dr.* **• 926-5881 • Tuesday–Friday 9–5, Saturday 10–5, Sunday 1–5. Closed Monday • Adults $1.50, seniors and children (4–17) $1.25, under 4 years old free • W variable**

This is a living history museum containing seven pioneer cabins from the early and mid-1800s that were moved to the site, restored, and furnished with period tools and furnishings. Interpreters dressed in pioneer costumes demonstrate old crafts, such as spinning and candle making. Milling equipment was installed into one of the cabins to convert it to a grist mill. There is also a staffed reproduction of a blacksmith shop from the period.

MODERN ART MUSEUM OF FORT WORTH

1309 Montgomery Street (76107) at Camp Bowie Blvd., in the Cultural District 738-9215 • Tuesday–Friday 10–5, Saturday 11–5, Sunday 12–5. Closed Mondays and holidays • Free • W+

Chartered in 1892 as the Fort Worth Public Library and Art Gallery, the Modern is the oldest art museum in Texas. The focus here is on modern and contemporary American and European art, including paintings, sculptures, and works on paper. Represented in the permanent collection are works by Picasso, Pollock, Rothko, Stella, Warhol, and Motherwell. Contemporary sculpture is on view outdoors on the museum grounds. The Modern offers a series of free lectures and performances on Tuesday evenings at 7 P.M. September–November and February–April. Museum store. Plans are in the early development stage to build a new Modern to the east of the Kimbell at University and Camp Bowie.

THE MODERN AT SUNDANCE SQUARE

410 Houston at the corner of 4th Street • 335-9215 • Monday–Wednesday 11–6, Thursday–Saturday 11–8, Sunday 1–5 • Free • W+

This branch of The Modern features both exhibits from the permanent collection and temporary traveling exhibits. It is located in a spacious downstairs store in the historic Sanger Building, which was built in 1929 and is listed in the National Register of Historic Places. Museum store.

SID RICHARDSON COLLECTION OF WESTERN ART

309 Main Street (76102) in Sundance Square • 332-6554 Tuesday–Wednesday 10–5, Thursday–Friday 10–8, Saturday 11–8, Sunday 1–5. Closed Monday and major holidays • Free • W+

On permanent display in this large one-room gallery are 60 paintings and bronzes by premier western artists Frederic Remington and Charles M. Russell. Reflecting the American West, the works are the legacy of late oilman and philantrophist Sid W. Richardson. Self-tour with a free gallery guidebook. Gift shop.

STOCKYARDS COLLECTION AND MUSEUM

131 East Exchange Avenue, in the Stockyards' Livestock Exchange Building, Suite 111–114 • 625-5087 • Monday–Saturday 10–5. Closed Sunday • Free (donations accepted) • W

More a collection for browsing than a tidy museum, the rooms contain a widely diverse assortment of memorabilia and artifacts, most of which are related in some way to the history of the Stockyards. These include saddles, antiques, and photographs. Gift shop.

TANDY ARCHAEOLOGICAL MUSEUM

2001 West Seminary Dr., in the library of the Southwestern Baptist Theological Seminary • 923-1921 • Open library hours, call for times Free • W

The items in the permanent collection date from about 1500 B.C. to the seventh century A.D. and consist of artifacts uncovered at digs in biblical sites in Israel. Visitor parking at the Memorial Building.

VINTAGE FLYING MUSEUM

505 NW 38th Street (76106), Hangar 33-S, adjacent to Meacham Airport
624-1935 • Saturday 10–5, Sunday 12–5 • $3 donation

This is an antique aircraft restoration facility that literally builds "museums that fly." Tours cover displays of vintage aircraft, land vehicles, and support equipment in various stages of preservation.

HISTORIC PLACES

EDDLEMAN McFARLAND HOUSE

1110 Penn Street (76102), south off West 7th • 332-5875 • Monday–Friday, tours on the hour 10–1 • Adults $2.50, children free

Built in 1899, in an area once called Quality Hill, this is one of the last of Fort Worth's elegant Victorian homes of the cattle barons. Its finely crafted woodwork and other architectural details remain largely unaltered from their original state. Listed in the National Register of Historic Places. Another Victorian home in the National Register is the **Pollock–Capps House,** at 1120. Built in 1898, it has been converted to offices.

PIONEER REST CEMETERY

626 Samuels, northeast of downtown • Open daily 9-dusk • W

This cemetery was started in 1850 to bury two children of Major Ripley Arnold, the officer who established Camp Worth. Arnold, reputedly a strict disciplinarian of his troops, was killed by one of his men at Fort Graham, near Hillsboro, Texas, in 1853 and his body brought back here to be buried with his children. Also buried here are General Edward H. Tarrant, after whom the county is named, and Ephraim M. Daggett, who was sometimes called the Father of Fort Worth in recognition of his importance in the city's early days. The graves of the pioneers are in the rear of the cemetery. After this small cemetery was filled, the latter-day Fort Worth giants and sinners were buried in **Oakwood Cemetery,** on Grand Avenue between downtown and the Stockyards. These included prominent cattle barons, like oilman/rancher W.T. Waggoner, who in the early 1900s gave each of his three children 90,000 acres of oil-rich land and 10,000 head of cattle.

ST. PATRICK'S CATHEDRAL COMPLEX

1206 and 1208 Throckmorton Street • 332-4915 • W

Built of white Texas stone, the Gothic Revival cathedral was completed in 1892. The oldest ecclesiastical building in the city, it contains the original hand-painted stained glass windows from Germany and a bell that has been in use since 1889. The church and St. Ignatius Academy next door, built in 1889, are in the National Register of Historic Places. The late William J. Marsh, organist at the cathedral for many years, composed the state song, "Texas, Our Texas."

STOCKYARDS NATIONAL HISTORIC DISTRICT

North Main from 23rd to 28th streets, north of downtown • W variable

The Stockyards, once the second largest in the country, played a major role in the growth of Fort Worth. Cattle pens extended for nearly a mile when the big meat packers established plants. In 1911, the area was incorporated as Niles City, a community composed almost entirely of the Stockyards that was set up as a defense by the meat packers to keep their tax haven from being annexed by Fort Worth. With a population of only 650 and property values of $25 million, Niles City's per capita wealth led to it being called the Richest Little Town in the World. But the meat packers lost in the courts, and in 1922 Fort Worth annexed Niles City. In that eleven years, more than 160 million head of livestock were processed through here. The whole district is in the National Register of Historic Places, and it looks a lot like it did a hundred years ago, with many of the buildings nearly a century old. But today those old-timers exist side by side with a thriving entertainment complex that plays up their age to keep alive the spirit of the Old West. **The Livestock Exchange Building,** for example, built in 1904, is now the appropriate location for The Stockyards Collection and Museum. **The Thannisch Building,** built in 1907, is now The Stockyards Hotel. And **The Cowtown Coliseum,** a structure built in 1907 that made the history books as the home of the first indoor rodeo, still has Wild West shows and professional rodeo competitions most weekends. The district has a number of restaurants, bars—including Billy Bob's, the world's largest honkytonk—and shops selling everything western from art and antiques to boots and cowboy hats. At 26th and Stockyards Boulevard is the impressive "Texas Gold" sculpture, depicting a herd of seven longhorn steers.

TARRANT COUNTY COURTHOUSE

100 West Weatherford at north end of Main • 884-1726 • Open to the public Monday–Friday during business hours • W

Built between 1893 and 1895 of Texas pink granite and marble, the courthouse's Renaissance Revival style was designed to resemble the Texas Capitol building. It cost over $400,000, and this extravagance so incensed the taxpayers that in 1894, before the building was completed, they voted out the county commissioners who voted for it. Free tours are available. Listed in the National Register of Historic Places.

THISTLE HILL

1509 Pennsylvania Avenue (76104), at south end of Summit Avenue 336-1212 • Monday–Friday 10–3, Sunday 1–4. Closed Saturday. Tours begin on the hour • Adults $4, seniors and children (7–12) $2 • W downstairs only

This mansion was built in 1903 as a wedding present from cattle baron W. T. Waggoner to his daughter Electra. Electra was considered a little eccentric. She set a record by being the first customer of Neiman-Marcus to spend more than $20,000 in that store in one day. She never wore the same dress twice, came back from Europe with a butterfly tattoo, and spent three hours a day in a milk bath. The house, which Electra sold in 1910, contains eighteen rooms, a fourteen-foot-wide oak grand stairway, with Tiffany-style windows on the landing and oak-paneled halls. The new owner, Winfield Scott, made several changes, the most prominent of which are the limestone columns on the front porch, which he had brought in from Indiana on special railcars. Tours last about an hour. Parking and the entrance are in the rear on Pruitt Street.

OTHER HISTORIC BUILDINGS

The following downtown buildings are among those in the city also listed in the National Register of Historic Places: **Hotel Texas** (1921), now the Radisson Plaza Hotel; **Blackstone Hotel** (1929), 601 Main; **Burk Burnett Building** (1914), 500 Main; **Knights of Pythis Hall** (1903), 313 Main; **First Christian Church**

(1914), 612 Throckmorton; **Fort Worth Club Building** (1925), 306 West 7th; **Neil P. Anderson Building** (1921), 411 West 7th; **Bryce Building** (1910), 909 Throckmorton; **W. T. Waggoner Building** (1919), 810 Houston; **Flatiron Building** (1907), 1000 Houston; **U.S. Post Office Building** (1933), Lancaster and Jennings; **Texas and Pacific Terminal Complex** (1928), West Lancaster; and **The Union Passenger Station** (1899), 1601 Jones Street. In addition, **Elizabeth Boulevard** between 8th and College, once called Silver Slipper Row, is also listed in the Register as a historic district. The history of all these are included in the Downtown Fort Worth Walking Tour map available from the Convention and Visitors Bureau.

OTHER POINTS OF INTEREST

THE CLIBURN ORGAN

Broadway Baptist Church, 305 West Broadway (76104) • 334-8211 • W
The largest organ in the state of Texas, it has 10,615 pipes. The largest is thirty-seven feet long with a diameter of seventeen-and-one-eighth inches, and the smallest pipe is eight inches long with a "speaking length" of five-sixteenth inch. The $2.5 million organ is designed for both church and concert use, which means it can produce a variety of sounds to fulfill a symphonic breath of color and form. It is officially named the Rildia Bee O'Bryan Cliburn Organ, in memory of the mother and principal teacher of famed pianist Van Cliburn, who is a member of the church. There is no set schedule for performances. Call for information.

FORT WORTH BOTANIC GARDEN

3220 Botanic Garden Dr. (76107) at University Drive, in the Cultural District just north of I-30 • 871-7689 • Daily 8 A.M.–sundown. • General admission free, admission fees for Conservatory and Japanese Garden • W variable
An 18-foot floral clock graces the entrance to this Botanic Garden, the oldest garden in Texas. It displays more than 150,000 plants representing more than 2,500 native and exotic species in 110 acres of special gardens and natural settings. Seasonal plantings provide color throughout the year. In late April and October, visitors can enjoy more than 3,400 roses reaching peaks of bloom in the rose gardens. The Fragrance Garden is designed for the visually impaired, but all can enjoy the fragrant leaves to touch and smell. The two areas that have admission fees are the Japanese Garden and the Conservatory. The seven-and-one-half acre Japanese Garden features waterfalls and pools with Koi (imperial carp) fish, a teahouse, and Meditation Garden surrounded by evergreen shrubs, trees, and spring flowers or colorful fall foliage. Open daily April–October and every day but Monday, November–March. Hours vary. Adults $2 weekdays, $2.50 weekends and holidays; seniors 50¢ discount, children (4–12) $1. Ticket office, 871-7685. The Conservatory, which displays tropical plants, is open daily all year. Adult admission $1, seniors and children (4–12) $0.50. Hours vary. Information on tours and programs, 871-7682. Visitors number more than 600,000 annually. The headquarters of all affiliated state garden clubs, and the Texas Garden Club, is located here.

FORT WORTH NATURE CENTER AND REFUGE

9601 Fossil Ridge Road (76135), off Hwy. 199 (Jacksboro Hwy.), four miles west of Loop 820, on Lake Worth • 237-1111 • Tuesday–Saturday 9–5, Sunday 12–5. Closed Monday and major holidays • Free • W call ahead

There are buffalo here, and if you're sharp-eyed you may also see white-tailed deer, armadillos, wild turkeys, egrets, and herons roaming the prairies, forest, and marshes amid an abundance of wildflowers on this 3,500-acre sanctuary that remains much as it was 150 years ago. Nature programs, maps, and interpretive exhibits are available at the Hardwicke Interpretive Center. Hike the twenty-five-mile trail system or canoe the Trinity River. Birdwatchers say it's a crossroads for both eastern and western species.

FORT WORTH WATER GARDENS

Between Houston and Commerce streets, downtown south of the Convention Center • 871-8700 (Parks and Recreation Dept.) • Free • W

This $6 million, 4.3-acre park of terraced concrete and cascading water is spread over four-and-one-half blocks of downtown. The Gardens depict a miniature mountain scene enhanced with rivers, waterfalls, and pools, except the mountains only rise a little above street level while the pools go down forty feet. Each minute, 19,000 gallons of water flow, fall, sparkle, gurgle, spray and then recirculate through the five major water features to do it all again. The biggest feature is the Active Water Pool, in which 10,500 gallons of water per minute cascade from the upper edge, down multiple tiers, and into a pool surrounded by stepping stones. If you're a little adventurous, you can walk the table-sized stepping stones down into the center.

FORT WORTH ZOO

1989 Colonial Parkway (76110), off University Dr. one mile south of IH-30 871-7050 (24-hour info line) • Open daily, usually 10–5; weekend and holiday hours change seasonally (call) • Adults $7, seniors $3, children (3–12) $4.50, under 3 free. Half-price admission on Wednesdays • W+ but not all areas

One of the Top Five Zoos in America, this zoo is the home of one of the largest animal collections in the Western Hemisphere, with nearly 5,000 exotic animals including lowland gorillas, cheetahs, bears, and Komodo dragons. Features include colorful bird exhibits, an exciting birds-of-prey display, a world-famous reptile collection, an aquarium, and an insect exhibit. The oldest continuous zoo site in Texas, it draws more than a million visitors a year. The zoo is renowned for creating natural habitats for the animals, as if they were in the wild. Premier exhibits include: the World of Primates, a climate-controlled tropical rain forest where you can literally come face-to-face with intriguing gorillas, orangutans, and chimpanzees through large viewing windows; Asian Falls, with its vast array of Asian wildlife including tigers, sun bears, elephants, and rhinos; Raptor Canyon, where these majestic birds of prey can fly above and around you; and TEXAS!, a recreated nineteenth-century pioneer town complete with both wild and domestic animals indigenous to the state. What is reportedly the world's longest miniature train ride connects the zoo with Trinity Park (*see* Kids' Stuff, below).

HERITAGE PARK

Bluff and Main streets, north of Tarrant County Courthouse • 871-8700 (Parks and Recreation Dept.) • Always open • Free • W variable

This restful park is located on the bluffs above the Trinity River at the approximate site of the original Camp Worth. You can walk among water walls and waterfalls and follow paths down to get a bird's-eye view of the Trinity

River Valley to the north. Most of the 112-acre park is down the bluff. Hiking and biking trails. Boat and recreation center (293-4355), in the Tandy parking lot down on the river.

LAKE WORTH

Off Hwy. 199 (Jacksboro Hwy.) or Loop 820 at northwest end of city
871-8700 (Parks and Recreation Dept.) • Always open • Free • W variable
This 3,560-acre city-owned lake has city parks and commercial facilities for fishing, boating, and other water sports as well as picnicking on the shoreline. Meandering Drive wanders almost all around it, offering many scenic vistas. Location of Fort Worth Nature Center (see above).

LORD'S SUPPER DISPLAY

2500 Ridgmar Plaza (76150), in the Radio and Televison Commission
Building of the Southern Baptist Convention • 737-6251 • Monday–Saturday
12–5, Sunday 1–5 • Free • W+
This is a life-sized interpretation in wax of Leonardo da Vinci's famous painting "The Last Supper." With the work of a mother and daughter team, both named Katerine Stubergh, it took approximately eighteen months to complete. A taped narration is given in English and Spanish.

SUNDANCE SQUARE DOWNTOWN ENTERTAINMENT DISTRICT

Downtown, Throckmorton to Calhoun and 2nd to 5th streets
Surrounded by modern skyscrapers, this fourteen-block historic entertainment district has red-brick paved streets and courtyards that add to the early 1900s architecture that has been restored or replicated and now houses a collection of restaurants, live theaters and movie theaters, nightclubs, art galleries, and specialty shops. Named after the Sundance Kid, who, with his partner Butch Cassidy, hid out in high fashion in the nearby Hell's Half Acre. One of the more fascinating aspects of Sundance Square is the extensive *trompe l'oeil* (fool the eye) paintings of Richard Haas, especially the three-story Chisholm Trail Mural on the south side of the building at 400 Main, which appears to have depth although it is a flat picture. When the new Nancy Lee and Perry R. Bass Performance Hall is fully operational, it will be the center of the many attractions in Sundance, occupying most of the block at Commerce and 4th. This will be the capstone of the successful master plan launched by Bass Brothers Enterprises in 1982 to revitalize the decaying downtown and create a vibrant marketplace for living, working, shopping, and entertaining. While popular in the daytime, the area livens up even more in the evenings. The sidewalks and street corners of Sundance are filled with strolling musicians, mimes, caricature artists, and other entertainers each Friday and Saturday evening throughout the year.

SPORTS AND ACTIVITIES

Auto Racing

TEXAS MOTOR SPEEDWAY

North of Fort Worth at intersection of IH-35W and Hwy. 114 (P.O. Box 500,
76101-2500) • 215-8500 • Admission varies • W+, but not all areas

This 1.5-mile speedway is the site of both major NASCAR and Indy Racing League events, including a number of 300- and 500-mile races. The track also plays host to major C&W and other celebrity concerts.

College Sports

(*See* Colleges and Universities, below.)

Equestrian

COWTOWN CORRALS

500 Northeast 23rd Street (76106), south end of the Stockyards • 740-0582 or Metro 817-429-9993
Horseback rides for both beginners and experienced riders along the Old Chisholm Trail. Trail rides, by reservation, leave six times daily. Pony rides for children less than 7 years old.

WILL ROGERS EQUESTRIAN CENTER

One Amon Carter Square (76107), in Will Rogers Memorial Center in the Cultural District • 871-8150 • Admission varies • W+
This is one of the nation's premier equestrian centers and the site of more than two dozen horse shows each year, ranging from the annual Miniature Horse Show (there are 200 breeders and 4,000 miniature horses registered in Texas) to the National Cutting Horse Association Super Stakes.

Fishing

BOB'S CAT FISHING PONDS

7712 Davis Blvd., North Richland Hills • 428-6608 • W
Your luck should be good here since the ponds are stocked weekly (usually on Thursday). Normally open daily during daylight, but best to call ahead. Admission plus fees per pound of catch.

Golf

CARSWELL GOLF COURSE

6520 White Settlement Road (76114) • 738-8402 • Eighteen holes. Call for green fees.

CASINO BEACH ACADEMY

7464 Jacksboro Hwy. (76135) • 237-3695 • Nine holes. Call for green fees.

IRON HORSE GOLF COURSE

6200 Skylark (North Richland Hills) • 485-6666 • Eighteen holes. Call for green fees.

MEADOWBROOK MUNICIPAL GOLF COURSE

1815 Jensen Road (76112) • 457-4616 • Eighteen holes. Green fees: weekdays $10, weekends/holidays $12.

PECAN VALLEY MUNICIPAL GOLF COURSE

6400 Pecan Valley Dr. (P.O. Box 26632, 76126) • 249-1845 • Thirty-six holes. Green fees (eighteen holes): weekdays $10, weekends/holidays $12.

ROCKWOOD GOLF COURSE

1851 Jacksboro Hwy. (76114) • 624-1771 • Twenty-seven holes. Green fees (eighteen holes): weekdays $10, weekends/holidays $12

ROCKWOOD PAR 3 GOLF COURSE

1524 Rockwood Park (76114) • 824-8311 • Nine-hole par 3 course. Call for fees

SYCAMORE CREEK GOLF COURSE

100 North University Dr. (76107) • 871-8748 • Nine holes. Call for green fees

TIMBER-VIEW GOLF CLUB

4508 East Enon (76140) • 478-3601 • Eighteen holes. Call for green fees

Z. BOAZ GOLF COURSE

3240 Lackland Road (76116) • 738-6287 • Eighteen holes. Green fees: weekdays $10, weekends/holidays $12

Ice Skating

THE ICE AT TANDY CENTER

Fort Worth Outlet Square, One Tandy Center, Houston Street between 2nd and 3rd • 878-4800 • Admission $3.75, skate rental $1.25
A popular downtown rink for both skaters and watchers. Public skating sessions usually Monday–Friday 11–5 and 7:30–10 P.M., and Saturday–Sunday 1–5.

In-line Skating

DRY ICE METROPLEX IN-LINE HOCKEY AND SKATING CENTER

8851 Grapevine Hwy. (North Richland Hills) • 788-1051 • W variable
Both hockey and public skating for in-line skaters. Skate rentals available. Open Monday–Saturday.

Rodeo

COWTOWN COLISEUM

121 East Exchange Avenue (76106), in the Stockyards • 625-1025 or Metro 654-1148 • Admission $8–$10 • W
Constructed in 1907 to house the Fort Worth Stock Show, it was home of the first indoor rodeo in 1918 and now features professional cowboy and cowgirl rodeo events every weekend from April–September and occasionally during other months. Shows at 8 P.M.

SOUTHWESTERN EXPOSITION AND LIVESTOCK SHOW AND RODEO

(*See* Annual Events, below.)

Tennis

DON McLELAND TENNIS CENTER

1600 West Seminary (76115) • 921-5134
Fourteen lighted outdoor courts and two covered courts. The two indoor courts are available for $20 for 1½ hours. Other courts are $2.50 per person before 5 P.M. and $3 per person after 5 P.M.

MARY POTISHMAN LARD TENNIS CENTER

3609 Bellaire North (76109), on Texas Christian University campus • 921-7960

Five-court indoor tennis complex, 22 lighted outdoor courts. Covered courts $20 for 1½ hours anytime. Outdoor courts $2.50 per person for 1½ hours until 5 P.M. weekdays, $3 per person after 5 P.M. and on weekends. Additional charge of $1 for reservations on outdoor courts only.

RICHLAND TENNIS CENTER

Loop 820 at Holiday Lane exit (North Richland Hills) • 581-5763

All sixteen courts are lighted. One sunken court with tournament seating. Rates: $2.50 per person for 1½ hours.

COLLEGES AND UNIVERSITIES

TARRANT COUNTY JUNIOR COLLEGE (TCJC)

1500 Houston Street (76102), district office • 515-7851

The four campuses in this county junior college system include two in Fort Worth: the **South Campus** (5301 Campus Drive, north of I-20 and west of I-35W 76119, 515-4861); and the **Northwest Campus** (4801 Marine Creek Drive, north of Loop 820, 76179, 515-2900). There are about 8,000 students at the South Campus and almost 4,000 at the Northwest campus enrolled in both academic and technical programs. TCJC ranks first in Texas and twenty-first in the nation in the number of associate degrees awarded annually. Visitors are welcome at the campus art galleries, open Monday–Friday 8–5 during the academic year. Additionally, the performing arts departments at both campuses offer a spring and fall schedule of widely ranging entertainment, including stage productions and musical concerts.

TEXAS CHRISTIAN UNIVERSITY (TCU)

2800 South University Dr. (TCU Box 297050, 76129) between Cantey and West Berry • 921-7800 or 921-7810 (campus events information) • W variable

This university has an enrollment of 7,000 students studying seventy-nine undergraduate majors and six fields of doctoral study in the schools of business and education and the colleges of arts and sciences, nursing, and fine arts and communication. TCU is an independent, self-governing university affiliated with the Christian Church (Disciples of Christ), a mainstream Protestant denomination that emphasizes understanding among the world's religions. Among the many interesting buildings on the 237-acre campus is the **Robert Carr Chapel** (east side of University Dr.), which features a distinctive pulpit in the shape of a wine chalice; and **Jarvis Hall** (west side of University Dr., just south of Cantey), built in 1911, is the only original campus structure whose Neo-Georgian exterior is largely preserved. **The Mills Glass Collection,** in the Faculty Center in Reed Hall (west side of University Dr., 921-7808), with its more than 2,500 examples of early American pressed glass, art glass, blown glass, cut glass, and porcelain is open to visitors. Another collection open to visitors is the **Oscar Monnig Meteorite Collection,** one of the finest private meteorite collections in the Southwest, containing more than 400 different meteorites. It is on display in a small gallery in the front lobby of the Sid Richardson Physical Sciences Building (east side of University at Bowie). Student, faculty, and traveling art exhibitions are held in the **J.M. Moudy Exhibition Hall** (east side of University Dr. at Cantey, 921-7601). A number of music, theater, and dance productions are put on here during the school year, including plays by the drama department and concerts by the TCU Orchestra and TCU Jazz Band. Public lectures and eminent guest speakers are also featured. The new **F. Howard and Mary D. Walsh Center for the Performing Arts** is under development on the west side of University at Cantey. When completed, this 50,000-square-foot facility will wrap around the back of the adjacent 1,200-seat **Ed Landreth Auditorium,** providing a new recital hall, rehearsal halls, and a studio theater. The intimate recital hall in the Walsh Center will complement the Ed Landreth Auditorium, one of the finest acoustical halls in the area, which contains a world-class concert pipe organ and serves as the host site for dozens of performances, including the Van Cliburn International Piano Competition (*See* Annual Events, below). Visitors are also welcome at intercollegiate sports events on campus. The TCU Horned Frogs compete in the Western Athletic Conference, the largest conference in NCAA Division 1A athletics. Football is played in the **Amon Carter Stadium** (Stadium Dr. and Cantey). Men's and women's basketball games are held in the **Daniel-Meyer Coliseum** (Stadium Dr.), and baseball, volleyball, and most other sports events are held at various locations on campus. For schedules and ticket information, call 922-FROG (922-3764). Limited visitor parking is available near the student center (west side of University Dr.) and the coliseum (Stadium Dr.). Visitors may pick up a campus map and view an extensive photographic history of the university in the **Dee J. Kelly Alumni and Visitors Center** (Stadium Dr. near the athletic complex).

TEXAS WESLEYAN UNIVERSITY
1201 Wesleyan (76105), between East Vickery and East Rosedale • 531-4444, Metro 817-429-7010, outside Texas 800-580-8980 • W+, but not all areas

Founded in 1890 by the Methodist Episcopal Church South, it was originally named Polytechnic College, which has the literal meaning "many arts and sciences." This concept has remained central to the mission of the university, which now has close to 3,000 students enrolled in programs leading to undergraduate degrees in the arts, humanities, science, business, and education, and graduate degrees in business, education, law, dentistry, and nurse anesthesia.

The campus is located on approximately seventy-five acres just four miles southeast of downtown Fort Worth on Polytechnic Heights, one of the highest points in the city. Visitors are welcome at a number of events, most of which are free. Art exhibits are held in the gallery in the **Law Sone Fine Arts Center** (1201 Wesleyan). Hillard Hall, also in The Fine Arts Center, is the location for performances of the Wesleyan Singers, the Jazz Ensemble, Wind Ensemble, the annual spring musical, and other voice and instrumental recitals. The location of theater performances vary but do include the intimate Firestation studio theater in the former fire station and city hall of Polytechnic Heights (531-4990). University varsity sports events open to visitors include men's soccer, basketball, baseball, and tennis, and women's volleyball, basketball, softball, and tennis. Game locations vary. Call 531-4210. Visitor parking is available at several locations on the campus.

PERFORMING ARTS
ALIVE AT FIVE SUMMER CONCERTS
Sundance Square • 339-7777 • Free • W

The "five" is five o'clock, the starting time of these free summer concerts, usually held on Thursday evenings 5–10, in the parking lot facing the Chisholm Trail Mural, between 3rd and 4th streets and Houston and Main. Entry by ticket, but free tickets are available in Sundance Square and through sponsors.

CARAVAN OF DREAMS PERFORMING ARTS CENTER

312 Houston Street (76102) in Sundance Square • 877-3000 or Metro 817-429-4000 • Admission varies • W+, but not all areas
This four-level entertainment complex includes a nightclub, live theater, and dance facilities. The nightclub, located on ground level, is a premier live performance venue, attracting national music acts in blues, rock, and jazz.

CASA MANANA THEATRE

3101 West Lancaster (76107), at University Dr., at east end of Cultural District 332-2272 • Admission varies • W+
It was originally started in the early 1930s as an outdoor summer theater. Amon Carter reportedly hired famed showman Billy Rose at $100 a day (a tidy sum during the Depression) to put on the first show. Rose shocked some citizens and pleased others by bringing in celebrated fan dancer Sally Rand as one of the headliners. In 1958 the old theater was replaced by the present geodesic dome, one of the first commercial uses of Buckminster Fuller's architectural creation. The 1,800-seat dome theater gained fame as the home of the world's first permanent musical theater-in-the-round. For years, the Casa Manana concentrated on summer musicals. Musicals still make up most productions; however, now the theater also puts on an occasional dramatic work, celebrity concerts, touring companies, and children's theater (*see* Kids' Stuff, below) on a year-round schedule.

CASA'S THEATRE ON THE SQUARE

109 East 3rd Street (76102), in Sundance Square • Tickets average $16–$20 332-3509 • W (elevator)
This intimate, 130-seat theater upstairs in the Knights of Pythias Building mostly features touring shows on weekends. Shows are usually Thursday–Friday at 8, Saturday at 5 and 9, and Sunday matinee.

CIRCLE THEATRE

230 West 4th Street (P.O. Box 470456, 76102) • 921-3040 Tickets average $12–$16
The professional theater troupe performing in this intimate, downstairs theater usually presents six productions a year with the emphasis on Broadway and off-Broadway shows.

CLIBURN CONCERTS

Van Cliburn Foundation, 2525 Ridgmar Blvd., Suite 307 (76116) • 738-6536, tickets 335-9000 • Admission
Begun in 1976, this annual concert series presents some of the world's finest artists in recital. This is one of the activities of the Van Cliburn Foundation, which also sponsors concerts by past winners of the Van Cliburn International Piano Competition, which it holds every four years. (*See* Annual Events, below) The concerts in Fort Worth are usually given one evening a month in the Ed Landreth Auditorium at Texas Christian University.

FORT WORTH DALLAS BALLET

6845 Green Oaks Road (76116) • 763-0207 (Fort Worth) or 214-696-3932 (Dallas) • Admission varies

This is not a merger of the Fort Worth and Dallas ballet companies, as the name may imply, but rather an expansion of the performances of the professional Fort Worth Ballet to Dallas to fill in the void left when the Dallas Ballet dissolved in 1988. Fort Worth performances are held in the Fort Worth/Tarrant County Convention Center Theatre and will move to the new Bass Performance Hall when that facility is fully developed. Dallas performances are at the Music Hall in Fair Park.

FORT WORTH/TARRANT COUNTY CONVENTION CENTER

1111 Houston Street (76102), just north of IH-30 • 884-2222 Admission varies • W+

Sure, there are lots of conventions and trade shows here (some open to the public), but there's a lot more going on, ranging from major concerts to ice hockey and ice shows. The 3,000-seat theater is presently home of the Fort Worth Opera and the Fort Worth Symphony, both of which will move to the Bass Performance Hall when that facility is ready for them.

FORT WORTH OPERA ASSOCIATION

3505 West Lancaster (76107), office • 731-0833 • Tickets $10–$45

This association sponsors the oldest continuing opera company in Texas, presenting three or four productions in its fall and winter season. Most company members are local professionals, but the association frequently brings in well-known artists for lead roles. Until the Bass Performance Hall facilities are ready, performances are usually given in the convention center's JFK Theatre or the Scott Theatre.

FORT WORTH SYMPHONY ORCHESTRA

4401 Trail Lake Drive (76109), administrative office • 921-2676 office, 926-8831 box office • Tickets $6–$34

This professional symphony orchestra puts on seven master concerts a year, interspersed with several pops concerts in its September–May season. It also gives six children's concerts. Until the Bass Performance Hall facilities are ready, performances are usually given in the Fort Worth/Tarrant County Convention Center's JFK Theatre. The core of the symphony orchestra is the **Fort Worth Chamber Orchestra,** composed of thirty-six full-time professional musicians recruited from across the United States. In addition to the symphony season, the chamber orchestra puts on concerts throughout the year at The Ed Landreth Auditorium on the campus of Texas Christian University. It was the first chamber orchestra to tour the People's Republic of China after the cultural revolution (1983).

FORT WORTH THEATER

3505 West Lancaster (76107) • 738-7491 • Admission varies

The city's oldest theater company offers two seasons: Main Stage and The Studio series. The Main Stage is entertainment served family style. The Studio series productions are designed to showcase a variety of playwrights and directors.

HIP POCKET THEATRE

1627 Fairmont Avenue (76104) • 927-2833 • Tickets $8–$14.

Known for its innovative and original works, this theater group performs a wide range of productions, from musicals to comedy and spoofs, in a variety of locations including its summer theater under the stars in the Oak Acres Amphitheatre.

JUBILEE THEATRE

506 Main (76102), in Sundance Square • 338-4411 • Tickets $8–$16 • W+

One of only two theaters in Texas that showcases black performers, this troupe is the only African-American theatre in the Metroplex that offers a full season of shows, which range across drama, comedy, and musicals.

ED LANDRETH AUDITORIUM

Texas Christian University, University and West Cantey • 921-7810, campus events information • W+

The 1,200-seat Ed Landreth Auditorium, considered one of the finest acoustical halls in the area, contains a world-class concert pipe organ and serves as the host site for dozens of guest performances, including the Van Cliburn Foundation Concerts and the Van Cliburn International Piano Competition (*see* Colleges and Universities—Texas Christian University, above, and Annual Events, below).

STAGE WEST

3055 South University Dr. (76109) at Berry, next to TCU campus • 784-9378 (STG-WEST) • Tickets $13–$16 • W+

This professional regional theater puts on nine plays in two subscription series that run through the entire year. The Center Stage Series offers six plays that are well-known and basically mainstream, ranging from classics to Broadway shows. The three plays in the Adventure Series, which are interspersed, are more on the cutting edge of theater and run two to three weekends.

TEXAS BOYS CHOIR

2925 Riverglen (76109) • 924-1482 or Metro 817-429-0066 • Tickets $5–$8

Founded in 1946, this choir has built an international reputation, made thirty-five records and won two Grammys. Boys from 8 years to change-of-voice are eligible to participate. The two main groups in the choir are the professional touring choir, which has performed all over the United States and in a number of foreign countries, and the resident performing choir, which performs at many area festivals and usually gives at least one local concert a year.

TEXAS GIRLS CHOIR

4449 Camp Bowie Blvd. (76107) • 732-8161

Not to be outdone by the boys, this choir also makes national and overseas tours. There are about 200 girls ranging in age from 8 to 15 divided into six choirs, with the top two being the concert choirs that put on about 100 performances annually. Some of these are free concerts at churches, malls, and hospitals, while other local concerts are held in performance halls with admission.

WILL ROGERS AUDITORIUM

Will Rogers Memorial Center, 3401 West Lancaster (76107), in the Cultural District • 332-2272 • Admission varies • W+

The auditorium has 2,856 seats and hosts touring Broadway productions, celebrity shows, and classical concerts.

SHOPPING

ANTIQUE SHOPS

There are a number of antique shops scattered throughout the city, including several that gather a number of dealers under one roof. Two of these conglomerate antique and collectible dealers are **Stockyards Antiques** and **The Antique Colony.** Stockyards Antiques is in a converted 1890s hotel at 1332 North Main, at Northside (624-2311), where the 30,000 square-foot building houses 125 shops. There are 100 shops in The Antique Colony, 7200 Camp Bowie Blvd. at the intersection with Hwy. 183/Southwest Blvd. (731-7252).

FORT WORTH OUTLET SQUARE

Throckmorton and 3rd, just west of Sundance Square • 390-3716 • W variable (elevator)

The name "Square" is loosely used here, because it's actually the indoor mall retail space between the two towers of the Tandy Center building. But the "Outlet" part of the title is appropriate since it has about three dozen upscale retail stores featuring outlet savings on brand-name products. Anchor stores are Computer City (naturally, it's a Tandy Corporation chain) and Spiegel. Other stores cover the gamut of products from clothing for men, women, and children, to jewelry, luggage, and vitamins. Park at the Tandy lot and take the subway right into the "Square" (see OFFBEAT). Food court.

HULEN MALL

4800 South Hulen (76132), at Loop 820 (IH-20) • 294-1200 • W variable

Dillard's, Foley's, and Montgomery Ward anchor more than 125 specialty shops, mostly national chain stores, in this two-level mall. Outside parking for more than 3,500 cars and garage parking for another 1,000. Luby's Cafeteria and a food court.

RIDGMAR MALL

2060 Green Oaks Road (76116), on IH-30 and Hwy. 183 • 731-0856 • W variable

The major stores in this two-level mall are Dillard's, Neiman-Marcus, Penney's, and Sears. They anchor more than 130 other specialty stores—mostly representatives of national chains—a cafeteria and fast food outlets.

WESTERN WEAR

This is where the West begins, and to be in the West you have to wear Western clothes, or at least something that pays tribute to both the cowboy heritage and the cowboy's fine sense of utilitarian wear, like hats that keep off the sun and rain, long-wearing jeans, or boots that help the rider keep his seat. Among the better-known Western wear stores in the city are: the collection of shops on East and West Exchange in the Stockyards; **Luskey's Western Wear,** 101 Houston at Weatherford, downtown (335-5833); **Justin Boot Company Factory Out-**

let, 717 W. Vickery Blvd. (654-3103); and **Ryon's Saddle and Ranch,** 2601 North Main, just north of the Stockyards (625-2391).

KIDS' STUFF

BURGER LAKE

1200 Meandering Road (76114), off Hwy. 183 (River Oaks Blvd.) southeast of Lake Worth • 737-3414 • Admission $5, children 5 and under free • W

This one-acre spring-fed swimming pool with a sand bottom and two sand beaches is in a seventeen-acre park. Open early May through Labor Day, 9 A.M. to dark. Picnic tables and grills.

CASA MANANA PLAYHOUSE

3101 West Lancaster (76107), at University Dr., at east end of Cultural District 332-2272 • Admission varies • W+

The Playhouse is a professional children's theater troupe that puts on children's plays in the domed Casa Manana Theatre. The group usually puts on a play a month from October through May, with each performance running two or three weekends. Single tickets $6.25.

MOUNTASIA FAMILY FUN CENTER

8851 Grapevine Hwy. (North Richland Hills) • 788-0990 • W variable

In addition to a thirty-six-hole miniature golf course, there are bumper boats, go-carts, batting cages, and video games in a large clubhouse. Separate charges for each activity. Open seven days.

NRH$_2$0 FAMILY WATER PARK

9001 Grapevine Hwy. (North Richland Hills), across from Tarrant County Junior College campus • 656-6500 • Mid-May to mid-September Adults $9.95, children (3–11) $7.95, under 3 free • W

Truly a family park with something for every age. For toddlers, it offers a water playground complete with a life-sized train engine, toddler-sized water slides, and entertainment every day. Teens and adventurous adults can try their skills with the wave pool, three twisting water slides, and a two-person tube slide. And for those who want relaxation more than thrills, there's the gentle Endless River.

PAWNEE BILL'S WILD WEST SHOW

Cowtown Coliseum, 121 East Exchange, in the Stockyards • 625-1025 Admission • W variable

Every Saturday from late April through September, this family show turns the coliseum back in time to the days of Buffalo Bill, with more than seventy animals, expert ropers and riders, trick shooters, a bull-whip artist, authentic prairie wagons, and even a stagecoach holdup.

PONY RIDES

Cowtown Corrals, 500 Northeast 23rd Street (76106), south end of the Stockyards • 740-0582 or Metro 817-429-9993

Rides available in the arena for children under 7 years old at $10 an hour.

TRAIN RIDE IN THE PARKS

**2100 Colonial Parkway in Forest Park (76110) • 475-1233 or 336-3328
Tuesday–Sunday, late May–Labor Day. Closed Monday • Children 12
and under $1.62, adults and youths $2.16**

Billed as one the world's longest miniature train rides, the two ornate, scaled-down trains carry passengers on a five-mile round trip from the Forest Park Depot to Trinity Park Duck Pond and back. Weekdays the train runs on the hour. Saturday, Sunday, and holidays it runs every forty-five minutes. Tuesday–Friday 11–5, Saturday–Sunday 11–6. Off-season, it operates 11–5 on Saturday, Sunday and holidays only.

OFFBEAT

TANDY SUBWAY

Downtown • Free • W

The only privately owned subway in the world, it was originally intended to carry Tandy employees from the stations in the nearby riverside parking lots to their workplaces in the headquarters buildings. But, thanks to the Tandy Corporation, you don't have to be a Tandy employee to take advantage of the free ride to avoid the hassle of downtown parking. The one-car trains run at frequent intervals between the 3,000 free parking spaces in the Tandy lots along the Trinity River (entrance at north end of Henderson) to the downstairs of the Fort Worth Outlet Square in the Tandy Building. Trains operate Monday–Friday 5:30 A.M.–10:30 P.M., Saturday 8 A.M.–10:30 P.M., and Sunday 11:30 A.M.–7 P.M. Parking in the Tandy lots is also free. Just make sure to remember which station you parked your car by.

ANNUAL EVENTS

Fort Worth Convention and Visitors Bureau Events Hotline, 332-2000. For events information in Sundance Square, 339-7777.

January–February

SOUTHWESTERN EXPOSITION AND LIVESTOCK SHOW AND RODEO

Will Rogers Memorial Center, 3301 West Lancaster (76107), in the Cultural District • Mid-January–early February • 877-2400 • General admission: adults $5, children (6–16) $2 • W+ but not all areas

The nation's oldest livestock show is now more than a century old. Usually scheduled for about seventeen days, starting mid-January and ending the first week in February, it is the biggest annual event in the city, drawing approximately 800,000 visitors. Highlights include an all-Western parade downtown, days and days of judging approximately 19,000 head of livestock ranging from pigeons and rabbits to bulls and horses, livestock auctions, commercial exhibits, a carnival midway, plus the nation's top cowboys and cowgirls competing and name entertainers performing at the rodeo. Rodeo performances nightly at 8 with matinees on weekends. Rodeo tickets $14–$16. Shuttle buses run weekends from noon to midnight from Billy Bob's Texas lot in the Stockyards, $1 one way.

April

MAIN STREET ART FESTIVAL

Main Street, downtown • Thursday–Sunday in mid-month
336-ARTS (336-2787) • Free • W variable

The brick-paved Main Street is blocked off from the courthouse, south nine blocks, almost to the convention center, to become the site of the Southwest's largest art festival. The area is filled with outdoor arts and crafts shows with more than 200 participating artists. Also loads of food and live entertainment with more than 400 entertainers performing almost continuously on three stages. Thursday–Saturday it goes on from late morning to midnight, Sunday to 8 P.M.

May

MAYFEST

Trinity Park • Thursday–Sunday closest to May 1 • 332-1055
Admission • W variable

Fort Worth's own rite of spring started out as a loosely organized community-wide picnic on the banks of the Trinity River in the early 1970s. The community still comes—or at least about 350,000 people—but it's now definitely more organized, with areas featuring sports, arts, a variety of entertainment, and fireworks. There's also a children's area and activities.

MASTERCARD COLONIAL GOLF TOURNAMENT

Colonial Country Club, 3735 Country Club Cir. (76109) • Usually third week in month • 927-4280 or 927-4281 • Admission • W call ahead

The nation's top golfers on the PGA tour compete in this nationally televised tournament for over $1 million in prizes. The invitation-only tournament is more than fifty years old. Fort Worth's native son, Ben Hogan, won the first one in 1946 and went on to win four more Colonial titles, so the course—rated one of the ten toughest on the tour—is called Hogan's Alley. Admission is free Monday and Tuesday for the practice rounds. Passes sell for $85 for the entire tournament; $35 per day for Wednesday (Pro-Am), Saturday, and Sunday; and $25 a day for Thursday and Friday. Attendance averages about 140,000.

May–June Every Four Years

VAN CLIBURN INTERNATIONAL PIANO COMPETITION

Van Cliburn Foundation, 2525 Ridgmar Blvd., Suite 307 (76116) • 738-6536

Technically, since it only takes place every four years, this is not an annual event; however, it earns a listing here because it is considered one of the most important music competitions in the world. In 1958, the young Texas pianist Van Cliburn won one of the most prestigious piano competitions in the world, the Tchaikovsky International Piano Competition in Moscow. His victory lead to the organization of this competition to seek out other world-class concert pianists. First held in 1962, the competition has been repeated every four years since then, with the tenth competition held in May–June 1997. The next competition, the eleventh, will be held in 2001.

June

CHISHOLM TRAIL ROUND-UP AND CHIEF QUANAH PARKER COMANCHE POW WOW

Stockyards National Historic District, North Main and Exchange
Friday–Sunday in mid-month • 625-7005 • Admission • W variable

The Old West lives again in this three-day celebration of the famous cattle drives that put Fort Worth on the map. A tradition that started in 1977, the festival now draws about 150,000 visitors. Activities include: a trail ride; street fair; authentic Native American exhibitions and dances; continuous live C&W entertainment on four stages; barbecue and chili cook-offs; a parade on Saturday; live gunfights and whip artistry demonstrations; armadillo, pig, and chuckwagon races; and street dances Friday and Saturday. A children's area features entertainment, a petting zoo, rides, and games.

June–July

SHAKESPEARE IN THE PARK

Trinity Park Playhouse, Trinity Blvd. and 7th Street, off Camp Bowie Blvd.
Two or three weeks late in June and early July • 923-6698 • Tickets $6–$12
W variable

A tradition for more than two decades is Fort Worth's outdoor presentation of the Bard's best. One of Shakespeare's plays is performed every night except Monday over a two- or three-week period in late June and early July in this open-air theater. Children 12 and under free. Also available, by reservation, is the Elizabethan Feast, offering a menu of dinner packages. Go early, bring a blanket or a chair to sit on, and enjoy.

August

PIONEER DAYS

Stockyards National Historic District, North Main and Exchange
Friday–Sunday, weekend before Labor Day • 626-7921 • Admission $5,
parking $6 • W variable

Fort Worth salutes its pioneer heritage and the early days of the cattle industry with this Western wingding. Old West doings include: demonstrations of pioneer skills; staged gunfights and a gunfight competition; a stunt show; rodeos, including a ranch rodeo for real ranch cowboys; Wild West shows in the coliseum; a Western melodrama (extra charge); and continuous music on four stages. Children's area includes a Root Beer Garden.

October

OKTOBERFEST

Fort Worth/Tarrant County Convention Center, 1111 Houston Street, just
north of I-30 • First Saturday–Sunday in month • 924-5881 • Adults $6,
seniors and children (7–16) $4, children 6 and under free • W+

If you can't go to Munich for Oktoberfest, try this miniature version of the famed beer festival. There's plenty of oompah music to dance to, as well as German and international foods. Also performing and visual arts make this an annual family festival in the true German spirit. And if you prefer other types of music, you'll probably be able to hear them on one of the five stages. Because this is a fund-raiser for the symphony, many groups representing both the local music scene and performing arts help out with their entertainment talents.

FORT WORTH INTERNATIONAL AIR SHOW

Alliance Airport, north of city at I-35W and Hwy. 170 (International Air Show, P.O. Box 821, 76101) • Saturday–Sunday in early or mid-month 870-1515 • Adults $10, children 6 and older $5, under 6 free • W variable

Fort Worth's place in aviation history is celebrated with heart-stopping displays of aerial aerobatics, stunt flying, wing-walking, and parachute team drops. On the ground there are displays of all types of military and civilian aircraft, as well as exhibits recounting the history of aviation.

RED STEAGALL COWBOY GATHERING & WESTERN SWING FESTIVAL

Stockyards National Historic District, North Main and Exchange Friday–Sunday late in month • 884-1945 • Admission • W variable

This annual gathering usually attracts about 35,000 to the three-day festival celebrating the cowboy way of life in both its reality and myth. The activities include ranch rodeos, in which real cowboys compete in everyday cowboy skills, such as branding, bronc riding, sorting, and team roping, as well as some definitely-not-everyday skills, like wild-cow milking. Also chuck wagon cooking, recitations of cowboy poetry, and musical entertainment that emphasizes Western swing at five locations throughout the Stockyards.

RESTAURANTS

ANGELO'S BAR-B-QUE

2533 White Settlement Road (76107) at Vecek • 332-0357 • Lunch and dinner Monday–Saturday. Closed Sunday and major holidays • $ • No Cr • W+

Angelo's started serving hickory-smoked brisket of beef and pork ribs in 1958 and since then has earned a reputation that not only keeps bringing in customers but has virtually turned Angelo's into a shrine for barbecue lovers. If you can't decide among the choices on the simple list of plate dinners, try a combo plate of any two meats. Beer and wine.

THE BALCONY OF RIDGLEA

6100 Camp Bowie Blvd. (76116) at Winthrop, in Ridglea Village Shopping Center • 731-3719 • Lunch Monday–Friday, dinner Monday–Saturday. Closed Sunday and major holidays • $$ • Cr • W (elevator)

This elegant upstairs restaurant offers seating in its mirrored dining room or on the glassed-in balcony that gives the restaurant its name. The chef-owner offers a continental menu. Children's menu. Jackets suggested for dinner. Pianist Friday and Saturday evenings. Bar.

THE BUFFET AT THE KIMBELL

3333 Camp Bowie Blvd., Kimbell Art Museum in the Cultural District 332-8451 • Lunch Tuesday–Sunday, light dinner Friday 5:30–7:30. Closed Monday • $ • Cr • W+

The cafeteria-style restaurant setting itself is nothing special, but you are just steps away from the most elegant surroundings of the art treasures in this museum. And the food, although light lunch fare, offers a variety of nonstandard choices of sandwiches, soups, salads, and simple-but-sweet desserts. Friday evenings, the light dinner buffet is served with live music (reservations recommended). Beer and wine.

CARSHON'S DELICATESSEN

3133 Cleburne Road (76110) near West Berry • 923-1907 • Breakfast and lunch Tuesday–Sunday 9–3. Closed Monday and major holidays • $ • No Cr

Almost three-quarters of a century after it was started as a kosher meat market in another location in 1928, Carshon's is now famed as a kosher-style deli that offers everything you'd expect in a deli, from chicken soup to a huge selection of old-fashioned two-handed sandwiches and plate lunches. Beer and wine.

CATTLEMEN'S STEAKHOUSE

2458 North Main (76106), in the Stockyards, just north of Exchange Avenue 624-3945 • Lunch and dinner daily • $–$$ • Cr • W call ahead

Founded in 1947, this restaurant has earned a place among the traditions of the Stockyards. As the name says, the big draw is the steaks, which are charcoal broiled and come in all sizes from an eight-ounce filet to an eighteen-ounce sirloin. Other choices include seafood and barbecued ribs. Bar.

CELEBRATION

4600 Dexter Avenue (76107), at Camp Bowie and Hulen • 731-6272 Lunch and dinner daily • $–$$ • Cr • W

In most restaurants that tout home cooking, the "home" was probably an orphanage, but here it is like Mom used to make, especially if Mom had been to a distinguished cooking school. Fried chicken, pot roast, seafood; all simply prepared and served in large portions with salad, fresh vegetables family style—which means seconds on most entrees if you want them—and homemade desserts. Children's menu. Bar.

EDELWEISS RESTAURANT

3801-A Southwest Blvd. (76116) on the Old Weatherford traffic circle 738-5934 • Dinner Tuesday–Saturday. Closed Sunday–Monday • $$ • Cr • W

The decor in this 350-seat restaurant is that of a German beer hall, and the atmosphere varies, so you can choose between cozy corners with candlelight to being just a step or two short of an Oktoberfest party. Owner/chef from Germany means true German food. Band plays everything from polkas to waltzes for dancing nightly. Children's menu. Bar. Same location more than thirty years.

8.0 RESTAURANT

111 East 3rd (76102), in Sundance Square • 336-0880 • Lunch and dinner daily $–$$ • Cr • W

Steaks, seafood, pasta, and Tex-Mex items are all on the menu, but in addition to the routine choices, each category has its own unique specialties. Another plus is that there are no preservatives, hormones, antibiotics or any other bad junk in the meat products served here, and everything else is made as pure and healthy as possible. Even the water and ice are filtered. The bar is a popular meeting place at night, so it can be noisy. Check out the wall murals by local artists.

JOE T. GARCIA'S MEXICAN DISHES

2201 North Commerce (76106), near the Stockyards • 626-4356 • Lunch and dinner daily. Closed some major holidays • $–$$ • No Cr • W (through patio)

In 1935, Joe T. Garcia opened part of his home as a Mexican restaurant. Customers walked through the kitchen to get to the dining room and got beer from the family refrigerator. Now, the family still operates the restaurant, but over more than sixty years, the family has expanded the house until it fills about half a city block with what is probably the best-known Tex-Mex restaurant in the city. If the weather's nice, the garden patio is the best place to be. Enchiladas, tacos, fajitas, chile rellenos; all the standard Tex-Mex dishes are on the menu. Actually, they're not on the menu, at least not on a printed one since there is none; the waiters spout it off for you. Strolling mariachis enhance the atmosphere on weekends. Bar. For what localites tout as the best place to get a Tex-Mex breakfast, there's **Joe T. Garcia's Mexican Bakery** with two locations, one around the corner from the restaurant at 2140 North Main and the other at 1109 Hemphill.

HEDARY'S LEBANESE RESTAURANT

3308 Fairfield (76116), in the 6323 Shopping Center of Camp Bowie Blvd. Lunch Tuesday–Friday, dinner Tuesday–Sunday. Closed Mondays. • $$ Cr • W

You've heard of *tabbuli* and *falafil* and *hummus*, but you're not sure exactly what they are, much less traditional Lebanese dishes called *sujak* or *shish tawuk*. Not to worry; Hedary's menu explains every dish in detail so you can order with competence. Beer and wine. Lebanese music.

JUANITA'S RESTAURANT

115 West 2nd (76102), in Sundance Square across from The Worthington Hotel • 335-1777 • Lunch and dinner daily. Closed major holidays $ • Cr • W

It looks like a classy Victorian restaurant you'd find in New York back in the early 1900s, but the menu is Tex-Mex, or maybe *nouvelle* Tex-Mex, with a touch of Cajun blended in. The standards are here—enchiladas, tacos, fajitas—however, specialties also include chile butter chicken, and quail braised in tequila. Latin/Mexican background music.

LE CHARDONNAY

2443 Forest Park Blvd. (76110), near TCU campus • 926-5622 Lunch and dinner daily. Closed major holidays. • $$–$$$ • Cr • W+

Take a chef-owner schooled in French cooking and expose him to southwestern ingredients, and you have the core of the menu in this restaurant that resembles a cozy Paris bistro with an outdoor terrace. Escargot, pates, steak Parisienne, duck, potato-crusted red snapper, and zesty lamb are just a few of the items that result from this combination. Children's menu. Bar.

MICHAEL'S

3413 West 7th (76107) • 877-3413 • $$–$$$ • Cr • W

The chef-partner titles his menu Contemporary Ranch Cuisine. That includes steaks, of course, from chicken fried to New York strip, but it also translates into entrees, like ranch-roasted pork tenderloin with roasted corn and red chile salsa cream sauce, or Michael's ranch-baked crab cakes with lite ancho chile cream sauce. Bar.

ON BROADWAY RISTORANTE

6306 Hulen Bend Blvd. (76132), in Hulen Point Shopping Center • 346-8841 Lunch Monday–Friday, dinner daily • $–$$ • Cr • W+

Grilled chicken and thin-crusted pizza with shrimp are just a couple of the items on the predominently Northern Italian menu that set this *ristorante* a cut above the normal strip-center Italian restaurant. Pastas, steaks, and seafood entrees include out-of-the-ordinary specialties like trout with a shrimp garnish in a tomato-wine-butter sauce. Bar.

REFLECTIONS

The Worthington Hotel, 200 Main Street (76102), north end of Sundance Square • 882-1765 • Dinner Monday–Saturday. Closed Sunday • $$$ Cr • W+

The name comes from the reflecting pools that are the centerpiece of this dining room, located on the mezzanine level. The atmosphere of subdued elegance, a chef who is creative and consistent, artistic presentation of palate-pleasing dishes, and unobtrusively efficient service combine to make the fine dining here a culinary occasion to reflect on. The menu offers American and regional dishes with a French influence. A fixed price menu ($28.95 including tax and tip) features a three-course meal. Semi-formal dress. Bar. Reservations suggested. Complimentary validated valet parking at hotel.

REATA

500 Throckmorton Street (76102), Bank One Tower • 336-1009 • Lunch and dinner Monday–Saturday. Closed Sunday • $–$$ • Cr • W+

Go for the panoramic view—it's on the thirty-fifth floor—but stay for the food, which is upscale cowboy cuisine. Named for the ranch in the movie *Giant,* the menu appropriately features steaks. But these steaks aren't steer-tough and burned to a crisp, as was the custom in the old ranch days; these—the pan-seared pepper-crusted tenderlion, for example—are tender and cooked to your liking. Also a selection of Tex-Mex and seafood entrees. Bar.

RUFFINO'S ITALIAN RESTAURANT

2455 Forest Park Blvd. (76110), near TCU campus • 923-0522 • Lunch and dinner Monday–Saturday. Closed Sunday • $$–$$$ • Cr • W+

Classic Italian fare is served in this cozy *trattoria*-style restaurant. Veal, chicken, beef, and seafood entrees all with tasty sauces. If you're really hungry try the family-style dinner for two, which runs from antipasto through pasta and entree to dessert. Beer and wine.

SAINT-EMILION

3617 West 7th (76107), near the Cultural District • 737-2781 • Dinner daily $$–$$$ • Cr • W+

The decor of this brick-home restaurant is so country French it could have been transplanted directly from a French village. And the menu follows through with well-crafted entrees, including such culinary delights as seafood in a puff pastry, veal medallions, duck, lamb, and fresh fish flown in daily from the Northeast. Fixed price dinner available (about $29). Bar.

CLUBS AND BARS

BILLY BOB'S TEXAS

**2520 Rodeo Plaza (76106), in the Stockyards • 624-7117 or
Metro 817-589-1711 • Admission • W+**

Known as the world's largest honky-tonk, Billy Bob's has room for 6,000 people, two dance floors, and forty bar stations and is the only nightclub in the nation with an indoor arena where every weekend professional rodeo cowboys try to ride bulls that don't want to be ridden. Live country music is played every night, with major country artists performing in concert most weekends. The Academy of Country Music and the Country Music Association have both awarded it the title of Club of the Year several times. Sunday–Thursday, general admission $1 before 6 P.M., $3 after; Friday–Saturday $1 before 5 P.M., $5.50–$8.50 after. Live music begins at 8 P.M. every night. Friday and Saturday: bull-riding at 9 and 10, and name entertainment begins at 10:30. Shops, arcade games, restaurant. Free parking during the day, pay parking at night.

CARAVAN OF DREAMS PERFORMING ARTS CENTER

**312 Houston Street (76102) in Sundance Square • 877-3000 or
Metro 817-429-4000 • Admission varies • W+, but not all areas**

This downstairs club is the Fort Worth mecca for jazz and blues fans. That's not all it books, but it's the main program most of the time. The club is small, so when a top name is booked, you'd best get your tickets early. Or you can just enjoy the ambiance and view from the rooftop grotto bar.

WHITE ELEPHANT SALOON

**106 East Exchange Avenue (76106), in the Stockyards • 624-1887
Cover on weekends**

The 1887 in the phone number isn't just a coincidence. A permanent place in Fort Worth's history was ensured for the saloon, which was then located downtown, when its owner, gambler Luke Short, outdrew and killed former marshal "Long Hair" Jim Courtright in 1887. There have been changes since 1887, of course, but today's saloon still recalls the Old West with its long, wooden stand-up bar with brass footrail. The saloon has been listed in *Esquire* magazine's 100 Best Bars in America. Upstairs is a cabaret theater, where the Cowtown Opry performs every Saturday (admission), and next door is the White Elephant Beer Garden, open April–October with live music and dancing on weekend nights.

ACCOMMODATIONS

($ = under $80, $$ = $81–$120, $$$ = $121–$180, $$$$ = $181–$250, $$$$$ = over $250)

Room tax 13%

AZALEA PLANTATION

1400 Robinwood Drive (76111) • 838-5882 or 800-68-RELAX (800-687-3529) • $$

This bed and breakfast offers four rooms with private baths and two private cottages with mini-kitchens. Free local phone calls. Fax and copy service available. Free continental breakfast weekdays, breakfast buffet weekends. Free outside parking.

ETTA'S PLACE

**200 West 3rd at Houston in Sundance Square (76102) • Metro 817-654-0267
$$$ • W+ elevator and some rooms • All no-smoking except for outside
terraces**

The ten units in this bed and breakfast include four suites and are located on
the second to fifth floors of the building, around the corner from the Caravan of
Dreams. Private baths. Children and pets accepted. Check in 3 P.M. Check out
noon. Inside access to rooms. Local phone calls free. Cable TV. Modem link in
rooms. Fax and copier service. Full breakfast. Reserved spaces in parking lot
across street ($5). Named after Etta Place, commonly known as the girlfriend of
the Sundance Kid.

GREEN OAKS PARK HOTEL

**6901 West Freeway (76116), off I-30 at Green Oaks exit • 738-7311 or
800-772-2341 in Texas, 800-433-2174 outside Texas • $$ • W+ 4 rooms
No-smoking rooms**

A two-story hotel with 282 units, including 55 suites ($$$) and 124 no-smok-
ing rooms. Senior, weekend, and other discounts available. Children 12 and
under stay free in room with parents. Pets OK (deposit $20). Check in 3 P.M.
Check out noon. Inside and outside access to rooms. Charge for local calls.
Cable TV with free premium channel and pay channels. VCR available. Cap-
tioned TV, visual alarms, and special phones for the hearing impaired. Wet bar
in rooms. Coffee available in lobby. Room service. Two outdoor pools, sauna,
exercise room. Two lighted tennis courts and health club facilities. Public golf
course adjacent. Business services available. One-day dry cleaning. Free full
breakfast. Free newspaper in restaurant. Restaurant serving all meals (dinner
under $12). Lounge with entertainment and dancing. Free outside parking. On
11.5 acres. Across from Ridgmar Mall.

HOLIDAY INN FORT WORTH CENTRAL

**2000 Beach Street (76103), off I-30 at Beach Street exit • 534-4801 • $$
W+ 2 rooms • No-smoking rooms**

The 185 units in this two- and three-story inn include nine suites, two with
kitchens ($$$–$$$$) and 120 no-smoking rooms. Senior and other discounts
available. Children 19 and under stay free in room with parents. Check in 3 P.M.
Check out noon. Inside and outside access to rooms. Charge for local calls. Cable
TV with HBO and pay channels. Captioned TV and visual alarms for the hearing
impaired. Coffeemakers in rooms. Modem link in rooms. Bell service. Room ser-
vice. Outdoor pool, sauna, exercise room, one lighted tennis court. Business ser-
vices available. One-day dry cleaning. Playground. Restaurant serving all meals
(dinner $12–$30). Lounge with occasional entertainment and dancing. Free out-
side parking. Free transportation to downtown and Stockyards.

HOLIDAY INN NORTH

**2540 Meacham Blvd. (76106) • 625-9911 or 800-465-4329 • $$ • W+ 3 rooms
No-smoking rooms**

This six-story inn has 247 units, including six suites ($$$–$$$$) and 168 no-
smoking rooms. Senior discount and package plans available. Children stay
free in rooms with parents. Check in 3 P.M. Check out noon. Inside access to
rooms. Charge for local calls. Cable TV with Disney and pay channels. VCR

available. Visual alarms and special phones for the hearing impaired. Wet bar in suites. Coffee available in lobby. Modem link in rooms. Fire intercom system. Bell service. Room service. Indoor pool, sauna, exercise room. Gift shop. Self-service laundry. One-day dry cleaning. Restaurant serving all meals (dinner $8–$19). Lounge with DJ for dancing. Free outside parking.

LA QUINTA WEST

7888 I-30 West (76108) off Cherry Lane exit • 246-5511 or 800-531-5900
$ • W+ 2 rooms • No-smoking rooms
The three floors of this La Quinta have 106 units that include two studio suites ($–$$) and sixty-five no-smoking rooms. Senior and other discounts available. Children 18 and under stay free in room with parents. Pets OK. Check in 2 P.M. Check out noon. Outside access to one hundred rooms, inside access to six. Local phone calls free. Cable TV with HBO and Disney and pay channels. Captioned TV and special phones for the hearing impaired. Free coffee in lobby. Modem link in rooms. Outdoor pool. One-day dry cleaning. Free continental breakfast. Free outside parking. Restaurant adjacent.

MISS MOLLY'S HOTEL

109½ West Exchange Avenue (76106), in Stockyards Historic District,
just west of Main • 626-1522 or 800-99MOLLY (800-996-6559) • $$–$$$
No-smoking
This upstairs bed and breakfast has eight rooms, one with private bath ($$$), all no-smoking. Free local calls on hall phone. Free continental breakfast. Free outside reserved parking. Don't expect B&B cute and cozy here. More cowboy rough and ready. Old-style rooming house (once a bordello) with three baths down the hall. In the heart of Stockyards action, which can be noisy until the wee hours.

RESIDENCE INN BY MARRIOTT

1701 South University Drive (76107), *take University exit off I-30,*
***go south ½ mile* • 870-1011 • $$–$$$ • W+ 2 suites • No-smoking suites**
Sixty-four of the 120 one- and two-bedroom suites with kitchens in this two-story all-suites inn are no-smoking. Senior, weekend, and other discounts available. Children stay free in room with parents. Pets OK ($5/day). Check in 3 P.M. Check out noon. Outside access to rooms. Charge for local calls. Cable TV with HBO. Captioned TV, visual alarms, and special phones for the hearing impaired. Coffeemakers in rooms. Modem link in rooms. Outdoor heated pool. Guest memberships available in Harris Hospital Health/Fitness Center. Self-service laundry. One-day dry cleaning. Free continental breakfast. Free newspaper. Free outside parking. Free transportation within ten-mile radius. Free grocery shopping service. In the Cultural District.

STOCKYARDS HOTEL

109 East Exchange Avenue at Main (76106), in Stockyards Historic District
625-6427 • $$$ • No-smoking rooms
There are four suites ($$$$–$$$$$) and several no-smoking rooms among the fifty-two units in this three-story hotel. Package plans available. Children 12 and under stay free in room with parents. Pets OK ($50 deposit). Check in 3 P.M. Check out noon. Inside access to rooms. Charge for local calls. Cable TV. Captioned TV for the hearing impaired. Wet bar in some rooms. Coffeemakers

in rooms. Modem link in rooms. Bell service. Room service. Copy service available. Free newspaper in restaurant. Restaurant serving all meals (dinner $12–$30). Lounge with entertainment. Valet parking $5. Restored historical hotel built in 1907. Western decor includes saddle-topped stools in bar.

THE TEXAS WHITE HOUSE

1417 Eighth Avenue (76104) • **923-3597 or 800-279-6491** • **$$**
No smoking in house
   The three rooms in this bed and breakfast are all on the second floor. All with private baths. No children. Free local phone calls (phone in room on request). TV in room on request. Secretarial services available. Full breakfast and afternoon snacks. Free outside parking.

THE WORTHINGTON

200 Main Street (76102), downtown at Sundance Square • **870-1000 or 800-477-8274** • **$$$–$$$$** • **W+ 15 rooms** • **No-smoking rooms**
   This 12-story hotel has 504 units including 44 suites ($$$$$) and 50% of the rooms designated as no smoking. Senior, weekend, and package plans available. Children 12 and under stay free in room with parents. Concierge floor. Small pets OK. Check in 3 P.M. Check out noon. Inside access to rooms. Charge for local calls. Cable TV with free premium channel and pay channels. Captioned TV, visual alarms, and special phones for the hearing impaired. In-room honor bar. Modem link in rooms. Fire intercom system. Bell service. Room service. Indoor pool, sauna, exercise room. Athletic club and tennis (fee). Business services available. Gift shop. One-day dry cleaning. Restaurant serving all meals (dinner $12–$30) (*see also* Restaurants–Reflections). Bar. Garage: self-parking $7, valet $10. Hotel spans three city blocks. Excellent views of the city from upper floor rooms.

GAINESVILLE

Cooke County Seat • **14,518** • **(940)**
   The "Forty-niners" heading west to seek gold in California followed the route leading through Gainesville and helped to settle the area. In 1850 the county seat of the two-year-old county was moved here. From 1858 until 1861 the Butterfield Stage provided semi-weekly mail and passenger service to the town on a 2,795-mile route between St. Louis and San Francisco.
   Though most Texans favored secession, when it became an issue in the 1860s Cooke County voted against it. When Texas joined the Confederacy, some of these anti-secessionists formed a secret society to work for Union victory. In 1862, a Confederate spy infiltrated the group and obtained a list of members. The Texas militia arrested more than 150 of them. This started what is known as "The Great Hanging," a three-week reign of terror during which Confederate extremists tried the Unionists in "citizen courts" and had more than 40 of them hanged.
   From the 1930s through the mid-1950s, the Gainesville Community Circus grew from a fund-raiser burlesque circus to become the largest circus of its kind

anywhere in the world. Members of the circus troupe, all volunteer local residents, performed in Texas, Oklahoma, and New Mexico. A 1954 fire destroyed much of the circus equipment but a smaller version of the circus continued another ten years.

The economy is now built on aircraft fabrication, agriculture, and ranching. There are so many quarter horse ranches in the area that the Chamber of Commerce refers to it as "The Quarter Horse Capital of the World."

TOURIST SERVICES

GAINESVILLE AREA CHAMBER OF COMMERCE

101 S. Culberson at California, 1 block east of IH-35 (P.O. Box 518, 76241) 665-2831, http://www.nortexinfo.net/gvchamber • W

TEXAS TRAVEL INFORMATION CENTER

Approximately 1 mile north on IH-35 • 665-2301 • Open daily 8–5 • W+

One of 12 roadside visitor centers operated by the Texas Transportation Department on key highways entering the state. Trained travel counselors can provide a wealth of free information, official highway maps, and other travel literature on Texas.

MUSEUMS

MORTON MUSEUM

210 S. Dixon at Pecan • 668-8900 • Tuesday–Saturday 12–5, Sunday 2–5 Free • W ramp at side

The 1884 city hall-fire station building was converted to a museum in 1968. Changing exhibits relate to county history including the Gainesville Community Circus.

HISTORIC PLACES

Well-preserved nineteenth-century homes originally built by cotton and cattle barons are concentrated along S. Denton, Lindsay, and Church streets. Among the oldest are the **Stewart-Laird House,** 319 S. Denton, built in 1882; the **Cloud-Stark House,** 327 S. Dixon, built in 1885; and the **Stevens-Smith House,** 329 S. Denton, built in 1885. The homes are all privately owned and not open to the public. A free map-brochure, "A Historical Tour of Gainesville," is available from the Chamber of Commerce.

OTHER POINTS OF INTEREST

FRANK BUCK ZOO

Leonard Park, California just west of IH-35 • 665-7332 • Daily: summer 9:30–7; winter 10–5. Park always open • Free • W variable

Famous wild animal hunter Frank "Bring 'em Back Alive" Buck was born here in the 1880s so they named this small zoo after him. The old circus calliope wagon stands just inside the entrance.

COLLEGES AND UNIVERSITIES

NORTH CENTRAL TEXAS COLLEGE

1525 W. California, about 1 mile west of IH-35 • 668-7731 • W+ But not all areas
About 3,500 students are enrolled in both academic and technical/vocational programs. Visitors are welcome at intercollegiate athletic events and at art department productions. A Children's Theater workshop is held each summer. The campus planetarium is sometimes open to the public.

PERFORMING ARTS

BUTTERFIELD STAGE PLAYHOUSE

201 S. Denton and Main • 665-3361 • Adults $6–$10
This nonprofessional group puts on about five productions during the September-to-May season held in a 100-seat theater on the top floor of the old Carnegie Library Building.

SHOPPING

GAINESVILLE FACTORY SHOPS

4321 IH-35N • 668-1888 • Open daily • W
Here are more than 80 shops including Reebok, Dansk, and Ann Taylor offering discounted items. There is a food court and playground for kids.

RESTAURANTS

($ = under $7, $$ = $8–$17, $$$ = $18–$25, $$$$ = over $25 for one person excluding drinks, tax, and tip.)

MAIN STREET PUB

216 W. Main • 668-4040 • Open daily 11–11 • $$ • W • Cr
Try the trout, a specialty of this restaurant located downtown near antique shops and boutiques.

ACCOMMODATIONS

($ = under $45, $$ = $46–$60, $$$ = $61–$80, $$$$ = $81–$100, $$$$$ = over $100) Room tax 13%

HOLIDAY INN

600 Fair Park Blvd., about 1 mile south of junction of IH-35 and California
665-8800 or 800-HOLIDAY (800-465-4329) • $–$$ • W+ 1 room
No-smoking rooms
This two-story inn has 118 rooms including ten no-smoking. Cable TV with HBO. Room phones (charge for local calls). Small pets OK. Restaurant. Private club (guests automatically members, membership for nonguests $10). Outdoor pool.

BEST WESTERN SOUTHWINDS

2103 N. I-35 (southbound take exit 498-B, northbound exit 499) 665-7737 • $
Built on one level, the motel has 35 rooms. Cable TV with HBO. Room phones (no charge for local calls). Pets limited. Restaurant adjacent. Outdoor pool.

GARLAND

Dallas County • 195,000 • (972)

According to the local stories, the city was originally founded in the late 1880s to settle a feud between Embree and Duck Creek, two rival towns barely a mile apart, over the location of the post office. It's said that the feelings ran so high that a man from one town dared not go "courting" in the other without courting trouble. Finally, in 1887, a local judge came to a Solomon-like decision and persuaded Congress to locate the post office between the towns. The post office was named in honor of the then Attorney General A. H. Garland and gradually the people abandoned both of their towns and moved to start a town around the post office. By the time World War II started, Garland had already begun to change from an agricultural-based economy to an industrial community. After the war, the industrial base stayed and grew and the city grew with it. And grew, and grew! As a result, Garland's 57 square miles tucked into the northeast corner of Dallas County is now a highly diversified industrial, high tech center and the ninth largest city in Texas.

TOURIST SERVICES

GARLAND CONVENTION AND VISITORS BUREAU

200 Museum Plaza, (4th and State) 75040 • 205-2749 • Monday–Friday 8:30–4:30 • W

You can pick up free brochures, maps, and specific information about Garland and the surrounding area and get help with hotel/motel accommodations. Located in the Landmark Museum (*see* Points of Interest).

POINTS OF INTEREST

HERITAGE PARK

4th and State, east of City Hall

The area east of City Hall is informally referred to as Garland's Heritage Park. It contains the old Santa Fe Railroad Depot, with a railroad passenger car, and a historic home. The depot is now the home of the Landmark Museum that features a small collection of Garland memorabilia. The Pullman car, which dates from the early 1900s, is being restored. Next door is the Pace House, a one-story frame house that is considered an excellent example of a Texas Victorian style farmhouse. Only the museum is open to the public (Monday–Friday 8:30–4:30. Free).

LAKE RAY HUBBARD

Take IH-30 east to the lake • **214-670-0936 • Open at all times**
Fee and non-fee areas • W

This 22,745-acre lake offers facilities for boating, fishing, waterskiing, picnicking, and camping (fee). Several marinas rent boats. *The Texas Queen* excursion boat (722-0039) operates from Elgin B. Robinson Park on the lake. The double-decked paddlewheeler offers both daytime tours and dinner cruises.

WOODLAND BASIN NATURE AREA

2332 East Miller Road at Lake Ray Hubbard • Free • 205-2750 (Garland Parks and Recreation) • W

A quarter-mile wooden boardwalk jutting into the marshy area of Lake Ray Hubbard provides an ideal platform for observing the marsh inhabitants, from armadillos to waterfowl.

SPORTS AND ACTIVITIES

Golf

FIREWHEEL GOLF PARK

600 Blackburn Road (75040) • 205-2795 • Two 18-hole courses. Green fees: weekdays $17, weekends $24

The Old Course has been ranked number one among public courses in Texas and the newer Lakes Course is ranked 12th.

Softball

JERRY CARTER SOFTBALL COMPLEX

Audubon Park, 550 Oates Rd. (75043), *exit Oates Rd. off I-635,* *go east to park* **• 613-7729 • W**

This complex is set up for softball tournaments with five softball fields arranged in a "wagon wheel" configuration, all identical and all fenced at 300 feet. Recognized as one of the best in the state, this complex hosts state and national tournaments.

WINTERS SOFTBALL COMPLEX

Winter Park, 1330 Spring Creek Drive (75040) • 276-5483 • W

Another softball tournament facility with three identical back-to-back fields with 300-foot fences. Adjacent to the softball complex is the 11 field Winters Soccer Complex.

Tennis

GARLAND TENNIS CENTER

1010 West Miller Road (75047) • 205-2778

The fee for using any of the 14 lighted courts is $1.50 per person for 1½ hours.

PERFORMING ARTS

GARLAND CENTER FOR THE PERFORMING ARTS

300 North 5th at Austin (P.O. Box 469002, 75046) • 205-2790 (information and tickets) • W+

This center houses two complete theaters and is home to organizations that stage everything from touring Broadway shows to symphony concerts. The Garland Civic Theatre (349-1331) usually puts on six productions in its September-to-May season. It also produces the Children on Stage Program which has its own season each year. Garland Summer Musicals (205-2780) presents one musical in June and one in July. The Garland Symphony Orchestra (553-1223) is a professional orchestra offering six subscription concerts in its October-through-May season.

GARLAND COUNTRY MUSIC ASSOCIATION
605 West State Street (75040) • 494-3835 • W
This association sponsors what's known locally as the "Big G Jamboree"—an every Saturday night performance of local and visiting western, gospel, and bluegrass groups.

KIDS' STUFF

SURF AND SWIM
Audubon Park, 440 Oates Road, *exit Oates Rd. off I-635, go east to park*
686-1237 or 205-2757 • Open daily June–September • Adults $4.50,
youths 5–17 $3.25, seniors $2.75, children 4 and under free • W
The "surf" here is a wave-action pool that produces four-foot waves. This municipal pool has grass beaches, pecan groves, shaded picnic tables, bath houses, a snack bar, and tube and raft rentals.

ANNUAL EVENTS
July

STAR SPANGLED 4TH
Three days including July 4th • Historic Downtown Square: State, Main,
and 5th streets • (P.O. Box 469002, 75046) • 205-2632 • Admission free • W
Just about every community in the country has a Fourth of July celebration, but Garland celebrates this historic event for three days from 10 to 10 with a lineup of shows and concerts featuring national talent, other continuous entertainment, choreographed fireworks nightly, a midway, a children's area, arts and crafts booths, and a wide variety of special exhibits and demonstrations.

GLEN ROSE

Somervell County Seat • 1,900 • (254)
The history of this area literally extends from the age of the dinosaurs into the nuclear age—from the 100-million-year-old tracks in Dinosaur Valley State Park to the Comanche Peak Nuclear Power Plant.
The town was named in 1872 for a small glen and the abundance of wild roses in the area. It soon became the county seat. During the 1920s and 1930s Glen Rose was a booming health resort. About the same time during Prohibition, the woods around the town sheltered a prosperous moonshine business, making Glen Rose the "Whiskey Woods Capital" of Texas.
Legend has it that in the 1870s a dying citizen named John St. Helen confessed to his lawyer that he was really John Wilkes Booth. St. Helen recovered only to later commit suicide. Witnesses who knew Booth confirmed that marks on St. Helen's body were identical to those they knew on Booth's.

TOURIST SERVICES

GLEN ROSE-SOMERVELL COUNTY CHAMBER OF COMMERCE
P.O. Box 605, 76043 • 897-2286 or fax 897-7670

MUSEUMS

SOMERVELL COUNTY HISTORICAL MUSEUM

Elm and Vernon • 897-4529 • June–Labor Day: Monday–Saturday 10–5; Labor Day–May: Saturday 10–5, Sunday 1–5 • Free (donations) • W

The historical and geological exhibits tell the story of Somervell County and include a genuine moonshiner's still from Prohibition days.

HISTORIC PLACES

SOMERVELL COUNTY COURTHOUSE

On the square, open business hours

This Romanesque Revival and Second Empire-style limestone courthouse was built in 1893. Its small size is appropriate for the third-smallest county in the state. Listed in the National Register of Historic Places.

OTHER POINTS OF INTEREST

COMANCHE PEAK NUCLEAR POWER PLANT

Take FM 56 north to plant. Visitors Center about 1 mile inside front gate **897-5554 or Fax 897-5715 • Visitors center open Monday–Saturday 9–4 Free • Group tours by reservation only • W**

The Visitors Center offers several interactive displays and a 10-minute video explaining how nuclear power is made. Included is a view of a control room simulator in which reactor operators are trained, as well as a driving tour providing an up-close view of Comanche Peak Power Plant. Nearby **Squaw Creek Lake** (*take TX 144 north about 4 miles*) provides cooling water for Comanche Peak Nuclear Power Plant. It is also used for boating, fishing, swimming, sailing, wind-surfing, picnicking, and camping (fee). The reservoir is also noted for scuba diving. For information write: Squaw Creek Park, 2300 Coates Rd., Granbury 76048, 254-573-7053.

DINOSAUR VALLEY STATE PARK

Take US 67 to FM 205 at west end of town, then northwest about 4 miles to Park Rd. 59 **• 800-792-1112 or 897-4588 • Open daily 7–10 for day use, at all times for camping. Visitor's Center with dinosaur exhibit 8–5 • Admission W+ but not all areas**

About a hundred million years ago massive dinosaurs left their tracks in the lime mud of an ancient sea. You can see these tracks that were uncovered by the Paluxy River. They are attributed to three types of dinosaurs: the 20- to 30-foot-long, two-legged *Acrocanthosaurus,* the 30- to 50-foot-long *Pleurocoelus,* and a third type which has not been fully identified. The best time to see the tracks is in summer. Two full-scale fiberglass models of dinosaurs—not the same types, but relatives of the types that made the tracks—help you appreciate the size of these monsters. The 1,523-acre park has tent and RV campsites (fee), primitive camping, a nature and hiking trail, visitors center, and picnic area. Swimming and fishing are permitted in the Paluxy River.

FOSSIL RIM WILDLIFE CENTER

On US 67, about 3 miles southwest of Glen Rose, turn left at sign, go about 1.5 miles to the Wildlife Center **• 897-2960 • Open daily 9 until 2 hours before** sunset. **Closed Thanksgiving and Christmas and may be closed occasionally in January and February due to weather. Call ahead • Admission • W variable**

Fossil Rim is home to over 60 species of exotic animals, including several on the endangered species list. Visitors tour 2,700 acres of open range land in their cars on a winding, nine-mile paved road. Except for the cheetah and red wolf, which live in spacious, fenced-in compounds, all of the other 1,100 animals roam freely, and many come right up to your car. There is a cafe with a scenic overlook, petting and picnic areas, and nature gift shop. Ask about behind-the-scene tours of endangered species, educational camps and programs, and special events such as star watches and moonlight safaris (897-2960).

For a unique adventure, overnight accommodations ($$$$$) are available, reached via a separate entrance. Turn left onto County Road 2010 off US 67 about a half mile beyond the Wildlife Center sign. Both the elegant, antique-filled **Lodge at Fossil Rim** or **The Foothills Safari Camp's** more rustic deluxe tents offer gourmet meals. For reservations, call **Nature Escapes** (897-4933).

PERFORMING ARTS

THE PROMISE

Texas Amphitheatre, crossroads off US 67 and TX 144 • 897-4341 or 800-687-2661 • Fridays and Saturdays June–October. Show times: 8:30 Adult admission: VIP $19, regular $16, economy $12; children $8

This contemporary musical drama is a not-to-be missed spectacular portraying the life of Jesus Christ. Sets were designed by Peter Wolf, a sparkling moat spans the width of the stage, and the costumes and voices are magnificent! Write: P.O. Box 2112, 76043 or call 897-4253.

SPORTS AND ACTIVITIES

Canoeing

A popular local sport on the Brazos River. Tres Rios Park is two miles east on County Rd. 312 at the joining of the Brazos and Paluxy Rivers and Squaw Creek with camping and cabins. Write: P.O. Box 2112 (76043) or call 897-4253.

ANNUAL EVENTS

BLUEGRASS FESTIVALS

There are many bluegrass events held during the year at which mostly professional musicians play bluegrass almost continuously. They are held at **Tres Rios RV Park,** two miles east on County Rd. 312 (897-4253), and at **Oakdale Park** on TX 144 about three miles south of US 67 (P.O. Box 548, 897-2321). Both parks have camping, cabins, pool, and pavilion. Several other events are held at Oakdale Park along with the Bluegrass Festivals.

RESTAURANTS

($ = under $7, $$ = $8–$17, $$$ = $18–$25, $$$$ = over $25 for one person excluding drinks, tax, and tip.)

HAMMOND'S BARBECUE

On US 67W • 897-3321 • Thursday–Sunday 11–8 , but call ahead and confirm hours • $–$$ • Cr • W
Beef cooked slowly over hickory makes this barbecue worthwhile.

ACCOMMODATIONS

($ = under $45, $$ = $46–$60, $$$ = $61–$80, $$$$ = $81–$100, $$$$$ = over $100) Room tax 13%

INN ON THE RIVER

205 S. W. Barnard off the town square • 972-424-7119 or 800-575-2101 Fax: 972-897-2929 • $$$$$ • All no-smoking rooms and suites • No pets or children under 16. • W 1 room
Casually elegant with some antiques, this historic 1919 bed and breakfast inn has 19 rooms and three suites with private baths, feather beds, and down comforters. Full breakfast in dining room with view of beautiful grounds and Paluxy River. A four-course gourmet dinner ($30) available Friday and Saturday nights. Outdoor pool, picnic tables. Two conference centers. Caters to corporate conferences weekdays, individual travelers weekends.

GRANBURY

Hood County Seat • 5,001 • (817)
Named by the Texas Legislature after Confederate General Hiram Granbury, Granbury started as a small settlement in 1854, and became the county seat in 1871.

Prosperity came with the Fort Worth and Rio Grande Railroad in 1887, and many of the buildings on the square today were built around that time.

By the early 1900s, the town began a decline that lasted until the late 1960s. Then, Mary Lou Watkins, a grand-niece of the Nutt brothers, who had helped found the town, restored and reopened the Nutt House, a hotel and restaurant on the square. Inspired, others also began restoring buildings, including the Granbury Opera House (*see* Performing Arts). Thanks to the town's spirited preservation efforts, the square was listed on the National Register of Historic Places in 1974—drawing visitors from far and wide, as it does today.

TOURIST SERVICES

GRANBURY CONVENTION AND VISITORS BUREAU

100 N. Crockett, 76048 • 573-5548 or 800-950-2212 or fax 573-5789 Open daily. Located on the corner of the square

HISTORIC PLACES

ACTON STATE HISTORIC SITE (ACTON CEMETERY)
Take US 377 east to FM 208, then south and east to Acton • **Free** • **W**
The smallest state park in Texas, this is the resting place of Elizabeth P. Crockett, widow of the Alamo hero Davy Crockett.

HOOD COUNTY COURTHOUSE HISTORIC DISTRICT
Bounded by Houston, Bridge, Crockett, and Pearl Streets
When it was listed in the National Register of Historic Places, the U.S. Department of the Interior described it as " . . . one of the most complete examples of a late-nineteenth-century courthouse square in Texas." The restored **Hood County Courthouse,** built in 1890, contains the original, working Seth Thomas clock.

OTHER HISTORIC BUILDINGS
Panter Post Office, 111 N. Baker, is the oldest building in town, built around 1773. **First Presbyterian Church,** 309 W. Bridge, was built in 1897. The original bell still hangs in the steeple. **Nutt House,** 319 E. Bridge, is a plantation-style home built in 1879. The term "Nutt House" originated here but later transferred to the hotel on the square. Some of the historic homes are open during the Granbury Candlelight Tour the first weekend in December.

OTHER POINTS OF INTEREST

LAKE GRANBURY
Mainly south and east of town • **573-5548 (Visitors Center)**
Open at all times • **Free** • **W variable**
The 8,700-acre lake almost surrounds the city. It is 30 miles long and has 103 miles of shoreline with both public and commercial facilities for fishing, swimming, boating, and other watery sports. The *Granbury Queen Riverboat* is a replica of a Mississippi paddlewheel riverboat, offering hour-long sightseeing cruises on weekends, dinner/dancing cruises, Saturday only; and group sightseeing and luncheon charters during the week, April through December. Location: one mile south of the US 377 bypass on TX 144, 573-6822 or 800-720-6822. Senior citizens and children discounts.

Swimming, picnicking, a play area for children, and a public boat ramp are also available at the City Beach off E. Pearl St., six blocks from the square.

PERFORMING ARTS

COUNTRY LOVE FAMILY THEATER
404 N. Houston, 2 blocks north of the square • **573-5525 or Metro 817-279-9999**
Admission $–$$, discounts for seniors, children, and groups • **W +**
Year-round family entertainment (country, Fifties, and gospel music) in a 400-seat theater on Friday and Saturday nights in the former sanctuary of the First Baptist Church. Snacks and full meals available from 6 until show time (7:30) and at intermission in adjoining dining hall ($–$$). No-smoking.

GRANBURY OPERA HOUSE

133 E. Pearl, south side of square • 573-9191 or Metro 817-572-0881
Admission $–$$, children, senior, and group discounts
Built in 1886, and reopened in 1975 after being vacant for six decades, the Granbury Opera House has drawn capacity audiences ever since. Open from February through mid-December, the professional company's productions include musicals and plays. June through August, shows are Thursday through Sunday; the rest of the year, Friday through Sunday.

SHOPPING

The square is filled with gift, antique, and dress shops and restaurants.

ANNUAL EVENTS

July

HOOD COUNTY JULY 4TH CELEBRATION

On the square, Shanley Park, and City Beach • 573-5548 (Visitors Center)
July 4 and either day before or after • Free • W variable
The usual July 4 events plus arts and crafts, fun runs, banjo pickin', and a performance at the Opera House.

October

HARVEST MOON FESTIVAL

On the square • 573-5548 (Visitors Center) • Usually third weekend in October • Free • W variable
Juried arts and crafts show, sidewalk sales by local merchants, music, entertainment, and food.

RESTAURANTS

($ = under $7, $$ = $8–$17, $$$ = $18–$25, $$$$ = over $25 for one person excluding drinks, tax, and tip.)

CUCKOO'S NEST RESTAURANT

110 Pearl, on the square • 573-9722 • Lunch and dinner Tuesday–Sunday. Closed Monday • $–$$ • Cr • W (club only)
This restaurant, upstairs in a restored building, has antiques, an aquarium, and a view of the square. Country-fried and marinated rib-eye steaks are favorites. First-floor club with entertainment, Wednesday through Saturday.

HENNINGTON'S CAFE AT THE NUTT HOUSE HOTEL

E. Bridge and Crockett, northeast corner of the square • 573-8400• Lunch and dinner Wednesday–Sunday; closed Monday and Tuesday • $$–$$$ plus gourmet chef's table $75 and up per person• AE, MC, V • W
Granbury's legendary Nutt House Dining Room is now the location for Hennington's Cafe, an upscale eatery acclaimed for its Black Angus beef and fresh seafood since opening on the square in 1995. Renowned Chef Brian Hennington, and his wife, Lori, converted their former site at 110 N. Crockett into Hennington's Famous BBQ Palace. Gourmet burgers and homemade fries are specialties, too. The Henningtons formerly owned the Deep Ellum Cafe in Dallas.

ACCOMMODATIONS

($ = under $45, $$ = $46–$60, $$$ = $61–$80, $$$$ = $81–$100, $$$$$ = over $100)
Room tax 13%

HENNINGTON'S AT THE NUTT HOUSE HOTEL
E. Bridge and Crockett, northeast corner of the square • 573-5612 • $–$$
   The hotel has nine rooms and one suite ($$$$) upstairs in the original building where rooms have a lavatory but share three baths, the suite has a private bath; five rooms with private baths in the annex.

PLANTATION INN
1451 E. Pearl (Bus US 377) • 573-8846 or fax 579-0917 • $$–$$$
   This two-story inn has 53 units including four suites ($$$–$$$$). Cable TV. Room phones (no charge for local calls). Pets. Two outdoor pools. Free continental breakfast in the lobby. On the lake with boat ramp.

THE LODGE OF GRANBURY
400 E. Pearl, 2 blocks east of the square • 573-2606 • $$$$$
   The one- and two-story lodge offers 48 one- and two-bedroom units. Cable TV with HBO. Room phones (no charge for local calls). Small pets OK. Restaurant. Private club. Outdoor pool, spa, four lighted tennis courts, exercise room. On the lake with boat docks.

Bed and Breakfast

THE CAPTAIN'S HOUSE
123 W. Doyle St., 76048 • 579-6664 or 579-LAKE • $$$ • No smoking inside
   Built in the 1870s, this beautifully restored Victorian home has three suites with private baths, a common room with a TV and books, and a backstairs entrance. Balconies overlook the lake. Bring your boat or fishing gear. A cottage is also available at 204 S. Travis. This B&B offers unique touches such as an optional lunch or brunch—in addition to a continental-plus breakfast. Next door is another picturesque B&B: **The Doyle House** (573-6492), which has three suites available.

GRAND PRAIRIE

Dallas and Tarrant Counties • 105,000 • (972)
   During the Civil War, A. M. Dechman, a trader who was in charge of the commissary at Fort Belknap, had his wagon break down near a prairie home. Ever the trader, Dechman swapped his disabled wagon, the team of oxen, and $200 in Confederate money to the settler for about 240 acres of land. After the war, a town grew up here that was named after him. In the 1870s, still the trader, he traded land in Dechman to get the Texas and Pacific Railroad to come to his town. The railroad did, but in the process the town was renamed Grand Prairie because it sits on a vast expanse of grassland between two large bands of timber known as the Cross Timbers.
   The town grew slowly until the opening of several large defense plants in World War II spurred population growth. Today it is mostly a residential city with some light industry.

TOURIST SERVICES

GRAND PRAIRIE TOURIST INFORMATION CENTER

Belt Line Road near Lone Star Park (75050), north of I-30
Metro 972-263-9588 or 800-288-8386 • Daily 9–5 • W+

Travel counselors are available to assist with directions, lodging, information, and discount coupons for Grand Prairie and all the Metroplex. Visitor information can also be obtained from the Grand Prairie Chamber of Commerce, 900 Conover Drive, 75051 (264-1558) and Grand Prairie City Hall, 317 College Street, 75050 (237-8000).

PLACES OF INTEREST

JOE POOL LAKE

Trinity River Authority • 817-467-2104 • *From I-20 take Great Southwest exit south. This becomes Lake Ridge Parkway and leads to Lynn Creek Park and Loyd Park* • W variable

The shoreline of this 7,470-acre lake is still being developed. It already has two Trinity River Authority (TRA) parks and one state park. The TRA day-use **Lynn Creek Park** (5700 Lake Ridge Parkway, 75052, Metro 817-640-4200) offers rental boats, water bikes, skis, and tubes. **Loyd Park** (3401 Ragland Road, 75052, Metro 817-467-2104) includes a 3-mile hiking and an off-road bike trail, and a camping area. The largest park is **Cedar Hill State Park** (P.O. Box 2649, Cedar Hill 75106, 291-3900). *From I-20 take FM 1382 exit, go south four miles to state park on the lake.* Day use admission $3. Among the facilities at this 1,850-acre park are boat and jet ski rentals, two lighted fishing jetties, a fishing barge, five miles of hiking trails and 12 miles of mountain bike trails, a swim beach, playgrounds, and campsites. **The Penn Farm Agricultural History Center** is also located in this park. The farm is architecturally significant as a set of rural farm buildings used by a single family for over 100 years. For information call 291-3900. Admission.

MOUNTAIN CREEK LAKE

Grand Prairie Parks and Recreation Department • 237-8100 • From Hwy 303 (Pioneer Parkway) take FM 1382 (Belt Line Road) to Marshall Drive then east to lake • W

This 2,710-acre lake is primarily for power generating use; however, boating and fishing are allowed. Horsepower limits on boats.

THE PALACE OF WAX AND RIPLEY'S BELIEVE IT OR NOT!

601 East Safari Parkway (75050). *From I-30 exit north at Belt Line Rd.; the museums can be seen from the highway* • Metro 972-263-2391 • Open daily at 10. Closed Thanksgiving, Christmas, and New Year's Day • Single admission $9.95 for adults and $6.95 for children 4–12. Combination ticket $12.95 for adults and $9.95 for children • W

These two unusual museums share a large onion-domed building that looks like something from an Arabian fantasy. The Palace of Wax exhibits life-sized figures from real and reel Hollywood, history, fantasy, and religion. There are also displays showing how the wax artist created the figures. The eight galleries in Ripley's display some of the bizarre oddities and fascinating facts that Robert Ripley collected on his travels to 198 countries during the 1930s. There are a number of hands-on exhibits and others that let visitors experience an earth-quake and a Texas tornado. Some of these more active exhibits may be frightening to small children. Gift shop and game area.

TRADERS VILLAGE

2602 Mayfield Road (75052). *Take Mayfield exit off Hwy. 360, go east*
Metro 972-647-2331 • Saturday–Sunday 8 to dusk • Free (parking $2) • W

A Texas-sized flea market occupies this 106-acre complex. First opened in 1973, it now attracts more than 1,600 dealers to set up in the bazaar that includes open lots, covered sheds, and enclosed buildings. Crowds of 45,000 to 60,000 bargain hunters come here each weekend to buy everything from antiques to garage sale items. There are children's rides, an arcade area, food vendors, stroller and wheelchair rentals. Over two dozen free special events are scheduled throughout the year (see ANNUAL EVENTS). The RV park is the largest in the Metroplex.

SPORTS

Golf

FUN CITY

I-20 and FM 1382 (3990 Westcliff, 75052) • 262-0022

A 9-hole par-3 course that's being expanded to 18 holes. Nine holes $5. Also batting cages.

GRAND PRAIRIE MUNICIPAL GOLF COURSE

3202 Southeast 14th St. (75052) • Metro 972-263-0661

Three nine-hole courses. Green fees: $13.50 weekdays, $15.50 weekends.

RIVERSIDE GOLF CLUB

3000 Riverside Drive (75050) at Hwy. 360 • Metro 817-640-7800

Eighteen holes. Green fees (includes cart): $48 weekdays, $58 weekends.

TANGLE RIDGE GOLF CLUB

818 Tangle Ridge Drive (75052), south of Joe Pool Lake • 972-299-6837

Although this is a city 18-hole championship course, it resembles a country club course. Green fees: $35 weekdays, $45 weekends. Club house with dining room.

Horse Racing

LONE STAR PARK AT GRAND PRAIRIE

2200 North Belt Line (75050), *take Belt Line exit off I-30 then ½ mile north*
263-RACE (263-7223) • Admission • W

Texas' newest Class 1 racecourse, Lone Star Park offers thoroughbred racing April–July and thoroughbred and quarter horse racing October–November. Seven-story enclosed grandstand seats 8,000. Race day general admission $2, club house admission $5, self-parking $2, valet parking $5. Reserved seating available. Restaurants. Simulcasting from tracks around the country Wednesday through Monday in the Post Time Pavilion. On non-racing days, admission to this pavilion is $1, self-parking $1, valet parking $5.

ANNUAL EVENTS

April

PRAIRIE DOG CHILI COOKOFF AND WORLD CHAMPIONSHIP OF PICKLED QUAIL EGG EATING

**Saturday–Sunday early in month • Traders Village, 2602 Mayfield Rd.
Metro 972-647-2331 • Free (parking $2) • W**

If nothing else, the title ranks right up there with the longest titles of any Texas event. Fortunately, that's not all there is to this tongue-in-cheek tribute to "Texas Red" and some of the activities are as colorful as its title. Non-cooking contests include the Original Anvil Toss and the Cuzin Homer Page Invitational Eat-and-Run Stewed Prune Pit Spitting Contest, and the Pickled Quail Egg Eating Contest in which the winner eats the most in 60 seconds. Free, continuous entertainment. Free dance Saturday night. About 80,000–85,000 people usually attend over the two days.

June

ANTIQUE AUTO SWAP MEET

**Saturday–Sunday early in month • Trader's Village, 2602 Mayfield Rd.
Metro 972-647-2331 • Free (parking $2) • W**

Usually about 600 collectors, vendors, and car buffs from across the country show off, horse trade, and sell cars, parts, accessories, and auto memorabilia.

August

WESTERN DAYS

**Wednesday–Saturday early in month • Various locations
Metro 972-263-9588 or 800-288-8386 (Grand Prairie Tourist Information
Center) • Free (admission to rodeo)**

The activities start mid-week but the big ones are on the weekend starting with a Professional Cowboys Rodeo Association (PCRA) rodeo on Friday night. Saturday features a pancake breakfast, parade, and another rodeo that night. Other events include country and western dancing.

September

NATIONAL CHAMPIONSHIP INDIAN POW WOW

**Saturday–Sunday weekend after Labor Day • Trader's Village,
2602 Mayfield Rd. • Metro 972-647-2331 • Free (parking $2) • W**

Representatives from dozens of Native American tribes from across the U.S. take part in this colorful celebration of culture and heritage that's open to the public. Tribal dance contests, arts and crafts, cultural heritage demonstrations, and Native American food are among the features. Sponsorship by the Dallas/Fort Worth Inter-Tribal Association ensures authenticity of all aspects of the celebration.

RESTAURANTS

($ = under $12, $$ = $12–$30, $$$ = over $30 for one person excluding drinks, tax, and tip.)

THE OASIS AT JOE POOL LAKE

5700 Lake Ridge Parkway (75052), near the Lynn Creek Marina
Metro 817-640-7676 • Lunch and dinner daily • $ • Cr • W

A major attraction here is that the restaurant floats on Joe Pool Lake with outside deck seating available. The menu includes seafood, steaks, pasta, and burgers. Children's menu. Entertainment on Friday and Saturday evenings in the upstairs bar.

ACCOMMODATIONS

($ = under $80, $$ = $80–$120, $$$ = $121–$180, $$$$ = $181–$250, $$$$$ = over $250)

Room tax 13%

HAMPTON INN DFW AIRPORT

2050 North Hwy. 360 (75050), exit east at Carrier Parkway • 988-8989 or
800-HAMPTON (800-426-7866) • $ • W+ 2 rooms • No-smoking rooms

Seventy-five percent of the 140 rooms in this four-story inn are no-smoking. Senior and weekend discounts available. Children under 18 stay free in room with parents. Pets OK. Check in 3 P.M. Check out noon. Inside access to rooms. Local phone calls free. Cable TV with free movies. Visual alarms for the hearing impaired. Free coffee in lobby. Modem link in rooms. Fire intercom system. Outdoor pool, exercise room. Public golf course nearby. Fax and copy services available. Self-service laundry. One-day dry cleaning. Free continental breakfast. Free newspaper in lobby weekdays. Restaurant adjacent (dinner under $12). Free outside parking. Free transportation to and from D/FW Airport and area restaurants within five mile radius.

LA QUINTA INN

1410 Northwest 19th St. (75050), at I-30 • 641-3021 or 800-531-5900 • $
W+ 2 rooms • No-smoking rooms

This two-story La Quinta has 122 units that include two suites ($) and 70% no-smoking rooms. Senior, weekend, and other discounts available. Children under 18 stay free in room with parents. Pets OK. Check in 2 P.M. Check out noon. Outside access to rooms. Local phone calls free. Cable TV with Showtime and the Disney channels and pay channels. Captioned TV for the hearing impaired. Free coffee in lobby. Modem link in rooms. Outdoor pool. Fax service available. One-day dry cleaning. Free continental breakfast. Restaurant adjacent (dinner under $12). Free outside parking.

HOMEGATE STUDIOS & SUITES

1108 North Hwy. 360 (75050), at Avenue J • 975-0000 • $ • W+ 7 rooms
No-smoking rooms • Extended stays only. Three night minimum

All of the 139 rooms in this three-story property come with kitchenette and 50 are no-smoking rooms. Children stay free in room with parents. Check-in 11 A.M. Check out 11 A.M. Outside access to rooms. Local phone calls free. Cable TV with pay channels. Coffeemakers in rooms. Modem link in rooms. Exercise room. Fax and copy services available. Self-service laundry. One-day dry cleaning. Free outside parking. Managed by Wyndham Hotels.

GRAPEVINE

Tarrant County • 33,000 • (817)

Although founded in 1845, it wasn't until 1854 that the community leaders felt there were enough settlers to justify a town which they named after the wild mustang grapes that grew profusely in the area.

Today, more than 50 million people a year come to Grapevine, but most don't know it, not realizing that when they land at the huge Dallas-Fort Worth International Airport, that airport lies almost entirely within the city limits.

Grapevine is rich in history. The Main Street, for example, with its famed "Opry House," historical museum, and 38 other restored historic sites, has earned a listing in the National Register of Historic Places. In keeping with the city's name, several wineries have settled here. Another recent addition is the new Grapevine Mills Mall, a value mall that is expected to draw up to 16 million bargain shoppers annually.

TOURIST SERVICES

GRAPEVINE CONVENTION AND VISITORS BUREAU

One Liberty Park Plaza (Main at Texas), 76051 • Metro 817-481-0454 or 800-457-6338 • Monday–Friday 8–5 • W (ramp in rear and elevator)

Brochures, maps, and other detailed information and assistance are available. Located upstairs in the re-creation of the 1891 Wallis Hotel.

GRAPEVINE VISITOR INFORMATION CENTER

701 South Main, 76051 (in 1901 Cotton Belt Railroad Depot) • 424-0561 Sunday–Friday 1–5, Saturday 10–5 • W

Information available on both the Grapevine area and other attractions in Texas. Co-located with the Grapevine Historical Museum.

INDUSTRY TOURS

DELANEY VINEYARDS AND WINERY

2000 Champagne Blvd. 76051 (Hwy. 121 at Glade Rd.) • 481-5668 Tuesday–Saturday 10–5 (Closed Sunday–Monday) • Tour $5 • W+

The building and landscaping of this winery are designed to reflect a classic French-inspired style from the eighteenth century. You can wander around on your own, but if you want the one-hour guided tour, they start on the hour from noon to 4 P.M. A tasting of five wines made here for $7.

MUSEUMS

GRAPEVINE HERITAGE CENTER COMPLEX

701–707 South Main, 76051 • 424-0516 (Grapevine Heritage Foundation: Metro 817-481-0454 or 800-457-6338) • Depot Museum Sunday–Friday 1–5, Saturday 10–5 • W

On this three-acre site are several restored buildings including the 1901 **Cotton Belt Depot,** the 1888 **Cotton Belt Railroad Grapevine Section Foreman's House,** the reconstructed **Millican Blacksmith's Shop,** where the town smithy worked from 1909 to 1959; and the **Bragg House,** a tenant farmer's house built in 1907. The depot museum features exhibits on city history. Reverting to its original status, the depot now also serves for the daily excursions of the **Tarantula Steam Train** (*see* Kids' Stuff). A more up-to-date addition to the complex is the **Heritage Artisan's Center** where skilled artisans demonstrate craftsmanship techniques used over 150 years ago.

OTHER POINTS OF INTEREST

DALLAS/FORT WORTH INTERNATIONAL AIRPORT

**P.O. Drawer DFW, D/FW Airport, 75261 • 972-574-8888
Open at all times • W+**

D/FW Airport is the world's second busiest airport with about 2,600 passenger flights daily. Larger than the island of Manhattan, the airport is located in Grapevine, halfway between the two cities for which it is named. All the passenger facilities at D/FW including terminals, rental car offices, parking lots, and the airport hotel are located along a central north-south highway, called International Parkway. This leads to highways 114 and 635 on the north and 183 and 360 on the south. Two things to know about the parkway are: it is a toll road with fees ranging from 50 cents, if you're just passing through, up to a couple of dollars if you enter and stay for several hours; and all exits off the parkway within the airport are to your left.

The airport itself is worth a visit as an attraction. If you're flying out, plan to arrive early enough to give yourself time to take a leisurely self-guided tour during which you can see this monster airport in operation while you relax and watch everyone else bustling to catch a plane. Ride the Air Trans to get around. Air Trans is a small train system that runs between the terminals, the parking areas, and the Hyatt Regency DFW Hotel. (Kids'll love the ride itself.) If you didn't get a chance to go to one of the wine tasting rooms in Grapevine, you can catch up by going to Terminal 2E where, opposite Gate 6, you'll find the La Bodega Winery, the nation's first winery in an airport.

GRAPEVINE LAKE

**About one mile north of downtown Grapevine, *from Main Street, go northeast on Hwys. 121/26 to Visitor Area* • Grapevine Lake Project, 110 Fairway Drive, 76051 • 481-4541 • Most areas open at all times
Fee and non-fee areas • W**

This 7,380-acre U.S. Army Corps of Engineers' lake is 19 miles long with seven developed parks and five undeveloped ones along its 146 miles of tree-lined shoreline. Now the fourth busiest lake in Texas, facilities are available for boating, fishing, swimming, water-skiing, wind surfing, hiking, trail bike riding, picnicking, and camping.

GRAPEVINE MILLS VALUE MALL

Hwy. 121 and International Parkway (FM 2499), two miles north of D/FW Airport • W+

This is a mega-mall under development. When fully occupied it will have about 15 major anchor stores and more than 200 specialty stores in 1,905,000 square feet, enough to cover 34 football fields. Most of these are value retailers, a collective name for manufacturers and fashion outlet shops, off-price retailers, catalogue stores, and discount merchandisers. It is expected to become a tourist destination attracting more than 16 million visitors annually.

WINE TASTING ROOMS

La Buena Vida Vineyards • 416 East College, 76051, off Main • 481-9463
Open Monday–Saturday 10–5, Sunday 12–5 • W

La Buena Vida, one of Texas' oldest producing wineries, was the first to establish a winery and tasting room in Grapevine. Most of the wine is made in Springtown, Texas, but the limestone building here does contain an antique grape press and a fermentation tank, a small winery museum, and tasting room. You can taste four wines for $5. **The Homestead Winery** may be open by the time you read this. Check with the Convention and Visitors Bureau for location and hours. (*See also* Delaney Winery and La Bodega Winery.)

SPORTS AND ACTIVITIES

Golf

GRAPEVINE MUNICIPAL GOLF COURSE

3800 Fairway Drive (76051), off Hwy. 26 on north side of Grapevine Dam
Metro 817-481-0421

Eighteen hole championship course rated among the top 20 municipal courses in Texas. Green fees: Weekdays $14, weekends/holidays $16. Designed by Byron Nelson and Joe Finger, it has been listed in the top 50 municipal courses in the nation.

HYATT BEAR CREEK GOLF AND RACQUET CLUB

Hyatt Regency DFW, International Parkway on D/FW Airport (P.O. Box 619014, D/FW Airport 75261-9014) • 972-453-1234 or 800-233-1234

The facilities include two 18-hole championship courses; west course ranked in the top ten public courses in the U.S. by *The Wall Street Journal;* east course in the top 25.

TOUR 18 GOLF COURSE

(*See* Side Trips)

Tennis

HILTON ATHLETIC AND TENNIS CLUB

DFW Lakes Hilton, 1800 Hwy. 26E, 76051 • 481-6647

Six lighted outdoor tennis courts and two indoor, plus two racquetball courts.

HYATT BEAR CREEK GOLF AND RACQUET CLUB

Hyatt Regency DFW, International Parkway on D/FW Airport (P.O. Box 619014, D/FW Airport 75261-9014) • 972-615-6808

Four outdoor lighted tennis courts and three indoor, plus nine racquetball courts.

PERFORMING ARTS

THE GRAPEVINE OPRY

Palace Theatre (308 South Main) • 481-8733 • Adults $8.25–$9.25, children $5.25–$6.25 • W

There's a foot-stompin'-hand-clappin' country and western music show here every Saturday night at 7:30. In the early years, The Opry featured rising stars like Willie Nelson, Ernest Tubb, and the Judds. There still are occasional specials with nationally known artists, but most of the family entertainment is a variety showcase for local and regional musicians and other performers. A gospel country music showcase is held the fourth Friday of each month.

THE RUNWAY THEATRE

217 North Dooley Street, 76051 (just north of Northwest Hwy.) • 488-4842
Adults $9, seniors and children $7, matinees $6 • W
This community theatre has been the home of the End of the Runway Players since 1983. The players put on about eight productions a year, mainly comedies and musicals, in the September through July season.

KID'S STUFF

ACT ONE CHILDREN'S THEATRE

3100 Timberline Drive, 76051 (Southwest of the D/FW runways) • 488-7572
Adults $7, children $6 ($1 less for advance purchase) • W
Children's plays are put on here on Friday and Saturday evenings with each production running about three weekends.

TARANTULA STEAM TRAIN EXCURSIONS

Cotton Belt Depot (707 South Main) • 625-Rail (625-7245), Metro 817-654-0898
or 800-952-5717 • Adults: about $20, children (3 to 12) about $10 • W call ahead
The Tarantula Steam Train makes daily round-trip excursions to the Fort Worth Stockyards. Weekdays the train departs Grapevine at 10 A.M. riding the 21 miles of track to arrive at the Stockyards at 11:15. There are a couple of hours for riders to explore the Stockyard attractions (*see* Stockyards listings in Fort Worth) before the return trip leaves at 2 P.M. arriving at its home base in Grapevine at 3:15. Sundays the excursions run from 1 to 5:30 P.M. Tarantula's primary steam locomotive, No. 2248, operates Wednesday through Sunday. Originally built in 1896 and fully restored, it pulls carefully restored passenger cars and touring coaches dating from the 1920s.

SIDE TRIPS

TOUR 18 GOLF COURSE

8718 Amen Corner, Flower Mound 75028, *from Grapevine, take Hwy. 121*
North to FM 2499 to FM 1171, then west 6 miles **• 430-2000 or 800-946-5310**
Tour 18 is promoted as the only golf course in the world where each of the 18 holes is a careful simulation of one of the greatest holes from a celebrated golf course like Augusta, Cherry Hill, Doral, Sawgrass, and Firestone. Green fees, which include golf cart and driving range balls are: Monday–Thursday $65, Friday–Sunday and holidays $75.

ANNUAL EVENTS

MAY

MAIN STREET DAYS—THE GRAPEVINE HERITAGE FESTIVAL

Third weekend (Friday–Sunday) • Main Street Historic District • 481-0454 or 800-457-6338 (Convention and Visitors Bureau) • Adults and teenagers $5, seniors and children 6–12 $1, weekend pass $7 • W

Grapevine's celebration of its prairie heritage is geared to living history with demonstrations of heritage arts and crafts, plus re-enactors and storytellers to make the past come to life. The roster of entertainment includes continuous music ranging from C&W to Rock on three stages, plus special entertainment Friday and Saturday nights and a street dance Saturday night. There's also a small Children's Midway.

SEPTEMBER

GRAPEFEST

Second full weekend (Friday–Sunday) • Main Street Historic District • 481-0454 or 800-457-6338 (Grapevine Convention and Visitors Bureau) • General Admission: adults $5, weekend pass $7, seniors and children 6–12 $1 • W

One of the largest wine festivals in the Southwest, GrapeFest's premier event is a black-tie Texas Wine Tribute Gala held on Saturday night featuring a gourmet dinner paired with award-winning Texas wines ($75 per person). At the same time, on Main Street the festivities start that evening with entertainment on three stages, a wine tasting, and wine auction. Saturday and Sunday, $10 will buy you a souvenir wine glass you can use during one of several wine-tasting sessions each day. Nonstop entertainment, plus wine seminars, storytelling, sports tournaments, a vintage and classic car display, vineyard tours, a carnival, and arts and crafts show.

RESTAURANTS

($ = under $12, $$ = $12–$30, $$$ = over $30 for one person excluding drinks, tax, and tip.)

DORRIS HOUSE CAFÉ

224 East College Street, 76051, 1 block east of Main • 421-1181 • Lunch Tuesday–Friday, Dinner Tuesday–Saturday. Closed Sunday–Monday. Reservations suggested Friday–Saturday dinner • $$–$$$ • Cr • W

The house specialties include roasted smoked duck or rack of lamb. Other entrées include a selection of fresh seafood, chicken, and steak. A *prix fixe* three course dinner is offered for about $25. Bar drinks served at the table. The setting is a restored 1896 home with a hand-carved staircase and six fireplaces.

ACCOMMODATIONS

($ = under $80, $$ = $80–$120, $$$ = $121–$180, $$$$ = $181–$250, $$$$$ = over $250)

Room tax 12%

DFW LAKES HILTON

1800 Hwy 26E, 76051, 2.5 miles north of D/FW Airport • 481-8444 or 800-445-8667 or 800-645-1019 (Reservations) • $–$$$ • W+ 8 rooms No-smoking rooms

This nine-story Hilton's 395 units include 11 suites ($$$$–$$$$$) and 317 no-smoking rooms. Senior and weekend discounts and package plans available. Children free in room with parents. Concierge floor Sunday–Thursday. Check in 3 P.M. Check out noon. Inside access to rooms. Charge for local calls. Cable TV with free HBO and pay channels. In-room honor bar. Coffeemakers in rooms. Modem link in rooms. Bell service. Room service. Heated indoor and outdoor pools, sauna, exercise room, indoor and outdoor tennis courts, racquetball. Private stocked lake. Business services available. Gift shop. One-day dry cleaning. Free newspaper. Coffee shop. Restaurant serving all meals (dinner $12–$30). Bar/lounge with entertainment and dancing on weekends. Free parking. Valet parking available. Free airport transportation. On 40 acres.

HYATT REGENCY DFW

International Parkway on D/FW Airport (P.O. Box 619014, D/FW Airport 75261-9014) • 972-453-1234 or 800-233-1234 • $$$–$$$$ • W+ 17 rooms No-smoking rooms

Located within the D/FW airport, this 12-story Hyatt offers 1,367 units that include 49 suites ($$$$$). Senior discount and golf package plans available. Children under 18 free in room with parents. Concierge floor. Check in 3 P.M. Check out noon. Inside access to rooms. Charge for local calls. Cable TV with free HBO and pay channels. VCR available. Captioned TV and visual alarms for the hearing impaired. Modem link in some rooms. Bell service. Room service. Outdoor heated pool, sauna, exercise room. Membership available in Hyatt Bear Creek Golf and Racquet Club, a 335-acre resort located at the south entrance to the airport, with two golf courses and tennis and racquetball courts. Free shuttle to Bear Creek. Business services available. Gift shop. One-day dry cleaning. Restaurants serving all meals (dinner $12–$30). Bar/lounge with entertainment and dancing. Valet parking ($9). Two tower buildings, one on each side of International Parkway, connected by covered walkways. East tower also connected to American Airlines Terminal.

GREENVILLE

Hunt County Seat • 23,071 • (903)

Greenville, founded in 1850 as the county seat of newly formed Hunt County, is named after Thomas Green, who had been a private at San Jacinto and was killed while serving as a general in the Confederate Army during the Civil War.

The land in this area is known as the Blackland Prairie because the earth is a rich black color and provides a fine base for a variety of crops. When the railroads arrived in 1880, they opened up the markets, and the town was soon known as the Cotton Capital of Texas. Greenville cotton was so highly regarded by cotton spinners in Manchester, England, that they paid premium prices for it.

Cotton is still an important crop here, but now an expanding industrial base includes companies producing a variety of products ranging from fruitcakes to the sophisticated communications equipment used on Air Force One.

The Audie Murphy Room of the Walworth Harrison Library is a memorial to the most-decorated soldier in World War II, who enlisted in Greenville on his eighteenth birthday. Displays feature pictures and mementos of his life.

TOURIST SERVICES

GREENVILLE CHAMBER OF COMMERCE
2713 Stonewall at Crockett (P.O. Box 1055, 75401) • 455-1510 • W

MUSEUMS

AMERICAN COTTON MUSEUM
600 I-30 East • 454-1990 • Tuesday–Friday 10–5, Saturday 10–5, Sunday and Monday 1–5 • Adults $3.50, children and seniors $2
This small museum tells the history of the cotton industry in Hunt County. Exhibits range from an assortment of labor-saving devices used by sharecroppers to the spectacular Maid of Cotton wardrobe. The museum even hosts an authentic cotton field you can visit.

HISTORIC PLACES

Central Christian Church, Wesley and Washington, is a red brick structure with a tin roof, built in 1899. Ask at the church office during business hours to go inside and see the colorful stained-glass windows. **Bourland-Stevens-Samuell House,** 1916 Stonewall, was erected in 1883 using part of the earlier Stevens house built in 1854. The **General Hal C. Horton Home,** 3925 Moulton, built in 1885, was the first two-story brick home erected in Greenville. These are all private homes, not open to the public.

SPORTS AND ACTIVITIES

MUNICIPAL GOLF COURSE
Wright Park, US 69 about .4 miles southeast of I-30 • 457-2996
9-hole course. Greens fee: $6. Also lighted tennis courts in park

SHOPPING

ANTIQUES
There are about a dozen antique shops in town. The Chamber of Commerce offers a free map and brochure with listings.

MARY OF PUDDIN HILL
4007 I-30 at Division St., exit 95 • 455-2651 • Open Monday–Saturday 9–5, November 15 till Christmas: Sunday 1–5 • W+
This is primarily a mail-order fruitcake and candy business—they send out more than 1.6 million catalogs a year—but they also have a small store attached to the larger plant. Mary Horton Lauderdale and her husband, Sam, started this business in 1948 when they were students trying to live on the GI Bill. They baked pecan fruitcakes from a recipe handed down by Mary's great-grandmother and sold 500 of them that first year. Today the fruitcakes are still mixed by hand and still follow the same basic recipe. Plant tours are usually held in fall. Call for schedule.

SIDE TRIPS

LAKE TAWAKONI

Take SH 34 south to Quinlan, then SH 35 east (left) to the lake. Approximately 16 miles • 447-3020 (Lake Tawakoni Area Chamber of Commerce) • Open at all times • Free • W variable

The 37,700-acre reservoir makes this one of the larger lakes entirely within Texas. It spreads over three counties and has 200 miles of shoreline dotted with marinas, RV parks, and camps. Wind Point Park on the northeastern shore offers facilities for boating, fishing, swimming, picnicking, and camping (fee). For information contact Lake Tawakoni Area Chamber of Commerce, P.O. Box 1810, Quinlan 75474.

ANNUAL EVENTS

August

HUNT COUNTY FAIR

Hunt County Fairgrounds, *from US 69 take FM 1570 south of town* 455-1510 (Chamber of Commerce) • Saturday to Saturday in middle of August • Admission • W variable

A typical county fair with livestock show and sale, arts and crafts show, homemaking contests, pet show, and entertainment.

October

COTTON JUBILEE

American Cotton Museum • 455-1510 • Dates vary

Arts, crafts, and a quilt show spotlighting cotton.

RESTAURANTS

($ = under $7, $$ = $8–$17, $$$ = $18–$25, $$$$ = over $25 for one person excluding drinks, tax, and tip.)

THE SPARE RIB

7818 Wesley, just south of I-30 • 455-0219 • Lunch and early dinner daily $ • MC, V • W

Hickory-smoked barbecue is the main event here. You can get beef, chicken, ham, pork, or hot links. It's all cooked inside, so the whole place has the warm smell of barbecued meat. And for dessert there's fried ice cream.

YEN JING CHINESE RESTAURANT

5113 Wesley in Town South Shopping Center • 454-7413 Lunch and dinner daily • $–$$ • Cr • W

The decor is what you'd imagine a Chinese restaurant should look like, with gilt and red dominating, Chinese paintings and carvings, dragon ceiling tiles, Chinese music in the background, and the chatter of the Chinese staff in the kitchen. The menu offers a wide variety of vegetable, beef, pork, fowl, and seafood entrées, all cooked Mandarin style.

ACCOMMODATIONS

($ = under $45, $$ = $46–$60, $$$ = $61–$80, $$$$ = $81–$100, $$$$$ = over $100)
Room tax 11%

BEST WESTERN GREENVILLE

1216 I-30 at US 69 • 454-1792 or 800-528-1234 • $–$$ • W+ 2 rooms
This two-story Best Western has 100 rooms, 50 no-smoking. Cable TV with HBO. Room phones (no charge for local calls). Private club (guests automatically members, membership available for nonguests). Outdoor pool. Free coffee in lobby.

HOLIDAY INN

1215 I-30 at US 69 • 454-7000 or 800-HOLIDAY (800-465-4329) • $$ • W+ 1 room
The two-story inn has 134 rooms, 102 no-smoking rooms. Cable TV with HBO and the Movie Channel. Room phones (no charge for local calls). Small pets OK. Restaurant. Private club with DJ and live entertainment Monday through Saturday (guests automatically members, temporary memberships available for nonguests). Outdoor pool, spa, weight room.

HILLSBORO

Hill County Seat • 8,500 • (254)
This has been the county seat since the county was formed in 1853. Both county and city are named for George Washington Hill, one of the many Tennesseans who came to Texas at the time of the revolution against Mexico. He served as secretary of war during Sam Houston's second term as president of the Republic.

TOURIST SERVICES

HILLSBORO CHAMBER OF COMMERCE

**115 N. Covington (P.O. Box 358, 76645) • 582-2481 or 800-445-5726 or
fax 582-0465• W**
Located two blocks north of the square in the restored Missouri, Kansas & Texas Railroad Depot built in 1892.

MUSEUMS

THE HAROLD B. SIMPSON HILL COLLEGE HISTORY COMPLEX

In the old library. *Take TX 22 east from IH-35 to college* **• 582-2555, Ext. 242
Monday–Friday 9–3 when college is in session (closed noon–1) • Free • W
Designated visitor parking**
The two major parts of this complex are the **Confederate Research Center and Museum** and the **Audie Murphy Gun Museum.** The research center houses an extensive collection on the military history of the Confederacy, especially Hood's Texas Brigade. Displays include a doll house reproduction of **Tara** from **Gone With the Wind.** The Audie Murphy section displays memorabilia from the life of the most decorated combat soldier of World War II.

HILL COUNTY CELL BLOCK MUSEUM

120 N. Waco • 582-8912 • 2nd and 4th Saturdays April–November, 10–4 • Free

Completed in 1893, this old jail is now a museum of Hill County history and listed on the National Register of Historic Places. Elvis Presley spent a night here on a charge of "drunk and disorderly."

HISTORIC PLACES

Hill County Courthouse on the Town Square was completed in 1891, replacing the previous brick building that burned. This Texas version of French Second Empire style, flamboyantly including both Italianate and Classical Revival architectural elements, led people to call it both a "monstrosity" and a "cathedral." The Courthouse burned again on New Year's Day, 1993! Its exterior has been restored to its original state, work continues inside. It is still listed on the National Register of Historic Places. The **Hillsboro Residential Historic District** is bounded by Corsicana on the north, Franklin on the south, Pleasant on the west, and Thompson on the east.

SPORTS AND ACTIVITIES

HILLSBORO COUNTRY CLUB

**North end of Country Club Dr., off Old Brandon Rd. • 582-8211
9-hole course open to visitors. Greens fee: weekdays $7.50, weekends and holidays $12.50**

COLLEGES AND UNIVERSITIES

HILL COLLEGE

Take TX 22 east from IH-35 **• 582-2555 • W variable • Designated visitor parking**

About 2,000 students are enrolled in academic and vocational/technical programs at this two-year community college. Visitors are welcome at the History Complex (*see* Museums), sports events, rodeos, drama productions, music recitals, and concerts.

SIDE TRIPS

LAKE WHITNEY AND LAKE WHITNEY STATE PARK

Take FM 22 west about 15 miles through Whitney to lake. (*see* **Clifton**)

ANNUAL EVENTS

BOND'S ALLEY ARTS AND CRAFT FESTIVAL

Courthouse Square • 582-2481 (Chamber of Commerce) • Saturday and Sunday of second full weekend in June • Free • W variable

Bond's Alley, adjacent to the courthouse, is an alley connected to local history. More than a hundred booths display the works of artists and craftsmen from all over the Southwest. Included is a book fair, Sunday barbecue, street dance, entertainment, and the Heritage League Homes Tour. This is the only alley in the state to boast a Texas Historical Marker.

SHOPPING

HILLSBORO OUTLET CENTER

Take exit 368A or 368B off IH-35 • 582-9205 • **Open 10–8 Monday–Saturday and 11–6 Sunday • W + wheelchairs and strollers can be rented from Outlet Office (behind Subway) or any Information Center**

Almost 100 designer factory outlets, including men's and women's fashions, music, entertainment, furnishings, and more. Shop till you drop.

RESTAURANTS

($ = under $7, $$ = $8–$17, $$$ = $18–$25, $$$$ = over $25 for one person excluding drinks, tax, and tip.)

CZECH-AMERICAN RESTAURANT

57 W. Franklin • 582-3400 • Lunch only 11–2 Monday–Saturday • $ • Cr • W

A tradition in the Central Texas town of West for about 20 years, this family-operated restaurant now also has a location on the first floor of the historic Majestic Theatre downtown. Besides Czech specialties, Texas favorites like chicken-fried steak is available. A second location is at the Hillsboro Outlet Center (10–8 Monday–Saturday and 11–6 on Sunday).

ACCOMMODATIONS

($ = under $45, $$ = $46–$60, $$$ = $61–$80, $$$$ = $81–$100, $$$$$ = over $100)
Room tax 13%

BEST WESTERN HILLSBORO INN

I-35, exit 368A • 582-8465 or 800-528-1234 • $ • No-smoking rooms

This two-story motel has 52 rooms, including two no-smoking. Satellite TV. Room phones (no charge for local calls). Small pets OK. Restaurant next door. Outdoor pool. Coffee in rooms.

RAMADA INN

I-35, exit 368A • 582-3493 or 800-2-RAMADA (800-272-6232) • $–$$ • W+ 2 rooms • No-smoking rooms

The two-story Ramada offers 100 units that include one suite ($$$) and six no-smoking rooms. TV with free in-room movies. Room phones (charge for local calls). Pets OK. Restaurant. Private club (guests automatically members). Outdoor pool.

Bed and Breakfast

TARLTON HOUSE

211 N. Pleasant • 800-823-7216 • $$$$–$$$$$ • No smoking in the house

In this 1895 Queen Anne-style Victorian three-story home, eight rooms have private baths, plus two suites. TV. No pets. Full country breakfast. Rooms are beautifully furnished with antiques. Listed in the National Register of Historic Places. Package specials such as stress relief, golf, and murder mystery weekends.

IRVING

Dallas County • 160,000 • (972)

The city owes its origin to Julius O. Schulze, a railroad surveyor, and his survey team rodman, Otis Brown, who recognized the opportunity that railroads brought to communities. In 1902, while surveying a railway route west of the Dallas county line, Schulze and Brown paid $2,169.30 for approximately 74 acres on which they built a town they named after Washington Irving, a popular writer of the time.

During the early years, Irving lived in the shadow of Dallas and grew slowly. The 1950 census listed the population at only 2,621. But, in the 1970s things started happening. In 1971, the Texas Stadium was built as the home of the Dallas Cowboys; in 1974, the Dallas/Fort Worth International Airport opened with its eastern border in Irving's city limits and the major highways between the airport and Dallas passing through the city. That same decade saw the beginnings of the 12,000-acre planned community of Las Colinas.

Although Irving is a corporate center and the home of more than 400 multinational companies, its convenient location next to D/FW Airport has led to the hotel/motel industry being the largest private employer with more than 7,000 people employed in the 52 hotels/motels.

If you want to go to Dallas for the day, but don't want to drive all the way in, you can take the Trinity Railway Express, a commuter train that runs from the South Irving Station at Rock Island Road and O'Connor Road about 15 times a day on weekdays. It makes it to the Dallas Union station in 16 minutes for $1 each way with transfers to either the Dallas Area Rapid Transit buses or the DART Light Rail System (see DALLAS).

TOURIST SERVICES

IRVING CONVENTION AND VISITORS BUREAU

3333 North MacArthur Blvd., Suite 200 (75062), in the Irving Arts Center, 1 mile north of Hwy 183 or 3 miles south of Hwy 114 • 252-7476 or 800-2-IRVING (247-8464) • Monday–Friday 8–5 • W+

Free information for visitors, plus this office sometimes has special discount coupons for area attractions.

COMMERCIAL TOUR SERVICES

LAS COLINAS WATER TAXI CRUISES

Smith Landing on the Mandalay Canal • 869-4321 • Adults $3.25, seniors $2.75, children (3 to 13) $1.75

Scenic tours of the Mandalay Canal in Las Colinas in an authentic Venetian water taxi (power boat, not a gondola). Cruises go throughout the Urban Center then across the 125-acre Lake Carolyn.

THE MOVIE STUDIOS AT LAS COLINAS TOUR

North O'Connor Rd. at Royal Lane (Building One in Dallas Communications Complex. Follow signs to tour) • 869-FILM (869-3456) • Adults $11.95, seniors (over 65) $9.95, children (4–12) $6.95

Get a glimpse of TV and movie production techniques and see how filmmakers create illusions in this hour-long tour. The state-of-the-art studios here in the Dallas Communications Complex have been used for a number of major films. Open daily year round. Gift shop.

TEXAS STADIUM TOURS

2401 East Airport Frwy. (75062), at junction of Hwys. 183 and 114 and Loop 12) 579-1414 • Adults $5, seniors and children (under 12) $3 • W

All tours leave from the Official Dallas Cowboys Pro Shop just outside Gate 8 every hour on the hour Monday–Saturday 10–3 and Sunday 11–3. The hour-long tours include a view from the stands that seat 64,000, a brief walk on the field, a view of the Dallas Cowboys' locker room, a walk-through of the Stadium Club and a view of a private suite. Gift shop.

OTHER POINTS OF INTEREST

DALLAS-FORT WORTH INTERNATIONAL AIRPORT

Part of the D/FW Airport lies within the western boundary of Irving. You can watch airport activity and takeoffs and landings from the observation deck set up just off the airport grounds at 30th and Carbon in Founder's Plaza. For details on the airport, see Other Points of Interest in Grapevine.

LAS COLINAS URBAN CENTER

One of the world's best-known urban developments, Las Colinas (Spanish for "the hills") is a 12,000-acre master-planned community. In addition to office towers housing corporate offices for hundreds of multinational companies employing 70,000 workday residents, there are large single-family and apartment villages for 25,000 full-time residents.

Following is a listing of the major places of visitor interest in Las Colinas.

Dallas Communications Complex (869-0700). 6301 North O'Connor Rd. This 125-acre development is the premiere film facility in the Southwest housing more than 120 communications-related companies servicing film, television, and other commercial projects. Only the Las Colinas Movie Studio Tour is open to visitors.

Las Colinas Flower Clock. Hwy 114 and O'Connor Rd. A huge, working clock with the hands set against the clockface of live flowers.

Las Colinas Equestrian Center (*see* Sports).

Mandalay Canal. A gently winding canal designed to resemble an old-world waterway with cobblestone walkways, a few dozen shops and restaurants, and Venetian-style motorboats serving as water taxis (Taxi 869-4321).

Marble Cows. The stampeding Mustangs of Las Colinas have gathered all the fame, but on Bluebonnet Hill, at Hwy. 114 and Rochelle Rd., is another group of Las Colinas' animals, five marble cows that are a tribute to the ranches that once dominated the area.

Mustangs of Las Colinas (869-9047). 5205 North O'Connor Blvd. in Williams Square. This is the world's largest equestrian sculpture; a bronze of nine wildly galloping mustangs rushing through a flowing stream. Each horse is one-and-a-half times life-size and weighs between a ton and a ton-and-a-half. A free exhibit area in the lobby of West Tower of Williams Square includes a short film about the creation of this impressive work.

SPORTS AND ACTIVITIES

Boating

LAKE CAROLYN BOAT RENTALS

Mandalay Canal in Las Colinas • 869-4342 • Monday–Friday 4–8 P.M., Saturday noon to 10, Sunday noon to 5.

Want your own little sunset cruise or picnic on the water? You can rent an electric powered boat that holds up to five adults for $25 an hour or one that holds up to eight adults for $35 an hour and cruise the waters of the 125-acre Lake Carolyn on your own. Reservations suggested.

Equestrian

5 BAR K STABLES

Off Tom Braniff Dr., west of Texas Stadium • 579-1140 • Daily 9 A.M to ½ hour before sundown

Located on the Elm Fork Ranch, this is a full equestrian center with rental horses for adult riders and ponies for children and more than 100 acres of scenic riding trails.

LAS COLINAS EQUESTRIAN CENTER

600 West Royal Lane (75039), across from the Dallas Communications Complex • 869-0600 • W

English riding and jumping are the sports at this 42-acre center that's often called a country club for horses. Site of numerous shows including the prestigious annual National Equestrian Grand Prix. Visitors welcome to watch training. Riding lessons available.

Football

DALLAS COWBOYS

1 Cowboys Parkway (75063) (Headquarters) • 579-5000 (Tickets)

The name says Dallas, but Irving's Texas Stadium is the home field for the Dallas Cowboys (*see* Commercial Tours). When they play there, the stadium is usually packed solid with fans because the Cowboys have brought home such a long string of play-off and Super Bowl Championships that they've become a national phenomenon earning the title "America's Team."

Golf

TWIN WELLS GOLF COURSE

2000 East Shady Grove (75060) • 438-4340 • 18 holes. Green fees: weekdays $16.50, weekends $22

Ice Hockey

DALLAS STARS

211 Cowboys Parkway (75063) (Headquarters) • 214-GO-STARS (214-467-8277)

Texas' only National Hockey League team, the Stars play their home games in Reunion Arena in Dallas, but they practice on the rink at their headquarters in the Dr Pepper StarCenter Ice Arena.

Ice Skating

DR PEPPER STARCENTER ICE ARENA

211 Cowboy Parkway (75063), in Valley Ranch off MacArthur Blvd. approximately 3.5 miles north of I-635/LBJ Freeway • 214-GO-SKATE (214-467-5283)
   This facility has two full-sized ice rinks. In addition to being the practice rink for the Dallas Stars, it also is home for the Dallas Junior Hockey Association, a senior hockey league, a figure skating club, and a speed skating club. Public skating is available when the rink is not otherwise booked.

COLLEGES AND UNIVERSITIES

NORTH LAKE COMMUNITY COLLEGE

5001 North MacArthur Blvd. (75038) • 273-3000 or 273-3184 • W
   Located on 276 wooded acres in the Las Colinas area, its architecturally interesting campus includes a nine-acre lake. The college offers technical/vocational and academic programs to approximately 10,000 students. Daytime visitor parking is on Liberty Circle. Visitors are welcome to student drama and music productions (Theater information 273-3569).

UNIVERSITY OF DALLAS

1845 East Northgate Dr. (75062) at Tom Braniff Dr. • 721-5000 • W
   This catholic university is located on an 800-acre campus just northwest of Texas Stadium on hills that overlook the Dallas skyline. It has an enrollment of about 3,000 undergraduate students in its College of Liberal Arts and more in its graduate schools. The university offers an on-going series of free lectures by speakers of national repute. Visitors are also welcome at student athletic events and drama and music performances (Theater information 721-5061). Designated visitor parking areas.

PERFORMING ARTS

Arts Hotline and Arts Center Box Office: 252-ARTS (252-2787).

IRVING ARTS CENTER

3333 MacArthur Blvd. (75062), 1 mile north of Hwy 183 or 3 miles south of Hwy. 114 • 252-7558 or Metro 972-256-4270 • Office open Monday–Friday 8–5 • W+
   Home of more than 20 Irving-based arts and cultural organizations, this complex includes two art galleries featuring contemporary and traditional works by established and emerging artists. It also is the site for theater and concert programs in its two state-of-the-art performance theaters. The galleries and some of the performances are free.
   Some of the music and performing arts organizations that use this center are **Irving Ballet** (252-7558), **Irving Chorale** (484-8580), **Irving Community Concert Association** (255-7161), **Irving Community Concert Band** (438-6259), **Irving Community Theater** (594-6104), **Irving Symphony Orchestra** (831-8818), **Las Colinas Symphony Orchestra** (580-1566), **Lyric Stage** (554-8534), **Metro Players** (255-8747), and the **New Philharmonic Orchestra of Irving** (780-1079).

ANNUAL EVENTS

MAY

GTE/BYRON NELSON GOLF CLASSIC

Wednesday–Sunday in middle of month • Four Seasons Resort and Club, 4150 MacArthur Blvd. (Mailing address: 400 South Houston #350, Dallas 75202-4811) • 214-742-3896 • Admission $40–$100 • W

About 150 top golf professionals compete in this annual classic, the only PGA tour event named after a golfer—a Texas golfer, of course. The four-day tournament has the largest attendance of any golf event in Texas, usually attracting more than 200,000 fans, and is the largest charity fund-raiser on the PGA tour.

MAY

LAS COLINAS SOUTHWEST SHOW JUMPING CLASSIC

Five days in middle or late in month • Las Colinas Equestrian Center, 600 Royal Lane at O'Connor (75039) • 869-0600 • Admission • W variable

Skilled riders from all over the United States compete in this event.

May or June

CANALFEST

Saturday and Sunday • Mandalay Canal, Las Colinas • 556-0625 Ext. 117 Free • W

This spring celebration on the canal walk is designed to be a true "Venetian Carnival" with a boat parade, arts and crafts, clowns and magicians, and a variety of musicians and other performers.

RESTAURANTS

($ = under $12, $$ = $12–$30, $$$ = over $30 for one person excluding drinks, tax, and tip.)

CAFÉ CIPRIANI

220 East Las Colinas Blvd. (75039), across from the Omni Mandalay Hotel 869-0713 • Lunch Monday–Friday, dinner Monday–Saturday. Closed Sunday $$ • Cr • W+ (elevator)

The menu is gourmet Italian. Dishes are selected from several regions of that country with the emphasis on Northern Italian cuisine. Bar.

CAFÉ ON THE GREEN

Four Seasons Resort and Club, 4150 North MacArthur Blvd. (75038) 717-0700 • Breakfast, lunch, and dinner daily. Sunday brunch 11:30–3 $$–$$$ • Cr • W+

(Note: Many of the luxury hotels in Irving have excellent restaurants. This one is just a sample.)

The specialties here are New American Cuisine with the emphasis on lighter, healthier fare. A buffet is available at all meals. The dinner buffet ($30) offers a wide selection of hot and cold items from appetizer to desserts. Children's menu. Bar.

JINBEH JAPANESE RESTAURANT

301 East Las Colinas Blvd. (75039), east of O'Connor Road • 869-4011 • Lunch Monday–Friday, dinner Monday–Saturday. Closed Sunday • $–$$ • Cr • W
   Entrées include a wide selection of beef, chicken, and seafood cooked in tempura or hibachi style. Children's menu. Bar.

ACCOMMODATIONS

($ = under $80, $$ = $80–$120, $$$ = $121–$180, $$$$ = $181–$250, $$$$$ = over $250)

Room tax 11%

FOUR SEASONS RESORT AND CLUB

4150 North MacArthur Blvd. (75038), 2 miles south from MacArthur exit off Hwy. 114 • 717-0700 or 800-332-3442 • $$$–$$$$$ • W+ rooms • No-smoking rooms
   There are 307 units in the nine floors in this luxury resort including six suites ($$$$$) and a large number of no-smoking rooms. In addition there are 50 villa-style rooms off the golf course including six suites. Weekend discounts and a number of package plans available. Children under 18 stay free in room with parents. Small pets OK. Check in 3 P.M. Check out noon. Inside access to rooms. Charge for local calls. Cable TV with pay channels. VCR available. Visual alarms for the hearing impaired. Modem link in rooms. Fire intercom system. In-room honor bar. Coffeemakers in villa rooms. Free coffee in lounge in morning. Bell service. Room service. Four pools (1 indoor, 3 outdoor), 176,000-sq.-ft. indoor sports complex adjoining, two golf courses, 12 tennis courts (four indoor), racquetball, squash, European-style spa. Business services available. Gift shop, barber and beauty shops, and golf/sports retail stores. One-day dry cleaning. Restaurant. Free newspaper. Child Care Center and children's programs. Lounge. Outside parking. Valet parking available. Top-notch resort on 400 acres of lush grounds. Rated one of best hotels in the United States in *Conde Nast Traveler's* magazine Readers Choice Awards.

HOLIDAY INN/HOLIDOME SELECT D/FW AIRPORT SOUTH

4440 West Airport Freeway (Hwy. 183) (75062), take Hwy. 183 from south exit of D/FW Airport, Valley View exit • 399-1010 or 800-360-2242 • $$–$$$ W+ 6 rooms • No-smoking rooms
   This inn has 409 units on four floors that include seven suites ($$$) and 301 no-smoking rooms. Senior, weekend, and other discounts and package plans available. Children under 18 stay free in room with parents. Concierge floor. Check in 3 P.M. Check out noon. Inside access to about 95% of rooms. Charge for local calls. Cable TV with free premium channel. Visual alarms for hearing impaired. Wet bar in suites. Coffeemakers in rooms. Modem link in rooms. Fire intercom system. Bell service. Room service. Holidome: indoor recreation facility includes heated indoor/outdoor pool, exercise equipment, sauna, games. Outdoor pool. Room key provides entrance to Irving Fitness Center. Copy and fax services available. Gift shop. Self-service laundry. One-day dry cleaning. Free newspaper. Children's play area in Holidome. Restaurants serving all meals (dinner under $12 to $30), children under 12 eat free from special menu. Lounge with DJ, dancing. Outside parking. Free airport transportation, free shuttle to Irving Mall available.

HOMEWOOD SUITES HOTEL-LAS COLINAS

4300 Wingren Road, 75039 (Wingren exit off Hwy. 114) • 556-0665 or 800-225-4663 • $–$$ • W+ 6 suites • No-smoking suites

The 136 suites with kitchens on the three floors of this all-suite hotel include 115 no-smoking. Senior, weekend, and other discounts and Dallas Cowboy packages available. Children stay free in room with parents. Pets OK ($50 fee). Check-in 3 P.M. Check out noon. Inside access to 114 suites, outside to 22. Local phone calls free. TV with pay channels and VCR. Visual alarms for the hearing impaired. Modem link in rooms. Fire intercom system. Heated outdoor pool, exercise room and sport court. Business services available. Convenience store. Self-service laundry. One-day dry cleaning. Free continental breakfast. Free beer and wine Monday–Thursday 5–7 P.M. Free newspaper. Free shuttle service within 5 mile radius. Outside parking.

OMNI MANDALAY HOTEL AT LAS COLINAS

221 East Las Colinas Blvd., 75039 • 556-0800 or 800-The-Omni (800-843-6664) $$$$ • W+ 5 rooms • No-smoking rooms

This 27-floor luxury hotel has 410 units that include 96 suites ($$$$–$$$$$) and 100 no-smoking rooms. Weekend and other discounts and occasional package plans available. Check-in 3 P.M. Check out noon. Inside access to rooms. Charge for local calls. Cable TV with free premium and pay channels. VCR available. Captioned TV, visual alarms, and special phones for the hearing impaired. Coffeemakers in rooms. Modem link in rooms. Fire intercom system. Bell service. Room service. Heated lakeside pool, sauna, exercise room, bicycles available for rent. Guest memberships available in local golf and health clubs. Business services available. Gift shop. One-day dry cleaning. Free newspaper. Playground, programs for children, and babysitting available. Restaurant serving all meals (dinner $12–$30). Lounge with entertainment. Outside and garage parking. Valet parking available ($6). On five acres of lakefront. Named on *Conde Nast Traveler's* magazine Gold List of top 500 hotels in the world.

SHERATON GRAND HOTEL AT D/FW AIRPORT

4440 West Carpenter Freeway (Hwy. 114) (75063) at Esters exit 929-8400 or 800-325-3535 • $$–$$$ • W+ rooms • No-smoking rooms

The 300 units in this 12-story hotel include seven suites ($$$–$$$$) and a majority of the units are no-smoking. Package plans available. Concierge floor. Check-in 3 P.M. Check out noon. Inside access to rooms. Charge for local calls. Cable TV with free premium channel and pay channels. VCR available. Captioned TV, visual alarms, and special phones for the hearing impaired. Coffeemakers in rooms. Modem link in rooms. Bell service. Room service. Indoor/outdoor heated pool, sauna, exercise room. Business services available. Gift shop. One-day dry cleaning. Restaurants serving all meals (dinner approximately $15). Bar. Free outside parking. Free airport transportation.

WYNDHAM GARDEN HOTEL-LAS COLINAS

110 West Carpenter Freeway (Hwy. 114), (75039) O'Connor Rd. exit 650-1600 or 800-WYNDHAM (800-996-3426) • $$$ • W+ 2 rooms No-smoking rooms

The 168 units in this three-story Wyndham includes 45 suites ($$$) and 111 no-smoking rooms. Senior, weekend, and other discounts available. Children

18 and under stay free in room with parents. Check in 3 P.M., Check out noon. Inside access to rooms. Refrigerators in some rooms. Charge for local calls. Cable TV with free premium channel and pay channels. VCR available. Captioned TV and special phones for hearing impaired. Coffeemakers in rooms. Modem link in rooms. Bell service. Room service for dinner. Indoor heated pool, sauna, exercise room. Guest memberships available in nearby athletic club. Copy and fax service available. One-day dry cleaning. Free newspaper. Restaurant serving all meals (dinner under $12–$30). Bar. Outside parking.

McKINNEY

Collin County Seat• 21,283 • (972)

When the Texas Legislature created this county in 1846, they directed that it be named Collin after Collin McKinney, one of the Committee of Five that drew up the Texas Declaration of Independence, who lived here. They also directed that the county seat be called Buckner and that it be no more than three miles from the geographic center of the county. A few years later, in 1848, it was determined that Buckner was outside the legal geographic limit for the county seat, so the legislature decreed that the seat of county government had to be moved. Appropriately enough, the settlement closest to the geographic center of the county was one founded by Collin McKinney, so they named it after him. The residents of Buckner moved their homes and other buildings three miles east to the new town of McKinney, and Buckner soon reverted back to farmland.

The proximity of Dallas/Fort Worth International Airport to the south has played a significant role in expansion of both industrial and retail business.

TOURIST SERVICES

McKINNEY CHAMBER OF COMMERCE

1801 W. Louisiana (P.O. Box 621, 75069) • 542-0163 • W

MUSEUMS

BOLIN WILDLIFE MUSEUM

1028 N. McDonald (TX 121), just south of TX 380 • 542-0163 • Monday–Friday 9–12, 1–4. Closed Saturday and Sunday • Free • W+ but not all areas.

Most of the exhibits are trophies from rancher and oilman W. Perry Bolin's worldwide hunting expeditions. One section is devoted to Texas wildlife—from the armadillo to the wild turkey. An audio and light tour leads visitors through the exhibits. Upstairs are displays of an old-time parlor, kitchen, and bedroom.

HEARD NATURAL SCIENCE MUSEUM AND WILDLIFE SANCTUARY

Take TX 5 south about 2 miles, then east 1 mile on FM 1378 • 562-5566
Monday–Saturday 9–5, Sunday 1–5 • Adult $3, children $2 • W

This museum tells the natural history of North Central Texas, presents changing exhibits of antique and contemporary nature prints, and displays an extensive and colorful collection of seashells. Outside is a 287-acre sanctuary for native wildlife species and native vegetation, including about 150 species of wildflowers. Guided tours of the sanctuary are available by reservation only Monday through Saturday. One of the shorter trails is paved for wheelchair visitors.

OLD POST OFFICE MUSEUM

105 Chestnut at Virginia • 542-0163 • Tuesday 1–5 or by appointment • Free
  The Collin County Historical Society has converted this 1911 post office into a museum filled with pioneer artifacts reflecting the history and development of the county.

HISTORIC PLACES

CHESTNUT SQUARE

311 Chestnut • 562-8790 • Tuesday 1–4 • $2 • W variable
  A collection of several homes from the mid-1800s that have been restored by the Heritage Guild. The oldest is the **Faires House,** built in 1853. The **Taylor House,** built in 1863, was once a stage stop where travelers stayed in the attic for 25¢ a night, earning it the name of "Two-bit Taylor House." These are usually part of the annual Christmas Tour of Homes (*see* Annual Events).

OTHER HISTORIC HOMES

  Among the other homes in town built during the 1800s are the **Howell House,** 909 Howell, built in 1865; the **Tuck Hill,** at 616 W. Virginia, built in 1877; and the **Aron-Harris-Hill House,** at 525 W. Hunt, built in 1889. The **Gough-Hughston House,** at 1206 W. Louisiana, built in 1898, is probably the best-known older home in town because it was used as a set in the movie *Benji*.

OTHER POINTS OF INTEREST

LAKE LAVON

Take US 380 east or FM 546 southeast about 8 miles to lake • 442-5711
Always open • Free • W variable
  See Plano.

SPORTS AND ACTIVITIES

Golf

MUNICIPAL GOLF COURSE

TX 121 north of US 380 • 542-4523 • 9-hole course. Greens fee: weekdays $6, weekends $7.50

SHOPPING

  The Old Courthouse Square hosts more than 70 antique and specialty stores including local crafts, ladies' fashions, coffee shops and bakeries.

THIRD MONDAY TRADE DAYS

US 380W, about 2 miles west of US 75 • 542-7174 • Friday–Sunday before the third Monday of each month • Free • W variable
  The emphasis is on antiques, and several hundred vendors take part in this monthly open-air flea market set on 25 acres. But there are a lot of other things besides antiques to bargain for.

ANNUAL EVENTS

December

CHRISTMAS TOUR OF HOMES

Various locations • 542-0136 (Chamber of Commerce) • Usually first Saturday and Sunday in December • Adults $5, children 5 to 12 $2

The tour includes the four historic homes in Chestnut Square—all decorated for a Victorian Christmas—and a selection of privately owned homes. Map available at the Chamber of Commerce.

MESQUITE

Dallas County • 110,000 • (972)

Mesquite officially became a town in 1873 when the Texas and Pacific Railroad bought 50 acres along its planned right of way for $15. The T&P plotted 40 acres for a town and 10 acres for the depot, siding, and cattle pens. For a time, the depot was all that was there. But, slowly, the early settlers and new arrivals moved into the town. Growth remained slow. As late as 1950 the population had only reached about 1,700, and city phones still went through a switchboard operator who knew everyone in town and would take messages for those who weren't home.

Then the vitality and growth of Dallas and the Metroplex started to spill over. With the opening of Interstates 20, 30, 80, and 635, Mesquite became a crossroads town. People and businesses moved in. In 1950 the corporate limits of the town were less than a square mile, about the same size as when it was founded in 1873. By 1960 it was almost 21 square miles, and the population had zoomed to 27,256. Today, the city limits encompass about 42 square miles, and the population is about 110,000.

In a *Money* Magazine survey, Mesquite ranked as one of the ten safest cities in the United States.

TOURIST SERVICES

MESQUITE CHAMBER OF COMMERCE AND VISITORS BUREAU

617 North Ebrite, one block west of Galloway, between Municipal Way and Main (P.O. Box 850115), 75185 • 285-0211 • Monday–Friday 8–5

An array of free brochures on Mesquite, the Metroplex, and Texas are available here.

POINTS OF INTEREST

LIGHT CRUST DOUGHBOYS HALL OF FAME AND MUSEUM

105 Broad, 75149 in McWhorter and Greenhaw Hardware in Old Town Square • 285-5441 • Free • W

This band lays claim to being the longest continually performing western swing group in America. Started in the 1930s by Fort Worth mill magnate W. "Pappy" Lee O'Daniel as a marketing gimmick to help sell both his Light Crust Flour, which they did, and his political campaign for governor, which he won. The original band included Bob Wills, who went on to become a Texas music legend. The Doughboys still perform today and the Texas Legislature has named them the official music ambassadors for the state. The small museum, which features memorabilia of the group, is located in the front of the old-fashioned hardware (and music) store owned by Art Greenhaw, one of the present members of the band. Open store hours.

SAMUELL FARM

100 East Hwy. 80, 75149, *exit at Belt Line Road then take south frontage road*
670-7866 or 800-670-FARM (670-3276) • Daily 9–5, closed major holidays
Adults and children 12 and over $3, children (3 to 11) $2, under 3 free
W (no W restrooms)

Operated as a turn-of-the-century working farm, its 340 acres offer visitors a variety of both farm and park experiences. There are five small well-stocked fishing ponds (bring your own fishing gear) and farm animals around for close-up viewing and petting. There are four-and-a-half miles of hiking trails, picnic areas with grills, and a camping area. Rental horses available for one-hour guided trail rides for $12 (Reservations required 670-8551).

SPORTS AND ACTIVITIES

Auto Racing

DEVIL'S BOWL SPEEDWAY

1711 Lawson Road, 75181, exit Lawson Road from Hwy. 80, go south
222-2421 • General admission: adults $10, children 12–15 $5, 6–11 $2,
under 6 free • W

They hold a variety of vehicle races on this unique D-shaped one-half mile track including World of Outlaws Sprint Cars, Super Sprints, late models, and street stocks. Grandstand seating for 10,000 and more than 1,000 reserved seats available at the finish line. Races March to November.

Golf

MESQUITE GOLF COURSE AND LEARNING CENTER

825 North Hwy. 67 (75150) (I-30 and Northwest Drive) • 270-7457
18 holes. Call for green fees.

TOUR PLAY GOLF CENTER

2920 Gus Thomasson Road (75150) • 270-4800 • 9 holes.
Green fees: weekdays $7, weekends/holidays $11, juniors $6.

TOWN EAST EXECUTIVE GOLF COURSE

3134 North Belt Line (75182) • 226-1959 • 9-hole par 3 public course.
Call for fees.

Rodeo

MESQUITE CHAMPIONSHIP RODEO

1818 Rodeo Drive (75149), *exit Military Parkway (exit 4) off I-635* **• 285-8777**
or 800-833-9339 • Friday and Saturday evenings April–September
Adults $8, seniors $7, children (12 and under) $3 • Parking $2 • W

It started modestly in 1958 when 5,000 fans turned out for the premier performance. The fans haven't stopped coming since. Today, this has probably become the best-known rodeo in the nation with an average attendance of about 300,000 a season, plus another three million who see the rodeos on cable TV, earning Mesquite the official title of "The Rodeo Capital of Texas."

Every Friday and Saturday night at 8, the rodeo kicks off with a colorful grand entry of cowboys and cowgirls riding to the tune of "The Eyes of Texas Are Upon You." From then on the show explodes with all the traditional cowboy competitions, including bull and bronco riding, calf roping, and steer wrestling. Other events include ladies' barrel-racing, a calf-scramble for kids, and half-time entertainment. Don't worry if you don't know anything about rodeo. The announcer explains each event before it starts. And to make sure you get a good view, there are TV monitors hanging from the ceiling to give you close-ups and replays of each ride. The all-weather arena seats 6,000, and there are air-conditioned suites on the third level that can be leased by the night. A pre-rodeo hickory-smoked barbecue dinner is served in the Bull's Eye Pavilion for $8.50 for adults and $5.50 for children. There are also pony rides and a petting zoo for kids, and a gift shop. Off-season and off-days, the arena is used for concerts, wrestling, and other events.

Tennis

WESTLAKE TENNIS CENTER

700 Gross Road, 75150 (across from Evans Community Center) • 289-5326

Six outdoor lighted courts and three covered courts. Outdoor courts $1.25 per person for 1½ hours, covered courts $6–$10 for 1½ hours.

COLLEGES AND UNIVERSITIES

EASTFIELD COMMUNITY COLLEGE

3737 Motley Dr., 75150 off IH-30 • 860-7002 • W+ but not all areas

The architectural design of the buildings on this 244-acre campus has won several awards. Visitors are welcome to the college's Performing Artists and Speakers Series, which brings in distinguished speakers as well as theater groups that put on plays for both adults and children.

PERFORMING ARTS

MESQUITE ARTS CENTER

1527 North Galloway (75149), next to Municipal Center. *Take Hwy 80 east to Galloway exit, then south* **• 216-8122 • W+**

The facilities in this building include a state-of-the-art concert hall seating 492, an intimate community theater, two art galleries, and a rehearsal hall which is also used for small recitals. A few of the organizations that use this center are the Mesquite Civic Chorus (216-8124), Mesquite Community Theater (216-8126), and the Mesquite Symphony Orchestra (216-8127).

MESQUITE OPRY

Texan Theatre, 214 West Davis Street, 75149, in the Old Town Square 285-8931 • Admission • W

You can hear traditional country and gospel music here every Saturday night starting at 8. Both professional and home-grown local talent perform.

KIDS' STUFF

CELEBRATION STATION

4040 Towne Crossing Blvd., 75150, southwest corner of intersection of I-30 and I-635 • 279-7888 • Open daily. Call for seasonal hours • W

This family entertainment park has go-karts, bumper cars, and kiddie carnival rides, plus miniature golf, batting cages, video games, shows, and a food court. Admission is free, buy tokens for all rides and games. Located at what's known locally as the "Spaghetti Interchange" of two interstates.

ANNUAL EVENTS

July

MESQUITE BALLOON FESTIVAL

Last Friday–Sunday in month • Paschall Park, 1001 New Market Road (75149), one mile east of I-635 (P.O. Box 850115, 75185-0115, Mesquite Chamber of Commerce) • 285-0211 • Free admission. Parking $3 • W

This has been the biggest event on the city's calendar since 1986. More than 50 colorful hot air balloons are the main attraction, but there are also arts and crafts vendors, a carnival, and almost continuous entertainment.

PLANO

Collin County • 181,000 • (972)

The birth of this city can be traced back to settlers who put down roots here in 1845. About a year later, William Forman started a sawmill and gristmill, and a settlement grew up around it. At first the town was named after President Millard Fillmore, but when the post office said that name couldn't be used, it was changed to Plano, reflecting its location on what was then open plains.

As late as the 1960 census, the population of this community was only 3,695 and there were still working farms and ranches within the city limits. Then, in the 1970s, several large firms moved in and others followed, causing the city's population to explode to 72,331 in the 1980 census. Since then it has more than doubled again.

The hot-air balloons that local enthusiasts fly over the city and the annual Balloon Festival held in the fall have inspired many to call Plano "The Balloon Capital of Texas."

A *Money* magazine survey ranked Plano as one of the ten safest cities in the United States.

TOURIST SERVICES

PLANO CONVENTION AND VISITORS BUREAU

2000 East Spring Creek Parkway in the Plano Center (P.O. Box 860358, 75086-0358), *take Spring Creek Parkway east off US 75* • 422-0296 or 800-81-PLANO (800-817-5266) • Monday–Friday 8–5 • W+

The bureau is in the sales and booking office just inside the convention center entrance.

MUSEUMS

ART CENTRE OF PLANO

1039 East 15th Street at Avenue K (75074) • 423-7809 • Tuesday–Saturday 10–6 • Free • W+

The three galleries in this building feature works of local, national, and international artists. The ArtCentre Theatre is co-located. (*See* Performing Arts, below.)

HERITAGE FARMSTEAD MUSEUM

1900 West 15th Street (75075), at Pitman Drive, about one-and-a-half miles west of exit 29 off US 75 • 881-0140 • Adults $3.50, seniors and children (3–12) $2.50 • W (downstairs in house only)

This four-acre living history museum depicts early Texas farm life on what was once a 360-acre farm that was worked until 1972. Listed in the National Register of Historic Places, the Farmstead features the Farrel-Wilson family house, a meticulously restored 14-room Victorian-style home built in 1891, and 12 outbuildings, including the smokehouse and a windmill. Guides dressed in period costumes give one-hour tours beginning on the hour and starting with an audio-visual orientation of the farm. Summer hours: Tuesday–Friday 10–2, Saturday–Sunday 1–5. Winter hours: Thursday–Friday 10–2, Saturday–Sunday 1–5. Gift shop.

INTERURBAN RAILWAY STATION MUSEUM

901 East 15th Street in historic downtown • 461-7250 (Parks and Recreation Dept.) • Tours Saturday 1–5 or by appointment • Free (donations welcome) • W

From 1908 to 1948, this was a station on the Texas Electric Railroad's Interurban Line. The Interurban's impact on rural life was dramatic as it ended the isolation of distant farm families. This restored building is the only station remaining from the Sherman-Dallas section of the line. The museum's exhibits relate to both railroad and city history. Outside, not open to the public, is an electric railway car, which was used as a railway post office. Individual tours may be arranged by calling the Parks and Recreation Department during business hours.

SPORTS

Golf

CHASE OAKS GOLF CLUB

7201 Chase Oaks Blvd. • 517-7777 • Two courses: an 18-hole and 9-hole. Green fees for 18 holes: weekdays $47, weekends $57

PECAN HOLLOW MUNICIPAL GOLF COURSE

4501 East 14th Street (75074) • 423-5444 • 18 holes. Green fees: weekdays $13, weekends $16

RIDGEVIEW RANCH GOLF CLUB

2701 Ridgeview Drive • 390-1039 • 18 holes. Green fees: weekdays $22, weekends $30

Ice Hockey/Ice Skating

ICE BOUND ENTERTAINMENT CENTER
**4020 West Plano Parkway at Coit (P.O. Box 260277, 75026-0277)
612-8760 • W**
This two-story entertainment center features two indoor ice rinks for public skating and ice hockey, a gym, aerobics area, and food concessions. Admission free, but there is a fee for public skating.

Tennis

HIGH POINT TENNIS CENTER
421 Spring Creek Parkway (just west of North Central Expressway) • 461-7170
Twenty-two lighted courts. Fees are $2.50 per person for 1½ hours.

COLLEGES AND UNIVERSITIES

COLLIN COUNTY COMMUNITY COLLEGE
**2800 East Spring Creek Blvd. and Jupiter Rd. (75074) • 881-5790
W+ but not all areas**
The college provides about 5,000 students with both academic and technical/vocational programs on the 115-acre campus. Visitors are welcome to the Art Gallery (K208), which is open Monday–Thursday 9–5:30, Friday 9–2 (881-5873); and the five-play October–June season of the highly regarded Quad-C Theater (881-5809). Musical events open to the public include jazz concerts. The highlight of the jazz year is the annual Jazz Festival in March, which is the largest jazz festival in North Texas and a showcase for a number of the best area jazz ensembles plus special guest musicians.

PERFORMING ARTS

COLLIN COUNTY COMMUNITY COLLEGE
(See above)

PLANO CIVIC CHORUS
881-5653
The season usually includes three or four major local concerts at the Collin County Community College and other citywide locations.

PLANO CHAMBER ORCHESTRA
2701-C West 15th Street, Suite 187 (75075) • 985-1983
The 35-member professional orchestra performs about nine concerts in its October–April season with most featuring guest artists or guest conductors. Most performances are in the theater of the Fellowship Bible Church, 850 Lexington.

PLANO REPERTORY THEATRE
**ArtCentre Theatre (box office in ArtCentre, 1039 East 15th Street)
422-7460 • W**
The six plays presented in this group's year-round season usually include several classic American dramas, a comedy, and a musical. The group also puts on a children's program and a popcorn-throwing melodrama in the summer.

KIDS' STUFF

THE CLASSICS THEATRE

3015 West 15th Street (75075), at Independence • 596-8948 • W

About four national theatre touring plays for children are presented each year in this theatre which is located in the northwest corner of a strip shopping center.

MOUNTASIA FANTASY GOLF

2400 Premier Drive, west off US 75 between Park and Parker • 424-9940

Fifty-four holes of miniature golf taking players through caves, waterfalls, and over obstacles. Also bumper boats and video games.

SIDE TRIPS

LAKE LAVON

Take Parker Road (FM 2514) east about 7 miles to St. Paul, then St. Paul Road to Collin Park on the lake **• 442-5755 • Always open • Free • W variable**

There are four large parks for camping and a number of day-use parks on this 21,400-acre Army Corps of Engineers' lake. Marinas with boat rentals, swimming, fishing, waterskiing, picnicking, and motorcycle-riding trails. Caddo Park is equipped for handicapped. For information write: Reservoir Manager, P.O. Box 429, Wylie, TX 75098

SOUTHFORK RANCH

3700 Hogge Road, Parker (75002), *from US 75 (exit 30) take Parker Road east about 6 miles to Hogge Road (FM 2551) then south to entrance* **• 972-442-7800 Open daily 9–5 • Adults $6, seniors $5, children $4 • Free parking • W variable**

The myths of the TV show "Dallas" live on here. This ranch was the exterior setting for that TV series, which had a 13-season run from 1978 to 1990. Since the show was seen by millions all over the world, this white colonial-style plantation home is probably as recognizable as The White House. Tour the small museum featuring show memorabilia and the grounds on your own. There's a tram, if you don't want to walk.

ANNUAL EVENTS

SEPTEMBER

PLANO BALLOON FESTIVAL

Three day weekend late in month • Bob Woodruff Park, 2601 San Gabriel, east from Park Blvd. exit off US 75 • 867-7566 • Free • Park parking $6, shuttle from remote parking $2 • W variable

For the most breath-taking view go to the Mass Ascension event, which is when all the balloons, now up to around 100, take to the sky. This usually takes place the Saturday evening or Sunday morning of this consistently eye-filling festival. From a small beginning of a scattering of balloons and a few spectators close to 20 years ago, the festival now draws about 300,000 spectators who watch balloonists from all over the country pilot the balloons. During all this, there's also continuous entertainment on two stages, exhibits, demonstrations, and an arts-and-crafts show. Remote-site and handicapped parking is available at the DART East-Side Transit Center on Archerwood Drive, between Park and

Parker, just east of US 75. Parking is free, but to get from the parking lot to the festival, you'll have to take a shuttle bus which costs $2 round-trip.

OFFBEAT

Hot-Air Balloon Flights

IN THE AIR

1004 East 15th Street (75074), in historic downtown • 612-8852 • W

Want a bird's-eye view of Plano? This store books hot-air balloon flights and also sells everything—from t-shirts to books—on the growing sport of ballooning. About a third of the 90 or so professional balloon pilots in the Metroplex live in the Plano area, and most are available to take you up to silently float in the breeze. Flights, usually scheduled at sunrise and sunset when the light winds are best, last an hour or so. They fly every day of the year, weather permitting. Most of the balloons carry four passengers. How much? About $150 per passenger. AirVenture Balloon Port (1791 Millard, Suite D 75074, 422-0212) also books flights.

RESTAURANTS

PLANO CAFÉ

1915 North Central Expressway (US 75), Suite 500, southwest corner at Park Lane • 516-0865 • Lunch and dinner Monday–Saturday, dinner only Sunday $$ • Cr

The management refers to this as a European-style bistro, but the menu entrées range from Continental to American cuisines. Everything is sautéed or grilled, nothing fried. Beef, chicken, pork, lamb, seafood, and vegetarian specialties. Children's menu. Bar.

SEA GRILL

2205 North Central Expressway (US 75), Suite 180, west side between Park and Parker • 509-5542 • Lunch Monday–Friday, dinner daily • $$–$$$ • Cr

The chef-owner here cooks seafood medium-rare so as not to overcook and spoil the natural flavors. Overall, the menu features seafood dishes that range from New American to French to Asian cuisines. A few beef and chicken entrées on the menu, too. Bar.

ACCOMMODATIONS

($ = under $80, $$ = $80–$120, $$$ = $121–$180, $$$$ = $181–$250, $$$$$ = over $250)

Room tax 13%

COURTYARD BY MARRIOTT

4901 West Plano Parkway at Preston Road (75093) • 867-8000 or 800-321-2211 (reservations) • $$ • W+ 2 rooms • No-smoking rooms

This three-story Courtyard has 149 units including 12 suites ($$$) and 123 no-smoking rooms. Senior and other discounts available. Children 17 and under stay free in room with parents. Check in 3 P.M. Check out 1 P.M. Inside access to rooms. Charge for local calls. Cable TV with HBO and pay channels. Visual alarms for the hearing impaired and special phone available at front desk. Modem link in rooms. Fire intercom system. Heated outdoor pool, exercise room. Guest memberships available for nearby sports club. Fax and copy services. Self-service laundry. One-day dry cleaning. Coffee in lobby, special hot water dispenser for coffee in rooms. Restaurant for breakfast only (under $10.) Free newspaper. Bar (weekday evenings). Free outside parking.

HAMPTON INN

4905 Old Shepard Place (75093), off Preston Road north of Plano Parkway 519-1000 or 800-HAMPTON (800-428-7866) • $ • W+ 7 rooms No-smoking rooms

Eighty percent of the 131 rooms in this five-story inn are no-smoking. Senior, weekend, and other discounts available. Children under 18 stay free in room with parents. Check in 2 P.M. Check out noon. Inside access to rooms. Local phone calls free. Cable TV with HBO, Disney, and pay channels. Captioned TV, visual alarms, and special phones for the hearing impaired. Coffeemakers in rooms and free coffee in lobby. Modem link in rooms. Fire intercom system. Outdoor pool, exercise room. Fax and copy services. One-day dry cleaning. Free continental breakfast. Free social hour Tuesday–Wednesday evenings. Free newspaper. Free shuttle transportation within five miles. Free outside parking.

HARVEY HOTEL PLANO

1600 North Central Expressway (US 75), exit 29 (15th Street) • 578-8555 or 800-922-9222 • $$–$$$ • W+ 3 rooms • No-smoking rooms

This three-story hotel has 279 units including 12 suites ($$$) and 186 no-smoking rooms. Senior, weekend, and other discounts and package plans available. Children 18 and under stay free in room with parents. Small pets OK ($125 deposit). Check in 3 P.M. Check out 1 P.M. Inside access to rooms. Charge for local calls. Cable TV with pay channels. VCR available. Captioned TV, visual alarms, and special phones for the hearing impaired. Coffeemakers available on request, free coffee in lobby. Modem link in rooms. Bell service. Room service. Outdoor pool, exercise room. Fax, copy, and printing services available. Gift shop. Self-service laundry. One-day dry cleaning. Free newspaper. Restaurant serving all meals (dinner under $12). Bar. Free outside parking.

RICHARDSON

Dallas and Collin Counties • 78,000 • (972)

In 1842, the Jackson family came from Tennessee and settled on land where Richland College is now located. Other settlers moved in, eventually forming a town they proudly named after John C. Breckenridge, who later served as vice president of the United States from 1857–1861. After the Civil War, the railroads became the driving force in the development of the West. Unfortunately, Breckenridge was not in any railroads plans, so, in 1872, John Wheeler lured the Houston and Texas Railroad to the area by giving land for a right-of-way and a townsite. Showing his political savvy, Wheeler named the new town after E. H. Richardson, the railroad contractor who built the line.

As late as 1950, Richardson's population stood at about 1,300. Then, in 1951, Collins Radio opened a Richardson office and the door to the electronic age. Today, the city is the home to more than 500 high-tech and telecommunications companies, and the area along the North Central Expressway is called the Tele-com Corridor®.

TOURIST SERVICES

RICHARDSON CONVENTION AND VISITORS BUREAU

411 Belle Grove Drive (75080), *from I-75, exit Arapaho, take South access road to Belle Grove, first right* • **234-4141 or 800-777-8001** • **Monday–Friday 8:30–5** • **W+**

Brochures, maps, directions—everything you'd expect from a convention and visitors bureau—and more.

POINTS OF INTEREST

OWENS SPRING CREEK FARM

1401 East Lookout (75081), off Plano Road between Renner and Campbell 235-0192 • **Open daily 9–12 and 1–4** • **Free** • **W variable**

The main building on this 56-acre farm is a small museum with exhibits depicting both life in the 1920s and how the Owens' family, who has been known in Texas for its sausages for well over 60 years, started out in that business. In the barn there are antique wagons and in the corrals are tiny Shetland ponies and a team of huge Belgian horses, which weigh an average of 2,300 pounds. There are also a number of farm animals, some of which can be petted. Guided tours are Monday–Friday 9–3.

SPORTS AND ACTIVITIES

Golf

THE PRACTICE TEE

2950 Waterview (75080), next to UT-Dallas campus • **235-6540 9-hole par 3 course. Call for fees.**

SHERRILL PARK MUNICIPAL GOLF COURSE

2001 Lookout Drive (75080) • **234-1416**

36-holes. Green fees (18 holes): weekdays $14, weekends/holidays $17. Ranked as the #4 municipal course in the state by *The Dallas Morning News.*

Tennis

TENNIS CENTER

1601 Syracuse Drive (75081) in Huffhines Park • **234-6697**

Ten lighted courts. Fees: $1.50 per person for 1½ hours.

COLLEGES AND UNIVERSITIES

RICHLAND COLLEGE

12800 Abrams Road (75243), just north of LBJ Freeway (I-635) • **238-6194 W+ but not all areas**

The 259-acre community college campus has an enrollment of about 13,000 in its academic and technical/vocational programs. Visitors are welcome at plays, dance and music concerts, recitals, the art gallery, the greenhouse and demonstration garden, and shows at the planetarium.

UNIVERSITY OF TEXAS AT DALLAS

2601 North Floyd Road (75080), at Campbell Road • News and information 883-2293 • W+ but not all areas

Established in 1969 as a graduate school only, the 500-acre university campus has added undergraduate levels over the years, and it now also offers a variety of undergraduate degrees. Visitors are welcome at the Visual Arts Gallery (883-2787), as well as at concerts, plays, and films (arts events line 883-ARTS/883-2787). The McDermott Library Special Collections Gallery features new art exhibits (883-2570) and displays its Wineburgh Philatelic Research Collection, one of the country's top resources on stamps and stamp collecting, and its History of Aviation Collection, which traces aviation history. Check at the gate for visitor parking.

PERFORMING ARTS

RICHARDSON COMMUNITY BAND

P.O. Box 832964, 75083 • Metro 972-851-9784

The band is composed of about 60 musicians who perform free concerts year-round, including a summer biweekly outdoor concert series Sunday evenings on the lawn of the Richardson Civic Center (411 W. Arapaho).

RICHARDSON SYMPHONY ORCHESTRA

333 West Campbell Road, #210 (Office) (P.O. Box 831675, 75083) • 234-4195

This 70-member professional orchestra performs four classical and two pops concerts in its October through April subscription season.

RICHARDSON THEATRE CENTER

718 Canyon Creek Square (75080), at Custer Road and Lookout behind the supermarket • 699-1130 • W

They put on five shows a year in this small 80-seat theater.

RICH TONES CHORUS

P.O. Box 832978, 75083 • 234-6065

More than 125 women make up this award-winning Sweet Adelines chorus that sings four-part harmony barbershop style in concerts in various locations in Richardson and the surrounding area.

RICHLAND COLLEGE

See Colleges and Universities, above.

UNIVERSITY OF TEXAS AT DALLAS

See Colleges and Universities, above.

KIDS' STUFF

RICHARDSON CHILDREN'S THEATRE

525 West Arapaho #20 (75080) (office) • 690-5029

The acting company consists of a professional troupe and children and youths ages 5–16 who have successfully completed acting workshops. Six productions are performed each year at the UT-Dallas Theatre (Floyd and Campbell W+).

ANNUAL EVENTS

Special events hotline 238-4021

April

WILDFLOWER! ARTS & MUSIC FESTIVAL

Weekends late in month (four nights and two days) • Greenway Office Park, US 75 and Campbell Road (office: 1405 Exchange St, 75081) • 680-7909 Admission to some events • W variable

If Mother Nature cooperates, when this festival starts the city will be in full bloom with over 90 acres of wildflowers in parks, along roadsides, in street medians, and along US 75. Bus tours leave the festival area to view many of these areas. The festival itself includes "A Taste of Richardson," where a number of local restaurants provide the food for dining, dancing, and entertainment; a Battle of the Bands, with the bands made up of some of the area's top corporate executives, and non-stop music on four other stages; arts and crafts; a car show; carnival; police motorcycle rodeo; children's activities; fireworks; and a laser show. The Richardson Symphony also presents its annual concert with a patriotic theme.

May and October

COTTONWOOD ART FESTIVAL

Saturday–Sunday • Cottonwood Park, 1321 West Belt Line Road, one block east of Coit Road (office: 711 West Arapaho Road, 75080) • 231-4624 • Free W variable

Artists from across the country participate in this twice a year arts-and-crafts show. Held for close to 30 years, it has built a reputation for the high quality of work presented. Music, children's programs, and food.

RESTAURANTS

($ = under $12, $$ = $12–$30, $$$ = over $30 for one person excluding drinks, tax, and tip.)

CAFÉ BRAZIL

2071 North Central Expressway (75080) • 783-9011 • Breakfast, lunch and dinner daily • $–$$ • Cr • W

One of four in the Metroplex, this small chain serves all meals, but is most consistently listed as one of the best breakfast spots in the Dallas. And breakfast is available all day.

SWAN COURT

2435 North Central Expressway (US 75) (75081), at Campbell • 235-7926 Lunch Monday–Friday, dinner Monday–Saturday. Closed Sunday • $$ Cr • W

A supper club setting with a continental menu that features seafood, steaks, veal, chicken, and pasta. Bar. Live music and dancing Monday–Saturday.

ACCOMMODATIONS

($ = under $80, $$ = $80–$120, $$$ = $121–$180, $$$$ = $181–$250,
$$$$$ = over $250)
Room tax 13%

HAMPTON INN

1577 Gateway Blvd. (75080), *from exit 26 Campbell Road off US 75, go west to*
Gateway • **234-5400 or 800-426-7866** • **$** • **W+ 5 rooms** • **No-smoking rooms**
   This four-story inn's 130 units include one suite ($$) and 98 no-smoking
rooms. Senior and weekend discounts available. Children 18 and under stay
free in room with parents. Check in 2 P.M. Check out noon. Inside access to
rooms. Local phone calls free. Cable TV with HBO, Disney, and pay channels.
Free coffee in lobby. Modem link in rooms. Outdoor pool. Guest memberships
available for nearby health club. Free local fax. One-day dry cleaning. Free continental breakfast. Free newspaper. Free outside parking.

HAWTHORN SUITES HOTEL

250 Municipal Drive (75080), *from US 75 exit 26, Campbell Road, take south*
access road to Municipal Drive • **669-1000 or 800-527-1133** • **$$$–$$$$**
W+ 2 rooms • **No-smoking rooms**
   All 72 units in this two-story hotel are suites with kitchens, and 36 of them
are no-smoking. Senior and weekend discounts and package plans available.
Pets OK ($50 deposit). Check in 2 P.M. Check out noon. Outside access to suites.
Charge for local calls. Cable TV with HBO. Coffeemakers in rooms. Modem
link in rooms. Room service. Outdoor pool. Guest memberships available for
nearby gym. Fax and copy services available. Self-service laundry. Free break-
fast buffet. Free cocktails. Free newspaper. Free outside parking.

OMNI RICHARDSON HOTEL

701 East Campbell Road (75081), east off I-75 exit 26 • **231-9600 or**
800-THE OMNI (800-843-6664) • **$$–$$$** • **W+ 5 rooms** • **No-smoking rooms**
   This 17-story Omni has 342 units, of which ten are suites ($$$–$$$$) and 294
are no-smoking. Senior, weekend, and other discounts available. Children free
in room with parents. Concierge floor. Check in 3 P.M. Check out noon. Inside
access to rooms. Charge for local calls. Cable TV with free premium channel
and pay channels. Modem link in rooms. Fire intercom system. Bell service.
Room service. Outdoor heated pool, sauna, exercise room. Guest memberships
available for health club and for golf. Gift shop. Restaurant serving all meals
(dinner $12–$30). Lounge with CD jukebox and dancing. Free outside parking.

SHERMAN

Grayson County Seat • **31,601** • **(903)**
   The town was established as the county seat with the founding of the county
in 1846, and named for Sidney Sherman, one of the leaders at the Battle of San
Jacinto and the man usually credited with coining the famous cry "Remember
the Alamo! Remember Goliad!" The original location of the town proved
unsuitable, and in 1848, it was moved five miles east. Some say the move was
necessary because of a lack of water and wood, but others claim it was agitated
by several men who owned land around the new townsite.

Transportation has always played a key role in Sherman's growth. The town was put on the map in 1857 when John Butterfield picked it for a stop on his St. Louis to San Francisco stage line. In the early 1870s the Houston and Texas Central Railway connected the town to Houston, opening up markets. But prosperity went to the heads of the town fathers. They had already gone along with the custom of paying a subsidy to get the first railroad to come to town, but in 1872, when Missouri, Kansas & Texas Railway (KATY) wanted a subsidy to come in from the north, the town fathers refused to pay. They figured that they were the only game in the county, so the KATY would have no choice but to make Sherman its destination. Instead, the KATY started its own town of Denison.

Industry came to town in 1891. Among the first companies were the Sherman Oil and Cotton Company, which processed cottonseed into an edible oil, and the Sherman Seamless Bag Mill. The successors to the original oil company eventually became part of Anderson-Clayton, and the successors to the bag mill were eventually taken into the Burlington Industries fold. Both of these international companies have plants in town and have been joined by a number of other Fortune 500 companies to make today's Sherman an industrial center.

TOURIST SERVICES

SHERMAN CHAMBER OF COMMERCE/CONVENTION AND VISITORS BUREAU

307 W. Washington, Suite 100 (P.O. Box 1029, 75090) • 893-1184 • W

MUSEUMS

RED RIVER HISTORICAL MUSEUM

301 S. Walnut at E. Jones • 893-7623 • Tuesday–Friday 10–12, 1–4:30; Saturday and Sunday 2–5 • Adults $2, seniors and students $1

Located in a 1914 Carnegie Library building, which is listed in the National Register of Historic Places, the museum exhibits tell the story of Grayson Glen Eden, the main house of a famed mid-1800s plantation on the Red River that was dismantled in the 1940s before the rising waters of the then-forming Lake Texoma could lap over it. Other exhibits include a collection of models of World War II aircraft, a turn-of-the-century country store, and a patent medicine collection.

HISTORIC PLACES

There are several late nineteenth-century buildings and homes in Sherman. A "Historical Driving Tour of Sherman" brochure is available from the Chamber of Commerce. Among the historic homes in the brochure are **C. S. Roberts House,** 915 S. Crockett, built in 1896; **Heritage Row,** 300 to 1300 blocks of S. Crockett, built between 1883 and the early 1900s; **Joiner-Omohundro House** (1892) and the **Taylor-Totten House** at 618 and 1118 S. Travis, respectively; **N. A. Birge House** (1896) at 727 W. Birge; **Mattingly House** (1892) at 1506 N. Alexander; and the **Ely-Eubanks House** (1896) at 709 W. Washington. These are all private homes not open to the public.

WEST HILL CEMETERY
Lamar and Woods

Occupying 125 acres and containing more than 28,000 graves—close to the city's present population—this cemetery, started in 1859, contains a number of historical markers. In addition to the city founders who are buried here, it also contains the grave of Olive Ann Oatman Fairchild. Indians captured her in Arizona in 1851, when she was 13, and marked her as a slave with a blue, cactus-needle tattoo on her chin that she bore the rest of her life. Ransomed by the Army in 1856, she married and settled in Sherman with her husband, who founded one of the city's first banks. Many of the grave sites have huge monuments. The mausoleum windows were made by Tiffany and bear the signature.

OTHER POINTS OF INTEREST

HAGERMAN NATIONAL WILDLIFE REFUGE
Refuge Headquarters off FM 1417 about 6 miles north • 786-2826
Always open • Free • W variable
See Denison.

SPORTS AND ACTIVITIES

Golf

GRAYSON COUNTY COLLEGE GOLF COURSE
West Campus, northwest of intersection of FM 691 and FM 1417 • 786-9719

The only golf course in Grayson County open to the public. 18-hole course. Greens fee: weekdays $7, weekends $10.

COLLEGES AND UNIVERSITIES

GRAYSON COUNTY COLLEGE
6101 Grayson Dr. *From US 75 go west on FM 691 to college* **• 465-6030 • W Variable**
See Denison.

AUSTIN COLLEGE
900 N. Grand between Brockett and Richards • 892-9101 or in Texas 800-442-5363 • W+ but not all areas

Founded by Presbyterians in Huntsville in 1849, this is the oldest college in Texas operating under its original charter. It was the first college in the state to grant a graduate degree, the first to start a law school, and the first to have a national fraternity. Named for Stephen F. Austin, it included Sam Houston and Anson Jones, two of the presidents of the Republic of Texas, among the first trustees. A bell donated by Sam Houston hangs in the present chapel. Post-Civil War problems and yellow fever epidemics caused the college to move to Sherman in 1876. Today, most of the 1,200 students pursue a four-year program in education. Visitors are welcome to intercollegiate athletic events, plays, recitals, and concerts by the drama and music departments, and monthly art exhibits at the gallery in the Ida Green Communications Center. Tours of the campus can be arranged Monday through Friday through the admissions office.

PERFORMING ARTS

SHERMAN COMMUNITY PLAYERS

Finley Playhouse, 500 N. Elm • 829-8818 (box office) or 893-8525
Admission $6 • W
Started in the 1940s, this group now operates with a professional director and non-professional casts to put on about five or six productions a year in the October–June season.

SHERMAN SYMPHONY

892-9101, Ext. 251 • Admission $5–$6
This combined professional/non-professional orchestra puts on about four concerts a year, most with guest artists. Performances are usually at the Wynne Chapel on the campus of Austin College (900 N. Grand).

SHOPPING

Antiques

The Chamber of Commerce offers a free map of more than a dozen antique shops in the area. Most are clustered downtown between Houston and Jones and Rusk and Willow streets.

HARING ART CENTER

120 E. Mulberry near Travis • 892-3113 • W
Ernie Haring not only runs an art supply store, he is also probably the most popular watercolorist in the area. A number of his landscape watercolors, painted all over the world, are for sale in his shop.

KELLY SQUARE

115 S. Travis on the square • 892-4971 • W downstairs only
Parking in lot on E. Lamar
A renovated 1870 building converted into a three-story grouping of about 24 specialty shops selling art, antiques, clothing, and handmade items, and two restaurants.

SIDE TRIPS

LAKE TEXOMA AND DENISON DAM

Take US 75 north to Denison, then 75A north about 4 miles to the dam. About 13 miles from Sherman • **465-4990 (Army Corps of Engineers) • Always open**
Free • W variable
See Denison

ANNUAL EVENTS

April

PRESERVATION LEAGUE TOUR OF HOMES

893-1184 (Chamber of Commerce) • Weekend late in April • $5
Five or six of the many historic buildings in town are opened to the public for this tour. Tickets and brochures listing the open houses are available in advance from the Chamber of Commerce (*see* Tourist Services).

September

RED RIVER VALLEY ARTS FESTIVAL

Sherman Municipal Building, Rusk and Pecan • 893-1184 (Chamber of Commerce) • Third weekend in September • Free • W+ but not all areas.

The festivities include an art show, craft booths and craft demonstrations, children's activities, and musical entertainment. Also a shuttle bus to Sherman Historical Museum's open house. Featured entertainment is usually early in the evening, and guests are encouraged to bring picnic suppers to eat on the lawn while watching.

ACCOMMODATIONS

($ = under $45, $$ = $46–$60, $$$ = $61–$80, $$$$ = $81–$100, $$$$$ = over $100)
Room tax 10%

GRAYSON HOUSE/BEST WESTERN

2501 S. Texoma Parkway • 892-2161 • $$–$$$$ • W+ 2 rooms
No-smoking rooms

The two-story Ramada has 144 rooms including 90 no-smoking. Cable TV. Room phones (no charge for local calls). Pets OK. Private club (guests automatically members). Restaurant. Outdoor pool and spa. Coffeemakers in some rooms. Free newspaper.

TERRELL

Kaufman County • 12,490 • (972)

The first settlers arrived in 1848, but the town wasn't founded until 1873. That was when the route of the Texas and Pacific Railroad was laid out through the area to take advantage of a large underground lake that ensured adequate water supply for the trains. Two men from Kaufman, C. C. Nash and John G. Moore, lost no time in capitalizing on the opportunity to develop a new town on the prairie. Nash provided the money, $1,600, and Moore took off on horseback to Uvalde, where he purchased 320 acres at $5 an acre. The railroad turned the town into the trading center it remains today.

TOURIST SERVICES

TERRELL VISITOR CENTER

Tanger Outlet Center • I-20 at Hwy. 34 • 563-3520 • Open Monday–Thursday 10–5, Fri. 11–5, Saturday 10–7, Sunday 1–4

MUSEUMS

TERRELL HERITAGE MUSEUM

207 N. Frances • 563-6082 • Wednesday 10–4 and Sunday 1–4 • Free

The museum is upstairs in the old Carnegie Library building, which was the city's library from 1904 to 1984. The historic collection of artifacts, pictures, clothing, tools, and other memorabilia depicts pioneer life in the area. The gallery of the Kaufman County Art League is downstairs.

SILENT WINGS MUSEUM

Terrell Municipal Airport, TX 34 north of I-20 (follow signs to museum)
563-0402 • Tuesday–Saturday 10–5, Sunday 12–5. Closed Monday
Free (donation) • W

The "silent wings" are the wings of the military gliders used to carry airborne troops into combat in World War II. The centerpiece of the displays in this museum is a restored WACO CG-4A combat transport glider, which could carry 13 fully equipped troops or a Jeep. Other displays include a Jeep, weapons, and other mementos of that war, photos following the life of glider pilots from training to combat, and ten dioramas depicting World War II battle scenes. World War II combat and training films are shown on request in the museum's theater. The museum is operated by the Military Glider Pilots Association.

HISTORIC PLACES

HISTORIC HOMES

Several historic homes have been preserved from the era when Terrell was a bustling railroad and cotton center. They include the **Griffith-Cox Home,** 803 First, built in 1883; the **Matthew Cartwright House,** 505 Griffith Ave., built in 1883; the Queen Anne-style Sites House, 605 N. Frances built in 1895; the **Jarvis-Pruitt Home,** 505 Pacific, built in 1887; the **Fields-Speer Home,** 506 Griffith built in 1893; and the **McClung-Summonds Cottage,** 201 Lawrence, built in 1893. They are all private homes and are not open to the public.

DR. L. E. GRIFFITH HOME

805 First

The exact date of construction of this house is unknown. Dr. Griffith came to Texas in 1836, and architectural details indicate it could have been built as early as 1853, making it the oldest house in Terrell. Tours may be arranged by appointment through the Chamber of Commerce (563-5703).

1880s PRIVATE RAILROAD CAR

Ben Gill Park, W. Moore St. (US 80W) • Admission

This railroad car is a memorial to the railroads, which played such an important part in the beginnings of Terrell. It is being restored to its original grandeur by the Terrell Police Officers' Association.

PERFORMING ARTS

TERRELL CIVIC THEATRE

115 N. Adelaide • 563-1307 or 563-5487 • Admission

Located in the old City Hall building, this community theater group puts on four to six productions in a season running from September to June. The small theater seats about 80.

SIDE TRIPS

LAKE TAWAKONI
Take US 80 east to FM 429, then northeast approximately 15 miles to lake
**(903) 447-3020 (Lake Tawakoni Chamber of Commerce) • Always open
Free • W variable**
This 36,000-acre lake offers facilities for boating, fishing, waterskiing, and camping (fee). There are a number of commercial marinas, motels, restaurants, and other recreational facilities along the 200 miles of shoreline. It is usually rated among the top ten fishing lakes in the state and has been the site of the U.S. Bass World Championship Tournament.

WALTER C. PORTER FARM
Take FM 986 (Poetry Rd.) 2 miles north to farm
One of Texas' most famous farms, it has been designated a national landmark as the birthplace of the USDA's Agricultural Extension Service. It started in 1903 when Walter C. Porter agreed to allow Dr. Seaman A. Knapp to experiment on his crops as a demonstration for other farmers. The experiments resulted in increased yields, which inspired the U.S. secretary of agriculture to set up a demonstration system, which led to the present extension service operating in rural areas all over the nation. There are no tours available, but visitors can view the historic landmark.

ANNUAL EVENTS

TERRELL SPRING HERITAGE JUBILEE
**Ben Gill Park, W. Moore St. (US 80W) • 563-5703 (Chamber of Commerce)
Last weekend of April • Admission to some events • W but not all areas**
Activities include a chili cookoff, arts-and-crafts fair, Junior Livestock Show, the Heritage Tour of Homes (fee), and other contests and entertainment.

WEATHERFORD

Parker County Seat • 18,000 • (817)
The first settlers came about 1854, designating Weatherford as the county seat two years later. The county was named for state legislator Issac Parker, the uncle of famous Comanche captive Cynthia Ann Parker. The town was named after Jefferson Weatherford, a state senator. The Parker County Courthouse on the square (599-6591), built in 1886, is open Monday through Friday 8–5. The original recorded cost of the white limestone building was $55,555.55.

In 1858, Oliver Loving of Parker County organized the first recorded Texas cattle drive to northern markets. After the Civil War he and Charles Goodnight established the Goodnight-Loving Trail from Texas to New Mexico organizing cattle drives from Weatherford to Kansas. Loving is buried in the Greenwood City Cemetery in the 200 block of Soward.

Fans of the late entertainer Mary Martin may see her childhood home at 314 W. Oak, now a private residence not open to the public. A life-sized (5 foot 4 inch) bronze statue of Martin as Peter Pan stands outside the library at 1214 Charles St. (off Bowie). The library contains a collection of Martin memorabilia.

Parker County watermelons, averaging 100 pounds each, won gold medals at the St. Louis World's Fair in 1904. Now peaches and other orchard fruits, vegetables, peanuts, and pecans contribute more to the local economy. Local produce is for sale at the Farmers' Market on Fort Worth Street (US 80/180) about three blocks east of the courthouse. Ranching, a fast-growing horse industry, and light industry are also mainstays of the economy.

TOURIST SERVICES

WEATHERFORD CHAMBER OF COMMERCE

401 Fort Worth St., about 2 blocks east of the courthouse (P.O. Box 310, 76086) 594-3801 • W

POINTS OF INTEREST

LAKE WEATHERFORD

From US 80/180 east take FM 1707 north to lake. About 7 miles from town **594-6905 (Marina) • Open at all times • Free • W variable**
This 1,210-acre municipal lake with a 19-mile shoreline offers facilities for boating, fishing, water sports, and picnicking.

SPORTS AND ACTIVITIES

RAILS TO TRAILS TRAILWAY

Take FM 51 north to FM 920 west about 2 miles to Cartwright Park **• 594-3801 (Chamber of Commerce) • W variable**
Once a railroad corridor, this 22-mile-long trail connects Weatherford with Lake Mineral Wells State Park (*see* Mineral Wells). It is for hike, bike, equestrian, and wheelchair use.

COLLEGES AND UNIVERSITIES

WEATHERFORD COLLEGE

308 E. Park at College Park Dr. • 594-5471 • W+ but not all areas
This two-year community college founded in 1869 is the oldest continuously operated junior college in the state. Visitors are welcome at drama and music productions and intercollegiate sports events. College tennis courts behind the gymnasium are open to the public when not used for classes.

SHOPPING

FIRST MONDAY TRADE DAYS

US 80/180 about 3 blocks east of courthouse • 594-3801 (Chamber of Commerce) • Friday–Sunday before the first Monday of each month Free • W variable
Bargain hunters find over 400 vendors selling everything from livestock to trinkets. Free street parking is available when you can find it.

ANNUAL EVENTS

June

PARKER COUNTY SHERIFF'S POSSE FRONTIER DAYS AND RODEO

Sheriff's Posse Rodeo Arena, 2 miles west of the courthouse on US 180W **594-3801 (Chamber of Commerce) • Last full week in June • Admission to rodeo • W variable**

The main event is the Sheriff's Posse Rodeo that runs nightly. There's also a parade, cutting horse competitions, livestock show and sale, and street dances.

ACCOMMODATIONS

($ = under $45, $$ = $46–$60, $$$ = $61–$80, $$$$ = $81–$100, $$$$$ = over $100) *Room tax 13%*

BEST WESTERN SANTA FE INN

1927 Santa Fe Dr., just north of I-20 exit 409 (Clear Lake Rd.) • 594-7401 or 800-528-1234 • $$ • W+ 1 room • No-smoking rooms

This two-story Best Western has 45 rooms including four no-smoking. Cable TV with HBO. Room phones (no charge for local calls). Small pets OK. Restaurant. Outdoor pool. Free coffee.

COMFORT INN

809 Palo Pinto, US 80/180 about .7 miles west of courthouse • 599-8683 • $$

The two-story inn has 42 rooms including 21 no-smoking rooms and three mini-suites. Cable TV with HBO. Room phones (no charge for local calls). Small pets OK. Outdoor pool. Free Continental breakfast.

HAMPTON INN

2524 S. Main, IH-20 exit 408 and TX 51/171 • 599-4800 or 800-426-7866 • $$$ W+ 1 room • No-smoking rooms

This three-story inn has 56 units including three suites ($$$$$) and 42 no-smoking rooms. All rooms have refrigerators and coffeemakers. Microwave ovens available on request. Cable TV with HBO. Room phones (no charge for local calls). Outdoor pool and hot tub. Coin-operated laundry. Free Continental breakfast.

HOLIDAY INN EXPRESS

2500 S. Main, IH 20 exit 408 and TX 151 • 599-3700 or 800-465-4329 • $$$ W+ 2 rooms • No-smoking rooms

There are 45 units in this two-story Holiday Inn including 33 no-smoking rooms and two suites ($$$$$). All rooms have refrigerators and coffeemakers. Microwave ovens available on request. Cable TV with HBO. Room phones (no charge for local calls). Outdoor pool and hot tub. Coin-operated laundry. Free Continental breakfast.

South Texas

BEAUMONT

Jefferson County Seat • 114,000 • (409)

Beaumont burst into the national and international headlines in 1901 when Spindletop blew its top and the second oil gusher in the world blew in.

The city goes back to about 1825 when Noah and Nancy Tevis settled on the banks of the Neches River on a land grant from the Mexican government. In 1835, Tevis sold 50 acres to Henry Millard for a townsite, but Millard went to fight against Mexico. Nancy provided more land and laid out Beaumont. The city was chartered in 1838 and became the county seat.

Millard is credited with naming Beaumont. Some say it's named for the French words "beautiful mountain," for the small hill near here. But, the average elevation is only 24 feet above sea level, so more credence is given to Millard's wife's maiden name of Beaumont.

Beaumont became a port on the Neches and a lumbering center, and later rice farming was an important industry.

Then came Spindletop.

Patillo Higgins had been obsessed for years with getting financial backing to drill under a mound known as Spindletop. He brought in Anthony Lucas, an Austrian engineer, and then went broke. Lucas secured several financiers and started drilling. On January 10, 1901, with the drill down to 1,160 feet and no sign of oil, the crew shut down to change the bit. Suddenly the well erupted with oil shooting 200 feet in the air. It blew for over a week, pouring more than 800,000 barrels of oil on the ground. Finally the drillers capped the well, and the boom was on.

Hundreds of oil companies were formed, but the few that survived were the parents of the present Exxon, Mobil, and Texaco corporations.

Today, Beaumont, Orange, and Port Arthur together are called The Golden Triangle.

TOURIST SERVICES

BEAUMONT CONVENTION AND VISITORS BUREAU

801 Main near College, in City Hall (P.O. Box 3827, 77704) • 880-3749 or 800-392-4401, e-mail: bmtcvb@satnet or web site: http://www.beaumontcvb.com W+

Free brochures and self-guided driving tour. It also operates the Visitors Information Center at the Babe Zaharias Museum, I-10 at Gulf exit, 833-4622, Monday through Saturday 9–5, closed Sunday.

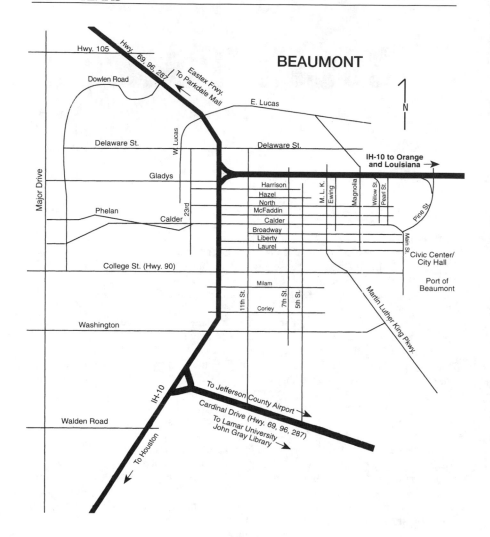

PORT OF BEAUMONT OBSERVATION DECK
1255 Main • 832-1546 • Monday–Friday • Free

Located on the deep-water Neches River ship channel, 42 miles inland from the Gulf of Mexico, this is one of the busiest ports in Texas. It handled all materiel for Desert Storm. Check with security guard at the main gate. Tours are by reservation.

BIRD'S-EYE VIEW

MARY AND JOHN GRAY LIBRARY
Lamar University (400 Martin Luther King Parkway) • 880-8118
Open during school term, hours vary • Free • W
  You can see all the way to Port Arthur from the eighth floor. On the seventh floor is a replica of Congressman Jack Brooks' office in Washington. After serving in the Texas Legislature, Brooks served 40 years in the U.S. Congress. Usually open Monday through Friday 9–4.

MUSEUMS

ART MUSEUM OF SOUTHEAST TEXAS
500 Main • 832-3432 • Monday–Friday 9–5, Saturday 10–5, Sunday noon–5. Closed Monday • Free • W
  This museum has a permanent collection of paintings, sculpture, mixed media, and art library. There are traveling exhibits during the year.

BABE DIDRIKSON ZAHARIAS MEMORIAL MUSEUM AND VISITOR INFORMATION CENTER
I-10 at MLK exit • 833-4622 • Open daily 9–5 • Free • W+
  Mildred "Babe" Didrikson Zaharias grew up in Beaumont. The museum, designed with the five Olympic circles, displays the memorabilia of the "Babe's" outstanding athletic career, which earned her the Associated Press title "Woman Athlete of the Year" six times.

BEAUMONT POLICE MUSEUM
255 College • 880-3825 • Monday–Friday 8–4:30 • Free
  A collection of weaponry and other paraphernalia used by Beaumont police, including some confiscated from the city's crime element, is on display.

EDISON PLAZA MUSEUM
350 Pine, behind the Gulf States Utilities Bldg. • 839-3089 • Monday–Friday 1–3:30. Tours by appointment • Free • W downstairs only • Visitor parking in Gulf States employees' lot
  Thomas Alva Edison is credited with 1,093 inventions, and examples of many of these are on display, including a replica of the original light bulb. Appropriately housed in the restored 1929 Travis Street Power Substation, the exhibits tell the story of the electric industry, stemming from Edison's genius. Gift shop sells Edison-related items.

GLADYS CITY SPINDLETOP BOOMTOWN
On the Lamar University Campus at intersection of University Dr. and US 69/96/287, Highland Ave. exit • 835-0823 • Tuesday–Sunday 1–5, Saturday 9–5. Closed Monday • Admission • W
  This is a reconstruction of the boom town that appeared almost overnight when Spindletop blew in. All that is missing is the sea of mud, the smell of oil, and the excited crowds of boomers who jammed the streets. The monument is the Lucas Gusher Monument, a memorial to these boomers.

JOHN JAY FRENCH MUSEUM

2995 French Rd. off Delaware • 898-3267 • Tuesday–Saturday 10–4 • Admission
The oldest house in Beaumont was built in 1845. French, a tanner and merchant from Connecticut, built this two-story Greek Revival house, opened a tannery nearby, and began trading. Gift shop.

THE McFADDEN-WARD HOUSE

1906 McFaddin, Visitors Center on Calder at 3rd • 832-2134 • Tuesday–Saturday 10–4, Sunday 1–3. Closed Monday • Admission $3
Built in 1906, this is one of the best-preserved, large-scale examples of Beaux Arts Colonial mansions in the nation. This 12,800-square-foot house reflects the lifestyle of the wealthy Southeast Texas family who owned and managed ranches, rice farms, and oil fields. It is elegantly furnished with silver, rare furniture, oriental rugs, European porcelains, and American Brilliant Period cut glass. It is listed in the National Register of Historic Places.

TEXAS ENERGY MUSEUM

600 Main • 833-5100 • Tuesday–Saturday 9–5, Sunday 1–5 • Admission • W Variable
This modern exhibit used to be The Western Company Museum in Fort Worth. Robotic displays and a gushing oil well are of the same caliber of exhibits at the Smithsonian.

FIRE MUSEUM OF TEXAS

400 Walnut, downstairs in Beaumont Fire Department • 880-3917 Monday–Friday 8–4:30 • Free (donations) • W
For visitors who always dreamed of being a fireman, there's a demonstration pole to slide down. The oldest piece of fire fighting equipment is a fire rattle from Boston that was used to alert villages of night fires in 1653. Beaumont and Texas A&M are the two largest fire fighters' training facilities in the world.

SPORTS AND ACTIVITIES

Golf

BAYOU DIN GOLF COURSE

LaBelle Rd. • 796-1327 • 18-hole course. Greens fee: weekdays $11.50, weekends $8

TYRRELL PARK MUNICIPAL GOLF COURSE

Babe Zaharias Dr. • 842-3220 • 18-hole course. Greens fee: weekdays $8, weekends $9

Tennis

BEAUMONT MUNICIPAL ATHLETIC COMPLEX

6455 College • 838-0783 • Free, except a metered charge for lighting at night

COLLEGES AND UNIVERSITIES

LAMAR UNIVERSITY

4400 Martin Luther King Parkway • 880-7011 • W+ but not all areas Visitor parking lot at entrance

About 7,500 students are enrolled at this campus. For visitors, the Dishman Art Gallery on the corner of Lavaca and Martin Luther King exhibits works by art students and has an eclectic permanent collection. Open Monday through Thursday 7:30–4:30, Friday 7:30–noon (880-8137). Indoor sports events and concerts are held in the Montagne Center (880-8615). Drama students stage productions during the school year in the University Theater (880-2250). The Gladys City Spindletop Museum is also on the campus (*see* Museums).

PERFORMING ARTS

JULIE ROGERS THEATRE FOR THE PERFORMING ARTS

765 Pearl at Forsythe, across from Civic Center • 838-3435 • Admission • W+

This is the cultural events center and the home of the Beaumont Symphony Orchestra, the Civic Ballet, the Ballet Theatre, and the Civic Opera.

SHOPPING

OLD TOWN

Between Laurel and Harrison avenues and 11th and 2nd streets

This was a picturesque neighborhood of large homes even during the oil boom. Many of the homes are now converted to shops featuring antiques, art, gifts, jewelry, and fashions.

SIDE TRIPS

ROY E. LARSON SANDYLAND SANCTUARY

Take US 96 north to Silsbee, then west about 2.5 miles on TX 327.
Approximately 25 miles from Beaumont **• 1-409-385-4135 • Open daily during daylight hours • Free**

There are six miles of trails through the 2,276 acres of pine and hardwood forest, and the creek offers an easy one-day canoe trip. No camping.

SUPER GATOR AIRBOAT SWAMP TOURS

Take I-10 east to Orange, exit 878 at Cypress Lake. (*See* **Orange.**)

ANNUAL EVENTS
April

NECHES RIVER FESTIVAL

Various locations • 835-2443 • 9 days starting on a Saturday near the end of April • Mostly free • W variable

More than 40 events go on ranging from art shows, flower shows, and museum tours to the Queen's Ball and speedboat races.

OFFBEAT

"EYE OF THE WORLD" MINIATURE HISTORY MUSEUM

J. & J. Steakhouse, 6685 N. 11th (west side of US 96/69/287 freeway)
898-0801 • Free

Enclosed in glass are scenes from the Bible and world history made from bits of wood, pipe cleaners, cigar boxes, and other scrap. An early owner, John Gavrelos, spent 25 years creating the world in miniature.

ROADSIDE ARCHITECTURE TOUR

Driving tour of one of the earliest motel chains, Alamo Plaza Courts; first drive-in restaurants, Pig Stands; and unique neon signs and buildings. Directions and brochure from the Visitors Center.

RESTAURANTS

($ = under $7, $$ = $8–$17, $$$ = $18–$25, $$$$ = over $25 for one person excluding drinks, tax, and tip.)

CARLO'S

2570 Calder between 9th and 10th • Lunch and dinner Monday–Friday, dinner only on Saturday. Closed Sunday • $$ • Cr • W

The name is Italian, the owner is Greek, and the menu is both, plus steaks and seafood. All served with candlelight and soft music. Bar.

DAVID'S UPSTAIRS

745 N. 11th in the Gaylynn Shopping Center • 898-0214 • Dinner Monday–Sunday • $$–$$$ • Cr

Dining in a New Orleans atmosphere with entertainment nightly makes David's a top draw in Beaumont. Chicken, seafood, steaks, stuffed oysters, fresh *paté,* and *escargot* add to the eclectic menu. Bar and extensive wine list.

GREEN BEANERY

2121 McFaddin at 6th, in Old Town • 833-5913 • Lunch Monday–Saturday. Closed Sunday • $ • AE, MC, V

The lunch menu features crepes, quiche, pasta, sandwiches, and salad plates. Gourmet dinner one weekend a month by reservation only. Beer and wine. Sharing this 1910 house are several specialty shops.

PATRIZI'S

2050 I-10S between College and Washington • 842-5151 • Lunch Sunday–Friday, dinner daily • $$ • Cr • W+ • Children's plates

The Patrizi's restaurant served Beaumont from another location from 1948 to 1980. They serve fine Italian dishes with hearty servings. Also, seafood, veal, poultry, and beef are on the menu. Bar.

SARTIN'S

6725 Eastex Freeway • 892-6771 • Lunch and dinner daily • $–$$ • Cr Reservations for 6 or more • W variable • Children's plates

Sartin's may be gone from Sabine Pass, but it's alive and well in Beaumont. Here is great seafood with a Cajun flair in a real downhome atmosphere.

ACCOMMODATIONS

($ = under $45, $$ = $46–$60, $$$ = $61–$80, $$$$ = $81–$100, $$$$$ = over $100) Room Tax 13%

BEAUMONT HILTON

2355 I-10S (Washington exit) • 842-3600 or 800-HILTONS (800-445-8667) $$$–$$$$$ • W+ 10 rooms • No-smoking rooms

The nine-story Hilton offers 284 units, including suites and 223 no-smoking rooms. Cable TV with HBO and pay channel. Room phones (charge for local calls.) Guest membership at the World Gym and Country Club. Free airport transportation. Two restaurants, lobby bar and comedy club. Outdoor pool, fitness center. Free newspapers and shoeshine.

BEAUMONT PLAZA HOLIDAY INN

950 I-10S (Walden exit) • 842-5995 or 800-HOLIDAY (800-465-4329)
$$$–$$$$$ • W+ 5 rooms • No-smoking rooms
The eight-story atrium lobby hotel offers 253 units that include 77 suites; 75% no-smoking rooms. Satellite TV with pay channel. Room phones (charge for local calls). Guest memberships available at the Brentwood Country Club and World Wide Gym. Pets allowed, deposit required. Free Airport transportation. Full restaurant and lobby bar. Indoor pool, exercise room, game room, sauna, and whirlpool. Free newspaper.

BRAZOSPORT

Brazoria County • 80,000 • (409)
Brazosport is not a city itself, but a loose confederation of nine cities and towns clustered on the coast near the mouth of the Brazos River. Interlocking like pieces of a jigsaw puzzle are Brazoria, Clute, Freeport, Jones Creek, Lake Jackson, Oyster Creek, Richwood, and the beach communities of Quintana and Surfside.

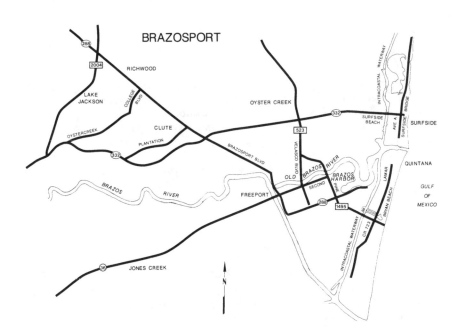

The cities have separate governments, but have joined together in one independent school district and one Chamber of Commerce. One of the peculiarities of the patchwork make-up of this composite city is that each part has its own version of the local option liquor law. As a result some of the cities are wet and some dry and in some cases wet and dry coexist on each side of a boundary street.

As a recreational area, Brazosport has a lot to offer in activities in the multi-cities as well as on the beaches. In addition to the two major beach communities, there are miles of quiet beaches, most of which you can drive on to find your own private spot. It is also a birdwatchers' paradise, having ranked #1 in the North American Christmas Count 14 times in the past 20 years.

In addition to the miles of beaches and other attractions, perhaps Brazosport's biggest draw is for fishermen. Deep-sea, surf, jetty, and small boat inshore fishing are all available.

Generally a low-cost recreation area, Brazosport appears to have one big handicap. It is the home of Texas' fastest growing petrochemical/industrial complex, which averages about a mile and a half in width and stretches along for about nine miles starting right behind the beach communities. As a result, this complex is the backdrop for everything you see or do in the area. The good news is that most visitors get used to it quickly and don't even notice it after a day or two. (If you want to tour one of the plants, call Dow Chemical 238-9222.)

TOURIST SERVICES

SOUTHERN BRAZORIA COUNTY CONVENTION AND TOURIST BUREAU

Clute, in Chamber of Commerce Building, 420 TX 332, approximately .5 mile from TX 288-B interchange • 265-2508 • Monday–Friday 9–5

MUSEUMS

MUSEUM OF NATURAL SCIENCES, NATURE CENTER, AND PLANETARIUM

Lake Jackson, 400 College Dr. on campus of Brazosport College • (Museum) 265-7831, (Nature Center/Planetarium) 265-3376 • Tuesday–Saturday 10–5, Sunday 2–5. Closed Monday • Free • W+ but not all areas

The cornerstone of this museum is its seashell collection that is reputed to be one of the most comprehensive on the Gulf Coast. There are also sections devoted to area archaeology, fossils, rocks, and minerals, and Touch Tables for children of all ages. The Nature Center has displays on plants and wildlife, and there is a three-fourths of a mile nature trail on the grounds. The planetarium periodically has shows open to the general public. This is part of the Brazosport Center for the Arts and Sciences, which is also the home of the Brazosport Art League, the Brazosport Music Theater, and the Little Theatre.

OTHER POINTS OF INTEREST

BRYAN BEACH STATE RECREATION AREA

From Freeport, take FM 1495 to end at Bryan Beach, then right and down beach approximately 2 miles (4-wheel drive recommended) • 737-1222 (Galveston Island State Park) • Open daylight hours • Free

This 878-acre undeveloped peninsula park is bordered by the Gulf, the Brazos River Diversion Channel, and the Intracoastal Waterway. It offers a quiet beach for fishing, birdwatching, beachcombing, and primitive camping. There are no facilities and no roads in the area. High tides can dictate whether cars can get in or out over the beach driving route, so the surest way to get there is by small boat.

MYSTERY MONUMENT

Freeport, TX 227 (400 block of Brazosport Blvd.) at head of Old Brazos River
Open at all times • Free • W

Forty tons of wood, iron, and rigging, proud bow still held high, this shrimp trawler looks eager to return to the Gulf waters that were her home for almost three decades. The 60-foot craft was once the undisputed wood-hull queen of the Gulf shrimp fleet from Mississippi to the Mexican border. Now a monument to the pioneers of the Texas shrimping industry, she got her name when her first owners thought it a mystery how they'd pay for her.

SEA CENTER TEXAS

300 Medical Dr., Lake Jackson (77566) • 292-0100 • Tuesday–Friday 9–4,
Saturday 10–5, Sunday 1–4 • Admission • W

The buildings in this saltwater fish hatchery house redfish and speckled trout broodfish, producing over 20 million fingerlings annually. In addition, the hatchery visitors center includes two "touch tanks" for children and three aquariums featuring fish found in Texas bays, rivers, and lakes; fish caught off Texas beaches and jetties; and fish found offshore in the Gulf.

SURFSIDE BEACH

Follow TX 332 to its eastern end **• W variable**

Located on the site where Santa Anna signed the treaty that gave Texas its independence, this is the major beach community in Brazosport. Facilities for swimming, sailing, surfing, sunning, fishing, and all the other beach activities are available here. There are also several places to eat, bars, small motels, and other beach-type businesses here. Driving is permitted on much of the beach but you need a permit to park there. Permits cost $8 a year and are for sale at most beach stores. A mile of pedestrians-only beach is located between First and Thirteenth streets.

SPORTS AND ACTIVITIES

Fishing

Brazosport is an excellent jumping-off place for deep sea fishing. From the Freeport jetties to the 100-foot depth where the big ones bite is only about three hours by boat. A number of record fish have been caught offshore. Surf, jetty, and small boat inshore fishing are also popular as is crabbing in the more than 100 miles of waterways in the area. During the summer the local marinas and organizations offer an almost continuous string of fishing tournaments. Several charter boat outfits are listed in the phone book, but the only party boats are operated by Captain Elliott's at 1010 W. 2nd in Freeport (233-1811). A 12-hour (6 A.M. to

6 P.M.) deep-sea party boat trip costs about $50 (children 12 and under $30) plus $7 for tackle rental. There is also a fishing pier at San Luis Pass (233-6902) off County Rd 257 north of Surfside. A list of fishing locations and boat ramps is available from the Visitors and Convention Bureau (see Tourist Services).

KIDS' STUFF

MODEL TRAIN MUSEUM

418 Plantation Dr., Lake Jackson • 299-0152 • Saturday 10–3, Sunday 1–4 Admission • W

The major display here is a 12′ × 32′ HO scale model of Brazoria County in the year 1955, just as the trains were being converted from steam to diesel. It's built only three feet off the ground to give small children a good view.

SIDE TRIPS

BRAZORIA NATIONAL WILDLIFE REFUGE

Approximately 4 miles east of Surfside • 849-6062 (Access difficult, call for directions)

More than 425 wildlife species, including 270 bird species, use the refuge during all or part of their life cycles. Public access is limited due to lack of facilities, but the refuge is open on a limited basis for birdwatching, wildlife photography, nature observation, fishing and hunting. For information write Refuge Manager, P.O. Drawer 1088 (1212 N. Velasco), Angleton 77515.

SAN BERNARD NATIONAL WILDLIFE REFUGE

Approximately 10 miles southwest of Freeport on County Rd. 306 off FM 2918 849-6062 • Open daily dawn to dusk

The blue and snow geese make this 24,454-acre refuge one of their winter homes. Permissible activities include birding, wildlife studies and photography, hiking, and limited hunting and fishing. For information write Refuge Manager, Brazoria National Wildlife Refuge Complex, P.O. Drawer 1088 (1212 N. Velasco), Angleton 77515.

ANNUAL EVENTS

July

GREAT TEXAS MOSQUITO FESTIVAL

Clute Community Park, Brazoswood Dr. between Dixie Dr. and Old Angleton Rd. • 265-8392 (Clute Parks and Recreation) • Thursday–Saturday last weekend in July • Free • W variable

Mosquitos are dear to the heart of Texans because wildcatters often use them to drill for oil. This festival celebrates these playful little bugs with entertainment, an arts-and-crafts show, cookoffs, a carnival and all the other things you'd expect. What makes it unique are events like the Mosquito Calling Contest, the Mosquito Juice Chug-a-Lug, and a Mosquito Song Writing Competition, all under the watchful stinger of a 25-foot tall mosquito called Willy Manchew.

RESTAURANTS

($ = under $7, $$ = $8–$17, $$$ = $18–$25, $$$$ = over $25 for one person excluding drinks, tax, and tip.)

WINDSWEPT SEAFOOD RESTAURANT

Oyster Creek, 105 Burch Circle. *Take TX 523 toward Oyster Creek and follow signs* • **233-1951** • **Lunch and dinner Sunday–Friday, Dinner only on Sunday $$ • Cr • W • Children's plates**

There's a wide variety of seafood choices on the menu, but the best deal in the house may be the all-you-can-eat fried or broiled shrimp for about $12. Also worth catching is the moderately priced seafood buffet lunch Wednesday, Thursday, and Friday. Private Club membership $5.

ACCOMMODATIONS

($ = under $45, $$ = $46–$60, $$$ = $61–$80, $$$$ = $81–$100, $$$$$ = over $100)

Room tax 10%

RAMADA-LAKE JACKSON INN

Lake Jackson, 925 TX 332W • **297-1161 or 800-544-2119** • **$$$** • **W+ 2 rooms No-smoking rooms**

The two-story Ramada has 146 rooms that include 33 no-smoking rooms. Children under 17 stay free in room with parents. Package plans and senior discount available. Cable TV with HBO and pay channel. Room phones (charge for local calls). Small pets OK. Restaurant, room service, private club open seven nights with occasional entertainment (guests automatically members, temporary membership for non-guests $5). Indoor heated pool. Guest memberships available in local racquet club. Free coffee in lobby. Free newspaper. Same-day dry cleaning.

COUNTRY HEARTH INN

Freeport, 1015 W. 2nd • **239-1602** • **$$** • **W+ 2 rooms** • **No-smoking rooms**

This two-story Inn has 40 units that include one suite ($$$$$) and four no-smoking rooms. Children under 17 stay free in room with parents. Senior discount. Cable TV with HBO. Room phones (local calls free). Small pets OK. Outdoor pool. Free coffee in lobby. Free two-hour manager's reception every evening. Free continental breakfast. Self-service laundry and same-day dry cleaning.

LA QUINTA INN

Clute, 1126 TX 332W • **265-7461 or 800-531-5900** • **$–$$** • **W+ 2 rooms No-smoking rooms**

This two-story La Quinta has 136 units that include one suite ($$) and 36 no-smoking rooms. Children under 18 stay free in room with parents. Senior discount. Cable and satellite TV with Showtime and pay channel. Room phones (local calls free). Small pets OK. Restaurant adjoining. Outdoor pool. Free breakfast. Same-day dry cleaning.

BROWNSVILLE

Cameron County Seat • 130,000 • (956)

Brownsville could also be called Bargainsville because it offers the opportunity for low-cost vacationing and shopping in both the largest American and Mexican cities in the Rio Grande Valley.

Although separated by a national boundary, Brownsville and Matamoros (population half million plus) share a common Spanish culture. Matamoros was a full-blown city long before Brownsville existed and its customs and heritage lapped over to its younger sister. So strong is this feeling of a common bond that many of the residents on both sides of the Rio Grande think of the two cities as one.

Brownsville originated as a fort in 1846, a fort that was the spark that ignited the fuse that led to the Mexican War. A major cause of that war was a dispute over whether the Nueces River or the Rio Grande was the border between Texas and Mexico. The Mexicans said the Nueces while the government of the new Republic of Texas claimed the Rio Grande. The festering dispute was carried with Texas when it entered the Union, elevating it to a major issue between the United States and Mexico. In 1846, as a statement of the American claim, General Zachary Taylor deliberately built a fort on the Rio Grande across from Matamoros. The Mexicans considered this an invasion and attacked the fort—and the war was on. Among the first casualties was Major Jacob Brown. The fort, and then the city, was named after him.

Today life is much quieter along the border. Brownsville is the southernmost city on the U.S. mainland. The subtropical climate, tempered by cool—and surprisingly dry—Gulf breezes, encourages a leisurely lifestyle. It also encourages year-round gardens of bougainvillea, hibiscus, oleander, and roses (to name just a few), all set against a background of stately palms, banana and citrus trees, bamboo, and the ubiquitous oak and mesquite. And scattered around the town are the *resacas*, the lagoons left behind as, over the centuries, the then untamed Rio Grande jumped from one course to another.

TOURIST SERVICES

BROWNSVILLE CONVENTION AND VISITORS BUREAU INFORMATION CENTER

**US 77/83 at FM 802 (P.O. Box 4697, 78523) • 546-3721 or 800-626-2639
Monday–Saturday 8:30–5, Sunday 9–4 • Free • W+**

In addition to free brochures and information, the following publications are for sale: *Birder's Guide to Brownsville* ($1.50), *Fishing Guide to the Brownsville Area* ($1.50), and the *Guide to Historic Brownsville* ($2). These are also available by mail.

BRO-MAT TOURS

233-1900

Personalized 3–3½ hour tours of Matamoros leave daily at 9 A.M. and 2 P.M. Minimum of four persons. Two for $35, three or more $15 each. Pick ups at hotels.

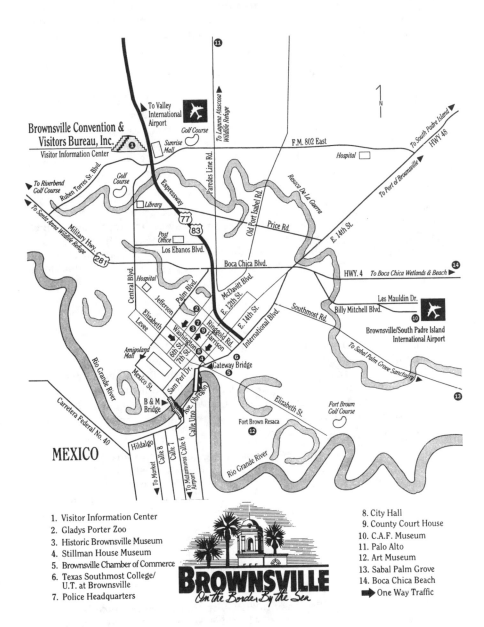

1. Visitor Information Center
2. Gladys Porter Zoo
3. Historic Brownsville Museum
4. Stillman House Museum
5. Brownsville Chamber of Commerce
6. Texas Southmost College/ U.T. at Brownsville
7. Police Headquarters

8. City Hall
9. County Court House
10. C.A.F. Museum
11. Palo Alto
12. Art Museum
13. Sabal Palm Grove
14. Boca Chica Beach
➡ One Way Traffic

BROWNSVILLE
On the Border, By the Sea

GRAY LINE TOURS

761-4343

Regularly scheduled tours of Matamoros are offered both mornings and afternoons Monday through Saturday. You can book at most hotels/motels and travel agencies. The tours last about 3½ hours and cost about $13 per person.

HISTORIC BROWNSVILLE TROLLEY TOURS

Convention and Visitors Bureau Information Center
546-3721 or 800-626-2639 • W+

A replica of an early 1900s trolley is used for these two hour tours at 10 and 1, Monday–Saturday. Monday tours are of the Port of Brownsville, a deep-water port connected to the Gulf of Mexico by a 17-mile ship channel. Tuesday–Saturday tours are of historic downtown and include a stop at one of the city's museums. Adults $6, seniors, children under 12, students, and guests in wheelchairs $3. Trolley seating is tight.

TOUR GUIDES IN MATAMOROS

Licensed, English-speaking tour guides can be hired at the Tourist Information booth located on the right just across the Gateway International Bridge. They charge about $25 for a car-full and they provide the car. The regular tour lasts about 2½ hours, but you can personalize it almost any way you want. To be sure your guide is licensed, ask to see the wallet-sized permit from the Mexican Tourism Department.

MUSEUMS

BROWNSVILLE ART LEAGUE MUSEUM

230 Neale Dr. (78520) • 542-0941 • Monday–Friday 9:30–3
Free (donations accepted) • W+

Although it is dedicated to exhibiting the arts of the Rio Grande Valley, the permanent collection also includes works by Chagall, Daumier, Samuelson, and Whistler. The League's headquarters is next door in the Neale House, the oldest frame building in the city.

CASA MATA MUSEUM

Matamoros, Santos Degollado between Guatemala and Panama • Usually open Tuesday–Sunday 9:30–5:30. Closed Monday • Admission

This small, thick-walled fort, built in the early 1800s, now serves as a city museum. The Spanish labels on the exhibits may be hard to decipher; however, many of the items on display tell a story that often needs no further explanation. With a little diligence you can pick out a few words of international understanding that indicate the significance of many of the documents and artifacts, such as a *charro* suit that once belonged to Pancho Villa and the names on the photographs of patriots of the Mexican Revolution.

CONFEDERATE AIR FORCE MUSEUM

955 Minnesota (78523) at Brownsville/SPI Airport, *from Boca Chica Blvd. take Billy Mitchell Blvd. to Minnesota* • 541-8585 • Monday–Saturday 9–5, Sunday noon–4 • Adults $5, seniors $4, children $3 • W+

The home of the Rio Grande Valley Wing of the Confederate Air Force (CAF) that offers displays of fully operational vintage military aircraft from WWII and the Korean War as well as memorabilia, equipment, and uniforms. If you've never heard of the CAF, there's a continuous showing of a video on the history of this unique organization. Gift shop and lounge open to public.

CORN MUSEUM (MUSEO DEL MAIZ)

Matamoros, Avenida Constitucion and 5th • 6–3763 • Tuesday–Sunday 9:30–5 • Free • W

The domestication of corn was an important factor in the growth of civilization in Mexico and Central America. Using more than a dozen large tableaus and displays, this museum traces the history of corn, its utilization, and importance. Guided tours are available.

HISTORIC BROWNSVILLE MUSEUM

641 E. Madison • 548-1391 • Monday–Saturday 10–4:30, Sunday 2–5 • Adults $2, children 50¢ • W

This is a private museum owned and operated by an historic association dedicated to telling the history of the Brownsville area. Housed in a 1928 Southern Pacific Railroad depot, its permanent collection includes historical documents, photos and prints, furniture, and clothing. Outside is a small engine used by the Rio Grande Railroad connecting Brownsville and Port Isabel in the 1870s. Gift shop.

STILLMAN HOUSE AND MUSEUM

1305 E. Washington • 542-3929 • Monday–Friday 10–12 and 2–5. Closed Saturday–Sunday • Adults $2, children 50¢ • W

One of the oldest buildings in the city, this one-story pink brick house was built in 1850 by Charles Stillman, who bought 3,000 acres at two cents an acre and laid out the city of Brownsville. Many of the furnishings and memorabilia inside were donated by the Stillman family in New York and date to the mid-1800s. The oldest items are a grandfather clock and a Wedgwood chandelier from 1770. The house is listed in the National Register of Historic Places. Street parking is a problem here. There is a small lot next door, but if it is filled, parking is usually available at Adams and 14th.

HISTORIC PLACES

FORT BROWN

600 International, just east of Gateway International Bridge • W

During the 102 years from its founding in 1846 until it was closed in 1948, this border post saw a lot of action. Its very construction in an area of dispute between Mexico and the United States was one of the immediate causes of the Mexican War. General Zachary Taylor first called it Fort Texas Across from Matamoros, but renamed it in honor of Major Jacob Brown who died defending the fort. It was fought over and occupied by both sides in the Civil War and, as a border post, helped defend the area against bandits well into the 1900s. The post hospital, now used as the Texas Southmost College administration building, was where Dr. W. C. Gorgas started his research that eventually led to his important contribution to the control of yellow fever. Other fort buildings still standing include the post commander's home, guard house, the medical laboratory, the cavalry barracks, and the morgue. The University of Texas at Brownsville is also located on the fort grounds.

OTHER HISTORIC BUILDINGS

Brownsville has more than a dozen buildings listed in the National Register of Historic Places. For a complete listing of these and other historic buildings in both Brownsville and Matamoros, see the *Guide to Historic Brownsville,* for sale at the Convention and Visitors Bureau Information Center ($2).

MEXICAN WAR BATTLEFIELDS

National Historic Sites Visitors Center, 1623 Central Blvd., Ste. 213 (78520) 541-2785 • Monday–Friday 8–5. Closed federal holidays • W
Marker commemorating the battle of Palo Alto in small park at intersection of FM 1847 and FM 511. Marker for battle of Resaca de la Palma on FM 1847 between Price and Coffeeport

When Texas entered the Union, it brought with it a long-standing border dispute with Mexico. The dispute led President Polk to send General Zachary Taylor with an army of about 4,000 troops to Corpus Christi and deployed the navy along the coast of Mexico. When the diplomatic efforts didn't resolve the problem, Polk ordered Taylor into the disputed territory.

Then Mexican troops wiped out an American cavalry patrol and laid siege to Fort Texas which Taylor had established across from Matamoros. On May 7, 1846, Taylor left from his supply base at Point Isabel (now Port Isabel) with about 2,300 troops to reinforce the fort. The next morning, at Palo Alto, some ten miles from the fort, the Americans clashed with a Mexican force of about 6,000. Taylor's light horse artillery was a major factor in the battle. Dashing from position to position, the "Flying Artillery," under the command of Major Samuel Ringgold, laid down deadly fire that overcame the almost three-to-one odds and forced the Mexicans to withdraw. One of the nine Americans killed in the battle was Major Ringgold. More than 300 Mexicans were killed.

When Taylor pressed on the next morning, the Mexican Army was waiting, dug into a strong position in a dry streambed called Resaca de la Palma. In this second battle, the Americans once again drove off the Mexicans. This time about 120 Americans were killed or wounded and the Mexican Army lost over a thousand. Among the American infantry company commanders in this second battle was Second Lieutenant Ulysses S. Grant who later noted that the Mexican soldiers were brave, but poorly led. On May 13, 1846, war was declared against Mexico.

Plans are in the works to develop a fully operating park that includes both battlefields as well as the Fort Texas (Fort Brown) site within the context of the Mexican War. Under mandate from Congress, exhibits must cover the war from both countries' perspectives.

PALMITO RANCH BATTLEFIELD

Marker on TX 4, approximately 12 miles east of downtown

While the Mexican War battles around Fort Brown were fought before that war was officially declared, the Civil War battle of Palmito Ranch was fought about six weeks after that war was officially over. The word of Lee's surrender had not reached the 300 Confederate soldiers from Fort Brown when they went out to successfully drive off about 1,600 Union troops trying to capture the cotton stored in the Brownsville warehouses. Coincidentally, this Civil War battle took place on May 12 and 13, 1865, the 13th being the same date that war had been declared against Mexico just 19 years before.

OTHER POINTS OF INTEREST

GLADYS PORTER ZOO

Ringgold and 6th • 546-2177 (activities recording) or 546-7187 • Gates open daily 9–5 with extended hours on weekends and in the summer (once inside, visitors may remain until dark) • Adults $6, children (2–13) $3 • W+ Guarded parking lot at entrance $2. Free lot across street

Zoo professionals consistently ranked this zoo as one of the best in the country proving that good things do come in small packages. Although the ingenious design and landscaping give the appearance of open spaces, the more than 1,500 mammals, birds, and reptiles from five continents are actually squeezed into only 31 acres. Viewing the zoo will take you through four major areas of the world: Africa, Asia, Australia and Indonesia, and tropical America. In each, the animals live in miniaturized naturalistic habitats on islands or in large open areas separated from visitors by moats or waterways—no bars or cages. The Children's Zoo includes both an animal nursery for viewing newborns and a petting zoo stocked with barnyard animals. Other exhibits include a free-flight aviary, bear grottos, and California sea lions. Tour train makes a half-hour narrated tour Sunday afternoons between 1:30 and 3:30. Adults $1, children (2–13) 50¢. Strollers and wheelchairs available for rent. Gift shop.

MATAMOROS

To call Matamoros direct from Brownsville, dial 011-52-881 and then the 5-digit local number

Named for Father Maiano Matamoros, a hero killed in the 1810 revolution, the town came into prominence in the 1860s when the Confederates used it as a shipping point for getting around the Union blockade and the French helped conservative Mexicans put Maximilian on the Mexican throne bringing many Europeans to the area. Money poured in, great mansions and buildings like the recently restored *Teatro de la Reforma* were built.

Today, with a population of close to half a million, Matamoros is one of Mexico's 15 major cities and the largest city on both sides of the border in the Rio Grande Valley.

You can get to Matamoros over either of two toll bridges. The main one is the Gateway International Bridge at the end of International Boulevard. Further south, at Perl Blvd./E. 12th is the privately owned old railroad bridge that is open for vehicle and walking traffic. Buses and taxis also run across the bridges. Both bridges come out on *Avenida Alvaro Obregon,* a major street with many shops and restaurants listed in this guide, so it is easy to just walk across.

You can get a Matamoros map at the Brownsville Convention and Visitors Bureau Information Center and the Mexican Tourism office located inside the building on the Matamoros side of the Gateway bridge right after you pass the Mexican customs office (phone 2-3630). It is sometimes staffed with English-speaking personnel. A little further on, on the right hand side of the street, is a booth housing licensed guides (*see* Tourist Services). There are also taxi stands in this area. Before you hire a guide or a taxi, make sure you settle on a fair price. Most of the drivers and guides are honest and genuinely friendly, but there are always some out to stick it to the *turista.*

An inexpensive way to get around Matamoros is by maxi-cab. You'll usually find a herd of them gathered on the first street to the left after you cross the

Gateway Bridge. These are small passenger vans that follow definite routes within the city, but will stop almost anywhere to pick up or let off a passenger. They cost pennies to ride and go to the markets and other places of tourist interest. The destination of each maxi-cab is marked on the front, and with a map and an understanding of a few, simple Spanish words you should be able to get around. For example, if you want to go to the Juarez Market (*see* Shopping) look for a cab marked *Mercado*. To get back to the bridge from almost anywhere in the city, look for one marked *Puente* (bridge). Simple—and fun!

SABAL PALM AUDUBON CENTER

Off FM 1419 (Southmost Road), ½ mile west of FM 3068 (P.O. Box 5052, 78523) 541-8034 • October–May: Tuesday–Sunday 9–5. Closed Monday and major holidays. June–September: only Saturday–Sunday 9–5 • Adults $3, children (over 6) $1

Sabal Palms once grew profusely along the edge of the Rio Grande in small stands or groves extending about 80 miles upstream from the Gulf of Mexico. Today only a small portion of that forest remains, protected on the 527 acres of this Audubon sanctuary on the river. Wildlife viewing areas and two half-mile trails open sunrise to sunset. Self-guided trail guides may be borrowed or purchased at the Visitors Center.

SPORTS AND ACTIVITIES

Birdwatching

More than 370 bird species, including many tropical bird species seen nowhere else in the United States, share the refuges and wild places in and around Brownsville. A colorful *Birder's Guide* is available from the Brownsville Convention and Visitors Bureau ($1.50).

Within the city there's a good chance you'll spot the red-crowned parrot, Brownsville's most abundant parrot and the city bird. They gather in roosting groups at dusk and its not uncommon to see flocks of a dozen or more moving from tree to tree. The yellow-headed parrot is also here and can often be seen on Los Ebanos one block west of Central, about an hour before dusk.

Golf

BROWNSVILLE GOLF AND RECREATION CENTER

North side of FM 802 between US 77/83 and FM 1847 • 541-2582 • 18 holes Green fees $8.50

FORT BROWN MUNICIPAL GOLF COURSE

Off Elizabeth Street east of International Blvd. • 542-9861 • 18 holes Green fees $7.50

RANCHO VIEJO COUNTRY CLUB

Approximately 9 miles north of downtown on US 77/83 • 350-4000 ext. 620 or 800-531-7400 • Two 18-hole courses • Green fees $56

RIVER BEND RESORT

About 3 miles west of downtown on US 281 • 548-0192 • 18 holes Call for green fees

VALLEY INTERNATIONAL COUNTRY CLUB
McAllen Road off FM 802 • 548-9199 • 18 hole and 9 hole par 3
Green fees: weekdays $13.25, weekends/holidays $16.50

PERFORMING ARTS

CAMILLE LIGHTNER PLAYHOUSE
One Dean Porter Park, across from Gladys Porter Zoo • 542-8900 • W
This community theater presents five or six plays and musicals by the local theater group during the September though May season. The 301-seat proscenium theater has been operating for more than 30 years. The theater is also used for concerts and other activities.

SHOPPING

To call Matamoros direct from Brownsville, dial 011-52-881 and then the 5-digit local number

AMIGOLAND MALL
301 Mexico at Palm • 546-3788 • W+ but not all areas
Dillard's, Penney's, and Ward's anchor the more than 60 other stores and a food court in this mall, which is near the Rio Grande between the two bridges to Matamoros.

BARBARA DE MATAMOROS
Matamoros, 37 Avenida Alvaro Obregon, about 4 blocks south of Gateway International Bridge • 2-5058
Looking for a life-sized brass monkey? Or how about a colorful larger-than-life *papier-mache* macaw on a perch? These are just a few of the originals elegantly displayed, and elegantly priced, in this shop. There are also ceramics, jewelry, and other selected items from the interior of Mexico. Upstairs is a fashionable boutique featuring clothing of Barbara's design.

DON BREEDEN ART GALLERY
2200 Boca Chica • 542-5481
Wildlife paintings and drawings in various media are the specialty of artist-owner Don Breeden.

MERCADO JUAREZ
Matamoros, Matamoros at Calle Nueve (9th St.) • W variable
There are two markets here: the old on one side of the street and the new market on the other. Each is made up of many small shops under a low roof. You'll find both the gaudy and the good here. The key is to know what you want, how much it costs elsewhere, and how much you're willing to pay. Then bargain. Just remember, the shopkeepers here are both hard-sell salesmen and bargaining experts. Even if they knock the price down, they always make a profit. However, you can at least have fun at the game and lower the price a bit—perhaps a lot.

SUNRISE MALL
2370 North Expressway 77/83 at FM 802 • 541-5302 • W+ but not all areas
Beall's, K-Mart, and Sears anchor about 50 other shops, a Luby's cafeteria, and a food court.

ANNUAL EVENTS

February

CHARRO DAYS FIESTA

Various locations in Brownsville and Matamoros • 546-3721 or 800-626-2639 (Convention and Visitors Bureau) • Thursday–Sunday of last weekend in February • Admission to some activities • W variable

A *grito,* the Mexican cowboy's yell of exuberance, usually opens this two-country fiesta. *Charro* refers to landowning Mexican horsemen whose formal attire was the traditional black or striped pants covered with fancy chaps, a bolero jacket with ornamental embroidery, and a sombrero covered with silver or gold filigree. The *charro* traditions and costume have been adopted by a number of *charro* associations on both sides of the border, and it is the spirit of the *charro* coupled with that of the hell-bent for pleasure Mexican cowboy who rides to town to spend his hard-earned wages that set the theme for this celebration. Festivities include day and night parades, fiestas, dances, floor shows, sports events including a *charreada* (Mexican rodeo). Many participants and spectators wear traditional Mexican dress.

RESTAURANTS

($ = under $7, $$ = $8–$17, $$$ = $18–$25, $$$$ = over $25 for one person excluding drinks, tax, and tip. To call Matamoros direct from Brownsville, dial 011-52-881 and then the 5-digit local number.)

THE DRIVE-IN

Matamoros, Sexta (6th) and Hidalgo, approximately 1 mile southwest of Gateway International Bridge • 2-0022 • Lunch and dinner daily • $–$$$ Cr • W

Don't let the name fool you—you can't drive in. In fact, inside the crystal chandeliers, red plush seats, an aviary with tropical birds, and the extensive continental menu will quickly dispel any lingering thoughts of fast food. The menu offers choices that include *chateaubriand,* lobster, frogs legs, shrimp, steaks and, of course, Mexican dishes. But be aware that the kitchen's efforts can be erratic. Bar.

GARCIA'S

Matamoros, Obregon near the bridge • 2-3929 • Lunch and dinner daily $–$$ • MC, V

Like Phoenix rising from the ashes of the fire that destroyed the popular restaurant near the bridge, Garcia's is back and many among its long-term devotees say both the food and the service are even better than before. The extensive menu includes steaks, turkey, lobster, crab, quail, and Mexican dishes. Bar with musicians.

PALM COURT RESTAURANT

2200 Boca Chica, about 1 block east of Expressway 77/83 • 542-3575 • Lunch only Monday–Saturday • $–$$ • AE, MC, V • W

The interior of this restaurant is designed to give the illusion of eating in an elegant open court—provided you can find a courtyard with a crystal chandelier. The menu offers salads from fresh fruit to shrimp, soups including *gaspacho* and *tortilla,* sandwiches from chicken or tuna salad to a super sub, and entrées that include *lasagne, quiche,* and chicken *crepes,* plus luscious desserts like coco mocho pie and Manhattan cheesecake. No smoking area. Beer and wine.

PANCHO VILLA'S

Matamoros, 55 Avenida de la Rosa • 6-4840 • Lunch and dinner daily $$ • MC, V
The specialty of the house is called *Basto Corte de Fajita Sin Filetar,* which the menu very loosely translates as "A big chunk of meat taken the way the man of the revolution cooked it." Charbroiled meats (*carnes asadas*) that include steaks and chicken, dominate the rest of the menu, but it also offers some seafood. Old photos of Pancho Villa and other revolutionaries look down at you from the walls. Limited parking in front. Bar.

ACCOMMODATIONS

($ = under $45, $$ = $46–$60, $$$ = $61–$80, $$$$ = $81–$100, $$$$$ = over $100. To call Matamoros direct from Brownsville, dial 011-52-881 and then the 5-digit local number.)

Room tax 13%

COMFORT INN

825 N. Expressway (US 77/83) (78521) • 504-3331 or 800-328-5150 • $$$ W+ 2 rooms • No-smoking rooms
This two-story inn has 53 units that include two suites ($$$$$) and 10 no-smoking rooms. Children under 17 stay free in room with parents. Senior discount and package plans available. Cable TV with HBO. Room phones (local calls free). Coffeemakers in rooms and free coffee in lobby. Fire intercom system. No pets. Free continental breakfast. Outdoor pool. Guest memberships available for health club. Self-service laundry, same-day dry cleaning.

FOUR POINTS ITT SHERATON

3777 N. Expressway (US 77/83) (78520) • 350-9191 or 800-325-3535 • $$$ • W+ 4 rooms • No-smoking rooms
The two-story Sheraton has 140 units that include two suites ($$$$$) and 20 no-smoking rooms. Children under 17 stay free in room with parents. Cable TV with HBO and pay channel. Room phones (charge for local calls). Fire sprinklers in rooms and fire intercom system. Small pets OK. Restaurant, room service, lounge open seven nights with entertainment nightly. Two pools (one outdoor and indoor-outdoor heated pool), outdoor whirlpool and exercise room. Guest memberships available for golf. Free airport transportation to Brownsville and Harlingen. Free coffee Monday–Friday and free newspaper. Same-day dry cleaning.

HOLIDAY INN FORT BROWN RESORT

1900 E. Elizabeth (P.O. Box 2255, 78520) • 546-2201 or 800-465-4329 • $$–$$$ No-smoking rooms
This two- and three-story hotel has 168 units that include four penthouse suites ($$$$$) and 12 no-smoking rooms. Children under 18 stay free in room with parents. Senior discount and package plans available. Cable TV with HBO.

Room phones (local calls free). Coffeemakers in rooms. Fire intercom system. No pets. Two restaurants, room service, club open seven nights with entertainment nightly. Two outdoor pools, outdoor whirlpool, two lighted tennis courts. Guest memberships available in health club and for golf. Playground. Free airport transportation to Brownsville and Harlingen. Same-day dry cleaning. Located on 17 acres within walking distance of Gateway International Bridge.

HOWARD JOHNSON HOTEL

1945 N. Expressway (US 77/83) (78520), just south of FM 802 • 546-4591 or 800-446-4656 • $$$ • W+ 1 room • No-smoking rooms
This two-story hotel has 159 rooms that include 16 no-smoking rooms. Children under 12 stay free in room with parents. Senior discount. Satellite TV with Showtime and pay channel. Room phones (local calls free). Pets OK. Restaurant, room service, lounge open seven nights with entertainment Monday–Saturday. Outdoor heated pool, exercise room, outdoor whirlpool. Guest memberships available in health club. Free airport transportation to Brownsville and Harlingen. Self-service laundry, same-day dry cleaning.

LA QUINTA

55 Sam Perl (southern extension of 12th St.) (78520) • 546-0381 or 800-531-5900 $–$$ • W+ 2 rooms • No-smoking rooms
The two-story La Quinta offers 143 units that include 20 no-smoking. Children under 18 free in room with parents. Senior discount. TV with Showtime. Room phones (local calls free). Small pets OK. Free continental breakfast. Restaurant next door. Outdoor pool. Free coffee in lobby. Same-day dry cleaning. Located between the two bridges to Matamoros.

RAMADA LIMITED

1900 E. Elizabeth (78521) • 541-2921 or 800-6232 • $$$ • W+ 1 room No-smoking rooms
The 104 rooms in this three-story Ramada include 55 no-smoking rooms. Children under 17 stay free in room with parents. Senior and weekend discounts and package plans available. Cable TV with HBO. Room phones (local calls free). Free coffee in lobby. No pets. Free continental breakfast. Lounge with entertainment and dancing. Guest memberships available for tennis and golf. Self-service laundry, same-day dry cleaning. Free airport transportation.

TRAVELERS INN

2377 N. Expressway (US 77/83) (78521) • 504-230 or 800-633-8300 • $$–$$$ • W+ 5 rooms • No-smoking rooms
The 124 units in this two-story inn include 11 suites ($$$$–$$$$$) and 77 no-smoking rooms. Children under 18 stay free in room with parents. Senior discount available. Cable TV with HBO. Room phones (local calls free). Free coffee in lobby. Fire intercom system. No pets. Outdoor pool. Self-service laundry, same-day dry cleaning.

CLEAR LAKE AREA

Harris and Galveston Counties • 147,000 • (713) and (281). All numbers (713) unless otherwise noted

Encompassing about 125 square miles, this area consists of the Southeast area of Houston known as Clear Lake City and eight small cities around Clear Lake and on Galveston Bay. The cities, most of which flow into each other without definitive borders other than city limits signs, are Clear Lake Shores, El Lago, Kemah, League City, Nassau Bay, Seabrook, Taylor Lake Village, and Webster. Some of these, like League City and Webster, started out as farm and ranch towns in the mid and late 1800s—a colony of Japanese farmers at Webster is often credited with providing the seeds that sparked the Gulf Coast rice industry. Seabrook and Kemah, on the other hand, took advantage of their locations on Galveston Bay to establish a commercial fishing industry. Kemah also diversified for a time, joining Galveston as a gambling center from the early 1920s until gambling was closed down in the late 1950s.

Agriculture and fishing are still important, but the economic complexion took on a rosier hue in 1961 when the National Aeronautics and Space Administration (NASA) established what was then called the Manned Space Center in the heart of this area. This sparked a boom. Today, NASA/Johnson Space Center and the high-tech businesses generated as spin-offs from the space program form the core of the economic base.

TOURIST SERVICES

CLEAR LAKE • NASA AREA CONVENTION AND VISITORS BUREAU

1201 NASA Rd. 1 (Houston 77058) • 488-7676 or 800-844-LAKE (800-844-5253), fax: 713-488-8981, email: clearlk@texasusa.com• Open daily 9–5 • W

GATEWAY VISITORS CENTER

1849 Gulf Freeway South (League City 77573). On I-45 southbound access road. Take Calder Rd. exit (Exit 22) • 332-8822 • Open daily 9–5 • W+

POINTS OF INTEREST

ARMAND BAYOU NATURE CENTER

8600 Bay Area Blvd. behind the Johnson Space Center east of Red Bluff Rd. near University of Houston-Clear Lake • 474-2551 • Wednesday 9–dusk, Thursday–Friday 9–4, Saturday dawn–4, Sunday noon–dusk. Closed Monday, Tuesday and major holidays • Adults $2.50, children (5–17) $2 • W variable

Much of the 1,900 acres is wilderness on a bayou preserved in its natural state for nature study. You can explore on hiking trails or rented canoe. Facilities include an Interpretive Center with hands-on exhibits, a reproduction of a Charruco Indian Village, and a farm restored to its turn-of-the-century condition. Demonstrations and tours on weekends. Call for schedule.

CLEAR LAKE *QUEEN*

NASA Rd. 1 at Clear Lake Park • 333-3334 • W lower deck only

The *Queen* is a three-deck paddlewheel boat built from an adaptation of plans from one of America's premier riverboat builders of the 1800s. Excursion cruises Saturdays and Sundays and dinner cruises Friday, Saturday, and holiday evenings. Call for schedule and fares.

SPACE CENTER HOUSTON

NASA/LYNDON B. JOHNSON SPACE CENTER • NASA Rd. 1 about 3
miles east of I-45 • 244-2100, Website: http://www.jsc.nasa.gov/pao/sch/
Daily usually 9–6. Closed Christmas • Adults $8.75, children (3–12) $5.25
W+ but not all areas

This center is probably as close as most of us will ever get to the physical and
emotional sensations of manned space flight while still planted firmly on the
ground. Located on a 123-acre site just inside the gate of the Johnson Space
Center, the seven major attractions give visitors a feel for the adventures of
space flight.

At the **Mission Status Center** you'll be briefed on what's going on in NASA
the day of your visit, with live camera shots of Mission Control, action at the
Kennedy Space Center, or even aboard the space shuttle if one is in orbit at the
time. You can touch a moon rock, walk through Skylab, and see a film on the
history of man's reach for the stars at the **Starship Gallery.** You can stand on an
exact duplicate of the Flight Deck at the **Space Shuttle Mock-up** and imagine
what it's like to fly in space. A guided NASA Tour on a tram will take you to
Mission Control, astronaut training areas, and other facilities of the Johnson
Space Center itself. In the **Space Center Theater** you'll feel you're actually in a
film on astronaut training shown on a huge screen 80-feet wide and five stories
tall. Then, with all this experience as back-up, you can try your hand at repair-
ing a satellite on the air-bearing floor of **The Feel of Space** section. Here, you
also find out how objects in the vacuum of space feel to an astronaut and see
what it'd be like to live and work aboard a space station. And in the **Space Center Plaza,** in addition to meeting and hearing talks by astronauts and space center scientists, during missions, a large screen video will turn the plaza into a
giant theater where you can witness space history in the making. Restaurants
and gift shop.

SPORTS AND ACTIVITIES

Boating

With 17 marinas and more than 7,000 boats of all kinds from small sailboats
to yachts, the Clear Lake area lays claim to being the third largest recreational
boating center in the United States. Most of the marinas offer boat rentals and
several offer yacht charters. There are also several sailing schools. For details,
contact the Convention and Visitors Bureau (*see* Tourist Services).

Fishing

JUDY BETH

Kemah, 601 2nd • 334-3760 • Adults $12, children 11 and under $9. Call for
schedule

This party fishing boat makes four-hour trips out in Galveston Bay twice
every day from March through November. (Closed December–February.) Rod
and reel rentals available.

SHOPPING

OLD SEABROOK ARTS AND ANTIQUE COLONY

Downtown Seabrook • 474-4451 • W variable
More than two dozen shops, galleries, and studios in a five block radius feature antiques, collectibles, jewelry and estate items, original art, shells, and nautical gifts.

SIDE TRIPS

BAYOU WILDLIFE PARK

Take I-45 south to FM 517, then west (right) about 6 miles, look for entrance sign on south side of road **(P.O. Box 808, Rt 6, Alvin 77511) • 337-6376**
April–August: daily 10–5, September–March: Tuesday–Sunday 10–4, Closed Monday. Closed Thanksgiving, Christmas, and New Year's Day • Adults $8, children (3–12) $5.50 • W variable
A narrated tram ride takes you over 86-acres of a natural habitat for a variety of animals and birds including camels, giraffes, ostriches, a rhino, and an alligator farm. Some of the animals will come up to the tram for feeding. Children's barnyard, petting zoo, and pony rides in summer.

ANNUAL EVENTS

September

HOUSTON INTERNATIONAL IN-THE-WATER BOAT SHOW

Watergate Arena, Kemah • 488-7676 (Convention and Visitors Bureau) or 334-1511 • Friday–Sunday near end of September • Admission • W variable
This claims to be the largest in-the-water boat show in Texas, with all kinds and all sizes of boats, nautical equipment and clothing on display and for sale. Entertainment.

RESTAURANTS

($ = under $7, $$ = $8–$17, $$$ = $18–$25, $$$$ = over $25 for one person excluding drinks, tax, and tip.)

LOUIE'S ON THE LAKE

Seabrook, 3813 NASA Rd. 1 • 326-0551 • Lunch and dinner daily
Reservations suggested on weekends • $$–$$$ • Cr • W • Children's plates
If you have a hearty appetite for seafood, try the Seafood Platter that piles up helpings of shrimp, stuffed shrimp, oysters, frog legs, and catfish, your choice of either deep fried or broiled. An even better deal for the seafood lover is the daily lunch ($$) or dinner ($$$) buffet. Also grilled steaks and chicken. Bar. Silent film stars Mary Pickford and Douglas Fairbanks once owned a home on this spot.

ACCOMMODATIONS

($ = under $45, $$ = $46–$60, $$$ = $61–$80, $$$$ = $81–$100, $$$$$ = over $100)
Room tax 12%

AMERICAN HOST HOTEL

**2020 NASA Rd. 1 • 332-3551 or 800-872-8847 • $$–$$$ • W+ 1 room
No-smoking rooms**

This two-story hotel's 128 units include three suites ($$$–$$$$) and 20 no-smoking rooms. Senior discount. Cable TV. Room phones (local calls free). No pets. Free transportation to Houston-Hobby Airport. Restaurant and lounge. Fire sprinklers in rooms. Outdoor pool, indoor whirlpool, physical fitness center. Free continental breakfast. Across from Johnson Space Center and adjacent to Nassau Bay Shopping Village.

HOLIDAY INN-NASA

1300 NASA Rd. 1 • 333-2500 or 800-HOLIDAY, Website: http://www.holiday-inn.com/ • $$$ • W+ 2 rooms • No-smoking rooms

This four-story inn's 226 units include three suites ($$$$$) and 60 no-smoking rooms. Senior discount. Satellite TV with Cinemax and pay channel. Room phones (charge for local calls). Free outside kennel for pets. Restaurant and lounge. Outdoor pool, exercise room, playground. Coffeemakers in most rooms. Limited number of refrigerators available for rooms on request.

NASSAU BAY HILTON AND MARINA

**3000 NASA Rd. 1 • 333-9300 or 800-634-4320, Web site:
http://www.hilton.com/reservations/index.html • $$$–$$$$$ • W+ 4 rooms
No-smoking rooms**

The 244 units in this 14-story Hilton include three suites ($$$$$) and 34 no-smoking rooms (two floors). Cable TV with pay channel. Room phones (charge for local calls). No pets. Free transportation to Houston-Hobby Airport. Restaurant and lounge. Fire sprinklers in rooms, fire intercom. Outdoor heated pool, outdoor whirlpool, exercise room. Some covered parking. 83-slip marina with boats available for rent or charter. All rooms with view of Clear Lake.

RAMADA SOUTH/NASA

1301 NASA Rd. 1 • 488-0220 or 800-255-7345 • $$$–$$$$ • No-smoking rooms

This two-story Ramada has 200 units that include 40 no-smoking rooms. Senior discount. Cable TV. Room phones (charge for local calls). Pets OK. Restaurant and lounge. Outdoor pool.

CORPUS CHRISTI

Nueces County Seat • 275,000 • (512)

The residents of Corpus Christi obviously love their bay. Why else would they put a picture window in their art museum so visitors could pause from looking at man-made art and look out at the natural beauty of the bay? Why else build a marina close enough to the downtown office buildings so boat owners can walk down and relax with a sail at the end of the day?

The city owes its religious name to Spanish explorer Alonso Alvarez de Pineda. In 1519, on the religious feast day of Corpus Christi (The Body of Christ), he discovered "a beautiful bay," which he named after the day. Eventually the name carried over to the city. Today, most Texans shorten that name to Corpus, but the abbreviated version is frowned on by many residents of the city.

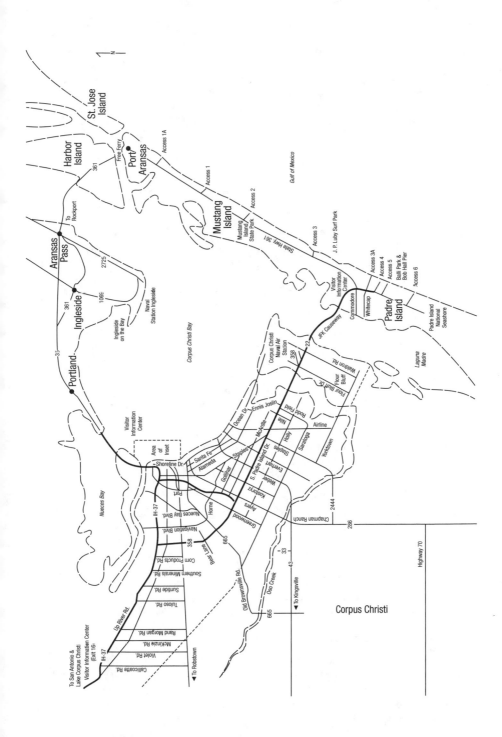

Corpus Christi

It was 1839, more than three centuries after Pineda's discovery, that a frontier trading post was set up near what is now the 400 block of Broadway and a colony slowly grew up around it. The Mexican War gave the colony its first spurt of growth. While waiting for the diplomats to try their hand at settling the Texas border dispute with Mexico, General Zachary Taylor and a small army was sent here to be ready to move south if diplomacy failed. The army set up a tent city in what is now Artesian Park near downtown. Diplomacy did fail, so Taylor and his men moved off to war, but by then Corpus Christi was established as a supply point. When the Mexican War ended it continued this mission supporting operations in the West.

It was another U.S. government decision in the 1920s that really put the city on the map. That was to make Corpus Christi a deep-water port. The dredges turned it into what is still the deepest port on the Texas coast. This soon attracted the petrochemical and other industries. Fortunately, the city was already established before the refineries and other industrial complexes moved in, so the plants were built on the ship channel instead of the bay. As a result the major plants are relatively hidden from downtown and other tourist areas. And, in spite of this industrial base, the city has repeatedly won recognition for being pollution-free.

Often called "The Texas Riviera" or "The Sparkling City by the Sea," the city itself sits like a quarter moon hugging the bay. From the air it looks long and thin, as if everyone were trying to get as close to the water as possible. On the north is Corpus Christi Beach, also called North Beach, a small resort area. Immediately behind and south of this beach, on both sides of the Harbor Bridge, is the bustling port. South of the bridge, along the bay is downtown with a concentration of major hotels as well as the business district and the cultural center at Bayfront Plaza. To the west of downtown is the industrial area. The major residential, shopping, and small business section of the city is southeast of both downtown and the industrial area. Connecting the two areas is Ocean Drive, a seven-mile scenic bay-view drive along a street lined with stately homes. And furthest south are Padre Island and the Gulf.

TOURIST SERVICES

CORPUS CHRISTI AREA CONVENTION AND VISITORS BUREAU

1201 N. Shoreline, in Greater Corpus Christi Business Alliance Building, 1 block north of where the extension of IH-37 ends at Shoreline (P.O. Box 2664, 78403) • 882-5603 or 800-766-2322 • Monday–Friday 8:30–5 • Free • W

If closed, you can pick up brochures and other tourist information at the **Tourist Information Center** on I-37 coming into the city at Exit 16 in Nueces River Park (241-1464), open every day 9–5, or in the **Padre Island National Seashore Headquarters** at 14252 SPI Dr. (949-8743). This one is usually open normal business hours every day June through August, closed Sunday September through May. Brochures and tourist information are also available at the Corpus Christi Museum (*see* Museums).

FLAGSHIP AND *GULF CLIPPER* SIGHTSEEING CRUISES

People's St. T-Head and Shoreline Blvd. (P.O. Box 1292, Portland, TX 78374) 884-1693 or 884-8306 • Morning, afternoon, evening, and moonlight cruises Times and prices vary by cruise and season. Daily in summer, closed Tuesday rest of year • W

The *Flagship,* a scaled-down version of an old Mississippi showboat, carries up to 400 passengers on an hour to an hour-and-a-half narrated tour of the bay and the harbor giving a view of the bayfront skyline and a close-up of operations of the port. (Day trips in high season: Adults $6, children 11 and under $3.50.) The weekend early evening cruises and the Saturday moonlight cruise feature a live band. The *Gulf Clipper* is a smaller vessel that occasionally alternates with the *Flagship.*

GRAY LINE TOURS

289-7113 • Make tour reservations at most hotels, motels, and travel agencies Tours $10–$28

In season, the two-and-a-half hour city tour usually starts at 10 A.M. daily except Sunday. The "Loop Tour," which lasts about four hours, goes around the bay through Padre Island, Port Aransas, and Aransas Pass. It is given by appointment with minimum of six passengers.

REGIONAL TRANSPORTATION AUTHORITY'S SPECIAL BUSES

Printed schedules are usually available at hotels/motels and various locations in the Bayfront area • Monday–Saturday on a seasonal schedule. For latest call 289-2600

B Trolley Scenic Trail. A motorized trolley with polished brass and wooden seats that operates on a Bayfront route with stops at major sights. Adults 50¢ (25¢ on Saturdays), children 6 and under free.

CC Beach Shuttle. From late May to early September, this free shuttle bus operates daily from 10:30 A.M. to 6:30 P.M., traveling around Corpus Christi Beach with service to and from the Water Taxi, Texas State Aquarium, USS Lexington, and other attractions. Just flag the driver down anywhere along the route.

The Tide. Look for the buses with the fish painted on the side. This route covers downtown, major hotels, Convention Center, Bayfront Arts and Sciences Park, and Texas State Aquarium. Daily. Adults 50¢ (25¢ on Saturdays), children 6 and under free.

Water Taxi. This passenger transport ferry travels across the ship channel between the barge dock on Shoreline and Corpus Christi Beach. It operates daily from 10:30 A.M. to 6:30 P.M. from late May to early September. Fare $1 each way, children five and under free.

BIRD'S EYE VIEW

You can get an excellent sky-high view of the shoreline and bay from the restaurants and lounges atop the Marriott and Radisson Marina hotels (*see* Accommodations). A lower-level view of the shoreline and port can be seen from the observation roof of the Texas State Aquarium.

MUSEUMS

A Corpus Christi Fun Pass Book provides a reduced price combination of tickets for admission to the Corpus Christi Museum of Science and History and the Columbus Fleet, the Texas State Aquarium, and the USS Lexington Museum on the Bay. Adults $21, seniors $16.50, youths (13–17) $19, children (5–12) $11. Children 5 and under free.

ART MUSEUM OF SOUTH TEXAS

1902 N. Shoreline in Bayfront Arts and Sciences Park • 884-3844 • Tuesday–Saturday 10–5, Sunday 12–5. Closed Monday • Adults $3, seniors $2, students (13–18) and children (2–12) $1. Free admission on Tuesdays • W+

Starkly austere in design, this building is worth seeing just for itself as it stands out, white and crisp, against the background of green park lawn and sparkling bay waters. Bronze-tinted glass is used on all exterior windows and doors so there will be no distortion of color of the works of art on display inside. Since the museum has only a small (but growing) permanent collection, it emphasizes traveling exhibits that cover a wide variety of periods and media. At Christmas time, as part of the Harbor Lights Festival, the museum is transformed by a forest of decorated Christmas trees. Gift shop.

CORPUS CHRISTI MUSEUM OF SCIENCE AND HISTORY: WORLD OF DISCOVERY

1900 N. Chaparral (78401) in Bayfront Arts and Sciences Park • 883-2862 Monday–Saturday 10–5, Sunday noon–5 • Adults $8, seniors $6.50, youths (13–17) $7, children (6–12) $4, children 5 and under free • W+

Under the collective title of the World of Discovery, this museum now includes the Museum of Science and History, the Ships of Christopher Columbus, and the Xeriscape Learning Center and Design Garden. The Museum emphasizes interactive exhibits that let visitors touch and explore subjects that include the impact of Christopher Columbus' voyages on science and natural history with displays focusing on energy, birds, gems and minerals, and shells. Artifacts from a Spanish ship that sank off Padre Island in 1554 is one of the many other major exhibits that range from dinosaurs to present day "Reptiles of South Texas." For those curious about what all that maze of pipes and tanks is in a refinery, a scale model in the Earth Sciences section explains it all. The Children's Wharf is a hands-on area for children 3–7 (and their parents). Treasure Hunt, a children's seek-and-find game is held every Saturday at 1:30.

Full-sized authentic re-creations of the three ships of the Columbus fleet, built by the government of Spain and sailed to be seen by millions around the world, are permanently docked here in a re-created fifteenth-century shipyard behind the museum building. Visitors can go below deck inside the Santa Maria and watch actual restoration work being done on the Pinta and Santa Maria by a master shipwright and his journeymen in dry dock.

The Xeriscape Center is an outdoor educational area designed to teach water and energy conservation through landscaping with native plants.

ASIAN CULTURES MUSEUM AND EDUCATIONAL CENTER

1809 N. Chaparral • 882-2641 • Tuesday–Saturday 10–5. Closed Sunday–Monday • Adults $4, seniors $3.50, youths (6–15) $2.50, 5 and under free • W+

The daily life, history, religion, and art of Japan and other Asian countries are the focal points here. Its collection of *Hakata* dolls is reportedly the largest private collection in the United States. There is also a collection of *Noh* and *Kabuki* masks and a bigger-than-life bronze statue of Buddha that is more than 200 years old. Gift shop.

TEXAS STATE AQUARIUM

2710 N. Shoreline Blvd. Corpus Christi Beach by the Harbor Bridge (P.O. Box 331307, 78463) • 881-1200 or 800-477-GULF • Monday–Saturday 9–6, Sunday 10–6 (closes at 5 in winter). Closed Thanksgiving and Christmas • Adults $8, seniors and youths (12–17) $5.75, children (4–11) $4.50, 3 and under free • W+

This is the first major aquarium in the country to focus on ecosystems of the Gulf of Mexico and the Caribbean Sea. Designed to be a world-class aquarium, it lives up to that rating with interactive exhibits that let the visitor experience plant and animal life presented in intricately reproduced settings of their natural environments. The aquarium is being built in phases on 7.3 acres. When the final phase is completed in 2000, it will have the largest collection of Gulf marine life anywhere. The first phase, costing more than $31 million of the projected $60 million-plus project, is the Gulf of Mexico Exhibit Building. Here visitors are engulfed (no pun intended) in an underwater journey that stretches from the coastal marshlands out across the barrier islands and past the oil rigs to the colorful Flower Gardens Coral Reef located about 115 miles off the Texas coast. You can watch divers feed exotic fish, play the role of a city mayor as a simulated hurricane threatens the coast, get eye-to-eye with a shark, and get your hands wet as you feel a variety of sea creatures in the Sea Star Discovery Pool. A collection of playful North American river otters and endangered sea turtles are featured in a re-creation of their natural habitats in Conservation Cove. Activities include dive shows and shark and ray touch times. Despite its title, this is not a state-owned facility. Designated the "official Aquarium of Texas" by the 69th Legislature, it is operated by the private, nonprofit Texas State Aquarium Association. Gift shop.

USS LEXINGTON MUSEUM ON THE BAY

2914 N. Shoreline Blvd. Corpus Christi Beach next to the Texas State Aquarium (P.O. Box 23076, 78403-3076) • 888-4873 or 800-LADY-LEX (800-523-9539) • Daily Memorial Day–Labor Day 9–8, rest of year 9–5. Closed Christmas • Adults $8, seniors $6, children (4–12) $4, children 4 and under free • W (hangar deck only)

Commissioned in 1943, the USS Lexington served longer, set more records, and earned more decorations than any aircraft carrier in U.S. naval history. During World War II, the Lex was called the "Blue Ghost" by Tokyo Rose because the carrier repeatedly made lies of reports that it was sunk. Now a floating naval museum, it offers visitors a choice of five tour routes, educational exhibits, restored aircraft, and a collection of historical memorabilia. Tours include the hangar deck; the 910-foot-long flight deck, which is larger than three football fields and displays vintage aircraft; the bridge; the captain's and admiral's quarters; engine room; and sick bay. Other exhibits include a high-tech jet fighter flight simulator ($3.50). During high season, helicopter rides are offered from the flight deck (call for schedule and prices). Tours involve a lot of walking and climbing stairs (ladders) between decks and ducking through narrow passages. Food court and Ship's Store.

HISTORIC PLACES

CENTENNIAL HOUSE

411 N. Upper Broadway • 882-8691 or 992-6003 • Wednesday 2–5 (when flag is flying) and by appointment for groups • Adults $2, children (6–12) $1, 5 and under free • W

Built in 1849, this house is the oldest standing structure in the city. During the Civil War it served as a hospital for both the Confederate and Union forces. It received its name because it was 100 years old when the Texas Historical Commission presented its medallion in 1949. It is listed in the National Register of Historic Places. Note the address—Broadway is on two levels and this is on the upper level.

HERITAGE PARK

1600 Block of N. Chaparral between Hughes and Fitzgerald • 883-0639 (Multicultural Center in the Galvan House at 1581 N. Chaparral) • Free self-guided tours: adults $3, seniors $2, children $1 • W variable

Nine Victorian homes were moved from various locations in the city to this historic district known as Old Irishtown. Now restored, most of these historic homes serve as offices for organizations. Two of the buildings, however, are set up for the public: the **Sidbury House,** located at 1609, was built in 1893 and is listed in the National Register of Historic Places, and the **Galvan House,** at 1581, was built in 1908 and is now used as a Multicultural Center and the starting point for guided tours. Tea room and gift shop.

OTHER POINTS OF INTEREST

ART CENTER OF CORPUS CHRISTI

100 N. Shoreline (78401) • 884-6406 • Tuesday–Sunday 10–4. Closed Monday • Free • W+

You can frequently watch artists at work here and they have shows and exhibits of local and area artists working in all media. Exhibits usually change monthly. Gift shop and gourmet sandwich and salad restaurant.

BAYFRONT ARTS AND SCIENCES PARK AND BAYFRONT PLAZA

North end of Shoreline Blvd. • Open at all times • W variable

Art, drama, science, history, and music are all concentrated on these few acres near the Harbor Bridge. The Art Museum of South Texas stands at the water's edge. Facing it across the lawn is the Corpus Christi Museum. In the adjoining plaza are the Convention Center, Selena Auditorium, and the Harbor Playhouse. Nearby is an observation point where you can see the traffic on the ship channel and the Texas State Aquarium across the water.

CORPUS CHRISTI BEACH

North of downtown off US 181 across Harbor Bridge

Old timers still call it "North Beach" and speak of its 1930s heyday when it was the home of gambling casinos and amusement parks. But then it lost the gambling and its glamour and turned into an eyesore. The city and the Army Corps of Engineers restored it in the late 1970s. Now hotels, motels, and condos line much of the one-and-a-half mile beachfront and the Texas State Aquarium is located here.

CORPUS CHRISTI BOTANICAL GARDENS

8545 S. Staples at Yorktown (78413) • 852-2100 • Tuesday–Sunday 9–5. Closed Monday, Thanksgiving, Christmas, and New Year's • Visitors Center free, gardens: adults $2, seniors $1.50, children (5–12) $1, 4 and under free • W

The gardens stretch along the bank of Oso Creek in the city's southwest quadrant. Surpassing 180 acres, the gardens are being opened in stages and include a nature trail, gardens of subtropicals, beds of seasonal color, a vegetable demonstration area, children's garden, picnic areas, an information center, and a gift shop. A good place for birdwatching. Guided tours available September–May.

CORPUS CHRISTI ZOO

CR 33 of Weber (P.O. Box 2611, 78403) • 814-8000 • Daily 10–5 • Adults $5, seniors $2.50, children (3–12) $3, children 2 and under free • W+ but not all areas

This small zoo is in the early stages of development. Located on 145 acres it already has a variety of animals on display ranging from big cats to wolves. It also boasts of having the largest Children's Zoo in the country with animals, a petting area, an animal care nursery, and pony rides. Programs include frequent animal shows.

THE INTERNATIONAL KITE MUSEUM

Best Western Sandy Shores Resort, 3200 Surfside on Corpus Christi Beach 883-7456 • Daily 10–5 • Free • W

Tucked in a corner of this resort hotel, this small museum is a celebration of the fascinating history of kites from their origin in the Orient to today. If you want, you can buy a kite in the Kite Shoppe and take it right out on the beach to fly it.

MARINA AND YACHT BASIN

Shoreline Dr. along the Seawall between Starr and Kinney • W variable

This downtown marina is built around three small, man-made peninsulas that take their names from their alphabetical shapes and the streets that lead to them: the Peoples Street T-Head, the Lawrence Street T-Head, and the Cooper's Alley L-Head. In addition to the pleasure craft berthed here, there are also a floating restaurant, sightseeing boats, charter and party fishing boats, and the commercial shrimp fleet, where you can usually buy fresh shrimp and fish right off the boats. In season, you'll also find rentals of aqua bikes, sailboards, sailboats, jet skis, paddle boats, and other water sports equipment.

PADRE ISLAND NATIONAL SEASHORE AND MALAQUITE BEACH

Approximately 25 miles south of JFK Causeway on Park Rd. 22 • 949-8068 Park open at all times. Visitor's Center daily 9–6 Memorial Day–Labor Day, varied hours rest of year • Entrance fees: $4 per vehicle (good for 1 week), $2 for hikers, bikers, or bus riders • W variable

Padre Island, stretching 113 miles from Corpus Christi on the north almost to the Mexican border on the south, is the longest in the string of barrier islands protecting the Texas coast. The island ranges in width from a few hundred yards to about three miles and is separated from the mainland by Laguna Madre, a generally shallow body of water with a maximum width of ten miles.

A little more than 80 miles, starting near the north end of the island, has been designated a National Seashore administered by the U.S. Department of the Interior. Commercial development is restricted to the two ends of the island.

Malaquite Beach is the only developed area within the National Seashore itself. There is a pavilion with visitors center and facilities for swimming, picnicking, and primitive camping ($5 per night). There are also nature trails and the park rangers and naturalists conduct a number of programs for visitors during the summer.

The paved road continues for a few miles past Malaquite, but from then on you need a 4-wheel drive vehicle (with water and other safety supplies). With one of these, you can venture south for more than 50 miles to the Mansfield Cut. Hiking and primitive camping is also permitted, but requires a great deal of planning because there is no water and no shade. For your own safety, you are required to check in at the ranger station before going into the area past Malaquite Beach.

For general information, contact the National Park Service's Padre Island Headquarters on the mainland at 9405 S. Padre Island Dr., Corpus Christi 78418 (937-2621), open normal business hours Monday–Friday. The phone number at Malaquite Beach is 949-8068.

THE SEAWALL

Shoreline Dr.

More than 2.5 miles long, this 14-foot high seawall was designed by sculptor Gutzon Borglum and built just before World War II (1939–1941) while he was still putting the finishing touches to his most famous project, Mount Rushmore. What is unique about this seawall is that it steps down into the water. The steps are wide enough to sit—or doze—on, and many people working in the nearby buildings find it an ideal place for a brown-bag lunch while watching the seagulls and other shorebirds. The sidewalk atop the seawall is up to 20 feet wide, making it a favorite track for joggers, roller skaters, and bicyclists, as well as strollers. You can also rent pedal-powered two-person surreys with the fringe on top. A number of gazebo-type shelters have been built along the seawall. Called *Miradores del Mar,* they provide shady spots to watch the bay. The largest, called *Mirador de la Flor,* at the entrance to the Peoples Street T-head, is dedicated as a memorial to Tejano singer Selena Quintanilla-Perez.

SPORTS AND ACTIVITIES

Birding

Brown pelicans and the rare masked duck are among the more than 500 species of birds that have been documented in the Corpus Christi area. These include seabirds, shorebirds, songbirds, game birds, raptors, and marsh waders with seasonal migrations by birds from Central and South America and the Arctic. For additional information contact the Coastal Bend Audubon Society, P.O. Box 6211, 78411 (882-7232) or the Convention and Visitors Bureau (*see* Tourist Services).

Fishing

Fishing the area's inshore waters is made easy by the many fishing piers and jetties. Surf fishing is good from the beaches on Padre and Mustang Islands. For wade fishing the Laguna Madre and Cayo del Oso (near the Naval Air Station) are both reportedly excellent. Party boats for bay fishing operate from the Peoples Street T-Head. These usually run four-hour trips morning, afternoon, and evening. The fare is about $15 per adult and $10 for children under 11. Bait is furnished and tackle is available for rent. Charter boats are also available for private fishing parties. Most deep-sea charters operate out of Port Aransas, which is really Corpus Christi's outlet to the Gulf (*see* Port Aransas). A list of party and charter boats and fishing guides operating from Corpus Christi, Port Aransas, Aransas Pass, and Rockport-Fulton and a list of fishing piers and jetties is available from the Corpus Christi Convention and Visitors Bureau (*see* Tourist Services).

Greyhound Racing

CORPUS CHRISTI GREYHOUND RACE TRACK

5302 Leotard (P.O. Box 9087, 78469) I-37 between Navigation and McBride 289-9333 or 800-580-RACE (800-580-7223) • Clubhouse $2, general admission $1 • Evening races Tuesday–Saturday, matinee races Wednesday, Saturday–Sunday • W varied

A $21-million complex offering year-round pari-mutuel greyhound racing with 450 race programs—300 evening and 150 days of both matinee and evening programs with 13 races per program—scheduled during the year. Simulcast races Monday, Tuesday, and Thursday.

Sailing

Almost any Wednesday starting around 5:30 P.M., the downtown marina and yacht basin looks like mad confusion with crews hustling to make their boats ready and dozens of sailboats dodging each other as they jockey to get into the bay. But there's actually a method to the madness, for what they're all doing is making ready to take off in the weekly sailboat races. You can watch them from the yacht basin or the Seawall.

If you want to sail yourself, small sailboats and catamarans are available for rent, in season, at the yacht basin as are captained and bare boat (no crew) charters. For a list of rental and charter companies throughout the area, contact the Convention and Visitors Bureau.

Stock Car Racing

CORPUS CHRISTI SPEEDWAY

241 Flato Rd., near Agnes • 289-8847 • Closed November–February (851-2383 off season) • Adults $7, children under 12 free with adult • W

Opened in 1945, this is the oldest racing complex in Texas. Races are held every Saturday from March through October on the quarter-mile, high-banked, oval, asphalt stock car track. (Call for times.)

Windsurfing

OLEANDER POINT

Cole Park, 2000 block of Ocean Dr.

It goes by several names: windsurfing, sailboarding, or boardsailing; but it's all the same sport of riding an enlarged surfboard equipped with a sail. With consistent winds of 15 to 25 miles per hour blowing across the warm waters of the bay—which are generally warm enough not to require a wetsuit—and a mild climate that offers the possibility of sailing 12 months a year, Corpus Christi is vying to become the nation's windsurfing capital. To draw the board-sailors, the city built a breakwater at Oleander Point and created what is claimed to be "the only city-sanctioned surfboard park in the world." It has also promoted windsurfing competitions at various locations on the bay, including the annual Windsurfing Regatta.

PERFORMING ARTS

CATHEDRAL CONCERT SERIES

Corpus Christi Cathedral, 505 N. Upper Broadway (78401) • 888-7444 • W+
   The series usually includes about four free concerts by choral and musical groups at the cathedral and one or two special benefit performances of plays or major musical organizations at other locations including Selena Auditorium ($10–$50).

CORPUS CHRISTI SYMPHONY

Selena Auditorium • 1901 N. Shoreline • 882-4091 • Admission varies • W+
   Usually seven or eight concerts are given during the October through April season. The Symphony also performs at some of the free Sunday evening concerts in Cole Park during the summer. The Corpus Christi Ballet also occasionally performs in this auditorium.

HARBOR PLAYHOUSE

1 Bayfront Park (78401) • 882-7469 • Admission varies • W+
   The local theater group puts on about a half dozen productions here ranging from drama to musicals during its August through May season plus a melodrama series during the summer. The Youth Theatre usually has two productions for children in the fall and two in the spring. The Playhouse is also used for musical events. This is Texas' oldest continually performing community theater.

SHOPPING

PADRE STAPLES MALL

5488 South Padre Island Drive (78411) • 991-5718 • W+ but not all areas
   Bealls, Dillard's, Penney's, and Foley's anchor about 100 stores, a food court, Luby's Cafeteria, and a movie theater in this mall. Covered parking. Stroller rentals. For the kids there's a colorful, old-fashioned, two-deck Italian-built carousel.

PILAR

3814 S. Alameda at Doddridge (78411), in Lamar Park Center • 853-7171 • W
   A distinctive women's shop brimming with selections from all over the world including embroidered dresses, wearable art, nubby woolens and cottons, jewelry, folk art, rugs, and tapestries.

SUNRISE MALL

Airline at South Padre Island Dr. • 993-2900 • W+ but not all areas
   Wards and Sears are the main anchors for about 100 stores, a food court, restaurants, a movie theater, and a model train club's display in this two story mall. Covered parking. Stroller rentals.

WATER STREET MARKET
309 N. Water St. (78401) • W
A grouping of several specialty shops in the Bayfront area convenient to the major hotels. One of the shops is Totally Texas (883-1682) where you'll find a wide selection of Texas-related gifts and novelty items including armadillo purses, chili pepper jewelry, and bluebonnet pottery.

ANNUAL EVENTS
April

BUCCANEER DAYS
Various locations in the city • 882-3242 • 2 weeks starting in middle of the month • Free (admission to some events) • W variable
For almost 60 years, the city has been celebrating the 1519 discovery of Corpus Christi Bay with this festival. The festivities kick off with a four-day PRCA rodeo and include the traditional capture of the city by pirate girls (actually the contestants in the Buc Days beauty contest) who make the mayor "walk the plank." Other activities include the junior parade, the illuminated night parade, fireworks, a carnival, music festivals, street dance, sports events on both land and sea, arts-and-crafts show, and a sailboat regatta.

September

BAYFEST
Shoreline Blvd. and Bayfront Arts and Sciences Park • 887-0868 • Usually last weekend in September or first in October • Free • W variable
It began as a bicentennial celebration and since then this three-day family fall festival has mushroomed into a major event drawing more than 350,000 visitors. Activities include arts and crafts show, fireworks, a boat parade and a street parade, a sailboat regatta, and the "Anything-That-Can-Float-But-A-Boat Race."

October

TEXAS JAZZ FESTIVAL
Various locations in the city • 883-4500 • Three-day weekend Most activities are free • W variable
Jazz musicians, many of them famous, donate their time to come here from all over the country to put on this festival. Activities include free clinics, concerts, and jam sessions, a scenic jazz festival cruise (pay) on Friday evening, and a Jazz Mass on Sunday.

RESTAURANTS
($ = under $7, $$ = $8–$17, $$$ = $18–$25, $$$$ = over $25 for one person excluding drinks, tax, and tip.)

Putting On The Ritz

REPUBLIC OF TEXAS BAR AND GRILL
Omni Marina Hotel, 900 N Shoreline Dr. (78401) • 886-3515 • Dinner only Monday–Saturday. Closed Sunday • $$$–$$$$ • Cr • W+
Steaks and chops are the major entrées on the menu, and they are so sure of the quality and preparation of their steaks here they offer a money-back guar-

antee if yours isn't up to your expectations. Also chicken, wild game, and seafood entrées. All with a 20th floor bird's-eye view of Corpus Christi Bay. Bar. Complimentary valet parking in hotel garage.

American

ELMO'S CITY DINER AND OYSTER BAR

622 N. Water at Starr • 883-1643 • Lunch and dinner daily • $$ • Cr • W Children's plates

Except for the shape, all the traditional standards of an old-time diner are here—the checkerboard black and white tile, stainless steel, and neon decor. The fare includes burgers and poorboys and "blue plate specials," but it also goes upscale with entrées like flounder filet stuffed with crab and shrimp stuffing, and mesquite roasted prime rib of beef. Look for hometown girl Farrah Fawcett as a teenager in old yearbook photos on the wall. Bar.

Italian

MARCO'S AT LAMAR PARK

3812 S. Alameda at Doddridge in Lamar Park Center • 853-2000 • Lunch Monday–Friday, dinner Monday–Saturday. Closed Sunday • $$ • Cr • W

Many Italian restaurants in Texas specialize in cuisine of Sicily and Southern Italy so most Texans think Italian food is always flavored with tomato sauces. There are several southern dishes like this on owner-chef Marco's Tuscany menu, but it also ranges the whole Italian peninsula offering a variety of that country's creative cuisines that depend more on butter and a variety of spices to enhance the flavor. Candlelight atmosphere. Live music for dancing Friday. Bar.

Seafood

ELMO'S STAPLES STREET GRILL

5253 S. Staples, near South Padre Island Dr. • 992-FISH (992-3474) • Lunch and dinner Monday–Friday and Sunday, dinner only Saturday • $$ • Cr • W

The dining area in this highly popular seafood house is tiered so you can watch the cooks at work behind the long counter, grilling the seafood over coals made from mesquite wood and stir-frying the vegetables. In addition to the local catch from the Gulf, seafood is also frequently flown in from the other two coasts. If you're not into seafood, they also use the grill to make *fajitas*. Bar.

LANDRY'S

600 N. Shoreline at Peoples St. T-Head • 882-6666 • Lunch and dinner daily $$ • AE, MC, V • W • Children's plates

A restored quarters barge turned into a floating restaurant offers such entrées as baked flounder fillet in lemon-pepper sauce, and a combination plate of broiled fish, shrimp, oysters, and scallops. Other seafood entrées come fried, grilled, blackened, or baked. There's an early bird special nightly from 5 to 7 and all day Sunday. Good view of the bayfront skyline or the bay. Bar.

THE LIGHTHOUSE

444 N. Shoreline at the Lawrence St. T-Head • 883-3982 • Lunch and dinner daily • $$ • Cr • W elevator

Casual dining with a menu that ranges from u-peel-em shrimp to oysters *en brochette* and steak sandwiches to the catch of the day. But the real catch of the day—or night—here is the wide-angle view of the bay. This makes it a favorite spot for watching the sailboat races held early every Wednesday evening in season. Bar.

SNOOPY'S PIER

13313 S. Padre Island Dr., actually off S. Padre Island Dr. under the east end of the JFK Causeway • 949-8815 • Lunch and dinner daily • $–$$ • No Cr • W

The decor is strictly "old fishermen's hangout," which it was; the dress is whatever you're wearing, and the menu is simple, mostly shrimp, the local catch of the day, and burgers. Sit outside on the deck and enjoy the evening breeze and watch the sun set over the water. Bar.

WATER STREET SEAFOOD COMPANY

309 N. Water, in rear of courtyard at Water St. Market • 882-8683 • Lunch and dinner daily • Reservations taken for large parties only • $$ • Cr • W Children's plates

For starters there are appetizers like *ceviche,* or a quarter-pound of Blue Crab Cocktail (in season), or oysters on the half shell. And the entrée menu is just as varied with choices like Red Snapper Nueces, sauteed snapper filet topped with shrimp and blue crabmeat in a browned butter sauce, or, if you prefer your seafood deep fried, the combination dinner includes shrimp, oysters, crab cake, soft shell crab, and frogs legs. Daily specials on the blackboard. Bar.

ACCOMMODATIONS

Note: Most accommodations in Corpus Christi have seasonal rates. Rate symbols used are for high season which is during the summer months. Ask about lower rates in low season.

($ = under $45, $$ = $46–$60, $$$ = $61–$80, $$$$ = $81–$100, $$$$$ = over $100)

Room Tax 13%

Hotels And Motels

BEST WESTERN SANDY SHORES RESORT

3200 Surfside, on Corpus Christi Beach north of Harbor Bridge (Box 839, 78403) 883-7456 or 800-528-1234 • $$$–$$$$$ • W+ 5 rooms • No-smoking rooms

This resort has a two-story section around the pool and a seven-story section on the beach. The 253 units include six suites ($$$$$) and 14 no-smoking rooms. Children under 12 stay free in room with parents. Senior discount. Limited covered parking. Cable TV with HBO and pay channel. Room phones (local calls free). Pets OK (extra charge). Restaurant and snack shops, room service, lounge open seven nights with entertainment Tuesday–Saturday. Outdoor heated pool, indoor saunas and whirlpool. Sports courts. Guest memberships available for country club. Self-service laundry, same-day dry cleaning. Gift shop. Map for joggers available. International Kite Museum located here (*see* Other Points of Interest). On the beach.

OMNI BAYFRONT HOTEL

900 N. Shoreline (78401) • 887-1600 or 800-THE-OMNI (800-843-6664) $$$$–$$$$$ • W+ 8 rooms • No-smoking rooms

The 20-story Omni has 474 units including 28 suites ($$$$$) and 25 no-smoking rooms. Children under 18 stay free in parent's room. Senior discount and package plans available. Weekend rates in off-season. Free garage parking. Cable TV with HBO and pay channel. Room phones (charge for local calls). Fire sprinklers in rooms and fire intercom system. No pets. Two restaurants, room service, and lounges open daily. Indoor/outdoor heated pool with bar in season, exercise room, whirlpool, sauna, racquetball court. Memberships available for guests in several golf clubs. Same-day dry cleaning. Free airport transportation. On the bayfront.

OMNI MARINA HOTEL

707 N. Shoreline (78401) • 882-1700 or 800-THE-OMNI (800-843-6664)
$$$$–$$$$$ • W+ 4 rooms • No-smoking rooms

This 20-story hotel has 346 units that include 19 suites ($$$$$) and 21 no-smoking rooms. Children under 18 stay free in room with parents. Senior discount, weekend rates, package plans available. Free garage parking. Cable TV with HBO and pay channel. Room phones (charge for local calls). Fire sprinklers in rooms and fire intercom system. Restaurant, room service, lounge open seven nights. Indoor/outdoor pool, indoor whirlpool, sauna, exercise room. Guest memberships available in country club. Sundeck. Free airport transportation. Same-day dry cleaning. On the bay front.

HOLIDAY INN-EMERALD BEACH

1102 S. Shoreline • 883-5731 or 800-465-4329 • $$$$–$$$$$
W+ 1 room • No-smoking rooms

This is a five- and seven-story inn that has 368 units including four suites ($$$$$) and 39 no-smoking rooms. Children under 18 stay free in room with parents. Senior discounts and package plans available. Cable TV with Showtime and pay channel. Room phones (charge for local calls). Two restaurants (one seasonal), lobby bar, lounge open seven nights with DJ. Indoor heated pool, children's pool, exercise room, whirlpool, and sauna. Guest memberships available in country club. Free airport transportation. Children's playground. Same-day dry cleaning. Gift shop. This is the only bayfront hotel/motel located on the beach on the bay.

HOLIDAY INN-GULF BEACH RESORT

15202 Windward Dr. • 949-8041 or 800-465-4329 • $$$$–$$$$$ • W+ 2 rooms
No-smoking rooms

This six-story inn offers 148 units including two suites ($$$$$) and 30 no-smoking rooms. Children under 19 stay free in parent's room. Senior discount and package plans available. Cable TV with premium and pay channel. Room phones (local calls free). Pets OK ($10). Restaurant, room service, lounge open daily with live entertainment Wednesday–Sunday in high season. Outdoor pool with bar. Guest memberships available in country club. Self-service laundry, same-day dry cleaning. Located on the beach on the Gulf.

OTHER ACCOMMODATIONS

Condominiums and Beach Houses

There are a number of agencies in the Corpus Christi area that handle condominium and beach house rentals. In most cases a minimum stay is two days with rates ranging from about $60 up to $250 a day. Weekly and monthly rates are available. For further information, contact the Convention and Visitors Bureau (*see* Tourist Services).

DEL RIO

Val Verde County Seat • 35,000 • (830)

Del Rio, the largest city between San Antonio and El Paso, was originally named San Felipe del Rio (St. Phillip of the River). That name survived more than two centuries, until the 1880s when the Post Office suggested shortening it to Del Rio to avoid confusion with another Texas town named San Felipe de Austin.

There are some 400 archaeological sites in Val Verde County. Indian pictographs painted on the walls of area caves have been dated back some 8,000 years.

Like most towns in semi-arid regions, Del Rio came into being because of the San Felipe Springs that gush forth from a subterranean river at a rate of more than 90 million gallons a day. The first real settlement grew up here after the Civil War when a group of ranchers moved in and dug an irrigation system based on the springs.

Irrigated farming is still important; however, it was soon discovered that sheep and goats could thrive on the sparse vegetation in the surrounding hills and today Del Rio claims to be the wool and mohair capital of the world. Other Texas cities, like San Angelo, contest that claim, but there's no doubt that Val

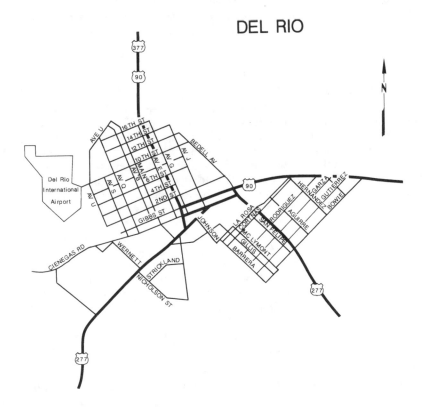

DEL RIO

Verde County is among the top producers in the state of sheep, lamb, wool, and mohair.

An outstanding feature of downtown Del Rio is the number of native limestone buildings. These were constructed by Italian stonemasons who came to build the city after finishing construction of Fort Clark at Brackettville and the stone embankments for the Galveston, Harrisburg and San Antonio Railroad, which reached Del Rio in 1882. Some of the Italians also planted vineyards and built a winery, which is now called the Val Verde Winery, the oldest winery in Texas.

About three miles south, across the Rio Grande, is the Mexican city of Acuña with a population of roughly 120,000.

TOURIST SERVICES

DEL RIO CHAMBER OF COMMERCE • 1915 Ave. F (78840), in rear of Civic Center • 775-3551 • W

DEL RIO-ACUÑA TOURS

US 90W (HCR#3, Box rr, 78840) • 775-6484 or 800-LAKEFUN (800-525-3386) W call ahead

Five-and-a-half hours of historic Del Rio and Ciudad Acuña, Mexico, start at 10:30 A.M. daily. Includes shopping and dining in Mexico.

HIGH BRIDGE ADVENTURES

Box 816, Comstock, 78837 • (915) 292-4495 • Tours $20–$25

Tours are on a pontoon boat holding six passengers that cruises the rivers to see the Indian pictographs and the highest bridge in Texas. Tours last three to four hours.

MUSEUMS

WHITEHEAD MEMORIAL MUSEUM

1308 S. Main at Wallen • 774-7568 • Tuesday–Saturday 9–4:30, Sunday 1–5 P.M. Closed Monday and major holidays • Adults $2, children 50¢ • W variable

In the 1870s the Perry Mercantile building was the largest store between San Antonio and El Paso. In 1962, it was given to the city for a museum by the Whiteheads, a local ranching family. Since that time, the museum has grown to include seven buildings on several landscaped acres. The entrance to the grounds is through the Hacienda, which houses the Visitors Center, a gift shop, and the chapel. The Perry Store is now an exhibition area for pioneer history. Another building features both black history and the story of the Seminole Indian Scouts. A replica of the Jersey Lilly, the saloon/court operated by the famous (or infamous) Judge Roy Bean is also on the grounds and behind it are the graves of the Judge and his son, Sam. Bean dispensed his own brand of justice that made him a legend as "The Law west of the Pecos." Other buildings on the grounds contain exhibits on prehistoric man and the Indians who lived in the area. Guided tours are available.

OTHER POINTS OF INTEREST

AMISTAD LAKE AND AMISTAD NATIONAL RECREATION AREA

Take US 90 northwest about 10 miles • 775-7491 (National Park Service Office, 4121 US 90W) • Open at all times • Nominal boating use fee • W variable

The eagle is a symbol of both the United States and Mexico, so it's appropriate that at the center of the joint U.S.-Mexican Amistad Dam across the Rio Grande are seven-foot-high bronze U.S. and Mexican eagles. You can drive into Mexico across the toll-free road atop the six-mile-long dam from 10–6 daily. An unstaffed National Park Service Visitors Center, near the customs station on the dam, is opened all year.

The dam impounds an international lake that reaches 78 miles up the Rio Grande, 25 miles up the Devils River, and 16 miles up the Pecos River with more than 67,000 water surface acres (44,000 acres are in Texas) and 851 miles of shoreline (547 in Texas).

More than 1,200,000 visitors come to the U.S. recreation area every year. There are facilities for boating and houseboating (rentals available), fishing, swimming, water skiing and other water sports, limited hunting, nature study, primitive camping, and picnicking. Park facilities are mostly on the east end of the lake. There are also several commercial campgrounds along the shoreline.

You can fish on both sides of the international boundary that runs through the lake, and there is no closed season, but a Texas fishing license is required in U.S. waters and a Mexican license in Mexican waters. Check with the park headquarters or the Chamber of Commerce on where to get both these licenses on the American side. The phenomenal visibility of the water most of the year makes this lake a choice for scuba shops across the state to bring their students for check-out dives.

In addition to a map/brochure of the area, the National Park Service offers a brochure outlining a self-guided tour of the major attractions in the Pecos River District including the Indian pictographs at the Panther and Parida Caves. For information contact Superintendent, Amistad National Recreation Area, Star Route #2, Box 5-J, Hwy 90W, Del Rio 78840.

CIUDAD ACUÑA

Take Garfield Ave. (Spur 239) west approximately 3 miles to International Toll Bridge • To call directly from Del Rio to Acuña, dial 011-52-877 and then the number.

This city of about 120,000 is named for Manuel Acuña, a romantic poet of the Mexican Revolution. On the tree-lined central plaza, called *Plaza Benjamin Canales*, is the *Palacio Municipal* (City Hall), from the balcony of which Presidents Eisenhower and Lopez Mateo spoke to the people in 1960 when they met to conclude the agreement to build Amistad Dam. Tourist shopping is near the bridge, especially along *Avenida Hidalgo*. Many shopkeepers speak English and almost all deal in American dollars. Several restaurants and nightclubs in Acuña are popular with American visitors. You can drive your car over, but if you do it's suggested you pick up Mexican auto insurance at one of the insurance agencies in Del Rio. Or you can park near the bridge and walk across (it's about ¾ mile to the shopping area), take a taxi, or take the bus, which runs every 30 minutes.

VAL VERDE WINERY

100 Qualia • 775-9714 • Monday–Saturday 9–5 • Free tour

This is the oldest winery in Texas, started in 1883 by Frank Qualia, an Italian immigrant, and still operated by the Qualia family. For years it was the only licensed winery in the state. The tour takes about 20 minutes and covers winemaking from growing the grapes to bottling. You will see the vineyard (look for the geese that are used for weeding), storage vats, aging room, and other facilities. A variety of wines are produced here, including the *Lenoir*, which was the first wine produced by the winery in the 1880s, and all are usually available for tasting (and sale).

SPORTS AND ACTIVITIES

Golf

SAN FELIPE GOLF COURSE

Hwy. 90 • 774-2511

Rated one of best 9-hole courses in Texas. Green fees $20–$25.

House Boating

LAKE AMISTAD RESORT & MARINA

US 90W at Diablo East Recreation Area (P.O. Box 420635, 78842) • 774-4157

Fifty-six and 50-foot houseboats are available for rent at this Amistad National Recreation Area concession. Each accommodates up to ten people and is equipped with bunk beds, stove, oven, refrigerator and ice chest, barbecue grill, cooking and eating utensils, and a shower. No special boat license is required but you must take instruction on the safe operation of the boat and its equipment from the concessionaire before setting out. Boat prices vary with the season. Other watercraft also for rent. There is also a damage deposit required and you pay for your own gas.

SHOPPING

(To call directly from Del Rio to Acuña, dial 011-52-877 and then the number.)

LANDO CURIOS

Ciudad Acuña, 290 Hidalgo • 2-1269

Mexican crafts, liquor, jewelry, and brass items are just a few of the things you'll find here. Free parking with purchase.

LA RUEDA (THE WHEEL)

Ciudad Acuña, 215 Hidalgo East • 2-1260

The wagon wheel that hangs over the shop entrance is old, but inside much of the stock is modern Mexican designer clothes for women, priced from about $50 to $200.

PANCHO'S MARKET

Ciudad Acuña, 299 Hidalgo East • 2-0466

If you get weary shopping this store for leather goods, liquor, jewelry, clothes, etc., etc., you can take a break in the lounge in the rear. They also advertise prompt curb service.

SIDE TRIPS

SEMINOLE CANYON STATE HISTORICAL PARK

Take US 90 west about 45 miles to Park Rd. 67, just east of the Pecos River Bridge • **(915) 292-4464** • **Open daily 8–10 for day use, at all times for camping** **$2 per person** • **W+ but not all areas**

In the canyon of this 2,173-acre park is Fate Bell Shelter that contains some of North America's oldest pictographs—some believed to be painted 8,000 years ago and considered by many experts to be among the most important rock art finds in the New World. Guided tours of this ancient rock art are conducted Wednesday through Sunday at 10 and 3, weather permitting. Some moderately strenuous hiking is involved, so persons taking the tour should be in good physical condition and wear comfortable shoes. The Visitors Center exhibits depict the life-style of early man based on the rock art and artifacts found in the area. There are picnic areas, RV and tent campsites (fee), and a six-mile (round-trip) hiking trail that leads to a scenic overlook 200-feet above the Rio Grande. For information contact Park Superintendent, P.O. Box 820, Comstock, TX 78837. Just west of the park, on US 90, is the Pecos River Bridge. At 273-feet above the river's normal waterline, this is the highest highway bridge in Texas.

ANNUAL EVENTS

October

FIESTA DE AMISTAD

Various locations in Del Rio • 775-3551 (Chamber of Commerce)
Usually week nearest October 24th • Most events free • W variable
A highlight of this bi-national fiesta is the International Parade from Del Rio to Ciudad Acuña, reportedly the only parade in the world that starts in one country and ends in another. Other activities during the week include the *Senorita Amistad* and Miss Del Rio pageants to choose the Mexican and U.S. ladies who will reign over the Fiesta, the *Abrazo* (friendship embrace) Ceremony, an open house and air show at Laughlin Air Force Base, an arts and crafts show, a bicycle race and a 10K International Run.

RESTAURANTS

($ = under $7, $$ = $8–$17, $$$ = $18–$25, $$$$ = over $25 for one person excluding drinks, tax, and tip. To call directly from Del Rio to Acuña, dial 011-52-877 and then the number.)

ASADERO LA POSTA

Ciudad Acuña, 348 Allende • 2-7427 • Breakfast, lunch, and dinner daily
$–$$ • MC, V • Parking lot across street
Roasted and grilled steaks, beef ribs, and other meats are the house specialty in this cozy, brick-walled restaurant. A special *fajita* plate with onions, quesadillas, and guacamole goes for about $5. Organ music on Friday and Saturday nights. Bar.

AVANTI'S

600 East 12th • 775-3363 • Lunch and dinner Tuesday–Saturday • $–$$ • W+
The chef-owner dishes up Italian food with a difference, like Vodka Pasta. Grilled salmon is usually available on weekends. Beer and wine.

CRIPPLE CREEK SALOON

US 90W about 1 mile north of the "Y" with US 277/377 • 775-0153 • Dinner only Monday–Saturday. Closed Sunday • $$ • MC, V • W • Children's plates
Outside the log cabin-style building there's a small animal farm to entertain the kids. Inside, the kitchen dishes up entrées that include a variety of

mesquite-grilled steaks, swordfish steaks, lobster, shrimp, king crab, catfish, frog legs, and quail. Bar.

CROSBY'S

Ciudad Acuña, 195 Hidalgo • 2-2020 • Breakfast, lunch, and dinner daily $-$$ • MC, V • W

Started in the 1930s, it's still going strong and holding onto its reputation of being one of the best places to eat in Acuña. Inside the etched glass entrance, old photos from the Mexican Revolution and masks from Oaxaca decorate the walls. The menu includes both continental and Mexican entrées ranging from *cabrito* and *fajitas* to seafood, quail and a house specialty: Portuguese Chicken. Bar and piano bar.

LANDO'S RESTAURANT AND BAR

Ciudad Acuña, 270 Hidalgo • 2-5975 • Lunch and dinner daily • Reservations recommended on weekends • $$ • MC, V • W • Secure parking in rear

The walls are covered with elegant wallpaper, the ceiling is mirrored, and there's a chandelier to round out the plush atmosphere. The menu features both Mexican and continental entrées.

MEMO'S

804 E. Losoya • 775-8104 • Lunch and dinner Monday–Saturday, dinner only Sunday • Reservations suggested for Tuesday and Thursday night jam sessions • $-$$ • W

One of the people in the many celebrity photos that line the walls of this Mexican restaurant is always Moises (Blondie) Calderon. Blondie (whose black hair was blonde when he was young), runs the family's restaurant when he's in town, but he is also the band leader and piano player for C&W singer Ray Price, making him a celebrity in his own right. When he's not on the road, Blondie and his local band play on Tuesday and Thursday nights. The food? Well, the family has been serving up Tex-Mex and American dishes here since 1936, so it must be pleasing the customers. Bar.

ACCOMMODATIONS

($ = under $45, $$ = $46–$60, $$$ = $61–$80, $$$$ = $81–$100, $$$$$ = over $100) Room tax 13%

BEST WESTERN INN OF DEL RIO

810 Ave. F (US 90W) • 775-7511 or 800-528-1234 • $$ • No-smoking rooms

This two-story Best Western has 62 rooms including six no-smoking. Senior discount. Cable TV with HBO. Room phones (local calls free). Pets OK (pet charge $3/day). Outdoor pool and whirlpool. Free airport transportation. Free coffee in lobby, free cocktail hour, and free full breakfast. Self-service laundry, same-day dry cleaning. Boat parking.

RAMADA INN

2101 Ave. F. (US 90W) • 775-1511 or 800-2-RAMADA • $$-$$$ No-smoking rooms

A two-story Ramada has 95 units including one suite with jacuzzi ($$$$$) and 27 no-smoking rooms. Children under 18 stay free in room with parents. Package plans available, senior discount, and weekend rates. Cable TV with

HBO and VCR rentals. Room phones (local calls free). Pets OK (pet deposit required). Restaurant, room service, lounge open seven nights with occasional entertainment on weekends. Outdoor heated pool and whirlpool, exercise room. Free transportation to airport and bridge. Self-service laundry and same-day dry cleaning. Boat parking, beauty shop.

Bed and Breakfasts

THE 1890 HOUSE

609 Griner Street (78840) • **775-8061 or 800-282-1360** • **$$$–$$$$$**
Two-story Victorian-style home with four rooms, antique furnishings.

INN ON THE CREEK

Rose Avenue (78840) • **774-6198 or 800-838-7897** • **$$$$$**
One-story home with three guest rooms just outside city limits on San Felipe Creek.

JOHNSON'S LA MANSION DEL RIO

123 Hudson Drive (78840) • **775-9543** • **$$$$–$$$$$**
In the historic Foster House, next to Val Verde Winery. Two-story, four rooms.

GALVESTON

Galveston County Seat • **72,000** • **(409)**
Two miles off the Texas Coast, Galveston Island offers everything from luxury hotels to a carnival-style playland at Stewart Beach Park. There is something to do here, rain or shine. You can swim in the Gulf or water-ski the bayous, wear your bathing suit as you shell and eat shrimp at a restaurant on the seawall or dress up for more formal dining in one of the several first class restaurants, shop on The Strand, admire the intricate craftsmanship of the woodwork in the Bishop's Palace, stroll a tree-shaded street in a historic district, or a path through a rain forest in a glass pyramid at Moody Gardens. Despite an ever-lengthening list of things to do, the two biggest draws for visitors are still the ageless ones: sun and sea. The city is located on one end of a 32-mile long barrier island, which means there are miles and miles of beaches. Visitors often think the gray sand is dirty. Not true. Galveston is in the outwash fan of the Mississippi River; the color comes from river silt mixed with the sand.

Galveston's colorful history goes back to 1528 when it was discovered by Cabeza de Vaca, a Spanish explorer. The discovery, however, was made when he was shipwrecked and kept prisoner for six years by the Karankawa Indians, a fact that may belie that vanished tribe's reputation for cannibalism. The island's name is courtesy of Spanish officials (soldiers were stationed on the island in the mid-1700s) who named it after their boss, Count Bernardo de Galvez. He never even saw the place.

The flags changed—Spanish, French, Mexican—but the island stayed the same until Jean Lafitte, the buccaneer, set up his base there in 1817. Lafitte, who had become an American hero when he came to the aid of General Andrew Jackson at the Battle of New Orleans in the War of 1812, founded the town of Campeche. This was literally a pirates' den from which he and his men ravaged the Spanish ships in the Gulf. He stayed until 1821 when the U.S. Government

GALVESTON

forced him to leave after his men made the undiplomatic mistake of capturing an American ship.

With the pirates gone, settlers arrived from all over. During the Texas War for Independence, Galveston was one of the temporary capitals of the provisional government, and a Galvestonian, Samuel May Williams, was a major financial backer of that revolution. It was also the home port of the Texas Navy's four ships, which prevented a Mexican blockade of the breakaway Republic's coast. After the Texans won, Michael B. Menard bought most of the eastern end of the island from the new government for $50,000 and laid out the townsite with the streets much as they exist today.

The first Customs House was established here in 1836, with Gail Borden, who later invented condensed milk, as Collector of the Port. It is said that Borden also was locally famous for occasionally riding down The Strand on a pet bull.

By the late 1800s, Galveston's natural deep water port had become the third largest in the nation, and The Strand, named after a similar commercial street in London, became known as the "Wall Street of the Southwest." Fortunes were made, elegant homes were built, and the city became a cultural center. Unfortunately, geography is often destiny, and in 1900 disaster struck in the form of a huge hurricane that lashed the low-lying island with devastating winds and tidal waves. At least 6,000 perished in what is still listed as the greatest natural disaster ever to strike North America. The flourishing port, as well as most buildings on the island, was destroyed.

Undaunted, the survivors started to rebuild. But first they had to work out a way to protect their island from future hurricanes. The plan they decided on would take heroic efforts, high purpose, perseverance, and years to complete. They started by building the seawall (originally less than four miles long, now more than ten). Then, behind this protective barrier, they worked for eight years dredging sand from the waterways and using it to raise more than 2,000 buildings and all the streets by some 3 to 17 feet. This prodigious project was severely tested by a storm in 1915 that was reportedly worse than the one in 1900. There were some casualties and some buildings were lost, but overall, the seawall held and the raised city survived.

Not long afterward, Galveston became known as the "Oleander City" because it is home to the world's most extensive collection of that flower. More than 60 varieties still grace the island's green spaces and in spring the city is saturated in color with blooms in a multiple of hues including white, reds, pinks, creams, and yellows. Unlike many seaside resorts, Galveston's mild, semitropical climate, to say nothing of its many events and attractions, makes the island a popular year-round destination.

TOURIST SERVICES

Galveston Island is geared for tourists. Detailed information is available at the Convention and Visitors Bureau and The Strand Visitors Center, but you'll find brochures popping up almost everywhere that give information on sights to see and places to go, and a wide variety of tours are available.

GALVESTON ISLAND CONVENTION AND VISITORS BUREAU

2106 Seawall at 21st (77550), in the Moody Civic Center • 763-4311 or 800-351-4236, Web site: http://intergate.com/wwwmarket/galveston/ or http://www.galvestontourism.com/ • Open daily 8:30–5 • Free W+ back entrance

GALVESTON HISTORICAL FOUNDATION

2016 Strand Street (77550) • Voice 765-7834, fax 765-7834, e-mail: ghf@phoenix.net
The foundation has the low-down on all of the island's many historical attractions as well as events like the annual historic church and home tours.

CARRIAGE TOURS

You can usually hire one of these horse-drawn carriages near The Strand Visitors Center. They offer narrated tours through The Strand, the historic districts, or just about anywhere else you want to go as long as it isn't hazardous to the horse and you're willing to pay for it. **Classic Carriage Tours,** 1604 Ave. M (762-1260), operates every day in summer, but usually only on weekends or during special events, like Dickens on the Strand, in winter. Prices depend on the route and the number of passengers.

THE COLONEL PADDLEWHEELER

At Moody Gardens. *Take Seawall Blvd. to 81st, then right to Jones, left to Hope Blvd. Next to airport* **• 744-1745 • Web site: http://www.moodygardens.com/ 763-4666 • April–Labor Day: 2-day cruises daily, dinner/jazz cruise Tuesday–Saturday, moonlight cruise Saturday only. Cruises on weekends only**

September–March. Call for times • Day cruises: adults $8, children (4–12) $4, dinner/jazz cruises: adults: $24, children (under 12) $15, moonlight cruise: adults only $8 • W • Free parking Strand at 25th.

Actually a floating period museum built in Mississippi for the nonprofit Moody Foundation at a cost of $3 million, this authentic reproduction of an 1860s stern wheeler is named in honor of Colonel W. L. Moody, a Virginian who came to Texas in 1854 to practice law. The Colonel is 152 feet long and holds up to 800 passengers on its three public decks. Sightseeing cruises last about two hours. Call for information on sailing times.

GALVESTON HISTORICAL FOUNDATION TOUR SERVICE

2016 Strand • Web site: http://www.galvestontourism.com/ • 765-7834
Fees vary by tour • W

Now that the members of the foundation have helped save much of historic Galveston, they welcome the opportunity to show visitors around. Call for details on their various tours.

GALVESTON ISLAND TROLLEY

216 28th, loops from the Moody Civic Center at Seawall and 21st to the Strand area and back • For schedule information call 765-7992 (Convention and Visitors Bureau) • Adults 60¢ each way, children and seniors 30¢

These are replicas of the fixed-rail commuter trolleys used here in the early 1900s. The round trip up Rosenberg Ave. from the Seawall to the Strand and back takes about one hour, and you can get on or off at any stop.

THE STRAND VISITORS CENTER

2016 Strand • Website: http://www.galvestontourism.com/ • 765-7834
Open daily 9:30–5. Extended hours in summer. Closed Christmas and Thanksgiving • Free • W ramp to see free movie

This should be your first stop when you hit The Strand. It's another project of the Galveston Historical Foundation whose office is upstairs.

TREASURE ISLAND TOUR TRAIN

Departs from Moody Civic Center, Seawall and 21st • 761-2618 • Daily. Number of tours vary from two a day in low season to nine a day in summer. Call for tour times • Adults about $4, children about $2.50 • W

A pink-awninged, open-air train carries up to 64 passengers on a leisurely 17-mile narrated trip that takes about an hour-and-a-half to cover the highlights of both old and new Galveston.

BIRD'S-EYE VIEW

AMERICAN NATIONAL OBSERVATION AREA

American National Insurance Building, 20th and Market • 766-6642
Monday– Saturday 10–5, Sunday noon–5 • Adults $2, children (7–18), seniors $1, children 6 and under free • W

You can see the historic districts and much of the island from this observation area on the 20th floor of Galveston's tallest building.

ISLAND (FLIGHT) CENTER

2115 Terminal Drive, Scholes Field Executive Terminal • 740-1223
(Call for directions)

See the island from the air. Light planes can give you a bird's-eye view of the city and a wide area around it on a one-hour flight that costs about $60 for up to three passengers.

MUSEUMS

GALVESTON COUNTY HISTORICAL MUSEUM

2219 Market (Ave. D) • 766-2340 • Memorial Day to Labor Day: Monday–Saturday 10–5, Sunday noon–5, rest of year closes one hour earlier • Donation $1

Housed in a narrow old bank building, built in 1919, the exhibits in this compact museum tell the story of Galveston County, the Civil War Battle of Galveston, and the devastating 1900 hurricane. There is also an exhibit on Nicholas Clayton, the architect who changed the face of the city in the late 1800s by designing such landmarks as the Bishop's Palace, Old Red, and about 50 other buildings that survived the 1900 hurricane. The museum is downtown, so parking space can be difficult to find. Try parking on the less-trafficked streets to the east or between the museum and The Strand.

LONE STAR FLIGHT MUSEUM

2002 Terminal Dr. (Scholes Field) • 740-7722, e-mail: rcecil@avdigest.com Open daily 10–5, except closed Thanksgiving and Christmas • Adults $6, children under 13 and seniors $2.50 • W+

Thirty-four splendidly restored vintage aircraft from this museum's growing collection are on display in the 68,000-sq.-ft., air-conditioned hangar. Most are flyable World War II era aircraft and include a B-17 Flying Fortress, a B-25, and a P-38. Gift shop.

MOODY MANSION AND MUSEUM

2618 Broadway • 762-7668 • Tours Monday–Saturday 10–4, Sunday 1–4:30 Adults $6, seniors $5, children 6–18 $3, under 6 free • W ground floor only

On a boulevard known for its handsome residences, the Moody Mansion stands out as one of the finest. The 32-room limestone and brick building, built around 1895, was acquired by William L. Moody, Jr., after the Galveston hurricane of 1900. Entrepreneurs in the cotton trade and banking, the Moodys became one of the wealthiest and most powerful families in Texas. The mansion was one of the first houses in Texas to be constructed on a steel frame, and it also was equipped to take advantage of the first electrical power plant in the state. Restored to its original splendor by the Moody Foundation, it is furnished to reflect activities that may have taken place on the day and evening of Mary Moody Northern's debut party, December 12, 1911. Tours take about one hour. Gift shop.

THE RAILROAD MUSEUM

123 Rosenberg (25th St) at the west end of The Strand • 765-5700 • Open daily 10–5, Wednesday 10–4, except Thanksgiving and Christmas • Adults $5, children $2.50, seniors $4.50 • W+ • Free parking at entrance on Santa Fe Place, 1 block west of Rosenberg

Located in the old art deco Santa Fe railroad station, two of the museum's prize exhibits are the waiting room, set up with more than 30 life-sized sculptures of travelers frozen in a moment in time in the 1930s, and the largest collection of vintage railroad locomotives and cars in the Southwest is displayed on the station's tracks. Other attractions include an imaginative sound and light show that covers the island's history from its discovery to the present, and a working scale model of the Port of Galveston (that kids can pop their heads up in plastic bubbles in the middle of and watch the model trains run around them). Among the collection of rail cars is the "Anacapa," a luxurious private car from the 1920s.

TEXAS SEAPORT MUSEUM AND *ELISSA*

**Pier 21 off water (Port Industrial Blvd.), near The Strand • 763-1877
Open daily 10–5, extended hours in summer • Admission
Museum W+, *Elissa* W deck only • Parking nearby**

The story of the search for the *Elissa,* an iron-hulled sailing vessel, is almost as fascinating as a visit to the ship itself. The Galveston Historical Foundation wanted a ship to represent that city's role as an important nineteenth-century port. The long search ended in Piraeus, Greece, where they found the *Elissa,* a 150-foot square-rigged barque that had called at Galveston several times in the 1880s. She was a tramp merchant ship carrying cargoes to more than a hundred different ports from the day she was launched from a Scottish shipyard in 1877 until 1970 when she made her last voyage carrying a load of smuggled cigarettes. Towed back to Galveston, she was restored at a cost of more than $4.5 million. *Elissa,* now a National Historic Landmark, is the third-oldest ship afloat—giving way only to England's Cutty Sark and the Star of India berthed in San Diego. Although well over a century old, she still is sailed at least once a year, which may make her the only operational nineteenth-century sailing ship in the world. A multimedia show in the museum theater gives you a simulated experience of sailing this tall ship. The museum also features exhibits depicting the maritime history of Galveston and a viewing platform where you can watch the activities in the working port. A second multimedia show, *The Great Storm,* tells the story of the 1900 disaster. Call 765-7834 for information. Gift shop.

HISTORIC PLACES

The Galveston Historical Foundation's properties include Ashton Villa, the Texas Seaport Museum and *Elissa,* the Galveston County Historical Museum, the St. Joseph's Church Museum, and the 1839 Williams Home. Discount combination tickets for visits to several of these historic places are available at The Strand Visitors Center or any of the Foundation properties.

ASHTON VILLA

2328 Broadway • 762-3933 • Open Monday–Saturday 10–4 and Sunday 12–4, except Thanksgiving and Christmas • Tours daily: Monday–Saturday 10–4, Sunday noon–4. Extended hours in summer • Adults $4.50, children and seniors $3.50 • W first floor • Parking in rear

This gracious Italianate mansion was built in 1859 during Galveston's reign as the leading seaport of the Southwest. The three-story structure is furnished with possessions of the James M. Brown family, the original owners, and other authentic antiques of the mid-1800s. The hour-long tour covers the dramatic history of Victorian Galveston and the part the Brown family and this home played in that era when it was a focal point for local society. It includes the gigantic projects of building the seawall and raising the elevation of the city. The Villa is listed in the National Register of Historic Places. Gift shop.

THE BISHOP'S PALACE

1402 Broadway • 762-2475 • May 31 to Labor Day: tours Monday–Saturday 10–5, Sunday noon–5, rest of year: tours Wednesday–Monday 12–4, closed Tuesday
Adults $5, children over 13 $3, under 13 $1, seniors $4 • Parking on street

Beautiful examples of the attention to detail that was the hallmark of the old-time craftsmen abound in Galveston, but nowhere is there a greater concentration of them in one place than in the Bishop's Palace. This grandiose home is often considered the crowning achievement of the well-known Galveston architect Nicholas Clayton, whose body of work left a lasting stamp on the city. Completed in 1886, it cost an estimated quarter of a million dollars and took seven years to build. The American Institute of Architecture included this home on its list of the hundred most architecturally significant buildings in the United States, the only residence in Texas to receive this honor. Originally called the Gresham House, after the first owner, its name was changed in 1923 when the Catholic Diocese of Galveston-Houston purchased it for the bishop's residence, a role it still serves when the bishop is in Galveston. The tour lasts approximately one hour.

EAST END HISTORIC DISTRICT

11th to 19th between Mechanic (Ave. C) and Broadway (Ave. J)

This area is where the well-to-do of the city lived from the late 1800s through the early 1900s. A few homes here date back as far as the 1850s, but most were built between 1875 and the turn of the century. The entire district is listed in the National Register of Historic Places and designated a National Historic Landmark. The best way to enjoy the architectural beauty of this 40-block district is to stop first at the Convention and Visitors Bureau or The Strand Visitors Center and pick up a riding and walking tour map.

1839 SAMUEL MAY WILLIAMS HOME

3601 Ave. P (Bernardo de Galvez) • 765-1839 • Open daily except
Thanksgiving and Christmas: Monday–Saturday 10–4, Sunday noon–4
Adults $3, children 7–18 $2.50, under 7 free • W

One of the oldest houses on the island, it is a prime example of a early 1800s prefabricated house—built in Maine then carefully taken apart and shipped to Galveston where it was reassembled. It was the home of a relatively unknown man who worked behind the scenes in the War for Texas Independence and is often called both the Father of the Texas Navy and the Father of Texas Banking. The home comes to life through a multi-image show and audio presentations in each room that tell the story of Williams and his place in Texas history.

SILK STOCKING HISTORIC DISTRICT

Along 24th and 25th between Ave. L and Ave. O

Its name supposedly came from the time when only the well-to-do ladies could afford silk stockings, and most of the ladies in the district were well-to-do. Excellent examples of nineteenth-century architecture in this district include the **Sweeny-Royston House** at 24th and Ave. L, designed by popular architect, Nicholas Clayton, and listed in the National Register of Historic Places.

STRAND HISTORIC DISTRICT

20th to 25th between water (Ave. A) and Mechanic (Ave. C)

Many cities have lost the battle to save their downtown areas from urban rot. Galveston is one city that won that battle. Instead of tearing down the old buildings, the civic-minded have turned the very age of the buildings into a tourist attraction. The restoration of most of the iron-front buildings in just a six-block section of this avenue has led to a rebirth of the whole area. When King Cotton reigned supreme and Galveston was the port on the Texas coast, the Strand was rightly called the "Wall Street of the Southwest." No longer lined with banks, cotton brokers, and commercial houses, it is now a sightseers' and shoppers' delight with shops and restaurants for every taste and pocketbook. To get the most from your visit, stop first at The Strand Visitors Center (*see* Tourist Services) and pick up a walking tour brochure.

OTHER POINTS OF INTEREST

GALVESTON ISLAND STATE PARK

West Beach, 14901 FM 3005 (Seawall Blvd.) near 13 Mile Rd. • Web site: http://www.tpwd.state.tx.us/park/parks.htm • 737-1222 • $2 per person per day W but not all areas

The 2,000 acres of this park cut across the narrow center of the island taking in a 1.6 mile beach on the Gulf on one side and the marshes on Galveston Bay on the other. Facilities are provided for surf-fishing on the beach and wade-fishing in the marshes, swimming, picnicking, camping (fee), birdwatching, and nature walks. The Mary Moody Northern Amphitheater, which features outdoor musicals in summer, adjoins the park on the bay side. For information write Route 1, Box 156A, Galveston 77551.

MOODY GARDENS

Take Seawall Blvd. to 81st, then right to Jones, left to Hope Blvd. Next to airport • 744-1745, Web site: http://www.moody gardens.com/ • Hours of **various facilities differ, call • Admission to some facilities • W+**

The Moody Foundation is currently developing a world-class education, recreation, and therapy complex. The 142-acre, $150-million project is scheduled to be completed in eight phases, with the year 2006 as the target date for completion. Currently open to the public is the 50,000-square foot **Moody Convention and Conference Center; Palm Beach,** a sparkling white sand beach with fresh water lagoons and tropical setting; **Seaside Safari,** an animal-assisted therapy facility that offers year-round public tours of its exotic grounds; the **Rainforest Pyramid,** a huge greenhouse growing replicas of the major tropical forests of the world, and an IMAX theatre with 3-D capabilities; and **The Discovery Pyramid,** an interactive outer space experience.

PORT OF GALVESTON

Along Water Street on north side of the island from 9th to 41st

Banana boats, shrimpers, grain carriers, container ships, and even cruise ships—they all use this port that claims to have the fastest access to the open seas of any major American port. For a better understanding of port operations, see the working scale model in the Railroad Museum (*see* Museums, above).

ROSENBERG LIBRARY

2310 Ave. I (Sealy), immediately behind Ashton Villa • 763-8854 • Monday–Thursday 9–9, Friday–Saturday 9–6 • Free • W ramp in alley • Parking at Ave. H (Ball) and 24th

The Rosenberg is the oldest Texas public library in continuous operation and one of the oldest in the Southwest. It also houses several art and history galleries, a rare book room, and the Galveston and Texas History Center. The extensive archives of the history center include Galveston newspapers starting in 1844 and a letter from Andrew Jackson to Sam Houston. Among the architectural drawings on file are those of Nicholas Clayton who designed approximately 120 buildings in the city between 1872 and the early 1900s, including the Bishop's Palace. Some of the special facilities have different open hours from the main library. Call for schedule.

THE SEAWALL

Starting near the east end of the island and stretching about 10 miles west

In addition to its protective role, the seawall is also a monument to the spirit of the Galvestonians who say this city is worth saving at any cost. After the devastating hurricane of 1900, in which more than 6,000 died, the city decided to build the seawall and, using sand dredged from the bayous and waterways, raise the elevation of the entire city. Those projects took eight years, but they worked and are still working. The first seawall was less than four miles long, but it has been slowly lengthened over the years and now protects about one third of the island from the Gulf's surf. One of the engineers who worked on the original design was Brigadier General Henry M. Roberts, who is more famous for his *Robert's Rules of Order*. The solid concrete wall was constructed to the height of 17 feet above mean low tide. Seawall Boulevard, behind it, is one of the island's best known streets and is lined with hotels, motels, restaurants, and shops. The seawall also claims the title of the world's longest continuous sidewalk, which makes it great for strolling, jogging, bicycling, skateboarding, and roller skating.

SEAWOLF PARK

Take 51st St. causeway to Pelican Island, continue on approximately 2 miles **744-5738 • Open daily dawn to dusk • Parking $2; fishing: adults $2, children $1; tour of ships: adults $2, children $1 • W+ except for ship tour**

Fishing from the rocks or the 380-foot fishing pier, an imaginative children's playground, picnic areas, a snack bar, an observation deck, and two World War II combat ships to explore—all are available in this park. One of the ships you can climb all over is the submarine *USS Cavalla*. The other is the *USS Stewart,* a destroyer escort that had the unusual distinction of sailing under both the U.S. and Japanese flags in World War II. Originally a U.S. ship, the Navy had attempted to scuttle her to prevent capture by the Japanese. Refloated by the Japanese, they sent her out as one of their own. Reports of an enemy ship that "looks like one of ours" were explained when the *Stewart* was found in Japan at the end of the war. From the upper level of the three-level pavilion you can see the Port of Galveston, the University of Texas Medical Branch, the many ships plying the Houston Ship Channel, the Bolivar Ferry on its route from Point Bolivar to its landing on Galveston Island, and the Texas City Dike.

SPORTS AND ACTIVITIES
Birdwatching

Galveston is noted for the wide variety of species observed including black shouldered kites, American oystercatchers, roseate spoonbills, herons, white-wing doves, and white and brown pelicans. Nearby Bolivar Flats is famous for waders and shorebirds including flocks of avocets. Galveston Island State Park has observation points for birdwatchers (*see* Other Points of Interest).

Boating

You can boat in Galveston Bay, the bayous, or the Gulf. For information on boat rental and charter firms, marinas, and public and commercial boat ramps contact the Convention and Visitors Bureau (*see* Tourist Services).

Fishing

Take your pick. There's fishing in the bay, the surf, off the piers, the jetties, and offshore in the Gulf. Some 52 varieties of saltwater fish populate the warm waters along and offshore from the island. Several charter and party boats operate daily from the docks around Pier 19 and the Yacht Basin. Several commercial piers and numerous rock groin piers extend well into the Gulf from the beachfront. Most commercial piers charge about $2, are lighted for night fishing, and have rental tackle and bait available. For fishing information contact the Convention and Visitors Bureau (*see* Tourist Services).

Greyhound Racing

GULF GREYHOUND PARK
LaMarque, 1 block east of I-45 South at FM 2004 and FM 1764 (Exit 15)
986-9500 800-ASK-2WIN • Tuesday–Sunday evenings at 7:30, Wednesday,
Saturday–Sunday matinees at 1:30. Closed December 24 and 25 only
Grandstand $1, lounge level $4, clubhouse level $4. Parking $1, valet
parking $3 • W+ but not all areas
You have your choice of four levels, all enclosed and air conditioned, on which to watch the dogs run. The grandstands, seating about 6,000, are on the first two levels. A lounge seating 500 is on level three and the clubhouse, seating 1,900, on level four. And with more than 300 teller windows, there should be no problem placing a bet.

Scuba Diving

Many good spots are near the offshore oil rigs that sit out in the Gulf from one to fifty miles away. The watery wonderland of the 500-acre live coral reef National Marine Sanctuary called the Flower Garden Banks is 120 miles offshore. For information contact any of the dive shops listed in the phone book.

Swimming

There are 32 miles of Gulf beaches on Galveston Island, and every mile is public. Lifeguards are provided at designated areas by the Galveston County Sheriff's Department Beach Patrol. There is an admission charge at some parks. Restrooms and other facilities are available at the following parks:

R. A. Apffel Beach Park, Seawall and Boddecker (extreme eastern end of island), 763-0166. Facilities include an 11,000 square foot recreation center.

Stewart Beach Park, Seawall near Broadway, 765-5023 (*see* Kids' Stuff). Pavilion and amusement park.

Galveston County Beach Pocket Parks: *Beach Park #1,* FM 3005 at 7½ Mile Road; *Beach Park #2,* FM 3005 at 9½ Mile Road; *Beach Park #3,* FM 3005 at 11 Mile Road.

Galveston Island State Park, FM 3005 (Seawall Blvd.) at 13 Mile Road (*see* Other Points of Interest).

And if the Gulf doesn't satisfy you, you can go to the man-made **Palm Beach at Moody Gardens.** *(Take Seawall Blvd to 81st, right on Jones, left on Hope Blvd.* Admission. Phone 744-PALM.) Sparkling white sand from Orlando, Florida was brought in by ocean barges for this beach located on crystal-clear freshwater lagoons complete with tropical landscaping. Also Texas-sized Jacuzzis, volleyball courts, paddleboats, and a children's area with water slides. Open daily May through Labor Day.

COLLEGES AND UNIVERSITIES

GALVESTON COLLEGE

Administration: 4015 Ave. Q; Fort Crockett Campus: 5001 Ave. U (*take 53rd north from Seawall to Ave. U)* • 763-6551 • W variable

This community college offers a wide variety of academic and vocational/technical programs to its more than 2,400 students. Visitors are welcome at musical concerts and at drama productions given in the Upper Deck Theatre, a 150-seat arena theater on the third floor of the Fort Crockett building. There are usually four or five productions during the October–May season, including some dinner theater performances at the San Luis Hotel. For information and reservations call 744-9661.

TEXAS A&M UNIVERSITY AT GALVESTON

Mitchell Campus: *take 51st St. causeway north to Pelican Island, campus on right;* Fort Crockett campus: Ave. U and 51st, next to Galveston College campus • 740-4400, Web site: http://www.tamu.edu/ • W variable

This branch of A&M trains students in marine-oriented programs and as officers for the U.S. Merchant Marines. The biggest attraction for visitors is the training ship *Chauvenet.* A former U.S. Navy hydrographic research vessel, the 393-foot ship serves as a dormitory and floating classroom in winter, and the summer training ship for the maritime cadets at the school who are required to complete three cruises in preparation for Merchant Marine licensing. The ship is usually in port from early September to late April and visitors are welcome aboard on most weekend afternoons. For information, contact the Public Information Office at 740-4559.

THE UNIVERSITY OF TEXAS MEDICAL BRANCH (UTMB)

Between Strand and Market from 4th to 14th. Visitor Information Center at 6th and Market • Voice: 772-3800, fax: 772-6424, Web site: http://www.utmb.edu • W variable

Starting with a class of 23 in 1891, UTMB now has about 2,100 students enrolled in its four schools: School of Medicine, School of Nursing, School of Biomedical Sciences, and School of Allied Health Sciences. The largest, as well as the oldest, medical school in the state, it offers a full spectrum of health care services in its seven hospitals and 85 specialty and sub-specialty outpatient clinics. The major architectural attraction on the campus is another structure designed by Nicholas Clayton, the **Ashbel Smith Building** at 916 Strand. Fondly called "Old Red," for its red sandstone exterior, it was completed in 1890 and is listed in the National Register of Historic Places. A visit to this building is included in the UTMB campus tours usually offered weekdays between 9 and 4.

PERFORMING ARTS

GALVESTON ISLAND OUTDOOR MUSICALS

Mary Moody Northern Amphitheatre, Galveston Island State Park, FM 3005 (Seawall Blvd.) at 13 Mile Rd. • 737-3440, Web site: http://www.intergate.com/wwwmarket/galveston/theater/ • Usually mid-May to late-August, Monday–Saturday at 8 P.M. • Adults $10–$22, children $4–$10 W call ahead

This 1,800 seat outdoor theater is the setting for the revivals of big and classic Broadway musicals that are especially appropriate for the large outdoor stage like "The Sound of Music" and "Fiddler on the Roof." The amphitheatre restaurant, decorated with theater memorabilia, is open before the show.

THE 1894 GRAND OPERA HOUSE

2020 Post Office (Ave. E) near 21st • 765-1894 or 800-821-1894, Web site: http://intergate.com/wwwmarket/galveston/opera • Admission depends on event • AE, MC, V • W+

Painstakingly restored, this grand old building is now as close in design as possible to the original house where Sarah Bernhardt, Paderewski, Anna Pavlova, George Burns and Gracie Allen, and other greats performed. It features double curved balconies and no seat is further than 70 feet from the stage. Everything from ballet and opera to rock and pop concerts and classic films are performed here now. The **Galveston Symphony** performs most of its concerts here during its September to May season. Open Monday–Saturday 9–5 and Sunday noon to 5 for self-guided tours (Admission). Conducted tours can be arranged for groups. Parking is a slight problem during major productions. It's first come, first park on the street, or there is a pay garage at 21st and Market (Ave. D).

STRAND STREET THEATRE

2317 Ship Mechanic Row (Ave. C) • 763-4591 • Admission varies by performance • W

Galveston's only year-round, professional repertory company produces about seven shows a year in this intimate playhouse that seats 110. Most are dramas and comedies, but occasionally they put on a musical. Performances are usually Thursday through Saturday at 8 and a Sunday matinee.

SHOPPING

BASTIEN'S

2317 Strand • 765-9394

If your appreciation of the beauty of stained glass is heightened after visiting the Bishop's Palace or some other Victorian home in Galveston, this is the place to go. Usually there are only small, decorative stained glass pieces on display—among the giftware of crystal, lace, and potpourri—but larger pieces can be made to order. The studio is in the rear, and sometimes you can watch the artists at work through the half door.

DON ROUSE'S WILDLIFE GALLERY

2314 Strand • 763-1391 • W

They claim this is Texas' largest selection of wildlife art and gifts, and they may be right. The favorite subjects seem to be ducks and other waterfowl, which appear on everything from doormats to collector plates to jewelry to duck stamp prints.

HENDLEY MARKET

2010 Strand • 762-2610 • W

This next-door neighbor of The Strand Visitors Center is worth a drop-in. Housed in one of the city's oldest commercial buildings, the shop offers a delightfully eclectic collection of Victorian clothing (a place to go for authentic costumes for the annual celebration of "Dickens on the Strand"), tintypes, old photos, South American folk art, Mexican toys, antiques, and old maps, books, and magazines.

THE OLD PEANUT BUTTER WAREHOUSE

100 20th, just north of The Strand • 762-8358 • W variable

You can still get peanut butter here, in the Peanut Pantry, but most of the items in this 22,000-square-foot assemblage of shops are antiques, collectibles, gifts, and souvenirs.

KIDS' STUFF

STEWART BEACH PARK

Seawall at Broadway • 765-5023, Web site: http://www.galveston.com/ W variable

It's like a miniature Coney Island. Attractions include water slides, bumper cars and bumper boats, miniature golf, go-karts, pavilion with bathhouse, restaurant, and concessions. The amusement area is open daily from 9 to 8:30 in summer and 9 to dusk in winter, except from November to mid-February when it's closed. Cost of rides vary. Parking $5.

SEASIDE SAFARI

Moody Gardens. *Take Seawall Blvd to 81st, then right on Jones and left on Hope Blvd.* **• 744-PETT • Daily 10–5 except closed Thanksgiving, Christmas, and New Year's • Admission • W+**

Designed to provide animal-assisted therapy, this facility also offers year-round tours. Developed around an African theme, Seaside Safari offers a stimulating, educational, and "fun" 45-minute tour. A llama, pigs, goats, sheep, and an African hedgehog are just a few of the animals to see here. The manicured topiary gardens, mineral and crystal deposits, and luscious landscaping add to the enjoyment of the tour.

SIDE TRIPS

BOLIVAR PENINSULA

This peninsula is a narrow strip sandwiched between the Gulf and East Galveston Bay that goes for about 30 miles from Port Bolivar, across the Houston Ship Channel from Galveston, to High Island. To reach it, take the free Bolivar Ferry from the north end of Ferry Rd. in Galveston. The only road on the peninsula is TX 87, which actually goes all the way along the coast from Port Bolivar to Sabine Pass, but because it is built just behind an eroding beach, it's not always open past High Island. At High Island TX 87 intersects with TX 124, which goes north past the Anahuac Wildlife Refuge to Winnie at I-10. The four small towns on the peninsula—made up mainly of beach houses—are Crystal Beach, Gilcrist, High Island, and Port Bolivar. Fishing and other beach activities are the main things here.

CLEAR LAKE AREA

Armand Bayou Nature Center
Bayou Wildlife Park
Clear Lake *Queen*
  See Clear Lake.

ANNUAL EVENTS

February

MARDI GRAS FESTIVAL

Various locations around the city • Approximately two weeks in February ending the Sunday before Ash Wednesday • 763-4311 (Convention and Visitors Bureau) • Free. Admission to some events • W variable

It's not as big as the New Orleans bash *yet*, but it's growing and already draws close to a quarter million spectators and participants. The two weeks of pre-Lenten festivities include ten parades, masked balls, art exhibits, pageants, costume contests, and entertainment. The biggest night is the final Saturday before Ash Wednesday when the Grand Night Momus Parade goes from Seawall Blvd. to the Strand, and a series of costumed and masked balls are held.

May

HISTORIC HOMES TOURS

765-7834 (Galveston Historical Foundation) • Web site: http://www.galveston.com/ • 2 weekends early in month $14 (Advance sale tickets $12) • W variable

Seven or eight restored nineteenth-century homes are usually on each tour. These are private homes not normally open to the public. You must get from home to home on your own, but at each home you are given a guided tour. Tied in are special events and activities that are either free or discounted to ticket holders.

November

GALVESTON ISLAND JAZZ FESTIVAL

Various locations • 763-1894 or 763-7080 • Friday–Sunday in mid-month Most day activities free. Night performances admission varies with performer • W variable

Nationally famous jazz greats are among the musicians who play during this three-day festival. Free concerts are put on in Old Galveston Square on The Strand and other outdoor locations. Other shows (admission) are held at places like the 1894 Grand Opera House and on the paddlewheeler *The Colonel*. Many of the larger hotels/motels feature jazz performances in their lounges.

December

DICKENS ON THE STRAND

Strand Historic District • 765-7834 (Galveston Historical Foundation)
Usually first Saturday–Sunday in month • Adults $6, children (over 6) $3
(lower prices for advance sale tickets) • W variable

A pre-Christmas festival in which The Strand area is turned into an authentic re-creation of its namesake in London as it was during the nineteenth century. Free entertainment is provided almost continuously on seven stages scattered throughout the area, and you'll likely see English bobbies chasing pickpockets, street performers and street vendors, two parades a day, strolling carolers, and Scrooge and other characters from Dickens's stories wandering through the crowd. The streets are blocked off to car traffic and only horse-drawn vehicles, other "beasts of burden," and bicycles are allowed. The thousands of volunteers who work on the festival wear period costumes and you can get in free if you wear a Victorian costume—and there are prizes for the best. The Dickens Handbell Festival, held Saturday evening near The Strand Visitors Center, is reportedly the world's largest outdoor handbell event.

OFFBEAT

COLONEL BUBBIE'S STRAND SURPLUS SENTER

2202 Strand • 762-7397 • Monday–Saturday 10–4 "usually"

This warehouse-type building, designed by Nicholas Clayton (who else?), is stacked with surplus from the armed forces of more than 50 different countries. REAL military surplus—no fakes here—with bargains like wool sweaters from the British Navy, shorts from the German Army, and Danish Army sheepskin hats. Few countries skimp on quality in military uniforms, so all-wool and 100 percent cotton items abound. There's not much space inside, the packed aisles are narrow and twisting, but a visit to Colonel Bubbie's bonanza is an experience every bargain shopper should have.

RESTAURANTS

($ = under $7, $$ = $8–$17, $$$ = $18–$25, $$$$ = over $25 for one person excluding drinks, tax, and tip.)

Putting on the Ritz

THE MERCHANT PRINCE

Tremont House, 2300 Ship's Mechanic Row • 763-0300 • Breakfast and lunch daily, dinner Wednesday–Sunday • $$–$$$$ • Cr

The light that falls from the glass ceiling, 65 feet above, casts a warm glow over the dining room with tables surrounding a fountain. The tasteful decor and elegance carries over to the mostly continental menu that offers gourmet choices from pasta to seafood. Bar.

THE WENTLETRAP

2301 Strand at Tremont • 765-5545 • Lunch and dinner Monday–Saturday, Sunday brunch • Reservations suggested for dinner on weekends • $$$–$$$$ Cr • W

There is a bright and airy feeling to the restored 1871 building that is the home of this restaurant. The staff is well-trained and attentive and the continental menu is equal to the ambiance. Selections vary by season, but among the seafood choices you are likely to find Trout Capucine (sauteed with mushrooms, shrimp and capers). Other choices include Veal Oscar (topped with king crab and hollandaise) and rack of lamb. Valet parking. Jackets required for men at dinner. Bar.

Italian

NASH D'AMICO'S PASTA AND CLAM BAR

2328 Strand • 763-6500 • Lunch and dinner daily • $$–$$$ • AE, MC, V

The homemade pasta comes in a variety of forms from fettuccine to ravioli and combined with seafood, chicken, or veal to make up entrées that offer the taste of Italy. The setting was once a staid old bank building but now is decorated in keeping with the space age. Bar.

Mexican

EL NAPALITO

614 42nd St. between Church (Ave. F) and Winnie (Ave. G). *Take Broadway to 41st, then right on 41st, left on Winnie and right on 42nd* **• 763-9815 Breakfast and lunch Tuesday–Sunday. Closed Monday • $ • No Cr • W**

Another café where the attention is given to the food not the decor. Definitely not in the tourist area, and because 42nd is not a through street, a little hard to find, but, if you are a Tex-Mex devotee, you'll welcome the Martinez family cooking of classics like *huevos rancheros* for breakfast or chicken mole or chile relleno for lunch. Beer and wine coolers.

Seafood

BENNO'S ON THE BEACH

Seawall at 12th • 762-4621 • Lunch and dinner daily • $–$$ • MC, V • W

It may look like a fast food place, but the emphasis here is definitely on feed not speed. One of the best buys on the beachfront is their boiled shrimp served with seasoned corn. Almost everything is done with a touch of Cajun, but if you want more than just a touch of that spicy cuisine try the Peppered Shrimp or Cajun Crabs. Beer.

CHRISTIE'S BEACHCOMBER

Stewart Beach, Seawall and 4th • 762-8648 • Lunch and dinner Monday–Saturday • $$ • MC, V • W

Two things that set this restaurant apart are its location right on the beach and its luncheon buffet that has long been a favorite of both locals and visitors making return trips to the island. Bar.

CLARY'S

8509 Teichman, across from the *Galveston Daily News. Take Teichman exit off I-45* **• 740-0771 • Lunch and dinner Monday–Friday, dinner only Saturday, closed Sunday and last 2 weeks in November • Reservations suggested $$–$$$ • MC, V • W call ahead**

There's a Cajun touch to many of the dishes, like Shrimp au Seasoned, but the spices are so expertly handled that it's more of a pleasant hint than the more common overpowering spicy taste. The seafood platter, broiled or grilled, is a house specialty, but you have to ask for it; it's not on the menu. Jackets suggested for men at dinner. Bar.

GAIDO'S

3828 Seawall • 762-9625 • Lunch and dinner daily • $$–$$$$ • AE, MC, V W • Children's plates

This family restaurant has something in common with the stately Hotel Galvez—they both opened in 1911 and are still going strong. If you don't believe it, just look at the line to get in on weekends. The lure, of course, is the emphasis put on making the best possible use of fresh local seafood instead of the frozen or processed product. The freshest catch is always listed on typed sheets in the menu. If you're over 65, they offer a moderately priced senior dinner that includes everything from appetizer to dessert. An indication of the high esteem Galvestonians hold for this restaurant's founder is on the street sign outside—39th St. is also called Mike Gaido Blvd. Bar.

ACCOMMODATIONS

Hotels and Motels

As a beach resort, Galveston has high and low seasons. Rates given are for a double in high season, which runs from about the middle of May to the middle of September and during certain special events like Mardi Gras. Rates usually drop considerably in low season.

($ = under $45, $$ = $46–$60, $$$ = $61–$80, $$$$ = $81–$100, $$$$$ = over $100)

Room tax 13%

FLAGSHIP HOTEL

2501 Seawall • 762-9000 or 800-392-6542, e-mail: flagship@galveston.com $$$$–$$$$$ • W+ 5 rooms • No-smoking rooms

This seven-story hotel has 230 units that include nine suites ($$$$$) and 25 no-smoking rooms. Children under 18 stay free in room with parents. Package plans and senior discount available. Cable and satellite TV with HBO and Showtime. Room phones (charge for local calls). Pets OK ($50 deposit). Two restaurants, room service, lounge open seven nights with entertainment Tuesday–Saturday. Outdoor pool and sauna. Guest memberships available for golf. Free transportation anywhere on the island. Same-day dry cleaning. On a steel and concrete pier jutting out into the Gulf, reportedly the only hotel in America built entirely over water.

HOTEL GALVEZ-GRAND HERITAGE

2024 Seawall • 765-7721 or in Texas 800-392-4285, e-mail: galvez@phoenix.net
$$$$–$$$$$ • W+ 4 rooms • No-smoking rooms

This eight-story hotel has 228 units including three suites ($$$$$) and 34 no-smoking rooms. Children under 12 stay free in room with parents. Package plans and senior discount available. Cable TV with HBO and pay channel. Room phones (charge for local calls). No pets. Restaurant, room service, lounge open seven nights with entertainment six nights in high season. Outdoor pool and indoor pool, indoor whirlpool, sauna, game room. Guest memberships available in country club and racquet club. Free transportation on the island. Same-day dry cleaning. Gift shop. Often called the Grand Old Lady of Galveston, this luxury hotel, built in 1911, has been restored to recapture its colorful past.

HOLIDAY INN ON THE BEACH

5002 Seawall • 740-3581 or 800-HOLIDAY, Web site: http://www.holiday-inn.com/ • $$$$–$$$$$ • W+ 2 rooms • No-smoking rooms

This eight-story Holiday Inn offers 178 units that include two suites ($$$$$) and 30 no-smoking rooms. Children under 18 stay free in parent's room. Package plans and senior discount available. Cable TV with HBO. Room phones (charge for local calls). No pets. Restaurant, room service, lounge open seven nights with entertainment Tuesday–Saturday. Outdoor pool, exercise room, and sauna. Self-service laundry and same-day dry cleaning. Gift shop. All rooms have Gulf view.

LA QUINTA MOTOR INN

1402 Seawall • 744-1500 or 800-392-5937, Web site:
http://www.hyatt.com/Travel Web/lq/common/home.html • $$$
W+ 6 rooms • No-smoking rooms

The three-story La Quinta offers 117 units that include two suites ($$$$$) and 38 no-smoking rooms. Children under 18 stay free in room with parents. Package plans and senior discount available. Cable TV with HBO. Room phones (local calls free). Pets OK. Restaurants adjacent. Outdoor pool. Free coffee in lobby. Free news magazine in rooms. Same-day dry cleaning.

SAN LUIS HOTEL

Seawall and 53rd • 744-1500 or 800-392-5937 • $$$$–$$$$$ • W+ 5 rooms

This 16-story hotel has 244 units that include two suites ($$$$$). Children under 12 stay free in room with parents. Package plans and senior discount available. Cable TV with pay channel. Room phones (charge for local calls). Fire sprinklers and fire intercom system in rooms. No pets. Restaurant, lounge open seven nights with entertainment on weekends. Outdoor heated pool with swim-up bar, outdoor whirlpool, two lighted tennis courts. Guest memberships available in country club and racquet club. Gift shop. Limited covered self-parking area and valet parking ($5).

THE TREMONT HOUSE

2300 Ship's Mechanic Row between 23rd and 24th (Mechanic St. renamed for this one block) • 763-0300 or 800-874-2300, e-mail: tremont@phoenix.net
$$$$$ • W+ 12 rooms • No-smoking rooms

The four-story Tremont has 117 units that include 15 suites ($$$$$) and nine no-smoking rooms. Children under 18 stay free in room with parents. Package plans and senior discount available. Cable TV. Room phones (charge for local calls). Fire sprinklers and fire intercom in rooms. No pets. Restaurant (*see* Restaurants), lobby bar with piano Wednesday–Sunday. Irish Pub across street with entertainment on weekends. Guest memberships available in country club and health club. Free transportation on the island in a London cab or a limo. Free shoeshines and free newspaper. Same-day dry cleaning. Gift and other shops. Complimentary valet parking. Historical restoration of 1870 hotel with Victorian-inspired guest rooms, one block from The Strand.

Condominiums

There are several condominiums with units in the rental pool that may be rented for short periods, usually with a two-night minimum. For information, contact the Convention and Visitors Bureau (*see* Tourist Services) or try "Galveston Island Online" at its Web site: http://www.phoenix.net/%7Eafactory/accom/accom.html).

Bed & Breakfast

The bed and breakfast phenomenon, which is spreading throughout the United States, has taken hold in Galveston's historic districts and each season the number of B&Bs increases. For an up-to-date list, contact the Convention and Visitors Bureau (*see* Tourist Services). Five of the bed and breakfast inns can also be booked through Bed and Breakfast Reservations, P.O. Box 1326, 77553 (762-1668 or 800-628-4644).

Beach Houses

Most rental houses are located on the island west of 100th St. Some may be rented for as short a time as two nights, but most rent by the weekend or the week. Everything from one- to five-bedroom houses are available, some on the beach and some on the bay. They range from no-frills beach houses to luxury homes. For a list of agencies that rent these homes contact the Convention and Visitors Bureau or try the Web site: http://intergate.com/wwwmarket/galveston/beach/.

GOLIAD

Goliad County Seat • 1,946 • (512)
This small town, a storehouse of early Texas history, had its beginning in 1749 when the Spanish moved a mission and a presidio (fort) here from the Guadalupe River. Among the things the missionaries taught the Indians was cattle raising. At times the mission herds reached as many as 30,000 head, supplying meat to Spanish settlements in a large area of what is now southern Texas and northern Mexico.

Independence was the theme in several battles that took place in and around the presidio. In 1829 the name of the village outside the presidio was changed from La Bahia to Goliad and this name became a battle cry in the Texas Revolution.

The Texian colonists seized the presidio on October 9, 1835, just days after the first battle of the Revolution was fought at Gonzales. That December the Texians in Goliad adopted the first Declaration of Texas Independence, which was soon suppressed as premature by the leaders of the Revolution. They also raised a flag of independence, which showed a severed arm and bloody sword, meaning that they would rather lose an arm than give in to the tyranny of Santa Anna's regime. In March, 1836, the Mexican Army defeated Colonel James Walker Fannin's force nearby at the Battle of Coleto. Fannin and his men were taken back to Goliad and held at the presidio with some other Texian prisoners. Then, on Palm Sunday, Fannin and more than 300 other Texian soldiers were executed in what has become known as the Goliad Massacre, an event that led to the battle cry "Remember the Alamo! Remember Goliad!"—a cry that is said to have inspired the Texas Army to victory at the Battle of San Jacinto.

Today Goliad's economy is based on oil, agribusiness, and, as would be expected with its wealth of historic sites, tourism.

TOURIST SERVICES

GOLIAD COUNTY CHAMBER OF COMMERCE

Market and Franklin, in Market House Museum (P.O. Box 606, 77963)
645-3563 or 800-848-8674• Monday–Friday 9–12, 1–5

A free Chamber brochure includes a map of the city, information on historical sites, and a walking tour of the courthouse area.

MUSEUMS

MARKET HOUSE MUSEUM

Market and Franklin • 645-3563 • Monday–Friday 9–12, 1–5; Saturday 10–12, 1–4 • Free • W

Built by the city in 1871, it contained stalls that were rented to farmers to sell their produce and meat. It became a firehouse in 1886, and turned into a museum depicting the early days of Goliad. It is also the office of the Chamber of Commerce.

HISTORIC PLACES

FANNIN BATTLEGROUND STATE HISTORIC SITE

Take US 59 east 9 miles, then go south (right) on Park Rd. 22 • 645-2020
Open daily 8–5 • $2 per vehicle

This 13-acre park with picnic areas marks the site where the Mexican Army caught up with Colonel James Walker Fannin and his force of about 400 on their retreat from Goliad. General Sam Houston had ordered Fannin to withdraw to Victoria shortly after the fall of the Alamo, on March 6, 1836. For reasons still unknown, Fannin delayed his retreat and he was overtaken near Coleto Creek and surrounded by the Mexicans. After a day of fighting, Fannin surrendered. A week later, on Palm Sunday, Santa Anna had Fannin and most of his men executed at Goliad.

FANNIN MONUMENT AND GRAVE

Loop 71 off US 183 south of Goliad, behind Presidio de la Bahia
Open at all times

After the Palm Sunday massacre, the bodies of Fannin and his men were stripped and partly burned. On June 3, 1836, the remains were buried with military honors in a common grave, which is now marked by this monument. It is estimated that about 342 men are buried here.

GENERAL ZARAGOZA BIRTHPLACE

US 183 about 2 miles south, near entrance to Presidio La Bahia • 645-2282
Open by appointment • Free

This reconstructed building commemorates the birth in Goliad in 1829 of Mexican hero Ignacio Zaragoza. In 1862, already a general at the age of 33, he was ordered to hold a pass near Puebla against Maximilian's French army. With about 4,000 poorly armed irregulars, he faced 8,000 battle-tested soldiers of the elite Zouave and routed them. The battle took place on May 5, and that date is now celebrated in both Mexico and the Mexican-American communities in Texas as Cinco de Mayo. (*See* Annual Events.)

GOLIAD STATE HISTORICAL PARK

US 183 about 1 mile south • 645-3405 • Open daily 7–10 for day use, at all times for camping • Adults $2, children free • W+ but not all areas

The major historic site in this 2,208-acre park is the Mission Nuestra Senora del Espiritu Santo de Zuniga (Mission of Our Lady of the Holy Spirit of Zuniga). Originally established near Lavaca Bay in 1722 along with the Presidio de La Bahia, it was moved to its present site in 1749. At the peak of its success it controlled vast expanses of land between the Guadalupe and the San Antonio rivers, and possessed huge herds of cattle that were used to supply settlements in Mexico and Texas. It was restored by the Civilian Conservation Corps in the 1930s. The park offers facilities for picnicking and camping (fee). Across the highway from the park there is a swimming pool operated by the city (admission).

PRESIDIO LA BAHIA

US 183 about 2 miles south • 645-3752 • Open daily 9–4:45 • Adults $3, children $1• W

The fort was built here in 1749 to protect the nearby missions and a 300-square-mile section of New Spain. It became what is probably the most fought-over fort in Texas. Soon after the start of the Texas War for Independence, the rebelling Texians succeeded in capturing the fort in October 1835, and it was here that the first—premature—Declaration of Texas Independence was signed. In March 1836 Colonel Fannin led his men out of the fort in a retreat that ended when his force was captured and brought back here to be executed on the order of General Santa Anna.

Historical restoration of the fort was completed in 1967. Operated by the Catholic Diocese of Victoria, it contains a museum displaying memorabilia of the Texas Revolution and artifacts uncovered during the restoration that indicate nine levels of civilization at the site. Religious services are held in the fort chapel on Sundays. Several times a year historical groups present living history programs re-creating life at the presidio at various times in its history.

GOLIAD COUNTY COURTHOUSE HISTORIC DISTRICT

Town Square

Surrounding the courthouse are a number of pioneer Texas and Victorian structures, making this a good example of an early Texas courthouse square. The limestone courthouse was constructed in 1894. On the lawn is the famed "Hanging Tree," and nearby, at Franklin and Market, is Fannin Park Plaza, which includes a cannon from the Texas Revolution and a memorial to Colonel Fannin and his men.

OTHER HISTORIC BUILDINGS

A number of historic buildings in Goliad have survived both natural and man-made disasters, including modernization. These are not open to the public. The oldest include: **Vivian Taylor House** (1840), Melrose Rd.; **Boyd House** (1846), 203 W. Market; **Captain Barton Peck House** (1852), Hill and Post Oak; **Seidel Hotel** (1854), Market and Fannin; **Boatwright-Maetze House** (1855), 205 E. Garden; **Lasater House** (1860), 203 W. Pearl; and the **Dill-Pryor Lea House** (1860), Chilton and Franklin.

SIDE TRIPS

COLETO CREEK RESERVOIR AND REGIONAL PARK

Take US 59 east about 14 miles • 575-6366 • Open daily • Admission W variable

Facilities are available for boating, fishing, swimming, waterskiing, picnicking, and camping (fee). For information and camping reservations write: Coleto Creek Park, P.O. Drawer 68, Fannin TX 77960.

ANNUAL EVENTS

March

PRESIDIO LA BAHIA LIVING HISTORY REENACTMENT

Presidio La Bahia on US 183 • 645-3752 • 4th weekend of March • Admission

Texas Revolutionary days at the fort and massacre are reenacted. Memorial service.

May

FIESTA ZARAGOZA

Goliad County Fairgrounds, US 183 about 1 mile south • 645-3327
Weekend closest to Cinco de Mayo (May 5) • Admission to dance • W variable

Festivities in honor of Goliad being the birthplace of General Ignacio Zaragoza, the Mexican hero whose victory over the French on May 5, 1862, is celebrated as Cinco de Mayo. Activities include an arts and crafts fair, dance, barbecue, folk dancing, and carnival.

December

CHRISTMAS IN GOLIAD

Courthouse square • 645-3563 • 1st weekend in December

Arts, crafts, food, entertainment on the courthouse square. Las Posadas at dusk.

ACCOMMODATIONS

ANTLERS INN

1013 W. US 59 • 645-8215 • $

This small two-story motel has 35 rooms. Cafe.

HARLINGEN

Cameron County • 52,000 • (210)

The town, named for a city in the Netherlands, was founded by Lon C. Hill in 1903, decades after the settlement of the wild West, but Harlingen's early days were reminiscent of those shoot'em-up times. At first it was peaceful. The railroad came to town in 1904 and by 1907 miles of canals had been dug to irrigate thousands of acres of farmland. But a few years later the chaos of the Mexican Revolution spilled over and bandit raids became commonplace. A company of

Texas Rangers and a unit of U.S. Customs mounted patrol were moved in. With all those guns around, the railroad people started to call the town "Sixshooter Junction." Rumor has it that there were more sidearms than citizens and the law was generally regarded as the thing you carried in your holster. Eventually, the bandit situation became so terrifying that the National Guard was called in to join forces with the Rangers and order was finally restored.

Today Harlingen is at the crossroads of U.S. Highways 77 and 83, four-lane thoroughfares linking the rest of Texas to the Valley. It is a processing, distribution, and marketing center for the major citrus orchards and vegetable farms of the fertile Rio Grande Valley.

In the works are plans for the Arroyo Colorado State Recreation Area to be developed in an area about 15 miles northeast of the city.

TOURIST SERVICES

HARLINGEN CHAMBER OF COMMERCE

311 E. Tyler at 3rd St. (P.O. Box 189, 78551) • 423-5440 • Monday–Friday 8–5 • W

In addition to providing maps, brochures, and other information on the city and the valley, this office is the outlet for tickets for just about anything going on in Harlingen.

TEXAS TRAVEL INFORMATION CENTER

2021 W. Harrison (Junction US 77 and US 83) • 428-4477 • Open daily 8–5 Free • W+

One of 12 roadside information centers operated by the Texas Department of Transportation on key highways entering the state. Bilingual travel counselors can provide a wealth of free information, official highway maps, and tons of other travel literature on the Rio Grande Valley and the rest of Texas. Even if you're not interested in all the goodies available, this is an excellent rest stop. The building is cool and quiet, the restrooms are clean, and there is a small reflecting pool in a courtyard outside that is relaxing just to sit by.

MUSEUMS

RIO GRANDE VALLEY HISTORICAL MUSEUM COMPLEX

Boxwood and Raintree off Loop 499, Harlingen Industrial Air Park, near Valley International Airport • 423-3979 • Tuesday–Friday 9–noon and 2–5, Sunday 2–5. Closed Saturday, Monday, and major holidays • Free (donation) W variable

This is really four museums in one. The **Historical Museum** building features the cultural and natural history of the Lower Rio Grande Valley. One outbuilding is the restored nineteenth-century **Paso Real Stagecoach Inn** that charged thirty-five cents a night for meals and a bed. It was used until 1904 when the railroad came to the Valley. Another building is Harlingen's first hospital, built in 1923, now restored as a medical museum. The fourth building is the **Lon C.**

Hill Home. Built in 1905 by the city's founder, this home was the headquarters of the Hill Plantation. Hill believed that irrigation would bring prosperity to the region. By 1907 he had 26 miles of canals in operation and 5,000 acres under irrigation. This house was visited by such notables as William Jennings Bryan. Hill's wife and the youngest of their nine children died in a typhoid fever epidemic just before the house was completed.

TEXAS AIR MUSEUM

FM 106, one mile east of Rio Hondo (P.O. Box 70, Rio Hondo, 78583)
748-2112 • Daily 9–4 • Adults $4, teens (12–16) $2, 11 and under $1 • W+
The history of flight from early days to present is presented here. A highlight is a large exhibit of German Focke-Wulf FW-190 aircraft. Gift shop.

OTHER POINTS OF INTEREST

MARINE MILITARY ACADEMY AND TEXAS IWO JIMA WAR MEMORIAL

320 Iwo Jima Blvd., across from Valley International Airport • 423-6006
Open daily except for school holidays • W variable
If you've ever wanted to see a Marine Corps precision drill or parade, but couldn't get to the real thing, this academy offers a good substitute. Students at this private military prep school wear uniforms similar to the U.S. Marines and follow the customs and traditions of the Corps. Check the Public Affairs Office for parade and activities schedule at which visitors are welcome. **The Iwo Jima War Memorial** on the campus is always open to visitors. This is the original working model used to cast the famous bronze memorial that stands in Arlington National Cemetery. The 32-foot-high figures are shown erecting a 78-foot steel flagpole from which a cloth flag flies 24 hours a day. (The Marine placing the flag pole in the ground was Corporal Harlon H. Block, from Weslaco in the Valley, who was later killed in battle). Across from the monument is a small museum with WWII memorabilia and a gift shop.

SHOPPING

HAND OF MAN STAINED GLASS

1201 W. Jackson at South K St. (entrance on South K) • 428-4562 • W
This is both a custom shop and a stained glass hobbyist's supply store. Stained glass for sale frequently includes salvaged windows from old houses.

SUGAR TREE FARMS

Bass Blvd. off US 83W • 423-5530 • Usually open November–April,
depending on harvest season • W
This shop is a typical example of the many in the area that sell local and imported citrus and fruits. You can buy by the pound, the sack, or the gift pack. They also sell fresh squeezed orange juice, nuts, dried fruits, imported glazed fruits, honey, jellies, and aloe vera products.

SIDE TRIPS

LAGUNA ATASCOSA NATIONAL WILDLIFE REFUGE

Take FM 106 east approximately 25 miles until it dead-ends, then north (left) about 2 miles to park headquarters • **748-3607** • **Open daily dawn to dusk Free • W variable**

The 45,000 acres in this coastline sanctuary lie on the Laguna Madre behind Padre Island. It is the southernmost refuge in the United States on what's called the Great Central Flyway along which waterfowl and other birds migrate annually between Canada and the Gulf. It is also the largest parcel of land in the Rio Grande Valley preserved for native plants and animals. Its name in Spanish means "muddy lagoon." More than 300 species of birds have been recorded here. The visitors center, located near the entrance, is open daily from 10–4 from October through April; on weekends only September and May. It is closed June through August. Bayside and lakeside tour roads provide ample opportunities for wildlife observation and photography. These are open daily from 7 to 7 year round. There are also walking trails. For information contact Refuge Manager, P.O. Box 450, Rio Hondo 78583.

ANNUAL EVENTS

October

RIOFEST

Fair Park, Valley Fair Blvd. • **425-2705** • **Three-day weekend in mid-October $2 admission • W variable**

This cultural arts festival features artists and artisans and almost continuous musical entertainment set up in a tent city. In the "Art in Action" area you can witness the evolution of art from mind to creation. A celebrity guest star performs during at least one evening's entertainment.

November

RIO GRANDE VALLEY BIRDING FESTIVAL

Harlingen Municipal Auditorium Complex, 1201 Fair Park Blvd. (P.O. Box 3162, 78551-3162) • **423-5440 or 800-531-7346** • **5 days in mid-month $35 for all events. Single tickets $3–$8**

The theme is the "Tropical Birds of the Border" and there are plenty of them to see from hummingbirds and herons to falcons and hawks. The festival includes field trips to wildlife refuges and other birding locations, lectures, seminars, and a trade fair.

RESTAURANTS

($ = under $7, $$ = $8–$17, $$$ = $18–$25, $$$$ = over $25 for one person excluding drinks, tax, and tip.)

LONE STAR

Palm Blvd., 1 mile east of US 83 • **423-8002** • **Lunch and dinner daily $–$$ • AE, MC, V • W**

Barbecue is the name of the game here and the mesquite-smoked offerings include ribs, brisket, and chicken. And if someone in your party doesn't like barbecue, the menu also has a few seafood and Tex-Mex items. Bar.

VANNIE TILDEN BAKERY

203 E. Harrison at S. 2nd (Downtown) • 423-4602 • Breakfast and lunch only Monday–Saturday, Closed Sunday • $ • No Cr • W

As soon as you walk in you're face-to-face with temptation in the form of pastry delights on display in an old wooden display case. You can give into temptation and fill up on pastries and coffee or have a regular full breakfast or breakfast tacos. For lunch there are soups, salads, sandwiches, chili, chicken 'n' dumplings, plus daily specials. They've been in business since 1930.

ACCOMMODATIONS

($ = under $45, $$ = $46–$60, $$$ = $61–$80, $$$$ = $81–$100, $$$$$ = over $100)

Room tax 13%

BEST WESTERN HARLINGEN INN

W. Expressway 83 at Stuart Place Rd. • 425-7070 or 800-528-1234 • $–$$ W+ 1 room • No-smoking rooms

This two-story Best Western has 102 units that include one suite ($$$$) and 20 no-smoking rooms. Children under 12 stay free in room with parents. Weekend rates. Cable TV and rentals. Room phones (local calls free). No pets. Restaurant, room service, lounge open Monday–Saturday with entertainment Wednesday–Saturday. Outdoor heated pool. Free airport transportation. Same-day dry cleaning.

DAYS INN

1901 W. Tyler at junction of US 77 and 83 • 425-1810 • $$–$$$ • W+ 1 room No-smoking rooms

The two-story Holiday Inn has 148 units that include six suites ($$$) and 15 no-smoking rooms. Children under 18 stay free in room with parents. Package plans available, senior discount, and weekend rates. Satellite TV with Showtime and pay channel. VCR rentals. Room phones (local calls free). Pets OK. Restaurant, room service, lounge open seven nights with entertainment Monday–Saturday. Outdoor heated pool. Guest memberships available in health club. Free airport transportation. Self-service laundry and same-day dry cleaning.

LA QUINTA MOTOR INN

1002 S. Expressway 83 at M St. exit • 428-6888 or 800-531-5900 • $ W+ 4 rooms • No-smoking rooms

The two-story La Quinta has 130 rooms that include 39 no-smoking. Children under 18 stay free in room with parents. Senior discount. Cable TV with Showtime and pay channel. Room phones (local calls free). Small pets OK. Restaurant adjacent. Outdoor pool. Guest memberships available in health club. Free airport transportation. Free coffee in lobby. Self-service laundry and same-day dry cleaning.

KINGSVILLE

Kleberg County Seat • 29,000 • (512)

The early history of Kingsville is really the history of Captain Richard King and his descendants and the growth of the world-famous King Ranch.

King, who had spent most of his early life on riverboats, came to the Rio Grande in 1847, at the age of 23, to captain one of the river steamboats that supplied our army during the Mexican War. In the early 1850s, King bought part of a Spanish land grant called the Santa Gertrudis, and started what was to be one of the largest ranches in the world. After Captain King died, his widow, Henrietta, put up considerable acreage of the ranch to help finance the building of the St. Louis, Brownsville and Mexico Railroad. One of the provisions of her financing was that the new town of Kingsville would be the railroad headquarters. She selected the site for the town on a spot near the center of the original Santa Gertrudis Land Grant and personally directed the laying out of the streets of the townsite. On July 4, 1904, the railroad made its first trip to the new town of Kingsville.

The King Ranch and the railroad were two of the three ingredients that came together to put Kingsville permanently on the map. The other ingredient was the successful sinking of wells by Robert Kleberg, Sr., in 1899, which provided a permanent source of water in the arid country.

TOURIST SERVICES

KINGSVILLE VISITOR INFORMATION DEPOT

1501 N. 77 Bypass at Corral • 592-4121 • Monday–Friday 9–5, Saturday–Sunday 10–3 • W

KINGSVILLE CONVENTION AND VISITORS BUREAU

635 E. King, at 11th St. (P.O. Box 1562, 78363) • 592-8516 or 800-333-5032 Monday–Friday 8–5 • W+

MUSEUMS

JOHN E. CONNER MUSEUM

821 Santa Gertrudis at Armstrong on campus of Texas A&M University-Kingsville • 595-2819 • Monday–Saturday 9–5. Closed Sunday and some university holidays • Free • W+

Displays emphasize the bicultural heritage of South Texas ranging from fossils and the findings at the La Paloma Mammoth site to chronological history and current economic development. The ranching section features one of the largest collections of cattle brands and branding irons in the state. There are changing exhibits monthly and Brown Bag Luncheon Lectures are given each Tuesday from November to April. Gift shop.

KING RANCH MUSEUM

Henrietta Memorial Building, 405 N. 6th • 595-1881 • Monday–Saturday 10–2, Sunday 1–5 • Adults $4, children (5–12) $2.50 • W

What was once the town's ice factory has been transformed into a museum that features King Ranch memorabilia including items like the family's horse-drawn wagons and coaches and custom cars. Award-winning photos of ranch operations in the 1940s by Toni Frissell cover most of the walls. A self-guided tour takes about an hour.

OTHER POINTS OF INTEREST

KING RANCH
SH 141 approximately 2.5 miles west (P.O. Box 1090, 78364) • 592-8055
Visitors Center open Monday–Saturday 9–4, Sunday 12–5 • Call for tour
schedule • Adults $6, children (over 5–12) $2.50 • W

In 1853, Richard King, captain of a steamboat on the Rio Grande, went with friends to Corpus Christi for the Lone Star State Fair. On the way they stopped at Santa Gertrudis Creek in the wild area south of Corpus Christi known as the Wild Horse Desert. This was an oasis, the first water they had seen in more than 100 miles. King and a friend, Texas Ranger Captain Gideon Lewis, formed a partnership to set up a cattle ranch with headquarters at the oasis. King purchased part of the Spanish land grant, called the Santa Gertrudis, which included the creek. This area was so sparsely settled then he had to go to Mexico to buy the cattle to stock his land and find men to work the ranch. But, this was the start of what was to become one of the largest and most famous ranches in the world.

During the Civil War, the King Ranch became a way station on the Cotton Road, the lifeline of the southern states over which thousands of bales of cotton were hauled south to Mexico to trade for war materials. After the war, more than 100,000 head of cattle carrying the famous "Running W" brand followed the trails to northern markets. And at every occasion, King bought more land. Prior to his death in 1885, he had increased the ranch size to about 600,000 acres.

Later purchases by his widow, Henrietta, and son-in-law, Robert Kleberg, brought the ranch to its maximum size of 1,125,000 acres. At one time the King Ranch holdings included close to 10 million acres in seven countries around the world. At present the ranch has shrunk to a mere 825,000 acres spread over several counties from north of Kingsville south to Raymondville. Covering more than 1,300 square miles, it is larger than the entire state of Rhode Island and its fences, if laid out in a straight line, would reach from Kingsville to Boston. The ranch is listed as a National Historic Landmark.

Among the achievements of the ranch are the improvement of the herds that eventually led to the production of a new breed of cattle called the Santa Gertrudis—a cross between the Indian Brahman and the British Shorthorn. There are about 40,000 Santa Gertrudis among the 60,000 head of cattle on the ranch today. It is also the home of a stable that in the past produced several Kentucky Derby winners—including Assault, winner of the Triple Crown in 1946—but now concentrates on breeding and training championship quarter horses.

Bus tours leave from the Visitors Center, just inside the main gate. The tours take about one-and-a-half hours to cover the ranch headquarters area. Among the stops is one at the cattle pens where you might see cowboys actually working the cattle, if that's on the day's work schedule. The tour also drives by the stud barns and the auction arena of the Quarter Horse Division and the main house. Guided wildlife tours and special programs for birders are also available.

COLLEGES AND UNIVERSITIES

TEXAS A&M UNIVERSITY-KINGSVILLE
University Blvd. • 593-2111 • W+ but not all areas • Visitor parking available
all over campus

About 6,200 students attend this university. The 240-acre campus includes a 1,000-seat theater, the Caesar Kleberg Wildlife Research Institute, the Ben Bailey

Art Gallery, an observatory with a sixteen-inch reflecting telescope, and an indoor arena for English and Western horseback riding. Visitors are welcome to sports events, recitals and other musical performances, and theatrical productions. The John E. Conner Museum (see above) is also on campus.

SHOPPING

KING RANCH SADDLE SHOP

201 E. Kleberg • 595-5761 or 1-800-282-KING (800-282-5464) • W

The saddle shop is the outgrowth of the shop established by Captain King to outfit his ranch hands. It's located in the Ragsland Building, the first mercantile building in town, built in 1904 and now listed in the National Register of Historic Places. The shop offers a custom line of leather goods all branded with the ranch's Running W. Also Western wear, as they call it, for horses and people.

ANNUAL EVENTS

January

TUFF HADEMAN PROFESSIONAL BULL RIDERS CHALLENGE

J. K. Northway Exposition Center, Dick Kleberg Park, south edge of city between Bus US 77 and US 77 Bypass • Usually Thursday–Saturday of first week • 595-8591 or 800-333-5032 (Convention and Visitors Bureau) Admission • W

Professional bull riders from all over the country come here to compete for national standing and qualify for the national finals.

February or March

SOUTH TEXAS RANCHING HERITAGE FESTIVAL

Various locations in the city • 593-2819 or 800-333-5032 (Convention and Visitors Bureau) • Friday–Saturday late in February or early March Admission to some events • W variable

One of the highlights of this festival is the Ranch Rodeo on both days in which real cowboys compete. Other events include campfire poetry/music and storytelling, folk art by ranch craftsmen and artisans, special exhibits at the Conner Museum, a cowcamp cooked meal, a chuckwagon cook-off, and a Saturday night dance.

April

KING RANCH WILD GAME LUNCH AND TEXAS CACTUS FESTIVAL

King Ranch and downtown Kingsville • 595-5761 or 800-333-5032 (Convention and Visitors Bureau) • Friday–Sunday in mid-month Admission to some events • W variable

There are some seminars on cactus on Friday, but the major events start on Saturday both at the King Ranch and downtown. The King Ranch festivities include a wild game lunch, 12-mile cowboy trail ride, hay rides, music, entertainment, and activities for kids. At the downtown festival you can enjoy Tejano, country, mariachi and other music, food booths offering a "Taste of South Texas," and a variety of demonstrations and competitions. The festival continues on Sunday.

June

GEORGE STRAIT TEAM ROPING AND CONCERT

J. K. Northway Exposition Center, Dick Kleberg Park, south edge of city between Bus US 77 and US 77 Bypass • 592-8516 (Convention and Visitors Bureau) • Admission • W

Country and Western singing star George Strait and his brothers compete in the three days of team roping by teams from all over the country. The event winds up with a Saturday night concert by Strait.

RESTAURANTS

($ = under $7, $$ = $8–$17, $$$ = $18–$25, $$$$ = over $25 for one person excluding drinks, tax, and tip.)

KING'S INN

Take US 77 south about 11 miles, then east (left) on FM 628 about 9 miles **297-5265 • Lunch and dinner daily • Reservations recommended on weekends • $$–$$$ • Cr • W**

This is yet another proof that a restaurant in the middle of nowhere will draw customers as long as it feeds them well. It's about 20 miles from Kingsville, and many more from Corpus Christi, but they come from both places. So many come that, if you don't have reservations, especially on weekends, be prepared to wait. The menu is by word-of-waiter and includes a wide variety of seafood. Most of it is sold by the pound and served family style. If you have a group, you can order a pound of this and a pound of that and share. Beer.

ACCOMMODATIONS

($ = under $45, $$ = $46–$60, $$$ = $61–$80, $$$$ = $81–$100, $$$$$ = over $100)
Room tax 13%

B BAR B RANCH INN

SH 77 (RR1, Box 457, 78363), about 8 miles south, follow sign • 296-3331 $$$–$$$$$ • All no-smoking

Six of the seven rooms in this bed and breakfast have private baths. No children under 12. Package plans available. Satellite TV. Room phones. Kennel for pets. Outdoor pool. Free full breakfast. Dinner available Friday–Saturday by reservations (approximately $25). Gift shop. On 220-acre working ranch.

BEST WESTERN KINGSVILLE INN

2402 E. King (SH 141) at US 77 Bypass • 595-5656 or 800-528-1234 • $$ • W+ 1 room • No-smoking rooms

The 50 rooms in this two-story Best Western include 23 no-smoking. Children under 12 stay free in room with parents. Senior discount. Cable TV with HBO. Room phones (local calls free). Pets limited. Free continental breakfast. Outdoor pool. Free coffee in lobby. Same-day dry cleaning.

HOLIDAY INN KINGSVILLE

3430 SH 77 (78363) • 595-5753 • $$ • W+ 2 rooms • No-smoking rooms

This two-story inn has 75 units that include one suite ($$$$$) and 56 no-smoking rooms. Children 18 and under stay free in room with parents. Senior discount available. Cable TV with HBO. Room phones (charge for local calls).

Small pets OK. Outdoor pool. Restaurant. Lounge. Self-service laundry. Same-day dry cleaning.

QUALITY INN

221 SH 77 Bypass (78363) • 592-5251 • $–$$ • W+ 1 room • No-smoking rooms
The 65 rooms in this two-story inn include 50 no-smoking. Children 18 and under stay free in room with parents. Senior and weekend discounts and package plans available. Cable TV with a premium channel. Room phones (local calls free). Small pets OK ($20 deposit). Coffeemakers in rooms and free coffee in lobby. Outdoor pool and exercise room. Free continental breakfast, free cocktail. Restaurant nearby. Lounge with dancing. Free airport transportation. Same-day dry cleaning.

LAREDO

Webb County Seat • 156,000 • (956)
Laredo was one of the first settlements in Texas not established as a mission or a *presidio* (fort). It was settled in 1755 by three Spanish families led by army officer Don Tomas Sanchez de la Barrera y Gallardo. He named it after the city of the same name in Spain. The original site was on the river near what is now St. Augustin Plaza.

By 1836, after the successful revolutions in Mexico and Texas, a census showed there were 2,000 citizens in Laredo and ranching and farming were thriving. During the next ten years Laredo was virtually the capital of a no-man's land. Mexico contended that the boundary with the new Republic of Texas was the Nueces River while the Texans claimed it was the Rio Grande. In 1840, some of the Mexican citizens in the disputed area, charging that the government in Mexico City neglected them, formed a coalition of three northern Mexican states and southwest Texas and set up an independent Republic of the Rio Grande with Laredo as the capital. This rebellion lasted 283 tumultuous days before it was crushed by the Mexican Army. During that time the flag of the short-lived republic flew over Laredo, giving it the distinction of having seven flags fly over it, while the rest of Texas had six.

The boundary dispute was settled by the Mexican War, which set the Rio Grande as the border. After that war many Laredoans moved to the section of the city south of the river to preserve their Mexican citizenship and renamed it Nuevo Laredo. This is now the larger of the sister cities with a population of well over a quarter of a million.

Most of the residents of the sister cities consider that they live in one city that just happens to exist on both sides of an international border, a city they often refer to as *Los Dos Laredos* (The Two Laredos).

TOURIST SERVICES

LAREDO CONVENTION AND VISITORS BUREAU

**501 San Agustin (78040), downtown adjacent to Old Mercado Square Plaza
795-2200 or 800-361-3360 • Monday–Friday 8–5, Saturday 9–1 • W**
In addition to providing free maps, brochures, and detailed information on both Laredo and Nuevo Laredo, the bureau conducts a Laredo Trolley Tour. Call for schedule and fare.

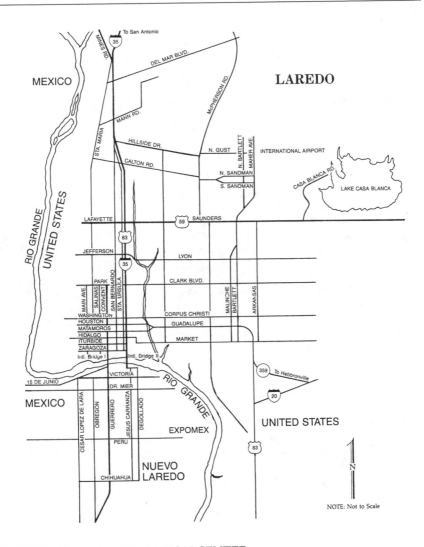

TEXAS TRAVEL INFORMATION CENTER
I-35 about 6 miles north • 722-8119 • Open daily 8–5 • Free • W+

One of 12 roadside visitor centers operated by the Texas Department of
Transportation on key highways entering the state. Bilingual travel counselors
can provide a wealth of free information on the Laredo area and the rest of
Texas. Located on the north-bound side of I-35. For southbound visitors, there
is a parking lot off I-35 with a walkway over the highway to the center.

HISTORIC PLACES

SAN AGUSTIN PLAZA
Downtown, San Agustin and Zaragosa

Many of Laredo's historic building are clustered on or near this plaza, which
was the center of the Spanish colonial town and is a National Historic District.

These include **St. Augustine Church,** 214 San Bernardo on the Plaza, established in 1778 with the present structure completed in 1872 on the site of two previous churches; the **Ortiz House,** 915 Zaragosa, various parts of which date from the late 1700s to the 1870s; **Capital Building of the Republic of the Rio Grande,** 1009 Zaragosa, with the back three rooms built in the 1790s; the **Bruni-Cantu Building,** 1101 Zaragosa, built in 1884 (now the Tack Room Restaurant of the La Posada Hotel); and the **Benavides-Vidaurri House** and **Leyendecker House** at 202 and 204 Flores, built in the 1870s.

MUSEUMS

MUSEUM OF THE REPUBLIC OF THE RIO GRANDE

1003 Zaragoza, on San Agustin Plaza • 727-3480 • Tuesday–Saturday 9–4, Sunday 1–4. Closed Monday • Free • W

By 1840, northern Mexico had become the center for opposition to the government in Mexico City, which paid little attention to this remote area and failed to protect the settlers from marauding Indians. In January 1840, the settlers in three northern states of Mexico banded together in Laredo and formed the Republic of the Rio Grande. Their capitol was this small rock building, built in 1834. About 300 Texans, from the newly established Republic of Texas, joined the army of this new republic. Mexican forces moved to crush the revolutionaries and there followed several months of bitter battles in which first one side and then the other was victorious. It ended on November 6, 1840, when the revolutionaries were granted amnesty and surrendered. The Republic of the Rio Grande had lasted 283 days and just about all that is preserved of it is in this building.

OTHER POINTS OF INTEREST

LAKE CASA BLANCA STATE PARK

5102 Bob Bullock, about 1 mile north of Hwy. 59 (P.O. Box 1844, 78044) 725-3826 • Daily 7 A.M.–10 P.M. • Adults and children 14 and older $3, 13 and under free • W

Located on the shores of a 1,100-acre lake, this park is still under development. It offers facilities for boating, fishing, picnicking, swimming, water-skiing, tennis, basketball, volleyball, and camping (reservations 389-8900, fee).

LAREDO CENTER FOR THE ARTS

500 San Agustin Ave. (78040) • 725-1715 • Tuesday–Saturday 9–5, Sunday 1–5. Closed Monday • W+ but not all areas

The center presents a changing monthly art exhibit featuring international as well as local artists. Its other offerings include an eclectic mix of juried art shows, jazz concerts on the patio in the spring, a citywide photo contest, poetry readings, and festivals.

NUEVO LAREDO

Take I-35 south across International Bridge #2 or Convent St. south across International Bridge #1 • To call from Laredo, dial 011-5287 plus the 6-digit local number

This bustling city of more than a quarter of a million people offers bargain shopping, inexpensive dining, nightclubs, professional baseball, and occasional bullfighting. Because the downtown areas of each city come right up to the bridges, the simplest way to go over is walk. You can park your car in the free lots along the river below Riverdrive Mall (off Zaragoza St.) and walk across Bridge #1 at Convent St., which connects with *Avenida Guerrero*, a major shopping street in Nuevo Laredo. You can also drive over, but first be sure your insurance covers your car in Mexico. Parking is often difficult in downtown Nuevo Laredo. The *Nuevo Laredo Chamber of Commerce* at 810 Guerrero (12-7926 or 12-7707) usually has someone who speaks English on duty.

SPORTS AND ACTIVITIES
Baseball

MEXICAN LEAGUE
West Martin Field, 2200 Santa Maria in Laredo (795-2080) and La Junta Stadium in Nuevo Laredo (12-1331) • Admission • W
The professional Mexican League team, *Tecolotes de los Dos Laredos*, plays on both sides of the border during the regular season.

Bullfighting

PLAZA DE TOROS LAURO LUIS LONGORIA
Nuevo Laredo, 4111 Avenida Monterrey • 1-888-240-8460 (direct from U.S.) or 795-2200 or 800-361-3360 (Laredo Convention and Visitors Bureau) Admission $4–$10 depending on sunny or shady side and fame of matadors W variable
There's no regular schedule here, but the season usually starts on Washington's birthday and lasts through September with bullfights most often held on Sundays and major American holidays.

Golf

CASA BLANCA MUNICIPAL GOLF COURSE
3900 E. Casa Blanca Lake Rd. (78041) • 724-1899 • 18 holes • Green fees: weekdays $10, weekends/holidays $12

COLLEGES AND UNIVERSITIES
LAREDO COMMUNITY COLLEGE
West end of Washington St. • 721-5140 (Public Information) • W variable
Occupational/technical and academic programs are offered to about 5,000 students on the 196-acre campus of this community college. A number of the older buildings on campus are the remains of Fort McIntosh. Established in 1849, this fort anchored the center of the chain of forts along the border that ran from Fort Brown at the mouth of the Rio Grande to Fort Bliss in El Paso. During the Civil War, the post was occupied by Confederate troops who protected the cotton routes to Mexico after the Union forces took control of the south Texas coast from Corpus Christi to Brownsville. In 1910, one of the first airfields in the United States was established here. The fort was closed in 1947. Today most of the remaining old fort buildings, including former officers' quarters and the one

remaining barracks building, are used by the college. Visitors are welcome to sports events, opera workshops, and other music, dance, and theater productions in the Kazen College Center.

TEXAS A&M INTERNATIONAL UNIVERSITY

5201 University Blvd. (78041) • 326-2320 • W+ but not all areas

The state's newest four-year university offers both undergraduate and graduate degrees for about 2,500 students in the liberal arts and sciences, education, and business, with a special focus on developing an international academic agenda for the state of Texas. The 300-acre campus is still in the early stages of development but already features award-winning architecture. Campus tours are available.

PERFORMING ARTS

CIVIC CENTER

2400 San Bernardo (78040) • 795-2080 • W+

Events here include concerts ranging from Country and Western to the Laredo Philharmonic, as well as a variety of other entertainment.

LAREDO LITTLE THEATRE

602 Thomas Ave. (78041), 1 block west of the airport • 723-1342
Adults $8, seniors/students $6 • W

This theater group traces its history back to 1911 when Market Hall was the scene of what was then reported as a spectacular musical presentation. The only live theater in Laredo, it puts on five productions each year ranging from drama to musicals.

LAREDO PHILHARMONIC ORCHESTRA

500 San Agustin (Laredo Center for the Arts) (P.O. Box 1399, 78042) • 727-8886
Admission $10–$15

During its October–July season, this professional orchestra puts on a number of concerts in both the Laredo Civic Auditorium and Christ Church Episcopal in Laredo and in Nuevo Laredo's *Teatro de la Ciudad.* Some of the concerts are with the Philharmonic Chorale and other area choirs as well as the Laredo Youth Orchestra.

SHOPPING

(To call Nuevo Laredo from Laredo, dial 011-5287 plus the 6-digit local number.)

BLUE GATE ANTIQUES

3002 N. Meadow • 727-4127 • W

The stock here includes china, crystal, silver, oriental porcelains, jewelry, and some early American furniture.

DEUTSCH'S

Nuevo Laredo, 300 Guerrero • 12-2066 • W

This jewelry store is best known for its custom-made gold and silver jewelry. Unlike most Nuevo Laredo tourist area shops that seem to be always open,

Deutsch's has limited hours just four or five days a week, so if you're interested in buying you may have to make an appointment.

THE GLASS SHOP

503 Calle Ocampo, Nuevo Laredo • 12-8525

Hand-blown glassware made in the nearby glass factories are for sale here, most at bargain prices.

MALL DEL NORTE

5300 IH-35, just north of Calton Rd. • 724-8191 • W

In addition to the anchor stores of Dillard's, Foley's, Sears, and Wards, there are about 125 other stores, a food court, and a movie theater.

RIVERDRIVE MALL

1600 Water St. (78040), just west of International Bridge #1 • 724-8241 • W

This is a small, two-level mall with about 50 stores and fast-food places anchored by Bealls, Penney's, and Weiner's. Its free 1,600 space parking area is a good place to park when walking across the bridge. It also has a studio for a local TV news program you can watch through a large window.

MARTI'S

Nuevo Laredo, 2923 Victoria at Guerrero • 12-3337 • W variable

Probably the best-known shop in Nuevo Laredo, Marti's offers a wide assortment of hand-picked items that includes unique designer clothes, jewelry, perfumes, antique and custom furniture, crystal, pottery, tableware, woven rugs and blankets, and tapestries. Everything is of the highest quality—with prices to match.

NUEVO MERCADO DE LA REFORMA

Nuevo Laredo, Guerrero at Belden • W ground floor only

It's called the New Market because it replaced the old one that was burned down when someone accidently tossed a match into a fireworks shop. The one-block, two-story market is a collection of shops selling souvenirs and tourist doodads, clothing, jewelry, toys, leather goods, baskets, candy, and a wide variety of other items. Bargain hunting here can be fun—the merchants expect you to haggle on price, and the careful shopper may find some treasures hidden among the junk.

OSCAR'S ANTIQUES

1002 Guadalupe at Hendricks • 723-0765 • W

American, European, and Mexican furniture are featured here. There are also Pre-Columbian artifacts and Spanish colonial architectural columns and doors.

RAFAEL DE MEXICO

Nuevo Laredo, 3902 Reforma (Mexico Hwy 85) near the El Rio Motor Hotel • W

You'll find a wide variety of gifts, arts and crafts here, even Christmas tree ornaments, in season. But Rafael's is best known as a builder of custom-made furniture. No phone, but message can be left at 14-2588.

KIDS' STUFF

LAREDO CHILDREN'S MUSEUM

**Laredo Community College, west end of Washington St. • 725-2299
Thursday–Saturday 10–5, Sunday 1–5 • Children 2–12 $1, children under 2
free, adults $2 • W downstairs only, ramp on side**

The purpose of this museum is "to create that spark of curiosity that ignites a lifelong passion for learning through educational exhibits that motivate the individual's sense of inquiry and inspiration." That may sound a little pompous, but the many exciting hands-on exhibits—from blocks and toys to computer games—definitely spark the fun of learning at every age from toddler on. Next door, in the old Guard House, is an a model train running in a model of Laredo. Here the children can crawl under the train table and pop their heads up in plexiglass turrets in various parts of the display and watch the trains speed around them. Gift shop.

ANNUAL EVENTS

February

GEORGE WASHINGTON'S BIRTHDAY CELEBRATION

**Various locations in Laredo and Nuevo Laredo • 795-2200 or 800-361-3360
(Convention and Visitors Bureau) • 10 days in mid–February • Admission to
some events • W variable**

It's doubtful that our First President ever heard of Laredo, but that doesn't stop the people here from celebrating his birthday in a grand manner—something they've been doing since 1898. Among the many activities are parades, pageants, fireworks, concerts and dances, entertainment by Mexican celebrities, sports contests, and a carnival. One highlight is the Jalapeño Festival that includes a contest to see who can eat the most of what locals call "border grapes" and a "Some Like It Hot" recipe contest.

RESTAURANTS

($ = under $7, $$ = $8–$17, $$$ = $18–$25, $$$$ = over $25 for one person excluding drinks, tax, and tip. To call Nuevo Laredo from Laredo, dial 011-5287 plus the 6-digit local number.)

Dinner For Two

TACK ROOM

**1000 Zaragoza (La Posada Hotel, San Agustin Plaza) • 722-1701 • Dinner only
Monday–Saturday. Closed Sunday • $$$–$$$$ • Cr**

This cozy, upstairs restaurant, with its racing stable motif, is housed in a charming restoration of a nineteenth-century house that once also served as Laredo's telephone exchange. The menu leans toward beef dishes and Baby Back Spare Ribs, but there are also several seafood selections. Piano bar downstairs.

Barbecue

COTULLA-STYLE PIT BAR-B-Q

**4502 McPherson, south of Calton Rd. • 724-5747 • Breakfast and lunch
Tuesday–Sunday, closed Monday • $ • AE, MC, V • W with assistance
Children's plates**

Elsewhere in Texas, tortillas filled with a variety of ingredients are known as breakfast tacos, but in Laredo they go by the name mariaches. This restaurant offers almost two dozen choices of fillings for this morning favorite and has made it into an all-day best seller. Not far behind in popularity is the pit barbe-cue—brisket cooked over mesquite coals for hours—and *fajitas*. The menu also offers a wide choice of Mexican entrées and some fried seafood dishes. No-smoking area. Beer.

Italian

FAVORATO'S

1916 San Bernardo • 722-9515 • Lunch and dinner Tuesday–Sunday. Closed Monday • $$–$$$ • Cr • W

Although it has a reputation as one of the better Italian restaurants in Laredo, there is really only a small part of the menu listing Italian entrées. The rest offers a wide variety of steaks, seafood, and continental cuisine. Bar.

Mexican

LA PALAPA

5300 San Dario, northbound access road of I-35 by Mall del Norte • 727-7115 Lunch and dinner daily • $–$$ • Cr • W with assistance

There is a variety of border cuisine with both Tex-Mex and Mexican entrées on the menu, but the specialty is beef and chicken *fajitas* broiled over mesquite that can be bought by the plate or by the pound. Bar. Another location in Nuevo Laredo at 3301 Reforma, Mexico Hwy. 85 (12-9995).

MEXICO TIPICO

Nuevo Laredo, 934 Guerrero • 12-1525 • Lunch and dinner daily • $ • No Cr W • Parking in rear

The charcoal broiler sits in a place of honor in the courtyard patio under a big sombrero, giving testimony that the specialties here are grilled meats, including *cabrito*. They are also known for their small sandwiches, called *tortas,* made from hard Mexican rolls filled with meat and *guacamole* and other fillings. *Mari-achis* play nightly. Bar.

VICTORIA 3020

Nuevo Laredo, 3020 Victoria, just west of Avenida Matamoros • 3-3020 Lunch and dinner daily • $$–$$$ • Cr • W with assistance

The cuisine in this former town mansion is interior Mexican, often a far-cry from border Tex-Mex. Examples are shrimp in a tequila-based sauce and *pollo pibil yucateco*—a spiced chicken breast steamed in a banana leaf and served on rice with a special sauce. There are also a number of mesquite-grilled entrées on the menu. Bar.

Seafood

MARISCOS EL PESCADOR

3919 San Dario • 724-8958 • Lunch and dinner daily • $$ • Cr • W downstairs only

This two-story restaurant features a wide variety of seafood prepared Mexi-can style, such as red snapper baked with onions and tomatoes. Bar.

ACCOMMODATIONS

($ = under $45, $$ = $46–$60, $$$ = $61–$80, $$$$ = $81–$100, $$$$$ = over $100.
Laredo Room tax 14%

EXECUTIVE HOUSE HOTEL

7060 N. San Bernardo (78041) (Del Mar exit off IH-35) • 724-8221 • $ • W+ 3 rooms • No-smoking rooms

The two-story Executive House has 137 units including two suites ($$–$$$) and 30 no-smoking rooms. Children under 18 stay free in room with parents. Senior discount. Coffeemakers, microwaves, and refrigerators in rooms. Cable TV with HBO. Room phones (local calls free). No pets. Restaurant, room service, lounge open Monday–Saturday. Outdoor pool. Free transportation to airport and bridge. Same-day dry cleaning.

FAMILY GARDENS INN

5830 San Bernardo (78041) (Mann Rd. exit off IH-35) • 723-5300 or 800-292-4053 $$–$$$ • W+ 1 room • No-smoking rooms

This two-story inn has 170 units in two buildings that include 18 suites ($$$$) and 38 no-smoking rooms. Children under 18 stay free in room with parents. Senior discount. Cable and satellite TV with HBO. Room phones (local calls free). Pets OK (kennel–$25 deposit). Restaurant open for lunch and dinner, room service, lounge open Monday–Saturday. Outdoor pool, three outdoor whirlpools, playground. Convenience store. Package store. Free airport transportation. Free coffee, free newspaper, and free breakfast. Self-service laundry, same-day dry cleaning. Microwaves and refrigerators in some rooms. Upstairs rooms in main building have large porches. Seventy rooms in Garden Square building built around garden with waterfall.

HOLIDAY INN-CIVIC CENTER

800 Garden St. (78040) (US 59 exit off IH-35 southbound. Entrance on Santa Ursala, southbound I-35 access road) • 727-5800 or 800-HOLIDAY • $$$ • W+ 2 rooms • No-smoking rooms

This 14-story Holiday Inn has 202 units that include three suites ($$$$–$$$$$) and 104 no-smoking rooms. Children under 17 stay free in room with parents. Senior discount. Satellite TV with HBO. Room phones (local calls free). Fire sprinklers in rooms. Pets OK. Restaurant, room service, lounge open daily with live entertainment Monday–Saturday. Outdoor pool, outdoor whirlpool, and exercise room. Free transportation to airport and bridge. Free coffee in rooms. Self-service laundry, same-day dry cleaning. Gift shop. Free parking in four-story garage. Good view of downtown from upper floors on south side.

LA POSADA HOTEL

1000 Zaragoza (78040) at San Agustin Plaza • 722-1701 or in TX 800-292-5659 or outside TX 800-531-7156 • $$$–$$$$

The two- and four-story La Posada has 208 units that include 57 suites ($$$$$). Children under 18 stay free in room with parents. Senior discount and package plans available. Cable and satellite TV with HBO and pay channel. Room phones (charge for local calls). No pets. Three restaurants (two dinner only), room service, three bars and lounges with live entertainment in one lounge Tuesday–Saturday. Two outdoor pools, one with swim-up bar. Free transportation to airport, train station, and country club. Guest memberships available in country club. Same-day dry cleaning. Valet parking in underground garage ($3 a day). Concierge floor ($$$$$). Part of hotel complex is in converted 1916 high school. Next to International Bridge #1.

LA QUINTA MOTOR INN

**3610 Santa Ursala (78041) IH-35 at Hwy. 59 • 722-0511 or 800-531-5900 • $$$
W+ 4 rooms • No-smoking rooms**
    The two-story La Quinta has 152 units that include two suites ($$$) and more than 100 no-smoking rooms. Children under 12 stay free in room with parents. Senior discount. TV with Showtime. Room phones (local calls free). Pets OK. Restaurant next door. Outdoor swimming pool. Free continental breakfast. Free coffee in lobby. Free national news magazine in rooms. Same-day dry cleaning.

RED ROOF INN

**1006 W. Colton Rd. (78041), Exit 3A off IH-35 • 712-0733 or 800-THE ROOF
(800-843-7663) • $$–$$$ • W+ 7 rooms • No-smoking rooms**
    The 150 rooms in this four-story inn include 105 no-smoking. Children under 18 stay free in room with parents. Package plans available. TV with Showtime and pay channel. Room phones (local calls free). Small pets OK. Restaurants within walking distance. Outdoor pool. Free continental breakfast. Free coffee in lobby. Free newspaper weekdays. Same-day dry cleaning.

McALLEN

Hidalgo County • 105,000 • (956)
    The city is named for John McAllen, who came to the area from Scotland in the 1850s, settling south of present day McAllen in what is now the town of Hidalgo.
    The county was plagued by bandits and cattle rustlers until the 1890s when Sheriff John Closner established law and order, surprisingly, according to reports, without the use of guns. Meanwhile, John McAllen had continued to increase his land holdings and by 1904 owned 80,000 acres. At that time he founded a town he called West McAllen, although no one was really sure what it was west of. In 1907, James Briggs, another land developer, bought 8,000 acres from Sheriff Closner (at $3 an acre) and founded East McAllen. There was not much going on in either town, both struggling to survive, but still a rivalry grew. East won out when the enterprising members of the newly formed Businessman's Club installed a horse trough to attract cowboys and ranchers to stop to water their horses and buy supplies. As a result, West McAllen literally dried up and died.
    Water again proved a major factor in the city's fortunes when the Rio Bravo Irrigation Company dug canals and soon had more than 27,000 acres of land ready for irrigation. With fertile soil, water, and a mild climate allowing two and sometimes three crops a year, agriculture boomed to become the number one industry in the area.
    Agriculture is still number one, but McAllen's economy is also boosted by the expanding industrial base in the McAllen Foreign Trade Zone and the Maquila (Twin-Plant) operations in Reynosa. Another boost comes from the thousands of "Winter Texans" who come down from the mid-West and Canada to avoid the cold winters in "The Texas Tropics."

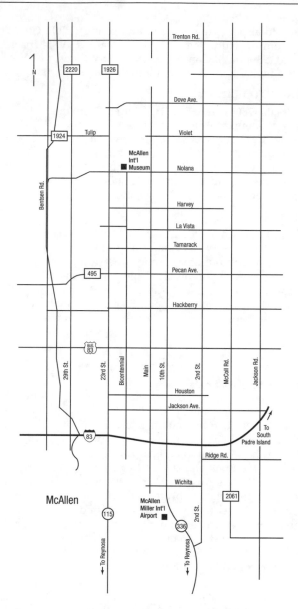

About ten miles south of the city is the Mexican city of Reynosa, which is a major industrial and oil refining center with a population estimated to be more than half a million (*see* Other Points of Interest).

TOURIST SERVICES

McALLEN CONVENTION AND VISITORS BUREAU

Chamber of Commerce Building, 10 N. Broadway, just north of BUS 83 (P.O. Box 790, 78505) • 682-2871 or 800-250-2591 • Monday–Friday 8:30–5 • Free parking behind building • W+

SANBORN'S VIVA TOURS

2015 S. 10th Street (P.O. Box Drawer 519, 78505-0519) • 682-9872 or 800-395-8482 • W

Although best known for its many extended tours of Mexico and South Texas, Sanborn also conducts occasional one-day tours visiting sights along the border, as well as birding tours. Prices for these range from $36 to $99. There are a number of other tour operators in McAllen, but Sanborn's has been doing it here since 1948. Tour catalog available.

MUSEUMS

McALLEN INTERNATIONAL MUSEUM

1900 Nolana (78504) at north end of Bicentennial • 682-1564 • Tuesday–Saturday 9–5, Sunday 1–5. Closed Monday • Adults $1, students and children 25¢ • W+

The permanent collection, used in rotating exhibits, includes Mexican folk art, masks and textiles; contemporary American and regional prints, and the Caton collection of sixteenth- to nineteenth-century European paintings. The Science Hall features a weather station as well as "hands-on" exhibits. The museum hosts some 20 traveling exhibitions annually. Gift shop.

OTHER POINTS OF INTEREST

REYNOSA, MEXICO

Take TX 336 (10th St.) or Loop 115 (23rd St.) south about 10 miles to the International Bridge. To call dial 011-52892 plus the 5-digit local number.

Founded in 1749, Reynosa is now a city of more than half a million that offers visitors bargain shopping, inexpensive dining, nightlife, sightseeing, and, occasionally, the opportunity to attend a bullfight. You can drive over, but first be sure you have insurance covering your car in Mexico and also realize that parking can be difficult in the downtown area. Or you can park your car in pay lots on the American side and walk over. You can also take a bus from the Valley Transit Bus Station at 120 S. 16th in downtown McAllen to the bridge or the Reynosa bus station. Buses depart every 20 or 30 minutes. The last bus departs Reynosa for McAllen at 11 P.M. For information call 686-5479.

There is a tourist information booth (phone 2-1308) at the end of the bridge just past the Mexican customs office. English speaking counselors are available and you can get a map of Reynosa and a variety of brochures on the city. There are usually licensed guides near the bridge. Before you hire one, ask to see their wallet-sized license from the Mexican Tourism Department and make sure you settle on the details of the tour and the fee before starting out.

Many of the shops and restaurants in Reynosa are in the *Zona Rosa* (Pink Zone), within an easy walk from the bridge. If you need assistance, an English-speaking policeman is usually on duty at the Tourist Branch Police Precinct in the *Zona Rosa*. If you want to go to the Main Plaza or the Zaragoza Market (*see* Shopping) it might be best to take a taxi, making sure you first fix the fare with the driver.

SPORTS AND ACTIVITIES

Baseball

The *Parque Beis-Bol* on the Monterrey Highway in Reynosa is the home of the Reynosa Broncos of the Mexican League. In addition to the regular season games, the team often plays exhibition games in the winter. For the schedule call the Reynosa Chamber of Commerce at 2-3734.

Birding

Because of its location on a system of continental flyways, some of the best birding areas in the country are in the lower Rio Grande Valley. (*See* Santa Ana National Wildlife Refuge, Bentsen-Rio Grande State Park, and Texas Tropics Nature Festival.)

Bullfighting

The bullfighting schedule is erratic and information about it is usually only released just before each event. For information try the McAllen Convention and Visitors Bureau (682-2871 or 800-250-2591) or the Reynosa Chamber of Commerce (2-3734).

Golf

EDINBURG MUNICIPAL GOLF COURSE

300 W. Palm Drive, Edinburg • 381-1244 • 18 holes • Green fees: $9

MARTIN'S VALLEY RANCH GOLF COURSE

Expressway 83, approximately 5 miles west of Mission • 585-6330 • 18 holes Green fees: $10.25

MONTE CRISTO GOLF COURSE

US 281 approximately 2½ miles east of Edinburg • 381-0964 • 18 holes Green fees: $12

PALM VIEW GOLF COURSE

Ware Rd., south of Expressway 83, McAllen • 687-9591 • 18 holes Green fees: $10.25

SEVEN OAKS RESORT AND COUNTRY CLUB

Los Ebanos Rd., Mission, approximately ¼ mile south of BUS 83 • 581-6262 18 holes • Green fees: $13.50

SHARY MUNICIPAL GOLF COURSE

2201 Mayberry, Mission • 580-8770 • two 9-hole courses Green fees: 18 holes $9.50

Square Dancing

Various locations • 682-2871 (Convention and Visitors Bureau)
The McAllen area claims the title of "Square Dance Capital of the World" because of the number of dancers and dances, and the number of callers and round dance cuers who either live in the Valley or winter here and set the pace

for this popular pastime. Each January and February, the McAllen Chamber of Commerce sponsors what it modestly calls "The World's Largest Beginners Square Dance Class," a five-week schedule of free Monday morning square dance classes that has attracted as many as 500 new dancers at a time. With all this activity going for it, it's no wonder that it's possible to dance somewhere in the area just about every hour of the day and well into the night, any day of the week. A schedule of dances, workshops, and classes is available at the Convention and Visitors Bureau. Each February, about 2,000 dancers bow to their partners during the annual Texas Square Dance Jamboree (tickets $7.50) held in McAllen Civic Center.

PERFORMING ARTS

McALLEN PERFORMING ARTS
Civic Center, 1300 S. 10th Street (78501) • 631-2545 • W+

This nonprofit organization brings in professional touring productions and entertainment during its October–April season. Performances are usually in the Civic Center. Single tickets range from $25–$45 depending on the production.

SOUTH TEXAS SYMPHONY
P.O. Box 2832, 75802-2832 • 630-5355 or 800-373-5810

There are about 75 professional musicians in this orchestra that gives concerts at University of Texas branch in nearby Edinburg and at the McAllen Civic Center.

WINTERSTAGE
Civic Center, 1300 S. 10th Street • 682-2781 or 800-250-2591 (Chamber of Commerce) • W+

For more than a dozen years, from December through February, the Chamber of Commerce has sponsored a series of concerts and other events geared to the tastes of the Winter Texans. These range from Mexican folkloric dancing through jazz and the McAllen Town Band concerts to an international travel show. Tickets $5–$7.50, depending on event.

SHOPPING

To call Reynosa dial 011-52892 plus the 5-digit local number.

GABII'S
Reynosa, 1097 Avenida Los Virreyes (Pink Zone) • 2-3433

Mexican designer dresses are among the fine items in this woman's clothing store. Also folk art and crafts and gifts from Mexico and Central and South America. Branch store in Texas Country Market, McAllen.

KLEMENT'S GROVE
FM 1924 (3 mile line) and Taylor Rd., west of McAllen. *Take Taylor Rd. north off Bus 83* **• 682-2980 • Open Monday–Saturday in citrus season (October–April). Closed Sunday • W**

Get your fresh fruit from baskets in the store or pull a little kid's wagon out into the grove and pick your own citrus right off the tree (in season). Gift fruit packs available. They also have mesquite and wildflower honey, pecans and pecan brittle, fruitcakes, and fresh-baked pies.

LA PLAZA MALL

2200 S. 10th Street (78503), next to Miller International Airport • 687-5251
W+ but not all areas
More than 110 specialty shops and a food court are anchored by Dillard's, Foley's, Penney's, and Sears.

TEXAS COUNTRY MARKET

807 S. Jackson, Pharr (78503), just south of Expressway 83 • 702-0127
Closed Monday • W
A number of shops under one roof selling a variety of items including leather goods, jewelry, folk art, clothing, and gifts. The Texas Emporium sells Texas souvenirs and there's a branch of Gabii's (see above). The Holbrook Family Country Music Dinner Theater is also here. For program and schedule call 787-3686.

ZARAGOZA MARKET

Reynosa, Hidalgo and Matamoros, just south of the Main Plaza • W variable
A typical tourist-oriented border market with dozens of small shops where bargaining over price is a way of life. For the smart shopper, there are some bargain treasures among the tourist souvenirs. It closes at sundown. Hidalgo Street is a pedestrian mall between the market and the Main Plaza.

SIDE TRIPS

BENTSEN-RIO GRANDE STATE PARK

P.O. Box 988, Mission 78572. *Take US 83 west to Inspiration Rd. exit in Mission, continue west 3 miles, then take FM 2062 south 3 miles to park* **585-1107 or 800-792-1112 (Texas Parks and Wildlife) • Open daily 8 A.M.–10 P.M. • Admission • W**
Birders from all over the United States come to this 588-acre park in the Rio Grande to observe its abundant and unusual variety of tropical resident and migrating northern birds. More than 290 bird species have been recorded in the park and another 74 sighted nearby. Facilities available for camping, picnicking, hiking, and boating and fishing on a 60-acre lake. Park store with bike rentals.

OLD CLOCK MUSEUM

Take BUS 83 east to Pharr **• 929 E. Preston (78577) • 787-1923**
Monday–Friday 1–5 • Free (donations are given to charity) • W
James Shawn started collecting clocks in the mid-1960s. His collection, which now numbers close to 2,000 timepieces, antique phonographs, and clock accessories, soon outgrew his home and he opened this museum next door. Now operated by the nonprofit Institute of Horological Research, it is one of only five such museums in the nation. Highlights of the collection include more than 200 clocks in numbered cases casted by famed foundryman Nicolas Müller from 1846 on. The numerous cuckoo clocks are especially popular with children.

SANTA ANA NATIONAL WILDLIFE REFUGE

Take US 83 Expressway east to Alamo, then FM 907 south approximately 7 miles to US 281, then east (left) about .25 miles to entrance **• 787-3079 • Trails**

open sunrise to sunset, Visitors Center: weekdays 8–4:30, weekends 9–4:30
Free • W+ Visitors Center and a trail for the handicapped

Most of the 2,080 acres are in subtropical native growth demonstrating how the area looked before the development of agriculture in the early 1900s. Because the lower Rio Grande Valley is on the convergence of two major flyways, Central and Mississippi, the refuge provides habitat for an amazing diversity of bird species, many of which cannot be found elsewhere in the United States. (Frontera Audubon Society operates a hot line for recent sightings of rare species throughout the Valley—565-6773). A birdwatcher's checklist of well over 390 species is available at the Visitors Center. Also at the Center are maps and brochures, slide programs, films, and exhibits on the refuge and area wildlife. There are three nature trails, including one paved. During the winter tourist season the Valley Nature Center operates a tram tour that lasts about one-and-a-half hours and costs $2 for adults and $1 for children.

For information write Refuge Manager, Route 2, Box 202A, Alamo 78516.

SHRINE OF LA VIRGEN DE SAN JUAN DEL VALLE

400 N. Nebraska (78589), just south of US 83. *Take US 83 Expressway east to San Juan exit* • 787-0033 • Open daily 6 A.M.–8 P.M. • Free • W

You don't have to be a Catholic to appreciate this impressive shrine. Built at a cost of $5 million, paid mostly by small donations, the church has a spacious interior seating 1,800, a gigantic ceramic altar, the statue of the Virgin of San Juan enshrined in a niche in the center of a 100-foot wall, and colorful stained-glass windows. Outside, one of the world's largest mosaics adorns the north face of the building, and there are life-sized bronze figures denoting the stations of the cross.

ANNUAL EVENTS

January–February

RIO GRANDE VALLEY INTERNATIONAL MUSIC FESTIVAL

Various locations in the Valley • 686-1456 • Admission varies with event
W variable

A week of musical events featuring orchestras, like the Fort Worth Symphony, and well-known guest performers. For information write P.O. Box 2315, McAllen, 78501.

March

SPRINGFEST

Various locations around city • 682-6221 • Nine days early in March
Free. Admission to some events • W variable

The activities during this fiesta include a parade, beauty pageant, antique car show, a variety of bands and other entertainment, a dance, German Night, sports tournaments, and Fiesta in the Park with arts and crafts and food booths. For information contact McAllen International Spring Fiesta, P.O. Box 720264, 78504.

April

TEXAS TROPICS NATURE FESTIVAL

Civic Center, 1300 S. 10th Street • 682-2781 or 800-250-2591 (Chamber of Commerce) • Thursday–Sunday near end of month • Admission varies with event • W+ (Civic Center only)

With seminars, field trips, and classes, this festival celebrates the Valley's bio-diversity. Events include bird and butterfly seminars and field trips on both sides of the Rio Grande, native plant seminars and tours, nature-observation boat rides on the Rio Grande, and a nature photography workshop. Featured speakers include nationally known naturalists. Seminars cost about $3, guest speaker presentations $5, and most field trips $15–$20.

December

CANDLELIGHT POSADA

Archer Park, just north of BUS 83 between Broadway and Main Friday–Saturday of first weekend in month • 682-2781 or 800-250-2591 (Chamber of Commerce) • Free • W variable

La Posada means inn or lodging and the central theme of this festival is a re-enactment of the search of Mary and Joseph for a place to spend the night. This is highlighted at the Posada procession downtown on Friday evening. Other events and activities include a live Nativity scene, folklorico dancers, band and choir concerts, and other entertainment on two stages at Archer Park.

OFFBEAT

LOS EBANOS FERRY

Los Ebanos • *Take US 83 west past Mission about 14 miles to FM 886, then south about 3 miles* **• Daily 8–4 • Car and passengers $1**

The only remaining hand-pulled ferry across the Rio Grande connects the Texas side with the dirt road leading to the tiny town of Diaz Ordaz, Mexico. The ferry's anchor cable has been tied to a tree near the river for more than 50 years, and the tree is estimated to be 250 years old. You can make the round trip as a passenger for about half a dollar and, if you want, get some exercise helping the Mexican crew pull the rope.

RESTAURANTS

($ = under $7, $$ = $8–$17, $$$ = $18–$25, $$$$ = over $25 for one person excluding drinks, tax, and tip. To call Reynosa dial 011-52892 plus the 5-digit local number.)

American

TOM AND JERRY'S

401 N. 10th (78501) at Date Palm • 687-3001 • Lunch and dinner Monday–Saturday • $ • Cr • W

The setting is simple: an old brick house on the corner with an enclosed porch, a patio, and bench seats. The menu is simple, too: several types of burg-ers, beef or chicken fajitas, the ever-popular chicken-fried steak, chili, hot dogs, and only one dessert—French cream cheese cake. Also in Mission at 2415 E. Griffin Parkway (581-2375) and on South Padre Island at 3212 Padre Blvd. (761-8999). Beer and wine.

Continental

LA CUCARACHA

Reynosa, Aldama and Ocampo, about 3 blocks SW of bridge • 2-0174
Lunch and dinner daily • $$–$$$ • Cr • W

The menu at this plush restaurant includes Chateaubriand and lobster thermidor, but most popular are the inexpensive two-meat special dinners that you can top off with a flaming dessert. Entertainment. Dancing nightly except Monday. Secured valet parking. Bar.

LA MANSION DEL PRADO

Reynosa, Emilio Portes Gil at Mendez, about 5 blocks SE of the bridge
2-9914 • Lunch and dinner daily • $–$$ • MC, V • W

Alambres (*shish kebob*), beef medallions with sherry sauce, chicken *chichingaro* and other traditional Mexican dishes are on the menu, as well as large steaks, and a variety of seafood. Note the intricate tile work throughout the restaurant. Private parking. Bar.

Italian

IANNELLI RISTORANTE ITALIANO

N. 10th (78501) at LaVista • 631-0666 • Lunch and dinner daily • $–$$
Cr • W

All the traditional southern Italian dishes are available here including seven different spaghetti dishes and a variety of other home-made pastas. Or you can try a deep dish vegetarian pizza. Other choices include a variety of chicken, veal, and seafood entrées. Bar.

Mediterranean

ESPANA

701 N. Main Street (78501) • 618-5242 • Lunch Monday–Friday, dinner
Monday–Saturday. Closed Sunday • $$–$$$ • Cr • W

The menu truly roams around the Mediterranean Sea with choices like French onion soup, *Gaspacho Andalusia*, classic Greek salad, Seafood Barcelona, *Paella*, Moroccan Sandwich, Chicken *Milanesa* and *Pasta Primavera*. Located in a poshly renovated old house. Bar.

Mexican

JOHNNY'S MEXICAN FOOD

1012 Houston (78501) • 686-9061 • Breakfast, lunch and dinner daily • $
AE, MC, V • W

This no-frills Mexican restaurant north of the border offers most of the typical Mexican and Tex-Mex choices from breakfast tacos and *migas* to *cabrito* and *chili rellenos*. Also steaks and vegetarian dishes. Bar.

MARIA BONITA RESTAURANT AND BAR

1621 N. 11th Street (78501) • 687-7181 • Lunch and dinner Monday–Saturday.
Closed Sunday • $$ • Cr • W+

There's some Tex-Mex on the menu, but most entrées feature real Mexican cuisine such as Cabrito al Pastro, Chile Relleno, and Pollo en Mole. Beef, poultry, and seafood. Children's menu. Musical entertainment at dinner. Bar.

SAM'S

Reynosa, Allende at Ocampo, 1 block west of the bridge • 2-0034 • Lunch and dinner daily • $–$$ • Cr • W

The two-meat dinner here runs around $7. You can do better on price in this border city, but they've been serving it up to diners since 1932 so they must be doing it better than the competition in some way. The menu also features a number of Northern Mexican dishes. Expect to be serenaded by *mariachis*. Parking lot on corner. Bar.

Oriental

LOTUS INN

1120 N. 10th (78501) at Kendlewood • 631-2693 • Lunch and dinner daily $–$$ • Cr • W

The selection of Hunan and Mandarin specialties includes choices like hot and sour soup, citrus chicken, Mandarin lamb, and Imperial Shrimp with water chestnuts. Behind this white, Chinese-style building is a large patio for pleasant outdoor dining. Bar.

Seafood

RICO'S

Reynosa, 585 P. Diaz at Mendez, about 2 blocks SW of the Main Plaza 2-2315 • Breakfast, lunch, and dinner daily • $–$$ • DIS, MC, V • W

Shrimp seems to be the name of the game in this no-frills seafood restaurant. They make it in a half dozen different ways, all good. A good place to eat when visiting the Zaragoza Market or the Main Plaza. Bar.

ACCOMMODATIONS

($ = under $45, $$ = $46–$60, $$$ = $61–$80, $$$$ = $81–$100, $$$$$ = over $100) Room tax 13%

DOUBLETREE CLUB HOTEL, CASA DE PALMAS

101 N. Main (78501), just north of BUS 83 • 631-1101 or 800-274-1102 • $$$ W+ 16 rooms • No-smoking rooms

This three-story hotel has 158 units that include several suites ($$$$$) and 52 no-smoking rooms. Children under 18 stay free in room with parents. Package plans available and senior discount. Satellite TV with HBO and pay movies. Room phones (charge for local calls). Fire sprinklers in rooms. No pets. Restaurant, room service, and bar. Outdoor pool, exercise room. Covered parking. Free airport transportation, free coffee, free newspaper, two complimentary drinks per guest, free full breakfast, late night snacks available in lounge. Charmingly restored, Spanish-style hotel originally built in 1918. Designated a Texas Historical Landmark.

EMBASSY SUITES

1800 S. 2nd (78501) off US 83 Expressway *(take 2nd St. exit westbound, 10th St. exit eastbound)* • 686-3000 or 800-EMBASSY • $$$$$ • W+ 10 suites No-smoking suites

This nine-story Embassy offers 168 two-room suites including 60 no-smoking. Children under 17 stay free in room with parents. Package plan available.

AARP discount. Satellite TV with HBO and pay movies. Room phones (charge for local calls). Coffeemakers in rooms. Fire sprinklers in rooms. No pets. Restaurant, room service, and lounge open seven nights with entertainment Monday–Saturday. Heated indoor pool, children's pool, whirlpool, exercise room, sauna. Free transportation to airport and mall. Complimentary two-hour cocktail party and full breakfast. Free newspaper. Self-service laundry and same-day dry cleaning. Gift shop. Suites have microwaves and small refrigerators. Top three floors are private condominiums.

HILTON McALLEN

2721 S. 10th (78503), across from the airport • 687-1161 or 800-346-2878 or 800-HILTONS (800-445-8667) • $$$ • W+ 1 room • No-smoking rooms
The five-story Hilton has 150 units that include one suite ($$$$$) and 32 no-smoking rooms (one floor). Children under 18 stay free in room with parents. Senior discounts and weekend rates. Satellite TV with pay channel. Room phones (charge for local calls). Fire sprinklers in rooms. Small pets OK (pet deposit $50). Restaurant, room service, and lounge open seven nights. Outdoor heated pool, outdoor whirlpool and lighted tennis court. Free transportation to airport and mall. Free coffee in morning. Same-day dry cleaning.

HOLIDAY INN-CIVIC CENTER

200 W. Expressway 83 (78501) (take 2nd St. exit westbound, 10th St. exit eastbound) • 686-2471 or 800-465-4329 • $$$ • W+ 1 room • No-smoking rooms
This two-story Holiday Inn has 173 units that include two suites ($$$$$) and 35 no-smoking rooms. Satellite TV with two free movie channels and pay movies. Room phones (local calls free). Pets OK in rooms outside the Holidome. Restaurant. Holidome with game room, putting green, whirlpool, sauna, and indoor/outdoor pool. Two tennis courts. Coffeemakers in rooms. Free transportation to airport and mall.

PORT ARANSAS

Nueces County • 2,450 • (512)
Texas 361 hops from island to island on the six-mile causeway that connects the mainland city of Aransas Pass with Port Aransas, which is located on the northern tip of Mustang Island. But the highway stops just short of its target and you have to take a free five-minute ferry ride across the Corpus Christi Ship Channel for the last thousand yards. The ferries, operated by the Texas Department of Transportation, are in service 24 hours a day.

Today, Port Aransas is a town with a split personality—still basically an unsophisticated fisherman's haven but its cottages and bait shops are now intermingled with luxury condos and some of the better restaurants on the coast. This combination draws close to six million visitors a year.

TOURIST SERVICES

PORT ARANSAS AREA CHAMBER OF COMMERCE/TOURIST BUREAU

421 W. Cotter near Cut-Off Rd. (P.O. Box 356, 78373) • 749-5919 or 800-45-COAST (452-6278) • Monday–Saturday 9–5 • Free • W

THE PORT A SHUTTLE
289-2600

For a free tour of the town, or to just get around, take this bus/trolley which makes a 50-minute shuttle route covering all the major streets and places of interest every day of the year from 10 A.M. to 5:30 P.M. Route maps area available at the Chamber of Commerce and City Hall, and you can flag down the trolley anywhere on its route.

BEACH WALK ADVENTURES
749-7053

A free guided beach walk is conducted by a local shell expert on the fourth Friday of the month (weather permitting). Meet at 9 A.M. on the beach at Access Rd. 1A. Bring water and a container for your shells.

NATURE BOAT TOURS
Woody's Sports Center, 136 Cotter Ave. (78373) • 749-6969 • Daily at 2 and 4 P.M. • Adults $15, seniors $12, children (12 and under) $10

The 49-passenger *Duke* is used to explore the waters around Port Aransas for dolphins and water and shore birds on these two-hour tours. During the tour, the crew pulls in a shrimp trawl net and dumps the catch in a tank where you can observe the crabs, shrimp, and fish that inhabit the local waters. (After the talk, the catch is put back into the water.) The *Duke* also makes 1½-hour sunset cruises where freshly steamed shrimp cocktails are served while the ship anchors by the Lydia Ann Lighthouse as the sun sets ($15).

OTHER BOAT TOURS

From mid-November to March 31st, a five-hour narrated tour is available from Fisherman's Wharf to take you on a 60-mile round trip to see the whooping cranes and other birds and animals that spend the winter at the Aransas National Wildlife Refuge. Other sightseeing and sunset cruises are available most of the year from both Fisherman's Wharf and Deep Sea headquarters. For information contact the Chamber of Commerce (*see* Tourist Services).

POINTS OF INTEREST

ART CENTER FOR THE ISLANDS
345 N. Alister St. (P.O. Box 1175, 78373) • 749-7334 • Tuesday–Sunday (Call for hours). Closed Monday and major holidays • Free • W

Located in a building behind Pelican's Landing Restaurant, the center offers an ongoing series of art exhibitions. In addition, it holds a sand sculpture competition in the spring. The building houses a working studio and classroom where one-day workshops ($25–$45) are frequently given in a variety of art forms including music and writing. Gift shop.

THE BEACHES

The Gulf side of Mustang Island is one long beach. The width varies, but here at Port Aransas, at low tide it is generally wide enough to almost lay out a football field between the water's edge and the dune line. Annual permits to park on the beach are available at most stores in town for $6.50. The money goes to a good cause—keeping the beaches clean. The 167-acre Port Aransas Park is at the northernmost point of the island. Operated by Nueces County Parks and

Recreation Department (10901 S. Padre Island Dr., Corpus Christi, 78418, 749-6117) it has restrooms, showers, a 1,240-foot-long lighted fishing pier, and 75 RV campsites (fee) with electricity and water. Primitive camping is permitted on the beach.

PORT ARANSAS BIRDING CENTER

North end of Ross Ave., *from Cut-Off Rd., follow signs to center* • **749-5959 or 800-45-COAST (800-452-6278) (Chamber of Commerce)** • **Open daylight hours only** • **W (Boardwalk)**

This flat marshy area attracts hundreds of species of shorebirds and migratory birds, including hummingbirds in spring and fall. They can be viewed from the boardwalk that goes out over the flats and the observation tower. In addition to the birds, two resident alligators call the place home and can occasionally be seen basking in the sun. Free guided nature tours are held here each Wednesday at 10:30 A.M., weather permitting (749-5307 or Chamber of Commerce 749-5919). There is also a boardwalk and observation gazebo for birders at **Port Aransas Wetland Park** on SH 361 about one-fourth mile south of Avenue G.

SAN JOSE ISLAND

Jetty Boat at Woody's Boat Basin off Cotter St. • **749-5252** • **Daily departures at frequent intervals from 6:30 A.M. to 6 P.M.** • **Adults $7.50, children $4**

St. Jo's, as it's called locally, is a private island; however, the area near the jetty and the beaches is open to the public. Accessible only by boat, it has NO facilities, just miles and miles of unsullied and uncrowded white sand beach for swimming, fishing, picnicking, surfing, or some of the best shelling on the coast. It takes about 15 minutes on the jetty boat and your ticket is good for any return trip during the day. If you're going to be there awhile, as a minimum, take food, drinks, and sunscreen.

UNIVERSITY OF TEXAS MARINE SCIENCE INSTITUTE

At the beach end of Cotter St. across from the Port Aransas Park • **749-6711 Visitors Center open Monday–Friday 8–5 September–May, daily in summer (Saturday 9–5, Sunday noon–4)** • **Free** • **W+**

Just about everything to do with the ecosystem of the Texas coastal zone from the natural phenomena to the impact that man has on the coast is under study here. A brochure is available in the Visitors Center for a self-guided tour of the seven aquaria and other exhibits. Educational films 11 A.M. and 3 P.M. (except Fridays).

SPORTS AND ACTIVITIES

Birding

More than 450 species of birds frequent the Texas coast, and many of them can be seen in Port Aransas. In addition to its own birding center, the area is listed as a major site on the Great Texas Coastal Birding Trail, developed by Texas Parks and Wildlife, and holds an annual Celebration of the Whooping Cranes (*see* Annual Events).

Fishing

The numbers of strictly sun-and-surfers may be increasing, but fishing is still the name of the biggest game at Port Aransas, where they boast it's the place "where they bite every day." If you want to prove or disprove that you can do it in the surf, on the jetties or piers, in the bay, or offshore. Two city piers, one at Roberts Point Park and the other at the north end of Station St., offer free fishing in the ship channel and it only costs 50¢ per person and $1 a pole to fish off the 1,200-foot Horace Caldwell Pier on the Gulf in Port Aransas Park, which is open 24 hours every day. Several boats offering bay and deep sea fishing are located on the ship channel. The Chamber of Commerce (*see* Tourist Services) offers an up-to-date list of both party and charter boats. During the summer there's a fishing tournament just about every week, including two for women only and the three-day Deep Sea Roundup (*see* Annual Events).

Scuba Diving

Boats offering offshore scuba diving trips with dive masters that last from five hours to two or three days are offered at Copelands (134 W. Cotter Ave., 749-7464) and Dolphin Docks (300 W. Cotter Ave., 749-6624). All divers must bring proof of certifications. Some require that you bring your own equipment; others rent.

PERFORMING ARTS

PORT ARANSAS COMMUNITY THEATRE

White St. at Alister • 749-6067 • Tickets $5–$8 • W

From late April to October, this community troupe puts on about six productions in its outdoor theater under the stars and another one or two dinner theatre productions in January and February in various indoor locations ($18–$20). Productions run from hit Broadway comedies, dramas, and musicals to cabaret shows to Shakespeare.

SIDE TRIPS

MUSTANG ISLAND STATE PARK

TX 361 approximately 14 miles south of Port Aransas • 1-749-5246 • Open daily 8–10 for day use, at all times for camping • $2 per day per vehicle • W+ but not all areas

This 3,704-acre park slices a cross section of Mustang Island between Corpus Christi Bay and the Gulf and includes five miles of Gulf beach frontage. Facilities are available for fishing, swimming, picnicking, nature walks, and camping (fee). Birdwatching is excellent. For information write to Box 326, Port Aransas 78373.

ANNUAL EVENTS

February–March

CELEBRATION OF WHOOPING CRANES AND OTHER BIRDS

Civic Center (710 W. Ave. A) and other locations • 749-5919 or 800-45-COAST (800-452-6278) (Chamber of Commerce) • Thursday–Sunday end of February/

beginning of March • **Registration fee $5, separate fees for most events.
Some events free • W+ (Civic Center only)**
Scheduled to coincide with the height of the migratory season, the program
includes guided shorebird bus tours, a variety of boat tours to see both the
whooping cranes and other birds and nature sights, exhibits, demonstrations,
and workshops. The registration fee also gets you in to hear a number of naturalists and other scientists give presentations at the University of Texas Marine
Science Institute.

July

DEEP SEA ROUNDUP

**Marina and other locations • 749-5919 (Chamber of Commerce)
Friday–Sunday early in month • Admission to some onshore events**
One of the reasons anglers love Port Aransas is the many fishing tournaments
held here. The first one, called the Tarpon Rodeo, took place in 1932. Of the 22
contestants, about half were women who won most of the prizes. The tournament was kept going even after the tarpon were overfished; they just switched
to calling it the Roundup, which makes it the oldest of all the fishing tournaments on the Texas Coast. Onshore there's an Activity Day with fun and games
for all ages.

OFFBEAT

TARPON INN

200 E. Cotter • 749-5555
The original was built in 1886, but fire and hurricanes knocked it and several
replacements out. The present barracks-like building was built in 1925 and is
listed in the National Register of Historic Places. The inn is best known for its
collection of thousands of tarpon scales on display in the lobby. Each scale is
marked with the fisherman's name and hometown and the date the tarpon was
caught. The prize of the collection is that of President Franklin D. Roosevelt,
dated May 8, 1937. The tarpon, once a prize sport fish in these waters, is now
rarely seen.
There are 24 rooms for rent (call for rates). They are air conditioned, but otherwise are basic, no-frills accommodations. The real lure here is living a little bit
of history and enjoying the gentle Gulf breezes on the wide second-story veranda. Restaurant.

RESTAURANTS

*($ = under $7, $$ = $8–$17, $$$ = $18–$25, $$$$ = over $25 for one person excluding
drinks, tax, and tip.)*

CASTAWAYS

**320 N. Alister St. at Beach • 749-5394 • Lunch and dinner daily. Closed
Tuesday in winter • $–$$$ • Cr • W**
The better part of the lengthy menu is devoted to seafood. Depending on the
type, you can order fried, grilled, sauteeded, or baked. Also steaks, chicken,
and pasta entrées, burgers, sandwiches, and children's menu. They'll cook your
catch and serve it with French bread or hush puppies for $4.75 to $6.50,
depending on your choice of cooking method. Bar.

CRAZY CAJUN SEAFOOD RESTAURANT

Station and Beach Streets • 749-5069 • $–$$ • Dinner only Monday–Friday, lunch and dinner Saturday–Sunday • Cr • W+ • Children's plates
The special here is The Hungry Cajun, which serves two with a combination of a half pound of shrimp, a half pound smoked sausage, new potatoes, corn on the cob, crab, and crawfish. It's all boiled in a blend of Cajun spices, your choice, from mild to lava hot, then dumped in the middle of your table on butcher paper. You can also get the ingredients as a la carte entrées, plus gumbo, red beans and rice, dirty rice, and Jambalaya. Beer and wine.

SEAFOOD AND SPAGHETTI WORKS

710 Alister at Ave. G • 749-5666 • Dinner daily • $$ • Cr
Children's plates • W through kitchen
The menu in this geodesic-domed restaurant has been pleasing diners for close to 20 years. It offers pasta, pizza, steaks, chicken and veal, and a variety of imaginative seafood entrées including shrimp prepared seven ways. Bar.

TORTUGA FLATS

821 Trout, across from Woody's Sport Center • 749-5255 • Lunch and dinner daily • $–$$ • AE, MC, V • W ramp in rear
Take your food out on the porch and watch the activities in the boat basin as you munch away on menu items that include charbroiled fresh fish, shrimp *flautas*, Cajun *Boudin*, "hamburguesas," *ceviche*, grilled marinated chicken, and shrimp and crab salads. Live entertainment Friday and Saturday evenings. Bar.

TROUT STREET BAR AND GRILL

104 W. Cotter Ave. • 749-7800 • Lunch and dinner daily • $$–$$$
Cr • W
A wall of windows and a porch offer waterfront views to diners. The menu includes a number of choices with a Cajun flair such as Tequila Shrimp and Grilled Red Snapper with Angelique Sauce. With the exception of specials and the catch of the day, most seafood entrées are fried. Also steaks and chicken. Two bars, one with big screen TV. Live music on weekends.

ACCOMMODATIONS

There are several small motels in Port Aransas, most of which cater to families and fishermen. But the majority of available accommodations in the town and on Mustang Island are rental units in condominiums.
($ = under $45, $$ = $46–$60, $$$ = $61–$80, $$$$ = $81–$100, $$$$$ = over $100)
Room tax 13%

MOTELS

Rates given are for a double in high season (summer, Spring Break and Easter holiday). Low season rates are usually considerably lower. Addresses are in zip code 78373.

ALISTER SQUARE INN

122 S. Alister St. • 749-3000 or toll free 888-749-3003 (reservations only)
$$$–$$$$ • W+ 2 units • No-smoking rooms

All 50 units in this two-story inn are suites, some with kitchenettes, with 20 designated as no-smoking. Children stay free in room with parents. Package plans available. Cable TV with free premium channel. Room phones. No pets. Free continental breakfast. Restaurants nearby. Outdoor heated pool. Guest memberships available in Padre Island Country Club. Self-service laundry.

SEASIDE MOTEL

Sandcastle Dr. at the beach (P.O. Box 519) • 749-4105 or 800-528-1234 • $$–$$$

This three-story motel has 54 units that include 20 one-bedroom condominium units ($$$$). Children under 12 stay free in room with parents. Package plans available and senior discount. TV and room phones (local calls free). Pets OK ($25 pet deposit). Coffee shop. Outdoor pool. On the beach.

CONDOMINIUMS

Rates are high season for two persons in the smallest-sized apartment available. All P.O. Box numbers are in zip code 78373. A complete list of condominiums with rental units is available from the Chamber of Commerce (*see* Tourist Services).

ARANSAS PRINCESS

**720 Beach Access Rd. 1-A (P.O. Box 309) • 749-5118 or 800-347-1819 • $$$$$
No-smoking units**

The eight-story Aransas Princess has 32 two- and three-bedroom units in the rental pool of which ten are no-smoking. Cable TV. Room phones (local calls free). No pets. Two outdoor heated pools, outdoor whirlpool, two tennis courts, sauna. Guest memberships available in country club. One covered parking space for each unit. Minimum stay two nights on weekends, three nights over holidays. Deposit of $100 for all stays less than one month. On the beach.

CLINE'S LANDING

**1000 N. Station St. (P.O. Box 1628) • 749-5274 or 800-999-7651 • $$$$$
No-smoking unit**

There are about 21 two- and three-bedroom units including three no-smoking in the rental pool at the seven-story Cline's Landing. Cable TV. Room phones (local calls free). No pets. Outdoor heated pool, outdoor whirlpool, two tennis courts, marina, and playground. Electronic security gate. Minimum stay three nights with reservations in summer. On the ship channel.

PORT ROYAL

6317 SH 361, about 7 miles south (P.O. Box 336) • 749-5011 or in TX 800-242-1034, outside TX 800-847-5659 • $$$$$ • W+ 1 unit • No-smoking units

There are three 4-story buildings at Port Royal with about 175 one-, two- and three-bedroom units in the rental pool including 15 no-smoking units. Cable TV with HBO. Room phones (local calls free). No pets. Restaurant, room service, lounge open seven nights with entertainment in high season. Five-hundred-foot lagoon-style outdoor pool with two swim-up bars, four outdoor whirlpools, and two lighted tennis courts. Guest memberships available in country club. Covered parking for most units. Whirlpool tub with steambaths in all units. Convenience store, boutique, gift shop. Two night minimum on weekends and three nights over major holidays in high season. On the beach.

SANDCASTLE

800 Sandcastle Dr., off 11th St., *take G Ave. south to 11th, then west to* *Sandcastle Dr.* **(P.O. Box 1688) • 749-6201 or 800-727-6201 (reservations only) • $$$$–$$$$$ (Efficiency)**

Most of the 184 efficiencies, one- two- and three-bedroom apartments in this five-story condominium are in the rental pool. All have balconies. Cable TV with free premium channel. Room phones (charge for local calls). No pets. Outdoor pool. Two lighted tennis courts. Guest memberships available in the Padre Island Country Club. Self-service laundry. Some covered parking. On the beach.

PORT ARTHUR

Jefferson County • 61,145 • (409)

On the shores of Lake Sabine, Port Arthur is in a "back-to-the-future" mode, which is good news for visitors. While refineries are still a part of the scene, diversification has replaced oil as Port Arthur's lifeblood. For more than a decade, this multifaceted, multicultural city has been returning to the tourism base it began with before Spindletop spawned refinery development. Only nine miles from the Gulf of Mexico, the city also lives up to its name as a port—a fact often brought home to the visitor by the startling sight of tankers and other large ships that appear to be gliding down a nearby street. What they're doing, of course, is sailing the Sabine-Neches Ship Channel that flows through the city.

Port Arthur emerged in the late 1890s when Arthur Stillwell pushed his Kansas City, Pittsburgh, and Gulf Railroad down from the north and dredged a canal from

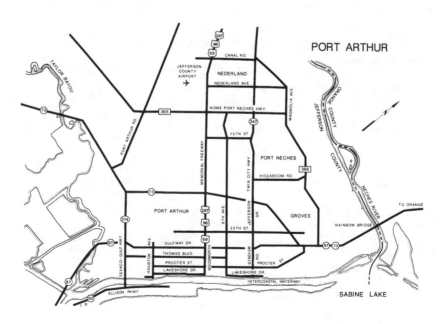

Lake Sabine to the Gulf. Stillwell said he chose this location as his Gulf terminus because of advice of "Brownies" from the spirit world, and in dreams he saw the city exact in every detail. Unfortunately for Stillwell, he ran out of money and went for help to John "Bet-a-Million" Gates. Before Stillwell knew it, all that remained of his interests was the city with his first name. "Bet-a-Million" really reaped the harvest of Stillwell's foresight in 1901 when Spindletop blew in just ten miles north of the city.

Prominent among the mix of cultures in the city are the Louisiana Cajuns. The Cajuns brought with them their distinctive cooking and the philosophy of "Let the good times roll" when work is done. Then there are the good ole boy Texans, the urban cowboys, Southern gentlefolk, Hispanics, African Americans, and the Vietnamese. The polygot population is also laced with descendants of the Dutch who are centered in Nederland, a city in its own right but molded right in with Port Arthur.

TOURIST SERVICES

PORT ARTHUR CONVENTION AND VISITORS BUREAU

3401 Cultural Center (TX 73 near 9th Ave., inside the Civic Center) • 985-7822 or 800-235-7822, fax: 985-5584 • W+

BIRD'S-EYE VIEW

CITY HALL OBSERVATION BALCONY

444 4th St. • 983-8115 • Monday–Friday 8–5 • Free • W+

You can see the Intracoastal Waterway, Pleasure Island, Sabine Lake, Lakeshore Drive, the downtown area, and the acres and acres of refineries.

MUSEUMS

LA MAISONS DES ACADIENS AND DUTCH WINDMILL MUSEUM

Tex Ritter Park, 1500 Boston near 17th St., 5 blocks west of Twin City Hwy, Nederland • 722-0279 (Nederland Chamber of Commerce) • Thursday–Sunday 1–5 • Free

It's an unusual group: a park dedicated to the memory of country singing star Tex Ritter containing two small museums commemorating the Cajuns and the Dutch. The Acadian house is a replica of an early home of the French immigrants who settled in Louisiana after being forced out of Nova Scotia by the British in the eighteenth century. Their descendants are the Cajuns. The 40-foot high replica of a Dutch windmill features memorabilia of Tex Ritter and the Dutch and other nationalities who settled the area. Gift shop.

MUSEUM OF THE GULF COAST

700 Proctor • 982-7000 • Monday–Friday 10–2 or by appointment • Free • W

Exhibits tell the story of the city and the Gulf Coast. Its American Pop Culture exhibit pays tribute to the contributions made in music, sports, arts, and entertainment by people who lived on the coast. These include Janis Joplin, Tex Ritter, Clarence "Gatemouth" Brown, "Bum" Phillips, and Babe Didrikson Zaharias.

HISTORIC PLACES

POMPEIIAN VILLA

1953 Lakeshore near Richmond • 983-5977 • Tours by appointment • Fee • W

Sometimes called the "Billion Dollar House," it was built in 1900 for Issac Ellwood, "the Barbed-Wire King," but he soon sold it to James Hopkins, President of the Diamond Match Company. Hopkin's wife didn't like Port Arthur, however, so he traded it to George Craig, banker, for ten percent of the stock in the newly formed Texas Company—a forerunner of Texaco. Craig never thought the oil company would survive, but it did and now his stock would be worth close to a billion dollars.

Refurbished with antiques that might be typical of the furnishing used by the Craig family, it is listed in the National Register of Historic Places.

ROSE HILL MANOR

100 Woodworth at Lakeshore • 985-7292 • Tours by appointment • Free • W ramp in rear

Another home in the National Register of Historic Places and one of the oldest landmarks in the city, this mansion was built in 1906 by Rome H. Woodworth, an early mayor.

VUYLSTEKE DUTCH HOME

1831 Lakeshore • 982-7822 (Convention and Visitors Bureau)
Tours by appointment • Free

Built in 1906 in Dutch style by the Dutch Consul to Port Arthur, the home has been restored to its original condition with original furnishings.

OTHER POINTS OF INTEREST

PLEASURE ISLAND

Take TX 82 over Martin Luther King-Gulfgate Bridge **• 982-4675 (Pleasure Island Commission)**

This 3,500-acre island located between the 400-foot wide Sabine-Neches Ship Channel and 100-square-mile saltwater Sabine Lake is being developed to live up to its name. Facilities include a concert park, a marina, picnic areas, lighted fishing pier, yacht club, boat launches, RV parks and free camping areas, condos, restaurants, bars, and a beach club. More plans are on the drawing board.

PORT OF PORT ARTHUR

East end of Houston St. near 4th • 983-2029 • Free • W

Small in size, it still has all the normal port activities. A highlight, especially in action, is a 75-ton gantry crane named "Big Arthur."

RAINBOW BRIDGE

Over the Neches River on TX 87 north of city

Completed in 1938, this is the tallest bridge on the Gulf coast, rising to the height of a 20-story building and clearing the river by 177 feet. This amazing clearance is due to over-diligent designers who wanted to ensure that everything afloat at the time could pass under it. The "tallest" ship then was a U.S. Navy dirigible tender with a huge dirigible mooring mast on its aft deck. Ironically, by the time the bridge was built the ship was out of service. The height does make for a spectacular view for everyone but the driver who may compare it to driving a roller coaster. The new Memorial Bridge to the east has only 133-feet navigational clearance, but its claim to fame is that it was the first cable-stayed bridge built on a Texas highway.

THE REFINERIES

West and south of downtown along TX 82, 87, and 73 • 800-235-7822 (Convention and Visitors Bureau) • Group tours only, by appointment • W

This is what Port Arthur calls "the world's largest oil refinery-petrochemical complex," so it's worth seeing up close. For group tours, call two weeks in advance.

SPORTS AND ACTIVITIES

Birdwatching

Port Arthur is located on the Central Flyway for waterfowl, so during the migratory season, birds are everywhere. Pleasure Island is one of the more accessible places to observe them. Not as accessible, but also not as disturbed by civilization are:

McFaddin Marsh National Wildlife Refuge, along the Gulf coast west of Sea Rim State Park. Office at Shell Oil Company Rd. off TX 87. Refuge Headquarters/U.S. Fish and Wildlife at McFaddin 409-971-2909.

Texas Point National Wildlife Refuge, Sabine Pass. Also contains one of the densest populations of American alligators in Texas. Refuge Headquarters/U.S. Fish and Wildlife at McFaddin 409-971-2909.

J. D. Murphree Wildlife Management Area, TX 73 approximately five miles west of Port Arthur 736-2551.

Fishing

Port Arthur is triply blessed because it offers lake, river and bayou, and Gulf fishing. For a complete list of guides and charter boat services contact the Convention and Visitors Bureau (800-235-7822).

Golf

BABE DIDRIKSON ZAHARIAS MEMORIAL GOLF COURSE

75th St. just off US 69 • 722-8286

18-hole course. Green fees $6–$7.

PORT GROVES GOLF CLUB

5721 Monroe Blvd., Groves • 962-4030

Nine-hole course open to the public. Green fees about $2.50 for 9 holes; weekends $3.50.

COLLEGES AND UNIVERSITIES

LAMAR UNIVERSITY AT PORT ARTHUR

1500 Proctor near Stillwell • 983-4921 • W variable

About 1,500 students are enrolled in technical and vocational courses. Visitors are welcome at the Gates Memorial Library, which contains the school library and rare book collection. This Renaissance-style building was donated by the wife of John "Bet-a-Million" Gates who had it designed by the same architects who designed New York's Grand Central Station. Also open to the public are frequent shows put on by visiting entertainers in the Ruby Ruth Fuller Building. Call 724-0886 for show schedule.

SHOPPING

SNOOPER'S PARADISE

5509 East Parkway in Cambridge Square (39th St. exit off TX 73), Groves 962-8427 • W

Here are 26,000 square feet filled with European furniture and other antiques from the nineteenth century.

SIDE TRIPS

SABINE PASS BATTLEGROUND STATE HISTORICAL PARK

Take TX 87 south about 14 miles to Sabine Pass, then south about 1.5 miles on FM 3322 • **971-2559 (Sea Rim State Park) • Open at all times • W**

It sounds like a Texas tall tale—but it's true. On September 8, 1863, a Union fleet numbering some 20 vessels and several thousand men tried to invade Texas through Sabine Pass. Facing them was Company F of the Texas Heavy Artillery, which consisted of a lieutenant—a young barkeep from Houston named Dick Dowling—and some 40 Irish dockworkers, and six cannons set up in unfinished earthworks reinforced with railroad iron and ships' timbers. In less than an hour, Dowling wound up with all six of his cannons and no casualties while the Union force lost two gunboats, 65 men killed, wounded, or missing, and 315 captured. The Union fleet returned to New Orleans. Here are picnic sites, restrooms, a boat ramp, and a statue of Dowling.

SEA RIM STATE PARK

About 14 miles west of Sabine Pass on TX 87 • 971-2559 • March–October open daily 8–10 for day use; November–February open daily 8–5 for day use; at all times for camping but gates close at day-use closing hours • Fee per vehicle per day • W+ but not all areas

This is the only marshland park in Texas. The highway divides the 15,109-acre park into two distinct areas. South, on the Gulf, is the Beach Unit with three miles of wide, sandy beach and a little over two miles of a biologically important zone where the salt tidal marshlands meet the Gulf. Here is the park headquarters, observation deck, camping area (fee) and Interpretive Center. The Marshlands Unit has a boat ramp, canoe and pirogue trails, observation platforms, and blinds. Don't forget the insect repellent. Airboat rides sometimes available. For information write Park Superintendent, P.O. Box 1066, Sabine Pass 77655.

ANNUAL EVENTS

January

JANIS JOPLIN BIRTHDAY BASH

Port Arthur Civic Center • 800-235-7822 (Convention and Visitors Bureau) Saturday closest to Joplin's Birthday (January 19) • Admission varies • W

An all-star tribute to the world-famous music of the Golden Triangle and Gulf Coast area. Enjoy live musical entertainment featuring a combination of styles representative of Southeast Texas including country, Cajun, and rhythm and blues.

February

MARDI GRAS SOUTHEAST TEXAS STYLE

Downtown Port Arthur Arts and Entertainment District • 800-235-7822 (Convention and Visitors Bureau) • Thursday–Sunday of the weekend preceding Ash Wednesday • Admission varies • W
    Billed as a "family affair," Mardi Gras festivities include masked balls, art exhibits, pageants, contests, parades, arts and crafts, ethnic foods, a kiddie land, and a fireworks finale. Four days of continuous entertainment feature headliner performers and more than a dozen bands.

April

PLEASURE ISLAND MUSIC FESTIVAL

Pleasure Island Music Park • 800-235-7822 (Convention and Visitors Bureau) Last Friday, Saturday, and Sunday in April • Admission • W
    Music is continuous with all types represented. During the day there are groups performing on stages throughout the park. At night there's a big name show on the main stage. Also there's an arts-and-crafts show, contests, a children's tent, and games.

RESTAURANTS

CHANNEL INN

Sabine Pass, TX 87 at entrance to Sabine Pass • 971-2400 • Lunch and dinner $$ • MC, V • W • Children's plates
    This restaurant grew out of the owner's decision to branch out from just pulling in seafood on his commercial fishing boats. A feature here is "platter service," which is all you can eat from platters of barbecued crabs, frog legs, catfish, stuffed crab, fried shrimp, and gumbo. Oysters in season, extra. Beer and wine.

DOROTHY'S FRONT PORCH

Nederland, 100 Holmes Rd. • 722-1472 • Lunch and dinner Tuesday–Sunday. Closed Monday • Reservations suggested • $$
    What started as a tiny restaurant on Dorothy and Cooper Borrough's front porch has grown to a 5,000-square-foot building. Catfish is the big item and it comes fried in peanut oil, mesquite smoked, broiled several ways, or blackened.

ESTHER'S CAJUN SEAFOOD AND OYSTER BAR

TX 87 at foot of Rainbow Bridge • 962-6268 • Lunch and dinner daily Reservations suggested • $$ • Cr • Children's plates
    Overlooking the marshes and marina on the Neches, Esther's became famous overnight when *Texas Monthly* wrote a magnificent article about her restaurant. It's all great Cajun cooking, particularly the seafood. Beer and wine.

ACCOMMODATIONS

($ = under $45, $$ = $46–$60, $$$ = $61–$80, $$$$ = $81–$100, $$$$$ = over $100)
Room tax 13%

HOLIDAY INN PARK CENTRAL

Memorial Hwy (US 69) at 75th St. • 724-5000 or 800-HOLIDAY • $$–$$$ • W+ 2 rooms • No-smoking rooms

This four-story Holiday Inn offers 164 units that include four suites ($$$) and 16 no-smoking rooms. Satellite TV with HBO. Room phones (charge for local calls). Guest memberships available in YMCA. Pets OK. Free transportation to airport and golf course. Restaurant and lounge. Outdoor pool, outdoor spa. Free coffee and newspaper. Municipal golf course and jogging track across street.

RAMADA INN

3801 TX 73 (9th Ave. exit) • 962-9858 or 800-2-RAMADA (800-272-6232) $$ • W+ 5 rooms

The two-story Ramada has 125 units including two suites ($$$$$). Cable TV. Room phones (no charge for local calls). Guest memberships available in YMCA and Wellness Center. Pets OK. Free transportation to airport and around city. Restaurant and lounge. Outdoor pool, jogging track, and two lighted tennis courts. Free coffee in lobby. Some rooms with kitchenettes.

PORT LAVACA

Calhoun County Seat • 10,886 • (512)

Soon after Texas became a state, Calhoun County was formed, named after John C. Calhoun, a senator from South Carolina who had used his influence to get Texas admitted as a slave state. Port Lavaca was named the county seat.

Then a competing port grew up on the peninsula to the south. It was called Indianola, and by 1856 it had taken so much business away from Port Lavaca that the county seat was moved there. Port Lavaca remained a backwater until two devastating hurricanes in 1875 and 1886 virtually wiped Indianola from the map. Then the shipping business and the county seat were moved back to Port Lavaca, where they remain to this day.

Today Port Lavaca is still a port, serving the major petrochemical and other industrial plants scattered up and down the nearby coast as well as both commercial and sport fishermen. Its location on protected Lavaca Bay also attracts enthusiasts for boating and all types of water sports.

TOURIST SERVICES

PORT LAVACA-CALHOUN COUNTY CHAMBER OF COMMERCE

Bauer Community Center, 2300 TX 35, just west of the Causeway (P.O. Box 528, 77979) • 552-2959 • Monday–Friday 8:30–12, 1–5 • W+

MUSEUMS

CALHOUN COUNTY MUSEUM

301 S. Ann • 552-2661 • Tuesday–Friday 1:30–4:30, Saturday 10–2. Closed Sunday • Free • W

One of the exhibits in this museum is a scale model with four dioramas of scenes in the town of Indianola as it looked in 1875 before it was destroyed by hurricanes. Also on display is the original Fresnel lens from the 1852 Matagorda Island Lighthouse, which, except for a time during the Civil War, served as a guiding beacon for ships until 1977. The museum is in the restored 1896 county jail building and old public library complex.

OTHER POINTS OF INTEREST

PORT LAVACA STATE FISHING PIER AND PIER PARK

TX 35 at the Causeway • 552-4402 • Fishing pier open daily, summer 6 A.M to midnight, winter 8 A.M. to midnight; park always open • Fishing $1 per device + tax • W variable
This lighted fishing pier is built on the pilings of the old causeway from Port Lavaca to Point Comfort. It extends more than half a mile into the bay and local anglers claim it's a great place to catch speckled trout, flounder, and redfish. A fee is charged for fishing, but if you just want to stroll out and enjoy the view, that's free. The adjoining park has RV spaces (fee), a swimming pool (fee), a playground, restrooms, and showers.

PORT LAVACA LIGHTHOUSE BEACH AND BIRD SANCTUARY

TX 35 at the Causeway • $2 per car, no charge for walk-ins • W variable
The only natural sand beach in the area, it includes a Wetlands Walkway made entirely of recycled plastics equaling approximately 2 million milk cartons.

SPORTS AND ACTIVITIES

Fishing

Landlubbers can fish off the lighted state pier or the pier at Lighthouse Beach or from the many other area beaches. Or you can go out in a boat on the bay or the Gulf. Most of the guides and charter boats operate out of nearby Port O'Connor and are listed with the Port Lavaca-Calhoun County Chamber of Commerce (*see* Tourist Services).

One of the richest fishing tournaments on the Gulf is held in Port O'Connor each year, usually in mid-July. This is the Poco Bueno Invitational Offshore Fishing Tournament, a deep-sea contest in which prizes can reach over a quarter million dollars. Sorry, but it is invitational and to be one of the hundred or so who get invited you need a deep-sea fishing reputation plus a big boat and big bucks.

SIDE TRIPS

INDIANOLA

Take TX 238 (Austin St.) southwest about 2 miles to TX 316, then take 316 about eight miles to the Indianola site
What you can see here is a historical marker, a monument, and a beach park. What you can't see is the ghost of a town that once was one of the most bustling ports on the Gulf.

In the 1840s, huge piers stretched out half a mile into the Gulf. In addition to the tons of cargo that went through the port, this was the main port of entry for new colonists coming to Texas, including the Germans who arrived with Prince

Carl zu Solms-Braunfels to found the inland cities of New Braunfels and Fredericksburg. Indianola became so prosperous that the county seat was moved here from Port Lavaca.

The town survived Union shellings and capture and recapture by both sides during the Civil War, yellow fever epidemics, and two hurricanes—in 1866 and 1875—that partially destroyed it and killed more than 900 people. The people felt it was too prosperous to let die, so they rebuilt only to be struck by a third hurricane and tidal wave that swept over it in 1886 leveling it. This time there was no rebuilding. There wasn't even anything left to move when they returned the county seat to Port Lavaca.

The 22-foot granite monument here is not to the people who withstood the three lashings from the elements before finally giving up, but to the French explorer, Rene Robert Cavelier Sieur de laSalle, who landed here in 1685.

There are covered picnic tables, barbecue pits, a boat ramp, and RV hook-ups at the little beach park and an assortment of rental cabins, bait shops, and other small businesses along the beach.

MATAGORDA ISLAND STATE PARK

P.O. Box 117, Port O'Connor 77982-0117 (Texas Parks and Wildlife office) 983-2215

A barrier island, Matagorda stretches nearly 38 miles southwest from Pass Cavallo, near Port O'Connor, to the Aransas National Wildlife Refuge. The U.S. Department of the Interior owns most of the island, but Texas Parks and Wildlife Department (TPWD) manages the nearly 45,000 acres. About 36,000 of these acres are set aside as a wildlife management area to protect endangered species. Most of the rest is open to the public as a state park. However, this island is still in its near-natural state—no condos, no T-shirt vendors, in fact, no drinking water, no electricity, not much of anything except miles and miles of pristine beach where you can go swimming, fishing, picnicking (bring your own food and water), shell collecting, or bird watching. There are also 80 miles of beach, roadway, and mowed pathways for hiking and bicycling.

A passenger ferry runs between the State Park Docks at 16th and Maple in Port O'Connor and the island three times a day every Saturday, Sunday, and holiday. A shuttle vehicle is available to take visitors the 2.5 miles across the island to the Gulf beach. Ferry fare is $8 for adults and $4 for children 12 and under. The shuttle is $2 for adults and $1 for 12 and under. Reservations are recommended.

ANNUAL EVENTS

June

SUMMERFEST

Bauer Community Center and Lighthouse Beach on TX 35 • 552-2959 (Chamber of Commerce) • Friday–Sunday of Memorial Day weekend Free (admission to dances) • W variable

A Friday night dance at the Community Center kicks off this weekend festival that includes a variety of entertainment, beauty pageant, carnival, and swimming and diving competitions, and many other activities on the beach. There's also another dance on Saturday night.

TEXAS WATER SAFARI

Seadrift, Bayfront Park • Free • W variable

Billed as the "World's Toughest Boat Race," this event challenges teams to paddle non-stop 260 miles from San Marcos to Seadrift against a 100-hour deadline. Any muscle-powered craft can be used—and everything from racing sculls to kayaks to pedal-powered boats have been—but most teams stick to standard aluminum canoes, often rigged with lights for night travel. Trophies are awarded in several categories, from being first to being first over-40, solo, or novice. Those who survive the grueling trip down the San Marcos and Guadalupe rivers to cross the finish line here at Seadrift also earn the much-coveted Water Safari patch.

RESTAURANTS

($ = under $7, $$ = $8–$17, $$$ = $18–$25, $$$$ = over $25 for one person excluding drinks, tax, and tip.)

THE PANTRY

702 N. Virginia • 552-1679 • Lunch Monday–Friday. Closed Saturday–Sunday • $ • Cr • W

There are about a dozen tables in this cozy restaurant set up in the rear of the Greenhouse Flower Shop. The blackboard menu lists soups, sandwiches, salads, and the daily special, which may be roast beef, or a seafood, or chicken dish. There are also items listed—like lasagna and banana split pie—which don't sound diet or low-fat but are.

ACCOMMODATIONS

($ = under $45, $$ = $46–$60, $$$ = $61–$80, $$$$ = $81–$100, $$$$$ = over $100)
Room tax 13%

CHAPARRAL MOTEL

2086 TX 35 • 552-7581 • $ • W+ 2 rooms

There are 53 rooms in this two-story motel. Children under 12 stay free in room with parents. Senior discount. Cable TV with HBO. Room phones (local calls free). No pets. Restaurant adjoining. Outdoor pool. Free continental breakfast. Same-day dry cleaning.

DAYS INN

2100 N. TX 35 • 552-4511 or 800-325-2525 • $ • W+ 1 room No-smoking rooms

The 99 units in this Days Inn include one suite ($$$) and ten no-smoking rooms. Children under 18 stay free in room with parents. Senior discount. Cable TV with HBO. Room phones (local calls free). Coffeemakers in rooms. Pets OK. Restaurant, room service, lounge open seven nights with occasional entertainment. Outdoor pool. Free coffee in restaurant. Self-service laundry and same-day dry cleaning. Small refrigerators in some rooms.

ROCKPORT AND FULTON

Rockport: Aransas County Seat • 4,753 • (512)
Fulton: Aransas County • 783 • (512)

These adjoining towns have grown together until most visitors now think of them as one. Located on a peninsula that rivals anything on the coast for natural beauty and protected by the barrier of San Jose Island, both are important commercial and sport fishing centers and popular resort communities.

Also considered part of this resort area is the small town of Lamar which sits just across the LBJ Causeway (SH 35) on the east side of Copano Bay. Established in 1838, shortly after the Texas Revolution, Lamar was one of the first towns settled in this area. It was during that Revolution that an unusual incident occurred near here in which a land force captured several enemy ships. It started when a company of mounted Rangers surprised and captured a merchant ship that was carrying supplies for the Mexican Army. They then used this ship as a decoy to lure in and capture two other Mexican supply ships. For this exploit, this company of Rangers became known locally as the Horse Marines.

This area has been known as an art community for several years. Today, it is home to approximately 150 artists, several commercial art galleries, photography studios, and numerous art-related shops.

TOURIST SERVICES

ROCKPORT-FULTON AREA CHAMBER OF COMMERCE VISITORS CENTER

404 Broadway (78382) • 729-6445 or 800-242-0071 or 800-826-6441
Monday–Friday 9–5, Saturday 9–2 • W

Among the free area map and many brochures available here are two walking tour guides: *Historical Walking Tour of Downtown Rockport* and *Take a Gallery Walk*. A *Historical Driving Tour* audiocassette tape is also available for use in your car ($3 deposit).

BOAT TOURS

Several boats operating out of here offer tours to Aransas National Wildlife Refuge, usually from November 1st through early March when the whooping cranes are there. Fares run about $25 for adults and $14 for children 12 and under. Although most skippers will take walk-ons, in the height of the whooping crane season *all* the boats fill up fast so reservations are strongly recommended. For a complete list of the tour boats, contact the Chamber of Commerce (see above).

MUSEUMS

TEXAS MARITIME MUSEUM

1202 Navigation Circle, BUS 35 at Rockport Harbor (P.O. Box 1836, 78381)
729-1271 • Tuesday–Saturday 10–4, Sunday 1–4. Closed Monday and some
major holidays • Adults $4, children 4 to 12 $2, under 4 free
W+ main floor only

Perhaps because of its cowboy image, few people realize that Texas is a maritime state with hundreds of miles of coastline, 12 deep-water ports, and a history that goes from Spanish treasure ships to the Texas Navy to the modern treasures of black gold brought up by offshore oil rigs. This museum is dedicated to overcoming that lack of understanding by preserving our maritime heritage and explaining its impact on our lives. Exhibits include artifacts from shipwrecks of Spanish ships dating back to 1554, paintings of all the sailing ships in the Texas Navy, and detailed coverage of the steamboat river trade. Gift shop.

HISTORIC PLACES

FULTON MANSION STATE HISTORIC STRUCTURE

Fulton Beach Rd. at Henderson, about 3 miles north • 729-0386
Wednesday–Sunday 9–noon and 1–4; last morning tour at 11:15, last
afternoon tour at 3:15 • Adults $4, children (6–12) $2, under 6 free
W first floor and basement only, lift in rear

When cattle baron George Fulton built this 30-room mansion in the mid-1870s, he used his engineering background to make it what we would now call "state-of-the-art." The exterior is French Second Empire, but inside, the house had a central heat and ventilation system, hot and cold running water, flush toilets, and gas lights fueled by a gas plant in the rear of the house. In the larder, water was circulated through concrete troughs to cool perishable food. The mansion has been restored to its original splendor by the Texas Parks and Wildlife Department. Visitors are requested to wear flat, soft-soled shoes to prevent damage to floors. Because this is a major tourist attraction in the area, in summer you might want to call first to find out the waiting time. Gift shop. For information write Park Superintendent, P.O. Box 1859, Fulton 78358.

OTHER POINTS OF INTEREST

THE BIG TREE OF LAMAR

Lamar. *Take SH 35 north across the LBJ Causeway to Park Rd. 13, then right (east) to sign, then left to tree* **• Open at all times • W**

While not the biggest tree in the state—that title goes to a bald cypress in East Texas—this Texas Champion coastal live oak earns its title as The Big Tree. Its trunk is more than 35 feet in circumference, it stands at a height of 44 feet above the ground and has a crown spread of 89 feet. The Big Tree is estimated to be well over 1,000 years old.

GOOSE ISLAND STATE RECREATION AREA

Lamar. *Take SH 35 north across the LBJ Causeway to Park Rd. 13, then east (right) and follow signs to entrance* **• 729-2858 • Open daily 8–8 for day use, at all times for camping • $2 per person per day • W+ but not all areas**

Starting on the mainland, this 314-acre park extends out onto a peninsula and several islands located in the conjunction of Aransas, Copano, and St. Charles bays. Facilities are available for boating, fishing, swimming, water skiing, picnicking, and camping (fee). For information write Park Superintendent, Star Route 1, Box 105, Rockport 78382.

ROCKPORT BEACH PARK

Rockport Harbor off BUS 35 • Open 5 A.M.–11 P.M. • 729-9293 (attendant on duty) or 729-2213 (City of Rockport) • Parking $3, walk-ins free • W variable

The heart of this park is the more than a mile of sandy beach on the shallow waters of Aransas Bay. Facilities include picnic cabanas, a fitness trail, saltwater swimming pool, playgrounds, lighted fishing pier, water ski area, pavilions with showers, restrooms, and concessions that rent water sports equipment including paddleboats and jet skis. For birders, there's an observation platform overlooking Little Bay.

ROCKPORT CENTER FOR THE ARTS

902 Navigation Circle (78382), at Rockport Harbor • 729-5519 • Tuesday–Saturday 10–4, Sunday 1–4. Closed Monday and major holidays • Free • W+

Housed in the attractive 1890s Bruhl/O'Connor home set against a backdrop of the harbor, this center could itself be the subject for the artist's brush. Inside are four galleries where local artists show ther work and three studio classrooms. During the year changing exhibits range from traditional to modern art in several media.

THE WINDSWEPT LEANING TREES

Mostly along Fulton Beach Rd., Fulton

These live oaks appear to be hanging on in a fight with the elements for survival. Sculpted into bent and twisted shapes by the constant winds, at times they look like creatures bowing gracefully toward the earth, and, at other times, like a Disney version of a witch's forest.

SPORTS AND ACTIVITIES

Birdwatching

Close to 500 different species of birds have been spotted in the Rockport area. A *Bird Sightings* bulletin board is kept at the Chamber of Commerce Visitors Center. For $2.17 by mail, you can get the 16-page area *Birder's Guide* from the Chamber of Commerce (*see* Tourist Services). This colorfully illustrated and comprehensive guide includes a loop driving tour that takes in most of the birding spots in the area and a seasonal checklist of birds. It also lists local birding groups and birding hotlines (e.g., Coastal Bend Bird Hotline 512-364-3634). The Connie Hagar Bird Sanctuary and the newer Connie Hagar Cottage Sanctuary are both in town.

Boating

Boating is excellent in all the area bays, and the Gulf is just a short trip away through Aransas Pass. Sunfish sailboat races are scheduled in Little Bay every Tuesday evening from May through August. There are also several sailboat regattas held during the summer and the race/cruise to Port Isabel is held annually over Labor Day weekend.

Fishing

Without leaving land, you can fish from the jetty at Rockport, the private fishing piers owned by many of the motels on the shoreline, the Fulton public pier, or the Copano Bay Fishing Pier (*see* below). Party boats operate out of Rockport harbor for bay fishing with fares running about $22–$25. For information on these and on charter boats and guides for both bay and offshore fishing, contact the Chamber of Commerce (*see* Tourist Services). The Chamber also offers a 20-page area "Fishing Guide" by mail for $1.50.

COPANO BAY STATE PARK FISHING PIER

SH 35 N at the LBJ Causeway, approximately 5 miles north of Rockport 729-8633 • Open at all times, weather permitting • $1 per fishing apparatus • W

Waste not, want not. That seems to be the excellent policy followed by the Texas Parks and Wildlife Department when it came to salvaging the old bridge to Lamar after the new causeway was built. The bridge has been converted into lighted piers extending from both north and south sides (taking out the old drawbridge in the middle) for a total length of over a mile and a half. Snack bar, bait and tackle shop, and restrooms on both sides; public boat ramp on the south side.

Golf

ROCKPORT COUNTRY CLUB

101 Champions Dr. (78382) • 729-4182

Eighteen hole, semi-private course, designed by Ben Crenshaw, and rated one of the top 50 courses in Texas by *The Dallas Morning News*. Green fees approximately $50.

SIDE TRIPS

ARANSAS NATIONAL WILDLIFE REFUGE

Take TX 35 north to FM 774 then northeast (right) to Austwell, then south (right) about 7 miles on FM 2040 to Refuge; **approximately 38 miles from Rockport • (512)286-3559 • Open daily sunrise to sunset. Closed Thanksgiving and Christmas. Wildlife Interpretive Center open daily 8:30–4:30 • Entrance free upon registering • W variable**

With about 70,000 acres, this is the largest national wildlife refuge in Texas. It is also the winter home of the whooping crane. These birds, which stand over five feet tall, migrate in October or November each year from their summer home in Canada. Only 21 whoopers were known to exist in the world in the early '40s when the U.S. and Canada started a joint program to save the bird from extinction. Slowly the efforts are paying off. Though still an endangered species, more than 100 whoopers usually winter in this colony alone. Their habitat is in the marshland along the shore so they cannot be seen from the refuge roads. The best way to see them is from the refuge observation tower or on one of the boat tours (*see* Tourist Services). But there's a lot more to see than just the whoopers. With the Central and Mississippi migratory flyways merging in the area, 392 species of birds have been spotted here. On the 16-mile loop drive you may see many species of birds, plus deer, coyotes, javelina, wild turkeys, armadillo, and even alligators. There are also over seven miles of walking trails and picnic areas. According to the park rangers, the most rewarding time to visit is November through March when both the migratory waterfowl and the whoopers are there. Picnic area. For information write P.O. Box 100, Austwell, 77950.

ANNUAL EVENTS

March

FULTON OYSTERFEST

Fulton Navigation Park at Fulton Harbor • 800-242-0071 (Chamber of Commerce) • First full Friday–Sunday weekend in March • Free • W variable

A gumbo cookoff and oyster-shucking and oyster-eating contests are just a few of the events in this festival sponsored by the Fulton Volunteer Fire Department. It also includes an arts and crafts show, entertainment, dances, a carnival, and, of course, lots of food booths including some selling—guess what?

July

JULY 4th WEEKEND

Various locations • 729-6445 or 800-242-0071 or 800-826-6441 (Chamber of Commerce) • 3 or 4 days on weekend including July 4th • Parking at Beach Park $3 • W variable

Highlights of this weekend include a patriotic boat parade on Little Bay, an airshow and fireworks over the Rockport Beach Park, a static aircraft display at the Aransas County Airport, and an art festival at the Harbor Festival Grounds next to the beach park.

August

FIESTA EN LA PLAYA

Rockport Harbor Festival Grounds • 729-6445 or 800-242-0071 or 800-826-6441 (Chamber of Commerce) • Saturday–Sunday of Labor Day weekend • Free W variable

This is a fiesta with a Hispanic flavor that features *Tejano* concerts, mariachi bands, folkloric and other dancers, piñata breaking and jalapeño eating contests, arts and crafts show, and plenty of Tex-Mex food.

September

HUMMER/BIRD CELEBRATION

Various locations • 800-242-0071 (Chamber of Commerce) • Thursday evening through Sunday of second weekend after Labor Day • Fees for individual programs/lectures and bus and boat field trips, or variety of combination passes • W variable

Close to 500 species of birds have been recorded in this area and one of them is the hummingbird, which migrates here each fall in great numbers. Although the hummer is the focus of this weekend's activities, there are speakers, programs, and workshops on many other birds including, of course, the whooping crane. Bus and boat tours to see the birds are available.

October

ROCKPORT SEAFAIR

Downtown and Rockport Harbor • 800-242-0071 (Chamber of Commerce) Usually weekend preceding Columbus Day • $1 Entrance fee • W variable

A land parade, boat regattas, water shows, arts-and-crafts booths, crab races, a beauty pageant, a gumbo cookoff, live entertainment, a carnival, and a variety of contests (including the "Anything That Floats But a Boat Race") keep things moving at this two-day event. But the biggest draw remains the fresh shrimp, oysters, and other seafood cooked up and sold at the food booths operated by local civic groups.

RESTAURANTS

($ = under $7, $$ = $8–$17, $$$ = $18–$25, $$$$ = over $25 for one person excluding drinks, tax, and tip.)

THE BOILING POT

Fulton Beach Rd., just north of the Fulton Mansion • 729-6972 • Lunch and dinner Friday–Sunday, dinner only Monday–Thursday • $–$$ • MC, V, DIS • W

You're furnished a bib and a small mallet (for the crabs). Then the boiled Cajun-style crabs, shrimp, and crawfish, mixed with chunks of spicy sausage and potatoes or corn on the cob, are dumped on butcher paper on the table in front of you and you go at it. Beer, wine, and champagne.

CHARLOTTE PLUMMER'S SEA FARE

202 Fulton Beach Rd. at Fulton Harbor • 729-1185 • Lunch and dinner daily and Sunday brunch • $$ • AE, MC, V • W+

The specialty is broiled and baked seafood with frying pretty much confined to the seafood platters. If you have three or more in your party you might want to try the Seafare Special, which includes shrimp steamed in beer, fish, oysters, and crab cakes—all served family style. Because they don't take reservations, the waiting can back up at times. Beer and wine.

CRAB-N RESTAURANT

City by the Sea, SH 35 about 5 miles west of Rockport (P.O. Box 998, Aransas Pass, 78335) • 758-2371 • Dinner only daily • $$–$$$ • Cr • W

Guests can drive-up or boat-up to this waterside restaurant. Naturally, the menu emphasizes seafood with entrées like grilled amberjack with crab and shrimp buttercream sauce, and sautéed crab cakes with lump crab and roasted pecan relish. Also some steaks and chicken choices. Seniors and children's menus. Bar.

KLINE'S CAFÉ

106 S. Austin (P.O. Box 101, 78381) • 729-8538 • Breakfast, lunch, and dinner Friday–Tuesday. Closed Wednesday–Thursday • $–$$ • No Cr • W

The dinner menu includes a number of seafood entrées, like stuffed flounder and a seafood platter with crab, scallops, oysters, fried fish and fried shrimp. Tuesday night features all-you-can-eat fried fish. But you can also get chicken, steaks, chops, and some Tex-Mex entrées as well as soups, salads, and sandwiches. Beer and wine.

ACCOMMODATIONS

($ = under $45, $$ = $46–$60, $$$ = $61–$80, $$$$ = $81–$100, $$$$$ = over $100)

(Rates are for a double room in high season. Off-season rates are usually lower, sometimes considerably so.)

Room tax 12%

BEST WESTERN ROCKPORT REBEL

800 Block of SH 35 N, Fulton (P.O. Box 310, Fulton 78358) • 729-8351 or 800-528-1234 • $–$$ • W+ 1 room • No-smoking rooms

This two-story Best Western has 72 units that include 24 kitchen unit suites ($$$$) and 24 no-smoking units. Children under 12 stay free in room with parents. Senior discount. Satellite TV with HBO. Room phones (local calls free). Pets OK ($25 pet deposit). Restaurant with room service. Outdoor pool. Free coffee in lobby and free newspaper. Self-service laundry and same-day dry cleaning.

DAYS INN

1212 Laurel at Broadway (SH 35), just north of the harbor • 729-6379 or 800-248-1057 or 800-DAYS-INN (800-329-7466) • $–$$ • No-smoking rooms

This two- and three-story inn has 29 rooms including two no-smoking. Children under 12 stay free in room with parents. Senior discount. Cable TV. Room phones (local calls free). Pets OK. Outdoor heated pool. Free continental breakfast.

HUMMINGBIRD LODGE AND EDUCATIONAL CENTER

5652 FM 1781 (HCO-1 Box 245, 78382), 6 miles north of Rockport just south of LBJ Causeway • 729-7555 or toll free 888-827-7555 • $$$–$$$$

There are eight guest rooms with private baths in this one-story bed and breakfast lodge. Package plans available. Cable TV. Outdoor pool. Seventy-two foot porch. Free gourmet breakfast. Other meals available ($8–$16). On nineteen-acre preserve at the tip of Live Oak Peninsula. Naturalist on staff. Guided nature walks and bird classes available (fee). Write or call for free newsletter.

LAGUNA REEF HOTEL

1021 S. Water St., entrance on Austin • 729-1742 or in Texas 800-248-1057 $$$ • W+ 1 room • No-smoking rooms

The 21 hotel rooms and 49 one- and two-bedroom suites ($$$$–$$$$$) in the four-story Laguna Reef include 32 no-smoking. Senior discount. Cable TV. Room phones (charge for local calls). Coffeemakers in suites. Small pets OK ($40 deposit). Outdoor pool. Small beach and 1,000-foot lighted fishing pier. Free continental breakfast. Self-service laundry.

SANDOLLAR RESORT

SH 35, approximately 5 miles north of Rockport (H.C.R. Box 30, Rockport 78382) • 729-2381 • $–$$$

There are 49 motel rooms in this one- and two-story resort that runs between SH 35 and Fulton Beach Rd. Cable TV. Room phones (local calls free). Pets OK. Restaurant, lounge open seven nights with entertainment occasionally. Two outdoor pools. Free coffee in office. Self-service laundry. Playground. Marina and 500-foot lighted fishing pier. Some kitchenettes. Also 76 RV hook-ups, almost all in the shade, costing about $10 a night.

SOUTH PADRE ISLAND AND PORT ISABEL

South Padre Island • Cameron County • 2,028 • (956)
Port Isabel • Cameron County • 4,894 • (956)

As you leave the mainland city of Port Isabel on the Queen Isabella Causeway, Texas' longest bridge, South Padre rises in front of you like a glowing island in the sun, luxurious and dreamlike. Here is the sun-bleached essence of the modern summer resort: a long, white beach—rated by some travel writers as one of the ten best beaches in the world— towering resort hotels and condominiums that offer all the pleasures of resort living, and a wide variety of activities for those who want more than just lazying on the sand or watching the sunset. Tourism is king here, accounting for close to one hundred percent of the island's business. Statistical evidence of this can be seen in the fact that there are about 1,500 hotel/motel rooms and close to 3,500 condominiums for rent.

Each year more than 2.5 million visitors come to play at the shore and enjoy the casual life known as "island-style," which blends small town ambiance with sophisticated living and dining.

The town of South Padre is on the southern tip of Padre Island, a narrow strip of land—in reality a giant sandbar—running parallel to the coast for more than a hundred miles from Corpus Christi on the north to this beach resort town.

The "South" in the name came to be when the Mansfield Cut, about 34 miles north, was completed in 1964, chopping Padre Island into two parts. Most of the land north of the cut is part of the Padre Island National Seashore (*see* Corpus Christi). South of the cut it's private land, but only about five miles on the southernmost end have been developed into the town with the same name as the island. To the east is the Gulf of Mexico with its white-tipped waves. To the west are the calm waters of Laguna Madre. And only about 30 miles south is Mexico.

Overall, South Padre is a getaway island with all the conveniences. And Port Isabel, on the mainland, once known only for its fishing and as the gateway to South Padre, is coming into its own as the home port of day cruise ships and the home city of several fine restaurants.

TOURIST SERVICES

SOUTH PADRE ISLAND CONVENTION AND VISITORS BUREAU

600 Padre Blvd. (78597), just north of the Causeway • 761-6433 or in U.S. and Canada 800-SO-PADRE (800-767-2373) in Mexico 95-800-SO-PADRE Monday–Friday 8–5, Saturday and Sunday 9–5 • Free • W

DOLPHIN WATCH BOAT TOURS

Tours to see the dolphins in the Bay are offered aboard the *Diver 1* (761-2030), the *Fish Tales* (943-3185), and the *Xcape!* (761-2212). Most tours last 1½ to 2 hours and cost $15 for adults and $10 for children 12 and under. *Diver 1* and *Xcape!* also offers nature tours and the *Diver 1* has sunset and moonlight cruises.

GRAY LINE TOURS

P.O. Box 2610, (78597) • 761-4343 or 800-321-8720 • Monday–Friday 8–6, Saturday–Sunday 8–3 • Tours $15–$99

They run daily six-hour sightseeing and shopping tours to nearby Matamoros, Mexico ($15–$25) and one-day ($30) and two-day ($99) tours to Monterrey, Mexico. Also golf tours and Ecotours of the Rio Grande Valley. Tours can be booked through most hotels/motels.

BIRD'S EYE VIEW

PORT ISABEL LIGHTHOUSE

Port Isabel, 421 Queen Isabella Blvd. • 943-2262 • Wednesday–Sunday 10–4. Closed Monday–Tuesday • Adults $2, students (12–18) $1, (7–12) 50¢, children 6 and under free.

Sitting in the middle of one of the state's smallest parks is the only lighthouse on the Texas coast that's open to the public. Completed in 1853, this guardian of the coast cast its light up to 16 miles out into the Gulf for more than half a century, until it was closed in 1905. From the top, on a clear day you can see almost forever. At least you'll get an unobstructed view of Port Isabel, the Causeway, South Padre Island, and well out into the Gulf. But this bird's-eye view doesn't come easy. To reach the top you have to climb more than 70 winding steps including three short ladders. On the grounds is an exact replica of the lighthouse keeper's cottage, originally built in 1855, which now houses the Port Isabel Chamber of Commerce (800-527-6102).

MUSEUMS

PORT ISABEL HISTORIC MUSEUM

Port Isabel, 317 Railroad at Tarnava (mailing address: 305 E. Maxan St, 78578) 943-7602 • Wednesday–Saturday 10–4, Sunday 1–4. Closed Monday–Tuesday Adults $3, seniors $2, students (13–18) children (12 and under) 50¢ • W+

The museum is housed in one of the oldest structures in Port Isabel, the historic Charles Champion Building, which dates from the 1890s. At one time, the building was the center of the community with its general store, post office, railroad depot, and the only telephone in town. The two-story museum now features interactive exhibits telling the story of the area. The second-floor exhibits tell the history of the Champion family, who were among the early settlers in the area.

POINTS OF INTEREST

ISLA BLANCA PARK (CAMERON COUNTY PARK)

South of Causeway at southern end of the island (P.O. Box 2106, 78597) 761-5493 • Open daily 6 A.M.–11 P.M., office open daily 8 A.M.–10 P.M. $3 per vehicle per day • W variable

In addition to containing one of the two RV camping areas on South Padre, this park also has over a mile of beach, marina, boat ramps, a fishing jetty, picnic areas, marine science exhibits, a bike trail, the Chapel by the Sea, a Coast Guard station, and restaurants.

QUEEN ISABELLA CAUSEWAY

Between Port Isabel and South Padre Island • Open at all times

Measuring 2.6 miles, this causeway across Laguna Madre Bay is in the record books as Texas' longest bridge. At the center the span is 73 feet above mean high tide permitting seagoing ships to pass underneath. It was built to withstand threefold hurricane force winds. About 6.5 million vehicles cross it each year.

UNIVERSITY OF TEXAS/PAN AMERICAN COASTAL STUDIES LAB

Isla Blanca Park (P.O. Box 2591, South Padre Island 78597) • 761-2644 Sunday–Friday 1:30–4:30. Closed Saturday • Free ($3 per vehicle for entrance to park) • W+

Research at this lab focuses on the coastal ecosystems of southern Texas and northern Mexico with emphasis on Laguna Madre and Padre Island. On display in aquariums are many species of marine life found in local waters, including Kemp's ridley sea turtles, stingray, redfish, grouper, snapper, and bighead sea robins. If you find shells on the beach, you can compare them to ones in the lab's extensive collection. If you find one you can't match, the lab's experts will identify it for you.

SPORTS AND ACTIVITIES

Boating and Windsurfing

Small craft can use the waters of the Laguna Madre while larger craft are just minutes away from the waters of the Gulf. Sailboats can be rented by the hour or the day and lessons are available. Charter boats for short term—like a sunset cruise—or long term are also available. For listings contact the South Padre Island Convention and Visitors Bureau (800-SO-PADRE).

Good winds and warm waters have combined to lure windsurfers, or boardsailers, to the island and make this a growing sport here. *Windsurfing* magazine has rated South Padre as one of the ten windsurfing destinations in the U.S. (*see* Annual Events).

Fishing

South Padre offers anglers a full range of opportunities. You can pay big bucks to go out in the Gulf after trophy game fish on a high-powered charter boat, pay a lot less for a half-day on a party boat in the bay or a day-long party boat trip in the Gulf, wade fish on the flats of Laguna Madre or in the surf, or just throw a line from a jetty or one of the two fishing piers. For information on fishing, party boats, charter boats, and guides contact the South Padre Island Convention and Visitors Bureau (800-SO PADRE) or the Port Isabel Chamber of Commerce (943-2262).

Golf

SOUTH PADRE ISLAND GOLF CLUB

Laguna Visa (mailing address 77 Santa Isabella, Laguna Vista 78578), *from Port Isabel go west on SH 100 to CR 510, then north* • **943-5678**
  Eighteen-hole course with 27 more in the planning stages. Green fees $35–$45.

Horseback Riding

ISLAND EQUESTRIAN CENTER

Andy Bowie County Park, north off Park Rd. 100 (P.O. Box 3633, 78597) 761-HOSS (761-4677) or 800-761-HOSS • Daily 8 A.M to dusk • $20–$25 hour
  Horses are available for all levels of riders for riding on the beach. Guides and instruction free. Pony rides for children under 6.

KIDS' STUFF

JEREMIAH'S

100 Padre Blvd., just south of the Causeway • 761-2131 • Open daily at noon in season, weather permitting
  This water park features seven waterslides for kids of all ages, a pollywog pond for small children, sundecks, video games, a snackbar, and a full-service bar for adults. The clue here is "If the flags are flyin', we're slidin'."

SIDE TRIPS

CASINO ISABELLA

1250 Port Rd. (78578) in Port Isabel • 943-GAME (943-4263) • Adults $24

As its name says, the ship is a floating casino featuring slots, bingo, and other games of chance. Sailings are Saturdays at 8 P.M. and Sundays at 10 A.M. Ticket includes one meal and a free cocktail. Both sailings can be tied together with a cabin for up to four in a Weekender Special for $99 per person. Reservations required and may be made Wednesday–Saturday 10–6.

ISABEL CORTES FERRY SERVICE LIMITED

Port Rd., Port Isabel (mailing address: 1200 W. Hwy 100, Suite 7A, Port Isabel) 943-2331 • W+ 1 cabin

The ocean-going ferry *M/V Regal Voyager* carries up to 400 passengers and 250 vehicles between Port Isabel and Puerto Cortes, Honduras, every week. It leaves Port Isabel on Sunday evening and arrives in Honduras early Wednesday. After an 8–10 hour stop-over it leaves Wednesday night, arriving in Port Isabel on Saturday. Fares range from $109 one way to $189 round trip for an economy double without private bath to $149 one way and $249 round-trip for a standard double. Fares include all meals. Nightly entertainment, small casino, and movie theater. Passenger vehicle fare is $684 one way, $325 for return.

ANNUAL EVENTS

March

SPRING BREAK

Various locations on the island • 761-6433 or 800-SO-PADRE (800-767-2373) (Convention and Visitors Bureau) • Last weekend in February through first week in April • Most events free • W variable

When you get right down to it, this is a big, boisterous beach bash for tens and tens of thousands of college students from all over the country who convene here when their schools close down for Spring Break. Organized activities include sports events, contests of all kinds, and many other events aimed at keeping the young crowd happy (so they will come back again), and their boundless energy in check (so they will leave the town in one piece when they depart).

May

SOUTH PADRE ISLAND WINDSURFING BLOWOUT

At "The Flats," just north of the Convention Center • 761-6433 or 800-SO-PADRE (800-767-2373) Convention and Visitors Bureau • First weekend in May • Free to spectators • W variable

This event is the largest amateur windsurfing tournament in the U.S. attracting surfers from across the country, Canada, and Mexico. Participants compete in course slalom races and long-distance races.

August

TEXAS INTERNATIONAL FISHING TOURNAMENT

Headquarters at South Point Marina, Port Isabel and Charlie's Paradise Bar (90 Park Rd.) on South Padre • 943-TIFT (943-8438), 943-6452 • Usually first weekend of August • Free to spectators • W variable

This is the second-oldest fishing competition on the coast, bowing only to the Deep Sea Roundup at Port Aransas. Trophies and awards are given for both bay and offshore fishing. Entry fees range from about $15 for children under 12—every child who catches a fish and weighs it in gets a trophy—to about $75 for adults. The entry fee includes social events most nights during the tourney.

OFFBEAT

SEA TURTLE, INC.

5805 Gulf Blvd. (P.O. Box 2575, 78597) • 761-2544 • Programs for visitors: Tuesday and Saturday at 10 A.M., weather permitting. Group tours at other times by arrangement • $2 donation • W

Shows designed to educate the public on the plight of Kemp's ridley sea turtle and other endangered sea turtles are held in the home of Ila Loetscher, the octogenarian "Turtle Lady" who has dedicated her life to saving and rehabilitating injured turtles. Although rarely active in the shows now, the Turtle Lady's enthusiasm for the project is still carried on by the volunteers. In her earlier years, Ms. Loetscher was one of the first woman pilots in the United States.

THE SONS OF THE BEACH

P.O. Box 2694, 78597 • 761-6222

During Spring Break 1987, more than 5,000 volunteers constructed what was then the world's longest sand castle on South Padre Island, a structure that measured more than two miles in length earning a place in the *Guiness Book of World Records*. The project was organized and guided by sand castle building wizards "Amazin' Walter" McDonald and Lucinda "Sandy Feet" Wierenga, founders of The Sons of the Beach (S.O.B.s). On Sundays, year-round, the S.O.B.s can be found building their intricate sand castles with towers, spiraling staircases, and gravity-defying arches on the beach in front of Boomerang Billy's (2612 Gulf Blvd.). They also give private lessons in sand castle building.

RESTAURANTS

($ = under $7, $$ = $8–$17, $$$ = $18–$25, $$$$ = over $25 for one person excluding drinks, tax, and tip.)

Dinner For Two

GRILL ROOM AT THE PANTRY

708 Padre Blvd. in Franke Plaza • 761-9331 • Dinner only Wednesday–Sunday (Days vary by season, call to confirm) • Reservations suggested • $$–$$$ • Cr • W

Among the seafood entrées are Red Snapper *Provence*, lump crab St. Charles, and a variety of shrimp dishes. The menu also offers beef, lamb chops, and grilled quail. All served in a cozy and comfortable dining room. The Pantry, attached, is open for breakfast and lunch from 10–4 and offers deli sandwiches and light lunch items ($) for your picnic basket, as well as gourmet foods. Bar.

THE YACHT CLUB

Port Isabel, 700 Yturria, about 2 blocks north of SH 100 • 943-1301
Dinner daily • Reservations suggested • $$$ • Cr • W

It hasn't been a yacht club since the Depression, but it still retains the air of substance—nothing cheap and nothing ostentatious—that one associates with old money. The cuisine carries out this promise at a more moderate cost than expected, featuring fresh seafood with just a dash of beef entrées. A house specialty, when available, is red snapper throats, a dish that will please the seafood-lover despite its unpleasant name. The full snapper fillet is available broiled, blackened or grilled. The wine list offers over 100 selections. Children's menu. No-smoking area. Bar.

Brewpub

PADRE ISLAND BREWING COMPANY

3400 Padre Blvd. • 761-9585 • Lunch and dinner Tuesday–Sunday, dinner only Monday • $$–$$$ • Cr • W+

The main draw is the 16 different handcrafted ales and lagers brewed here (about $3 a pint). But to go with them you can order a variety of soups and salads, sandwiches, burgers, pizza, baskets of fried seafood, and dinner entrées that include beer-batter shrimp, grilled swordfish, grilled quail, and baby back ribs. Second-floor deck. Bar.

Home Cooking

ROVAN'S BAKERY, RESTAURANT & BBQ

5300 Padre Blvd. • 761-6972 • Breakfast, lunch, and early dinner Wednesday–Monday (6 A.M.–6 P.M.). Closed Tuesday • $–$$ • No Cr • W+

Long famed for its variety of bountiful breakfasts (served all day), they also serve reasonably priced specials including all-you-can-eat buffets for about $6 (Saturday prime rib buffet $9). Also sandwiches, seafood, steaks and chops, barbecue, and fresh-from-the-oven bakery goodies. Gift shop.

Italian

MARCELLO'S ITALIAN RISTORANTE

Port Isabel, 101 N. Tarnava at SH 100, about 2 blocks from the Causeway
943-7611 • Lunch and dinner Monday–Friday, dinner only Saturday–Sunday
Reservations suggested • $–$$$ • Cr • W • Children's plates

All the familiar Italian standbys are on the menu here. There's a variety of pasta dishes including spaghetti with *pesto* sauce, lasagna, linguini with white or red clam sauce, *cannelloni, fettucini Alfredo,* and several veal and chicken entrées, plus *Sicilia-* and *Napolitana*-style pizza. They also offer fresh seafood choices like *scampi linguini* and flounder filet *parmigiana.* Live music Friday–Saturday nights. Bar.

Seafood

BLACKBEARD'S

103 E. Saturn, off Padre Blvd. 2 miles north of the Causeway • 761-2962
Lunch and dinner daily • No reservations • $–$$ • Cr • W (ramp)

Although well-known by the beach crowd for its burgers, sandwiches, and steaks, the main order of business is seafood. The top of the line is the Seafood Platter Supreme, which includes shrimp, stuffed crab, stuffed shrimp, fish, and scallops for about $16. Bar.

PIRATE'S LANDING

Port Isabel, 100 Garcia St. off SH 100 at the Lighthouse • 943-FOOD (943-3663) • Lunch and dinner daily • $–$$ • Cr • W+

Located next to the historic Port Isabel Lighthouse, this waterfront restaurant overlooks the tranquil Laguna Madre and South Padre Island. The menu offers a variety of seafood that comes from their own boats. Enclosed deck. Children's plates. Bar.

SEA RANCH RESTAURANT

1 Padre Blvd., at entrance to Isla Blanca Park • 761-1314 • Dinner daily (lunch daily January–February) • Reservations suggested on weekends $$–$$$ • Cr • W • Children's plates

Located next to the Sea Ranch Marina, this waterside restaurant specializes in fresh seafood ranging from *cerviche* to red snapper (and snapper throats) to lobster tails. But it also offers steaks, chicken, burgers, deli sandwiches, and Mexican food. No smoking area. Bar.

SCAMPI'S RESTAURANT AND BAR

206 W. Aries at Laguna • 761-1755 • Dinner daily • Reservations suggested $$–$$$$ • Cr • W downstairs only

If you can start off with an appetizer your choices include Oysters Rockefeller, Crab Nachos, or Peel-Your-Own Shrimp. Because the restaurant's name in Italian means shrimp, there is a variety of shrimp dishes on the menu including shrimp and fettucini and their award-winning Peanut-Butter Shrimp. Entrées also include Flounder Maurice and Flounder Georgette. For variety there are some steak and chicken dishes. Patio dining in good weather. Lounge upstairs.

ACCOMMODATIONS

($ = under $45, $$ = $46–$60, $$$ = $61–$80, $$$$ = $81–$100, $$$$$ = over $100)

Rate symbols are for high season (Spring Break and summer). Off-season rates are substantially lower.

Room Tax 13%

BAHIA MAR RESORT AND CONFERENCE CENTER

6300 Padre Blvd. (P.O. Box 2280, 78597) • 761-1343 or 800-99-PADRE (800-997-2373) • $$$–$$$$

This 12-story resort has 200 hotel rooms and 137 two- and three-bedroom condominium units ($$$$$) on 15 acres of beachfront property. Children under 12 stay free in room with parents. Package plans available. Cable TV with HBO. Room phones (charge for local calls). No pets. Restaurant. Two outdoor pools (one heated), outdoor whirlpool, two lighted tennis courts, putting green. Guest memberships available in country club and health club. Self-service laundry and same-day dry cleaning. Gift shop. On the beach.

DAYS INN

3913 Padre Blvd. • 761-7831 or 800-329-7466 • $$$–$$$$ • W+ 2 rooms
No-smoking rooms
   The 57 rooms in this two-story Days Inn include ten no-smoking rooms. Package plans and senior discount. Cable TV. Room phones (charge for local calls). Pets OK ($25 deposit). Outdoor pool, outdoor whirlpool. Free coffee in lobby and free continental breakfast. Self-service laundry. All rooms have kitchenettes (but no plates or utensils).

HOLIDAY INN SUNSPREE RESORT

100 Padre Blvd., just south of Causeway • 761-5401 or 800-465-4329
$$$$–$$$$$ • W+ 5 rooms • No-smoking rooms
   The four- and six-story Holiday Inn offers 227 units that include eight suites ($$$$$) and no-smoking rooms. Children under 12 stay free in room with parents. Package plans and senior discount available. Cable TV with premium channel and pay channel. Room phones (charge for local calls). No pets. Restaurant, club open seven nights with entertainment in season. Two outdoor pools (one heated), wading pool, outdoor whirlpool, four tennis courts, and rental water sports equipment. Self-service laundry and same-day dry cleaning. Gift shop. On the beach.

PADRE SOUTH RESORT

1500 Gulf Blvd. at Harbor (P.O. Box 2338, 78597) • 761-4951 • $$$–$$$$$
W+ 2 rooms
   The 87 units in this eight-story building include 62 efficiencies and 25 two-bedroom suites, all with kitchens. Children to age 10 stay free in room with parents. Senior discount and package plans available. Cable TV with HBO. Room phones (local calls free). No pets. Outdoor pool. Guest memberships available for golf. Self-service laundry and same-day dry cleaning. On the beach.

SHERATON FIESTA SOUTH PADRE ISLAND BEACH RESORT

310 Padre Blvd., south of Causeway • 761-6551 or 800-325-3535 • $$$$$
W+ 4 rooms • No-smoking rooms
   The 12-story Sheraton offers 248 units including 45 two-bedroom condominiums ($$$$$) and 24 no-smoking rooms. Children up to 17 stay free in room with parents. Package plans and senior discount available. Cable TV with pay channels. Room phones (charge for local calls). No pets. Two restaurants, room service, and club with live entertainment every night in season. Indoor/outdoor heated pool with pool bar in season, outdoor whirlpool, and four lighted tennis courts. All units have balconies with Gulf view. Free newspaper. Self-service laundry and same-day dry cleaning. Gift shop. On the beach.

RADISSON RESORT SOUTH PADRE ISLAND

500 Padre Blvd., just north of Causeway • 761-6511 or 800-333-3333
$$$$$ • No-smoking rooms
   The two-story hotel section of the Radisson Resort offers 128 hotel rooms, including 22 no-smoking, and 58 two-bedroom condominium units ($$$$$). Children under 18 stay free in room with parents. Package plans and senior discount available. Cable TV with HBO and pay channel. Room phones (charge for

local calls). No pets. Restaurant, room service, and club open seven nights with live entertainment every night. Two outdoor pools, three outdoor whirlpools, four lighted tennis courts. Guest memberships available in private golf club. Self-service laundry in 12-story condominium tower. Same-day dry cleaning. Gift shop. Limited covered parking. Ten acres on the beach.

THE YACHT CLUB HOTEL
Port Isabel, 700 Yturria, about 2 blocks north of TX 100 • 943-1301 • $$–$$$
This two-story hotel has 24 units including four suites ($$). Cable TV. No pets. Restaurant (*see* Restaurants, above), bar. Outdoor heated pool. Free continental breakfast. A classic, built in the 1920s and restored to close to its original condition.

Bed and Breakfast

BROWN PELICAN BED AND BREAKFAST
**207 W. Aires at Laguna (P.O. Box 2667, 78597) • 761-2722 • $$$$–$$$$$
W+ 1 room • All no-smoking**
This two-story B&B has eight rooms all with private baths, most with covered porches. Children over 12 welcome. No pets. Free continental breakfast. Rooms furnished with antiques and collectibles.

OTHER ACCOMMODATIONS

There are twice as many condominium units on South Padre Island as there are hotel and motel rooms and thousands of the condo apartments are available for rent. High season rates for a two-bedroom condo start at about $125 a day and go up to $300 or more with the location and number of amenities matching the price. Weekly rates are usually available.

Fortunately, finding a condo rental on South Padre is easy because almost all the rental units are listed with rental agencies. For a current listing of condominium units and rental agencies, contact the South Padre Island Convention and Visitors Bureau (800-SO PADRE, 800-767-2373).

VICTORIA

Victoria County Seat • 60,584 • (512)
Its location near the coast made the area around present-day Victoria a crossroads for early explorers. Cabeza DeVaca and La Salle were among those who tramped through this country. In 1722, the Spanish established a mission and fort just to the northwest. Both were later moved to the site of the present city of Goliad, but the area is still called Mission Valley.

Settlers moved in and out of the area until a permanent settlement was founded in 1824 by 41 Mexican families led by Martin De Leon. Some accounts say he named it after Mexican President Guadalupe Victoria; others say the original name was *Nuestra Señora de Guadalupe de Jesus Victoria.*

The settlement prospered from the sale of cattle and horses, most of which were wild descendants of animals abandoned when the mission moved, giving Victoria claim to the title "The Cradle of the Cattle Industry in Texas."

Most of the Mexican settlers fought on the side of the Texians in the Texas Revolution. The Victoria militia, part of Sam Houston's army, was led by De Leon's son-in-law. After the war, Victoria was established as one of the original counties under the republic, and the town was the third in Texas to receive a charter.

Agriculture was the mainstay of the area—Victoria is still one of the leading cattle counties in the state—until the 1930s when the oil and gas industries came here, followed by the chemical industry in the 1950s. Although inland, the city has water access to the Gulf and the rest of the country via the 35-mile Victoria Canal.

The city is an architectural treasure with almost 100 structures listed in the National Register of Historic Places. The city's newspaper, *The Victoria Advocate,* was founded in 1846, making it the second oldest in the state.

TOURIST SERVICES

VICTORIA CONVENTION AND VISITORS BUREAU
700 Main Center (P.O. Box 2465, 77902) • 573-5277 or 800-926-5774

MUSEUMS

McNAMARA HOUSE HISTORICAL MUSEUM
502 N. Liberty • 575-8227 • Tuesday–Sunday 1–5 • Free
This Victorian Gothic-style frame home was built in 1876 for W. J. McNamara, a prominent businessman who dealt in cotton and hides. It contains period rooms, and features both permanent and changing art and local history exhibits. The house is listed in the National Register of Historic Places.

NAVE MUSEUM
306 W. Commercial • 575-8227 • Tuesday–Sunday 1–5 • Free • W
Royston Nave was a Texas painter of portraits and landscapes who was acclaimed in New York art circles in the 1920s. Much of his work was painted in and around Victoria. This Greco-Roman building was built in 1931 by his widow to display his paintings. Contemporary art and traveling exhibits are also featured here.

HISTORIC PLACES

A booklet, *A Walking and Driving Tour of Old Victoria,* is available free from the Victoria Convention and Visitors Bureau (*see* Tourist Services).

MEMORIAL SQUARE
400 Block E. Commercial at Wheeler
A number of pioneer citizens and Texas Revolution and Civil War soldiers were buried here. The main items of interest on the square today are a Southern Pacific steam locomotive that made its last run right into Memorial Square in 1957 and a Dutch wind gristmill.

Historic Homes

More than 30 of the many historic homes in the city are listed in the National Register of Historic Places. Most were built in the late 1800s and early 1900s, but some are pre-Civil War. Many of the oldest homes were later expanded or renovated. These include: **Ledbetter-Phillips-Proctor-Austin-Welder House,** 604 N. Craig, the first portion built in 1844 and later expanded; **Pickering House,** 403 N. Glass, built on the coast in the 1850s and moved to Victoria, and renovated in 1911; **Phillips House,** 705 N. Craig, built in 1851 and stuccoed in 1893; **Callender House,** 404 W. Guadalupe, built in 1855 and later expanded; **Fox House,** 708 Power, with an original part built in the 1860s and later incorporated into the larger house in the 1890s; **Levi-Welder House,** 403 N. Main, built around 1860 with the porch added in the early 1900s. All are private homes not open to the public.

Other Historic Buildings

OLD VICTORIA COUNTY COURTHOUSE

101 N. Bridge • Monday–Friday 8–5 • Free

This Romanesque-Revival limestone structure was completed in 1892. It was designed by J. Riely Gordon, an architect well known during this period for his public buildings. Although a new courthouse has been built, parts of this one are still in use. The second-floor courtroom has been fully restored.

OTHER POINTS OF INTEREST

THE CHANCERY

1300 block of Mesquite • 573-0828 • Monday–Friday 9–4 • Free • W variable

This building houses the administrative offices of the Roman Catholic Diocese of Victoria; however, it is open to all visitors. Among the highlights of the building are the stained-glass windows. The small Chancery museum has exhibit areas divided into sections ranging from the Indian occupation to the present.

RIVERSIDE PARK AND ROSE GARDEN

Red River • 572-2763 (Parks and Recreation) • Daily 6–11 • Free • W variable

Located on the west side of the city, this 562-acre park is bordered by more than 4 miles of the Guadalupe River. Facilities include picnic areas, playgrounds, sports fields, public boat ramps, and an 18-hole golf course (*see* Sports and Activities). At one time Victoria was called "The City of Roses." A reminder of this is the park's Rose Garden which features more than 1,000 rosebushes representing more than 100 varieties. The Texas Zoo is in the south section of the park (see below).

TEXAS ZOO

Riverside Park, entrance on Memorial Dr. • 573-7681 • Daily 9–5
Adults $2, children $1 (under 2 free) • W+ but not all areas

Now there are animals representing around 90 species of native animals exhibited in their natural habitat. These range from armadillos and alligators to ocelots and raccoons, plus there's an observational beehive.

VICTORIA BOTANICAL GARDENS

3003 N. Vine • 578-8867 • Free

Gardens feature roses, herbs, wildflowers, butterfly, and hummingbird gardens.

SPORTS AND ACTIVITIES

Golf

RIVERSIDE GOLF COURSE
Riverside Park • 573-4521
18-hole municipal course. Open Tuesday–Sunday. Call for green fees.

Tennis

Public courts are available at Stroman High School, 3002 E. North; Victoria High School, 1110 Sam Houston; Victoria College, 2200 E. Red River; and the H.E.B. Municipal Tennis Center, 2905 E. North. Call the Parks and Recreation Department (572-2763) for times and fees.

COLLEGES AND UNIVERSITIES

VICTORIA COLLEGE
2200 E. Red River • 573-3291 • W variable
A two-year community college providing academic and vocational programs. Visitors are welcome at concerts performed by the choral groups, concert band, and jazz band, and the tennis courts are open to the public. The **University of Houston-Victoria** (2302 E. Red River, 573-3151), a two-year upper-division university which shares the campus, also holds musical events open to the public.

PERFORMING ARTS

Information on cultural events, including those listed below, can also be obtained from the Victoria Cultural Council, City Hall, 105 E. Juan Linn, 572-ARTS.

VICTORIA COMMUNITY THEATER
206 E. Constitution • 576-6277 • Admission • W
This group usually puts on shows and a musical during its September–May season and a melodrama in the summer.

VICTORIA SYMPHONY ORCHESTRA
576-4500 • Admission
Most of the September-through-May season concerts are performed at the Victoria College auditorium.

SIDE TRIPS

COLETO CREEK RESERVOIR AND REGIONAL PARK
Take US Hwy 59 southeast about 12 miles to sign (*See* Goliad)

ANNUAL EVENTS

May

BACH FESTIVAL
Various locations • 572-2787 (Victoria Cultural Council) • Several days late in month • Admission • W variable

The European tradition of concert festivals featuring Bach's music is carried on here, as well as the works of other classical composers.

October

CZECH HERITAGE FESTIVAL

Sun Valley Ranch, Hwy. 87 N • 575-0820 • Sunday late in October Admission $5

Czechs celebrate their heritage with dancing, music, and food. Czech-English polka mass, and arts and crafts.

RESTAURANTS

FOSSATI'S

302 S. Main • 576-3354 • Lunch Monday–Friday • $ • MC, V

Locals know where to get their deli sandwiches. And they've been chowing down for years in this old-time deli in an old building.

THE CORRAL

3502 Houston Hwy. (US 59) • 576-1277 • Lunch and dinner daily • $–$$ • AE, MC, V • W

It opened in 1952 as a barbecue place and continued concentrating on barbecue until the mid-1980s. Now the menu has been expanded to include steaks, seafood, and chicken entrées. Bar.

ACCOMMODATIONS

($ = under $45, $$ = $46–$60, $$$ = $61–$80, $$$$ = $81–$100, $$$$$ = over $100)

Room tax 13%

BEST WESTERN INN

2605 Houston Hwy. (US 59) • 578-9911 or 800-528-1234 • $ • No-smoking rooms

This two-story Best Western has 104 rooms, including 33 no-smoking, cable TV with HBO, room phones, pets OK, restaurant nearby, outdoor pool, free coffee, free newspaper.

HOLIDAY INN

2705 E. Houston Hwy. (US 59 BUS) • 575-0251 or 800-HOLIDAY • $$ • W+ 3 rooms • No-smoking rooms

This inn has 228 units, including 14 suites ($$–$$$) and 30 no-smoking rooms, cable TV with Showtime and pay channel, room phones, pets OK, free transportation to airport and mall, lounge, restaurant, Holidome with heated indoor/outdoor pool, exercise room, spa, sauna, free coffee, free newspaper.

LA QUINTA MOTOR INN

7603 N. Navarro at Hallettsville Hwy. (US 77N) • 572-3585 or 800-531-5900 $$ • W+ 6 rooms • No-smoking rooms

The two-story La Quinta has 130 rooms, including 32 no-smoking, cable TV with HBO and pay channel, room phones (local calls free), small pets OK, restaurant adjacent, outdoor pool, free coffee in lobby. Senior discount.

RAMADA INN

3901 Houston Hwy. (US 59) • 578-2723 or 800-228-2828 • $–$$ • W+ 2 rooms No-smoking rooms

The inn has 126 rooms, including 12 no-smoking, cable TV with HBO, room phones, guest memberships available for golf at country club, small pets OK, free airport transportation, lounge, restaurant, outdoor pool, outdoor spa.

WESLACO

Hidalgo County • 26,500 • (956)

The name is composed from the initials of the W. E. Stewart Land Company, which sold a parcel of land to the town's developers in 1919. For a time, in the early 1940s, Weslaco was known as the "City with the Neon Skyline." The neon lights of downtown were darkened during World War II. One of the casualties from the city in that war was Corporal Harlon Block, a Marine who was killed shortly after being photographed as one of the men in a photo that made history—the planting of the flag on Iwo Jima (*see* Harlingen—Marine Military Academy).

In 1997, Weslaco was designated a main street historical city, one of five in Texas.

Because of its location in the heart of the vast Rio Grande Valley agricultural belt, the citrus, sugar, vegetable, and cotton industries all have major facilities in the area.

TOURIST SERVICES

RIO GRANDE VALLEY PARTNERSHIP

US 83 Expressway and FM 1015 east of city • (P.O. Box 1499, 78596) • 968-3141 Monday–Friday 8:30–5 • W

This is the information center for all the cities and towns in the lower and central Valley from South Padre on the east to Falcon Lake on the west.

WESLACO AREA CHAMBER OF COMMERCE AND TOURISM CENTER

1710 E. Pike, North Access Rd. of US 83 Expressway, exit Pike/Airport (P.O. Box 8398, 78596) • 968-2102 • Monday–Friday 8–5 • W

MUSEUMS

WESLACO BI-CULTURAL MUSEUM

521 S. Kansas, next to library • 968-9142 • Wednesday–Thursday 1–3, Friday 10–12, 1–3 • Free • W

The exhibits relate to the daily life of early Spanish and Anglo settlers and the dual culture of the area. Displays range from an ox cart to a silver glove stretcher used to stretch the fingers in kid gloves. Staffed by volunteers, so the hours sometimes vary from those posted.

OTHER POINTS OF INTEREST

VALLEY NATURE CENTER

301 S. Border, in Gibson Park just south of BUS US 83 • 969-2475 Monday–Saturday 9–1. Closed Sunday and holidays • Free • W

In the building are exhibits on native birds and other nature items from this area ranging from insects to rocks. Outside is a four-acre park filled with native flora, all nicely labeled. Guided tours are available if you call in advance. Gift shop.

SIDE TRIPS

NUEVO PROGRESO, MEXICO
Take FM 1015 south about 7 miles to International Bridge
    Benito Juarez Avenida, the main shopping street of this border town, starts right at the bridge. The majority of the stores and restaurants are in the first few blocks, so you can park on the Texas side (about $1) and walk across. Just a block from the bridge, on your left, is Arturo's (*see* Restaurants) and a little further on, upstairs, is the Garcia Gomez Restaurant. Both are consistently popular with border-crossers from Weslaco.

RESTAURANTS

($ = under $7, $$ = $8–$17, $$$ = $18–$25, $$$$ = over $25 for one person excluding drinks, tax, and tip.)

ARTURO'S
Nuevo Progreso, about 1 block south of the International Bridge
Lunch and dinner daily • $–$$ • MC, V • Secured parking
    This plush-looking restaurant has red jacketed waiters, tablecloths, cloth napkins, and even that rarity among silver settings in most Texas restaurants—salad forks. The menu offers both Mexican and American entrées with so many choices that it could be broken up and the pieces used as full menus in several different restaurants. Don't expect a gourmet meal—the kitchen isn't up to it—but you'll certainly get your money's worth, and then some. Bar.

CIRO'S
318 W. Pike Blvd., in Palm Plaza Shopping Center, between South Access
Rd. of US Expressway 83 and W. Pike • 969-2236 • Lunch and dinner daily
$–$$ • MC, V
    There are almost a dozen shrimp entrées on the menu that go from the simple *Camaron a la Pancha* (broiled in butter) to *Camaron Veracruzano* (with tomato sauce, tomato, onions, pimentos, olives, capers, jalapeños, parsley, garlic, wine and other spices). They also have red snapper and other fish, meats including steaks, *fajitas,* a variety of Mexican plates, and even Kosher ribs.

MILANO'S ITALIAN RESTAURANT
2900 W. Pike Blvd., just west of Milano's Rd. • 968-3677 • Dinner only
Tuesday–Sunday. Closed Monday • $$ • Cr • W
    They've been pleasing customers with Neapolitan-style Italian cuisine here since 1955. If you want a taste of why, try the pasta combination platter, which includes lasagna, ravioli, manicotti, and spaghetti. No-smoking area. Beer and wine.

ACCOMMODATIONS

($ = under $45, $$ = $46–$60, $$$ = $61–$80, $$$$ = $81–$100, $$$$$ = over $100)
Room tax 13%

BEST WESTERN PALM AIRE MOTOR INN

415 S. International, US 83 Expressway and FM 1015 • 969-2411 or in TX 800-248-6511, outside TX 800-528-1234 • $$–$$$ • No-smoking rooms
   The 201 units in this two-story Best Western include two suites and 20 no-smoking rooms. Children under 12 stay free in room with parents. Satellite TV with HBO. Room phones (local calls free). Fire intercom system. No pets. Restaurant, room service, lounge open Monday–Saturday with entertainment Wednesday–Saturday. Three outdoor pools, outdoor whirlpool, exercise room, lighted tennis court, weight room, racquetball courts, sauna, steam room. Free breakfast. Self-service laundry and same-day dry cleaning. Shops.

WEST COLUMBIA

Brazoria County • 4,700 • (409)
   In 1824, Josiah H. Bell, a friend of Stephen F. Austin and one of the original 300 families that made up Austin's colony, moved to his land grant on the Brazos River and founded the town of Marion, which soon became known as Bell's Landing. He had always intended this to be merely a port town and depot for supplies, so two years later he cut a two-mile road through the woods and established the town of Columbia.
   After the Texans won their independence from Mexico, they had a difficult time picking a place to set up the capital of the new nation. Columbia was chosen because it had a hotel and several rooming houses offering more accommodations for government officials than almost every other town in the area. It also had one of the few newspapers.
   The first Congress met here on October 3, 1836. In its short session it accomplished much. It ratified the constitution, elected Sam Houston the first president, with Mirabeau B. Lamar as vice-president, and selected Stephen F. Austin as secretary of state, appointed committees, provided for the army and navy, created a judiciary, a postal department, a land office, established a financial system, and, in general, took the first steps to get the new government rolling. It also decided to move the capital and hold the next session in the growing town of Houston.
   During this same period, the captured Mexican General Santa Anna was held prisoner here from shortly after his capture until his release in late 1836. And on December 27, 1836, Stephen F. Austin died here of pneumonia.
   After the government moved, Columbia declined. Bell's Landing became the more prosperous town and people started calling it Columbia. The original Columbia then became known as West Columbia. It wasn't until the 1920s that the post office straightened out the confusion over the name interchange by designating what was originally Bell's Landing as East Columbia.
   Today East Columbia has declined to a quiet village whose chief claim to fame is a number of historic buildings. West Columbia, on the other hand, has built up its economy and become a trade center based on farming, ranching, and oil.

TOURIST SERVICES

WEST COLUMBIA CHAMBER OF COMMERCE

247 E. Brazos at Broad in Columbia Historical Museum (P.O. Box 837, 77486)
345-3921 • Monday–Friday 9–1

HISTORIC PLACES

AMMON UNDERWOOD HOME

East Columbia • Call Chamber of Commerce for appointment
and directions (345-3921)

The Ammon Underwood Home is one of the oldest frame houses still standing in Texas. The original portion of it, a two-story log house, was built in 1835 by colonist Thomas W. Nibbs. In 1838, young Ammon Underwood, in a business venture with Mrs. Catherine Carson, bought the house, enlarged it, and opened a boarding house. Shortly after Underwood married Mrs. Carson's daughter, Rachel, and shortly after that, the widowed Mrs. Carson married Gail Borden, Sr., who later invented the canned milk process. Their descendants continued to live in the house until 1958.

VARNER-HOGG STATE HISTORICAL PARK

Take FM 2852 (13th St.) about 2 miles north off TX 35 (Brazos Ave.) • 345-4656
Open for tours Wednesday–Saturday 10–11:30 and 1–4:30, Sunday 1–4:30.
Closed Monday–Tuesday • Adults $3, children $1.50

The name refers to the first and last owners: Martin Varner, one of the Old Three Hundred of Austin's Colony, who built the original cabin in the late 1820s (he also built a rum distillery that Austin said produced the first "ardent spirits" made in the colony), and former Texas governor James S. Hogg, who bought the plantation in 1901. The main house was built in the 1830s by the Patton family. There were several owners between the Pattons and Hogg. Soon after Hogg purchased the house, he became convinced that there was oil under the property and drilled several wells trying to find it. He died in 1906 without hitting oil, but 14 years later he was proven right when the West Columbia field was brought in. A photo on display in the house shows the mansion surrounded by a forest of derricks. Oil soon became the cornerstone of the Hogg family wealth. The house was donated to the state in 1958 by Miss Ima Hogg who also furnished it with her collection of historic furnishings that would have been available to an antebellum family of means. Picnic sites are available in the park.

OTHER POINTS OF INTEREST

REPLICA OF FIRST CAPITOL

14th St. and Hamilton, 1 block north of Brazos (TX 35) • For appointment call
345-3921 (Chamber of Commerce) • Free

About 1833 Leman Kelsey built a story-and-a-half clapboard store near this location. When Columbia became the capital of the Republic of Texas in 1836, this building was one of the two that housed the first Congress. The shed room in the rear served as Stephen F. Austin's office during the brief period he served as secretary of state before his death in December 1836. In 1837 the government moved to Houston. The 1900 hurricane destroyed the Kelsey store. This replica was built in 1977.

ANNUAL EVENTS

April

SAN JACINTO FESTIVAL

At Capitol replica and various locations in town • 345-3921 (Chamber of Commerce) • Usually weekend in middle of month • Most events free W variable

The festivities include a Bar-B-Que Cookoff, arts and crafts show, a parade, dances, sports tournaments, a historical skirmish by the Brazoria Militia, entertainment, and the Belle of the Brazos Pageant. There are also historical tours of Brazoria County and many local people dress in period clothing.

ACCOMMODATIONS

($ = under $45, $$ = $46–$60, $$$ = $61–$80, $$$$ = $81–$100, $$$$$ = over $100)
Room tax 10%

COUNTRY HEARTH INN

714 Columbia (TX 36) • 345-2399 • $ • W+ 2 rooms • No-smoking rooms

The two-story inn offers 40 units that include one suite ($$$$) and four no-smoking rooms. Satellite TV with HBO. Room phones (no charge for local calls). Guest memberships available in country club. Pets OK. Outdoor pool. Complimentary Continental breakfast, complimentary two hours of cocktails in evening, free coffee in lobby.

Panhandle

ABILENE

Taylor County Seat • 106,000 • (915)

The county is named for Edward, James, and George Taylor, brothers who died at the Alamo, and Abilene, the major city in this and 22 surrounding counties, still exhibits a great deal of the true Old West spirit common to the defenders of the Alamo.

Abilene was founded in 1881 as a railhead for the Texas and Pacific Railroad, which cut short the long cattle drives that previously had to go on to Dodge

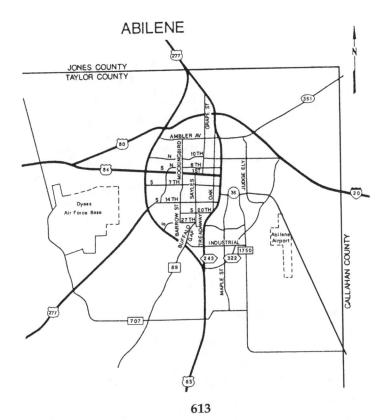

ABILENE

City. It was named after Abilene, Kansas, but the lawlessness of the early days soon gave way here to the influence of religious fundamentalists. It was called the buckle of the Bible Belt—a title it still holds, with three church-affiliated colleges and the great number of churches located here.

Today, agriculture, ranching, manufacturing, oil, and military installations provide a broad base for its economy, with two enclosed shopping malls and several shopping centers, a much-used civic center and an expo center, medical facilities which include a medical center, a good selection of accommodations and restaurants, and a variety of recreational facilities ranging from a state park to a zoo. The city is also an important cultural center, with a fine arts museum, several performing theater groups, and a philharmonic orchestra.

Downtown historic Hickory Street (the 500 to 700 blocks) offers unique crafts, antique, and specialty shops in old homes. Nearby Buffalo Gap is home of a growing historic village as well as several shops and fine restaurants. Not far from the city are the ruins of Fort Phantom Hill, built in 1851 as one of the chain of forts that guarded the frontier against Indian and outlaw raids.

TOURIST SERVICES

ABILENE CONVENTION AND VISITORS BUREAU & VISITOR INFORMATION CENTER

Visitor Information Center at I-20 and FM 600 (P.O. Box 2281, 79604, Web site http://www.abilene.com/visitors) • 676-7241 or 800-727-7704 • W

MUSEUMS

MUSEUMS OF ABILENE

102 Cypress at N. 1st • 673-4587 • Tuesday–Saturday 10–5, Sunday 1–5
Adults $2, children 12 and under $1. Free Thursday 5–8:30 • W

Three museums housed together offer visitors the opportunity to see all types of art and historical and scientific exhibits. The Fine Arts Museum's exhibitions range from the classics to abstract in a variety of media; a blend of fine art, crafts, and popular and commercial art. The historical museum covers Abilene's history in light of recent events, and the Children's Museum teaches the principles of science, the uses of technology, and aspects of daily living. There are usually 18 to 20 exhibitions a year. Some are traveling exhibits, some from the museum's permanent collection, and occasionally, an invitational exhibit put together by the museum staff. There is also a sculpture garden on the outdoor patio.

MUNICIPAL ART GALLERIES

These are two small galleries in civic buildings: the Red Carpet Gallery in the civic center and a mini-gallery at the Taylor County Courthouse. Their purpose is to enhance the public buildings, expose Abilenians to various art forms, and provide artists with the opportunity to exhibit their work. Exhibits change approximately every two months.

HISTORIC PLACES

FORT PHANTOM HILL RUINS

On FM 600 14 miles north of I-20 • Open daily dawn to dusk • Free

The ruins are on private property, but the owner keeps them open to the public. There's not much to see here now; only a few buildings and a dozen chimneys remain of the fort that once housed five infantry companies of the U.S. Army. Built in 1851 to stop Indian raids, it was staffed by foot soldiers, not cavalry, which may be why it was completely ineffective against the swift Comanche horsemen who simply ignored the post on their lightning strikes in the area. In addition, there was no good drinking water nearby. As a result, the fort was abandoned in 1854. Shortly after the troops were withdrawn, the fort mysteriously burned. Ironically, the ruins are only a couple of miles from Lake Phantom Hill, which today supplies much of Abilene's drinking water. The fort was later used as an outpost by the Texas Rangers, then by the Confederate Army, as a station on the Butterfield stage line, and as a U.S. Army outpost again in the Indian Wars of the 1870s.

OTHER POINTS OF INTEREST

ABILENE STATE PARK

Off FM 89 approximately 16 miles southwest • 572-3204 • Open daily 8–10 for day use, at all times for camping • $3 per day per person, 13 and up

This 490-acre park offers facilities for picnicking, tent and trailer camping, and hiking on a nature trail. There is also a swimming pool open from noon to 8 P.M. Wednesday–Sunday starting Friday before Memorial Day through Labor Day. Although not a part of the state park, Lake Abilene is adjacent. This 595-acre lake offers free day-fishing and boating.

ABILENE ZOO

In Nelson Park, SH 36 at Loop 322 • 672-9771 • Monday–Friday 9–5, Saturday, Sunday, holidays 9–7 • Closed Thanksgiving, Christmas, and New Year's Day • Adults $3, children 3–12 and seniors $1 • Strollers

Many of the more than 900 animals in this 13-acre zoo are in moat-type exhibit areas rather than cages. The objective of the zoo is to compare animals native to the Plains of the American Southwest to those of a similar habitat in Africa. So the Texas Plains section is home to bison, pronghorn, javelina, coyote, and wild turkeys, while the African Veldt area has an intermingling of zebra, gnu, and ostrich. Elephants, lions, giraffes, monkeys, and birds complete the African collection. A herpetarium houses over 70 different species of reptiles and amphibians from both American and Africa. The Discovery Center compares habitats in the southwestern United States and Mexico with similar regions a world away in Africa and Madagascar. There is a picnic area and gift shop, and strollers may be rented at the main gate. This zoo is small enough to see in a brief visit, while still offering plenty to occupy you for a long time.

LINEAR AIR PARK

Dyess Air Force Base • I-20 from east or west, by US 277 from north and by US 83/84 or US 277 from south • 696-5609 or 696-2196 • Open daylight hours, but closed during military exercises. Stop at main gate for a pass • Free

There are 31 World War II, Korean conflict, and Vietnam conflict aircraft on display outdoors. The air park was originated by the Texas Museum of Military History. Dyess AFB holds an open house annually in late April or early May, usually with an air show by a wing of the Confederate Air Force (see Midland) and/or the USAF Thunderbirds.

LAKE FORT PHANTOM

**Off FM 600 10 miles northeast • 676-6207 • Open at all times • Free
W but not all areas**

With more than 4,246 acres and 29 miles of shoreline, this is the largest of the Abilene area lakes and the most popular with fishermen, who find it great for walleye and crappie. Facilities around the lake include marinas, public boat ramps, primitive campsites, a swimming beach, and a model airplane field.

SPORTS AND ACTIVITIES

Golf

MAXWELL MUNICIPAL GOLF COURSE

1002 S. 32nd, east of Treadaway • 692-2737 • 18-hole course. Green fees: weekdays $9.20, weekends and holidays $11.87

Tennis

ROSE PARK TENNIS CENTER

S. 7th and Mockingbird • 676-6292 • 15 lighted tennis courts, pro shop, dressing areas • Monday–Thursday 9–9, Friday-Saturday 9–5, Sunday 1–5 $2 for 2 hours on first-come, first-served basis

COLLEGES AND UNIVERSITIES

ABILENE CHRISTIAN UNIVERSITY

1600 Campus Court • 674-2000 • W but not all areas • No roads through campus; visitor parking all around it

Affiliated with the Church of Christ, this university was founded in 1906 and now has an enrollment of approximately 4,000, which makes it one of the largest private universities in the Southwest. The Shore Art Gallery in the Don H. Morris Center and the Women for ACU Museum located at 1602 Campus Court are open to the public. In addition to major sports, other activities the public is invited to attend include the Sing Song in February followed by the Bible lectureship and the homecoming musical in the fall.

HARDIN-SIMMONS UNIVERSITY

2200 Hickory at Ambler • 670-1000 • W but not all areas • Limited visitor parking on campus

This Baptist institution, founded in 1891, has an enrollment of approximately 2,100. Intercollegiate sports include an annual student rodeo. The concert band and concert choir, as well as other musical organizations in the music department, give public concerts periodically in the Woodward-Dellis Recital Hall; and plays ranging from the classics to experimental are performed at the university's Van Ellis Theater. There is an art gallery in the art building, which is also open to the public.

McMURRY UNIVERSITY

S. 14th and Sayles • 691-6200 • W but not all areas • Visitor parking in center of campus, near the stadium

This Methodist college, which opened in 1923, is the smallest of the three colleges and universities in Abilene, with an enrollment of about 1,400. The campus center is built underground for energy efficiency. Every October the various college organizations get together and build a realistic Indian tepee village and perform Indian dances and rituals for the public.

PERFORMING ARTS

ABILENE COMMUNITY THEATRE

801 S. Mockingbird at Rose Park • 673-6271 • Admission varies • W
This theater usually hosts about five productions a year, including a summer musical. Children's theater is also performed here occasionally.

ABILENE PHILHARMONIC ORCHESTRA

310 N. Willis, Suite 108 • 677-6710 or 800-460-0610 • Admission
Performances are held in the civic center, and the September through April season includes both classical and pops concerts, with the orchestra backing guest performers.

PARAMOUNT THEATRE

352 Cypress • 676-9620 • Adults $4, seniors, students and military, children $3 • W ground level only
Restored by the Abilene Preservation League, this classic-style movie theater from the 1930s is now used for such things as a classics film series and other special performances, including dance and opera. Listed in the national Register of Historic Places, the theater's interior decor resembles a courtyard with a ceiling of twinkling stars and floating clouds.

ABILENE REPERTORY THEATRE

825 N. 2nd east of Cypress • 672-9991 • Admission varies • W
Variety of community performances put on by local actors and directors. Normally have about six shows a year.

SHOPPING

ART REED CUSTOM SADDLES

904 Ambler at Pine • 677-4572 • W
Art Reed is one of the few saddlemakers around who makes his own saddle trees, so his saddles are truly "made from scratch." For more than 30 years he has made Western saddles, tack, chaps, and belts for repeat customers and those who come, drawn by word of mouth. His saddles are mostly for ranchers and working cowboys, and a working saddle starts at about $1,500. But don't expect a rush job. His backlog usually runs four to six months. He also carries English saddles, but doesn't make them.

BELL CUSTOM-MADE BOOTS

2118 N. Treadaway near Ambler • 677-0632 • W
Alan Bell specializes in custom boots with belts to match. Prices start at about $450 for a calfskin and go up to around $2,500. The waiting period usually runs about six to eight months.

CENTER FOR CONTEMPORARY ARTS

1140-1/2 N. 2nd near Cypress • 677-8389 • Tuesday–Friday 11–2, Saturday–Sunday 1–4

This is more a local artist's exhibit area than a commercial gallery, but most of the art is for sale. Located on the second floor, one side of the space is devoted to the individual artists' studios—with artists working with everything from classical media to found items—and the other side is the exhibit space. Juried shows are held here throughout the year.

CRAFTER'S GALLERY

Brookhollow Shopping Center, 2540 Barrow at 27th • 695-3257 or 800-588-2723 • W

The estimated 100 crafters here offer just about any kind of craft item imaginable in this browser's delight that has been dubbed Texas' largest arts-and-crafts mall. Located in the back is the Gallery Cafe and Pie Shop.

JAMES LEDDY BOOTS

926 Ambler at Pine • 677-7811 • W west side entrance

Leddy is one of the better known names among bootmakers in Texas, and family members have stores all over the state. At this shop, custom-made work boots start at about $525 and dress boots at $450 and go up to around $3,500. James also makes belts and billfolds to match. At a rate of about eight pairs of boots a week, his backlog usually runs about eight months. He will gladly give a tour of the shop to individuals but prefers notice for group tours.

SIDE TRIPS

BUFFALO GAP HISTORIC VILLAGE

Buffalo Gap. *From Abilene on FM 89, turn right on Elm, or follow signs* 572-3365 • March 15–November 15: Monday–Saturday 10–7, Sunday noon–7; November 16–March 14: Friday–Saturday 10–6, Sunday noon–6 • Adults $4.25, seniors $3.25, students $1.75

Talk about being an avid historian, Dr. R. Lee Rode of Abilene not only studies history, he is also helping relive it by continually adding to and restoring this small village of historic homes that he owns. Among the buildings here now is the Taylor County Courthouse and Jail (1879), which has Civil War cannonballs tucked in between the sandstone building stones for added support. Upstairs there is an original jail cell and a museum with a large gun collection. Other buildings include a railroad depot built in 1881 and moved in from Clyde, the first blacksmith shop in Abilene, and the Nazarene Church, which was built in Buffalo Gap in 1902, a few blocks from its present location.

ANNUAL EVENTS

March

ABILENE RAILROAD FESTIVAL

Downtown from N. 1st at Cypress to Abilene Civic Center • 676-3775 Second weekend in March • W but not all areas

Except for the model train exhibit, this is an outdoor festival with lots of family activities such as the Hobo Cookoff.

April

BUFFALO GAP ARTS FESTIVAL

Perini Ranch, FM 89 1.25 miles past Buffalo Gap • 673-4587 • Usually the last weekend in April • Admission • W variable

This is truly art under the oaks. Proceeds benefit the museums of Abilene, so it is well supported by the local art community. In addition to art booths and an art auction, entertainment includes a variety of musical events ranging from mariachis to barbershop singing; skits, square dancing, fun activities for children.

May

WESTERN HERITAGE CLASSIC AND RANCH RODEO

Taylor County Expo Center, SH 36 • 677-4376 • Second weekend in May Admission • W but not all areas

This event celebrates both the Old West and modern ranch life. Events include a ranch rodeo, campfire cookoff, a blacksmiths' competition, a trail ride, a Western art show, and Friday and Saturday night Western dances.

September

WEST TEXAS FAIR AND RODEO

Taylor County Expo Center, SH 36 • 677-4376 • Starts first Friday after Labor Day • Admission • W but not all areas

Events include assorted livestock and horse shows, a rodeo, agricultural and horticultural exhibits, tractor pulls and other contests, a parade, entertainment, and a carnival midway.

RESTAURANTS

($ = under $7, $$ = $8–$17, $$$ = $18–$25, $$$$ = over $25 for one person excluding drinks, tax, and tip)

American

TUCSON'S

3370 N. 1st, just east of Willis • 676-8279 • Lunch and dinner daily • $–$$ AE, MC, V • Children's menu

A touch of just about everything from gourmet burgers to steaks, sandwiches, salads, and even a few Mexican dishes. Casual dining. Only the steaks get in the $$ price range. Bar.

Barbecue

JOE ALLEN'S PIT BAR-B-QUE

1233 S. Treadaway • 672-6082 • Lunch and dinner Monday–Saturday. Closed Sunday • $ • AE, MC, V • W

When Joe Allen was a county extension agent, he cooked barbecue to raise money for the 4-H clubs. When he decided to leave that job in 1980, it was only natural that he would open this restaurant. Abilene welcomed the switch, and Joe's mesquite-smoked briskets, ribs, ham, and sausage are still favorites in the city today. He'll also cook a steak if you want it. Beer.

HAROLD'S BAR-B-Q

Walnut and 13th • 672-4451 • Lunch and early dinner Monday–Saturday. Closed Sunday • $ • No Cr

This would be a typical neighborhood barbecue place—a small, cinder block building with the major decoration a display of baseball trophies—if it wasn't for the line up of customers who come here from all over town to squeeze in to eat Harold's oak wood-cooked barbecue and hot-water corn bread for lunch.

Mexican

CASA HERRERA

4109 Ridgemont Dr. • 692-7065 • Lunch and dinner daily • $ • DIS, MC, V W • Parking in rear

Mexican decor with tile-topped tables and *charro sombreros* on the wall. Along with Tex-Mex, there are several low-cholesterol items on the menu. Located in the Garden Plaza of the Burro Alley shopping center.

JUDY'S MEXICAN FOOD CAFE

Buffalo Gap, FM 89 • 572-3731 • Lunch Tuesday–Sunday, dinner Friday–Saturday. Closed Monday • Reservations suggested • $ • No Cr W call ahead

Judy offers what she calls bunkhouse cooking with country class—usually five entrées—in this tiny place tucked between a store and an art gallery. Judy greets and treats everyone who comes in—regulars and newcomers alike—as if they were part of her happy family. BYOB.

Oriental

HOUSE OF HUNAN

3106 S. Clack • 695-9282 • Lunch and dinner daily • $-$$ • Cr • W

The decor is simple, but the menu is huge and offers a wide variety of selections of beef, poultry, pork, and seafood with the spicy dishes marked HOT. Bar.

Steaks

PERINI'S RANCH STEAKHOUSE

Buffalo Gap, off FM 89 on way to Abilene State Park • 572-3339 • Dinner only Wednesday–Thursday, lunch and dinner Friday–Sunday. Closed Monday–Tuesday • Reservations recommended on weekends • $$-$$$ • MC, V • W

The setting is ranch rustic, and the specialty of the house is a 16-ounce Ranch Roast Ribeye served with garden-fresh salad, and either cowboy potatoes or ranch beans. They also offer a variety of other steaks, and baby back ribs, all cooked over mesquite. Private club (temporary membership $3). This is the site of the Buffalo Gap Art Festival (see Annual Events) and a chili cookoff over Labor Day weekend.

ROYAL INN STEAK HOUSE

4695 S. 1st (US 80, just west of US 277) • 692-3022 • Breakfast, lunch, and dinner daily • $$-$$$ • Cr • W • Children's menu

They've been up at the top of the list of where to get a good steak in Abilene for a long time, so they must be doing something right. Also seafood, chicken, and ham and an extensive wine list. The plush dining room, with its low ceiling and chandeliers, adds to the pleasure of eating here. Bar.

ACCOMMODATIONS

($ = under $45, $$ = $46–$60, $$$ = $61–$80, $$$$ = $81–$100, $$$$$ = over $100)
Room tax 13%

BEST WESTERN COLONIAL INN

3210 Pine at I-20 • 677-2683 or 800-528-1234 • $ • No-smoking rooms
   All on ground level, this inn has 105 units including two suites ($$$) and 24 no-smoking rooms. Children under 12 stay free in room with parents. Senior discounts. Cable TV with HBO. Room phones (no charge for local calls). Pets OK. Airport transportation. Restaurant. Outdoor pool.

EMBASSY SUITES

4250 Ridgemont (behind the mall of Abilene) • 698-1234 or 800-EMBASSY (800-362-2779) • $$$–$$$$ • W 4 suites • No-smoking suites
   This three-story Embassy has 176 suites including three executive suites with Jacuzzis ($$$$$) and 124 no-smoking suites. Children under 12 stay free in room with parents. Senior discount. Cable and Showtime and pay channel. Room phones (charge for local calls). Fire sprinklers in rooms. Pets OK. Free airport transportation. Restaurant and lounge with live entertainment. Heated indoor pool, whirlpool, sauna, steambath. Free full breakfast and two hours of free beverages in evening.

HOLIDAY INN EXPRESS

SH 351 at I-20 • 673-5271 or 800 HOLIDAY (800-465-4329) • $$ • W 1 room No-smoking rooms
   A two-story Holiday Inn with 160 rooms including 80 no-smoking. Children under 18 stay free in room with parents. Senior discount. Satellite TV with free in-room movies. Room phones (no charge for local calls). Pets OK. Free airport transportation. Outdoor pool. Free continental breakfast.

KIVA INN

5403 S. 1st (BUS US 83/84) just west of US 277 • 695-2150 or in Texas 800-592-4466 • $–$$ • W 1 room • No-smoking rooms
   The 200 units in this two- and three-story hotel include six suites ($$$-$$$$) and 15 no-smoking rooms. Children under 16 stay free in room with parents. Senior discount. Cable TV. Room phones (charge for local calls). Free airport transportation. Restaurant and lounge. Indoor and outdoor pools, children's pool, garden atrium, wet/dry saunas, whirlpool, putting green, video and sports game areas.

LA QUINTA MOTOR INN

3501 FM 600 at I-20 • 676-1676 or 800-531-5900 • $$ • W 2 rooms No-smoking rooms
   This two-story La Quinta has 106 rooms including 50 no-smoking. Children under 18 stay free in room with parents. Senior discount. Cable TV with Showtime and pay channel. Room phones (no charge for local calls). Small pets OK. Outdoor pool. Free continental breakfast and coffee in lobby.

RAMADA INN

3450 S. Clack (access road of US 83/84, Winters Freeway) • 695-7700, 800-676-7262, or 800-2-RAMADA (800-272-6232) • $$$ • W • No-smoking rooms
The two-story Ramada has 150 rooms including 40 no-smoking. Children under 18 stay free in room with parents. Senior discount. Cable TV. Room phones (no charge for local calls). Pets OK. Restaurant and lounge with DJ. Outdoor pool. Coffee in lobby.

ALBANY

Shackelford County Seat • 2,040 • (915)
Called "The Home of the Hereford" in honor of the early introduction into Texas of that popular cattle breed. Beef cattle, sheep, horses, and hogs account for most of this county's agricultural income. Albany puts on the Fort Griffin Fandangle, one of the best-known annual events in the state. The local newspaper, *The Albany News,* has files dating back to its founding in 1883.

TOURIST SERVICES

CHAMBER OF COMMERCE

In the old railroad depot, S. Main and Railroad (P.O. Box 185, 76430) 762-2525 • Closed Monday
Map available for a self-guided tour of the historic district.

MUSEUMS

OLD JAIL ART CENTER

S. 2nd near Walnut • 762-2269 • Tuesday–Saturday 10–5, Sunday 2–5. Closed Monday • Free • W+ downstairs
Built in 1878, this expanded old jail building houses an exceptional permanent collection of art including works of Picasso, Modigliani, Klee, and others. The Arts of the East gallery exhibits 34 Chinese terra-cotta tomb figures dating from 206 B.C. to 907 A.D.

HISTORIC PLACES

FORT GRIFFIN STATE HISTORICAL PARK

Approximately 15 miles north on US 283 • 762-3592 • Day use and camping $2 per person• W+ but not all areas
Fort Griffin was established in 1867 to give more protection to settlers during the federal reoccupation of post-Civil War Texas. Troops from Fort Griffin fought in all decisive campaigns of the 1870s. The fort was abandoned in 1881. At the visitor's center of this 506-acre park is an exhibit on the fort's history. On the grounds are a restored bakery, replicas of several of the fort's original buildings, and ruins of others. Fort Griffin, home of the State Longhorn Herd started by author J. Frank Dobie, produces some of the famed Bevo mascots for the University of Texas at Austin. Other facilities include 20 campsites, most with water and electricity, picnic area, playground, and nature trail.

HISTORIC BUILDINGS

Ledbetter Picket House, City Park, S. Main at S. 1st. This restored frontier ranchhouse built in the 1870s near Fort Griffin contains items from the Ledbetter Salt Works founded in 1860. **Shackelford County Courthouse,** S. Main and S. 2nd. Construction started in 1883 and was budgeted at $27,000. By the time it was finished, a year later, the final cost was $49,000.

ANNUAL EVENTS

FORT GRIFFIN FANDANGLE

Prairie Theater, Cook Field Rd. approximately 1 mile west of courthouse 762-2525 (Chamber of Commerce) • Last two weekends in June • Admission $5–$15 • W

Well past its 50th anniversary, the Fandangle is an annual outdoor extravaganza put on by local town folks. Of the town's 2,500 population, about 300 have roles and another couple hundred work behind the scenes. The resulting musical makes the heritage of West Texas come to life on the stage. The pageant includes everything from galloping cowboys to antique automobiles. Other activities around town entertain visitors, too. Box seats are available for $15, but must be purchased in blocks.

ACCOMMODATIONS

($ = under $45, $$ = $46–$60, $$$ = $61–$80, $$$$ = $81–$100, $$$$$ = over $100) Room tax 13%

ALBANY MOTOR INN & RV CAMPGROUND

US 180 at 283 • 762-2451 • $ • W 2 rooms • No-smoking rooms

All on ground level, this motel has 28 rooms, 13 full hook-up RV spaces and 6 tent spaces. Children under 7 stay free in room with parents. Satellite TV. Room phones (no charge for local calls). Dog kennels and game cleaning area.

AMARILLO

Potter County Seat; also in Randall County • 161,000 • (806)

This flat country, the southernmost part of the American Great Plains, was called the *Llano Estacado,* or staked plains, by Spanish explorers.

To the east, running down through the Panhandle, a series of canyons forms the escarpment of the plains. These canyonlands are the most interesting topographical feature of the region and provide some of the most beautiful vistas; they are also interesting archaeologically, providing evidence of human occupation 12,000 years ago.

It is true cowboy country, and proud of its heritage. One may still see Stetsons and boots on the streets of Amarillo, especially at the Livestock Auction (see Other Points of Interest). Several regional ranches welcome visitors and provide a first-hand view of cowboy life. And, using Amarillo as a base, one can explore the Panhandle. Almost every town has a museum and many have yearly rodeos. Here you can experience the heritage of the American frontier.

At the same time, Amarillo is a cultural and medical center and boasts a symphony and ballet, modern accommodations, fine restaurants, and beautiful parks.

Amarillo (the name is the Spanish word for "yellow") grew up at the junction of the Fort Worth & Denver City Railroad and the Atchison, Topeka & Santa Fe. By the early 1890s, the city was the world's greatest cattle shipping market; sometimes there were 50,000 head in the area. At about the turn of the century

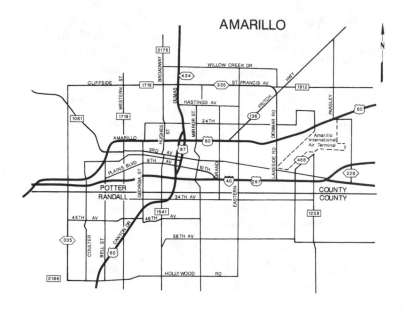

settlement increased; farming began in earnest and the region soon developed into a major wheat belt. Today it produces grain, sorghum, cotton, vegetables, and other crops, including about two million pounds of sunflower seeds each year. Gas was discovered near here in 1918 and petroleum in 1921. The extraction of helium from natural gas began in 1929. Amarillo calls itself Helium Capital of the World, because natural reserves here and in adjacent states contain more than 90% of the world's known supply.

TOURIST SERVICES

AMARILLO CONVENTION AND VISITORS BUREAU

1000 S. Polk at 10th (P.O. Box 9480, 79105) • 373-7800 or in Texas 800-692-1338 Monday–Friday 8–5 • W

In the restored Lee and Mary E. Bivins Home (see Historic Places), the bureau provides city maps, brochures, and advice for the visitor. The *Entertainment Guide* lists concerts, exhibits, and special events throughout the city. Since almost every town has a local museum, ask for the excellent little brochure, *Area Museums*, before you set out. You can also get information about rodeos in the area that coincide with your visit, and about local ranches that welcome visitors.

TEXAS TRAVEL INFORMATION CENTER

I-40 between Lakeside and Airport exits • 335-1441 • Open 8–5 every day except major holidays • W

Operated by the Texas Department of Transportation, the travel information center may be reached directly if you are going east, or by parking and taking an overpass if you are going west. Trained travel counselors offer a wide selection of free maps, literature (including the state travel guide), and expert help in charting routes anywhere in Texas.

HISTORIC PLACES

LEE AND MARY E. BIVINS HOME

1000 S. Polk (Amarillo Convention and Visitors Bureau) • 373-7800 • Free • W

This massive three-story house is a West Texas version of late Georgian Revival-style with a rather eclectic combination of architectural features. Built in 1905, it was originally the home of the family of Lee Bivins, a prominent pioneer. You can browse through the house when you stop by for information from the Visitors Center. A brochure describes the building and its furnishings, maintained by the Junior League.

HARRINGTON HOUSE

1600 S. Polk • 374-5490 • Tours by reservation only, Tuesday and Thursday 10–12:30 on the half hour, April through December • Free

This neoclassical mansion, built in 1914 by cattlemen John and Pat Landergin, owes its name to the Harringtons, a prominent local family who acquired it in 1940, took pains to preserve it, and deeded it to the Panhandle–Plains Historical Society. In 1995, at Mrs. Harrington's request, it was conveyed to the Amarillo Area Foundation and converted to a nonprofit foundation. Tours are limited to four people over 14 years of age and reservations are required. Entrance is at the rear, off 16th St. Visitors are asked to wear soft-soled shoes which will not damage the exquisite rugs and eighteenth-century *parquet de Versailles* flooring.

MUSEUMS AND ART GALLERIES

AMARILLO MUSEUM OF ART

Amarillo College Main Campus, 2200 S. Van Buren at 22nd. *Three blocks south of I-40 and two blocks east of Washington* **• 371-5050 • Tuesday–Friday 10–5; Thursday to 9:00, Saturday and Sunday 1–5. Closed major holidays Free (Donation) • W+**

Part of a three-building complex designed by Edward Stone, who also did the Kennedy Center in Washington, D.C., this handsome complex includes a theater, sculpture court, and outdoor amphitheater. The privately supported main Arts Center building has three levels surrounding an interior atrium and topped by a large skylight. More than 20 art exhibits are held here annually ranging from ancient to contemporary. The center's permanent collection emphasizes twentieth-century American art and includes the works of Georgia O'Keefe, Fritz Scholder, Franz Kline, Elaine de Kooning, and Jack Boynton. It also includes an extensive collection of photos taken in the 1930s and '40s and more recent cowboy photos made by Martin Schreiber. Gift shop. Although there are some designated parking spaces, parking can be a problem when college is in session.

AMERICAN QUARTER HORSE HERITAGE CENTER & MUSEUM

2601 I-40E at Quarter Horse Drive • 376-5181 • Monday–Saturday 10–5 (9–5 in summer), Sunday 12–5 • Adults $4, seniors $3.50, children $2.50, under 6 free • W+

This stunning 35,600-square-foot building is a tribute to the more than 369,000 quarter horses in Texas and almost two-and-a-half million worldwide who are registered in the computer files of the American Quarter Horse Association Headquarters (next door). At the entrance to the building, huge sculptures of the quarter horse adorn the roof; the motif reappears throughout the interior. Begin your visit at the theater, where a professionally produced video dramatizes the history and importance of the quarter horse in American life; the rodeo shots are spectacular. Then you can visit the art gallery, museum, and library. But one of the best exhibits is the hands-on area for youngsters in which interactive exhibits (including a talking horse) provide information on choosing, caring for, training, and showing your quarter horse. An outdoor arena is used for demonstrations during warm weather. Gift shop.

DON HARRINGTON DISCOVERY CENTER AND PLANETARIUM

Amarillo Medical Center Complex, 1200 Streit • *Take Coulter exit off I-40, go north to Wallace, then right and follow signs to Garden Center and Discovery Center* **• 355-9547 • Tuesday–Saturday 10–5, Sunday 1–5. Closed Mondays and major holidays; hours extended during summer Free • W+ • Planetarium shows Saturday and Sunday, September–May; seven days, June–August. Call for times (Not recommended for children under 6) • $2 • W+**

A well-planned "hands-on" science museum for children of all ages. Although it is designed especially for groups (and you are likely to find a class visiting) it is just as much fun for a child and family. Exploration Gallery contains physical science exhibits; Construction Zone reveals architectural elements of all kinds of structures; Kidscovery has special interactive exhibits for children 2–6. Kids get to play with water (and observe the dynamics); to weigh and measure themselves (a voice announces the results), to create music and reproduce the sounds of different instruments with their feet, and to participate in other experiments that are both educational and fun. One area has changing exhibits; others are permanent. During warm months, special exhibits and events are scheduled on the outside patio. The planetarium propels visitors into space and presents detailed audio-visual projections of our changing earth, the world of the single cell, views of the heavens. Gift shop. The Helium Monument is located in front near the parking lot.

OTHER POINTS OF INTEREST

AMARILLO GARDEN CENTER

1400 Streit at Medical Center Park • *Take Coulter exit off I-40, go north on Coulter, right on Wallace, then follow signs* **• 352-6513 or fax: 352-6227 Monday–Friday 9–5. Center closed last two weeks in December. Gardens open at all times • Free • W**

This small center makes maximum use of its two acres, with a rose garden, an iris bed and a rock garden, as well as a special fragrance garden for the vision impaired. The greenhouse serves patients at nearby medical center with garden therapy work.

ENGLISH FIELD AIR AND SPACE MUSEUM

2014 English Rd. *(Highway 60 East to English Rd., next to control tower)* **335-1812 • Daily during summer, weekends rest of year • Free • W**

A small but exciting array of aircraft and space exhibits. Group tours by appointment.

HELIUM MONUMENT

Opposite Don Harrington Discovery Center, 1200 Streit • *Take Coulter exit off I-40, go north to Wallace, then right and follow signs to Discovery Center* **Open at all times • Free • W**

Built in 1968 to celebrate the centennial of the discovery of helium, the stainless steel structure is a modernistic model of the helium atom. In the columns are time capsules scheduled to be opened in 1993, 2018, 2068, and 2968. Sealed inside are over 4,000 items of everyday living, including a bankbook for a $10 account drawing 4% interest, due to be worth over one quintillion dollars when opened in 2968. Recordings (activated when you press a button) give information about helium and the monument.

LIVESTOCK AUCTION

At Western Stockyards, S. Manhattan at E. 3rd • *Take Grand exit off I-40E, go north to E. 3rd, then left (west) to Manhattan* **• 373-7464 • Sales Tuesday starting at 9 • Closed weeks of July 4 and Christmas • Free**

The largest cattle auction in Texas, selling over 600,000 head of cattle annually. You will rub shoulders with cowboys and cattlemen and experience the excitement of sale day. Auctions are now held via satellite video, and buyers can call in their bids from home or office, but you will still see plenty of Stetsons, boots and jeans on the premises. If you are not in town on auction day, you are still welcome to visit the building. Plan to grab breakfast or lunch at the Stockyard Cafe (see Restaurants). Reservations for tours are strongly encouraged on sales days.

THOMPSON MEMORIAL PARK

US 87/287 north between NE 24th and Hastings • 378-3036 Open at all times • W

The 610-acre park includes an olympic-sized pool, a 36-hole municipal golf course, two small lakes, Storyland Zoo, and Wonderland Park, along with rolling lawns and shady trees, picnic areas, ball fields: in short, a perfect setting for a family day out.

SPORTS AND ACTIVITIES

Baseball

AMARILLO DILLAS

Play at Dick Bivins Stadium • Call 342-3455 for schedule

Golf

COMANCHE TRAILS GOLF COURSE

4200 South Grand • 378-4281 • 18-hole course. Green fees: weekdays $7, weekends $9

PRESTON WEST PAR 3 GOLF COURSE

Hollywood and Coulter • 353-7003 • 18-hole course • Greens fee: $7 weekdays, $9 weekends

SOUTHWEST GOLF CLUB
Hollywood Rd. exit on Canyon Expressway • 355-7161 • 18-hole course. Greens fee: weekdays $7, weekends and holidays $9

ROSS ROGERS GOLF COURSE
722 N.E. 24th, adjacent to Thompson Park • 378-3086 • 36-hole course. Greens fee: weekdays $7, weekends and holidays for 18 holes $9

Hockey

AMARILLO RATTLERS
Play at Civic Center • Call 378-3096 for schedule

Tennis

MUNICIPAL TENNIS CENTER
Stephen F. Austin Middle School, 26th and Elmwood • 378-4213 • 11 courts; fees charged only in summer, $1 per person, $1.50 after 5:30 P.M. Pro shop, lessons. Courts also at Memorial Park near Amarillo College, Washington at 24th and Thompson Park, US 87/287 near NE 24th and in most city parks.

Ranches

Some area ranches now welcome visitors for special events and provide a first-hand view of cowboy life; there are also "dude" ranches that take overnight guests. Inquire at the Convention and Visitors Bureau about "Ranch Roundups."

COWBOY MORNING & COWBOY EVENING
Figure 3 Ranch, at Palo Duro Canyon, Route 1, Box 69, Claude 79019-9712 *Take 1541 south 4 miles, 1151 east 9 miles, 1258 south 21 miles; allow about an hour* • 1-800-658-2613 or 1-806-944-5562 • Daily during summer; weekends spring and fall when sufficient demand. Reservations required • Cowboy Morning: Adults $19, children $14.50, under 4 free; Cowboy Evening: $22.50 adults, $14.50 children, under 4 free • W

This is the oldest of the "ranch events" in the Amarillo region, and has become enormously popular; reservations are sometimes made months in advance. When you call you will be given detailed directions on how to get to the ranch and what time to be there. Horse-drawn wagons meet you at the ranch gates and carry you to the site, on the rim of Palo Duro Canyon. There, you will be given a huge cowboy breakfast (flapjacks, steak, biscuits and gravy, eggs, and all the accompaniments) or steak dinner with traditional fixings (beans, potato salad, etc.) all prepared on a campfire by cooks who know their stuff. Then, working cowboys give a demonstration of roping, branding, cow-chip tossing and other cowboy skills and games, often inviting guests to join in. All the while, you will revel in the breathtaking view of Palo Duro Canyon, which is at its most colorful in early morning and evening. (Take a sweater or light jacket.) Reservations can be hard to get on short notice during the busy summer season, but it is worth calling to see if they can fit you into a group. (Wheelchairs can be placed on the wagons, but guests in wheelchairs often prefer to follow the wagon in their cars; the site itself is level.)

COLLEGES AND UNIVERSITIES

AMARILLO COLLEGE

Main campus at 2201 S. Washington • *Take Washington exit off I-40* **• 371-5000 • Other campuses at 6222 W. 9th Ave. and 1206 S. Polk • W**

A community college, established in 1929, which offers classes from Country and Western dancing to business and technical/vocational fields. About 6,000 students are enrolled in associate degree and college preparation programs and another 24,000 in community programs that include a ski school with its own (very gentle) slope. In addition to the **Amarillo Arts Center** (see Museums), a small **Panhandle Sports Hall of Fame** in the second floor lobby of the Technology Building is open to visitors. **Amarillo College of Fine Arts** presents frequent programs (371-5340). Information and guided tours are available at the College Union Building, which is near the 24th St. overwalk.

PERFORMING ARTS

AMARILLO GUNFIGHTERS

Rusty Spur Outpost • *18 miles south on I-27, then 10 miles east on SH 217, ranch is .5 mile before park entrance* **• 379-7667 or 488-2406 • Adults $5, children $3 • Schedule varies; call ahead • W variable**

Working cowboys, all volunteers, present entertaining drama on the rim of beautiful Palo Duro Canyon; sometimes there is barbecue; some weekend nights, cowboy poets perform by the campfire. Fine family entertainment. Programs are by arrangement, but usually there is room for visitors; call to find out what is happening during your visit.

AMARILLO LITTLE THEATRE

2019 Civic Circle, near I-40 and Georgia, across from Wolfin Village Shopping Center • 355-9991 • September–May • Admission • W

Started in 1927, this is perhaps the longest continually performing little theater in the nation. It usually presents four productions annually including musicals, drama, and children's shows in a modern theater that seats 456 persons.

AMARILLO OPERA

Amarillo College, 2201 S. Washington • *Take Washington exit off I-40* **371-5340 • Call for schedule**

Amarillo Opera presents several productions each year, in English, with local and guest performers.

AMARILLO SYMPHONY

Symphony office in Chamber of Commerce Building, 1000 S. Polk • 376-8782 Performs in Civic Center Music Hall • Admission • W+

This 90-member professional symphony orchestra usually gives seven major classical and pops concerts during its September-to-April season, several with nationally known guest artists and occasional guest conductors. Each Christmas season, *The Nutcracker* is performed with the Lone Star Ballet.

CIVIC CENTER

3rd and Buchanan • Ticket office 378-3096 • W+
Besides being the home of the Amarillo Symphony and convention center for the city, the Civic Center hosts concerts by touring musical groups and other shows in either its 2,400-seat auditorium or 5,000-seat coliseum.

KAWAHIDI INDIAN DANCERS

Kiva **at Plains Blvd. and Bellaire off I-40W. Performances also at other locations and events • 358-6253 or 354-5013 or 353-1505 • Call for performance times, schedules • Adults $5, students $3 (no reservations) • W**
This unique troupe of Boy Scout Explorer Post youngsters presents Native American dances in costume and with music, carefully researched for authenticity. Besides appearing locally, they go on national and even international tours throughout the year. Programs are presented at their own *kiva* (they are hoping to build a new, larger facility), and at other sites and are scheduled for festival and special events around the region. During the summer, the boys are often on tour. Different programs are prepared for different seasons of the year. Call for current schedule.

LONE STAR BALLET

Office in Chamber of Commerce Building, 1000 S. Polk (P.O. Box 1133, 79105) 372-2463 • Performs in the Civic Center Auditorium, October–April $6–$18 • W+
Formed in 1975 by the dance corps from the outdoor musical *Texas!* and scholarship students from West Texas State University, the company performs *The Nutcracker* at Christmas and gives other concerts throughout the year, sometimes with visiting touring companies.

SHOPPING

Malls

Western Plaza Shopping Center, I-40 and Western, 355-8216. **Westgate Shopping Mall,** I-40 and Coulter, 358-7221. **Wolfin Square Village,** I-40 at Georgia, 358-2420.

Art

James M. Haney Gallery, 3714 Olsen Blvd., 358-3653, classical, Western, Southwestern Art. **Castleberry Western Art,** 6666 W. Amarillo Blvd., 359-6253. **Colony,** 2606 Wolfin Ave., 352-2782. **Gamble's Frames & Art,** 414 15th St., 655-7323, art by Danny Gamble and others; hand-thrown pottery. **La Fleur,** Westgate Mall, 352-1737. **Webb Galleries,** 2816 W. 6th St., 342-4044. **Wells Justin Cowboy Art Gallery,** 2710 SE 3rd, 373-0889.

Western Wear and Gear

Bob Marrs Stockman's Saddle Shop, 2710 E. 3rd at Nelson, just west of the stockyards, 383-7711, saddles, chaps and tack. **Hilltop Boot and Saddle,** 4624 River Rd. *(Take Hastings exit off US 87/287 north of Thompson Park, then east 1 block to River Rd.)* 383-0501, belts, wallets, boots and other small items. **Oliver Saddle Shop,** 3016 Plains *(between Georgia and Western)*, 372-7562, custom saddles, pack equipment and chaps, name belts and billfolds, Western tack.

Boots n Jeans Western Wear, 4225 S. Georgia, 353-4368: name-brand boots, hats, Western wear. Luskey's Western Store, 2455 Wolfin Square at I-40W and Georgia, 353-4341. Cavender's Boot City, 7900 I40W, *across from Westgate Mall*, 358-1400. Tejas Western Outlet, 3701 Plains Blvd., 356-6692. Texas Trading Company, *4 miles west on I-40, Exit 60 (W. Arnot Rd.) South*: authentic reproductions, rare artifacts or souvenirs.

Miscellaneous

Old San Jacinto *(Sixth Street between Western and Georgia)* • Open daily, some shops open Sundays • 374-0459 • W varied

Old U.S. Route 66, a major highway for business and tourists for many years, goes through Amarillo, and part of the route is being restored and amplified with small shops, restaurants, used book stores, crafts stores and (mostly) antique shops and collectibles—a browser's delight. Plans are afoot to make the area even more attractive to pedestrians with plantings and walkways. Parking now is mostly on the street; some sidewalk areas are uneven—but improvements are being made all the time. There are shops for refreshments, including an old-fashioned soda shop.

KIDS' STUFF

DON HARRINGTON DISCOVERY CENTER AND PLANETARIUM

(See Museums and Art Galleries)

STORYLAND ZOO

Thompson Park, off US 87/287 at NE. 24th • 383-6141 ask for Storyland Zoo
Open daily, during daylight savings time 10–7, rest of year 9–5:30 • Free • W

Fairy tales form the theme for the exhibits at this clean and pleasant children's zoo (adults are welcome, but will have to stoop to get through the grotto entrance) featuring mostly animals native to the Panhandle—raccoons, rabbits, foxes, barnyard animals and birds. But there are also a few larger and more exotic beasts, including sheep from Europe and Africa, llamas, and monkeys. A petting zoo is available for the youngest visitors during the summer. Concessions and food for the animals can be purchased. Note: the best times to visit this (or any) zoo are early in the morning and early evening, when the animals are being fed. Picnic area.

WONDERLAND PARK

Thompson Park, off US 87/287 at NE. 24th • 383-4712 • Hours and days vary throughout the year, call ahead • Admission 50¢, separate charges for rides • W

Wonderland Park has been for many years an exceptionally clean, pleasant, safe, and well-maintained amusement park to which visitors can take their children with confidence. It has something for youngsters from the tiny tots through the teens, with 32 attractions including 22 rides ranging from a merry-go-round and haunted house to the Big Splash log flume ride, the Texas Tornado, a double-loop roller coaster, and the Rattle Snake River Raft Ride. For some attractions, riders must be a certain height; on others, even the tiniest will be secure. There's also an 18-hole miniature golf course.

SIDE TRIPS

CAL FARLEY'S BOYS RANCH AND OLD TASCOSA

Take FM 1061 northwest about 36 miles to US 385, then right (north) about 2 miles to Spur 233 • **372-2341 or 800-687-3722** • **Daily 8–5** • **Tours from Boys Center, first building on right** • **Free** • **W variable**

Tascosa boomed, then busted in 1887 when the railroad passed it by. During its heyday, these dusty streets saw the likes of outlaws and gunfighters like Billy the Kid, Pat Garrett, and Len Woodruff (who left three of his victims in Boot Hill Cemetery here). The courthouse of Old Tascosa, now the Julian Bivins Museum, pays tribute to those days when West Texas was truly the untamed American frontier.

In 1939, Cal Farley, a prizefighter, established Boys Ranch to rescue orphaned and troubled boys and give them a fresh start on life. The ranch, on a pleasant, tree-filled spot along the Canadian River breaks, looks like a small private college. It is almost a self-contained community for its more than 400 residents, who do much of the ranch work themselves in addition to their school duties. Each September there's a **Boys Ranch Rodeo** (Labor Day, adults $3.50–$4.50, children 6 to 12 $2.50–$3.50 • W). This is a highlight of the year for the boys; everyone participates either in the rodeo or behind the scenes, and about 10,000 spectators come every year to watch the fun. The smaller boys race stick ponies, but the older ones take part in real rodeo events. Visitors are always welcome, especially for the rodeo and when school is not in session. **Girls Ranch** in Whiteface (45 miles west of Lubbock on SH114, 229-6361) is part of the same organization. To visit either ranch, you are encouraged to call in advance to arrange a tour. Usually one of the residents will be your escort, and you will be invited to share a meal.

CAPROCK CANYONS STATE PARK

Three miles north of Quitaque on SH 86, approximately 100 miles southeast of Amarillo • *Go south on I-27, then east on US 86 through Silverton to Quitaque; then north on FR 1065* • **455-1492** • **Open at all times $3–$5**

One of the best-kept secrets in the Panhandle, this out-of-the-way park, little known either by natives or visitors, has stunning views of mountains, canyons, waterways, and native flora and fauna. The park has a headquarters building, and an interpretive center and archaeological site, where artifacts illustrate the history of the canyon for 250 million years or so. Campsites (fees) range from fancy, with electrical hookups, to primitive; the park even has equestrian campsites so that you can bring your horse. The 120-acre lake has facilities for swimming, fishing, and boating. For the explorer and hiker, the 14,000 acres of parkland contain 25 miles of trails which can be traversed either on foot or by horse, and eight miles of mountain trails. Buffalo and antelope are on display, and when you get into the remoter areas, you have a good chance of seeing other wild animals that abound in this park.

On the way is Turkey, home of the Bob Wills Day reunion each April and the Hotel Turkey (not rated), a 1927 hotel restored as a bed & breakfast (806) 423-1151.

ANNUAL EVENTS

January

"SUPER BULL" BULL RIDING

Amarillo Civic Center, 3rd and Buchanan • 378-4297 • $8, $10, and $12 • W+
For a true taste of the Old West, try this bull-riding event.

March

"BEST OF TEXAS"

**Amarillo Civic Center, 3rd and Buchanan • 374-0802 or 378-4297
Admission • W+**
Top merchants bring antiques, fashion, arts and crafts to Amarillo, along with food, silent auction, other events.

May

FUNFEST

Thompson Park, off US 87/287N and 24th St. • 374-0802 • Memorial Day weekend • Adults $4, seniors $3, children under 8, $2 • W
Three-day festival of games, entertainment and food sponsored by the Junior League and the City of Amarillo Parks and Recreation Department. More than 70,000 men, women, and children come each year to hear top-flight name entertainment and take part in or watch the marathon and half-marathon, volleyball and golf tournaments, bicycle races, talent contest and many children's activities. Fun for the whole family.

June

COORS RANCH RODEO

**Tri-state Fairgrounds, 3rd and Grand • *Take Grand exit north off I-40*
376-7767 • About $10 • W**
Cowboys from more than a dozen ranches compete in bronc riding, wild cow milking, cattle branding, team penning, in this authentic Western tradition.

July

OLD WEST DAYS & RANCH RIDERS RODEO

Will Rogers Range Rider Rodeo Arena *(intersection of Bell Ave. and Amarillo Blvd. West)* • 355-2212 • 7:30 nightly • Adults $8, children $3, under 6 free • W
Sponsored by the Chamber of Commerce and Will Rogers Range Rider Rodeo Arena, this annual event features a parade, a dress-up contest, and other fun events, with the traditional rodeo events in the evenings.

September

BOYS RANCH RODEO

See Cal Farley's Boys' Ranch (Side Trips) for details of this event.

ANNUAL TRI-STATE FAIR

Fairgrounds, 10th and Bell St. • 376-7767 • Usually beginning the third Monday in September • Adults $3, children $1, evening concerts priced separately • W • Parking $2

Midway, rides, games, food, concerts, shows, animals, and more. Big C&W stars entertain nightly in the coliseum (tickets about $12).

October

TASTE OF THE ARTS

Westgate Mall Center Court • *I-40 at Coulter Exit* • 373-7800 • Free • W

Arts groups of all kinds: artists, performers, dancers, music, theater, opera and exhibits from local and area museums. Sponsored by the Arts Committee of the Amarillo Chamber of Commerce.

November

WORLD CHAMPIONSHIP RANCH RODEO

Amarillo Civic Center, 3rd and Buchanan • 358-7383 Tickets $12, $10, and $8 • W+

Real cowboys, who actually earn their living on working ranches, compete in bronc riding, wild cow milking, team doctoring, branding, and penning, and a wild horse race.

December

AMARILLO FARM & RANCH SHOW

Amarillo Civic Center, 3rd and Buchanan • 378-4297 • Free • W+

One of the largest such shows in the nation, with more than 700 booths welcoming 40,000 visitors yearly.

RESTAURANTS

($ = under $7, $$ = $8–$17, $$$ = $18–$25, $$$$ = over $25 for one person excluding drinks, tax, and tip.)

American Eclectic

BIG TEXAN STEAK RANCH

7701 I-40E *(North on I-40 access, between Whitaker and Lakeside exits)* 372-7000 • Lunch and dinner daily • $–$$ • Cr • W+

If you haven't visited the Big Texan, you haven't visited Amarillo. For years, tourists have been stopping in at this Texas legend. With old-fashioned, down-home Texas atmosphere and food, this place is legendary for its 72-oz. steak, free if you can eat it in an hour. Texas hors d'oeuvres include rattlesnake, calf fries, buffalo, rabbit, chicken, sausage, and barbecued ribs. Portions are generous. Waitpersons are cheerful and attentive; the decor is remarkable. Often the Big Texan sponsors special events, such as the Cowboy Poets' Breakfast, Texas "Opry," Country/Western concerts, family events.

THE BREW PUB

3705 Olsen • 353-2622 • Lunch and dinner, daily • $–$$ • Cr • W

Craft beers, steaks, cheeseburgers, pizza, chicken in a pleasant, upbeat atmosphere. Informal. Caters to young professionals and students.

CAJUN MAGIC

2201 Paramount • 359-4762 • Lunch and dinner, daily • $$–$$$ • Cr • W

Crawfish, pan-fried oysters, po'boys, all fairly mild, with hotter *etouffes, jambalaya,* and blackened dishes. Stuffed mushrooms and catfish are good. Pasta dishes, *beignets,* chicory coffee, Dixie beer. Live jazz some nights. Bar.

CALICO COUNTY

2410 Paramount • 358-7664 • Lunch and dinner • $–$$ • Cr • W+

Almost everything is chicken-fried—steak, pork chops, chicken livers and gizzards, even corn on the cob—then served as an entrée, in a sandwich or salad. Bar.

COUNTRY BARN

1805 Lakeside Dr. • North access road on I-40E at Lakeside exit • 355-2325 Lunch and dinner, Monday through Saturday, dinner only Sunday. Closed some holidays • $$–$$$ • Cr • W

You'll find traditional Texas fare with a countryfied atmosphere that's locally popular, with quick, pleasant service. Specializes in steaks, tender and cooked to order; Tex-Mex and chicken dishes, some "lite" dishes, children's menu. Music, dancing on weekends. Beer/wine list.

OHMS GALLERY CAFE

Atrium Plaza, 619 S. Taylor • 373-3233 • Lunch Monday–Friday, dinner Friday–Saturday. Closed Sunday • $–$$ • No Cr • W

Upscale eatery featuring exotic teas and coffees, beer and wine, live entertainment on weekends. British dishes, pie, light pasta dishes, lamb and pork entrées, and stews. Cafeteria-style gourmet lunches and dinners, live music on weekends, featured artist every month. Espresso, Victorian decor.

OYSTER BAR

4150 Paramount • 354-9110 • Lunch and dinner. Closed Sunday • $–$$ • MC, V

Popular for seafood, including oysters on the half shell, boiled shrimp, po'boys. Beer and wine.

STOCKYARD CAFE

100 S. Manhattan • 374-6024 • Breakfast and lunch Monday–Saturday, dinner Friday and Saturday. Closed Sunday • $–$$

When you visit the stockyards, stop by for steak, sandwiches, homemade pie. Unpretentious and satisfying for farmers, ranchers, and cowboys as well as tourists.

Asian

BLACK STONE CAFE

202 W. 10th • Downtown, near Convention and Visitors' Bureau, Civic Center • 372-7700 • Breakfast, lunch and dinner Monday–Saturday • $–$$ Cr • W

This plain, downtown eatery features "American" breakfasts, and Thai/Chinese lunches and dinners, in an unpretentious setting; lunch (Thai/Chinese) buffet on weekdays. Popular with downtown workers, who often pick up lunch to take back to the gang at the office.

THE KING AND I

2300 Bell • 355-1016 • Lunch and dinner daily • $–$$ • V, MC • W

A more upscale Thai restaurant specializing in soups and stir-fry dishes, some quite spicy.

MY-THAI

2029 Coulter • 355-9541 or 352-9014 • Lunch and dinner daily • $–$$ No Cr • W

Chinese-Thai menu from mildly seasoned to very hot; hearty soups. Lunch specials are a bargain, or for dinner you might choose Sea Food Delight, with beef and scallops. Wonderful version of hot and sour soup, made with coconut milk; crisp spring rolls.

Continental

ITALIAN DELIGHTS

2710 W. 10th Ave. • 372-5444 • Lunch and dinner, Tuesday–Saturday, lunch only Monday. Closed Sunday • $ • No Cr • W

This modest little restaurant is popular for for *lasagna,* chicken *marsalas* and eggplant *parmigiana* as well as other traditional and pasta dishes. Half orders available.

SCARPELLI'S

6010 W. 34th • 358-8750 • Closed Sunday and Monday, espresso bar open every day • $$–$$$ • Cr • W

Definitely worth trying, Scarpelli's is a tiny grotto, so reservations for dinner are recommended. Filletto di garberi e carciofi, rib eye rossini with forest mushrooms, garlic prawns with ravioli primavera, salmon, veal, penne giambotte. Espresso bar serves light foods all day.

Mexican

LA FIESTA

2200 S. Ross, off I-40, 45th and Bell at Bell Plaza • 374-3689 Lunch and dinner Monday–Saturday. Closed Sunday • $$ • Cr • W

Near the American Quarter Horse Heritage Center and Museum. Fajitas, quesadillas, enchiladas, hot tamales, chiles rellenos. Tex-Mex, steaks, chicken dishes from the grill. Imported beers and margaritas.

RESTAURANTE LOS INSURGENTES

3531 West 15th St. • 353-5361 • Lunch and dinner Monday–Saturday, closed Sunday • $–$$ • Cr • W+

Long-standing eatery continues to be popular with local folks because of its well prepared, good food. Classic mole poblano, chicken cooked in a rich chile and chocolate sauce; el platillo, a flat enchilada smothered in chili and topped with a fried egg and cheese, homemade tamales and chiles rellenos. Mexican beer.

RUBY TEQUILLA'S MEXICAN KITCHEN

2108 Paramount • 358-7829 • Lunch and dinner daily • $–$$ • Cr • W

Ruby's has been around for a while with liberal portions, a large menu, and conservative cuisine served in a renovated warehouse. Popular locally. Bar.

ACCOMMODATIONS

($ = under $45, $$ = $46–$60, $$$ = $61–$80, $$$$ = $81–$100, $$$$$ = over $100)
Room tax 13%

BEST WESTERN AMARILLO INN

**1610 Coulter, off I-40W, near Medical Center • 358-7861, 1-800-528-1234,
or fax 806-352-7287 • $$ • W+ 1 room • No-smoking rooms**
   This two-story motel has 103 units, including five suites ($100 plus). Children under 18 stay free with parents. Rates higher in summer, lower in winter. Senior rates. TV with cable, HBO. Room phones (no charge for local calls). Pets OK ($10 deposit). Restaurant on premises, breakfast and dinner, room service. Indoor pool, hot tub. Meeting rooms, business amenities. Free continental breakfast.

BIG TEXAN STEAK RANCH MOTEL

**7703 I-40E between Lakeside and Whitaker exits • 372-5000, 800-657-7177,
or fax: 806-371-0099 • $$ • W+ 1 room • No-smoking rooms**
   A Western motif fronts this two-story motel with 55 units, including the Cattle Baron's suite, with wet bar. Children under 18 stay free in room with parents. Rates higher in summer, lower in winter. Senior discount. Cable TV with HBO. Room phones (no charge for local calls). Pets OK. Restaurant (see Restaurants), club, entertainment. Texas-shaped outdoor heated pool. Free airport transportation. Free continental breakfast. Special events in restaurant include Cowboy Poets' Breakfast, Country/Western concerts, Texas "Opry."

FAIRFIELD INN

**6600 I-40W • 351-0172, 1-800-228-2800, fax 806-351-0172 • $$ • W+ 4 rooms
No-smoking rooms**
   The new Fairfield Inn has 76 units with eight suites (higher rates for suites). Kids under 18 stay free in parents' room. Senior, AAA, government rates available. Rates higher in summer. Check-out time is noon. TV with cable and HBO. Room phones (no charge for local calls). Room sprinklers. Indoor pool, hot tub, game room. Free coffee in lobby; free continental breakfast. Business services available. Free newspaper.

HAMPTON INN

**1700 I-40 East at Ross/Osage exit • 372-1425, 1-800-HAMPTON,
or fax: 806-379-8807 • $–$$ • W+ 2 rooms • No-smoking rooms**
   The two-story Hampton has 116 units. Rates are higher in summer, lower in winter. Children under 18 stay free with parents, senior discounts are available. Pets OK. TV, cable with premium channels. Pool. Complimentary continental breakfast. Restaurant next door. Check-out noon.

HOLIDAY INN EXPRESS

**3411 I-40 West (79109) • 356-6800, 1-800-HOLIDAY, or fax: 806-356-0401
$$$ • W+ 2 rooms • No-smoking rooms**
   This two-story motel has 97 rooms and two suites (suite rates higher), with wheelchair-accessible rooms on the first floor and non-smoking rooms. Check-out time is noon. Rates are higher in summer. TV with cable and HBO; room phones (no charge for local calls). Pets not permitted. Restaurant next door.

Outdoor pool, exercise room. Free airport transportation, newspaper, continental breakfast.

HOLIDAY INN HOLIDOME

1911 I-40 East at Ross/Osage exit (79102) • 372-8741, 1-800-465-4329, fax: 806-372-2913 • $$–$$$$ • W+ 5 rooms • No-smoking rooms

This four-story motel has 247 units and one suite; special rates for seniors, government workers, and others. Children under 19 stay free in room with parents. Rates lower in summer, higher in winter. Five rooms are wheelchair-accessible. Check-out time is noon. TV, cable and HBO, room phones (no charge for local calls). Pets OK. Restaurant on premises; room service available. Lounge. Indoor pool, whirlpool, meeting rooms, and free airport transportation. Ask about B&B special.

LA QUINTA INN EAST

1708 I-40E at Ross/Osage exit (Another La Quinta at 2108 Coulter, near Medical Center) • 373-7486 or 1-800-531-5900, or fax: 806/372-4100 • $–$$ • W+ 6 rooms • No-smoking rooms

The two-story La Quinta has 130 rooms, cable TV with Showtime. Room phones (no charge for local calls). Small pets OK. Outdoor pool. Rates are higher in summer, lower in winter. Restaurant (Denny's) next door. Free coffee, free continental breakfast. Business amenities. Senior discount.

RADISSON INN AIRPORT

7909 I-40E • 373-3303, 1-800-333-3333, or fax: 806-373-3353 • $$–$$$ W+ 1 room • No-smoking rooms

This two-story motel, near the airport, has 206 units and a honeymoon suite. Children under 18 stay free with parents; other family plans, senior discounts, are available. Summer rates are higher. Cable TV. Room phones (no charge for local calls). Fire sprinklers. Pets permitted with $100 deposit. Restaurant, lounge, nightclub; dancing Saturday nights. Indoor heated pool, exercise room, game room. Free airport transportation. Meeting room, free newspaper. Business amenities. Electronic door locks. Same-day valet service.

RAMADA INN EAST

2501 I-40 East • 379-6555, 1-800-245-5525, or fax: 806-372-7355 • $$$–$$$$ • W+ 1 room • No-smoking rooms

The three-story Ramada has 185 units and 18 suites. Family plans available; kids free in parents' room. Rates are lower in winter. Senior discounts. Check-out noon. TV, limited cable. Room phones (no charge for local calls). Fire sprinklers in room. Pets OK with $30 deposit. Lounge, entertainment. Indoor pool, hot tub, sauna. Free airport transportation. Free continental breakfast, newspaper.

TRAVELODGE EAST

3205 I-40E (another at 2035 Paramount, 353-3541) • 372-8171, 1-800-578-7878, or fax: 806-372-2815 • $–$$ • W+ 3 rooms • No-smoking rooms

This two-story motel has 96 units, with three rooms equipped for wheelchair patrons. Rates are higher in summer, lower in winter. Check-out time is noon. Room phones (no charge for local calls); room fire sprinklers. Pets OK. Restaurant, lounge. Outdoor heated pool. Free coffee.

WESTAR SUITES

6800 I-40W (Bell St. exit) • 358-7943, or fax: 806-358-8475 • $$$ • W+
No-smoking rooms
The two-story Westar has 126 suites with kitchens, no-smoking rooms. Children under 18 free in parents' room. Rates higher in summer, lower in winter. Cable TV with premium channels. Heated pool, whirlpool, hot tub. Business amenities. Complimentary continental breakfast. Health club privileges. Picnic tables, grills. Senior discount available. Room phones (no charge for local calls).

BRECKENRIDGE

Stephens County Seat • 5,665 • (254)
This is a city named after a U.S. vice president in a county named after a Confederate vice president. However, Breckinridge (spelled with an *i*), who was Buchanan's vice president, sided with the South in the Civil War, and for a short time near the end of the war was the Confederate Secretary of War. The oil boom hit here in 1918, briefly turning the city into a boom town. But that soon died out, and today the area has a balanced economic base of agriculture, oil, manufacturing, and petrochemical production.

TOURIST SERVICES

BRECKENRIDGE CHAMBER OF COMMERCE

**2410 W. Walker, US 180 approximately 1.5 miles west of town
(P.O. Box 1466, 76424)** • 559-2301 • W

MUSEUMS

BRECKENRIDGE AVIATION MUSEUM

**Stephens County Airport, approximately 2.2 miles south on US 183
559-3201** • Monday–Friday 9–5 • Free • W
The museum serves as the headquarters of the Big Iron Squadron of the West Texas Wing of the Confederate Air Force (see Midland). It features a collection of some 20 World War II aircraft as well as memorabilia from that war and the Korean and Vietnam wars. The annual air show is held here.

LIBRARY AND FINE ARTS CENTER

207 N. Breckenridge (US 183N) • 559-6602 • **Monday–Friday 11–5 and special hours on weekends when there is a special exhibit on display** • W+
The art exhibits change about every four to six weeks and feature both local artists and traveling shows.

SWENSON MEMORIAL MUSEUM

116 W. Walker, near US 180 at US 183 • 559-8471 • **Tuesday–Saturday 10–12, 1–5. Closed major holidays** • Free • **Small parking lot in rear off Elm St.**
Housed in an old bank building (with a research library in the vault), this museum tells county history with a series of permanent small dioramas and temporary exhibits that change every few weeks. Among the many displays are a pre-Civil War hearse and a music room filled with old pianos, organs, and radios. **The J.D. Sandefer Oil Museum Annex,** in another building nearby, retells the story of the oil boom days in exhibits and pictures.

OTHER POINTS OF INTEREST

HUBBARD CREEK LAKE

US 180 approximately 4 miles west • 559-9103 (Store)
Open at all times • Free

This is a water source for Breckenridge and several other cities, and one of the larger lakes in West Texas with nearly 17,000 surface acres and more than 130 miles of shoreline. Water sports available include fishing, boating, sailing, waterskiing, and swimming. In addition to residential areas, there are camping areas (call for reservations), motels, and marinas around the lake.

LAKE DANIEL

US 183 south about 9 miles • Open at all times • Free

This lake is Breckenridge's principal water supply. It is undeveloped, but offers excellent fishing.

SPORTS AND OTHER ACTIVITIES

Golf

BRECKENRIDGE COUNTRY CLUB

US 180 at western city limits • 559-3466 • Private 9-hole club, but visitors welcome to play. Greens fee $5 weekdays, $7.50 weekends.

SIDE TRIP

POSSUM KINGDOM STATE PARK

Box 70, Caddo, 76429 • *From Breckenridge take US 180 east to Caddo and then go north on Park Rd. 33 approximately 17 miles* • 549-1803
Open at all times • Adults $3, under 12 free • W+ but not all areas

Created in the late 1940s, this lake has more than 20,000 acres of the clearest water in the Southwest and more than 310 miles of shoreline. The 1,529-acre park is on the south shore and contains picnic areas, campsites (call for reservations), dumpstation, six cabins, double boat ramp, canoe and paddleboatrentals, playground, and park store. Part of the official state longhorn herd is here. Possum Kingdom is a deep lake, and, in addition to the usual water sports, it offers scuba diving in depths up to 150 feet. The private areas around the lake are well developed with residences, campsites, marinas, lodges, restaurants, and other commercial establishments.

ANNUAL EVENTS

May

STEPHENS COUNTY FRONTIER DAYS

Breckenridge City Park and Stephens County Agriculture and Community Center • 559-2301 (Chamber of Commerce) • $5

Celebrate the county's heritage at the Stephens County Ranch Rodeo and Junior Rodeo. There are arts and crafts, gun and knife show, and bit and spur show. Fiddlers and storytellers provide entertainment during this 3-day event.

ACCOMMODATIONS

($ = under $45, $$ = $46–$60, $$$ = $61–$80, $$$$ = $81–$100, $$$$$ = over $100)
Room tax 13%

BRECKENRIDGE INN
3111 W. Walker (US 180) • 559-6502 or 800-270-8290 • $
All 40 rooms are on ground level. Cable TV and HBO. Room phones (no charge for local calls). Pets OK. Restaurant adjacent. Guest memberships available in local private clubs. Outdoor pool, hot tub. Free continental breakfast.

RIDGE MOTEL
2602 W. Walker (US 180) • 559-2244 or 800-462-5308 • $ • No-smoking rooms
This 1- and 2-story motel has 47 rooms. Cable TV. Room phones (no charge for local calls). Pets OK. Private supper club with automatic membership for guests. Guest memberships available in local private clubs. Restaurant adjacent. Outdoor pool. Free coffee in office.

CANYON

Randall County Seat • 11,365 • (806)
Canyon is a pleasant small college town. Its major attractions are West Texas A&M University, with the excellent Panhandle-Plains Historical Museum, and nearby Palo Duro Canyon State Park, where the award-winning historical drama *Texas!* is presented each summer.

The main event that led to the settlement of this region by farmers and ranchers was the final defeat of the Native Americans under their legendary chief Quanah Parker, in the mid-1870s. Son of a Comanche chief and a white woman captive, Parker led a last, futile attempt to resist white domination in what is described as the last Indian battle in Texas. The U.S. Cavalry, led by Col. Ranald S. Mackenzie, surprised the Indians in Blanco Canyon, destroyed their villages and captured their horses so that they were forced to return to the reservation in Oklahoma. Quanah Parker remained a hero to his people and later counted among his friends such men as Theodore Roosevelt.

A short time later, Charles Goodnight established the first ranch in the Panhandle near Palo Duro Canyon. Two years later the T-Anchor Ranch headquarters was established by his brother-in-law, Leigh Dyer. The city of Canyon evolved from that ranch.

TOURIST SERVICES

CANYON CHAMBER OF COMMERCE
308 17th St. (P.O. Box 8, 79015) • 655-7815 or 800-999-9481 • W
Arrangements can be made here to visit regional ranches.

MUSEUMS

PANHANDLE-PLAINS HISTORICAL MUSEUM

On campus of West Texas A&M University, 2401 4th Ave. 1 block east of US
87 • 656-2244 • Monday–Saturday 9–5 (June–August 9–6), Sunday 2–6
Free • W variable

It takes several hours to do justice to this truly outstanding facility, Texas'
oldest and largest state-supported museum. The emphasis is on the unique history and character of this region from prehistoric days through the years of
farming and ranching, to the importance of the region's petroleum industry. In
one area you can trace the history of the state from the Paleozoic Era (fossils) to
the present. The Hall of the South Plains Indian portrays the character and life
of the Native Americans. Leigh Dyer's cabin and the T-Anchor Ranch House
illustrate the coming of white settlers, followed by Pioneer Town, a visualiza-
tion of life in a small West Texas town. In the Petroleum Wing you can follow
the path of oil from fossilized sea creatures to your car's tank. Also on display is
an exhibit of antique vehicles along with an extensive gun collection of nearly
1,000 weapons. On the second floor is an art gallery, with both permanent and
changing exhibits. Gift shop.

OTHER POINTS OF INTEREST

PALO DURO CANYON STATE PARK

Take SH 217 east 12 miles to Park Rd. 5 • 488-2227, reservations 512-389-8900,
information 800-792-1112, fax: 806-488-2556 • Summer: daily 6–10; Winter:
daily 8–10 • $2–$5 • W variable

Cutting jaggedly down through the Texas Panhandle from north to south is
the escarpment of the Great American Plains, a series of canyons whose wild
natural beauty is only beginning to be appreciated. Palo Duro is the largest and
best-known of these and provides perhaps the most beautiful vistas. Named for
the juniper that still grows in abundance, Palo Duro is 120 miles long, 20 miles
wide at its widest, and more than 1,100 feet from the rim to the lowest elevation. The State Park, which is almost 16,000 acres, contains only a small part of
the canyon.

According to geologists, visitors can step back 90 million years in time as
they descend into the canyon. Although not found in the abundance found by
the first white explorers, native plants and animals may still be seen. Early
morning and late evening, when changing colors are most dramatic, are the
best times to appreciate the landscape.

The park has an interpretative center, shaded picnic shelters, the Goodnight
Trading Post (488-2760), horseback riding, a dugout, and the narrow-gauged
Sad Monkey Railroad ($1.50, 488-2222), which makes frequent trips for visitors.
Sites are available for tent and trailer camping (fee). And you can engage in
rock climbing, exploring, studying the native plants and animals, or just enjoying the breath-taking vistas. Note: mornings and evening can be quite cool,
even in summer. Also, sudden downpours can cause flash flooding. Check with
a park ranger for current conditions. The musical drama *Texas!* is presented
here at the Pioneer Amphitheater during the summer.

COLLEGES AND UNIVERSITIES

WEST TEXAS A&M UNIVERSITY

US 87 and S. 2nd Ave. • 656-0111 • W variable • Visitor parking near Administration Building on 3rd Ave.

Part of the Texas A&M system, the University has six schools and colleges that include art and sciences, agriculture, business, education, fine arts, and the graduate school. Information and guided tours are available at the Administration Building, which is on the left just past the entrance gates. The university is proud of its fine arts programs. Visitors are welcome to visit the art gallery in Mary Moody Northern Hall (8–5 weekdays, 656-2799), and attend concerts and stage productions in the Branding Iron Theater of the Fine Arts Building (656-2798), or the Amarillo Civic Center (656-3701). You are also welcome at intercollegiate sports events.

PERFORMING ARTS

TEXAS! A MUSICAL DRAMA

Pioneer Amphitheatre, Palo Duro State Park • *Take SH 217 12 miles east to Park Rd. 5, then follow that to the amphitheater* • 655-2185 • June–August, 8:30 P.M. • W • $7–$16 • Reservations required

Nightly except Sunday from late June through late August you can relive the exciting story of pioneer life in the Texas Panhandle in this professional musical drama written by Pulitzer prize-winning author Paul Green. More than a million visitors from every state and 83 foreign countries have attended the production. The company of 80 actors and singers recreate life in the 1880s: the struggles of the settlers, the life of the cowboys, the grief of the Native Americans, and the coming of the railroads. Barbecue is available before the show (about $6 person, starting at 6:30 P.M.). Entrance to the park is free with your ticket after 6 P.M., before that you'll have to pay the car entrance fee. Ticket center is at 2010 4th Ave. in Canyon. You can arrange shuttle bus service from most Amarillo hotels.

ANNUAL EVENTS

December

OLD FASHIONED CHRISTMAS

**Panhandle-Plains Historical Museum, 2401 4th Ave. • 656-2244
Usually first weekend in December • Free • W**

A Christmas party with Santa Claus and entertainment, refreshments, demonstrations of pioneer crafts, and the museum's Pioneer Village filled with civic leaders portraying the early settlers. Usually Thursday and Friday evenings and Sunday afternoon.

RESTAURANTS

($ = under $7, $$ = $8–$17, $$$ = $18–$25, $$$$ = over $25 for one person excluding drinks, tax, and tip.)

RAILROAD CROSSING STEAKHOUSE

1303 23rd St. (US 87) at 14th Ave. • 655-7701 • Lunch and dinner daily except major holidays • $–$$ • Cr • W • Children's menu

This locally popular eatery specializes in tender steaks, but you can also get chicken and some seafood entrées.

BANGKOK CUISINE

2321 4th Ave. (near campus, museum) • 655-7073 • Lunch and dinner, Monday–Friday. Closed Saturday and Sunday

Small, unpretentious restaurant on the edge of the campus, and next door to the museum, serves Thai/Chinese cuisine, all-you-can-eat specials, lunch buffet, spicy and mild dishes from the menu.

ACCOMMODATIONS

($ = under $45, $$ = $46–$60, $$$ = $61–$80, $$$$ = $81–$100, $$$$$ = over $100) Room tax 10%

HUDSPETH HOUSE (BED & BREAKFAST)

1905 4th Ave. • 655-9800 or 800-999-9504 • $$–$$$ • No-smoking

Artist Georgia O'Keefe once lived in this restored Victorian house built with lumber from an old cotton gin and furnished with antiques. Three stories, eight units, seven baths. TV. Whirlpool and exercise room. Telephone only in common room. Full breakfast (other meals may be arranged in advance). Smoking only in common room. Picnic tables and grills.

DALHART

Dallam County Seat, also in Hartley County • 6,398 • (806)

Starting in the 1880s this whole area was part of the XIT Ranch, at that time the largest ranch in the world under fence—6,000 miles of fence. The XIT came into being when some out-of-state investors contracted to built a $3 million granite capitol building in Austin in exchange for three million acres of land. The spread covered parts of what is now nine counties, averaging about 27 miles wide and 200 miles from the north to the south fence. At its peak it ran about 150,000 head of cattle and employed about 150 cowboys. The investors, however, were not interested in being in the cattle business, and by 1912 the cows were all sold and eventually the land was divided up and sold. Dalhart is proud of the cowboy mystique and the legend of the XIT, which lives on in the annual XIT Rodeo and Reunion and the XIT Museum.

TOURIST SERVICES

DALHART CHAMBER OF COMMERCE

102 E. 7th St. (P.O. Box 967, 79022) • 249-5646, fax: 806-249-4945 • W

In addition to maps, literature, and information about the area, ask about the community theater in an art deco building being restored and the schedule of melodramas and other productions by this local theater group.

MUSEUMS

XIT MUSEUM
**108 E. 5th between Denver and Denrock • 249-5390 • Monday–Saturday 10–5
Free (Donation) • W**
This regional museum, in a restored art deco building, tells the story of the XIT
Ranch and of Dalham and Hartley counties through pictures, documents, and
exhibits. These include a 1900 parlor, bedroom, and kitchen; a cook's wagon, and
an antique gun collection. A collection of Native American artifacts and a Peter
Hurd painting are proud possessions. The Pioneer Chapel, with furnishings from
the first six churches in the city, is often a setting for local weddings.

OTHER POINTS OF INTEREST

EMPTY SADDLE MONUMENT
On a traffic island near underpass on US 87N and US 385
According to local legend, an XIT cowboy passed away just before the annual
reunion, and his widow asked if his horse could be in the parade in his memory. Since then, a horse with an empty saddle traditionally leads the annual
parade. The monument is a tribute to all departed XIT cowboys.

SIDE TRIPS

LAKE RITA BLANCA
Take US 87 south to FM 281, then turn right (west) to the lake • **249-6393**
Open at all times • Free • W variable
Boating, tent and RV camping (fee), fishing (get permit at boat house), and
picnicking on this 560-acre lake, which is the site of the XIT Rodeo and
Reunion.

SHOPPING

JUNIOR GRAY'S SADDLE SHOP
310 E. 7th, between Keeler and Scott • 249-2054 • W
Junior, a community fixture, prefers to make saddles for working cowboys,
but he'll make fancy ones, too. His wife does other leather work, such as chaps
and belts.

ANNUAL EVENTS

August

XIT RODEO AND REUNION
Rita Blanca Park. *Take US 87 south to FM 281 then right (west) to the park*
**249-5646 • First Thursday, Friday, and Saturday in August • Admission to
rodeo and nightly dance • W**
Billed as the "world's largest amateur rodeo," this event has been held for
more than a half century and includes a free barbecue where thousands chow
down on more than six tons of beef. Other highlights include the opening parade,
a junior rodeo, the 5K "Empty Saddle Run," and pony express. An antique car
show is part of the celebration, and each evening C&W stars headline the show
and dance (Admission).

ACCOMMODATIONS

($ = under $45, $$ = $46–$60, $$$ = $61–$80, $$$$ = $81–$100, $$$$$ = over $100)
Room tax 11%

BEST WESTERN NURSANICKEL

Corner US 87S • 249-5637 or 800-528-1234 • $–$$$ (higher rates in summer and during rodeo) • No-smoking rooms
   The two-story Nursanickel has 55 rooms of which half are no-smoking. Cable TV. Free movie channel. Room phones (no charge for local calls). Small dogs OK. Restaurant (locally popular). Outdoor heated pool. Free coffee.

COMFORT INN

US 54E • 249-8585 • $–$$ • W+ 1 room • No-smoking rooms
   The Comfort Inn has 36 units, with wheelchair room and no-smoking rooms. Cable TV, heated pool, airport, bus depot transportation. Free coffee. Pets OK. Restaurant adjacent.

DAYS INN

701 Liberal, US 54 East • 806-249-5246 or 1-800-DAYSINN • $$–$$$$ (higher rates in summer and during rodeo) • No-smoking rooms
   The two-story, 43-unit Days Inn is the newest motel in Dalhart, features many amenities, and is user-friendly for business travelers, with data ports in every room, fax and photocopier available in lobby. Interior corridors. Family vacation plans available. Senior discounts available. Two wheelchair rooms, one room for hearing-impaired. Check out time 11 A.M. TV, HBO, VCRs in every room. Small pets OK. Phones (no charge for local calls). Airport transportation available. Indoor pool, hot tub, exercise rooms, fitness facilities. Free full breakfast. Electronically monitored parking lot.

EASTLAND

Eastland County Seat • 3,641 • (254)
   Named for Captain William Mosby Eastland, who went on the ill-conceived and ill-fated Mier Expedition in 1842. After being captured by Santa Anna, Eastland drew one of 17 black beans used to select those to be executed when Santa Anna decreed that every tenth man would die. Today the area economy is based on oil, ranching, farming, and manufacturing. The county ranks third in the state in peanut production.

TOURIST SERVICES

EASTLAND CHAMBER OF COMMERCE

102 S. Seaman • 629-2332 • W

POINTS OF INTEREST

KENDRICK RELIGIOUS PAGEANT, DIORAMA & MUSEUM

US 80 approximately 5 miles west • 629-8672 • Daily 10–5, except closed second and third weeks in September • Adults $2.50, children $2 • W

There are over 140 life-sized figures in the 24 scenes from the Old and New Testament in the wax museum. Audio narration and guided tours last about an hour and a half. A 325-foot outdoor stage is used for two-hour presentations of Bible stories with live performers and live animals every Thursday and Friday night at 9, from mid-June through mid-August (admission $3). An Easter Sunday predawn pageant has been presented free here for more than 20 years.

LAKE LEON

About 7 miles southeast via FM 570 and FM 2214 • **629-2332**
(Chamber of Commerce) • **Open at all times** • **Free** • **W variable**
A 1,590-acre lake offering boating and fishing, marina, RV hookups, cabins for rent, and an exotic animal ranch.

"OLD RIP" THE HORNED TOAD

Top of steps on Main St. side of county courthouse • **Open at all times** • **Free**
This is the stuff that Texas legends are made of. In 1897, during the dedication of the cornerstone of the new courthouse, the townfolk put a live horned toad into the cornerstone along with memorabilia. In 1928, when the courthouse was torn down to build the new one, the cornerstone was opened. The toad they thought was dead came to life. Named "Old Rip" after Rip Van Winkle, he became an instant celebrity. He was exhibited all over the U.S. including a visit with President Coolidge in Washington. "Old Rip" died—for sure—less than a year after coming out of his tomb. His embalmed body is displayed in a glass-topped casket in the outside wall of the new courthouse.

POST OFFICE MURAL

Post Office, 400 block of E. Main
Marene Johnson, Eastland's postmaster from 1957 to 1968, spent $15,000 and countless hours using 11,217 stamps to create this 6-by-10-foot mural. Depictions include the Great Seal of the United States and a map of Texas. The mural is just to the left as you enter the building.

FRITCH

Hutchinson County • **2,964** • **(806)**
Ranchers in southern Hutchinson County were so happy to see the Rock Island Railroad come south in 1926 that they named the town after one of its company officers, H. C. Fritch. Fritch then was a cattle shipping point; today it is better known as the gateway to Lake Meredith and the Alibates Flint Quarries National Monument.

At the monument, one of many archaeological sites throughout the Texas Panhandle, evidence of human occupation goes back 13,000 years. The earliest known humans in the Americas, simply called "Humanos," are believed to have been related to the Pueblo people of New Mexico and Arizona. It is not known whether they moved from this region, were destroyed, or were absorbed by later Native Americans. What is known is that they traded goods, including the flint quarried here, along vast trade routes that stretched west to California and south to Mexico.

TOURIST SERVICES

FRITCH CHAMBER OF COMMERCE

104 N. Roby at Broadway (SH 136) under the watertower in the museum
(P.O. Box 406, 79036) • 857-2458 • W

NATIONAL PARK SERVICE HEADQUARTERS

419 E. Broadway (SH 136) • 857-3151

MUSEUMS

LAKE MEREDITH AQUARIUM AND WILDLIFE MUSEUM

Broadway (SH 136) and Robey, under the watertower • 857-2458
Tuesday–Saturday 8:30–6. Closed Sunday • Free • W

A fine small museum, with six excellent life-size dioramas picturing local
wildlife in their natural habitats: bobcats, pronghorn antelopes, wild turkeys,
raccoons, coyotes, and an eagle. In addition, five aquariums display a variety of
fish found in the lake. Exhibits of original art, mostly by local and regional
artists, change throughout the year.

OTHER POINTS OF INTEREST

ALIBATES FLINT QUARRIES NATIONAL MONUMENT

Take TX 136 south to sign at Alibates Rd., follow signs to monument
857-3151 (National Park Service Headquarters) • Guided tours only,
daily 10 and 2 in summer and on weekends in spring and fall, rest of year by
appointment only • Free

For thousands of years, the early inhabitants of this region came here to mine
the flint to use for their own tools and weapons and to trade for goods with
other people. It was an early, and very valuable, form of currency. Flint, which
is as hard as the best steel, remained a prime material for implements from the
time of the mammoth hunters until iron became readily available to the Plains
Indians in the nineteenth century. This 92-acre site, the only national monument in the state of Texas, commemorates the importance of flint. Besides the
quarries, one can see the ruins of the permanent villages built by the flint miners. The mile-and-a-half tour trail is rugged and steep in places, and is recommended only for those in good physical condition and dressed for hiking. You
are advised to bring a hat for protection from the sun, and a container of water.
The tour ends with a flint-chipping demonstration.

LAKE MEREDITH

*Take SH 136 to FM 687 and follow this to Sanford Dam, local roads lead to
different areas of the lake* • 857-3151 (National Park Service Headquarters)

At places two miles wide and 14 miles long, Lake Meredith has 16,500 surface
acres and more than 100 miles of shoreline. Much of the shoreline has been developed by the National Park Service into eight recreational areas. Visitors can
swim, fish, boat, and water ski or enjoy on-land sports such as golf, tennis, and
racquetball. Canyons and bluffs around the lake are equipped for both picnicking
and camping.

GRAHAM

Young County Seat• 9,014 • (940)

Founded in 1872 by the Graham brothers, who were salt merchants. Prior to that, in the 1850s the area was an Indian Reservation, but the Comanches and others who lived here were moved to Oklahoma in 1859. Eight miles north is the site of the Warren Wagon Train Massacre in which seven teamsters were killed. This massacre is especially important because it stirred General William T. Sherman, who was making a tour of the frontier at that time, to order Colonel Ranald Mackenzie (a general himself during the Civil War) to go after the Indians. This order led to the ultimate defeat of the Indians in Texas. Manufacturing and oil well servicing are important in the area's economy today.

TOURIST SERVICES

GRAHAM CHAMBER OF COMMERCE

Elm and 3rd (P.O. Box 299, 76450) • 549-3355 or 800-256-4844 • W

HISTORIC PLACES

A booklet directory of historic sites in Young County is available from the Chamber of Commerce ($1). Among the historically important buildings in Graham are **A.P. McCormick Home,** 710 Cherry St., built in 1876, it now houses an antique shop; **Beckham-Bell Home,** 710 Grove near 2nd, built in 1878; **Church Of Christ,** Grove and 2nd, originally built as a Baptist church in 1885.

OTHER POINTS OF INTEREST

LAKE EDDLEMAN AND LAKE GRAHAM

Take US 380 north approximately 4 miles • **Open at all times** • **Free**

Connected by a canal, these two lakes have a surface area of 2,600 acres. Together they offer the opportunity for boating, fishing, swimming, waterskiing, and camping.

SIDE TRIPS

FORT BELKNAP

Approximately 11 miles west on SH 61 • 846-3222 • Fort open most days, museum: Monday, Tuesday, and Thursday–Saturday 9–5, Sunday 1:30–5. Closed Wednesday • Free • W

Fort Belknap, anchor of a chain of forts stretching from the Red River to the Rio Grande, was founded in 1851 and abandoned in 1876 after the Indians were finally defeated. Restoration of this historical site started in 1936. The 20-acre grounds contain the restored commissary, magazine, corn house, kitchen, and two infantry barracks. Two museums feature frontier artifacts and ladies' clothing (1851 to present), including several inaugural gowns of Texas' first ladies. There are picnic sites and 12 RV spaces with electric hookups (three-day limit).

POSSUM KINGDOM LAKE STATE PARK

Take SH 16 southeast about 20 miles **(see Breckenridge).**

ANNUAL EVENTS

WILD WEST POSSUM FEST

Fireman's Park at SH 67 and 380 • 800-256-4844 (Chamber of Commerce)
Fourth Saturday in September • $2 per person • W

Entertainment includes music, arts and crafts booths, children's activities, Backyard BBQ & Chili Cook-Off, Heritage Village, and the World Championship Turtle Race.

ACCOMMODATIONS

($ = under $45, $$ = $46–$60, $$$ = $61–$80, $$$$ = $81–$100, $$$$$ = over $100)
Room tax 13%

THE GATEWAY INN

1401 SH 16S • 549-0222 • $–$$ • No-smoking rooms

The 87 units include seven kitchenettes ($$$) and 14 no-smoking rooms. Cable TV. Room phones (no charge for local calls). Restaurant. Automatic guest membership in private club (non-guests $7 fee). Outdoor pool. Hot tub. Coffeemakers in rooms.

RODEWAY INN

1919 SH 16S • 549-8320 or 800-880-9551 • $–$$$ • W+ 1 room

Half of the 41 rooms are no-smoking rooms. Room phones (no charge for local calls). Cable TV. Hot tub. Outdoor pool. Complimentary continental breakfast.

JACKSBORO

Jack County Seat • 3,412 • (940)

Settled in 1855, the area suffered from Indian raids until Fort Richardson was built here in 1867. Both the county and the city are named for the Jack brothers, one of whom became famous when he was arrested with William Travis by the Mexicans in 1832. His arrest led to the dispute between the colonists and the Mexicans at Anahuac that was really the first shots of the Texas Revolution. In 1871 Jacksboro was the site of the first trial of Indians in a white man's court. Three Kiowa chiefs—Satank, Satanta, and Big Tree—were arrested for the Warren Wagon Train Massacre. On the way to Jacksboro, Satank tried to escape and was killed. The other two were sentenced to hang but later paroled. Satanta went back on the warpath, was recaptured and imprisoned. He committed suicide in Huntsville Penitentiary. Big Tree also went back to his old ways, was recaptured, pardoned, and became a Baptist missionary working among his people. This massacre led to the Army's final campaigns against the Indians that settled the Texas frontier. Today, oil field services and agribusiness form the economic base of this area. Fort Richardson State Park is on the city's south side, and the downtown square contains historic old buildings including the old Fort Richardson Hotel, built in 1899, and the first bank building in the county.

TOURIST SERVICES

JACKSBORO CHAMBER OF COMMERCE

100 S. Main and Belknap (P.O. Box 606, 76458) • 567-2602 • W
Located in the old Fort Richardson Hotel

HISTORIC PLACES

FORT RICHARDSON STATE HISTORICAL PARK

US 281 (within city limits) approximately .5 mile from courthouse • 567-3506
Open daily 8–5, summer weekends until 7, for day use, Interpretative Center
hours vary • Adults $2, under 12 free • W+ but not all areas

This was the northernmost of the line of forts established in Texas after the
Civil War to stop the Indian raids. Among its commanding officers was Ranald
Slidell Mackenzie of the Fourth Cavalry, one of the West's most successful Indian fighters, who later forced the Indians back onto their reservations after winning the Battle of Palo Duro. Parts of the fort have been restored. There is an
Interpretative Center explaining the fort's history. The recreational facilities at
the park include campsites with water and electricity (fee), picnic areas, a
nature trail, 9-mile multi-use trail, and a small fishing pond.

OTHER POINTS OF INTEREST

LAKE JACKSBORO AND LOST CREEK RESERVOIR

Take SH 59 approximately 1 mile north • 567-6321 • Open daily • Free

These lakes offer facilities for camping, picnicking, fishing, and boating.

ANNUAL EVENTS

March

RATTLESNAKE SAFARI ROUNDUP

Armory building at Lake Jacksboro, SH 59 • 567-2602 (Chamber of
Commerce) • Usually a weekend in March • Admission • W

The actual dates depend on when the rattlers start stirring, because the
roundup means going out and catching them (volunteers only). There are
snake handling demonstrations, and you can buy snakeskins or eat fried rattlesnake meat.

July

TWIN LAKES SUMMER FEST

Twin Lakes Park, SH 59 • 567-2602 (Chamber of Commerce) • Independence
Day • Admission • W

Celebrate the 4th of July with arts and crafts and food booths, participatory
water sports, entertainment, fireworks display.

ACCOMMODATIONS

($ = under $45, $$ = $46–$60, $$$ = $61–$80, $$$$ = $81–$100, $$$$$ = over $100)
Room tax 13%

BEST WESTERN JACKSBORO INN

US 281 and SH 199 approximately 1.5 miles south • 567-3751 • $

The inn has 49 rooms. Cable TV with HBO. Room phones (no charge for local calls). Pets OK. 24-hour restaurant next door. Outdoor pool.

LUBBOCK

Lubbock County Seat • 191,523 • (806)

Lubbock is a clean, pleasant city with an informal, small town atmosphere. It enjoys fine weather nearly all year, and the dry, clear air is rarely very hot in summer or very cold in winter.

Although this is one of the most recently settled areas of the country, it is possibly the oldest community in Texas, if not in the New World. Archaeological evidence of human occupation at the Lubbock Lake Landmark goes back 12,000 years, to the Clovis Period. More recently, the area was occupied by Native Americans, followed by buffalo hunters, soldiers of fortune, ranchers and farmers.

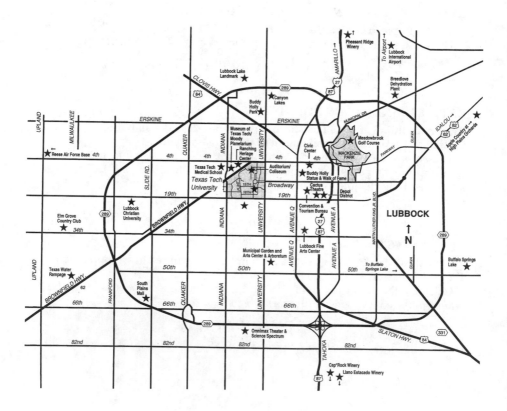

Lubbock calls itself the "Hub City" because it was once the hub of railroad lines and is still the hub of several highways. Medicine, education, and hi-tech industry are important to the local economy, but agriculture, distribution, and retail trade are still vital. Lubbock is an agribusiness center, one of the largest inland cotton markets in the nation. Other agricultural products include cattle, wheat, grain sorghum, sunflower seeds and oil. Wine is a new and growing industry whose products are receiving very favorable notice. Agriculture on such a scale requires irrigation by means of the Ogallala Aquifer, a vast underground reservoir. Windmills are almost a regional art form.

Music Legends

Lubbock has always nurtured more than its share of creative artists, especially musicians. Buddy Holly, legendary rock 'n' roll pioneer, grew up here, and went on to inspire a generation of musicians, including The Beatles (who acknowledged their debt to Buddy Holly and the Crickets). Other legendary names include Bob Wills (from Turkey, which celebrates each spring with Bob Wills Day), Mac Davis, John Denver, Joe Ely, Roy Orbison, Don Williams, the Gatlin Brothers, Tanya Tucker, Terry Allen, Butch Hancock, Jimmie Dale Gilmore, the Nelsons and the Maines Brothers. Nearly any night, local musicians entertain enthusiastic audiences in local clubs, and it would be a shame to leave West Texas without experiencing the lively night life.

Other art forms are also popular in Lubbock, which has a number of small theater groups and art galleries. And there are always plays, lectures, concerts and other cultural events. To learn what is happening during your visit, check Bill Kerns' entertainment section in Friday's *Avalanche Journal*.

Lubbock has several pleasant parks, the largest of which is Mackenzie, which is part of the Canyon Lakes Project. In *playa lakes* (small depressions in which rainwater collects), you can see hundreds of the thousands of Canada geese, sandhill cranes and other migratory waterfowl who winter over in this region. Devoted birders will find even more at **Muleshoe Wildlife Refuge,** 60 miles northwest of Lubbock (Hwy. 214 between Enochs and Needmore).

TOURIST SERVICES

VISITORS AND CONVENTION BUREAU

Lubbock Chamber of Commerce, 14th and Ave. K (P.O. Box 561, Lubbock, TX, 79408) • 747-5232 or 800-692-4035 • Weekdays 8–5 • W

Ask for self-guide tour brochure *Historic Homes and Buildings Tour*, beautifully illustrated by local artist Virginia Thompson and published by the Lubbock Heritage Society.

MUSEUMS AND ART GALLERIES

LUBBOCK FINE ARTS CENTER

2600 Avenue P • 767-2686 • Monday–Friday 9–5, Saturday 10–4. Closed Sunday • Free • W

This small, nonprofit center sponsors about 12 exhibits a year from various collections, often eclectic and unusual and frequently showcasing local and regional artists.

TEXAS TECH MUSEUM AND MOODY PLANETARIUM
4th and Indiana • 742-2490 • Tuesday–Saturday 10–5 (to 8:30 on Thursday), Sunday 1–5. Closed Mondays, major holidays • Free (Donation) • W+

An excellent, well-maintained complex that hosts thousands of visitors each year, the museum also offers an academic program in museum science and has an extensive natural science research laboratory (not open to the public). The DeVitt Wing houses permanent galleries with exhibitions related to the West Texas region and arid and semi-arid lands, (a field of exceptional interest to Texas Tech researchers). A balcony gallery (accessible by elevator) is used for exhibits; otherwise everything for the visitor is on the first floor. Notable exhibits include African Art, Taos/Southwest collection, early Texas cultures, Pre-Columbian collection. A recent acquisition is the Diamond M Collection, brought from Snyder, which focuses on the American West, and includes 40 paintings from a group of early twentieth-century illustrators, including N. C. Wyeth. Part of this collection is the fascinating Jades & Ivories exhibit. The museum also has a collection of Mexican Indian costumes and an unusually large collection of historical fashions. A hands-on area for children focuses on the natural sciences. The small museum shop has interesting jewelry, books, cards, and science projects. Moody Planetarium shows are at 3:30 Tuesday through Friday, 7:30 Thursday evenings, and 2 and 3:30 on Saturday and Sunday.

RANCHING HERITAGE CENTER
4th and Indiana • 742-2498 • Tuesday–Saturday 10–5, Sunday 1–5 Free (Donation) • W+

This 14-acre restoration, surrounded by berms to block out modern surroundings and traffic noise, includes an orientation building and some 30 structures, brought to this site from their original locations and restored as nearly as possible to their original condition. They are furnished authentically and illustrate ranching from the 1830s through the 1920s. Exhibits include a primitive log cabin, a stone ranch house, a half-dugout, windmills (including a Waupun, unusual in that the blades face away from the wind), an 1890s schoolhouse, a bunkhouse, and barns, a blacksmith shop and a large Victorian-style home. A steam locomotive and depot illustrate the importance of cattle ranching and shipping to the area. In the visitor orientation center are exhibits of saddles, wagons, branding irons, and Western art. From time to time special events are scheduled, such as Candlelight Christmas, when docents in costume demonstrate frontier skills from blacksmithing to candle-dipping. Gift shop.

OTHER POINTS OF INTEREST

BUDDY HOLLY'S STATUE AND WALK OF FAME
8th and Avenue Q on island in entrance road to Civic Center • 767-2241 Open at all times

Visitors come from all over the world to visit the hometown of legendary pioneer rock star Buddy Holly, who was killed in an airplane crash in 1959. This larger-than-life bronze statue of Lubbock's famous son stands in a flower-planted centerpiece between the Lubbock Memorial Center fountain and the Civic Center. The Walk of Fame consists of bronze plaques that honor West Texans who have made a significant contribution to the entertainment industry, including Waylon Jennings, Mac Davis, and Jimmy Dean. (Buddy Holly's grave is in the Lubbock Cemetery at the east end of 34th St. Take the first left inside the cemetery and the grave is about 50 yards down on the right. It is a flat stone decorated with a guitar and musical notes.) Guide available at Civic Center.

HISTORIC DEPOT DISTRICT

19th St. at I-27 (Avenue H has been renamed Buddy Holly Ave. here)
Open at all times

This section of old downtown Lubbock, around the restored railroad depot, is being lovingly restored and promoted as an entertainment district. Buddy Holly's birthday is celebrated here in early September with a music festival featuring local, regional, and big-name entertainers, and visitors come from England (where there are a lot of Buddy Holly fans), as well as throughout the U.S. The district includes restored **Cactus Theater,** 747-7047; **Kyle's 88-Key Cafe,** (lunch and dinner, music every evening, closed Sunday) 763-8888; **Hub City Brewery,** sandwiches and brews, 747-1535; **Stubb's Barbecue,** a West Texas legend, 747-4777; **Einstein's,** sandwiches, etc. 762-5205; **Clousseau's,** cigars and martinis, 749-5282. New places are opening all the time. Check it out.

THE CLUB SCENE

Lubbock has a wealth of live entertainment frequently featuring local artists performing in clubs, restaurants, and coffeehouses. Some C/W clubs have dancing. Many are family-friendly; others are more rowdy. Coffee houses are no-drinking and no-smoking and may have poets and writers, as well as musicians. Check the *Avalanche Journal,* the Caprock *Sun* or *Lubbock Magazine,* to see what is happening during your visit; then call to find out whether the venue is suitable for your family.

LUBBOCK LAKE LANDMARK STATE HISTORICAL PARK

Northeast edge of the city near the intersection of Loop 289 and Clovis Road (US 84) just west of Indiana • 765-0737 or 741-0306 • Tuesday–Saturday 9–5, Sunday 1–5. Closed Mondays and major holidays • 90-minute tours at 9:30 and 1:30 • Adults $2, children 6–12, $1 • W+ but not all areas

Located in a meander of the Yellowhouse Draw, the Lubbock Lake Landmark is believed to be the only site in North America containing deposits related to all the cultures known to have existed on the Southern Plains. Artifacts and tools dating back 12,000 years to early Clovis man and Folsom man have been uncovered here, along with remains of mammoth, extinct horse, camel, bison, and six-foot armadillo. The new Robert A. Nash Interpretive Center houses museum exhibits, a children's educational center, an auditorium, gift shop, and administrative offices. A three-quarter-mile self-guided trail leads around the 20-acre excavation area and provides interpretive wayside exhibits. The remainder of the 300-acre site may be seen along a three-mile trail meandering through Yellowhouse Draw with shade shelters and interpretive exhibits. Picnic areas.

MACKENZIE PARK

302 I-27 north of 4th St., entrances off E. Broadway and Avenue A • *Take Broadway east to Park Rd. 18* **• 767-2687 • Free • W**

Named for Colonel R. S. Mackenzie, who routed the last Native Americans from the region, this 500-acre park has picnic and camping facilities, fishing, a swimming pool, a golf course, and **Joyland Amusement Park** (see KIDS'

STUFF). At **Prairie Dog Town,** visitors can observe the cute little critters, along with burrowing owls and an occasional rabbit, in an enclosed concrete area (which is not entirely successful in containing them). The park is part of Yellowhouse Canyon Lakes, which runs from North University and Marshall southeast to 29th and contains waterfalls, boat launching places, fishing piers, picnic tables, foot bridges, and hiking/biking trails. Each summer, the Great Yellowhouse Canyon Raft Race draws rafting enthusiasts on homemade boats to the river.

MUNICIPAL GARDEN AND ARTS CENTER AND ARBORETUM

4215 University at 42nd • 797-4520 or 767-3724 • Monday–Friday 9–5, Saturday and Sunday 1–5 • Free • W+

The Arts Center is set in a 90-acre arboretum that emphasizes the flora that grows well in this area and some rare species. Regional art shows appear here and there are exhibits of local artists the rest of the time. Art classes, flower shows, and programs on horticulture are also held. A scent-garden walk provides special pleasure to the visually impaired. Restored St. Paul's on the Plains Episcopal Church is on the grounds.

SPORTS AND ACTIVITIES

Golf

ELM GROVE GOLF COURSE

6800 34th St. • 799-7801 or 799-1346 • 18-hole course. Greens fees: weekdays $10, weekends $13, after 2 P.M. $6

MEADOWBROOK GOLF COURSE

Mackenzie State Park (See Other Places of Interest) • 765-6679 • 36-hole course • Greens fees: weekdays $10–$14, weekends $14–$18.

PINE VALLEY GOLF COURSE

111th and Indiana • 748-1448 • 18 holes, 9 lighted • Green fees: weekdays $10, weekends $13

SHADOW HILLS GOLF CLUB

6002 3rd • 793-9700 • 18-hole course • Greens fees: weekdays $14, weekends $17.25, after 2 P.M. $7.75

Baseball

THE CRICKETS

Play at Dan Law field (off I-27 north) • Tickets $5, $6, and $7 • 749-2255

The young hometown team is a source of local pride and games are usually well-attended.

Tennis

Lubbock Municipal Tennis Center • 3030 66th St. • 792-0749 • 12 lighted courts with spectator bleachers in a park setting adjacent to a lake. Closed on major holidays and in bad weather. Fees depend on day and time.

COLLEGES AND UNIVERSITIES

LUBBOCK CHRISTIAN UNIVERSITY

**5601 W. 19th St., approximately 1.5 miles east of Loop 289 • 796-8800 • W
Visitor parking marked**

A four-year university affiliated with the Church of Christ, with a current enrollment of close to 1,200. Visitors are welcome to theatrical productions, musical performances, and sports activities.

TEXAS TECH UNIVERSITY

Main entrance at Broadway and University • 742-1299 • W most areas

Texas Tech University occupies a spacious 1,837-acre campus with Spanish-style architecture and well-groomed grounds and gardens. When you enter you must stop at a kiosk where an officer will issue you a visitor's pass and map of the campus and indicate where you can park. Ask about tours, which are scheduled regularly when classes are in session. The **Peter Hurd mural** in Holden Hall is noteworthy. Visitors are welcome to **athletic events** including the rodeo (742-3341) and **theatrical and musical productions** (742-3601). The Architecture building houses the **FOVA** (Forum on the Visual Arts), a gallery with faculty and student works (Architecture Building, 18th and Flint; parking can be a problem when classes are in session.) Texas Tech is proud of its new **International Cultural Center** (Indiana between 4th St. and Brownfield Highway) (742-2974), which contains the **International Center for Arid and Semi-Arid Land Studies** and the **Center for Vietnam Studies**, probably the largest collection of Vietnam-era materials in the world, aside from the national archives. Also on campus, in a brand new building adjacent to the University Library, is the **Southwest Collection** (742-3749), a unique archives. The TTU Health Sciences Center, with schools of Medicine, Nursing and Allied Health, is West of the University campus, beyond the museum.

PERFORMING ARTS

Community theaters appear (and sometimes disappear) regularly in Lubbock; check the Friday *Avalanche Journal* or Caprock *Sun* to see what is current.

BALLET LUBBOCK

1500 Broadway, Ste. 703 • 740-0505 • $10–$14 • W+

Ballet Lubbock usually presents two concerts a year including the *Nutcracker* during the Christmas season. Performances are at the Civic Center.

AVALON THEATRE

2405 34th St. • 785-5815 • About $5

Live theater, varied schedule. Productions are usually on weekends. Some experimental theater.

CACTUS THEATER

1812 Buddy Holly Avenue (Old Avenue H, off I-27 and 19th St. in Depot District) • 747-7047 • Admission varies, $5–$20, depending on event

Theater, musical, and other special events, weekends and other times; very popular are "Best of the . . . 40s, 50s, or whatever nights.

FAIR PARK COLISEUM

In Mackenzie Park, off I-27 east on 82 • 744-9557
Prices vary for different events
 A variety of rodeos, concerts, and other major events throughout the year.

GARZA THEATER

Post, *approximately 42 miles southeast on US 84* • 495-4005 • $7 for adults, $4 for children under 12 • W
 Very popular community theater presents a variety of works each year, usually on Friday, Saturday, and Sunday afternoon and evening. Sometimes barbecue is served before the performance. The house is frequently sold out, so reservations are a good idea.

LUBBOCK CHORALE

742-2272 • About $12
 Presents three or four concerts each year, usually at Hemmle Recital Hall on the Texas Tech University campus.

LUBBOCK COMMUNITY THEATER

112 Broadway • 741-1640 • About $5
 Live theater productions throughout the year, usually on weekends.

MUNICIPAL AUDITORIUM-COLISEUM

Sixth Street and Boston Avenue • 770-2000 • W
 Major events sports, rodeos, concerts, etc., throughout the year as well as graduations and other special events.

LAB THEATER

Texas Tech University • 742-3601 • $3–$6
 Experimental theater by TTU University students; several productions during academic year.

LUBBOCK MEMORIAL CIVIC CENTER

1501 6th St. • Ticket office 765-9441 • W+
 A killer tornado reduced this area of Lubbock to rubble on May 11, 1970 and a complex of modern buildings replaced those destroyed. The "memorial" in the name of the Civic Center honors citizens who died in the tragedy. Plays, symphonies, concerts, touring companies, special films, antique shows, dog shows, and the annual Arts Festival appear here.

LUBBOCK SYMPHONY ORCHESTRA

For tickets call Select-a-seat, 770-2000 • $11.25, $15.25 and $18.75 • W+
 This 80-musician professional orchestra presents classical and pops concerts, several with guests artists, usually in the Lubbock Civic Center.

SHOPPING

Antiques

Antique Mall Of Lubbock, 7907 W. 19th, approximately 3 miles west of Loop 289 (796-2166). Also, along 34th Street, between Avenue Q and Indiana Ave.

Malls

Most major stores and chains are located in or near **SOUTH PLAINS MALL,** S. Loop 289 and Slide; newer, upscale shopping venues may be found along 82nd Street between Indiana and Slide.

Art

Charles Adams Gallery, Kingsgate North, 4210 82nd St. (788-1008). **ARTary,** 4509 Clovis Highway. **Baker Company,** 1301 13th St. (763-2500). **James VirMar Gallery,** 2714 50th St. (796-2147). **White Buffalo Gallery,** 6400 Indiana Ave at KK's Antique and Collectible Mall.

Western Wear

Boot City, 6645 19th St. (797-8782) and 2610 50th St. (791-3522); **Branding Iron,** 3320 34th St. (785-0500). **Dollar Western Wear,** 5007 Brownfield Highway (793-2828); **Luskey's Western Store,** 2431 34th St. (795-7106); **Tejas Western Outlet,** 5715 19th (793-6297).

Miscellaneous

Cactus Alley, 2610 Salem near Brownfield W. This charming mini-mall, in an enclosed courtyard, has a number of small shops that sell an array varying from women's and children's clothing to toys, miniatures, soaps, gourmet foods, clocks, decorated eggs, vintage clothing. There is also a Mexican Restaurant, *La Cumbre* **(see Restaurants).**

KIDS' STUFF

DISCOVERY ZONE FUNCENTER

5011 Slide Rd. (corner of Slide and 50th St.) • 792-5437 • ages 1–12 • $5.99, parents play free • Open daily, 11–8 • W+

Indoor workout center for kids, with slides, ball bins, obstacle course. Mini-zone, maxizone areas.

JOYLAND AMUSEMENT PARK

Mackenzie Park 4th and Avenue A • 763-2719 • $10

Family entertainment center includes 23 rides on nine acres, including miniature train, bumper cars, carousel, music express, water slide, rollercoaster, and watercoaster. Opens at 2, spring and fall; all day during summer.

SCIENCE SPECTRUM AND OMNIMAX

2579 S. Loop 289 (Indiana exit) • Omnimax 745-6299, Science Spectrum 745-2525 • Monday–Friday 10–5:00, Saturday 10–6, Sunday 1–5:30 Combination tickets $9 for adults, $7 for students under 16 and seniors; lower for either facility alone • W+

Science Spectrum features more than 100 hands-on scientific exhibits throughout the year, with interactive exhibits including Computer Fun, Bubble over with Fun, Kidspace, especially for preschoolers, hands-on flight exhibit, the Whisper Dish, Money Center, Science Theater, aquariums with variety of underwater life, special traveling exhibitions and demonstrations. Science shop has unusual toys, books, souvenirs and science kits. Screenings daily on the giant screen at the Omnimax Theater. Call for schedule.

TEXAS WATER RAMPAGE

Brownfield Hwy. (US 82) and Spur 327, approximately 3 miles southwest of city • 796-0701 • Daily 12–7 during summer, weekends May and September. Closed rest of year • $12.75 (discounts often available) • W+ call ahead

This water park features two Twin Twister 63-foot water slides; a wave pool with a pneumatic system that creates waves only on the surface; Whaler's Bay, with safety-coded activities for youngsters; Paradise Cove, for adults (separate from the children's pool but near enough to keep an eye on the kids); Rio Rampage, a 72-foot lazy river down which folks raft on inner tubes so peacefully that they often fall asleep; a soft slide for the tiniest visitors, and a covered picnic area. Refreshments are available at concession stand.

SIDE TRIPS

BUFFALO SPRINGS LAKE

Take FM 835 (continuation of 50th St.) east about 4 miles past Loop 289E **747-3353 • Open daily year round • Fees $1 • W but not all areas**

A recreation area on 1,200 acres around a lake of about 225 surface acres with seven miles of shoreline. Boating, fishing, waterskiing. On shore are picnic areas and sites for both tent and RV camping (fees). Two sandy beaches and a water slide are offered. A self-guiding nature trail and Audubon interpretive center will fascinate nature lovers. The trail, about 1.7 miles round trip, descends 155 feet from the canyon rim to the stream, with rest stops along the way. Bike trails.

CROSBYTON

Approximately 40 miles east of Lubbock on US 82

At the **Crosby County Pioneer Memorial Museum,** 101 Main (675-2331), are exhibits showing the settlement of this community that straddles the edge of the caprock. In late summer, the historical drama *God's Country* is performed in **Blanco Canyon Amphitheater** (10.5 miles north on FM 651. 675-2331). Five miles beyond Crosbyton on US 82 is **Silver Falls,** a roadside park, with picnic area, trails, and glimpses of native flora and fauna.

PLAINVIEW

Approximately 60 miles north on I-27 • 296-0819 (Chamber of Commerce)

Plainview is a lively, growing town along the interstate. On the campus of **Wayland Baptist University** (296-4735) is the **Llano Estacado Museum,** with exhibits on pre-history and pioneer days (free); and, in the basement of the library, the new **Abraham Family Art Gallery,** with changing exhibits and the **Harrell Theater** (296-4742), which has concerts and theater events throughout the year. Downtown Plainview is looking for a revival with antiques and other shops. And check out **McDonald's Trading Post,** 1401 S. Columbia, with 60,000 square feet of machinery, tools, hardware, farming and ranching equipment— you name it. Accommodations and restaurants are available locally.

POST

42 miles southeast on US 84 • 495-3724 (Chamber of Commerce)

Post, established as a "model" community by the cereal king, has become a lively center for visitors. **Old Mill Post Days** (Thursday–Sunday, the first weekend of every month) attract shoppers and buyers from the region and beyond. **Garza Theater** (see Theaters) presents professional productions year round. **Tower Theater** (495-3461 or 894-3552) also schedules stage shows and concerts. Post has interesting and unusual shops, restaurants, and B&Bs.

Wineries

Lubbock is justifiably proud of the growth of a local wine industry, and Texas wines are beginning to receive highly favorable notice in national and international competitions. The region, at a 3,200-foot elevation, provides warm days and cool nights which, experts say, are ideal for premium grape growing. Local wineries welcome visitors with tours and tastings.

LLANO ESTACADO

Take US 87 south to FM 1585, then go 3.2 miles east • **745-2258**
Monday–Saturday 10–5, Sunday 12–5
The oldest and best-known winery has won more awards than any vineyard in Texas. Complimentary tours and wine tasting Monday through Saturday, 10–5, Sundays 12–5, beginning every half hour (other tours can be arranged by appointment). Last tour begins at 4 P.M.

PHEASANT RIDGE

Off FM 1729 north of Lubbock. *From I-27, exit on FM 1729 and go*
2 miles east, 1 mile south • **746-6033** • **Tours and tastings on weekends**
by appointment only • **W**
Named after the numerous pheasants in the area, this limited-production winery, sometimes called a boutique winery, specializes in only a few types of wine.

CAP*ROCK

Approximately 5 miles from Loop 289. *Go south on US 87 (Tahoka Highway),*
to Woodrow Road • **863-2704** • **Monday–Saturday 10–5, Sunday 12–5**
Free • W+
The third largest winery in the state, located in an opulent building, is popular for tastings, parties, and special events.

ANNUAL EVENTS

March

CORK & FORK AFFAIR—TASTE OF LUBBOCK

Lubbock Civic Center • 794-7533 • Admission • W+
Lubbock restaurateurs present the best of their foods and wines.

ABC RODEO

Lubbock Memorial Coliseum • 4th and Boston (at the edge of the TTU
campus) • 796-4074 • $8 and $12 • W
A fine rodeo, always well-attended and lively. Check for location, which may change soon.

April

LUBBOCK ARTS FESTIVAL

Fairgrounds • 744-2781 • Usually three-day weekend in late April
$2 children under 12 free • W+
This annual Celebration of the Arts offers an opportunity to view and purchase fine, juried artwork, and each year more than 85,000 people take advantage of the

opportunity. There are also crafts demonstrations and booths, continuous entertainment on four stages, and evening performances by national entertainment stars (fee). Special children's area with activities inviting active participation. Food booths give festival-goers a chance to taste foods from all over the world.

May

CINCO DE MAYO

Buddy Holly Park, University Ave. south from Loop 289 north, part of Yellowhouse Canyon Lakes Park • 791-3545 or 784-0261 • Free • W
  Yearly celebration is marked by mariachi bands, spicy Mexican food and kiddie rides. Commemorates the Mexican peoples' joining forces to battle the French government, shortly after Mexico received its independence from Spain. A family celebration.

June

JUNETEENTH CELEBRATION

Mae Simmons Park, Yellowhouse Canyon Lakes Park, off Martin Luther King, Jr., Blvd., east of I-27 • 744-0766 • Free
  Texans celebrate the day word of the Emancipation Proclamation arrived in Texas with this yearly celebration, featuring gospel music, speeches, games, and family fun.

July

4th ON BROADWAY

Broadway, from the entrance to the TTU campus • 749-2929
  Day-long celebration of our country's independence with live performers, vendors, a parade through downtown Lubbock, food, and music.

August

GOD'S COUNTRY

Blanco Canyon Amphitheater • *East on US 82, then 10.5 miles north on FM 651* **• 675-2331**
  Historical drama shows the settlement of Crosby County, from the buffalo hunters and soldiers to Quakers and Europeans and, especially, the story of the family of Hank Smith, the first white settler of the county. In natural amphitheater at the edge of the canyon.

September

BUDDY HOLLY'S BIRTHDAY

Historic Depot District • *19th St. exit off I-27, west on 19th one block to Buddy Holly Avenue (Avenue H), and environs* **• 749-2929 • Admission charges to some venues • W but not all areas**
  Lubbock celebrates the birthday of its favorite son with music, live entertainment, street acts, various vendors, in the historic Depot District. Usually one cover charge gets you into all clubs.

FIESTAS DEL LLANO

Lubbock Civic Center (747-5232) • Free, variable costs for booths • W+

Three-day celebration of Mexico's independence from Spain, features dances, mariachi bands, Mexican food, booths, children's activities.

NATIONAL COWBOY SYMPOSIUM

Civic Center, 1501 6th • 795-2455 • Free • W+
The largest event of its kind in the nation, this symposium is a mixture of scholarship and fun, and attracts people from working cowboys to scholars to articulate the heritage of the cowboy through storytelling, poetry, music, scholarly papers, exhibits, demonstrations, and panel discussions. Barbecue ($7) and chuckwagon breakfast ($5) are available.

September–October

SOUTH PLAINS FAIR

Fair Park and Fair Park Coliseum, 105 E. Broadway • 763-2833 • One week in late September or early October • Adults $3, children 6–11 $1. Parking $2 • W variable
All you expect from a big fair: a midway, horse and livestock shows, industrial and military exhibits, flower festival, women's and educational exhibits, and lots of contests. Top C&W entertainers perform at the coliseum every night (admission and ticket information 744-9557).

October

FARMER STOCKMAN SHOW

Lubbock city farm, East 50th (FM 385) • 747-7134 • Free • W variable
Three-day trade show features the latest in farming, stock raising attracts industry leaders from a wide area.

October–November

TEXAS TECH INTERCOLLEGIATE RODEO

Lubbock Municipal Auditorium • 742-3341 • Usually Thursday–Saturday late in October or early November • Admission • W
Rodeoing started at Tech in 1940 and has been an intercollegiate sport here since 1950. At this event, teams from more than a dozen colleges in Texas and New Mexico compete for top honors in everything from bareback bronc to bull riding.

November

HOLIDAY HAPPENING

Lubbock Memorial Civic Center • 794-8874 • Various charges for different events • W+
Sponsored by the Junior League, this yearly event features all kinds of gifts and Christmas decorations as well as entertainment and special events for adults and children.

December

LIGHTS ON BROADWAY AND CAROL OF LIGHTS

Broadway from Texas Tech campus to downtown
The lighting of thousands of lights on the university buildings around Memorial Circle, which is accompanied by singing of Christmas carols and

other special events in mid-December, is the beginning of a special celebration that features horse-drawn rides, shops and booths all along Broadway from the university entrance to downtown.

RESTAURANTS

($ = under $7, $$ = $8–$17, $$$ = $18–$25, $$$$ = over $25 for one person excluding drinks, tax, and tip.)

American Eclectic/Texan

COUNTY LINE

FM 2641 .5 miles west of I-27 north of city • 763-6001 • Dinner only, daily No reservations • $$ • W call ahead • Children's menu

The County Line, in its bucolic setting in the Canyon north of town, has been popular for years with local couples and families, especially for romantic and "special" occasions. Before being served, diners can stroll along the small lake, admiring the ducks, peacocks, and other half-tame wildfowl, or meet friends for drinks on the patio. There are several dining rooms, with country appointments and exposed beams. Menu features barbecued beef, chicken, ham, sausage, ribs, with beans, slaw, and other traditional fixings, home-made bread. On pleasant nights, there may be a waiting line; best arrive early. Bar.

JAZZ

3703-C 19th St. (in hospital district) • 799-2124 • Lunch and dinner daily $$ • W

Small, popular restaurant near the medical center and Texas Tech campus, features Cajun seasonings: red beans and rice, crawfish, gumbo, blackened fish, other Louisiana favorites. Some dishes are pretty hot. Bar. Live entertainment many evenings.

GARDSKI'S LOFT

2009 Broadway • 744-2391 • Lunch and dinner, daily. Closed major holidays • $$ • Cr

In a 50-year-old mansion near Texas Tech and downtown Lubbock, Gardski's Loft is a favorite lunch or after-the-theater spot, with gourmet hamburgers, aged steak, soft tacos. Garden decor, often crowded at lunch time. Beer and wine.

GRAPEVINE CAFE AND WINE BAR

2407 19th St. (off-street) • 744-8246 • Lunch daily, dinner Tuesday–Sunday. Closed Monday evening • $–$$ • W

George has been a Lubbock restaurateur for years, and is a favorite with local people. This little restaurant, tucked into a corner near the major 19th St/University Ave. intersection, is frequented by Tech faculty, downtown professionals, especially for lunch. Seafood, crepes, pasta, salads, soups, house dressing, subtle sauces. Half orders available. Wine.

MESQUITES

Down the alley at 1211 University, near Broadway (rear entrance at 2419 Broadway) • Breakfast Monday–Friday, lunch and dinner daily • $$ • Cr Street parking only

Down the alley and across the street from the campus, this is a popular spot with students. Pleasant, outdoorsy atmosphere. Barbecued brisket, ham, ribs, sausage, chicken, and hot links, steaks, burgers, some Tex-Mex. Onion rings are special. Half orders. Bar.

OTTO'S & THIBODEAUX'S

4119 Brownfield • 795-2569 • Lunch and dinner daily • $–$$ • Cr

New York strip, rib eye steaks, surf and turf, steak teriyaki, with a touch of Cajun. Also (upstairs) Otto's Attic Store (797-0710). Godiva coffees.

RONNIE'S

5206 82nd St. • 798-0276 • Lunch and dinner daily. Closed major holidays $$–$$$ • Cr • Children's menu

Ronnie's has a devoted clientele among Lubbock people. Beef dishes, especially Stroganoff and Chateaubriand, are outstanding, chicken and fish entrées well-prepared with subtle seasonings. Nice selection of desserts.

Asian

CHINA STAR

1919 50th (50th and Avenue T) • 749-2100 • Lunch and dinner six days. Closed Sundays • $$ • Cr

An excellent buffet, moderately priced especially for lunch; more than 30 dishes (a few are spicy) well-prepared and kept hot, cold, crisp, or whatever they are supposed to be. You can also order from the menu. Beer/wine.

DELHI PALACE

5401 Aberdeen • 799-6772 • Lunch and dinner daily • $$–$$$ • Cr • W

In an out-of-the-way corner near South Plains Mall, this very good Indian restaurant serves consistently good food: lamb, chicken, all-vegetable dishes from mild to hot, curries, Tamboor-roasted meats. Novices might enjoy a sampler of appetizers—Bararchi Ki Pasand and Tandoori Khoobiyan (Tandoori chicken, lamb kabobs, and shrimp). Pleasant atmosphere. A good plan for groups is to order a number of meat and vegetable dishes and share. Lunch buffets are popular and good.

THAI THAI

5101 Quaker • 791-0024 • Lunch and dinner, six days. Closed Tuesdays $ • No Cr • W

Of several Thai restaurants in Lubbock, this is an excellent choice: fine food in an unpretentious atmosphere; curries, noodles, salads, and soups ranging from mild to very hot. Consistently good.

Continental

CHEZ SUZETTE

4423 50th St. in Quaker Square Shopping Center • 795-6796 • Lunch and dinner Monday–Friday, dinner only Saturday. Closed Sunday and major holidays • $$–$$$ • Cr • W

A Lubbock tradition, this popular, upscale restaurant, tucked into a small shopping center off 50th St., features French/Italian cuisine, specializing in Chateubriand, snapper in puff pastry, paté, French onion soup. Own baking. Special occasion menus (Valentine's Day, Bastille Day). Children's menu. Bar and wine list.

FRENCHMAN INN

4409 19th St. (just off Quaker) • 799-7596 • Dinner. Closed Sundays
Reservations strongly recommended • $$$ • W

A small restaurant, off the beaten path, ordinary on the outside, cozy on the inside, where gourmet meals are lovingly cooked to order (menu is posted on chalkboard as you enter); wonderful appetizers include soup of the day, sausage, paté; entrées include fish, beef, pork, lamb dishes, lovingly, individually prepared, with fantastic sauces. A dining experience. Bring your own wine; they will pour.

ORLANDO'S

2402 Avenue Q (also at 6951 Indiana) • 747-5998 • Lunch and dinner daily
$$ • Cr

Locally owned, Orlando's is consistently popular with the community and has opened a second location on South Indiana, just inside the Loop. Specializes in lasagna, fettucine, tortellini. Soups, sandwiches, and salads are good choices for lunch. Child's menu; senior discounts. Live entertainment some evenings. Popular also for lunch.

Mexican

ABUELO'S

82nd and Quaker • 794-1762 • Lunch and dinner daily • $$–$$$ • Cr • W

With a charming setting and atmosphere, Abuelo's is very popular with local families. Patrons may wait to be seated in the courtyard, by the fountain. On summer evenings there is often live entertainment. Standard Tex-Mex fare, but with some outstanding dishes. Bar, courtyard lounge.

JOSIE'S

212 University Ave. • 747-8546 • Breakfast, lunch, and dinner,
Monday–Saturday. Sunday lunch • $ • No Cr • W

Modest, low-priced and very popular locally, Josie's traditional dishes are consistently wonderful and this unpretentious restaurant is nearly always crowded. The breakfast burritos are to die for. Other locations at 4105 Brownfield Highway (796-0192), 5101 Aberdeen (793-7752), and 1308 50th St. (741-0588).

LA CUMBRE

2610 Salem (in Cactus Alley) • 796-5006 • Lunch and dinner • $–$$ • Cr • W

We enjoy this small restaurant, pleasant but unpretentious, in Cactus Alley. Relatively mild Tex-Mex is the rule, traditional fare, well prepared—but for best results, order from the Gourmet Section of the Menu. Huge, fluffy dessert sopapillas are favorites, especially with fresh strawberries.

SANTA FE RESTAURANT

401 Avenue Q • 763-6114 (another location at 5501 Slide Rd., 796-3999)
Lunch and dinner daily. Closed Sundays and major holidays
$$–$$$ • Cr • W

Pleasant atmosphere, locally popular, always dependable, close to downtown, Civic Center, Texas Tech. Specializes in consistently good American and Mexican dishes; very pleasant atmosphere. Children's menu; senior discounts. Beer and wine.

TACO VILLAGE

1712 3rd St. (just off Avenue Q) • 762-4457 • Lunch and dinner daily • $ • W

A no-nonsense family establishment, arguably the best Mexican food in town; well-prepared meals served promptly and without pretense. Convenient to downtown and Civic Center area, but you have to look for it.

ACCOMMODATIONS

($ = under $45, $$ = $46–$60, $$$ = $61–$80, $$$$ = $81–$100, $$$$$ = over $100)

Room tax 13%

ASHMORE INN AND SUITES

4019 South Loop 289 (Quaker exit) • 785-0060 or 1-800-785-0061, fax: 806-785-6001 • $$–$$$ • W+ 5 rooms • No-smoking rooms

New, two-story Ashmore Inn, on the growing southern rim, has higher rates during some premium weekends (graduation, football), but also has some weekend specials. Children under 12 stay free with parents. Senior discounts are available. The Ashmore has 100 units, including 16 suites. Check-out time is noon. TV with cable and HBO. Room phones (no charge for local calls). Fire sprinklers. Complimentary hospitality hour. Outdoor pool, exercise room, Jacuzzi. Free coffee in rooms, *USA Today;* free cocktails; free continental deluxe breakfast. Self-service laundry. Free airport transportation. Business amenities. Superior soundproofing, interior corridors, electronic locks.

BARCELONA COURT

5215 South Loop 289 (Slide Rd. exit) • 794-5353 or 1-800-222-1122, fax: 806-798-9398 • $$$–$$$$ • W+ 3 rooms • No-smoking rooms

The three-story Barcelona has 161 suites. Children under 12 free in room with parents. Senior discounts. Cable TV with HBO. Room phones (charge for local calls). Heated outdoor pool, sauna, Jacuzzi. Free airport transportation, cocktails, breakfast. Self-service laundry. Gift shop. Shopping, restaurants, clubs nearby.

COMFORT SUITES

5113 South Loop 289 (Slide Rd. exit) • 798-0002, 800-228-5150, fax: 806-798-0035 • $$–$$$$ (higher rates during premium weekends—graduation, football games) • W+ 3 rooms • No-smoking rooms

Brand new Comfort Suites is conveniently near South Plains Mall, with lots of shopping, restaurants, nearby. Two-story facility has 65 units. Senior discounts available. Children under 13 stay free with parents. TV with cable, HBO. Room phones (no charge for local calls). Room fire sprinklers. Outdoor heated pool with whirlpool; Jacuzzi. Free coffee in rooms; complimentary deluxe breakfast, *USA Today.* Self-service laundry.

COURTYARD BY MARRIOTT

4011 South Loop 289 (Quaker exit) • 795-1633, 800-321-2211, fax: 806-795-1633 • $$–$$$$ • W+ 1 room • No-smoking rooms

This new three-story facility has 75 units including ten suites, Check-out time is 1 P.M.; check in 3 P.M. TV with cable, HBO, CNN, E-Span. Room phones with data ports (no charge for local calls). Room fire sprinklers. Full buffet breakfast.

Irons and ironing boards. Lounge open evenings. Senior discounts. Indoor pool, hot tub. Free coffee, tea, apples, newspaper. Self-service laundry. Business amenities available to Courtyard Club members (apply at any Courtyard).

FAIRFIELD INN

4007 South Loop 289 (Quaker exit) • 795-1288 or 800-228-2800, fax: 806-795-1288 • $$ (executive suites $$$) • W+ 2 rooms • No-smoking rooms
The brand new three-story Fairfield Inn has 64 units, including some executive-king suites. Senior discounts, and children under 18 stay free with parents. Check-out time is noon; check-in time is 3 P.M. TV with cable, HBO in all rooms. Room phones (no charge for local calls). Room fire sprinklers. Indoor heated pool, spa. Free coffee in lobby; free continental breakfast.

FOUR POINTS BY ITT SHERATON

505 Avenue Q • 747-0171, fax: 806-747-9243 • $$$–$$$$ • W+ 2 rooms No-smoking rooms
This downtown motel, near the Civic Center, has six stories and 145 rooms and four suites. Children under 18 stay free in room with parents. Senior discounts. Cable TV, in-room movies. Room phones (charge for local calls). Restaurant and bar on premises. Indoor pool. Free newspaper and coffee. Free airport transportation. Rates higher some weekends. Refrigerators and minibars in suites.

HAMPTON INN

4003 South Loop 289 (Quaker exit) • 765-1080 or 800-HAMPTON, fax: 806-795-1376 • $$ • W+ 4 rooms • No-smoking rooms
The new three-story Hampton Inn has 81 rooms. Higher rates some weekends. Senior discounts available. TV with cable, HBO. Room phones (no charge for local calls). Check-out time is noon. Indoor pool. Coffee in lobby, free newspaper.

HOLIDAY INN LUBBOCK PLAZA

3201 South Loop 289 (at Indiana) • 797-3241 or 1-800-HOLIDAY, fax: 806-793-1203 • $$$$ • W+ 4 rooms • No-smoking rooms
The two-story Lubbock Plaza has 203 units including eight suites ($$$$$). Children under 18 stay free with parents. Senior discounts are available. Check-out time noon; check-in time 3. TV with cable and on-cable video. Room phones (charge for local calls). Pets OK. Two restaurants (Recipes, Beethoven's), two lounges (Oliver's, Fountain Court); room service. Indoor pool, wading pool in atrium; exercise room, dry sauna. Pyramid Fitness Center and Racquetball Club next door, free to Plaza guests. Business amenities, meeting rooms. Free coffeemakers in some rooms; free newspaper, self-service laundry.

HOLIDAY INN CIVIC CENTER

801 Avenue Q • 763-1200 • 1-800-HOLIDAY • $$$–$$$$ • W+ 2 rooms No-smoking rooms
The six-story Holiday Inn is near the Civic Center in downtown Lubbock. It has 295 units, including some suites (higher rates for suites). Senior rates are available. Kids under 18 stay free with parents. Check-out time is noon; check-in time is 2. TV with cable, on-command video, movies available. Room phones (charge for local calls). Room sprinklers. Pets OK. Restaurant, The Greenery, on premises; room service. Lounge, Brass Banjo, open evenings. Indoor pool, pool service, sauna, whirlpool, Jacuzzi, exercise room. Convention, business ameni-

ties. Free coffee in suites; newspaper. Ask about B&B rates. Self-service laundry; free airport transportation.

LA QUINTA MOTOR INN
601 Avenue Q • **763-9441, fax: 806-747-9325** • **$$$–$$$$** • **W+ 4 rooms**
No-smoking rooms
   La Quinta, near downtown and Civic Center, has 137 rooms and three suites, two stories. Children under 18 stay free with parents. Room phones (no charge for local calls). Pets OK. TV with cable. Pool. Free coffee, free continental breakfast. Restaurant next door. Check out noon. Business amenities available. Senior, other discounts.

LUBBOCK INN
3901 19th St. • **792-5181 or 1-800-545-8226, fax: 806-792-1319** • **$$–$$$**
W+ 2 rooms • **No-smoking rooms**
   The Lubbock Inn, not a chain, is across from the Texas Tech University campus and near the hospital district. It has 119 rooms, 28 with kitchens, on three floors. Children under 12 stay free with parents. TV with cable, premium channels, VCR available. Heated pool. Senior discounts. Restaurant open 6–11; room service. Lounge. Check-out, noon. Meeting rooms, business amenities available. Bellhops, sundries. Free airport transportation. Bathroom phones, some refrigerators.

RESIDENCE INN BY MARRIOTT
2551 Loop 289 (Indiana exit) • **745-1963, fax: 748-1183** • **$$$$** • **W+ rooms**
No-smoking rooms
   The two-story Residence Inn has 80 kitchen suites, many of which are non-smoking. Senior discounts are available. Room phones (no charge for local calls). Senior discounts. Cable TV, premium channels. Children free in parents' room. Heated pool, whirlpools. Free airport transportation; free continental breakfast; coin laundry. Meeting rooms, business amenities, valet, tennis, refrigerators. Private patios, balconies, picnic tables, grills.

MINERAL WELLS

Palo Pinto and Parker Counties • **15,256** • **(940)**
   This town went crazy over water. In 1878, J. A. Lynch dug a well on his property that produced foul-smelling water his family was afraid to drink. But when they did, his wife felt that it relieved the pain of her rheumatism. The word spread and people started to take the waters for medicinal values. A boom started in 1880 with the opening of a new well. When the water made better a woman the townspeople called crazy, they named the well the "Crazy Woman's Well." Later they called it the "Crazy Well." True or not, the story holds up when one realizes that the water contains some of the ingredients of present day tranquilizers.
   From then on everything was "crazy." There was a Crazy Hotel, Crazy Park, laundry, theater, and even a radio show called "The Crazy Gang." By 1920 there were about 400 mineral wells operating here. Health seekers came from all over to drink the mineral waters and take therapeutic baths. Capping the boom in 1929, just before the start of the Great Depression, the Baker Hotel was built at a cost of $1.2 million and was a copy of the famed Arlington Hotel in Hot Springs, Arkansas. This now-empty 415 room, 14-story hotel still domi-

nates the skyline, though several tries to sell and restore it have failed. The Crazy Water Hotel is now a retirement home.

During the Vietnam conflict, the U.S. Army operated the world's largest primary helicopter training base here at Camp Wolters. That camp, closed in 1973, is now an industrial park and the home of the local branch of Weatherford College.

TOURIST SERVICES

MINERAL WELLS CHAMBER OF COMMERCE

511 E. Hubbard St. (P.O. Box 1408, 76068-1408) • 325-2557 or 800-252-6989 • W

OTHER POINTS OF INTEREST

BAT WORLD

217 North Oak • 325-3404 • September–May, second Saturday and third Sunday of each month, 2 P.M. or by appointment • Adults $8, under 12 $4 • W

This bat sanctuary and living museum provides a lifetime home in a natural habitat setting for bats that are permanently injured, used in research, or confiscated from illegal trading. Some 75 bats represent 12 species. Bat house plans are available.

LAKE MINERAL WELLS STATE PARK & TRAILWAY

Take US 180 east approximately 4 miles • 328-1171 • Open at all times
Adults $3, under 12 free • W+ but not all areas

The 2,809 acres include a 646-acre lake that offers boating, fishing (lighted fishing pier), and swimming. Boats, canoes, and paddleboats are available for rental. There are areas for tent and RV camping (reservations needed for weekend camping), picnicking, hiking, and an equestrian camping area with parking for 20 horse trailers. The multi-use Trailway, a 22-mile-long converted railroad corridor, connects Mineral Wells with Weatherford. Popular with rock climbers.

SIDE TRIPS

LAKE POSSUM KINGDOM

Take US 180 west about 26 miles to SH 16, then north about 14 miles to lake area. (See Breckenridge)

OLD JAILHOUSE MUSEUM

Palo Pinto, 5th and Elm 2 blocks south of courthouse • 659-3781
June–August, Saturday and Sunday 2–4 or by appointment

Housed in a two-story sandstone block jail built in the early 1880s, this small museum concentrates on telling the story of the growth of the county.

ANNUAL EVENTS

October

CRAZY WATER FESTIVAL

At junction of US 180 and US 281 • 325-2557 (Chamber of Commerce)
Second weekend in October • Free • W

For two days they celebrate the good old times when Crazy Well water was the town's main claim to fame. Activities include non-stop entertainment, arts and crafts and food booths, sports tournaments, and contests and demonstrations.

ACCOMMODATIONS

($ = under $45, $$ = $46–$60, $$$ = $61–$80, $$$$ = $81–$100, $$$$$ = over $100)
Room tax 13%

RAMADA LIMITED
4103 US 180 East • 325-6956 or 800-272-6232 • $$–$$$ • W+ 1 room
No-smoking rooms
   This inn has 31 units including one suite ($$$). Children 18 and under stay free in parents' room. Cable TV with HBO. Room phones (no charge for local calls). Free Continental breakfast.

QUANAH

Hardeman County Seat • 3,325 • (940)
   The town is named after the last of the great Comanche war chiefs, Quanah Parker, the son of a Comanche chief and a white woman captive. His mother, Cynthia Ann Parker, had been taken captive when she was nine years old and later accepted the Indian life. She was recaptured by Texas Rangers in 1860, but her two sons got away. Despondent and unhappy with her return to civilization, Cynthia Ann died in 1864. Quanah became chief at the time when the Indians on the South Plains were struggling for the survival of their old way of life. He repeatedly led his braves against the U.S. Army, Texas Rangers, and settlers who were moving into his people's hunting grounds. Finally, after Colonel R. S. Mackenzie's campaigns against him in the 1870s, he foresaw inevitable defeat and took his people to the reservation. Even there he was a great leader and became a rancher. He also negotiated with the government in the interest of his people and counted President Theodore Roosevelt among his friends. A story that shows his wisdom concerns his many wives. Some government men told him that polygamy was against the white man's law and pressured him to go home and tell all but his favorite wife to leave. Quanah thought about this for a time and then said, "You tell 'em."
   Today, agribusiness and manufacturing play important roles in the local economy.

TOURIST SERVICES

QUANAH CHAMBER OF COMMERCE
220 S. Main (P.O. Box 158, 79252-0158) • 663-2222 • W

MUSEUM

HARDEMAN COUNTY HISTORICAL MUSEUM
101 Green St., 2 blocks west of Main (SH 6) • 663-5272 • Monday–Friday 2–6
Free • W Downstairs only
   This old stone building built in 1891 as the Hardeman County Jail is now a museum devoted primarily to local history. An exhibit in memory of native-son astronaut Ed Givens contains items on loan from NASA.

OTHER POINTS OF INTEREST

COPPER BREAKS STATE PARK

Take SH 6 approximately 13 miles south to Park Rd. 62 • **1-839-4331**
**Open daily 8–10 for day use, at all times for camping • Adults $2,
under 12 free • W+ but not all areas**

The park contains 1,933 acres that primarily consist of juniper breaks and grass covered mesas bounded on the south by the Pease River. A 60-acre lake offers swimming, boating, and fishing. Facilities include an Interpretive Center, both tent and RV campsites (fee), a nature trail, a hiking trail, picnic areas, playground, and an outdoor amphitheater where interpretive programs are given during summer months. Part of the Texas longhorn herd is kept here.

MEDICINE MOUNDS

**Southeast; can be seen from US 287 east near Quanah SH 6 south between
Quanah and Copper Breaks State Park • On private property, drive-by view
only**

These four cone-shaped mounds rise about 350 feet over the flat plains. The Indians believed that these were the dwelling places of Great Spirits who could cure their ills and help them in hunting the buffalo and fighting their enemies.

ANNUAL EVENTS

September

FALL FESTIVAL

**Downtown courthouse square • 663-2222 (Chamber of Commerce)
Second Saturday in September • Free • W**

Live entertainment and seminars on local Comanche Indian history highlight this event. Family fun includes arts and crafts, game and food booths, tractor and classic car shows, museum tours, quilt show, and street dance.

RESTAURANTS

($ = under $7, $$ = $8–$17, $$$ = $18–$25, $$$$ = over $25 for one person excluding drinks, tax, and tip.)

MEDICINE MOUND DEPOT

US 287E • 663-5619 • Lunch and dinner daily • $$ • Cr • W

Mesquite-broiled steaks and Mexican food served in the historic 1910 depot moved here from Medicine Mound.

DUTCH'S RESTAURANT

US 287W • 663-2435 • Breakfast, lunch, and dinner daily • $ • Cr • W

Good food cooked home-style. Southwestern murals painted by a local artist adorn the walls. Gift area.

ACCOMMODATIONS

($ = under $45, $$ = $46–$60, $$$ = $61–$80, $$$$ = $81–$100, $$$$$ = over $100)
Room tax 11%

CASA ROYALE INN
1400 W. 11th (US 287W) • 663-6341 • $–$$ • W+ 2 rooms
The two-story inn has 40 rooms. Cable TV. Room phones (no charge for local calls). Pets OK. Restaurant. Playground. Outdoor pool, indoor hot tub.

QUANAH PARKER INN
US 287W • 663-6366 • $ • No-smoking rooms
The one-story inn has 41 rooms including six no-smoking. Cable TV. Room phones (no charge for local calls). Pets OK, free breakfast.

SNYDER

Scurry County Seat • 12,700 • 915
Not long after Pete Snyder started a trading post here in 1876, outlaws set up buffalo hide huts around his post. Then there was a range war, which culminated when cowboys locked the sheriff in his own jail. After a new sheriff tamed the wild bunch with a pool cue, the town quieted down. Snyder's first oil well was completed in 1948, and Scurry County became one of the nation's top oil-producing counties, boosting Snyder's population from 4,000 to above 15,000, and turning many parts of the city into shanty towns. When the boom ended, the citizens got together to clean up the city, and in 1969, Snyder was judged an All-American City by the National Municipal League.

TOURIST SERVICES

SNYDER CHAMBER OF COMMERCE
2302 Avenue R (P.O. Box 840, 79549) • 573-3558 • W use rear entrance

MUSEUMS

SCURRY COUNTY MUSEUM
Western Texas College, southern edge of town, off College Ave. (SH 350)
573-6107 • Monday–Friday 10–4, Sunday 1–4, or by appointment
Free • W but not all areas
Collections relate to buffalo hunting, farming and ranching, medicine, banking, and current oil technology.

OTHER POINTS OF INTEREST

WHITE BUFFALO STATUE
Courthouse lawn, College and 25th St.
This life-size statue commemorates the buffalo herds that once roamed the area, and the rare albino buffalo shot by J. Wright Mooar, who claimed that he had killed over 22,000 buffalo. In 1995, the Chamber and interested citizens constructed a White Buffalo Park on Deep Creek, near the site where the buffalo was shot, on the ranch now owned by Mooar's granddaughter. Tourists are invited to visit the site, 5 miles northwest of Snyder.

PRAIRIE DOG TOWN

Located at Towle Memorial Park on South College Avenue, you can watch prairie dogs practicing their antics.

DEEP CREEK WALKING PATHS

A half mile of walking paths constructed along downtown Deep Creek, taking in a small park and bird sanctuary.

COLLEGES AND UNIVERSITIES

WESTERN TEXAS COLLEGE

6200 S. College, south edge of town • 573-8511 • W but not all areas
Visitor parking south side of campus

This two-year college has a nine-hole golf course (open to the public) that's used as a practical laboratory for the school's Golf and Grounds Management Program—one of only three accredited golf course management schools in the nation. Other programs include technical/vocational and academic courses. In addition to the Scurry County Museum (which is on campus) and the golf course, visitors are welcome to theater department productions and intercollegiate sports events that include basketball, rodeo, judo, and, of course, golf.

ANNUAL EVENTS

June

LEGENDS OF WESTERN SWING FESTIVAL

Scurry County Coliseum • Third week of June, Wednesday through Saturday • Admission • W

The music begins at noon, lasts until midnight, and gathers in the best of western swing musicians for the enjoyment of the crowds who bring their lawn chairs, or use the seating in the coliseum, to listen and dance and catch up on their visiting. For information, call 573-3558 (Chamber of Commerce).

July

JULY FOURTH

Snyder celebrates our national holiday with a prayer breakfast, a parade, food, arts and crafts, fireworks at dusk, a carnival, and a street dance.

October

WHITE BUFFALO FESTIVAL

Downtown in the square • First weekend in October • W

Festivities begin Friday night on the Mooar Ranch with a chuckwagon-cooked steak dinner, buggy rides, and a melodrama, while buffalo graze nearby. Saturday goings-on include a big parade, foods, crafts, art, face-painting, and entertainment all day long, capping off the evening with a street dance. Tickets for Friday night are $25 each, but Saturday is free.

ACCOMMODATIONS

($ = under $45, $$ = $46–$60, $$$ = $61–$80, $$$$ = $81–$100, $$$$$ = over $100)
Room tax 12%

WAGON WHEEL DUDE RANCH AND B&B

5996 CR 2128 *From Snyder go 8 miles on Hwy 84 to FM 1142, turn right, go 3 miles to CR 2128, turn left, go 1 mile to ranch entrance on right* • **573-2348, e-mail wheonwr@snydertex.com, Web page http://www.wagonwheel.com**
$ • 13 No-smoking rooms • W
   This 15-unit dude ranch and B&B offers horseback riding, fishing, paddleboats, etc. in a beautiful setting. Children can stay in room with parents for $15 per child.

WILLOW PARK INN

US 180 at US 84 • **573-1961 or 800-854-6818** • **$$–$$$** • **W 1 room**
No-smoking rooms
   The two-story motel has 44 units that include four no-smoking rooms and one suite ($$$). Children under 12 free in room with parents. Senior discount. Cable TV with HBO. Room phones (no charge for local calls). Small dogs OK. Restaurant serving breakfast and dinner. Indoor heated pool, hot tub, and kiddie pool.

PURPLE SAGE MOTEL

1501 East Coliseum Dr. • **1-800-545-5792** • **45 rooms, 25 no-smoking**
$–$$ • **W 2 rooms**
   Children under 12 stay free in room with parents, extra charge for extra beds.

AMERICAN MOTOR INN

573-5432 • **51 rooms** • **$** • **3 non-smoking.**
   Children under 12 free in rooms. Room phones (no charge for local calls). Small pets OK. Restaurant.

GREAT WESTERN MOTEL

800 E. Coliseum • **1-800-496-6835** • **$** • **56 rooms, 10 no-smoking**
   Room phones, no charge for local calls.

SWEETWATER

Nolan County Seat • **12,000** • **(915)**
   In the 1870s, buffalo hunters frequently camped along Sweet Water Creek because its waters were clean and sweet-tasting when compared to the surrounding streams that tasted of gypsum. A dugout trading post was opened in 1877 that was the start of this city. But Sweetwater had a hard time getting officially organized. Declared the county seat in 1881, it was first incorporated as a town in 1884. Because of the severe blizzard and drought in 1885–1886, many people left the area and the town charter lapsed. It was revived in 1897, but two years later the charter was declared null and void. Finally, in 1902, the town was fully incorporated.
   During World War II the Women's Air Force Service Pilots (WASP) training program was conducted at nearby Avenger Field, now the site of Texas State Technical College-Sweetwater (TSTC). Avenger Field, the first and only all-women military flying school in the world, trained female pilots for every kind of flying mission short of combat, releasing male pilots for overseas duty. Of 1,830 accepted into the program from 25,000 applicants, 174 won their wings.

WASPs flew 60 million miles on operational duty and 38 lost their lives serving their country. A Walk of Honor on the TSTC campus and a life-size bronze statue recognize these brave women.

The Sweetwater Commercial Historic District, with more than 26 sites representing architectural styles from the early 1900s, is listed in the National Register of Historic Places.

Sweetwater was named an All-American City in 1988.

TOURIST SERVICES

SWEETWATER CHAMBER OF COMMERCE

810 E. Broadway (P.O. Box 1148, 79556) • 235-5488 or 800-658-6757

MUSEUMS

CITY-COUNTY PIONEER MUSEUM

610 E. 3rd, 1 block off Broadway • 235-8547 • Tuesday–Saturday 2–5. Closed Sunday, Monday and holidays • Free (donation) • W

The museum is housed in the partially restored home of Judge and Mrs. Ragland, built in 1909. Among the more than 20 exhibit areas are an art gallery that tells history through art, a saddle shop that displays outstanding examples of leather craft, a reconstructed courtroom, a pioneer schoolroom, a history of the WASPs at Avenger Field, and Indian and pioneer artifacts that portray the lives of the early settlers and the development of the area.

OTHER POINTS OF INTEREST

LAKE SWEETWATER

Take TX 70 south about 3 miles, then east (left) on FM 1856 and go approximately 5 miles • 235-4648 (Lake store) • Open daily: November–April 7–7, May–October 7–9 • $2 person or $2 family • W variable

This 640-acre lake in a large park offers facilities for fishing, boating, boat rentals, both tent and RV camping ($8 fee), picnicking, swimming, water skiing, and nature trails.

SPORTS AND OTHER ACTIVITIES

Golf

SWEETWATER COUNTRY CLUB

1900 Country Club Drive off 17th (north near Santa Fe Lake) • 235-8093 18-hole private course open to visitors. Green fees: weekdays $15, weekends $20

LAKE SWEETWATER MUNICIPAL GOLF COURSE

FM 1856 at Lake Sweetwater • 235-8816 • 18-hole course. Green fees: $9 for 18 holes, $7 for 9 holes

PERFORMING ARTS

SWEETWATER LITTLE THEATRE

400 Locust St. • 235-5488 • Admission

Productions range from comedy to serious drama for this all-volunteer group with about four shows a year, usually performed at the Municipal Auditorium.

SHOPPING

LEN BOWDEN CUSTOM BOOTS

1912 E. Broadway on BUS I-20 • 235-3428 • W

Len is a one-man shop and the only thing he makes is Western boots. Prices begin at $395, and it takes about four months for delivery.

ANNUAL EVENTS

March

SWEETWATER JAYCEES RATTLESNAKE ROUNDUP

Nolan County Coliseum, north end of Elm • 235-5488
Usually second weekend in March • Admission • W

How does four or five tons of rattlesnakes strike you? Well, that's about what they catch on their annual snake hunts at this, the world's largest rattlesnake roundup. This Texas tradition started in 1958, when the Jaycees organized a rattlesnake hunt to help the rattler-plagued ranchers and farmers. Festivities over the long weekend include a parade, the Miss Snake Charmer Queen Contest, snake hunts, weigh-ins, professional snake-handling demonstrations, snake milking for medical research, a rattlesnake eating contest, a chili-brisket cook-off, a rattlesnake dance (for people), guided tours for non-hunters, in areas where snakes can be seen in their natural habitat, and prizes for the most and the largest Western diamondbacks caught. To hunt, you must register, have proper equipment, and stick to strict rules on how you catch the snakes.

RESTAURANTS

($ = under $7, $$ = $8–$17, $$$ = $18–$25, $$$$ = over $25 for one person excluding drinks, tax, and tip.)

ALLEN'S FAMILY-STYLE MEALS

1301 E. Broadway, about a mile east of downtown • 235-2060 • Lunch only
Tuesday–Sunday • $ • No Cr • W

Since 1952. A family-style restaurant where parties are seated together to fill each of the large tables and then the food is passed around. Meals include as many as five salads, three meats, nine vegetables, and dessert.

ACCOMMODATIONS

($ = under $45, $$ = $46–$60, $$$ = $61–$80, $$$$ = $81–$100, $$$$$ = over $100)
Room tax 13%

BEST WESTERN SUNDAY HOUSE INN

701 SW Georgia at I-20 exit 243/244, I-20 west of SH 70 • 235-4853 or
800-528-1234 • $ • W 2 rooms • No-smoking rooms

This two-story motel has 131 rooms including 35 no-smoking. Children under 10 stay free in room with parents. Senior discount. Cable TV. Room phones (no charge for local calls). Small pets OK. Outdoor pool. Coffee in reception area.

HOLIDAY INN

500 W. I-20 just west of SH 70 • 236-6887 or 800-HOLIDAY (800-465-4329) $–$$ • W 2 rooms • No-smoking rooms

The two-story Holiday Inn has 107 rooms including 24 no-smoking. Children under 19 stay free in room with parents. Senior discount. Cable TV with Showtime and pay channel. Room phones (no charge for local calls). Pets OK; 24-hr. restaurant in motel. Guests are automatically members in private club when they charge purchases on room. Cash-paying customers must first obtain a 24-hour membership for $3.50. Outdoor pool. Playground. Self-service laundry.

RANCH HOUSE MOTEL

301 S. Georgia, I-20 and TX 70 • 236-6341 • $

This two-story motel has 50 rooms. Children under 14 stay free in room with parents. Senior discount. Cable TV. Room phones (no charge for local calls). Pets OK (kennels). Restaurant. Outdoor pool. Nine stalls and a corral for horses, horse trailer parking.

MOTEL 6

510 W. I-20 • 235-4387/800-4-MOTEL 6 (800-466-8356) • $ • W+ 5 rooms No-smoking rooms

Two-story motel has 79 rooms, including 49 no-smoking. Children under 17 stay free in room with parents. Cable TV. Room phones (no charge for local calls). Small pets OK. Outdoor pool.

COMFORT INN

216 S. Georgia (I-20) • 235-5234 or 800-228-5150 • $$–$$$ • W+ 2 rooms

This two-story motel has 44 rooms, 32 no-smoking. Children under 18 stay free in room with parents. Cable TV. Room phones (no charge for local calls). Pets allowed with deposit. Pool. Restaurant. Senior discount.

WICHITA FALLS

Wichita County Seat • 102,000 • (940)

The falls on the Wichita River that this city was named after were destroyed in a flood years ago. But now a new falls has been built, once again giving meaning to the name. The original falls were probably only about five feet tall. The new falls—three-tiered and 54 feet tall—are located on the river in the northern part of town just off I-44 near the river bridge and the Sheraton Hotel.

Part of Wichita Falls' history is tied up in a poker game that took place in New Orleans in 1837. In that game John C. Scott won a number of land certificates for over 12,000 acres in what is now Wichita County. The certificates lay in a trunk for 17 years. When his heirs heard a railroad would be coming through their land, they had the townsite surveyed. The railroad didn't come through until 1882, then the town grew with it. By the early 1900s the town boasted over 100 businesses of which 21 were saloons. Oil discoveries in 1911 and 1918 found the city a hub of the North Texas oil boom.

WICHITA FALLS

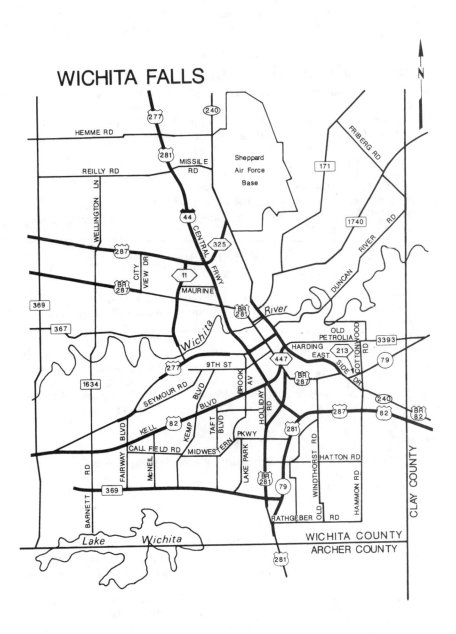

Oil-related industries, agribusiness, and manufacturing are a major part of the economy stimulated by nearby Sheppard Air Force Base. After a devastating tornado in 1979, the city quickly recovered. In 1981 it was one of ten cities in the nation, and the only one in Texas at that time, to be named an All-American City.

TOURIST SERVICES

TEXAS TRAVEL INFORMATION CENTER
900 Central Freeway (IH-44) • 723-7931 • Open daily 8–5 • W+
One of 12 tourist bureaus operated by the Texas Departmentof Transportation on key highways entering the state. Trained travel counselors can provide a wealth of free information, official highway maps, and tons of other state travel literature on the area and the rest of Texas.

WICHITA FALLS/WICHITA COUNTY MULTIPURPOSE EVENTS CENTER
1000 5th (76301) • 716-5500
http://www.viewscape.com • http://www.wf.net • W+
A state-of-the-art facility to accommodate convention and meeting needs. Call for visitor information or site tour.

MUSEUMS

KELL HOUSE MUSEUMS
900 Bluff between 8th and 9th • 723-0623 • Group tours Tuesday, Wednesday, and Sunday 2–4 or by appointment • Adults $3, children $1 W downstairs only
A Texas Historic Landmark, this home was built in 1909 by one of the city's founders. It has been restored and contains original family furnishings and other items from the period. The house is noted for its high ceilings, oak floors, and ornate woodwork. There is also an extensive collection of period clothing. The one-hour guided tour tells the history of both the house and of Wichita Falls. For ten days in early December, it becomes the city's Santa House and is open to the public. Call for hours.

WICHITA FALLS AREA FIRE AND POLICE MUSEUM
Ave. H and Giddings • 767-2412 • Saturday 12–4 or by appointment Free • W downstairs only
Located in a fire station built in 1925, this museum has displays of fire and police memorabilia dating back to the 1880s. Guided tours available or you can wander through the two floors on your own.

WICHITA FALLS MUSEUM AND ART CENTER
#2 Eureka Circle, off Midwestern Parkway between Taft and Maplewood 692-0923 • Tuesday–Friday 9:30 A.M–4:30 P.M., Thurday until 7:30, Saturday 10–5 • Adults $3, children $2 • W+
The major museum in town, it gives a broad view of art, history, and science. Among the more than 350 prints in its permanent print collection is the *Boston Massacre* by Paul Revere. Another holding is the first map of America made in America. Call for hours and admission to planetarium and laser light shows.

OTHER POINTS OF INTEREST

LAKE ARROWHEAD STATE PARK

Take US 281 north to FM 1954, then east for 8 miles. Approximately 18 miles southeast of town • **528-2211** • **Open daily 8–10 for day use, at all times for camping** • **Adults $2, under 12 free** • **W+ but not all areas**

The lake itself covers approximately 13,500 acres and has 106 miles of shore-line. It was formed over an oilfield and there are oil derricks in the water. The waters around these structures are especially good for fishing. The recreation area consists of 524 acres and provides facilities for boating, fishing, swimming, waterskiing, picnicking, and tent and RV camping, as well as nature trails.

LAKE WICHITA

Off SH 79 at south edge of town • **766-2383** • **W variable**

A close-in small lake, 2,200 acres, that is popular for swimming, fishing, sailing, and picnicking.

LUCY PARK

Off Seymour Hwy., entrance on Sunset • **761-7495** • **Free** • **W variable**

The Wichita River runs through this large park and there are trails connecting the park to the waterfall. In addition to hike-and-bike and jogging trails, there are a public swimming pool, picnic areas, playing fields, duck pond, and Lucyland, a playground with imaginatively designed equipment that kids like.

SPORTS AND ACTIVITIES

Golf

RIVER CREEK GOLF COURSE

FM 1177, Burkburnett • **855-3361** • **18 holes.**
Greens fee: $8 weekdays, $9 weekends

WEEKS PARK GOLF CENTER

4400 Lake Park Dr. • **767-6107** • **18 holes.**
Greens fee: $11 weekdays, $13.50 weekends

Tennis

HAMILTON PARK TENNIS CENTER

3101 Hamilton • **766-2321** • **12 lighted courts**
$1.50 per person days; $2 evenings; $1 weekends and holidays

WEEKS PARK TENNIS CENTER

4101 Weeks Park Dr. • **322-6600** • **9 lighted courts**
$1.50 per person days; $2 evenings, $1 weekends

COLLEGES AND UNIVERSITIES

MIDWESTERN STATE UNIVERSITY

3410 Taft • **689-4000** • **W+ but not all areas**

Founded in 1922, MSU offers associate, baccalaureate, and master's degrees on a beautiful 170-acre campus where Spanish architecture predominates. Visitors are invited to attend activities presented by the art, drama, and music departments. Other events include the annual Fantasy of Lights display (see Annual Events) and seasonal sporting events.

PERFORMING ARTS

BACKDOOR THEATRE

501 Indiana • 322-5000 • Main stage productions $10, dinner theater $25 Closed Sunday and Monday • W call ahead

This is a nonprofit community theater combined with a dinner theater. Together they put on about a dozen productions each year, with about half performed on the main stage and half in the dinner theater.

MEMORIAL AUDITORIUM

1300 7th • 716-5506 • W

The symphony and ballet perform here, as well as traveling performers ranging from C&W, chamber music, rock and roll, comedians, and magicians.

PARKS AND RECREATION OUTDOOR CONCERT SERIES

761-7495 • Free • W

The Brown Bag concert series is held Fridays in April and May at the noon hour on the Kemp Public Library lawn at 14th and Lamar. The outdoor Lawn Chair Series is presented each Tuesday evening starting at 7:30 P.M. on the stage at the Sheraton Hotel amphitheater across from the falls at 100 Central Freeway.

WICHITA FALLS BALLET THEATRE

3412 Buchanan • 322-2552 • Admission

Founded in 1963, the WFBT is recognized nationally as an Honor Company for consistent artistic and technical excellence.

WICHITA FALLS SYMPHONY

322-4489 • Admission

This orchestra puts on about six concerts a year at Memorial Auditorium with both local artists and guest performers.

WICHITA THEATER AND OPERA HOUSE

10th and Indiana • 723-9037 • Admission

Home of the Texas Gold Country Music Show, it features old-time country and gospel music.

KIDS' STUFF

FUNLAND AMUSEMENT PARK

2006 Southwest Parkway • 767-7911 • Admission • Open weekday evenings and weekends from spring to fall • W

A small park that's mostly for younger children. Train ride, carnival-like rides, miniature golf, and an arcade.

PUTT-PUTT GOLF AND GAMES

4415 Westgate • 692-4144 • Admission • Monday–Thursday 11 A.M.–9 P.M., Friday 11 A.M.–Midnight, Saturday 10 A.M.–midnight, Sunday noon–9

Miniature golf, arcade, go-karts, batting cages, and more.

THE PLEX

4131 Southwest Parkway • 696-1222 • Admission • Tuesday–Thursday 3:30–9, Friday 3:30–midnight, Saturday 11 A.M.–midnight, Sunday noon–9
    Try the Laser Trek Arena, miniature golf, go-karts, bumper boats, batting cages, and more.

SIDE TRIPS

TRAILS AND TALES OF BOOMTOWN USA

Railroad Depot, 102 West 3rd St. in Burkburnett, north on IH-44 at exit 240 569-0460 • Admission • June–October Friday and Saturday or call for private tour information year round
    Housed in the historic 1907 depot in Burkburnett, Trail and Tales offers narrated bus tours of sites where the oil boom happened: Fowler's Folly, outdoor oil museum, Nesterville, and other historic sites. There is also a video at the depot for those who don't take the tour.

ANNUAL EVENTS

April

SPRING FLING

Wichita Falls Museum and Art Center, #2 Eureka Circle off Midwestern Parkway • 692-0923 • Admission • Usually held the last weekend in April W • Additional parking across street at Midwestern State University
    A regional arts and crafts festival featuring the juried works of about 80 artists and craftsmen from all over the U.S., Mexico, and Canada. Also planetarium shows, music and dance performances, and entertainment for kids.

June

RED RIVER RODEO

Mounted Patrol Arena, FM 369 • 592-2156 • $12 box seats, $8 reserved seats, $6 general admission • Second weekend in June
    Many current and previous PRCA champions compete in this rodeo. There's also a parade, barbecue, and a dance every night.

TEXAS-OKLAHOMA JUNIOR GOLF TOURNAMENT

Various golf courses • 767-6107 • Charge for registration. Spectators free Third full week in June • W
    Entries include more than 600 young men and women from 16 states. Golfers must be 18 or under.

August

HOTTER 'N' HELL HUNDRED BICYCLE RIDE AND FESTIVAL

Multipurpose Events Center, 1000 5th St. • 692-2925 http://www.wtr.com/hhh • Call for registration information • Spectators free
    The largest sanctioned century ride in the United States. Thousands of serious, as well as recreational riders, bike from 10 kilometers to 100 miles.

TEXAS RANCH ROUNDUP

Mounted Patrol Arena, FM 369 • 322-0771 • $7–$10 reserved seats
Third weekend in August • W

This is a team competition to pick the best working cowboys from a dozen or more of the largest and most historic ranches in Texas. Events reflect actual ranch working conditions and include cutting out calves, wild cow milking, a wild horse race, team branding, and ranch cooking contest. There's an evening dance.

September

FALLS FEST

Lucy Park • 692-9797 • Date varies • Admission • Parking along Seymour Hwy., shuttle buses provided • W

A family event with two stages featuring continuous live entertainment. Other activities include bike races, contests, media olympics, children's olympics, and children's area in Lucyland for kids under 10.

October

DEPOT SQUARE HERITAGE DAYS

8th and Indiana • 723-0623 • Date varies

For two days, a four-block area in the heart of the Depot Square Historic District is transformed into a 1900s street scene. More than 200 antiques dealers, artists, craftsmen, and food vendors sell their wares in this turn-of-the-century setting.

December

FANTASY OF LIGHTS

Midwestern State University campus, 3410 Taft St. • 689-4000 • Free

It started back in the 1920s when Mrs. L. T. Burns turned her yard into a Christmas fairyland of lights. On her death the display was given to the university. Now it has grown to 32 displays with 20,000 lights outlining campus buildings. An estimated 250,000 people see this display each year.

OFFBEAT

LITTLEST SKYSCRAPER

7th just past Ohio in alley behind Farmers Market at the railroad tracks

It's amazing the trouble that some con artists will go to in order to put across a scam. According to the story, a con man built this building that stands 10 by 16 feet at its base and 40 feet tall, took pictures of it from an angle that made it appear huge against the city skyline, and then peddled shares in his skyscraper around the country. Some say he neglected to tell potential investors that the building plans were in inches rather than feet. By the time the scam was discovered he was long gone. His sucker bait remains, on a downtown alley.

ACCOMMODATIONS

$ = under $45, $$ = $46–$60, $$$ = $61–$80, $$$$ = $81–$100, $$$$$ = over $100)
Room tax 13%

FOUR POINTS BY SHERATON HOTEL
**100 Central Freeway (IH-44), Texas Travel Information Center exit • 761-6000
or 800-325-3535 • $$–$$$ • W+ 2 rooms • No-smoking rooms**
   This six-story hotel has 176 units that include ten suites ($$$$–$$$$$) and 17
no-smoking rooms. Satellite TV with The Movie Channel and pay channel.
Room phones (charge for local calls). Fire sprinklers in rooms and fire inter-
coms. Pets OK. Free airport transportation. Lounge and lobby bar. Indoor pool,
whirlpool, health club. Free morning coffee.

HOLIDAY INN
**401 Broad (IH-44) • 766-6000 or 800-HOLIDAY (465-4329) • $$–$$$$
W+ 3 rooms • No-smoking rooms**
   This four-story Holiday Inn has 241 units including 26 suites ($$$–$$$$$) and
75 percent of the rooms are no-smoking. Cable TV with pay channel. Room
phones (charge for local calls). Free airport transportation. Restaurant. Lounge
with DJ. Indoor and outdoor pools, children's pool and play area, indoor
whirlpool, and coin-operated washer and dryer.

LA QUINTA MOTOR INN
**1128 Central Freeway (IH-44) at Maurine exit • 322-6971 or 800-531-5900
$–$$ • W+ 2 rooms • No-smoking rooms**
   This two-story inn has 139 units and 41 no-smoking rooms. Cable TV with
Showtime. Room phones (no charge for local calls). Pets OK. 24-hour restaurant
next door. Outdoor pool. Free coffee in lobby in morning.

West Texas

ALPINE

Brewster County Seat • 5,637 • (915)

In the early 1880s, when steam locomotives needed water, the railroad signed a contract to use the local spring owned by the Murphys. As part of the deal the spring owners got to name the community growing up around them. Naturally, they named it Murphyville. But in 1888, the people of the little town outvoted the Murphys and—looking at the nearby mountains—changed the name to Alpine.

This is the county seat of Brewster County, the largest county in Texas with nearly 6,000 square miles—larger than the state of Connecticut. The town sits at an elevation of 4,481 feet in a wide valley at the foothills of the Davis Mountains.

TOURIST SERVICES

ALPINE CHAMBER OF COMMERCE

106 N. 3rd between Ave. E and Holland (US 90) • 837-2326 • W

The Alpine Chamber not only provides information on local businesses, it also serves as a gateway to the Big Bend and Davis Mountains regions and provides information on area parks, accommodations, activities, and itineraries.

BIG BEND TRANSPORTATION

304 E. Holland Ave • 837-7143

In country where a grocery run can be hundreds of miles, this shuttle operation provides an invaluable service for solitary travelers as well as groups needing buses. Call for rates from El Paso and Midland/Odessa as well as within the Big Bend.

MUSEUMS

MUSEUM OF THE BIG BEND

Sul Ross University, US 90E • 837-8143 • Tuesday–Saturday 9–5, Sunday 1–5. Closed Monday • Free (donations) • W

The thrust of this museum is the exhibition of historical materials that relate to the Big Bend region. Exhibits trace regional history by contrasting the cultures of the Indians, Spanish, Mexicans, and Anglo-Americans who lived here.

OTHER POINTS OF INTEREST

WOODWARD RANCH

Take SH 118 south about 16 miles to sign, then about 1.5 miles to house
364-2271 • Open at all times • W variable

This ranch is a rock hunter's paradise, with more than 70 varieties of cutting stones for the picking, including gemstones such as red plume and pom pom agates, amethysts, and opal—all for 50¢ a pound if you pick 'em yourself (the ranch experts will tell you where the best prospecting is). You can also buy specimens at the rock store for $1 a pound and up. The 4,000-acre ranch has a camping area with RV hook-ups (fee).

COLLEGES AND UNIVERSITIES

SUL ROSS STATE UNIVERSITY

US 90E • 837-8059 • W+ but not all areas • Visitor parking at Administration Building

Sitting on a hill on the east side of town, the campus overlooks Alpine and the surrounding mountains. Visitors are invited to attend a full slate of athletic events that include intercollegiate rodeo. The Music Department stages band and choir concerts and the Art Department has rotating art exhibits in the Art Gallery. The Museum of the Big Bend is also on campus (*see* Museums).

SHOPPING

APACHE TRADING POST

Take US 90 west about 1.5 miles • **837-5149 • W**

In this large log cabin you'll find a good selection of souvenirs and gifts that includes Indian-made turquoise and silver jewelry and Mexican and Indian pottery. They also stock books related to the region and aeronautical charts. They are the map headquarters for this area.

ARTS AND CRAFTS MALL OF THE BIG BEND

101 W. Holland across from Amtrak • 837-7486 • W

Over 100 different artists, artisans, craftsmen, and other exhibitors have booths, counters, corners, even nooks with their wares. At the high end of the price scale are antiques, sterling, china, and cowboy memorabilia. On the less expensive side are books, antique bottles, brain teasers, hand-blown crystal, gourmet food products, paintings, photos, pottery, even a year-round Christmas booth.

BIG BEND SADDLERY

E. Highway 90 • 837-5551 or 800-634-4502 • W

Founded in 1905, this saddle shop still serves its original clientele of local ranches and cowboys who ride the range. Big Bend Saddlery is also well-known outside the Trans-Pecos as a Western outfitter. Tally books, chuck boxes, and bed rolls are a few of the hundred-plus items listed in their extensive catalog, which is available free of charge in the store.

FRONT STREET BOOKS
121 E. Holland Avenue at Fourth St. • 837-3360 or 800-597-3360 • W
Continuing the tradition of the independent bookseller, Front Street carries an extensive selection of new and used books featuring the Big Bend, Chihuahuan Desert natural history, and the West. National bestsellers, the *New York Times*, and *The Wall Street Journal* are also available, as is an intriguing assortment of out-of-print and antiquarian titles.

J. DAVIS STUDIO/PORTABLE ART
510 W. Holland • 837-3812 • W
Inlaid stoneware vessels are John Davis's forte. The advantages of stopping by his studio and seeing his wares locally are numerous: lower prices than what you'll pay at Joan Cawley's Gallery in Santa Fe, a broader selection, and the opportunity to view his wife's Portable Art. Robin Brown's hand-dyed and block-printed fashions are available nationally at Nordstrom's, the Smithsonian Museum Shop, and Jane Smith's in Aspen and Santa Fe. Just blocks from her factory, you can buy Portable Art by Robin Brown for all ages, sizes, and sexes.

KIOWA GALLERY
105 E. Holland Ave. at Fifth St. • 837-3067 • W
The success of the Kiowa parallels the rise of the Big Bend as haven for artists and artisans. Local artists are represented in a an ever-changing number of media—sculpture, bronze, pottery, furniture, watercolor, pen and ink, and oil. Easy-to-find, the western wall of the Kiowa features a sensational 17' x 81' Stylle Read mural of Milton Faver crossing the Rio Grande in 1873.

OCOTILLO ENTERPRISES
205 N. Fifth St. • 837-5353 or 800-642-0427 • W
Owner Judith Brueske wrote a 50-page study on the Marfa Lights that is a bestseller locally. In addition to an extensive selection of books for adults and kids, her shop also stocks beads, gems, and minerals.

QUETZAL IMPORTS
302 W. Holland Ave. at Seventh St. • 837-1051 • W (on east side)
Travel to Mexico with a stop at Quetzal, which features Talavera ceramics, Tarahumara Indian crafts, folk art, and home furnishings.

SIDE TRIPS

MARATHON
31 miles east of Alpine via US 90 • 800-884-4243 (Gage Hotel)
This former stop on the Southern Pacific was named for its likeness to the Plains of Marathon in Greece. The town has gained international prominence thanks to the presence of the Gage Hotel, which has been featured in *Conde Nast Traveler*, the *New York Times*, and dozens of other publications. A growing number of galleries and crafts shops make Marathon a popular day trip or multi-day getaway.

MARFA
26 miles west of Alpine via US 90 • 915-729-4942 (Marfa Chamber)
One look at the Presidio County Court House and Marfa will be forever etched in your memory. Home to the Marfa Lights, site of the filming of the

1956 classic *Giant,* and the final residence of minimalist Donald Judd whose Marfa-based Chinati Foundation houses much of his work, Marfa is more than a side trip and can become a destination in itself.

RESTAURANTS

($ = under $7, $$ = $8–$17, $$$ = $18–$25, $$$$ = over $25 for one person excluding drinks, tax, and tip.)

LA CASITA
1104 E. Avenue H east of south Highway 118 • 837-2842 • Lunch and dinner daily • $ • MC, V
Once 11:30 rolls around, La Casita fills up. The generous portions of Tex-Mex favorites make this hard-to-find family-owned eatery a favorite of locals and a find for persistent travelers. Beer and wine.

THE OUTBACK
300 S. Phelps west of south Highway 118 • 837-5074 • Lunch and dinner daily • $–$$$ • AE, DIC, MC, V • W
This restaurant serves a little bit of everything and all ably prepared: Italian food, Mexican food, sandwiches, and burgers. Beer and wine.

PONDEROSA INN RESTAURANT
E. Highway 90 • 837-3321 • Breakfast, lunch, and dinner daily • $ • W
Alpine's leading coffee shop specializes in honest American fare. Bigger-than-life breakfasts and daily luncheon specials are two of the top reasons to stop by Louis Gordon's local institution.

REATA ALPINE
203 N. Fifth St. across from First National Bank • 837-9232 • Lunch and dinner Monday–Saturday. Closed Sunday • Reservations recommended $$–$$$ • AE, MC, V
Known nationwide for its innovative style and use of indigenous foods, Reata Alpine and its sister restaurant, Reata Fort Worth, have made transformed cowboy cooking into a culinary style that has been featured in *Food and Wine, Travel and Leisure, Martha Stewart Living, Texas Monthly,* and *Chile Pepper.* Located in a nineteenth-century territorial adobe, a visit to the restaurant is mandatory if only to view the 30-foot-tall mural off the back patio. Private club (temporary memberships are available).

ACCOMMODATIONS

($ = under $45, $$ = $46–$60, $$$ = $61–$80, $$$$ = $81–$100, $$$$$ = over $100)
Room tax 13%

BEST WESTERN ALPINE CLASSIC
2401 E. Highway 90 • 837-1530 or 800-528-1234 • $$–$$$ • W+ 2 rooms • No-smoking rooms
This two-story motel has 64 rooms including eight suites and 40 no-smoking rooms. Pool and hot tub. Free continental breakfast. Government, senior, and student rates available.

CORNER HOUSE BED & BREAKFAST

801 E. Ave. E. • 837-7161 or 800-585-7795 • $–$$$ • Smoking on porch only

In addition to its welcoming decor, the Corner House is home of Scots-born world traveler Jim Glendinning, who makes a point of advising his guests on the ins and outs of any visit to the Big Bend and beyond. Built in 1937 and restored in 1993 by Glendinning, it has five rooms, and the tariff includes a healthy to ample breakfast. Note that Glendinning also serves breakfast only to nonguests daily from 7:30 A.M. to 10:30 A.M.

HOLLAND HOTEL

209 W. Holland (US 90E) • 837-3455 or 800-535-8040 • $–$$

This historic three-story hotel has 12 renovated rooms with more being added. Two suites ($$$$) include a penthouse with outdoor deck. Cable TV, some with VCR. Some rooms have phones (no charge for local calls). Pets limited. Restaurant and private club (guests automatically members. Temporary membership $3 for party of 4). Free continental breakfast in room. Coffeemakers, refrigerator, microwave in most rooms. Room service. Free transportation to airport. Amtrak station across the street. Self-service laundry.

RAMADA LIMITED

2800 W. Highway 90 • 837-1100 or 800-272-6232 • $$ • W+ 4 rooms • No-smoking rooms

This two-story motel has 61 rooms including two suites and 42 no-smoking rooms. Pets OK. Free continental breakfast. AAA, AARP, government, and student rates available.

SUNDAY HOUSE INN

US 90E • 837-3363 • $ • W+ 1 room

The two-story inn has 80 units. Cable TV with HBO. Room phones (no charge for local calls). Pets OK. Restaurant and private club (guests automatically members. Temporary membership for non-guests $4). Outdoor pool. Free coffee in morning.

BIG BEND NATIONAL PARK

Brewster County • 477-2251 • $10 per vehicle per week

Encompassing more than 700,000 acres, this wilderness park is the largest park in Texas, filling the corner of the state where the Rio Grande River makes a sweeping bend to the northeast before turning back east. The river's route through the park runs for 107 miles; an additional 100+ miles below the park is designated the Rio Grande Wild and Scenic River. Although the park lies within the Chihuahuan Desert, its varied topography includes the forested Rio Grande floodplain, cool mountain highlands, and plunging canyons as well as hundreds of square miles of desert with scenic mountain backdrops. Rain falling on the mountains percolates through underground aquifers and emerges as springs on the desert floor, supporting abundant wildlife including 75 species of mammals, about 400 species of birds, and 65 species of amphibians and reptiles. More than 1,000 plant specimens have been identified here including 60 forms of cacti.

Two paved roads lead into the park. From Marathon, take US 385 about 69 miles to the Park Headquarters at Panther Junction. It's 102 miles from Alpine via Texas 118 to Park Headquarters. Or, if you want to follow the Rio Grande, take Farm Road 170 east from Presidio through Lajitas and Terlingua until it meets Texas 118 at Study Butte. Then follow that route to the west entrance and on to Park Headquarters 22 miles beyond.

Within the park itself are more than 100 miles of paved roads going to all the main areas, and many more miles of improved dirt roads that are normally accessible with passenger cars. Check the posting of road conditions at Park Headquarters and any of the ranger stations within the park. If you want to try the unimproved backcountry roads you'd best have a four-wheel drive, high clearance vehicle. Small, inexpensive booklets on sale at Park Headquarters contain maps and driving tours of the roads within the park, giving mile-by-mile instructions on what to look for.

Visitor Centers

There are four staffed visitor centers in the park, but some may not be open during winter months. The Park Headquarters at Panther Junction is open year round and has a large relief map that will help you understand more clearly the topography of the park and help you lay out your visit. All of the ranger stations provide park maps; information on current road, weather, hiking trail and camping conditions; and information on activities within the park. Regularly scheduled activities such as hiking (trail maps are available for a small fee), guided horseback trips and nature walks, and evening slide programs are provided by the park naturalists.

There are three campsites with facilities (fee) in the park: the Basin, Cottonwood Campground (near Castolon, on the western side of the park), and Rio Grande Village (on the eastern side of the park). The Basin is not accessible to trailers over 22 feet long nor to large motorhomes due to steep grades and winding roads; check with a ranger before attempting the climb if you are in doubt. Only the concession-operated trailer park at Rio Grande Village has hook-ups. The only showers and washateria are also located here. All campgrounds are on a first-come-first-served basis. There are also backcountry roadside campsites without facilities scattered along the improved and unimproved dirt roads throughout the park. These are free, but you must get a permit from any ranger station. On busy holidays and weekends, the campsites with facilities are often full, so you should make alternate plans.

Due to the vast size of this park (it's 65 miles north to south, 50 miles east to west), much of your time can be spent driving from one attraction to the next. However, the ever-changing view of the mountains is itself one of the park's main attractions. Roadside exhibits every few miles highlight aspects of the Chihuahuan Desert and break up the drives. Major points of interest include Green Gulch, the drive from Panther Junction to the Basin, along which black bears have been seen in recent years; the Basin, a depression surrounded on all sides by mountains that shield it from the sun and, with its mile-high altitude, make it a pleasant refuge from summer heat; the Castolon Historic District, a U.S. Army post built during the troubles with Mexico in the 1910s and now converted to a trading post and ranger station; and the Hot Springs Historic District, a popular bathing spot on the Rio Grande where a hot spring pours its water into the river. Spectacular views of the Rio Grande can be obtained by

(continued on page 694)

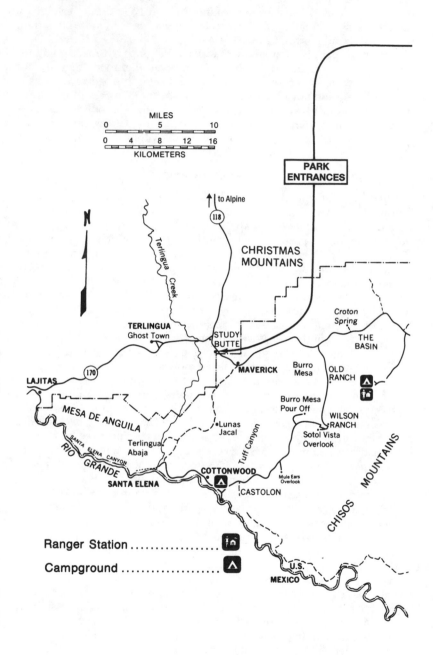

MILES
0   5   10

0   4   8   12   16
KILOMETERS

PARK
ENTRANCES

↑ to Alpine
118

N

CHRISTMAS
MOUNTAINS

Terlingua Creek

Croton
Spring

THE
BASIN

TERLINGUA
Ghost Town

STUDY
BUTTE

MAVERICK

Burro
Mesa

OLD
RANCH

170

LAJITAS

Burro Mesa
Pour Off

MESA DE ANGUILA

WILSON
RANCH

Lunas
Jacal

Sotol Vista
Overlook

Terlingua
Abaja

Tuff Canyon

RIO GRANDE

SANTA ELENA CANYON

COTTONWOOD

Mule Ears
Overlook

CHISOS MOUNTAINS

SANTA ELENA

CASTOLON

Ranger Station ....

Campground ....

U.S.

MEXICO

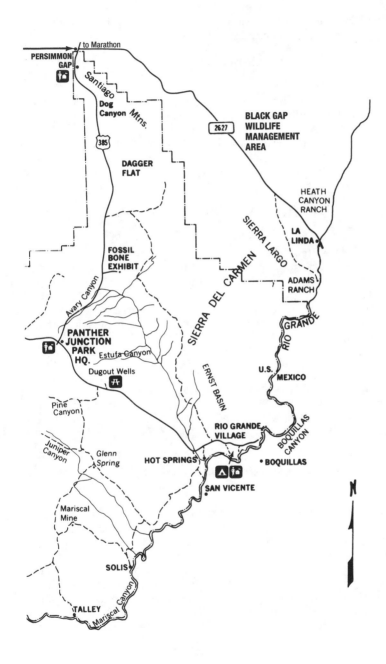

(continued from page 691)
hiking into Santa Elena and Boquillas canyons. Numerous short hiking trails lead from parking areas to other historic and scenic locations near roads.

BIRD'S-EYE VIEW

THE LOST MINE TRAIL

Trailhead starts at Panther Pass on the Basin Rd.

The views along this route are superb regardless of whether you take a 30-minute hike or go the full 4.8 miles (round trip). Park your car at the trailhead, spend a quarter for the self-guiding booklet, and hit the trail. It starts at 5,600 feet and goes up to 6,850 feet. Views of Casa Grande, the Sierra del Carmens, and Juniper and Pine canyons make it unforgettable. Best of all, the walk back is downhill (unlike the Window Trail).

HISTORIC PLACES

CASTOLON

Via Ross Maxwell Drive (paved road)

Tremors from the Mexican Revolution were felt along the Rio Grande, and the U.S. Cavalry responded by establishing a tiny cavalry post at Castolon. Barracks, officers' quarters, and other structures were completed by 1920 but never used for military purposes. Today, the barracks houses a trading post and the officers' quarters serve park personnel. Remnants of the Big Bend's only cotton gin stand outside the trading post.

GLENN SPRING

Almost nine miles from the north end of Glenn Spring Rd. (improved). Check with park personnel for road conditions and exact directions

A steady supply of water made Glenn Spring an important stop on the Comanche Trail and for early settlers including H. E. Glenn, a Big Bend pioneer and Indian fatality.

MARISCAL MINE

Almost 20 miles from the east end of River Rd. Accessible by high clearance or four-wheel-drive vehicles only. Check with park personnel for road conditions and exact directions

The Big Bend area abounds in mineral deposits. The Presidio Mine near Shafter (on the far side of the Big Bend Ranch State Natural Area) produced more silver and gold than any mine in Texas history. And the Chisos Mine near Terlingua was a national leader in cinnabar (quicksilver) production. The Mariscal Mine also produced cinnabar and was the only commercial mine within the bounds of what is now the park. The mining facilities have been designated a National Register Historic District. In addition to dilapidated commercial Historic District. In addition to dilapidated commercial buildings and rock houses, the most visible remnants are a Scott furnace and a concrete condenser.

OTHER POINTS OF INTEREST

HOT SPRINGS

From near the Rio Grande Village, drive two miles down the improved dirt road to the Hot Springs parking lot. Park and then hike a quarter of a mile to the springs

J. O. Langford left Alpine in 1909 looking for better health and brought his wife and daughter, Lovie, to these hot springs. The springs spew over 250,000 gallons of 105° water daily, and you don't have to pay the dime he charged to enjoy them.

SANTA ELENA CANYON

Via Ross Maxwell Drive

If you don't have the opportunity to float the canyon (*see* Sports and Activities), be sure to either stop at the parking lot to enjoy the vista or hike the two-mile self-guided trail into the canyon's mouth. At 1,500 feet high, the sheer walls are not quickly forgotten. Neither is the silence. The first part of the hike crosses Terlingua Creek (occasionally muddy). Concrete stairs switchback into the canyon before descending to the river.

THE WINDOW

Chisos Basin • W

The Window is the sole drainage for the Basin and regularly offers unforgettable sunsets in addition to a pleasant hike which is paved and wheelchair accessible. It can be reached on foot via the Window Trail (2.8 miles) or on horseback.

SPORTS AND ACTIVITIES

Birding

Because of its location on the north-south flyway and its position along the dividing line between Eastern and Western species, Big Bend offers more species of birds than any other national park. At last count, nearly 450 species had been identified including the only U.S. sightings of the Colima Warbler. More than 75% of these fly through, and the remaining 100 or so actually nest.

The top birding spot is the Rio Grande Village with the Basin a close second.

Driving Tours

The Big Bend Natural History Association in conjunction with the National Park Service produced two excellent (and inexpensive) guides for on-road and off-road touring: *A Road Guide to Paved and Improved Dirt Roads of Big Bend National Park* and *A Road Guide to Backcountry Dirt Roads of Big Bend National Park*. They provide a complete list of routes, points of interest, and guidelines. It's best to register at a ranger station and check your vehicle before any off-road trips.

An excellent first tour is the 30-mile Ross Maxwell Scenic Drive (paved). This route includes views of the Basin (framed by the Window) and Mule Ears Peaks and stops at historic Castolon and the Santa Elena Canyon overlook and Nature Trail.

Fishing

No fishing license or permit is required within the National Park.

Hiking/Backpacking/Camping

Only overnight trips require a backcountry permit (free of charge and available at any ranger station). Get a copy of the Big Bend Natural History Association's *Hiker's Guide to the Trails of Big Bend National Park*. This 28-page booklet includes 36 hikes of all distances and in all parts of the park.

Horseback Riding

For details on riding in the park, contact park headquarters and ask for the park's *Regulations and Information Regarding Use of Personal Horses* (915-477-2251).

SPRING CREEK RANCH

17 miles north of Persimmon Gap on US 385 • 376-2260

Fresh from 18 years at the Chisos Remuda, Lynn and Cathey Carter have set up their own outfit off US 385 between Marathon and the park's north entrance. They offer overnighters, multi-day rides, and music by their son Craig's popular Spur of the Moment Band.

TURQUOISE TRAILRIDES

Study Butte • 371-2212

Just west of the park in Study Butte, these wranglers offer hourly, half and full day trips. The most popular excursions are to a pre-Columbian Indian camp and the combo trips in conjunction with local rafting companies.

Mountain Biking/Cycling

All of the park's paved and primitive roads are open to cyclers, but none of the trails are. Recommended rides include the River Road (west to east) and Old Ore Road.

River Rafting

The most common float trips in order of length and with approximate times are Black Rock Canyon (½ day), Colorado Canyon (full day with lunch stop), Santa Elena Canyon (one to three days), Mariscal Canyon (one to three days), Boquillas Canyon (three days), and the Lower Canyons (a week). There are three ways to ride the river:

- bring your own equipment
- rent equipment at Study Butte, Terlingua, or Lajitas
- hire a guide service

By far the most common way to run the river is with one of the local guide services listed here:

- Big Bend River Tours (800-545-4240)
- Desert Sports (888-989-6900)
- Far Flung Adventures (800-359-4138)
- Texas River Expeditions (800-839-7238)

A backcountry use permit is required for any river excursion. Backcountry use permits are free and are available at all Big Bend National Park Visitor Centers.

SHOPPING

NATIONAL PARK CONCESSIONS

Basin • Castolon • Panther Junction • Rio Grande Village

Each store stocks essentials you were sure you brought. The Rio Grande Village Store caters to the RV campground and offers a coin laundry and showers in addition to groceries and general merchandise. The Basin store has the widest selection, including meats, fruits, canned goods, and hiking supplies.

STUDY BUTTE STORE
Study Butte • 371-2231 • W
A sampling of the inventory includes cold beer, shotgun shells, aspirin, antacids, band aids, Dramamine, fresh produce, meats, canned vegetables and other groceries, videos, and pesticides. For motorists, there are jumper cables, gas, diesel, motor oil, transmission fluid, and fuel cans.

RESTAURANTS

($ = under $7, $$ = $8–$17, $$$ = $18–$25, $$$$ = over $25 for one person excluding drinks, tax, and tip.)

BIG BEND MOTOR INN RESTAURANT & STORE
Study Butte • 371-2483 • Breakfast, lunch, and dinner daily • $–$$ • Cr
The main reason to stop here for a burger, some Mexican food, or a chicken-fried steak is because it's 80 miles to Alpine and 30 miles to Big Bend National Park.

CHISOS BASIN LODGE RESTAURANT
477-2291 • Breakfast, lunch, and dinner daily • $–$$ • AE, MC, V • W
The dining room is only open for meals and includes mainstays like burgers, steaks, and a good chef's salad. The coffee shop stays open all day making sandwiches, malts, milk shakes, and the like.

ROADRUNNER DELI
By the Study Butte Store • 371-2364 • Breakfast and lunch daily • $
Plenty of fresh coffee, hearty sandwiches, and delicious cheesecake. You can't go wrong at breakfast: good omelets, breakfast sandwiches, muffins, and scones. Call or stop by to order a picnic basket for two or twenty. They also offer the only cappuccino and espresso down south.

ACCOMMODATIONS

($ = under $45, $$ = $46–$60, $$$ = $61–$80, $$$$ = $81–$100, $$$$$ = over $100) Room tax 13%

CHISOS MOUNTAIN LODGE
Chisos Basin • Big Bend National Park • 477-2291 • $$$–$$$$$ • W+ 3 rooms No-smoking rooms
The only lodging in the park is located in the heart of the Chisos Mountains. There are 72 units in this two-story complex including six stone cottages with bath and three double beds and the newer Casa Grande Lodge, which has 26 no-smoking rooms and handicap access. Amenities include the Chisos Mountain Lodge Dining Room, a gift and curio shop, and free parking. Pets are welcome, but the maid staff doesn't service rooms with pets inside. The property runs 100 percent occupancy during the high seasons: October to New Year's and during Spring Break.

BIG BEND RANCH STATE PARK

PRESIDIO AND BREWSTER COUNTIES • (915)
The largest component of the Texas Parks and Wildlife system, at more than 265,000 acres, the Big Bend Ranch exceeds the size of all other Texas state parks combined. Run for most of the 20th century as a private ranch, it was acquired by the state of Texas in 1988.

TOURIST SERVICES

BARTON WARNOCK ENVIRONMENTAL EDUCATION CENTER
HCR 70, Box 375 • Terlingua (79852) • 424-3327 • Daily 8 A.M. to 4:30 P.M. Admission
The Warnock Center sits several hundred yards east of Lajitas and is the eastern gateway to the State Natural Area. Its gift shop offers numerous books on the Big Bend and Trans-Pecos as well as maps and other items. Bus tours of the Big Bend Ranch leave here and travel 136 miles round trip compared with the 74-mile tour from Fort Leaton.

FORT LEATON STATE HISTORICAL PARK
Three miles east of Presidio along FM 170 • 229-3613 • P.O. Box 1180 Presidio (79845) • Daily 8 A.M. to 4:30 P.M. • Admission • W
Fort Leaton serves as the western gateway to the Big Bend Ranch State Park and stands almost 60 miles west of the Warnock Center along FM 170. Tours of Fort Leaton include 25 of the fort's 40 rooms with exhibits and programs detailing the history of the Spanish, Mexican, Texas, and American colonizers. Trading post.

OTHER POINTS OF INTEREST

SOLITARIO
This classic geologic dome was uplifted by an intrusive igneous body and runs about eight miles east to west and nine miles north to south. Contact the Warnock Center or Fort Leaton for information on tours and access.

SPORTS AND ACTIVITIES

Bus Tours
The most popular way to see most of the park is via one of the two bus tours operated by Texas Parks & Wildlife. Tours depart the first and third Saturdays of the month on air-conditioned buses complete with restroom. Reservations and a deposit are required. Contact TP&W central reservations at 512-389-8900, or at the Warnock Center (915-424-3327) or Fort Leaton (915-229-3613). A discount is available to Texas Conservation Passport holders. Each tour begins at 8:00 A.M.

Fishing
Fishing along the Rio Grande is allowed. Unlike the national park, however, a fishing license and a park permit are required. Trotline and jug fishing are discouraged.

Hiking and Camping

The expansion of the park's system is underway. As new trails such as Cinco Tinajas open (in 1997), they will be incorporated into future editions of the *Big Bend Ranch State Park Trail Guide,* produced by the Texas Parks & Wildlife Department and available at the Warnock Center or Fort Leaton.

River Rafting

Refer to River Trips under **Big Bend National Park** for a complete listing of guide services, trips, and suggestions. As in Big Bend National Park, you can run the river on your own or with a commercial service. Within the State Natural Area, access is offered at seven points. In order, heading west from the Warnock Center, they are Contrabando Canyon, Grassy Banks, Madera Canyon, Colorado Canyon, and Arenosa (combination to lock required). Each of these is right off of FM 170 and is marked on maps. Some have primitive campsites with self-composting outhouses, but none offer potable water, electricity, or much shade.

Seminars

Seminars at the Big Bend Ranch last two or three days, cost from $50 to more than $500, and range from desert survival to rock art to useful plants of the Chihuahuan Desert. Call 915-229-3416 or fax 915-229-3506 for more information.

RESTAURANTS AND ACCOMMODATIONS

See separate listings under **Big Bend National Park** and **Lajitas** and **Terlingua.**

BIG SPRING

Howard County Seat • 23,093 • (915)
Water was the reason for Big Spring's beginnings. The town is named after the natural spring gushing from Sulphur Draw, a dramatic formation in a sudden rise of land. It produced the greatest supply of water within 60 miles. Before the coming of the Europeans and later the settlers bringing cattle from East Texas, this was the watering hole for both the Plains animals and the Comanche and Shawnee Indians. In the mid-1800s, the spring gained fame as a popular campsite on the Overland Trail to California and the Santa Fe Trail.

The town remained nothing but a tent village until the coming of the Texas & Pacific Railroad in 1881. Then, once again because of the abundant water supply, it became a railroad center. Railroading was its principal industry until the 1920s when oil was discovered; however, today the economy is based primarily on cotton and oil. The big spring is now the site of a local city park (*see* Other Points of Interest–Comanche Trail Park).

Big Spring is also famous for being the home of what might be called the first of the big Texas spenders, the Earl of Aylesford. The English nobleman came to town in 1883, shortly after the building of the railroad, and arrived with about a dozen people in his entourage. The local hotel didn't have room for his party, so he bought the hotel and rearranged the occupancy of the rooms to accommodate his guests and servants. Once, in order to throw a party for the whole town, he bought a saloon. The next day, according to the story, he gave it back to the people he bought it from. When he couldn't get the choice cuts of meat he liked, he built a butcher shop. It was made of stone and was the first permanent building in town. The building still stands at 121 Main. The story of his leaving is as strange as his coming. One night about a year and a half after he arrived in town, he got up from a card game, said "Bye, boys," and then laid down and died. He was 36. The Earl is buried in England, but his legend remains alive in Big Spring.

TOURIST SERVICES

BIG SPRING AREA CHAMBER OF COMMERCE

215 W. 3rd and US 87 (P.O. Box 1391, 79721) • 263-7641 • W

HISTORIC PLACES

POTTON HOUSE

Gregg St. (BUS US 87) at 2nd • 263-0511 • Tuesday–Saturday 1–5. Closed Sunday and Monday • Adults $2, seniors and children 12 and under $1 (includes ticket to tour Heritage Museum)

This restored Victorian home was built of Pecos sandstone in 1901. Among its significant features are the fish scale shingles on the gables, and the iron fence. Inside are original furnishings and personal belongings of the Potton family. The home is listed in the National Register of Historic Places.

MUSEUMS

HERITAGE MUSEUM

510 S. Scurry at W. 6th • 267-8255• Tuesday–Friday 9–5, Saturday 10–5. Closed Sunday, Monday, and holidays. Adults $2, seniors and children 12 and under $1 (includes tour of Potton House) • W but not all areas

The windmill outside the museum indicates its purpose to preserve and portray the heritage of Howard County. Permanent exhibits explore that heritage from the first Indians 12,000 years ago to the present. Its collection of longhorn cattle horns, with the handtooled leather holders, is the largest in the region. There are also collections of paintings and artifacts emphasizing frontier history.

OTHER POINTS OF INTEREST

BIG SPRING STATE PARK

Off FM 700 just west of downtown • 263-4931 • Open daily: April 1–October 31, 8–10; November 1–March 31, 8–8 • $3 person 12 and up, seniors born before September 1930 free • W but not all areas

Locally, this 370-acre park is known as "Scenic Mountain" because of the 200-foot limestone-capped mesa that overlooks the city and provides a bird's-eye view. There is also a three-mile scenic drive around the park. Facilities include an interpretive center, picnic sites, a playground, nature trails, and a prairie dog town.

COMANCHE TRAIL PARK

Whipkey Dr. off US 87 just south of FM 700 • 263-8311 (City Parks Department) • W variable

The original "big spring" is in this 479-acre park. The park also has a swimming pool, nine lighted tennis courts, an 18-hole municipal golf course, a small fishing lake, baseball fields, playground, hike-and-bike and nature trails, a flower garden, and campsites with hookups (fee). The amphitheater here seats 7,000. It was built of native limestone during the Depression. All the rocks were cut and shaped by hand.

SANDHILL CRANE SANCTUARY
S. First and Jones St. off Hwy 80 going west
Also called One-Mile Lake because of its distance from downtown, this is one of a series of *playa lakes*—shallow lakes mainly filled with rainwater. The lake provides nesting and feeding grounds in the winter for thousands of sandhill cranes, which stand in the brackish water safe from predators.

COLLEGES AND UNIVERSITIES

HOWARD COLLEGE
1001 Birdwell Ln. at 11th • 264-5000 • W, but not all areas
This two-year community college provides both academic and technical/vocational courses for approximately 3,500 students. The 120-acre campus includes a large agricultural research and demonstration center and a 20-acre rodeo arena. Visitors are welcome to athletic events, including the Rodeo Club's participation in intercollegiate rodeo and the four or five drama productions presented each school year. Located on Birdwell St. is the Dorothy Garrett Coliseum, a 90,000-square-foot facility that hosts athletic events, concerts, and other community activities such as exhibition games, special contests, and even circuses.

SOUTHWEST COLLEGIATE INSTITUTE FOR THE DEAF
FM 700W and Ave. C, located in Industrial Park on the old Air Force Base 264-3700 • W
The only junior college for the hearing-impaired in the world, this two-year school offers both academic and vocational programs, some in conjunction with Howard College. Among the activities visitors may attend are drama productions given in sign language with interpreters for those who need assistance with ASL.

ANNUAL EVENTS

March

RATTLESNAKE ROUNDUP
Howard County Fairgrounds, off FM 700N just west of Big Spring State Recreation Area • 263-7641 (Chamber of Commerce) • Usually mid–March Adults $3, children $2 • W
They do about everything you can do with a rattlesnake here: they hunt it, they demonstrate how to handle it, they milk it for the venom, and they skin it. Then they use the various parts for everything from hatbands and belt buckles to fried snacks. The participants in the roundup usually catch more than a ton-and-a-half of the rattlers, and prizes are given for the heaviest snake caught. There's also an arts-and-crafts show.

June

BIG SPRING COWBOY REUNION AND RODEO

Howard County Rodeo Bowl, Fairgrounds, off FM 700 just west of Big Spring State Recreation Area • 263-7641 (Chamber of Commerce) • Wednesday–Sunday late in June • Admission • W • Free parking

Festivities include a parade, street dance, cowboy poetry reading Saturday afternoon, and professional rodeo every night with top rodeo competitors from surrounding ranches, as well as the professionals.

September

HOWARD COUNTY FAIR

Fairgrounds, off FM 700 just west of Big Spring State Recreation Area 394-4439 • First Monday in September through Saturday • Adults $2, children over 6 $1 • W • Free parking

A typical bustling county fair with a livestock show and sale, a flower show and judging, agricultural products show and judging, cake and pie judging, a fiddler's contest, a calf roping, a barbecue and chili cookoff, a carnival, and nightly entertainment.

RESTAURANTS

($= under $7, $$= $8–$17, $$$= $18–25, $$$$= over $25 for one person excluding drinks, tax, and tip.)

BIG JOHN'S FEED LOT

802 W. 3rd, 2 blocks west of Gregg • 263-3178 • Lunch only Monday–Saturday. Closed Sunday • $ • AE, V, MC, DIS • W

The simple menu, handwritten on paper sacks, touts barbecue beef, ham, and German sausage. The building is hodgepodge rustic with the counter up front where you can buy barbecue by the pound and homemade pies. The restaurant is in the rear.

LA POSADA

206 NW 4th, just east of Gregg • 267-9112 • Lunch and dinner Tuesday–Sunday. Closed Monday • $ • Cr but not DIS • W • Children's menu

The building is Mexican hacienda-style and so is the food. They also own a tortilla factory and a Mexican bakery, so the tortillas, chips, and bakery products are all fresh from the ovens. Beer and wine.

ACCOMMODATIONS

($ = under $45, $$ = $46–$60, $$$ = $61–$80, $$$$ = $81–$100, $$$$$ = over $100) Room tax 13%

BEST WESTERN

IH-20 at US 87N • 267-1601 or 800-528-1234 • $ • W 2 rooms • No-smoking rooms

The two-story motel has 152 units including two suites ($$) and 90 no-smoking rooms. Children under 12 stay free in room with parents. Cable TV with pay channel. Room phones (no charge for local calls). Small pets OK. Restaurant next door. Outdoor heated pool. Free coffee and continental breakfast in lobby. Motel is part of a Rip Griffin Truck Stop complex.

COLORADO CITY

Mitchell County Seat • 8,051 • (915)

In 1881 the Texas & Pacific Railroad came to Colorado City, making it one of the largest cattle shipping points in the region and the first real boomtown in West Texas. Soon afterward, Isaac Ellwood and J. F. Glidden, inventors of barbed wire, came. Ellwood later bought the Renderbrook ranch near Colorado City and established the famous "Spade" brand. By 1884, the population was around 10,000, and a group of businessmen got together and built what was then the finest hotel between Fort Worth and El Paso. But a combination of severe drought and competition from other shipping points soon took the bloom off the boom. Today, Colorado City's economy is based on agriculture, oil, and cattle.

TOURIST SERVICES

COLORADO CITY AREA CHAMBER OF COMMERCE

157 W. 2nd at Oak (P.O. Box 242, 79512) • 728-3403 • Web page: http://camalott.com/~tmcn/colocity.html • E-mail commerce@bitstreet.com • W

HISTORIC PLACES

MITCHELL COUNTY HERITAGE HOUSE

425 Chestnut • 728-8841 or 728-3403 • Summer: Saturday–Sunday 2–5 or by appointment • Free (donations) • W

In 1883, shortly after the railroad came to town, this one-story home was built of bricks from local kilns. Now restored, it is one of the few structures remaining from the town's earliest days.

MUSEUMS

HEART OF WEST TEXAS MUSEUM

340 E. 3rd • 728-8285 • Tuesday–Saturday 2–5. Closed Sunday–Monday Free (donations) • W downstairs only, enter back door

The earliest exhibit in this museum is a collection of prehistoric bones. But most of the displays are devoted to tracing the early settlement and growth of the city. Among the nearly 5,000 historical items in the museum's collection is a 1877 horse-drawn hearse.

OTHER POINTS OF INTEREST

LAKE COLORADO CITY STATE PARK

Take TX 263 southwest 7 miles to FM 2836, then right (west); 11 miles from town **• 728-3931 • Adults $3, children 12 and under free. Seniors born before September 1930 free • W but not all areas**

There's more than a mile of beach in this 500-acre park by the 1,600-acre lake on a tributary of the Colorado River. Other facilities include boat ramps, three fishing piers, picnic areas, and campsites with hookups (fee). The lake water temperature is warmer than that of the surrounding coldwater lakes due to the circulation through a nearby power plant. This not only increases the number of days that swimmers and skiers can enjoy the lake, but it also provides a longer annual feeding and growing period for native species of bass, catfish, and redfish.

WALL OF BRANDS

Downtown Colorado City, near the railroad
This wall depicts the long history of ranching in the area through the brands registered with the county clerk.

PERFORMING ARTS

COLORADO CITY PLAYHOUSE

337 Walnut • 728-3491 or 728-3403 (Chamber of Commerce) • Admission • W
This community theatrical group puts on about four productions a year. The theater is the old Colorado City Opera House, which was built in 1900 and wound up as a boarding house before it was returned to its original use. It was restored into a 160-seat theater by the playhouse group, entirely with volunteer labor and financing through the production of plays.

SHOPPING

CANDYLAND AND NUT DEPOT

IH-20E in the Woods Boots Complex • 728-3195
Pottery, gourmet candy, souvenirs, and a variety of unusually flavored peanuts such as nacho cheese, hot and spicy, and Cajun.

WOODS BOOTS

IH-20E • 728-3722 • W
Thousands of pairs of boots from about 30 different manufacturers in a wide variety of leathers are available here. Also Western wear and hats.

ANNUAL EVENTS

July

AMERICAN JUNIOR RODEO ASSOCIATION RODEO

Mitchell County Fairgrounds. *Take old US 80 west 1 mile* **• 728-3403 Admission • W**
With more than 300 contestants from all over, this is a lively junior rodeo. To round out events there's also a parade, a barbecue supper, and a rodeo queen contest.

October

RAILHEAD ARTS AND CRAFTS FAIR

Mitchell County Fair Barn. *Take old US 80 west 1 mile* **• 728-3403 • Free • W**
The "Railhead" refers back to the days when Colorado City was one of the largest shipping centers west of Fort Worth. Craftsmen display and market handmade quilts, antique barbed wire, paintings, and other items. Other highlights include demonstrations of various crafts, a turkey shoot, calf roping contest, and entertainment.

RESTAURANTS

($ = under $7, $$ = $8–$17, $$$ = $18–25, $$$$ = over $25 for one person excluding drinks, tax, and tip.)

FORT WOOD CAFE

IH-20E inside fort complex • 728-8322 • Lunch and dinner Monday–Saturday, lunch only Sunday • $ • MC, V • W • Children's menu
  The decor is rustic Western, with the tried-and-true West Texas favorites of steaks, seafood, Mexican dishes, and burgers.

ACCOMMODATIONS

($ = under $45, $$ = $46–$60, $$$ = $61–$80, $$$$ = $81–$100, $$$$$ = over $100)

Room tax 13%

DAYS INN

SH 208 at IH-20W • 728-2638 • $ • No-smoking rooms
  The two-story motel has 52 units including six no-smoking rooms. Children under 12 free in room with parents. Senior discount available. Cable TV with HBO. Room phones (no charge for local calls). Pets OK. Restaurant adjacent. Outdoor pool.

VILLA INN

2310 Hickory Street • 728-5217 • $ • No-smoking rooms
  One-story, with 40 units, including 15 no-smoking rooms. Cable TV. Pets okay. Restaurant adjacent. Outdoor pool.

EL PASO

El Paso County Seat • 475,394 • (915)
  If you have ever had a vacation ruined by a lack of sunshine, El Paso is the place for you. Sitting on Texas' border with Mexico and New Mexico, it is the only major desert city in the state. As such, it averages about seven inches of rain a year, and the local Chamber of Commerce is continuously boasting of statistics such as "only 50 days without sunshine in 18 years."
  In addition to being the sunshine champ of the state, El Paso is unique in a number of other ways. It is the largest city directly on the U.S.–Mexican border, the westernmost city in the state, and it is closer to the capitals of New Mexico, Arizona, and the state of Chihuahua, Mexico than it is to its own capital in Austin. Then, if you consider El Paso and Juarez (its sister city across the trickling Río Grande) as one metropolitan area (which local advertisers do) and throw in the immediately adjoining section of New Mexico, we have another stamp of uniqueness. This is the only metropolitan area in Texas with two race tracks that offer parimutuel betting: Juarez and Sunland Park. If that's not enough, El Paso also claims to be the place where the first margarita was served.
  It was in 1598, twenty-two years before the Pilgrims landed at Plymouth Rock, that a Spanish colonizer, Juan de Oñate, led an expedition north from Santa Barbara, Mexico to New Mexico. It was a large party with several hundred colonists and several thousand head of livestock. Pushing across the Chi-

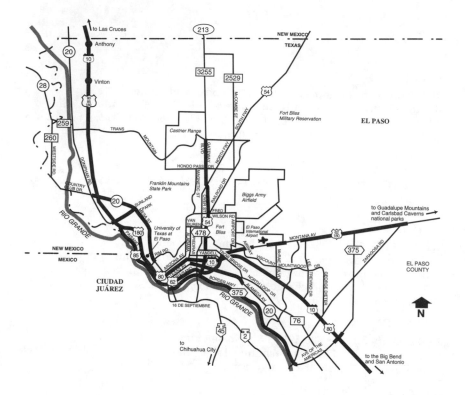

huahuan Desert, they crossed the Río Grande near where San Elizario stands today. Oñate named the area *El Paso del Río del Norte*—crossing of the River of the North. The party moved on, but this was the beginning of the recorded history of the area.

It was in the mid-1600s that a settlement finally took hold with the construction of the mission of *Nuestra Señora de Guadalupe* (Our Lady of Guadalupe) on what is now the main plaza in Juarez. This mission became the heart of the village called *El Paso del Norte*, which became a principal rest stop on the journey between Chihuahua City and Santa Fe. The village received a boost in population in 1680, when Spanish colonists fled the Pueblo Revolution in northern New Mexico. Whether by force or by choice, they were accompanied by some of the Pueblo Indians, including the Tiguas, who are still in El Paso and now lay claim to being the oldest identifiable ethnic group in Texas. The Tigua Indian Reservation is one of only three reservations in Texas.

The Texas Revolution came and went with little effect on this isolated town. It wasn't until Texas entered the Union and the United States went to war to support the Texan's claim of the Rio Grande as the southern border that the people here paid any real attention to that river's role as a dividing line. The political division was finalized in the Treaty of Guadalupe Hidalgo, which ended the Mexican War in 1848.

The Mexican side of the river retained the name El Paso del Norte. For a while, the settlement north of the river was called Magoffinsville, then Franklin, and finally El Paso.

El Paso was, and is, the key pass in the best all-weather route to the West Coast. So when the California gold rush hit in 1849, there was enough traffic for two major stage companies to set up stations here.

Fort Bliss, now a major U.S. Army post, began about this time as a campsite for soldiers chasing the marauding Apaches. By 1861 it was a regular fort and, along with all the other posts in Texas, it was surrendered to the Confederacy. Then in late 1862 it fell to Federal troops from California (but not before the Confederates burned down the fort buildings) and remained in Union hands for the rest of the war.

Meanwhile, during our Civil War, the French invaded Mexico and set Maximilian on the throne as emperor. Mexican President Benito Juarez moved his government to El Paso del Norte. Juarez, with strong American political support, threw out the French in 1866 and executed Maximilian. In honor of this victory, El Paso del Norte was renamed Ciudad Juarez in 1888.

The Wild West

El Paso was truly the Wild West. The Apaches continued to raid the area until as late as 1879, and the easy crossing of the river at this point made it a favorite of both American and Mexican bandits and gunman.

The tiny town of about 700 was finally opened up to the world when the Southern Pacific, laying tracks from California, reached El Paso in 1881. It was soon followed by the Santa Fe and, across the river, the Mexican Central. Quickly the population jumped to several thousand, and the town became even wilder, with the streets echoing to the escapades of Billy the Kid, Wyatt Earp, Bat Masterson, and John Wesley Hardin, the one they said was the fastest gun of them all. Most of these famous gunmen went on to other places, but Hardin, who claimed to have killed 40 men, was killed here in 1895. He is buried in Concordia Cemetery near downtown.

Even after the era of the gunfighters, things didn't quiet down completely. There always seemed to be a revolution or a plot of some kind going on in Juarez. Sometimes it spilled across the border, but mainly El Paso became a center for soldiers of fortune seeking jobs. When Pancho Villa was on the loose in northern Mexico, General Blackjack Pershing's U.S. Army expedition that went after him was based at Fort Bliss.

It's still the West here, but no longer so wild. With local boot factories making more than a million pair of cowboy boots a year and factories pouring out jeans and other Western clothing, El Paso can at least lay claim to being the Western *Wear* capital of the Southwest. The city is also a center for agribusiness, manufacturing, and the refining and processing of copper ore, oil, and natural gas. A major portion of the rapidly developing *maquiladora* industry is centered in the El Paso-Ciudad Juarez area. And the tiny campsite that grew into Fort Bliss is now the center for all air defense activity in the U.S. Army and the Free World, pumping hundreds of millions of dollars a year into the local economy.

The Wandering Border

Through most of its history, the Rio Grande was a wandering river. It frequently flooded and cut new channels. Because it was the official border, pieces of land were constantly swapped between the two countries. This made for a continuing source of irritation. Finally, in 1968, President Lyndon Johnson and Mexican President Gustavo Diaz Ordaz signed a treaty that confined the river to a concrete channel. The land that the meandering river had kept in dispute was turned into the Chamizal National Memorial on the El Paso side of the river and Chamizal Park on the Juarez side.

Although the river is a political boundary, the people on both sides seem to regard the sister cities as just one big international city separated by the minor inconvenience of a border crossing.

To place a direct dialed international call to Juarez from El Paso, dial 011-52-16 and the six-digit local number. To place an operator-assisted call, dial 01-52-16 and the six-digit local number. A pay phone call to Juarez costs about $1. To place a call from Juarez to El Paso, dial 8 then the seven-digit U.S. number. Juarez pay phones accept the U.S. dime. The area code for all of neighboring New Mexico is 505.

El Paso is the only major city in Texas on Mountain Time, so it is one hour earlier than the rest of the state. In addition, Juarez does not observe daylight savings time, so for half the year the time is different in the two cities.

Police officers in Juarez are instructed to help visitors in case of any problem, so don't hesitate to ask them for directions or help.

For questions about declarations and duties you can reach the U.S. Customs Bridge/Americas at 534-6795.

Because it is serviced by major airlines, El Paso is also a good jumping-off place for the New Mexican ski resorts, like Cloudcroft and Ruidoso.

TOURIST SERVICES

EL PASO CIVIC CONVENTION AND TOURIST CENTER
**1 Civic Center Plaza (79901), on Santa Fe • 534-0696 or 800-351-6024
Monday–Friday 8–5 • W+**

One of the more helpful brochures available here, *Historic Missions* covers a tour of the city's mission trail. Pay parking in the garage under the Civic Center.

MEXICAN TOURIST INFORMATION CENTER
Juarez, Tourism Department, Municipal Building (*Unidad Administrativa Municipal*) • Av. Malecon and Francisco Villa, near the Stanton St. bridge 011-52-16-152301 or 011-52-16-140837

English-speaking counselors can provide you with maps, brochures, and hotel information about Juarez and the rest of Mexico. With two-weeks notice they can mail this information to the United States. You can contact the Mexican Consulate in El Paso at 533-4082. The American consulate in Juarez can be reached at 011-52-16-134048.

TEXAS TRAVEL INFORMATION CENTER
At Anthony, on IH-10 at the New Mexico state line • Approximately 19 miles northwest of downtown El Paso • 886-3468 or 800-452-9292 • Open daily 8–5 W (W+ restrooms nearby)

One of 12 travel information centers operated by the Texas Transportation Department on key highways entering the state. The 800 number will connect you with one of these centers. The local number will connect you directly to the El Paso center. Trained travel counselors can provide a wealth of free information, official highway maps, and tons of other state travel literature on El Paso/Juarez and the rest of Texas. Anthony itself is worth a stop-over because it is a town divided, with part in Texas and part in New Mexico. Wet 'N Wild Water World, a water amusement park the kids'll love, is also here.

EL PASO-JUAREZ TROLLEY

1 Civic Center Plaza • 544-0061 or 800-259-6284 • Daily except New Year's, Easter, Thanksgiving, Christmas

For self-paced tours, the trolley offers the Border Jumper, colorful red and green trollies, that follow an international circuit of shops, restaurants, and attractions. Departs Civic Center Plaza hourly, free shuttle service from major hotels. All day ticket $7.50, children 3 and under free.

TOUR BUS COMPANIES

The following offer regularly scheduled daily half-day sightseeing or shopping tours of El Paso or Juarez or a full-day tour of both cities. Pick-ups at the major hotels/motels. Prices range from about $5 for the tour to the race track up to $18 for the full-day tour. Children generally half price. Group tours also available.

Around and About Tours • 300 Shadow Mountain, #815 • 833-2650
Golden Tours • 332 N. Clark • 779-0555
Si El Paso Tours • 711 Coer d'Aline Circle • 581-1122
Sunset Coaches • 1317 W. Main Dr. • 533-8300

BIRD'S-EYE VIEW

MURCHISON PARK ON SCENIC DRIVE

Take Stanton or Mesa to Rim Road, then turn east. Rim Road becomes Scenic Drive. Murchison Park is approximately 2 miles from the start of Rim Road
Open at all times • Free • W but not all areas

The parking lot is small but the view is grand, especially near sunset. Another good time is after dark when the sister cities come alive with lights. From this vantage point, at 4,222 feet above sea level, you can see most of El Paso and Juarez as well as parts of New Mexico. There are 12 tablets here explaining the view by sections—from Fort Bliss on the east to the University of Texas at El Paso on the west—and giving some of the history of the area. An interesting tidbit is that there are fossils of prehistoric fish embedded in the rocks some 200 feet above this park.

MUSEUMS

AMERICANA MUSEUM

5 Civic Center Plaza, Santa Fe St., Convention and Performing Arts Center
542-0394 • Tuesday–Friday 10–5 • Free • Pay parking at Civic Center Garage • W+

This small museum is dedicated to the study and display of American pre-Columbian, tribal, historic, and contemporary Western art of the Americas. The emphasis is on using pottery to show the cultural history of the region. Displays include several full-scale models of Indians making pottery and performing other daily chores. Gift shop.

CHAMIZAL NATIONAL MUSEUM

800 S. San Marcial and Delta • 532-7273 • Daily 8–5 • Free • W+

Part of the National Park Service's memorial commemorating the peaceful settlement of the long-standing border dispute between the U.S. and Mexico. Permanent displays trace the details of the joint survey, which took eight years during the 1850s, and the reasons for the misunderstandings between the two countries. A 28-minute film also covers this history. There is a small gallery that features traveling exhibits of artists from both sides of the border. The 500-seat theater is used for a number of special events, including several important festivals (*see* Annual Events).

EL PASO CENTENNIAL MUSEUM

University of Texas at El Paso, University Ave. and Wiggins • 747-5565
Tuesday–Friday 10–4:30, Saturday and Sunday 1–5 • Free • W+ (ramp in rear)

Its name comes from the fact it was built in 1936 as part of the state's centennial celebration. The museum focuses on the human and natural history of the region. Displays range from geological and paleontological specimens to Indian pottery and the Josephine Clardy-Fox fine art collection. There is also a collection of almost 600 glass plate negatives dating from 1880 to 1897 that show scenes from Santa Fe to Chihuahua. One gallery is devoted to changing exhibits of photographs, paintings, and folk art. The gift shop has a large collection of books with the emphasis on archaeology. Outside the building, enclosed in its own glass case, is Engine No. 1, a steam locomotive of the El Paso and Southwestern Railroad.

EL PASO MUSEUM OF ART

1211 Montana between Brown and Noble • 541-4040 • Tuesday–Saturday 9–5, Thursday 9–9, Sunday 1–5 • Free • W+ (ramp in rear)

The heart of this museum, which is located in a Greek Revival mansion expanded with exhibit wings, is the Kress Collection that was donated by merchant Samuel H. Kress in the late 1950s. This collection traces the subjects, media, and techniques used by the European masters from 1300 to 1800. Included in the collection of 57 paintings and two sculptures are works of Di Pietro, Lippi, Tintoretto, Murillo, Van Dyke, Canaletto, and others. There is also a collection of American paintings that features a Gilbert Stuart portrait of George Washington and Frederic Remington's *Sign of Friendship*. The museum's active changing exhibition program includes as many as 20 special shows a year.

EL PASO MUSEUM OF HISTORY

12901 Gateway West, IH-10E at Americas Ave. exit, approximately 15 miles east of downtown • 858-1928 • Tuesday–Friday 9–5, Saturday–Sunday 1–5 • Free • W

This started out as the Cavalry Museum. Now its focus is El Paso history, with a number of life-size dioramas depicting the people and events that shaped the city during the last 400 years. Gift shop.

FORT BLISS AIR DEFENSE ARTILLERY MUSEUM

Fort Bliss, Pleasanton Rd. near Sheridan (Building 5000) • 568-4518 • Daily 9–4:30 • Free (donations) • W+ but not all areas (ramp in rear)

Outside is a large display of U.S. and foreign antiaircraft weapons from World War II cannons to today's sophisticated air defense missiles. Inside, photographs, weapons, dioramas, models, and audio-visuals tell the story of the birth and development of weapons systems to protect ground units from enemy aircraft and missiles. Gift shop.

FORT BLISS MUSEUM

Fort Bliss, Pershing and Pleasanton Rds. (Building 5054) • 568-4518 or 568-2804 Daily 9–4:30 • Free • W (W+ restrooms in building across street)
These adobe buildings are a representation of Fort Bliss as it appeared from 1854 to 1868 at the location know as "Magoffinsville," which is now part of downtown. A walk through three of the buildings moves you progressively through the history of the fort during the century from 1848 to 1948. One of the displays is a terrain model of the five former locations of the fort and its present location. A unique thing about the museum is it flies a reproduction of a 30-star flag—the only one authorized to fly officially in the country—to reflect the 30 states in the Union in 1848 at the time of the fort's beginnings as a cavalry outpost.

MUSEO DE ARTE Y HISTORIA

Juarez, Centro Comercial ProNaF, Av. Lincoln • 011-52-16-131708 Tuesday–Sunday 11–7 (Juarez time). Closed Mexican holidays • Adults 50¢, students with ID and children free • W
This small museum is located in the midst of the ProNaF shopping area. Exhibits include pre-Columbian and contemporary art and artifacts.

MUSEUM OF THE NONCOMMISSIONED OFFICER

Biggs Army Airfield, Fort Bliss, SSG Sims St. and Barksdale (Building 11331) 568-8646 • Monday–Friday 9–4, Saturday and Sunday noon–4 • Free • W
This museum offers a 200-year journey through the history of the noncommissioned officer—the NCO. Starting with the American Revolution, the exhibits portray the evolution of the NCO from a strictly combat soldier to today's mid-level manager. There are artifacts of NCO life from the Civil War to the present.

WILDERNESS PARK MUSEUM

4301 Transmountain Rd. and Gateway South • 755-4332 • Tuesday–Sunday 9–5 • Free • W+ but not all areas
Through dioramas, exhibits, and a series of stunning murals, the museum portrays human adaptation to the southwestern desert environment from prehistoric times to the present. Includes full-scale dioramas of cliff dwellings and exhibits on hunting and gathering and a "time-tunnel" series of murals that depict the interaction of humans and environment in the Southwest through history. Set in a 17-acre park with a mile-long nature trail.

YSLETA DEL SUR TIGUA INDIAN CULTURAL CENTER

Tigua Reservation, 305 Yaya Lane • 859-5287 • Tuesday–Sunday 9–4 Free (donations) • W+
Visitors can watch tribal artisans creating pottery, baking bread, or performing ceremonial dances. Exhibits trace the history of the Tigua tribe. The restaurant is famous for its chili and other spicy specialties (*see* Restaurants). Gift shop.

HISTORIC PLACES

CHURCH OF THE IMMACULATE CONCEPTION

Campbell near Myrtle

This church was constructed in 1892 on this small rise to protect it from what was then the annual flooding of the Rio Grande.

CONCORDIA CEMETERY

Just north of the IH-10/Gateway North interchange (locally called The Spaghetti Bowl)

This is El Paso's "Boot Hill." The graves of many members of the town's pioneer families are here, but better known are the graves of a number of gunfighters, including the notorious John Wesley Hardin. Hardin, reportedly the fastest gun of his time, claimed he killed 40 men. His end came when he was shot in the head by lawman John Selman, who later also died with his boots on and is buried here. There is also a special section for the Chinese coolies who died while constructing the railroad here.

HART'S MILL SITE AND OLD FORT BLISS

1700–1900 W. Paisano Dr.

The adobe building at 1720 W. Paisano is all that remains of the water-powered gristmill built by Simeon Hart in 1849. The remaining building was the residence he built in 1854. The well-known La Hacienda Café now occupies the building (*see* Restaurants). Just down the street are several buildings remaining from the fifth location of Fort Bliss. From 1880 to 1894 the fort was located here on the bank of the Río Grande. There are two officers' quarters, at 1838 and 1844 W. Paisano, and the former guardhouse at 1932.

LOS PORTALES

San Elizario, San Elizario Plaza, off FM 258 (Socorro Rd.)

Built as a residence sometime about 1855, this adobe building saw use as the county courthouse (when San Elizario was the first county seat of El Paso County), an elementary school, and apartments before being rehabilitated in 1967. It was near here that the Spanish expedition under Juan de Oñate reached the Rio Grande in 1598 and celebrated one of America's first thanksgivings, now the subject of an annual reenactment (*see* Annual Events).

MISION NUESTRA SEÑORA DE GUADALUPE

Juarez, Av. 16 de Septiembre, at the Plaza

The Mission of Our Lady of Guadalupe was completed in 1668, more than 100 years before the American Revolution. It has adobe brick walls more than four feet thick as well as beautifully carved ceiling beams and altar.

SAN ELIZARIO PRESIDIO CHAPEL

San Elizario, FM 258 (Socorro Rd. approximately 5 miles east of the Socorro Mission) • 851-2333

The Presidio (fort) was established here by the Spanish in the early 1770s and the original chapel built a few years later to service both the garrison and the tiny village that grew up around it. That chapel was destroyed and the present one, built in 1883, still is an active Catholic church.

SOCORRO MISSION

FM 258 (Socorro Rd.) at Nevarez • 859-7718

When the Spanish and Indians fled the Pueblo Revolt in New Mexico in 1680, some of them came here and built this mission and town. The first mission, which was built of adobe and completed in 1681, was destroyed by the rampaging Rio Grande, as was its successor. The present church was built around 1843 using some of the roof beams salvaged from one of the earlier churches, beams that were hand-carved by the Piro Indians. Replacement beams are dated with the year they were installed. According to the legend, the hand-carved statue of St. Michael was "miraculously" delivered to the church more than 150 years ago. It was being transported from Mexico to a church in New Mexico when the ox cart carrying it was "miraculously" mired in the Rio Grande and could only be pulled out after the statue was removed. The parishioners decided this meant the statue should stay in their church, so they kept it. The church, still in use, is reputedly the oldest continuously active parish in the United States.

UNION STATION

700 San Francisco Ave., *Exit IH-10 at Downtown exit, take Mesa St. south to Paisano, follow Paisano St. west to station* • Daily 11–7, except closed holidays • W

The El Paso Union Station stands at the eastern entrance to the storied pass that gave the city its name. Three American and one Mexican railways formed the nation's first international union station, where passengers could change from one line to another. Completed in 1905 and restored in the 1980s, the building is an architectural masterpiece best appreciated from the inside. It serves both as the local Amtrak station and as offices of the Sun City Transit Company.

YSLETA MISSION

Zaragosa and Alemeda, next to the Tigua Indian Reservation • 859-9848

Founded in 1681 by the Spanish and Tigua Indians who fled the Pueblo Revolt in New Mexico. This church was built in 1908 on the original foundation after floods and fire destroyed several earlier churches on this site. The official name of the church is Our Lady of Mount Carmel, but there is a statue of St. Anthony in a niche outside because he is the Tiguas' patron saint. The adobe Ysleta Mission rectory, at 9501 Socorro Rd., is also one of the oldest buildings in El Paso County.

OTHER POINTS OF INTEREST

ASCARATE PARK

6900 Delta • 778-5337 • W but not all areas

A large city park with a lake for boating and fishing and facilities for baseball, handball, volleyball, and picnicking. There is also a golf course (*see* Sports and Other Activities) and Western Playland Amusement Park (*see* Kids' Stuff).

CHAMIZAL NATIONAL MEMORIAL

800 S. San Marcial at Delta • 532-7273 • W+ (electric carts available)

This 55-acre park commemorates the peaceful settlement of a long-standing border dispute between the U.S. and Mexico. It is operated by the National Park Service. Immediately opposite it, across the river, is Mexico's Chamizal Federal Park, 750 acres that include a museum (*see* Museums), a botanical garden, and various recreational facilities.

EL PASO ZOO

4001 Paisano at Evergreen, across from the City Coliseum • 521-1850 for further information • Open daily 9:30–4:00 weekdays, 9:30–5 weekends and holidays • Adults $2, senior citizens and children (3–11) $1, under 3 free W+ but not all areas • Free parking across street

An 18-acre zoo makes the most of the approximately 460 mammals, birds, and reptiles that live here. The reptile collection, for example, was originally set up to exhibit only local reptiles, but now has been expanded to include many exotic species including American alligators. An interesting indoor exhibit contrasts the animal communities of the Central American rain forest with those of the local Chihuahuan Desert. Early each afternoon the white light in this exhibit fades into red light that simulates darkness to the animals and permits observance of the nighttime behavior of the exhibit's inhabitants, including a bat flight and emerging two-toed sloths. These activities usually occur shortly after the light switch.

FORT BLISS/U.S. ARMY AIR DEFENSE ARTILLERY CENTER

Main Post, east of US 54 (Gateway North) and west of the El Paso International Airport, between Fred Wilson Rd. and Montana 568-4505/4601 (Public Affairs Office) • Free • W variable

What started out in 1847 as a small camp for cavalry trying to keep the Indians in check has grown into one of the largest military installations in Texas. The 1.2 million-acre reservation is now the center for all the air defense activity throughout the U.S. Army and much of the free world. It is the home of more than 14,000 troops. Military personnel from 25 allied nations train here. This is the sixth location that the post has occupied in the El Paso area. Several of the earlier posts were wiped out by the changing course of the temperamental Rio Grande. The fifth location was rendered unusable when the railroad barons, who ruled the West in the 1880s, used their influence to lay tracks right through the center of the post. The present post was opened in 1893 and about 20 of the buildings erected at that time are still in use. This is an open post and visitors are welcome. There are three military museums open to the public on the post (*see* Museums). Other activities open to the public include spectator sports. Some missile firings are also open. For information on firing dates, times, and locations call the Public Affairs Office at 568-4320.

LINCOLN STATUE

Juarez, Av. Lincoln near the ProNaF, just south of Chamizal Federal Park

It is rare to find a statue of an American president in a foreign country. President Lincoln and President Juarez of Mexico were of the same era. This statue commemorates the common bonds between those two great men and the two countries.

McKELLIGON CANYON PARK

McKelligon Rd. off Alabama •565-6900 • Free • W

A park in the heart of the Franklin Mountains that offers facilities for picnicking or hiking on the three-mile Senda Mañana trail. The cliff-enclosed amphitheater here is the summer home of the musical *Viva! El Paso* (*see* Performing Arts).

PLAZA MONUMENTAL DE TOROS
Juarez, Av. 16 de Septiembre near Boulevard Lopez Mateos and the Pan American Hwy.

There is a statue of bulls on the outside and professional bullfights inside. The season usually runs on Sundays from about Easter to Labor Day, but the scheduling is erratic and the matadors are rarely well known. The easiest way to attend a bullfight is by going with one of the tour bus companies (*see* Tourist Services).

SIERRA DEL CRISTO REY
Take Sunland Park exit off IH-10 to Doniphan

On a 4,576-foot summit in New Mexico, near where that state comes up against Texas and old Mexico, stands a 27-foot-high figure of Christ on the Cross that looks out over El Paso. The statue was carved in 1940 from Cordova cream limestone quarried near Austin and is a replica of the one that overlooks Río de Janeiro, Brazil. On the Feast of Christ the King, the last Sunday in October, thousands of pilgrims make the long climb up the two-and-a-half-mile switchback foot trail to the top. Other visits should be made only in very large numbers. **Local authorities warn that gangs and thieves prey on individuals or small groups in this relatively inaccessible area.**

TIGUA INDIAN RESERVATION
119 S. Old Pueblo Rd. off Alemeda, about 14 miles east • 859-3916
Daily 8–5 • Free (donations) • W+

The Tigua Indians operate what they call a living history pueblo on the only Texas Indian reservation located within a major city. The Tiguas were one of the Pueblo tribes that came here with the Spanish settlers fleeing the Pueblo uprising in New Mexico in 1681. As such, they are the state's oldest identifiable ethnic group. Although many people thought the Tiguas had disappeared by the 1950s, they had maintained their tribal government in secret and had preserved traditional dances and customs. In the late 1960s the Tiguas were "discovered" and officially recognized as a tribe both by the state and national governments. Now there are more than 600 Tiguas connected with the small, 37-acre reservation. Some spend their days showing visitors what daily life was like in the old pueblo with demonstrations that include dances (summer weekends, call for times and admission), weaving, jewelry and pottery-making, and baking Indian bread in igloo-shaped adobe ovens. The reservation includes an arts and crafts center, where jewelry, pottery, and souvenirs are for sale; the Ysleta del Sur Mission (*see* Historic Places), a museum (*see* Museums), and one restaurant (*see* Restaurants). Since 1993, the Tiguas have also operated Speaking Rock Casino. Located on the mission grounds, it offers slots, card games, and bingo.

TRANSMOUNTAIN ROAD
Loop 375 • *Take US 54 (Gateway North) north or IH-10W to intersect*

As its name implies, this road cuts across the Franklin Mountains. At its highest point it is just under a mile in altitude, which makes it one of the highest roads in the state. It is the east-west connection between US 54 on the eastern side of the mountains and IH-10 on the western side, and the views when descending are impressive on both sides. The Wilderness Park Museum is on the eastern side (*see* Museums).

SPORTS AND ACTIVITIES
Baseball
EL PASO DIABLOS
Cohen Stadium, 9700 Gateway North • 755-2000 • General admission $4 Parking $2 • W but not all areas
Minor league baseball in the Texas League.

Basketball
UNIVERSITY OF TEXAS AT EL PASO (UTEP) MINERS
Special Events Center, Mesa and Baltimore • 747-5265 • Admission • W+ but not all areas
Regular season plus the annual Sun Bowl Tournament in December. No general admission tickets are sold. The Lady Miners team usually plays here.

Bullfighting
PLAZA MONUMENTAL DE TOROS
Juarez, Av. 16 de Septiembre near Río Grande Mall • 011-52-16-131656 $5–$18 • W but not all areas
As a major city, Juarez is on the major professional bullfighting circuit, but the scheduling tends to be erratic. Fights are usually held early on Sunday evenings between Easter and Labor Day. Another, smaller arena is the Plaza de Toros Balderas at Francisco Villa and Abraham Gonzalez. This one is for amateurs. For information on when the fights are held, check with the tour bus companies (see Tourist Services).

Charreada (Mexican Rodeo)
CHARRO ASSOCIATION RODEOS
Juarez, Lienzo Charro Lopez Mateos Arena, on the Pan American Hwy. at Av. del Charro • Sundays 4:30 • $5
The Charros, Mexico's urban cowboys wearing the striking costumes of the 1800s, perform feats of horsemanship most Sunday afternoons. Occasionally, admission-free *charreadas* are also held at the Chamizal National Memorial, S. San Marcial and Delta (532-7273).

Football
UNIVERSITY OF TEXAS AT EL PASO (UTEP) MINERS
Sun Bowl Stadium, Sun Bowl Dr., UTEP • 747-5234 • W+ but not all areas
No general admission tickets are sold. The UTEP Miners play a regular season against such opponents as the New Mexico State Aggies and the Rice Owls. The Northwest Sun Bowl is played here every December.

Golf
ASCARATE GOLF COURSE
Ascarate Park 600 Delta Dr. • 772-7381. County course. 18 main holes, 9 executive holes. Green fees: Weekdays $10, weekends $13 for 18 holes, $10 for nine.

CIELO VISTA MUNICIPAL GOLF COURSE
1510 Hawkins • 591-4927. City course. 18 holes. Green fees: Weekdays $14.07, weekends $17.86

CAMPESTRE GOLF COURSE, JUAREZ COUNTRY CLUB
Juarez, Av. Senecu. 011-52-16-173439. 18 holes. Green fees: Weekdays $20, weekends $30

PAINTED DUNES
12000 McCombs Rd. and Hwy 54. 821-2122. 18 holes. Green fees: Weekdays $19, weekends $23

Horse Racing

SUNLAND PARK RACETRACK
Sunland Park Dr. exit off IH-10W about 5 miles west of downtown
505-589-1131 • Admission • Pay parking • W+ but not all areas

This track, just across the state border in New Mexico, offers thoroughbred and quarter horse racing Friday, Saturday, and Sunday at 1 from October through May. Televised races from Ruidoso Downs May through September and from Albuquerque State Fair during September.

COLLEGES AND UNIVERSITIES

EL PASO COMMUNITY COLLEGE
919 Hunter • 775-2000 or 594-2126 (Public Relations) • W+ but not all areas

The 20,000 students attending three campuses take classes in both occupational and continuing education and academic programs. Visitors are welcome at cultural programs, theater and music performances, art shows, and the guest speaker program.

UNIVERSITY OF TEXAS AT EL PASO (UTEP)
Take Shuster Ave./UTEP exit off IH-10W • 747-5000 • W+ but not all areas
Get visitor parking permit from guard post at main entrance on University just off Sun Bowl Dr.

What started out in 1913 as the State School of Mines and Metallurgy is now a full-blown university with six colleges and a graduate school. There is no longer a mining department, but a doctorate can be earned in geological sciences. Enrollment is over 14,000.

One of the most striking things about the campus is the architecture. The style is derived from that of the lamaseries of the Himalayan kingdom of Bhutan near Tibet and is said to be the only example of this ancient architecture to be found in the Western Hemisphere. Characteristics include gently sloping outer walls, overhanging hipped roofs, and brick-and-tile trim between deeply indented upper windows. The inspiration for this unique architectural theme came from the wife of the first dean of the school who saw photographs of Bhutan in a 1914 issue of *National Geographic*.

In addition to sporting events (*see* Sports and Activities), visitors are welcome to theater performances, musical programs, ballet, and opera offered year round by the Theatre Arts Department (747-5146) and the Music Department (747-5606) (*see* Performing Arts). Many of these are free. Art exhibits are scheduled by the Department of Art in the Fox Fine Arts Center (747-5181) and the Union Gallery (747-5481). The library also has permanent exhibits of works by Jose Cisneros and Tom Lea. The Centennial Museum is on campus (*see* Museums).

PERFORMING ARTS

CHAMIZAL NATIONAL MEMORIAL PARK THEATER

S. San Marcial and Delta • 534-6668 • W+ (electric carts available)

Variety is really the spice of life in this 500-seat theater. The theater's objective is to provide diverse and alternative entertainment, which means everything from big Broadway musicals to Indian dancers, opera, and Spanish language plays. About 35% of the more than 150 productions in the average year are either bilingual or in Spanish. Many of the programs are free or have low admissions. During the summer, from June 1st to September 1st, the *Music Under the Stars* program is held on the grounds each Sunday evening at 8. It's free, but bring your own seating.

EL PASO CONVENTION AND PERFORMING ARTS CENTER

Santa Fe and San Francisco, 1 Civic Center Plaza • 534-0609 or 800-351-6024 • W+ but not all areas

The theater in this modernistic complex seats more than 2,500 and plays host to the El Paso Symphony, the ballet, and dozens of touring stage and musical events each year. Next door is the Grand Hall, which seats up to 6,000. It is the frequent site of trade shows and popular music concerts.

EL PASO PLAYHOUSE

2501 Montana • 532-1317 • Admission • W but not all areas

The performers here are a community theater group that puts on mostly contemporary plays with the emphasis on comedies. Performances are Friday and Saturday evenings and Sunday matinee. Reservations required.

EL PASO SYMPHONY ORCHESTRA

Convention and Performing Arts Center, Santa Fe and San Francisco (Office with Chamber of Commerce) • 532-8707 • Admission • W+

The 80-musician orchestra, which is now more than 50 years old, normally plays an eight concert season, from September through April, in the Performing Arts Center Theater or Grand Hall. It also puts on Young People's Concerts throughout the year and a summer concert series. Tickets range from $6–$23, reservations required.

EL PASO PRO MUSICA

6557 N. Mesa • 833-4400 • Admission

A chamber orchestra and choir that holds a series of concerts from October through April. They perform all over town, mostly in churches. There is also a children's choir that performs with the *Pro Musica* at Christmas.

UTEP THEATERS

University of Texas at El Paso, *take Schuster Ave./UTEP exit off IH-10W* 747-5146 • Admission • W to W+ depending on theater

All three theaters on the UTEP campus welcome visitors. The University Playhouse and the Studio Theater are both in the Fox Fine Arts Center (747-

5118) on Sun Bowl Dr., and the Union Dinner Theater is in the Student Union building (747-5481).

VIVA! EL PASO

McKelligon Canyon Amphitheatre, McKelligon Canyon off Alabama
565-6900 • Admission $7–$14 • W call ahead

This lavish outdoor summer production celebrates the 400-year history of the border area with song, dance, and drama. Discounts available for students, seniors, military, and groups. Performances are at 8:30 P.M. Wednesday through Saturday evenings during June and August. Barbecue dinner available.

SHOPPING

El Paso

FACTORY OUTLETS AND DISCOUNT STORES

Because boots and Western wear are the output of several factories in town, it's natural for many factory outlet stores to specialize in these items. The following list is just a sampling of these stores in El Paso. For a full list, check the Yellow Pages.

Cowtown Boot Co. Factory Outlet, 11401 Gateway West, 593-2929
El Paso Saddleblanket Co. Warehouse Outlet, 601 N. Oregon, 544-1000
Farah Manufacturing Outlet, 8889 Gateway West, 593-4444
Justin Boot Store, I-10 at Hawkins, 779-5465
Tony Lama Factory Store, 7156 Gateway East, 772-4327

Juárez

Juárez, as the fourth largest city in Mexico, is larger in size and population than its sister city, El Paso. As in most border towns, the shops that cater to English-speaking tourists are clustered along the streets leading from the bridges that span the border. In this case those streets are Avenida Juárez leading from the Santa Fe bridge, and Avenida Lincoln at the Cordova crossing near the Chamizal. There are also a number of interesting shops along the long Avenida 16 Septiembre, which runs between and connects the two, but they are not as tightly clustered as those on the two primary shopping streets. Border towns are hagglers' paradises, and Juárez is no exception, although several of the better shops now have fixed prices. However, you won't get a discount unless you ask.

JUÁREZ TOUR

EL PASO-JUÁREZ TROLLEY CO.

1 Civic Center Plaza • 544-0061 or 800-259-6284 • Daily on hourly circuit
Adults $11, children 4 to 12 $8.50

Certain less tiresome than a walking tour, the trolley tour crosses the Río Grande into Juárez and will appease almost every rider with its selection of varied sites. Reasons to take the trolley rather than your own vehicle include no insurance hassles, no parking problems, and, most of all, no delay at the bridge coming back across (getting over is easy). Head to the El Paso-Juárez Trolley Company office at the Convention Center or if you're staying at one

CIUDAD JUÁREZ

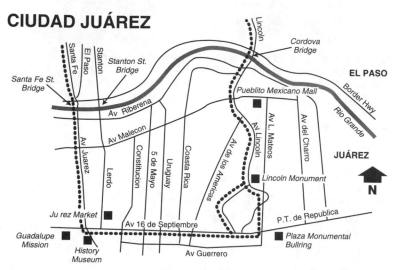

•••••• El Paso-Juárez Trolley tour route.

of the following hotels, call in advance for a complimentary shuttle: the Airport Hilton, Embassy Suites, Holiday Inn Sunland Park, Howard Johnson, and the Quality Inn.

KIDS' STUFF

EL PASO ZOO

(*See* Other Points of Interest)

INSIGHTS—EL PASO SCIENCE CENTER

505 N. Santa Fe • 542-2990 • Tuesday–Saturday 9–5, Sunday 12–5 Admission • W

This science museum, across from City Hall, is a joy for those who want to touch and do. There are about 80 hands-on exhibits that draw children (and most adults) into the "magic" of science. Among the favorites is one in which the child appears to defy gravity.

WESTERN PLAYLAND

Ascarate Park, Delta and Alemeda • 772-3914 • General admission $2 + $1.75/ ride or $15 for all rides • Call for seasonal hours • W but not all areas or rides

A 25-acre amusement park beside the lake in Ascarate Park with about 50 rides and attractions. Among the more popular rides are the roller coaster and the miniature train that circles the park.

WET 'N WILD

Anthony, IH-10W at exit 0 • 886-2222 • Adults $16, children 4–12 $14, under 4 free. Observers $11

Water amusement park with a volcanic garden theme.

SIDE TRIPS

HUECO TANKS STATE HISTORICAL PARK

Take US Hwy 62/180 (Montana St.) 24 miles east to Ranch Rd. 2775, then north *Approximately 32 miles from El Paso* • **1-857-1135** • **Daily for day use and camping** • **$2 per person per day** • **W but not all areas**

"Hueco" (pronounced way-co) is the Spanish word referring to the hollowed-out rock basins that trapped water so precious to ancient desert travelers. Archaeologists believe that humans visited this water hole as early as 10,000 years ago. Many of them, including the Apaches, left thousands of paintings on the rocks. It is estimated that there are at least 2,000 pictographs—or paintings—scattered about in the 860-acre park. (Unfortunately, modern visitors have also left their mark in the form of spray-painted graffiti.) In addition to the natural tanks and other interesting cave and rock formations and ruins of a stagecoach station, this oasis also has picnic sites, campsites (fee), and a playground. Guided tours of the rock art are available in summer and there are self-guided tour maps for the off-season.

INDIAN CLIFFS RANCH

Take IH-10 east approximately 30 miles to Fabens exit, then north about 5 *miles on FM 793* • **544-3200** • **W but not all areas**

This combination of the New and the Old West is a good place for a brief getaway from city life. There are trail rides and horsedrawn hayrides and wagon trains at the ranch's replica of a frontier fort, called Fort Misery. There is also a small zoo, a playground, and the Cattleman's Steak House (*see* Restaurants) that ranks among the best in or out of the city. Call for prices on rides.

ANNUAL EVENTS

February

SOUTHWESTERN INTERNATIONAL LIVESTOCK SHOW AND RODEO

El Paso County Coliseum, 4200 E. Paisano at Boone • **532-1401** • **First full week in February** • **$5–$12** • **W but not all areas**

About 1,500 exhibitors from seven states show off close to 3,000 animals as they vie for prizes, and 600–700 cowboys and cowgirls compete in one of the top-purse PRCA rodeos in the country. For entertainment there are big name C&W stars and rodeo specialty acts.

March

SIGLO DE ORO DRAMA FESTIVAL

Chamizal National Memorial Theater, S. San Marcial and Delta • **532-7273, Ext. 102** • **Usually first two weeks in March** • **Free** • **W+**

The *Siglo de Oro* is the name given to the period from the late sixteenth through the mid-eighteenth centuries, which is the Hispanic golden age of the arts. In the schools throughout the Spanish-speaking world the works of the master playwrights of that time, such as Miguel de Cervantes and Lope de Vega, are taught much as Shakespeare is taught in English-speaking schools. This international cultural festival celebrates that age with performances in Spanish of the masterpieces of classic Hispanic drama presented by theater groups from such diverse places as Spain, Mexico, Latin and South America, Puerto Rico, New Mexico, New York, and El Paso.

April

JUAN DE OÑATE FIRST THANKSGIVING REENACTMENT

Chamizal National Memorial • S. San Marcial and Delta • 532-7273 Ext. 102
Last Sunday in April • Free • W+

In 1598 Oñate's band of exhausted settlers bound for New Mexico reached the Río Grande after crossing the desert of northern Mexico. They held a feast of Thanksgiving, which El Pasoans proudly claim as the first in the New World. Costumed actors reenact the event.

July–August

INTERNATIONAL FESTIVAL DE LA ZARZUELA

Chamizal National Memorial • S. San Marcial and Delta • 532-7273 Ext. 102
Last weekend in July and first two weekends in August • Adults $4.50,
children, seniors, handicapped and military $3.50 • W+ but not all areas
(electric carts available)

The *Zarzuela* is a Spanish operetta, and this festival provides an outstanding feast of the genre. Top companies from Latin America perform.

September

DIEZ Y SEIS DE SEPTIEMBRE CELEBRATION

Juarez, Av. 16 de Septiembre, and Chamizal National Memorial in El Paso
532-7273 Ext. 102 • Free • National Memorial W+ but not all areas (electric
carts available)

Most of the events are in Juarez starting late on the evening of September 15. But at the Chamizal on the U.S. side on the 15th the festivities include a *charreada* or Mexican rodeo at 3 P.M. At 6 P.M. the *Grito* or "shout" that began the Revolution is delivered by the Consulate General of Mexico in El Paso, followed by music and dancing. The big parade and other festivities marking the anniversary of Mexico's independence from Spain are in Juarez on the 16th. Bring your own seating to outdoor programs.

October

AMIGO AIRSHOW

Biggs Army Airfield (Fort Bliss) • 545-2864 • Two days early in October
Adults $10, children $6 • W but not all areas

Promoted as the "Circus in the Sky," this airshow normally features professional and military precision flying teams, aerobatic acts, parachute jumping, and static aircraft displays and demonstrations.

BORDER FOLK FESTIVAL

Chamizal National Memorial, S. San Marcial and Delta • 532-7273 Ext. 102
Three-day weekend early in October • Free • W+ but not all areas (electric
carts available)

A weekend of traditional folk music, dancing, and crafts from the U.S. and Mexico to celebrate the peaceful settlement of the Río Grande border dispute between the two countries. Some performances are given in the theater, but most are on several open-air stages on the grounds. Bring your own seating to outdoor programs. There is usually a Mexican *charreada* (rodeo) one afternoon.

KERMEZAAR

Grand Hall, El Paso Convention and Performing Arts Center, Santa Fe and San Francisco • 532-1162 • Three days in mid-October • Adults: $4, children $1, under 6 free • W+ • Parking downtown or in Center's underground garage
   A major arts-and-crafts show with participants from all over the Southwest. The emphasis is on paintings, but there is also sculpture, graphics, ceramics, textiles, photography, and jewelry.

November–January

NORTHWEST SUN BOWL FESTIVITIES

All over the city • 533-4416 or 800-351-6024 (Convention and Visitors Bureau) Admission • W variable
   Almost everything that goes on in El Paso from before Thanksgiving until well after Christmas is somehow connected to this major festival. The highlights are the Sun Bowl Parade (which is the city's biggest parade and normally held on Thanksgiving Day), the Northwest Sun Bowl Football Classic and Basketball Classic, and the Coronation and Ball. There are also a number of other sports tournaments and talent shows and the like to round out the activities.

RESTAURANTS

($ = under $7, $$ = $8–$17, $$$ = $18–$25, $$$$ = over $25 for one person excluding drinks, tax, and tip.)

   El Paso and Juárez call themselves jointly the Mexican Food Capital of the World. But there's a lot more to dining in these two cities than just this spicy cuisine. Up until a few years ago the local wisdom was to go to Juárez for oriental food and seafood; El Paso for barbecue, Italian, and steaks; and both sides of the border for Mexican. In general, this may still be true, but it is no longer such a rigid rule. With the opening of several new restaurants, the choice is now wide for all types of cuisine on both sides of the Río Grande. Use the 011 phone numbers to call from El Paso to a Juárez restaurant. The following is just a sampling of the many good restaurants in the twin cities.

DOME GRILL

Westin Paso del Norte Hotel, 101 S. El Paso • 534-3010 • Lunch and dinner Monday–Saturday • $$–$$$$ • Cr • W+
   You'll find all the standard hearty dishes here—prime rib, steaks, and roast turkey, for example—but you'll also find *nouvelle cuisine* that lives up to its advance billing. A place to go for variety and refined dining. Bar.

American

IRON TENDER

1270 Giles, just south of McRae exit off IH-10 • 592-4186 • Lunch Monday–Friday, dinner daily • $–$$$ • Cr • W
   The name refers to the cowboy who tended the branding iron, so the decor is ranch and the main offering is steak. Each entrée includes the house's steak soup, a soup almost as thick as gravy with pieces of steak in it. However, this is

not just a steakhouse since there are also several chicken and seafood entrées on the menu. Lounge with live entertainment on weekends.

Barbecue

BILL PARKS BAR-B-Q

3130 Gateway East between Piedras and Copia • 542-0960 • Lunch and dinner Tuesday–Saturday. Closed Sunday–Monday • $ • MC, V • W

As in any Texas city, there are more barbecue places than you can shake a stick at, but this one has kept its loyal patrons and remains a local favorite. The decor is typical barbecue-joint, with chrome dinette chairs and beer signs. And the meat is the usual ribs, brisket, and links. But what sets it apart are the southern style vegetables that fill out the plate, like black-eyed peas, fried okra, and greens. There's also sweet potato pie. Beer and wine.

STATE LINE

1222 Sunland Park Dr. just past Doniphan • 581-3371 • Lunch and dinner daily • $–$$$ • AE, DIS, MC, V • W+

The atmosphere is from the '40s and if your group orders the family-style barbecue platter you may think the prices are too, because you get a lot for your money. In addition to the full-line of barbecue choices there's also homemade bread and homemade ice cream. Patio. Bar.

German

GUNTHER'S EDELWEISS

11055 Gateway West near Lomaland exit off IH-10 • 592-1084 • Lunch and dinner Tuesday–Sunday. Closed Monday • $$ • Cr • W • Children's and seniors' plates

There's a mountain scene on the wall behind the oompah band, cuckoo clocks, stags' heads, a variety of *schnitzels* and other German dishes, and enough beer and wine (both German and domestic) to give this the flavor of a Bavarian inn. The hearty entrées include a salad plate with a sampling of several German-style salads such as potato and pickled red cabbage. And the German bread is a temptation all by itself. Bar.

Italian

ARDOVINO'S

206 Cincinnati Avenue • 532-9483 • Lunch and dinner Monday–Saturday. Closed Sunday. Reservations for large groups only • $–$$ • AE, MC, V • W

An El Paso tradition since 1960, Ardovino's is ranked as one of the best 100 independent pizzerias nationwide and serves tried-and-true favorites, such as pepperoni and salami, as well as pizzas garnished with capers, smoked salmon and fennel, and ricotta. In addition to thin crust pizza, Ardovino's other specialties include minestrone soup, an excellent antipasto salad, a cold cut plate, and a wide selection of sandwiches during the day. As with any self-respecting Italian cucina, tiramisu, spumone, cappuccino, and espresso are menu mainstays. Everything can be prepared to go, and picnic baskets are a specialty. Beer and wine.

BELLA NAPOLI

6331 N. Mesa near Leon • 584-3321 • Lunch and dinner Wednesday–Sunday. Closed Monday–Tuesday • $–$$ • AE, MC, V • W

Typical old-fashioned Italian restaurant with checkered tablecloths, candles in the wine bottle, cheese and crushed red pepper shakers on the tables, and Neapolitan dishes on the menu. A local favorite is chicken Jerusalem. Half orders available for children. Bar.

ITALIAN KITCHEN

2923 Pershing • 565-4041 • Lunch and dinner Monday–Saturday. Closed Sunday • $–$$ • AE, MC, V

They don't lavish much on atmosphere here, but they sure put their attention on the kitchen. The veal scallopini is just one good example of what that kitchen can produce, and the pasta dishes just add to its reputation. Beer and wine.

Mexican

FORTI'S MEXICAN ELDER

321 Chelsea at Paisano exit off IH-10 • 772-0066 • $–$$ • Lunch and dinner daily • Cr • W • Children's plates

The local favorites, among the many choices on the menu here, are the *carnitas, fajitas,* and the *tacos al carbon.* The restaurant name doesn't refer to an elder member of the family but to the name of a tree.

JULIO'S CAFE CORONA

Juárez, 16 de Septiembre & Av. de las Americas • 011-52-16-133397 Lunch and dinner daily • $–$$ • MC, V • W • Children's plates

This has been touted as the best Mexican food in town. Even those who strongly disagree with that rating will still usually concede that it is consistently among the best. (They also concede that, at times, the service can be the slowest on either side of the border.) Specialties include *Boquillas,* black bass a la Vera Cruz, and *Tlalpeno,* a spicy chicken soup with avocados. Some devotees of Mexican cuisine argue that Julio's on the American side (8050 Gateway East, 591-7676) features better food than the Juárez edition. Bar.

LA HACIENDA CAFE

1720 W. Paisano beneath the Yandell overpass • 532-5094 • Lunch and dinner Tuesday–Sunday. Monday 11–4• $ • Cr • W

Set on the banks of the Río Grande, this adobe building is all that remains of a water-powered gristmill constructed by Simeon Hart in 1849. The building was the residence he built in 1854. Among the favorites here are the steak *tampiqueña* and the huge combination plate. The *chiles rellenos* are different, but delicious. Bar.

WYNGS 'N SPIRITS

Tigua Indian Reservation, 122 S. Old Pueblo Rd. • 859-3916 • Lunch and dinner daily • $–$$ • W+ but not all areas

The food here is a Tigua version of Mexican cuisine, which means enchiladas and flautas, but also chile verde con carne, a savory beef stew full of green chiles and jalapeños. There is also freshly baked bread from the reservation's adobe ovens. Bar. For a late breakfast and lunch there is also the older restaurant on the reservation that is open daily. It emphasizes the Tigua-Mexican meals, but also has hamburgers and French fries.

New Mexican

GRIGGS GOURMET NEW MEXICAN FOOD

9007 Montana • 598-3451 • Lunch and dinner daily • $–$$ • MC, V • W+
Children's plates

The recipes here, which were passed down through the Griggs' family for more than a hundred years, are basically Mexican dishes without the fire. Not that they are bland, just that they do not use mouth-searing peppers. Another location at 701 S. Mesa Hills (584-0451). Bar.

Oriental

MANDARIN GARDEN

6404 N. Mesa • 581-8199 • Lunch and dinner daily • $–$$ • AE, DIS, MC, V • W

The menu here includes Mandarin entrées, but the emphasis is on Szechuan cooking, which means many of the dishes are hot. These are clearly marked, however, and there are enough choices among the milder entrées to satisfy most tastes. Beer and wine.

ASIA PALACE

9099 Gateway West near Hunter • 590-2220 • Lunch and dinner daily • $–$$$
AE, MC, V • W

The atmosphere here is heightened by the Chinese decor of keyhole doors, black lacquered furniture, and red and gilt trim everywhere. The cuisine is Cantonese and the menu offers a profusion of choices.

SHANGRI-LA

Juarez, 133 Av. de las Americas • 011-52-16-133978 or 130033 • Lunch and dinner daily • $–$$ • Cr • W

Shangri-La has lived up to its reputation as one of the best Chinese restaurants on either side of the border for more than 30 years. Allow yourself a lot of time to look over the huge menu here that lists dozens of offerings of mostly Cantonese dishes. Bar.

UNCLE BAO'S

9515 Gateway West in Sunray East Shopping Center • 592-1101
Lunch and dinner daily • $–$$ • Cr • W+

Who can resist a menu that includes such imaginative dishes as "The Dragon Teasing the Phoenix" (spicy chicken and lobster) or "Lover's Shrimp"? The extensive menu even includes lamb entrées. About half the entrées are spicy hot.

Seafood

MARTINO'S

Juarez, 412 Av. Juarez • 011-52-16-123370 • Lunch and dinner daily
$$ • No Cr • W

This is another Juárez restaurant that has been around for years and has built a well-deserved reputation. The lengthy menu features continental cuisine with a seafood section that is longer than the entire menu in most seafood restaurants. Stuffed black bass is a local favorite. Bar.

Steaks

BILLY CREW'S DINING ROOM

1200 Country Club Rd. (Santa Theresa, New Mexico) • 505-589-2071
Lunch and dinner daily • Reservations for large parties suggested
$$$–$$$$ • Cr • W+
Custom-cut steaks are the attraction here. You pick out your favorite type steak, have it cut to your order, and tell them how to grill it. And if your eyes are bigger than your stomach, you can always get a doggy bag and enjoy the leftovers the next day. Also seafood, chicken, and a wine list with more than 400 wines of the world. Bar.

CATTLEMAN'S STEAKHOUSE

Fabens, Indian Cliff Ranch • *Take IH-10 east about 30 miles to Fabens exit,* *then north on FM 793 to ranch* • 544-3200 or 1-764-2283 • Dinner daily. Lunch Sunday • Reservations for groups of 15 or more only • $$–$$$ • Cr • W+
The decor is Old West, with leather tack and saddles and other ranch paraphernalia. Worth the drive since the desert ranch setting is the star here, with even the big steaks taking second place to the sunset view. As to the steaks, they have all types and sizes up to and including a two-pound T-bone. Get there early if you want to try for a window seat. Bar. (*see* Side Trips.)

ACCOMMODATIONS

($ = under $45, $$ = $46–$60, $$$ = $61–$80, $$$$ = $81–$100, $$$$$ = over $100)
Room tax 14%

BEST WESTERN AIRPORT INN

7144 Gateway East • 779-7700 or 800-528-1234 • $–$$$ • No-smoking rooms
The two-story Airport Inn has 176 units including 20 no-smoking rooms and 15 suites with wet bars and refrigerators ($$). Satellite TV with HBO, room phones (no charge for local calls). Guest memberships available in local health club. Small pets OK. Free airport and mall transportation. Restaurant nearby. Heated pool. Free Continental breakfast. Free coffee in lobby. Self-service laundry.

CLIFF INN

1600 Cliff Dr. *From IH-10W take East Cotton exit, north on Cotton to Arizona,* *then west to Cliff Dr.* • 533-6700 or 800-333-CLIF (800-333-2543) • $$$–$$$$ W+ 4 rooms • No-smoking rooms
The Cliff Inn has 78 units including 38 kitchenettes, four suites ($$$$), and ten no-smoking units. Cable TV with HBO. Room phones (charge for local calls). No pets. Airport shuttle service. Restaurant and lounge. Outdoor pool with Jacuzzi, lap pool, and tennis courts. Free continental breakfast. Self-service laundry.

DAYS INN

9125 Gateway West between Viscount and McRae exits off IH-10 • 593-8400 or 800-325-2525 • $–$$ • W+ 5 rooms • No-smoking rooms
The Days Inn has 114 units including one suite ($$$$$) and one wing of 40 no-smoking rooms. Satellite TV with the Movie Channel. Room phones (free

local calls). Small pets OK. Free airport transportation. Restaurants nearby. Outdoor pool and whirlpool. Free Continental breakfast.

EL PASO AIRPORT HILTON

2027 Airway at El Paso International Airport • 778-4241 or 800-HILTONS (800-284-4837) • $–$$$$$ • W+ 7 rooms • No-smoking rooms
    The four-story Airport Hilton has 272 units including 151 suites with refrigerator and wet bar, and some no-smoking units. Cable TV with Showtime. Room phones (charge for local calls). Pets OK. Free airport transportation. Restaurant and lobby bar and lounge. Fire sprinklers in rooms. Health club with sauna and Jacuzzi. Outdoor heated pool. Free newspaper. Some suites have private outdoor Jacuzzi. Executive level offers free continental breakfast, free hors d'oeuvres, business facilities, and private exercise room.

EL PASO MARRIOTT

1600 Airway at Montana at El Paso International Airport • 779-3300 or 800-228-9290 • $$$$–$$$$$ • W+ 6 rooms • No-smoking rooms
    The six-story Marriott has 296 units including 13 suites ($$$$$) and some no-smoking floors. Cable TV with HBO and pay channel. Room phones (charge for local calls). Pets OK. Free airport transportation. Two restaurants and lounge. Fire sprinklers in rooms. Indoor/outdoor heated pool, whirlpool and sauna, health spa, putting green. Concierge level with private lounge.

EL PASO TRAVELODGE-CITY CENTER

409 E. Missouri between Kansas and Campbell • 544-3333 or 800-578-7878 $–$$ • W+ 2 rooms • No-smoking rooms
    This Travelodge has 110 units including two suites ($$$–$$$$) and nine no-smoking rooms. Cable TV with HBO. Room phones (charge for local calls). No pets. Free daytime airport transportation. Restaurant and lounge. Outdoor heated pool. Coffeemakers in rooms. Same day laundry/dry cleaning. Inexpensive downtown location with view of Franklin Mountains on north side and city on south side.

EMBASSY SUITES

6100 Gateway East, off IH-10 between Geronimo and Trowbridge exits 779-6222 or 800-EMBASSY (800-362-2779) • $$$–$$$$$ • No-smoking rooms
    The 185 units in this eight-story Embassy are all suites of which 18 are no-smoking suites. Satellite TV with the Movie Channel. Room phones (charge for local calls). Pets OK with $50 deposit. Free airport limo. Indoor pool, sauna, Jacuzzi and exercise room. Complimentary breakfast and cocktail hours. Coffeemakers in rooms. Gift shop. Top-floor restaurant/lounge has bird's-eye view across border into Mexico.

HOLIDAY INN AIRPORT

6655 Gateway West at Airway • 778-6411 or 800-HOLIDAY (800-465-4329) $$–$$$ • No-smoking rooms
    The two-story Airport Holiday Inn has 203 units that includes some no-smoking rooms. Satellite TV with Showtime and pay channel. Room phones (charge for local calls). Guest memberships available for local health club. No pets. Free airport and mall transportation. Coffee shop and lounge. Outdoor pool, children's wading pool, and game room. Gift shop.

HOLIDAY INN SUNLAND PARK

900 Sunland Park Dr. and IH-10W, approximately 1 mile from Sunland Park
833-2900 or 800-HOLIDAY (800-465-4329) • $$–$$$$ • W+

This two-story Holiday Inn has 178 units including nine suites ($$$$–$$$$$). Cable TV with HBO. Room phones (charge for local calls). Free airport transportation. Coffee shop and dinner only restaurant. Lounge. Fire sprinklers in rooms. Outdoor pool, Jacuzzi, and game room. Guest memberships available in golf and tennis clubs. The rooms are clustered in nine small buildings.

PARK PLACE

325 N. Kansas at Main • 533-8241 • $$$–$$$$

The 12-story Park Place has 119 units including five suites ($$$$$). Cable TV. Room phones (charge for local calls). Pets OK. Free airport transportation. Restaurant and lounge. Outdoor pool. Free hors d'oeuvres in evening. Gift shop.

CAMINO REAL PASEO DEL NORTE

101 S. El Paso, across street from Convention and Performing Arts Center
534-3000 or 800-769-4300 • $$$–$$$$$ • W+ 14 rooms • No-smoking rooms

This 17-story hotel has 375 units including 32 suites (with prices ranging up to $950) and 30 no-smoking rooms. Executive club floor. Free garage parking. Cable TV. Room phones (charge for local calls). Small pets OK. Free airport transportation. Two restaurants, room service, lounge, and disco. Fire sprinklers in rooms. Outdoor heated pool and health club. All normal hotel amenities and services. Built in 1912, this landmark hotel has been brought up-to-date with an extensive renovation.

FORT DAVIS

Jeff Davis County Seat • 1,212 • (915)

Located in the Davis Mountains at an altitude of 5,050 feet, Fort Davis is the highest town in the state. It has also been called "The best tiny town in Texas" by *Texas Monthly* magazine.

Although located in the Chihuahuan Desert of West Texas, the Davis Mountains usually receive more than 20 inches of rain a year so they are often green and lush. They are also high enough to offer relatively cool days and nights when the rest of Texas is sweltering in the summer heat. From Fort Davis you can take a loop drive through these scenic mountains. To do this take SH 17 south to SH 166, then west to SH 118 and then southeast back to 17 and Fort Davis. Along the way on this 74-mile loop you'll see Mount Livermore (at 8,382 feet the second highest peak in the state), Mount Locke (topped by the McDonald Observatory), Madera Canyon, and several beautifully sited roadside parks with dramatic mountain backdrops.

TOURIST SERVICES

FORT DAVIS CHAMBER OF COMMERCE

#1 Town Square across from the Court House • 79734 • 426-3015 or 800-524-3015

Located in the historic Union Mercantile Building, the Fort Davis Chamber has complete information on the town and the numerous attractions in the vicinity such as the UT McDonald's Observatory, Davis Mountains State Park, and the Big Bend.

MUSEUMS

NEILL MUSEUM

Court and 7th (7 blocks west of the courthouse) • 426-3969 • Open June 1–Labor Day, Tuesday–Saturday 10–5, Sunday 1:30–5. Closed Monday After Labor Day by appointment or by chance • Admission
 Located in the Truehart house, which was built in 1898, this museum is listed in state and national registers of historic places. The five rooms open to the public feature an antique doll collection of more than 350 dolls, along with a doll house built in 1730. The home is also a bed and breakfast inn.

OVERLAND TRAIL MUSEUM

About 2 blocks south of Fort Davis National Historic Site and 2 west of SH 17/118 • 426-3904 • Open Tuesday and Friday 1–6 and Saturday 10–6 Admission
 Named for the historic trail that once passed by its door, this small museum has exhibits depicting local history.

HISTORIC PLACES

FORT DAVIS NATIONAL HISTORIC SITE

SH 17/118 at north edge of town • 426-3225 • Open daily: 8–5 in winter, 8–6 in summer. Closed Christmas • $2 person • W+ variable (electric carts available)
 The fort was established in 1854 to protect travelers who used the San Antonio-El Paso road on the southern transcontinental trail west. After Federal troops abandoned the post at the outbreak of the Civil War, Confederate troops occupied it. But inadequate numbers of troops and mounting Indian attacks forced them to abandon it also in 1862. The Indians then moved in and destroyed the buildings. The Army reactivated the post in 1867, constructing new buildings of stone and adobe. Most of the troops that served here then were black infantry and cavalry who the Indians respectfully called "Buffalo Soldiers." Until it was closed in 1891, Fort Davis played a major role in controlling the Indians and bandits on the southwestern frontier and opening up the West. The historic ruins of the fort were acquired by the National Park Service in 1963 and since then there has been a continuing effort to preserve and restore. The 460-acre site encompasses approximately 25 original structures and the foundations and ruins of dozens of others. A visitor center and museum in a restored barracks contains exhibits and a slide show of the fort's history. Five buildings are restored and refurbished to the 1880s period. A sound re-creation of an 1875 dress Retreat Parade movingly echoes over the parade ground at scheduled times with the bark of commands, the rattle of sabers and rifles, and the spine-tingling bugle calls.
 During the summer, park rangers and volunteers dressed as soldiers, officers' wives, or servants provide information and bring the fort to life. Visitors are free to roam the grounds at their own pace on a self-guided tour. There are no organized guided tours. There is a shaded picnic area at the fort and several

miles of hiking trails around it, including one leading to the Davis Mountains State Park approximately three and a half miles away. Fort Davis is an outstanding example of a southwestern frontier military post.

OTHER POINTS OF INTEREST

CHIHUAHUAN DESERT RESEARCH INSTITUTE

Approximately 3 miles south on SH 118 • Visitor Center open April 1st–September 1st, Monday–Friday 1–5, Saturday–Sunday 9–6 • 1-837-8370 (Headquarters in Alpine) • Free • W variable

The Chihuahuan Desert is a vast area that stretches from northern Mexico up through West Texas and parts of New Mexico and Arizona. This research institute's headquarters is at Sul Ross University at Alpine, promotes the understanding of this desert region through scientific research and public education. This Fort Davis location's 507 acres include an arboretum and desert garden with a collection of more than 500 species of plants from the region, including 95% of the cacti that grows in the desert. There are also about two, and, a, half miles of nature trails.

DAVIS MOUNTAINS STATE PARK

Take SH 17/118 north one mile to intersection, then take SH 118 west about three miles to Park Rd. 3 **• 426-3337 • Open daily 8–10 for day use, at all times for camping • $3 per person per day, weekends $4 per car • W+ but not all areas**

The park is located between the desert plains grasslands of lower elevations and the piñon juniper-oak woodlands of intermediate elevations in the Davis Mountains. Consequently, the plants and wildlife of the park represent both areas. There are hiking trails, an amphitheater, picnic areas, and a Skyline Drive in the park. The main facility is **Indian Lodge,** a hotel styled after the southwestern pueblos. The lodge has 39 rooms, many with walls 18 inches thick, and all with air conditioning, TV, and phone. The rooms in the original part of the building were built by the Civilian Conservation Corps (CCC) and have cedar furnishings hand-made in a CCC workshop in Bastrop. There is also a heated swimming pool and restaurant. The lodge is open all year except for two weeks in January. Double rooms cost from $55–$85 and must be paid for by MasterCard, Visa, or check. Reservations are advised (P.O. Box 786, 79734; 426-3254). Campsites are available without and with hookups from $6–$13 a night.

McDONALD OBSERVATORY

Highway 118, 17 miles north of Fort Davis • 426-3640 • UT McDonald Observatory • P.O. Box 1337, Fort Davis (79734) • Visitor's Center open daily 9–5 except Thanksgiving, Christmas, New Year's Day • Longer hours during summer for star parties

William Johnson McDonald, a prosperous Paris, Texas, banker, willed to the University of Texas over $1,000,000 in 1925 for the creation of an observatory.

Recognized around the world for its research excellence, the University of Texas has once again focused attention upon the McDonald Observatory with the announcement that UT has joined with Penn State University as principal partners in the construction of a massive new scope atop adjacent Mount Fowlkes, the William P. Hobby–Robert Eberly Telescope. Unlike more traditional optical telescopes, the Hobby-Eberly Telescope will be a *spectroscopic survey telescope* or SST. Spectroscopic astronomy measures the amount and composition of wavelengths (or colors) of light from astronomical objects.

The W. L. Moody, Jr., Visitor's Information Center, located at the base of Mount Locke, offers astronomy exhibits, films, a gift shop, and a bookstore. The Center is open year-round from 9 A.M. to 5 P.M. Observatory tours and solar viewing take place each afternoon at 2 P.M., and each morning at 9:30 A.M. in March, June, July, and August (weather permitting). Hosted Star Parties occur every Tuesday, Friday, and Saturday evenings at differing times throughout the year. Because of the seasonal variance in time of sunset, the beginning times change monthly. Call for exact times.

MARFA GHOST LIGHTS

Take SH 17 about 21 miles south to Marfa, then US 90 east about 9 miles to viewing area

There are reports of these mysterious lights as far back as the late 1800s, and they are still seen today. If you want to try your luck, after dark scan the southwestern horizon toward Chinati Peak, using a distant red tower light as a marker. Any light that appears and disappears to the right of the marker is a Marfa Ghost Light.

SHOPPING

JAVELINAS AND HOLLYHOCKS

Main Street in the Limpia West Building • 426-2236

This retail establishment defies a simple description by stocking an eclectic assortment of giftables. To wit: nature-related gifts and toys, an extensive bath section, a wide selection of books including local lore, Texana, and children's, and plenty of knickknacks for kids of all ages.

THE TOMATO BARN

Main Street at Fifth • 426-9096

Almost 50 percent of Texas' tomato crop is harvested a few miles south of Fort Davis on Highway 17. This tiny store is one of the few local outlets for this fresh produce and specializes in mail order nationwide.

SIDE TRIPS

BALMORHEA STATE PARK

Approximately 35 miles north on SH 17 • 375-2370 • Park and pool open all year • Park: weekdays $3 per day per person, weekends $4; Pool: free • W No pets, no glass

The claim is that this is the world's largest spring-fed swimming pool—1¾ acres, 25 feet deep, with a capacity of 3,500,000 gallons. The water temperature remains at 72 to 76 degrees year round. Concession stand and bathhouse. Tent and RV campsites from $7 to $12. The San Solomon Springs Courts is an 18-unit motel; double $35. Kitchen units $5 extra. Reservations advised in summer. Call 512-389-8900 for reservations.

RESTAURANTS

($ = under $7, $$ = $8–$17, $$$ = $18–$25, $$$$ = over $25 for one person excluding drinks, tax, and tip.)

HOTEL LIMPIA DINING ROOM

SH 17/118 downtown • 426-3241 • Lunch and dinner Tuesday–Sunday. Closed Monday, gift shop open daily • $$ •W • Children's menu

This restaurant stakes its reputation on fresh food served family style in generous portions. As part of their dedication to freshness, the owners maintain their own herb garden on the premises. The menu changes frequently but always includes fresh-baked biscuits and desserts. Vegetarian entrées available. Private club with $3 temporary membership good for three days for group of four. Reservations recommended on weekends.

ACCOMMODATIONS

($ = under $45, $$ = $46–$60, $$$ = $61–$80, $$$$ = $81–$100, $$$$$ = over $100)

Room tax 13%

HOTEL LIMPIA

Town Square (P.O. Box 822, 79734) • 426-3237, 800-662-5517 • $$–$$$ No smoking in rooms

This historic two-story hotel has 36 units in five historic buildings including two suites ($$–$$$$), and a cottage on four acres a short distance away at the foot of Sleeping Lion Mountain. Cable TV with HBO. No room phones. Pets OK ($5 deposit). Restaurant. Free coffee in morning. Sprawling porches and verandas plentifully supplied with rocking chairs make this a porch-sitter's paradise.

THE VERANDA COUNTRY INN BED AND BREAKFAST

210 Court Avenue • 426-2233 or 888-383-2847 • $$–$$$$$ • No smoking

The Veranda is a spacious historic inn built in 1883 and surrounded by walled gardens and courtyards. Located a single block west of the Jeff Davis County Court House, it has eight rooms and a separate carriage house. A full breakfast is included with each night's stay.

WAYSIDE INN BED AND BREAKFAST

Four blocks west of Main Street (turn at Stone Village Grocery) 426-3535 or 800-582-7510 • $$–$$$$$

This country house (1941) has five bedrooms ($$) downstairs, each with private bath, and two larger bedrooms upstairs that share a bathroom and can be rented as a suite ($$$$$). Antique and contemporary quilts, furnishings old and new, and Anna Beth and Jay Ward's full country breakfast can be found inside. The private side entrance is for guests returning from star parties, the Marfa Lights, or a day on the river.

INDIAN LODGE

(*See* Davis Mountains State Park.)

FORT STOCKTON

Pecos County Seat • 8,524 • (915)

The large springs in the area, later called Comanche Springs, were a stopping place for Indians long before the white man arrived. In 1859, a cavalry post was established near the springs at the crossing of the San Antonio-El Paso Trail and the Comanche War Trail to protect travelers. As the area became settled, the post outlived its usefulness and was closed in 1886. But by then the railroad had come, and the town of Fort Stockton was well established.

The drought of the 1950s brought an end to the historic springs. For seven years the average rainfall was under four inches and the springs dried up.

Today Fort Stockton is a center for the natural gas and oil industry, ranching, and irrigated farming. A new venture in the area is the Domaine Cordier Vineyard, which produces the award-winning St. Genevieve wines. Located about 30 miles east on IH-10, the vineyard is owned by the University of Texas and is on land that studies show is comparable to that in the Napa Valley of California. There are about 1,000 acres under cultivation now.

TOURIST SERVICES

FORT STOCKTON CHAMBER OF COMMERCE

222 W. Dickinson Blvd. (US 290 at US 385) • (Drawer C, 79735)
336-2264 or 800-336-2166 • W

Tours of the Domaine Cordier Winery leave the chamber office at 10 A.M. on Wednesday–Saturdays; $8 per person. Reservations recommended.

MUSEUMS

ANNIE RIGGS MEMORIAL MUSEUM

301 S. Main (FM 1053) across from the Courthouse • 336-2167
September–May: Monday–Saturday; June–August: Monday–Saturday 9–8,
Sunday 1:30–8 • Adults $1, children, 6–12, 50¢ • W

This adobe block building was a hotel managed by Annie Riggs from its opening soon after the turn of the century until her death in 1931. The 14 rooms now house a varied collection that ranges from a 22,000-year-old Mammoth tusk, found about eight miles from the museum, to a "Lazy Man's Butter Churn," which used the jostling of a wagon to churn the butter. Among the other items of local history on display are a safe with a hidden keyhole, a model of the old fort, and the desk at which a famed local sheriff was sitting when he was assassinated.

HISTORIC PLACES

OLD FORT STOCKTON

Bounded by Water St., Fifth St., and Spring Dr. • Museum open Monday–
Saturday 10–1, 2–5 •Free • W

Three of the original seven buildings in Officers' Row are still standing, as is the Guardhouse, which bears the date 1867 on the cornerstone.

OTHER HISTORIC PLACES

A self-guided historic tour map is available from the Chamber of Commerce and there are special signs on the city streets giving directions to historic places.

Grey Mule Saloon, 200 block of S. Main., was built and operated by the infamous Sheriff A. J. Royal in the 1880s. Royal ruled with such terror that, in 1894, six leading citizens drew lots to choose his assassin. Now a private business. **Old County Jail,** 400 block of S. Main, was built in 1884. **St. Joseph's Church,** 400 block of S. Main, was the first church in Fort Stockton, built in 1875. **St. Stephen's Church,** Spring Dr., was built in Pecos in 1872 and moved to Fort Stockton in the 1950s. **Zero Stone,** County Courthouse lawn, was placed here in 1859. This stone was the zero reference point for surveyors running lines over much of West Texas.

OTHER POINTS OF INTEREST

PAISANO PETE STATUE

Main St. just south of US 290

The world's largest roadrunner, the symbol of Fort Stockton, is 10 feet tall and 22 feet long.

SPORTS AND ACTIVITIES

Golf

PECOS COUNTY GOLF COURSE

US 285N across from Civic Center • 336-2050 • 18-hole course. Green fees: Weekdays $10, weekends $15.

ANNUAL EVENTS

July

WATER CARNIVAL

Comanche Springs Pool in Rooney Park off Spring Dr. • 336-2264 (Chamber of Commerce) • Thursday–Saturday evenings of third weekend in July Admission • W

Water may be scarce in West Texas, but Fort Stockton leads the way in showing how to make the most of what's available with this annual show the town has been putting on since 1936. The show is built around a different theme each year and features synchronized swimming, dancing, and musical numbers staged in and around the olympic-sized pool. As many as 300 local citizens of all ages make up the cast.

RESTAURANTS

($ = under $7, $$ = $8–$17, $$$ = $18–$25, $$$$ = over $25 for one person excluding drinks, tax, and tip.)

SARAH'S

106 S. Nelson near W. Division • 336-7700 • Lunch and dinner Monday–Saturday • $–$$ • AE, MC, V • W but not all areas • Children's plate

This Mexican restaurant is now the oldest restaurant in Fort Stockton owned and operated by the same family in the same location. If you like a sampling of several dishes, try "Sarah's Café Special." Beer and wine.

ACCOMMODATIONS

($ = under $45, $$ = $46–$60, $$$ = $61–$80, $$$$ = $81–$100, $$$$$ = over $100)
Room tax 13%

BEST WESTERN SUNDAY HOUSE

3200 W. Dickinson (US 290W) • 336-8521 • $–$$ • No-smoking rooms

The two-story Sunday House has 111 rooms including some no-smoking. Satellite TV with HBO. Room phones (no charge for local calls). Small pets OK. Restaurant. Private club (guests automatically members, non-guest temporary membership $4). Outdoor pool. Free coffee in lobby. Steambaths and Jacuzzis in some rooms.

COMFORT INN

2601 IH-10W (US 285) • 336-9781 or 800-592-4515 • $ • No-smoking rooms

This two-story inn right on the highway has 97 rooms including 30 no-smoking, and one suite ($$$). Cable TV with HBO. Room phones (no charge for local calls) Outdoor pool. Free continental breakfast.

ECONO LODGE OF FORT STOCKTON

800 E. Dickinson Blvd. • 336-9711 • $–$$ • No-smoking rooms

Located on Fort Stockton's main street, the two-story Econo Lodge has 87 units including some no-smoking, and two suites ($$$). Satellite TV with HBO, Room phones (no charge for local calls). Two outdoor pools. Restaurant. Free hot breakfast.

GUADALUPE MOUNTAINS NATIONAL PARK

Culberson and Hudspeth Counties • Mountain Time • (915)

Unlike many national parks, Guadalupe Mountains has almost no appreciable development either in its vicinity or within the park itself. Come prepared. Enormous salt flats and rugged mountain ranges surround this already desolate area. The nearest gas station is 35 miles north across the New Mexico state line near Carlsbad Caverns National Park. Conveniences such as service stations and restaurants are even more distant in Texas: 75 miles south in Van Horn and 110 miles west in El Paso. Commercial air service and rental cars are available in Carlsbad, New Mexico (55 miles), El Paso (110 miles), and Midland-Odessa (170 miles). The nearest air strip is 34 miles north at White's City (800-228-3767). Improved but not paved, it's seven-tenths of a mile long.

Most of the park's limited development borders Highway 62-180 along the park's eastern edge. The Pine Springs Visitor Center, the nearby Pine Springs Campground, and the Ranger Station at McKittrick Canyon are all accessible via paved or improved dirt roads from this highway. Highway 62-180 is the route that the TNM&O Bus Line (806-765-6641) travels (ask for the Pine Springs stop). Some of the more remote areas, Dog Canyon, for instance, are more than 100 miles by car even though as the crow flies they are less than 15. Because of the lack of development, most of the highest country in Texas remains as pristine as it was when Spanish explorers first encountered the Mescalero Apache in the sixteenth century. More than half the park, 46,850 acres, has been mandated as wilderness area.

Almost all of the present park is former ranch land that was donated expressly for a national park or acquired with cooperation of ranch owners. The oldest structures standing are ranch headquarters, such as the Williams Ranch, which can be accessed only by four-wheel-drive roads or the Frijole Ranch (and nearby Manzanita Spring) right off Highway 62-180.

TOURIST SERVICES

SUPERINTENDENT, GUADALUPE MOUNTAINS NATIONAL PARK
HC 60 • Box 400 • Salt Flat, TX • 79847-9400 • 828-3251 • Monday–Friday 8 A.M. to 4:30 P.M.

There is no park entrance fee although campground use fees are charged. Use this address and phone number when contacting the Park Service for information; however, don't go to Salt Flat, Texas, if visiting Guadalupe National Park is on the agenda (you'll only find a cafe and a post office). The visitor centers and ranger stations are located on the eastern and northern portions of the national park.

PINE SPRINGS VISITOR CENTER
Highway 62-180 • 828-3251 • Daily 8 A.M. to 4:30 P.M.

Located adjacent to the Pine Springs Campground, this Visitor Center provides the full gamut of information, activities, and resources. Brochures and trail maps on the park, books covering regional history and natural sciences, exhibits, and a slide program are all available. Rangers not only provide the latest details on trails, campgrounds, and special conditions but also offer guided hikes and nightly programs at the Pine Springs Campground Amphitheater (seasonally).

McKITTRICK CANYON VISITOR CENTER
Four miles west of Highway 62-180 from a turnoff 7.5 miles northeast of Pine Springs • Access closed nightly

This is the gateway to McKittrick Canyon, where you can learn about this Texas treasure and one-of-a-kind relic forest before you begin your day hike. No overnight camping is permitted in McKittrick Canyon.

DOG CANYON RANGER STATION
Located at the Dog Canyon Campground, this remote facility can be reached by foot via the Pine Springs or McKittrick Canyon Trails or by car via SH 137, a paved road, which extends west 59 miles from Highway 285 approximately 12 miles north of Carlsbad. Even phone lines go the long route. Although the ranger station is in Texas, it has a New Mexico number (505-981-2418). The distance from the Pine Springs Visitor Center is 12 miles by foot and 105 miles by vehicle.

BIRD'S-EYE VIEW

ATOP GUADALUPE PEAK

8,749 feet above sea level

The top of Texas is less than five miles from the Pine Springs Visitor Center, and that means views of the Chihuahuan Desert and the mountains of three states: Chihuahua, New Mexico, and Texas.

Directions, information, and trail maps are all available at the Visitor Center. On a clear day, vistas of more than 100 miles including the Davis Mountains and Mexico are not uncommon as are views of the Sierra Diablos directly south and the Delaware Mountains to the southeast. Of course, right in front of you is the *El Capitan* escarpment.

SIDE TRIPS

CARLSBAD CAVERNS NATIONAL PARK

Take US 62/180 north 35 miles to White's City, NM, and park entrance 505-785-2232 or 505-785-2107 (recorded info line) • Visitor Center open 7–7 (summer) 8–5:30 (winter) • Admission • W variable

One of the most spectacular caverns in the world.

LAJITAS AND TERLINGUA

Brewster County • (915)

Lajitas, site of an old trading post and now a resort community, and Terlingua, a reborn ghost town that first hosted what is probably the world's best known chili cookoff, are neighbors in the remote area near the Río Grande and the western entrance to Big Bend National Park.

The Río Grande crossing at Lajitas (La-HEE-tahs) was used by Indians for hundreds of years. Pancho Villa also used it in the early 1900s and in 1916. As a result, General John J. Pershing established a cavalry outpost here. In 1977, the Mischer Corporation came to Lajitas and built The Cavalry Post Motel on the actual foundations of Pershing's cavalry post as part of the development of a new resort community.

Terlingua had its heyday in the late 1800s and early 1900s when quicksilver (mercury) mines were operating there. When the mines were booming its population reached close to 2,000. The town lasted until the price of mercury dropped in 1942. Then it became a ghost town, but a ghost town watched over by a nonprofit corporation intent on its preservation and restoration.

The route to both communities is either on the scenic FM 170 from Presidio, some 50 miles west, or SH 118 from Alpine, which is about 80 miles to the north.

MUSEUMS

BARTON WARNOCK ENVIRONMENTAL EDUCATION CENTER

Lajitas, FM 170 • 424-3327 • Daily 8–4:30 • Admission • W

Formerly the Lajitas Desert Garden and Museum, the Warnock Center now is part of the state parks system and serves as one of the two entry points to the Big Bend Ranch State Natural Area (*see* Big Bend). Outside there is a two-acre Desert Garden with exhibits of cactus and other plants native to the Chihuahuan Desert. Book store and gift shop.

SPORTS AND ACTIVITIES
Bicycling

DESERT SPORTS
Four miles west of Highway 118 on Highway 170 • 371-2727 or 888-989-6900
Stop by Desert Sports for mountain bike rentals (including helmet), guided day and multi-day rides throughout the Big Bend country, as well as to make use of their full-service bike shop, which stocks tubes, tires, and other cycling accessories. Call or ask about the combination peddle and paddle trips.

Horseback Riding

LAJITAS STABLES
Lajitas, FM 170 • 888-508-7667 (day) or 424-3438 (night)
Guided one-day to multi-day trail rides, ranging from $14 to $60 for an all-day ride. Overnight trips start at $100 per day. Combination river trip/horseback trips, wagon rides, and steak cookout also available. Access to 100,000+ scenic acres.

River Rafting

The Río Grande weaves its magic for over 1,200 miles between Texas and Mexico, and the canyons carved by the river offer some of the most beautiful scenery in the state. The catch is that the only way to see most of the canyons is by boat. Float trips down the Río Grande are rarely whitewater experiences; most of the year the few rapids are quite tame. If you are experienced you can do it yourself in your own raft or rent one locally and arrange for shuttle service. Backcountry Use Permits are required if you are going to float within the Big Bend National Park. These may be obtained at any Park Ranger Station or at the Lajitas Trading Post, which also rents equipment.

For safety and convenience, most visitors use one of the several good commercial outfitters with guide services in the area. The outfitters take care of all the details and provide everything needed (including waterproof boxes for your camera and gear) except clothing and personal items. They conduct a variety of trips from half-day float trips (about $50 per person) to overnights (about $90 up) and trips that last several days. Following is a list of the better known outfitters.

Big Bend River Tours, Box 317, Lajitas 79852 • 424-3219 or 800-545-4240.
Far Flung Adventures, Box 31, Terlingua 79852 • 371-2489 or 800-359-4138.
Texas River Expeditions, Box 583, Terlingua 79852 • 371-2633.

Shopping

LAJITAS TRADING POST
Lajitas, under the hill • 424-3234 • W
This store has been in continuous operation since it opened as a trading post in the late 1800s, making it the oldest business in town. Its eclectic frontier decor makes some people mistake it for a museum, but it is an active general store stocking everything from boom boxes to *bombillas* (chimneys for kerosene lamps). The store is the unofficial community center for people from both sides of the river. A meal of crackers, bologna, cheese, and chiles eaten on the front porch, a tradition among the regulars, is known as a Lajitas lunch.

TERLINGUA TRADING COMPANY
Downtown Terlingua • 371-2234 • W

Big Bend books, jewelry, T-shirts, gourmet foods, and all sorts of Mexican imports are for sale in the former headquarters of the Chisos Mining Company. Stop in for a look around or just to buy a cold one, which is best enjoyed while seated on the store's front porch with an eye to the Chisos Mountains.

SIDE TRIPS

BIG BEND NATIONAL PARK AND BIG BEND STATE NATURAL AREA
(See separate listing.)

ANNUAL EVENTS

November

TERLINGUA WORLD CHAMPIONSHIP CHILI COOKOFFS
Terlingua • First weekend in November • Admission • W

What started in 1967 as a publicity stunt to promote a book called *A Bowl of Red* by *Dallas Morning News* columnist Frank X. Tolbert has grown to the point that two and sometimes three rival groups, all claiming to be the true chili cookoff, descend on Terlingua each November. Thousands of spectators drive and fly in from all over the country and the world to cheer on their favorites. Local accommodations can't handle the crowds so, if you intend to attend, make motel or camping reservations early, early, early.

OFFBEAT

For an experience, take a leaky ferryboat across from Lajitas to Paso Lajitas, a tiny Mexican village. Many of the villagers commute to work daily in Lajitas. One restaurant caters to tourists, Dos Amigos, and Mexican food doesn't get any more authentic than this. Go well before dark and pay the ferry operator on the return trip; there are no overnight accommodations, and the villas don't accept American Express either.

RESTAURANTS

($ = under $7, $$ = $8–$17, $$$ = $18–$25, $$$$ = over $25 for one person excluding drinks, tax, and tip.)

STARLIGHT THEATRE
Downtown Terlingua • 371-2326 • Dinner only daily • $–$$ • W

The restored movie theater of the Chisos Mining Company has a new lease on life as a dinner theater serving steaks, chicken, burgers, and Mexican specialty dishes in "Adobe Deco" surroundings. Lite menu and vegetarian entrées available. Bar.

ACCOMMODATIONS

($ = under $45, $$ = $46–$60, $$$ = $61–$80, $$$$ = $81–$100, $$$$$ = over $100)
Room tax 6%

BIG BEND MOTOR INN

Study Butte, SH 118 at FM 170 (P.O. Box 336, Terlingua 79852) • 371-2218 or 800-848-2363 • $$–$$$ • W+ 2 rooms

The one-story motel's 45 units include four duplexes with kitchens ($$$$–$$$$$) and a cottage ($$$$$). Special rates for chili cookoff weekend. Cable TV. Restaurant nearby. Outdoor pool. Self-service laundry.

LAJITAS ON THE RIO GRANDE

Lajitas, on the boardwalk (Star Route 70, Box 400, Terlingua 79852) 424-3471 • $$$

This resort development includes 81 rooms in a small hotel and three motels in the complex, plus a group bunkhouse. Individual houses and condos are also available for rent for $100–$195 in high season. Rooms available with phones and satellite TV. The resort also offers a restaurant, RV and tent camping spaces. Available to all guests are a swimming pool, nine-hole golf course, and tennis courts. They even have their own airstrip. Small pets OK. High season March–June and October–November. Rates slightly lower rest of year.

MISSION LODGE

Study Butte, SH 118 at FM 170 (P.O. Box 169, Terlingua 79852) • 371-2555 or 800-848-2363 • $$ • W+ 2 rooms

This one-story motel has 36 units. Cable TV. Restaurant nearby. Special rates for chili cookoff weekend.

LANGTRY

Val Verde County • 30 • (915)

For a brief time in 1883 this town was famous for the link-up near here of the Southern Pacific and the Galveston, Harrisburg, and San Antonio railroads, opening up a southern route for transcontinental rail service. But it wasn't that event that made Langtry famous. Judge Roy Bean did that. Fact and fiction have mingled into legend when it comes to this man. We do know Bean operated a tent saloon that followed the railroad construction. When the Texas Rangers and the railroad people made him a justice of the peace, he took his job seriously and called himself "The Law West of the Pecos." He ruled with a six-shooter and frontier horse sense, laced with a sense of humor. His courtroom was also his saloon and he often fined the guilty a round of drinks for everyone in the court. Bean was fascinated by a famous English music hall performer, Lillie Langtry, internationally known as "The Jersey Lily." He claimed he named the town after her (railroad historians say it was named after a railroad construction foreman) and wrote numerous letters to Miss Langtry inviting her to "her town." Finally she accepted his invitation but, unfortunately, before she actually made her visit in 1904, the Judge died.

JUDGE ROY BEAN VISITOR CENTER

From US 90 take Loop 25 approximately 1 mile • 291-3340 • **Daily 8–5 except closed Thanksgiving, December 24–25, and January 1 • Free • W**

There are three parts to this center. The center building is staffed by travel counselors from the Texas Department of Transportation who can provide information, maps, and brochures on the whole state. There are also six dioramas with audio programs that highlight both the facts and the legends about Judge Roy Bean. Out back is the second of the saloons in which Bean ruled as JP, complete with the sign that calls it "The Jersey Lilly," spelled incorrectly with two "l"s instead of one. The final part is an impressive cactus garden with more than a hundred species of plants native to the Southwest. Signs identify the plants and provide information about Indian and pioneer use of them.

PECOS RIVER BRIDGE OVERLOOK

East bank of Pecos River on US 90 near Comstock, approximately 18 miles east of Langtry • Free • W

At 273 feet above the river's normal water line, this is the highest highway bridge in Texas. Looking north from the overlook you can see the bridge. It was near here that the Southern Pacific and the Galveston, Harrisburg, and San Antonio railroads met to complete the southern transcontinental rail route. The view to the south includes the mouth of the Pecos emptying into Amistad Reservoir on the Río Grande. The mountains beyond are in Mexico.

SEMINOLE CANYON STATE HISTORICAL PARK

Comstock, Park Rd. 67 off US 90, east of Pecos River Bridge. Approximately 20 miles east of Langtry • 292-4464 • Daily 8–10 for day use, at all times for camping • $2 per person per day • W+ but not all areas

In the canyon of this 2,173-acre park is Fate Bell Shelter, which contains some of North America's oldest pictographs—believed to be painted as long as 8,000 years ago. These paintings are considered by many experts to be among the most important rock art finds in the New World. Guided tours (fee) are conducted at 10 and 3 Wednesday through Sunday, weather permitting. Persons planning to go on the tour should be in good physical condition. The park visitor center contains exhibits depicting the life-style of early man based on rock art and artifacts found in the area. There are picnic areas, RV and tent campsites (fee), and a three-mile hiking trail that leads to a scenic overlook of the Río Grande. Visitors can also ride mountain bikes on the hiking trail.

MIDLAND

Midland County Seat • 111,439 • (915)

The city and county were originally called Midway because of their location midway between Fort Worth/Dallas and El Paso.

It took the town a long time to get rolling. At first it was just a junction of many trails, including the Comanche War Trail. It was wild enough at that time to be the site of the last Comanche raid into Texas. The railroad came through in 1881, and Midland became a brief stopping place where the passengers on the Texas and Pacific could get out and stretch their legs. Sheepherders and cattlemen came and the county was established. The first big population jump came when oil was discovered in the vast Permian Basin in the 1920s. Surprisingly, the first oil well in Midland County itself wasn't brought in until 1945, but by then the production and administrative end of the oil business had settled in the city and the population boomed. In fact, it doubled every decade from 1920 to the 1960s. And the surge isn't over. According to the U.S. Census Bureau, in the first half of the 1980s, Midland was the fastest growing city in the nation, increasing its population by 38 percent in just five years.

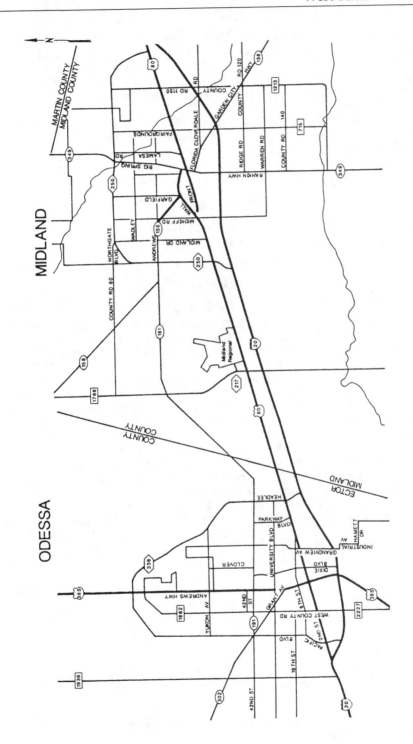

In 1995, the joint populations of Midland and Odessa and the immediate surroundings were lumped together for a total of 250,000 and given a Metropolitan Statistical Area (MSA) designation. The new designation, along with a new highway (Loop 250) circling the city, brought in big-name, big-city retail interests offering a variety of restaurants, discount houses, and other shopping opportunities.

Today Midland has a big-city skyline and remains headquarters of much of the West Texas oil activity. It offers its citizens and visitors several recreational and cultural opportunities such as a minor league baseball team, museums (including the outstanding Permian Basin Petroleum Museum), a community theater, symphony orchestra and chorale, and a community college.

TOURIST SERVICES

MIDLAND CONVENTION AND VISITORS BUREAU

109 N. Main (P.O. Box 1890, 79702) • 683-3381,
e-mail: bpartain@computek.net • W

MUSEUMS

CONFEDERATE AIR FORCE FLYING MUSEUM

Midland International Airport, 9600 Wright Dr. (P.O. Box 62000, 769711-2000) 563-1000 • Monday–Saturday 9–5, Sunday and holidays 12–5. Closed Christmas • Adults $6, children 13–18 and seniors $5, children 6–12 $3, under 6 free • W

Located in the 70-acre Confederate Air Force (CAF) headquarters complex, the American Airpower Heritage Museum is internationally recognized for its collections of World War II aircraft as well as artifacts and memorabilia of that war ranging from uniforms to weapons from the Allied and Axis countries. The museum has 145 WWII planes of 69 different types, about 20 of which are on display here at all times. The display changes four times a year. CAF's "Ghost Squadron" includes an almost complete collection of American WWII combat aircraft plus several rare and classic aircraft of the Royal Air Force (RAF), German *Luftwaffe,* and the Imperial Japanese Navy.

The main attractions are the restored planes in the display hangars and on the CAF ramp. Here, on a typical day, you may find a Supermarine MK IX Spitfire, Piper L-4 Grasshopper, Cessna UC-94, Vultee BT-13 Valiant, and a Republic P-47 Thunderbolt, side by side. All are clearly marked with detailed information. CAF's planes and pilots have participated in several movies, advertisements, videos, and TV documentaries. Among the CAF movie production credits are *The Enola Gay Story, Hindenburg, 1941, Close Encounters of the Third Kind, Tora!Tora!Tora!,* and *Fat Man and Little Boy.*

For the aircraft buff, the World War II historian, and children (young and old), this is a don't miss museum. Gift shop.

MUSEUM OF THE SOUTHWEST

1705 W. Missouri at J St. • 683-2882 or 570-7770 • Tuesday–Saturday 10–5, Sunday 2–5. Closed Monday • Free • W downstairs only, ramp in rear.

MARIAN BLAKEMORE PLANETARIUM

W. Indiana and K St., across street from museum. Shows Tuesday 7:30 P.M. and Sunday 2 and 3:30. Admission • W

Dedicated to the collection, preservation, and interpretation of Southwestern art and culture, the museum is housed in a large attractive home built in 1934. The art collection includes works by the Taos Society of Artists and contemporary sculpture by Allan Houser and Doug Hyde. Travelling exhibits change about every six weeks. Gift shop. The planetarium is part of the museum. Programs change bi-monthly.

PERMIAN BASIN PETROLEUM MUSEUM

1500 IH-20W at SH 349 • 683-4403 • Monday–Saturday 9–5, Sunday 2–5
Adults $3, seniors $2.50, children 6–high school $1.50, preschoolers free • W but not all areas

This is the largest museum in the U.S., possibly the world, devoted to telling the story of the oil industry. A good place to start to understand that story is at the audio-visual show just inside the entrance that gives an introduction to both oil exploration and the museum itself. Throughout the museum are other audio-visual shows that take the technical aspects of the oil business and break them down into understandable terms in interesting and exciting ways. This is a "hands-on" museum that is a delightful mixture of education and entertainment. You can spin a wheel of fortune to try to beat the odds and hit a gusher, walk through a time-tunnel that takes you on an undersea trip along the Permian-age reef as it existed 230 million years ago and see the plants and animals that time turned into oil, or experience a dangerous well blowout and see what the oil field firefighters must do to extinguish the blaze. The world's largest collection of antique drilling equipment is set up outside in the oil patch.

OTHER POINTS OF INTEREST

HALEY MEMORIAL LIBRARY

1805 W. Indiana at L St., 682-5785 • Monday–Friday 9–5 • Free • W

Basically, this is a research library with collections emphasizing Texas and Southwestern history. But it also exhibits a noteworthy collection of art, photographs, and artifacts relating to the horseback tradition of the range country. Foremost among the historical items is one of the original bells from the Alamo Mission, cast in 1722.

SPORTS AND ACTIVITIES

Baseball

MIDLAND ANGELS

Angel Stadium, 4500 N. Lamesa Rd., north end of Hogan Park • 683-4251
General admission $3 • W but not all areas

This Double-A farm team of the California Angels plays about 65 home games in the April through August season.

Golf

HOGAN PARK GOLF COURSE

3600 N. Fairground Rd. • 685-7360 • 27-hole course • Green fees: Weekdays $8.50, weekends $12

Polo

MIDLAND POLO CLUB

N. Garfield, north of Loop 250 • 684-6493 • Matches most Sundays May/June–October. Admission free except for special fund-raising matches

Tennis

There are a number of Midland Parks and Recreation Department courts throughout the city. For information call 685-7355.

COLLEGES AND UNIVERSITIES

MIDLAND COLLEGE

3600 N. Garfield, north of Wadley • 685-4500 • W but not all areas

A two-year community college offering both academic and vocational programs to approximately 4,100 students. Among points of interest to visitors are the art gallery, in the Allison Fine Arts Building (685-4640), and the campus multi-purpose Chaparral Center (685-4585), where, in addition to the home games of the school's basketball team, they hold a number of other events including pop artist concerts and the circus.

PERFORMING ARTS

MIDLAND-ODESSA SYMPHONY AND CHORALE

Performances alternate between Midland and Odessa locations • 563-0921 or 563-5269 • Admission • W

Formed in 1962 by joining the Odessa and Midland symphony associations, the Midland-Odessa Symphony and Chorale plays classical concerts alternately at Midland and Odessa, with 65 members, 45 of whom are teaching professionals, and guest artists from around the nation. Annually they offer 11 subscription concerts (individual tickets usually available) and one outdoor concert.

THEATRE MIDLAND

2000 W. Wadley, just east of Garfield • 682-2544 or 682-4111 • Admission • W

Using local talent and professional directors, Theatre Midland has been rated one of the top ten community theater groups in the nation. The season usually consists of six productions in the large proscenium-thrust stage theater and two productions in the smaller theater-in-the-round. Theatre Midland also serves as the teaching and laboratory facility for the theatre arts program at Midland College, an innovative association between the academic and public communities.

YUCCA THEATRE

208 N. Colorado near Texas • 682-4111 • Admission • W

This restored and converted old movie house is part of the Midland Community Theatre. The most popular Theatre Midland productions get extended runs here. And in the summer, there's the Summer Mummers, a group that puts on old-fashioned melodramas where you can cheer the hero (or heroine) and boo and throw popcorn (nothing harder, please) at the villain.

SHOPPING

ESCENTS CANDLE CO.

2401 W. Indiana • 570-5163 • W

This small company creates candles that smell like white cake baking, old-fashioned flowers, sachets, or other reminders of yesteryear.

KIDS' STUFF

DENNIS THE MENACE PARK

Garfield and Missouri • Open daily until dusk • Free • W

A duplicate of the original in Monterey, California (home of Hank Ketchum, Dennis' creator), this three-acre park is the type playground kids love, with strange things to climb on and playhouses.

FREDDA TURNER DURHAM CHILDREN'S MUSEUM

1705 W. Missouri at J • Tuesday–Saturday 10–5, Sunday 2–5. Closed Monday 683-2882 • Free • W

Exhibitions and educational programs designed for young people to have hands-on experiences. Tours by reservation.

ANNUAL EVENTS

May

CELEBRATION OF THE ARTS

Midland Center and Centennial Plaza, Wall and Loraine • 687-1149 First weekend of May • Adults $2, children to 17 $1, under 5 free • W

Arts festival featuring arts and crafts, over 100 visual and performing artists, food, and a large children's activity area. Street dance Saturday night (Adults $5).

September

SEPTEMBERFEST

Museum of the Southwest, 1705 W. Missouri • 683-2882 • Usually second weekend in month • Admission • W downstairs only (ramp in rear)

Juried artists and craftsmen from all over the nation exhibit and sell their art at this museum fund-raiser. Also featured is a variety of ethnic music from polkas to *mariachis* as well at C&W, bluegrass, and jazz. Kids' area with pony rides and petting zoo. And, of course, food booths.

October

CONFEDERATE AIR FORCE AIRSHOW

Midland International Airport, 9600 Wright Dr. • 563-1000 • Second weekend in October • Advance admission: Adults $7, children 6–12 $3; gate admission $1 additional • W • Parking fee

The Confederate Air Force's World War II demonstration takes you back to the time when America rallied behind a single cause. Some of the major air battles of WWII are re-enacted by the CAF "Ghost Squadron." These include The Battle of Britain, Pearl Harbor, Wake Island, Flying Tigers, Thirty Seconds Over Tokyo, Midway, Schweinfurt, Ploesti, Marianas Turkey Shoot, D-Day, and V-J Day.

MIDLAND JAZZ CLASSIC

Various locations • 683-5208 or 682-5334 • Admission • W
A four-day festival that is held whenever in the month they can get the best collection of jazz musicians to come to town. A ticket for the whole week of jazz concerts goes for about $150.

RESTAURANTS

($ = under $7, $$ = $8–$17, $$$ = $18–$25, $$$$ = over $25 for one person excluding drinks, tax, and tip.)

Cajun

JAZZ, A LOUISIANA KITCHEN

2215 N. Midland Dr., Suite 2A, in the Mesa Verde Shopping Center 689-7777 • Lunch and dinner Monday–Saturday 11–10:30, Sunday brunch 11–3 $$–$$$ • Cr • W
This is where you come in West Texas to get a taste of the Big Easy, from *beignets* to crawfish *etoufee*, and to hear the best in jazz, both local and imported. The motto is *Laissez le bon temps rouler*—let the good times roll, and the atmosphere is Cajun all the way. The music starts at 8:30 weeknights, and at noon for Sunday brunch.

Italian

LUIGI'S

111 N. Big Spring at W. Wall • 683-6363 • Lunch and dinner Monday–Friday, dinner only Saturday • $$ • AE, DIS, MC, V • W • Children's plates
This small *trattoria* has been serving Italian dishes, such as veal *scaloppine* and eggplant *parmigiana* on traditional red-checked tablecloths for more than a quarter of a century. The decor is mainly photos of Theatre Midland productions from the 1940s to the present. Bar.

Mexican

LA BODEGA

2700 N. Big Spring • 684-5594 • Lunch and dinner Monday–Thursday 11–10. Weekends 11–10:30 (Bar 11–2) • $$–$$$ • Cr • W downstairs
In 1972, 22 Texans persuaded Austrian chef Alois Munzer to leave the ski slopes in New Mexico and come to Midland to begin a restaurant. They hired architect Frank Welch to design the building—a towering *bodega* (Spanish for "Warehouse"), and Mr. Munzer proceeded to teach his chefs to cook a type of Mexican cuisine unique in the southwest. Twenty-five years later, La Bodega is still one of the most popular spots in West Texas.

Eat inside, where the white stucco walls are hung with reprints of 1910 Mexican photos, or in the enclosed fountain courtyard, or at a leather-topped table in the domed atrium bar upstairs.

MANUEL'S COUNTRY STORE & DELI

3905 S. Hwy 349, *3½ miles south of Wall Street, on Big Spring Street which becomes Highway 349* • 682-2258 • Monday–Saturday 6–8:30 • $
Proprietors Manuel and Manuela Muñoz serve breakfast Tex-Mex style: the tortillas are homemade daily, as is everything else they serve. This place is a

favorite of actor Tommy Lee Jones, as well as several sports figures and long-time oilfield hands, ranch-hands, farmers, and other Midlanders.

Seafood

WALL STREET BAR AND GRILL

115 E. Wall • 684-8686 • Lunch Monday–Friday, Sunday brunch, dinner daily $$ • Cr • W

The long wooden 1867 bar and pressed-tin ceiling give this downtown restaurant an atmosphere all its own, but it's the menu that brings them back. Steaks and seafood are the main entrées, with the emphasis on seafood.

Steak

CATTLEMAN'S STEAKHOUSE

3300 N. Big Spring at Wadley • 682-5668 • Lunch and dinner Monday–Friday, dinner only Saturday • $$ • Cr • W • Children's plates

There are steaks and steaks and a long list of seafood—most at prices lower than the beef. Pictures of the Confederate Air Force and Western scenes decorate the walls. Bar.

ACCOMMODATIONS

($ = under $45, $$ = $46–$60, $$$ = $61–$80, $$$$ = $81–$100, $$$$$ = over $100)

Room tax 13%

HILTON

117 W. Wall at Loraine • 683-6131 or 800-722-6131 • $$$–$$$$ • W+ 3 rooms No-smoking rooms

The eleven-story Hilton has 249 units including eight suites ($$$$$) and 150 no-smoking rooms. Children under 18 stay free in room with parents. Senior discount. Cable TV with Showtime and pay channel. Room phones (charge for local calls). No pets. Free airport transportation. Garage parking. Restaurant and cafe. Fire sprinklers in rooms. Outdoor heated pool. Exercise room. Gift and flower shops. Free newspaper. Free coffee in lobby. One-day dry cleaning.

HOLIDAY INN COUNTRY VILLA

4300 W. BUS 20 east of Midland Dr. • 697-3181 or 800-HOLIDAY (800-465-4329) • $$–$$$ • W 1 room • No-smoking rooms

The two-story Holiday Inn has 280 units including two suites ($$$$$) and 47 no-smoking rooms. Children under 12 stay free in room with parents. Senior discount and family plans available. Cable TV with pay channel. Room phones (charge for local calls). Pets OK. Free airport transportation. Restaurant and lounge. Holidome with indoor heated pool, whirlpool, saunas, game room, miniature golf, and kids' play area. Free coffee in morning.

PLAZA INN

4108 N. Big Spring (Hwy 349) • 686-8733 or 800-365-3222 • $$ • W+ 6 rooms No-smoking rooms

This three-story motel has 113 units including 50 no-smoking rooms, cable TV, room phones, outdoor pool with small spa, game room, and complimentary breakfast. Children under 16 stay free in room with parents. Corporate and senior discount available. Free airport transportation.

RAMADA HOTEL

3100 W. Wall at Powell • 699-4144 or 800-2-RAMADA (800-272-6232) • $$–$$$ W 3 rooms • No-smoking rooms

The three-story Ramada has 200 units including three suites ($$$–$$$$$) and 100 no-smoking rooms. Children under 18 stay free in room with parents. Senior discounts and family plans available. Cable TV. Room phones (charge for local calls). Pets OK. Free airport transportation. Restaurant and lounge. Indoor heated pool, whirlpool, and exercise room. Free newspaper.

MONAHANS

Ward County Seat • 8,101 • (915)

Monahans came to be because John Thomas Monahans, a surveyor for the Texas and Pacific Railroad, which was being built west from Fort Worth in the 1880s, dug a well and found a plentiful supply of water. So the town grew up around the water stop. Later, another precious liquid, oil, led to a population boom here during the late 1920s. Today Monahans is a trading center for a large oil and cattle region. The importance of oil to the city is evidenced by the several pump jacks sitting side by side just off downtown on SH 18 a block north of US 80. These draw oil from slant wells that go under the city hall, the courthouse, and other buildings in the heart of downtown. One way the city has used its oil money for the benefit of both citizens and visitors is by building a multipurpose facility that includes a large indoor swimming pool. The facility is part of the local school district, but is open to the public, for a moderate fee, several times a week when not needed for school activities (see listing below).

TOURIST SERVICES

MONAHANS CHAMBER OF COMMERCE

401 S. Dwight at 4th, 79756 • 943-2187 • W

MUSEUMS

MILLION BARREL MUSEUM

.25 mile south of BUS Loop 20 on Museum Blvd. • 943-8401 • Tuesday– Saturday 10–6, Sunday 2–6. Closed Monday • Free (donations)

The centerpiece of this museum is a hole in the ground, a million barrel oil tank built by Shell Oil in 1928 when the nearby Hendricks field was flowing wildly and storage capacity was badly needed. The open, concrete tank measures 522 feet by 425 feet (large enough to hold almost five football fields) with walls rising to a height of 35 feet. But seepage plagued the tank and it was abandoned as soon as the development of pipelines ended the need for it. The museum complex includes exhibits on the railroad, the oil industry, and local agriculture. It also includes the Holman Hotel, a Texas Historic Landmark building built in 1909, the first Ward County jail, and an amphitheater with covered seating.

OTHER POINTS OF INTEREST

MONAHANS SANDHILL STATE PARK

Take IH-20 east approximately 5 miles to Park Rd. 41 • 943-2092 • Daily 8–10 for day use only • $2 per adult• W+ but not all areas

With almost 4,000 acres of wind-sculpted sand dunes up to 50 feet high, this is the Sahara of Texas. The park is only a small portion of a dune field that extends 200 miles, into New Mexico. The park itself contains dunes that are still active, which means they grow and change shape in response to seasonal prevailing winds. The shinoaks that grow here are part of one of the largest oak forests in America—but the plants are rarely more than three feet tall. The oaks stabilize the area where they grow by sinking roots that frequently go as deep as 90 feet. The trees also produce large acorns that provide food for the desert wildlife. The park's headquarters/interpretive center has exhibits depicting this wildlife as well as botanical, archaeological, historical, and geological features of the sandhills area. Facilities include sites for tent and RV camping with hookups (fee), a shaded picnic area, and a concession renting disks for sandsurfing.

RATTLESNAKE BOMBER BASE MUSEUM

Pyote, 15 miles west of Monahans • 389-5691 • Saturday 9–6, Sunday 2–6, or by appointment

The small museum contains memorabilia from when this was a major B-17 and B-29 training base during World War II. This later became home to the *Enola Gay*, the plane that dropped the first atomic bomb on Hiroshima.

SPORTS AND ACTIVITIES

MULTI-PURPOSE COMPLEX

605 S. Betty • 943-3222 • Monday–Friday 6–2 and 4–10, Saturday 10–6, Sunday 1–6 • Fee varies with facility used • W+ but not all areas

The facilities in this complex include an indoor swimming pool, two gymnasiums, racquetball courts, weight room, and aerobics room. Call first to determine hours open to the public.

ACCOMMODATIONS

($ = under $45, $$ = $46–$60, $$$ = $61–$80, $$$$ = $81–$100, $$$$$ = over $100)
Room tax 13%

BEST WESTERN COLONIAL INN

702 W. IH-20 and SH 18 (exit 80) • 943-4345 or 800-528-1234 • $–$$

This one-level Best Western has 93 units. Cable TV. Room phones (no charge for local calls). Small pets accepted in limited number of rooms. Restaurant. Outdoor pool.

TEXAN INN

806 IH-20W • 943-7585 • $ • No-smoking rooms

The two-story Howard Johnson has 47 units including five suites ($$$) and nine no-smoking rooms. Cable TV with HBO. Room phones (no charge for local calls). Small pets OK. Private club (automatic membership for guests, temporary membership $3 for non-guests). Outdoor heated pool. Free newspaper. Free coffee in morning.

ODESSA

Ector County Seat • 125,000 • (915)

Odessa is another city that started out as a stopover on the Texas and Pacific Railroad's push westward in the early 1880s. There are two stories about how the city got its name. One is it was named after an Indian princess who wandered into the railroad camp. The other is it was named by Russian railroad workers who thought the flat prairies resembled the landscape of their homeland on the steppes of the Ukraine. The county, like many in Texas, is named after a Confederate officer, Matthew D. Ector.

The Permian Basin oil boom hit in the late 1920s and now the Basin produces nearly one fifth of the nation's crude oil, natural gas, and gas liquids. Odessa, with the largest inland petrochemical complex of its kind in the nation, has become known as the petroleum service capital of the area, reportedly providing more oilfield technology than any other city in the world. The Permian Basin Oil Show, held here every other year, draws over half a million visitors.

The city satisfies a wide spectrum of recreational and cultural interests with parks, museums, theatrical productions and, in association with nearby Midland, a symphony and chorale. Soaring has become increasing popular in the area with the prevailing air currents offering the sailplane enthusiast fine flight conditions.

Every city has its boosters, but Odessa has a group that puts its money where its mouth is—traveling all over the country, and even overseas, catering barbecue dinners to spread the word about the town. A volunteer organization of the Chamber of Commerce, the Odessa Chuck Wagon Gang has catered these barbecue beef meals, with pinto beans and all the other trimmings, to as many as 30,000 at the Grand Ole Opry Fan Fair in Nashville and put out the feedbag for thousands of others from Washington D.C. to California and from Norway to Canada.

TOURIST SERVICES

ODESSA CONVENTION AND VISITORS BUREAU

700 N. Grant (P.O. Box 3626, 79760) • 333-7871 • Web page http://www.odessa.edu/city/ • e-mail: ecodev@global.net • W (ramp in rear)

HISTORIC PLACES

WHITE-POOL HOUSE

112 E. Murphy, 1 block east of S. Grant • 333-4072 • Tuesday noon–3, Wednesday–Friday 10–3, Saturday by appointment, Sunday call for hours Free (donation) • W downstairs only

Built in 1887 by the Charles White family, Quakers who came from Indiana, the two-story red brick house is the city's oldest structure. A photo of the house taken in 1889 was used in land company brochures to attract settlers to the county. Some rooms depict the 1890s, when the Whites lived in the house, and others depict the 1930s when the Pool family occupied it.

MUSEUMS

ELLEN NOEL ART MUSEUM OF THE PERMIAN BASIN

**4909 E. University between E. Loop 338 and John Ben Shepperd Parkway
368-7222 • Tuesday–Saturday 10–5, Sunday 2–5 • Free • W**

This is an independent art museum located on the campus of the University of Texas of the Permian Basin. The museum features rotating exhibitions of historical and contemporary art for all ages. Gift shop.

PRESIDENTIAL MUSEUM

622 N. Lee at 7th • 332-7123 • Tuesday–Saturday 10–5 • Free • W • Free parking on south side of building

This is the only museum in the country dedicated exclusively to the office of the president. Exhibits range from George Washington's era to the present. Also on display is a collection of dolls representing the First Ladies dressed in miniature copies of their inaugural gowns. Gift shop.

OTHER POINTS OF INTEREST

METEOR CRATER

Take US 20 west approximately 1.8 miles past Loop 338 to FM 1936 exit off IH-20 and follow south IH-20 frontage road to sign indicating crater, which is then 2 miles to the south • **Free**

A six-foot-deep hole that spans 500 feet across still remains from an iron meteorite weighing 1,000 tons that crashed into the earth more than 20,000 years ago. The site is the second largest meteor crater in the U.S. and the sixth largest in the world.

WORLD'S LARGEST JACK RABBIT

Corner of 8th and Sam Houston • Free

Another Texas-sized mascot, this jumbo jack rabbit, an eight-foot-tall statue, is one of the most popular photo attractions in the city.

SPORTS AND ACTIVITIES

ODESSA JACKALOPES PROFESSIONAL HOCKEY

**Ector County Coliseum, 42nd and Andrews Highway • 552-PUCK (552-7825)
October–March • Admission • W**

This professional hockey team is a member of the Western Professional Hockey League. The Jackalopes play from October through March, with games split between home and nine other locations.

The team also offers public skating and youth hockey, hockey camps and clinics, and professional ice shows.

TWIN CITIES SPEEDWAY ENTERTAINMENT CENTER

606 S. County Rd. 1300 (about 10 miles east, between Midland and Odessa)
Turn right at Coors Rd., cross railroad tracks and follow signs • **570-0650
Mid-April–first weekend in October • Admission**

Activities include car races, tractor pulls, and car thrill shows.

WATER WONDERLAND

BUS 20 between Odessa and Midland • 563-2200 • Admission varies
W but not all areas • May–September

Water, water, everywhere, and all of it moving. This is the nearest thing to Six Flags to be found in West Texas. It is also the home of Permian Basin BMX racing.

COLLEGES AND UNIVERSITIES

ODESSA COLLEGE

201 W. University at Andrews Hwy. • 335-6400 • W but not all areas
Visitor parking on University

This is a junior college with an enrollment of about 5,000 in both academic and vocational/technical programs. In addition to spectator sports, visitors are welcome to attend theater productions, concerts, and art shows. The Options Gallery is located in the Learning Resources Center (335-6640). The school's $6 million sports complex is open to the public when not in use for classes or athletic events. The Globe of the Great Southwest Theatre is on the south side of the campus (*see* Performing Arts).

UNIVERSITY OF TEXAS AT THE PERMIAN BASIN

4901 E. University between John Ben Shepperd Parkway and Loop 338
552-2020 • W but not all areas

There are more than 2,100 students enrolled in this four-year university and graduate school. Visitors are welcome to intercollegiate sports activities and the art gallery located on the third floor.

PERFORMING ARTS

GLOBE OF THE GREAT SOUTHWEST THEATRE AND ANNE HATHAWAY COTTAGE

Odessa College, 2308 Shakespeare Rd. • 332-1586 • W • call ahead

The Globe is a nearly authentic replica of the home of William Shakespeare's acting company, the Globe Theatre in London. Like the original Globe, it was specifically built to house performances of Shakespeare's plays, and the plays are performed throughout the year, culminating in the annual Odessa Shakespeare Festival each spring (*see* Annual Events). The theater also regularly hosts community theater performances, the Brand New Opree, and the annual Renaissance Faire each May. The Anne Hathaway (Cottage) Library, named after Shakespeare's wife, replicates as close as possible her cottage in Shottery, England. The cottage has four large rooms, each with antique period decor. The Great Hall has an open-fire stove, large Tudor table, and upholstered Elizabethan chairs.

MIDLAND/ODESSA SYMPHONY AND CHORALE

Office at Terminal, between Midland and Odessa • 563-0921 • Admission • W

Formed in 1962, this is a professional orchestra that performs both a masterworks and a pops season of concerts, as well as a concerts by the Everest Quartet and the Lone Star Brass Quintet. A 100-voice volunteer chorale and the Symphony Pops singers perform regularly under the direction of the MOSC conductor. Call for concert information and location.

ODESSA BRAND NEW OPREE

Odessa College, Globe of the Great Southwest Theatre, 2308 Shakespeare Rd. 332-1586 • First Saturday evening of each month starting at 7 • General admission $3, reserved $5 • W call ahead

The family-oriented Opree is an opportunity to enjoy professional and amateur entertainers of gospel and C&W music from Texas and other states.

PERMIAN PLAYHOUSE

2750 N. Grandview and University • 362-2329 • Admission • W

A community theater staging six membership productions a year, plus several special shows. They also have a children's theater.

SHOPPING

RED DOOR ANTIQUES

2750 N. Grandview and University • 366-2911 or 366-0983 • W

This is the largest single-dealer antique store in West Texas. Inside is an antique buff's delight with jewelry, silver, cut glass, china, fine furniture, and primitives.

SIDE TRIPS

MONAHANS SANDHILLS STATE PARK

Take IH-20 west about 26 miles to Park Rd. 41 • 943-2092 (*see* **Monahans**)

ANNUAL EVENTS

January

SANDHILLS HEREFORD AND QUARTER HORSE SHOW AND RODEO

Ector County Coliseum, 42nd and Andrews Hwy. • 366-3541 • First week in January • Admission • W

This rodeo is the kickoff for the year-long competition on the Professional Rodeo Cowboys Association (PRCA) circuit. Top name entertainers perform nightly at the dance afterwards.

March/April

ODESSA SHAKESPEARE FESTIVAL

Odessa College, Globe of the Great Southwest Theatre, 2308 Shakespeare Rd. 332-1586 • Adults $8, seniors and students $6 • W call ahead

Professional and collegiate productions of the Bard's works performed in celebration of Shakespeare's birthday (April 23).

May

RENAISSANCE FAIR

Odessa College, Globe of the Great Southwest Theatre, 2308 Shakespeare Rd. 332-1586 • Usually first week in May • Admission

The fair is a traditional outdoor show representing the festivities of the fourteenth century in England. It features traditional Renaissance games, food, handcrafts, and dances. Costumed participants take part in jousting, archery, and other events.

September

PERMIAN BASIN FAIR AND EXPOSITION

Ector County Coliseum, 42nd and Andrews Hwy. • 366-3541 • Wednesday–Sunday in mid-September • Admission • W
Old-fashioned country fair with livestock shows, quilt and food judging, arts and crafts, contests, a carnival, and outdoor stage entertainment.

RESTAURANTS

($ = under $7, $$ = $8–$17, $$$ = $18–$25, $$$$ = over $25 for one person excluding drinks, tax, and tip.)

Tex-Mex

DOS AMIGOS

47th and Golder • 368-7556 • Lunch and dinner Tuesday–Saturday • Open some Sundays for scheduled bull rides, call. Closed Monday • $ • MC, V • W
Owner Ronnie Lewis converted a horse barn into a Tex-Mex eatery that is the site of bull rides once a month. Decorated with antiques, the restaurant creates a nostalgic step back in time. Top name entertainers perform on the outdoor stage. Bar.

Oriental

SHOGUN STEAK HOUSE

3952 E. 42nd, upstairs in Santa Fe Square • 368-4711 • Lunch and dinner Sunday–Friday, dinner only on Saturday • $–$$ • Cr • W (elevator) Children's plates
The lunch buffet is an excellent way to sample the Japanese delicacies. One of the specialties here is *Teppen Yaki* in which the chef prepares the dinner on a grill set in a table while the guests sit around and watch the show.

Steaks

THE BARN DOOR AND PECOS DEPOT

2140 N. Grant (Andrews Hwy) at E. 23rd • 337-4142 • Lunch and dinner Monday–Saturday. Closed Sunday • $$ • AE, MC, V • W • Children's plates
A gay-nineties-style restaurant, it is decorated with antiques and specializes in beef dishes with a few seafood and Tex-Mex entrées. Each entrée includes a complimentary soup and fresh hot bread and a block of cheddar cheese. Attached to the restaurant is the Pecos Depot Lounge. This is the original Santa Fe Railroad depot from Pecos, Texas, built in 1892.

HARRIGAN'S

2701 John Ben Shepperd Parkway at University • 367-4185 Lunch and dinner daily • $–$$ • Cr • W
Mesquite-grilled prime rib and a variety of steaks and hamburgers dominate the menu, but there is also chicken, seafood, and Tex-Mex. Bar.

ACCOMMODATIONS

($ = under $45, $$ = $46–$60, $$$ = $61–$80, $$$$ = $81–$100, $$$$$ = over $100)
Room tax 13%.

DAYS INN

3075 E. BUS Loop 20 just east of John Ben Shepperd Parkway • 335-8000 • $
W 1 room • No-smoking rooms
The three-story Days Inn has 96 rooms including 29 no-smoking rooms. Children under 18 stay free in room with parents. Senior discount. Cable TV with HBO. Room phones (no charge for local calls). Small pets OK. Free airport transportation. Restaurant and lounge. Outdoor pool. Free breakfast.

EXECUTIVE INN

2505 E. 2nd, east of Grandview • 333-1528 • $
The two-story Executive Inn has 44 rooms. Children under 10 stay free in room with parents. Senior discount. Cable TV with HBO. Room phones (no charge for local calls). Free coffee.

HILTON

5200 E. University at Loop 338 • 368-5885 or 800-533-0214 or 800-HILTONS (800-445-8667) • $$$ • W 2 rooms • No-smoking rooms
The eight-story Hilton has 194 units including six suites, two with Jacuzzis ($$$$$), and 15 no-smoking rooms. Children stay free in parents' room. Senior discount and family plan available. Satellite TV with movie and pay channels. Room phones (charge for local calls). Free airport transportation. Restaurant, lobby bar, and lounge with live entertainment Monday–Saturday. Outdoor heated pool and Jacuzzi. Guest memberships in local health club available. Free *USA Today*. Closest hotel to University of Texas at the Permian Basin.

HOLIDAY INN CENTRE

6201 E. BUS Loop 20, east of Loop 338 • 362-2311 or 800-HOLIDAY (800-465-4329) • $$$ • W 3 rooms • No-smoking rooms
The three-story Holiday Inn has 274 units including six suites ($$$$$) and 70 no-smoking rooms. Children under 19 stay free in room with parents. Senior discount and family plan. Cable TV with Showtime and pay channel. Room phones (charge for local calls). Small pets OK. Free airport transportation. Restaurant and lounge with DJ nightly. Holidome containing indoor/outdoor heated pool, whirlpool, wet and dry sauna, exercise area, miniature golf, and playground.

LA QUINTA

5001 E. BUS 20 at Loop 338 • 333-2820 or 800-531-5900 • $$ • W 2 rooms No-smoking rooms
The two-story La Quinta has 122 rooms including 48 no-smoking rooms. Children under 18 stay free in parents' room. Senior discount. Cable TV with Showtime. Room phones (no charge for local calls). House broken pets OK. Restaurant next door. Outdoor pool and small picnic area. Free morning coffee.

OZONA

Crockett County Seat • 3,181 • (915)

In addition to being the only town in a county larger than the state of Delaware, Ozona is also the largest unincorporated town in the nation. All of its business is taken care of by the county officials. The county is one of the nation's top wool and mohair producers, with more than one million pounds of each marketed annually. Oil and gas are other sources of income. At one time, Ozona claimed to have more millionaires per capita than any other city in the country.

TOURIST SERVICES

OZONA CHAMBER OF COMMERCE

1110 Ave. E (P.O. Box 1135, 76943) • 392-3737 • W variable

MUSEUMS

CROCKETT COUNTY MUSEUM

404 11th St. (BUS US 290), in basement of courthouse annex • 392-2837
Monday–Friday 9–5 • Free (donations)

Exhibits tell the history of the county from prehistoric times to the present. There are artifacts from the Indians, the Spanish, nearby Fort Lancaster, and the old Chihuahua Trail. Gift shop.

HISTORIC PLACES

CROCKETT COUNTY COURTHOUSE

404 11th St. at Ave. D • Free • W

Designed by Oscar Ruffini, this two-story structure was built in 1902 of native limestone.

CROCKETT COUNTY JAIL

Ave. D behind Courthouse

Built in 1892 with quarters for the sheriff's family downstairs and the jail upstairs. Still in use as jail.

EMERALD HOUSE

11th St. (BUS US 290) east of town in Memorial Fair Park

Emerald was the first town in the county. The people abandoned the town and moved to Ozona after that town became the county seat in 1891. This house was one of those moved when the town moved and is now the oldest dwelling in the county.

OTHER POINTS OF INTEREST

DAVY CROCKETT MONUMENT

Courthouse Square

This statue honors the hero of the Alamo for whom the county was named. There are many legends about this frontiersman, and also legends about the statue. One is that it was made for the town of Crockett but accidentally shipped to the Crockett County seat, Ozona. At the time the town of Crockett didn't have the money to pay to have it reshipped there, so the statue stayed.

PECOS

Reeves County Seat • 12,069 • (915)

Today, Pecos is a commercial center for ranching, farming, and oil production. One of its best-known products is the Pecos cantaloupe. But at the same
time it is a city intent on preserving its heritage from the Old West. Established
in 1881 when the Texas and Pacific Railroad put a stop here, the town started
out wild and woolly with gunmen like Billy the Kid and Clay Allison roaming
the streets. To "Pecos" a man in those days meant to kill him, then weigh down
the body with rocks, and toss it in the river. Much of this frontier history is on
exhibit in the West of the Pecos Museum. Another part of that heritage the
town continues to celebrate is its annual rodeo, which is more than a century
old. Pecos claims it gave birth to the world's first rodeo when cowboys from
several of the area ranches held some rip-roarin' contests on the Fourth of July
in 1883 to settle who was the best roper and rider.

TOURIST SERVICES

PECOS CHAMBER OF COMMERCE

1115 Cedar (US 285) (P.O. Box 27, 79772) 445-2406 • W

MUSEUMS

WEST OF THE PECOS MUSEUM

**120 E. 1st at Cedar (US 285) • 445-5076 • Tuesday–Saturday 9–5. Closed
Sunday–Monday. Closed December 18–25 • Adults $3.50, seniors $2.50, teens
$1, children 6–12 50¢ • W first floor only**

The old Orient Hotel, built in 1904 and once touted as the best hotel between
Fort Worth and El Paso, and the adjoining "Number 11 Saloon," built in 1896,
are now the home of this museum that depicts the colorful frontier history of the
area. That history includes a double killing in the saloon soon after it opened.
Bronze markers have been placed on the floor where the two men fell. In the
hotel there are about 30 rooms filled with exhibits. In addition to showing what
life in the hotel was like, they depict local life ranging from pioneer homes to the
elected Queens of the Rodeo. In the courtyard and park out back are a variety of
horse-drawn buggies and wagons, the oldest house in Pecos, the old jail and
hanging tree, a replica of Judge Roy Bean's "Jersey Lilly Saloon" (*see* Langtry),
and the grave of gunfighter Clay Allison. During Pecos' cantaloupe season, mid-
July to September, sliced cantaloupe is served to museum visitors.

OTHER POINTS OF INTEREST

MAXIE PARK

South of IH-20 between Tolivar and Cothrun

A small park featuring colorful cacti and other plants, plus a small zoo with a
variety of animals including deer, antelope, Mexican burros, and prairie dogs.

SPORTS AND ACTIVITIES

Golf

REEVES COUNTY GOLF COURSE

88 Starley Drive, behind Pecos Valley Country Club • 447-2858 • 12-hole course. Green fees: Weekdays $5, weekends $7

ANNUAL EVENTS

July

WEST OF THE PECOS RODEO

Rodeo Arena and various places in town • 445-2406 (Chamber of Commerce) Four days usually including July 4th • Admission to rodeo and some events W variable

On the Fourth of July, 1883, cowboys from the area ranches had a steer roping and bronc riding contest to see who was best, with prizes to the winners. Now, more than a century later, they celebrate this as the world's first rodeo. There are a number of events that make up rodeo week. Among them is a "Night in Old Pecos," the Golden Girl of the Old West Pageant, a rodeo parade, Old Timers' Reunion, Sheriff's Posse Bar-B-Q, and dances after the rodeo. And at the rodeo, in addition to the standard bone-rattling events, there is a wild cow milking contest and a wild mare race.

ACCOMMODATIONS

($ = under $45, $$ = $46–$60, $$$ = $61–$80, $$$$ = $81–$100, $$$$$ = over $100) Room Tax 13%

QUALITY INN

4002 S. Cedar, IH-20 and US 285 • 445-5404 or 800-332-5255 • $$ No-smoking rooms

The newly remodeled two-story inn has 96 rooms, including 50 no-smoking. Cable TV. Room phones (no charge for local calls). Pets OK. Restaurant. Private club (guests automatically members, temporary membership for non-guests $3). Outdoor pool and wading pool.

SAN ANGELO

Tom Green County Seat • 98,458 • (915)

It started out about 1870 as a cluster of gambling houses, saloons, brothels, and trading posts across the North Concho River from Fort Concho. The fort had been established a few years before in 1867, and the soldiers there called the settlement simply "Over the River." The fort was closed in 1889, but the village lived on, first as Santa Angela and then becoming the city of San Angelo, which is today the largest primary wood producer in the nation as well as a center for farming, ranching, and oil production.

Today "Over the River" is also called "The Oasis of West Texas" because of the river. After a flood in 1936, the Concho was tamed with a series of dams. But damming the river caused it to stagnate and become polluted. In the 1970s,

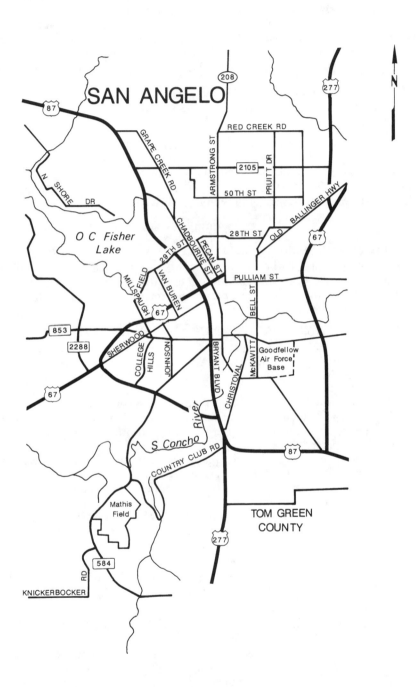

it was a smelly eyesore when a group of citizens joined together to try to revitalize the dying river and turn it into an asset to the community. With the backing of the people, evidenced by passage of a bond issue for river beautification in 1980, they have succeeded. Today parks and gardens line the river. Through the downtown area are four miles of hike and bike trails, 14 water fountains, picnic tables, a golf course, and turn-of-the-century lighting. And the water is clean and clear.

This river is also famed for the Concho pearl. At least 12 varieties of mussels inhabit the Concho system, and one of these varieties occasionally produces. (*See* Offbeat.)

TOURIST SERVICES

SAN ANGELO CONVENTION AND VISITORS BUREAU

500 Río Concho Drive (76903) • 653-1206 or 800-375-1206
Web page http://www.sanangelo-tx.com/cc_tourw.htm • W

MUSEUMS

E.H. DANNER MUSEUM OF TELEPHONY

Officers Quarters #4 at Fort Concho, 213 E. Ave. D • 481-2646
Monday–Friday 8–5 • Free with admission to Fort • W variable
The exhibits of antique instruments and equipment in this museum trace the evolution of the telephone.

FORT CONCHO NATIONAL HISTORIC LANDMARK

213 E. Ave. D • Weekdays: 481-2646 • Tuesday–Saturday 10–5, Sunday 1–5
Closed Thanksgiving and Christmas • Adults $2.00, students $1.25, seniors and military $1.50, children under 6 free • Tickets at headquarters building W but not all buildings
The fort was closed in 1889, but because of its solid construction many of the buildings have withstood the test of time and are still standing. A concerted effort to restore and revitalize the old fort has paid off. It is now considered among the best preserved of the frontier forts.

Among the buildings around the quadrangle parade field are several barracks, officers' quarters, headquarters, commissary, and the school. Exhibits in these buildings tell the history of the development of the West and of Fort Concho's role in that development.

Fort Concho is owned by the city, and its staff and volunteers have gone to great lengths to help visitors relive history. Everything is as close to the original as possible. Guided or independent tours usually take about one and a half hours. For information call 481-2646.

Several festivals and special events take place on the fort grounds, including Christmas in Old Fort Concho (*see* Annual Events).

MISS HATTIE'S MUSEUM

18½ E. Concho • 655-1166 • Tuesday–Saturday 10–5 • Admission $3
Tickets at Needful Things, next door
At the turn of the century, East Concho was a street of saloons with several bordellos nestled in among them. This was one of the houses of ill-repute. It is faithfully restored and includes original furnishings and original and reproduc-

tions of the clothes worn—and not worn—by the "soiled doves" who entertained ranchers, cowboys, businessmen, and soldiers here.

ROBERT WOOD JOHNSON MUSEUM OF FRONTIER MEDICINE

213 E. Avenue D, inside the reconstructed Post Hospital, in the John and Sally Meadows Historical Complex on the ground of Fort Concho 481-2646 • Tuesday–Saturday 10–6, Sunday 1–4 • Admission included in tour of Fort Concho

Here, the tools of the frontier physician and surgeon trace the history of medicine from the late 1860s to the 20th century. Behind the hospital is a replica of a tuberculosis isolation bungalow, typical of the type built at the sanitorium at Carlsbad, just north of San Angelo, which housed tuberculosis patients in the 1930s and 1940s.

SAN ANGELO MUSEUM OF FINE ARTS

Fort Concho, E. Ave. C and Burgess, in Quartermaster Building • 658-4084 Tuesday–Saturday 10–4, Sunday 1–4 • Adults $2, children, seniors and military $1, under 6 free • W downstairs only

Exhibits change frequently and cover all art periods and a variety of media. There are usually three to six exhibits.

HISTORIC PLACES

CONCHO AVENUE

Just east of Chadbourne

This was the first block to be laid out in the town, and at one time this area was home to over 35 saloons and brothels. From 20 to 26 E. Concho, three one-story masonry structures built in the mid-1880s represent San Angelo's first surge of permanent buildings. Upstairs at 18 is where Miss Hattie's brothel operated for almost half a century; across the street is a furniture store in the building that once housed a livery stable, carriage factory, and saloon.

OTHER POINTS OF INTEREST

CACTUS HOTEL

36 E. Twohig

This was Conrad Hilton's fourth hotel. Built in 1929, it was the largest, most ornate, and the most expensive ($900,000).

The hotel, with its 14 stories, lavish decorations and elegant crystal ballroom, has been revitalized as the city's cultural center. The San Angelo Symphony, The Civic Ballet, and the Cultural Affairs Council are housed in the hotel.

The San Angelo Museum of Fine Arts, Children's Museum and Gift Shop are located on the first floor. In the lobby and on the mezzanine are shops, a turn-of-the-century barber shop, a restaurant, and a coffee house. For more information call 655-5000.

CIVIC PARK LILY POND

Beauregard and Park Street

Rare and exotic waterlilies grow here, including a species that was extinct in Texas for almost 70 years, the ancient Blue Lotus of the Nile.

EL PASEO DE SANTA ANGELO

Downtown San Angelo to Fort Concho

A combination of public and private dollars helped create this heritage trail linking the past and future of San Angelo—an open mall and marketplace that includes pathways, two pavilions and a tiered plaza connecting Fort Concho National Historic Landmark, the Historic Orient-Santa Fe Railroad depots, and the Concho River. Visitors can walk from the Celebration Bridge to Fort Concho along a pecan-shaded walkway accented by fountains, reconstructed ranch buildings, and windmills.

GOODFELLOW AIR FORCE BASE

Fort McKavett Rd. between Paint Rock Rd. (FM 388) and S. Chadbourne (FM 1223) • 654-3876 (Public Affairs Office)

This Air Training command base provides intelligence and cryptology training for personnel from all the armed services. Group tours may be arranged by calling the Public Affairs Office.

LAKE NASWORTHY

Take Knickerbocker (FM 584) southwest approximately 6 miles • 944-3812 (Lake Ranger) • Open at all times • $1 per vehicle weekends and holidays March 1–Labor Day • Other times free

A 1,596-acre lake that is a companion to the larger Twin Buttes Reservoir (see below). Camping (fee), picnicking, fishing, swimming, and other water sports.

SAN ANGELO NATURE CENTER

7409 Knickerbocker • 942-0121 • Adults $2, $1 children 3–18 • Call for hours

Located on the shore of Lake Nasworthy, the center features native plant gardens, and a natural science and natural history museum.

SAN ANGELO STATE PARK

The San Angelo State Park features 7,000 acres of recreational and leisure activities. Located at O. C. Fisher Reservoir, the park has abundant camping facilities and RV hookups. San Angelo State Park is situated northwest of San Angelo. For additional information, call 949-4757.

PRODUCERS' LIVESTOCK AUCTION AND STOCKYARDS

1131 N. Bell • 653-3371 • Tuesday–Friday

This is the nation's number one sheep market and one of Texas' largest cattle markets. Sheep sales are on Tuesday and Wednesday and cattle sales on Thursday and Friday. Stockyards Cafe is open Monday–Friday.

TWIN BUTTES RESERVOIR

Take US 67 west approximately 5 miles • 949-7187 • Open at all times • $1 per vehicle weekends and holidays March 1–Labor Day • Other times free

An impoundment of the Middle and South Concho rivers with a 8.1-mile-long earth-filled dam, one of the longest of that type dam ever built by the Bureau of Reclamation. On the 500 acres are facilities for camping (fee), picnicking, boating, fishing, swimming, and other water sports. Adjoins Lake Nasworthy (see above).

SPORTS AND ACTIVITIES

Golf

CITADEL ON THE CONCHO GOLF COURSE
At the junction of Pullium Street and Loop 306 • 657-0629
San Angelo's newest public golf course. 27 holes, 128 sand traps and 4 sets of tees.

LAKESIDE GOLF COURSE
Mathis Field, south of San Angelo Municipal Airport • 949-2069 • 9-hole course • Green fees: daily $3.25

RIVERSIDE GOLF CLUB
900 W. 29th • 643-6130 • 18-hole course • Green fees: Weekdays $8, weekends $9

SANTA FE GOLF COURSE
Santa Fe Park • 657-4485 • 9-hole course • Green fees: Weekdays $5, weekends $6

COLLEGES AND UNIVERSITIES

ANGELO STATE UNIVERSITY
2601 W. Ave. N, Administration Building between Johnson and Rosemont 942-2248 • Adults $4, children $1.50 • W but not all areas
Visitor parking marked
More than 6,000 students are enrolled in both undergraduate programs. In addition to football and other intercollegiate sports, visitors are welcome to the art gallery in the University Center and the Planetarium. The Planetarium is one of the largest and most technologically advanced in the state. It is located in the Nursing-Physical Science Building on Vanderventer just west of the high-rise residence halls (942-2188). There are usually two shows a week: Thursday 8 P.M. and Saturday 2 P.M.

ANGELO CIVIC THEATRE
1936 Sherwood Way • 949-4400 • Adults $7.50–$10, students and seniors $5–$10 • W call ahead
Five or six productions a year including dramas, comedies and musicals.

SAN ANGELO SYMPHONY ORCHESTRA
658-5877
This is a professional orchestra that presents a fall-to-spring season of symphony and pops concerts, frequently with well-known guest artists, occasionally performs with the Symphony Chorale. Most symphony performances are at the City Auditorium, 72 W. College, and pops concerts are at the San Angelo Coliseum, 50 E. 43rd.

SHOPPING

CONCHO AVENUE

The first street in San Angelo, Concho Avenue is still a great place to shop, with antique and clock shops, designer fashion stores, a working saddle shop, and lunch at a sidewalk cafe or tearoom.

In addition to shopping along San Angelo's historic Concho Avenue, San Angelo offers shopping throughout downtown.

OLD CHICKEN FARM ART CENTER

2505 Martin Luther King Blvd.• *Take US 87 N to 23rd, then 1 block east to Martin Luther King* • **653-4936** • **Tuesday–Saturday 10–5** • **W but not all buildings**

This chicken farm was converted in the 1970s to studios for about a dozen artists working in a number of media including paintings, photography, fiber, metal, glass, clay, and wood. Visitors are invited to watch the artists at work. Works for sale range in price from about $2 to $500.

KIDS' STUFF

NEFF'S AMUSEMENT PARK

River Plaza Place • **653-3014** • **Open mid-March until school begins again Admission**

A small amusement park on the Concho River with a variety of rides and amusement games for children of all ages.

CHILDREN'S ART MUSEUM

First floor of the Cactus Hotel, 36 E. Twohig • **659-4391**
Tuesday–Friday 1–5, Saturday 10–5, Sunday 1–5 • **Admission $2, free on Tuesdays, children under 2 free, discounts for seniors and military**

The museum focuses on activities that require some real thought and encourage creative problem solving.

ANNUAL EVENTS

March

SAN ANGELO STOCK SHOW AND RODEO

Coliseum Fairgrounds • **653-7785** • **First weekend in March**
Stock Show: adults $1, children 50¢, rodeo $6.25

Entries come from all over Texas to this stock show. Rodeo most nights.

June

FIESTA DEL CONCHO

One of the most fun-filled and unique summer events in San Angelo, this attraction has grown in popularity over the years. Among the crowd's favorites are children's activities booths, arts-and-crafts booths, armadillo races and all types of food. Continuous entertainment for all ages, stretching from the Concho River to the El Paseo de Santa Angela. For information call 655-4136.

The highlight of this fiesta week is the river parade on Saturday night with floats to provide a nighttime extravaganza. Other activities throughout the week include a street parade, talent shows, fiddler's contest, a dance under the stars at Fort Concho, arts and crafts fair, armadillo races, boat rides, contests on and off the river, musical entertainment, and special activities for children.

November

COWBOY ROPING FIESTA

Coliseum Fairground, 43rd and Coliseum Dr. • 653-7785 • First weekend in November • Admission • W but not all areas
  Some of the best calf and steer roping in the country.

December

CHRISTMAS AT OLD FORT CONCHO

Fort Concho, 213 E. Ave. D • 657-4441 • First weekend in December Admission • W but not all buildings
  Visitors will find the 20 historic buildings at the fort aglow with thousands of flickering candle *luminarias.* Each building is decorated to represent Christmas at a different time in the past. Highlights include a colorful historical Christmas pageant presented each evening featuring about 200 costumed actors, singers, and dancers; heritage chapel services; strolling *mariachis;* choirs; horse-drawn wagon rides; and shopping for unique gifts displayed by more than 100 merchants and artisans. As many as 40,000 people attend this event each year. Proceeds benefit the fort restoration project.

CONCHO CHRISTMAS CELEBRATION

  The El Paseo de Santa Angela and the River Walk are arrayed with Christmas lights from November 29 to December 31 each year. Over a million Christmas lights are lit each night with large-scale animated scenes. The giant community Christmas party includes tours, Santa Claus, entertainment, and a large Christmas card display.

OFFBEAT

CONCHO PEARL

  The Concho River is aptly named because it is the River of Shells. At least 12 varieties of mussels inhabit the Concho system. However only one species (*Cyrtonaias tampicoensis*) produces pearls. The pearl begins as an irritant, often a microscopic parasite, which finds its way inside the mussel's shell. The mussel coats the irritant with layers of shiny nacre, eventually producing a natural pearl. Freshwater pearls are found in many areas of the country, but none grow with the consistency of beautiful pastel colors and luster as those found in the San Angelo area. Legend has it that several pieces of the crown jewels in Spain contain some of the earliest examples of fine pearls from the Concho. The pearls can be found is most of the city's large jewelry stores.

RESTAURANTS

($ = under $7, $$ = $8–$17, $$$ = $18–$25, $$$$ = over $25 for one person excluding drinks, tax, and tip.)

Oriental

CHINA GARDEN

4217 College Hills Blvd. at Loop 306 • 949-2838
Lunch and dinner daily • $–$$ • Cr • W • Children's plates
   Extensive menu goes beyond Chinese to American steaks and seafood. What it may lack in oriental authenticity it makes up for in ample portions. Bar.

Steaks

ZENTNER'S STEAKHOUSE

2715 Sherwood Way • 942-8631 • Lunch and dinner daily • $$
Cr, but not DIS • Children's plates
   A steak-and-potato lover is in high cotton here. That's what they serve in large portions at reasonable prices. Bar.

ZENTNER'S DAUGHTER

1901 Knickerbocker, across from the stadium • 949-2821
Lunch and dinner daily • $$ • Cr • W • Children's plates
   Don't be confused by the name—the Zentners running the local steak houses are not related. The West Texas favorite here is chicken-fried steak. A specialty is what they call "Tenders," a small premium steak that goes for about $10.95 for one, up to $18.95 for two people. You can also get a K.C. steak for $24 that is enough to feed the whole family. There is a touch of seafood, chicken, ham, etc., on the menu, but here steak is king. Bar.

ACCOMMODATIONS

($ = under $45, $$ = $46–$60, $$$ = $61–$80, $$$$ = $81–$100, $$$$$ = over $100)
Room tax 13%

BEST WESTERN INN OF THE WEST

415 W. Beauregard • 653-2995, 800-582-9668 or 800-528-1234 • $
No-smoking rooms
   This two- and three-story Best Western has 75 rooms including 13 no-smoking. Children under 12 stay free in room with parents. Senior discount. Cable TV with HBO. Room phones (no charge for local calls). Small housebroken pets OK. Restaurant and lounge. Small indoor heated pool. Coffee in rooms.

DAYS INN

4613 S. Jackson • 658-6594 • $ • W 2 rooms • No-smoking rooms
   The 113-room motel includes 21 no-smoking rooms and two suites ($$). Senior discount. Cable TV with HBO. Room phones (no charge for local calls). Restaurant. Outdoor pool. Free coffee in lobby.

EL PATIO MOTOR INN

1901 W. Beauregard at Milton • 655-5711 or 800-677-7735 • $
W 1 room • No-smoking rooms
   This two-story motel has 100 rooms, including 20 no-smoking. Children under 12 free in room with parents. Senior discount. Cable TV. Room phones

(no charge for local calls). Pets OK. Restaurant. Outdoor pool. Free coffee in lobby.

HOLIDAY INN CONVENTION CENTER HOTEL

441 Río Concho Dr. on the river walk • 658-2828 or 800-HOLIDAY (800-465-4329) • $$–$$$ • W 2 rooms • No-smoking rooms

This six-story hotel has 149 rooms, including 60 no-smoking, and three suites ($$$$$). Children under 19 stay free in room with parents. Senior discount. Cable TV with pay channel. Room phones (no charge for local calls). Pets OK. Lounge with live entertainment Tuesday–Saturday. Fire sprinklers in rooms. Indoor heated pool and hot tub. Coffeemakers in rooms.

LA QUINTA INN

2307 Loop 306 S. at Knickerbocker • 949-0515 or 800-531-5900 • $–$$ W 2 rooms • No-smoking rooms

The two-story La Quinta has 170 rooms, including 69 no-smoking. Children under 18 stay free in room with parents. Senior discount. Satellite TV with Showtime. Room phones (no charge for local calls). Small pets OK. Restaurant. Outdoor pool and Jacuzzi. Free coffee in lobby.

SONORA

Sutton County Seat • 2,751 • (915)

There were two interesting legal incidents in the early years of this town after its founding in 1890. First, to avoid the rowdiness of other frontier towns, a clause was put in each deed prohibiting the premises from being used to sell liquor. But one deed slipped by without that clause, and a saloon opened. The second incident was of greater importance to the early settlers. Not long after the town was settled, it was discovered that there was a survey error and the land the town was built on was actually owned by a New York company. The result was the citizens had to repurchase their own homesites to straighten out the titles.

The world's longest fenced cattle trail once operated from here. It was a right-of-way owned by the Fort Worth and Río Grande Railroad, but it was a railroad without rails. Cattle were moved through a fenced lane 250 feet wide and 100 miles long from Sonora to the railhead at Brady. The railroad itself did not come to town until 1930. Cattle are still important here, but today this city is better known as a center for the production of wool and mohair. Oil-related industries also contribute significantly to the economy. The main tourist attraction here is the famed Caverns of Sonora.

TOURIST SERVICES

SONORA CHAMBER OF COMMERCE

706 SW Crockett, BUS US 290 near 6th St. (P.O. Box 1172, 76950) 387-2880 • Monday–Friday 9–12 and 1–5

HISTORIC PLACES

SUTTON COUNTY COURTHOUSE

Water Ave. between Oak and Poplar • 387-2711
Open regular county office hours • Free • W

There have not been any major attempts to modernize, so this Second Empire design building is still pretty much as it was when it was built in the early 1890s. A time capsule buried in the lawn in 1986 is scheduled to be opened in 2036.

OTHER POINTS OF INTEREST

CAVERNS OF SONORA

Take IH-10 west about 8 miles to FM 1989 (exit 392), then south about 6 miles
387-3105 • Summer 8–6, winter 9–5. Closed Christmas • Admission

Although it is a relatively small cave, it is ranked by cave experts as being among the world leaders for sheer beauty, color, and delicacy of formations. In fact, Bill Stephenson, founder of the American Speleological Society, called it ". . . the most indescribably beautiful cavern in the world." The tour, which takes about one-and-a-half hours to cover about 1.5 miles, starts out rather dull because it moves through the dead part of the cavern. But once the active part of the cavern is reached the beauty makes up for the boring walk in. The walk is relatively easy most of the way, but the exit requires climbing many stairs (usually with stops at landings) so save energy for that. Tours leave every 30 minutes, or sooner if 12 people are waiting. Snack bar, gift shop, and campgrounds with hookups (fee).

SPORTS AND ACTIVITIES

Golf

SONORA MUNICIPAL GOLF COURSE

Golf Course Rd., north access road on IH-10 west of US 277 • 387-3680
9-hole course. Green fees: Weekdays $10, weekends and holidays $12.

ANNUAL EVENTS

June

WOOL AND MOHAIR SHOW

Langford Memorial 4-H Center, US 290W just east of IH-10 • 387-3101
(County Extension Agent) • Thursday–Saturday in mid-June • Free • W

Ranchers from all over the area bring their wool and mohair to be judged in this prestigious show. The National 4-H Wool Judging Show is held at the same time and teams come from all over the nation.

August

SUTTON COUNTY DAYS AND PRCA RODEO

Courthouse lawn and Sutton County Park on US 290W • 387-2880 (Chamber of Commerce) • Usually Thursday–Saturday before Labor Day • Admission to rodeo and dance • W

Sutton County Days includes an Old Time Fiddler's Contest and other contests, a Friday night parade, arts and crafts and food booths, and the crowning of Miss Sutton County. The rodeo runs all three nights with an outdoor dance after the Friday and Saturday performances.

RESTAURANTS

($ = under $7, $$ = $8–$17, $$$ = $18–$25, $$$$ = over $25 for one person excluding drinks, tax, and tip.)

SUTTON COUNTY STEAKHOUSE

Golf Course Rd., exit 400 off IH-10 at Devil's River Motel • 387-3833
Breakfast, lunch, and dinner Monday–Saturday; breakfast and lunch only on
Sunday • $–$$ • AE, MC, V • W • Children's plates

This is not your usual interstate restaurant. Most of their clientele are local ranchers, cowboys, and oilfield roughnecks who want simple, good food in large portions. Testimony to the size of their portions is the large number of doggie bags carried out even by hearty eaters. Menu is varied, but steaks, seafood, and Texas-sized burgers are the mainstays. Their beef is always fresh, cut daily in their own butcher shop. "Dining Lite" specials available. Bar.

ACCOMMODATIONS

($ = under $45, $$ = $46–$60, $$$ = $61–$80, $$$$ = $81–$100, $$$$$ = over $100)

Room tax 13%

DEVIL'S RIVER MOTEL

Golf Course Rd., exit 400 off IH-10 • 387-3516 • $$ • W+ 3 rooms
No-smoking rooms

This one- and two-story motel has 99 rooms, including 33 no-smoking. Cable TV and HBO. Room phones (no charge for local calls). Pets OK ($2 charge). Restaurant. Outdoor pool. Self-service laundry. Free coffee in lobby.

Index

Abilene, 613–622
  accommodations,
    621–622
  annual events, 618–619
  historic places, 614–615
  history, 613–614
  lake, 616
  map, 613
  museums, 614
  other points of interest,
    615–616
  performing arts, 617
  restaurants, 619–621
  shopping, 617–618
  side trips, 618
  sports and activities, 616
  tourist services, 614
  universities, 616–617
  zoo, 615
Abilene Christian
  University, 616
Abilene State Park, 615
Accommodations. *See
  individual town/city
  listings*
Acton State Historic Site
  (Acton Cemetery),
  426–427
Addison, 310–314
  accommodations,
    313–314
  annual events, 312
  aviation tours, 310
  history, 310
  museums, 311
  other points of interest,
    311
  sports and activities, 311
  performing arts, 311
  restaurants, 312–313
  shopping, 312
  tourist services, 310

Admiral Nimitz State
    Historical Park, 194
Alabama-Coushatta Indian
    Reservation, 72
Alamo, 251
Alamo Community College
    district, 259
Albany, 622–623
Alibates Flint Quarries
    National Monument,
    648
Alpine, 686–690
  accommodations,
    689–690
  history, 686
  museums, 686
  other points of interest,
    687
  restaurants, 689
  shopping, 687–688
  side trips, 688
  tourist services, 686
  university, 687
Amarillo, 623–639
  accommodations,
    637–639
  annual events, 633–634
  college, 629
  historic places, 625
  history, 623–624
  kids' stuff, 631
  map, 624
  museums and art
    galleries, 625–626
  other points of interest,
    626–627
  performing arts, 629–630
  restaurants, 634–636
  shopping, 630–631
  side trips, 632
  sports and activities,
    627–628
  tourist services, 624

Amarillo College, 629
Amistad National
    Recreation Area,
    516–517
Angelina College, 76
Angelina National Forest,
    65, 76
Angelo State University,
    765
Anheuser-Busch Brewery,
    27
Annual events. *See
    individual towns*
Aransas National Wildlife
    Refuge, 591
Arlington, 314–322
  accommodations,
    320–322
  annual events, 319
  commercial tours, 314
  history, 314
  kids' stuff, 318–319
  lake, 316
  museums, 315–316
  performing arts, 317–318
  restaurants, 320
  shopping, 318
  side trips, 319
  sports and activities,
    316–317
  tourist services, 314
  university, 317
Art galleries. *See individual
    cities*
Astrodome, 28
Astroworld, 43
Attwater Prairie Chicken
    National Wildlife
    Refuge, 190
Austin, 135–169
  accommodations,
    164–169
  annual events, 156

bird's-eye view, 139
colleges and universities,
    148–150
historic places, 142–145
history, 135–137
kids' stuff, 155
lakes, 146
map, 136
museums and art
    galleries, 139–142,
    154–155
other points of interest,
    145
performing arts, 150–151
restaurants, 157–164
shopping, 151–154
sports and activities,
    147–148
Texas capitol, 143–144
tourist services, 137
walking tours, 137–139
zoo, 155
Austin College, 468
Balmorhea State Park, 732
Bandera, 169–171
accommodations, 171
annual events, 170
historic places, 170
history, 169
museums, 169
restaurants, 170–171
side trips, 170
sports and activities, 170
tourist services, 169
Baseball. *See also* Sports
    under individual
    town/city
Houston Astros, 32
Texas Rangers, 316
Basketball. *See also* Sports
    under individual
    town/city
Dallas Mavericks, 346
Houston Rockets, 32
San Antonio Spurs, 258
Bastrop, 171–173
Bastrop State Park, 172
Bat colony, 145
Battleship Texas, 43–44
Baylor University, 303
Beaumont, 475–481
accommodations,
    480–481
annual events, 479
bird's-eye view, 477

history, 475
map, 476
museums, 477–478
offbeat, 479–480
performing arts, 479
restaurants, 480
shopping, 479
side trips, 479
sports and activities, 478
tourist services, 475–476
tours, 479–480
university, 478–479
Bed and breakfasts
Alpine, 690
Austin, 168–169
Bastrop, 173
Belton, 175
Boerne, 178
Bonham, 325
Brady, 180
Brenham, 4
Bryan/College Station, 8
Canyon, 645
Center, 12
Chappell Hill, 13
Clifton, 327
Columbus, 191
Comfort, 193
Crockett, 19
Del Rio, 521
Fort Davis, 733
Fort Worth, 417, 418
Galveston, 539
Gonzales, 204
Granbury, 429
Hico, 205
Hillsboro, 444
Houston, 60
Huntsville, 64
Jefferson, 70
Lampasas, 220
Llano, 222
Mason, 229
Nacogdoches, 91–92
Navasota, 94
New Braunfels, 238
Salado, 244
San Antonio, 281
San Augustine, 117
South Padre Island, 603
Snyder, 675
Stephenville, 291
Waco, 307
Wimberley, 309
Woodville, 134

Belton, 173–175
accommodations, 175
annual events, 174–175
historic places, 173–174
history, 173
museums, 173
other points of interest,
    174
restaurants, 175
sports and activities, 174
tourist services, 173
university, 174
Belton Lake, 174, 214, 295
Bentsen-Rio Grande State
    Park, 566
Big Bend National Park,
    690–697
accommodations, 697
bird's-eye view, 694
historic places, 694
history, 690–691
maps, 692–693
other points of interest,
    694–695
restaurants, 697
shopping, 696–697
sports and activities,
    695–696
visitor center, 691, 694
Big Bend Ranch State Park,
    698–699
Big Spring, 699–702
accommodations, 702
annual events, 701–702
colleges, 701
historic places, 700
history, 699–700
museums, 700
other points of interest,
    700–701
restaurants, 702
tourist services, 700
Big Spring State Park, 700
Big Thicket National
    Preserve, 1
Billy Bob's Texas, 415
Blinn College, 3
Blue Bell Creameries, 2
Boerne, 175–178
accommodations,
    177–178
annual events, 177
historic places, 176
history, 175–176
museums, 176

other points of interest, 176
restaurants, 177
side trips, 176–177
tourist services, 176
Bonham, 322–325
accommodations, 325
annual events, 325
historic places, 323
history, 322
museums, 322–323
other points of interest, 323–324
side trips, 324–325
tourist services, 322
Bonham State Recreation Area, 324
Brady, 178–180
accommodations, 180
annual events, 179
history, 178
lake, 179
museums, 178
other points of interest, 179
restaurants, 179–180
sports and activities, 179
tourist services, 178
Brazoria National Wildlife Refuge, 484
Brazos Bend State Park, 44, 111
Brazosport, 481–485
accommodations, 485
annual events, 484
history, 481–482
kids' stuff, 484
map, 481
museums, 482
other points of interest, 482–483
restaurants, 485
side trips, 484
sports and activities, 483–484
tourist services, 482
Breckenridge, 639–641
Brenham, 1–4
accommodations, 4
annual events, 3
college, 3
history, 1
historic places, 2
lake, 3

other points of interest, 2–3
restaurants, 4
shopping, 3
side trips, 3
tourist services, 1–2
Breweries
Anheuser-Busch Brewery, 27
Celis Brewery, 145
Brownsville, 486–496
accommodations, 495–496
annual events, 494
historic places, 489–490
history, 486
map, 487
museums, 488–489
other points of interest, 491–492
performing arts, 493
restaurants, 494–495
shopping, 493
sports and activities, 492–493
tourist services, 486, 488
tours, 486, 488
zoo, 491
Brownwood, 180–182
accommodations, 182
annual events, 182
history, 180
museums, 181
performing arts, 181
restaurants, 182
side trips, 181
tourist services, 180
university, 181
Bryan Beach State Recreation Area, 482–483
Bryan/College Station, 4–8
accommodations, 8
history, 4
map, 5
museums, 6
performing arts, 7
restaurants, 7–8
sport, 6
tourist services, 6
university, 6–7
winery, 6
Buchanan Dam, 182–184
Buffalo Gap Historic Village, 618

Burnet, 184–185
Caddo Lake State Park, 69, 81
Caddo-LBJ National Grasslands and Wildlife Management Area, 324–325
Caddoan Mounds State Historical Park, 17, 115
Canyon, 641–644
Caprock Canyons State Park, 632
Carlsbad Caverns National Park, 738
Carthage, 8–10
accommodations, 11–12
annual events, 10
college, 9
historic places, 9
history, 8
lake, 10
points of interest, 9
side trips, 9–10
tourist services, 8
museums, 9
Cascade Caverns, 176
Castroville, 186–188
Caverns
Carlsbad Caverns National Park, 738
Cascade Caverns, 176
Inner Space Caverns, 200
Longhorn Caverns State Park, 185
Natural Bridge Caverns, 235, 266
Celis Brewery, 145
Center, 10–12
annual events, 11
historic places, 10
history, 10
tourist services, 10
museums, 10
side trips, 11
Chamizal National Memorial, 713
Chappell Hill, 12–13
accommodations, 13
annual events, 13
historic places, 13
history, 12
museums, 12
tourist services, 12

Cibolo Wilderness Trail
and Agricultural
Heritage Center, 176
Clear Lake Area, 497–500
accommodations,
499–500
annual events, 499
history, 497
points of interest,
497–498
restaurants, 499
shopping, 499
side trips, 499
sports and activities, 498
tourist services, 497
Clifton, 326–327
College Station. *See*
Bryan/College Station
Colleges. *See also*
Universities
Alamo Community
College district, 259
Amarillo College, 629
Angelina College, 76
Austin College, 468
Blinn College, 3
Collin County
Community
College, 459
Dallas County
Community
College District,
348–349
Eastfield Community
College, 456
El Paso Community
College, 717
Galveston College, 531
Grayson County
College, 379
Hill College, 443
Houston Community
College system, 33
Howard College, 701
Kilgore College, 71
Laredo Community
College, 555–556
McLennan Community
College, 304
Midland College, 746
Navarro College, 329
North Central Texas
College, 420
North Lake Community
College, 448

Odessa College, 754
Panola College, 9
Paris Junior College, 104
Richland College, 463
San Antonio College, 259
Southwest Collegiate
Institute for the
Deaf, 701
Tarrant County Junior
College (TCJC), 401
Texarkana College, 123
Texas College, 128
Texas State Technical
College, 304
Tyler Junior College, 128
Victoria College, 606
Weatherford College, 473
Western Texas College,
674
Wiley College, 80
Collin County Community
College, 459
Colorado City, 703–705
Columbus, 188–191
accommodations, 191
annual events, 190
golf, 190
historic places, 189
history, 188
museums and historic
homes, 189
restaurants, 190
side trips, 190
tourist services, 188–189
Comal River, 232
Comfort, 191–193
Congress Avenue Bridge
Bat Colony, 145
Conroe, 14–16
accommodations, 16
annual events, 15–16
history, 14
lake, 14
points of interest, 14–15
side trips, 15
theater, 15
tourist services, 14
Cooper Lake State Park,
118
Copper Breaks State Park,
672
Corpus Christi, 500–515
accommodations,
513–515
annual events, 511

bird's-eye view, 503
historic places, 506
history, 500, 502
map, 501
museums, 503–505
other points of interest,
506–508
performing arts, 510
restaurants, 511–513
shopping, 510–511
sports and activities,
508–510
tourist services, 502–503
zoo, 507
Corsicana, 327–330
Cotton Bowl, 337
Southwestern Bell
Cotton Bowl
Classic, 358–359
Crockett, 17–19
accommodations, 19
annual events, 18
history, 17
lake, 18
historic places, 17
restaurants, 18
side trips, 17–18
tourist services, 17
Crosbyton, 660
Dalhart, 644–646
Dallas, 330–376
accommodations,
370–376
annual events, 358–361
bird's-eye view, 335
clubs and bars, 369–370
colleges and universities,
348–349
historic places, 342–343
history, 330, 332
kids' stuff, 356–357
map, 331
museums, 336–337,
338–341
offbeat, 358
other points of interest,
343–346
performing arts, 349–355
restaurants, 362–369
shopping, 355–356
sports and activities,
346–348
tourist services, 333
tours, 334–335
zoo, 345

Dallas County Community College district, 348–349
Dallas Cowboys, 447
Dallas Mavericks, 346
Dallas Stars, 347, 447
Davis Mountains State Park, 731
Davy Crockett National Forest, 17–18, 76
Dealey Plaza National Historic Landmark District/Kennedy Assassination Site, 342
Del Rio, 515–521
  accommodations, 520–521
  annual events, 519
  history, 515–516
  lake, 516–517
  map, 515
  museums, 516
  other points of interest, 516–518
  restaurants, 519–520
  shopping, 518
  side trips, 518–519
  sports and activities, 518
  tourist services, 516
  winery, 517–518
Denison, 377–380
  accommodations, 380
  annual events, 379–380
  college, 379
  historic places, 378
  history, 377
  lake, 378–379
  museums, 377
  other points of interest, 378–379
  restaurant, 380
  shopping, 379
  sports and activities, 379
  tourist services, 377
Denton, 381–385
  accommodations, 384–385
  annual events, 384
  historic places, 381
  history, 381
  lake, 383
  museums, 381
  offbeat, 383
  performing arts, 383
  restaurants, 384

  side trips, 383
  sports and activities, 382
  tourist services, 381
  universities, 382–383
Dining out. *See individual town/city*
Dinosaur Valley State Park, 424
East Texas Baptist University, 80
Eastfield Community College, 356
Eastland, 646–647
Eisenhower State Recreation Area, 378
El Paso, 705–729
  accommodations, 727–729
  annual events, 721–723
  bird's-eye view, 709
  colleges and universities, 717–718
  historic places, 712–713
  history, 705–708
  kids' stuff, 720
  map, 706
  museums, 709–711
  other points of interest, 713–716
  performing arts, 718–719
  restaurants, 723–727
  shopping, 719
  side trips, 721
  sports and activities, 716–717
  tourist services, 708–709
  zoo, 714
El Paso Community College, 717
Enchanted Rock State Natural Area, 16
Fair Park, 335–338
Fairchild State Forest, 114
Fannin Battleground State Historic Site, 540
Farmers Branch, 385–386
Farmers Branch Historical Park, 385
Fiesta, 267
Food. *See* Restaurants *under individual town/city*
Football. *See also* Sports *under individual town/city*
  Dallas Cowboys, 447

Northwest Sun Bowl Festivities, 723
Southwestern Bell Cotton Bowl Classic, 358–359
Fort Belknap, 649
Fort Brown, 489
Fort Concho National Historic Landmark, 762
Fort Davis, 729–733
  accommodations, 733
  historic places, 730–731
  history, 729
  museums, 730
  other points of interest, 731–732
  restaurants, 733
  shopping, 732
  side trips, 732
  tourist services, 729–730
Fort Davis National Historic Site, 730–731
Fort Griffin State Historical Park, 622
Fort Hood, 213
Fort Leaton State Historical Park, 698
Fort Martin Scott, 195
Fort Parker State Park, 83
Fort Richardson State Historical Park, 651
Fort Sam Houston, 252
Fort Stockton, 734–736
Fort Worth, 387–418
  accommodations, 415–418
  annual events, 408–411
  art galleries, 391–394
  bird's-eye view, 390
  clubs and bars, 415
  colleges and universities, 401–402
  historic places, 394–396
  history, 387–389
  kids' stuff, 407–408
  lake, 398
  map, 387
  museums, 391–394
  offbeat, 408
  other points of interest, 396–398
  performing arts, 402–406
  restaurants, 411–414
  shopping, 406–407

sports and activities, 398–401
tourist services, 389–390
tours, 390
zoo, 397
Fredericksburg, 193–199
accommodations, 198–199
annual events, 197–198
historic places, 194–195
history, 193
museums, 194
park, 196
restaurants, 198
shopping, 196
side trips, 196–197
tourist services, 194
Fritch, 647–648
Fulton. *See* Rockport and Fulton
Fulton Mansion State Historic Structure, 589
Gainesville, 418–420
Galleria
Dallas, 355
Houston, 39
Galveston, 521–539
accommodations, 537–539
annual events, 534–535
bird's-eye view, 524–525
colleges and universities, 531–532
historic places, 526–528
history, 521–523
kids' stuff, 533
map, 522
museums, 525–526
offbeat, 535
other points of interest, 528–529
performing arts, 532
restaurants, 535–537
shopping, 532–533
side trips, 534
sports and activities, 530–531
tourist services, 523–524
Galveston College, 531
Galveston Island State Park, 528
Gambill Goose Refuge, 105
Garland, 421–423
Garner State Park, 297

George Bush Presidential Library and Museum, 6
Georgetown, 199–200
Glen Rose, 423–426
Golf courses
Abilene, 616
Amarillo, 627–628
Arlington, 316–317
Austin, 147–148
Beaumont, 478
Belton, 174
Brady, 179
Breckenridge, 640
Brownsville, 492–493
Bryan/College Station, 6
Columbus, 190
Corsicana, 328
Dallas, 346–347
Del Rio, 518
Denison, 379
Denton, 382
El Paso, 716–717
Fort Stockton, 735
Fort Worth, 399–400
Garland, 422
Grand Prairie, 431
Grapevine, 436
Greenville, 440
Hillsboro, 443
Houston, 32
Huntsville, 62
Irving, 447
Kerrville, 210
Killeen, 214
Lampasas, 219
Laredo, 555
Llano, 221
Lubbock, 656
Marble Falls, 225
Mason, 228
McAllen, 564–565
McKinney, 453
Mesquite, 455
Midland, 745
Nacogdoches, 89
Navasota, 93
New Braunfels, 233
Palestine, 100
Paris, 104
Pecos, 760
Plano, 458
Port Arthur, 581
Richardson, 463
Rockport, 591

San Angelo, 765
San Antonio, 258
San Marcos, 283
Sherman, 468
Sonora, 770
South Padre Island, 597
Stephenville, 289
Sweetwater, 676
Temple, 294
Texarkana, 122
Victoria, 606
Waco, 302–303
Wichita Falls, 681
Goliad, 539–542
accommodations, 542
annual events, 542
historic places, 540–542
history, 539–540
museums, 540
side trips, 542
tourist services, 540
Goliad State Historical Park, 541
Gonzales, 201–204
accommodations, 204
annual events, 203–204
historic places, 202
history, 201
museums, 201
side trips, 203
tourist services, 201
Goose Island State Recreation Area, 589
Governor Hogg Shrine State Historical Park, 109
Governor's Mansion, 142
Graham, 649–650
Granbury, 426–429
Grand Prairie, 429–433
accommodations, 433
annual events, 432
history, 429
lakes, 430
places of interest, 430–431
restaurants, 432–433
sports, 431
tourist services, 430
Grapevine, 434–439
accommodations, 438–439
annual events, 438
history, 434
kids' stuff, 437

museums, 434–435
other points of interest,
    435–436
performing arts, 436–437
restaurants, 438
side trips, 437
sports and activities, 436
tourist services, 434
tours, 434
Grayson County College,
    379
Greenville, 439–442
Guadalupe Mountains
    National Park,
    736–738
Guadalupe River State
    Park, 177
Gus Engeling Wildlife
    Management Area,
    100–101
Hagerman National
    Wildlife Refuge, 378
Hardin-Simmons
    University, 616
Harlingen, 543–547
    accommodations, 547
    annual events, 546
    history, 543–544
    map, 543
    museums, 544–545
    other points of interest,
        545
    restaurants, 546–547
    shopping, 545
    side trips, 546
    tourist services, 544
Henderson, 19–21
    annual events, 21
    historic places, 20
    history, 19
    lake, 21
    museums, 20
    shopping, 20
    side trips, 21
    tourist services, 20
Hico, 204–206
Highland Lakes, 206
Hill College, 443
Hill Country State Natural
    Area, 170
Hillsboro, 442–444
Historic places
    Abilene, 614–615
    Albany, 622–623
    Amarillo, 624–625

Austin, 142–145
Bandera, 170
Belton, 173–174
Big Bend National Park,
    694
Big Spring, 700
Boerne, 176
Bonham, 323
Brenham, 2
Brownsville, 489–490
Carthage, 9
Castroville, 186
Center, 10
Chappell Hill, 13
Colorado City, 703
Columbus, 189
Comfort, 191–192
Corpus Christi, 506
Corsicana, 328
Crockett, 17
Dallas, 342–343
Denison, 378
Denton, 381
El Paso, 712–713
Fort Davis, 730–731
Fort Stockton, 734–735
Fort Worth, 394–396
Fredericksburg, 194–195
Fulton, 589
Gainesville, 419
Galveston, 526–528
Georgetown, 199
Glen Rose, 424
Goliad, 540–542
Gonzales, 202
Graham, 649
Granbury, 426–427
Greenville, 440
Henderson, 20
Hillsboro, 443
Huntsville, 61–62
Jacksboro, 651
Jasper, 65
Jefferson, 68
Kerrville, 209
La Grange, 216–217
Lampasas, 219
Laredo, 553–554
Llano, 221
Lockhart, 223
Marble Falls, 225
Marshall, 80
Mason, 227
McKinney, 453
Mexia, 83

Mount Vernon, 86
Nacogdoches, 89
Navasota, 93
New Braunfels, 232
Odessa, 752
Orange, 95
Ozona, 758
Palestine, 98–99
Paris, 103
Port Arthur, 580
Rockport and Fulton,
    589
Round Rock, 239
Rusk, 113–114
Salado, 242–243
San Angelo, 763
San Antonio, 251–254
San Augustine, 116
San Marcos, 282
Seguin, 286
Sherman, 467–468
Sonora, 770
Sulphur Springs, 118
Taylor, 291–292
Temple, 294
Terrell, 471
Texarkana, 121–122
Tyler, 127
Uvalde, 297
Victoria, 604–605
Waco, 301
West Columbia, 611
Hockey. *See also* Sports
    under individual
    town/city
    Dallas Stars, 347
Horse racing
    Austin, 148
    El Paso, 717
    Grand Prairie, 431
    Houston, 30
    San Antonio, 258
    Weatherford, 473
Hotels. *See*
    Accommodations
    under individual
    town/city
Houston, 21–60
    accommodations, 56–60
    annual events, 45–48
    art galleries, 40
    Astrodome, 28
    Astroworld, 43
    bird's-eye view, 23–24

colleges and universities, 33–34
history, 21–23
kids' stuff, 42–43
map, 22
museums and art galleries, 24–27
other points of interest, 27–31
performing arts, 34–39
restaurants, 48–55
shopping, 39–42
side trips, 43–45
sports, 31–33
tourist services, 23
Houston Astros, 32
Houston Baptist University, 33
Houston Community College system, 33
Houston Livestock Show and Rodeo, 45–46
Houston Rockets, 32
Howard College, 701
Howard Payne University, 181
Hueco Tanks State Historical Park, 721
Huntsville, 61–64
accommodations, 63–64
annual events, 63
historic places, 61–62
history, 61
lake, 62
museums, 61
restaurants, 63
side trips, 62–63
sports, 62
tourist services, 61
university, 62
Huntsville State Park, 62
Incarnate Word University, 259–260
Independence, 64
Indian reservations
Alabama–Coushatta, 72
Tigua, 715
Inks Lake State Park, 183
Inner Space Caverns, 200
Irving, 445–452
accommodations, 450–452
annual events, 449
colleges and universities, 448

history, 445
other points of interest, 446
performing arts, 448
restaurants, 449–450
sports and activities, 447–448
tourist services, 445
tours, 445–446
Jacksboro, 650–652
Jasper, 65–66
accommodations, 66
historic places, 65
history, 65
lakes, 65–66
restaurants, 66
shopping, 65
side trips, 65–66
tourist services, 65
Jefferson, 66–70
accommodations, 69–70
annual events, 69
historic places, 68
history, 66–67
lake, 69
museums, 67–68
other points of interest, 68
side trips, 69
tourist services, 67
JFK assassination site, 342
Jim Hogg State Historic Park, 114
John F. Kennedy Memorial, 345
Johnson City, 207–208
Juarez, Mexico, 719–720
Kennedy Assassination Site, 342
Kerrville, 208–212
accommodations, 212
annual events, 211
golf, 210
historic places, 209
history, 208
museums, 209
other points of interest, 209–210
restaurants, 211
side trips, 210–211
tourist services, 209
Kerrville Schreiner State Park, 210
Kilgore, 70–71
accommodations, 71

college, 71
history, 70
museums, 70–71
other points of interest, 71
tourist services, 70
Kilgore College, 71
Killeen, 212–215
accommodations, 215
annual events, 214
golf, 214
history, 212
museums, 213
other points of interest, 213
performing arts, 214
restaurants, 214–215
side trips, 214
tourist services, 213
King Ranch, 549
Kingsville, 548–552
accommodations, 551–552
annual events, 550–551
history, 548
museums, 548
other points of interest, 549
restaurants, 551
shopping, 550
tourist services, 548
university, 549–550
La Grange, 215–218
annual events, 217
historic places, 216–217
history, 215
museums, 216
restaurants, 218
side trips, 217
tourist services, 216
Laguna Atascosa National Wildlife Refuge, 546
Lajitas and Terlingua, 738–741
Lake Arrowhead State Park, 680–681
Lake Bonham Recreation Area, 324
Lake Brownwood State Recreation Area, 181
Lake Casa Blanca State Park, 554
Lake Colorado City State Park, 703–704

Lake Livingston State Park, 72
Lake Mineral Wells State Park & Trailway, 670
Lake Ray Roberts State Park, 383
Lake Whitney State Park, 326–327
Lakes
  Amistad Lake, 516–517
  Bachman Lake Park, 343
  Belton Lake, 174, 214, 295
  Brady, 179
  Buffalo Springs Lake, 660
  Canyon Lake, 235
  Fayette Lake, 217
  Grapevine Lake, 435
  Houston County Lake, 18
  Hubbard Creek Lake, 640
  Joe Pool Lake, 430
  Lake Arlington, 316
  Lake Austin, 146
  Lake B. A. Steinhagen, 65
  Lake Bastrop, 172
  Lake Bob Sandlin, 84–85, 86, 107
  Lake Brazos, 302
  Lake Buchanan, 183
  Lake Conroe, 14
  Lake Crook, 103
  Lake Cypress Springs, 86
  Lake Daniel, 640
  Lake Eddleman, 649
  Lake Fork Reservoir, 109
  Lake Fort Phantom, 616
  Lake Georgetown, 200
  Lake Graham, 649
  Lake Granbury, 427
  Lake Jacksboro, 651
  Lake Lavon, 453, 460
  Lake Leon, 647
  Lake Lewisville, 383
  Lake Livingston, 62
  Lake Lyndon B. Johnson (LBJ), 225
  Lake Marble Falls, 225
  Lake McQueeney, 287
  Lake Meredith, 648
  Lake Mexia, 83–84
  Lake Monticello, 84

Lake Murvaul, 10
Lake Nacogdoches, 90
Lake Nasworthy, 764
Lake O' The Pines, 69
Lake Palestine, 101, 129
Lake Pat Mayse, 105
Lake Quitman, 109
Lake Ray Hubbard, 421
Lake Rita Blanca, 645
Lake Sam Rayburn, 66, 76
Lake Somerville, 3
Lake Striker, 21
Lake Sweetwater, 676
Lake Tawakoni, 441, 472
Lake Tejas, 133
Lake Texoma, 379
Lake Travis, 146
Lake Tyler, 129
Lake Tyler East, 129
Lake Weatherford, 473
Lake Welsh, 85
Lake Whitney, 326–327
Lake Wichita, 681
Lake Worth, 398
Lake Wright Patman, 123
Lost Creek Reservoir, 651
Medina Lake, 170, 187
Mountain Creek Lake, 430
Stillhouse Hollow Lake, 174, 214, 243
Waco Lake, 302
Lamar University
  at Beaumont, 478–479
  at Port Arthur, 581–582
Lampasas, 218–220
Langtry, 741–742
Laredo, 552–561
  accommodations, 560–561
  annual events, 558
  colleges and universities, 555–556
  historic places, 553–554
  history, 552
  kids' stuff, 558
  map, 553
  museums, 554
  other points of interest, 554–555
  performing arts, 556
  restaurants, 558–559

  shopping, 556–557
  sports and activities, 555
  tourist services, 552
Laredo Community College, 555–556
Leon Springs, 267
LeTourneau University, 74
Livingston, 72
Llano, 220–222
Lockhart, 222–224
Lockhart State Park, 223
Longhorn Caverns State Park, 185
Longview, 73–75
  accommodations, 74–75
  annual events, 74
  history, 73
  museums, 73
  other points of interest, 73
  restaurant, 74
  tourist services, 73
  university, 74
Lost Maples State Natural Area, 170
Lubbock, 652–669
  accommodations, 667–669
  annual events, 661–664
  history, 652–653
  kids' stuff, 659–660
  map, 652
  museums and art galleries, 653–654
  other points of interest, 654–656
  performing arts, 657–658
  restaurants, 664–667
  shopping, 658–659
  side trips, 660–661
  sports and activities, 656
  tourist services, 653
  universities, 657
  winery, 661
Lubbock Christian University, 657
Lubbock Lake Landmark State Historical Park, 655
Luckenbach, 197
Lufkin, 75–77
  accommodations, 77
  annual events, 77
  college, 76
  history, 75

museum, 75
other points of interest, 76
performing arts, 76
restaurants, 77
side trips, 76
tourist services, 75
zoo, 76
Lyndon B. Johnson Library, 141
Lyndon B. Johnson National Historic Park, 207
Lyndon B. Johnson State Historic Park, 208
Maps. *See individual towns/cities*
Marathon, 688
Marble Falls, 224–226
Mardi Gras Festival, 534, 583
Marfa, 686–689
Marshall, 78–82
accommodations, 82
annual events, 81–82
colleges and universities, 80
historic places, 80
history, 78
map, 79
museums, 78
other points of interest, 80
shopping, 81
side trips, 81
tourist services, 78
Martin Creek Lake State Park, 9, 21
Mary Kay World Headquarters and Museum, 311
Mason, 226–229
accommodations, 229
annual events, 228
golf, 228
historic places, 227
history, 226
museums, 227
other points of interest, 228
restaurants, 229
tourist services, 226
Matagorda Island State Park, 586

Matamoros, Mexico, 491–492
McAllen, 561–571
accommodations, 570–571
annual events, 567–568
history, 561–562
map, 562
museums, 563
offbeat, 568
other points of interest, 563
performing arts, 565
restaurants, 568–570
shopping, 565–566
side trips, 566–567
sports and activities, 564–565
tourist services, 562–563
McKinney, 452–454
McKinney Falls State Park, 145–146
McLennan Community College, 304
McMurry University, 616–617
Mesquite, 454–457
Mexia, 83–84
Mexico
Juarez, 719–720
Matamoros, 491–492
Nuevo Progreso, 609
Reynosa, 563
Midland, 742–750
accommodations, 749–750
annual events, 747–748
college, 746
history, 742, 744
kids' stuff, 747
map, 743
museums, 744–745
other points of interest, 745
performing arts, 746
restaurants, 748–749
shopping, 747
sports and activities, 745–746
tourist services, 744
Midland College, 746
Midwestern State University, 681
Mineral Wells, 669–671

Mission Tejas State Historical Park, 18
Monahans, 750–751
Monahans Sandhill State Park, 751
Montgomery, 15
Motels. *See Accommodations under individual town/city*
Mount Pleasant, 84–85
Mount Vernon, 86–87
Museums. *See individual town/city*
Mustang Island State Park, 574
Nacogdoches, 87–92
accommodations, 91–92
annual events, 90–91
golf, 89
historic places, 89
history, 87
lake, 90
map, 88
museums, 88–89
performing arts, 90
restaurants, 91
shopping, 90
side trips, 90
tourist services, 87
university, 90
NASA/Lyndon B. Johnson Space Center, 498
National forests
Angelina National Forest, 65, 76
Davy Crockett National Forest, 17–18, 76
Sabine National Forest, 11, 66
Sam Houston National Forest, 15, 63
National memorials and monuments
Alibates Flint Quarries National Monument, 648
Chamizal National Memorial, 713
National parks
Amistad National Recreation Area, 516–517
Big Bend National Park, 690–697

Carlsbad Caverns
National Park, 738
Fort Davis National
Historic Site,
730–731
Guadalupe Mountains
National Park,
736–738
Lyndon B. Johnson
National Historic
Park, 207
San Antonio Missions
National Historical
Park, 252
National Scientific Balloon
Facility, 99
National Wildflower
Research Center, 146
National wildlife refuges
Aransas NWR, 591
Attwater Prairie Chicken
NWR, 190
Brazoria NWR, 484
Hagerman NWR, 378
Laguna Atascosa NWR,
546
San Bernard NWR, 484
Santa Ana NWR,
566–567
Natural Bridge Caverns,
235, 266
Natural Bridge Wildlife
Ranch, 235–236, 266
Navarro Historical Site, 253
Navasota, 92–94
accommodations, 94
annual events, 93
golf, 93
historic places, 93
history, 92
museums, 92
side trips, 93
tourist services, 92
New Braunfels, 229–238
accommodations,
237–238
annual events, 236
golf, 233
historic places, 232
history, 229–231
kids' stuff, 235
map, 230
museums, 231
other points of interest,
232–233

performing arts, 234
restaurants, 236–237
shopping, 234
side trips, 235
tourist services, 231
Noah's Land Wildlife Park,
203
North Central Texas
College, 420
North Lake Community
College, 448
Northwest Sun Bowl
Festivities, 723
Nuevo Progreso, Mexico,
609
Odessa, 752–757
accommodations, 757
annual events, 755–756
colleges and universities,
754
historic places, 752
history, 752
museums, 753
other points of interest,
753
performing arts, 754–755
restaurants, 756
shopping, 755
side trips, 755
sports and activities,
753–754
tourist services, 752
Odessa College, 754
Orange, 94–98
accommodations, 97
annual events, 97
historic places, 95
history, 94
museums, 95
other points of interest,
96
performing arts, 96
restaurants, 97
shopping, 96
side trips, 97
tourist services, 95
Our Lady of the Lake
University, 260
Ozona, 758
Padre Island National
Seashore and
Malaquite Beach,
507–508
Palestine, 98–101
accommodations, 101

annual events, 101
historic places, 98–99
history, 98
lake, 101
museums, 98
other points of interest,
99
side trips, 100–101
sports and activities, 100
tourist services, 98
Palmetto State Park, 203
Palo Duro Canyon State
Park, 642
Panola College, 9
Paris, 102–106
accommodations, 106
annual events, 106
college, 104
historic places, 103
history, 102
lakes, 103, 105
museums, 102–103
other points of interest,
103
performing arts, 104
shopping, 104–105
side trips, 105
sports and activities,
103–104
tourist services, 102
Paris Junior College, 104
Park Chalk Bluff, 297
Paseo del Rio (River Walk),
256
Pecos, 759–760
Pedernales Falls State Park,
208
Performing arts. See
Symphonies and
individual towns/cities
Pittsburgh, 106–108
annual events, 107
history, 106–107
lake, 107
offbeat, 107–108
restaurants, 108
side trips, 107
tourist services, 107
Plainview, 660
Plano, 457–462
accommodations,
461–462
annual events, 460–461
history, 457
kids' stuff, 460

lake, 460
museums, 458
offbeat, 461
performing arts, 459
restaurants, 461
side trips, 460
sports, 458–459
tourist services, 457
Port Aransas, 571–578
accommodations,
576–578
annual events, 574–575
history, 571
offbeat, 575
performing arts, 574
points of interest,
572–573
restaurants, 575–576
side trips, 574
sports and activities,
573–574
tourist services, 571–572
Port Arthur, 578–584
accommodations, 584
annual events, 582–583
bird's-eye view, 579
historic places, 580
history, 578–579
map, 578
museums, 579
other points of interest,
580–581
restaurants, 583
shopping, 582
side trips, 582
sports and activities, 581
tourist services, 579
university, 581–582
Port Lavaca, 584–587
Possum Kingdom State
Park, 640
Post, 660–661
Presidential libraries
George Bush, 6
Lyndon B. Johnson, 141
Quanah, 671–673
Quitman, 109–110
Restaurants. *See individual
town/city*
Reynosa, Mexico, 563
Rice University, 33
Richardson, 462–466
accommodations, 466
annual events, 465

colleges and universities,
463–464
history, 462–463
kids' stuff, 464
performing arts, 464
points of interest, 463
restaurants, 465
sports and activities, 463
tourist services, 463
Richland College, 463
Richmond. *See* Rosenberg-
Richmond
River Walk (Paseo del Rio),
256
Rockport and Fulton,
588–594
accommodations,
593–594
annual events, 591–592
historic places, 589
history, 588
museums, 588–589
other points of interest,
589–590
restaurants, 592–593
side trips, 591
sports and activities,
590–591
tourist services, 588
Rosenberg-Richmond,
110–113
accommodations, 113
annual events, 112
history, 110
museums, 111
restaurants, 112–113
side trips, 111–112
tourist services, 110
Round Rock, 238–239
Round Top, 239–242
Rusk, 113–115
annual events, 115
historic places, 113–114
history, 113
other points of interest,
114–115
performing arts, 115
side trips, 115
tourist services, 113
Rusk State Park, 114–115
Sabine National Forest,
11, 66
Sabine Pass Battleground
State Historical Park,
582

Salado, 242–244
Sam Houston National
Forest, 15, 63
Sam Houston Race Park, 30
Sam Houston State
University, 62
San Angelo, 760–769
accommodations,
768–769
annual events, 766–767
historic places, 763
history, 760, 762
kids' stuff, 766
map, 761
museums, 762–763
offbeat, 767
other points of interest,
763–764
performing arts, 765
restaurants, 767–768
shopping, 766
sports and activities, 765
tourist services, 762
university, 765
San Angelo State Park, 764
San Antonio, 245–281
accommodations,
277–281
annual events, 267–269
art galleries, 263–264
bird's-eye view, 249
colleges and universities,
259–261
historic places, 251–254
history, 245–247
kids' stuff, 265–266
map, 245
military bases, 256
missions, 251–253
museums, 249–251
offbeat, 269
other points of interest,
254–258
performing arts, 261–262
restaurants, 269–276
shopping, 262–265
side trips, 266–267
sports and activities,
258–259
terrain and climate, 247
tourist services, 248
tours, 247–249
San Antonio College, 259

San Antonio Missions
National Historical
Park, 252
San Antonio Spurs, 258
San Augustine, 116–117
San Bernard National
Wildlife Refuge, 484
San Jacinto Monument, 45
San Marcos, 281–285
accommodations,
284–285
annual events, 283–284
historic places, 281
history, 281
other points of interest,
282–283
restaurants, 284
sports and activities, 283
tourist services, 281
university, 283
Santa Ana National
Wildlife Refuge,
566–567
Schlitterbahn, 235
Sea Rim State Park, 582
Sea World of Texas, 257
Sebastopol House State
Historical Park, 286
Seguin, 285–288
accommodations, 288
annual events, 287–288
historic places, 286
history, 285
museums, 285
other points of interest,
286
performing arts, 287
restaurants, 288
shopping, 287
side trips, 287
sports and activities, 287
tourist services, 285
university, 287
Seminole Canyon State
Historical Park,
518–519, 742
Sherman, 466–470
accommodations, 470
annual events, 469–470
colleges, 468
historic places, 467–468
history, 466–467
museums, 467
other points of interest,
468

performing arts, 469
shopping, 469
side trips, 469
sports and activities, 468
tourist services, 467
Shopping. *See individual
cities*
Six Flags Astroworld, 43
Six Flags Fiesta Texas,
257–258
Six Flags Over Texas, 319
Snyder, 673–675
Sonora, 769–771
**South Padre Island and
Port Isabel,** 594–603
accommodations,
601–603
annual events, 598–599
bird's-eye view, 595–596
history, 594–595
kids' stuff, 597
museums, 596
offbeat, 599
points of interest, 596
restaurants, 599–601
side trips, 598
sports and activities, 597
tourist services, 595
Southern Methodist
University, 349
Southfork Ranch, 460
Southwest Collegiate
Institute for the Deaf,
701
Southwest Texas State
University, 283
Southwestern Bell Cotton
Bowl Classic, 358–359
Southwestern University,
200
Space Center Houston, 498
Sports and recreation. *See
individual sports and
cities*
St. Edward's University,
148–149
St. Mary's University, 260
State Capitol Complex,
143–144
State Cemetery, 144
State Fair of Texas, 361
State forests
Fairchild State Forest,
114

W. Goodrich Jones State
Forest, 14
State parks
Abilene State Park, 615
Acton State Historic Site,
426–427
Admiral Nimitz State
Historical Park, 194
Balmorhea State Park,
732
Bastrop State Park, 172
Bentsen-Rio Grande
State Park, 566
Big Bend Ranch State
Park, 698–699
Big Spring State Park,
700
Bonham State Recreation
Area, 324
Brazos Bend State Park,
43–44, 111
Bryan Beach State
Recreation Area,
483
Caddo Lake State Park,
69, 81
Caddoan Mounds State
Historical Park, 17,
115
Caprock Canyons State
Park, 632
Cooper Lake State Park,
118
Copper Breaks State
Park, 672
Davis Mountains State
Park, 731
Dinosaur Valley State
Park, 424
Eisenhower State
Recreation Area,
378
Enchanted Rock State
Natural Area, 196
Fannin Battleground
State Historic Site,
540
Fort Griffin State
Historical Park, 622
Fort Leaton State
Historical Park, 698
Fort Parker State Park,
83
Fort Richardson State
Historical Park, 651

Galveston Island State Park, 528
Garner State Park, 297
Goliad State Historical Park, 541
Goose Island State Recreation Area, 589
Governor Hogg Shrine State Historical Park, 109
Guadalupe River State Park, 177
Hill Country State Natural Area, 170
Hueco Tanks State Historical Park, 721
Huntsville State Park, 62
Inks Lake State Park, 183
Jim Hogg State Park, 114
Kerrville Schreiner State Park, 210
Lake Arrowhead State Park, 680–681
Lake Casa Blanca State Park, 554
Lake Colorado City State Park, 703–704
Lake Livingston State Park, 72
Lake Mineral Wells State Park & Trailway, 670
Lake Ray Roberts State Park, 383
Lake Whitney State Park, 326–327
Lockhart State Park, 223
Longhorn Caverns State Park, 185
Lost Maples State Natural Area, 170
Lubbock Lake Landmark State Historical Park, 655
Lyndon B. Johnson State Historical Park, 208
Martin Creek Lake State Park, 9, 21
Matagorda Island State Park, 586
McKinney Falls State Park, 145–146
Mission Tejas State Historical Park, 18

Monahans Sandhill State Park, 751
Mustang Island State Park, 574
Palmetto State Park, 203
Palo Duro Canyon State Park, 642
Pedernales Falls State Park, 208
Possum Kingdom State Park, 640
Rusk State Park, 114–115
Sabine Pass Battleground State Historical Park, 582
San Angelo State Park, 764
Sea Rim State Park, 582
Sebastopol House State Historical Park, 286
Seminole Canyon State Historical Park, 518–519, 742
Texas State Railroad State Historical Park, 99–100, 115
Tyler State Park, 128
Varner-Hogg State Historical Park, 611
Washington-On-The-Brazos State Historical Park, 131–132
Stephen F. Austin State University, 90
Stephenville, 289–291
Stillhouse Hollow Lake, 243
Stockyards National Historic District, 394–395
Sul Ross State University, 687
Sulphur Springs, 117–120
  accommodations, 119–120
  annual events, 119
  historic places, 118
  history, 117
  museums, 118
  other points of interest, 118
  shopping, 119
  tourist services, 118
Sun Bowl, 723

Sweetwater, 675–678
Symphonies
  Abilene, 617
  Amarillo, 629
  Austin, 150
  Corpus Christi, 510
  Dallas, 353
  El Paso, 718
  Fort Worth, 404
  Houston, 36
  Laredo, 556
  Lubbock, 658
  McAllen, 565
  Midland-Odessa, 746, 754
  Richardson, 464
  San Angelo, 765
  San Antonio, 262
  Sherman, 469
  Tyler, 129
  Victoria, 606
  Wichita Falls, 682
Tarleton State University, 289
Tarrant County Junior College, 401
Taylor, 291–292
Temple, 292–296
  accommodations, 295–296
  annual events, 295
  historic places, 294
  history, 292–293
  museums, 293
  performing arts, 294
  restaurants, 295
  shopping, 295
  side trips, 295
  sports and activities, 294
  tourist services, 293
Terlingua, 738–741
Terrell, 470–472
Texarkana, 120–124
  accommodations, 124
  annual events, 124
  college, 123
  historic places, 121–122
  history, 120–121
  kids' stuff, 123
  lake, 123
  museums, 121
  other points of interest, 122
  performing arts, 123
  restaurants, 124

side trips, 123
sports and activities, 122
tourist services, 121
Texarkana College, 123
TEXAS! A Musical Drama,
  643
Texas A&M International
  University, 556
Texas A&M University
  at College Station, 6–7
  at Galveston, 531
  at Kingsville, 549–550
Texas Christian University,
  401–402
Texas College, 128
Texas Lutheran University,
  287
Texas Motor Speedway,
  382, 398–399
Texas Ranger Hall of Fame
  and Museum, 301
Texas Rangers, 316
Texas Renaissance Festival,
  15, 47–48, 93
Texas Southern University,
  33–34
Texas Sports Hall of Fame,
  302
Texas Star Ferris Wheel,
  338
Texas State Railroad State
  Historical Park,
  99–100, 115
Texas State Technical
  College, 304
Texas Tech University, 657
Texas Wesleyan
  University, 402
Texas Woman's University,
  382
Tigua Indian Reservation,
  715
Toledo Bend Reservoir, 11
Topsey Exotic Ranch and
  Drive Through Park,
  214, 219
Tower of the Americas, 249
Trinity University, 260
Tyler, 125–131
  accommodations, 131
  annual events, 129–130
  colleges and universities,
  128–129
  historic places, 127
  history, 125–126

map, 125
museums, 126
other points of interest,
  127–128
performing arts, 129
restaurants, 130
shopping, 129
side trips, 129
tourist services, 126
zoo, 127
Tyler Junior College, 128
Tyler State Park, 128
Universities. *See also*
  Colleges
  Abilene Christian
    University, 616
  Angelo State University,
    765
  Baylor University, 303
  East Texas Baptist
    University, 80
  Hardin-Simmons
    University, 616
  Houston Baptist
    University, 33
  Howard Payne
    University, 181
  Incarnate Word
    University, 259–260
  Lamar University
    at Beaumont, 478–479
    at Port Arthur,
    581–582
  LeTourneau University,
    74
  Lubbock Christian
    University, 657
  McMurry University,
    616–617
  Midwestern State
    University, 681
  Our Lady of the Lake
    University, 260
  Rice University, 33
  Sam Houston State
    University, 62
  Southern Methodist
    University, 349
  Southwest Texas State
    University, 283
  Southwestern
    University, 200
  St. Edward's University,
    148–149

St. Mary's University,
  260
Stephen F. Austin State
  University, 90
Sul Ross State
  University, 687
Tarleton State
  University, 289
Texas A&M
  International
  University, 556
Texas A&M University
  at College Station, 6–7
  at Galveston, 531
  at Kingsville, 549–550
Texas Christian
  University, 401–402
Texas Lutheran
  University, 287
Texas Southern
  University, 33–34
Texas Tech University,
  657
Texas Wesleyan
  University, 402
Texas Woman's
  University, 382
Trinity University, 260
University of Dallas, 448
University of Houston,
  34
University of Mary
  Hardin-Baylor, 174
University of Mexico at
  San Antonio, 260
University of North
  Texas, 382–383
University of
  St. Thomas, 34
University of Texas
  at Arlington, 317
  at Austin, 149–150
  at Dallas, 464
  at El Paso, 717–718
  at Permian Basin, 754
  at San Antonio, 260
  at Tyler, 128–129
University of Texas
  Health Science
  Center at San
  Antonio, 261
University of Texas
  Medical Branch,
  531–532

West Texas A&M
    University, 643
Uvalde, 296–298
Varner-Hogg State
    Historical Park, 611
Victoria, 603–608
    accommodations,
        607–608
    annual events, 606–607
    college, 606
    historic places, 604–605
    history, 603–604
    museums, 604
    other points of interest,
        605
    performing arts, 606
    restaurants, 607
    side trips, 606
    sports and activities, 606
    tourist services, 604
    zoo, 605
Victoria College, 606
W. Goodrich Jones State
    Forest, 14
Waco, 299–307
    accommodations,
        306–307
    annual events, 305
    bird's-eye view, 299
    colleges and universities,
        303–304
    historic places, 301
    history, 299
    kids' stuff, 304
    lakes, 302
    map, 300
    museums, 299, 301
    other points of interest,
        302
    performing arts, 304
    restaurants, 305–306

shopping, 304
sports and activities,
    302–303
tourist services, 299
Waco Lake, 302
Walter C. Porter Farm, 472
Washington, 131–132
Washington-On-The-Brazos
    State Historical Park,
    131–132
Weatherford, 472–474
Weatherford College, 473
Weslaco, 608–610
West Columbia, 610–612
West End Historic District,
    342–343
West End Marketplace, 356
West Texas A&M
    University, 643
Western Texas College, 674
Wichita Falls, 678–685
    accommodations,
        684–685
    annual events, 683–684
    history, 678, 680
    kids' stuff, 682–683
    lakes, 681
    map, 679
    museums, 680
    offbeat, 684
    other points of interest,
        681
    performing arts, 682
    side trips, 683
    sports and activities, 681
    tourist services, 680
    university, 681
Wildlife management areas
    Caddo-LBJ National
        Grasslands and
        WMA, 324–325

Gus Engeling WMA,
    100–101
Wiley College, 80
Wimberley, 307–309
Wineries
    Austin, 154
    Bryan/College Station, 6
    Buchanan Dam, 183
    Del Rio, 517–518
    Fredericksburg, 197
    Grapevine, 434, 436
    Lubbock, 661
    Orange, 96
Woodville, 132–134
    accommodations, 134
    annual events, 133
    history, 132
    lake, 133
    museums, 132
    restaurants, 133–134
    shopping, 132–133
    side trips, 133
    tourist services, 132
Zoos
    Abilene, 615
    Austin, 155
    Brownsville, 491
    Corpus Christi, 507
    Dallas, 345
    El Paso, 714
    Fort Worth, 397
    Gainesville, 419
    Houston, 29
    Lufkin, 76
    San Antonio, 257
    Tyler, 127
    Victoria, 605
    Waco, 302

The Sounds of Texas

The whole concept of Texas music would be a stretch, if it weren't true. No other state can make a claim to having a "sound," and what qualifies as Texas music encompasses a pretty broad range of music. The seven selections here reflect Texas' reputation as a musical crossroads, as do the artists who perform the songs. Each and every one is a real working musician who puts his or her magic on display in honky tonks, supper clubs, coffeehouses, and dancehalls every weekend night all around the state.

♪ **Joe Carr and Alan Munde's "Windy Days, Dusty Skies"** sums up the experience of living in the wide open spaces on the High Plains of West Texas, which both know more than a little bit about. That's because both members of this virtuoso guitar duo are instructors at South Plains College in Levelland, one of only two institutes of higher learning in the United States where a student can earn degrees in country music and bluegrass.

♪ Endless horizons are just as intriguing to **Kimberley M'Carver** in the lyrical **"Texas Home."** She's a purebred Texas songster and the latest in a long line of acoustic guitarists who perform their own original compositions, having matriculated at Anderson Fair, the storied Houston folk music club that fostered the careers of Townes Van Zandt, Guy Clark, Nanci Griffith, and Lyle Lovett, among others.

♪ Also from Houston are **Lil' Brian Terry and the Zydeco Travelers.** This electrifying young band of twentysomething musicians raised on zydeco, has a sound that infuses the best of blues, soul, and hip hop into the traditional music of the French-speaking blacks who emigrated from southwest Louisiana and southeast Texas to Houston after World War II. On **"H-Town Zydeco"** they sing the praises of their hometown, serving up a funky rhythm guaranteed to move any pair of dancing shoes.

♪ **Tish Hinojosa,** who grew up in San Antonio and lives in Austin, pays homage to Texas as a musical melting pot with **"San Antonio Romeo."** The song is a variation of "San Antonio Rose," the Bob Wills & His Texas Playboys classic, that remains a standard of western swing, an original Texas style that is still hugely popular more than eighty years after it was invented.

♪ **Clarence "Gatemouth" Brown** knows a few things about swing himself. **"Strolling with Bones"** honors Brown's one-time mentor, Aaron "T-Bone" Walker of Dallas, the man who originated electric blues guitar and made it swing. Gatemouth got his career break back in the forties when he picked up T-Bone's guitar during a set break to entertain a packed house at Houston's storied Bronze Peacock Club. It was the first of a long string of electric guitar "battles" between the two players that spanned three decades.

♪ **"Viva Sequin"** is a peppy instrumental celebrating the town of Sequin, just east of San Antonio, written by Santiago Jimenez, one of the fathers of Tex-Mex conjunto accordion. Here, it is performed by Santiago's son **Flaco Jimenez,** regarded as the best and best known contemporary Tex-Mex accordionist by virtue of recording more than thirty albums, making frequent worldwide tours as a solo act, and performing as a sometimes member of the Texas Tornadoes.

♪ **Brave Combo's "Charanga Y Mambo"** blends two distinctive south-of-the-border sounds into one irresistible dancehall crowd-pleaser—what the band calls, nuclear polka. It includes Czech music (they're the featured entertainment at the annual Westfest in the central Texas town of West), and German music (BC also performs at the annual Muensterfest in the North Texas town of Muenster).

Absorbing a variety of different sounds and influences to create something wholly original, as does Brave Combo, explains Texas music as well as anything. You may have a hard time putting your finger on it, but believe me, once you hear it, you'll know what it is, and you won't be able to keep still. So, see you on a dancefloor, somewhere, anywhere in the Lone Star State.

JOE NICK PATOSKI

Joe Nick Patoski is a senior editor at Texas Monthly magazine and has been writing about Texas and Texas music for 25 years. Patoski's articles have appeared in Rolling Stone, Creem, and Country Music among other publications. He coauthored the book Stevie Ray Vaughan: Caught in the Crossfire *(Little, Brown), and authored the book* Selena: Como la Flor *(Little, Brown).*